DATE DUE

			PRINTED IN U.S.A.

CLASSICAL
AND MEDIEVAL
LITERATURE
CRITICISM

Guide to Gale Literary Criticism Series

For criticism on	Consult these Gale series
Authors now living or who died after December 31, 1959	*CONTEMPORARY LITERARY CRITICISM (CLC)*
Authors who died between 1900 and 1959	*TWENTIETH-CENTURY LITERARY CRITICISM (TCLC)*
Authors who died between 1800 and 1899	*NINETEENTH-CENTURY LITERATURE CRITICISM (NCLC)*
Authors who died between 1400 and 1799	*LITERATURE CRITICISM FROM 1400 TO 1800 (LC)* *SHAKESPEAREAN CRITICISM (SC)*
Authors who died before 1400	*CLASSICAL AND MEDIEVAL LITERATURE CRITICISM (CMLC)*
Black writers of the past two hundred years	*BLACK LITERATURE CRITICISM (BLC)*
Authors of books for children and young adults	*CHILDREN'S LITERATURE REVIEW (CLR)*
Dramatists	*DRAMA CRITICISM (DC)*
Hispanic writers of the late nineteenth and twentieth centuries	*HISPANIC LITERATURE CRITICISM (HLC)*
Native North American writers and orators of the eighteenth, nineteenth, and twentieth centuries	*NATIVE NORTH AMERICAN LITERATURE (NNAL)*
Poets	*POETRY CRITICISM (PC)*
Short story writers	*SHORT STORY CRITICISM (SSC)*
Major authors from the Renaissance to the present	*WORLD LITERATURE CRITICISM, 1500 TO THE PRESENT (WLC)*

ISSN 0896-0011

Volume 26

CLASSICAL
AND MEDIEVAL
LITERATURE
CRITICISM

Excerpts from Criticism of the Works of World
Authors from Classical Antiquity through the
Fourteenth Century, from the First Appraisals
to Current Evaluations

Amy K. Crook
Jelena O. Krstović
Daniel G. Marowski
Editors

GALE

DETROIT • LONDON

Library of Congress Catalog Card Number 88-658021
ISBN 0-7876-2405-5
ISSN 0896-0011
Printed in the United States of America

10 9 8 7 6 5 4 3 2 1

Contents

Preface vii

Acknowledgments ix

Preface

Since its inception in 1988, *Classical and Medieval Literature Criticism* has been a valuable resource for students and librarians seeking critical commentary on the writers and works of these periods in world history. Major reviewing sources have assessed *CMLC* as "useful" and "extremely convenient," noting that it "adds to our understanding of the rich legacy left by the ancient period and the Middle Ages," and praising its "general excellence in the presentation of an inherently interesting subject." No other single reference source has surveyed the critical reaction to classical and medieval literature as thoroughly as *CMLC*.

Scope of the Series

CMLC is designed to serve as an introduction for students and advanced readers of the works and authors of antiquity through the fourteenth century. The great poets, prose writers, dramatists, and philosophers of this period form the basis of most humanities curricula, so that virtually every student will encounter many of these works during the course of a high school and college education. By organizing and reprinting an enormous amount of commentary written on classical and medieval authors and works, *CMLC* helps students develop valuable insight into literary history, promotes a better understanding of the texts, and sparks ideas for papers and assignments. Each entry in *CMLC* presents a comprehensive survey of an author's career, an individual work of literature, or a literary topic, and provides the user with a multiplicity of interpretations and assessments. Such variety allows students to pursue their own interests; furthermore, it fosters an awareness that literature is dynamic and responsive to many different opinions.

CMLC continues the survey of criticism of world literature begun by Gale's *Contemporary Literary Criticism (CLC)*, *Twentieth-Century Literary Criticism (TCLC)*, *Nineteenth-Century Literature Criticism (NCLC)*, *Literature Criticism from 1400 to 1800 (LC)*, and *Shakespearean Criticism (SC)*. For additional information about these and Gale's other criticism series, users should consult the Guide to Gale Literary Criticism Series preceding the title page in this volume.

Coverage

Each volume of *CMLC* is carefully compiled to present:

- criticism of authors and works which represent a variety of genres, time periods, and nationalities

- both major and lesser-known writers and works of the period (such as non-Western authors and literature, increasingly read by today's students)

- 4-6 authors or works per volume

- individual entries that survey the critical response to each author, work, or topic, including early criticism, later criticism (to represent any rise or decline in the author's reputation), and current retrospective analyses. The length of each author or work entry also indicates relative importance, reflecting the amount of critical attention the author, work, or topic has received from critics writing in English, and from foreign criticism in translation.

An author may appear more than once in the series if his or her writings have been the subject of a substantial amount of criticism; in these instances, specific works or groups of works by the author will be covered in separate entries. For example, Homer will be represented by three entries, one devoted to the *Iliad,* one to the *Odyssey,* and one to the Homeric Hymns.

Starting with Volume 10, *CMLC* will also occasionally include entries devoted to literary topics. For example, *CMLC*-10 focuses on Arthurian Legend and includes general criticism on that subject as well as individual entries on writers or works central to that topic—Chrétien de Troyes, Gottfried von Strassburg, Layamon, and the Alliterative *Morte Arthure.* Presocratic Philosophy is the focus of *CMLC*-22, which includes general criticism as well as essays on Greek philosophers Anaximander, Heraclitus, Parmenides, and Pythagoras.

Organization of the Book

An author entry consists of the following elements: author heading, biographical and critical introduction, principal English translations or editions, excerpts of criticism (each preceded by a bibliographic citation and an annotation), and a bibliography of further reading.

- The **Author Heading** consists of the author's most commonly used name, followed by birth and death dates. If the entry is devoted to a work, the heading will consist of the most common form of the title in English translation (if applicable), and the original date of composition. Located at the beginning of the introduction are any name or title variations.

- A **Portrait** of the author is included when available. Many entries also feature illustrations of materials pertinent to the author or work, including manuscript pages, book illustrations, and representations of people, places, and events important to a study of the author or work.

- The **Biographical and Critical Introduction** contains background information that concisely introduces the reader to the author, work, or topic.

- The list of **Principal Works** and **English Translations** or **Editions** is chronological by date of first publication and is included as an aid to the student seeking translated versions or editions of these works for study. The list will focus primarily on twentieth-century translations, selecting those works most commonly considered the best by critics.

- **Criticism** is arranged chronologically in each entry to provide a useful perspective on changes in critical evaluation over the years. All titles by the author featured in the critical entry are printed in boldface type to enable the user to ascertain without difficulty the works being discussed. Also for purposes of easier identification, the critic's name and the publication date of the essay are given at the beginning of each piece of criticism. Anonymous criticism is preceded by the title of the journal in which it appeared. Publication information (such as publisher names and book prices) and parenthetical numerical references (such as footnotes or page and line references to specific editions of works) have been deleted at the editors' discretion to provide smoother reading of the text. Many critical entries in *CMLC* also contain translations to aid the users. Footnotes that appear with previously published pieces of criticism are reprinted at the end of each essay or excerpt. In the case of excerpted criticism, only those footnotes that pertain to the excerpted text are included

- A complete **Bibliographic Citation** provides original publication information for each piece of criticism.

- Critical excerpts are also prefaced by **Annotations** providing the reader with information about both the critic and the criticism, the scope of the excerpt, the growth of critical controversy, or changes in critical trends regarding an author or work. In some cases, these notes include cross-references to excerpts by critics who discuss each other's commentary. Dates in parentheses within the annotation refer to a book publication date when they follow a book title, and to an essay date when they follow a critic's name.

- An annotated bibliography of **Further Reading** appears at the end of each entry and lists additional secondary sources on the author or work. In some cases it includes essays for which the editors could not obtain reprint rights. When applicable, the Further Reading is followed by references to additional entries on the author in other literary reference series published by Gale.

Topic Entries are subdivided into several thematic rubrics in which criticism appears in order of descending scope.

Cumulative Indexes

Each volume of *CMLC* includes a cumulative **author index** listing all authors who have appeared in Gale's Literary Criticism Series, along with cross references to such biographical series as *Contemporary Authors* and *Dictionary of Literary Biography*. For readers' convenience, a complete list of Gale titles included appears on the page prior to the author index. Useful for locating an author within the various series, this index is particularly valuable for those authors who are identified with a certain period but who, because of their death date, are placed in another, or for those authors whose careers span two periods. For example, Geoffrey Chaucer, who is usually considered a medieval author, is found in *Literature Criticism from 1400 to 1800* because he died after 1399.

Beginning with the tenth volume, *CMLC* includes a cumulative index listing all topic entries that have appeared in the Gale Literary Criticism Series *Classical and Medieval Literature Criticism, Contemporary Literary Criticism, Literature Criticism from 1400 to 1800, Nineteenth-Century Literature Criticism,* and *Twentieth-Century Literary Criticism.*

Beginning with the second volume, *CMLC* also includes a cumulative nationality index. Authors and/or works are grouped by nationality, and the volume in which criticism on them may be found is indicated.

Title Index

Each volume of *CMLC* also includes an index listing the titles of all literary works discussed in the series. Foreign language titles that have been translated are followed by the titles of the translations—for example, *Slovo o polku Igorove (The Song of Igor's Campaign)*. Page numbers following these translated titles refer to all pages on which any form of the title, either foreign language or translated, appears. Titles of novels, dramas, nonfiction books, and poetry, short story, or essay collections are printed in italics, while those of all individual poems, short stories, and essays are printed in roman type within quotation marks. In cases where the same title is used by different authors, the author's name or surname is given in parentheses after the title, e.g. *Collected Poems* (Horace) and *Collected Poems* (Sappho).

Critic Index

An index to critics, which cumulates with the second volume, is another useful feature of *CMLC*. Under each critic's name are listed the authors and/or works on whom the critic has written and the volume and page number where criticism may be found.

A Note to the Reader

When writing papers, students who quote directly from any volume in the Literary Criticism Series may use the following general forms to footnote reprinted criticism. The first example pertains to material drawn from a periodical, the second to material reprinted from books.

Rollo May, "The Therapist and the Journey into Hell," *Michigan Quarterly Review,* XXV, No. 4 (Fall 1986), 629-41; excerpted and reprinted in *Classical and Medieval Literature Criticism,* Vol. 3, ed. Jelena O. Krstovic (Detroit: Gale Research, 1989), pp. 154-58.

Dana Ferrin Sutton, *Self and Society in Aristophanes* (University of Press of America, 1980); excerpted and reprinted in *Classical and Medieval Literature Criticism,* Vol. 4, ed. Jelena O. Krstovic (Detroit: Gale Research, 1990), pp. 162-69.

Suggestions Are Welcome

Readers who wish to make suggestions for future volumes, or who have other comments regarding the series, are cordially invited to write or call the editors (1-800-347-GALE, Fax: (313) 961-6815).

Acknowledgments

The editors wish to thank the copyright holders of the excerpted criticism included in this volume and the permissions managers of many book and magazine publishing companies for assisting us in securing reproduction rights. We are also grateful to the staffs of the Detroit Public Library, the Library of Congress, the University of Detroit Mercy Library, Wayne State University Purdy/Kresge Library Complex, and the University of Michigan Libraries for making their resources available to us. Following is a list of the copyright holders who have granted us permission to reproduce material in this volume of *CMLC*. Every effort has been made to trace copyright, but if omissions have been made, please let us know.

COPYRIGHTED EXCERPTS IN *CMLC*, VOLUME 26, WERE REPRODUCED FROM THE FOLLOWING PERIODICALS:

Japanese Journal of Religious Studies, v. 8, March-June, 1981. © Copyright 1981 by the Nanzan Institute for Religion and Culture. Reproduced by permission.—*Journal of Folklore Research,* v. 20, June-December, 1983. Reproduced by permission.—*Proceedings of the British Academy,* 1934. Reproduced by permission.

COPYRIGHTED EXCERPTS IN *CMLC*, VOLUME 26, WERE REPRODUCED FROM THE FOLLOWING BOOKS:

Anthes, Rudolf. From "Mythology in Ancient Egypt" in *Mythologies of the Ancient World.* Edited by Samuel Noah Kramer. Anchor Books, 1961. Copyright © 1961 by Doubleday, a division of Bantam Doubleday Dell Publishing Group, Inc. All rights reserved. Used by permission of Doubleday, a division of Bantam Doubleday Dell Publishing Group, Inc.—Branston, Brian. From *Gods of the North.* Thames and Hudson, 1955. Copyright 1955 by Brian Branston. All rights reserved. Reproduced by permission.—Buxton, Richard. From *Imaginary Greece: The Contexts of Mythology.* Cambridge University Press, 1994. © Cambridge University Press 1994. Reproduced with the permission of Cambridge University Press and the author.—Caldwell, Richard. From *The Origin of The Gods: A Psychoanalytic Study of Greek Theogonic Myth.* Oxford University Press, 1989. Copyright © 1989 by Oxford University Press, Inc. All rights reserved. Used by permission of Oxford University Press, Inc.—Crossley-Holland, Kevin. From an introduction to *The Norse Myths.* Pantheon Books, 1980. Copyright © 1980 by Kevin Crossley-Holland. All rights reserved. Reproduced by permission of the author. In the United States and Philippines by Pantheon Books, a division of Random House, Inc.—Edinger, Edward F. From *The Eternal Drama: The Inner Meaning of Greek Mythology.* Edited by Deborah A. Wesley. Shambhala Publications, Inc., 1994. © 1994 by Edward F. Edinger. All rights reserved. Reproduced by arrangement with the publisher.—Gadd, C. J. From "Babylonian Myth and Ritual" in *Myth and Ritual: Essays on the Myth and Ritual of the Hebrews in relation to the Culture Pattern of the Ancient East.* Edited by S. H. Hooke. Oxford University Press, 1933. © Oxford University Press, 1933. Reproduced by permission of Oxford University Press.—Gantz, Jeffrey. From the introduction to *Early Irish Myths and Sagas.* Translated by Jeffrey Gantz. Penguin Books, 1981. Reproduced by permission of Penguin Books, Ltd.— Harris, Joseph. From "Eddic Poetry" in *Old Norse—Icelandic Literature: A Critical Guide.* Edited by Carol J. Clover and John Lindow. Cornell University Press, 1985. Copyright © 1985 Cornell University. All rights reserved. Used by permission of Cornell University Press. All additional uses of this material—including, but not limited to, photocopying and reprinting—are prohibited without the prior written approval of Cornell University Press.—Irani, K. D. From "The Socioeconomic Implications of Conflict of Gods in Indo-Iranian Mythology" in *Ancient Economy in Mythology: East and West.* Edited by Morris Silver. Rowman & Littlefield Publishers, Inc., 1991. Copyright © 1991 by Rowman & Littlefield Publishers, Inc. All rights reserved. Reproduced by permission.—Kerényi, C. From *Essays on a Science of Mythology: The Myth of the Divine Child and The Mysteries of Eleusis.* By C. G. Jung and C. Kerényi. Translated by R. F. C. Hull. Bollingen Series, XXII, Princeton University Press, 1949. Copyright 1949 by Bollingen Foundation. Renewed 1977 by Princeton University Press. Reproduced by permission.—Kirk, G. S. From *The Nature of Greek Myths.* Overlook Press, 1975. Copyright © G. S. Kirk, 1974. Reproduced by permission.—Littleton, C. Scott. From "The 'Kingship in Heaven' Theme" in *Myth and Law Among the Indo-Europeans: Studies in Indo-European Comparative Mythology.* Edited by Jaan Puhvel. University of California Press, 1970. Copyright © 1970 by the Regents of the

PHOTOGRAPHS AND ILLUSTRATIONS APPEARING IN *CMLC,* VOLUME 26, WERE RECEIVED FROM THE FOLLOWING SOURCES:

Celtic Mythology

INTRODUCTION

Once a diverse cultural group that extended throughout western Europe and even farther south and east, the Celts are today generally associated with the northwestern locales of Wales, Scotland, Cornwall, Brittany, the Isle of Man, and especially Ireland, where individuals of Celtic ancestry predominate. Linked with the Insular branch of Celtic culture, these areas are contrasted with those of the Continental Celts, who occupied the region known as Gaul (today approximately occupied by modern France). In his *Commentaries* of the first century B. C., the Roman emperor Julius Caesar, then governor of Gaul, recorded his assessments of Celtic religion, mentioning some of their nearly four hundred appellations for divine beings and other specifics of their culture. As Celtic Gaul was absorbed by the Roman Empire, the continental Celts nevertheless continued to practice their native religion and culture until Christianity took firm hold in the region, as it had in the remainder of Europe, by the fifth century A. D. By this time, however, the newly-converted Christian monks in the Insular north, particularly in Ireland, had undertaken measures to preserve their heritage by transcribing manuscript copies of the ancient tales of Celtic gods and heroes. In their manuscripts, many of which where lost in the ensuing centuries of invasion, these scribes recorded the rich mythology of iron-age Ireland.

Preserved for centuries through oral tradition, the stories in these texts were popularly "rediscovered" in 1760 when Scottish poet James Macpherson published his *Fragments of Ancient Poetry*. He claimed that the poems were translations of verse composed by the third-century Gaelic poet Ossian (Oisín), but the works were shortly thereafter labeled bogus by scholars. Nevertheless, Macpherson's "translations" stirred considerable popular and scholarly interest in all things Gaelic—a Celtic language of ancient Ireland that has since evolved into modern Irish, Manx, and Scots Gaelic dialects. A little over a century later, in the 1890s, an Anglo-Irish movement known as the Irish Literary Revival—led by poet William Butler Yeats, playwright Lady Isabella Augusta Gregory, and other prominent Irish literary figures of the era—spawned a renewed interest in the subject of Celtic mythology by re-introducing its themes, characters, and culture into modern works of Irish literature written in English.

In the contemporary era, scholars have attempted to reconstruct the culture and history of the Celts through what remains of their mythological literature, but have encountered several barriers. One such obstacle has been the long-standing conflation of ancient Irish myth and history. Until the mid-nineteenth century many scholars tended to view the heroes and gods of Celtic mythology as actual historical figures whose activities had simply been exaggerated or "mythologized" over the centuries. This practice (termed euhemerism) has since been largely forsaken and modern scholars no longer construe such figures as Fionn mac Cumhaill and Conchobar mac Nessa as real men of the past, nor regard the extant mythological texts as having any true historical currency.

Further complications for scholars have appeared as the result of the structure of Celtic culture itself. As Georges Dumézil observed of other Indo-European cultures, Celtic society was generally organized into three parts, consisting of groups of warriors (led by the tribal king), priests, and farmers/freemen. Members of the priestly class, called Druids, acted as intermediaries between ordinary individuals and the gods. Revered for their knowledge and wisdom, the Druids legislated in the spiritual realm and were the bearers of the Celtic religious system—which features an amoral ethic that thoroughly disavows good or evil in individual actions and offers a pervasive belief in metempsychosis, or the transmigration of the soul after death. The historical Druids, like their mythological counterparts who often wielded magical powers and were largely characterized as seers with superhuman clairvoyance, demonstrated an aversion to the written word. Thus, their knowledge was transmitted orally, leaving no written record of the ancient sagas until they were first transcribed in the Christian era.

Despite the scarcity of written texts and a legacy of euhemerism in Celtic studies, scholars have been able to preserve and codify considerable portions of Celtic myth using two key manuscripts, both from the twelfth century—the *Lebor Gabála Érenn*, literally "The Book of the Taking of Ireland" and the *Dindshenchas*, sometimes rendered as "The History of Places." The former presents a mythological history of Ireland, while the latter amounts to a mythic geography of the island. The work describes Ireland as a pentarchy, divided into five provinces: in the north Ulster, Connacht in the west, Munster to the southwest, in the southeast Leinster, and Mide (corresponding to modern Meath, site of the mythological Tara, the seat of the ancient Irish High King) in the center. In addition to these geographical distinctions, scholars have also outlined four story cycles in Celtic mythology. These include: 1) The Kings Cycle; 2) The Mythological Cycle; 3) The Fenian Cycle; and 4) The Uliah or Ulster Cycle, also called the "Red Branch" Cycle.

The Kings Cycle focuses on a series of "historical" kings, while the Mythological Cycle is concerned with Ireland's mythic prehistory. Derived in large part from the *Lebor Gabála Érenn*, the Mythological Cycle describes a series of heroes and peoples who were said to have invaded ancient Ireland. The first of these, Fintan, dates to the time of the Biblical Flood. He was followed by the hero Partholón, who along with his kinsmen battled the demonic Fomoire (one-armed and one-legged monstrosities). The next group of settlers, the Fir Bolg, reputedly divided the island into its five provinces, or *cóiceds,* and ushered in an era of relative peace. They were later defeated by the Tuatha Dé Danann (literally "The People of the Goddess Danu") at the First Battle of Mag Tuired. Suffering the loss of his arm during the battle—grounds for abdication according to Celtic cultural mores—the Tuatha Dé Danann King Núadu stepped down in favor of Bres (whose father was Fomoire and mother Tuatha). Seven years later the Fomoire and Tuatha collided again, this time under the leadership of Balor and the divine Lug, respectively, in the Second Battle of Mag Tuired. Lug defeated Balor and the Fomoire, but the Tuatha later acquiesced to a final group of invaders, the Sons of Míl (corresponding to the modern Irish), whose King, Eremon, forced the Tuatha Dé Danann underground into the so-called *sídh,* or faery mounds, which dot the Irish mythological landscape and serve as entrances to a magical subterranean otherworld.

By far the most popular of the Celtic story cycles, the Fenian Cycle, takes its name from its warrior-hero Fionn mac Cumhaill (sometimes anglicized as Finn MacCool). Considered the "exemplary hero of Ireland," Fionn mac Cumhaill eventually becomes leader of the *fiana*, an elite band of hunter-warriors. Masterful in battle, Fionn possesses the peculiar ability to see clearly into the future and into the past by sucking his thumb—a power granted him when he touched the Salmon of Knowledge, procured by his tutor, the Druid Finegas. The Fenian canon also includes the famous story of *Tóruigheacht Dhiarmada agus Ghráinne*, translated as "The Pursuit of Diarmaid and Gráinne," as well as the tales of Fionn's father, Oisín, who plays an important role in the Fenian tale *Agallamh na Senórach*, "The Colloquy of the Old Men."

The Ulster Cycle features the exploits of the northern King Conchobar mac Nessa and the youthful hero Cú Chulainn. The central story of the cycle, the *Táin Bó Cuailnge*, or "The Cattle Raid at Cooley"—sometimes described as the "Irish *Iliad*"—details an attack on the kingdom of Conchobar mac Nessa by the army of

Queen Medb of Connacht in order to steal the famed Brown Bull of Ulster. With all the warriors of Ulster waylaid by supernatural labor pains, Conchobar's nephew Cú Chulainn agrees to fight the attacking forces of Connacht single-handedly, engaging one champion per day. He defeats all of his opponents, but is later slain by trickery. Other important figures in the Ulster Cycle include the Druid Cathbad, King Fergus mac Roich, the troublemaker Bricriu, and the tragic Deirdre, who takes her own life rather than submit to the killer of her lover, Naoise.

Further sources of tales in the canon of Celtic mythology appear in two important early medieval manuscripts: *Lebor na hUidre*, "The Book of the Dun Cow," and *Lebor Laignech*, called "The Book of Leinster." The former, though fragmentary, contains thirty-seven mythic stories, while the latter includes complete texts of "The Cattle Raid at Fróech" and "The Cattle Raid at Cooley." Many more stories, culled from various sources, including the fourteenth-century text known as *The Yellow Book of Lecan*, have appeared in various modern editions and continue to delight and intrigue contemporary readers and scholars.

OVERVIEWS

Proinsias MacCana (1970)

SOURCE: Introduction to *Celtic Mythology*, The Hamlyn Publishing Group Limited, 1970, pp. 11-18.

[*In the following excerpt, MacCana explores the combination of unity and diversity found in the various branches of Celtic mythology.*]

The Sources

The earliest sources [of Celtic Mythology] are those relating to the Celts of the continent—mainly Gaul—and of Romanised Britain. Unfortunately they have serious shortcomings. Gaulish literature, being purely oral, disappeared with the Gaulish language: we have it on Caesar's authority that the druids of Gaul considered it improper to commit their learning to writing, and on this point he is substantially borne out by the Irish evidence. As a result, since mythology implies narrative of some sort or other, Gaulish mythology, properly speaking, is lost beyond recovery. There remains, of course, a considerable body of residual evidence, but, since by its very nature it is allusive rather than descriptive, or else is reported at second hand, the modern student is frequently in the uncomfortable position of working from the ambiguous to the unknown.

The evidence is of three types: dedicatory inscriptions such as occur throughout the territories occupied by the Romans, plastic representations of Celtic divinities, and observations by classical authors. In the first two categories the great bulk of the material belongs to the Roman period, and consequently it raises difficult problems of interpretation. For example, Gaulish sculpture developed under Greco-Roman influence and it is no easy task to determine precisely to what extent this influence may have affected the motifs of the sculpture as well as its form. As for the classical authors, it is a matter of scholarly opinion how much value should be placed upon their testimony. Most of them derive their information from earlier sources: even Caesar, who had a better opportunity than most to become acquainted with the Gaulish situation, is far from relying on his own experience and observation. And no doubt all of them were influenced to a greater or lesser degree by the forms and concepts of classical religion and mythology. These considerations have led some scholars to reject the classical evidence out of hand, which is probably an excess of scepticism. It should not be forgotten that a number of observations by the same classical authors on matters of Celtic custom and social organisation are corroborated by Irish literature: so closely in fact that certain early Irish tales might almost have been written to illustrate these comments on the continental Celts, and this few scholars would entertain as a serious possibility. The classical evidence therefore merits consideration, but it must be treated with extreme caution.

By way of contrast, the recorded testimony of Irish literature is later by a millenium or more, but, as we have seen, it has a conservative quality which more than outweighs the disparity in date. (The Irish language, despite the later date of its documents, seems in many respects to be more conservative than Gaulish, and the same may well hold true for the mythologies.) The writing down of Irish oral tradition had already commenced by the end of the sixth century, but time and the Viking raiders proved a ruthless combination and only a few manuscript fragments survive from the period before *c.* 1100. Then comes the first of a number of great manuscript compilations which between them preserve a wealth of varied material relating to the Irish past. These manuscripts are themselves relatively late, but they have been compiled from earlier sources and many of the individual items which they contain may be dated on linguistic grounds centuries earlier than their extant transcription. But, irrespective of their date of composition, it is beyond question that these texts contain a vast amount of pre-Christian matter.

Among the tales which formed an important part of the *filidh's* repertoire there are some which concern themselves explicitly with the supernatural world, and for that reason modern scholars sometimes refer to them as the Mythological Cycle. But this is a rather misleading title since in point of fact most early Irish narrative is mythological to a greater or lesser degree. There is much to be said for the native system of classification which groups the individual titles not by cycle but by theme: plunderings, cattle-raids, wooings, battles, voyages, adventures, elopements, etc. But for the sake of brevity the remaining tales may be divided into three broad categories: miscellaneous tales assigned to the reigns of various kings, historic and prehistoric (though this distinction has little relevance to the historicity of their content), the cycle of the Ulaidh or 'Ulstermen' with Conchobhar mac Nessa their king and Cú Chulainn their youthful hero, and finally the cycle of Fionn mac Cumhaill and the roving bands of warriors known as *fiana.*

The Ulster cycle was the literature of greatest prestige in the early period; it is heroic literature *par excellence* and it concerns itself with the activities and virtues that typify heroic society everywhere. By contrast, the Fionn cycle (or *fianaigheacht,* as it is often called) was more popular among the lower orders of society and correspondingly less highly esteemed by the *filidh,* and it is in fact only from the twelfth century, a watershed in Irish history and culture, that it bulks large in the literary record. Nevertheless, its roots lie deep in the pagan past. The great delight of the *fiana,* and their principal activity, is hunting, and this fact alone gives the cycle a quite different temper to that of the Ulster tales. It is predominantly a literature of the open air that ranges far and wide throughout the changing landscape of Ireland, and in due course it becomes a convenient vehicle for numerous nature lyrics.

To this varied collection of tales one must add the pseudo-historical material, and in particular the *Leabhar Gabhála,* 'The Book of Invasions', and the *Dinnshenchas,* 'The History of Places'. The former is a twelfth-century compilation which purports to describe the several invasions of Ireland from the time of the Deluge (and even before it!). It is weak on history but relatively strong on myth. The *Dinnshenchas,* which also belongs to the twelfth century in its definitive form, is a massive collection of onomastic lore 'explaining' the names of well-known places throughout Ireland. Marie-Louise Sjoestedt has characterised the two rather neatly: *Leabhar Gabhála* is the mythological pre-history of the country and the *Dinnshenchas* its mythological geography.

There is enough evidence to indicate that Wales also inherited a rich mythological tradition, but, unfortunately, it is poorly documented. Like Ireland, Wales has its great manuscript compilations, the earliest of them from about the end of the twelfth century, but they do not preserve such a wealth of material from the early period as do their Irish counterparts. This is especially true of prose literature, and the earliest surviving tales, *Culhwch and Olwen* and *The Four Branches,* were probably first written in the eleventh century. The four tales, or 'branches', of the *Mabinogi* constitute one of the most important sources for British mythology. They abound in mythological themes and motifs and their *dramatis personae* are the ancient gods of Britain. Nevertheless, they represent the mere debris of a tradition recast in a loose narrative framework by a talented author who was less interested in preserving sources than in producing an effective piece of literature. There is also a considerable volume of mythological matter scattered throughout the remainder of medieval literature, but clearly any semblance of an integrated mythological tradition had passed away long before the extant literature was recorded. What remains is an imbroglio of anecdotes, allusions, motifs and characters which under close scrutiny gradually reveal the outlines of a number of familiar mythological paradigms within a British setting.

The Welsh evidence derives a special interest from its close association with the great continental cycle of Arthurian romance. Welsh together with Breton literary tradition provided the many Celtic elements incorporated in the Arthurian romances of Chrétien de Troyes and his fellows, and not a little of the enduring fascination of these stories is due to their essentially mythological character. The original Arthur may well have been a historical person, but the King Arthur of medieval romance and his knightly entourage are much larger than life and share many of the mythological traits of the Irish hero Fionn mac Cumhaill and his *fiana.*

The Diversity of Celtic Mythology

To speak of 'Celtic mythology' is not to imply a close unity, but merely to recognise a tangible relationship based upon common inheritance. What we know of the mythology of the continental Celts hardly suggests a sustained correspondence with that of Ireland and Wales, and this cannot be due entirely to the unequal documentation. Even among the insular Celts the differences are, at first glance, much more evident than the underlying similarities. Nor is this very surprising, for a number of reasons: the several peoples in question do not derive from a single community of continental Celts; over the last two thousand years or more they have evolved somewhat differently in their social and cultural organisation; in the case of Britain and Gaul, but not of Ireland, they have been conditioned to the physical presence of Rome over a period of centuries; and, finally, it can safely be presumed that all have assimilated much of the religious thought and usage of the pre-Celtic inhabitants of their several areas.

These considerations go far towards explaining the wide discrepancies between the three visible branches of Celtic mythology. But by themselves they are not sufficient to account for the lack of unity and order which

is so evident within each separate branch. Instead, it has been argued that this incoherence simply reflects the decentralised structure of Celtic society, in which each tribe functioned as an independent political unit, the inference being that political autonomy was coupled with religious autonomy and that each tribe had its own special gods, which might, or might not, be common to neighbouring tribes. It may be that this is in fact one of the causes of what has been described as 'the local and anarchical character' of Celtic mythology, though its effects may well be exaggerated by a defective documentation dating in all cases from a period of drastic readjustment, when native religious usage was exposed to the influence of systems of greater sophistication and prestige.

The Celts being notoriously rich in paradox, it is perhaps not surprising to find that this local independence, which is such a feature of their political organisation, is in some respects counterbalanced by a highly developed sense of cultural affinity among the learned classes. Nowadays we know that what gave the Celts such unity as they possessed was not common racial origins but a common culture and environment. The classical ethnographers identified them—not infallibly it may be said—by their language, their shared characteristics, and their mode of life, as well as by their geographical location, and one can still sense something of this cultural coherence in the remarkable analogies, both of ideas and their expression, in the traditional literatures of Ireland and Wales. What is even more to the point, the druidic order existed throughout the Celtic world and its organisation appears to have been essentially the same in all areas. The cult of the centre to which its members attached such importance epitomises their professional solidarity and their assiduous fostering of an ideological unity transcending the political divisions within each nation or agglomeration of tribes. This is a persistent trait and nowhere is it evidenced more clearly than in post-Norman Ireland where the *filidh* conserved an astonishing cultural unity in a world of political strife and instability.

This faculty for combining unity with diversity, centripetal with centrifugal forces, is no less evident in the mythology. Here the externals present a bewildering variety. The nomenclature continually renews itself even when the underlying concepts remain undisturbed. The myths proliferate in endless narrative variants but their themes are constant and, so far as one can judge, in large measure common to the whole Celtic world. For instance, the theme of divine sovereignty which is such a permanent and such a fundamental element of Irish tradition was also familiar in Britain and in Brittany, though most of the literature to which it gave rise there is known only from occasional allusions. It is this underlying homogeneity that justifies us in speaking of one Celtic mythology rather than of several.

Jeffrey Gantz (1981)

SOURCE: Introduction to *Early Irish Myths and Sagas*, translated by Jeffrey Gantz, Penguin Books, 1981, pp. 1-27.

[*In the following excerpt, Gantz offers an overview of Celtic culture, history, society, religion, and literature.*]

> One day, in winter, Derdriu's foster-father was outside, in the snow, flaying a weaned calf for her. Derdriu saw a raven drinking the blood on the snow, and she said to Lebarcham 'I could love a man with those three colours: hair like a raven, cheeks like blood and body like snow.'
>
> 'The Exile of the Sons of Uisliu' (p. 260)

This passage, from one of the finest stories ever written in Ireland, evinces much of what Irish literature is: romantic, idealistic, stylized and yet vividly, even appallingly, concrete. Most of all, it exemplifies the tension between reality and fantasy that characterizes all Celtic art. In Ireland, this art has taken many forms: illumination (the books of Durrow and Kells), metal work (the Ardagh Chalice and the Tara Brooch), sculpture (the stone crosses at Moone and Clonmacnois), architecture (the Rock of Cashel and the various round towers), music (Turlough O'Carolan). But this tension manifests itself particularly in the literature of Ireland, and most particularly in the myths/sagas—no more precise description is possible, at least for the moment—that survive in Irish manuscripts dating back to the twelfth century.

There are many reasons why this should be so. To begin with, these stories originated in the mists of Irish prehistory (some elements must predate the arrival of the Celts in Ireland), and they developed through the course of centuries until reaching their present manuscript state; consequently, they manage to be both archaic and contemporary. Their setting is both historical Ireland (itself an elusive entity) and the mythic otherworld of the Síde (Ireland's 'faery people', who live in burial mounds called 'síde' and exhibit magical powers), and it is not always easy to tell one from the other. Many of the characters are partially euhemerized gods—that is, they are gods in the process of becoming ordinary mortals—so that, again, it is not easy to tell divine from human.

At bottom, this tension between reality and fantasy is not accidental to the circumstances of literary transmission and formation but rather an innate characteristic, a gift of the Celts. The world of the Irish story is graphic: blood spurts not only from the calf flayed for Derdriu but also from the lips of Anlúan as his head is thrown across a table (in 'The Tale of Macc Da Thó's Pig'); the 'hero' of 'Bricriu's Feast' is tossed from the balcony of his house on to a garbage heap;

the warriors of Ulaid (the Irish name for Ulster) are all but roasted in an iron house (in 'The Intoxication of the Ulaid'). Yet this story-world is also magically bright and achingly beautiful. Two pairs of lovers—Mider and Étaín (in 'The Wooing of Étaín'), and Óengus and Cáer Ibormeith (in 'The Dream of Óengus')—turn into swans. The hero of 'The Destruction of Da Derga's Hostel' can dispatch several hundred foes without even reaching for his weapons; Macc Da Thó's pig is so large that forty oxen can be laid across it. Myth obtrudes upon reality at every turn. In 'The Destruction of Da Derga's Hostel', a bird descends through a skylight, sheds his bird outfit and sleeps with the woman Mess Búachalla, thus fathering the story's hero, Conare Már; in 'The Wooing of Étaín', Mider's wife, Fúamnach, turns her rival Étaín into a scarlet fly; in 'The Wasting Sickness of Cú Chulaind', Cú Chulaind is horsewhipped and then healed by two women from the otherworld (shades of the German women in Fellini's *Casanova*). In these Irish stories, then, the pride and energy of reality are allied with the magic and beauty of fantasy—and the result is infused with a rare degree of idealism. In the otherworld of 'The Wooing of Étaín', not only are bodies white as snow and cheeks red as foxglove, but there is no 'mine' or 'yours'.

The Celts

The traditions of these early Irish stories originated with the Celts, an Indo-European group who are the ancestors of the Irish, the Scots, the Welsh, the Cornish, the Bretons and the people of the Isle of Man. When and where this group first appeared is, rather fittingly, an elusive, even controversial, question. The conservative view, and perhaps the most prevalent, is that the Celts surfaced with the beginning of the Iron Age in Europe, roughly 1000 B.C.; and this is certainly the earliest period in which the archaeological testimony affords positive proof. Myles Dillon and Nora Chadwick, however, propose to date the first Celtic settlements of the British Isles to the early Bronze Age (*circa* 1800 B.C.) and to identify the Beaker Folk as Celts.[1] Leon E. Stover and Bruce Kraig go further still: comparing the Classical descriptions of the Iron Age Celts with what they infer from burials at Stonehenge and Únětice (a cemetery near Prague), they propose to classify 'the Wessex and Únětician warriors as formative Celts' and conclude by claiming that the Celts 'emerged as a dominant people in Europe by the beginning of the third millennium B.C.'[2] The controversy is largely semantic. Wessex as presented by Stover and Kraig does look like an early form of what is described by Posidonius and Caesar, but then so does the heroic society of Homer's *Iliad,* and of course there is no linguistic evidence at all. Presumably, from the beginning of the third millennium on there developed, in Europe and subsequently in Britain and Ireland, heroic societies that gradually became, both culturally and linguistically, Celtic.

In any event, by the beginning or the early part of the first millennium B.C., the Celts clearly had emerged, not as a subset of their Slavic or Germanic or Italic neighbours but as a discrete Indo-European ethnic and cultural group; moreover, during the course of that millennium, they became the dominant people in non-Mediterranean Europe. From their homeland (probably in Bohemia), they expanded westward into France and Spain and, eventually, Britain and Ireland; southward into Italy; and eastward into Turkey, where they became the Galatians of St Paul. These early Celts took with them not only their chariots and their iron swords but also a distinctive geometric/linear art, called Hallstatt (after an important cemetery in Austria). By 500 B.C., a new art form had sprung up, this called La Tène (after a site in Switzerland); much less restrained than its predecessor, La Tène is a kind of baroque development, all curves and spirals and luxuriant plant and animal outgrowths. At this time, too, the Celts began to come under notice of the Classical authors: Herodotos, writing in the mid-fifth century, described the *Keltoí* as tall (by Mediterranean standards) and with light skin and hair and eyes, boastful and vainglorious but demonic in battle, childlike and ostentatious but hospitable, fond of hunting and feasting and music and poetry and glittering jewellery and bright colours; and his impressions were confirmed by subsequent accounts, particularly those attributed to Posidonius in the first century B.C.[3]

With their energy and warlike temperament, the Celts were able to expand quickly; by 390 B.C., they had sacked Rome, and by 279 B.C., Delphi. Many tribes settled in France, where the Romans called them Gauls, but their numbers also included the Boii (Bologna, Bohemia), the Belgae (Belgium) and the Helvetii (Switzerland); moreover, their settlements included Lutetia Parisiorum (Paris), Lugudunum (Lyon), Vindobona (Vienna) and Mediolanum (Milan), and they also named the Sequana (Seine) and the Danuvia (Danube). Unfortunately, Celtic tribal free-spiritedness was no match for Roman civic organization. Caesar's defeat of Vercingetorix, at Alesia in 52 B.C., signalled the decline of the Celts' hegemony in Europe; thereafter, they were overrun and assimilated. As a distinct entity, Celtic language and culture disappeared in Europe (though of course their influence persisted); in Great Britain, the Celtic tribes were driven back into Scotland, Wales and Cornwall (from where they eventually reclaimed Brittany) by the numerous incursions of Romans, Angles/Saxons and Normans.

Ireland was a different story. By virtue of its westerly and isolated geographic position, this island remained free of Roman colonization; thus, Irish society did not change appreciably until the advent of Christianity (in the fifth century) and the arrival of Viking raiders (some time thereafter). Consequently, the culture of the Iron Age Celts survived in Ireland long after it had been extinguished elsewhere. It is this conservatism that makes the early Irish tales, quite apart from their literary value, such a valuable repository of information about the Celtic people.

The Irish

As elusive as the date of the Celts' emergence in Europe is the date of their arrival in Ireland. Such megalithic tombs as Knowth, Dowth and New Grange, which now appear to date from the middle of the fourth millennium, testify to the presence of an indigenous, pre-Celtic culture; but how soon afterwards Celts—even formative Celts—appeared is open to controversy. If the Bell-Beaker people are viewed as proto-Celts, then one might say that they—assuming they reached Ireland as well as Britain—represent the beginnings of Celtic culture in Ireland; against this, archaeological evidence of large-scale immigration to Ireland between 2000 and 600 B.C. is wanting. If the indigenous population evolved into a Celtic one at the behest of a small number of aristocratic invaders, however, no such large-scale immigration would have been necessary. In any event, we know that Celts of the Hallstatt type reached Ireland by the middle of the sixth century and that Celts continued to migrate to Ireland and Britain until the time of the Belgic invasion in the first century B.C.

How and in what form they arrived is even more uncertain. According to Lebor Gabála (The Book of Invasions), our earliest copy of which dates from the twelfth century, Ireland was subjected to six invasions, those of Cessair, Partholón, Nemed, the Fir Bolg, the Túatha Dé Danand and the sons of Mil Espáne. Irish history being what it is, the particulars of the Lebor Gabála account are open to question; what matters is that Ireland was, or was felt to have been, settled by a succession of different tribes. That these people actually arrived in separate waves—as opposed to filtering in more or less continuously—is moot; but the early tales do reflect the existence of different ethnic groups.

The Ireland of these tales is apportioned into four provinces, called, perversely, *cóiceda,* or 'fifths': Ulaid (Ulster), Connachta (Connaught), Lagin (Leinster) and Mumu (Munster). The fifth province was probably Mide (Meath), though there is also a tradition, probably artificial, that Mumu was once two provinces. Either this fifth province was original and disappeared (while the word *cóiced* persisted), or else the original four provinces became five after the emergence of a new power centre. Mide, which encompassed both Bruig na Bóinde (New Grange) and Temuir (Tara), is the setting for the early mythological tales, and this argues for its status as an original province. On the other hand, Mide was also the territory of the Uí Néill, who by the fourth century had supplanted the Ulaid as the dominant power in Ireland; this argues for its being a later addition. Moreover, the name Mide, which means 'middle', looks palpably artificial—of course, the entire province set-up may be artificial.

In any case, there are, in the stories of this volume, four centres of action. Mide, with its numerous burial mounds, is the setting for the early mythological tales. It is peopled by the Túatha Dé Danand (the People of the Goddess Danu), who, though presented by Lebor Gabála as a wave of invaders, appear in these tales as the denizens of the otherworld, the Síde. They interact freely with the ordinary people of the mythological stories, and they also appear in some of the more historical tales. Ulaid, with its capital of Emuin Machae (near present-day Armagh), is the primary setting for the historical (insofar as any of the Irish tales are historical) sagas of the Ulster Cycle; its king is Conchubur son of Ness, but its champion is the mythic hero Cú Chulaind. The arch-enemies of the Ulaid (province names apply to the people as well) are the Connachta, who have their capital at Crúachu, in the west of Ireland. These people may well have originally occupied Mide, for their queen, Medb, is often identified as the daughter of the king of Temuir, and she may once have been a fertility goddess. It also seems more logical that Ulaid's foe should have been centred in adjacent Mide rather than in the distant west; and this in fact would have been true if the Ulster Cycle tales reflect the historical conflict between the Ulaid and the emerging Uí Néill of Mide. The tradition that the Connachta were the enemies of the Ulaid coupled with the fact that Connachta was now the name of Ireland's western province would have given the storytellers sufficient reason to move Medb and her husband, Ailill, from Temuir to Crúachu. Finally, there are the people of Mumu; they play a more peripheral role in the Ulster Cycle, but the king Cú Ruí son of Dáre does figure prominently in several tales.

When the events related in these stories might have taken place is yet another mystery. The Alexandrian geographer Ptolemy, who wrote in the second century A.D. but is believed to have drawn upon sources at least two hundred years older, provides evidence that Ireland was then Celtic-speaking; however, few of his names—and they are restricted both in number and in location—suggest those of our stories, so that one might suppose the people of these stories (insofar as they were real) had not yet appeared. At the other end, the milieu of the tales predates the advent of Christianity, while the circumstances of the Ulster Cycle must predate the Uí Néill appropriation of Emuin Machae. Kenneth Jackson has placed the formation of the Ulster tradition some-

where between the second century B.C. and the fourth century A.D., which seems entirely reasonable.

What Irish life was like during this period is, fortunately, *not* such a difficult question. On the one hand, we have the evidence of the Classical authors, Posidonius (via Diodorus Siculus and Strabo) and Caesar—evidence that was taken from Gaul and Britain but must surely have been valid for the Irish Celts as well. On the other, we have not only the evidence of the stories but also that of the Irish annals and genealogies and law tracts.

What emerges from the collation of this evidence is a culture of extraordinary vitality and beauty. Irish society exhibited the same tripartism that Georges Dumézil perceived elsewhere in the Indo-European world: a warrior class headed by a king; a priestly class (the druids); and a class of farmers and free men. The king of a *túath,* or tribe, was often subject to an over-king, to whom he gave assurances of allegiance and from whom he received some kind of support; the over-king, in turn, might have been subject to his provincial king. (The idea of a high king or king of Ireland is probably a fiction, fabricated by later peoples—notably the Uí Néill—to provide a historical justification for their claim to rule Ireland and perpetuated by the romanticism of subsequent tradition.) Kingship seems originally to have been sacral—indeed, the 'kings' in the mythological tales are barely euhemerized gods. In some traditions, the tribal king was ritually married to the tribal goddess (Medb, for example); in others, he had a sympathetic relationship with the land: if he were healthy and virile, the land would be fertile, while if he were blemished or impotent, the land would become barren. (This Wasteland idea is not, of course, exclusively Celtic.)

In 'The Destruction of Da Derga's Hostel', a druid partakes of the flesh and broth of a slaughtered bull and then lapses into a deep sleep, wherein he is expected to see the form of the new king. In later Irish history, however, the king was chosen from an extended family unit; and his position, continually contested by other family members (just as in fifteenth-century England), was far from secure. Curiously, the kings of the Irish stories are not battle leaders: either they betray vestiges of divinity (Cú Ruí, for example) or they have a young champion as heir and rival. Examples of this second pattern—which reflects the relationship of Agamemnon to Achilles and anticipates those of Arthur to Lancelot and Mark to Tristan—are legion: Mider temporarily loses Étaín to his foster-son Óengus; Conchubur loses Derdriu to the young warrior Noísiu and relinquishes supremacy in battle to Cú Chulaind; Cet rather than King Ailill is the champion of the Connachta.

The second class of Irish society, the priests, is more controversial. Popular notions of white-robed druids overseeing human sacrifices, cutting mistletoe with golden sickles and chanting spells over magic cauldrons persist—and not without reason. But Strabo points out that the druids

> concern themselves with questions of ethics in addition to their study of natural phenomena. And because they are considered the most just of all, they possess the power to decide judicial matters, both those dealing with individuals and those involving the common good. Thus they have been known to control the course of wars, and to check armies about to join battle, and especially to judge cases of homicide. When there is a large number of these last, they suppose there will be a large return from the land as well. And both they and others maintain that the soul and the cosmos are immortal, though at some time in the future fire and water will prevail over them.[4]

Diodorus, moreover, makes mention of

> certain *philosophoi* and religious interpreters, men highly honoured, whom they call Druids . . . It is their custom not to make any sacrifice without one of these *philosophoi,* since they believe that offerings should be rendered to the gods through the agency of those well acquainted with the divine nature (on speaking terms, one might say), and that requests for favours should likewise be made by these same men. In matters of war too the *philosophoi* are readily obeyed, they and the singing bards, and this by enemies as well as their own people. Often, in fact, when battle lines are drawn and armies close ground with swords and spears poised, they will step out into the middle and halt both sides, as if enchanting wild beasts. Thus even among the most savage barbarians, the spirit yields to the arts, and Ares reveres the Muses.[5]

Valuable as they are, these Classical accounts, at second hand and biased, should not be accepted at face value: the druids were, most probably, neither human-sacrificing savages nor great moral philosophers. Certainly, there is no evidence of either role in the Irish tales. In the mythological stories, druids are magicians: in 'The Wooing of Étain', Fúamnach, who has been reared by the druid Bresal, is able to turn her rival, Étaín, into first a pool of water and then a scarlet fly; in 'The Destruction of Da Derga's Hostel', Ingcél's druids bring about Conare's death by making him thirsty. The druids of the Ulster Cycle, however, are little more than wise old men (reminiscent of Nestor), though they claim some power of prophecy. Cathub and Senchae are greatly revered for their sagacity and for their peacemaking ('Bricriu's Feast' and 'The Intoxication of the Ulaid' fully confirm Diodorus's account of druidic intervention between combatants), but they display neither magical powers nor moral phi-

losophy. It seems that the process of becoming a druid was a protracted one—according to Caesar, it could take twenty years—and involved the study of myth/history, law, science, religion and philosophy. Since the Celts in general and the druids in particular were averse to writing their knowledge down (out of fear that it might be corrupted if outsiders found it, but doubtless also because of the druids' desire to preserve their privileged status), all this material had to be memorized. In short, the druids appear to have been the caretakers of whatever knowledge—from magic to science—their people possessed.

The third class of people were free men who farmed and herded. As the clients of a chieftain or other land-owner, they received rent of the land, perhaps some stock, and some protection from enemies; in return, they surrendered a portion of what the land yielded and did some kind of service for their landlord. The upper class of these tenant farmers took possession of the rented stock after seven years; the lower classes did not and were in effect serfs. At the bottom of the social scale were the slaves; these were often people captured from neighbouring tribes, but they do not appear to have been numerous.

Irish society, especially that of the historical tales, was an aristocratic one. The strongholds of the Ulster Cycle—Crúachu and Emuin Machae—are not cities but rather compounds where the king lives with his household and where he regales his chieftains with feasts and entertainments: poets, singers, musicians, jugglers. These strongholds may also have been centres for rounding up stock in autumn and for the holding of annual fairs, such as the one described at the beginning of 'The Wasting Sickness of Cú Chulaind': 'Each year the Ulaid held an assembly: the three days before Samuin and the three days after Samuin and Samuin itself. They would gather at Mag Muirthemni, and during these seven days there would be nothing but meetings and games and amusements and entertainments and eating and feasting.' And drinking. Such a lifestyle dictated an expansionist policy towards one's neighbours, since, in order to distribute wealth to their clients, kings and chieftains first had to accumulate it. Even in the mythological stories, the importance of land and possessions is patent: in 'The Wooing of Étaín', Óengus asserts his right to land from his father, the Dagdae, and it is the wealth of Bruig na Bóinde that enables him to compensate his foster-father, Mider, when the latter is injured.

The Irish year was divided into two parts: winter and summer. The first day of November, called Samuin, was both the first day of winter and the first day of the new year; the feast has since given rise to Hallowe'en/All Saints' Day and contributed the bonfire to Guy Fawkes celebrations. Samuin was a day of changes, of births and deaths; it was an open door between the real world and the otherworld. Óengus (in 'The Wooing of Étaín') dispossesses Elcmar of Bruig na Bóinde at Samuin, and he finds his beloved (in 'The Dream of Óengus') at Samuin. It is at Samuin that Da Derga's hostel is destroyed and Conare Már is slain (the death of a king at Samuin is so common as to suggest regeneration myths and ritual slaying); it is at Samuin that, in 'The Wasting Sickness of Cú Chulaind', beautiful birds appear at Mag Muirthemni and Cú Chulaind is entranced by Fand; it is at Samuin that, in 'The Intoxication of the Ulaid', the Ulaid charge off to the southwest of Ireland and are nearly burnt inside an iron house. Proinsias Mac Cana has called Samuin 'a partial return to primordial chaos . . . the appropriate setting for myths which symbolise the dissolution of established order as a prelude to its recreation in a new period of time';[6] and there can be no doubt that Samuin was the most important day of re-creation and rebirth in Ireland.

The first day of May, called Beltene, marked the beginning of summer; this feast has since given rise to May Eve/Walpurgisnacht and May Day. Beltene was a less important day, and, consequently, less information about it has survived; the name seems to mean 'fire of Bel' (Bel presumably being the Irish descendant of the continental god Belenos) or 'bright fire', and there is a tradition that cattle were driven between two fires on this day so that the smoke would purify them. In any case, the rites of Beltene were probably directed towards ensuring the fertility of land and stock. The Welsh hero Pryderi is born on the first of May, and this fact coupled with the unusual circumstances of his birth (the concurrent birth of colts, the otherworld visitor) suggests that Beltene was also a day when the real and the fantastic merged.

The beginnings of spring and autumn were also celebrated, but even less is known about these holidays. Imbolg, which fell on the first of February, seems to have been the beginning of the lambing season; it is also associated with the goddess Brigit (Briganti in Britain), whose successor, Saint Brighid, has her feast day, significantly, on the first of February. Lugnasad, which fell on the first of August, was named after the god Lug and seems to have been a harvest festival; if so, it was probably a late addition, since harvest time (that is, the end of the grazing season) in a pastoral (as opposed to an agrarian) community would have fallen closer to Samuin. In any case, the opening sentences of 'The Wasting Sickness of Cú Chulaind' show that the annual autumn round-up and assembly of the Ulaid took place at Samuin.

For Celtic and Irish religion, there is a wealth of evidence: the testimony of the Classical writers, especially Caesar; that of Gaulish sculpture and inscriptions; and that of the surviving Welsh and Irish myths. The resultant picture, however, is far from clear. Cae-

sar identifies a Gaulish pantheon headed by Mercury and including Apollo, Mars, Jupiter and Minerva; corroborating evidence is so absent, however, that one has to suspect he is simply pinning Roman tails on a Celtic donkey.[7] It is the Gaulish sculptures and inscriptions (we have no stories, unfortunately) that attest to the true nature of Celtic religion: no pantheon, but rather localized deities with localized functions; and this accords with what we know of the Celts politically, for they had little tolerance for centralized authority, even their own. The more widespread and possibly more important deities include Lugos (Mercury in Caesar, Lug in Ireland, Lleu in Wales; he gave his name to Lyon, Leiden and Liegnitz (Legnica), as well as to the Irish autumn festival of Lugnasad); Belenos, whose name means 'bright' and who might have been a rough counterpart to Apollo; Maponos (Mabon in Wales, the Macc Óc in Ireland; his name means 'great son'); Ogmios, whom Lucian describes as the Gaulish Herakles and as a god of eloquence;[8] Cernunnos, whose name means 'horned' and who presumably is the horned figure on the Gundestrup cauldron; and Epona, a goddess whose name means 'great horse'. Much attention has been given to the trio of Esus, Taranis and Teutates in Lucan[9] and to the sacrifices with which they allegedly were appeased (hanging, burning and drowning, respectively), but their true importance is uncertain. Evidence as to how these and other Celtic gods (who are literally too numerous to mention) related to each other—the kind of testimony we find in Greek mythology—is totally lacking.

The evidence of the Irish tales, our third and final source, is abundant, but it has suffered from faulty transmission, political distortion, historical overlays and church censorship; the result is no clearer than that from the continent. The Ireland of the tales comprises two worlds, 'real' and 'other'; but the line between them is not well demarcated. Even the location of the otherworld—which should not be confused with the Classical underworld—is uncertain: sometimes it is to the west, over the sea; sometimes it is in the southwest of Ireland (where it may be called the 'House of Dond', Dond being a chthonic deity); but usually it is found in the great pre-Celtic burial mounds of the Síde, of which the most important in the tales is Bruig na Bóinde, today's New Grange. The Irish otherworld is, not surprisingly, a stylized, idealized version of the real one: everyone is beautiful, and there is an abundance of beautiful things, and the joys of life are endless—hunting, feasting, carousing, perhaps even love. Paradoxically (of course), though this otherworld makes the real one seem a shadow by comparison, it is the Síde who are the shadows, for they have no physical strength for fighting; just as Pwyll, in 'Pwyll Lord of Dyved', is asked to fight on behalf of the otherworld ruler Arawn, so Cú Chulaind, in 'The Wasting Sickness of Cú Chulaind', is asked to fight on behalf of the otherworld ruler Labraid Lúathlám. The Síde are distinguished primarily by their power of transformation: they move invisibly, or they turn themselves (and others) into birds and animals. But they exert no moral authority, and, while they can injure and heal, they do not have that power over life and death characteristic of the Greek Olympians. Often they seem just like ordinary humans.

Relatively few of the names from Gaulish inscriptions reappear in Ireland—given the decentralized nature of Gaulish religion, this is not surprising. Lug is the major figure in 'The Second Battle of Mag Tured', but in the stories included in this volume he appears prominently only as the father of Cú Chulaind. The Macc Óc is a central character in both 'The Wooing of Étaín' and 'The Dream of Óengus', but he has been so thoroughly euhemerized that there is no trace of the Gaulish Maponos; and such names as the Dagdae, Mider, Bóand, Étaín, Cáer Ibormeith, Medb and Cú Ruí have no apparent continental counterparts. Many of the quasi-divine figures in these tales are associated with animals or with natural features. The name Bóand, for example, means 'white cow'; but Bóand is also the Irish name of the river Boyne. At the outset of 'The Wooing of Étaín', Bóand sleeps with the Dagdae, whose other name, Echu, means 'horse'; Frank O'Connor saw this 'love affair' between a horse god and a cow goddess as a reconciliation between Bronze Age invaders and the indigenous Neolithic civilization, which gives some idea of how old these stories might be.[10] Like Rhiannon in 'Pwyll Lord of Dyved', Macha of 'The Labour Pains of the Ulaid' is a euhemerized horse goddess; and the same may be conjectured of Étaín, whose epithet Échrade means 'horse troop'. A number of the Síde appear as birds: Mider and Étaín leave Temuir as swans, and Óengus (Mider's foster-son) and Cáer Ibormeith return to Bruig na Bóinde as swans; Conare Már's unnamed father discloses himself to Mess Búachalla in the form of a bird; and Fand and Lí Ban first present themselves to Cú Chulaind as birds.

Strabo's testimony, the evidence of lavish grave goods buried with the wealthy, and the identification of the Boyne burial mounds as the dwelling place of the Síde all suggest that the Irish did believe in a life after death. But the Irish otherworld was not simply an anticipated joyful afterlife; it was also—even primarily—an alternative to reality, a world that the hero might enter upon the invitation of a king or a beautiful woman. Inasmuch as this otherworld, no matter how beautiful, is not quite human (there is, for example, no winter), the hero never stays; but the alternative—and thus the tension—is always present.

Finally, there is the language, as beautiful and elusive as any aspect of Irish culture. Just as the Celts were a distinct Indo-European entity, so their languages formed an independent branch of the Indo-European language tree; nonetheless, Celtic is more like Italic (that is, the

Romance languages) than it is like any of the other Indo-European language groups, and many place and personal names in Gaulish are very similar to those in Latin. For example, the Gaulish suffix -*rix* (as in Vercingetorix) is the counterpart of the Latin word *rex,* both meaning 'king'.

In the British Isles, the Celtic languages divided into two groups, one spoken primarily in Britain (and comprising Welsh and, eventually, Cornish and Breton), the other spoken primarily in Ireland (and comprising Irish Gaelic and, eventually, Scottish Gaelic and Manx Gaelic). The most obvious (though not necessarily the most important or fundamental) difference between the two groups is that Indo-European q^u became *p* in the British languages (the word for 'four' was *petwar*) and *c* in the Irish group ('four' was *cethair*).

At the time our stories are purported to have taken place—which is to say any time before the fourth century—the Irish language probably looked a good deal like Gaulish and not so very different from Latin. By the time these stories were being written down, however—and this could have begun as early as the seventh century—drastic changes had taken place: many final syllables had dropped away, many medial vowels had disappeared and many medial consonants had been simplified or lightened. Thus, the word for 'horse', *equus* in Latin, had become *ech* in Ireland at this time. The language of the tales, then, is quite different from that of the time they describe; and this makes the correlation of the stories' proper names with those in earlier sources (such as Ptolemy's geography) even more difficult. Although the syntax of the new language was straightforward, the morphology was not: regular verb conjugations often looked wildly irregular, and word roots occasionally disappeared altogether. The principles of phonetic change were aesthetic rather than semantic; the resultant language was soft and subtle, verb poor but noun-and-adjective rich, static and yet vital.

Irish Storytelling

Irish literature—meaning whatever was written down in Irish—of this time encompassed a broad area, including history, genealogy and law tracts; but it is poetry and narrative prose that are relevant to the early Irish myths and sagas. The earliest poetry was alliterative and syllabic, with end-rhyme appearing later. In Welsh literature, there are epics told entirely through the medium of verse—the *Gododdin,* for example; in Ireland, however, the storytelling medium is invariably prose. Some of the very archaic poetry is essential to the tales in which it appears; thus, the rhetorics in the early part of 'The Cattle Raid of Cúailnge' help to clarify the relationship among Ailill, Medb and Fergus.[11] The poetry in 'The Exile of the Sons of Uisliu', on the other hand, reinforces the narrative, adds detail—mostly descriptive—and provides weight; but it could be omitted without loss of sense. Conceivably these myths/sagas were at one time recited entirely in verse; what remains, however, is largely decorative.

The earliest form of transmission must have been oral. Storytelling was a favourite entertainment among the Celts, and one version of 'The Voyage of Bran' states that Mongan (an Ulaid king who died about A.D. 625) was told a story by his *fili* (a kind of poet) every winter night from Samuin to Beltene. Presumably, the storytellers did not memorize entire tales—rather, they memorized the outlines and filled in the details extemporaneously. Eventually, perhaps as early as the seventh century, the tales began to be transcribed; and thereby two processes, rather opposite in effect, were initiated. In many cases, tales are reworked and acquire a literary veneer; this is certainly true of the Book of Leinster opening to 'The Cattle Raid of Cúailnge', and it would seem to apply to 'The Cattle Raid of Fróech' and to the concluding section of 'The Wasting Sickness of Cú Chulaind'. But these same tales have also deteriorated considerably by the time they reach our earliest (twelfth-century) surviving manuscripts. This deterioration is not likely to have originated with the storytellers themselves, for a long tale would naturally be prolonged over several evenings (which would be in the storyteller's interest, since during that time he would be enjoying his host's hospitality); and in any case, as James Delargy has pointed out, no audience would 'have listened very long to the story-teller if he were to recite tales in the form in which they have come down to us'.[12] The people who wrote these stories down, however, were—for the most part—not literary artists; and of course, they lacked the incentive of an appreciative (and remunerative) audience. Banquet-hall transcription cannot have been easy, and the scribe doubtless grew weary before the storyteller did; consequently, it is not surprising that spelling is erratic, that inconsistencies abound (this could also result from a storyteller's attempting to conflate multiple traditions) and that many tales deteriorate after a promising beginning. Some formulaic passages, such as in 'The Destruction of Da Derga's Hostel', are represented simply by 'et reliqua'. As manuscripts were recopied, moreover, additional errors inevitably appeared. Some areas are manifestly corrupt, and in the case of the archaic poetic sections it seems doubtful whether the scribes understood what they were writing. All this is hardly surprising—just consider the problems attendant upon the texts of Shakespeare's plays, only four hundred years old—but it should be remembered that what survives in the manuscripts, however beautiful, is far from representative of these stories at their best.

The Irish Manuscripts

The language of these tales varies considerably as to date; but at its oldest, and allowing for some degree of deliberate archaism, it appears to go back to the eighth

century; one may assume the tales were being written down at least then, if not earlier. Unfortunately, Scandinavian raiders were legion in Ireland at this time, and they tended to destroy whatever was not worth taking away; consequently, very few manuscripts predating A.D. 1000 have survived. Among the missing is the Book of Druimm Snechtai, which belonged to the first part of the eighth century and included 'The Wooing of Étaín', 'The Destruction of Da Derga's Hostel' and 'The Birth of Cú Chulaind'.

Of the manuscripts that have survived, the two earliest and most important for these tales belong to the twelfth century. Lebor na huidre (The Book of the Dun Cow) is so called after a famous cow belonging to St Cíaran of Clonmacnois; the chief scribe, a monk named Máel Muire, was slain by raiders in the Clonmacnois cathedral in 1106. Unfortunately, the manuscript is only a fragment: though sixty-seven leaves of eight-by-eleven vellum remain, at least as much has been lost. Lebor na huidre comprises thirty-seven stories, most of them myths/sagas, and includes substantially complete versions of 'The Destruction of Da Derga's Hostel', 'The Birth of Cú Chulaind', 'The Wasting Sickness of Cú Chulaind' and 'Bricriu's Feast' as well as an incomplete 'Wooing of Étaín' and acephalous accounts of 'The Intoxication of the Ulaid' and 'The Cattle Raid of Cúailnge'.

The second manuscript, which is generally known as the Book of Leinster, is much larger, having 187 nine-by-thirteen leaves; it dates to about 1160 and includes in its varied contents complete versions of 'The Cattle Raid of Fróech', 'The Labour Pains of the Ulaid', 'The Tale of Macc Da Thó's Pig' and 'The Exile of the Sons of Uisliu' as well as an unfinished and rather different 'Intoxication of the Ulaid' and a complete, more polished 'Cattle Raid of Cúailnge'. Two later manuscripts also contribute to this volume: the Yellow Book of Lecan, which offers complete accounts of 'The Wooing of Étaín' and 'The Death of Aífe's Only Son' and dates to the fourteenth century; and Egerton 1782, which includes 'The Dream of Óengus' and has the date 1419 written on it.

These manuscripts do not, of course, date the stories they contain. Our earliest complete version of 'The Wooing of Étaín' appears in the fourteenth-century Yellow Book of Lecan, yet we have a partial account in the twelfth-century Lebor na huidre, and we know from the contents list of the Book of Druimm Snechtai that the tale was in written form by the early eighth century. What we do not know—and probably never will—is whether the Druimm Snechtai version was very different from the one in the Yellow Book of Lecan, whether the tale assumed written form earlier than in the eighth century, and what the tale was like before it was first written down. Even the surviving manuscripts, which we are fortunate to have, are far from ideal:

obscure words abound, some passages seem obviously corrupt, and there are lacunae and entire missing leaves.

The Irish Material

Convention and tradition have classified the early Irish tales into four groups, called cycles: (1) the Mythological Cycle, whose protagonists are the Síde and whose tales are set primarily among the burial mounds of the Boyne Valley; (2) the Ulster Cycle, which details the (purportedly historical) exploits of the Ulaid, a few centuries before or after the birth of Christ; (3) the Kings Cycle, which focuses on the activities of the 'historical' kings; (4) the Find Cycle, which describes the adventures of Find mac Cumaill and his fíana and which did not achieve widespread popularity until the twelfth century. Although these categories are useful, it should be remembered that they are also modern (no particular arrangement is apparent in the manuscripts, while it seems that the storytellers grouped tales by type—births, deaths, cattle raids, destructions, visions, wooings, etc.—for ease in remembering) and artificial. Characters from one cycle often turn up in another: the Síde-woman Bóand is introduced as Fróech's aunt in the Ulster Cycle's 'Cattle Raid of Fróech'; the otherworld-figure Manandán appears in the Ulster Cycle's 'Wasting Sickness of Cú Chulaind' and in the Kings Cycle's 'Adventures of Cormac'; Ulaid warriors join the invaders in the Mythological Cycle's 'Destruction of Da Derga's Hostel'; Ailill and Medb, king and queen of Connachta, take part in the Mythological Cycle's 'Dream of Óengus'. Also, one should not suppose that the Mythological Cycle is populated exclusively by deities or that the other cycles are inhabited exclusively by mortals: many of the 'humans' are barely euhemerized gods, many of the 'gods' behave much like humans, and the two groups are often difficult to distinguish.

The material of these tales encompasses both impacted myth and corrupted history. Although Irish mythology does evince the tripartism detected by Georges Dumézil in other Indo-European cultures ('The Second Battle of Mag Tured' is on one level an explanation of how the priests and warriors—Dumézil's first two functions—wrested the secrets of agriculture from the third function, the farmers), its fundamental orientation seems more seasonal than societal, for the mythic subtexts of the tales focus on themes of dying kings and alternating lovers. (This strong pre-Indo-European element in Irish mythology probably derives both from the Celts' innate conservatism and from the fringe position of Ireland in the geography of the Indo-European world.) These themes are stated most clearly in 'The Wooing of Étaín' and 'The Exile of the Sons of Uisliu'. In the former story, Bóand passes from her husband, Elcmar, to the Dagdae (also called Echu) and then returns to Elcmar; Étaín goes from Mider to Óengus and back to Mider, from Echu Airem to Ailill Angubae and back

to Echu, and from Echu Airem to Mider and back (in some versions) to Echu. In the latter tale, Derdriu passes from an old king, Conchubur, to a young hero, Noísiu, and back to Conchubur after Noísiu's death; when Conchubur threatens to send her to Noísiu's murderer, she kills herself. Sometimes, the woman's father substitutes for the dying king (this variant appears in the Greek tales of Jason and Medea and Theseus and Ariadne): Óengus has to win Étaín away from her father in 'The Wooing of Étaín' and Cáer Ibormeith away from hers in 'The Dream of Óengus'; Fróech has to win Findabair from Ailill and Medb—but primarily, and significantly, from Ailill—in 'The Cattle Raid of Fróech', while Cú Chulaind has to win Emer from Forgall in 'The Wooing of Emer'. Sometimes, the dying king is absent, and the regeneration theme is embodied in the wooing of a mortal hero by a beautiful otherworld woman (whom he often loses or leaves): Cáer Ibormeith seeks out Óengus in 'The Dream of Óengus', Macha comes to Crunniuc in 'The Labour Pains of the Ulaid', Fand appears to Cú Chulaind in 'The Wasting Sickness of Cú Chulaind'. (This variant persists even into the Find Cycle, where Níam's wooing of Oisín becomes the basis of Yeats's 'The Wanderings of Oisín'.) And sometimes the theme treats only of the dying king: in 'The Destruction of Da Derga's Hostel', Conare Már is slain, at Samuin, in the hostel of a chthonic red god; in 'The Intoxication of the Ulaid', Cú Chulaind is nearly burnt, also at Samuin, in an iron house in the southwest of Ireland (where the House of Dond, an Irish underworld deity, was located). Centuries of historical appropriation and Christian censorship notwithstanding, these regeneration themes are never far from the narrative surface; and in their ubiquitousness is apparent their power.

As history, the early Irish tales verge upon wishful thinking, if not outright propaganda. The Ulster Cycle, however, does appear to preserve genuine traditions of a continuing conflict between the Ulaid (who appear to have concentrated in the area round present-day Armagh) and the Uí Néill (who were probably centred at Temuir, though for reasons suggested earlier they have been moved to present-day Connaught by the storytellers); in any case, it is a valuable repository of information about the Ireland of prehistory—what Kenneth Jackson has called 'a window on the Iron Age'[13]—with its extensive descriptions of fighting (chariots are still the norm) and feasting (an abundance of strong words and strong drink) and dress (opulent, at least for the aristocracy) and its detailing of such institutions as fosterhood, clientship and the taking of sureties. The important but not very surprising conclusion generated by this information is that the Irish society represented by the Ulster Cycle is still very similar to the Gaulish civilization described by Caesar; and there are good reasons to think it not very different from the Celtic world of an even earlier period.

What is surprising, though, is that these tales—which betray a natural and unmistakable bias towards the Ulaid and against the Connachta—do not more consistently depict Ulster society at its zenith. Cú Chulaind is the only true hero in the Ulster Cycle, and his deeds are more often superhuman than heroic; Conchubur, as early as 'The Boyhood Deeds of Cú Chulaind', serves notice that he will be largely a *roi fainéant;* and among the Ulaid warriors there is, 'The Cattle Raid of Cúailnge' excepted, more talk than action. Odder still, in many of the best-known and most important tales, there are clear instances of parody. In 'The Death of Aífe's Only Son', the Ulaid are awestruck by the feats of a seven-year-old boy; in 'The Tale of Macc Da Thó's Pig', Ulaid and Connachta are reduced to fighting over a dog (at least, in 'The Cattle Raid of Cúailnge', the bone of contention is a bull), and the Ulaid are ridiculed and put to shame by the Connachta champion; in 'The Intoxication of the Ulaid', Cú Chulaind loses his way and leads the Ulaid on a drunken spree across Ireland, while the two druids guarding Cú Ruí's stronghold bicker and quarrel; and in 'Bricriu's Feast', the wives of the Ulaid warriors squabble over precedence in entering the drinking hall, while Bricriu is accidentally flung out of his house and on to a garbage dump. Conchubur's treachery (equivalent to Arthur's murdering Lancelot) in 'The Exile of the Sons of Uisliu' eliminates any doubt: the society of the Ulster Cycle, for all the splendour that attaches to it, is a society in decline.

Notes

[1] Myles Dillon and Nora Chadwick, *The Celtic Realms* (New York: New American Library, 1967), pp. 1-2, 214.

[2] Leon E. Stover and Bruce Kraig, *Stonehenge: The Indo-European Heritage* (Chicago: Nelson-Hall, 1978), p. 141.

[3] Herodotos, 2:33.

[4] Strabo, *Geographia,* 4.4.4 (translation by Timothy Gantz).

[5] Diodorus Siculus, 5: 31.2, 4-5 (translation by Timothy Gantz).

[6] Proinsias Mac Cana, *Celtic Mythology* (London: Hamlyn, 1970), p. 127.

[7] Julius Caesar, *De bello gallico,* 6.17.

[8] Lucian, *Herakles,* 1.1.

[9] Lucan, *De bello civili,* 1.444-6.

[10] Frank O'Connor, *The Backward Look: A Survey of Irish Literature* (London: Macmillan, 1967), p. 242.

[11] A rhetoric is a dense, archaic poetic passage.

[12] James Delargy, *The Gaelic Story-teller* (London: G. Cumberlege, 1947), p. 32.

[13] K. H. Jackson, *The Oldest Irish Tradition: A Window on the Iron Age* (Cambridge: Cambridge University Press, 1964).

Jaan Puhvel (1987)

SOURCE: "Celtic Myth," in *Comparative Mythology,* The Johns Hopkins University Press, 1987, pp. 166-88.

[*In the following excerpt, Puhvel compares early Celtic mythology—from Julius Caesar's writings on the gods of Gaul, to Ireland's mythic history and the stories of the Ulster and Fenian Cycles—with the mythologies of other Indo-European cultures.*]

"The Dead prevailed in testimony over the Living, since preference was given to the written word." This denunciation of the dead letter as against vivifying live speech occurs in an Irish tale about the falsification of the inscribed name on a famous sword, a forgery that impressed the judges more than the rightful owner's oral testimony. It is a late reflex of the well-known druidic aversion to writing mentioned by Caesar in *De bello Gallico,* a priestly attitude not unlike that of the Vedic brahmins. Both cultures had early access to writing (India from age-old contacts with Mesopotamia, Gaul since the founding of Massilia [= Marseilles] and other Greek colonies on the "French Riviera" about 600 B.C.E.) but chose not to make large-scale use of it until a later period (Epic India and the coming of Christianity respectively; in the wake of Saint Patrick, Irish monks would scribble furiously all over western Europe, as if to make up for centuries of self-imposed Celtic illiteracy). This tabu against writing may be based on dogma that lingered in the farthest east-west reaches of the Indo-European continuum, as did the archaic items of vocabulary discussed in chapter 3 (Vedic *rāj-*: Gaulish *rīg-* 'king', etc.). Caesar reports druidic teachings of metempsychosis, and India was of course the prime and expanding locus of transmigrational lore. Perhaps the transmission of the sacred text was held to be analogous to the progress of the individual and collective soul, with each successive generation rejuvenating and reincarnating the Word. Such sanctification of orality contrasts with the codificational trends first in evidence in the ancient Near East. Likewise the evidence for open-air divine service makes an impression of expansiveness, as opposed to an ever more centripetal focusing on some boxed-in holy of holies. In this latter respect the northern peoples (Celtic, Germanic,

Baltic, Slavic) hewed to a seemingly old pattern, while Italy and Greece had already been strongly internalized by their Mediterranean-Near Eastern exposure.

Chapter 3 outlined the main phases of Celtic protohistory. It was the first great Indo-European migration traceable by historical as well as archeological means, but owing to its own essential illiteracy it remains hazily penumbral. Although the Celts managed to disperse themselves as far afield as Galatia (the old Hittite heartland in central Asia Minor), they were essentially ensconced in central and western Europe, with evanescent excrescences into Italy and Spain and more durable migrations into the British Isles. Pressed by Romanization and Germanic migrations, they were gradually squeezed to the northwestern fringes of Europe. The Celts are thus truly "marginal"; there were never other early Indo-Europeans to the west or north of them, and they were shielded by geography and choice against the impact of Mediterranean civilization. If sedentariness had been their virtue, coupled with early literacy, they would have been an extraordinary source for Western Indo-European archaism. As it is, one must arduously forage for scraps of their early traditions.

In moving westward through the Indo-European continuum, it appears that the social class divisions of priests, warriors, and cultivators, so pronounced in Vedic India in conjunction with pantheonic structures, and subsequently rigidified, played a much less pervasive part in Iranian tradition and were hardly in evidence in Greece and Rome. Despite some echoes here and there in religious, legendary, ideal, or real patterns, neither Greek (Dorian, Ionian, later Athenian) "tribal" divisions nor the Roman patrician: plebeian dichotomy preserved much of the prehistoric setup. Not so among the Celts, where Caesar separated the Gauls into *druides* (priests), *milites* (warriors), and *miserrima plebs* (wretched masses), or early Ireland, where the druids (cf. Vedic *brahmán-*), the *fláith* ('dominion'; cf. Vedic *ksatrám*), and the *bō airig* ('cow freemen'; cf. Sanskrit *ārya-ka-* and Avestan *vāstryō-fšuyant-*) are uncannily reminiscent of the Indo-Iranian kind. Unlike Germanic society, where the system had been broken by the virtual disappearance of the priestly class, the tripartite societal pattern lingered on in its insular Celtic holding tank, and by the end of the first millennium it experienced a remarkable recrudescence in Anglo-Saxon England. About 900, in his own Old English version of Boethius's *Consolation of Philosophy*, King Alfred the Great divided a ruler's subjects into *gebeðmen, fyrðmen,* and *weorcmen,* which Aelfric and Wulfstan echoed a century later by *oratores, bellatores,* and *laboratores.* Just as the Celtic-Germanic symbiosis in England had saved the tradition, the Norse superstrate on both sides of the Channel (culminating in the Norman invasion of 1066) facilitated its spread to the north of France during the eleventh century,

whence it expanded to form the basis of the medieval European and later three estates, which in France lasted as the basis of society down to the revolution of 1789. This is another illustration of the insidious power of Celtic persistence, not unlike its substratal ability to overhaul a seemingly triumphant Latin into subsequently unintelligible French (see chap. 3).

Our written knowledge of the Gaulish pantheon begins with Caesar (*De bello Gallico* 6.16-17), who credits the Gauls with plenty of religious practices and enumerates their gods in Roman interpretation, with brief characterizations: "Of gods they worship Mercury most" as the *omnium inventorem artium* 'inventor of all skills', next Apollo (dispelling disease), Mars (in charge of war), Jupiter (holding sway in the heavens), and Minerva (originator of arts and crafts). This is a strangely unhelpful grab bag, notable for the low ranking of "Jupiter" and the preeminence of "Mercury," whose functions seem to overlap with Minerva's at the end; but Caesar was not doing systematic ethnography; he was merely padding an otherwise meager annual military report to the Senate with curious detail about the natives of Gaul. Caesar's account acquires some systematic meaning only by comparison with subsequent sources. A century or so later the poet Lucan (*Pharsalia* 3.399-425) depicted a blood-spattered sacred grove at Massilia and (1.444-46) described human sacrifice among the Gauls:

> immitis placatur sanguine diro
> Teutates, horrensque feris altaribus Esus,
> et Taranis Scythicae non mitior ara Dianae

> harsh Teutates is cruelly propitiated
>   with blood,
> and dread Esus on savage platforms,
> and the altar of Taranis, a match for that of
>   the Scythian Diana[1]

Later commentators on Lucan supplied their own Roman interpretations for Teutates, Esus, and Taranis, either Mars, Mercurius, and Jupiter or Mercurius, Mars, and Dispater (the ruler of the Otherworld, whom according to Caesar the Gauls claimed as their ancestor). Caesar also mentioned huge wickerwork dummies inside which human victims were burned, which chimes with the information of Lucan's commentators that Teutates' victims were drowned in casks, those of Esus were hanged and lacerated, and those of Taranis were burned. At this point the names begin to be informative:

Teutātes (Toutates, Totates, Tutates) is derived from **tewta* 'people' (Old Irish *tūath,* Oscan *touto,* Gothic *thiuda*) and thus resembles in meaning the Umbrian Vofione and the Roman Quirinus.

Ēsus may mean simply 'Lord' and be cognate with Latin *erus* 'master' (with rhotacism); yet there is also the variant form *Aesus,* pointing to an original diphthong.

Taranis is cognate with the *u*-stem **taranu-* seen in Old Irish *torann,* Welsh *taran* 'thunder' (Taran is a man's name in the Welsh *Mabinogi,* and there was a Christianized Saint Taran in Brittany). The Celtic *taran-* is metathetic for *tanar-* (= Germanic **thunar-* 'thunder'), as seen in the inscription *J(ovi) O(ptimo) M(aximo) Tanaro* (Chester, England, 154 C.E.; *Corpus Inscriptionum Latinarum* 7.168).

People's god, lord, thunderer—this descriptively named triad does not sound very compatible with the Roman Jupiter, Mars, Quirinus, which explains the wretched results of the Roman interpretation. Teutates may somehow fit the third-estate or "collective" slot of Quirinus, but the relatively low estate of Caesar's "Jupiter" shows that Taranis is no head of the pantheon, rather a thunder-god with either wheel (= thunderball) or spiral (= thunderbolt) as emblem, of the order of the Norse Thor (< **Thunaraz*). Equating Esus with Mars makes no particular sense either, once it is clear that Taranis is no match for Jupiter. But the alternative interpretation of Esus as "Mercury" is interesting on several counts:

1. In Tacitus's Roman interpretation of the Germanic pantheon, too, "they worship Mercury most," and there "Mercury" reflects with certainty the great god **Wōðanaz,* the Norse Odin (see chap. 11).

2. Esus is homologous with the Norse Odin in receiving human sacrifices by hanging, whereas the victims of Teutates were drowned, in the manner of offerings to the Germanic fertility deities, for example, Tacitus's Nerthus (see chap. 11) or the man being plunged headlong into a vat in a cultic scene depicted in high relief on the inside of the Gundestrup cauldron, a Celtic silver-plated copper vessel found in a Danish peatbog (first century B.C.E.).

3. Granted "Mercury's" pride of place on Caesar's list, it is possible that "Mercury" = Esus is the high god of the Gaulish pantheon, above Taranis and Teutates.

Esus has mythologically significant iconography. The "Paris Altar," datable to the time of Christ and found in 1711 under the choir of the cathedral of Notre Dame de Paris (now in the Musée des Thermes at the site of the Roman baths of Lutetia Parisiorum), depicts on two sides Taranis (inscription *Jovis*) and *Volcanus,* and on a third the bearded, ax-wielding god Esus cutting a tree. The fourth panel shows a similar leafy tree protruding from behind a bull on whom three birds are perched, surmounted by the inscription *Tarvos Trigaranus* 'Bull with Three Cranes'. On an analogous relief from Trier (now in the Landesmuseum there) a woodcutter is felling a tree with a bull's head and

three birds on top of its foliage. At the basis of this depiction may lie some lost myth reminiscent of Indra's killing of Triśiras, as told in Yajurvedic texts and especially in book 5 of the *Mahābhārata,* how Indra struck down the adversary with his bolt, but then enlisted the services of a woodcutter who completed the slaying by severing the three heads with his ax, whereupon birds (woodcock, partridge, and sparrow) escaped through the three necks. Tricephalic representations are common in Celtic iconography, but in the absence of texts, the full meaning of the Gaulish scene is bound to remain opaque.

The figure of Esus can perhaps be brought together with the theonym *Lugus,* which lurks in toponyms (*Lugu-dunum* 'Lugus town' > Lyons in France, Leiden in Holland, etc.), and with the Irish Lug (discussed further below) who was the all-around man of skill (*samildānach;* cf. "Mercury" as *omnium inventor artium*). Lug was the father of Cúchulainn in Irish saga, even as Odin was the sire of prominent Norse heroes; likewise *Esugenus* 'Begotten of Esus' was a Gaulish name of nobility. When Lugudunum = Lyons became the capital of Gaul, Augustus fixed his own imperial feast day there on 1 August, which was the date of the festival of Lugnasad in Irish lore and presumably had been the holy day of the town's eponym; the emperor "usurped" the antecedent cult, much as later Notre Dame de Paris rose on the emplacement of a sanctuary of Esus and Taranis.

Esus-Lugus, Taranis, and Teutates as a triad receiving human sacrifices may thus roughly match the Scandinavian set of Odin, Thor, and Freyr in pagan Sweden, who were given human victims at Uppsala up to the Christianization in the eleventh century (see chap. II). They, like Jupiter-Mars-Quirinus, were a stylized Western Indo-European embodiment of the erstwhile tripartite pantheon, thus a match for the Eastern structure first glimpsed at Mitanni (Mitra-Varuna, Indra, Nāsatya; see chaps. 3 and 4). Around their axis swarmed the rest of the pantheon. "Mars" takes on more sense in two directions. There is epigraphic attestation of *Mars Teutates* (e.g., *Marti Toutati*) who, like the rural Roman Mars, seems more a patron of peace and fertility than a war-god, warding off plague, invasion, and blight alike. At the same time, "Mars" and "Mercury" alternated in Lucan's scholiasts as interpretations of Teutates and Esus, and in inscriptions both take similar epithets (e.g., Vellaunus, of unknown meaning). Thus "Mars" may hide yet another divine figure, structurally akin to Esus-Lugus and perhaps partially syncretized with him. One thinks here of the faded Vedic Mitra, Roman Diūs Fidius, and Scandinavian Tyr by the side of Varuna, Jupiter, and Odin, thus the god of covenants paired with the magical lord of oaths and bonds but subsequently eclipsed and almost absorbed by him (Mitra practically reduced to Varuna's dvandvamate, Diūs Fidius as an "allomorph" of Jupiter, Tyr "militarized" along with Odin in Scandinavia). "Mars" was likewise the Roman interpretation of the Germanic god *Tīwz (> Old Norse *Tyr*), as "Mercury" was of *Wōðanaz; a Latin inscription from northern England (third century C.E.) mentions Mars Thingsus, thus the Germanic god Tīw, the protector of the judicial assembly held on Tuesdays, even as the Scandinavian Tyr originally patronized the *thing* (Latin *Martis dies* came out in Germanic interpretation as *Tuesday;* see chap. II). The Gaulish name of such a "Mars" is not known, but he appears in Ireland as Nūadu beside Lug (see further below).

The rest of the Gaulish divine inventory can be characterized more in list fashion. "Apollo" does duty for both Borvo or Bormo (god of thermal healing waters; cf. the French name Bourbon) and Belenus 'Bright' or Grannus 'Sun' as solar deity (cf. Old Irish Beltene 'Brightfire', name of the Mayday feast, and *grīan* 'sun'). "Vulcanus" is attested in Gaul, but his native name is not; it may have been based on the word for 'smith' (as his Irish counterpart, the divine smith Goibniu, reflected *gobae* 'smith'; cf. MacGowan 'Smithson'). "Hercules" characterized the Gaulish Ogmios, according to Lucian (*Herakles,* chap. I) an aged, baldish, sun-blackened champion who literally held men spellbound by the ears with golden-tongued eloquence, matching the Irish 'sun-faced' strongman Ogma, who was credited with devising the Ogam notch script; elements of his myth may have resembled those of the Indo-European warrior hero embodied by both the Greek Herakles and the Norse Starkaðr (the former met up with Gêras 'Old Age' and was known as *Hercules Musarum;* the latter was both a *senex* and a great skaldic poet; cf. chap. 13). "Dispater" (*Dīs,* the Latin name for Hades, from *Dīves* 'Rich' translating Greek *Ploútōn* = "Pluto") cropped up in Lucan's scholiasts as the alternative cover for Taranis but more plausibly reflects a death-god. The Gaulish deity Sucellus 'Good Striker' or Silvanus 'Woodsman', depicted with mallet and cask, sometimes with wolfskin and dog, may be a representation of this "ancestor" figure, who can perhaps be thought of as a "first colonizer" on the lines of the Vedic Yama or as the otherworldly replica of the ruling deity, in the manner of Zeus Katakhthonios or the Norse Odin, who extended his dominion to include Valhöll. In any event belief in an afterlife was strong, for Gauls would lend money on terms of postmortem reimbursement.

"Minerva," with the epithet Belisama 'Brightest', is the cover term for a great goddess. Powerful female types stand out in Celtic mythical lore at both the divine and the saga levels. The transfunctional goddess has here come into her own. "Minerva" had a temple with "eternal flame" in third-century C.E. Britain and is identifiable with the British Celtic theonym Brigantia, formally identical with the Sanskrit feminine adjective *brhati* 'great, lofty' and with the Irish Brigit, the later

saint with her feast day of Imbolc (1 February) and her monastery with perpetual fire at Kildare. (Unlike the usual overlay, e.g., with the Virgin Mary superimposed on the sanctuary of Aphrodite at Cypriot Paphos, the Celtic deity was simply Christianized, name and all.) Triplicity or triunity is in evidence among the Celtic mythical females: Brigit herself had two synonymous "sisters," there was the triad of Irish Machas, and Gaul had the triple Mātres or Mātrae or Mātrōnae. Just as the Greek three-by-three Muses did not perturb Homer's Muse, the Matronae did not preclude a single great Matrona, embodied in a river (Matrona > Marne), whereas in Ireland the mother-goddess was the land itself (*Ēriu;* cf. the Indic Sarasvatī [river] vs. the Iranian Harahvaiti [land]). Matrona was the mother of the 'Divine Son', Maponos, matching Modron and her son Mabon in Welsh saga and the river-goddess Bō and (> Boyne) and her 'Young Son' (Mac Ōc = Oengus) in Irish lore. In addition the Gaulish male deities had "consorts," somewhat as in Roman or Indic religion (Rosmerta 'Foresighted' for "Mercurius," Nemetona 'Shriner' for "Mars," Damona 'Cow' for Borvo, Sirona 'Star' for Grannus, Nantosuelta 'River-?' for Sucellus, and so forth).

There were the taurine Tarvos Trigaranus and an antlered god Cernunnos 'Horned One', the latter sitting cross-legged in the inside of the Gundestrup cauldron with a ram-headed snake in his left hand and torques in his right hand and around his neck, surrounded by a wolf, a stag, and a bull. But females were more prominent among the theriomorphic type, though their animal nature tended to be mitigated: Epona 'Mare' (surnamed Regina 'Queen') had shed her presumable original hippomorphism and was depicted riding sidesaddle, much like her Welsh saga version Rhiannon (< *Rīgantō na* 'Queen') in the *Mabinogi.* Like many Celtic deities, she was not free of an otherworldly tinge; horses appear to have been important to that place, as they were in Greek and Hittite myth (see chap. 8). Dea Artio was a bear-goddess (cf. the Greek Artemis), and Dea Arduinna rode on boarback. Cathubodua (*Corpus Inscriptionum Latinarum* 12.2571) is matched by the ornithomorphous Irish *Bodb (catha)* '[Battle] Crow' and such other bird-shaped battle-goddesses as Morrīgan 'Great Queen'. A kind of animal totemism is also discernible (names like Boduognatus 'Crowson'), reaching over into Ireland (Cūchulainn [*cū* 'dog'], Oisīn [*oss* 'stag']), although it need be no stranger than Leo, Wolf, or Björn as men's names in the Latin and Germanic orbits.

The bulk of the Gauls seem to have belonged linguistically to the branch later known as "British" (still surviving in Welsh and Breton), whereas the Irish (and Scottish) represent the "Gaelic" variety (the differences resemble those between the Oscan-Umbrian and Latin types of Italic, e.g., in the treatment of original labiovelars [*qu* sounds], which developed into labials [*p* sounds] in British and Oscan but were retained in Gaelic and Latin: Welsh *pump,* Oscan *pompe,* but Irish *cōic,* Latin *quinque* 'five'). Apart from names, the records of insular myth postdate Christianization. Ireland has the edge here for several reasons. It was a backwater of tradition, escaping Roman invasion and sheltered from Christianity until the mission of Saint Patrick (who died in 461). On the other hand, its monastic converts fast developed a zealous literacy that was pious and antiquarian-minded at the same time, leaving a record the Welsh material from the High Middle Ages (such as the *Mabinogi*) can only remotely emulate. The separate developments were conditioned by geographic isolation and linguistic split alike (Irish and Welsh were no longer mutually intelligible).

Ireland had its own "mythic geography," made up of the five *cōiced* 'fifths', comprising Ulster in the north, Connaught in the west, Munster in the south(west), and Leinster in the (south)east, all in relation to Mide 'Middle' (county Meath, the site of Tara, seat of the *ard-rī* 'high king'). This is an inherited structure with a clear parallel in ancient India, where the 'five tribes' (*páñca krstáyah* or *carsanáyah*) typically express the *ārya* or even human totality (*páñca* equaling *viśve* 'all'; cf. the Hittite *pankus* 'plenary assembly', and English *fist* > **pnkʷstis* 'a fivefold', namely the sum of the *five fingers* [< **pénkʷe penkʷros*]). Presumably in India, too, the ethnocentric seat of power and the four outlying cardinal divisions formed the basis of the quinary system (cf. the Chinese "Kingdom of the Middle"). The fivefold division of the community survives elsewhere, too, especially with tribes that have recently emerged from the obscurity of prehistory—for example, the five demes of Sparta or the Philistine pentapolis of Gaza, Askalon, Ashdod, Gath, and Ekron. The partition of the Irish year into quarters, punctuated by the great feasts of Samain (1 November, New Year, Day of the Dead, later All Saints' Day), Imbolc (1 February), Beltene (Mayday), and Lugnasad (1 August), maybe at least proto-Celtic, for *Samonios* is attested also on the Gaulish "Calendar of Coligny"; in this system the "markers" fall in the interspaces of the solstices and equinoxes, thus in the "center" of each quarter.

Central to the Irish myth tradition are the epic reflections of the old Celtic gods, the Tūatha Dē Danann 'People of the Goddess Danu'. Traditions about them can be culled from various antiquarian texts, such as the *Dindshenchas* ('Place Traditions') or *Cōir Anmann* ('Fitness of Names', dealing with onomastic etymology), but especially in the *Lebor Gabāla Ērenn* ('Book of Conquests of Ireland'), a legendary history compiled in the twelfth century, and the *Cath Maige Tuired* 'Battle of Mag Tuired'. The monkish redactors have fitted the Tūatha into a whole string of legendary invasions of Ireland, starting biblically with a certain Cessair, a granddaughter of Noah, and antedating the Flood. The only survivor of the flood was Cessair's

husband Fintan, who led a subsequent ichthyo- or ornithomorphic open-ended life as an observer of Irish history. The next settler was Partholōn with his followers, a culture hero who cleared the land and instituted custom and also had a first conflict with the Fomoire, monstrous archenemies each with a single arm and leg who loom large in the sequel. Partholōn and his folk perished in a plague and were succeeded by Nemed and his people. After their leader's death the Fomoire imposed on them crushing tribute, leading to revolt, decimation, and emigration of the remnants to the south and the north. The descendants of the first group ultimately returned as the Fir Bolg, who are credited with the division of Ireland into *cōiceds* and a golden age reminiscent of Hesiodic and Avestan descriptions (soft showers, plentiful harvest, no falsehood). The northern emigrants, equally descended from Nemed's people, returned later as the Tūatha and defeated the Fir Bolg in the First Battle of Mag Tuired. Besides the mother figure Danu (or Anu), they comprised her brother Dagda 'Good God' (also known as Ollathair 'Allfather'), the latter's daughter Brigit, Ogma the champion, Goibniu the smith, Dian Cēcht the healer, and Nechtan (onomastic match of the Latin Neptūnus, whose story is elaborated in chap. 16). Their king was Nūadu, who lost his arm in the battle against the Fir Bolg. They brought along four magical objects: the spear of Lug, the sword of Nūadu, the cauldron of Dagda, and the Great Fāl. The first two were talismanic weapons that ensured victory, the cauldron guaranteed a full meal at all times, and the Great Fāl would cry out whenever mounted by the true king of Ireland (matching in kind the Scottish Stone of Scone under the coronation chair of the British sovereign).

At this point the Fomoire reappear. They seem to be a shadow presence all along—the perennial foe and yet linked intimately to the society they antagonize; in chapter 7 we were reminded of them in the context of the ambivalent relations of Iran and Turan. When Nūadu abdicates the kingship because of his physical handicap, Bres ('Beautiful'; son of a Fomoire father and a Tūatha mother) is elected to succeed him on the urgings of the women; here one is reminded of the Etruscan period in Roman legendry down to the Republican War, when even Brutus the Liberator was (conversely) a Tarquin on his mother's side (even as in Iran Khosraw's mother was the daughter of the king of Turan). Bres turns out to be a poor choice, for he favors the Fomoire, forces menial tasks on the Tūatha champions, and lacks the generosity essential to a successful Irish king. Culinary abundance and other entertainment decline under his niggardly regime, and he draws the fatal ancient equivalent of a poor press, namely lampooning by the poets of the Tūatha. When his resignation is demanded, Bres with his twisted loyalties musters his Fomoire allies for assistance.

The stage is thus set for a showdown. The Tūatha regroup against their own failed king. Nūadu has a new prosthetic silver arm made by Dian Cěcht and the latter's son Miach and is hence rehabilitated to resume the kingship with the epithet *Argatlām* 'Silver Hand'. At this point the young Lug arrives at Tara (he too was part Fomoire, daughter's son of Balor, the Fomoire champion) and impresses everyone with his range of expertise, to the point that Nūadu cedes his leadership to him. Seven years of preparations culminated in the great Second Battle of Mag Tuired. During the slaughter Dian Cěcht and his three children used magic arts (singing spells over corpses thrown into a healing well) to revive the dead of the Tūatha, thus furthering their victory. Lug circumambulated the enemy host on one foot and with one eye closed, a magic circuit that mimed the single-leggedness of the foes in general and Balor's "evil eye" in particular. The latter shared with Cūchulainn and assorted Norse berserks the contortionist trick of sucking in one eye and expanding the other to a monstrous, paralyzing gaze, only in Balor's instance it took four men to raise the resulting heavy lid. At that instant Lug shot a sling stone through the opening and forced the eye backward through Balor's head, so that its evil was vented instead at the Fomoire themselves. Thus died Balor (having earlier slain Nūadu), and the Tūatha triumphed. This marked the end of the Fomoire, while Bres was reprieved in return for becoming a governmental advisor in matters of agriculture. But the peace era of the Tūatha was not to last either, for a final invasion by the "Sons of Mīl," that is, the Irish under their king Eremon, forced them to retire to the *síde,* the fairy mounds, and thus perpetuate their influence from a subterranean spirit world. This is a unique tandem approach by levels to ethnogenesis and Christianization. The gods once held sway over the land, and in a sense they still do, despite yielding the surface of the Hibernian soil to the folk and to a new cult and being retired to what is sometimes called the "lower mythology." In subtlety the Irish solution outshines downright demonization of the onetime pagan gods in Christianized cultures.

Sound method requires that this material be confronted first with other Celtic, in this instance Welsh, traditions before resorting to extra-Celtic comparisons. Our main sources are the *Four Branches* of the *Mabinogi* and such other tales as *Lludd and Lleuelys* and *Culhwch and Olwen.* Far more than Irish tradition, this literature is caught up in the more cosmopolitan world of medieval romances and international folktales, nor did its authors have the same feeling for native myth that still guided the Irish compilers. The frequently fantastic narrative rarely yields systematic matter for comparison but can nevertheless be probed for incidental relevant lore.

Clear parallels to the Tūatha occur in the Welsh material. The *Fourth Branch* concerns the family of Dōn (cf. Danu) with her brother Math (cf. Dagda), ruler of Gwynedd (North Wales). Math could live only if his feet were held in a maiden's lap, except in time of war. Through the machinations of two sons of Dōn the incumbent foot holder was disqualified for loss of maidenhead. At length Math interviewed a new candidate, Dōn's daughter Aranrhod, who had to step over a magic wand as proof of her virginity, but in doing so dropped a male child (the sea-god Dylan) and a second object that was put in a chest. The latter turned out to be another son whom Aranrhod would not name until tricked to do so, and he became Lleu Llawgyffes 'Lleu the Deft-Handed', a match for the Irish Lug Samildānach 'Lug the Many-Skilled'. Aranrhod likewise swore to deny him weapons and spouse but was also induced unwittingly to countermand this ban. Lleu eventually became lord of Gwynedd. Gofannon 'Smith' (cf. Goibniu) and Amaethon 'Plowman' (both with the "augmentative" *-no-* suffix) were further sons of Dōn. Amaethon is mentioned in *Culhwch and Olwen,* which is also the attested source for Lludd Llawereint, the Welsh match for Nūadu Argatlām (*Lludd < Nudd* by alliterative assimilation to the epithet *Llaw-ereint,* literally 'Hand [of] Silver'). The tale of *Lludd and Lleuelys* tells of Lludd, king of Britain (popular etymon of London, known in Welsh tradition as Caer Lludd 'Lludd-town'; cf. names like Ludgate), and his brother Lleuelys who had married his way to the throne of France. Three calamities afflicted Britain under Lludd: the advent of a people called the Coraniaid, armed with such advanced eavesdropping capabilities that no secrets were safe, a terrible dragon fight every Mayday, attended by a blood-curdling cry that debilitated people, animals, and nature at large, and an ongoing mysterious disappearance of provender from the royal larder. Brother Lleuelys (in whose name we recognize Lleu), "a man of great and wise counsel," supplied the remedy: a poison specifically calibrated to exterminate the Coraniaid, a means of talismanic entombment of the dragons for ever after, and the arrest of the magical purloiner of food and drink, who not only made restitution but reformed to become the king's faithful retainer (in modern times he might have become his castle security consultant). Thus Lleuelys helps Lludd overcome a tripartite set of afflictions, the kind we have seen from India to Iran to Rome, consisting of miscarriage of language or violation of verbal sanctity (botched formulas, lies, spells, oath breaking, eavesdropping), breach of communal peace (invasion, armed attack, mayhem, unsettling screams), and loss of physical resources (blight, plague, famine, theft). The regime of Bres in Ireland, relieved by the intervention of Lug taking over from Nūadu, was likewise characterized by breakdown of verbal trust (Bres plotting with the Fomoire against the Tūatha), debilitation of warriors (Ogma reduced to carrying firewood), and shortage of victuals (unfair tribute of crops and produce to the Fomoire, the stingy foodways of Bres himself). The formula seems to be inversely replicated in the series of invasions, where Partholōn's and Nemed's people were decimated by plague and famine, the Fir

Bolg and the Tūatha were conquered by force of arms, and according to druidic prophecy, the Sons of Mīl will perish by fire and water after a breakdown of law and social order. In the principal Old Irish legal corpus, the *Senchus Mōr,* disease/famine, warfare, and breach of covenant are singled out as the threefold causes of calamity, even as in Plato's *Republic* (413b-14a) Socrates lists theft, spells, and violence as reasons for alienation from truth. Underlying the stories of Nūadu (genitive Nūadat) and Lug and that of Lludd and Lleuelys we may thus discern a Celtic myth of Lugus bringing relief to Nōdons; the latter is attested in dedications from Lydney (cf. Lludd!) in Gloucestershire bordering South Wales (*Deo Nodonti*) and seems to mean 'Fisher' (cf. Gothic *nuta* 'fisherman', from **nudōn[s]*), the probable ancestor of the Arthurian "Fisher King" of the Grail legend, whose maiming resulted in the Waste Land.

Other *Branches* of the *Mabinogi* are less amenable to comparison, but the mythic background is still palpable. In the *First Branch,* Pwyll, lord of Dyfed (South Wales), whose name means 'Wisdom', also mysteriously acquires condominium in the Otherworld (Annwn; cf. the Arthurian Avalon) before meeting and marrying the Lady on the White Horse, Rhiannon 'Queen' (who was compared above to the Gaulish horse-goddess Epona Regina). Their son Pryderi was kidnapped at birth and was found and reared by Teyrnon (< **Tigernonos* 'Lord'), the events being linked with the birth of a horse. The *Second Branch* deals with the brood of Llyr 'Sea', notably the giant Brān ("The Blessed", *Bendigeid-fran*), Manawydan, and their sister Branwen, and the misadventures resulting from the latter's unhappy marriage to the king of Ireland. Here the Irish connection is felt in more than the plot, for the main characters match in name the Irish god Manannān Mac Lir ('Son of the Sea') and such Otherworld-farers as the hero of the "Voyage of Bran" (cf. Saint Brendan). Sea voyages and Otherworld notions are often interlinked in Celtic lore, implying Elysian isles or sunken paradises in the West (*Mag Mell* 'Field of Pleasure', *Tīr na n-ōg* 'Land of the Young', Land of Lyonnesse, City of Is, etc.), but in fairytale fashion the Otherworld can also be entered by a kind of on-the-spot enchantment—through the looking glass, so to speak—without any visible or distant boundaries. In the *Second Branch* battle between the Welsh and the Irish, the latter made good field use of their "Cauldron of Rebirth" to revive the casualties, a close parallel to Dian Cēcht's restorative well in the Second Battle of Mag Tuired. Only seven Welshmen survived, including Manawydan; Brān's severed head was buried as a talisman at London, facing the Continent, where it has warded off invasion of Britain at least since 1066. The *Third Branch* ties together the first two (Manawydan marrying Pwyll's widow Rhiannon, whose son Pryderi is now lord of Dyfed; together they have to fight off an evil spell cast on the land by a certain Llwyd), while in the *Fourth Branch,* in addition to the family saga of Dōn, Pryderi's death is told, tied to a gift of horses, a last leitmotif alluding back to the mythology of his mother Rhiannon. In this way the *Mabinogi* still yields vague echoes of Celtic myth, in confirmation of the Irish and even Gaulish material.

Essaying extra-Celtic comparisons for the insular tradition, we find the Irish pair Nūadu and Lug (or their Welsh counterparts Lludd and Lleu) homologous with Scaevola and Cocles of the Roman Republican War, marked by loss of a hand and one-eyed battle magic respectively. On the divine level this means comparability with the Germanic pair *Tīwz and *Wōðanaz, in Old Norse terms Tyr and Odin, the former having given up his right hand in order to bind the wolf, the latter sacrificing an eye to gain magical powers. The ascendancy of Lug over Nūadu parallels the eclipsing of Tyr by Odin in Norse tradition. Ogma seems to embody the warrior level, with his club matching Thor's hammer (and Feridun's *gurz*), while the third estate is reflected by Bres, the agricultural expert and popular favorite elected king by the women's vote. That he has to be put in his place by a violent conflict indicates that the Second Battle of Mag Tuired contains elements of the Indo-European myth of the "war of the divine classes" (Indra vs. Aśvins, Romans vs. Sabines, Äsir vs. Vanir, discussed in chaps. 4, 9, and 11). Yet while the Fomoire in addition to Bres himself seem to be to a degree "Sabinic" (soil oriented, intermarrying with the Tūatha, etc.), as a group they are not integrated by the conflict but rather are eliminated from the scene. Hence more than a divine skirmish and conciliation took place at Mag Tuired. The Fomoire also have a definite demonic tinge, that of a monstrous and oppressive archenemy who is yet too close for comfort and sooner or later requires a showdown with eschatological overtones. The Indic and Iranian gods versus demons, the Norse gods versus giants, the Roman patriots versus Tarquins, and such modern mutations as communism versus capitalism are all fair parallels (cf. the "end struggle" of the Internationale). Dian Cēcht's resurrective battlefield well has its analogue in ancient India, where Kāvya Uśanas, serving as sorcerer of the demons, kept reviving the dead in the ongoing conflict against the gods. But while Ragnarök and communism hold out a postconflict millennium, India eschewed eschatology, contenting itself with a mere epic resolution in the *Mahābhārata* (see chap. 5). In Ireland too the epicized triumph of the Tūatha proves transitory. Even as the Pāndavas move on to posthumous heaven, the Tūatha are retired to the mounds in favor of a new set of men. But Ireland is not yet through with mythological surprises. The king of the Sons of Mīl, Eremon, is etymologically the equivalent of the Gaulish Ariomanus, reflecting the same personified **aryomn* 'Aryanness' as is seen in the Vedic Aryamán and the Iranian Airyaman. In addition, very specific traits connect Eremon with both of the latter. The dossier of Eremon in the *Lebor Gabála* involves his role as builder of causeways and royal roads. In the *Historia Britonum* of Nennius, the *Book of Leinster,* the *Book of Lecan,* and some other sources, Eremon arranged a protection against poisoned enemy arrows that consisted of pouring cow's milk into furrows on the battlefield. He also provided wives to his allies and arranged for hereditary succession in favor of the Irish, his own people. All three features are distinctly "Aryamanic" in Indo-Iranian terms: Aryaman is connected with roads and pathways from the *Rig-Veda* onward. Airyaman invented the *gaomaēza* ritual of decontamination and healing, consisting of filling furrows with bovine excretions, specifically urine. Aryaman, Airyaman, and Vidura (the epic transposition of Aryaman; see chap. 5) are all connected with marriage rituals. The Indo-Iranian *Aryaman was clearly a satellite of *Mitra, a kind of hypostasis of the Mitra type proper, an abstraction expressing the self-sense of the community and championing the operation of communal welfare and health, especially in terms of marital compacts and rituals of healing. In Celtic tradition, a linear downward projection has replaced the "timeless" level of coexistence of figures such as Mitra and Aryaman. Eremon is in fact a diachronic hypostasis of Nūadu as king of the "next" layer of settlers, appropriately closer to mankind proper, even as Aryaman was in contrast to Mitra. Thus Celtic theology seems to have perpetuated, at the far end of the Indo-European continuum, a match for the Mitra-Aryaman structure at the other extremity—a notable instance of the "archaism of the fringe."

The perceptive mythological ear may pick up further Celtic : Indic echoes. Aranrhod's triple withholding of name, weapons, and spouse from the young Lleu recalls Devavrata's renunciation of kingship and marriage in the *Mahābhārata* in return for a new name (Bhīsma; see chap. 5); since Bhīsma incarnates Dyaus, something of the Indo-European sky-god *Dyēws may still lurk in the Celtic Lugus-Lug-Lleu (he was worshiped on mountaintops, for example, at the Lugnasad in Ireland, and with the colossal statue erected by the Gaulish Arverni on the peak of Puy de Dôme in the Massif Central range in the Auvergne). Students of ancient India are reminded of the Vedic three-stepping world measurer Visnu in the triple-leaping Irish Saint Moling, and of the all-encompassing Krsna-Visnu of the *Bhagavadgītā* when the bard of the Sons of Mīl, Amairgin, takes possession of the soil of Ireland with a lay in which he equates everything with himself. The death-god Donn, first of the Tūatha to die and the post-mortem receiver of mankind, has traits in common with the Vedic Yama. The nine or so forms of marriage listed in Irish and Welsh traditions resemble the *Laws of Manu* by several varieties of family-centered and wealth-related "honorable" union at the beginning and stealthy rape or "mockery" at the end,

separated by free-will and abduction marriages closely resembling the Indic *gāndharva* and *rāksasa;* in this instance the Indic and Celtic multiplicity contrasts with the reductionistic tripartite stylization seen in Roman law (chap. 9).

In the *Lebor Gabála* the female figures (Danu, Brigit) are in the background; this is a man's world, perhaps owing to skewing by the monkish compilers. Important women are more to the fore in the Welsh tales (Modron, Rhiannon, Aranrhod), but they hardly do full justice to the notable goddesses of the Gaulish pantheon either. To find proper insular reflections of the female component in Celtic myth one must turn to the Irish sagas and to folklore. Danu-Anu, Brigit, Ēriu, Bōand, the three Machas, Bodb, Morrīgan have flitted past in the pages above. They, augmented by Medb, reflect aspects of the Indo-European transfunctional goddess, but with specific Celtic emphases. Sacrality, "untaintedness" is not much in evidence. Instead there is embodiment of "sovereignty" in the secular sense, and nary a virgin in sight. There is hypertrophy of the "amazonal" and fertility components, but these have often been tucked under the umbrella of "sovereignty" to yield domineering warrior-harridans and fountains of sexuality alike. Some figures were a bit "provincial" (B and local to Ulster, Medb in Connacht with a "double" in Leinster, Brigit in Leinster, Anu in Munster with her two breasts embodied by the twin hills of county Kerry known as *Dá Chích Anann* 'Paps of Anu'; see fig. 9), but names like Medb (< *Meduā*, Bodb (< *Boduā*), and Brigit (< *Brigantia*) are paralleled in Gaul and Britain; they all reflect a pan-Celtic type. Those that have more "myth" to their name, such as Medb, the Machas, and Bōand, will have their stories told in chapters 14, 15, and 16.

The world of Irish saga in its imaginative and anarchic fluidity is even harder to explore for comparative mythology than the lucubrations of the "Mythological Cycle" centered on the *Lebor Gabála.* But while the latter may with reservations be called a "chronicle-epic" on the lines of Livy, the sagas of the "Ulster Cycle," with their alternating prose narrative and direct-speech verse, and the story and ballad versions of the "Fenian Cycle" can be characterized as remnants of heroic epic art. Folktale motifs proliferate, stock themes abound,[2] and yet the sagas have an ancient flavor that makes one suspect their core of a mythical residue. What they lack in direct mythological concern is compensated for by sheer untouched native archaism and by the absence or mitigation of any clerical distortions.

The "Ulster Cycle" purports to be "tribal," involving the Ulaid (Ulstermen) with their king Conchobor Mac Nessa residing at Emain Macha ('Twins of Macha'), near the later Christian capital of Ard Macha ('Hill of Macha', Armagh). It is a reflection of Celtic Iron Age warrior society, untainted by Roman, let alone Christian, influences. It bears notable resemblance to the heroic late Bronze Age traditions depicted in the Homeric poems. Conchobor's courtiers included the druid Cathbad, the conciliatory sage Sencha, the oversexed champion Fergus Mac Roich with his outsized phallus, and the trickster and troublemaker Bricriu. The old king grew himself a young wife, Deirdre ("of the sorrows"), whose elopement with Noise brought death to Noise and his brothers and desperate suicide upon herself; the story is of a Celtic triangle type also seen in the Fenian (Finn : Gráinne: Finn's nephew Diarmaid) and Arthurian traditions (Mark : Yseult : Mark's nephew Tristan; Arthur : Guinevere : Lancelot). Underlying it is the willful, strong female divine figure of Celtic myth, epitomized in saga form by Queen Medb, who takes and discards mates at will but whose power play no longer matches her sex drive in courtly intrigue, so that she trails "fate" and disaster in her wake. The chief driving forces in this company were aristocratic honor and the craving for fame, and the main pastimes included feasting, feuding for primacy over the "hero's portion," and intertribal fighting, especially with Connacht under Medb over a great bull whom the latter coveted (*Táin Bó Cuailnge* 'Cattle Raid of Cooley'). Into this circle was born Conchobor's nephew Sétanta, sired by Lug and synchronized with the birth of twin foals (cf. Pryderi in the *Mabinogi*). Tutored and trained by the best teachers (Amairgin, Cathbad, Sencha, Fergus), Sétanta took on the name Cúchulainn ('Culann's dog') in atonement for one of his "boyhood deeds" (killing the hound of the smith Culann). Like Achilles, he alacritously chose a short life of fame and in short order developed into a full-blown berserk, complete with contortions (*riastrad:* eye trick, mouth stretched from ear to ear, hair standing on end as if by static electricity, magic halo [*lúan láith* 'warrior's moon'] over his head), but also subject to the multiple *geis* or tabu that shadows the Irish hero. He killed a murderous triple adversary (three sons of Nechta Scéne) but thereupon in his frenzy attacked Emain Macha itself (shades of Horatius slaying the three Curiatii then turning on his own sister). Conchobor confronted him not with champions but with a phalanx of naked women; when this vanguard embarrassed his youthful modesty, the men grabbed him and cooled him off in successive tubs of cold water (one burst, one boiled, the third merely warmed). Now a full-fledged champion, he had to ward off single-handed Medb's cattle raid into Ulster, until the other men could recover from their annual "childbed sickness" (a couvadelike travesty of travail induced by a curse of the Third Macha; cf. chap. 15). Later he enrolled for some adult education from the divine instructresses Scáthach 'Modest', her daughter Uathach 'Terrible', and Aife 'Fair', who sound suspiciously trifunctional on the pattern of the Greek Euphrosyne, Aglaia, and Thaleia (it must be an ancient set, for 'modesty' is not otherwise a notable component of Celtic transfunctional triads). Uathach

advised Cúchulainn to wring from her mother Scáthach at swordpoint a triple set of boons: instruction in warfare, Uathach's hand in wedlock, and a foretelling of his future, for Scáthach was also a prophetess. Instead the hero ended up begetting upon Aife a son Conlae, whom he later unwittingly slew in combat, in enactment of the Rustam : Sohrab pattern of filicide (cf. chap. 7). His own end came by being caught between two *geasa* when his enemies served up roast dog on his passage: he could neither pass up a meal nor eat dog, which might be his totem. A statue of him collapsing, with the death crow perched on his shoulder, adorns the main post office in Dublin. His head was retrieved by his brother-in-arms, Conall Cernach, chiming with the well-documented Celtic cult of human heads (cf., e.g., Brán's head buried at London).

Even this quick glance at some salient points of the "Ulster Cycle" points up the scattered but palpable mythical elements in the heroic narrative. The same is true of the "Fenian Cycle," but with a difference. It is not "localized," though mostly southern (Leinster and Munster), not centered at some heroic court; in fact it is almost extrasocietal with its free-roaming band (*fiana*) of fighters and hunters beholden only to themselves, an epic-romantic Irish body of tradition about ancient initiational warrior brotherhoods still marked by a free-will autonomy resembling that of Indra and the Maruts. First codified in the *Acallam na Senórach* 'Parley of Oldsters' in the twelfth century and fueled by James Macpherson's Ossianic fancies in the eighteenth, it has proved durable with storytellers and balladeers until modern times, especially in the southwest (Munster). Much nature lyricism enters into the epic material, Finn-Fingal himself (with his son Oisín-Ossian and grandson Oscar) being not only a warrior but a seer (*fili*) and a bard (*fáith*, cognate with Latin *vátēs*). He had his "boyhood deeds" like Cúchulainn, and like Conchobor he suffered marital infidelity at the hands of his willful wife and his nephew Diarmaid, the fellow with the irresistible 'love spot' (*ball seirc*); when the latter was mortally gored during a boar hunt in Sligo, Finn begrudged him his magic healing waters, thus declining to save him (even as Kay Us withheld his elixir from the dying Sohrab in the *Shāh Nāma*). Despite the folktale aura, Finn's divine origins are probable (*Vindos 'White', cf. the Welsh Gwyn son of Nudd as a magical hunter and fighter, and theophorous continental place-names like *Vindobona* 'Vienna'); he may in fact be an allonymous saga version of Lug, and so may Cúchulainn, the "son of Lug." Lugus-Lug-Lleu is, as we have seen, homologous with the Germanic *Wōðanaz, the patron of the Germanic warrior bands, who had part demonic (giant) ancestry, even as Lug was part Fomoire. It would be nice to report that *Lugos means 'Bright', as is sometimes alleged, beside *Vindos 'White', but more probably it matches Gaulish *loûgos* 'raven' and thus provides another analogue to *Wōðanaz with his ravens. But the intra-Irish similarities of Lug and Finn are themselves patent; just as Lug the spear wielder killed Balor with his evil eye, the eight-year-old Finn with the help of a magic spear vanquished a one-eyed fire-breathing marauder who would burn down Tara on every Samain; thus he secured his position within the brotherhood, but he had to deal even later with an antagonist Goll ('One-Eyed') Mac Morna (also called *Aed* 'Fire'), who before his birth had killed his father Cumaill. Lug was of consummate skill, while Finn had his "thumb of knowledge" that imparted preternatural insight (even as Odin had his magic of runes). Altogether Finn strengthens the case for a Celtic magician-god *Lugos, in many respects (part-demonic ancestry, secret knowledge, one-eyedness, magical warrior character, perhaps raven connection) similar to the Germanic *Wōðanaz; his saga reflections are not only Lug and Lleu but Cúchulainn and Finn, and even Arthur (the boar hunter of *Culhwch and Olwen*), who resembles Finn in many respects.

The "Historical Cycles" deal with royal persons who sometimes interact with figures such as Medb (e.g., Ailill, Lugaid, Conn, Art, and Cormac); these are dealt with in chapter 14. In other instances, such as Suibhne Geilt 'Sweeney the Madman', the saga itself is of direct relevance to Indo-European warrior myth (see chap. 13).

Notes

[1] That is, the Artemis Taurica of the Crimea, to whom strangers were sacrificed, as in Euripides' play *Iphigenia in Tauris.*

[2] Some of these have parallels in India, such as the magically potent "act of truth" in Irish lore and the analogous *satyakriyā,* resorted to by Damayantī and Sītā (for the latter, see chap. 5), or even the romantic commonplace of the "love sight unseen" (*sercc ēcmaise: adrstakēma*) afflicting the likes of Nala and Damayantī, Oengus, and Findabair (in the *Tāin Bō Froich*).

CELTIC MYTH AS LITERATURE AND HISTORY

W. B. Yeats (1898)

SOURCE: "The Celtic Element in Literature," in *Writings on Irish Folklore, Legend and Myth*, edited by Robert Welch, Penguin Books, 1993, pp. 189-200.

[*In the following essay, originally published in 1898, Yeats discusses the importance of Celtic myth and folklore to modern European literature.*]

I

Ernest Renan[1] described what he held to be Celtic characteristics in *The Poetry of the Celtic Races.* 'No race communed so intimately as the Celtic race with the lower creation, or believed it to have so big a share of moral life.' The Celtic race had 'a realistic naturalism', 'a love of nature for herself, a vivid feeling for her magic, commingled with the melancholy a man knows when he is face to face with her, and thinks he hears her communing with him about his origin and his destiny'. 'It has worn itself out in mistaking dreams for realities', and 'compared with the classical imagination the Celtic imagination is indeed the infinite contrasted with the finite'. 'Its history is one long lament, it still recalls its exiles, its flights across the seas.' 'If at times it seems to be cheerful, its tear is not slow to glisten behind the smile. Its songs of joy end as elegies; there is nothing to equal the delightful sadness of its national melodies.' Matthew Arnold,[2] in *The Study of Celtic Literature,* has accepted this passion for nature, this imaginativeness, this melancholy, as Celtic characteristics, but has described them more elaborately. The Celtic passion for nature comes almost more from a sense of her 'mystery' than of her 'beauty', and it adds 'charm and magic' to nature, and the Celtic imaginativeness and melancholy are alike 'a passionate, turbulent, indomitable reaction against the despotism of fact'. The Celt is not melancholy, as Faust or Werther[3] are melancholy, from 'a perfectly definitive motive', but because of something about him 'unaccountable, defiant and titanic'. How well one knows these sentences, and how well one knows the passages of prose and verse which he uses to prove that wherever English literature has the qualities these sentences describe, it has them from a Celtic source. Though I do not think any of us who write about Celtic things have built any argument upon them, it is well to consider them a little, and see where they are helpful and where they are hurtful. If we do not, we may go mad some day, and the enemy of Celtic things root up our rose garden and plant a cabbage garden instead.

I am going to make a claim for the Celt, but I am not going to make quite the same claim that Ernest Renan and Matthew Arnold made. Matthew Arnold, and still more Ernest Renan, wrote before the activity in the study of folk-lore and of folk literature of our own day had begun to give us so many new ideas about old things. When we talk to-day about the delight in nature, about the imaginativeness, about the melancholy of the Celt, we cannot help thinking of the delight in nature, of the imaginativeness, of the melancholy of the makers of the Icelandic *Eddas,* and of the *Kalavala,*[4] and of many other folk literatures, and we soon grow persuaded that much that Matthew Arnold and Ernest Renan thought wholly or almost wholly Celtic is of the substance of the minds of the ancient farmers and herdsmen. One comes to think of the Celt as an ancient farmer or herdsman, who sits bowed with the dreams of his unnumbered years, in the gates of the rich races, talking of forgotten things. Is the Celt's feeling for nature, and for the 'lower creation', one of those forgotten things? Because we have come to associate the ancient beliefs about nature with 'savage customs' and with books written by men of science, we have almost forgotten that they are still worth dreaming about and talking about. It is only when we describe them in some language, which is not the language of science, that we discover they are beautiful.

II

Once every people in the world believed that trees were divine, and could take a human or grotesque shape and dance among the shadows of the woods; and deer, and ravens and foxes, and wolves and bears, and clouds and pools, almost all things under the sun and moon, and the sun and moon, not less divine and changeable: they saw in the rainbow the still bent bow of a god thrown down in his negligence; they heard in the thunder the sound of his beaten water-jar, or the tumult of his chariot wheels; and when a sudden flight of wild duck, or of crows, passed over their heads, they thought they were gazing at the dead hastening to their rest; while they dreamed of so great a mystery in little things that they believed the waving of a hand, or of a sacred bough, enough to trouble far-off hearts, or hood the moon with darkness. All old literatures are full of this way of looking at things, and all the poets of races, who have not lost this way of looking at things, could have said of themselves, as the poet of the *Kalavala* said of himself, 'I have learned my songs from the music of many birds, and from the music of many waters.' When a mother in the *Kalavala* weeps for a daughter, who was drowned flying from an old suitor, she weeps so greatly that her tears become three rivers, and cast up three rocks, on which grow three birch trees, where three cuckoos sit and sing, the one 'love, love', the one 'suitor, suitor', the one 'consolation, consolation'. And the makers of the sagas made the squirrel run up and down the sacred ash tree carrying words of hatred from the eagle to the worm, and from the worm to the eagle; although they had less of the old way than the makers of the *Kalavala,* for they lived in a more crowded and complicated world, and were learning the abstract meditation which lures men from visible beauty, and were unlearning, it may be, the impassioned meditation which brings men beyond the edge of trance and makes trees, and beasts, and dead things talk with human voices.

The Celts, though they had less of the old way than the makers of the *Kalavala,* had more of it than the makers of the sagas, and it is this that distinguishes the examples Matthew Arnold quotes of the Celts' 'natural magic', of their sense of 'the mystery' more than of 'the beauty' of nature. When Matthew Arnold thought he was criticising the Celts, he was really criticising the ancient religion of the world, the ancient worship of nature and the troubled ecstasy before her, the belief that all beautiful places are haunted, which it

brought into men's minds. The ancient religion is in that marvellous passage from the *Mabinogion*[5] about the making of 'Flower Aspect'. Gwydion and Math made her 'by charms and illusions' 'out of flowers'. 'They took the blossoms of the oak, and the blossoms of the broom, and the blossoms of the meadow-sweet, and produced from them a maiden the fairest and most graceful that man ever saw; and they baptized her, and called her Flower Aspect'; and one finds it in the not less beautiful passage about the burning Tree, that has half its beauty from calling up a fancy of leaves so living and beautiful, they can be of no less living and beautiful a thing than flame: 'They saw a tall tree by the side of the river, one half of which was in flames from the root to the top, and the other half was green and in full leaf.' And one finds it very certainly in the quotations he makes from English poets to prove a Celtic influence in English poetry; in Keats's 'magic casements, opening on the foam of perilous seas in faerylands forlorn'; in his 'moving waters at their priestlike task of pure oblations round earth's human shore';[6] in Shakespeare's 'floor of heaven', 'inlaid with patens of bright gold'; and in his Dido standing 'on the wild sea banks', 'a willow in her hand', and waving it in the ritual of the old worship of nature and the spirits of nature, to wave 'her love to come again to Carthage'.[7] And his other examples have the delight and wonder of devout worshippers among the haunts of their divinities. Is there not such delight and wonder in the description of Olwen in the *Mabinogion:* 'More yellow was her hair than the flower of the broom, and her skin was whiter than the foam of the wave, and fairer were her hands and her fingers than the blossoms of the wood-anemony amidst the spray of the meadow fountains.' And is there not such delight and wonder in—

> Meet we on hill, in dale, forest or mead,
> By paved fountain or by rushy brook,
> Or on the beached margent of the sea?[8]

If men had never dreamed that maidens could be made out of flowers, or rise up out of meadow fountains and paved fountains, neither passage could have been written. Certainly, the descriptions of nature made in what Matthew Arnold calls 'the faithful way', or in what he calls 'the Greek way', would have lost nothing if all the meadow fountains or paved fountains were nothing but meadow fountains and paved fountains.[9] When Keats wrote, in the Greek way, which adds lightness and brightness to nature:

> What little town by river or sea-shore
> Or mountain built with quiet citadel,
> Is emptied of its folk, this pious morn;[10]

When Shakespeare wrote in the Greek way:

> I know a bank whereon the wild thyme blows,
> Where oxlips and the nodding violet grows;[11]

When Virgil wrote in the Greek way:

> Muscosi fontes et somno mollior herba,

and

> Pallentes violas et summa papavera carpens
> Narcissum et florem jungit bene olentis
>   anethi;[12]

they looked at nature without ecstasy, but with the affection a man feels for the garden where he has walked daily and thought pleasant thoughts. They looked at nature in the modern way, the way of people who are poetical, but are more interested in one another than in a nature which has faded to be but friendly and pleasant.

III

Men who lived in a world where anything might flow and change, and become any other thing; and among great gods whose passions were in the flaming sunset, and in the thunder and the thundershower, had not our thoughts of weight and measure. They worshipped nature and the abundance of nature, and had always, as it seems, for a supreme ritual that tumultuous dance among the hills or in the depths of the woods, where unearthly ecstasy fell upon the dancers, until they seemed the gods or the god-like beasts, and felt their souls overtopping the moon; and, as some think, imagined for the first time in the world the blessed country of the gods and of the happy dead. They had imaginative passions because they did not live within our own straight limits, and were nearer to ancient chaos, every man's desire, and had immortal models about them. The hare that ran by among the dew might have sat upon his haunches when the first man was made, and the poor bunch of rushes under their feet might have been a goddess laughing among the stars; and with but a little magic, a little waving of the hands, a little murmuring of the lips, they too could become a hare or a bunch of rushes, and know immortal love and immortal hatred.

All folk literature, and all literature that keeps the folk tradition, delights in unbounded and immortal things. The *Kalavala* delights in the seven hundred years that Luonaton wanders in the depths of the sea with Wäinämöinen in her womb, and the Mahomedan king in the *Song of Roland,*[13] pondering upon the greatness of Charlemaine, repeats over and over, 'He is three hundred years old, when will he weary of war?' Cuchulain in the Irish folk tale had the passion of victory, and he overcame all men, and died warring upon the waves, because they alone had the strength to overcome him; and Caolte, in his sorrow for his companions, dead upon the plain of Gabra, stormed the house of the Gods at Asseroe, and drove them out and

lives there in their stead. The lover in the Irish folk song bids his beloved come with him into the woods, and see the salmon leap in the rivers, and hear the cuckoo sing, because death will never find them in the heart of the woods.[14] Oisin, new come from his three hundred years of faeryland, and of the love that is in faeryland, bids St Patrick cease his prayers a while and listen to the blackbird, because it is the blackbird of Darrycarn that Fionn brought from Norway, three hundred years before, and set its nest upon the oak tree with his own hands.[15] Surely if one goes far enough into the woods, there one will find all that one is seeking? Who knows how many centuries the birds of the woods have been singing?

All folk literature has indeed a passion whose like is not in modern literature and music and art, except where it has come by some straight or crooked way out of ancient times. Love was held to be a fatal sickness in ancient Ireland, and there is a love-poem in *The Songs of Connacht* that is like a death cry: 'My love, O she is my love, the woman who is most for destroying me, dearer is she for making me ill than the woman who would be for making me well. She is my treasure, O she is my treasure, the woman of the grey eyes . . . a woman who would not lay a hand under my head . . . She is my love, O she is my love, the woman who left no strength in me; a woman who would not breathe a sigh after me, a woman who would not raise a stone at my tomb . . . She is my secret love, O she is my secret love. A woman who tells me nothing . . . a woman who does not remember me to be out . . . She is my choice, O she is my choice, the woman who would not look back at me, the woman who would not make peace with me . . . She is my desire, O she is my desire: a woman dearest to me under the sun, a woman who would not pay me heed, if I were to sit by her side. It is she ruined my heart and left a sigh for ever in me.'[16] There is another song that ends, 'The Erne shall be in strong flood, the hills shall be torn down, and the sea shall have red waves, and blood shall be spilled, and every mountain valley and every moor shall be on high, before you shall perish, my little black rose.'[17] Nor does the Celt weigh and measure his hatred. The nurse of O'Sullivan Bere in the folk song prays that the bed of his betrayer may be the red hearthstone of hell for ever.[18] And an Elizabethan Irish poet cries (I quote him from memory, but I can hardly have forgotten the bitterest curse in literature): 'Three things are waiting for my death. The devil, who is waiting for my soul and cares nothing for my body or my wealth; the worms, who are waiting for my body but care nothing for my soul or my wealth; my children, who are waiting for my wealth and care nothing for my body or my soul. O Christ, hang all three in the one noose.'[19] Such love and hatred seek no mortal thing but their own infinity, and such love and hatred soon become love and hatred of the idea. The lover who loves so passionately can soon sing to his beloved like the lover in the poem by AE, an exquisite Irish poet of our days, 'A vast desire awakes and grows into forgetfulness of thee.'[20] When an early Irish poet calls the Irishman famous for much loving and a proverb, a friend[21] has heard in the Highlands of Scotland, talks of the lovelessness of the Irishman, they may say but the same thing, for if your passion is but great enough it leads you to a country where there are many cloisters. The hater who hates with too good a heart soon comes also to hate the idea only; and from this idealism in love and hatred comes, as I think, a certain power of saying and forgetting things, especially a power of saying and forgetting things in politics, which others do not say and forget. The ancient farmers and herdsmen were full of love and hatred, and made their friends gods, and their enemies the enemies of gods, and those who keep their tradition are not less mythological. From this 'mistaking dreams', which are perhaps essences, for 'realities' which are perhaps accidents, from this 'passionate, turbulent reaction against the despotism of fact', comes, it may be, that melancholy which made all ancient peoples delight in tales that end in death and parting, as modern peoples delight in tales that end in marriage bells; and made all ancient peoples who like the Celts had a nature more lyrical than dramatic, delight in wild and beautiful lamentations. Life was so weighed down by the emptiness of the great forests and by the mystery of all things, and by the greatness of its own desires, and, as I think, by the loneliness of much beauty; and seemed so little and so fragile and so brief, that nothing could be more sweet in the memory than a tale that ended in death and parting, and than a wild and beautiful lamentation. Men did not mourn because their beloved was married to another, or because learning was bitter in the mouth, for such mourning believes that life might be happy were it different, and is therefore the less mourning; but because they had been born and must die with their great thirst unslaked. And so it is that all the august sorrowful persons of literature, Cassandra and Helen and Brunhilda, and Lear and Tristram, have come out of legends and are indeed but the images of the primitive imagination mirrored in the little looking-glass of the modern and classic imagination. This is that 'melancholy a man knows when he is face to face' with nature, and thinks 'he hears her communing with him about' the mournfulness of being born and of dying; and how can it do otherwise than call into his mind 'its exiles, its flights across the seas', that it may stir the ever-smouldering ashes?[22] No Gaelic poetry is so popular in Gaelic-speaking places as the lamentations of Oisin, old and miserable, remembering the companions and the loves of his youth, and his three hundred years in faeryland, and faery love: all dreams withering in the winds of time lament in his lamentations: 'The clouds are long above me this night; last night was a long night to me; although I find this day long, yesterday was still longer. Every day that comes to me is long . . . No one in this great world is like

me—a poor old man dragging stones. The clouds are long above me this night. I am the last man of the Fianna, the great Oisin, the son of Fionn, listening to the sound of bells. The clouds are long above me this night.'[23] Almost more beautiful is the lamentation of Leyrach Hen, which Matthew Arnold quotes as a type of the Celtic melancholy, and which I prefer to quote as a type of the primitive melancholy: 'O my crutch, is it not autumn when the fern is red and the water flag yellow? Have I not hated that which I love? . . . Behold, old age, which makes sport of me, from the hair of my head and my teeth, to my eyes which women loved. The four things I have all my life most hated fall upon me together—coughing and old age, sickness and sorrow. I am old, I am alone, shapeliness and warmth are gone from me, the couch of honour shall be no more mine; I am miserable, I am bent on my crutch. How evil was the lot allotted to Leyrach, the night he was brought forth! Sorrows without end and no deliverance from his burden.'[24] There are an Oisin and a Leyrach Hen still in the hearts of the Irish peasantry. 'The same man,' writes Dr Hyde in the beautiful prose which he first writes in Gaelic, 'who will to-day be dancing, sporting, drinking, and shouting, will be soliloquising by himself to-morrow, heavy and sick and sad in his own lonely little hut, making a croon over departed hopes, lost life, the vanity of this world, and the coming of death.'[25]

IV

Matthew Arnold asks how much of the Celt must one imagine in the ideal man of genius. I prefer to say, how much of the ancient hunters and fishers and of the ecstatic dancers among hills and woods must one imagine in the ideal man of genius. Certainly a thirst for unbounded emotion and a wild melancholy are troublesome things in the world, and do not make its life more easy or orderly, but it may be the arts are founded on the life beyond the world, and that they must cry in the ears of our penury until the world has been consumed and become a vision. Certainly, as Samuel Palmer wrote, 'Excess is the vivifying spirit of the finest art, and we must always seek to make excess more abundantly excessive.'[26] Matthew Arnold has said that if he were asked 'where English got its turn for melancholy and its turn for natural magic,' he 'would answer with little doubt that it got much of its melancholy from a Celtic source, with no doubt at all that from a Celtic source is got nearly all its natural magic.' I will put this differently and say that literature dwindles to a mere chronicle of circumstance, or passionless phantasies, and passionless meditations, unless it is constantly flooded with the passions and beliefs of ancient times,[27] and that of all the fountains of the passions and beliefs of ancient times in Europe, the Slavonic, the Finnish, the Scandinavian, and the Celtic, the Celtic alone has been for centuries close to the main river of European literature. It has again and again brought 'the vivifying spirit' 'of excess' into the arts of Europe. Ernest Renan has told how the visions of purgatory seen by pilgrims to Lough Derg—once visions of the pagan underworld, as the hollow tree that bore the pilgrim to the holy island was alone enough to prove—gave European thought new symbols of a more abundant penitence; and had so great an influence that he has written, 'It cannot be doubted for a moment that to the number of poetical themes Europe owes to the genius of the Celt is to be added the framework of the divine comedy.' A little later the legends of Arthur and his table, and of the Holy Grail, once the cauldron of the Irish god, the Dagda,[28] changed the literature of Europe, and it may be changed, as it were, the very roots of man's emotions by their influence on the spirit of chivalry and on the spirit of romance; and later still Shakespeare found his Puck and his Mab, and one knows not how much else of his faery kingdom, in Celtic legend; and Spenser, living in Celtic Ireland where the faeries were part of men's daily lives, set the faery kingdom over all the kingdoms of romance; while at the beginning of our own day Sir Walter Scott gave Highland legends and Highland excitability so great a mastery over all romance that they seem romance herself.[29] In our own time Scandinavian tradition, thanks to the imagination of Richard Wagner[30] and of William Morris, whose *Sigurd the Volsung* is surely the most epical of modern poems, and of the earlier and, as I think, greater Dr Ibsen, has created a new romance, and through the imagination of Richard Wagner, become the most passionate element in the arts of the modern world. There is indeed but one other element that is almost as passionate, the still unfaded legends of Arthur and of the Holy Grail; and now a new fountain of legends, and, as scholars have said, a more abundant fountain than any in Europe, is being opened, the great fountain of Gaelic legends; the tale of Deirdre,[31] who alone among the women who have set men mad was at once the white flame and the red flame, wisdom and loveliness; the tale of the Sons of Turran,[32] with its unintelligible mysteries, an old Grail Quest as I think; the tale of the four children changed into four swans, and lamenting over many waters;[33] the tale of the love of Cuchulain for an immortal goddess,[34] and his coming home to a mortal woman in the end; the tale of his many battles at the ford with that dear friend, he kissed before the battles, and over whose dead body he wept when he had killed him; the tale of the flight of Grainne with Diarmaid, strangest of all tales of the fickleness of woman;[35] and the tale of the coming of Oisin out of faeryland, and of his memories and lamentations. 'The Celtic movement', as I understand it, is principally the opening of this fountain, and none can measure of how great importance it may be to coming times, for every new fountain of legends is a new intoxication for the imagination of the world. It comes at a time when the imagination of the world is as ready, as it was at the coming of the tales of Arthur and of the Grail, for a

new intoxication. The reaction against the rationalism of the eighteenth century has mingled with a reaction against the materialism of the nineteenth century, and the symbolical movement, which has come to perfection in Germany in Wagner, in England in the Pre-Raphaelites,[36] and in France in Villiers de l'Isle-Adam,[37] and Mallarmé[38] and Maeterlinck,[39] and has stirred the imagination of Ibsen and D'Annunzio,[40] is certainly the only movement that is saying new things. The arts by brooding upon their own intensity have become religious, and are seeking, as some French critic[41] has said, to create a sacred book. They must, as religious thought has always done, utter themselves through legends; and the Slavonic and Finnish legends tell of strange woods and seas, and the Scandinavian legends are held by a great master, and tell also of strange woods and seas, and the Welsh legends are held by almost as many great masters as the Greek legends; while the Irish legends move among known woods and seas, and have so much of a new beauty, that they may well give the opening century its most memorable symbols.[42]

Notes

This essay, which first appeared in *Cosmopolis*, a journal of arts and letters, for June 1898, shows Yeats uniting his interest in folklore with his study of mythology, and integrating both with his sense of mission as an Irish writer above all else. Starting with Matthew Arnold and Ernest Renan, both of whom he has studied carefully, he argues that the 'Celtic' element is significant for modern literature because Irish folklore retains connections with the primary impulses of human nature that are evident in Irish and Celtic mythology. The argument evolves from Arnold but becomes quite different: Arnold holds that Celtic sensibility was crucial in order to make the Saxon or Germanic temperament more sensitive; whereas Yeats's contention is that the Celtic (therefore Irish) genius, as expressed in its folklore and mythology, is universal, therefore absolutely valid.

[1] Ernest Renan (1823-92), philologist, Celticist and historian of religion. Born in Brittany, he studied for the priesthood, but left the seminary and applied himself to a scientific investigation of Christianity. Author of *Vie de Jésus* (1863) and, in the field of Celtic studies, the influential essay of 1854. 'De la poésie des races Celtiques', translated by William G. Hutchinson in *Ernest Renan: The Poetry of the Celtic Races and Other Essays* (1896).

[2] Matthew Arnold published *On the Study of Celtic Literature* in 1867; Yeats takes his phrases from various parts of the work, but he does not distort Arnold's essential point.

[3] Johann Wolfgang von Goethe (1749-1832) wrote

Faust (Part I, 1808; Part II, 1832) and *The Sorrows of Young Werther* (1774).

[4] The *Kalevala* is an epic poem of Finland, based on the oral poetry of Karelia on the Finnish-Russian border, compiled by Elias Lönnrot (1802-84) and published in 1835. It was translated into English by John Martin Crawford in 1888. For the *Eddas,* see item 9, note 18.

[5] A collection of Welsh tales translated by Lady Charlotte Guest (1838-49). *On the Study of Celtic Literature* quotes passages describing the making of 'Flower Aspect', *Blodeuwedd,* from the fourth branch of the *Mabinogion.* The passage about the tree half in leaf recurs in the poem 'Vacillation', *Words for Music Perhaps and Other Poems* (1932), *CP,* p. 282.

[6] The two Keats quotations are from 'Ode to a Nightingale' and 'Bright star! Would I were steadfast as thou art'. 'Oblations' should read 'ablutions' and 'shore' should read 'shores'.

[7] This and preceding quotations from *The Merchant of Venice,* V, i.

[8] From *A Midsummer Night's Dream,* II, i.

[9] Arnold distinguishes four ways of 'handling nature'—the conventional, the faithful, the Greek and the Celtic: 'in the faithful way . . . the eye is on the object, and that is all you can say; in the Greek, the eye is on the object, but lightness and brightness are added; in the magical, the eye is on the object, but charm and magic are added.'

[10] From Keats's 'Ode on a Grecian Urn'. Yeats misquotes: 'mountain built' should be hyphenated, 'quiet' should be 'peaceful' and 'its' in line 3 should read 'this'.

[11] From *A Midsummer Night's Dream,* II, i.

[12] The first quotation from Virgil is from *Eclogue VII,* l. 45, '[You] mossy springs and grass softer than sleep . . . '; the second from *Eclogue II,* ll. 47-8: '[the beautiful Naiad] gathering pale violets and the heads of poppies / mingles the narcissus and the flower of the sweet-smelling fennel . . . '

[13] A medieval French romance that celebrates a victory of Charlemagne over the armies of Islam. The Mahomedan king is Marsile.

[14] Yeats is recalling a 'Love Song' from the Gaelic, based on Edward Walsh's translation of 'Éamonn an Chnoic' in *Irish Popular Songs* (1847), which he published in *Poems and Ballads of Young Ireland* (1888) but never reprinted. See Timothy Webb (ed.), *W. B.*

Yeats: Selected Poetry (1991), p. 230.

[15] The lay in which Oisín describes to St Patrick the origin of the blackbird of Derrycairn is amongst the best-known of the Ossianic lays or songs. They were edited in the *Transactions of the Ossianic Society* (1859 and 1861).

[16] From Douglas Hyde's *Love Songs of Connacht* (1893), pp. 134-5.

[17] A literal version of 'Róisín Dubh', best known in James Clarence Mangan's translation 'Dark Rosaleen'. Yeats's source possibly was Ferguson's literal translation in the *Dublin University Magazine* for August 1834.

[18] From 'The Dirge of O'Sullivan Bear' by J. J. Callanan, a poem based on Gaelic originals collected by Callanan in west Cork. The lines cursing the killers of O'Sullivan Bear read:

> May the hearth stone of hell
> Be their best bed for ever!

Yeats's source was T. Crofton Croker's *Researches in the South of Ireland* (1824).

[19] The poem is the Irish poem beginning 'Triúr atá ag brath ar mo bhás' and may be found in Tomás Ó Rathile (ed.), *Measgra Dánta II* (1927, reprinted 1977), p. 186. Ó Rathile argues that the author was probably a Franciscan called Francis O'Molloy, who wrote a *Grammatica Latino-Hibernica* in 1676.

[20] From 'Illusion', to be found in AE, *Collected Poems* (1919), p. 175. For AE, see headnote to item 14.

[21] In a note of 1924 Yeats reveals that the friend was William Sharp ('Fiona Macleod') (1855-1915), a Scottish writer who came under the influence of the Celtic revival of the late nineteenth century and who achieved some fame under his feminine pseudonym. Yeats also expresses the view that, though this proverb was probably invented, it remains true for all that.

[22] The phrases are from Hutchinson's translation of Renan. See note 1.

[23] A translation of this poem can be found in Lady Gregory's *Gods and Fighting Men* (1904), p. 460. The original she found in *The Book of the Dean of Lismore* (1862); Yeats follows Lady Gregory's mistranslation of the first line, which correctly should be: 'Tonight is long in Elphin'. Yeats provides a defiant version of this lament in *The Wanderings of Oisin* (1889), where Oisín turns aside from St Patrick's Christianity at the close (*CP,* p. 447).

[24] Quoted in Arnold's *On the Study of Celtic Literature* (see headnote and note 2 above) from *Canu Llywarch Hen* (*The Song of Llywarch the Old*), a cycle of Welsh poems about Llywarch and his sons, dating from the ninth or tenth century.

[25] From the opening paragraphs of Douglas Hyde's *Love Songs of Connacht.* For Douglas Hyde, see item 1, note 23.

[26] From a sketchbook of Samuel Palmer's, written 1823/4, quoted in A. H. Palmer (ed.), *The Life and Letters of Samuel Palmer* (London, 1892), p. 16. Palmer (1805-81), artist and engraver, was a disciple of William Blake.

[27] In 1924 Yeats added a note: 'I should have added as an alternative that the supernatural may at any moment create new myths, but I was too timid.'

[28] The vat the Daghda has beneath Newgrange, from which no one departs unsatisfied.

[29] In novels such as *Waverley* (1814), *The Antiquary* (1816), *Old Mortality* (1816) and *Rob Roy* (1817).

[30] Richard Wagner (1813-83), the German composer, based many of his operas on Nordic mythology; William Morris retold Norse material in *Sigurd the Volsung* (1876). For Morris, see item 42, note 2.

[31] Heroine of *Longes meic nUisnigh* (*The Exile of the Sons of Uisnech*) preserved in the *Book of Leinster* and elsewhere in a version of the eighth or ninth century. An early form of the story of Tristan and Isolde, it tells a tale of tragic doomed love, wandering and human malice. Deirdre's story is the basis of Yeats's play of 1907.

[32] *Oidheadh Chlainne Tuireann* (*The Death of the Children of Tuireann*) tells of the adventures of the children of Tuireann, as they discharge tasks imposed upon them by the son of a man they have killed. They eventually die in carrying out the duties laid upon them.

[33] *Oidheadh Chlainne Lir* (*The Death of the Children of Lir*) tells how the four children of Lir, one of the Tuatha Dé Danann (see glossary), are transformed through the sorcery of a jealous stepmother into four swans, and in this shape they live on the seas off Ireland until the coming of St Patrick.

[34] In *Serglighe Con Chulainn* (*The Wasting Sickness of Cuchulain*), preserved in the twelfth-century *Book of the Dun Cow,* Cuchulain is cast into a trance by two otherworld women who beat him; after a year in this state he is taken to the otherworld, where he fights for Fand's love against a host of the *sídh* on behalf of Labhraidh, himself one of the *sídh.* Having spent a

month with Fand, he is won back by Emer, his earthly wife. Yeats based his play *The Only Jealousy of Emer* (1919) on this tale. The friend is Ferdia; see glossary entry Tain Bo.

[35] See glossary entry Dermod.

[36] The Pre-Raphaelite Brotherhood was a group of artists and poets (D. G. Rossetti, Holman Hunt, William Morris among them) who developed a cult of simplicity, naïvety and medievalism in art. They flourished in the 1850s, but they continued to influence literature and painting for a considerable time after.

[37] Philippe-Auguste Villiers de L'Isle-Adam (1838-89), French writer and aesthete whose *Axël* (1890) was a formative symbolist visionary drama. .

[38] Stéphane Mallarmé (1842-98), an influential French symbolist poet, who experimented with the musical and suggestive possibilities of verse.

[39] Maurice Maeterlinck (1862-1949), Belgian playwright and symbolist.

[40] Gabriele D'Annunzio (1863-1938), Italian writer who experimented in a wide range of forms.

[41] In 1902 Yeats wrote 'Verhaeren'. Émile Verhaeren (1855-1916), Belgian poet and Rosicrucian, who united symbolism and social awareness. He knew Maeterlinck (see note 39 above).

[42] In 1902 he added: 'I could have written this essay with much more precision and have much better illustrated my meaning if I had waited until Lady Gregory had finished her book of legends, *Cuchulain of Muirthemne,* a book to set beside the *Morte d'Arthur* and the *Mabinogion.*'

Thomas F. O'Rahilly (1946)

SOURCE: "History or Fable?," in *Early Irish History and Mythology*, The Dublin Institute for Advanced Studies, 1946, pp. 260-85.

[*In the following essay, O'Rahilly traces the ways in which various Celtic gods, heroes, and myths have been treated as exaggerated but real figures and stories from ancient history.*]

1.—Euhemerists and Others

To our forefathers of a few centuries ago the history of Ireland appeared to be known, at least in outline, continuously from a couple of thousand years B. C. down to their own time. Nowadays we are naturally more sceptical. Before we can give credence to precise statements regarding events in remote times, we have to assure ourselves that these statements are based on contemporary, or nearly contemporary, records.

The critical evaluation of the sources of our knowledge of pre-Christian Ireland is of recent growth. About the middle of the last century those two great contemporary scholars, O'Donovan and O'Curry, still had almost unbounded confidence in the historical accuracy of most of our records relating to pre-Christian times. Thus in O'Donovan's opinion the Tuatha Dé Danann 'were a real people, though their history is so much wrapped up in fable and obscurity'.[1] A folk version of the myth of the birth of Lug, which he records, he regards as 'evidently founded on facts', while conceding that the facts have been 'much distorted'.[2] O'Curry seems to have accepted without question the history of Ireland as related in Lebor Gabála and elsewhere from at least the time of the 'Milesian' invasion onwards.[3] Even the story of the Second Battle of Mag Tuired, in which the mythical Tuatha Dé Danann vanquish the no less mythical Fomoire, he is inclined to regard as veracious.[4]

Euhemerism, that is, the treating of divine beings as if they were men of a far-off age, has long been a favourite method of manufacturing early history, in Ireland and elsewhere. Our Irish pseudo-historians were thoroughgoing euhemerists; so, too, were the inventors of the pre-Christian parts of our genealogies. By thus humanizing and mortalizing the divinities of pagan Ireland, they hoped to eradicate the pagan beliefs that still lingered on among many of their countrymen. Cormac mac Cuilennáin († 908) turns Manannán mac Lir into a skilful navigator who lived in the Isle of Man and who was afterwards deified by the Irish and the Welsh. Flann Mainistrech († 1056) devotes a poem (LL 11 a 19 ff.) to recounting the deaths of all the leading members of the Tuatha Dé Danann. Doubtless his intention was to emphasize their mortal nature, for he must have been well aware that many of the personages he mentions were really pagan deities.[5]

The euhemeristic method has several features which have ensured it a continued popularity in Ireland. It is easy to apply; it enables the uncritical writer to fill up the historical vacuum which he abhors; and it gives us the flattering notion that the records of our history reach back into a very remote past. Moreover with the lapse of time and the disappearance of pagan beliefs the original divine character of the euhemerized personages became increasingly difficult to recognize and was frequently quite forgotten. Accordingly it is not surprising to find that euhemerism still has its votaries. Thus, to take a rather extreme instance, a well-known scholar of our own day has argued that the god Oengus, of Bruig na Bóinne, was originally 'a real historical character who lived, probably, some time towards the beginning of the Bronze Age.' Similarly the goddess

Medb has been treated as 'a real historical character' by Eoin Mac Neill and others. One May readily concede that famous men (e. g. Brian Bóramha and his son Murchadh) have frequently been credited with fabulous achievements in the popular imagination of a later age. But that admission does not alter the fact that the euhemeristic method in general is worthless and misleading, and can throw light neither upon history nor upon religion. As Alfred Nutt wrote many years ago, 'the mythology of the Celts has suffered more than that of any other race from the euhemerising methods of investigation applied to it'.[6]

With euhemerism is usually associated rationalization, which would explain the supernatural as due to the misunderstanding or exaggeration, by simple or stupid people, of what was originally not supernatural at all. Among many of our population the belief long persisted that a supernatural personage had his dwelling beneath a local lake. Our early rationalizers tried to explain away this belief by averring that the site of the lake had once been dry land, and that, when the lake was formed by the bursting forth of water from a well, the dwelling of the local lord had been engulfed in the flood and he himself drowned therein. As an example of modern rationalization we may quote O'Donovan's opinion of the Tuatha Dé Danann: 'From their having been considered gods and magicians by the Gaedhil or Scoti who subdued them, it may be inferred that they were skilled in arts which the latter did not understand'.[7] Similarly O'Curry rationalizes the supernatural powers of the Tuatha Dé into their 'scientific superiority'.[8] We are indebted to a contemporary of these scholars for the following amusing explanation of Finn's custom of chewing his thumb in order to acquire occult knowledge. Finn, 'when in deep thought, seems to have been in the habit of biting his nails'; but the common people, observing the beneficial results of his meditations, distorted his unpleasant habit into the chewing of his thumb, which they regarded as 'some mysterious act necessary to his communication with the unseen world'.[9] The submarine Otherworld was sometimes conceived as a glass house in the sea; and into such a glass house the enchanter Merlin is said to have taken the thirteen treasures of Britain. An eighteenth-century Welshman, Lewis Morris, explains that 'this house of glass, it seems, was the museum where they kept their curiosities to be seen by everybody, but not handled', and he makes Merlin 'the keeper of the museum'.[10] Of all the methods applied to the interpretation of mythic material, the rationalistic method is surely the most absurd.

One sometimes hears the question asked: 'Where are we to draw the line between fact and fiction?' It would, no doubt, be very convenient if we could draw such a line: if we could, for instance, assume that before A.D. 200 we have fiction, and after that time fact.[11] Actually no such line can be drawn. Even in the accounts we possess of historical persons, like Colum Cille or Brian Bórama, fiction is blended with history or legend (i.e. semi-history). Speaking generally, however, we may say that our annalistic records, which begin immediately after the official introduction of Christianity in the year 431, give us fact. For the pre-Christian period contemporary records fail us; but fortunately we are not left completely in the dark. In early Christian Ireland the popular memory was extraordinarily tenacious and conservative regarding the various origins of the different strata of the population; and with the help of these popular traditions, which have been in part preserved, it is possible to trace our history, in some of its broad outlines, back to a period antecedent to the Christian era.

2.—Lebor Gabála

The history of pre-Christian Ireland as related in Lebor Gabála seems to have imposed itself easily on our ancestors. In the course of time the increasing antiquity of the record only strengthened its authority; and as late as the seventeenth century it was accepted unquestioningly as historical truth by scholars like the Four Masters, Keating,[12] and Duald Mac Firbis. Despite its generally spurious character, Lebor Gabála embodies some popular traditions concerning the Goidelic invasion and the names of the pre-Goidelic inhabitants (pp. 194, 197). One section of it, that relating to the Tuatha Dé Danann, owes its origin to a desire to reduce the deities of pagan Ireland to the level of mortal men. This part of Lebor Gabála misled d'Arbois de Jubainville[13] into treating the whole work as a mythological compilation, a kind of Irish theogony, into which he read the struggles of the 'gods of life and light' against the 'gods of death and night'. Actually Lebor Gabála is no more a mythological treatise than it is an historical one.[14]

While no one nowadays would accept all the fictions of Lebor Gabála,[15] its influence on opinion is by no means exhausted. The biggest fiction of the authors of Lebor Gabála, and a fiction which necessitated a long series of other fabrications to support it, was their claim that the dominant Goidels had been in occupation of Ireland from a very remote period; and it is precisely this 'pious fraud' that has been most readily accepted by many scholars in recent times. Sir John Rhys, as is well known, maintained that the Goidels were settled, not only in Ireland but also in Britain, from a remote antiquity;[16] indeed Rhys's theorizings are quite as imaginative and unsubstantiated as anything in Lebor Gabála. Even yet similar views are put forward from time to time by archæologists, who, chafing under the limitations of their science, too often succumb to the temptation to lend a specious semblance of reality to their speculations by linking them arbitrarily with the names of historical peoples.

Even scholars who are rightly sceptical regarding the historicity of most of the kings who are recorded as having reigned in pagan times seem to lose their caution when dealing with the alleged kings of Ireland during the early centuries of our era. Despite the fact that the story of Tuathal's birth and upbringing 'reads like a fairy tale', Mac Neill gives it sufficient credence to infer from it that there was probably 'a plebeian revolution' in Ireland in the second century A.D.[17] The same scholar regards Medb as an historical queen of Connacht who 'flourished just at the commencement of the Christian era'; and because the pedigree represents Tuathal as sixth in descent from Eochu Fedlech, Medb's father, he concludes that Tuathal flourished 'between A.D. 150 and A.D. 175'.[18] Likewise he regards Cormac ua Cuinn as an historical king, who conquered Tara from the Lagin.[19] During Cormac's reign, he writes, 'we trace the establishment in Ireland of permanent military forces, the Fiana, adopted no doubt in imitation of the Roman military organization'.[20] This idea that the Fiana, the hunting and fighting bands of Finn and Goll, were modelled on the Roman legions goes back to John Pinkerton, who wrote, as far back as 1814: 'His [i.e. Finn's] formation of a regular standing army, trained to war, in which all the Irish accounts agree, seems to have been a rude imitation of the Roman legions in Britain'.[21] Now the Fiana in question are indissolubly linked with Finn and Goll; and the only connexion they have with Cormac is that Finn and his fellows are often supposed to have lived contemporaneously with Cormac. The question of their historicity is bound up with the historicity of Finn and Goll; if these are mythical figures, so too are the Fiana, who have no existence apart from them.

3.—The Genealogies

The Irish genealogists did their work thoroughly. Not only did they provide every Irish family of importance with a pedigree which went back to Míl of Spain (or to Ith, Míl's uncle), but they also invented a pedigree of Míl's ancestors going back to Noah and thence to Adam. All this was accepted as indubitable truth by our native scholars. Mac Firbis in 1650, in the preface to his great genealogical compilation, stoutly affirms his belief in it.[22] So does Thady Roddy (Tadhg Ó Rodaighe), who, writing in 1700, boasts that 'all the familyes of the Milesian race' can trace their pedigree back to Adam.[23] As late as 1856 Eugene O'Curry is strongly inclined to make a similar claim, and deprecates the 'scepticism' with which some would regard such pedigrees.[24] In our own day one may still notice a certain reluctance among Irishmen to consign these imposing lists of ancestors to the scrap-heap. Mac Neill at one time held that 'the extant genealogies of great families are substantially accurate as far back as the Birth of our Lord.[25] A few years later, in 1908, he is decidedly more sceptical; he has not 'a shadow of doubt' that 'the authentic genealogies reach back in no instance beyond the year 300 A.D.'[26] Yet in 1919 we find him treating as historical the pedigree of the kings of Tara in the first and second centuries A.D.;[27] and in 1941 he treats the same pedigree as historical back to the middle of the third century.[28]

The fact is that no trust can be placed in the pedigrees of pre-Christian times. The pedigree-makers and the authors of Lebor Gabála worked hand in hand. Their object was the same, namely, to provide a fictitious antiquity for the Goidels and a fictitious Goidelic descent for the Irish generally (p. 162). Accordingly they filled out the pre-Christian part of the pedigrees of the kings of Tara and of Cashel with mythical or fanciful names, drawn in part from the traditions of the pre-Goidelic Érainn. It is sometimes argued that, because people have been known who could repeat their pedigree back for seven generations, the pedigree of King Loegaire († 463) must be trustworthy for at least a couple of centuries previous to his time.[29] Unfortunately the cases are not parallel. The record that we possess of the ancestors of Loegaire was not derived from Loegaire himself or from any contemporary of his, but forms part of a lengthy pedigree, invented several centuries after his death, in which his descent is traced back to the fabulous Míl. Moreover, as we have seen, the inventors of this and similar pedigrees were very far indeed from being animated by a desire for historical truth and accuracy; indeed one need not hesitate to say that their object was rather to disguise the truth.

The Laginian pedigree is instructive in this connexion. The death of Bresal, king of Lagin, is chronicled in AU under 435 and 436; he was thus an elder contemporary of Loegaire, king of Ireland. Elsewhere he is called Bresal Bélach, as in the pedigree, according to which he was grandson of Cathaer Már (or Mór).[30] Accordingly, Meyer places the *floruit* of Cathaer Már (whom he takes to have been an historical king) in the fourth century.[31] Actually, there can hardly be a doubt, Cathaer Már is the ancestor-deity of the Lagin, the Otherworld god from whom they claimed descent.[32] Hence we see that the compilers of the Laginian pedigree did not shrink from making a purely mythical personage grandfather of an historical king who lived in the early fifth century.

As Cathaer Már was ancestor of the Lagin, so Conn Cétchathach was ancestor of their enemies, the Goidels of the Midlands. Hence our pseudo-historians, without troubling on this occasion to adapt their implied chronology to that of the genealogists, thought it appropriate to make Cathaer and Conn contemporaries and rivals,[33] and so in the list of kings of Tara Cathaer appears as Conn's immediate predecessor. So in the tract on the Bórama Cathaer's grandson, Bresal Bélach, is said to have won a battle at Cnámross against Conn's great-grandson, Cairbre Lifechar, and to have slain three

of Cairbre's sons,[34] although according to the pedigree Cairbre Lifechar was five generations removed from Loegaire, who historically was Bresal's junior contemporary. On the other hand, as we have seen (p. 19), Failge Berraide or Failge Rot, who fought battles in 510 and 516, is said to have been a son of Cathaer Már, which would imply that Cathaer lived in the fifth century! It is vain to attempt to resolve these inconsistencies; the fact is that Cathaer Már, as a non-historical character, does not belong to any century more than another.

4.—The Ulidian Tales

Our earliest critic of any of the Ulidian tales is Aed mac Crimthainn, the twelfth-century scribe of the Book of Leinster, who records his opinion that 'Táin Bó Cualnge' includes fictitious and foolish things (*quaedam figmenta poetica . . . quaedam ad delectationem stultorum*), and is fable rather than history.[35] Many centuries elapse before we hear a similar critical voice. Keating and his contemporaries have no doubts about the historical character of the Ulidian tales. Concerning 'Táin Bó Cualnge' O'Curry wrote in 1855: 'Though often exhibiting high poetic colouring in the description of particular circumstances, it unquestionably embraces and is all through founded upon authentic historic facts'; and again: 'The chief actors in this warfare are all well-known and undoubted historical characters, and are to be met with not only in our ancient tales, but in our authentic annals also'.[36] Zimmer in 1884 affirmed his belief in the historicity of Ailill, Medb, Conchobar, Cúchulainn and Finn.[37] A few years later Meyer writes: 'Conchobor and Cuchulaind were, I believe, historical personages'.[38]

With greater insight Alfred Nutt wrote in 1888: 'This [viz. the Ulidian] cycle, in its origin almost if not wholly mythic, was at an early date (probably as early as the eighth century) euhemerised, and its gods and demi-gods made to do duty as historical personages living at the beginning of the Christian era'.[39] In his Hibbert Lectures, published in the same year, Rhys, like Nutt, regards the Ulidian tales as based on myth, not on history; but in his attempts to unravel the underlying myths and to explain the actors in them he is very much at sea. Thus he regards Cúchulainn as 'the Sun-god or Solar Hero';[40] and he takes Conchobar mac Nesa, Cormac mac Airt and Conaire Mór to be representatives of 'the Celtic Zeus'.[41]

The view of Rev. Edmund Hogan in 1892 approximates to that of O'Curry; he regards the characters of the Ulidian tales as 'real personages,' on the ground that there is mention of them in Irish documents from the eighth century onwards.[42] Windisch's view in 1905 is not very dissimilar. Concerning 'Táin Bó Cualnge' he writes: 'Es ist sehr wohl möglich, sogar wahrscheinlich, dass es einst einen König Conchobar von Ulster, eine Königin Medb von Connacht gegeben hat, dass Ulster und Connacht aus ähnlichen Anlässen, wie sie in der Sage geschildert werden, Krieg mit einander geführt haben, dass Helden mit den Namen, die in der Sage genannt werden, warum nicht auch ein Held Namens Cuchulinn, in solchen Kämpfen sich ausgezeichnet haben. Aber ein geschichtliche Genauigkeit in dem Berichte davon ist nicht zu erwarten. Dazu waltet in der Sage die Phantasie zu sehr vor'.[43]

The euhemeristic tendency is by no means extinct. Because myth has become attached to certain historical personages, it is supposed by those who have no deep acquaintance with Celtic mythology that characters like Cúchulainn and Fergus mac Roich were likewise historical.[44]

Actually the Ulidian tales are wholly mythical in origin, and they have not the faintest connexion with anything that could be called history, apart from the fact that traditions of warfare between the Ulaid and the Connachta have been adventitiously introduced into a few of them, and especially into the longest and best-known tale, 'Táin Bó Cualnge'. Cúchulainn, who in the Táin is assigned the role of defender of the Ulaid against their invaders, can be shown to be in origin Lug or Lugaid, a deity whom we may conveniently call the Hero, provided we bear in mind that he was a wholly supernatural personage, and not a mere mortal. The other leading characters, such as Cú Roí, Fergus, Briccriu and Medb, are likewise euhemerized divinities.[45]

5.—Finn and the Fiana

The other great cycle of storytelling, that of the Finnian tales (as we may call them), is concerned mainly with Finn mac Cumaill, his son Oisín, Diarmait mac Duinn (D. ua Duibne), and Goll mac Morna. Finn and his fellows are represented as a *fian*[46] or band of hunters and warriors; and the rivalry between Finn and Goll is rationalized into a contest concerning the *rígfhénnidecht* or leadership of the *fian*. Keating claims that Finn and his *fian* were real persons (FF ii, 324), though he admits that not a few of the tales told about them, such as 'Cath Fionntrágha', are fictitious romances (ib. i, 50; ii, 326). O'Curry's views are identical. 'It is quite a mistake', he writes,[47] 'to suppose Finn Mac Cumhaill to have been a merely imaginary or mythical character. Much that has been related of his exploits is, no doubt, apocryphal enough; but Finn himself is an undoubtedly historical personage, and that he existed about the time at which his appearance is recorded in the annals, is as certain as that Julius Caesar lived and ruled at the time stated on the authority of the Roman historians'.

John O'Donovan likewise held that Finn and his *fiana* were historical. 'I have always believed,' he writes,

'that Finn Mac Cumhaill was *a real historical personage,* and not a myth or a god of war. . . . He was the son-in-law of the famous Cormac Mac Airt monarch of Ireland, and the general of his standing army. He was slain in the year A. D. 284, according to the Annals of Tighernach, a period to which our authentic history unquestionably reaches'.[48] W. M. Hennessy, while accepting the popular opinion that 'a person named Find Mac Cumhaill did live' in the third century, held that 'his history has degenerated into a pure myth'.[49] The views of Windisch (in 1878) concerning Finn and his fellows resemble those of O'Curry, except that Windisch is sceptical as to the complete accuracy of the dates assigned to them in early Irish history.[50] As a curiosity may be mentioned the theory put forward by Zimmer in 1891, that Finn is in origin the Norseman Caittil Find who was slain in Munster in 857, and that the Finnian tales have their origin in popular recollections of the Norse invaders.[51] Contrast with this the conclusion reached by Alfred Nutt, that 'from the earliest date to which we can trace it, the Ossianic saga is romantic rather than historical; in other words, it narrates to a very slight extent events which ever actually happened, or which ever would happen'.[52]

Scottish scholars, as was to be expected, have also interested themselves in the question. W. F. Skene, in 1862, propounded the theory that the Feinne (*sic*) 'were of the population who immediately preceded the Scots in Erin and Alban'.[53] Equally extravagant is the theory of David MacRitchie, that the Fians (*sic*), the Picts and the 'fairies' are all 'historical people,' who were 'closely akin to each other, if not actually one people under three names'.[54] J. A. MacCulloch's view resembles that of Nutt. 'Little historic fact,' he writes, 'can be found in it' (viz. the Finn saga); and 'whether personages called Fionn, Oisin, Diarmaid, or Conan, ever existed [or not], what we know of them now is purely mythical'.[55]

Whereas the Ulidian tales are tied down geographically and are assigned to a definite period of pseudo-history, the Finnian tales are much more elastic in both respects, and in particular they possessed (unlike the Ulidian tales) a local adaptability, which contributed in no small measure to their increasing popularity. While Cúchulainn belonged to the Ulaid alone, Finn had no exclusive connexions with any tribe, and he and his *fiana* were free to indulge in war or the chase or adventure in any part of the country, so that eventually, as may be inferred from 'Acallam na Senórach', there was hardly a district in Ireland that did not acquire associations with them. In Gaelic Scotland, too, the stories of Finn and his *fiana* became thoroughly acclimatized.

Unlike the heroes of the Ulidian tales, Finn mac Cumaill and the members of his *fiana* are entirely ignored by the genealogists and by the authors of Lebor Gabála.

However, the growing importance of the Finnian tales and poems made it necessary to allocate a place in pseudo-history to Finn; and so we find the Irish World-Chronicle recording his death, just as it records the death of Cúchulainn. Finn is there said to have been slain by the Luaigni of Tara in the reign of Cairbre Lifechar.[56] His death at the hands of the *fian* of the Luaigni is also recorded by Cinaed ua hArtacáin.[57] His birth is assigned to the reign of Conn, or of Conn's predecessor Cathaer Már.[58] Elsewhere Finn is supposed to have lived in the reign of Cormac,[59] Conn's grandson. But the author of the compilation known as 'Macgnímartha Find', probably because of the difficulty he found in reconciling his sources, deliberately refrains from introducing any king of Ireland into his tale, and leaves Finn divorced from pseudo-history.[60]

While Finn's lifetime is made to extend over a period of four generations, from Conn Cétchathach to Cairbre Lifechar,[61] his son Oisín and his nephew Caílte were, by a later convention, supposed to have lived sufficiently long to have held converse with St. Patrick. This idea[62] of Oisín and Caílte surviving into Christian times proved very popular, and underlies 'Acallam na Senórach' (a long prose text interspersed with poems), as well as a great deal of later 'Ossianic' verse.[63]

Traditions of a hero of superhuman accomplishments, one of whose names was Finn, must have been known in various parts of the country; and it is possible to distinguish a Finn of Midland tradition, a Laginian Finn, and a Finn associated with the Érainn of Munster. In the pedigree of the kings of Tara, Finn is father of Eochu Fedlech,[64] while the pedigree of the kings of Lagin includes Finn Fili,[65] son of Rus Ruad. The Finn of romance (Finn mac Cumaill) was, however, disassociated from these, and various special pedigrees were invented for him. Sometimes he is made to descend from Nuadu Necht,[66] ancestor of the Lagin; at other times from Dáire,[67] son of Ded, ancestor of the Érainn. There is a similar fluctuation regarding his descent on the maternal side. Finn's mother is best known as Muirne, daughter of Tadg, son of Nuadu (or Nuadu Necht); but according to other accounts his mother was Torba or Tarbda, who was of the Érainn of Cermna (in Co. Cork).[68] Likewise there were at least two different accounts of Finn's death. Usually he is represented as having been slain at Brea, or Áth Brea, on the River Boyne;[69] but another tradition made his death take place in Luachair Dedad, in the south-west of Ireland.[70]

In 'Tochmarc Ailbe' Finn is represented as an officer in the service of Cormac, king of Tara, and as captain of Cormac's fighting-men (*ta sech ceithirne*).[71] He wedded Gráinne, Cormac's daughter; but as a result of her unfaithfulness he was temporarily banished from Tara. Later he was reconciled to Cormac, and wedded another daughter of his, named Ailbe. Here we probably have the Finn of Midland tradition. His close relations with Cormac are what one would expect, for reasons that will appear later. Naturally, when he is brought into association with a pseudo-historic king of Ireland, Finn's role has to be a subordinate one.

On the whole it is the Laginian Finn who is best known. According to Laginian tradition Finn compelled his maternal grandfather, Tadg mac Nuadat, to surrender Almu (the hill of Allen, near Kildare town); and in the later literature it is an established convention that Almu was Finn's principal residence.[72] In the legendary battle of Cnámross, in which Bresal Bélach defeated Cairbre Lifechar, king of Tara, Finn and his *fian* are said to have fought on the side of the victors.[73] Conversely Goll, who is Finn's enemy in the primitive myth, is associated with the Luaigni,[74] who were the fighting-men of the early kings of Tara; and as the Luaigni were said to have slain Cathaer Már,[75] king of the Lagin, so too they are said to have slain Finn.[76] Hence Conn Cétchathach, king of Tara, sometimes takes the place of Goll as enemy of the youthful Finn.[77]

Our storytellers may be forgiven for the fluctuating chronology they assign to Finn and his *fian,* for none of their alleged achievements has the remotest connexion with history. Finn and his fellows (Goll, Diarmait, Oisín, etc.) never existed. Finn is ultimately the divine Hero, Lug or Lugaid, just like Cúchulainn.[78] Lugaid, who was especially prominent in the traditions of the Érainn, appears in pseudo-history as Lugaid mac Con, who is the immediate predecessor of Cormac in the list of the kings of Ireland, and again as Lugaid Lága, who is likewise contemporary with Cormac, and who is represented as brother of Ailill Aulomm. We find early mention of the *fian* of Lugaid mac Con,[79] which we may regard as the forerunner of the *fian* of Finn. So we understand why the Finn of Southern tradition is represented as the friend and avenger of Lugaid mac Con.[80] Likewise we see the probable reason why Finn was made contemporary with Cormac. Finn's rival, Goll ('the one-eyed'), who was also called Aed ('fire'), is the sun-deity, who was also the lord of the Otherworld. The enmity between Finn and Goll mac Morna is but another version of the enmity between Lug and Balar, and between Cúchulainn and Goll mac Carbada. According to the primitive myth,[81] the newly-born Hero 'slew' or overcame the Otherworld deity. The latter had many appellations; here we need only mention that one of his names in Laginian tradition was Nuadu Necht. As it happens, the Laginian Finn, descended from Nuadu, has his counterpart in the Gwyn, son of Nudd, of Welsh mythical tradition.[82]

We have several versions of the myth of Finn's overcoming of the Otherworld-god. Two of them may be briefly mentioned here. In 'Acallam na Senórach' it is told how the youthful Finn slew Aillén mac Midgna of the *síd* (or Otherworld) of Finnachad, and how Goll had to surrender to Finn the leadership of the *fiana* of

Ireland (*rígfhéinnidhecht Éirenn*).[83] This deposition of the euhemerized Goll is admittedly an immediate consequence of Finn's victory over Aillén; and so the conclusion is sufficiently obvious, that the Aillén whom Finn overthrew was in reality Goll himself. Elsewhere[84] the personage whom Finn deposes is his maternal grandfather, Tadg mac Nuadat. The youthful Finn threatened Tadg with battle, and Tadg, unable to resist, surrendered Almu, where he lived, to Finn.

In pagan belief the deity Nuadu (of whom Tadg mac Nuadat was but an alias) was lord of the *síd* of Almu.[85] The primitive version of the rivalry between Finn and Nuadu would have told how Finn 'slew' Nuadu, as elsewhere he slays Aillén, and as Lug slays his maternal grandfather Balar; but when Nuadu had been euhemerized into an historical person, it was natural to assume that Finn, after overthrowing his maternal grandfather, deprived him of his property rather than his life. As the *síd* or Otherworld was above all a place of feasting,[86] we understand why Finn is represented as presiding over feasts in Almu. Similarly Finn's victory over Aillén means that he deposed the lord of the festive Otherworld; but in 'Acallam na Senórach' the myth has been adapted to pseudo-history, with the result that the feast no longer belongs to the *síd,* but is represented as the Feast of Tara (*feis na Temra*), which is being held by King Conn Cétchathach and is being assailed by the fire-breathing Aillén.

The hill of Almu (Allen), therefore, was a *síd* or hill within which the Otherworld, ruled by Nuadu, was believed to be located; and Finn's taking possession of it is merely a late euhemeristic inference from his victory over Nuadu in the pagan myth. Accordingly it is not a matter for surprise if those who have explored the hill of Allen in the hope of finding material evidence of Finn's residence thereon have returned disappointed. Thus O'Donovan writes in 1837: 'I traversed all the hill, but could find upon it no monuments from which it could be inferred that it was ever a royal seat. . . . And still, in all the Fingallian or Ossianic poems, this hill is referred to as containing the palace of the renowned champion, Finn Mac Cool, who seems to have been a real historical character that flourished here in the latter end of the third century'.[87] Later explorers of the hill have naturally had no better success.[88] Mac Neill, who (like the others) entirely misses the mythological significance of Finn, tries to explain away the absence of all traces of former habitation on the hill by suggesting that 'its military value must have consisted in its being a watching place from which the Leinster king in his stronghold of Ailinn might be warned of an enemy's approach'.[89] T. O'Neill Russell tried to get over the difficulty by suggesting[90] that our storytellers have confused Almu (the hill of Allen) with Ailenn (Knockawlin, near Kilcullen), which was at one time the residence of the kings of Leinster, so that Ailenn 'may have been the hill on which Finn Mac

Cumhaill had his dun'. This suggestion was taken up by Meyer, who, observing that Ailenn was assigned as residence to Finn Fili, mythical king of the Lagin, asserted that 'the connexion of Find mac Cumaill with the hill of Allen rests on a confusion with his namesake [Finn Fili] and of Alenn with Almu (Allen)'.[91] Actually there is no 'confusion' between Finn Fili and Finn mac Cumaill, who are always kept distinct, even though they are ultimately the same; nor is there ever any confusion in the literature between Ailenn and Almu. In his role of pseudo-historical king of Lagin, Finn Fili was inevitably thought to have resided in Ailenn, which was the residence of the kings of Lagin in early historical times. Finn mac Cumaill's residence on Almu is simply a way of saying that he overcame the god Nuadu, who ruled over the Otherworld within the hill. To look for traces of Finn mac Cumaill's *dún* on the hill of Allen is as vain as to try to discover Bodb Derg's residence on Slievenamon or Mider's on Croghan Hill. The Otherworld is impervious to archæological exploration.

6.—Conn Cétchathach. Cormac ua Cuinn.

Conn Cétchathach and Cormac ua Cuinn have been mentioned above as the two 'kings of Ireland' with whom Finn is most frequently associated. The Dictionary of National Biography treats these two personages as historical kings, and devotes several columns to an account of the doings of each of them. It may be worth while to examine their alleged historicity a little more closely.

Conn was one of the numerous names applied to the god of the Otherworld, from whom the Celts believed themselves to be descended, and after whom they were wont to name themselves, both as individuals and as tribes. Hence the Midland Goidels called themselves *Connacht(a),* 'descendants of Conn'. The pseudo-historians and the genealogists, following their custom, turned Conn into an Irish king, making him son of Fedlimmid Rechtaid,[92] son of Tuathal Techtmar.

As a common noun *conn* (*cond*) means 'sense, reason', and goes back to Celt. **kondo-,* IE. **kom-dho-.*[93] We may take it, therefore, that the name *Conn* was applied to the god in his capacity of god of wisdom.[94] Welsh tradition affords a close parallel in Pwyll, 'head of Annwfn', whose name (Welsh *pwyll,* 'sense, reason, prudence') is the counterpart of Ir. *ciall* and is synonymous with *conn.* In Gaul *Condos* and *Senocondos* are known to have been in use as personal names;[95] as the Otherworld deity was characterized at once by great age and great wisdom,[96] the latter name, meaning 'the wise old one',[97] would have been a very appropriate designation for him.

The word *conn* (*cond*) means also 'head' and (figuratively) 'chief'. A possible explanation of this is to see in it a secondary use of *conn,* 'reason', the head being the seat of reason. In any event a word meaning 'head' would be an appropriate designation of the Celtic Otherworld-deity.[98] On Gaulish monuments he is often represented as a triple-faced head, or as a triple head. Welsh tradition tells of the joyous feasting in the Otherworld island of Gwales, presided over by Bran's Head, and known as *yspydawt urdawl Benn,* 'the hospitality of the honourable Head'.[99] So it is possibly significant that Pwyll is called, not 'lord of the Otherworld', but 'head of the Otherworld', *penn Annwvyn.* Sufficient evidence remains to show that in pagan Ireland, too, there was a similar belief concerning the divine Head presiding at the Otherworld feast.[100]

A plain trace of the divinity of Conn is seen in the text 'Baile Chuinn Chétchathaig',[101] which purports to be a prophecy by Conn concerning the kings of Ireland who were to succeed him. Here Conn, as befits his name, is the god of foreknowledge and prophecy. It is interesting to observe the modifications introduced into 'Baile in Scáil',[102] a later and longer text on the same theme. This tells how Conn one day, after a magic mist had come upon him near Tara, found himself in the Otherworld, and how the lord of the Otherworld, who is here identified with Lug mac Ethlenn,[103] foretold to Conn the kings who were to succeed him. Here Conn is merely king of Tara, and as a mortal he no longer possesses the power of seeing into the future; hence it is necessary to transport him to the Otherworld in order that the future may be revealed to him.

Cormac, who is made grandson of Conn, is likewise, I have little doubt, a wholly unhistorical personage. His name,[104] the story of his birth and upbringing, and the story of his wedding Ethne Thoebfhota, all suggest his ultimate identity with the divine Hero, Lug or Lugaid. In Ernean tradition he appears as Cormac Conn Loinges, who in the Ulidian tales is very artificially made son of Conchobar, king of Ulaid.[105] As the kingship of Tara was taken over by the Goidels from the Érainn, so also, it would appear, was Cormac. The Goidelic Cormac is distinguished by being called Cormac ua Cuinn,[106] which practically means 'Cormac of the Goidels'. In the regnal lists he succeeds Lugaid mac Con, of the Érainn, as king of Tara,[107] and after this there is no further mention of the Érainn ruling in Tara. He is said to have been twice driven out of Tara by the Ulaid.[108] These 'exiles' (*loingis*) of Cormac have doubtless been inherited from the earlier Cormac Conn Loinges, though they may also be regarded as typifying vicissitudes in the warfare of the early Goidelic kings with their neighbours. We also hear of Cormac winning battles against each of the four provinces,[109] much like Tuathal.

Lug, in one of his functions, was the divine prototype of human kingship; and so Cormac has become an idealization of the first Goidelic king of Tara. In later

times his supposed reign had in retrospect something of the halo of the Golden Age, and under his rule, it was thought, Tara reached the summit of its glory.[110] He is said to have built the great *ráith* at Tara.[111] To him is attributed the compilation of a fictitious 'Saltair Temrach', and he is also credited with the authorship of 'Tecosca Cormaic', an Old-Irish text which professes to be a series of counsels given by him to his son Cairbre. Together with his mythical predecessors Conchobar and Morann, he is one of the three who believed in the true God before the coming of St. Patrick.[112] In no small measure, as Gwynn has shown,[113] this glorification of Cormac is of learned origin, suggested by the biblical descriptions of King Solomon and his house.

Just as Cormac, Goidelic king of Tara, is ultimately a borrowing of a legendary Ernean namesake, so his alleged son and successor, Cairbre Lifechar, is, as we have seen (p. 139 f.), a borrowing of the Laginian Cairbre whom we meet elsewhere as Cairbre Nia Fer, king of Tara.

Notes

[1] FM i, 23 n.

[2] ib. 18 n.

[3] See his MS. Materials, 446 ff. He has very exaggerated ideas of the antiquity of many of the texts he is dealing with. Thus of the tale of the First Battle of Mag Tuired he says: 'The antiquity of this tract, in its present form, can scarcely be under fourteen hundred years' (ib, 246).

[4] ib. 247 f.

[5] A generation or two before Flann's time Eochaid ua Flainn had composed a poem in which he names many of the Tuatha Dé; at the end of the poem he is careful to add: *cia dos·ruirmend nis·adrand,* 'though he (the author) enumerates them, he does not worship them' (LL 10 a 42; of ZCP xiv, 178 4).

[6] Folk-lore Record iv, 38 (1881).

[7] FM i, 24 n.

[8] MS. Materials 250.

[9] John H. Simpson, Poems of Oisin, Bard of Erin (1857), 207 n.

[10] Quoted by Rhys, Hibbert Lectures 1886, 155, n. 4.

[11] According to Mac Neill, 'neither history nor genealogy in Ireland, it may confidently be affirmed, is credible *in detail* beyond A.D. 300' (Celtic Ireland 57). The

implication is that our 'history' is trustworthy, even in detail, as far back as A.D. 300,—a view which will commend itself only to the credulous and the uncritical.

[12] Keating's credulity is shaken only with regard to the expedition of the lady Ceasair to Ireland forty days before the Flood (FF i, 146 ff.). Charles O'Conor, in 1766, criticizes Keating's work as 'a most injudicious Collection; the historical Part is degraded by the fabulous, with which it abounds' (Dissertations on the History of Ireland, p. x). Yet he himself accepts as historical the 'Milesian' invasion, and the subsequent kings of Ireland as enumerated in L. G., and also the heroes of the Ulidian tales and Finn mac Cumaill.

[13] Le cycle mythologique irlandaise et la mythologie celtique (1884 English translation by R. I. Best, 1903).

[14] Compare Meyer's animadversions on d'Arbois's view of Lebor Gabála: 'Die Zeit, wo man in diesem Machwerk die Urgeschichte Irlands sah, ist hoffentlich auf immer vorüber; es wäre aber auch an der Zeit, es nicht ohne weiteres als Fundgrube für irische Mythologie und Sagengeschichte zu benutzen' (Sitz.-Ber. der preuss. Akad. der Wissensch. 1919, 546).

[15] This statement, though true in substance, may yet be slightly misleading. In Ireland our tendency with regard to early Irish history is to accept as historical truth any statement, true or otherwise, that we have heard repeated sufficiently often; and if to-day, speaking generally, we are not prepared to swallow all the fictions of Lebor Gabála. one probable reason is that we are no longer sufficiently familiar with them.

[16] One of his guesses as to the date of their arrival was 'more than a millennium before the Christian era'.

[17] Phases of Irish History 119 f.

[18] ibid. 118.

[19] ib. 120 ff.

[20] Saorstát Eireann Official Handbook (1932), 45; and cf. Phases of Irish History 150, Jrnl. Cork Hist. and Arch Soc. 1941, 7 f.

[21] Inquiry into the History of Scotland ii, 77. This has been quoted approvingly by Petrie, Hist. and Antiqq. of Tara Hill (1839) p. 25, and by O'Donovan, FM i, 119 n. Macalister in adopting the same view gives free rein to his imagination: 'Cormac had ample opportunities of becoming acquainted with Roman methods of government, and with the machinery of empire. These methods he ambitiously set himself to imitate in his own kingdom. . . . He organized a standing army—a thing till then unheard of in Ireland. So deep was the impression produced by this innovation that the general entrusted with its organization has dominated the country's folk-lore ever since, in the person of the gigantic [sic] Find mac Cumhaill' (The Archaeology of Ireland, p. 21). Pokorny, Hist. of Ireland 25, echoes Mac Neill.

[22] O'Curry, MS. Materials 575, = Gen. Tracts 10.

[23] Miscellany of the Irish Arch. Society 120.

[24] MS. Materials 205.

[25] Ireland before St. Patrick 14. With regard to 'our lists of kings and their order of succession' he expresses the opinion that they 'are probably fairly authentic in the main as far back as 200 B.C.' (ibid.).

[26] ITS vii, p. xl.

[27] Phases of Ir. History 118.

[28] See the next note.

[29] So, relying on the fact that Cormac's name appears six generations earlier than that of Loegaire, Mac Neill writes: 'Reckoning by generations, we can thus date the floruit of Cormac and the main prominence of the Fiana about the middle of the third century' (Jrnl. Cork Hist. and Arch. Soc. 1941, p. 8).

[30] e.g. R 117 a 26. In the list of kings of Lagin, LL 39 b, Bresal Bélach occupies the first place.

[31] Zur kelt. Wortkunde §44, where Meyer suggests an impossible etymology of Cathaer.

[32] He is thus identical with Nuadu Necht. The name Cathaer, as I hope to show elsewhere, is a borrowing of an Ivernic (Hiberno-Brittonic) form of Celt. *Catutegernos, 'battle-lord'. The Otherworld deity was also the god of war.

[33] e.g. LL 24 a 11, R 124 a 26 (= LL 315 b 45), Fotha Catha Cnucha (RC ii, 86). See also Gwynn's discussion of Cathaer's date, Met. D. iii, 508 f. But in 'Esnada Tige Buchet' Cathaer is an elder contemporary of Cormac Conn's grandson (RC xxv, 24).

[34] RC xiii, 50; and cf. Met. D. iii, 130-132, RC xvii, 28.

[35] TBC Wi, p. 911.

[36] MS. Materials pp. 33, 41. O'Curry's confidence in 'our authentic annals' is to be noted. He was unaware that the Irish 'annals' previous to A.D. 431 are a concoction devoid of all historical value.

[37] Keltische Studien ii, 189.

[38] The Archaeological Review i, 68 (1888).

[39] Studies in the Legend of the Holy Grail 185. Cf. also The Archæological Review iii, 211. J. A. MacCulloch in 1911 ranges himself with Alfred Nutt: 'Though some personages who are mentioned in the Annals figure in the [Ulidian] tales, on the whole they deal with persons who never existed' (The Religion of the Ancient Celts 127). MacCulloch's conclusion is excellent, though he does appear to attach undue importance to the Irish 'Annals' (of the first century B.C.!).

[40] Rhys applies 'solar' methods of interpretation in all directions with incredible recklessness. The *gaí Bulga*, Cúchulainn's weapon, he interprets as 'the appearance of the sun as seen from the Plain of Murthemne when rising out of the sea to pierce with his rays the clouds above' (The Hibbert Lectures 1886, 481). In this inept explanation, as throughout the book, one can see the influence of Max Müller and his school, who imagined that all kinds of myths and mythical figures originated in solar or atmospheric phenomena.

[41] The equation of these three personages with the Celtic (or any other) Zeus is so absurdly inappropriate that one cannot but sympathize with Windisch's protest: 'Warum können jene drei irischen Könige, soviel auch über sie gefabelt worden ist, ihrem Kerne nach nicht historisch sein? (Das kelt. Brittannien 118).

[42] Cath Ruis na Ríg, p. x.

[43] TBC Wi, p. viii. Twenty-seven years previously, in 1878, Windisch had expressed very similar views (RC v, 79).

[44] In 1917 van Hamel expressed his belief in the historicity of Cúchulainn, Conn and Cormac (cf. ZCP xii, 451 f.). For more recent examples of the euhemeristic interpretation of Irish mythical material see H. M. and N. K. Chadwick, The Growth of Literature i, pp. 179, 236 (1932).

[45] For the moment I have to content myself with this bald summary of my views. The details and the proofs, which would fill many chapters, must be deferred to a later volume.

[46] Otherwise spelled *fiann;* and often used in the plural (*na fianna, fianna Érenn, fianna Finn*).

[47] MS. Materials 303.

[48] Ossianic Soc. iv, 285. Similarly O'Donovan asserts his belief that 'Diarmaid and Gráinne were historical personages, and that the romance of their running away is founded on historical facts' (letter of 1837, in Rev.

P. Walsh, The Placenames of Westmeath i, 53).

[49] RC ii, 87. This drew from Alfred Nutt the apposite rejoinder: 'So far from his history having degenerated into a myth, his myth has been rationalized into history,' Folk-lore Record iv, 39 (1881).

[50] RC v, 82 f.

[51] Kelt. Beiträge iii, in Zeit. für deutsches Alterthum, Bd. xxxv. Cf. Nutt's summary and criticism in Waifs and Strays of Celtic Tradition, iv, p. xxii ff. For a refutation of Zimmer's exaggerated views regarding Norse influence on Irish, see Meyer, Sitz.-Ber. der preuss. Akad. der Wissensch. 1918, 1042 ff.

[52] Waifs and Strays of Celtic Tradition iv, p. xxi.

[53] The Book of the Dean of Lismore, ed. M'Lauchlan, p. lxxvi ff. He identifies the 'Feinne' with the Cruithni of Scotland and the Tuatha Dé Danann of Ireland.

[54] See MacRitchie's book, Fians, Fairies and Picts (1893).

[55] The Religion of the Ancient Celts 144 f. Under the influence of Skene's theory, MacCulloch supposes, without any justification, that the Finn-saga was 'the saga of a non-Celtic people occupying both Ireland and Scotland' (ib. 146). Compare Mac Neill's view that 'the Fenian epic originated among the Galeoin who dwelt in the neighbourhood of Almu' (ITS vii, p. xxxii).

[56] RC xvii, 21; and cf. Ann. Clon. 61. The absence of the entry of his death in AI, 8 b, may be attributed to the abbreviating tendencies of the scribe.

[57] LU 4152 (= Met. D. ii, 12); RC xxiii, 310, §29. Gilla Coemáin records the slaying of Finn by the three sons of Urgriu (Trip. Life, ed. Stokes, 536.6.).

[58] Met. D. ii, 74; Fotha Catha Cnucha, RC ii, 86; and cf. Ac. Sen. 1678.

[59] e.g. Ac. Sen. 2381; Aided Finn, in Meyer's Cath Finntrága, p. 73.

[60] Mac Neill, ITS vii, p. xxix f., draws unwarranted conclusions from the absence of any reference to a king of Tara in 'Macgnímartha Find,' which he dates far too early ('about 900').

[61] According to the reckoning of the Four Masters, Conn began to reign in A.D. 123, and Cairbre Lifechar was slain in 284. In the same Annals Finn's death is dated 283. Meyer (Fianaigecht p. xxvii) says that in the tract on the Bórama 'Finn converses with Moling († 697), so that well-known historical [*sic*] personages

who lived centuries apart are brought together'. This is an error; in the tract in question Finn converses with his foster-brother, Molling Lúath, son of Fiachu mac Conga (LL, 297 a 1), an imaginary character, who is quite distinct from the seventh-century saint Molling who plays a part later in the tale (LL 305 a 22).

[62] It goes back at least to the twelfth century, being found in a poem ascribed to Caílte, LL 208 a 24, = Ériu i, 72.

[63] Compare the extravagant life-spans credited to various members of the *fiana* in an Ossianic poem, RC xvi, 26 f. Finn is said to have lived for 249 years, ibid.; for 230 years, Ac. Sen. 2537.

[64] In some versions of the pedigree this Finn is son of Finnlug (R 137 b 39; IT i, 121), in others he is son of Fintan, son of Finngoll, son of Finnlug (R 136 a 19, 144 a 15).

[65] Finn mac Cumaill is even more distinguished as a poet and seer (*fili*) than as a warrior; hence Finn Fili would have been a very appropriate name for him. So *Finnecis* (read *Finn Éces,* 'Finn the poet or seer') was a name for Finn mac Cumaill (Macgn. Find, RC v, 202, §22).

[66] ZCP viii, 560; R 118 a, = LL 311 c (quoted in Meyer's Fianaigecht, p. xvii); Laud 610 (quoted in Meyer's Cath Finntrága, p. 76). His connexion with the Uí Thairsig (of the Uí Fhailge) likewise links him with the Lagin (Cath Finntrága, *loc. cit.;* Ac. Sen. 6547 ff.).

[67] ZCP viii, 560; YBL 119 a 37; LL 379 a 35-37; ITS xxviii, 16, 18. So Dáire Derg is said to have been another name for Morna, father of Goll (RC v, 197).

[68] Meyer's Fianaigecht, pp. xxix (l. 19), 48; Gen. Tracts 148 (where *Chruithentuaith* is to be emended to *Érnaib*). We are told (ibid.) that this Torba or Tarbda was also mother of another Finn, called Finn mac Geoir (or Gleoir); doubtless the two Finns are ultimately one and the same. In 'Macgnímartha Find' Cumall marries successively Torba and Muirne (the mother of Finn), and Finn mac Gleoir is another name for Finn mac Cumaill (RC v, 197 f.). According to another account Finn's mother was Fuince, daughter of Dáire (Anecdota ii, 76).

[69] RC xvii, 21; xxiii, 328; Meyer's Cath Finntrága, p. 75; ZCP i, 464.

[70] Ac. Sen. 1766; RC xxiii, 328. 16. Compare Gilla in Chomded's statement that Finn was buried in Ard Caille in Múscraige Trí Maige, in the north of Co. Cork (Fianaigecht 46).

[71] ZCP xiii, 254. So also Meyer's Cath Finntrága, p. 73; ZCP i, 472.

[72] In 'Aided Finn' we are told that, after Cormac's death, Finn resided mainly in Almu (Meyer's Cath Finntrága p. 73. 30). Compare RC ii, 90 (Fotha Catha Cnucha), and *Almu Lagen, les na Fian, port ragnāthaig Find fīrfhial,* Met. D. ii, 72 (and Ac. Sen. 1262).

[73] RC xiii, 50.

[74] RC ii, 88; v, 197. In 'Cath Maige Léna' Goll and his men fight on Conn's side against the men of Munster.

[75] R 136 a 55; LL 24 a 11; Lr. na gCeart 204. In an Ossianic poem (ITS vii, 86) Goll boasts that he slew Cathaer in battle.

[76] Fianaigecht pp. xxii, 70, 98; RC xvii, 21; Meyer's Cath Finntrága, p. 75. See p. 274, n. 2.

[77] Cf. Fianaigecht 46, §8 (Gilla in Chomded); ITS vii, 33 f. In the Dindshenchas poem on Almu, Conn brings about Cumall's death, but is friendly to the youthful Finn, Met. D. ii, 74-76 (similarly Fotha Catha Cnucha, RC ii, 88-90). Ultimately Conn and Goll represent the one deity (cf. pp. 318-320).

[78] It should be added, however, that the name *Finn* (Welsh *Gwyn,* Celt. **Vindos*), meaning 'white', would be no less appropriate to the Otherworld-god than to the Hero. Compare the mythical names *Finn-goll* and *Finn-lug.* This may help to explain why Finn is represented as the rival of Diarmait for the hand of Gráinne, and is thus assigned a role which in primitive myth would belong to the Otherworld deity. On the other hand, making Finn the rival of Diarmait may equally well be a storyteller's invention, like making Gráinne daughter of Cormac ua Cuinn. We may compare the unfavourable light in which Conchobar mac Nesa, as wooer of Deirdre, is depicted by the author of 'Longes Mac nUsnig.'

[79] *Fian Maicc Con* is incidentally alluded to by Tírechán in his memoir of St. Patrick. See p. 201 f.

[80] Finn is said to have been Mac Con's *féinnid* or *fian*-leader; and after Ferches had slain Mac Con, Finn slew Ferches in revenge (Fianaigecht 38; and cf. San. Corm. 1084). In an account of the battle of Cenn Abrat Finn mac Cumaill fights on Mac Con's side (Anecdota ii, 76).

[81] This I hope to discuss at length on another occasion.

[82] It is, however, right to add that the Welsh traditions regarding Gwyn ab Nudd are few and fragmentary, and leave it by no means certain that Gwyn represents the Hero, like his Irish namesake Finn. In the *mabinogi*

of 'Branwen' there is mention of Heilyn, son of Gwyn Hen. This Gwyn Hen may, or may not, be the same as Gwyn ab Nudd; but his epithet, *hen,* 'old,' would be appropriate to the Otherworld deity, but not to the Hero.

[83] Ac. Sen. 1721 ff. Aillén used to burn Tara every *samain* with a fiery rock that issued from his mouth (see p. 110, n. 6, p. 111, n. 1). For a folk-version see Curtin, Myths and Folk-Lore of Ireland 213 ff.

[84] In the verse *dindshenchas* of Almu (Met. D. ii, 72 ff.), and in the derived prose-tale 'Fotha Catha Cnucha' (RC ii, 86 ff.).

[85] In Ac. Sen., 5119, Tadg mac Nuadat is a member of the Tuatha Dé Danann and dwells in the *síd* of Almu. In Meyer's Hail Brigit, p. 16, §19, Almu is 'the dwelling-place of Tadg, son of Nuadu Necht'. According to Met. D., ii. 72, Nuadu built a residence for himself on Almu, and his son Tadg inherited it; in this text, and in 'Fotha Catha Cnucha'. Nuadu and Tadg are reduced to the position of 'druids' of Cathaer Mór in order to accommodate the Finn story to pseudo-history.

[86] See p. 121 f.

[87] Quoted in ZCP, iv, 340.

[88] So W. M. Hennessy and J. F. Campbell (RC ii, 87), T. O'Neill Russell (ZCP iv. 339), and Lady Gregory (ITS vii, p. lix).

[89] ITS vii, p. lix. Lately the same scholar has written: 'The chief centre of the Fiana at Almhuin was a permanent military camp' (Jrnl. Cork Hist. and Arch. Soc. 1941, 7).

[90] ZCP iv. 341 f.

[91] Meyer, Hail Brigit p. 8 n.

[92] Fedlimmid Rechtaid is a mere name to us. He was possibly taken over from Laginian tradition. Fedlimmid Fortrén, whose name occurs in the mythical part of the Laginian pedigree, is called *Fedelmid Rechtaid* in a metrical version of the same (ÄID i, 28, §16, = *Fortren Fedelmid,* ib. 40, §18).

[93] Walde-Pokorny, i, 458; Pedersen, V. G. ii, 502.

[94] Mac Neill erroneously interprets *Conn* as 'the Free-man,' and, no less erroneously, takes *Leth Moga [Nuadat]* to mean 'the Slave's Half,' in contrast to *Leth Cuinn,* 'the Freeman's Half' (Celtic Ireland 61).

[95] See Holder, s.vv. *Condus, Senocondos.*

[96] Cf. *infra,* p. 318 f. Conn Cétchathach is called *Cond Crínna,* 'Conn the Wise', LL 364. 5, = Martyr. Tallaght

122. The word *crínna* (*crínda*), 'prudent, wise', is a derivative of *crín,* 'old, withered'. In Munster Irish *críonna* has come to mean 'old', for, as the Munster proverb has it, 'good sense only comes with age' (*Ní thagann ciall ruim aois*).

[97] Thurneysen's interpretation is 'den Verstand eines Alten habend' (Rom.-Germ. Kommission, 20. Bericht, 198).

[98] The head symbolizes the sun as well as wisdom. See *infra,* p. 300, n. 2.

[99] The storyteller (*mabinogi* of Branwen) rationalizes the tradition by supposing that Bran was dead, and that his head had been cut from off his body. In Norse mythology Odin has a double in the all-knowing Mimir; and we are told that, after Mimir's head had been cut off by the Vanir, Odin kept it alive by means of his spells and drew from it a store of hidden knowledge. The cutting off of Mimir's head is, of course, a piece of rationalization, analogous to that in 'Branwen'.

[100] It is thus that we can explain the Irish traditions of a severed head speaking at a feast, viz. the head of Lomna (San. Corm. *s. v.* 'orc tréith'), the head of Finn mac Cumaill (ZCP i, 464 f.), and the heads of Donn Bó and Fergal mac Maile Dúin (RC xxiv, 58 ff.).

[101] Edited by Thurneysen, Zu ir. Hss. u. Litteraturdenkmälern i, 48 ff.

[102] ZCP iii, 458; xiii, 372.

[103] The transference of the functions of the Otherworld deity to Lug is a mythological impossibility, and marks a redactor's mishandling of the original story. *A Scál,* meaning 'the Phantom' or the like, is an appropriate name for the Otherworld deity; so that *Baile in Scáil = Baile Chuinn.* (Compare *Scál Balb* as a name for Cian, the father of Lug, LL 9 a 43, RC xv, 317, xvi, 50.) In the text Lug is referred to as *a scál,* though he himself disclaims the name and says that he is 'of the race of Adam'.

[104] *Cor(b)mac* is from **Korbo-makkvos.* In *Maccorb* we have the same components reversed. Cormac's explanation of *corb* as 'chariot' (San. Corm. 204), suggested by *carbat,* can be dismissed as a fiction; but a discussion of the probable meaning of the word would occupy too much space here. Compare other names for the youthful Hero, viz. *Commac* (otherwise *Mac Con*), and *Macc ind Óc* (a corruption of **Maccon Óc*), = Welsh *Mabon.*

[105] See p. 130 ff.

[106] So nearly always in early texts. In late texts he is called Cormac mac Airt.

[107] Cf. SG i, pp. 255, 317.

[108] RC xvii, pp. 14, 16. He was driven out first by Fergus Dubdétach, and afterwards by Eochaid Gunnat (Meyer's Cath Finntrága, p. 72 f.); these two kings belonged to the Dál Fiatach. Another text speaks of his being driven out by Fiachu Araide, of the Dál nAraidi, and of his going into exile (*for longes*) to Fiachu Mullethan in Munster (ZCP viii, 314. 8-9). Another account says that he was banished by the Ulaid into Connacht (LL 328 f 18). Compare also his banishment 'across the sea': *loingeas mór Cormuic maic Airt tar magh rein fri re teora mbliadan* (RC xvii, 13; and cf. ZCP xiii, 375.22, 376.7).

[109] RC xvii, 13; and cf. ZCP xiii, 375 f.

[110] Cf. Met. D. i, pp. 14, 28-36; Aided Finn, in Meyer's Cath Finntrága, p. 73 (= SG i, 89 f.); IT iii, 85 f. Tara is pre-eminently the residence of Cormac: *ard-chathir Cormaic meic Airt,* Met. D. i, 14. Cormac brought the hostages of Ireland to Tara, ib. 16.

[111] RC xxv, 24-26.

[112] LU 4045-51. Elsewhere (Meyer, Death-Tales p. 8) there are only two such believers, Conchobar and Morann.

[113] Met. D. i, 70 ff.

Abbreviated References

A. (*or* Ann.) Clon. = *The Annals of Clonmacnoise,* translated by Conell Ma Geoghagan; ed. D. Murphy.

Ac. Sen. = *Acallamh na Senórach,* ed. Stokes (IT iv).

AI = *The Annals of Inisfallen* (facsimile).

ÄID = *Über die älteste irische Dichtung,* by K. Meyer (reprinted from Abhandlungen der königl. preuss. Akademie, 1913).

Anecdota = *Anecdota from Irish Manuscripts.*

FF = *Foras Feasa ar Éirinn,* by Keating; ed. Comyn and Dinneen (ITS).

FM = *Annals of the Kingdom of Ireland by the Four Masters,* ed. O'Donovan.

Gen. Tracts = *Genealogical Tracts,* i, ed. T. Ó. Raithbheartaigh.

Holder = *Alt-celtischer Sprachschatz,* by A. Holder.

IT = *Irische Texte,* ed. Windisch and Stokes.

ITS = Irish Texts Society.

L. G. = *Lebor Gabála,* in LL and later MSS. (At present being edited by R.A.S. Macalister for ITS).

LL = *The Book of Leinster* (facsimile).

Lr. na gCeart = *Leabhar na gCeart or The Book of Rights,* ed. O'Donovan.

LU = *Lebor na hUidre,* ed. Best and Bergin.

Mart. (*or* Martyr.) Gorman = *The Martyrology of Gorman,* ed. Stokes.

Met. D. = *The Metrical Dindshenchas,* ed. Edward Gwynn.

R = *Rawlinson B 502* (facsimile).

RC = *Revue Celtique.*

San. Corm. = *Sanas Cormaic,* ed. Meyer (Anecdota iv).

S. G. = *Silva Gadelica,* ed. S. H. O'Grady.

TBC Wi. = *Táin Bó Cúaluge,* ed. Windisch (from LL, etc.)

Trip. Life = *The Tripartite Life of Patrick with Other Documents relating to that Saint,* ed. Stokes. (The text of the Tripartite Life has been re-edited by K. Mulchrone.)

V. G. = *Vergleichende Grammatik der keltischen Sprachen,* by H. Pedersen.

Walde-Pokorny = *Vergleichendes Wörterbuch der indogermanischen Sprachen,* by A. Walde; ed. J. Pokorny.

YBL = *The Yellow Book of Lecan* (facsimile).

ZCP = *Zeitschrift für Celtische Philologie.*

Tomás Ó Cathasaigh (1985)

SOURCE: "The Concept of the Hero in Irish Mythology," in *The Irish Mind: Exploring Intellectual Traditions,* edited by Richard Kearney, Wolfhound Press, 1985, pp. 79-90.

[*In the following essay, Ó Cathasaigh explores the nature of the Irish mythological hero as an intermediate figure between gods and humans. In his view, the hero's accomplishments are balanced by his sym-*

bolic assertion of "the precariousness of man's position in the cosmos."]

Giambattista Vico claimed, as long ago as 1725, that "the first science to be learned should be mythology or the interpretation of fables."[1] Vico's words, and the work of modern mythologists in many fields—anthropology, depth psychology, the history of religions and literary criticism—have left little impression on the intellectual life of Ireland. Yet our manuscripts contain mythological texts whose abundance and archaic character make them unique in Western Europe. Insofar as our mythology has been at all rediscovered, credit must rest largely with our creative writers, and notably with Yeats whose use of myth in the creation of literature was hailed as "a step toward making the modern world possible in art."[2] The use of myth by Anglo-Irish writers stands in marked contrast to the practice of modern writers in the Irish language. There is a chiastic pattern here: Anglo-Irish writers trying to create a national literature in English have drawn upon the resources of the indigenous tradition, whereas those writers whose aim has been to create a modern European literature in Irish have for the most part turned away from traditional themes. Perhaps in their case the burden of the past was too strong in the language itself to allow them to exploit Irish myth for their own purposes.

But it is not primarily as a quarry for modern creative writers that Irish mythology lays claim upon our attention, but rather as a rich and complex body of material which is there and which calls for elucidation and interpretation. It is in that mythology that we can discover the native ideology of Ireland, for although the early Irish material includes a valuable wisdom literature the abstract formulation of philosophical and theological theories was not the Irish way. It was in their myths that they explored the nature of men and the gods, and a central task of criticism must be to uncover and to restate in abstract terms the configuration of the ideological patterns which underlie the myths. As the great French mythologist Georges Dumézil has put it: "A literary work does not have to set forth a theory: it is the hearer's or the reader's task to perceive the providential design which has arranged the events in the order in which the work presents them and with the results which it describes. Yet it is the design that justifies these events and results, and gives them a meaning."[3]

This "providential design" must be established by close study of the texts, but the general observation may be made that Irish myth is concerned above all with the relationship between man and the gods, and that the myth of the hero is used as a vehicle for exploring this relationship. In this respect, Irish myth shares the character of mythological systems in general. The situation can be stated in structuralist terms: a basic opposition in Irish myth is between man and god, and this oppo-

sition is mediated in the person of the hero. "Opposition" is used here in the sense of the discrimination of paired categories, and it is the structuralist view that every mythical system is built upon a sequence of such oppositions which are mediated by a third category which is abnormal or anomalous.[4] The hero belongs to this third category: he is at once the son of a god and of a human father; he is mortal and he lives out his life among men, but otherworld personages intervene at crucial moments of his life. The myth of the hero is exceptionally well represented in Irish sources, and the space at my disposal here allows only of a selective treatment. It seemed best to choose two of the more remarkable heroes of Irish tradition for extended discussion, and the two who are dealt with are the martial hero, Cú Chulainn, and the king-hero, Conaire Mór. In each case I concentrate on a single tale: for Cú Chulainn I restrict myself in the main to the early version of his 'Conception Tale', and for Conaire Mór to 'The Destruction of Da Hostel'. The necessarily summary account of these two texts may perhaps give some indications of the thematic content of the Irish versions of the myth of the hero, while the commentary is intended to elucidate the ideological framework within which they may be interpreted. Having considered the two texts, we go on to two other topics, one of which is thoroughly pagan, while the other shows an admixture of pagan and Christian elements. The first of these is the role of the god Lug in relation to mortal heroes, the second the election to kingship of Corc of Cashel.

The early version of *Compert Con Culainn* ("The Conception of Cú Chulainn") tells how a flock of birds repeatedly grazed to the roots the plain of Emain Macha, the ancient capital of Ulster. The warriors of Ulster gave chase to the birds and pursued them in nine chariots, Conchobor's daughter Dechtine serving as his charioteer. In the evening, three of the birds led the pursuers to the edge of Bruig na Bóinne (Newgrange), where night came upon the Ulstermen. It snowed heavily and the Ulstermen sought shelter. They found a new house where they were made welcome by a couple. The man of the house told them that his wife was in labour. Dechtine went to her and a boy-child was born. At the same time, a mare outside the house dropped two foals, and these were given to the child. By morning both the house and the birds had disappeared, and all that remained with the Ulstermen at the edge of Bruig na Bóinne were the child and the two foals. With these the warriors returned to Emain Macha.

Dechtine reared the child, but he fell ill and died. Then a man came to Dechtine in her sleep and said that he was Lug son of Eithniu. He told her that she would be pregnant by him; it was he who had brought her to Bruig na Bóinne, it was with him she had stayed the night, and the boy she reared was his son. It was that boy he had placed in her womb, and his name would be Sétantae.

Conchobor betrothed Dechtine to one Sualdaim mac Roich, but she was ashamed to go pregnant to Sualdaim's bed and carried out an abortion. Then she slept with Sualdaim: she conceived again, and bore a son, Sétantae, who was later given the name Cú Chulainn.[5]

The theme of the "waste land", with which *Compert Con Culainn (CCC)* opens, occurs frequently in Irish tradition: the laying waste of the land is the ultimate sanction of the gods. In *CCC* the land is laid waste by otherworld birds; in other texts this is done by otherworld horses and pigs; and the fruits of the earth will of themselves dry up when the land is ruled by an unrighteous king, who is unpleasing to the gods. The theme of the waste land implies the need for a fecundating hero who will restore vegetation to Emain Macha. In Irish tradition the fecundating role of the hero is seen most clearly in the lives of the king-heroes, who ensure the fertility of land and beast and man by their wise and judicious rule: we shall see presently that Conaire Mór exemplifies this. Cú Chulainn, on the other hand, is essentially a martial hero, the defender of his people against the enemy invader. But it has been argued that in the *Táin,* when he defends Ulster against the ravages of its Connaught enemies while Conchobor and the Ulstermen are undergoing their winter sleep, Cú Chulainn exemplifies the vigorous young male as the vital force in nature, and that this scenario represents an ancient vegetation myth, the basic theme of which is "the triumph of life and fecundity over death and decay, as suggested by seasonal change."[6] The occurrence of the theme of the waste land in *CCC* lends weight to that interpretation. In the immediate context of *CCC,* however, the theme presages the decisive intervention by the otherworld in the affairs of Ulster. It also has the function of inducing the Ulstermen to give chase to the birds, which lead them to Bruig na Bóinne.

Bruig na Bóinne is a localisation of the otherworld, one of the *síde* to which the gods were consigned when men came to share dominion of the land in Ireland. Thus, these *síde* (the singular is *síd*) were the abodes of the gods: they were located in the mounds of the earth (both natural formations and prehistoric tumuli), under the lakes, and on the islands of the ocean. The world of the *síde* was distinct from that of men, but contact between the two was frequent, and especially at Samain (November 1) when the *síde* were believed to be open, and their denizens free to wander abroad at will—beliefs which have persisted down to modern times. The prominence of the *síde* on the landscape doubtless contributed to the constant awareness among Irish country people of the imminence of the otherworld. Bruig na Bóinne, in particular, was originally the whole necropolis on the Boyne, but the name became specially attached to Newgrange, which is but one of the tumuli there. In our text, the Lord of Bruig

na Bóinne is Lug, the Irish reflex of a Celtic god who is commemorated in the names of a number of continental cities such as Lyons (from an earlier Lugudunum), Laon and Leyden. We have seen that when he later comes to Dechtine in her sleep, Lug explains that it was he who brought her to Bruig na Bóinne. And he brought her there, not on an errand of doom, but so that Sétantae might be brought into the world. Thus, Bruig na Bóinne is here the telluric womb from which emerges the saviour-hero of Ulster.

Cú Chulainn shares with mythical personages everywhere the characteristic of dual paternity: he is at once the son of a god (Lug) and of a human father (Sualdaim). What is remarkable in the case of Cú Chulainn is that he is conceived three times: in one manuscript text of *CCC* he is said to have been "the son of three years". The number three is of course everywhere invested with symbolic significance, and triplicity of gods and heroes is a very common theme in Irish myth. Cú Chulainn's threefold conception is one of the many expressions of this notion. Another one which may be noted here is the theme of threefold death, of which we have a number of examples in Irish texts and which will be mentioned again in connection with Conaire Mór. Triplicity is a feature also of Celtic iconography, both in Ireland and on the continent, its most striking expression being the head with three faces. In the particular case of Cú Chulainn, his triplicity is related to his destiny as a warrior, for his martial career is marked by a number of encounters with triple adversaries of one kind or another. One such encounter is his initiatory combat in which he ventures forth and defeats the three formidable sons of Nechta Scéne. This has been identified as a variant of an ancient mythical exploit in which a god or hero slays an adversary who is endowed with some form of triplicity: Dumézil compares Heracles, who conquers the three-headed Geryon, and who was conceived in one night three times as long as normal.[7]

But perhaps the most interesting feature of the threefold conception in *CCC* is its structural sequence. The boy is first begotten in the otherworld by Lug upon his otherworld consort; then at Emain by Lug upon Dechtine; and finally by Sualdaim upon Dechtine. There is thus a progression from fully divine to fully human parentage: in this sequence the hero recapitulates in his own life the history of man, since, if we may judge from the occurrence of deity names in their pedigrees, the Irish apparently believed themselves to be descended from the gods. Furthermore, this sequence gives us a singularly clear example of the manner in which the hero mediates between the gods and men: the second (or middle) conception, linked to the first by Lug and Dechtine respectively, mediates the opposition between the divine and the human. In this case at least the "meaning" of the triplicity of the hero is inseparable from the structure of the narrative.

The manner of Cú Chulainn's conception and birth marks him out for greatness. He is destined to save his people from the ravages of war: how he accomplishes this is shown in the *Tain*. There is a whole cycle of texts about Cú Chulainn telling how he was initiated into warrior status, how he overcame great obstacles to win Emer as his wife, how he journeyed to the otherworld, how he killed his only son, and, finally, how he met his tragic death. Taken together, these episodes make up Cú Chulainn's heroic biography from conception and birth to death. Rather than follow up these texts here, however, we turn now to our second hero.

Conaire Mór (Conaire the Great) is depicted in our sources as a prehistoric king of Tara. His biography is heroic, and it follows much the same basic pattern as that of Cú Chulainn. But Conaire is destined to be king, and, in contrast to the martial ethic which informs the cycle of Cú Chulainn, Conaire's life is presented in terms of the pacific ethic which was the basis of the Irish ideology of kingship. I have already referred to the fecundating role of the king who ensures the fertility of man and beast and land by his wise and judicious rule. The characteristic of the king which ensured fertility in this way was known as *fír flatha* ("Prince's truth"). "Truth" in this context is a broad term, embracing the notions of wisdom and justice, and, as well as fertility, it also secures seasonable weather and amity among men. In short, it is a cosmic force, and the doctrine of *fír flatha* places the king at the centre of the cosmos. This is the doctrine which is expressed in heroic terms in the life of Conaire Mór.

Our text for Conaire Mór is *Togail Bruidne Da Derga (TBDD)*.[8] The title is conventionally translated "The Destruction of Da Derga's Hostel", but the *bruiden* or "hostel" in question is a localisation of the otherworld. (It may be noted in passing the this *bruiden* gave its name to Bohernabreena, near Tallaght in County Dublin.)[9] It is in Da Derga's hostel that Conaire met his death, and the title of our tale is in keeping with the fact that much the greater part of it is devoted to that event and to those which led up to it. *TBDD* is nonetheless a biography of Conaire, dealing in turn with his conception and birth, his boyhood, his elevation to kingship, the Golden Age enjoyed in Ireland during his reign, and turning only then to the tragic story of his death. All of this resolves itself into three sections, which we shall consider in turn: the making of a king, the golden age, and the tragedy of a king.

The Making of a King

Conaire's mother Mess Buachalla was brought up in humble circumstances, but she was the daughter of a king and a beautiful goddess who was born in a *síd*. Mess Buachalla married Eterscélae king of Tara, but on the night before her marriage she saw a bird on the skylight coming to her. The bird left his "bird-skin" on the floor and ravished her. He told her that she would bear his son and that he should be called Conaire. So it came to pass, and Conaire was brought up as the son of Eterscélae. He was reared with three foster-brothers. Now Conaire had three "gifts" *(buada),* the gift of hearing, the gift of seeing and the gift of calculation, and he shared these gifts with his foster-brothers, giving one gift to each of the three.

When Eterscélae died and a successor was to be chosen, Conaire was told by his foster-father to go to Tara. He set out and when he reached Dublin he saw great speckled birds, which he pursued as far as the sea and onto the waves. They then cast off their bird-skins, and one of them identified himself to Conaire as Nemglan "the king of your father's birds". Nemglan instructed Conaire to go along the road to Tara stark-naked, bearing a stone and a sling. Meanwhile, it had been prophesied at a "bull-feast" (a solemn divinatory rite) that the person who arrived in this way would be the future king. So when Conaire appeared he was recognised as king. His nakedness was covered with royal raiment, he was placed in a chariot, and he bound the hostages of Tara (an act which signifies their submission to him). But the people of Tara objected to him, since he was young and beardless. Conaire refuted this objection, however, saying that a king was not disqualified by youth, provided that he be generous, and that it was his right from father and grandfather to bind the hostages of Tara. This utterance was greeted with enthusiasm by the people ("'Wonder of wonders', they cried"), and Conaire was invested with the kingship. Then the taboos of Conaire's reign are listed: these are prohibitions which were laid upon Conaire (perhaps by Nemglan, but the text is ambiguous at this point), and so long as they are honoured Conaire's reign is marked by prodigious peace and prosperity.

The begetting of Conaire Mór represents an otherworld intervention in the affairs of Tara. We are reminded of the otherworld birds in *CCC*, who summon the Ulstermen to Bruig na Bóinne. In *TBDD* the birds have a more direct role: Conaire is begotten by a god who appears in the guise of a bird; he is called to his destiny by the king of his father's birds, Nemglan; and his reign is called "the bird-reign" *(én-flaith)*. This otherworld intervention is an integral part of the election of Conaire to kingship, and it seems right to compare the sequence summarised above with the scenario which Dumézil has traced in the traditions concerning the primitive Hindu king Prthu. There were three stages in the election of Prthu: designation by the gods, recognition by the wise men and acceptance by the people.[10] These three elements occur in *TBDD*: Conaire is designated by the very manner of his conception; he is recognised as king when he arrives on the road to Tara in fulfilment of the diviner's prophecy; and he is accepted by the people when he successfully meets their objection to his youth and beardlessness. Each of these stages has its proper place in the structure, but it is in the last one that Conaire establishes his right to the kingship. This he does by delivering a true judgement on the matter of his own eligibility for kingship, a judgement which reveals his understanding that it is essential for a ruler *(flaith)* to be generous—a notion which is reflected in the Modern Irish *flaithiúil* "generous". This true judgement shows Conaire to be possessed of *fír flatha,* which, as we have seen, is the distinguishing characteristic of the rightful king.

The Golden Age

TBDD describes the state of peace and plenty which was enjoyed in Ireland during the reign of Conaire Mór. The ideal conditions which characterised his reign (and also that of Cormac mac Airt) are reminiscent of the otherworld in its beneficent aspect as it is depicted in Irish texts. They represent two different responses to the paradisal yearning, the otherworld being separated in space, the Golden Age in time from the storyteller and his audience. In Old Irish the word for "peace" is *síd,* which is a homonym of the word which (as we have seen) denotes a habitation of the gods. These homonyms were originally one and the same: I have argued elsewhere that the homonymy reflects the nexus between the otherworld and conditions in this world, as mediated in the person of the king. The otherworld is the source of the king's cosmic truth *(fír)* and peace is its symptom; the state of peace secured by the kings of the mythical past, whose kingship was sanctioned by the otherworld, is seen as a re-creation of the paradisal condition; and, as a material correlative to these abstract connections, the king would seem often to have been consecrated upon a *síd*.[11]

The Tragedy of a King

The golden age of peace and plenty depicted in *TBDD* is a measure of the beneficent role of the rightful king. In fulfilling this role the king is constrained by his *gessi* (taboos), and by the requirement to maintain the order based on cosmic truth. Conaire's tragedy is that he is faced with a conflict between his duty in these respects and his love for his foster-brothers, and that he puts love before duty. What happened is that Conaire's foster-brothers took to thieving in order to see what punishment the king might inflict upon them and how the theft in his reign might damage him. Conaire repeatedly refused to punish them. They were therefore emboldened to advance in crime from theft to marauding, the significance of this being that one of the taboos laid upon Conaire was that there should be no marauding during his reign. By failing to punish his foster-brothers for their earlier and less serious crime, Conaire caused the violation of one of his own taboos. And then, when the foster-brothers and their companions in crime were brought before him on the charge

of marauding, Conaire delivered a false judgment, decreeing that the others should be slain by their fathers, but that his foster-brothers should be spared. Conaire saw the injustice of his judgment and revoked it, saying, "The judgment which I have given is no extension of life for me." He ordained instead that all the marauders should be spared and banished overseas. Ironically, even the revised judgment proved "no extension of life" to Conaire, for in due course the marauders whom he had spared returned to destroy him in the *bruiden* of Da Derga.

All of this provides us with an Irish example of an old Indo-European theme which Dumézil has called the "sin of the sovereign", "which destroys either the raison d'etre of sovereignty, namely the protection of the order founded on truth . . . or the mystical support of human sovereignties, namely the respect for the superior sovereignty of the gods and the sense of limitations inherent in every delegation of the divine sovereignty. The king falls prey to one or other of these risks, which are at bottom reducible to the same thing."[12] Dumézil was not aware of the occurrence of this theme in Irish tradition, but his formulation stands as an excellent summary of Conaire's "sin" in *TBDD,* save that Conaire falls prey to both of the "risks" described by Dumézil. The taboos which have been laid upon him constitute in effect a contract with the otherworld, and his transgression of one of these taboos destroys the respect of the otherworld personages who have delegated sovereignty to him. In failing to punish his foster-brothers, and later in delivering a false judgment, Conaire destroys the respect for the order founded on truth.

No sooner has the king's judgment been given and the marauders departed than we hear that the perfect peace has broken down which had been enjoyed during Conaire's reign. The otherworld now takes on its malevolent aspect, and Conaire proceeds to transgress all the taboos which have been laid upon him. He sets out from Tara and finds that he cannot return, for the lands round about are full of raiders coming from every side, men roam about naked, and the land is all on fire. This is a sign that the law has broken down there. And so Conaire turns away and he takes the path which leads him to his doom in the *bruiden.* He encounters a number of malevolent otherworld beings on his way to the *bruiden,* and in the meantime his foster-brothers and their allies return to Ireland. They assail Conaire in the *bruiden,* which they set on fire three times. Conaire's head is cut off, and the severed head is given a drink of water which has been taken by his servant Mac Cécht from Uarán Garaid on the plain of Croghan in County Roscommon after a tour of the rivers and lakes of Ireland. The severed head thanks Mac Cécht, and Conaire dies.

Conaire dies by decapitation, but the elements of fire and water are also present: the *bruiden* is set on fire, and Conaire dies only after water has been poured into his throat and gullet. I suspect that we have a variant here of the motif of three-fold death. This is well-represented in Irish sources, and in its classic form comprises death by wounding, drowning and burning. Although Conaire is not drowned and it is not explicitly stated that he is burned, the elements of iron, water and fire are brought into play in the account of his death.

There is another instance of triplicity in *TBDD* which is made explicit, and which has a bearing on the interpretation of the text, namely the fact that Conaire's foster-brothers are three in number. Irish tradition presents examples of trios which are merely triplications of a single personality. Perhaps the best known of these is the trio in the Deirdre story: the three sons of Uisniu are at all times found together, and among them only Naoise has a definite personality. Áinle and Ardán are but shadows of Naoise, and they die when he dies.[13] The three foster-brothers in *TBDD* (who are themselves blood-brothers) are a somewhat different trio, for they are identical in appearance and dress, not only among themselves, but also with Conaire: the text says that all four were identical in their clothing, their weapons, and the colour of their horses. Moreover, it will be recalled that Conaire distributed his gifts (*buada*) to them: each one of them represents an aspect of his triple self and together they are his equal. These three personages are cast in Conaire's image and in *TBDD* they use his own "gifts" to destroy him: it is scarcely too much to suggest that they may be taken to represent the evil side of his nature. In this way they are a projection in corporeal form of "the enemy within". They too die at the destruction of the *bruiden*.

The "providential design" (to use Dumézil's term) which gives meaning to the tragic events of *TBDD* is that of the Irish ideology of kingship, and it will be clear by now that the otherworld is central to that ideology. Many Irish texts give expression to the underworld legitimation of sovereignty, but this notion is nowhere more explicitly stated than in *Baile In Scáil* ("The Phantom's Vision").[14] This tells how Conn Cétchathach was brought to an otherworld abode where he met a couple—a girl sitting on a chair of crystal and wearing a golden crown, and a man sitting on a throne. The man identifies himself to Conn as Lug and tells him that he has come to Conn to tell him the span of his sovereignty and of that of every prince that will come of him in Tara for ever. The girl is identified as the Sovereignty of Ireland, and she has a golden cup from which she gives Conn a drink of ale at Lug's instructions. And then she asks who next should be given a drink from the cup, and Lug names Conn's successor, and so the dialogue continues and we are given a list of those who will follow Conn in the kingship of Tara. This text is a version of the sovereignty myth, which

has to do with the espousal of the king to the goddess of sovereignty, and it shows that the kingship of Conn and his descendants at Tara has been conferred at the behest of the god Lug. It will be remembered that Lug was the divine father of Cú Chulainn, and now we find him presented as legitimator of the Dál Cuinn kings of Tara. The key to Lug's role is to be found in the story of the battle of Mag Tuired (now Moytirra, in County Sligo), *Cath Maige Tuired*.[15] This tale tells of the war of the gods, and in it we see Lug successively attaining pre-eminence in the domains of sovereignty, martial vigour and agricultural practice: those who are acquainted with Dumézil's work will recognise here the three terms of the tripartite structure which that scholar has established for Indo-European ideology.

Lug may be described as the hero among the gods. His heroic deeds in relation to kingship, martial vigour and agricultural practice were performed in the time of the gods, which preceded the appearance of man in Ireland. When men did come to share dominion of the land, the gods, as we have seen, retreated to the *síde*. Thenceforth, great deeds were to be performed by mortal heroes, such as Cú Chulainn, who differ from Lug in that, however great their achievements in life, they must die, and when they are dead they are dead.

What then is the relationship between the mortal hero and his divine predecessor who still inhabits the *síde?* It can be said, in the first place, as de Vries has argued, that the hero raises himself to the level of the gods.[16] Having performed his deeds in the time of the gods, Lug is by definition anterior to the mortal heroes: it follows that the other heroes are perceived within the system as replicating (in some measure) the heroic achievements of Lug. In the field of kingship, the great hero is Cormac mac Airt, who is the exemplary model of *fír flatha;* the Golden Age which was enjoyed in his reign was not brought to an end by any sin of the kind committed by Conaire Mór. In the field of martial vigour, Cú Chulainn is the outstanding figure. But the connection between Lug and Cú Chulainn or Cormac is not solely that of exemplary model and replicator. We know from *CCC* that Lug was progenitor to Cú Chulainn. And *Baile In Scáil* attests a connection of a somewhat different kind between Lug and Cormac. The latter was one of the Dál Cuinn kings of Tara, and one of those upon whom the drink of sovereignty was conferred at Lug's behest. In this act, Lug effectively bestows his otherworld consort, the Sovereignty of Ireland, upon Cormac for a stated period of years. As her spouse for the time being, Cormac is Lug's surrogate as king of Tara, while Cú Chulainn, for his part, is an incarnation of Lug.

. . . . .

What we find in the early Irish narrative texts is mythology and ideology refracted through literature, and it is worth noting that this literature would not have come down to us were it not for the labours of monastic scribes. Early Irish literature stems from the fruitful interplay of two sets of institutions, the native orders of learning and the monastic schools. The texts contain many survivals from Celtic and Indo-European culture, and these elements clearly must have been transmitted orally until such time as they were transferred into the written record. The written literature had its beginnings in the monasteries in the seventh century, and continued to flourish in them until the twelfth, and what survives to us today is the remains of that literature. The early Irish texts owe much to the vigorous oral tradition which not only preceded the written literature but continued unabated alongside, but the ecclesiastics' contribution to their extant condition must have been crucial and continuing. The creation and survival of the early Irish narrative texts show that the early Irish churchmen were not only open to, but deeply involved in the extra-ecclesiastical lore of their country.

It will be appropriate, therefore, to end with an instance of syncretism: this is an account of the election to the kingship of Cashel of Corc mac Láire (Corc son of the Mare), in which the basic pattern is similar to that of the election of Conaire in *TBDD*, but which is realised in partly Christian terms.[17] The designation by the gods here takes the form of designation by angels; the recognition of Corc by the wise men is here entrusted to swineherds to whom it has been revealed in a vision, though there is also a druid who discovers that Corc is to be king by means of druidic divination; the people assent to Corc's accession by answering "Amen" to his response to a blessing. As Dillon pointed out, this blessing, apart from a pious invocation, "is rather pagan than Christian in expression". This blessing and the king's solemn response to it show the power of the spoken word, as did Conaire's pronouncement on his eligibility to kingship. Finally, we may note that the king is bound to preserve his prescriptions, namely that he have truth and mercy; such a prescription *(buaid)* "is a thing or act which brings good luck, and which is therefore a duty or prescribed conduct, the reverse of *geis*";[18] we are reminded of the *gessi* which were laid upon Conaire.

The story of Corc also bears comparison with *Baile In Scáil,* for here the angels reveal the names of the kings who are to succeed Corc in the kingship of Cashel. In contrast to *Baile In Scáil,* however, this text shows the kings to have been legitimated by God, of whom the angels are of course messengers.

Corc of Cashel mediates between his people and God. The other texts which I have been discussing exemplify some of the ways in which Irish tradition presents the destiny of the hero who mediates between man and the pagan gods. The world-view of these texts is an anthropocentric one: man is the centre of the cosmos, and the fruits of the earth and the workings of the elements are contingent upon the physical and moral excellence of the king—and, in texts where the martial ethic prevails, upon that of the champion. But the hero is subject to constraints from within and without, and otherworld personages intervene at all the crucial moments in his career. These interventions may be benevolent or malevolent, reflecting the contradictory aspects of the otherworld. A benevolent god may function as progenitor and helper, a malevolent one as villain and destroyer. The burden of heroism is a heavy one, and is ultimately unenviable. While celebrating the achievements of the hero, Irish myth asserts the precariousness of man's position in the cosmos.

Notes

[1] Quoted by Terence Hawkes, 1977, *Structuralism and Semiotics,* London, p. 12.

[2] T. S. Eliot, quoted in F. O. Mathiessen, 1959, *The Achievement of T. S. Eliot,* Galaxy Editions, New York, p. 40.

[3] G. Dumézil, 1973, *The Destiny of a King,* Chicago, p. 115.

[4] Edmund Leach, 1969, *Genesis as Myth and other essays,* London, p. 11.

[5] Text edited by A. G. Van Hamel, 1933, *Compert Con Culainn and other stories,* Dublin. There is a translation by Thomas Kinsella, 1970, in *The Tain,* London, pp. 21-23.

[6] Tomás Ó Broin, 1961-63, *Éigse,* vol. 10, pp. 286-99.

[7] G. Dumézil, 1970, *The Destiny of a Warrior,* Chicago, p. 16.

[8] Text edited by Eleanor Knott, 1963, *Togail Bruidne Da Derga,* Dublin.

[9] T. F. O'Rahilly, 1946, *Early Irish History and Mythology,* Dublin, p. 121.

[10] G. Dumézil, 1943, *Servius et la Fortune,* pp. 33ff; cf. J. E. Caerwyn Williams, 1971, *The Court Poet in Medieval Ireland,* p. 19.

[11] *Éigse,* vol. 17, 1977-79, pp. 137ff.

[12] G. Dumézil, 1973, *The Destiny of a King,* pp. 111f.

[13] J. Vendryes, 1952, "L'unité en trois personnes chez les Celtes," *Chois d'Études Linguistiques et Celtiques,* Paris, pp. 233-46.

A Celtic cross.

[14] Myles Dillon, 1946, *The Cycles of the Kings,* Oxford, pp. 11ff.

[15] Edited and translated by Whitley Stokes, 1891, *Revue Celtique,* vol. 12, pp. 56ff.

[16] Jan de Vries, 1963, *Heroic Song and Heroic Legend,* Oxford, p. 241.

[17] Myles Dillon, 1952, *Ériu,* vol. 16, pp. 61ff., for text and translation.

[18] *Ibid.,* p. 72, note 6.

CELTIC RELIGION: DRUIDS AND DIVINITIES

Marie-Louise Sjoestedt (1949)

SOURCE: *Gods and Heroes of the Celts,* translated by Myles Dillon, Turtle Island Foundation, 1982, pp. 11-36.

[*In the following excerpt, originally published in 1949, Sjoestedt recounts the events of the "mythological period" of Irish prehistory as outlined in the* Lebor Gabála *and describes the characteristics of the continental Celtic gods in ancient Gaul.*]

A discussion of the mythological world of the Celts encounters at once a peculiar difficulty, namely, that when seeking to approach it you find that you are already within. We are accustomed to distinguish the supernatural from the natural. The barrier between the two domains is not, indeed, always impenetrable: the Homeric gods sometimes fight in the ranks of human armies, and a hero may force the gates of Hades and visit the empire of the dead. But the chasm is there nonetheless, and we are made aware of it by the feeling of wonder or horror aroused by this violation of established order. The Celts knew nothing of this, if we are entitled to judge their attitude from Irish tradition. Here there is continuity, in space and in time, between what we call our world and the other world—or worlds. Some peoples, such as the Romans, think of their myths historically; the Irish think of their history mythologically; and so, too, of their geography. Every strange feature of the soil of Ireland is the witness of a myth, and, as it were, its crystallization. The supernatural and the natural penetrate and continue each other, and constant communication between them ensures their organic unity. Hence it is easier to describe the mythological world of the Celts than to define it, for definition implies a contrast.

This omnipresence of the myth in Ireland is specially evident in two collections of stories, the *Dindshenchas* or "Tradition of Places," which is the mythological geography of the country, and the *Lebor Gabála* or "Book of Conquests," which is its mythological prehistory. The myths indeed involve both time and space, and the importance of remarkable places, the mystic virtues that belong to them, are closely bound up with events which happened during the period when other peoples, human or divine (one can hardly say exactly which), controlled the land now occupied by the Gaels, but which the Gaels possessed only in partnership with their mysterious forerunners.

This mythological period can be defined as "a period when beings lived or events happened such as one no longer sees in our days."[1] Christian texts sometimes betray this notion of a time when other laws than those we know governed the world. "In that fight," says the author of *The Battle of Mag Tured,* "Ogma the champion found Orna the sword of Tethra a king of the Fomorians. Ogma unsheathed the sword and cleansed it. Then the sword related whatsoever had been done by it; for it was the custom of swords at that time, when unsheathed, to set forth the deeds that had been done by them. And therefore swords are entitled to the tribute of cleansing them after they have been unsheathed. Hence also charms are preserved in swords thenceforward. Now the reason why demons used to speak from weapons at that time was because weapons were worshipped by human beings then; and the weapons were among the (legal) safeguards of that time."[2]

We see that the good cleric does not think of questioning the truth of a tradition of his time which must have seemed to him as fanciful as it does to us. At most he feels the need of explaining it by supposing the intervention of the power of demons. But how is it that weapons and demons have lost the power of speech? The scribe who copied the tale of Cú Chulainn and Fann gives the reason in these closing words: "That is the story of the disastrous vision shown to Cú Chulainn by the fairies. For the diabolical power was great before the faith, and it was so great that devils used to fight with men in bodily form, and used to show delights and mysteries to them. And people believed that they were immortal."[3]

In the same way the stone of Fál, a talisman brought to Ireland by the ancient gods, whose cry proclaimed the lawful king of Ireland, is silent today, "for it was a demon that possessed it, and the power of every idol ceased at the time of the birth of the Lord."[4]

We see that Christian Ireland preserved, as a legacy from paganism, the belief in a time when the supernatural was natural, when the marvellous was normal. This belief is indeed characteristic of a mentality common to folklore ("Once upon a time, when animals could speak . . .") and to various so-called 'primitive' peoples. So, in defining the mythological period, we have borrowed the words used by Lévy-Bruhl to describe the epoch of the *Dema,* those ancestral creators who figure in the mythologies of the natives of New Guinea.

The Book of Conquests is the story of the Irish *Dema,* retouched, no doubt, by clerics anxious to fit the local traditions into the framework of Biblical history, while its pagan quality has not noticeably been altered. We shall therefore summarize it, according to the texts;[5] and if we chance to include a secondary episode, it will not matter, from our present standpoint, provided that it be a product of the same mythical imagination and suppose the same type of notion as those elements that are most clearly native.

Tradition has little to say about the first race that inhabited Ireland, before the Deluge; and we may suspect it to be a late invention, intended to make up the number of six races corresponding to the six ages of the world. One of its leaders was Ladhra, who had sixteen wives and died "from excess of women." He was the first to die in Ireland. The whole race was destroyed by the Deluge.

Two hundred and sixty-eight years later (Irish annalists are never shy of exactitude), the race of Partholón landed. This name has been explained as a corruption of Bartholomeus,[6] and the legend as a product of the imagination of Christian monks. But whatever be the origin of the name, the mythical character of this personage cannot be doubted, as Van Hamel has shown.[7] He regards Partholón as a god of vegetation; but, apart from the fact that the activities of Partholón extend beyond the domain of agriculture, it is important to observe that here, as throughout the prehistoric tradition, we have to do not with a single god, one mythical individual, but with a whole race, of which Partholón is merely, as it were, a nickname. It is hard to define this race of Partholón in terms of Indo-European mythology. In the vocabulary of primitive mythology, we may identify it as the first race of those *Dema,* the ancestors (mythical, not human, according to Lévy-Brühl's useful distinction) who controlled the world, if they did not create it—the world of the Gael, of course, that is to say: Ireland.

When Partholón landed in Ireland, he found there only three lakes and nine rivers, but seven new lakes were formed in his lifetime. He cleared four plains and "he found no tiller of the soil before him." He brought with him the steward Accasbél who built the first "guest-house"; and Brea who built the first dwelling, made the first cauldron and fought the first duel; and Malaliach who was the first surety (guarantee is an essential part of the Celtic legal system), brewed the first beer from bracken, and ordained divination, sacrifice and ritual; Bachorbladhra, who was the first foster-father (fosterage was the basis of the Irish system of education); and finally the two merchants, Biobal, who introduced gold into Ireland, and Babal, who introduced cattle.

It was in Partholón's time that adultery was first committed in Ireland. Having left his wife alone with his servant, he found on his return that they had wronged him. He demanded his "honour-price," but his wife replied that it was she who was entitled to compensation, for it was the owner's responsibility to protect his property:

> *honey with a woman, milk with a cat,*
> *food with one generous, meat with a child,*
> *a wright within and an edged tool,*
> *one with one other, it is a great risk*[8]

And this was the first "judgment" in Ireland. Hence the proverb "the right of Partholón's wife against her husband."

The race of Partholón fought the first battle of Ireland against the Fomorians. The name (*Fomoire*) is a compound of the preposition *fo* 'under' and a root which appears in the German *Mahr,* name of a female demon who lies on the breast of people while they sleep (cf. Eng. 'nightmare'), in the name *Morrígan* (queen of demons), and perhaps in the name of the formidable Marats of the Veda. The Irish form means "inferior" or "latent demons." The myth presents the Fomorians as native powers constantly driven back to the limits of the world controlled by civilizing races, and always about to invade it and devour its produce. In Partholón's time they had lived for two hundred years in the islands near the coast, "having no other food." They fight against Partholón and his people "with one foot, one hand and one eye," a monstrous form, or a ritual posture (either interpretation seems possible), which has a magic value and a demonic significance. After seven days they are defeated and driven off. But we shall soon see them return, for the Fomorians never lay down their arms. They are like the powers of Chaos, ever latent and hostile to cosmic order.

On the feast of *Beltine,* the First of May, the race of Partholón was destroyed by a mysterious plague; but, by this time, the crafts and institutions by which Celtic society was maintained had already been established. How did this established tradition survive the destruction of the race? How was it transmitted to later peoples? The mythology, naturally incoherent, does not explain.

The race of Nemed, whose name means "sacred" (cf. Gaul [*nemēton*] 'sacred place'), then occupied Ireland, after the country had lain desert for thirty years. In their time four lakes were formed, two forts were built and twelve plains were cleared. But they were unable to control the Fomorians and finally became their vassals. The land into which Partholón had brought the precious herds of cattle became "a land of sheep," and every year on the Feast of *Samain,* the First of November, the people of Nemed had to deliver to their masters two-thirds of their corn, their milk and their children. After vain resistance and ruinous victories, they resolved to abandon Ireland.

The race of Partholón was followed by a fourth race, that of the *Fir Bolg,* who arrived on the Feast of *Lugnasad,* the First of August, the third great feast of the Celtic year. Various tribes came with them, *Gaileoin* and *Fir Domnann,* but all were "only one race and one power." Unlike their predecessors, these people did not disappear, but left descendants after them. The heroic sagas often mention these elements of the population as distinct from the ruling Gaels.[9] And here the mythology apparently preserves the memory of actual invasions of foreigners. Perhaps the *Gaileoin* are Gauls, the *Fir Domnann* the Dumnonii of Great Britain, the *Fir Bolg* the Belgac. Thus witnesses of a relatively recent past have come to be introduced between the fanciful Fomorians and the divine "Peoples of Dana": supernatural and human are blended in the crucible of the myth.

The races of Partholón and Nemed had been clearers of the plains. With the *Fir Bolg* we seem to emerge from the era of agrarian culture. No plains are said to have been cleared in their time, nor any lakes to have been formed. Their contribution is proper rather to a warlike aristocracy, for they introduced into Ireland the iron spearhead and the system of monarchy. It is said of their king Eochaid mac Eirc that "no rain fell during his reign, but only the dew; there was not a year without harvest." For (we add the connective on the evidence of several parallel passages), "falsehood was banished from Ireland in his time. He was the first to establish there the rule of justice." Thus there appears with the establishment of the first Celtic communities in Ireland the principle of association between the king and the earth—the king's justice being a condition of the fertility of the soil—which is the very formula of the magic of kingship.

The *Fir Bolg* were soon to be dispossessed by new invaders, the *Tuatha Dé Danann,* "Peoples of the Goddess Dana," who landed on the Feast of Beltine, and defeated the *Fir Bolg* in the First Battle of Mag Tured. They won the battle by their "talent," and this talent consisted of the power of magic (*draoidheacht*). In distant islands (the "islands of Northern Greece") they had learned "magic and every sort of craft and liberal art, so that they were learned, wise, and well skilled in every branch of these arts." From these islands they brought four talismans: the Stone of Fál, which screamed when the lawful king of Ireland placed his foot upon it; the sword of Nuada, of which the wounds were fatal; the spear of Lug which gave victory, and the Cauldron of the Dagda "from which none

parts without being satisfied." To these talismans and to their knowledge of magic, the *Tuatha* owe their supernatural power. They are "gods" because they are sorcerers. Moreover, among these *Tuatha* only the artisans, those who share this knowledge by which the divine race enjoys its power, are "gods." "They considered their artists to be gods (*dee*) and their labourers to be non-gods (*andee*)." And this distinction recurs in the epic formula: "the blessing of gods and non-gods upon you!" The divine race, like the human, includes, therefore, in addition to the privileged classes of warriors and initiated craftsmen, a common class which has no share in the magic hierarchy. It is characteristic that this profane element in society is the agricultural class. In this respect the race of the *Tuatha Dé Danann* differs from the preceding races, and in particular from that of Partholón, of which the agrarian character is so marked as to suggest a vegetation myth.

Having conquered the *Fir Bolg,* the *Tuatha Dé Danann* soon came into conflict with the Fomorians, to whom they were opposed in the Second Battle of Mag Tured. This battle, which is the subject of a long epic tale, is one of the dominant episodes of Irish mythology, and one of those most readily susceptible of varying interpretations. Some have found here a conflict between the forces of disorder and darkness and the forces of order and light, a sort of Celtic replica of the struggle of Chthónioi and Ouránioi. And this explanation does account for one aspect, and clearly the dominant aspect, of the rivalry which involved the two races. But we lose perspective by attributing this anarchical conflict of rival peoples to the essential antagonism of opposite cosmic principles; for the two parties were connected by a series of intermarriages so complex as to confuse even the native mythographers, and were forced into opposition by the same play of political events that governs the relations of human beings. In order to illustrate the conditions that govern this mythical world, we shall summarize the origins of the second Battle of Mag Tured.

In the course of a fight with the *Fir Bolg,* Nuada, king of the *Tuatha,* lost an arm. Any mutilation disqualifies a king, so another must be chosen. The chieftains select Bres (The Handsome), who is a son of the king of the Fomorians, but was reared by the *Tuatha* because his mother was one of them. But Bres lacks a sense of what is the first duty of a king, namely generosity. He does not grease the knives of the chieftains, and "however often they visited him their breath did not smell of beer." Worse still, he provides neither poets nor musicians nor acrobats nor jesters to entertain them. When their poet presents himself before Bres, he is offered neither bed nor fire, and receives only three dry biscuits on a small dish. Thereupon he pronounced the first satire (*áer*) ever to be pronounced in Ireland, the first of those rhythmic maledictions by means of which the poets, masters of the power of the word, can bring blotches on the face of a prince or sterility upon a whole province:

> *Without food upon his dish,*
> *without cow's milk upon which a calf grows,*
> *without a man's abode under the gloom of*
>   *night,*
> *without enough to reward poets, may that be*
>   *the fate of Bres![10]*

Enraged by his conduct, the chieftains demanded that Bres abdicate, and he invoked the aid of his father, who was king of the Fomorians. Thus the fight is joined, and above the battle of the warriors rages the struggle of wizards on either side who employ every resource of magic and countermagic. When the five chieftains who constitute the general staff of the *Tuatha* (Nuada, Dagda, Ogma, Goibniu and Dian Cécht) decide to declare war, their first care is to mobilize their artisans and make inventory of their magical resources. Their sorcerer promises to hurl against the enemy the twelve mountains of Ireland, their cup-bearer to drain the twelve lakes of Ireland, their druid to cause three showers of fire to rain upon the Fomorians, to deprive them of two-thirds of their valour and strength and to retain the urine of their men and of their horses. Throughout the battle Dian Cécht, "the leech," remains, chanting incantations with his three children, beside a well into which the bodies of slain warriors are thrown (for death by violence does not spare the race of the gods) and whence they emerge restored to life.

Thus a conflict, arising from the revolt of discontented chieftains, and spreading as a result of the appeal by the dispossessed king to his natural allies (circumstances which reflect in the myth political and domestic conditions familiar to Celtic society) ends in the victory of the divine invaders over the grim Fomorians, who are now finally expelled from the confines of what is to become the domain of the Gael.

The sixth and last race to invade Ireland is that of the "Sons of Míl," ancestors of the present inhabitants of the country. They landed on the Feast of *Beltine,* and the first three inhabitants that they met were the three eponymous goddesses of Ireland, Éire, Banba and Fódla. The circumstances of the meeting are remarkable. Éire, in welcoming the invaders, predicts that the island will belong to their descendants forever. The poet Amairgin thanks her, but Donn, the eldest of the Sons of Míl, says rudely: "It is not you that we must thank, but our gods and our magic powers." "What is that to you," said Éire, "for neither you nor your children will enjoy this island." Then she asked of Amairgin that the island should bear her name forever, and her sisters did likewise; and that is why the island has three names: Éire, Banba and Fódla. In accordance with the prophecy of the goddess, Donn was drowned before he had found a home in Ireland. He was buried

on an island off the west coast, since known as "The House of Donn." The descendants of the Sons of Míl follow him there after death.[11]

We see how Amairgin secured possession of the country for his race by conciliating its ancient goddesses, while Donn failed by his refusal to invoke other gods than his own. This episode illustrates the attitude of the Celts in religion, a willingness to adopt local cults and take advantage of the power that attached to them.

Nevertheless, the Sons of Míl demanded of the *Tuatha* "combat or sovereignty or agreement." The *Tuatha* gave them nine days' delay in which "to depart or to submit or to give battle." When they refused, the *Tuatha* appealed to the judgment of the poets of their adversaries: "for if they give an unjust judgment, our elements will kill them on the spot." We see that it is the poet, the sacred one, not the king or the warrior, who appears as arbiter. Amairgin decided that the Sons of Míl should re-embark and withdraw "as far as the ninth wave," that ninth wave which for the Celts had a magic power. When the invaders sought to return to shore they were prevented by a "druidic wind" raised by the *Tuatha*. (Druidic wind differs from natural wind in that it blows no higher than the ships' masts.) Then Amairgin sang an invocation to the great lady Éire:

> *I invoke the land of Ireland.*
> *Much coursed be the fertile sea,*
> *fertile be the fruit-strewn mountain,*
> *fruit-strewn be the showery wood, . . .* [12]

The wind abated so that the Sons of Míl were able to land. As he set his right foot on shore, Amairgin sang again:

> *I am the wind on the sea.*
> *I am a wave of the ocean.*
> *I am the roar of the sea.*
> *I am a powerful ox.*
> *I am a hawk on a cliff.*
> *I am a dewdrop in sunshine.*
>
> *
>
> *I am the strength of art.*
> *I am a spear with spoils that wages battle.*
>
> *
>
> *Who clears the stony place of the mountain?*
>
> *
>
> *Who has sought peace (in death?)*
> *seven times without fear?*
>
> *
>
> *Who brings his cattle from the house of*
>   *Tethra?*

*

*What man, what god forges weapons in a
   fort? . . .*
*Who chants a petition, divides the Ogam
   letters . . . ?*
A wise chanter.[13]

It has been suggested that this poem, which is a tissue of obscure formulas that puzzled even the mediæval commentators, echoes the druidic doctrine of metempsychosis; but it simply expressed the pride of the sorcerer, whose art has just brought him triumph over his enemies, and who now parades his talents and declares his power. For we know that one of the gifts which all primitive peoples attribute to their sorcerers is that of shape-shifting.

These two incantations of Amairgin mark with ritual pathos the solemnity of the moment when man proclaims his sovereignty over the earth, by virtue of the magic powers of the poets which have prevailed over the forces opposed to them. They illustrate too the dual attitude of man towards these forces: religion in the invocation, addressed to the eponymous goddess, the local "Mother," to obtain the fertility of the region of which she is still mistress; and magic in the explosion of pride on the part of the sorcerer who is the embodiment of the art which will enable him to prevail even against the gods. We shall find everywhere amongst the Celts the dialectic of these two attitudes, religion and magic. And if one of the two should be emphasized, it is the second. We have seen that the Irish regarded the gods as master magicians, so that the sacred and the magical are not distinct notions. Their relations with these gods are primarily relations of constraint, only secondarily of deference. We shall observe the same behaviour in the hero, always struggling against the supernatural and seeking to dominate it, to pursue it into its own territory and conquer it with mere weapons.

The Sons of Míl gave battle to the *Tuatha*, killed a great number of them, including the three eponymous goddesses, and put them to flight. The Book of Conquests declares that they were expelled from Ireland. But the common tradition, which is confirmed by modern folklore, contradicts this assertion. Like the *Dema* to whom we have compared them, the *Tuatha* "returned underground," where they continue to live, in those mounds where the peasant of today still believes them to dwell. We must now examine the status of the supernatural after the mythological period comes to an end, and the *modus vivendi* that was established between the two races destined to dwell together upon Irish soil.

. . . . .

While we depend on the witness of the insular Celts for the myths, we have for the images some documents concerning the Celts of the continent. These documents are of two sorts: texts of ancient writers, and Gaulish or Gallo-Roman inscriptions and monuments. The Latin and Greek texts are brief, categorical, and suggest conceptions analogous to those familiar in other mythologies; and therefore they are reassuring. The inscriptions (mere names or epithets of divinities) and the monuments (insofar as they are purely Celtic, for we must reckon with the possibility of Roman influence) give us only allusions which are not easy to interpret and which throw only a little light upon a world of obscure notions. One is tempted to use the texts as a starting point in order to explain the monuments, and so to fit the fragments of the puzzle into the ready framework that some paragraph of Caesar provides. But this temptation is to be avoided, for it is safer to wander without a guide in an unmapped country than to trust completely a map traced by men who came only as tourists and often with biased judgment. We shall proceed therefore as though no Greek or Roman had ever visited Celtic territory, and examine first the native documents. Then we shall be ready to compare our findings with what other writers have reported.

The first fact that strikes one is the multiplicity of the names of gods, and the fewness of the examples of each of them that occur. According to an early estimate, which is probably not subject to any notable correction, of the three hundred and seventy-four names attested in the inscriptions three hundred and five occur only once.[14] The names most frequently mentioned are those of the gods Grannos (nineteen times) and Belenos (thirty-one times), and the goddesses Rosmerta (twenty-one times) and Epona (twenty-six times). Names of Gaulish gods are legion, and the number has not been explained by those parallel processes of syncretism and expansion which elsewhere have resulted in defining and establishing the features of the gods. In the Gallo-Roman period, when the native cults became integrated in the imperial religious system, a single Roman deity represents a multiplicity of local gods whose memory is preserved in the epithet of the imported foreigner. Thus fifty-nine different epithets are joined to the name of Mars:[15] Mars Teutates is the Teutates that we know from Lucan; Mars Segomo is Segomo whose cult appears in Munster and whose name occurs in that of the Irish hero Nia Segamon (Champion of Segomo);[16] Mars Camulus is the disguise of a god Camulus, identical, no doubt, with Cumall, father of the hero Finn (see chapter VII); Mars Rudianos (The Red) recalls the name of the horse-god Rudiobos,[17] for the horse and the colour red are associated with the land of the dead and with gods of war throughout Celtic territory. This is evidenced by the red trappings of the *Morrígan* and by the three red horsemen from the kingdom of Donn, lord of the dead, whose appearance in *The Destruction of Da Derga's Hostel* announces his approaching doom to king Conaire.[18] Thus a multiplicity of local tribal gods whom he has supplanted, appears under the unity of the imperial cult of Mars.

The plurality of names over the whole territory suggests that these were tribal gods, the gods of communities or groups of communities, for their distribution seems to be political or geographic rather than functional. And this suggestion is confirmed by a useful observation made by Vendryes.[19] It is well known that one of the gods most frequently represented on Gaulish monuments is Tricephalus, a three-headed or three-faced god. We have thirty-two effigies of him, most of them from Northern Gaul. Fifteen of the more archaic examples were found in the territory of the Remi. We may therefore consider Tricephalus to be a god of the Remi, at least in origin. Again, the cult of the *Matres* is widespread in the Rhineland and especially among the Treviri. But in one instance we find Tricephalus represented on a stele at Trier, and he appears surmounted by the three *Matres* of the Treviri who seem to trample him under foot. This monument may be compared with a stele discovered at Malmaison, on which Tricephalus is associated with another group, the pair consisting of Mercury and his companion Rosmerta. But here the positions are reversed and Tricephalus seems to dominate the divine pair. Thus each of the two peoples has symbolized the triumph of their own god over foreign or hostile gods. No doubt Vendryes is right in regarding such evidence as an indication of the national character that the Remi attributed to their Tricephalus and the Treviri to their *Matres*.

This tribal character of the god is directly expressed in the name of a Gaulish god Teutates mentioned by Lucan: "and those who propitiate with horrid victims ruthless Teutates, and Esus whose savage shrine makes men shudder, and Taranis whose altar is no more benign than that of Scythian Diana."[20] Teutates has been supposed to be one of the great Gaulish gods, but this hypothesis is invalidated by the fact that he is mentioned elsewhere only in a single inscription, and was adored probably only by some obscure tribe. The name indeed means simply "(the god) of the tribe" (G. *touto-, teuto-*, Ir. *túath* 'tribe'),[21] a title which corresponds to a familiar formula of Irish sagas: "I swear by the god (or gods) by whom my people swear." Every Gaulish people had, then, its Teutates, and adored him each by a different name, or by one of the titles: *Albiorix* (King of the World); *Rigisamus* (Most Royal); *Maponos* (The Great Youth); *Toutiorix* (King of the Tribe); *Caturix* (King of Battle); *Loucetius* (The Brilliant One), which are perhaps no more than means of invoking the god without profaning his name, by a precaution analogous to that suggested by the Irish formula. How did these gods of peoples or tribes appear to the imagination of the Gauls? Without discussing the effigies in detail, we shall note some general features.[22]

First of all, the triple figures are important, gods with three heads or three faces and groups of three goddesses. The number three plays a large part in Celtic tradition; the "triad," a formula which combines three facts or three precepts, is a *genre* which dominates the gnomic literature of both Wales and Ireland, and triple personages or trios are prominent in the epic tradition of the two peoples.

Another notable fact is the more or less marked zoomorphic character of the effigies, sometimes expressed in a more evolved form of the same mythological type by association of an animal with the god. An example is furnished by Cernunnos (The Horned One), the god whose cult is most widely attested. He is represented with the horns of a ram or a deer, squatting on the ground. The posture recalls that of the Buddha, but it must have been habitual to the Gauls, whose furniture did not include any sort of chair. He is often accompanied by one or two horned serpents, and the horned god with a serpent recurs on the famous Gundestrup vessel. Certain variants present a female deity, or a three-headed figure, of the same type.

This zoomorphic element appears more clearly in the female than in the male effigies: one of the most familiar goddesses is Epona, whose name means "The Great Mare" and who appears on horseback accompanied by a mare with her foal, or feeding some foals; the Welsh Rhiannon, "The Great Queen," has been recognized as a mare-goddess comparable to Epona.[23] We find also a bear-goddess, Artio, and there can be no doubt that the name Damona, formed like Epona, means "The Great Cow" (cf. Ir. *dam* 'ox').

These female deities fill a big place in the religious world of the Gauls. They can be divided into two classes. The first is that of the tutelary goddesses,[24] who are connected with the earth itself and with local features, wells or forests, or again with the animals that frequent them, and who control the fertility of the earth, as is shown by the horn of plenty which is one of their attributes. Such are the *Matres* and Epona and the goddesses of water (Sirona in eastern Gaul and Brixia, the companion of Luxovius, the watergod of Luxeuil) or of forests (Dea Arduina of the Ardennes). The second class, which is smaller, is that of the goddesses of war: for example, Andarta of the Vocontii, or Andrasta who was invoked by Boudicca before she went into battle, or Nemetona whose name resembles that of Nemain, one of the three *Morrígna* of Irish tradition. The two types of which the one represents the powers of fertility, the other the powers of destruction, appear separately on continental territory. We find them confused in the persons of the same divinities in insular tradition, which represents in this respect, as in others, a less analytical and more archaic conception than the Gaulish.

Many of the goddesses often appear as companions of a god. Brixia and Luxovius have been cited; and Sirona is usually associated with Grannos, sometimes with Apollo; Nemetona appears on the monuments beside Mars, who has, no doubt, been substituted in these cases for some Celtic war-god; Rosmerta is likewise the companion of Mercury. But the pair who appear most frequently are Sucellos and Nantosuelta.

Sucellos, "The God of the Mallet," whose name means "Good Striker," has been identified with Dispater, ancestor of the Gauls, of whom Caesar tells us. The appearance of this bearded god, dressed in the short tunic which was the national costume of the Gauls, and expressing strength and authority and, at the same time, a certain benevolence, accords well with one's idea of a father-god, and recalls in many respects the chief god of the Irish, the Dagda. His attributes are the mallet, weapon of the "Good Striker," and the cup or dish, symbol of abundance, and here there is a striking parallel with the two attributes of the Dagda, the club which fells his enemy and the inexhaustible cauldron which ensures abundance to his people. These divinities have, therefore, the two characteristics that define the function of a father-god, who is at the same time a warrior, and therefore protector and nurturer. The name of the companion, Nantosuelta, is obscure, but the first element is recognizable as meaning "river" (cf. W. *nant* 'stream'). We find, then, on Gaulish soil an association of a father-god with a local river-goddess which is confirmed by an episode of Irish mythology in which the Dagda is associated with the Boyne, the sacred river of Ireland. Other pairs might be added to this class. In the region of Salzbach a "god of the mallet" is associated with the goddess Aeracura who appears with a horn of plenty or a basket of fruit, attributes of the *Matres*. In the mythology of the insular Celts we shall find again these pairs, consisting of the chief god and one of the *Matres,* and there is no doubt that they present one of the fundamental notions of Celtic religion.

Tribal gods and mother-goddesses: is it possible to go beyond this general characterization of the Gaulish divinities? Can one find the trace of a separation of functions and activities? The attempt has been made on the strength of a paragraph of Caesar which has been often quoted and which must again be quoted here. We declined to begin with this testimony, but it must now be considered.

Caesar uses these words: "Among the gods they most worship Mercury. There are numerous images of him; they declare him the inventor of all arts, the guide for every road and journey, and they deem him to have the greatest influence for all money-making and traffic. After him they set Apollo, Mars, Jupiter and Minerva. Of these deities they have almost the same idea as other nations: Apollo drives away diseases, Minerva supplies the first principles of arts and crafts, Jupiter holds the empire of heaven, Mars controls wars."[25]

Thus the great gods of the Celts would seem to correspond more or less exactly to the great gods of the Romans and would have divided among them, as these do, the various domains of human activity. Such a coincidence is *a priori* surprising. In view of the profound divergence in mentality and social structure which we observe as between Romans and Celts, one must wonder at such a similarity in their religious ideas; and a comparison of this text with the Gaulish documents confirms the suspicion.

If we consider the goddesses, we have noticed among the mother-goddesses divinities of water and forest, goddesses of fertility who protect certain animals, and goddesses of war, but nowhere a Minerva, patroness of the arts. This does not mean that some mother-goddess did not play this part. And indeed we shall find a patroness of the arts among the insular Celts in the triple Brigit. Caesar may have observed this quality in some Gaulish goddess unknown to us, or even in one of those we do know but not in this connection. The quality familiar to him, and therefore immediately intelligible, prompted a hasty identification calculated to satisfy him and to mislead us. Caesar's testimony is important inasmuch as it throws light on an aspect of the mother-goddesses which is confirmed by Irish tradition, and about which Gaulish tradition is silent. But by accepting it as it stands we should form a false notion of the complex goddesses of the Celts.

In the case of the gods we are in the same situation. We can well believe that Gaulish gods were warriors, artisans, healers, and that they presided over certain phenomena of the heavens. Which people has not attributed these various activities to its gods? But if we seek, for instance, the contrast between a god of war and a god of arts and crafts, then difficulties arise. This is illustrated by the contradictions of scholiasts who have tried to reconcile the independent evidence of Lucan with the system outlined by Caesar. In a passage cited above Lucan enumerates three gods adored by Gaulish tribes; Teutates, Esus and Taranis. There is nothing to suggest that these are three great Gaulish gods, still less that they are the three principal gods of the Gauls, a conception which, as we have seen, does not correspond to any reality. But in the light of Caesar's testimony, one is led to establish some equivalence between these gods and those that he has defined; and the scholiasts of Lucan have made the attempt.[26] The name Taranis, which means "Thunderer" (cf. Ir. *torann* 'thunder') indicates an identification with Jupiter. But, as between Esus and Teutates, which corresponds to Mars and which to Mercury? There is so little correspondence that the two scholiasts have answered the question in contradictory terms, so that we find both Esus and Teutates identified with each of the two Roman gods. We have seen that in fact Teutates is simply "the god of the tribe"; and he must have been regarded sometimes as a god of war and sometimes as a god of industry, according as he was invoked in times of war or peace. No doubt it was the same in the case of Esus, whose name may mean "master," if the comparison with Latin *erus* be correct.[27] Lucan describes him as the blood-thirsty master of warlike tribes, but on the altars of Trier and Paris he appears as the gracious patron of a peaceful corporation of builders.[28] Similarly the Irish Lug is an artisan of many talents, even a healer, but also a warrior whose spear never misses its mark. General and complete efficiency is the character of all the Celtic gods, and we see them fighting or giving help and counsel, according to the needs of their people.

However, there is one point in the testimony of Caesar which must be remembered, and it requires interpretation. It is the pre-eminence that he accords to the Gaulish Mercury over the other gods, including the lord of heaven. This conflicts so strongly with the notions that were familiar to him that we are bound to accept it; and, moreover, it is confirmed by insular tradition. But we must not rush to the conclusion that the Gauls distinguished a god of arts and crafts as opposed to a god of war, and preferred one to the other. The cult of Mars, who is adored under fifty-nine different titles, is no less widespread in Gallo-Roman Gaul than that of Mercury, who possesses only nineteen titles. We must rather suppose that the Gauls gave precedence in their divine world to the craftsperson over the warrior, and that both qualities could be combined, and were normally combined, in one divine person. This, at least, is how we should explain, in terms of Celtic mythology, the fact which impressed Caesar, and which he explained in Roman terms.

Some general characteristics have emerged from this rapid survey: the multiplicity of divine persons, sometimes in triple form, sometimes in animal form; tribal character, marked in the case of the gods; local character, especially in the case of the goddesses; the importance of female deities, goddesses of war or mother-goddesses; the frequent association of these females with tribal gods; the lack of differentiation of functions as among the gods; and the importance of the craftsperson in the celestial hierarchy. These characteristics appear only as shadows in our picture of the religious world of the Gauls, for our imperfect knowledge permits merely a sketch; but we shall observe them again, more clearly drawn, and emphasized by the rich colour of a living mythology, in the epic tradition of the insular Celts.

Notes

1 Lévy-Brühl, *La Mentalité Primitive,* 3.

2 *Revue Celtique,* 12, 107. 162.

3 R. I. Best and Osborn Bergin, *Lebor na Huidre* (Dublin, 1929) 4034.

4 R. A. S. Macalister and J. MacNeill, *Leabhar Gabhála,* 145.

5 R. A. S. Macalister, *Lebor Gabála Érenn.*

6 R. Thurneysen, *Zeitschrift für Celtische Philologie* 13, 141; 20, 375.

7 *Revue Celtique* 50, 217.

8 *Lebor Gabála,* III, 69; *ibid.* 41.

9 MacNeill, *Phases of Irish History,* 76.

10 *Revue Celtique* 12, 70.10 = *Lebor na Huidre* 561 [Tr.].

11 Meyer, *Sitzungsberichte der preussischen Akademie der Wissenschaften* 1919, 537.

12 *Leabhar Gabhála* 257 [Tr.].

13 *Leabhar Gabhála* 263 [Tr.].

14 Anwyl, *Trans. Gael. Soc. Inverness,* 26, 411.

15 Dottin, *Manule pour servir a l'étude de l'antiquité celtique,* 226.

16 MacNeill, *Phases of Irish History,* 127.

17 J. Loth, *Rev. Arch.* 22, 5e Sér. 210; Eva Wunderlich, *Rel.-Geschicht. Versuche,* 20, 46.

18 *Revue Celtique* 22, 36.

19 *Comptes rendus de l'Acad. des Inscriptions,* 1935, 324.

20 *Bellum Civile,* i, 444-46 (tr. Duff).

21 Vendryes, *Teutomatos, Comptes rendus de l'Acad. des Inscriptions,* 1939, 466.

22 For the images, see W. Krause, *Religion der Kelten (Bilderatlas zur Religionsgeschichte,* 17); S. Reinach, *Description raisonnée du musée de Saint-Germain-en-Laye, Bronzes figurés de la Gaule Romaine,* 137.

23 H. Hubert, 'Le Mythe d'Epona', *Mélanges Vendryes,* 187.

24 Daremberg-Saglio, *Dict. des Ant., s.v. Matres.*

25 *De Bell. Gall.,* vi, 17 (tr. Edwards).

[26] *Commenta Bernensia,* ed. Usener, 32.

[27] Ernout and Meillet, *Dict. Etym. de la langue latine* (2nd ed.), 310.

[28] St. Czarnowski, RC 42, 1.

Ward Rutherford (1978)

SOURCE: *The Druids and Their Heritage,* Gordon & Cremonesi, 1978, pp. 91-115.

[*In the following excerpt, Rutherford investigates the pantheon of Celtic gods, and the beliefs—notably in the transmigration of the soul after death—held by their intermediaries, the Druids.*]

While it is easy to understand the astonishment which seized the classical writers at the involvement of what they regarded as ministers of religion in such a multiplicity of functions, it is also easy to understand how it came about.

Societies like the Celtic, believing that they alone occupied the Great Cosmic Centre, the very point at which the numen reached out to make its contact with humanity, were convinced that it was their acts, more than anyone else's, which sustained life and kept the world on its axis. As Soustelle points out in describing the centrality of religious observance to Aztec life, it is only by rituals faithfully and meticulously carried out that cataclysm is averted and chaos kept at bay. Thus religion was by no means the extra duty, the hedging of one's bets with Providence, it had become for the Romans or was to become for Christians even in the so-called "Ages of Faith". This is why the Gauls appeared as incorrigibly superstitious to foreign observers of them.

The matrix of belief was their mythology. It was through this that men learnt that, as nothing happened without cause in their day-to-day existence, causative agencies were to be found in the Cosmos itself. The acts of the gods or their deliberate decisions were responsible for the genesis of the race, and through it of mankind; for the great crises of flood, earthquake and plague, even for such repetitive occurrences as the succession of the seasons or the rising of the sun in the morning. And merely to take these sequences for granted was a perilous act of *hubris.* The empirical facts of bad harvests, drought or disease among the livestock were there to prove that the gods were not mocked.

Between men and their gods, as myth described them, stood the Druids, at once mediators and interpreters, because they stood in a relationship with the gods so intimate it was as though they themselves partook of the divine character.

And for their part, too, the gods are magicians of an unassailable potency who in the use of their powers must be alternatively restrained or encouraged.

As this magical character provides something of the key to our understanding of them, so it also poses riddles of its own. Indeed, this entire area of Celtic deities is one fraught with queries. Caesar lists six "principal" gods to the Gauls: Dispater (or Pluto), Mercury, Mars, Apollo, Jupiter and Minerva. He makes no claim to comprehensiveness, but even if we add to his list the names of those Celtic gods who, from their incidence in place-names, epigraphy and mythology, we can be sure were worshipped over a wide area, we are still left far short of the 374 god-names made out by scholars of which no fewer than 305 occur only once.

That we are not dealing with an equal number of distinct deities is certain, if for no other reason because of the Celtic practice of using different names in different localities. The father-god *In Dagda* becomes *In Ruad Rofhessa,* "the Red One of Great Wisdom" in some places; *Eochaid Ollathair* in others. The last form introduces a *horse*-element, *eoch-* into the name which might well lead the unwary to conclude that here was a totally different being.

There were, too, the numerous territorial divinities, associated with specific geographical features, like Deva, goddess of the River Dee, or Clota, goddess of the Clyde. There are the many important European rivers whose names can be traced back to Celtic gods.

Then there were those which must have been purely tribal gods, whose existence can be inferred from the very nature of Celtic society and its constant internecine wars, but which is supported by the god-names found only in one area.

The necessary adjustments made, we are left, all the same, with a formidable total. How many could, with accuracy, be identified with the Druids? All, says Kendrick, and though one might agree in the sense that the Druids' objective was to dominate Celtic religion in all its facets, some clarification is needed. Somehow we must try to separate the strands of the tangled skein of this huge pantheon, and to do so have to go back as far as we can to the origins of their gods and, indeed, to the roots of the idea of deities itself.

The habitat of the shaman is, as we have seen, within the heart of nature and its forces. In trance, his guides are the spirits of those animals familiar to him either from observation or from the hunt. Indeed, the shaman's role comes into existence because of the need the hunter feels to "make peace" with the spirits of the creatures he kills. But in this world of ghostly-animals, as in that of living ones, it is the most potent animals who occupy the dominant positions: the fierce, courageous boar; the powerful and virile bull; the fleet reindeer; the bear; the horse; the eagle; perhaps the raven; the salmon. All are to be found in the Celtic supernatural, just as we find animal-headed gods among the Egyptians and the Hindus.

And in the ecology of the Other World, too, the lesser creatures play their subordinate roles: for example, the egret perches on the bull's back to cleanse it of vermin, as it is to be seen represented on a carved stone found in Paris in 1711.

Between the shaman and his "guides" special relationships would come to be forged: a "bull spirit", a "bear spirit" or an "eagle spirit" would become friend and benefactor. Dressing himself in the creature's likeness, that he might be recognizable, it would be this "spirit friend" that the shaman would seek out on his own travels through the Other World. The "guide" would show his own goodwill towards the living in a host of ways.

Hunters know of and often form special relationships with a single animal in a hunted species—usually a female—which will actually assist them in their task. It will act, quite voluntarily, as a decoy attracting other members of the herd to where the hunter lies in wait. Those of early times would probably have regarded such animals as supernatural allies and they may well offer a clue to the interpretation of legends about creatures like the "supernatural" boar, Twrc Trywth, or the mysterious white hart which appears in the Arthurian and other stories.

There are also, of course, the numerous stories of birds' becoming emissaries to lead the way to new pastures. Titus Livy (59 BC-AD 17) relates how Ambiganus, king of the Bituriges, among the most powerful of the Gaulish tribes (their name means, according to Markale, "Kings of the Earth"), growing old and believing his realm to be too big, instructed his nephews, Bellovesus and Sigoevsus, to seek out new lands for at least part of his people. They were to take with them such numbers as would make their progress and final settlement irresistible and their quest would be guided by the will of the gods, as manifested by the flight of birds. One can well envisage from the frequency with which avian couriers occur in Celtic myth that what Livy described was a well-established tradition.

For such favours as the shaman's guide displayed towards them, the tribe would want not only to show its gratitude, but also to ensure their continuance. Among other ways of honouring him would be by representations set up in prominent places where all might see and be reminded. The tribe might also take his name and display his likeness on its battle shields. He has become, we should say, a totem.

The road that leads from here to full deification may be long, but its final destination is inevitable. May it not be that the creature that bestows one favour bestows all? It calls for little discernment to see how close the Celts were to this totemic feeling. Lugh takes on the likeness of an eagle in one myth, that of a salmon in another. Angus, son of In Dagda, is himself sometimes given a horse-name and takes on the form of a swan.

But there are besides the wider questions, those for example of the origins of the tribes, of humanity, of life itself. May it not be that these, too, derive from some beneficent animal? To find communities tracing their ancestry back to a totemic animal is, of course, common enough.

There is the wolf which suckled Romulus and Remus, twin founders of Rome. The Scythian tribes traced their lineage in the same way. There are numerous Celtic mother-goddesses who are associated with animals: the cow; the pig; the bear. It may well be that the Arduinna, associated with the boar or Mathonwy, mother of Math, whose name associates her with the bear (Matu), were in origin tribal mother-deities who, in the course of time passed into a general, as it were racial, mythology.

But for the Celts, pride of place among these totemic creatures must surely be accorded to the horse. As one of the first great horse-using peoples, they had probably been introduced to it as beast of burden by the Scythians, though both races may well have hunted and eaten it or even grazed it and drunk mare's milk for centuries before they put it to other employment. The Indo-European word, *Ekuos,* is the base of the word for "horse" used in most languages, including the Greek *hippos* and the Latin *equus,* both probably derived from the Celtic. So one finds standing high among the *deae matres* of the Celts, the Gaulish Epona, "the Great Horse". Under her Welsh form of Rhiannon, she bears a child abducted at birth. As punishment she has to carry guests to the court of her husband, Pwyll, upon her back. Their offspring, meanwhile, is found outside the stable of a mare which has just foaled. The pregnant Macha, the Irish "Great Horse", curses the Ulstermen when they insist she takes part in a horse-race just before she is due to be delivered. As her chariot reaches the end of the field, she gives birth to twins, a boy and girl; as a consequence the place is called Emain Macha, "Twins of Macha" thereafter. In these stories one catches the hint of some early foundation myth in which the race and perhaps all living things sprang from the belly of a great, totemic mare.

Totems are a long way from the concept of gods, however, and Georges Dumezil in *Les Dieux des Indo-Européens* has pointed to the existence among the Indo-Europeans of a word, *deiwos,* used to describe creatures in the likeness of humans, but possessing superhuman powers. This is plainly the radical of most of the words for "god" in the European tongues: the Greek *theos,* the Latin *deo,* the Spanish, *dios,* the French *dieu,* for example.

As the title of his book implies, he goes further than this and claims to distinguish a group of deities common to all the Indo-European races. There are, thus, the gods of wealth and fertility; the divine warriors: Indra of the Hindus; Mars of the Romans; Thor of the Scandinavians. There are the gods of law and justice: Mitra; the Greek Zeus; Fides; Tyr. But standing in opposition to Mitra is Varuna; to Zeus, Uranus; to Fides, Jupiter; and to Tyr, Odinn (similar juxtapositions are also to be found in Persian religion and, as a matter of fact, in Babylonian). Varuna, Uranus, Jupiter, Odinn, are all designated by Dumezil as "the great, furious magical kings".

While not all scholars would agree with Dumezil's more far-reaching conclusions, most would unhesitatingly subscribe to the view that there are such marked similarities between many of the gods found among the Indo-European peoples as would postulate a common origin. It is for this reason that Caesar is able to render his six Gaulish gods in terms of their Graeco-Roman counterparts.

Dumezil's "magical kings" provide us I think, with a valuable key to the Celtic pantheon. As we know, only one mortal is qualified to enter the world of the spirits—the shaman—and the "magical kings", almost be definition, all have shamanic links. Odinn is actually nicknamed "the Great Shaman". By his sacrifice, he recapitulates the initiation, symbolical death and regeneration of the shaman. Even his reward takes the form of magical skill. What we have in Odinn, therefore, is a shaman joined with the world of spirits. If we admit to the degree of gods only beings in human likeness, it is surely the "shaman-become-god" who is its founder-member.

And if we can detect him among the Celtic gods we have, surely, one thread we can disentangle. Let us return to Caesar's six, which may well have come from Posidonius. The chief of these was, he says, Jupiter, though the one most venerated was Mercury, represented in countless images and regarded as inventor of the arts, director of travellers and as a powerful supporter of trade and commerce. Dispater was regarded as the common ancestor of the Gauls and it was on account of this that they measured time by nights rather than days and fixed the dates of festivals by the night.

When one tries to turn the list back into its Celtic originals, however, one is quickly led into the realm of conjecture. Jupiter must be Taranis. Apollo is, almost certainly, Belenos. Dispater is likely to be the horned-god Cernunnos.

With Mercury on the other hand we are faced by a choice: the obvious one is Lugh the Many Skilled, but on a stone discovered at Trèves in 1895 Esus is linked with Mercury. The problem is further confused by the Berne *scholiasts* who equate Esus with Mars, though the answer here is that they probably mean Mars not as war-god but as god of pastoralism and Esus certainly had his pastoral character. The god most often rendered as Mars is, in fact, Teutatis, and on the Gundestrup Cauldron he is certainly shown in association with warriors.

Minerva, the only one remaining, is sheer speculation and I can only hazard Epona, the horse-goddess.

My own form of Caesar's list would be, therefore: Taranis, Belenos, Cernunnos, Esus, Teutatis and ?Epona. And what we have is, undoubtedly, a group of six extremely powerful Celtic gods. Taranis is represented in numerous dedications. He is the god associated with the oaktree and hence with Druidism, a link made explicit by Pliny's description of the mistletoe-culling rite. He is, obviously, the god represented on the so-called "Jupiter-columns" found in north eastern and central Gaul where, often, he is portrayed holding a thunder bolt, like Jupiter, or a wheel, his other attribute. It is surely his name which is commemorated in the name of the isle of Taransay in Harris and in the chapel of Saint Tarran which stands on it.

The name Belenos occurs on thirty-two dedications and he was invoked over an area which runs from Northern Italy—the old Cisalpine Gaul—to the Shetlands. Cymbeline, the historical king on whom Shakespeare based his play is, correctly, Cuno-Belenos, the "Hound of Belenos". As we saw earlier, he is still associated, at least in name, with May Day festivals in many parts of the Celtic world.

For the Celtic Mercury I have settled on Esus in preference to Lugh because the latter comes from a totally different strain of deities, as I shall demonstrate shortly.

If we regard Esus as Mercury, we are forced to cast Teutatis as Mars, though the whole concept of war-god of the Celts as such may be an over-simplification. They never fought as a nation because they never were a nation. Usually they fought as tribes, sometimes in loose and unstable coalitions. One might, therefore, expect not one but many war-gods and there is evidence that this is the case. It accounts for the apparent confusion which seized the writers of the Gallo-Roman inscriptions, who in various places equate Mars not only with Teutatis, Esus, Cernunnos and Taranis, but also with such local deities as Cocidius, Rudiobus, Lenus, Corotiacus and Alator. But we know, in addition, that there were also powerful goddesses of war, like the Mórrígan. This apart, the most common translation of Teutatis is "God of the People" which would seem to make him something nearer to a giver of laws or a dispenser of justice.

Who then out of this list represents the "deified shaman" and hence the founder-god of the Celtic pantheon? In point of fact all have strong magical associations. Whether or not one is right in equating Esus with Mercury, we certainly know that the Roman god has a connexion with magic as the descendant of the Greek Hermes, who as Hermes Trimegistus, Hermes the Thrice-Great (a curiously Druidic-sounding epithet), supposedly provided the inspiration behind the "Hermetic system" used in alchemy, which later, taken over by orthodox science, was still being taken seriously as late as the time of Isaac Newton.

But Jupiter, equated wtih Taranis, is also a magician and sounds very much like a primal deity since his Latin name actually derives from "Father of the Gods".

But according to Dumezil, and the concept is elaborated by Eliade, the "magical king" is the "god who binds", that is to say who ties his worshippers to himself. In fact, one possible etymology of the word "religion" is through the verb *'religare'*, to tie together. The Hindu Varuna is associated with bonds in several of the Vedic hymns; so is the Norse Odinn, who on account of his ritual hanging of himself is sometimes called "God of the Rope" or "the Hanged". This would seem to give him a kinship with Esus in whose honour sacrificial victims were hanged and, in addition, there is equation often made between Odinn and Mercury.

Gods bear the marks of their creators and as Taranis, Esus and even Belenos are all super-magicians we can suppose their creators to have been magicians themselves, that is to say, the shamans or their successors the Druids.

But there is an even more convincing candidate for the role of "shaman-become-god" yet to be considered. This is Caesar's "Dispater", generally and most plausibly identified as Cernunnos. Strangely, he occurs less frequently than the other gods and is actually named only once, on an altar-stone found at Notre Dame de Paris. He has been tentatively identified, however, with a rock-carving in Val Camonica, Northern Italy and with representations found in Denmark, Rumania, Germany and Spain. At least one Celtic tribe appears to have derived its name from him and he may well be perpetuated in Cornwall, the Celtic name for which is Kernyw, as well as in such festivals as the Abbots Bromley stag-dance and the Breton *Pardon* of St. Cornely.

May he not also be the "Green Man" who in one form or other turns up with such regularity particularly in local legend? [In this connexion there is a fascinating study to be made of British pub names. No far from Lewes in Sussex is a "Green Man" whose sign shows a head complete with horns. And how about some of the others: The White Hart, to be found in almost every English town; The White Horse; or The Blue Boar?] One example may be Robin Hood, who traditionally wore green; there is a green giant in the Welsh *Dream of Rhonabwy;* while the festival of "The Lord of the Green Leaves" is kept by a community in Northumberland, described by Professor Ross, which still venerates the Celtic gods side by side with its Christian practices.

As Caesar tells us, it is he from whom the Gauls claim common descent, doing so by a "tradition preserved by the Druids". He is, on this evidence, a primary god.

He has been given the title of "Lord of the Animals" and the Gundestrup Cauldron shows him as squatting in the midst of various creatures. If one wished to represent the shaman surrounded by his animal-familiars, the Gundestrup picture is how one might well choose to do so. He even has his deer's antlers so that he may the better identify with them, as the shaman dresses himself in the likeness of that creature he seeks in spirit. Furthermore, he alone of the deities on the cauldron has eyes closed and wears the rapt expression of one entranced.

In his left hand he grasps his ram-headed serpent, but in his right he holds up what is indisputably an instrument of binding—a torc—while another encircles his own neck. The other gods on the cauldron's panels are similarly adorned, but it is Cernunnos alone who appears to be offering it. Thus, it may well be that the wearing of the torc, common to all classes of Celtic society may here have its origin. It was the symbol of their union with this all-important deity, who was father not only of mortals but also of the gods themselves. As a symbol of union, the wearing of a neck-ring is well-attested and is found, among other places, in the pre-Aryan cultures of India.

And if we pursue the Dumezilian vein further, there is another striking parallel. In terms of the space occupied on the cauldron, two gods predominate. The first is Cernunnos and his surrounding animals; the other, occupying the position facing him, is the one usually identified as Teutatis, the "God of the People" or "Ruler of the People", which seems to make him into Dumezil's "god of justice and the law". So once more we have the magical king opposed by the lawgiver as Varuna is opposed by Mitra or Odinn by Tyr.

But if he is so central to Druidism why are traces of Cernunnos less frequently found that those of other gods? Probably for this precise reason. To the Romans, out to expunge every vestige of Druidism, he would have seemed like its essence and, as they would no doubt have seen, since he was himself a kind of

Other World Druid, none but the Druids could ever invoke or mediate with him. What the Romans began the early Christians would certainly have continued. It is usually accepted that he was the prototype of the Western image of Satan. There is no reason why Satan should have been given horns unless his likeness is based upon some model. This Cernunnos could certainly provide. He inhabited a subterranean Other World and he had strongly magical—that is to say, witch-craft—associations. Reasons enough to seek his total extirpation.

We can say with assurance that Cernunnos belongs to a group of deities which can be directly linked with Druidism, a group whose other members, on the intimations of Caesar, of the Gundestrup Cauldron, of the Berne *Scholia* and of their frequent recurrence over a wide area also included Belenos, Teutatis, Taranis and Esus, besides, no doubt, a powerful *Magna Mater,* probably in the form of a horse-goddess, Epona, with all the fertility cult practices normally associated with the worship of this type of deity. All six bear characteristics which indicate that they are primal gods whose origins reach down to the deepest levels of Celtic, or possibly of Indo-European pre-history. They were, therefore, a group of gods carried by the Celtic migrants to the lands in which they established themselves.

To their number were added the various tribal and territorial deities who form the greater proportion of that host we can ascribe to the Celts.

However, their establishment in their new territories along the Atlantic seaboard led the Celts to adopt a new strain of gods, so powerful and important that they were rapidly accorded parity with the original ones. These were the *Tuatha De Danann,* the people (or tribe) of the goddess Dana, that great family held to be the pre-Celtic deities of Ireland, but which were obviously taken over by Druidism and spread throughout the Celtic world. Indeed, the spread is such that one is forced to ask oneself whether there had not been some contact with the worshippers of the *Tuatha De Danann* long before their migrations to the British Isles. As we have seen, it was Celtic custom to associate powerful feminine deities with rivers; the more important the river, the more powerful the goddess linked with it. Among the two most important must have been the Danube, where the Celts first emerged, and the Marne, where the discoveries at La Tène indicate that there must have been a thriving society. The Marne derives from Matrona, The Mother; the Danube, mentioned by Herodotus about the middle of the 5th Century BC, has plain links with Danu (or Dana), *déesse-foundatrice* of the *Tuatha,* and mother-goddess par excellence, "the source," in the words of Markale, "of a race of gods and heroes". As the Welsh Don, she is, besides being mother of Math, the mother of Gilvaethy

(Girflet in the Arthurian legends), of Arianrhod, mother of Lugh; of Amalthon the Labourer; of Hyveidd; and of the smith, Govannon, who is also the Irish Goibniu. So fertile is her womb that we can trace Cu Chulainn or even, with very little conjecture, Arthur back to it.

Admittedly controversy still surrounds the questions of whether Danu is one and the same as another goddess, Ana or Anu, but with the weight of opinion shifting forward the view that she was. A goddess called Anu is certainly to be found in Ireland where a hill in Kerry is called the "Paps of Anou" and she is especially associated with Munster. In Brittany, a mother-goddess called Ana survived as Saint Anne, its patron saint. It is generally asserted by Breton scholars that she was taken over from the pre-Celtic inhabitants of the peninsula. It accounts also for the wide distribution of St. Anne in place- and other names in Britain and elsewhere (the capital town of the Channel Island of Alderney, for example, is St. Anne's).

But we must not lose sight of another connexion: that between the two names Dana and Diana. In the latter, the first syllable may simply be an epithet meaning "god", in which case we would have something like "the goddess Ana". The cult of Diana, in origin a moon-deity, was extremely widespread in the ancient world and under the variants of her Greek name, Artemis, she goes back far into antiquity. She was to be found among the Etruscans who may themselves have borrowed her from Babylonic, certainly from Semitic, sources. Originally, she was associated with agriculture and hence with fertility, particularly that of women, though under the name Diana she was also the divine huntress, in which connexion a boar is one of her attributes (though, by name and in various other ways, Artemis is linked with the bear). The boar and huntresses are a recurrent motif of Celtic myth and iconography, occurring, among other places, on the partially defaced Ribchester stone dedicated to Maponos, "the Divine Son", and there are a number of Gallo-Roman inscriptions in which a local goddess is equated with Diana.

Her festival was on mid-summer's day June 24, and as we have seen, there are traces of customs practised on this day in both the Isle of Man and the Channel Islands. In the former, there is a direct, if tenuous link with Diana/Artemis in the wearing of mug-wort, *Artemisia vulgaris,* on St. John's Day, which is actually June 24. Throughout the Christian world, in the Middle Ages, St. John's Eve was an occasion for major festivity of a character singularly out of keeping with the somewhat austere nature of the Baptist himself, beheaded for refusing to moderate his condemnation of the incestuous King Herod. They included dancing in the streets, the lighting of public bonfires and, especially, uninhibited amatory displays by the young. It is hard to avoid the suspicion that the day corresponded with the festival of some important pagan deity, and this would help to explain why the church appointed it as the holy-day of one of its most august saints.

But who were the original invokers of the *Tuatha De Danann?* The generally accepted belief is that the pre-Celtic inhabitants of the British Isles were a people who had migrated from North Africa by way of the Atlantic seaboard of Europe, marking their progress by the building of the megaliths. For this, the myths themselves offer two interesting pieces of supportive evidence.

The first is the name of one of the central *Tuatha* deities, Lugh the Many Skilled. The Welsh form of his name, Lleu, means "lion" and that it was understood to mean this elsewhere is indicated by the name of the large French city Lyon, which derives from Lugdunum, "the fortress of Lugh". The use of "Y" to stand for the vowel-sound we today represent by "I" was no less common in Old French than in Old English, so that Lyon actually does mean "Lion". Lions are hardly creatures that the Indo-Europeans would have come into contact with and they would not, therefore, have taken one as a totem. On the other hand, they would certainly have been familiar enough to a people from North Africa.

The second piece of evidence is Diana/Artemis herself who, as we have already observed, undoubtedly had connexions with that general area. The Temple of Diana (actually, Artemis) at Ephesus was one of the Seven Wonders of the Ancient World and was still very much in use at the time of St. Paul.

But whether or not Dana/Ana is actually Diana, the fact remains that it is her offspring which figure most frequently and prominently in the myths. There are, to be sure, references in both those of Ireland and those of Wales which could be interpreted as hinting at the gods of the earlier phylum. In two of the Welsh stories, *Branwen Daughter of Llyr* and *How Culhwch Won Olwen* we have a Glinyeu ap Taran mentioned. There is also Beli the Great, son of Mynogan and Beli Adver, names certainly cognate with Belenos. Ross discusses a giant in the story of *The Lady of the Fountain* who, because of the power over animals he possesses, may be Cernunnos. Among the Irish stories, she suggests that he may lie concealed under the name of Conall Cernach in *The Driving-Off of Fraich's Cattle.* Here he displays power over serpents. This is congruous with the representation of Cernunnos on the Gundestrup Cauldron where he grasps a ram-headed serpent by the neck, but it also leads one to wonder whether St. Patrick's proverbial power over snakes may not, in fact, have had a pagan origin.

All these identifications have to be tentative, however, and the roles played in the stories are very subsidiary; sometimes they feature only as names in long lists. This is in contrast with the *Tuatha* deities: usually clearly labelled and playing key-roles. One must, naturally, take into account the confused state in which we have received the myths, though it would be very strange if the relegation of a group of important deities had been brought about by such inadvertence alone.

But we have, in addition, the evidence of the Christian festivals which were intended to supplant the earlier, pagan ones. Of these, two—the Feasts of Brigid and Lugh—both commemorate gods of the *Tuatha,* while almost all the myths surrounding Samain are associated with the same phylum of deities. The only exceptions are Beltain, the festival of Belenos, and the various, now purely local festivals traceable back to Cernunnos or, say, Epona, with the Padstow "Hobby-Horse" providing a good example. No surviving occasion can be traced to Esus, Teutatis or Taranis.

What was it about the life-style of the existing populations that so impressed the newly arrived Celts that they felt compelled to take over their gods? Undoubtedly it was the megaliths of which these aboriginals had been the builders, though even for them this had taken place in a past so remote that their constructors had ceased to be regarded as humans and had become gods.

Stories of the supernatural origins of the standing-stone are to be found wherever they occur. In the Channel Islands, particularly rich in them, the patois word, *"pouquelayé",* means "puck or fairy" and not only does island folklore ascribe their building to these supernatural creatures (who are by no means to be conceived of as the tiny beings of later tradition), it also regards the stones as their dwelling-place which mortals disturb at their peril. In Brittany, down to late times, the stones were the centres of cults, probably pre-Celtic in origin.

We know, too, that the Celts were fascinated by them, burying their dead in megalithic tombs, absorbing them into their mythology as the *sidhs* and depositing round them what, in Piggott's words "looks like more than picnic debris". (There are also, incidentally, indications that some of the shafts and enclosures associated wih Druidism in Britain pre-date those of the Continent, offering support for Caesar's statement that Britain was the birthplace of the order.)

Among the megaliths were to be found, of course, the great stone circles, including the most astonishing of all—Stonehenge. From the work of Professor Gerald Hawkins and others it is now recognized that this is an astronomical computer, using a base of nineteen years (actually, 19+19+18=56) to bring solar and lunar years into syncronization. From the Coligny calendar we also know this to have been the system employed by the

Druids. It is, therefore, likely that they used Stonehenge (which would be consistent, anyway, with archaeological data from other henges where signs of Celtic use have been found) and they could only have learnt its complex operation under the tutelage of the existing priesthood.

We can now assert confidently that these Stone-Age people were themselves sophisticated astronomers which, as already pointed out, means they must also have possessed a quite high degree of mathematical skill.

In my view it was through their contacts with this priesthood, which may itself have had links with the same shaman-magicians who so greatly influenced the Persian Magi, Brahmins and Babylonic priesthood, that the Druids acquired the knowledge which led writers like Diogenes to equate them with these other three bodies.

In any event, discovering a system of religious belief so much more highly developed than their own, the Druids could scarcely ignore its deities. They had to be absorbed into their own pantheon. This must have posed a problem, for gods are notoriously jealous and do not take kindly to supersession or demotion. The solution the Druids adopted was that employed by others, notably the Greeks with their large and complex Olympus of interrelated deities: all the gods, new as well as old, became the members of one vast family or clan whose stories were encapsulated in a cycle of myths.

One finds oneself asking, in fact, whether anything recognizable as Druidism, at least as it impressed Aristotle and, through him, Diogenes can actually have existed before this time.

Nonetheless, whatever the original personalities of the gods of this influx may have been, they would quickly have acquired the likeness of the people who were worshipping them.

The life of the gods differed little from that of men. They tilled the land like Amathaon or they wrought metal into weapons like Govannon. They feasted and they fornicated. They knew the pangs of desire and did not scruple to use any subterfuge to satisfy it.

Yet these activities merely filled the intervals of peace between the great battles in which they participated with the same rumbustious joy in violence as men. For them, it was no more than a game, played according to its own strict code of rules and none the worse because the stakes were the highest of all. And the gods, too, could suffer in the fray. Nuada lost his hand, and even death was no stranger. Carman died as a prisoner in the hands of the *Tuatha De Danann.* Brân survived

decapitation as a disembodied head. He and his seven companions lived a life of joyous feasting which lasted eighty years, before the head was finally laid to rest at White Hill in London.

What distinguished the divine from the human, then? The power of magic, naturally, and Ross has drawn attention to the expression of "withdrawn, inscrutable intensity" which characterizes almost all depictions of deities, even those which, artistically, are the most rudimentary. Nowhere is this more marked than on the faces which decorate the Gundestrup Cauldron. Yet they were capable of compassion, as well. When Cu Chulainn is wounded, Lugh, visible only to his favourite, comes to his side and not only comforts him and dresses his wounds, he even undertakes to replace him on the battlefield so that his forces' strength will not be depleted by his absence.

The gods were marked off from mere humans, all the same.

One of the archaeological mysteries surrounding the Celts is the frequent occurrence of "Janus" heads, that is to say heads made up of two or more, often three, faces. There are a number of possible explanations for this. One is that three was the sacred number of the Druids. Much of their learning is expressed in "triads". It is also possible that the three faces represent three aspects of the god. Thus, the triple representations of Macha, the Irish horse-goddess, is explained as being due to the fact that woman has three aspects: the mother, the virgin and "the devourer of men".

Powell suggests [in *The Celts,* 1958] that this tricephalism expressed the idea that the gods were conceived as "to the power of three". That is to say they had in all things thrice the power of men.

This undoubtedly applied to their stature. Hence we find the hillside figures as giants. Interestingly enough, the Cornish giant Gogmagog is described as being twelve cubits tall. This is equivalent to eighteen feet or three times the height of a tall man. And the Celts were themselves tall. Other nations saw them as a race of giants so that Diodorus ascribes the foundation of the Celtic nation to Hercules. They could hardly have seen themselves other than as large and, indeed, they attributed their military invincibility to this physical advantage.

Esteeming large stature, one would expect their gods to be giants. And this is how we find them. On the Gundestrup Cauldron they dwarf both mortals and animals. In the Welsh stories we constantly come across supernatural giants, Ysbaddaden in *How Culhwch Won Olwen;* the green giant, Iddawg in *The Dream of Rhonabwy;* the black giant in *Owein.* Brân carried musicians on his back across the water separating Ireland and Wales. From Ireland we have the god Dagda copulating with the Mórrígan with one foot on either bank of a river, while rivers themselves result from the urination of goddesses. Scottish legend, too, is replete with its giant gods.

It may well be that it is in the light of this we should interpret the sacrificial colossi in the image of a man mentioned by Caesar and Strabo.

And who could have built the megaliths but giants? No wonder the gods of Druidism as we see them represented look out on puny mortals with their cool, dispassionate gaze. The wonder is that they can be coerced into interesting themselves in the affairs of these mannikins at all.

A tradition associating the megaliths with giants is particularly persistent. In Geoffrey of Monmouth's *History of the Kings of Britain,* the British king Aurelius decides to set up a monument to those fallen in battle against the Saxon marauders. Merlin prevails upon him to fetch a group of enormous, magical stones from Ireland. These form, so Merlin tells him, 'The Giants Ring', and they were erected by titans, who brought them from Africa, at the time they ruled Ireland.

. . . . .

Now that we have gone some way in forming an idea of the Druidic pantheon, can we hope to find a unitary system of belief, something which we can properly speak of as "Druidism", as we speak of Buddhism or Hinduism?

Caesar mentions the belief in transmigration of the soul and interprets it as a means of inculcating fearlessness in battle as, in Celtic society, it must have been. Kendrik refers to it [in *The Druids: A Study of Celtic Prehistory,* 1927] as the sole Druidic doctrine to come down to us and this view is echoed, more or less, by most other writers. Even Markale, in his essay on the topic [*Les Celtes,* 1969], confesses to the difficulty of reconstructing a "Druidic" philosophy and what he himself has been able to piece together is couched in negative rather than positive terms. They did not, for example, accept the duality of Good and Evil, but understood their own lives and the universe itself as being guided by a single internal movement. There was, in consequence, no concept of reward or punishment in an afterworld.

Piggott mentions a triad quoted by Diogenes Laertius [in *The Druids,* 1965] as the summary of Druidic ethical teaching which bids believers to worship the gods, refrain from evil and maintain manly conduct. This is so all-embracing that there can hardly be a single creed to which it could not with slight modification, be applied. Much the same goes for the quotation from the

Irish 12th Century *Colloquy of the Elders.* Here St. Patrick, in an imaginary dialogue with the pagan hero, Caelte, is told that he and his people were sustained in life by "the truth that was in our hearts, the strength in our arms and the fulfilment in our tongues". This might come marginally closer to the sort of view one might expect from a member of a vigorous, heroic society, but it helps not at all in distinguishing Druidic doctrine from others.

Strabo mentions the belief that the universe, like men's souls, was indestructible, "but that fire and water will sometime or other prevail over them".

The truth is surely that the quest for an underlying doctrinal base is a vain one. Not even the classical religions can yield anything remotely resembling it. The most they offer is that honouring the gods will bring its own reward, and in general attitudes towards them are those summed up in Shakespeare's epigram, "As flies to wanton boys are we to the gods . . ." Even Tacitus can say only, "As to the acts of the gods, it seems holier and more reverent to believe than to know".

We must remind ourselves that the Druids are the direct descendants of shamans and that shamanism is not concerned with broad issues of causality, with rules of conduct applicable to all men. Certainly, there is no question of that subjection of human to divine will which to our eyes would be the hallmark of religion. They are concerned with the specific instance: the means whereby the hunter can secure his prey and protect himself from the malignity of its spirit; the banishing of whatever occult forces are causing the particular illness or, say, an epidemic among his cattle.

The "spirits" are, as I M Lewis says [in *Ecstatic Religion,* 1975], "amoral". They visit with affliction or grant favour without consideration of the character or conduct of the recipient. The same must go for the gods of the Druids as for those of similar cultures. In the Norse legend of the king "magically" sacrificed when the calf's-gut round his neck becomes a rope, we are given no hint that such a fate was deserved. Odinn has simply demanded repayment for his gift to Starkad and this is how he takes it. There are several parallels in Celtic myth.

It is only by means of ritual that men have the slightest chance of safeguarding themselves from the caprices of spirits or gods. This explains why it is even more essential to magic than religion. For religion ritual is a pure symbol: the smoke of incense rising skywards symbolizes the petitions of the faithful rising to the throne of God; it is not, of itself, those petitions. Magic's rituals, when performed correctly in every minutest detail, are per se effective. Their sole aim is to compel the obedience of those forces towards which they are directed.

From the Isle of Man comes the story of the lazy wife, one of several such to be found all over the Celtic world. Too idle to spin the wool her husband brings her, she one days receives a surprise visit from a giant. He undertakes to help her if she can only guess his name which, after several attempts, she does. By his sudden appearance, so typical of Celtic Other World beings, her visitor had made his true nature clear. The woman calls him, nonetheless, "Mollyn droat"—"the servant of the Druid"—and in that attitude sums up an entire attitude to deities.

Thanks to the work of T C Lethbridge we can now be sure that the giant, chalk-cut figures adorning so many of our hillsides are not only far more numerous than was previously supposed, but also that they are connected with Druidism—strangely enough similar ones are also to be found in India. The male figure at Cerne Abbas in Dorset is probably the Celtic Hercules, Ogmios, for example. The female horse-rider uncovered by Lethbridge at Wandlebury in Cambridgeshire has been identified by Sir Cyril Fox as Epona and the Uffington White Horse may also be a representation of her. The purpose of such figures can only have been, surely, the ritual one of "fixing" something of the divine essence upon the locality in which they are portrayed, in the same manner as the cave-artists of Lascaux or Schmidt's pygmy-hunter tried to "fix" the spirits of their quarries by their creations. As Frazer and others have pointed out, any representation is thought of as containing some part of the vital force of the original. It is for this very reason that natives in some remote areas will go to such lengths to avoid being photographed.

In much the same way the fertility of the land is ritually "guaranteed" when the territorial goddess is given her mortal mate, the new king.

Illness, too, is cured, not by any property inherent in the herb, but by the entire spell wrought over the "spirit" causing the illness, from the moment of gathering to its application to the patient. So Pliny tells us that in gathering *selago* (no translation has ever been agreed), it was necessary for the Druids involved to wear white robes and to stretch their right hands through the left sleeve "in the manner of a thief". Similar attitudes were held by the herb-doctors found until recently in the Channel Islands and still existing in the Isle of Man, where their treatments were so esteemed that the island legislature had to abandon a measure to control the practice of medicine because it would have abolished them. These practitioners, often spoken of as "the last of the Druids", insisted that one must never speak of picking, but always of "lifting" and that this must be done with a charm. The same lifting would not serve for more than one patient. For maximum therapeutic effect nine pieces of a herb were necessary, then seven, six might serve and in cases where

the plant was rare one might even use three—all, of course, are magical numbers.

In Jersey, there were similarly detailed prescriptions for the use of herbs. Among those most highly prized were vervain; L'Amy speaks of it as the "holy herb of the Druids", which besides being a panacea for all maladies, can break the spells of sorcerers and reconcile enemies. In its lifting care had to be taken to see not a single fibre of the root remained in the soil. A piece of the root was then cut off and hung round the patient's neck with a ribbon, while the rest of it was burnt. The foliage was hung on a chimney and, as it dried, the illness would disappear.

But quite apart from the essentially magical character of Druidism, the abstraction of ethical principles from its only "statement"—the myths—would have the effect of making them something other than what, to the eyes of the Celts as to other similar societies, they were. They would then become religious allegory, and they were nothing of the kind. The myth exists autonomously. It is not the retelling of events; it is the programme of the events themselves.

To understand this we have to understand that the conception of time held by many cultures, of which the Celtic was certainly one, was quite different from our own. Some hint of this is given in the old opening formula of the fairy-story: "Once upon a time . . ." The Breton story tellers, according to Markale, went still further, for they began: "Once upon a time, there was no time, and it was then that . . ." Thus there are not one but many "times" of which the "progressive" one known to us, that of irreversible change, is only one version.

But in contrast with this one, with events passing in an unending cavalcade, there was that one in which it was the observer himself who passed events, cyclically, in the same way that, for example, while sitting on a roundabout one might see a couple embracing and catch them repeatedly, frozen in their attitudes, with each revolution of the machine. Here events were recoverable or could be "revisited" and this was the time inhabited by the gods. It could be partly shared by their human intermediaries in trance—a sense of being "outside time" is a characteristic of this state. The rest of the human race came nearest to it only during the rituals of the high festivals.

Since myth is the event itself there can be no place for the kind of extrapolation which doctrine represents. The frequent visits of mythical heroes to the Other World, so constant a motif of, for example, the Welsh stories, are indicative only of the close intermeshing of mortal and immortal existences. Notwithstanding the evidence that the advance on Delphi partook in some degree of the character of just such an expedition to the Other World, it should not be supposed that these ventures were enjoined upon the faithful in the way that Muslims are enjoined to visit Mecca.

And so we are left with transmigration as the central and one persisting tenet of doctrine. In fact, as Max Weber makes clear [in *The Religion of India,* 1958], it is also the only discernible one in Brahminism, and in both cases it is obviously little more than a development of the shaman's image of a world haunted by the souls of the envious dead liable to take up their abode in the bodies of the living.

The difficulty lies in discovering the exact scope and form of a belief which, after all, is common to many religions (though usually traceable back to shamanistic sources). Its variations are as wide as those of the religions themselves. In some, the soul is said to move freely from human to animal habitation; in others, it always occupies a human body; in others, the cycle of birth-death-rebirth continues until redemption and Nirvana have been achieved; in still others, it lasts perpetually.

If we can trust Lucan, who speaks of the Druids as viewing death as "but the mid-point in a long-life", there seems to be the implication that men live, as it were, a double life. But there is no other reliable sanction for this.

Did it apply to all? Kendrick believed that survival was enjoyed only by the warrior-aristocracy and this seems to be the view taken by Markale. "It is only possible to declare." he says, "that there are certain examples of reincarnation in the Celtic myths, but always limited to certain persons." If, however, it was, as Caesar says, intended to overcome fear of death among warriors, then it must have been extended further, though we have no warrant for suggesting it was conditional, say, on death in battle.

Perhaps a clue to the nature of the belief lies at the other terminal of existence, birth, no less mysterious than death itself. We have already seen that the Celts, at least in the earliest times, had no concept of the male role in conception. In these circumstances, one explanation of pregnancy and birth would be that it came about through spirits taking up habitation in the uterus, a belief still held among some Pacific islanders.

But we have, as a matter of fact, fairly plain hints about the means by which, in Druidic belief, the spirit was thought to enter the womb: in *The Wooing of Etain,* Etain Echraide is abducted by the *sidh*-god Midir. Unfortunately there is already a woman installed in Midir's palace, the sorceress, Fuamnach, who takes Etain's arrival very much amiss and in a fit of jealously changes her into a blue-bottle. First chased out

to sea, she manages to fly back to land, where exhausted and battered by the winds, she finally lands on the roof of a house and falls through the smoke-hole into a cup. The house is, by chance, that of king of Ulster whose wife, taking a drink from the cup, swallows the fly. In due course, she becomes pregnant and bears a daughter who is Etain regenerate.

Nessa, mother of King Conchobhar, becomes pregnant after drinking water given to her by her husband, the Druid, Cathbadh. In the story of the begetting of the magic bulls of Cooley, who later became the object of the raid, we first encounter them as the two swineherds of rival *sidh*-kings, Ochall Ochne and Bodb. Dismissed when their pigs fail to fatten, the swineherds spend two years as birds of prey, then return to their original shapes; next they spend two years as water-creatures, living under the sea, then they become two stags, then warriors, then phantoms, then dragons and finally maggots which drop into a stream to be drunk by two cows, to whom they are reborn as the two bulls, Finntbennach Ai, the white and Donn Cuailnge, the brown.

The Irish bard, Tuan mac Cairll, like his Welsh counterpart, Taliesin, undergoes many metamorphoses in which he becomes, inter alia, a stag, a boar, a hawk and a salmon, and in this form is eaten by the wife of Cairill to be reborn in his ultimate shape.

In the case of Taliesin, the transformations are even more elaborate, as is told in a comic story. Kerridwen, wife of Tegi Voel of Penllyn, gives birth to a boy of such ugliness she decides, in compensation, to equip him with knowledge such as cannot fail to impress all who meet him. From the *Books of Fferyllt,* she discovers the recipe for a magical liquid which will impart inspiration and knowledge. The reference to the *Books of Fferyllt,* which means "a worker in metal", introduces a touch of alchemy, a theme pursued in the story. The liquid must distill for a year and a day until only three potent drops remain. This long process is tended by Gwyon Bach and the blind Morda. All goes well until almost the end and, when Gwyon spills a little of the hot liquid on his finger and, because of the pain, puts it to his mouth. He at once receives the enlightenment intended for Kerridwen's son, and realizing what he has done, flees. Now guarded only by Morda, the cauldron in which the magic liquid has been brewing bursts and the last of the precious subtance is lost.

An irate Kerridwen sets out to find Gwyon, who thanks to the ingestion of the liquid is able to change himself at will. He therefore becomes a hare the more easily to escape, but Kerridwen outwits him by becoming a greyhound. Gwyon then throws himself into a river and becomes a fish; again, Kerridwen trumps him: she becomes an otter. Gwyon responds by becoming a bird; Kerridwen, a falcon. At last, Gwyon turns himself into a grain of corn. In vain, for Kerridwen becomes a black hen and devours it. She duly becomes pregnant, but when the infant is born, she cannot bring herself to kill it, as she intended. Instead, she puts it into a bag of skin which she consigns to the waters. In due course, the bag is found by Elffin, son of Gwyddno, who saves the child and brings him up under the name of Taliesin.

In other words, as is plain from all these stories, regeneration occurs when a woman consumes the "spirit" which has been transformed into some suitable form.

The cauldron which here serves Kerridwen for alembic no doubt comes into the story more or less by chance. The cauldron was after all the principal cooking pot of the times. That it also served ritual functions is clear not only from the Gundestrup Cauldron, but from the numerous references in myth. In the *mabinogi* of *Manawydan Son of Llyr,* Pryderi, while hunting a magic white boar, comes upon a mysterious castle which his dogs, following the scent, enter. Pryderi, against Manawydan's advice, follows. In a magnificant interior court, he sees a golden bowl hanging by chains over a marble slab. He attempts to take it, but when he grasps it his hands stick to it and his feet to the marble slab, while he also loses the power of speech. The queen, Rhiannon, who goes in search of him, is similarly afflicted when she tries to grasp the bowl.

The storyteller goes on: "When the night came thunder rolled and a mist fell; the fortress vanished it, and they with it".

The castle is obviously a *sidh* and the incident represents yet another visit to the Other World. The story has undergone considerable redaction by scribes who had no idea of its deeper meaning. One likely change made by them was in the story's ending, since the present one introduces a bishop. A little light is cast when one recalls that Rhiannon is the Welsh equivalent of Epona/Macha, the horse-goddess, who is also a Great Mother, and that Pryderi may be Maponos who, of course, also appears in a boar-hunt in the story of Culhwch and is connected with hunting in the Ribchester altar-stone mentioned earlier. Maponos is often equated with Appolo, the sun-god, and this would certainly make sense of the golden bowl which the god and his mother try to repossess. Furthermore, the owner of the castle is Llwyd, which means gray, and the basic problem of the story is to discover the cause of a mysterious desolation which has fallen upon the land. The myth then is about the theft of the golden-bowl of the sun by the gray *sidh*-god of winter.

One important element is the fact that both Pryderi and Rhiannon are struck dumb by contact with the bowl. There are similarities in two other cauldron-myths. The cauldron which Brân attempts to steal from the Irish has the property that if one took "a man who has been slain today and throw him into it. . . . tomorrow he will fight as well as ever, only he will not be able to speak". The cauldron which Peredur is shown in the court of the King of Suffering is also used to restore the dead to life.

The cauldron's life-giving properties are, of course, shared by the sun, which after the gray desolation of winter quickens the dead seed.

It is this which connects it with transmigration, for Diodorus, drawing on Posidonius, tells that the Celts believe that when they died "after a definite number of years they live a second life when the soul passes to another body". In other words, there is between one life and another a period of fallowness, analogous to winter.

The similarity of the uterus to a cauldron is hardly one which could have escaped Celtic notice, if only because a woman in the final stages of pregnancy looks very much as if she had a bowl inside her. There are, to be sure, the numerous rustic jokes on the subject to be found almost everywhere in which an expectant woman is described as carrying a cooking pot, pitcher or something similar under her skirts.

One might hazard, therefore, that the Druidic doctrine of transmigration could be restated somewhat along these lines:

> Plants grow, flower and fruit through the summer. But *sidh*-god of winter seizes the magic bowl of the sun which gives them life and takes it to his castle, whereupon everything withers and dies. However, in death the plant drops its seeds upon the earth. Here it would remain, a dead thing were it not for the sun-god's courage. While hunting he is led by the magic boar (note the beneficent, totemic animal) to the winter-god's castle, which he bravely enters and where aided by his great mother, he repossesses the golden bowl, though not without many perilous adventures. When it returns to its proper place in the sky, the seed is quickened into life and the plant lives again.

> It is the same with men. As their winter comes and with it, death, their seed also falls, to remain in the Underworld until it is, under some guise, devoured by a woman to enter the cauldron of resurrection in her belly.

As the explanation of birth, these ideas would obviously have been modified as the male role came to be understood. (As we know, at this stage the man sees his own and not the woman's, function as the all-important one. His is the seed; she the mere soil into which it is implanted. From this stems patrilinear descent and with it the dominance of the male.) However, the idea would no doubt have persisted in myth where it would be seen as an example of "miraculous-birth" imbuing the child involved with supernatural qualities.

But could we, perhaps, have here the rudiments of an answer to another problem; the reason for the Celtic practice of severing heads? The custom is well-attested not only in the classical descriptions of the Celts, but also archaeologically and in myth down to late times. Herodotus describes their being set up on high staves, "so that the head sticks up far above the house, often above the chimney". He was told that it served thereby as "guardian of the whole house".

Archaeology has unearthed skulls in votive deposits, niches for them in buildings, stone and wooden representations of heads (all with a most uncanny look of death about them), as well as sculptured masonry, like the pillar at Entremont, Bouches du Rhône, whose principal sculpture was disembodied heads. Professor Ross has gone so far as to suggest that the adornment of houses and other buildings with representations of the human head, as for example in gargoyles or over-arches, is a survival of the practice.

It occurs in Scottish, Irish and Welsh myth—in the story of *Gereint and Enid,* for example, Gereint is about to behead an enemy but has his hand stayed. Among the numerous references in the Arthurian legend is that in Chrêtien de Troyes's version to *The Maiden of the Mule,* who demands from Lancelot the head of a recently slain enemy. When he gives it to her she evinces the greatest gratitude, promising to aid him whenever he is in need.

In folk custom there are the numerous curative wells, some of which, like *Tobar na Ceann* in the Outer Hebrides, actually have the word "head" in their names, while others have saints' names.

In former days many of these had a skull, said to be that of the saint, standing by them for use as a drinking vessel. This connects with references in both Herodotus and Livy to skulls used as goblets.

Herodotus tells us that the cranium was sawn off above the eyebrows, the interior cleaned and the exterior covered in calf-leather, if the owner were poor, or lined in gold if he were rich. Livy cites the example of the chief of the Boii, who, after capturing the Roman consul Postumius, had his skull gold-mounted and used it as a cup.

The examples of skulls dropped into wells and particularly their use for drinking water from curative wells, by associating them, in one way or another, with health or its restoration, also, of course, link them with the maintenance of life itself. But, like the seed head of a plant, standing at the plant's top, so the head and the skull tops the man. It is his "seed-head", the place where the potential for life resides. In the shamanic spirit flights, in the legends surrounding such ecstasy-cults as that of the Pythian Apollo, as well as in some found in Tibet and China, even in contemporary reports of so-called "out-of-the-body" experiences the spirit is said to leave and enter the body via the head.

By taking possession of an enemy's head, therefore, one can ensure that he is not reborn to seek revenge, but at the same time, because of its potential for life, it also has health-giving properties of its own.

There is still, however, one aspect of the teaching of transmigration which requires examination. This is the all important Druidic notion of equilibrium, another idea found in early Brahminism and even in ancient Chinese systems, which it seems to have entered by way of Taoism, itself strongly influenced by shamanism. In Celtic terms the notion is well illustrated in one of the Welsh stories, that of Peredur, who is the most likely prototype for Sir Percival or Parsifal in the later versions of the Arthurian legends.

While out adventuring, the young knight comes upon a very strange sight. He passes through a wooded valley, bisected by a river. On either bank, sheep graze, but those on the one bank are white, while those on the other are black. Whenever one of the white sheep bleats, one of the black wades through the river to emerge on the other side, white: whenever one of the black sheep bleats, a white sheep goes through the same process to arrive, black, on the far bank. That the river represents the divide between the world of living and dead is plain enough. It is a symbol to be found in many rivers from the Greek Styx to the Christian Jordan. The story makes it quite explicit, however, for on the river's bank there also stands a tree, one half of which is green with leaves, while the other half is aflame "from roots to crown".

The black and white sheep, then, represent the dead and the living respectively. One may hazard that the two remain roughly in balance, for, since they could summon one another, each could ensure that his numbers did not diminish. The world of living and dead are, therefore, inextricably bound one with another. When the transmigrating soul is summoned from the world of death to take up abode among the living once more, the world of the dead will, sooner or later, make its summons, too.

One would, of course, expect this concept to have some bearing on the practice of human sacrifice, indeed to provide a rationale for it. And, turning to Caesar, one finds this is the case. As an illustration of the extreme superstition of the Gauls, he tells us that those "suffering from serious disease, as well as those who are exposed to perils of battle, offer or vow to offer, human sacrifices, for the performance of which they employ the Druids". Thus, when the black sheep bleat, those of the white sheep who have reason to feel the call most likely to apply to them, try to find a substitute.

Conversely, birth itself is also a matter for awe, as this summoning of the black sheep to join the white will demand its requital.

Proinsias MacCana (1985)

SOURCE: "Early Irish Ideology and the Concept of Unity," in *The Irish Mind: Exploring Intellectual Traditions*, edited by Richard Kearney, Wolfhound Press, 1985, pp. 56-78.

[*In the following essay, MacCana searches the pre-Christian Druidic culture of Ireland for sources of the modern ideal of unity.*]

Sometime in the second half of the twelfth century one of the scribes of the *Book of Leinster* recorded there a recension of *Táin Bó Cuailnge* "The Cattle-raid of Cuailnge" that had been compiled earlier in the same century. And having copied the long heroic narrative of the *Táin* he went on to copy the hortatory tail-piece which, in one form or another, was a familiar feature of learned Irish storytelling—as it had once been of ancient Indian storytelling:

> A blessing on everyone who shall faithfully memorize the *Táin* as it is written here and shall not add any other form to it.[1]

But then, as if this abbreviated invocation of the story's magic potency had reminded him of its rank paganism, he immediately deferred to Christian orthodoxy by adding another codicil, this time in Latin and pedantically formal, disclaiming any personal interest in or responsibility for the narrative he had so faithfully transcribed:

> But I who have written this story, or rather this fable, give no credence to the various incidents related in it. For some things in it are the deceptions of demons, others poetic figments; some are probable, others improbable; while still others are intended for the delectation of foolish men.

This nice instance of medieval diglossia neatly epitomises the disparity between the cultural contexts of the two languages, Irish and Latin. On the one hand we have to do with a culture which is coeval with the Irish language and receives its only verbal expression through it, first orally and then from the late sixth century onwards both orally and in writing. It is a mythopoeic culture, innocent of secular chronology and

locating people and events in the past by reference to genealogical filiation or to the reigns of famous kings, whether legendary or historical. On the other hand there is the Roman and international culture which was introduced to Ireland with Christianity and the Latin language and which extended its influence with the spread of monasticism and the monastic schools from the first half of the sixth century onwards. It is the creation of a church rooted in finite time by the central fact of the incarnation and by its residual inheritance from imperial Rome, and in consequence it brought with it to Ireland a view of time and history, of secular and sacred, of artistic and religious categories, that was radically at variance with that of native Irish society. The events and phases of the Irish past, real or legendary, were fitted within the chronological framework of world history as formulated by Christian historians like Eusebius and Orosius, and monastic scribes began to make brief notes of significant happenings in the form of annals, which in the course of time developed into a relatively full chronological record of Irish political and socio-cultural history. Latin, which was almost exclusively the language of monastic history until the middle of the ninth century, provided continuing if not total access to the universal learning mediated by the Church and at the same time acted as a partial filter against the mythic cast of native thought and tradition. "The white language of Beatus" (*bélre bán biait*), as Latin is called in an early Irish legal tract, could be used not merely as a linguistic reference but also as shorthand for scriptural or canon law, or, in a still broader sense, for the whole range of ecclesiastical learning. It embodied a culture and patterns of thought foreign to those inherited from pre-Christian Irish society. Its ideology was exogenous, "universal" and, at least in a relative sense, innovational, whereas that of Irish was by contrast indigenous, self-contained and largely conservative.

The conservatism of early Ireland is a commonplace of historical commentary. Those concerned with the ordering of society set much store by time-hallowed precedent and by the maintenance of cultural continuity, and their preoccupation with the past was as pragmatic as it was philosophical. The kingship of each Irish kingdom was a reflex, or a replica, of the sacral kingship that was already old when the Indo-European community took shape, and even when Irish rulers owed their accession more to force of arms than to hereditary right they were always careful to legitimise their claim by reference to the primal myth and ritual of sovereignty. The simple political structure over which they presided lacked institutionalised machinery for enforcing the administration of justice, and in the absence of appropriate state sanctions the only power that could command permanent respect for the rule of law was the power inherent in immemorial custom, confirmed as it was by the wisdom of countless generations and by the sacred prestige of the professional class who were its custodians and interpreters. This fairly numerous yet exclusive corporation of priests, poets and lawmen controlled the whole range of sacred tradition—myth and ritual, epic, onomastics, genealogy, origin legend and law—and it is largely in consequence of their jealous safeguarding of tribal or national memory that the surviving records of Old, Middle and even Modern Irish preserve so much that is archaic, some of it every bit as old as the oldest testimony to Indo-European ritual and institutions.

Like extreme conservatism anywhere, the conservatism of druids and *fili* (the fraternity of poet-seers and savants associated with the druids) discouraged change and innovation in so far as they disturbed the stability of social and cultural norms, but where change was inevitable the native orders showed a remarkable capacity to live with it, to temper its novelty and to assimiliate it as quickly as possible to their own system of perennial verities. The coming of Christianity is itself perhaps the most striking instance of this. It might so easily have transformed or even eradicated the existing learning and institutions associated with paganism, and it did in fact bring about a confrontation with organised paganism which led to the extinction of the druidic order and the suppression of certain of the more unacceptable features of druidic doctrine and ritual; but when the dust had cleared away, say by the seventh century, it could be seen that the *fili* had assumed the mantle of the druids—discreetly adjusted to contemporary circumstance—and that native institutions and modes of thought had survived the change of religious orthodoxy relatively unscathed. The subtle *modus vivendi* which had evolved during the first century and a half of the Christian mission—and which continued to the period of church reform in the eleventh and twelfth centuries and, in a more restricted form, to the aftermath of the Elizabethan conquest—permitted the complementary coexistence of two ideologies, one explicitly Christian, the other implicitly and essentially pagan. In matters theological and doctrinal the former was backed up by the universal authority of the church, yet whenever its exponents—the clerics and other monastic scholars—extended their activities to encompass the several areas of profane learning they were immediately subject to the pull of traditional categories of knowledge and the ways of thinking that accompanied them. The attraction was all the stronger in that the monastic *literati* were themselves sprung from this traditional culture, and many of them must have belonged to those very families which over numberless generations produced the *fili* whose status and vocation were bound up with the responsibility of maintaining it. Against this kind of pervasive influence the civilisation opened up by the Church and by Latin could make only limited headway, affecting certain facets of the external expression of the Irish mind rather than its conceptual or analytical capacity.

The effect of the use of writing in the vernacular is a case in point. One knows that when a rich and cultivated oral tradition is introduced to writing it can be transformed in various ways. The very fact of its being recorded in more or less permanent form enables the actual process of composition to be accompanied by a continuing exercise of retrospection, elaboration and reference, which may in turn lead to a greater variety of style and complexity of thought than is possible in oral narrative or discourse. As has often been pointed out, the first and the essential step towards the achievement of Greek philosophy and science was the adoption of writing. In mastering its potential the Greeks perceived the limitations imposed by oral or poetic discourse, and set forth a clear opposition of style and significance between the *logos* that was the written language of science and reason and the *muthos* embodied in oral tradition:

> Prose composition—medical treatises, historical accounts, the speeches of the orators and the dissertation of the philosophers—represents not only a different mode of expression from that of oral tradition and poetic composition but also a new form of thought. The organisation of written discourse goes hand in hand with a more rigorous analysis and a stricter ordering of the conceptual material. As early as in an orator such as Gorgias or a historian such as Thucydides, the measured interplay of antithesis in the balanced rhetoric of written discourse functions as a veritable logical tool. By separating, positioning and opposing the fundamental elements of the situation to be described, term for term, it allows the verbal intelligence to obtain a grip on reality. The elaboration of philosophical language goes further, not only in the degree of the abstraction of concepts and in the use of ontological terminology (for example of Being, as such, or of the One), but also in its insistence on a new type of rigorous reasoning. . . . In form it is opposed to *muthos* in all the ways that argued demonstration differs from the narrative of the mythical story; and in fundamental significance it is also opposed, to the extent that the abstractions of the philosopher differ from the divine powers whose dramatic adventures are the subject of myth.[2]

However, like causes do not necessarily produce like consequences. Irish, a language like Greek with a rich and respected oral tradition, began to be written about the middle of the sixth century and thereafter produced the earliest written vernacular literature in Western Europe—and the most abundant until the twelfth century—yet this did not bring Irish literature and learning significantly closer to the spirit of rationalist and scientific enquiry which it led to in Greece. New genres or disciplines introduced with Latin had to struggle continually, and often ineffectually, to escape the pervasive influence of *muthos,* and history, like hagiography, tended to be conceived in the same terms as the traditional narratives of gods and heroes. Commentators relate the elaboration of Greek thought to the emergence of a written prose which permitted the development of an abstract language far removed from the epico-poetic timbre of oral tradition; yet Irish not merely had an extensive written prose but was somewhat exceptional in using prose rather than verse for the epico-mythic narrative, and still it never experienced the need to extend its use still further and to make of it a vehicle for a new kind of rigorous and speculative reasoning.

One reason for the disparity (apart from the fact that the Greek achievement is distinguished by its uniqueness) is the control exercised by the native men of learning, the *filí,* whose responsibility and corporate interest it was to maintain the traditional integrity of social organisation and the traditional concepts on which it depended. With certain exceptions they had little active part in the creation of a written literature, which was mainly the work of the monastic scriptoria, but the oral literature which constituted the official legacy of the past was virtually their monopoly, and this, be it remembered, must have been much more extensive and socially more effective than what has been transmitted in writing. It was not for nothing that the *filí,* some of whom must have been able to read and perhaps even to write already in the early Irish period, nonetheless accorded a certain very definite priority to the oral mode, as did the druids of Gaul before them or the Brahmans of India; the spoken word was not only in some respects more exclusive, as Caesar suggests, but it was also regarded as a living dynamic medium by contrast with the static character of writing, and it never wholly lost the magic associated with solem oral pronouncement in traditional societies.

Oral language is, by its very nature, more suited to narrative, description, ritual and imagery than to speculative discourse, and in the Irish context it would appear that this limitation was, by and large, accepted for the written literature as well. During its creative period, from about the seventh to the early tenth century, the authors of this literature were seemingly more concerned to refine what they received from oral tradition than to replace or transform it. In the event they produced an extraordinary harvest of lyric verse and of spare sinewy prose admirably adapted to hero tale or straight historical narrative; but in reading this literature one is generally conscious—and senses that its authors were still more conscious—of its continuing relationship to the oral tradition from which it is largely derived; only fleetingly did it achieve the kind of autonomy that written Greek had already attained by the fourth century BC, and for the specific reason that those who wrote it assumed for the most part the same basic postulates as those who cultivated the oral tradition. And this applied even to those monastic scholars writing in Latin, despite their access to foreign models, in

so far as they belonged to the same native cultural environment as the composers and transmitters of oral literature, as in fact most of them did.

It has sometimes been remarked that one of the admirable qualities of the Irish language (and literature) in all its periods is its peculiar concreteness of expression and imagery. It has also often been remarked by ethnologists that primitive thinking in general is more concrete than that of more literate and intellectual societies. The connection between the two has been made succinctly by the great German Celticist Rudolf Thurneysen in a review of the edition of an early Irish tract on grammar:

> The Irishman sees the grammatical schemata as concrete realities. There are few documents that give us so deep an insight into the mind of the early Irish—so completely different from our own—as these tracts, and yet they spring from the learned classes, acquainted with Latin grammarians. Only by comparison with them can we judge the powerful intellectual achievement a Johannes Eriugena has accomplished in the ninth century, schooled of course by the translation of Dionysius the Areopagite; he too erects a similar pyramidal construction, though it is logically built on a capacity for abstraction learned from the Greeks, without any loss of the Irish capacity for concreteness. Such a work in the Ireland of his day would have been impossible and remained incomprehensible. Apart from their piety the Irish certainly brought abroad with them their inclination to scholarship, which was not very widespread on the continent, and made them welcome as schoolmasters; but to develop their powers was something they could only do in closer proximity to the Mediterranean.[3]

Thurneysen refers here to grammar and philosophy, but as Frank O'Connor remarks, "He might have said with equal truth that a book like Bede's *History of the English Church* would in the Ireland of that time have been impossible and remained incomprehensible."[4]

The trouble is, if trouble it is, that the mode of theoretical thinking which has long been familiar throughout the educated world and which has its origin in the speculation of the Greeks did not take root in Gaelic Ireland. This was not, as we have seen, through lack of literacy nor indeed through any inherent inability to deal in theoretical concepts, but rather because traditional ideology (even in its somewhat restricted para-Christian form) and the social order were so closely intertwined as to be mutually dependent. The druids may have been extinguished as a religious and moral establishment by the Christian church but they left behind them a deep-rooted system of cultural values that flourished and eventually faded with Gaelic society itself. It is no longer possible, of course, to construct any adequate idea of the totality of the detail of their teaching in the pre-Christian period, for the simple reason that our only record of it was made by Christian redactors who could, and doubtless did, censor it by extensive omission as well as by revision. So far as the continental druids are concerned, it is clear that Posidonius and some later Greek and Latin writers exaggerated their intellectual sophistication as philosophers and theologians, but it is equally clear that the extant literature understates the form and content of druidic teaching in Ireland. It is idle to imagine how it might have developed had it passed into writing without the intervention of Christianity, but one can be fairly certain that here as in so many other instances Ireland would have found itself closer to India than to Greece, and that such druidic philosophy as might have emerged would have subordinated itself to the reality of the sacred in a way familiar to the Indians, but quite foreign to the rationalist spirit of the Greeks.

Until recently the very idea that the Irish druids might have been capable of producing a system of thought remotely comparable with that of India would have seemed inconceivable to most Celticists. Apart from the suppressed premise—to which most philologists were inherently prone—that any form of sustained and systematic thought was impossible in a non-literate society, there was the related assumption that the written remains of early Irish literature offer a reasonably full and accurate reflection of the pre-Christian socio-religious ideas of the learned and priestly classes. Neither supposition has much substance: the first has been effectively disposed of by Paul Radin and other anthropologists and the second is disproved not merely by its general improbability but also by the internal evidence of the extant literature; it is true that Irish monastic scribes and redactors were exceptionally liberal in recording native non-Christian tradition, but they were writing several centuries after the dissolution of druidism as the organised religion of the Irish people, and this remove in time combined with the need to uphold Christian orthodoxy made it quite impossible for them to reflect adequately the integral system of druidic teaching. Yet despite all the evidence of revision and suppression there remains a great deal of material bearing upon native institutions and ideology—sacred kingship, the otherworld, cosmic division and the provinces, status and functions of druids and *filid,* and so on—which presupposes the earlier existence of a complex system of socio-religious doctrine and practice consciously maintained and applied during many centuries. Georges Dumézil, who has done more than any other scholar to reveal the continuities of Indo-European ideology in Irish and other conservative traditions, has this to say of one particular instance of analogous tales of kingship in India and in Ireland:

> Certainly we have here, conserved on the one side by the Druids, on the other in the unwritten "fifth Veda" from which the post-Vedic narratives of India in large part derive, a fragment of Indo-European politico-religious philosophy, that is, some of the speculations made by the Indo-Europeans on the status and the destiny of kings. . . . As is typical in accounts from medieval Ireland, which no longer rely upon a religion or even upon a living ideology, the story of Eochaid, of his daughters Medb and Clothru and his grandson Lugaid, is still more laicized and worked over as literature ["plus littérarisée"]—despite the marvels which are still found in it. But the "lessons", as we have seen are the same.

Noting that the Indian analogue is in this case more structured than the Irish he continues:

> One may suppose that this latter, cut off from Druidic philosophy like all the epic texts and conserving from the ancient symbols only the interplay of figures and their behaviour, has reached us in an impoverished form. But the Indian comparison does afford a glimpse of its primary significance, its value as a structure.[5]

There are many such survivals in Irish literature, some of them like this one cast in an epic mould and therefore more or less secularised, or *littérarisé,* others embodying ritual or institutional forms and therefore more likely to retain their original religious definition as applied or canonical texts, but taken in the aggregate—and making due allowance for defective and selective transmission—they can hardly be seen other than as the residue of an earlier comprehensive and internally coherent system of politico-religious doctrine and speculation preserved and interpreted by the druids. Most of these survivals were in the form of myth and epic narrative or were closely connected with specific ritual or quasi-legal contexts, and as a result they perished in large measure together with the learned literature and with the aristocratic society which engendered it. But there were others which, while linked to traditional ritual and institutions, had at the same time a much wider cultural resonance and which for that reason have outlasted profound social and linguistic change to become part of the image of the "typical" Irishman particularly as it is perceived by the greater world outside. Take for example what one might call the motif of Irish, or Celtic, generosity, which goes back as far as the classical authors of antiquity and is still not quite extinct even in the age of commercialism and the Common Market. One can easily and validly explain it as a varying blend of external preconception and internal reality, yet at the same time one cannot wholly dissociate it from the functional role of liberality in early Irish and Celtic society, where, as an integral part of the communal honour-system it was more a social imperative than a personal virtue and where a ruler's open-handedness was one of the ritual touchstones of his worthiness for office. But to pursue this and kindred topics further would lead us towards modern sociology and away from medieval ideology.

Instead we shall concern ourself in the present context with an instance of cultural continuity which has more to do with political organisation and action and has the advantage of being more susceptible to clear demonstration.

. . . . .

One of the commonplace notions about the Celtic peoples in general, the Irish in particular, is that they were chronically incapable of unity of purpose and, as a corollary to this, that they lacked the sense of nationality (and *a fortiori* that of nationalism). Like most ethnic clichés this one is not wholly without substance: whatever of the second of its two assumptions—and we shall return to that presently—the first seems to be amply substantiated by the chronicle of Irish history, which from the annalistic perspective is little more than a catalogue of battles, burnings and killings and of continual strife and dissension, even in the face of external aggression. The inability of the Irish to make common cause against a common enemy becomes the more obvious in the context of the modern concept of nationalism, and it is significant that from the sixteenth or seventeenth century onwards the Irish themselves seem to betray a growing if still intermittent consciousness of this disunion as a defect, a negative factor in native society—as in the disillusioned realism of the poet who deplores *an dream bocht silte nár chuir le chéile* "the poor and ineffective mob who did not stand together."

And here surely we come close to the nub of the matter. One salutary lesson we have learned from anthropologists (and from some good cultural historians) is not to import our own inherited system of motivation and classification into our description of alien societies—and naturally this holds as true for the diachronic as for the synchronic dimension. In the primitive Irish view of things political cohesion and centralism were not in themselves necessarily a social good, nor did this attitude change radically with the rise of expansionist dynasties within the historical period. The underlying principal was one of coordination rather than consolidation. Over-kings there were, and provincial kings, but in the earliest documented situation the king *tout court* was the king of the petty or tribal kingdom, the *tuath,* and he and his kingdom constituted the central nexus, both ritual and political, in Irish society. One's *tuath* was one's *patrie* and beyond its boundaries one became an outlander, a foreigner (Old Irish *deoraid*), and however much this definition was overlaid by the effects of political expansionism within the historical period the concept of local loyalty and autonomy long remained an essential element of the Irish understanding of social organisation.

But kingdoms were not islands even in the earliest period for which we have documentary evidence, and

relations were maintained, through the persons of king, over-king and king of a province, by a system of treaties, bonds of allegiance—and by fighting. The structure of early Irish society was such that one could no more do without one's enemies than one could do without one's friends and in consequence the character and the effects of warfare were limited accordingly. Modern police and "security" forces, struggling to cope with urban unrest, are busy devising what they sometimes refer to as "harmless weapons"; by the same euphemism one might almost describe the endemic warfare of early Ireland as 'harmless', for, while it could be barbarous, its primary aim was not unlike that of the modern riot weapon: to sting and to stun but not to kill. It was not designed to destroy people or to annex territories, but to assert status or to claim redress for real or assumed breaches of established relations. Like the later faction fights it had a strong element of ritual, but it was essentially less destructive because it was less rigidly patterned and because in the long run its purpose, at least in theory, was to uphold social order and to bond the tribal kingdom. As in India the newly elected monarch had to carry out a successful cattle-raid as an integral part of the protracted ceremonial of royal inauguration, so in Ireland, though the procedure is less formally defined in the extant texts, he had to perform the *crech ríg* or "royal prey", and the whole symbolism of this ritual expedition underlines the normative and conservative function of the cross-border cattle-raid.

Two factors contributed towards this convention of limitation, one practical, the other ideological. Cattle-reiving in a cattle-rearing society can be a source of profit as well as of honour, but one thing it requires is that there be foreign or enemy territory within easy reach, and this in itself is frequently sufficient to neutralise the lust for territorial conquest. Secondly, where war was governed by the heroic ethic, as was largely the case in early Ireland, it often constituted its own justification and, as with the Indian *dharmavijaya* or "righteous conquest", it had for its reward honour and glory rather than annexation of territory. Where one or other of these factors operates—or both—there is almost always a tendency to limit the consequences of war—notably in regard to its extent, duration and range of target—by a body of restrictive convention or a more or less developed code of chivalry. One of the most demoralising effects of the Norse invasions, as D. A. Binchy has pointed out, was that they brought the Irish face to face with an enemy who ignored the traditional conventions: "Hence war as waged by the invaders was more 'total', to use a modern term; ancient taboos were ignored; no holds were barred. Before long the native kings themselves were using these ruthless and efficient fighters as allies in their own quarrels, and, inevitably, came to adopt the new tactics."[6]

Viewed then in purely Irish or even in Indo-European terms the obvious political disunity of the country did not entirely lack a social rationale. Moreover the Vikings themselves demonstrated most dramatically if unintentionally that it could function as an effective mechanism of defence against foreign aggression—at least until such time as the aggressors could mobilise sufficient forces and sophisticated weaponry to wage a war of total conquest: given the cellular, un-centralist structure of Irish civil organisation and the absence of complex organs of administrators it was possible to win victory after victory and slay king after king without achieving effective control over any considerable part of the country. In the event the Norse invaders faced up to the realities of the situation and, conscious of their own priorities, set about establishing a string of posts and trading settlements around the coast which were to stand for all time as the Achilles heel of the native order.

This is what happened on the level of historical fact; equally significant, however, if less tangible, was the psychic reaction produced by these events in the popular consciousness, in so far as this can be gauged accurately from their reflex in the literature. The Scandinavians do not figure as such outside the strictly historical and more particularly annalistic tradition before the eleventh century, but there can be little doubt that they are already present, disguised under the name Fomoire, in a number of earlier texts. These Fomoire are the race of demonic beings who exist somewhere beyond the sea, a perpetual menace to the familiar world of everyday reality. According to the account of the several mythical settlements of the country in *Leabhar Gabhála Éireann,* "The Book of the Conquest of Ireland", they opposed Partholán, leader of the second immigration, in the first battle that was fought on Irish soil and they strive continually to subvert cosmic order as represented by legitimate rule and sovereignty within the confines of Ireland. When the pagan, marauding Norsemen appeared around the Irish coast, the shock-waves created by their violent irruptions must have had a profound effect upon the whole populace in the vicinity of their landings and far beyond, and while the clerics, nobles and secular men of learning would have been only too well aware of the mortal character of the terror that threatened them, for the mass of the people, beset by report and rumour, it was all too easy to confuse these ravaging gentiles with the mythic forces of anarchy. And so, one should not be unduly surprised to find that, when the cycle of Fionn mac Cumhaill and his brotherhood of roving hunter-warriors develops a prolific written literature from the twelfth century onwards which obviously draws heavily on popular and semi-popular oral tradition, one of the motifs which keep recurring in it is that of the Fianna defending the Irish shore against the Lochlannaigh, as the Norsemen are generally known in the non-historical literature. Here we have the fusion of myth and history, the assimilation of the historical event to the mythic analogue that is a characteristic feature of a people *admodum dedita religionibus*— and what is important from our immediate point of view is that the dominating theme is the security and integrity of the land of Ireland as a whole, not of one or other of its constituent parts. As the divine Lugh, paragon of kingship and vindicator of the central sovereignty of Tara, had routed the hordes of Fomoire in the great mythic battle of Mag Tuired, so did Fionn mac Cumhaill and the Fianna repel the attacks of the marauding Lochlannaigh.

One could of course argue, if one wished, that in the latter case the notion of Fionn as the protector of Ireland is tied up with the elaboration of the propagandist fiction of the high-kingship as a political reality, particularly from the ninth century onwards, but while this was doubtless a contributory factor it was not a prime cause: the idea of Ireland as a single entity goes back much further in time, and indeed without its prior existence the political exploitation of the "high-kingship" would not have been possible. Here, as in so many other instances in the Irish past, history converges with mythic tradition and draws support from it. D. A. Binchy has stressed the enhanced reputation of the over-king of the Uí Néill dynasties as a result of their obstinate resistance to the Norsemen and the increased prestige of the Tara monarchy as the main focus of that resistance, and he sees here "a striking parallel with the fortunes of the House of Wessex, which, alone among the English kingdoms, maintained an unbroken resistance to the Danes, and eventually became the nucleus of the national monarchy."[7] He also observed that the Norse invasions evoked among the native population "that sense of 'otherness' which lies at the basis of nationalism". Yet if this was a notable step towards political unity, it was also by the same token a step towards the secularisation and politicisation of a spiritual datum of long standing. In ideological terms the sense of national identity and the concept of unity were already old when the Vikings first drew up their long ships on the Irish shore.

Eoin MacNeill once wrote that the Pentarchy—the division of Ireland into five provinces ruled by five kings of equal status—"is the oldest certain fact in the political history of Ireland", a statement so well supported by tradition as to be almost axiomatic. The corollary of this—as has since been argued with convincing logic by D. A. Binchy—is that the "high-kingship" as a political reality is late and largely spurious. However, if the pentarchy thus helps to discredit the notion of a supreme political monarchy, at the same time (by the kind of paradox that is not unfamiliar in the Irish context) it also has the effect of highlighting the underlying conceptual unity of the country. The word for a "province" in Irish is *cúigeadh,* Old Irish *cóiced,* literally "a fifth", and *cúig cúigidh na hÉireann* is still a familiar synonym for "the whole of Ireland"; and as the fraction presupposes the whole, so the five provinces, though politically discrete, are conceived as mere fractions of a single all-embracing totality coterminous with the land of Ireland. The pattern of a central province enclosed by four others representing the cardinal points cannot be explained otherwise than as a historical reflex of an ancient cosmographic schema, and one which has striking analogues in several of the "great traditions" of the world. This cosmography is implicit in many incidental details of the extant tradition, though only one fairly extended exposition of it survives, in a Middle Irish text on "The Disposition of the Manor of Tara". This defines the extent of the provinces and their attributes and it declares that a pillarstone with five ridges on it, one for each of the five provinces, was erected at Uisneach. The central province was known as Mide (from an older *Medion* "Middle") and within it stood the hill of Uisneach, supposedly the centre of Ireland, or as Giraldus Cambrensis puts it: *umbilicus Hiberniae dicitur, quasi in medio et meditullio terrae positus.*[8]

Here we have one of the most fundamental constituents of Irish, and indeed of Celtic ideology: the cult of the centre. The very notion of a centre naturally presupposes a circumference and an encompassed unity, and it is both remarkable and significant that the Celts should have recreated this cult wherever they established themselves as a distinct community or nation with reasonably well-defined borders. We have it on Caesar's authority that the Gaulish druids held an assembly at a holy place in the lands of the Carnutes which was believed to be the centre of the whole of Gaul, and to it came people from all parts to submit their disputes to the judgment of the druids. It seems likely that the *drunemeton* "oak-sanctuary" at which the council of the Galatians met had a similar role to the "holy place" of the Gauls, as no doubt had the great assembly, *Mordháil Uisnigh,* which is said to have been held at Uisneach on May-day. The social and ideological significance of such assemblies cannot be disregarded. Ferdinand Lot declared that the Gaulish gathering maintained a kind of ideal unity, both judiciary and political, among the Gauls, comparing its role to that of the temple of Delphi among the Greeks: "The Gauls had thus a sense of *celticité* as the Greeks had of Hellenism, in spite of the rivalries and wars that took place within these two nations. This the Romans understood full well, and they made use of the abolition of human sacrifice as a pretext for the persecution they carried out against druidism until it was exterminated."[9]

It should be said at once that Lot's comments conceal a fair amount of academic controversy and uncertainty: was the pursuit of the Gaulish druids as ruthless and thorough-going as some of our sources suggest, what were the real motives which inspired it, and what was the real extent of the druidic participation and influence in politics? For example, as part of the critical re-evaluation of the classical commentaries on the Gauls, especially Caesar's, it has been argued that the social and political importance of the druids has been exaggerated (as also indeed their religious and speculative sophistication). How one interprets the evidence in this regard depends very much, I fear, on one's scholarly background and presuppositions; certain it is that many of those who have cast doubt on Caesar's account—and not entirely without justification be it said—have been fortified in their conclusions by an almost total ignorance of the culture and social organisation of the insular Celts.

Essentially the druid was a religious not a political figure, but the distinction was easily blurred where the political structures were as simple as they were in primitive Ireland and no doubt had been in the other Celtic communities. In the small individual kingdom the few governmental functions required were at the disposal of the king and, given that the chief-druid of the *tuath* was the king's "chaplain" and counsellor and the interpreter of the law, it is inevitable that he should have exerted some influence on political policy within the *tuath* and, perhaps especially, in relations with neighbouring kingdoms; just how great his influence was in any particular instance must have depended as much on his adroitness and strength of personality as on the political power conferred by his office. By and large those who would make light of the druids' political role are those who believe that the Romans in seeking to suppress the druids were motivated by the desire to eradicate barbarism rather than to quell political opposition. The problem is that barbarism may mean different things to different people. For some, mainly the classically oriented, it was marked by savage practices, such as human sacrifice, which were incompatible with Roman civilisation, and this they deemed sufficient justification for its suppression. But historical situations can rarely be adequately interpreted in such simple terms. The civilising (or proselytising) impulse is a characteristic feature of empire-builders wherever they appear and no doubt it affected Roman policy regarding the druids, but it would be naive to suppose that a sodality like the druids, enjoying high social status and control over law, religion and sacred tradition, would not have been seen as a main source and organiser of opposition to the Roman conquest. Whatever of nationalism, cultural or political, professional solidarity and self-interest alone would have given them sufficient cause to defend the native ideology and institutions with which their own existence was wholly bound up, and the Romans, in common with other colonising powers before and after, were only too well aware that conquest to be permanent required acculturation and that a native learned class of prestige and influence could seriously hinder both one and the other. "Dès la conquête terminée," observed Joseph Vendryes, "le druidisme devait porter ombrage aux vainqueurs, parce qu'il représentait une force d'opposition. C'est en lui que s'incarnaient les traditions nationales. Il fallait le supprimer pour romaniser le pays."[10]

A millennium and a half later the same suspicion and animosity coloured the attitude of the British government towards the Irish "rhymers" who were the lineal descendants of the druids, and ultimately for the same reason: consciousness of cultural identity and commitment to its preservation is not overtly political, even among a professional elite, but they have profound political implications and a political potential which, given the right circumstances—the threat of foreign domination for example—can easily be transformed into an active and even decisive force. This is why the Romans and English distrusted druids and *filí* and acted more or less effectively to neutralise them.

The fact is, of course, that the *filí* of the fifteenth and sixteenth centuries, whatever of the Gaulish druids, lacked the capacity for effective political action on a national scale. The element of "realism" introduced by the Vikings does not appear to have seriously disturbed the basic assumptions which shaped the *filí*'s view of society and their own role within it; if indeed these assumptions were temporarily cast into doubt by the Vikings' lamentable lack of respect for convention, then they were certainly reaffirmed in the period of retrenchment which followed the Norse invasion and the reform of the Church. For the *filí* themselves personified the web of paradox and ambiguity that materialises so easily where the two planes of reality, the secular and the sacred, converge. According to the view of the world by which they were conditioned the spiritual concept of a national unity did not require an exact reflex in the realm of secular politics: in other words religious concept and political structure did not necessarily coincide. We have seen that the cosmographic schema of the four quarters and the centre occurs in several major traditions as well as in Irish, but, as Alwyn Rees has remarked,[11] in many respects these do not accord with actual political and geographical structures.

In Ireland, Tara was the ritual centre of sovereignty and consequently the king of Tara enjoyed a special prestige, but he was not in any real and practical sense king of all Ireland. Ideally, no doubt, religious and political entities would have formed a complete correspondence, but in practice, circumstances would as surely have hindered its full realisation. If we assume that Tara was established as the seat of sacred kingship *par excellence* by the Gaelic colonisers who seized dominion over large areas of the northern half, those who came to be known as Uí Chuinn "descendants of Conn Cétchathach", then obviously its spiritual precedence could only have become a political precedence

in so far as the Uí Chuinn or their later representatives succeeded in gaining effective control over the whole of Ireland. This they failed to do. In particular, the province of Munster came under the sway of a different set of Gaelic colonisers who, while they shared for the most part the same cultural heritage as the northern overlords, yielded nothing willingly to them in terms of political power.

Thus, while in principle one might expect the two orders to tally, they do not do so in practice, through the pressure of personal, tribal and dynastic interests (but also perhaps, as we shall see, because there is an inherent tension and conflict between the political and cultural-religious spheres in many pre-modern societies). It is true that some scholars have found difficulty in accepting this. Faced by the discrepancy between the religious concept of unity and the reality of political disunity, they have sought to resolve it by discounting the former. Joseph Vendryes laid great stress on the local character of Irish, and Celtic, religion. He pointed to the some four hundred deity names attested in Gaulish inscriptions, noting that the great majority of them occur only once. He also pointed to the formulaic oath which occurs a number of times in the tales of the Ulster cycle: *tongu do dia toinges mo thuath* "I swear to the god to whom my tribe swears", and related it to the name of the Gaulish deity *Teutates* mentioned by Lucan. The conclusion he arrived at was that Celtic religion lacked universal deities and was characterised by local cults and tribal deities. In this he was echoed by his brilliant student Marie-Louise, Sjoestedt.

It seems to me that both of them have in this instance misread the evidence and have as a result greatly exaggerated the inorganic character of Celtic religion. The features on which they base their conclusions come into clearer focus when we take account of the syncretism of Gaulish religion as represented in epigraphy and plastic art, the inadequacies of the Irish written tradition as a record of pagan belief and practice, the use of multiple names for a single deity, the confusion of divine epithets with deity names, and so on. That two such perceptive scholars should have so erred by taking the evidence at its face value requires some explanation. Perhaps the most likely one is that they were influenced by the teaching of their close neighbours in the Sorbonne school of sociology and most especially by the views of Emile Durkheim, father of modern comparative sociology, who maintained that religion was essentially a social phenomenon and that "primitive gods are part and parcel of the community, their form expressing accurately the details of its structure, their powers punishing and rewarding on its behalf."[12] Durkheim's theories in this regard were accepted widely, if not universally, and naturally they have been especially influential among French scholars. Vendryes and Sjoestedt can hardly have been unaffected by them, and if this has led as I suspect to their partially misrepresenting the character and structure of Irish religion it is not that Durkheim's views are wholly incorrect or irrelevant to the Irish situation, but that they have operated as an unstated and unquestioned premise and been applied without sufficient regard to the peculiarities of the context and to the deficiencies of the extant corpus of evidence. Irish religion is not unstructured, as Sjoestedt would have it ("we seek for a cosmos and find chaos"), but it is structured differently from Irish society, and to the extent that the two correspond it is not so much that religion reflects society as that it itself furnishes an ideal model towards which in given circumstances actual political structures may evolve or be consciously directed (as in the case of the Uí Neills' exploitation for their own expansionist ends of the cult of the central kingship of Tara). And the fact remains that despite the large ambitions of certain kings and dynasties, the impressive unionist and centralist theory so richly supported by myth and ritual was virtually impossible to translate into practical reality because, traditionally, there was no close correspondence between religious and political structures.

This disparity between the political and the cultural-religious is not in any way peculiar to Ireland. In universal terms one may see it as a particular manifestation of the combination or tension of oppositions which, like some complex system of systole and diastole, seems to be essential to the whole of human life and culture and which, as in the case of living speech, creates a fruitful interplay of conservation and change, of irregularity and uniformity: "L'humanité," as Claude Lévi-Strauss puts it, "est constamment aux prises avec deux processus contradictoires dont l'un tend à instaurer l'unification, tandis que l'autre vise à maintenir ou à rétablir la diversification."[13] But there are, and have been, other societies as well as Ireland in which this conjunction of opposites appears to express itself with particular clarity as a contrast or inequality of political and cultural-religious structures, and in some indeed this is so much the norm that the degree of political and administrative centralism stands more or less in inverse ratio to that of religious and cultural unity. M. Fortes and E. E. Evans-Pritchard have discussed the several variations on this relationship which they found among a number of African peoples in modern times:

> We may, therefore, ask to what extent cultural heterogeneity in a society is correlated with an administrative system and central authority. The evidence at our disposal in this book suggests that cultural and economic heterogeneity is associated with a state-like political structure. Centralized authority and an administrative organization seem to be necessary to accommodate culturally diverse groups within a single political system, especially if they have different modes of livelihood.

Naturally, centralised government may be found in societies of homogeneous culture, but:

> A centralised form of government is not necessary to enable different groups of closely related culture to amalgamate, nor does it necessarily arise out of the amalgamation.

It is a matter that has universal relevance for the analysis and classification of social organisation:

> Herein lies a problem of world importance: what is the relation of political structure to the whole social structure? Everywhere in Africa social ties of one kind or another tend to draw together peoples who are politically separated and *political ties appear to be dominant whenever there is conflict between them and other social ties* [my italics]. The solution of this problem would seem to lie in a more detailed investigation of the nature of political values and of the symbols in which they are expressed. Bonds of utilitarian interest between individuals and between groups are not as strong as the bonds implied in common attachment to mystical symbols.[14]

Its relevance for the Irish situation in particular is obvious, for when Fortes and Evans-Pritchard speak of "culture" and "other social ties" they include among these myths, rituals and all the other "mystical symbols" to which they attach such importance for the effective ordering of society. Basically what they are saying is that where there is cultural diversity unity must be maintained through centralist state-like structures, but that where there is cultural homogeneity these may be dispensed with. The position in early Ireland was that each individual kingdom was small enough not to require such structures, while in the country as a whole cultural-religious homogeneity was such that centralised government was unnecessary.

As in so many other contexts, here again one of the most striking analogues to the Irish situation, despite the glaring discrepancy in scale, is that of India. In the period before independence apologists for the Indian nationalist movement were much concerned to demonstrate the cultural homogeneity of the country as a justification for their claim to self-government. For that very reason their arguments and conclusions are suspect, or at least would be so if they were not confirmed by a good deal of informed objective opinion. When Radhakrishnan declares that "there is an inner cohesion among the Hindus from the Himalayas to Cape Comorin," he is saying in effect what virtually every serious student of India has said: that despite its teeming variety the huge continent of India shares in the same flexible, tolerant, comprehensive culture engendered of Hinduism. In the words of the *Oxford History of India,* "India beyond all doubt possesses a deep underlying fundamental unity, far more profound than that produced either by geographical isolation or by political superiority. That unity transcends the innumerable diversities of blood, colour, language, dress, manners, and sect."[15] It was most definitely not a political unity; indeed a stable, enduring political unity was something never achieved, even under the powerful Mauryan Empire, yet such was the integrating force of India's dominant culture that she was able to absorb an endless variety of peoples and traditions in a way that is hardly paralleled elsewhere in the world.

This almost axiomatic sense of belonging to a single comprehensive cultural environment colours the whole mainstream of the literary tradition, and what I said of Irish literature in this regard might be said, and indeed has been said, of its Indian counterpart: "The Indian epics and legends, in their manifold versions, teach that the stage for the gods was nothing less than the entire land and that the land remains one religious setting for those who dwell in it."[16] One of the many scholars who have stressed this capacity for integration is Louis Dumont ("By putting ourselves in the school of Indology, we learn in the first place never to forget that India is one . . ."). He views it in terms of a conflict between *dharma* "the moral law, moral and religious duty", and *artha* "material gain, the pursuit of the useful". *Artha* is the negation of *dharma,* but since society continues to be ruled by *dharma,* the art of politics is thus dissociated from the realm of values (a dissociation which is not unknown much nearer home, though lacking perhaps the same philosophical justification as in India). *Dharma* and *artha* must coexist, but they need not, and in a sense they cannot, coincide:

> It is not in the political sphere that the society finds its unity, but in the social regime of castes . . . The system of government has no universal value, it is not the State in the modern sense of the term, and as we shall see, the state is identical with the king. Force and interest work only for strife and instability, but these conditions may thrive without anything essential being put in question; much to the contrary, *social unity implies and entertains political division* [my italics].[17]

Early Indian society differed profoundly from the modern African societies discussed by Fortes and Evans-Pritchard, but clearly the principle succinctly enunciated by Dumont has relevance for the question posed and answered tentatively by them. When they say that "bonds of utilitarian interest between individuals and between groups are not as strong as the bonds implied in common attachment to mystical symbols," what they are saying in fact is that *artha* has less binding force than *dharma,* though naturally these precise terms are very much culture-bound and the social context to which they refer is infinitely more complex than the African one. The dissociation of *dharma* and *artha* has even more relevance for early

Irish society—not surprisingly in view of the cultural affinities between Ireland and India. It may lack the explicit documentation and elaborate rationale that it has in India, but it is implicit in the very fabric of history and tradition.

In both India and Ireland, then, culture—in the sense of belief, ritual and general tradition—was the transcendent force operating towards unity, but it was able to do so effectively only because there was in both countries a learned and priestly class which could assert the claims of orthodoxy. The druid or *file* had his local affiliations but at the same time he, and he alone, had free and untrammelled passage across tribal boundaries throughout Ireland. He had therefore, like the brahman, the mobility as well as the professional status and cohesion to propagate an accepted culture to all parts of the land and all segments of the population irrespective of ethnic origins. It might indeed almost be said of him, as has been said of the brahman, that "the destruction of tribal culture was a logical outcome, if not the conscious goal, of his ideology." In his residual role as priest and adviser to his royal patron the *file* was above all distinguished as praise-poet. This was one of his primary functions during the historical period, since praise-poetry was the medium *par excellence* for validating a rightful king and for setting forth in exemplary fashion the ideals of conduct which he should strive to maintain, and it is perhaps not surprising, in the light of what has already been said, that the topos of unity should crop up fairly frequently in these formal poems, some of which may have been odes composed for the occasion of the prince or chief's inauguration. In a poem addressed to Niall Óg Ó Néill, who was inaugurated chief of Tír Eoghain in 1397, the poet Tadhg Óg Ó hUiginn begins with the declaration:

> From the north comes succour;
> from Eamhain all quarters are joined in union;
> let the men of the north take Tara,
> they who came to her aid in the past.

and ends with a stanza that echoes and confirms the cosmographic allusion in the phrase *gach aird* "all points of the compass, all quarters":

> Niall Ó Néill of the nine fetters
> brings peace to the lands he unites;
> having established the five equal divisions,
> he goes forth to inspect the borders of
>   Ireland's territory.

Most of the examples of the theme of unification as a panegyric motif occur in the post-Norman period which saw the establishment of the hereditary schools of poetry run by a number of distinguished learned families. The work of these learned poets is dominated by praise-poetry—though this preponderance of the genre in the later as compared with the earlier period may be somewhat exaggerated by the fact that it was more consistently recorded; during the Old and Middle Irish period, when the writing of secular literature seems to have been virtually confined to the monastic scriptoria, it was hardly to be expected that panegyric verse should enjoy priority, whereas the position was quite the opposite from the thirteenth century onwards when the learned lay families themselves assumed responsibility for writing the poetry and began to compile "poem-books" (*duanairí*) which brought together the formal verse of individual poets or groups of poets or verse composed for individual patron families. This would help to account not only for the higher concentration of praise-poetry in the post-Norman period but also for the higher frequency of the unity theme as a praise motif. It is true that one might also explain the latter as a reflex of a growing unease and foreboding among the poets, who now saw the social order on which they depended being gradually eroded and threatened with total dissolution, but the rather formalised manner in which the motif is used in most instances also suggests something less topical and it seems reasonable to accept that it is in fact a very old ingredient of native praise-poetry which, for the reasons I have suggested, is better documented after the twelfth century.[18]

That it acquired a new and more urgent relevance during this period, and especially from the mid-sixteenth century onwards, is beyond question. For as long as Gaelic society remained relatively intact, so long could the combination of spiritual unity and political disunity continue without serious risk, since both were encompassed within a common, universally acknowledged ideology. So far as the poets were concerned, raiding and skirmishing among native chieftains was little more than a well-tried social lubricant that conferred certain benefits and carried few dangers for the system. This is why Eleanor Knott can write in the following terms of the poetry of Tadhg Dall Ó hUiginn, who died in 1591:

> He shows in most of his poems a calm acceptation of the contemporary strife, as though it were the natural order. Poetry flourished on it, and for him, like most bardic poets, the profession was the thing. The apprehensions and sorrows which troubled Irish poets of a slightly later period did not affect Tadhg Dall. Shadows palpable enough to us in his own poems portended no disaster to him. We may take him as a typical figure, thoroughly adapted in mind and customs to the existing order; utterly unaware of the imminent dawn of a new world.[19]

Warfare and strife were indeed part of "the natural order". So also was the traditional independence and mobility of the *file,* who, notwithstanding that he often formed close bonds of friendship and loyalty to a single patron, still set great value upon his own freedom to choose the subjects of his encomium. It is this, combined with a liberal dash of professional self-interest,

that accounts for the apparent opportunism and cynicism of the poets some of whom seem to opt for the highest bidder and to measure their praise more in terms of profit than of merit—a failing which is neatly ridiculed by one of their own number, Gofraidh Fionn Ó Dálaigh, who flourished in the fourteenth century.

But by the late sixteenth century the poets were faced with a very different kind of reality, one in which war was fraught with calamitous and possibly irrevocable consequences. The expansion of English power in Ireland meant cultural suppression as well as military conquest, and the ultimate outcome could only be the extinction of the native order. The poets, who were after all better placed than most, including their patrons, to take a global view of contemporary events, saw the signs and read them clearly. Tadhg Dall Ó hUiginn himself realised the inappropriateness of the traditional dissipation of energy and in his poem urging Brian Ó Ruairc to engage the English in all-out war he counsels a different mode of action; I quote from the convenient summary by Standish Hayes O'Grady:

> . . . in the sword alone all hope lies now, and the state of affairs is such that never were the five provinces less inclined to peace; but all will not serve unless there be union: from north to south, from sea to ocean; the components of a great and (supposing concord to prevail) a feasible army are recited: the poet's immediate hero being (according to the consecrated figure of speech) held forth as chief commander of the host.[20]

The nobles of Ireland, says the poet, "are being driven to the outskirts of Ireland, while troops of English are at its very centre (*'na glémheadhón*)," in other words the foreigner has established himself at the sacred spot which symbolises the unity of the country. The phrasing is eloquent in its brevity.

A hundred years later Dáibhí Ó Bruadair is scandalised by the bickering and dissension of the Irish leaders, declaiming his message with all the passion and solemnity that only he can bring to bear on such a subject. There is no cause to wonder, he says, that the English are successful, for they hold firm by their compact, unlike his fellow-Irishmen whose alliance falls apart at the pluck of a hair. The substance of his plaint is summarised in the title assigned to this poem in several of the manuscripts; it reads in translation: "The Shipwreck of Ireland, composed by Dáibhí Ó Bruadair on the misfortunes of Ireland in the year of the Lord 1691 and how the sins of her own children brought ruin and dispersion upon her in the month of October of that year: *Regnum in se divisum desolabitur.*"[21] Again in his poem to Patrick Sarsfield (no. 22) he shows himself preoccupied with the same anxiety:

> O King of the world, Thou who hast created
>   it
> and everything that stands upon it,
> redeem the land of Fodla from the peril of
>   this conflict
> and join her peoples together in mutual love

—to which a scribal note in one of the manuscripts adds the disillusioned comment, *Agus fáríor ní dearna* "But alas! He did not."

By the time of Dáibhí Ó Bruadair the great dissolution of the native order had largely been accomplished, a circumstance which goes some way to explaining the sombre cast of much of his verse. He realised the full implications of the cultural changes brought about by military defeat and the imposition of British rule and he was close enough to the old dispensation to appreciate in a way that was impossible for those who came after how much had been lost and never could be regained. The symbols of unity are occasionally invoked by later poets, but they have become mere stereotypes emptied of real significance, either in the political or in the cultural sphere. Throughout the visible history of Irish tradition the palpable mark of the cultural unity of the island was the learned, literary language fashioned and cared for by endless generations of druids and *filí;* now this linguistic cohesion was shattered, and with its shattering came the end not perhaps of a culture but certainly of an ideology. *Things fall apart; the centre cannot hold*—the atrophy of the archetypal symbolism of the centre and of the cosmographic vision of totality of which it is a part signifies the collapse of a subtle equilibrium between cultural cohesion and political segmentation that was, it would seem, already old when the Celtic peoples were born. This perhaps more than any other single event or innovation marks the end of traditional Irish society and—from the ideological point of view—the reversion from order to chaos.

. . . . .

These notes on the traditional concept of unity are not intended to be exhaustive nor do they follow through to the end the possible implications of the topic. One might, for instance, trace out the extremely important role of the land, the actual soil of Ireland, as the material basis for the concept of national unity, and the tensions and complications which later arise within Irish republican nationalism when "the people"—an entity which figures hardly at all in Irish tradition—becomes an integral part of the complex from the eighteenth century onwards. One might also reflect on the curious contradiction between the traditional view that cultural unity could dispense with political unity and the modern nationalist view which glorifies political unity in the face of cultural disparities.

But the primary motivation of republican nationalism lies further back in the English conquest and plantations of the sixteenth and seventeenth centuries and these had already by dint of suppression and expropriation profoundly altered the traditional concept of nationhood. That it survived the seventeenth century only as an etiolated memory is in the circumstances hardly surprising. What is much more remarkable is that the principle of discrepant political and cultural organisation, whose existence is endlessly implied in the literature but never explicitly described—unlike the Indian theory of the relationship of *artha* and *dharma* which it so much resembles—should have outlived the druids who propagated it as part of their ideological system, sustained more than a millennium of Christianity, and remained a living force in Irish tradition centuries after Vikings and Normans had shaken the social premises on which it was founded.

Notes

[1] *Táin Bó Cúalnge* from the *Book of Leinster,* ed. Cecile O'Rahilly, 1970, Dublin, pp. 136. 272.

[2] Jean-Pierre Vernant, 1980, *Myth and Society in Ancient Greece,* Brighton, pp. 187-89.

[3] *Zeitschrift für celtische Philologie* xvii, 279f.

[4] *The Backward Look,* 1967, London, p. 9. I quote O'Connor's translation of Thurneysen's German.

[5] G. Dumézil, 1973, *The Destiny of a King,* Chicago and London, pp. 115f, 106 = *Mythe et Epopée,* vol. 2, Paris, pp. 361f, 353.

[6] *The Impact of the Scandinavian Invasions on the Celtic-speaking Peoples c. 800-1100 AD,* ed. Brian Ó Cuiv, 1962, 1975, Dublin, p. 128.

[7] *Ibid.,* p. 129.

[8] *Top. Hib.,* ed. Dimock, p. 144. For the idea of Uisnech as the "navel" of Ireland; cf. *ós imlind Usnig* "above Uisnech's navel," *Ériu* 4, 150. 22.

[9] F. Lot, 1947, *La Gaule,* Paris, pp. 79f.

[10] J. Vendryes, 1948, "La Réligion des Celtes," *Mana: Introduction à l'histoire des religions,* 2, Paris, p. 294.

[11] A. Rees, 1966, *Proceedings of the International Congress of Celtic Studies 1963,* Cardiff, pp. 47f.

[12] This is how the central message of E. Durkheim, *The Elementary Forms of Religious Life* is summarised by Mary Douglas in her *Purity and Danger,* 1970, Pelican Books, p. 30.

[13] C. Lévi-Strauss, 1961, *Race et Histoire,* Paris, p. 84.

[14] M. Fortes and E. E. Evans-Pritchard (eds.), 1940, *African Political Systems,* Oxford, pp. 9f, 23.

[15] *Oxford History of India,* 1919, p. x.

[16] David G. Mandelbaum, 1970, *Society in India,* Univ. of Calif., ii, 401.

[17] Louis Dumont, 1970, *Religion, Politics and History in India,* The Hague, p. 78.

[18] It has been noted of other pre-modern societies that praise-poetry can fulfil a unifying function. Among the Zulu, for instance, praise of the chief, who personified his tribe, served to build up tribal loyalty and solidarity, and, when the various tribes were joined to form a Zulu nation, it helped to bind them together in a common loyalty. (Cf. Trevor Cope, 1968, *Izibongo: Zulu Praise-poems,* Oxford, pp. 32f.)

[19] Eleanor Knott, 1922, *The Bardic Poems of Tadhg Dall Ó Huigin,* London, vol. 1, p. xlv.

[20] Standish Hayes O'Grady, 1926, *Catalogue of Irish Mss. in the British Museum,* London, vol. 1, pp. 413f.

[21] John C. Mac Erlean, S.J., ed., 1917, *Poems,* London, vol. 3, p. 164.

FIONN MAC CUMHAILL AND THE FENIAN CYCLE

A. G. van Hamel (1934)

SOURCE: "Aspects of Celtic Mythology," in *Proceedings of the British Academy*, 1934, pp. 207-48.

[*In the following essay, van Hamel undertakes a comparative analysis of Celtic mythology, particularly of the Irish Fenian Cycle, in order to uncover the magical and religious undercurrents in the tradition.*]

Some scholars look upon a myth as an article of faith of pagan times. Others take it as an expression of the early religious mind in a symbolical form. However, neither dogmatism nor speculation belongs to the primitive properties of religion. Their influence, great though it may become in the course of evolution, is not in any degree underrated if precedence is given to an altogether different aspect of mythology, which is of a practical and, therefore, a more primitive character. Myths have an essential bearing upon the execution of the earliest religious functions, that is, upon the ritual intended for the obtaining of a gift or favour from a superior power. Where a god is worshipped, the myth is there to remind him of what he has done or allowed

on a previous occasion. At a more primitive stage some fictitious story of the past is recited so that fate, or whatever friendly or hostile powers might be involved, may react in accordance with the precedent. Whenever a supernatural force is raised by means of magic from a particular individual, the means resorted to is, again, the invocation of a sublime parallel. In this connexion myths appear in the introductory episodes of charms and incantations. These prefatory stories, where as a rule gods or demons are the agents, serve as an incentive to action, addressed to the powers invoked. Here we grasp the myth in its original significance, as we know it from the Anglo-Saxon charms and from those of the German Merseburg MS.

In Irish the verb usually rendered by 'to invoke' (*admuiniur*) has the literal meaning of 'to remind' or 'to call to mind'. In fact, 'to invoke' is an incorrect translation, as may be seen from the plain fact that the power 'invoked' is never identical with that to which the prayer is directed. The concluding verses of the text called the Elegy of Colum Cille contain a prayer to the Lord, but an 'invocation' of St. Columba; evidently the intention is to remind, on our own behalf, the deity of the merits of the saint. In an Old-Irish prayer to God, St. Patrick and his deeds are 'recalled'. We have an Irish spell of the same period for the cure of the eye, directed to God and Christ, with a reference to Bishop Ibar 'who heals'; it is clear that the bishop is not invoked, but only instanced. Very interesting in this respect is the Old-Irish prayer for long life. Its editor expressed his astonishment at the combination in this early text of a dedication to the Holy Trinity and the so-called invocation of pagan superhuman beings. However, the latter are only referred to as examples of a high age and propounded as such to the God of Christianity. This consideration, in fact, elucidates to a great extent the presumed confusion of paganism and Christianity in early times. In the sense 'to adore' the Irish language uses a Latin loan-word (*adraim*).[1]

In the most comprehensive text of the Irish Fenian Cycle, the Colloquy of the Ancients, we witness a scene which is perhaps more instructive than any other in this respect, since it reveals the paradigmatic power of a myth in full action. Two Munster princes request the assistance of Cáilte, one of the last surviving Fenian warriors, against three flocks of demoniacal birds. These demons harass their territory every year, destroying the crops and annihilating the game. The old hero complies, and as soon as the birds appear, pronounces a spell, which makes them return to the sea, and kill one another with their beaks of bone and their breath of fire. However, Cáilte has previously learned from St. Patrick, in whose company he is wandering over Ireland, that the day corresponds astronomically to that other day when, in the olden time, three mythical benefactors of his race succeeded in expelling an equal number of demoniacal foes. This allusion links the story of the scattered birds to what precedes in the text. For the mythical example of the three good and the three wicked divine beings is described there in an earlier passage. It ends in a spell cast upon the infernal demons, very much like that used by Cáilte against the birds. Evidently his success is due to the imitation of the exemplary myth. [The adjective 'exemplary', throughout this lecture, as applied to heroes or traditions, means a hero or tradition that had to be regarded by people in the early Celtic society as an example which must be imitated by them, or of whose example the deeds of other men must be regarded as a reflexion. It is nearly the same as 'model' but not quite.] There is an occult relation between the two events. The myth is not merely an anthropomorphic fiction, but a precedent, fraught with magical energy.

Our conclusion is confirmed by a study of the accessory elements of the myth under review. Before their expulsion by means of a spell the three wicked ones (they are named the Sons of Uar, 'Sons of Cold') have been harassing Finn's warriors for some time, but without success. Their antagonists, the three divine protectors, know how to ward them off; they are accompanied by a magical hound which guards Finn's rampart. In fact, the relations of these benefactors with their clients are of a very intimate character, although this has not been so from their first appearance. It has been necessary to incorporate them in the body of Finn's warriors, the so-called Fiann, and this could not be done until they had revealed their names and made themselves known as the Sons of the King of Iruath. Before this decisive moment their friendship was unreliable and their protection uncertain. They have even killed two young Ulster princes of the Fiann, whose curiosity had incited them to break the conditions of the divine protectors by spying them out during the night. Here is another instance of the paradigmatic meaning of a myth, although the magical connexion is failing. There is a pedagogic note instead. The two Munster princes at whose request the baleful birds are exterminated by Cáilte invite St. Patrick to their feast and pay the Gospel tribute. The example of the king's sons of Ulster is there to show what would have happened without this ready submission.[2]

Have we a right to regard the three benevolent Sons of the King of Iruath as gods of the Fiann? The question is not altogether irrelevant seeing the harm often caused by the lack of a well-defined terminology in mythological matters. If a distinction is made between gods and divinities, then the Sons of the King of Iruath are on the side of the gods, since there exists a continuous relation between them and their clients. A divinity is a supernatural being, exercising power in a world not identical with ours; it may influence human society, man will occasionally feel and realize its existence, but this contact was never intended by either of the two parties. The god, on the other hand, acts upon human affairs and intervenes whenever it is deemed necessary; man, from his side, seeks to approach him. As we shall see in the course of the present investigation, gods are rare in our sources of Irish paganism, and this must not be imputed to the imperfect state of our authorities, seeing the wealth of light they shed on other sides of early Celtic religion. This makes the appearance of the Sons of the King of Iruath in Fenian story only the more striking. In their case the relation established between the two parties is even expressed by a covenant and strengthened by magical guarantees. At the same time, these princes from fairyland lack one of the prominent characteristics of a real god: they do not endure. They protect as long as the magical vow—let us use the Irish word *geiss*—is not broken; then, they chastise and pass away. This is the natural consequence of the omnipotence of magic in the Irish conception of life. Broken magic means fate to the early Irish mind, for the human as well as for the divine world. The real god, as known from the mythology of other peoples, is always there; he cannot but exist and is bound to spend his favour or to exert his wrath until the moment when everything shall cease to be. What we find in Ireland is different. These immortals are but moved by the mechanism of magic, their personality is but little developed, and their presence is only temporary. Thus the use of the word 'a god' would be misleading and prejudicial to a deeper understanding of the facts. It must needs lead astray those students of comparative mythology who have no first-hand knowledge in the Celtic field. The Irish texts themselves use the word for 'a god' practically only in the oath. Here a lasting sanction is instrumental. Mythological figures of the type represented by the Sons of the King of Iruath may best be labelled 'divine magicians'. With a god they share the interest in human affairs, with a divinity the aloofness as soon as the magical bond is broken. The text of the Colloquy of the Ancients, as we have it, is incomplete. Our fragment does not tell us how the intercourse of the Fiann with the Sons of the King of Iruath ends. Fortunately the gap is filled by a Fenian ballad in the Book of Lismore.[3] When it is discovered that the death of the two Ulster princes is their work, Finn spares their lives on the condition that the wonderful hound shall henceforth be his. They pledge the sun and the moon, the land and the sea, that they will never bring it alive out of Ireland. Then they kill it and take the body with them on their way north. There is a pursuit but, of course, without success. The divine protectors pass again into the night of mystery from whence they came.

Now let us consider the manifestation of the magical energy in the Sons of the King of Iruath. Their virtues amount to these three: they protect in war, they provide abundance, and they heal diseases.[4] The whole of Irish literature is there to show that these are exactly the virtues that were expected to be present in beings gifted with a supernatural force, whether divine or human. Elves are in the possession of healing cauldrons or vessels of abundance, saints procure plenty and health by their word or their contact. The head of a buried hero is a security for the land. Princes touch the sick with their hands so that they may be cured. And when the ruler's valour and bounty form the eternal theme with endless variations of bardic poetry, we can only look upon this tradition as a reminiscence of the sacral nature of kingship. The Sons of the King of Iruath are in no way distinguished from other beings with a supernatural touch. Their attributes are of a general, not an individual character, and there is nothing personal about them. Here is another reason why they are no true gods.[5] Their hound is an animal of plenty that hunts the deer on its own account, just as Manannán's swine procure meat and his cows milk. Their pipe is a healing object and makes man sleep in spite of pains or wounds, owing to the well-known magical virtue of fairy-music.

Even the three magical gifts embodied in the three Sons of the King of Iruath are not represented by each of them separately, as appears from contradictions in the text. Moreover, these virtues are exercised not through personal strength or knowledge, but by mere magic. Spells and a venomous wind, emitted by the dog, are their means of protection. Abundance is also provided from the dog. It vomits fifty ounces of gold and fifty ounces of silver at the moment when Finn finds himself in the necessity to succour a company of indigent poets. Its masters need only pronounce the name of a beverage, and it comes forth from its mouth.

No less remarkable is the homage desired by these divine magicians from their clients. Adoration, the usual form of reciprocity for divine favour, is altogether absent. So is sacrifice. What is asked is actually the opposite thing: they shall not be provided with food by the Fiann, and the poorest hunting-grounds in the country shall be theirs. The third condition is that nobody shall disturb them during the night and, of the three, this is the only obligation that plays a part in the story: it is violated by the Ulster princes and thus causes their destruction. The two other provisions have no object but to display, and perhaps to maintain, the unequalled magical qualities of the dog. Secrecy, mystery, and privacy are what their activity is based upon, not reverence or worship.

Not only is the nature of the Irish divine magicians, at least in some respects, in straight opposition to that of gods, but the attitude of their human dependants is also of a very unusual character. They just have to let them alone. A nearer approach, even with perfectly friendly and humble intentions, would prove disastrous. Strange though this relation of man with the higher powers may appear, the reason is obvious as soon as it is realized that these powers can only communicate

with us by means of magic. From this the early Irish outlook derives its essence, which makes it so much a puzzle for those conversant with the conceptions of, say, the Greeks or the Scandinavians. Whenever magical bonds have been established between a group of humans and some superior being, things should be left as they are. The patron need not exert himself in the interest of his client, since the magic acts for him. Likewise, the dependant is sure to receive what he has been promised, for the patron cannot alter his obligations. The client has no reason to please his divine benefactor. All he should do is not to infringe the magical injunction.

The magical dog links the Sons of the King of Iruath to another triad of supernatural beings, even more famous in Irish mythology, namely, the Sons of Turill Picrenn. The pathetic story of their wanderings and hardships constitutes one of the most beloved themes of Irish literature. We have it in an early and in a later recension.[6]

Of these, the former has only come down to us fragmentarily, as an episode of the Irish Book of Invasions; the opening chapters are wanting. According to the later version, Ireland is attacked by a demoniacal host from overseas, and Lug, lord of the fairy host, sends three messengers in three different directions to collect help. One of them is Cian, his own father. On the way north he meets the three Sons of Turill Picrenn. Without any special reason they decide to attack him. He transforms himself into a pig and escapes. In the disguise of hounds they find him out and kill him with stones, although not without having allowed him to throw off his animal shape. Inevitably their wer-gild will be greater now, since they have not killed a pig, but a man. In the meantime, Lug has driven away the invaders and calls his men together at Tara. By a stratagem he discovers his father's murderers. They plead for their lives and Lug shows mercy. But he imposes upon them a number of supernatural tasks. It is here the earlier version sets in. They exert themselves to the utmost and perform the tasks with success. But when all care is over, they succumb. To this tragical end the story owes its popularity.

The first thing to be noticed is that, for this other triad, the name 'Sons of Turill Picrenn' is by no means general. In the Book of Invasions they are called the Sons of Delbaeth mac Ogma, a fairy prince. According to a separate tract in the Book of Leinster their father is another fairy lord, Bress mac Elathan. Evidently there was no fixed tradition as to their origin. Then, one of the tasks imposed upon them by Lug is the seeking of a dog that turns into wine every liquid contained in its skin; it belongs to the King of Iruath. Thus Lug, lord of the fairy host, acquires the dog very much in the same way as Finn, chief of the Fiann. Besides, there are some minor points where the two stories agree.

Lug's father, Cian, is stoned by his adversaries and, as a memory of this event, a vast plain of stones remains. Likewise, Finn's warriors pelt stones at the departing divine magicians and leave a stony desert behind. Evidently it was customary to connect the possessors of the dog of plenty, or rather their departure, in some way or other with the barrenness of rocks.

Are we to identify the Sons of the King of Iruath with the Sons of Turill Picrenn? The question is not well formulated. Of each of the two triads we have but one story. The two traditions differ a good deal. Lug receives the dog, and those who brought it die. Finn's possession of the dog is of a temporary nature and the original owners take it from him and vanish for ever. In one story it is asked: how did Lug acquire the animal of plenty, and this is but one single episode in a long list of tasks which are nearly all concerned with some magical object. The other tale is mainly about the way in which Finn lost the hound. This difference must be explained from the fact that Lug is a fairy lord, and Finn, in spite of his heroic dimensions, but a human being. In both cases there is a dog of plenty, which is owned by three supernatural beings and placed by them at the disposal of a representative of Irish chieftaincy. The two divine triads may as well be declared to be identical as not. Nobody ever believed in them in the strict sense of the word. Their stories are but the expression of an idea. The unity is to be seen in the underlying notion; but it gave rise to more than one development. From this very variance of aspects we infer the existence of what may be called a mythical complex.[7] Its principal personalities are the dog, the lord who receives its protection, and the three keepers.

Who are these three? They must by no means be regarded as servile spirits. In the Fenian tale they figure as honoured guests. When in the other story they must obey Lug's command, the sole cause is their obligation to procure the wer-gild for his murdered father. According to the Book of Invasions and a few other sources, they belong to the race of the Tuatha Dé Danann, a group of spirits or supernatural beings, which are usually regarded as a survival of an original Celtic Pantheon. However, all that speaks for this theory is the resemblance of some of their names to those of Gaulish gods. It receives but little support from the Irish tradition. Tuatha Dé Danann literally means 'the Tribes of the god (or goddess) Danu', which would seem to imply that the members of these tribes are no gods themselves. At the same time, in the Book of Invasions the three sons of Turill Picrenn, who procure the magical hound for Lug, receive the title of 'the three gods of Danu'. It would take us too far at present to inquire into the true nature of this Danu. The problem is not only of the etymological order. Evidently in one case Danu is the name of a divinity, whereas in the other Danu appears as a being that stands itself in the need of gods. At all events, for the Tuatha Dé Danann it is essential to have gods; but apart from this, tradition is uncertain. The current notion is that they had but one god, whose name is Danu; from this the denotation Tuatha Dé Danann was derived. But according to the concomitant tradition there were three gods, and those were the three Sons of Turill Picrenn, who provided their tribes with the dog of plenty and other magical objects. About Danu we know next to nothing. On the sons of Turill Picrenn, on the other hand, we have already succeeded in collecting some valuable materials. Now we can go a step farther and find our conclusion on the nature of a god in Irish paganism confirmed. The name of the Tuatha Dé Danann shows that these tribes receive the assistance of their gods continually, that they will never be deprived of their protection, bounty, and healing power. Even though their society is superhuman, they cannot do without the support of beings that are magically superior. But this support is lasting. This accounts for the use of the word 'god' in connexion with them. No doubt we were right in rejecting it with regard to the human world, with the only exception of the oath. The Tuatha Dé Danann are beings of the blest. Therefore they have a god or gods. In human society, which is essentially imperfect, there are none.[8]

Now it may be understood why the attitude assumed by the divine providers of plenty is so much different in the two traditions compared. To Finn and his warriors eternal bliss is unattainable. The Sons of the King of Iruath give them a chance to have the dog of plenty for themselves for ever. But it is a gift, bound to certain magical conditions. Later on, these are broken. We might add, it was fated that they should be so. The Fenian tradition, as represented by the Colloquy of the Ancients on one side, and the Fenian ballad on the other, is not consistent. Both authorities speak of a rising against the divine benefactors on account of the death of the two Ulster princes. The prose tale makes Finn ask for their names. These they reveal. What followed we do not know, owing to the fragmentary state of our text. But it may be assumed that subsequently they depart because of the forbidden question. The ballad is no more explicit on this point. All we hear is that the dog is killed by its masters when Finn has wrested the promise from them that it will never be removed alive from Ireland.

However, the circumstances under which the departure of the divine magicians is effectuated, or the causes that made them act so cruelly with regard to their former friends, are not of primary importance. They are but accessory embellishments. What really imports is the fundamental notion of the myth. On this there can be no doubt. We have learned it from our comparison with the story of the Sons of Turill Picrenn. For the Fenian host there are no gods yielding a protection that endures. There is no personal relation, no lasting friendship with any power directing our destiny. On this earth everything is bound by magic, and the risk that it should be broken, even unwillingly and ignorantly, is always there. Man is never sure of the morrow. The idea is generally human. What is characteristic of Irish paganism is the inference that this world has no gods. Their non-existence is the religious expression of the fact that life teems with misery and evil. Gods are a privilege of the world of the blessed spirits.

It is not incumbent upon us to judge of the moral or the philosophical standard of this fundamental religious conception. In itself, however, the incapability to represent a god as jealous, tricky, or cruel—and this is what it comes to with many other peoples—does not point to a low ethical level. This fact remains, even though the belief in the omnipresence of the blind mechanism of magic is in its consequences closely akin to fatalism.

So far it has been attempted to trace the religious foundation of a Fenian legend. The problem presented by traditions of this type cannot be dismissed with a mere reference to the obvious fact that they largely borrow from the folk-tale. Of course, elements such as animals or objects of plenty, conditioned protection, the forbidden question, and many others, cannot deceive us as to their origin. This statement, however, yields only a starting-point. The body of Fenian story is not a collection of folk-tales. Nor is the attachment of popular elements to Finn and his heroes fortuitous. It shows that Fenian story is representative of a conceptional complex which, owing to an inner affinity, could be partly expressed by certain commonplaces of the folk-tale. At the same time, it abounds with matter that has nothing to do with the folk-tale whatever, and the borrowed popular elements have all been linked to definite personalities, forming together well-characterized groups. Wherever the magical outlook is predominant, it is but natural for mythology to draw its images from the inexhaustible well of primitive popular tradition. But as soon as this happens, they acquire a fresh application, and sometimes even a new meaning. Under the outer evidence there must be some hidden psychological process. In order to reveal this it will be necessary first to examine the groups that attracted the popular elements under consideration.

We found the *motif* of the magical dog used in connexion with both the Tuatha Dé Danann and Finn's warriors. Of these, the latter group presents far greater difficulties to the critic than the former, who are evidently the spirits of the land and thus stand for a special chapter of Celtic religion. This it will be best to pass by in silence, since the problem of the Fiann is so much more tantalizing. The outstanding difference between the two groups is expressed by Cáilte, himself one of the Fiann, in these words: 'The Tuatha Dé

Danann are imperishable; but I belong to the Sons of Míl, and they are short-lived and perishable' (*Acc. na Sen.,* l. 3908). The Fenian warriors are both mortal and failing. We are perfectly justified in regarding them as human beings.

Still, there is something in Fenian tradition that makes us shrink from accepting this conclusion without any restriction. Professor John MacNeill's ingenious argument, which had the object of disclosing an historical foundation for this section of Irish literature, leaves us no better satisfied than the theory that the Fenian Cycle should be nothing but a mere body of folk-tales. It fails to elucidate the intermingling of historical and fictitious, mostly magical, elements. And should it be objected that a similar process is observed in the Ulster Cycle, then we might retort that then we had better look for an explanation there, too. Only a very few texts of the Fenian Cycle have come down to us from the Old-Irish period. Among them there is, indeed, one that tells us a good deal about the earliest historical connexions of Finn and his warriors; it is the story called 'The Youthful Exploits of Finn'. This, however, may be due to mere accident. Earlier texts may have been lost, and in historical saga youth stories do not generally belong to the primitive stratum. Besides, when the whole body of Fenian tradition is considered, the historical or pseudo-historical tales vanish as compared to those with a magical or even a mythical aspect, such as the numerous hunting traditions. In itself, a mythical origin with later historical connexions, varying according to the successive periods, is even more likely than the reverse. If the numerous allusions to the invasions and raids of the Vikings are regarded as the additions of a later period, then why should not an earlier time be responsible for the rare references to conflicts among Irish tribes? There is no branch of Irish literature where the tendency towards historicizing did not make itself felt.[9]

A glance at the early traditions of Britain settles the matter. Confining ourselves to the legends of King Arthur and his companions, we notice both in the general tendency and in multitudinous details such a perfect and striking agreement with those of the Irish Finn that it cannot be explained away by stating that obviously the two cycles took their subject-matter from the identical stock of popular notions. What to say, for instance, of Creiddylad, daughter of Lludd Silverhand, in one of the Welsh Mabinogion stories, who was 'the tallest maiden in the three islands and the three adjacent islands of the Strong' and for whom two famous heroes, on the authority of Arthur himself, wage the eternal battle; and of Bébind, daughter of Trén, of Fenian tradition, whom Finn's men compared to 'the mast of a full great high-topped ship', when she fled to them and made Cáilte defend her against a detested husband?[10] Or of the tombstone of Arthur's son Anir, measuring now 6, then 9, and sometimes even 12 or 15 feet, and that of the dwarf of Tara, in which the tallest man of Ireland as well as the tiniest babe found their due proportion?[11]

Let us inspect some prominent characteristics of the leading hero on both sides. Arthur is a great boar-hunter; as such he figures not only in one of the most primitive tales of the Mabinogion, but already in the ninth-century *Wonders of Britain*. In Fenian story boar-hunting is the perpetual *leitmotiv*. The boar is generally of a supernatural character; in some Irish traditions it comports itself exactly like the Welsh Twrch Trwyth.[12] The hounds are no less endowed with magical faculties. Arthur's dog Cafal leaves its footprint in the rock, Finn's dog Bran is conspicuous by its supernatural colouring.[13]

Arthur is also a fighter of monsters. His combat with Rhita the Giant, whose cloak was made of kings' beards, is recorded in the triads of Britain and in several other old sources; its memory still lingers on in present-day Welsh folk-tradition. The number of monsters slain by Finn is imposing. One of them was that of Loch Derg; it killed two thousand or more in a single day, but Finn gripped it by one of the joints and turned it upside down.[14]

If necessary, both Arthur and Finn intervene in the supernatural world. Between Gwynn, son of Nudd, in whom divine traits are now generally recognized, and his unrelenting adversary Gwythr, son of Greidawl, peace is established by Arthur. The Colloquy of the Ancients, likewise, contains more than one instance of a conflict among the Tuatha Dé Danann being decided by the intervention of Finn. From them Cáilte receives a liquid that preserves all past events fresh in the memory, as a reward for his constant assistance in repelling the plunderers that used to harass the land-divinities every seventh year.[15] Arthur's principal task is the warding-off of foreign invaders. Although we hear little or nothing about this in early Welsh poetry or the prose-tales, one of the original sections of Nennius's *Historia Britonum* enlarges upon it with evident preference. Finn defends the country against both demoniacal and human intruders. Among the former are the Fomore, or submarine demons, among the latter is Mílid, son of Tréchossach, the king of the great eastern world. The Lochlannachs, Finn's continual enemies, are usually regarded as the historical Norsemen, but their character is at the same time largely demoniacal. Sometimes Arthur's opponent is one of the British princes themselves, as in the case of Huail, son of Caw, whose ambition is a menace to the great ruler's empire.[16]

Arthur is also a great releaser of prisoners. Of this there are two instances in the Hunting of the Twrch Trwyth, apart from an allusion to a number of Arthur's own men, who had been captured by Gwynn ab Nudd and were afterwards restored to liberty by the king himself. Of the two other stories, the best known is that of Mabon, son of Modron, who was imprisoned at Gloucester (*Caerloyw*). This Mabon could not be liberated until his cousin Eidoel, son of Aer, had been released from his prison at Caer Glini. According to a life of St. Gildas, Arthur carried his wife, Queen Guinevere, home from Glastonbury after her abduction by Melvas. In one of the collections of early Welsh poetry, the Book of Taliessin, occurs an Arthurian poem, the so-called Harryings of Hell, which contains at least one record of a released prisoner. Evidently this very popular theme is a special Welsh, or British, development; its deeper meaning still remains obscure. It is less conspicuous in the Fenian tradition of Ireland, where the blessings of Roman rule never penetrated.[17]

There must be a common Celtic stock surviving in the Fenian and Arthurian cycles. They are both based on the same notions, and the resemblance of their constitutive elements is too strong to be accidental. When in the literature of two cognate peoples we find corresponding heroic figures of a very particular type, then there must be a common nucleus. This fact cannot be obscured by any special historical connexions on either side; these are not essential. At present we are not concerned with the evolution but with the origin and foundation of this typical Celtic form of hero-worship. We seek a formula expressive of what is fundamental in the nature of Celtic heroes like Finn and Arthur. Perhaps they are best indicated as the exemplary protectors of the land.

The better one becomes acquainted with Celtic pagan thinking, the more does one realize that there is always a religious undercurrent, which, through many branches, tends towards the central notion of the preservation and protection of the land, both from inside and outside. In Ireland the official historians created a system, according to which the successive groups of colonists wrung the island from their predecessors and from the Fomore, the demons of the surrounding sea. These unfriendly beings appear as the original owners, they are always on the watch and never loosen their grip completely. No fresh colony ever landed without their resistance. In this system there was no room for Fenian tradition, probably because official Milesian history was not interested in it. Still, Finn also has his fights with transmarine monsters and, as a matter of fact, all his activities are at bottom intended for the protection of the land.[18]

This protection assumes many forms. One that is comparatively difficult to understand, since for this a certain revolution in our modes of thinking is required, consists in what might be called the 'knowledge' of the land. The conservation of traditions as to how all the natural phenomena, such as the wells, plains, lakes, and rocks, came into being, and what happened near them, secures a command of the demoniacal guardian powers. This knowledge enables us to befriend them or, if they should be wicked, to appease or subdue them.[19] Protection of a simpler and a more primitive character is afforded by hunting and fighting. Living creatures embody a magic often more dangerous and more hostile to civilization than that of wild nature itself. Whosoever hunts the boar successfully, destroys those perils. Fighting is necessitated by human invaders, and of them the insular Celts had their share. Besides, there were always the demoniacal spirits of the wild, prone to thwart all human efforts, and the black forces of the waters all around.

Here we feel the eminent importance of magic. All kinds of protection are bound and dominated by it. However, no magic but entails other magic, as the protector needs protection himself. The result is a magical chain that would have no end but for the natural limits of all human reasoning. There is a graduation in accordance with the groups in which this continued magic manifests itself. This we must understand in order to grasp the deeper meaning of Celtic myths.

Highest rank those beings we have labelled 'divine magicians'; for the gods, invoked in the oath, are of too shadowy a nature. The Sons of Turill Picrenn and the Sons of the King of Iruath protect the spirits of the land and the warriors of Finn. But they cannot achieve this without falling back upon the Hound of Plenty. A similar correlation may be noticed in the Welsh mythical stories, even though but scanty remains have come down to us. Of Math, son of Mathonwy, lord of North Wales, it is said in the Mabinogion that he cannot make the circuit of his domain unless he is accompanied by the two sons of Don, Gwydyon and Gilfathwy. These are his divine magical protectors. For him they hunt the swine of Pryderi. For him Gwydyon even slays Pryderi. However, not by his own force but by the performance of magical practices (*hud a lledrith*). These are not described in the text, but the words suffice to prove that Gwydyon, although a divine being, is dependent upon magic himself.

Next in rank come the spirits of the land, the Irish Tuatha Dé Danann. In the official Irish protohistory they figure as the predecessors of the Gaedhil in the capacity of owners of the land. They have a society of their own, which leads its own life, uninfluenced by human society and, as a rule, not influencing it. Sometimes, however, relations arise, either of a friendly or a hostile character. The Tuatha Dé Danann dispose of various means to protect the land from evil powers. They defeat the ever-lurking sea-demons (*Fomore*) in the battle of Moytura. They have powerful physicians in their midst. However, they want magical protection themselves, and it is of many kinds. Theirs is the Feast of Goibniu, which prevents sorrow and disease, theirs the magical spear that keeps Finn awake in spite of the

fairy music of Aillén, son of Midna, who comes in the night to burn down the hall of Tara.[20] Their counterpart in Welsh tradition are the Children of Llyr, the central group in the so-called Four Branches of the Mabinogi. They are typical protectors of the land. Bran is the oldest of them; after his death his head is buried in the White Hill in London, and as long as it is left there, no plague will befall the Island of Britain. It was Arthur himself who disinterred the head, in order that the protection should be entirely his own work, and thus he paved the way for the Saxon conqueror. Bran's brother, Manawydan, is a famous destroyer of magic; he kills the demoniacal mice that ruin his wheat. At the same time, the Children of Llyr have surrounded themselves by numerous magical objects for their own preservation. Among these are the healing cauldron of Bran, which restores life to the killed warriors as soon as their bodies are thrown into it, and the birds of Rhiannon, whose song brings oblivion of troubles and disease.[21]

The third group is that of the heroes. Finn and his warriors are no divinities, they belong to a human race inhabiting Ireland and converse with princes and kings. Yet they have certain superhuman traits as, for instance, their extraordinary size, age, and valour. Therefore they may be styled heroes, on the condition that this word should not be taken in the sense of demi-gods. They are sublimated men, not dethroned or bastardized gods. Their manifold active protection has already been sufficiently illustrated. But they themselves receive protection, too. We saw them guarded by three divine magicians. Then, there is Créde the wonderful maiden who feeds the heroes during the battle of Ventry. An altogether different form of protection is that afforded by Finn's tooth of wisdom, which always reveals the truth, and his numerous *geasa* or magical injunctions that constitute an infallible security as long as they are not transgressed. Thus it is forbidden to Finn to see a dead man unless he has been killed in battle. As long as this *geiss* is not violated, Finn will remain victorious.[22] Finn's counterpart in Britain is, of course, King Arthur. The whole of his career is devoted to the protection of the land; no more need be said about this. That he was also magically protected is not quite so clear as we might expect. He believed so much in himself, that is, in his own supernatural qualities, that he scorned the bonds of magical security. According to one of the Welsh triads, this is the reason why he disinterred Bran's head and thus prepared the fall of Celtic Britain. On another occasion he defeats the demoniacal ravens of Owein by crushing the magical chessmen of his partner. The moves on the chessboard are a magical counterpart of the real events. Likewise, Caledfwlch, his sword, and Prydwen, his ship, are objects of supernatural qualities.[23]

As a last group there are the kings themselves. To them the actual work of protection is committed. This duty they perform actively by resisting the enemy. But this is not all. There is also a protection of a more mystical character, as appears, for instance, from their responsibility for a failure in the crops. In order to secure the prosperity of the land the Irish kings must not only be physically worthy of the kingship but must also refrain from transgressing certain negative magical obligations. The High-king of Ireland, for instance, must allow the sun to rise upon him on his bed at Tara. On the other hand, if the king protects his country by a strict observance of rules prescribed by fate, their latent energy guards him in its turn. This is clearly shown in the case of the Lia Fáil, the stone that utters a shriek as soon as the king, willed by destiny, sits down upon it. Henceforth he is magically safeguarded by its inherent power. Among the historical or pseudo-historical Irish kings of an exemplary character King Cormac, son of Art, is prominent. Similar conceptions are found in Britain. A blemished king is deemed incapable of providing sufficient protection and is debarred from succession on account of his defect. Such was the case of Iorwerth Drwyndwn (Flatnose), son of Owein Gwynedd. When King Vortigern realizes that he can stop the Saxon flood no longer, he ceases fighting and builds the Castle of Ambrosius in Snowdonia as a magical rampart for himself and his people. At the prayer of St. German it is destroyed by the fire of heaven; this fatal issue symbolizes the triumph of the personal God of Christianity over the blind magical powers of paganism. The British kings are also under the protection of some magical objects, the so-called Thirteen Jewels of Britain; amongst them are a cauldron of plenty and a sword that bursts into flame as soon as it is drawn by the wrong person. It is interesting to note that even the protection afforded by living beings is not precluded in the case of kings. This, in fact, must be the primary significance of the office of the foot-holder (*troediog*) at the Welsh, and of the king's bed-man (*fer leptha ríg*) at the Irish, court. King Conaire Mór of Tara sleeps with his legs upon the lap of a man and with his head in the lap of another; then he has dreams of value. St. Patrick enjoins that the king's bed-fellow shall always be a musician, obviously because of the blessed influence of music. That the foot-holder's function in Wales was of a similar nature, appears from the story of Math, King of Gwynedd, of whom it is said that, in time of peace, he could only live with his feet in the lap of a maiden. The underlying idea is that she imparts her vital force to the king and strengthens him magically. For the same purpose King Cadwallon uses his young nephew Brian. It is only after a sleep in his lap that the king finds himself mentally capable of rejecting the demands of his Northumbrian opponent.[24]

The forms in which the magical protection, both active and passive, manifests itself are much the same in the different groups. Their development presents an interesting problem which, however, lies outside our present scope. It might be surmised that the notion of magical protection attached primarily to actual kingship and was transferred to heroes and divinities. The mystical security emanates from objects and animals; sometimes from human or anthropomorphic beings. Even with these a personal and friendly relation is rare. The magic character is too strong for that.

The group that demands our present attention is that of the heroes. If they are no dethroned gods, but sublimated men, in what sense, then, must this term be taken? The concord of Arthurian and Fenian saga precludes the primary nature of the historical references. The Fenian complex must be largely unhistorical. In all cases where it accords with Arthurian tradition there is not one single trace of an historical basis. Hence a study of the possible historical elements will never take us to the core of the problem. It is the common insular Celtic complex that must be accounted for. Later accretions, of the historical, the romantic, or the mythical type, only prove the survival of its fundamental idea at a comparatively recent date. In Ireland the existence of Fenian saga in a literary form has been demonstrated for the ninth century.[25]

What, then, are the germs of Fenian tradition in Ireland? Even Celtic imagination is not boundless. It requires a starting-point. At the beginning there must be some sense, some inner reality. It is even likely that, for a long time, the contact with this was never completely lost. If we are ever to succeed in discovering this inner reality, it must be borne in mind that all literature has a social function as well as a psychological basis, and that in societies of a more primitive character religion stands for the life of the soul in all its aspects. What are the social and religious aspirations reflected by this strange body of Irish fiction?

Our answer to this question must be based upon the two main results of our examination of the texts. The social function of Fenian and Arthurian tradition, no less than that of the real myths, lies in the paradigmatic value of the stories, and its religious tendencies centre about the fundamental notion of the protection of the land. From these two starting-points the core can be approached. What protection means in the religious sense of the word we have attempted to establish. It implies the fighting of human and demoniacal enemies, the destruction of hostile magic, a complete command of the land by the knowledge of its secrets. Power as a consequence of knowledge must be taken in a far more literal and practical sense than in our own days. Whoever knows the events that have happened at a particular locality, is master of the place, and can turn its latent magical energy into the direction of his own interests. Knowledge of the land is a kind of insurance against failure. The more traditions we possess and the better we preserve them, the stronger will our position be against natural and supernatural adversaries. Hence the typically Irish notion of a 'powerful story', that is, a story-parallel whose recitation warrants success. It survived even in Christian times. Of the hymn called *Lorica Patricii* it is said that it preserves us from the imminent dangers of soul and body, provided it be piously recited. With regard to another semi-Christian semi-pagan story St. Patrick orders that there shall be neither sleep nor conversation during its recital, and that it shall not be told except to a few good people, so that it may be all the better listened to; in addition he ordains many other virtues for it.[26]

This notion of protective power inherent in a story attaches itself naturally to that of its paradigmatic value. The recitation under similar circumstances of a sequence of events of the past secures an identical issue. This holds good especially of stories where the acting personages are of a superhuman quality. All the tales of Finn's heroes are about some form of protection of the land. Hence the knowledge and preservation of Fenian tradition is in itself a safeguard for generations to come. It constitutes a special form of magical protection in itself and may be defined as a body of paradigmatic stories intended for the security of the native soil. The young have to learn them. The older generation, in its turn, will preserve and transmit them. A comprehensive body of paradigmatic traditions ensures an effective protection of the land.[27]

As a further illustration of this conclusion we may point to the important position assigned to apprenticeship. This is especially clear in the case of the heroical tales. The stories were not only intended to teach their lessons but to emphasize the necessity of profiting from them. The Colloquy of the Ancients is almost exclusively based upon this principle. St. Patrick and many other men besides—mostly princes and kings—visit Cáilte and ask about the happenings in the days of Finn. He never tires of teaching them, and the names of localities are his usual starting-point. His main object is to impart knowledge of the land. Apart from this general structure of the text, there are among the personalities figuring in it some typical representatives of the class of apprentices. One of them is Bran, son of Derg, a Munster prince (*Acc. na Sen.,* ll. 877 sqq.). He comes to Cáilte with the express wish to learn Fenianism (*fiannaigecht*) from him. The old warrior asks the young man how hunting is practised by his own people, and Bran gives an explanation of it, ending in the complaint: 'Sometimes we kill a deer, sometimes it escapes us'. Upon hearing this, Cáilte bursts into tears because of so much ignorance, and then organizes an exemplary hunt. Eight hundred deer are killed. From that day Bran knows how to hunt the deer. To this typical didactic story another lesson is attached. One of St. Patrick's clerics asks for a share of the game and the young prince is reluctant to comply. But Cáilte intervenes and reminds him of the moral

duty to give a part of his profit to the Church. This is, of course, only an addition dating from Christian times. But it shows that the Church also availed itself of the means provided by the paradigmatic character of Fenian tradition for the establishment of its own rights.

Another instance of Fenian apprenticeship may be seen in the long story of Cas Corach, the musician of the Tuatha Dé Danann, who joins Cáilte on his wanderings over Ireland and seizes every possible opportunity to increase his knowledge of localities and early events (*Acc. na Sen.,* ll. 3352 sqq.). The lessons learned cover the three departments of protection: the providing of safety, abundance, and health. Cas Corach being the minstrel of a divine race, he is already in the possession of the fairy music that enraptures the soul. What he still must learn is tradition. He gives the impression of being intended as an example for young artists, gifted with promising lyrical talents, but as yet lacking the indispensable amount of solid and massive knowledge.

In one of the ballads it is Finn himself who performs the function of the traditional apprentice. When out hunting with some of his men he sees emerging from the mist a tall warrior who holds a bird-crib of red gold in his hand and catches all the birds that pass him. Evidently he belongs to the type of the divine magicians. He invites Finn to follow him, but no sooner have the men entered his stronghold than an iron door is closed upon them. From that moment they receive no food. But Finn has learned his lesson well. Imitating what he has seen from the divine magician, he makes a hazel crib for each of his companions and thus saves their lives. The ballad shows that the didactic element is not limited to the Colloquy of the Ancients, but constitutes an essential trait of Fenian tradition.[28]

Finn is the exemplary hero of Ireland. Princes and nobles learn their office of protecting the land by studying and remembering his exploits. The historical connexions in which he appears are all of a secondary character. He makes his first appearance at Tara as an unknown boy (*Acc. na Sen.,* l. 1677). His name means 'White' and would suit anybody, like Dub, 'Black', or Derg, 'Red'. We have no right to identify Finn, because of his name, with the Welsh divinity, Gwynn ab Nudd. The British counterpart of Finn is Arthur. Nor is his name uncommon in the early records of Britain and Ireland. For Arthur, as for Finn, scholars have often advocated an historical origin. There may be historical elements in Arthurian tradition. But the foundations of the historical theory are still weaker in Arthur's than in Finn's case. Our earliest source, Gildas, never names him. Yet he would have been his contemporary. Next comes Nennius's *Historia Britonum*, where Arthur figures as a leader in war (*dux bellorum*), who defeats the Saxons in twelve successive battles. However, in an appendix, the *Mirabilia Britanniae*, he appears as the hero of a famous boar-hunting story and of other legendary traditions. It is true that the *Mirabilia* are probably of later origin than the *Historia* proper, but still they belong to the ninth century. If an historical Arthur ever existed, he must have been raised to the level of a legendary hero a few centuries after his death. Besides, the general likeness which links his saga to that of Finn proves that the complex was ready before it was attached to an historical person. At the very best some other British hero preceded Arthur at its head. But then it matters very little for our present argument whether he was originally called Arthur or by some other name. However, since the question of Arthur's historicity will probably never lose its attraction for scholars, it is well to point out that neither the expression *dux bellorum* in Nennius nor the twelve battles against the Saxons justify the assumption that he ever was a living man. Arthurian story shows that in Britain he performs the same function as Finn in Ireland. He protects the land in every possible manner. It was but natural to represent a hero of this type as the victor over the Saxons. At the present day hardly any scholar would maintain the theory that Finn actually was a great warrior of the ninth or the tenth century because he is represented as constantly repulsing the Norsemen. The two cases are completely parallel. *Dux bellorum*, leader in war, is no doubt a suitable title for a victorious general. But is it not equally appropriate as the title of the chief of a legendary warlike band like the Round Table or the Irish Fiann? In fact, the expressions used in the *Historia Britonum* and its description of Arthur's relations with the Saxons lose nothing of their force if we regard him, in accordance with all the remaining evidence, as the exemplary protecting hero of Britain and nothing else. There is not one single testimony that can be explained exclusively by the assumption of Arthur's historicity.[29]

Our quest has led us towards a general principle from which the whole of Arthurian legend can be understood in its outlines. Like Finn, Arthur hunts the boar and slays demons, monsters, and witches; he repulses the invaders from overseas, he provides wealth from his cauldron of plenty, he is always prepared to intervene whenever his warriors are in straits. Magically protected himself by the Thirteen Jewels of Britain, he applies his own supernatural power to the preservation of the land. By crushing a set of chessmen he scatters the ravens of Owein and overthrows the Saxons. His story teems with topographical lore, and the list of localities having Arthurian connexions is no less imposing than that of places with Fenian memories. If Arthur's activity for the deliverance of prisoners makes his legend depart in one respect from Finn's, it must be realized that this difference does not touch the core. In its essence the theme of the released prisoner has much in common with those Fenian tales where Finn liberates one of his heroes, or his divine allies, from the grip of some wicked demon. The transmitted Arthurian prisoner stories are far from perspicuous, owing to the extreme succinctness of the texts. Yet so much is clear that there is a considerable element of supernatural scenery in them. The dungeons opened by Arthur do not seem to belong to our visible world; they recall the fortresses of Irish demons or divinities. The prison referred to in the Taliessin poem is called *Caer Sidi*, and this *sidi* is singularly reminiscent of the Irish name of the fairies (*sídhe*). Mabon, son of Modron, is no doubt kept imprisoned at Gloucester; but the colouring of the narrative is far more suggestive of a mysterious locality than of an historical city. Who can tell us what body of tradition was associated with the famous site on the Severn? Weighing the evidence, we might suggest that the theme of the released prisoner has a fair chance of being part and parcel of the common insular Celtic stock, no less than all the other legendary elements under review. It is after all only its outer trappings that betray typically British conditions. In the later Irish Fenian ballads the same *motif* has been introduced. Besides, it is not absent from other sections of Irish literature.[30]

Nor is the notion of apprenticeship altogether unknown in Arthurian legend. It is present in the disguise of the theme of the 'preceding failure'. The Mabinogion story of Kulhwch and Olwen tells how Kulhwch is sent to Arthur's court and claims the king's assistance in the winning of Olwen as his bride (*Red Book Mab.*, pp. 113 sqq.). The great difficulty is to find her. Arthur's first embassy fails. Then the prominent heroes set out and trace her to her father's stronghold. Likewise, in the story called 'The Lady of the Fountain', Owein's great adventure at the magic well is preceded by a visit of a certain Cynon to the same locality. But Cynon was not destined to overcome the Black Knight, and turned home sorely afflicted (*Red Book Mab.*, pp. 170 sqq.). The text records the name 'story of failure' (*chwedl fethedig*) for this type of tradition, and thus furnishes a precious support for the theory that these negative illustrations form a separate group. There can be no doubt as to its meaning. It has a didactic and a pedagogic purpose: the apprentice should avoid failure by studying the career of those who did not fail in the same circumstances. The bonds of relationship uniting Arthurian and Fenian heroic saga are very close indeed. They have the same social function, which is of a religious character and differs but little from that of the mythical tales in the strict sense.

We are led towards a new interpretation of the Welsh term 'Mabinogi'. It has the advantage that it combines the two principal doctrines, which until now seemed irreconcilable. Against the theory that Mabinogi should mean 'a youth story' it may be argued that the Mabinogion collection, even in its narrowest limits, contains a good many episodes that are not about the hero's youth at all. On the other hand, to interpret it as 'the traditional material intended for a bardic apprentice' seems incompatible with the fact that Mabinogi is also used as a translation of the Latin *infantia*. It may now be suggested that in the term the two notions are to a certain extent combined. For the early Celtic mentality the didactic element is a constituent part of any story, owing to its paradigmatic character. Those that have to learn from it are not only the beginners among the bards, but the whole of the aristocratic younger generation. At the same time, this exemplary material is largely, though not exclusively, about youthful exploits; hence *Infantia Christi* could be translated by *Mabinogi Iesu Crist*. This apparent double meaning is a consequence of the Celtic didactic principle. An exemplary story is intended to impart the actual power of imitating its hero. Therefore, a *mabinogi* does not necessarily reveal the name of its principal figure in the title, as is the case in the 'Mabinogi of the Collar and the Hammer'. This was a tale about capture by means of magic, and it was meant as a magical help to prisoners. No title could better indicate its purport.[31]

Let us return to our main argument. It is, of course, not precluded that at least some tales should preserve ancient myths in the classical sense of the word, that is, traditions embodying a belief connected with gods, even though much of their original splendour should have faded away. Here lies a problem that at present must be left aside. Nor is it ripe for solution. Perhaps one day archaeology will throw its light on it. At all events, the number of possibly ancient myths, reminiscent of an almost forgotten Celtic Olympus, and surviving in insular Celtic literature, is comparatively small. The essential identity of Fenian and Arthurian legend shows that the religion of the land, and its expression in the form of paradigmatic hero-tales, continues a deeply rooted Celtic tradition. Of course there may also have existed other means of religious presentation. If the tendency to identify every personality in an Irish or Welsh story of magic and imagination with a god is no longer predominant in Celtic studies, yet the evidence for a common Celtic belief in certain divinities remains. It is not sufficient to point to such general similarities as the healing power and the wonderful craftsmanship of the Irish Tuatha Dé Danann and the Welsh Children of Llyr. This Llyr must be equated with the Irish Ler, and his son Manawydan with Manannán. But here the comparison ends. The traditions about these so-called gods never agree completely. Llyr or Ler, the Sea, is a shadowy figure; he may even have been chosen independently in Ireland and in Britain as a god to swear by, and then have become the father of a set of divine magicians. From a linguistic point of view the Irish name Manannán is not identical with the Welsh Manawydan. Scholars have sometimes equated the Welsh Lludd Silverhand with the Irish Nuadu Silverhand, accepting a change of *Nudd* into *Lludd* owing to the tendency to make the name alliterate with the epithet (*Llaw Ereint*). But the Welsh name of London, *Caerludd,* seems to forbid this construction.

It has already been observed that from such a very plain and natural name as Finn or Gwynn ('White') nothing can be inferred. More significant is the identity of the name of the Irish divinity Nuadu with that of the Welsh Nudd, which in a British inscription from Roman times has even come down to us in the older form *Nodons (Nodens).*

Why are these traces of common Celtic divinities so faint? There are two possible solutions. Either theism was but little more developed among the ancient Celts than with the later Britons and Irish, or it declined and religion returned to a more primitive stage amongst a population that had left the old home and settled down in the insular colonies. It is a well-known fact that colonizing groups are generally of a conservative character. Of the home traditions they stick to those that have the deepest roots in the national conscience, leaving behind what bears a late or a foreign stamp. Religious rites and social observances that either adopted a new appearance at home or faded away to mere formalism, will return to their original significance in entirely new circumstances and cut off from the continual influence of the old surroundings. Further, in the case of Britain and Ireland, there is the possibility of an influence exercised upon the Celtic colonists by the original population.

We turn our eyes to ancient Gaul for some more light. Do we find there the same sequence of oath-strengthening gods, divine magicians, spirits of the land, and exemplary heroes? Are there any traces of mythical and heroic lore intended as a guarantee for an undisputed possession of the land? Although Gaulish civilization, lying open to penetration from many sides, is far from uniform, and although it went through a rapid and vehement process of evolution in the last centuries before our era, yet Gaul was the starting-point of the Celtic tribes of Britain and Ireland. As late as Caesar's time the migration of Belgic population-groups had not yet come to an end.

There is plenty of literary and archaeological evidence that in ancient Gaul divinities were worshipped. There is, for instance, the 'god' *Lugus.* His name re-occurs in both Irish and British literary tradition as *Lug* or *Lleu.* More correspondences of this type can be cited. No doubt there is a possibility that the same name may have been chosen independently in different parts of the Celtic world for some divine being. This follows from the plain character of the names. Lugus derives his name from an animal, the lynx.[32] The Gaulish *Senacus,* which is identical with the Irish *Senach* and the Welsh *Hynog,* simply means 'the Aged One'. A similar meaning has *Sirona,* which returns in the Irish *Síorna Saeglach;* the etymon is the Irish adjective *sír,* Welsh *hir* 'long'. With the Gaulish *Segomo(n)* the name *Netta Segomonas* of an Irish ogam-inscription (later Irish *Nia Segamain*) has been compared; the interpretation is 'the Victorious One'. One of the most common elements in Gaulish proper names is *Boduo-*, and that this also denoted a divinity with an animal name appears from the Irish noun *bodb*, 'a scaldcrow' or 'a female war genius'. A famous correspondence of Gaulish and insular Celtic mythology is furnished by the Welsh *Mabon ab Modron.* In Gaulish this personality would be called *Maponos*, son of *Matrona,* and both names occur in more than one inscription. *Maponos* simply means 'the Youthful One' and *Matrona* 'the Motherly One'. Of all these equations none is of so stringent a character that it could not be accidental. The similarity of the Gaulish *Ogmios*, denoting, according to Lucian, 'the god of eloquence', and the Irish *Ogmae*, one of the Tuatha Dé Danann, is even misleading. Linguistic rules forbid their identification and *Ogmae* is but a derivation from *Ogam,* the name of the earliest Irish alphabet.

However, if credulity is a vice, hypercriticism is one, too. The correspondences demonstrate by their number what each of them would not prove by itself. The existence of a number of names for divine beings common to the continental and the insular Celts cannot be denied. Unfortunately the information regarding the true nature of these deities, furnished by either archaeological or literary sources, is deplorably poor. If the name symbolizes an outstanding quality, the divinity may have been of the exemplary type. This can be proved for Senacus, whose Irish counterpart Senach is 'invoked' in a prayer for long life, that is, he was exhibited to the life energy itself as an example of old age. For Sirona the Irish evidence is less conclusive, but it points in the same direction. Síorna Saeglach figures in the Annals of the Four Masters (*A. M.* 4169) as a prehistoric king of the race of Erimon who reached the age of one hundred and fifty years and defeated both the demoniacal Fomore and the human invaders from Ulster. Thus he appears as an exemplary protector, of the aged type, of a distinct population-group. If the associations attaching to these names were not different in Gaul from what they were in Ireland, then Segomo would be an exemplary victor in battle. Inscriptions with the name *Matrona* (Welsh: Modron) usually have it in the plural, and in a few instances *Lug* is also found in the old plural form *Lugoves.* This points to groups of divinities, not unlike the Irish Tuatha Dé Danann, and to the deification of the land. With these the singular form must be taken as a common noun rather than a proper name. Probably this remark applies also to other deities with names borrowed from animals. *Bodb* is not uncommon in the plural; in Gaul the name has only been preserved as a first element of compounds.

So far as the scanty evidence leaves room for conclusions, the mythological names represented both in Gaul and the islands denote either exemplary figures or group divinities. Apart from these, the Gaulish inscriptions reveal the names of a number of divine beings suggestive of a more individual character. Still it is very doubtful how much of all this is ancient. Gaulish society was, of course, far more complicated than that of other Celtic populations. It was continually in touch with Mediterranean civilization and under this influence it would naturally develop the notion of a god in the classical sense. The old divinities, in their various characters, could easily be raised to a higher standard. That this is what really happened, may be gathered from some of the names. If *Esus,* for instance, means 'the Good One', we cannot help being reminded of 'the Aged One' or 'the Victorious One'. *Teutates* is proved by the name itself to be an ancient tribal divinity; his primitive function can hardly have been anything but that of a protector, either divine or heroic. As to *Taranis* or *Taranos,* his name derives from a Celtic word (Welsh *taran,* Irish *torann*) denoting the thunder as an acoustic phenomenon.[33] In fact, he might be an ancient god in the typically Celtic sense of a strengthener of the oath. It is in the oath that the natural phenomena appear among the Celtic nations as superior powers interfering in human affairs. In this capacity Taranis would naturally be a common Celtic mythological figure, and this suggestion is confirmed by the proper name *Glifieu Eil Taran* for one of the companions of the Children of Llyr in Welsh mythological story.[34] It means 'Son of Thunder' and recalls the Irish name of a divinity 'Son of the Sun' (*Mac Gréine*), of whom we know that he was so called because the sun was his god or oath-strengthener.

In studying Gaulish religion the information supplied by the Roman authors, especially Caesar, must not be neglected. Yet it should be used critically as it contains a fair amount of *interpretatio romana,* or rather, *interpretatio pro Romanis.*[35] However, deities named by Caesar and attested by inscriptions cannot be fictitious; only the suitability of the Latin equations and the description of the god's function are open to doubt. Besides, there is always the possibility of survivals in Gaulish religion of notions or observances pertaining to the pre-Celtic inhabitants of the country, about whom we know next to nothing.

Of the great Gaulish gods, as enumerated by Caesar, Mars makes a very Roman impression. To him the spoils of battle are offered—Caesar has seen this with his own eyes—whereas in insular Celtic religion there is no trace of sacrifice. The archaeological evidence is not conclusive, and of literary there is none. That sacrifice could be introduced from foreign usage appears from the scene of Bran, son of Derg (*Acc. na Sen.,* ll. 920 sqq.), who begins by refusing to pay the tenth part of his game to the Church, but complies when Cáilte insists. Still, although the Gaulish Mars doubtless has adopted non-Celtic traits, there is some evidence that at the same time he represents an originally Celtic divinity. According to Caesar (*B. G.* 7. 2) the Gauls swear by their raised standards of battle, and this is their most solemn oath. This practice discloses the Gaulish Mars as an oath-strengthening god, whose primitive nature unfortunately escapes us. Of a similar character was, doubtless, Jupiter; he is naturally identified with the Gaulish Taranis, whose function we have traced already. When Caesar declares that he rules the sky, this is well in harmony with our interpretation, since in Irish the sun and the moon are frequently invoked for the confirmation of the oath.[36] As a result of Caesar's diplomatic relations with the Gaulish tribes, the oath-strengthening gods would naturally rank foremost in his opinion. Apart from Mars and Jupiter, Caesar names three more principal gods of Gaul; Mercury, the inventor of arts, Apollo, the healer of diseases, and Minerva, the teacher of crafts. The resemblance of these gods to the Irish Tuatha Dé Danann and the Welsh Children of Llyr springs to the eyes. Their individualities have crystallized from the collectivity of a similar group. Mercury evidently developed among trading people. The commercial men formed a social class with which the Romans were familiar, and this accounts for the prominent position assigned by Caesar to Mercury.

Caesar's five chief gods of Gaul represent two types of Celtic deities. This conclusion is based upon the actual evidence on both sides. Mars and Jupiter are originally oath-strengtheners, of the type that in Ireland is classed as 'gods', and Mercury, Apollo, and Minerva are benevolent and protecting divinities of the land. We cannot make out whether their individualities had already developed to a stage where the designation as 'gods' would be justified in our eyes. This depends upon the degree of romanizing on one side, and of Caesar's *interpretatio romana* on the other. Of Jupiter we know at least the Gaulish name. Was there, then, no hero-worship in Gaul, such as is so strikingly prominent in Ireland and Britain?

A most interesting figure is Heracles, although Caesar does not mention him. Lucian equates him with the Gaulish Ogmios, the god of eloquence, but without sufficient foundation. Diodorus Siculus, on the other hand, characterizes the Gaulish Heracles in a manner that recalls very strikingly the insular Celtic protecting-heroes, Finn and Arthur. He collects supporters, takes his place at the head of his troops, protects the land by abolishing lawlessness and subduing barbarous tribes; and as a centre for his protective activity he founds the city of Alesia. Obviously Alesia is to this Gaulish hero what the hill of Almu was to Finn and Caerleon to Arthur. The inference is that the character of the protecting exemplary hero belongs not only to the insular Celts but to the common Celtic stock. We do not know his Gaulish name. The Gaulish Heracles affords a precious confirmation of our argument concerning Finn and Arthur. The identification with the Greek Heracles is, of course, based upon the similarity of their exploits and upon the legend that in the course of his adventures the famous Hellenic hero also visited the shores of Gaul.[37]

We conclude with a remark on Apollo, the Healer. The interdependence of music and healing power is a commonplace in the Irish mythical stories. Fairy music is in itself a cure for all diseases. In North-British inscriptions Apollo has the surname of Maponos 'The Youth'. The combination of youth, healing-power, music, and heavenly bliss is typically Celtic. As a counterpart of the Gaulish Apollo Maponos let us remember the numerous youths of plenty among the Irish Tuatha Dé Danann.[38] In Gaul the belief in the magical energy of youth even had a social effect. There was a curious law (Caesar, *B. G.* 6. 18) that children, not yet capable of bearing arms, must not be seen publicly in the company of their fathers. This means that they form a separate group with, of course, its own religious symbol. Maponos seems to be their exemplary divinity, Maponos, or Mabon, who according to Welsh tradition was taken away, three days old, from between his mother and the wall. In Ireland there are also consecrated unions of the young, such as the noble youths of Ulster (in the Cú Chulainn cycle), or the yeomanry of the Tuatha Dé Danann, whose leader was Lug. The method of interpreting and expanding the sparse evidence on Gaulish religious thought from the Irish and Welsh material yields precious results, although our authorities are naturally silent regarding its magical basis.

The difficulty was to trace a central idea amidst the intricacies of insular Celtic tradition. Now that we have hit upon this, a wonderful light falls upon the Gaulish fragments too. Gaul had its mythical and heroic lore, much like the insular Celts; in Gaul the young formed a separate social class. They were the Gaulish apprentices. Their instruction was committed to the druids. These taught them many thousands of verses, says Caesar. Is it too bold to suggest that what Caesar calls a body of verse was in reality a collection of exemplary traditions, either in verse or prose, intended to prepare the young for their task of protecting the land from demoniac and human enemies? The highest grade was acquired not in Gaul, but in Britain. The best-gifted pupils used to cross the Channel and to remain away for many years. In Britain the druidical doctrine had been found originally (*disciplina reperta*). Commentators have asked why Caesar did not use the far more natural word 'invented' (*inventa*) instead of 'found' (*reperta*). The answer is that according to druidic belief their wisdom was not really an invention but an element of eternity, found existing at the moment when the first Celtic colonists landed on the British coast.[39] Here we recognize once more a fundamental idea that unites all the Celtic peoples and their store of paradigmatic tradition. It is the notion of the Land of Learning. The Tuatha Dé Danann received their potent knowledge from Greece; Cian, Lug's father, brought his home from Lochlann (or Norway); Cú Chulainn was sent to the Alps in the eastern world. To the Irish mind Greece, Norway, and the Alps were but names of fairy-land. The druids of Gaul, who had statues made for their divinities, transformed this mythical conception into a palpable reality. To them this fair island, rising from the sea, was the Land of Learning. Such it has remained for many of us up to the present day.

Notes

¹ Amra Choluim Chille, see *Lebor na Huidre,* ed. by R. I. Best and O. Bergin (Dublin, 1929), l. 1182; *admuniu[r] móritge meic Ethne ainm.* Ninine's Prayer, see *Thes. Pal.* ii. 322: *admuinemmar nóeb Patraicc . . . Dia lem la itge Patraicc.* Spell in the Stowe Missal, see *Thes. Pal.* ii. 250: *admuiniur epscop nIbar íccas . . . ronícca do súil sén Dée et C[ríst].* 'An Old-Irish Prayer for Long Life', ed. by K. Meyer (*A Miscellany presented to J. M. Mackay,* 1914, p. 228): *admuiniur m'argetnia nad ba nad beba . . . domthá aurchur n-aimsire ó Ríg inna n-uile.*

² The story is found in two episodes of the Colloquy of the Ancients, see *Acallamh na Senorach,* ed. by Whitley Stokes (Stokes and Windisch, Irische Texte, iv. 1, Leipzig, 1900), ll. 5452-631 and 6083-353; S. H. O'Grady, *Silva Gadelica,* ii. 233 sqq. The three Sons of the King of Iruath visit the Fiann, together with their hound, and promise to protect Ireland on three conditions, namely, that they shall not be approached during the night, that it shall not be attempted to provide them with any food, that the poorest game-country shall be allotted to them. Besides, they must never be questioned as to their true nature. This is accepted by the Fiann. In turn, the hound vomits gold and silver for them and the water in their drinking-horns is turned into mead (Stokes, ll. 5452-514). During the night the divine protectors hide themselves behind a wall of fire. One day, the two Ulster princes leap over it and see the hound, now no larger than a lap-dog, pouring the choicest drinks from its mouth into the drinking-horns. As soon as it perceives the princes it sends forth a fiery wind, which makes ashes of their bodies (ll. 5555-631). The Fiann are vexed at the mysteriousness of their protectors and conspire to kill them. From this they are dissuaded by Finn, who bids the three leave him, but allows them to remain when they have disclosed their names (ll. 6083-141). Then the Sons of Uar appear and desire a tribute from the Fiann. When this is refused, they threaten to extinguish the Fiann (ll. 6146-76). Finn tells his heroes to prepare each his own rampart. This he also does himself. The three Sons of the King of Iruath ward off the Sons of Uar from the Fiann and heal their wounds. Finn himself receives the protection of the hound, on condition that it shall never be lodged in one house with fire, arms, or an-

other dog; from this moment it turns round Finn thrice an hour, licks him, and diffuses a smell like mead and apples (ll. 6177-210). In the meantime, King Cormac of Tara, who has heard of the sufferings of Finn and his men, invites the Sons of the King of Iruath to his court and at his request one of them pronounces a charm, with the effect that the demons fly towards the sea and kill each other with their swords (ll. 6211-69). Then follows the story of the two Munster princes and Cáilte's spell (ll. 6270-353); the arrival amongst the Fiann of the princes is told in ll. 5895-909.

³ Edited by K. Meyer, *Zeitschr. f. celt. Phil.* iii. 433 sq.

⁴ The text contains two passages referring to the magical virtues of the Sons of the King of Iruath. Cf. *Acc. na Sen.,* ll. 5461-70: 'I shall discharge the watching of the Fianna of Ireland and Scotland', said one of them. 'Every stress of battle and combat that shall befall the Fiann, I shall ward it off for them all, let them all but keep still', said the other. . . . 'Every serious difficulty that shall arise before my lord, I shall remove it, and everything that shall be demanded from him shall be obtained from me,' said the third; 'and as for the hound, as long as there shall be any deer in Ireland, it shall discharge the hunting for the Fianna of Ireland every second night, and I shall do the like myself on the remaining nights.' *Acc. na Sen.,* ll. 6093-103; and Finn said: 'They possess three arts, and it would not be right for the men of the world to kill them because of these arts'. 'Should the men of the world be in sickness or disease,' said Cáilte, 'then one of the three would apply herbs to their ailments, so that they would be smooth and scarless. And whatever is asked of the second man is gotten from him. And as to the third man, let the wants of the world be told to him, and they will be satisfied without failing. And there was still more, as well as all these: he had a pipe, and the men of the world would sleep at its sound, however great their pains. And as to the hound,' said Cáilte, 'even though none of us should kill a deer or (other) animal, thanks to it we should never be in want.'

⁵ The only case where the Irish texts (with the exception of Aided Clainne Tuirill Picrenn, on which see note 6) use the word *dee,* 'gods', is in the name of the Tuatha Dé Danann and in the oath. 'Gods' are invoked in order that the oath may be sanctioned by them. Cf., for instance, *Lebor na Huidre,* l. 5504: *artungsa deu* (in the *Táin Bó Cualgne*), Book of Leinster, 55 a 12: *dothung mo deo da n-adraim (Táin Bó Cualgne,* ed. Windisch, l. 143), Book of Leinster, 108 b 18: *atbiursa mo dee* (in the text *Gessa agus ilberta bítis for Coin Culainn,* edited by Wh. Stokes, *Rev. celt.* xiv. 396 sqq.). Here a lasting relation is implied. The oath would be worthless if the god were at liberty to forsake the swearer. But the word *dee* is only used in the plural and there is no trace of personality in these 'gods'. When Keating says of Mac Cuill, Mac Cécht, and Mac

Gréine that they received their names because *Coll* (Hazel), *Cécht* (Plough), and *Grian* (Sun) were 'gods of adoration (*dee adartha*) to them', he probably gives his own interpretation.

[6] The early version has been published by Thurneysen, *Z. c. P.* xii. 239 sqq.; it consists of a poem and a prose commentary. Of the later recension there are editions by O'Curry (Atlantis iv. 1863), O'Duffy (Dublin, 1902), and Craig (Dublin, 1902). On the different forms of the name (*Tuirill, Tuireann, Piccrenn, Biccrenn, Picreo, Bicreo*) see Thurneysen, loc. cit.

[7] Or a *mytheme,* if it may be allowed to coin a new term which would prove very useful for the study of comparative mythology.

[8] It might be suggested that the revelation of a god for the human world was what made the early Irish embrace Christianity with so much fervour. To the Norsemen (and probably other Germanic tribes) the motive was different. They longed to be relieved from the wandering of the soul after death.

[9] See Duanaire Finn, *The Book of the Lays of Fionn,* edited by Eoin MacNeill, i (London, 1908), p. xxiv sqq. (Irish Texts Soc., vol. vii). Professor MacNeill has shown that the connexion with the high-kings of Tara, and with Conn of the Hundred Battles in particular, was not there at the earliest stage. At all events, the connexion with the subject races of Leinster, and of other provinces, is older. Hence the Fenian Cycle would reflect the epic tradition of the subject races of Ireland, which constituted two-thirds of the population. It would have been orally transmitted during the time when the Ulster epic was receiving its final shape at the hands of men of letters, who were the representatives of a new aristocracy. It is true that in 'The Youthful Exploits of Finn', Cumall, the chieftain's father, is slain by the race of Morna and the men of Conn, whereas his death is avenged on a chief of the subject race of the Luagni. The contradiction is removed by the assumption that originally the Luagni were responsible for Cumall's death also, in which case the story would preserve the memory of a conflict of subject races. But this does not prove that the historical connexion is the primitive element in Fenian tradition. The same objection applies to the argument that only the subject races were required to furnish a militia of the type of the Fiann. On the Viking traditions see R. Th. Christiansen, *The Vikings and the Viking Wars in Irish and Gaelic Tradition,* Oslo, 1931.

[10] See *Red Book Mabinogion* (Oxford, 1887), pp. 113, 134; J. Loth, *Les Mabinogion,* i (Paris, 1913), pp. 284, 331; *Acc. na Sen.,* ll. 5917 sqq.

[11] The tombstone of *Anir filius Arthuri militis* is described in the *Mirabilia Britanniae,* the appendix to

Nennius's *Historia Britonum,* see A. G. van Hamel, *Lebor Bretnach* (Dublin, 1932), p. 80. On the dwarf of Tara's grave see *Acc. na Sen.,* ll. 7978-93, and R. A. S. Macalister, *Tara, A Pagan Sanctuary of Ancient Ireland,* p. 58.

[12] See, for instance, *Duanaire Finn,* ii, ed. by G. Murphy (London, 1933), pp. 184 sqq.

[13] Cafal's footprint and tombstone occur in the *Mirabilia Britanniae.* Of Bran it is said that its sides were white, its tail purple, its legs blue, its paws green, and its nails pale red (*Duan. Finn,* ii. 198).

[14] For Rhita Gawr see Loth, *Les Mab.* i. 314 and ii. 303; Geoffrey of Monmouth, *Hist. Reg. Brit.,* ed. by A. Griscom (London, 1929), p. 473; T. Gwynn Jones, *Welsh Folklore and Folk-custom* (London, 1929), pp. 77-9. The ballad of Finn slaying the monster of Loch Derg: *Duan. Finn,* ii. 234 sqq.

[15] See *Red Book Mab.,* p. 134; *Acc. na Sen.,* ll. 7264 sqq.

[16] See *Lebor Bretnach,* p. 71; *Acc. na Sen.,* ll. 4774 sqq. On Arthur and Huail, son of Caw, see Baring-Gould and Fisher, *The Lives of the British Saints,* iii. 106.

[17] See *Red Book Mab.,* pp. 134, 128, 131 sqq.; E. K. Chambers, *Arthur of Britain* (London, 1927), pl 263; *Text of the Book of Taliessin,* ed. by J. Gwen. Evans (Llanbedrog, 1910), pp. 54 sqq.

[18] For Finn's battle against the Dogheads see *Duan. Finn,* ii. 20 sqq. The Dogheads number three thousand and land in the north. They kill many of the Fiann, but are at length beaten by Finn. The ballad describes 'each dog's tooth as large as a man's fist, and its circuit equal to a warrior's grasp'.

[19] The act of drinking from a particular well may have the deeper meaning of a communication with the earth and a magical enlightenment as to its secrets. This notion is found among both Britons and Irish. On their respective expeditions to Fairy Land both Owein, Arthur's knight, and Diarmaid, Finn's warrior, approach the spirits of the land by drinking from a magic well, with a magical drinking-horn (cf. J. Rhŷs, *Hibbert Lectures,* 1888, pp. 187 sqq.). Knowledge is a spiritualized form of communication.

[20] For the war of the Tuatha Dé Danann with the Fomore see the *Second Battle of Moytura,* ed. by Wh. Stokes (*Rev. celt.,* xii. 52 sqq.). The famous leech of the Tuatha Dé Danann was Dian Cécht, but he was outshone by his son, whom he slew out of envy (O'Curry in *Atlantis,* iv. 158). One of the most attractive members of their race is Cas Corach. He follows Cáilte and the Fiann,

until he receives the blessing of St. Patrick, and entertains his companions with his exquisite fairy-music (*Acc. na Sen.*, pass.). Aillén mac Midna, on the other hand, is of the wicked type; every year, on All-Hallows, he brings sleep over the Fiann with his music and sets the hall of Tara on fire (*Acc. na Sen.*, ll. 1662 sqq.). Finn himself, however, is saved by his magical spear (l. 1719). On the Feast of Goibniu see *Acc. na Sen.*, ll. 6402 sq. The Tuatha Dé Danann have other magical objects besides that enable them to conserve their blessed state, e.g. the so-called Four Jewels of the T.D.D., on which see V. Hull, *Z.c.P.* xviii. 73 sqq.

[21] Cf. *Pedeir Keinc y Mabinogi*, ed. by I. Williams (Cardiff, 1930), pp. 47 (Bran's head), 63 (Manawydan's mice), 34 (the healing cauldron), 46 (the birds of Rhiannon); J. Loth, *Les Mab.* i, pp. 129, 148, 149, 168.

[22] Créde provides milk and healing during the battle (*Acc. na Sen.*, ll. 829 sqq.). On the tooth of wisdom see R. D. Scott, *The Thumb of Knowledge* (New York, 1930), and on the *geasa* J. R. Reinhard, *The Survival of 'Geis' in Mediaeval Romance* (Halle, 1933).

[23] Arthur disinters Bran's head because he desires all the glory for himself; see Loth, *Les Mab.* ii. 242. The story of Arthur's game of chess occurs in Rhonabwy's Dream (*Red Book Mab.*, pp. 153 sqq.; Loth, *Les Mab.*, i. 364 sqq.); it affords an interesting instance of magic in the second power. Arthur's crushing of the chessmen causes the defeat of Owein's ravens and this, again, the discomfiture of the Saxons.

[24] On the magical obligations of kings see J. Baudiš, *Eriu*, viii. 101 sqq., and J. Reinhard, op. cit., 107 sqq. On the Thirteen Jewels of Britain: R. S Loomis, *Rom. Forsch.* xlv. 68 sqq. On foot-holders and bedmen at insular Celtic courts: J. Rhŷs, *Hibbert Lectures*, p. 305; O'Curry, *Manners and Customs*, iii. 143 sqq.; I. Williams, *Pedeir Keinc*, p. 67; Geoffrey of Monmouth, *Hist. Reg. Brit.* xii. 2 (ed. Griscom, pp. 513 sqq.).

[25] See K. Meyer, *Fianaigecht*, Dublin, 1910 (Todd Lect. Series, no. 16).

[26] See *Tripartite Life of St. Patrick*, ed. by Wh. Stokes, i (London, 1887), p. 48; *Eriu*, xi. 224.

[27] The technical term for this form of protection is *gress*, on which see *Eriu*, xi. 94 sqq.

[28] See *Duan. Finn*, ii. 60 sqq. The philosophy of this ballad (as of many other specimens of Fenian literature) recalls Plato's ideal world.

[29] *Dux bellorum* would make a very satisfactory equivalent for *rígféinnid*, the Irish title of Finn.

[30] On Caer Sidi see R. S. Loomis, *Speculum*, viii. 428sq. On Mabon's prison at Gloucester: W. J. Gruffydd, *Y Cymmrodor*, xlii. 129 sqq. Finn himself is imprisoned by a divine magician (*Duan. Finn*, ii. 60 sq.) and by a witch (*Béaloideas*, ii. 26 sqq.).

[31] A substantial account of the different doctrines relating to the name Mabinogion is found in the introduction to Prof. I. Williams's edition of *Pedeir Keinc y Mabinogi* (Cardiff, 1930), pp. xlii sqq. On p. xlix Prof. Williams remarks that in our texts the 'Mabinogi' traditions of different parts of Wales have coalesced, and that originally Gwynedd and Dyfed, Powys and Gwent had their own tales; cf. also I. Williams, *The Poetry of Llywarch Hen* (Sir John Rhŷs Mem. Lect. for 1932), p. 16. Similarly in Ireland each of the provinces originally had its own *fiannaigecht*, but in texts like the Colloquy of the Ancients and the Dindsenchas it was joined together. Here is another illustration of the inner affinity of the Irish and the Welsh material.

[32] Irish *lug* still denotes a lynx. In Welsh, *lleu* no longer occurs in this sense. But the evolution of *lleu* to *llew* 'a lion' (in the proper name *Llew Llawgyffes*), shows that the episode of how Llew Llawgyffes got his name (in the Mabinogi of Math ab Mathonwy), conveyed to the keepers of the tradition the notion that the name was that of a wild animal.

[33] The word is not related to Latin *tonare* or English *thunder*.

[34] See I. Williams, *Pedeir Keinc*, p. 44. The Red Book has the form *Gliuieri*.

[35] Cf. Caesar's *De Bello Gallico*, vi. 13 sqq.

[36] Cf. also the reply of certain Celtic envoys to Alexander the Great: 'We fear nothing save that perchance the sky may fall upon our heads' (R. A. S. Macalister, *Tara, A Pagan Sanctuary of Ancient Ireland*, p. 14).

[37] The passages in Lucian (*Heracles*, 1-5) and Diodorus Siculus (*Bibl.* iv. 19) are rendered by Dottin, *Manuel pour servir à l'étude de l'antiquité celtique*, 2nd ed., pp. 301 sq., 311 sqq. If Lucian's *Ogmios* has anything at all to do with the Gaulish counterpart of Heracles, then the figure having numerous chains linked to its tongue, and thus leading all those to whose ears the chains are attached, might symbolize the exemplary hero as the embodier of traditions to be imitated by those employed in the protection of the land. What Diodorus describes is evidently the career of the Gaulish equivalent of Heracles.

[38] One of the names of the Land of the Bliss in Irish is *Tír-na-nÓg*, 'the Land of the Young', not 'the Land of Youth' as it is usually rendered. A typical instance

of an Irish Apollo Maponos is Cas Corach, on whom see note 20.

[39] Likewise the roads of Ireland had been 'discovered' when Conn of the Hundred Battles was born (R. A. S. Macalister, op. cit., p. 78 sq.). The roads, as a vital organ of the land, are divine, eternal, and uncreated.

James MacKillop (1986)

SOURCE: "The Myth of Fionn mac Cumhaill in Irish Literature," in *Fionn mac Cumhaill: Celtic Myth in English Literature*, Syracuse University Press, 1986, pp. 1-36.

[*In the following essay, MacKillop studies the long and varied tradition surrounding the Irish mythological hero Fionn mac Cumhaill.*]

Although the English people had shared the British Isles with several Celtic peoples for fourteen centuries, English writers, by and large, did not discover the Celtic world until the sensational success in the 1760s of James Macpherson's *Poems of Ossian,* a bogus rendering of Scottish Gaelic ballads. Despite a critical rebuke from Dr. Johnson and much general controversy over their authenticity, the poems were widely read all over Europe and provided an introduction to Celtic literature for a score of important poets, critics, and tastemakers, including such diverse talents as Goethe, Blake, James Fenimore Cooper, and Matthew Arnold. Not many were taken by the intrinsic art of the poems; after all, Macpherson always described himself as a translator and virtually no one knew the language of the original. That they could be read at all was cause for celebration. Best of all for Macpherson's fortunes, *Ossian* appeared in the midst of a general European fashion for the primitive and ancient. In them, the reader could seize a literary tradition that had survived among somewhat backward people living on the fringes of modern society, a tradition so archaic that it provided a link between the present and the time of Homer.

The *Poems* was ascribed to Ossian because so many of the ballads Macpherson employed were composed in the persona of Oisín or Ossian, an old Celtic warrior and poet who sang the glories of a world recently lost to him. The most frequent subject of the poems, as Macpherson "translated" them, was Fingal, Ossian's father. In subsequent decades Fingal and Ossian would become widely celebrated figures in European literature, as would Ossian's son, the noble Oscar, whose name, for example, would be given to more than a half-dozen members of Scandinavian royal houses.

The Fingal of Macpherson's *Ossian* was based on a figure of traditional Gaelic literature, Fionn mac Cumhaill. . . . [There] was some confusion in the minds of Macpherson and his contemporaries about the relationship of the Irish and Scottish Gaelic languages, and thus many early commentators, no matter what they felt about Macpherson's "authenticity," thought that there should be a distinction drawn between the Scottish Fingal and the Irish Fionn. The desire of scholars to know the background of the Macpherson question helped to lead to the development, especially in France and Germany, of the academic study of the Celtic languages. By the end of the nineteenth century a sufficient number of manuscripts had been edited and translated to demolish the pretensions of Macpherson and, more importantly, to give the rest of the Western world an understanding of the extent, complexity, and beauty of literature in the Celtic languages. Most of the effort in this first chapter will be to determine just what kind of character Fionn was in Irish and Scottish Gaelic literature so we can understand what transformations he underwent as he became a figure in English literature.

The two centuries of scholarship since the time of Macpherson have also given us a better understanding of the relationship between Celtic and English literature. Although the Celtic languages provide a paucity of loan words to English, we now know that there has been a steady transmission of Celtic themes and characters into English literature since early medieval times. . . . [The] archetype of Fionn mac Cumhaill is one of the many from Irish and Welsh literatures which have been adapted in the Arthurian legends. As far as we know, Fionn first appeared in English literature under his own name in John Barbour's Lallans dialect *The Bruce* (c. 1375). In the next four hundred years, until the coming of Macpherson, Fionn appeared in a large number of English chronicles and pseudo-histories and also in a number of works of imaginative literature. . . . With the rise of English-language literature in Ireland, beginning in the early nineteenth century, we find almost a hundred depictions of Fionn mac Cumhaill. . . .

Myth

The suggestion that the disconnected narratives of Fionn mac Cumhaill and his Fianna constitute a mythology would undoubtedly seem a presumption to many modern readers, especially to the Irish, most of whom know him through the storytellers among their country cousins in the *Gaeltacht* or Irish-speaking areas. For them the "tale" or "legend" of Fionn might seem more suitable. Even academics, usually more tolerant of presumption, may balk, more because of their concern for the current debasement of the word "myth." In a much-cited passage of *Hero With a Thousand Faces* (1956), Joseph Campbell summarizes seven different definitions used in mid-century academia, many of which are not only mutually exclusive but contradictory as well. Because the present study is investigative and not polemical, I shall not seek to use one theory or definition against another but rather try to limit myself to the definitions of myth which have been used in the study of traditional literature.

In the eighteenth century, when the study of traditional literature began and the only traditional literature anyone studied was that of ancient Greece, the entire matter was much easier to handle. In the divisions of Greek literature made during the generation of Christian Gottlob Heyne (1729-1810) and Johann Gottfried Herder (1744-1803), "mythology" dealt with the origin of the world and of many, the vicissitudes of vegetation, weather, eclipses, the discovery of fire, and the mystery of death. Under this generalized definition, myth is distinct from legend in that the latter deals with figures people thought to have been historical, who may indeed have been, although their deeds are most likely invented or exaggerated. "Folktales" are purely imaginary and have no other aim than pure entertainment and thus make no real claim to credibility. All the stories of the Titans and the Olympians are therefore myths, from the narratives of creation found in Hesiod's *Theogony* to the romances of the gods, even those incorporating scandal such as the one describing Zeus's pederasty with Ganymede. The love of the non-Olympian Orpheus, on the other hand, may have been legendary, and the amatory and military conquests of King Theseus of Athens are more probably legendary. Many of the adventures of Odysseus, sometimes called myth because they are ancient, are actually folktales. The distinction is carried forth by Sir James Frazer and is given tacit support by such contemporary critics of myth as Northrop Frye. One of Frye's more succinct definitions of myth is "a story in which some of the chief characters are gods" [*Fables of Identity,* 1963].

Under the strictest application of the criteria drawn from Heyne and Herder, it is difficult to argue that there is any surviving body of Celtic mythology at all. The prohibition against putting sacred beliefs in writing in Druidic mystery cults, coupled with early Christianization (fifth century), which sought to destroy profane "pagan" texts, has denied us the hope of finding a Celtic text with a picture of belief comparable to what we find in Hesiod's *Theogony*. This is not to suggest that there was never a Celtic religion or mythology; the handful of studies of Celtic mythology and religion are based largely on archeological artifacts and interpolations and extrapolations of contemporary texts from Roman and Greek authors. Thus in speaking of Celtic gods we do not know if they were anthropomorphic personalities like the Greek, mere *numina* like the Roman, or something much less. Marie-Louise Sjoestedt, in *Gods and Heroes of the Celts,* remarks that it is often difficult to distinguish between gods and heroes in early Celtic narratives, apparently because the dichotomy between mortals and immor-

tals, an importation from the Mediterranean world, was not always honored by Celtic storytellers of different centuries, especially after Christianization.

Unquestionably, many storytellers have considered Fionn not only mortal but historical. This is a question considered more fully in the next chapter, but suffice it for the moment to say that a number of credulous, popular histories of Ireland, for example, Seumas MacManus' *The Story of the Irish Race* (1921), assert that Fionn is not the figment of anyone's imagination but a genuine historical personage. Among better-informed scholars the question of Fionn's historicity has not been seriously entertained since the late nineteenth century. What is significant in the Irish peasant's tenacious belief in Fionn's historicity is that the hero is usually portrayed as an immortal who always lives in the present. Even as late as 1969, E. Estyn Evans came upon a farmer in County Cavan who spoke of Fionn and his men in the present indicative. "He's not a giant," the man said. "He's only five-foot six."

Such evidence suggests that Fionn is much more than a character in folklore and is at least a legendary hero, similar in status to, say, King Arthur of Camelot. Before we can argue that Fionn is more than a mortal, we must consider the kind of evidence open to us. Traditional literature in Irish, as in other vernaculars, is of two modes, the written or "manuscript," transmitted by literate poets, storytellers, and scribes, and oral tradition, which is transmitted by the unlettered. The term "unlettered" did not carry the pejorative implications of being ignorant or uncouth in earlier centuries, especially in Ireland where there was a professional class of trained but illiterate story-tellers. As Gerard Murphy has pointed out in his Introduction to Volume III of *Duanaire Finn* (1953), the manuscript and oral traditions can be demonstrated to exist side by side in Irish at least since the eleventh century. The figure of Fionn mac Cumhaill is essentially the same in both, even though the different traditions usually portray different aspects of his personality. The question of which came first, oral or written, is still moot, even though it has been the subject of much scholarly dispute for more than one hundred and fifty years; abundant argument exists to support both sides of the question in Irish as well as in other vernaculars. The relevance of reviewing the two traditions here is that most of the support for the contention that Fionn had divine origin is found in manuscripts written by the learned class.

Quite a bit of scholar's ink has been spilled in the last hundred years on the question of Fionn's divinity. Although there is so little unambiguous evidence as to limit positive conclusions, the subject cannot be shrugged off. Our assumptions about Fionn's origins have much to do with the classifications of Fenian narratives. If Fionn were an historical figure, as uninformed popular opinion has long supposed, or if he were only an aggrandized figure from folk imagination, then perhaps the stories about him would best be classified as legends. But if the persona of Fionn includes elements of the supernatural, then contemporary scholarship is more justified in thinking of him as a mythical figure.

In many stories, admittedly, Fionn does not seem like a god. He cannot control the weather, travel through time, or bring fire. There are no surviving prayers in Fionn's honor, no incantations, shrines, or votive paraphernalia. On the other hand he has what appear to be divinities in his genealogy, he has magical powers to foretell the future, and he may be able to overcome death.

Some of the most persuasive arguments for Fionn's divinity were given by T. F. O'Rahilly in his landmark study, *Early Irish History and Mythology* (1946). In O'Rahilly's view Fionn was an anthropomorphized remnant of a Celtic god worshipped on the Continent and in the British Isles (pp. 271, 277-78). This same pre-Christian god was the original for the heroes of the other two cycles of Old Irish literature, Lugh Lámhfada and Cúchulainn. O'Rahilly's proposal has received wide acceptance from informed commentators but is based on linguistic and circumstantial evidence.

More compelling in O'Rahilly's discussion is Fionn's power of prophecy, which the hero can summon by chewing his thumb, an attribute he shares with Heracles, the Norse figure Sigurd, and the Welsh Taliesin. In a lengthy chapter devoted to prophecy and devination (pp. 318-40), O'Rahilly argues that Fionn was accorded the unique powers of *imbas forosnai* (roughly "foresight") and *teinm laída* (again, roughly, "break open the pith" or "superhuman intuition"). Within narratives Fionn wears his powers lightly. He does not exploit his gifts to win a high status in his society; instead, he is a leader among men because he excels at what all men can do—hunting and making poetry. When he does use his supernatural power, the effect is to disentangle him from a quandary or to free the narrative from an impasse. More significantly, Fionn's powers are the subject of debate between Patrick, when that saint becomes a figure in Fenian narrative, and the aged survivors of the Fianna, Oisín and Caoilte. Saint Patrick forbids the practice of *imbas forosnai* and *teinm laída* in an evangelized Ireland. The old Fenians lament the passing of pagan Ireland and champion the generosity and heroism of Fionn's time as against the Christian present.

The most certain divinity of Fionn's genealogy is Nuadu Argetlám, or "Nuadu of the Silver Hand," described in manuscript literature as the king of the Tuatha Dé Danann, the race of immortals who inhabited Ireland before the present generation of humanity arrived. Not only is Nuadu an immortal, but he is an Irish counter-

part of the British god Nodons, whose cult flourished in Roman Britain and whose temple ruin may be found at Lydney Park, Gloucester. Nuadu's divinity does not automatically pass on to Fionn, of course, as many early historical Irish, including the entire Eóganacht federation of families in Munster, also claimed the same descent. This is little different from genealogies of ancient Greece in which a distinguished family, such as Erichthonius and his progeny of Athens, claimed descent from the virgin Athena.

A final indication of the residual belief in Fionn's divinity is his ability to overcome death. Fionn does face death, according to different stories, under different forms, a subject considered later in this chapter. Whether he faces death on the battlefield at the hands of many, or alone and slain by a single assassin, he is somehow taken away to a hidden place where he "sleeps" and will return to his people when he is needed. The same is true, of course, of such heroic figures as Arthur and Barbarossa, who are not perceived as gods. Folklorists classify such stories under the "Sleeping Warriors" or "Sleeping Army" motif, index number E502 in the Aarne-Thompson classification. The promise of Fionn's return found more reverence in the popular mind: there are more than thirty-five locations, in both Ireland and Gaelic Scotland, where Fionn and his men are supposed to be sleeping. Readers of *Finnegans Wake* will recognize that Joyce took a little-known Dublin variant of this motif to help structure that narrative. Joyce felt, as others have, that Fionn's ability to conquer death was not separate from the rest of his adventures.

Indeed, Fionn overcomes death in two identities, as himself, and also as Mongan, an Ulster petty king of the seventh century, described in the eighth-century narrative *Imram Brain,* "The Voyage of Bran, Son of Febal" (edited by D. Nutt, 1895-97, vol. I, pp. 52; vol. II, pp. 6, 281). In a dispute with the court bard, Mongan allows himself to be portrayed as the reincarnated Fionn. The story is narrated by one of Mongan's warriors, alleging himself to be the reincarnated Caoilte. In the story Mongan/Fionn deals quickly with his enemies as, by implication, King Mongan will now.

The evidence when assembled does not prove Fionn's divinity, but it does suggest that if Fionn is not quite a god, he seems to be at least something more than a warrior-hunter-poet of a great mass of stories. Perhaps the safest judgment is that given by Alexander MacBain as long ago as 1894 [in *Transactions of the Gaelic Society of Glasgow*], when the impact of modern anthropology was first felt on the study of mythology:

> Fionn is, like Heracles, Theseus, Perseus, and other such persons of Greek Myth, a culture hero— probably originally a local deity raised to a national place. He is an incarnation of the chief diety of the

race—the Mercury, whom Caesar tells us the Gauls worship—a god of literary and mercantile character. His grandson Oscar is a reflection of the war god, and other characters of the Fenian band no doubt correspond to the other personages of the Gaelic Olympus.

MacBain's analysis makes two points, one explicitly and other implicitly. The first is that Fionn compares with three great heroes of Greek mythology, all of them having some links to the divine. The second is the use of the term "culture hero," which is probably more apt to a Celtic context than in a Greek one. "Culture hero" was first used to describe figures in non-European mythology, such as the Coyote of California Indians or Gluskabe of those in the Northeast. Among the North American Indians there is not a clear demarcation between heroes and gods; a culture hero, whether worshiped or not, is distinct from others by the useful or good things he or she brings. Prometheus, for example, is a culture hero because he is a firebringer, not because he is a Titan. Among the Celts, too, there is no clear line between mortals and immortals. Fionn's status can be grasped by seeing that he is the center of an immense cycle of narratives, much as Heracles is. Fionn is a hunter, poet, seer, and warrior; for those who follow him, he is a benefactor. The persistence of his persona over more than a thousand years argues that his stories offered more than momentary diversion beside the turf fire.

Some questions about the accuracy of speaking of the "myth" of Fionn mac Cumhaill remain. Because the present study purports to say something about English literature, it should acknowledge that the word "myth" has acquired new implications since Joyce's *Ulysses*, Crane's *The Bridge*, or for that matter *King Kong*. Can the narratives of Fionn mac Cumhaill strike a response from our unconscious minds? Do they draw on a character who evokes a memory of the continuity of human experience? In short, do the stories of Fionn *function* as myth as well as meet the tests that distinguish myth from mere legend or folklore? They do. The stories of the Fenian Cycle are not only ancient and continuous but various as well. They embody supposed attributes of the Gaelic peoples: heroic, romantic, ribald, and even absurd. The working-out of these characteristics and values, over centuries and in different genres, is the labor of the next four chapters. A shorter route to the importance of Fionn as an embodiment of the unconsciously held value systems and beliefs of a suppressed nation is given to us by Joyce in *Finnegans Wake*. In it Fionn is among the first residents of the monomyth, the single narrative strand that unites all human experience.

The Context of Irish Literature

Thus far we have established only the externals of the character of Fionn mac Cumhaill. We know he is a figure of traditional Irish literature, sufficiently widely known to be recognized in an allusion today, and we know there is good evidence he is derived from a Celtic god. Such information alone would hardly justify the attention we are giving him, so that it seems a fair question to ask, "Who is—or was—Fionn mac Cumhaill? What does he do that sets him apart from other figures in traditional literature?" The short answer to those questions is that he is the leading figure in one of the great epochs of Irish literature, the focus of several thousand narratives we have called the "Fenian Cycle." An outline of the development of Fionn's character, the major responsibility of this chapter, cannot begin without understanding the place the Fenian Cycle holds in Irish literature. For reasons to be considered later, many scholars prefer to call the cycle "Finnian," in part to denote Fionn's central role in it, or "Ossianic," to underscore Oisín's persona as narrator in many of the tales, especially those from oral tradition. The Fenian Cycle is one of four major branches of narrative in Irish secular literature. The other three are called "Invasions" or "Mythological Cycle," the "Red Branch" or "Ulster Cycle," and the "Cycle of the Kings."

Of the four cycles the "Mythological" is commonly judged to be the oldest. The titling of this cycle, which is sometimes also known as the "Invasions Cycle," indicates that it deals with the origins of Ireland, but it does not mean that the others are less "mythological." Many of the narratives here are pseudo-histories, dealing extensively with the five legendary invasions of Ireland as reconstructed in the *Lebor Gabála*, "The Book of Invasions." Characteristically, much of this cycle is taken up with the recitation of genealogies of rather implausible families (kings sired by animals, multi-armed and multi-headed warriors, etc.). As is so often the case with fabulous histories such as Hesiod's *Works and Days*, the men of earlier days appear to be the champions of glory whereas the men of the present appear to be witless, cowardly, and crude. It follows then that the leading figures of this cycle are not the victors of the fifth invasions, those humans called Milesians; instead, most of the stories concern the Tuatha Dé Danaan, "the tribe of the goddess Danu," the immortals from the fourth invasion who linger to haunt the usually unimaginative, often hapless Milesians.

The narratives of the Ulster or "Red Branch" Cycle appear to be of later composition than the "Mythological" and are the best-known of all four to English readers, largely through the efforts of W. B. Yeats and his contemporaries. Much richer in character and episode than the earlier materials, the narratives of the Ulster Cycle are the product of disciplined court poets and storytellers. Yeats liked to think of them as "aristocratic" because of the patronage of the arts and education by such northerners as Ruaidhrí Ó Conchubhair,

"Rory O'Connor" (fl. 1169), who founded a center of learning in Armagh. "Aristocratic" may seem a misleading description compared to French tastes at the opening of Versailles, but Ulster had been the leading province of Ireland long before the English invasion (1170), and the Ulster families were among the most cultivated in Ireland down to the time of the Flight of the Earls and the Cromwellian plantations of the seventeenth century. The Ulster Cycle includes not only the stories of Cúchulainn and Deirdre but also the "Irish Iliad," *Táin Bó Cuailnge.*

The cycle usually listed third is the Fenian, about which more later, and the fourth is made up of those stories about more or less historical figures that do not fit in the earlier three. Myles Dillon categorized these remainders as the Cycles of the Kings, if "king" is not too grand a translation for the Irish *rí,* denoting petty chieftains who ruled families in different parts of Ireland. The most celebrated of these kings was Brian Boru, who defeated the Danes at Clontarf (A.D. 1014). Other authorities have argued that the stories of Brian and his family should be called the Dalcassian Cycle, after their narrative region in what is now County Clare.

Assembling a Heroic Biography of Fionn Mac Cumhaill from Irish and Gaelic Literatures

The third cycle is usually called the "Fenian," although some informed commentators wince at the term. Despite the similarity of phonology, "Fenian" does not refer to Fionn at all but instead derives from a confusion of *féni,* denoting the oldest, purest, or aboriginal inhabitants of Ireland, and *féinn,* a variant of *fiann/fianna,* implying Fionn's band of merry men. There are many other fianna than Fionn's, however, and the very concept of an independent caste of warrior-hunters may be much older than Irish tradition, having antecedent in the Gaulish *gaesatae* as described by Polybius (second century B.C.) and Roman commentators. What makes the word "Fenian" much more unattractive is that it was coined (in 1804) by the scholarly charlatan, Colonel Charles Vallancey, a man who also argued that the Irish language was derived from Phoenician. Informed readers shunned the word, and it probably would have disappeared if not used by the Irish-American political leader, John O'Mahoney, who adopted "Fenian" for the Irish Republican Brotherhood about 1858. Perhaps because of its political associations, "Fenian" is a term many modern readers recognize easily. Like "Quaker" and "Jesuit," it has become the standard reference despite the implications of its origins.

Rival terms for the cycle are neither more authentic nor more descriptive. "Ossianic," for example, is a neologism derived from Macpherson's spelling of Oisín. At one time it was used to describe all the Irish literature that Macpherson pretended to translate; thus the first large-scale translations of early manuscripts were the *Transactions of the Ossianic Society* of Dublin, 1854-61. The term more accurately describes such works as the *Agallamh na Senórach,* "The Colloquy of the Elders," and subsequent ballad literature, beginning in the thirteenth century, in which Fenians surviving to the Christian era, usually Oisín or Caoilte, wrangle with Saint Patrick over the virtues of the old order.

As suggested earlier, the Fenian has been the most popular and widespread of all four cycles with Irish storytellers, in manuscript tradition and even more with unlettered storytellers. Alfred Nutt [in *Ossian and the Ossianic Literature,* 1910] suggested that as much as 60 percent of all Irish native fiction is from this cycle, and Fenian characters and themes are widely celebrated in lyric, chronicle, pseudo-history, and proverb. Narratives of Fionn and the Fianna have been recorded in all the counties of Ireland as well as in the other two parts of the trifurcated Goidelic branch of Celtic languages on the Isle of Man and throughout Gaelic Scotland. Several dozen place names, such as "Finn MacCool's Pebble," "—Fingerstone," "Fingals' Cave," can be found in many parts of both Ireland and Scotland. Likewise, virtually every dolmen in Ireland has been called "The Bed of Diarmaid and Gráinne," though those primitive constructs, each a miniature Stonehenge, would be unsuited for sleep, much less lovemaking. John V. Kelleher has suggested that such mythological allusions in Irish place names have no more meaning than the many "Lover's Leaps" and "Devil's Washtubs" on the American map. But the preponderance of place names, such as the frequent naming of Fionn's seat of power at the Hill of Allen in Kildare, and great number of times in the narrative that Fionn's men are called the "Leinster Fianna," suggest that the homeland of the hero is somewhere along a line running southwest of Dublin from central Kildare to the Leinster/Munster border. Despite this, there is never anything regional about his characterization; the various aspects of his character do not appear to have any geographical pattern. And although different genre, different modes of transmission, and the passing centuries have wrought many changes in the particulars of Fionn's appearance, the archetype of the hero, as Gerard Murphy has demonstrated, is recognizably continuous throughout. This is not to say that the differences in Fionn's portrayals are not significant; indeed, charting and analyzing the changes in their presentations, especially as they appear in English literature, is the principal work at hand. Nevertheless, proceeding further, I want to stress that there is a discernible coherence and continuity in Fionn's character despite the disparity in his portrayal from one narrative to another.

Much of what gives Fionn's portrayal apparent stability through the thousands of narratives in which he performs is borrowed from the traditional European portrayal of kings, especially as they appear in fairy tale and romance. In common with unnumbered counterparts, Fionn is a brave warrior and leader of men, a stalwart defender of his country against all invaders, steadfast in battle and generous in victory. But there are distinctions in Fionn's kingship; he is the king only of his immediate followers, a *rígfhénnid,* and his power is nearly always represented as distinct from that of the *ardríg,* "high king," who is resident at *Temhair,* or Tara, northeast of what is today Dublin. When Fionn is a young hero the high king is Cormac mac Airt ("Son of Art"), with whom he maintains generally poor terms. Cormac, incidentally, has a much better claim to historicity than does Fionn. The high king during Fionn's maturity is Cairbre or Cairbri ("of the Liffey"), Cormac's son, whose enmity for Fionn and his men grows with every episode.

In his separation and later isolation from royal power in Ireland, Fionn distinguishes himself from his counterparts in the other Irish cycles, Lugh and Cúchulainn. The French Celticist, Marie-Louise Sjoestedt, argued that Fionn's relegation to the countryside is what distinguished him most sharply from the more sophisticated hero, Cúchulainn. The myth of the Ulster hero is based on a heritage of an ordered society, of princes, scholars, and clerics, but the myth of Fionn derives from the men outside the tribe, the hunters, the woodsmen, and the soldiers-for-hire. Sjoestedt reminds us that the Fenian texts show that men are not born in the fianna; they acquire that status by choice and rigorous apprenticeship [*Gods and Heroes of the Celts,* 1949]. Lacking other scholarly conclusions about the fianna, she asserts that they were originally a band of men who lived by hunting and plunder, roving the countryside under the authority of their own leaders. They trained as hunters from May 1 to November 1, *Bealtaine* to *Samhain,* and quartered where they could in winter. In the eyes of what established authority there was, the fianna were indistinguishable from guerillas. They may have been Irish counterparts of the Norse *berserkirs.* As evidence she suggests that *fian* has cognates in Old High German, Slavonic, Avestic, and Sanskrit, in each instance with words merging the notions of hunting and warring (p. 83). Thus she thinks that the tales which portray the Fenian heroes as appointed defenders of their country against foreign invaders are of later origin. Although Sjoestedt did not know of his work, Reidar Christiansen, writing several years earlier, provided evidence for her thesis in *The Vikings and the Viking Wars in Irish and Gaelic Tradition,* where he demonstrated that the historical episodes from the Norse invasions had become imbedded in Fenian stories of much earlier provenience. Cúchulainn does not fight Norsemen because the Ulster Cycle represents a different concept of the hero which does not make allusion to the realities of the countryside. At his most exalted moment in Irish literature, in the *Táin,* Cúchulainn does battle with Queen Medb and her

warriors to retain possession of the Great Brown Bull of Ulster, all figures whose reality is no more likely than his. The distinction in Sjoestedt's summary is that: "The myth of Cúchulainn is the myth of the tribal man, the exaltation of heroism as a social function. The myth of the fianna is the myth of man outside the tribe, the release of gratuitous heroism. These two concepts do not contradict each other, but form an opposition like thesis and antithesis, two complimentary aspects of the racial temperament" (p. 90). And although she spoke only for Celtic tradition, Sjoestedt is also describing the Fionn mac Cumhaill of English literature, especially as he has been recreated in twentieth-century fiction such as *Finnegans Wake* and *At Swim-Two-Birds.*

In the Introduction to Volume III of *Duanaire Finn,* perhaps the most sustained and considerable study of Fenian literature ever published, Gerard Murphy agrees that two of Fionn's primary roles are hunter and warrior, which is demonstrated both in manuscript and oral texts from several centuries. Murphy also argues that Fionn's role of seer is as much a part of his character over a comparable period of time, although this is less of a distinction since his power has analogues in the careers of Heracles, Sigurd, and Taliesin, as we have mentioned before. Fionn's power of devination comes from "chewing" his thumb, or placing it behind his upper teeth, a curious ritual which has been the subject of considerable speculation, including an entire book on the subject of Robert Douglas Scott [entitled *The Thumb of Knowledge in Legends of Finn, Sigurd, and Taliesin,* 1930]. A character chewing his thumb, not identified as Fionn, also appears on a number of large Celtic Crosses from the early Christian period, as Françoise Henry has observed [in *Irish Art in the Early Christian Period to A.D. 800,* 1965].

A more important distinction, as Murphy shows us, is Fionn's ability to slay Aillén, "the Burner." According to the most frequently repeated story, Aillén harasses Cormac's court at Tara every November 1 at Samhain. As in *Beowulf,* none of the royal retainers can defeat the super-human power until the hero arrives from a land beyond the realm. Aillén burns down the palace and so might be seen as a more formidable opponent than Grendel, but Fionn's power proves to be greater. Fortunately, Aillén is not avenged by his mother. Again as in the Anglo-Saxon narrative, the hero wins the esteem of the royal household but does not become a part of it.

Although the oldest texts of the Aillén motif date only from the twelfth century, closer investigation of even earlier texts reveals that Fionn's opponents are non-human personalities whose "name, nickname, known character, habits, or story connect them either with fire in general, or more definitely with the Burner" (p. lxiii). For example, Fionn does battle with the three Fothadhs in a number of early romances, and further references to the Fothadhs, some of them highly ambiguous, can be found in narratives dating from as early as the seventh century. Although the Fothadhs are not always associated with fire in the narratives, an eleventh-century etymology of their name, viz. *fí-aeda,* i.e., "venom of fire," includes a description of them which translates, "They were a virulent fire in destroying clans and races." The genealogy of the Fothadhs includes, first, their father, Dáire Derg, or Dáire the Red, and their grandfather, Gnathaltach, whose epithet is *daig garg,* "fierce flame." The family line leads back ultimately to Nuadu, who is, coincidentally, Fionn's ancestor.

Another enemy of Fionn, who appears only in very early texts such as "Fionn and the Man in the Tree," is Dearg Corra moucu Dhaighre, whose name Murphy translates as "Red One of Corr[?] of the race of Flame." This "Red One," Murphy further explains, has the peculiar habit of jumping to and fro on the cooking hearth (p. 1xiv).

The traditional enemy of Fionn mac Cumhaill in the prose romances of 1400-1800, and of most literature in English, is not so easily associated with fire or "the Burner." He is Goll of the Clann Morna and the Connacht Fianna who, according to one of the better known narratives of the cycle, *Fotha Catha Cnucha,* "The Cause of the Battle of Cnucha," has killed Fionn's father, Cumhal, and taken command of all the fianna of Ireland. In one of the tasks the young hero must undertake to prove himself, Fionn overpowers Goll and becomes the head of the Fianna Éireann. In some stories Goll is known as Áed or Aodh ("flame" or "fire"). There is no question of Fionn's killing Goll in the romances, but there is a persistent enmity between the two all through narratives in the manuscript tradition. One instance in English literature where this enmity is continued is *Finnegans Wake,* where Goll mac Morna is portrayed as a mysterious, incomprehensible, but unavoidable opponent. The several stories from oral sources which portray Goll as admirable or as a bosom companion of Fionn do not obscure the animosity in the oldest tradition.

In sum, Murphy's study of the early materials on Fionn as compared with most recent folklore shows that the irreducible components in Fionn's heroic character are: (a) his powers to slay "the Burner" and subsequently to overpower Goll mac Morna and become head of the Fianna Éireann; (b) his skill as a hunter; (c) his bravery as a warrior, especially in defense of his people; and (d) his ability to see into the future by chewing his thumb, an ability that allows him to be seen as a prophet or seer. These may be the four roots of his personality as it appears in the literature, but early tales, especially those written before the twelfth century, and oral folklore, even that composed and recorded in the twentieth

century, do not develop personality of character as we understand those terms in the literature of the past three centuries. Nowhere is there a characterization of Fionn comparable to what we might have had if the myth had been adapted by Dickens, Balzac, or Strindberg. But to know anything of the fuller character of Fionn mac Cumhaill in Irish tradition, we must give some consideration to the vast, tangled body of ballad and romance composed, often extrapolated from earlier tales, between the twelfth and the eighteenth centuries.

Because the many narratives of Fionn mac Cumhaill are discontinuous, disparate, and widely dispersed, the full story of his adventures has never been told. There is no epic of Fionn; the closest approximation to epic in the whole cycle is the *Agallamhna Senórach,* which Oisín is the major figure and Fionn is a secondary character remembered from the distant past. Unlike Deirdre in "The Fate of the Sons of Usnech," or Cúchulainn in the *Táin* and two or three other narratives, Fionn does not appear as a major figure in any tale which has been of any great interest, either to critics or to adapters. I am excluding the "Pursuit of Diarmaid and Gráinne," in which Fionn plays a supporting role. Part of the continuity of Fionn seems to have been provided by the storyteller's feeling of having known the hero, as we have noted earlier, and his talent for expanding extemporaneously from the known. Unfortunately, there was no Malory in those times to weave together the known and the variants into one continuous fabric of narrative. The task is more difficult for a modern reteller of the tales in that he or she may now know too much about the hero, even though all the work of editing the texts has not been finished; nevertheless, the problem of determining the most authentic version of various stories would be an Herculean—if not Sisyphean—labor. As the eminent Norweigian folklorist Reidar Th. Christiansen has advised us, the mere description of the minutiae of difference between the manuscripts and their filiation is a superhuman task (pp. 46-47).

If a complete and totally coherent retelling of Fionn's adventures is a superhuman burden, we can rejoice that a number of earthbound scholars have given us an interim solution, a kind of scenario of events, based on the apparent life of the hero. I say "apparent" not merely because there is no evidence that such a figure as Fionn mac Cumhaill ever lived, but more because there is none to suggest that Irish storytellers ever considered the concatenation of his adventures in apparently chronological order. A storyteller, or shanachie (Irish: *seanchaidhe*), in Kerry in the fourteenth century might have told a tale of Fionn in his maturity, while another in Meath in the fifteenth century might have told one of the hero's youth. The time of mythographers is outside that of chronologers. The only vital date of any kind we have for Fionn is given for the hero's death at the Battle of Gabhra, A.D. 283, recorded in the *Annals* of Tigernach (d. 1088) and inter-leafed in the *Annals of the Four Masters* in the seventeenth century. The dating in chronicles and annals can be capricious, and those before the supposed date of the introduction of Christianity and literacy in A.D. 432 have little meaning. Within these severe limitations the most celebrated scenarist of Fenian narratives was Lady Gregory in *Gods and Fighting Men* (1904), more than half of which is given to this end. Her version is told in eleven chapters with sixty-four numbered episodes and is based largely on manuscript narratives which had recently been translated in such scholary Celtic journals as the *Transactions of the Ossianic Society* and *Revue Celtique,* as she acknowledged in rather incomplete footnotes. Where it suited her taste, she altered or augmented manuscript narratives with materials from oral tradition collected by Jeremiah Curtin, Douglas Hyde, and others, including some variants from Gaelic Scotland. Thus her final product was something never before seen anywhere, and it contained episodes which certainly would have sounded unfamiliar to almost any individual inheritor of Fenian tradition. Nonetheless, for her work in arranging these tales, and even more for *Cuchulain of Muirthemne* (1902), W. B. Yeats called her the Malory of the Irish Renaissance, a compliment as much indicative of the influence of her work as of its method of organization.

The extent of Lady Gregory's influence on English writing is a subject for consideration further elsewhere in this study, but for the moment we should acknowledge her dominance in a much smaller area, Fenian adventure fiction. Most of these works are of slight literary distinction and are remembered here because each of them attempted to fit the episodes associated with Fionn into a sequence. The first popular account in English of Fionn's adventures was Standish James O'Grady's *Finn and His Companions* (1892), a miscellaneous assortment of fantastic adventures, all taken from oral tradition. O'Grady's account is isolated in time and does not present any kind of developing or maturing hero as does Lady Gregory's. After *Gods and Fighting Men* there were five other novelistic accounts of Fionn's adventures. The first, Donald MacKenzie's *Finn and his Warrior Band* (1910), gave the stories a Scottish setting. A second portrayed the heroes in Irish Renaissance colorings with theosophic undertones: *Heroes of the Dawn* (1913) by Violet Russell, wife of George "AE" Russell. Two American authors who reshaped the narratives were Harold F. Hughes in *Legendary Heroes of Ireland* (1922) and Ella Young in *Tangle-Coated Horse* (1929); Young's version has been in print off and on for more than fifty years and is stocked in many public libraries. More recently, Rosemary Sutcliff produced an English (as opposed to Anglo-Irish) account in *The High Deeds of Finn MacCool* (1967). There is in addition a kind of fictionalized folklore collection by T. W. Rolleston, *The High Deeds of Finn MacCool* (1910), which sug-

gests by its title that it deals exclusively with Fenian matters while actually treating of several cycles. All six later collections have at least three qualities in common with Lady Gregory: they blend manuscript and oral narratives, they consider Fionn's adventures a lifelong story, and they avoid most of the unseemly presentations of the hero, thus subverting the irony present in many of the Irish originals. But unlike Lady Gregory's work the six are, in varying degrees, geared for juvenile readership, much as O'Grady's was. This may have resulted from the Victorian convention of having children read Scott and Cooper novels, the implication being that heroic narratives from the past provided suitable life models for the young.

Two other attempts to weld the Fenian narratives into a whole were not compiled to be considered works of literature themselves. One comes from T. F. O'Rahilly in his *Early Irish History and Mythology* (431, 1946, pp. 271-81) and is concerned with distinguishing myth from history in pre-Christian Ireland; understandably, O'Rahilly restricted himself to manuscript materials. Seán Ó Súilleabháin, on the other hand, devoted himself entirely to oral tradition in his *Handbook of Irish Folklore* (432, 1963, pp. 588-97), a guide for collectors of living traditions, in which he compiled a thirty-six episode résumé of Fionn's adventures.

This still leaves the question: Just what did Fionn *do*? Lacking a manageable, coherent outline of Fionn's career I now summon the audacity to compile one here, for my present purposes. One of the first assignments is to find the Fionn most attractive to English-language writers over a period of centuries. The complete adventures of Fionn in Old, Middle, and Modern Irish literature must wait for another book, one much longer than this. What is presented here is taken from a reading of eight authors: S. J. O'Grady, Gregory, MacKenzie, Russell, Hughes, Young, Sutcliff, Rolleston, O'Rahilly, and Ó Súilleabhan, with references to some significant histories of Irish and Gaelic literatures such as Douglas Hyde [*A Literary History of Ireland,* 1899], Aodh deBlacam [*Gaelic Literature Surveyed,* 1929], and Robin Flower [*The Irish Tradition,* 1947].

Within limits, then, here are eleven key chapters of the Fenian Cycle, especially as they relate to English literature.

Genealogy and Birth

Fenian lore begins with the founding of Fionn's family, the Clan Bascna (*Baiscne, Baoisgne, Basca,* etc.), which grows to become the core of the Leinster Fianna. Leinster is the easternmost of Ireland's four provinces. The rival family of the Clan Bascna is the Clan Morna which is centered in Connacht, the westernmost of Ireland's provinces.

In these narratives about the early rivalry of the families, the most important figure we encounter is Cumhal mac Trenmor, Fionn's father. Cumhal is killed at the Battle of Cnucha (modern: Castleknock, western County Dublin) by Goll mac Morna of Connacht, a catastrophe that brings a sharp reversal in the family fortunes; as a result, Cumhal's wife, Muirne of the White Neck, a great-granddaughter of Nuadu, flees into exile with the infant hero, Fionn mac Cumhaill.

The most important text in this chapter of Fionn's heroic biography is the manuscript tale, *Fotha Catha Cnucha,* "The Cause of the Battle of Cnucha," found in the oldest Irish codex, *Lebor na hUidre,* "The Book of the Dun Cow," dating from the early twelfth century. Although some variants of the story of Fionn's birth and departure into exile have been recorded in oral tradition, the genealogy and early life of Fionn has been of little interest to later storytellers, lettered or unlettered, and it has been ignored by English writers.

Boyhood Deeds of the Hero

After being reared in hiding, the youthful Fionn, then called Deimne, goes through a series of magical adventures which prepare him for his career as a great chief. The first of these is the Salmon of Knowledge episode: Finneigas, a druid, has been waiting for many years by the banks of a river for the appearance of the Salmon of Knowledge. In some versions Finneigas is waiting on the banks of the Boyne, a river rich in mystical associations ("Boyne" is from *Boann,* one of the principal early goddesses of Ireland), while other versions have the druid waiting at the falls of Assaroe on the Erne Estuary in County Donegal. There is perhaps no need to speculate on the significance of the salmon as the carrier of knowledge as there is a great body of lore associated with the fish all across the northern hemisphere, much of it identifying the characteristic leap of the salmon with inspiration, sexual energy, nimbleness, etc. The salmon has been especially important in Celtic tradition, both Goidelic and Brythonic, as a repository of Otherworldly wisdom. Finneigas succeeds in catching the long-awaited salmon and is proceeding to cook it when Fionn, quite by accident, burns his thumb on the salmon and nurses the burn in his mouth, thus inheriting the power of divination before the druid can.

Buoyant with the new confidence of his spiritual powers, Fionn sets about developing his physical skills and soon excels in running, jumping, swimming, handling of various weapons, and, in oral tradition, prowess in playing hurley or *camán,* Irish field hockey. While sporting with other young men, he acquires his heroic name when he is called "fionn," the Irish word for fair or white; Fionn is always represented as having blond hair and a fair, broad brow. He also acquires his special, magical sword from Lein (or Lochan), a smith of

the gods, his aegis, a banner showing the likeness of the golden sun half-risen from the blue floor of the sea, and, most mysteriously, he wins a bag made of crane skin, *corrbolg,* which may represent the beginnings of the insular alphabet, *ogham.* Capping his boyish adventures, as recounted earlier, he overcomes Goll mac Morna to become unchallenged head of the Fianna Éireann, then goes to Tara and slays Aillén, "the Burner."

The most important Irish manuscript tale of Fionn's youth is *Macgníamhartha Finn,* literally, "The Boyhood Deeds of Finn," found first in the medieval *Psalter of Cashel.* The sequence of events we have described has been fairly popular in oral tradition; variants are recorded as late as the twentieth century, but the story of the youth of Fionn tends to become confused with parallel stories of other heroes, especially Perceval and the Welsh hero Peredur.[2]

English adaptations of the story of Fionn's youth have been quite numerous, including early chapters in the several juvenile retellings of Fionn's adventures as well as separate chapters in more than a dozen collections of Irish stories and folk tales. The most distinguished of these is certainly that found in James Stephens' *Irish Fairy Tales* (1920), which despite its title, devotes more than half its bulk to Fenian stories. Not all English adapters have been so admiring, however; Caeser Otway, an anti-Catholic evangelist and first editor of the peasant novelist William Carleton, wrote a burlesque of the "Salmon of Knowledge" story in his *Sketches in Ireland* in 1827.

Fionn the Resplendent Hero

After joining the two warring fianna, those of Leinster and Connacht, into the Fianna Éireann, Fionn quickly establishes his hegemony over the forests, streams, and open places of the four provinces of Ireland with his seat of power at the Hill of Allen (also *Almu, Almhain,* etc.) in County Kildare in Leinster. Almost immediately we encounter the paradigm of Fionn's character which made him the admired hero of the Goidelic peoples. As Gerard Murphy has pointed out in *Duanaire Finn,* Fionn is a hunter, warrior, and seer. He is also a poet of some skill, indeed, several poems ascribed to him, the best known of which is "In Praise of May," are still included in anthologies of Irish poetry. In oral tradition he is also something of an incipient civil engineer, building the Giant's Causeway, cutting the pass at Glendalough, even working as far afield as the Grand Canyon in the southwestern United States. Though usually in the company of men, Fionn is occasionally portrayed as a lover; in manuscript tradition he is more restrained, as in *Cath Fionntrágha,* "The Battle of Ventry, or the White Strand," in which he is smitten with the invading princess of Greece, overcomes her, but cannot bear to take advantage of her. In oral tradition he is more bold; one tale collected in Ulster has him steal the clothes of the queen of Italy while she is bathing, and later sire three sons upon her.

We also read of the leading men in the Fianna Éireann, a host of immeasurable size. One text, *Airem Muintiri Finn,* "The Enumeration of Fionn's People," suggests that the hero was surrounded by thousands of warriors, but a closer reading of the narrative gives no more than thirty names. Across the breadth of Fenian literature, only six figures from the Fianna appear with any regularity. First, from his family, a son Oisín, and later his grandson, Oscar (also Osgar, Osca, etc.), often called by critics the "Galahad of the Cycle," and the embodiment of many of Fionn's aspirations reborn. The more prominent non-familial Fenian is Goll mac Morna, though his protryal ranges from the villainous in some manuscript tales to the moral and physical superior to Fionn in some folk tales. Caoilte (also Cailte, Keeltya, etc.) mac Ronain is the greatest runner and jumper of the Fianna and a survivor with Oisín until the time of Saint Patrick. Diarmaid O'Duibhne, a son-surrogate of Fionn's, is the greatest lover of the Fianna; no woman who sees his "love spot," *ball seirce,* can resist him, even if Diarmaid would wish otherwise. Finally, there is Conán Moal ("the bald"), a type for Falstaff and Thersites, a sharp-tongued scold, the butt of most Fenian pranks and, consequently, the comic relief in many early narratives.

Like popular heroes in much of world literature, Fionn is usually best at what all men must do. And yet Fionn, because of flaws which prefigure greater weaknesses to come, is frequently bested by his men. Diarmaid is more attractive to women. Caolite is a better runner and jumper. And both Oisín and Oscar often appear stronger and more virtuous.

Irish texts detailing Fionn's heroic adventures from both manuscript and oral traditions abound through all centuries in which Irish literature has been recorded. Indeed, many of the untranslated texts feature the heroic Fionn and his men in pursuit of wild boar, rescuing maidens and their mothers, performing in contests of strength and skill, many of which are distinguished one from the other only by specific topographical references, "The Chase of Slievenamon," for example. The most significant appearance of the heroic Fionn in English literature is, of course, in James Macpherson's *Poems of Ossian,* based on rearranged Highland Gaelic ballad collections, elements of which are cognate with Irish ballads. Along with Macpherson came a half-dozen or so imitators, James Clark, the McCallum brothers, and others. Portrayals of the heroic Fionn also appear in the translations of such early and reputable scholars as Charlotte Brooke, notably the "Lay of Moira Borb" in her *Reliques of Irish Poetry* (1789). And allusions to the heroic Fionn are common in the writings of English authors from Sir Walter Scott (in

Waverley and *The Antiquary*), and Thomas Moore, down to Padraic Colum. But as might be expected with the declining interest in heroic literature (Seán O'Faoláin speaks of a vanishing hero), most of the heroic depictions of Fionn mac Cumhaill in the past one hundred years have been found in juvenile literature. Surprisingly there are some specific omissions: there was no literature about Fionn produced by the Fenian movement, c. 1860-1900, despite the allusion in its naming.

Fionn the Defender of His Land and People

The most celebrated of Fionn's heroic roles in Irish literature is as a defender of Ireland. As Reidar Christiansen has shown in *The Vikings and the Viking Wars in Irish and Gaelic Tradition* (1931), there is an immense body of ballad literature based on historical predecents in which Fionn is portrayed doing battle with the savage Norsemen, or Lochlanns, as they are known in Irish, the men from beyond the sea. Norse influence in Ireland is the subject of a large chapter in every history of the island, and Norse influence infuses the culture of Gaelic Scotland at every level. Most informed commentators today agree that Fenian narratives predate the Norse invasions of the eighth century and after. One of the evidences for this is the Irish word for Scandinavians, *Lochlann,* cognate with the Welsh *Llychlyn,* was previously used for any invader, real or imagined, from beyond the Celtic world. Further, there is no longer much interest in the notion proposed by some German commentators, notably Heinrich Zimmer, that Fionn's characterization was borrowed from Norse invaders. The suggestion would not be worth commentary if James Joyce had not heard a précis of it from Zimmer's son in the early twenties and subsequently included Norse ancestry in the makeup of his Fionn archetype in *Finnegans Wake.*

Fenian stories in oral tradition, though dominated by Norse invaders when the stories are told in Ossianic frame, include a number of imaginative and allusive alternate invaders. For example, in a story called "The Chase of Glennasmol," Ireland is invaded by another Amazonian princess of Greece, armed with a repertory of tricks, including the Circe-like power of lulling the Fenians to sleep—after which she destroys a hundred of them. One of the best known manuscript tales which portrays Fionn as a heroic defender of Ireland is *Cath Fionntrágha,* "The Battle of the White Strand" (also called "The Battle of Ventry," using the contemporary place name on the Dingle Peninsula in County Kerry that appears to be a corruption of *Fionntrágha*). This narrative, one of the longest and most tedious in the cycle, appears to be an Irish instance of the international tale of the "everlasting fight" (Aarne-Thompson 2300, motif 211). In it Dara Donn, variously identified as the Holy Roman Emperor, Charlemagne, or the king of Norway, invades Ireland. Fionn leads the defenders at the "White Strand," Ventry Harbor in Kerry, and the battle rages on interminably amid much slaughter. For some reason not apparent in printed texts of the story, the battle at Ventry Harbor seized hold of the imagination of the peasant storyteller and would not let go. Perhaps the *Cath Fionntrágha* was an invitation to lively histrionics on the part of the storyteller.

Fionn the repeller of invasions has not translated well into English; perhaps because the hero's character is so static in many of these tales, or perhaps because writers in English do not find the defense of Ireland quite so compelling. James Macpherson includes several episodes of Fingal (Fionn) doing battle with Lochlanns in the *Poems of Ossian,* but of course the country defended is Scotland, as seen through a Tory perception.

The Bruidhean Tales

The warrior Fionn is much more vincible when pitted against the supernatural powers of druids, magicians, and the like. After his initial establishment of power in the slaying of the Aillén, Fionn is successful in defeating supernatural power in only a handful of stories, notably the early manuscript tale from "The Book of the Dun Cow," usually known as "Finn and the Phantoms." In this it takes Fionn and the Fianna an entire night to destroy an old hag with three heads on one thin neck, her husband with no head and an eye in the middle of his breast, and their equally charmless brood of nine children. In a whole series of tales, from both manuscript and oral tradition, Fionn is trapped in a magical dwelling and cannot get out without help. Following the conventions of those twelfth-century professional poets, the *filidh,* the stories of Fionn's entrapment always include with the same word, *bruidhean, bruidne,* etc., which cannot be precisely translated into English. The best approximations appear to be "palace," "hostel," or "dwelling" with Oz-like overtones of "enchanted" or "magical." Anne Ross has suggested that the *bruidhean* tales evoke the ancient Celtic mode of human sacrifice in which the victim is put inside a wicker container that is then set afire.

The most representative *bruidhean* tale is probably *Bruidhean Chaorthainn,* "The Hostel (or Palace, etc.) of the Quicken Trees," which Geoffrey Keating cited as long ago as 1633 to be typical of the "unhistorical" Fenian tales. Midac, the son of the villainous Colga of Lochlann, was a boy whom the Fianna had raised as one of their own after they had found him during the defeat of the invader. Upon reaching manhood Midac left the hospitality of the Hill of Allen and took up residence at his "hostel" or "palace" on the Shannon, a gift from the Fianna. Midac invites Fionn and his men to a banquet, only to lure them into the trap of his enchanted dwelling; once inside the men find that they

are fixed to their chairs and cannot cry for help from a window or raise themselves so much as one inch. Midac, it turns out, wants to contain Fionn while he conquers Ireland with the help of his grotesquely fantastic friends, Sinsar of the Battles, Borba the Haughty, etc. Fionn's children and grandchildren, some of them too young to attend the banquet, save the day, and slaughter the enemy as they ford a river; later, they pull their *paterfamilias* and the Fianna from their chairs, unharmed.

The *bruidhean* theme is found in texts as early as the tenth century and has been popular in both manuscript and oral traditions. Some of the better known manuscript tales are *Bruidhean Eochaid Bhig Dheirg,* "The Palace of Little Red Eocha," and *Bruidhean Cheis Choriann,* "The Enchanted Cave of Kesh Corran," this latter being among the most popular of all Irish prose romances of the late medieval period. Kesh Corran, incidentally, is the best known hideway of Diarmaid and Gráinne. On the contemporary map it refers to a cave about fifteen miles south of the town of Sligo, but in earlier times, it may have referred to all of County Sligo.

The popularity of the *bruidhean* has never found a counterpart among English writers. To be sure there are a fair number of translations, and at least a few of the collections of Irish traditional narratives include a *bruidhean* tale; the juvenile collections of Fenian tales, by Ella Young, and others, include at least one such tale, and there is one *bruidhean* story in Charlotte Brooke's *Reliques,* but that is the extent of it. The encumbered Fionn is not a part of English literature of the past one hundred years either as a pathetic, comic, or absurd figure.

Céadach and Other Helper Tales

Just as Arthur virtually disappears in a number of later Arthurian romances, especially those which center on the exploits of Lancelot, so too Fionn is peripheral to the action in a large body of tales found mostly in oral tradition which concerns various helpers of the Fianna. The most numerous of these concern a supernaturally gifted but benevolent helper, or *giolla,* usually named Céadach. Murphy summarizes and coordinates twenty-five of these in an appendix to *Duanaire Finn III* (pp. 177-88) and Bruford states that Cáedach tales present the most popular of any theme in all of Irish folk tradition and cites 128 versions from Irish and Highland sources [*Gaelic Folktales and Medieval Romances,* 1969, pp. 106-33].

In the tales where the helper named Céadach is actually an aid to the Fenians, his conventional task is to help defeat a magical or giant opponent who puts his arm down a chimney; Céadach cuts off the arm. This episode is, apparently at least, an analogue of the fight between Grendel and Beowulf, and may be, as the eminent Swedish folklorist, C. W. vonSydow, has argued [in *Duanaire Finn III,* 1953], the source for it.

More pertinent to our immediate interests are the other tales in which the Fianna is abused by the helper, such as *Tóraidheacht an Ghiolla Dheacair* (which may be translated as "The Pursuit of the Hard Gilly" or "The Difficult Servant"), and *Bodach an Chóta Lachtna,* "The Churl in the Gray Coat," both of which are found in seventeenth-century manuscript redactions and numerous oral variants. In the former an irritable and impudent servant coaxes the Fenians (but not Fionn) to sit on the swayed back of his enchanted roan and then runs off with them to the land beneath the waves. The Irish heroes are not only overpowered but also appear a bit absurd; in one Kerry variant they all pile on the back of the old horse and break it with their weight. The "Churl in the Gray Coat" is the sea god, Manannán mac Lir, in disguise; he takes up the challenge of "Ironbones," son of the prince of Thessaly to run a race when the Fenians cannot muster a man. To the chagrin of the heroes, the churl makes no effort to run very fast, and instead sits down to eat blackberries, but nevertheless wins the race handily.

Despite their great popularity in Irish, the helper tales are uncommon in English. Lady Gregory and her imitators include the stories as threads in the whole Fenian fabric, and the "Hard Gilly" story is in at least two dozen collections of Irish folk tales, but other than James Clarence Mangan's early (1840) adaptation of "The Churl in the Gray Coat" there has been no individual English-language interest in this series of episodes. English interest seems to focus on Fionn and Oisín, their rise, which we have just considered briefly, and even more their fall.

The Fenians in Disgrace

In a passage cited above, Marie-Louise Sjoestedt described how the historical fianna of Ireland lived on hunting and plunder. In time, it would appear, their demands on the non-military population became onerous. Not only did the warriors have to be fed, clothed and housed, but they demanded the first option on all virgins in the community before they could be given in marriage. Perhaps for these barely substantial historical reasons, or perhaps because of a cloyed taste for the heroic, Irish storytellers also include in their repertory a considerable number of tales in which Fionn mac Cumhaill and the Fianna Éireann are pictured as something other than admirable. This non-heroic literature is in two modes; in some the Fenians, and Fionn especially, appear to be vicious, despicable brutes who degenerate their heroic ideal in pointless violence leading to their destruction in The Battle of Gabhra or Gowra, recorded by the annalists as having occurred in A.D. 283. In a second mode Fionn, only rarely with an

accomplice or two, is made to appear just the opposite of what he is in the heroic literature; in this second mode he is cowardly and clumsy, but still something of a trickster.

Of the two non-heroic modes, the picture of Fionn mac Cumhaill as villain is less common in both Irish and English. The most important manuscript tale which portrays Fionn as a cruel rowdy is probably the *Bóramha,* "Boromian Tribute," although Fionn is not the only heavy in the piece. In oral tradition, perhaps because of the lesser refinements of audiences for the tales or perhaps because of the oral convention which frequently portrays Fionn as a giant, we find a crude and cruel Fionn more frequently.

The abused and comic Fionn is quite another matter indeed. As seen in the *bruidhean* and helper stories, the leader of the Fenians has a vulnerability to *contretemps.* The earliest reference to a comic Fionn is in an eighth-century manuscript where the hero is attacked by his son Oisín. David Krause has speculated in an insightful essay that a considerable body of literature has been lost, in which Oisín has focused his Oedipal anxieties in order to torment his father into a kind of farcial Laius. Such stories most probably were suppressed by clerical scribes. Be that as it may, in the literature which survives the comic and anti-heroic Fionn seems disproportionately a part of oral tradition, so much so that some scholars would identify that characterization with peasant humor. Whether the comic Fionn is as old as the eighth century, as Krause suggests, or only the creation of culturally dispossessed peasants after the Flight of the Earls in the seventeenth century, the comic Fionn is well established in English literature from the writing of William Carleton as early as the 1830s to our own time, in Flann O'Brien's *At Swim-Two-Birds* and Joyce's *Finnegans Wake,* both in 1939.

The Pursuit of Diarmaid and Gráinue

Of all the tales in the Fenian canon, the one with the greatest critical reputation is also the one which bears the closest analogies to international medieval romance narratives: *Tóruigheacht Dhiarmada agus Ghráinne,* "The Pursuit of Diarmaid and Gráinne." Not surprisingly, it has been adapted in English more often than other Fenian narrative, as a play, novel, narrative poem, and opera libretto. So much attention has been devoted to it that it almost deserves to be considered as a cycle by itself, especially as Fionn's role is nearly always supportive to the main characters, the lovers. In all but one or two versions Fionn is cast as a most unattractive, vengeful, jealous cuckold.

Gráinne is the coquettish young dauther of Cormac mac Airt, the high king at Tara. For the convenience of her father she has been betrothed, and in some versions actually married to the now aging Fionn mac Cumhaill, who, when all of the texts are coordinated, has had something like thirty wives. The action begins when the Fianna Éireann is invited to Tara for a wedding feast and Gráinne for the first time sees Diarmaid, a favorite of the band and a surrogate son to its leader. Diarmaid is not only a handsome physical specimen but he is endowed with a magical "love spot," *ball seirce,* which makes him—literally—absolutely irresistible to women. Gráinne is immediately taken with him and although Diarmaid does not reciprocate, the two lovers flee from Tara and spend as many as the next twenty years travelling all of Ireland; Scottish variants, understandably, extend the itinerary to Scottish locales. Fionn and his men eventually find the lovers, usually in northwestern Ireland, often at Kesh Corran, and the disappointed old bridegroom entices the young warrior to join his old comrades in a boar hunt. The reforged bond between the men is short-lived when Diarmaid is injured by the boar and Fionn desists from a chance to save him.

The exact parallels with the stories of Naoise and Deirdre in the Ulster Cycle and Tristan and Iseult in European literature need hardly be mentioned except to say that the differences, such as Diarmaid's hesitance as a lover, are ultimately more interesting than the parallels.

Nessa Ní Shéaghdha has shown in the introduction to the best contemporary edition of a manuscript text that part of the uniqueness of the tale is that it incorporates and extrapolates from earlier Fenian narratives, some dating from the tenth century. The manuscript scenario of the tale, summarized above, apparently took form in the seventeenth century, but folk variants continued to appear until the twentieth century.

As I have said, "The Pursuit of Diarmaid and Gráinne," has been adapted in English more often than any other Fenian tale; further, the adapters have included such distinguished figures as W. B. Yeats with George Moore, Lady Gregory, Sir Samuel Ferguson, the ninth Duke of Argyll, and Austin Clarke, as well as a dozen lesser known figures. The continued interest in the tale from writers in the different genres in both Irish and English is probably more indicative of the intrinsic merits of the narrative than of a public hunger for a villainous portrayal of the national hero of Ireland.

The Battle of Gabhra

Fionn and his men are recorded as having overcome many enemies and obstacles, animals, other Irish warriors, Lochlanners and other invaders, and when acting in unison, even supernatural powers. But the literature is divided on their success in the greatest of all heroic labors, the conquering of death. Many Irish storytellers never acknowledge that Fionn ever aged past maturity,

much less died. For example, in the early modern manuscript tale, *Bruidhean beg na hAlmhaine,* "The Little Brawl at Allen," Fionn performs feats of valor alongside his great grandsons Eachtach and Illan. In an oral tale of uncertain date, "The Chase of Slieve Guillean," Fionn is transformed into an atrophied old man by a jealous member of a trio of weird sisters reminiscent of *Macbeth.* Later, with the help of the Fianna and another of the sisters, Fionn is restored; if he cannot quite conquer death he can muster the power to resist it.

Yet the annalists record a date for his death, and at least two stories depict the end of Fionn mac Cumhaill and the Fianna. In an article [in *Zeitschrift für celtische Philologie* (1897)] that Kuno Meyer devoted to this subject we find that one version has Fionn decapitated (a significant mode of execution among the Celts from earliest times, as Roman writers observed) by Aiclech mac Dubdrenn at a battle named Áth Brea on the banks of the Boyne; this is first found in a tenth-century text by the poet Cinaed húa Hartacain and repeated by Tigernach (d. 1088) and subsequently by the "Four Masters" in the seventeenth century. This version is known to romance in at least one manuscript text, *Aided Finn,* "The Violent Death of Finn" (1892) and three fragments. But the far better known version in romance literature is given in the text of *Cath Gabhra,* "The Battle of Gabhra (Gowra)." Here the end of the Fenians is presented more dramatically. Along with the retreat from their heroic ideals which we suggested above, the Fenians begin to squabble among themselves; specifically, the Leinster Fianna revives the memory of wrongs it had suffered from the Clan Morna of Connacht at the Battle of Cnucha when Cumhal was killed. The reigning high king at Tara, Cairbre of the Liffey, resolves that he would rather die in ridding the country of the Fianna Éireann than try to rule an Ireland blighted by their immorality. Cairbre provokes the final conflict by killing Fionn's servant Ferdia, obliging Fionn to declare war. In the battle which ensues at Gabhra (Gowra, or on modern maps, Garristown in northwest County Dublin), the bloodbath is enough to rival that of the poorer Elizabethan horror dramas. The Fianna Éireann splits when Fer-tai of the Clan Morna falls in with Cairbre and fights his former comrades. Both sides use swords and spears, and the most common deaths are decapitations. Oscar, conventionally the most innocent of the Fenians, runs Cairbre through with his spear, and subsequently is killed by Cairbre's household guard within view of his grandfather. Fionn himself, although drawing blood on all sides with either hand, did not initially distinguish himself; he fulfills Cairbre's vision of him when he beheads the young son of Fer-tai, Fer-li, who stands alone against the host. One by one the Fenians fall, all except Oisín, who is not described at all, and Caoilte, the swiftest of runners, until Fionn stands alone. When the five sons of Urgriu come upon him with spears drawn Fionn knows he is defenseless and lets his aegis and shield drop to his feet, standing straight and unmoving as a pillar. Thus in death Fionn receives five wounds, not only like Christ but in keeping with conventions of Continental romance.

Although this version of Fionn's death is the best known in the early romances, it is by no means widely known or acknowledged across the body of the Fenian Cycle in Irish literature. Oral storytellers for the most part do not remember any tale in which Fionn is killed. Their view seems to be either (a) that he never engaged Cairbre in a final battle, or (b) he was wounded in an unnamed battle and now waits, "sleeping," at some specific spot, any of several caves all over Ireland and Gaelic Scotland, until he is again needed in the defense of his country. The reluctance of oral storytellers to speak of Fionn's death does not necessarily indicate a finicky unwillingness to deal with the distasteful, especially considering the buffoonish humor such tellers used to portray the anti-heroic Fionn. Instead, it seems more likely that folk tradition was presented with a dilemma by the Christian environment of Ireland, as seen in stories in the Ossianic frame. The reward of the unbaptized hero would be damnation. Yet even without the obstacle of revealed religion, storytellers seem to have difficulty in conceiving an end for Fionn and the Fianna. As Anton van Hamel points out [in *Proceedings of the British Academy* 20 (1934)] this is one of the distinctions between the Fenian and earlier cycles: "to Fionn and his warriors eternal bliss is unattainable."

Other than as a late chapter in Lady Gregory's work and that of some of her imitators, the story of Fionn's violent death in battle is unknown in English. Indeed, English writing knows of a different version of Fionn's death not found in Irish. Meredith Hanmer (1543-1604) records in his *Chronicle of Ireland* that Fionn died at an advanced age as a beggar in great poverty.[3] The greatest significance of Fionn's death to English literature is, of course, that one alluded to by Joyce in *Finnegans Wake;* this is a little known oral variant on the "sleeping warriors" myth which would place Fionn's head under Howth, his body under Dublin proper, and his feet stretching all the way to Chapelizod.

Oisín in the Land of Youth

Explanations of why Oisín did not stand with his father and comrades in their annihilation are varied. The best known today is that he was seduced by a beautiful fairy woman, Niamh of the Golden Hair, who leads him to the Tír na nÓg, "Land of Youth." Although voyages to the Land of Youth or the Ever-Young are common in Celtic literature, just what happens to the fortunate who go there is not always clear, as David Spaan's dissertation ["The Otherworld in Early Irish Literature," 1970] has shown. The only known Irish

text which treats with the narrative comes from an identifiable poet, Micheál Coimín (1676-1760), *Laoi Oisín i dTír na nÓg,* "The Lay of Oisín in the Land of Youth,"[4] which may mean that details have been individualized from a tradition we have lost. Coimín (anglice: "Comyn" or "Cummings") is airily unspecific about both Niamh and Tír na nÓg; apparently Oisín enjoys no sexual or other gustatory pleasures in the paradise of youth. For these or other reasons, Oisín grows bored after three hundred years and longs to return to the land of mortals. The Ireland he finds upon his return is domesticated and inhabited throughout by small men who bow to the authority of Saint Patrick and his bishops. As soon as Oisín, now a comparative giant, touches the earth when he tries to help some puny mortals lift a boulder, he is transformed to his actual age, thus appearing to be a semi-fossilized remnant of the past when he finally meets Patrick.

As Coimín's text is unique there is room for speculation that his narrative is the product of his own genius, especially as the name of Niamh is not associated with Oisín elsewhere in the cycle. Nevertheless, the episode of Oisín's survival to later times is extremely common in both manuscript and oral tradition. A completely loveless counterpart to Coimín's lay can be found in the oral narrative, *Fear ma dheiradh na Féinne,* "The Last of the Feni; or the Man Who Went to the Land of Youth" (1908). Whatever his entanglement with Niamh, the Oisín who survives from a lost heroic time to compose nostalgic poetry in the glamourless present has several counterparts elsewhere in Celtic literature. Llywarch Hên, a sixth-century Welsh poet, laments the ruin of the great halls of Cyndylan and Urien. Likewise, Myrddin, a possible ancestor of the Merlin of the Arthurian legends, is credited with poems celebrating the heroic past of Wales, often championing pagan ideals against Christian.

In any case, Fionn's role is completely subsidiary to Oisín's in this segment of the scenario. We see him in Coimín's text as a benign, not an abused father, an embodiment of all that the younger hero has lost in time. This flattering picture of the older Fionn is not as important for Irish literature as it is for English, as W. B. Yeats's "Wanderings of Oisin" (1889), based on early translations of Coimín, has established the picture of an authoritative, refined, and pagan Fionn which may supersede that of any other in the minds of those readers who know Irish mythology only from its use in English poetry.

The Colloquy of the Elders

The Elders of the *Agallamh na Senórach,* the only text in the cycle which might be called epic in breadth and length, are Oisín and Patrick.[5] As mentioned often before, an elderly Oisín tells Saint Patrick of the adventures of the Fenians in pre-Christian times in the early manuscript, and further, this frame serves in oral tradition for the retelling of hundreds of different narratives. As these narratives in fact recapitulate many of the portrayals of Fionn mentioned in the previous pages, there are no new roles for him to play here. David Krause, in his essay, "The Hidden Oisín," feels that Oisín in the *Agallamh* has inherited a pugnacity from his disputes with his father. Thus when Saint Patrick affirms his patriarchal prohibitions he simultaneously assumes the role of a surrogate father and becomes an analogue for Fionn. This does not mean that we have even the beginnings of evidence that Fionn is actually identifiable with Saint Patrick, although it is worth mentioning that Oisín frequently remarks that his father had predicted the saint's coming; further, both Irish and Scottish commentators have remarked on the confusion of Fionn and Saint Patrick in the folk traditions of their countries. Except in the mind of Joyce writing *Finnegans Wake,* the association of Fionn with Saint Patrick is probably not worth pursuing.

Perhaps because of the relatively great size of the text of the *Agallamh* or because of the popularity of the Ossianic frame in folk tradition, the scenario of the "Colloquy of the Elders" has had a separate tradition in English literature, almost independent from the rest of the cycle. Macpherson's *Poems of Ossian,* to name but one example, are named for Oisín because their "translator" perceived them to have been composed by their persona. During the heyday of the Irish Renaissance, 1890-1920, at least two dozen poems appeared in periodicals with names such as "Oisín and Saint Patrick." An American poet, Mary Grant O'Sheridan, produced an entire volume of verse in 1922, *Lays and Ranns from the Folk-Lore of the Gael,* which is in fact an unstructured and highly interpretive "recension" of the translation by S. H. O'Grady. Darrell Figgis, one of the more secular writers of revolutionary Ireland, produced a novel based on the *Agallamh* in 1923 entitled *The Return of the Hero,* in which Saint Patrick becomes an anti-clerical effigy (23). But quite apart from translations, adaptations, or Irish tradition, Oisín, alias Ossian, is one of the most widely distributed figures of Western literature, certainly in excess of any other character of Irish origin. Even in American poetry he can be found as far afield as in the poetry of Robinson Jeffers, who published a poem entitled "Ossian's Grave" in 1933.

Fionn mac Cumhaill in Summary: A Paradox

When confronted with the unfolding of heroic character in Irish tradition, Standish James O'Grady, nephew of the great translator, wrote in 1878 that "Heroes expand into giants, and dwindle into goblins, or fling aside the heroic form and gambol as buffoons." He was speaking of Fionn in particular, but he could have intended any of a number of figures in European tradition. What makes Fionn more distinctive is that the

different parts of his character exist simultaneously in tradition. Perhaps because of his broad social appeal or perhaps because he was never ossified in one perfected romance which superseded all others, Fionn has remained alive in tradition, far in excess of any other Irish traditional figure. Because he remained alive in tradition, unlike Cúchulainn or even Arthur, there was never any need to revive him. He was both contemporary, familiar, and perhaps less than heroic, as well as ancient, revered and patriarchal. In contrasting Fionn with Cúchulainn, Padraic Colum wrote, "He is a folk-hero, crafty as well as brave, vindictive as well as generous." He is, in short, neither a contradiction nor only an accumulation of discontinuous personalities but rather a paradox. . . .

Notes

. . . [2] The most pertinent passages from Brown's work are in vol. 18 (1920-21), 201-28, 661-73. Cf. Sheila McHugh, *"Sir Percyvelle": Its Irish Connections* (Ann Arbor: Edwards Brothers, 1946). This subject is treated at greater length in chapter 2, where Fionn is considered as a parallel to other European heroes, including Arthurian figures.

[3] Hanmer's *Chronicle* was published in 1633. Wilson M. Hudson, who has commented on the *Chronicle* in "Ossian in English Before Macpherson," *Studies in English* [Texas] 19 (1950): 125, thinks that the episode is new with Hanmer and is not based on a lost Irish original.

[4] Thomas Flannery provided the only scholarly edition in 1895 (Dublin: M. H. Gill), but the poem has been translated several times, the first as early as 1863. Curiously, Coimín's quite traditional composition (c. 1750) was just prior to Macpherson's *Ossian* (1760-63).

[5] The *Agallamh* has been translated several times; the most celebrated of these seems to be that of S. H. O'Grady in *Silva Gadelica* II (London: Williams and Norgate, 1892), 101-264. The best modern Irish edition is by Nessa Ni Shéaghdha, 3 vols. (Dublin: Oifig an tSoláthair, 1942-45).

FURTHER READING

Davidson, H. R. Ellis. *Myths and Symbols in Pagan Europe: Early Scandinavian and Celtic Religions.* Manchester: Manchester University Press, 1988, 268 p.
    Comparative analysis of pre-Christian religion in northwestern Europe.

Feehan, Ellen. "Frank Herbert and the Making of Myths: Irish History, Celtic Mythology, and IRA Ideology in *The White Plague.*" *Science-Fiction Studies* 19 (1992): 289-310.

Studies the architecture of Celtic mythology in Herbert's often neglected 1982 novel *The White Plague*.

Kearney, Richard. "Myth and Motherland." In *Ireland's Field Day*, pp. 61-80. London: Hutchinson, 1985.
Examines myth in Irish society from the literary use of myth by W. B. Yeats, James Joyce, Samuel Beckett, and others, to the IRA discourse of martyrdom.

Loomis, Roger Sherman. *Celtic Myth and Arthurian Romance*. New York: Columbia University Press, 1926, 371 p.
Detailed analysis of affinities between Arthurian romance and Irish and Welsh mythology.

MacCana, Proinsias. "Mythology in Early Irish Literature." In *The Celtic Consciousness*, edited by Robert O'Driscoll, pp. 143-54. New York: George Braziller, 1981.

O'Rahilly, Thomas F. *Early Irish History and Mythology*. Dublin: The Dublin Institute for Advanced Studies, 1946, 568 p.
Extensive study of pagan beliefs, mythology, and history in pre-Christian Ireland.

Warmind, Morten Lund. "Irish Literature as Source-Material for Celtic Religion." *Temenos: Studies in Comparative Religion* 28 (1992): 209-22.
Investigates the use of mythological material in the study of Celtic religion.

Yeats, W. B. *Writings on Irish Folklore, Legend and Myth*, edited by Robert Welch. London: Penguin Books, 1993, 457 p.
Anthology that includes Yeats's many essays on the subject of Irish mythology and folklore.

Eastern Mythology

INTRODUCTION

Mythology is one of the most ancient forms of literature, as well as one of the most pervasive. In the cultural traditions of Asia, it is primarily oral and thus particularly mutable and susceptible to intercultural influences, although myths have also been preserved through sculpture, painting, music, and drama. The essays collected here discuss narratives from diverse cultures, from ancient Egypt to Japanese Buddhism. If mythology can be understood as a series of responses to the human experience, common themes and figures across cultures are compelling evidence for the universal nature of certain concerns and interests. These legends not only describe the origins of the world, or the establishment of societies, but have normative force, as they are stories of heroes, gods, and royalty.

One major strand of the study of Eastern mythology attempts to ground these narratives in real conditions such as natural, socio-economic, and political events and processes. In this way mythology can be studied for its historical content and accuracy. For instance, in J. W. Kinnier Wilson's essay (see Further Reading), the legend of Gilgamesh is read as a transformative interpretation of certain naturally occurring phenomena. In another approach, mythology is treated as the expression of fundamental values and animating questions of a culture; C. J. Gadd's essay on Babylonian ceremonies of cyclical rejuvenation and Kelsey's examination of the snake as a figure of moral redemption in Buddhist mythology are examples of this hermeneutic path. Both methods of scholarship reflect the significance of myth as a cultural horizon, a heritage that structures and deeply influences the self-understanding of a society.

Asian myths have been preserved in a variety of ways: through oral repetition (and only recent recording), in written form, in ceremonial performances, and in painting, sculpture, and architecture. The highly developed and long-standing trade routes that traversed the continent and linked it to Europe and northern Africa served not merely to transport goods but to transmit cultural artifacts and ideas. Different versions of certain myths and recurring motifs have been linked to this economically-driven form of intercultural communication. The length and level of detail of the narratives also vary considerably, ranging from the few words that encapsulate the relatively simple plot of a Shinto tale, to the vast and sprawling epic of the *Mahabharata,* which in a hundred thousand couplets tells of a complex series of events that precipitate a cataclysmic war that involves numerous individual characters and intricate philosophical dialogue.

A great many tropes in Eastern mythology transcend cultural boundaries and much scholarly work has investigated the patterns and significance of cross-cultural figures, symbolism, and narrative events. In particular, the figure of the divine king appears in Egyptian as well as Babylonian and Southeast Asian mythology, and many divine figures possess some attribute of an animal, such as a serpent (related to the Chinese and Japanese dragon motif), bird (Horus, from Egyptian myth), or monkey (Hanuman, from Hindu mythology). Eastern mythology, as is typical of most mythological tales, has the characteristic of being composed by multiple and anonymous authors, generally over a long period of time, during which the narrative evolves, and often is spread over a wide geographical area — which also contributes to the existence of many different versions of the same tale.

For some early commentators, myth stood in opposition to the science of history as practiced by "enlightened" civilizations. Myth was thus regarded as the explanatory method of "primitive" Asian cultures, the romanticized and deified imaginings of those with no access to more objective accounts. Eastern mythology has also been closely tied to religious belief and practice, particularly in ancient Egyptian, Hindu, and Buddhist traditions. More recent scholarship has questioned the distinction between myth and history or science, and instead defined myth not by its supernatural content but by its cultural function. Eastern mythology in particular is strongly interwoven with traditional systems of government, social organization, and religion. To dismiss the centrality of what is called myth for these societies, some scholars claim, is to distort the relation of myth to reality; additionally, to portray science as fully disengaged from the functions of mythology is to misunderstand mythology. The commonality that links the diverse manifestations of mythology is concerned with quintessentially human questions: of origin and creation, of the order governing the natural world, and of what constitutes an ideal life. The answers to these questions, however, are deeply influenced by specific cultures; Eastern mythology thus reveals many divergent strands of thought and a profusion of cultural traditions.

HEROES AND KINGS

Rudolf Anthes (essay date 1961)

SOURCE: "Mythology in Ancient Egypt," in *Mythologies of the Ancient World*, edited by Samuel Noah Kramer, Anchor Books, 1961, pp. 15-92.

[*In the following essay, Anthes discusses the interconnected Egyptian myths of Osiris, Isis, and Horus, with specific consideration of the ceremonies that developed around these narratives.*]

[The] myth of Osiris must be discussed. The most significant of the Egyptian myths, it was not only popular with the Egyptians, but has even been known in Europe for two thousand years. Naturally, the story of the good king who was murdered by his covetous brother, his faithful widow who protected their son from the outside world and who brought him up in solitude, and the boy who eventually avenged his father and regained his kingdom appealed to people since everybody was ready to identify himself and his experiences with one or another of its features. The survival of the tale in Europe is due to another reason. The Roman mysteries of Isis, upon which the eighteenth-century idea of Osiris as expressed in Mozart's *Magic Flute* is based, featured the tale of Isis and her deceased husband in a spiritual rather than bodily aspect. Osiris was accepted as a mythological symbol by those who sought that ceremonial guidance to a religious experience which a predominantly rationalistic conception of religion could not offer to its followers.

To the best of our knowledge, the myth of Osiris was never written down by the Egyptians in a single comprehensive tale. The Greek authors were the first whose versions of the story have been directly transmitted. The Egyptian documents allude to it frequently in all kinds of religious texts, and they relate episodes in the form of ritual and tales. I should first like to deal with that form of the tale which is alluded to in our earliest source, the Pyramid Texts, and then discuss some of the major Egyptian elaborations on the myth. Finally, a hymn to Osiris from the time of the Empire may give an impression of how the Egyptian theologians of that period looked upon the myth.

We have already seen that the myth of Osiris originated in the genealogy of Horus. This might have been established in a ceremony such as the one which I have invented to illustrate the proceedings of the elevation to the throne in the earliest period. The elements of the myth, therefore, originated in two actions: the death of the king with his transformation into Osiris, and the installation of his son upon the throne, which meant the son's deification on earth as Horus. Evidently, no historical reminiscence of any

figure of the past was involved, and folklore, too, played little if any role in it. Moreover, a significant observation of Siegfried Schott should be mentioned here: The fact that our first knowledge of the myth of Osiris originates in the funerary rituals of the king should not lead us to conclude that this ritual was some sort of performance of the myth of Osiris. The proceedings of the funeral were prompted by the factual necessity of a ceremonial interment in the pyramid as befitted the king, and they inspired the incidental mythological allusions. However, these allusions fit into the pattern of a tale. While any change in the proceedings of the funerary rites was apt to add new details to the story, its basic facts appear well established in the Pyramid Texts. We have evidence that the myth of Osiris was then already understood to have happened in the past, notwithstanding the fact that it was experienced anew in every performance of the rites. In our understanding, the myth was about six hundred years old when the Pyramid Texts were first written down in stone, and the ritual underwent considerable changes during this period. The funeral rites were certainly rooted in the prehistoric period. Thus many elements of the ceremonies contributed to the final appearance of the tale.

According to the Pyramid Texts, the tale of Osiris runs about as follows: The king, Osiris, was killed by his brother, Seth, in Nedyt (or Gehesty). Isis and Nephthys, the sisters of Osiris, sought for the body, found it in Nedyt, and lamented over it. Isis restored Osiris to life temporarily so that he might get her with child. She then gave birth to Horus, suckled him, and brought him up in Khemmis, a place in the Delta. As a child, Horus overpowered a snake. He reached manhood through a ceremony which centered on the fastening of the belt, which Isis performed, and went out to "see" his father (*Pyr.* 1214-15). Apparently he found him. Then a court over which Geb presided was held at Heliopolis. Seth denied the murder of Osiris; presumably, too, the question arose whether or not Horus was the true heir to Osiris; in any event, Isis testified on behalf of her son by taking him to her breasts. Horus was made the king by the acclaim of the court. I have mentioned before that an additional story which centered on the Eye was fused with the main one: Seth stole the eye of Horus who subsequently became Osiris, when they fought at Heliopolis, and the younger Horus, the son of Osiris, regained it in a fight with Seth and took it to his murdered father, Osiris, to revive him. According to the first story, the kingdom which was lost by murder was reassigned to the right heir by the court. According to the second story, the sign of kingship, the Eye, was first taken away from its owner and then restored to him by means of fights. The fusion of these two tales was accomplished by introducing the son into the combat; furthermore, the second fight was vaguely associated with the court procedure, and Horus restored the Eye to his father at Gehesty, the very place where Osiris was slain, according to the first story.

Apparently, for reasons which are unknown to us, it was necessary to connect the idea of the Eye which was lost and then regained with the concept that the king was Horus and Osiris. In view of this interrelation we may venture the opinion that the idea of fights was not genuinely connected with the loss and recovery of the Eye; it was the criminality of Seth, originating in the concept of the slaying of Osiris, which might well have first suggested that the fate of the Eye was due to struggles with that evil character. In addition to the elements of the combined story as presented here, two other features are alluded to in the Pyramid Texts, which are not yet fused into the main story. First, the drowning of Osiris, which refers to his cosmic character as the vegetation which arises out of the inundation of the Nile; this, as we have seen, plays a role in the version of the tale of Osiris which is related in the "Memphite Theology." Second, references to the dismemberment of the body of the deceased king who was Osiris seem to be reminiscent of a very ancient burial custom, which was no longer practiced early in the third millennium; the dismemberment of Osiris by Seth is a significant element of the tale of Osiris chiefly in the versions which are transmitted from the Greek period.

A papyrus roll written about 1970 B.C. deals with a series of ceremonies which were performed in connection with the accession of King Sesostris I to the throne. The ceremony probably represents a much older tradition. I should like to present the contents on the basis of Sethe's first edition as well as Drioton's most recent interpretation, which is, however, preliminary in character. The papyrus presents, in a very sketchy manner, a text in forty-six parts and thirty-one illustrations. They feature individual scenes apparently in a logical sequence, which represent what we may call the action, as a pantomime. The actors are the king, his children, some officials, and men and women. Objects and activities include the slaughtering of a bull, the preparation and offering of bread, boats, branches of trees, the insignia of the king, the figure of the deceased king, et al. The pantomime appears to be accompanied by the acting out of mythological scenes with the actors speaking. The following translation of the main part of the eighteenth scene, which is illustrated with the "mena"-fight of two men without weapons, may exemplify the evidence: "(The) action (is): (the performance of a) mena-fight.——This (corresponds to): Horus fights with Seth.——Geb (addresses) Horus and Seth. Speech (of Geb): 'Forget (it).'——Horus, Seth, fight.——Mena-fight." Evidently, both text and picture are only notes which serve for the harmonizing of two different performances. The pantomime follows in logical sequence although it cannot be reconstructed as a whole. Each scene contains a verbal or figurative allusion which directs the selection of the corresponding scene of the mythological performance. The mythological scenes, consequently, do not follow in logical order. They do not represent either a continuous drama or a tale. Again, however, just as in the Pyramid Texts, we may try to use the mythological notes as elements for reconstructing the underlying narrative. This appears as the myth of Osiris: the slaying of Osiris, the fight for the Eye, and the proclamation of Horus as the king. It seems to run in summary as follows:

Seth and his followers killed Osiris. Horus and his sons sought for Osiris on the earth and in heaven with the help of fish and birds. Horus found his father and lamented over him. He addressed Geb in order to seek justice and promised his deceased father to avenge him. The children of Horus brought the body of Osiris. Then they bound Seth and put him under the body of Osiris to serve as a bier. Then Seth with his followers and Horus with his children fought and Geb first encouraged their fight. The eye of Horus was torn out and the testicles of Seth were torn off. Thoth gave the eye of Horus to both Horus and Seth. The eye of Horus escaped. It was caught by the children of Horus who brought it back to Horus. Eventually it was restored to Horus and healed by Thoth. The details of the fight and the Eye are not too well understood at present, and it should be mentioned that both the intervention of Thoth and the escape of the Eye of Horus are alluded to in the Pyramid Texts as well as here. The end of the tale appears clearer: Geb ordered Thoth to assemble all the gods. These in turn did homage to their lord, Horus. Apparently Geb proclaimed an amnesty by which the followers of Seth as well as the children of Horus regained the heads which they lost during the fight.

Abydos in Upper Egypt, where the kings of the first two dynasties were buried, was the main seat of the worship of Osiris. Its great festival featured the finding, burying, and bringing back to life of Osiris in a ceremonial performance. This festival is attested mainly about 1850 B.C. in the autobiographical inscriptions of those men who were commissioned by the king to participate in it. It appears to be an exception that, in the eighteenth century B.C., a king, Neferhotep, personally attended the performance and seems to have even participated in it in the role of Horus (Breasted, *Ancient Records* I, pp. 332-38). It is an open question whether this feast was repeated annually or only upon special occasions. The following reconstruction of the ceremony is based mainly on the inscriptions of the chancellor of Sesostris III, Ikhernofret (*ANET*, pp. 329-30): The standards of those gods who guarded Osiris in his holy chapel were brought from the temple in the "Procession of Upwawet." Upwawet (translated "he who finds or prepares the ways") was the canine deity of Asiut. He acted here as Horus when he went out to fight for his father. The enemies of Osiris were overthrown and those who rebelled against the Neshmet-boat of Osiris were driven away. Then, presumably on the second day of the feast, there took place the "Great

Procession," in which Osiris, the deceased god, was brought from the temple and placed in the Neshmet-boat, which floated on a lake. According to the Neferhotep inscription, it was here that Horus "joined" his father, that is, found him and made a great offering for him. The funeral procession was drawn up on the lake and on the land and proceeded to the tomb of Osiris in Peker, the ancient royal necropolis. The death of Osiris was avenged in a fight which took place on the island of Nedyt. A triumphant procession brought Osiris back to Abydos in a boat which was then called "the great one." At Abydos he was conducted into his holy chapel. The stress which is laid upon the fights in the narrations of this festival leads us to think that they actually were performed and, consequently, that the processions were accompanied with the lamentation and the jubilation of the onlooking population, just as on the corresponding occasions in the late period. The character of this ceremony differs basically from that previously discussed. There we saw royal ceremonies which were interpreted by mythological references; here, however, the subject of the performance was the very myth of Osiris and Horus who, as divine beings, were only reminiscent of their former identity with the king. No direct connection appears to exist between these different types of performances. The following attempt to find affinities for the Abydian ceremony may, however, throw some light on the character of the myth itself.

From about 1500 B.C. we know of a funeral rite which brought about the identification of the deceased with what we call a grain-Osiris, i.e., moist earth and grain molded in a clay form. The growing of the grain indicated the Osirian rebirth. The rite is attested in the funerals of both kings and commoners. It took place in the last month of the inundation season when the water started to recede. This was the same month in which, fifteen hundred years later, the festival of the resurrection of Osiris was celebrated in all the forty-two nomes of Egypt. These ceremonies centered around the finding of Osiris as did the Abydian celebrations, but Osiris now was represented by a grain-Osiris, and the jubilant cry, "We have found him, we rejoice," sounded loud throughout the country when the water of the Nile was mixed with the earth and the grain in the clay form. After Osiris was "found," the new grain-Osiris was taken in procession to the temple. There it was deposited in the upper chamber of that room of the temple which represented the tomb of Osiris, where it replaced its predecessor from the preceding year. The latter was prepared for burial and exposed in front of the tomb either upon branches of sycamore, which was the tree in which Hathor, and subsequently Nut, had been embodied since ancient times, or else it was placed inside a wooden cow representing the ancient heavenly cow which was Nut and subsequently Hathor. These ceremonies of the latest period appear closely related to the funerary rites of the grain-Osiris, and not

with the Abydian ceremonies of Osiris. As the god of vegetation who had deceased and was revived, Osiris appears only incidentally identified with the mythological character.

There exists, however, a certain affinity between the late ceremonies of Osiris and those which were performed in Abydos. Diodorus Siculus (*Bibliotheca Historica* I 87, 2-3) tells us that, according to some of his authorities, Anubis the dog was "a 'guard of the body' among those who were around Osiris and Isis; others, however, think that the dogs guided Isis during her search for Osiris." These two statements are confirmed by Egyptian sources. Anubis is the leader of those who guard the body of the deceased Osiris, according to the Coffin Texts, and together with the children of Horus he slays the enemies of Osiris according to a ritual of the late period. All this activity of Anubis is duplicated by the canine Upwawet, who is represented by the figure of a wolf standing upon a standard in Abydos where, according to pictures and the report of Ikhernofret, he was the first of the guardians in the chapel of Osiris and went forth in the "procession of Upwawet" to seek Osiris and to slay his enemies. Since the canines Upwawet and Anubis are interrelated and are sometimes substituted for each other, the fact that they acted alike in the service of Osiris can hardly be accidental. Another close parallel between the late mysteries of Osiris and the Abydian ceremonies is their virtual restriction to the finding, the burial, and the revival of the god. To be sure, it has been often assumed that the death of Osiris was represented in the ceremonies of Abydos but that it was not mentioned in the inscriptions because it was something secret and unspeakable. But this is hardly likely. The ceremony expressly starts with the departure of Horus in the guise of Upwawet to "fight for [or, to avenge]" Osiris, an expression which always indicates the activity of the son Horus for his deceased father. The departure of Upwawet mirrors that of Horus from Khemmis. Now, it is striking that the ceremonial reiteration of the extensive myth of Horus was restricted to the mere finding and resurrection of the god, just as it was in the late mysteries. Thus, the Abydian and the late ceremonies have something significant in common although the latter, which concern the god of vegetation, cannot possibly be traced back directly to the representation of the myth of the god who once was the deceased king. It is true that this agreement was possibly accidental. Abydos was the site of what was regarded as the tomb of Osiris and therefore the question of how his death occurred might have appeared less significant. Nor did the grain-Osiris ceremony pose the question of how the god died. However, the possibility that a historical reason for the conformity existed should be taken into consideration. It might be that the ceremony by which a deceased person was identified with vegetation goes back to earlier, and possibly prehistoric, times. Deposits of heaps of grain in tombs of commoners of the Early Dynastic period have been tentatively interpreted by Alexander Scharff as the prototype of the grain-Osiris. This interpretation of the grain deposits has been disputed for good reasons and must not be accepted as certain. Still, it is not altogether impossible, in spite of the lack of positive evidence, that the Osirian ceremonies at Abydos were influenced by agricultural rites as was the rite of the grain-Osiris. This brings up the further question of whether the identification of the deceased king with Osiris in the context of the lineage already had some prototype in popular belief. I am submitting to the reader this problem which cannot be solved with the available evidence, as an example of the difficulties confronting the student of Egyptian mythology.

There exist a number of additional features of the myth of Osiris and his family which throw light on the popularity which it enjoyed. I may mention the political implications which were given the fights between Horus and Seth. The hostile character of Seth, who ruled the desert outside of Egypt, and his affinity to the Asiatic storm god, eventually led to his identification as Apophis, although, according to the Coffin Texts, it was he who fought Apophis. The Hyksos who invaded Egypt about 1700 B.C. worshiped him more than any other Egyptian god. Later on, in retrospect, the Hyksos as well as the destructive Assyrians and the Persians who made Egypt a Persian satrapy, were identified with Seth. A myth recorded on the walls of the Ptolemaic temple of Horus at Edfu in Upper Egypt featured Horus as the victorious king who, on behalf of his father, Re, overcame Seth and his followers in Egypt and expelled them to Asia; this version of the myth was doubtless influenced by the experience of foreign invasions into Egypt. The character of Horus as a warrior developed mainly in the figure of Haroëris, "the great, or the elder Horus," who was regarded as the son of Re, in contrast to Harsiese, "Horus, the son of Isis," and Harpokrates, "Horus the child." The differentiation between Horus, the son of Re, and Horus, the son of Isis, is reminiscent of the fact that, in the ancient period, as we have seen, the king, Horus, was thought of as the bodily son of Atum and, at the same time, as the son of Osiris and Isis. However, Horus, the king, and Haroëris were clearly distinguished from each other as early as in the Pyramid Texts, as were several other forms of Horus, including Harakhty or Re-Harakhty.

Isis was looked on as an especially powerful magician, since it was she who revived her husband and protected her child against all the dangers of the wilderness. She still occurred as such in magical spells of the Christian period in Egypt. A longish tale which was recommended for use as a magical spell to "kill the poison—really successful a million times" is preserved from about 1300 B.C. and describes how she tricked Re into betraying his "name" to her, because, except for this name, "there was nothing that she did not know in heaven and earth." She created a serpent which bit Re as he took his evening walk. There was no remedy against the poison except for the magic of Isis, but Isis claimed that her magic was powerless in this case if she did not know Re's name. He tried to sell her many of his numerous names for this purpose, but the poison still burned "more powerful than flame and fire." Eventually, Re divulged his secret name to her, and Isis healed him with her spell, which, by the way, did not reveal the name (*ANET*, pp. 12-14). "He whose name is not known" occurs elsewhere in Egyptian religious literature as early as the Pyramid Texts. The tale of Isis indicates that this epithet was used for the highest god because he could not be submitted to magic, and not for any other reason.

In narrative fiction the separation of the world of the gods and the king on the one hand, and of non-royal individuals on the other, was, as a rule, observed. In the "Story of the Two Brothers" (*ANET*, pp. 23-25), the gods fashioned a woman for Bata, but then Bata was a divine being and not a mere mortal. This tale was written down about 1300 B.C., as were the other tales which we shall discuss. It is what we may call a semi-mythological tale. The names given to the two brothers, Bata and Anubis, are the names of deities and are so indicated in the writing, which makes it clear that the divine character inherent in them applies also to the two brothers themselves. The jackal-headed god Anubis and the very minor deity Bata are known from other sources but, in contrast to the two brothers of the tale, are in no way related, to the best of our knowledge. Neither the characters of the two brothers, nor the experiences which are related in the tale display any similarity to what we know about the gods whose names they bear. However, the tale contains several incidents which are clearly reminiscent of the story of Osiris. An essential part of the tale, the experiences of Bata and his wife in Byblos and in the palace of Pharaoh, is almost exactly like Plutarch's story of what happened to Isis when she sought for Osiris in these same places (*De Iside et Osiride,* Chap. 15). In contrast to this similarity of setting, however, the behavior of Bata's wife is just the opposite of that of the faithful Isis. Another story of the same kind, that of the two hostile brothers, Right and Wrong, is obviously reminiscent of the tale of Osiris: Wrong blinds Right, and the latter's son fights Wrong in court to avenge his father. Neither in this tale is the boy's mother reminiscent of Isis.

Besides these works of literature which are merely influenced by mythological motifs, there are others which are mythological in the strict sense of the word. We have already encountered some of them. The story of the sorceress Isis and the hidden name of Re is a good example; while it was recommended for use as a magical spell, it was doubtless composed for entertainment. The most sophisticated and most extensive example of this type of fiction is the story of the contest of Horus and Seth for the rule of Egypt (*ANET*, pp. 14-18). It adds considerably to our knowledge of mythological details since it relates at length episodes which are otherwise known only from allusions. Moreover, it throws some light upon the question of how mythological tales came into existence. All the characters of this tale are divine beings, as is to be expected in an Egyptian mythological text, but they are all very human, including the sorceress Isis.

The theme of the tale centers about the lawsuit between the clumsy, boorish fellow, Seth, who is introduced as the brother of Isis, and the clever child, Horus, who is assisted by his resourceful mother, Isis. The lawsuit deals, of course, with the inheritance of Osiris, the kingship in Egypt, which is claimed by Horus and Isis on the basis of the law, and by Seth on the basis of his strength and power. The court is the Ennead, the ancient court of Heliopolis, and is presided over by Shu, who is also called Onuris, "the bringer of her [i.e., the Eye] who was far away." Thoth, the recorder, is expressly described as the keeper of the Eye on behalf of Atum during the interregnum—the Eye, as we have seen above, being the royal Uraeus viper and crown, identical with Maat meaning law and order. Atum, who is also called Re, Re-Harakhty, "Re-Harakhty and Atum," the Lord of All, et al., is "the Great one, the Oldest one, who is in Heliopolis," and his consent is necessary for the validity of the decision of the court. The episodes occur because Atum favors the powerful Seth, while the court clearly decides in favor of the lawful heir, Horus. The tale opens with this decision of the court, and with the same decision the quarrel is finally brought to a happy end, with Horus crowned the king of Egypt. A characteristic feature of the end is the appearance of Seth here as in the "Memphite Theology" as a good loser. Once the decision is final, he agrees to it willingly and is then assigned to Re-Harakhty to be with him like a son, the frightful warrior in the sun boat. Between its beginning and end, the tale is replete with incidents which either delay or expedite the proceedings and decisions of the court. Atum hopes to find support for Seth in the goddess Neit, "the mother of the god," to whom Thoth writes a letter on behalf of the Ennead. In her answer Neit threatens to cause the sky to collapse if Horus is not made the king of Egypt. She recommends that the Lord of All compensate Seth by doubling his property and giving him Anat and Astarte, his (the Heliopolitan's) daughters. At another time, Re-Harakhty is placed in a situation where he cannot deny the right of Horus. Angry, as always, he blames the court for delaying the procedure and orders them to give the crown to Horus, but when they start to do so Seth throws a tantrum and the Heliopolitan gladly yields to his protest. Eventually, Thoth, the god of wisdom, recommends that the court ask the opinion of Osiris,

the old king who is in the realm of the dead and is thus prevented from performing his former office. Naturally, the answer of Osiris favors the claim of his son, Horus, and prompts the final decision.

The tale is a parody on delayed court procedures and red tape, and is spiced with gibes at the leading figures. Baba, definitely a minor deity but apparently a member of the court, insults Re-Harakhty by claiming, "Your chapel is empty,"—though, in fact, Re was always worshiped in the open and not inside a temple. This impudent remark, which offends even the other gods, enrages Re. He lies down on his back in his tent, and, like Achilles, sulks. Then his daughter, Hathor, enters and displays her naked beauty to his eyes. This gesture makes him laugh. Later on, however, Re-Harakhty shows his own impudence toward Osiris. For when Osiris boasts in his letter that he created barley and emmer which are indispensable for all life, Re answers him, "If you had never existed, if you had never been born—still, barley and emmer would exist." Osiris, however, keeps his temper, even though he appears sensitive about his banishment to the realm of the dead. He earnestly reminds Re of his spectral "messengers who do not fear either god or goddess," and intimates that mankind and the gods eventually rest in his kingdom beneath in accordance with the word which Ptah once spoke when he created heaven.

In addition to all this, a major part of the tale consists of interludes which are prompted either by the crafty Isis or the plodding, muscle-bound Seth. Seth boasts of his strength. Isis insults him. Seth refuses to attend the court as long as Isis is admitted. The court adjourns to an island, and the ferryman Anty is forbidden to ferry any woman over to it. Isis deceives him and induces Seth to concede unwittingly that his claim is unjustified. At the suggestion of Seth, both he and Horus engage in a contest for which they turn into hippopotami. After an initial failure, Isis succeeds in spearing the Seth-hippopotamus, but then, driven by sisterly love, she frees him and is promptly beheaded by her son, Horus—this detail, however, does not diminish in any degree her activity throughout the balance of the story. Horus hides, but Seth finds him and rips his eyes out, and Hathor heals them with milk of a gazelle. Then Seth tries to overcome Horus by sexually attacking him, for this would make Horus despicable to all the gods. Horus, however, thinking quickly, nullifies this attack without Seth's knowledge, while Isis ingeniously turns Seth's scheming back on himself: in the presence of all the gods, a golden disk, unmistakably engendered by Horus, arises out of the head of Seth. Seth then suggests another test, a fight in boats on the Nile, and again Isis helps Horus to victory. He sails downstream to Neit of Sais to urge her to bring about the final decision, which, however, as we have seen, is actually prompted by Osiris's favorable opinion.

All of these ludicrous episodes have a mythological background, or, putting it more cautiously, most of their details also occur more or less explicitly elsewhere in mythological texts. This makes us wonder how far such details are genuinely mythological, and how far they originated in the fanciful imagination of the storytellers. We may remember that it was the activity of literary men rather than theologians which appears to have played a significant role in the composition of the Coffin Texts. Two of the episodes enumerated above may be stressed here because of their etiological origin: the ferryman Anty is punished by the removal of the "forepart of his feet," the god Anty is "he with claws," a falcon. The story could then refer to an anthropomorphic image of the god in which the toes were replaced by claws, in accordance with a suggestion first proffered by Joachim Spiegel. An etiological tendency is also evident in the beheading of Isis. She then appears to the gods as a headless statue of flint or obsidian. This might well have referred to a local image of hers. However, her decapitation also occurs contemporaneously elsewhere, and Plutarch (*De Iside et Osiride,* Chap. 19) relates that Horus beheaded his mother because she freed Seth. According to Plutarch, her head was replaced by that of a cow, and this is thought to explain the appearance of Isis as the cow-headed Hathor.

The origin, aim, and composition of this tale might well be explained in a serious light, and the fact remains that it is a purely mythological tale with respect to all its elements and its final appearance. In spite of the gravity of the topic, however, neither the exalted station of the gods nor the calamities which befell them were taken seriously by those who enjoyed the story. The tale is unmistakably the humorous product of, presumably, generations of storytellers. They and their audience identified themselves with the characters of this tale, and the fact that these were actually the gods of Egypt might not have been a matter of great concern. Perhaps listening to a story like this one was like remembering the youthful pranks of a man of undisputed dignity, which could not do any harm to his authority. Whether we regard this tale as a joke or as blasphemy, one fact is certain: a thousand years and more after this tale of the gods was written down, the common people of Egypt clung to these same gods with a worship which was both fanatic and fetishistic, and the teachers and sages interpreted Egyptian mythology reverently in a manner which brought it worldwide recognition. The humorous story of the contest of Horus and Seth did no harm to the myth of Osiris and Isis.

The great hymn to Osiris which was engraved on the tombstone of a certain Amenmose about 1550 B.C. may conclude this discussion. In the first section of the hymn Osiris is invoked in his characters of the god who is worshiped in all temples; the personification of Egypt,

to whom Nunu yields the water of the Nile and for whom the beneficent north wind blows; the ruler of the starry sky; and the king of the deceased and the living. Throughout the hymn Osiris appears as the glorious ruler, terrifying only to his enemies. No allusion is made to the sinister aspect of his kingdom beyond, nor is the death of the god mentioned in the myth which is presented in the second and concluding part of the hymn. The glory of the kingdom of Osiris, the deeds of Isis, and the happiness of the kingdom of Horus are extolled. This is a paraphrase of the myth and at the same time the glorification of the kingship in Egypt, with both Osiris and Horus representing the kingship whose continuity is guaranteed by Isis, "the throne"; the author might well have been aware of the ancient meaning of these mythological figures. This part of the hymn, translated here with only a few minor omissions and introduced with the first line of the hymn, follows:

Praise to you, O Osiris, Lord of Eternity,
  King of the Gods. . . .
Great One, First of his brothers, Eldest of the Primeval Deities,
who established Maat (the law) throughout the two
  banks of the river,
who put the son upon the seat of the father,
whom his father, Geb, favors and his mother, Nut,
  loves,
great of strength when he overthrows the rebel,
mighty of arm when he kills his enemy. . . .
who inherited Geb's kingship of the Two Lands.
He (Geb) saw his virtue, he bequeathed to him the
  leadership of the countries,
                    that coming events might be
                    happy,
  He fashioned this country (Egypt) with his hand,
  its water, its wind, its herbs, all its herds,
  and whatever flies in the air and alights on earth,
  its worms, and its small game of the desert
  being rightly given to the son of Nut, and the Two
    Lands were pleased with this.
Who appeared on the throne of his father like Re
  when he shines forth in the horizon and gives light
  in the face of the darkness.
He brightened the sunlight with his plumes and inundated the Two Lands like the sun disk at dawn.
His crown, it pierced the heaven and mingled with
  the stars,
the leader of every god, clear of command,
whom the Great Ennead favors and the Little Ennead
  loves.
His sister protected him, she who repelled the enemies
and who caused the deeds of the mischief-maker to
  retreat by the power of her mouth,
she who is excellent of tongue, whose words do not
  fail, who is clear of command,
Isis, the mighty, who took action for her brother, who

sought him without tiring,
who roved through Egypt as the (wailing) kite without
  rest until she found him,
who provided shade with her feathers and created wind
  with her wings,
who made jubilation and brought her brother to rest,
who strengthened the weakness of him who was tired
  of heart,
who received his seed, who bore an heir,
who suckled the infant in solitude—the place where he
  was unknown—
who introduced him, when his arm was strong, into
  the hall of Geb,
while the Ennead rejoiced:
    "Welcome, O Son of Osiris, Horus, firm of heart,
      vindicated,
    Son of Isis, Heir of Osiris,
    for whom the proper court, the Ennead and the
      All-Lord himself, has assembled.
    The Lords of Maat are united in it,
    those who shun wrongdoing, and sit in the hall of
      Geb
    in order to give the office to its lord and the
      kingship to whom it should be rendered."
They found that the acclamation given to Horus was,
  "He is right."
The office of his father was given to him.
He came forth wearing the fillet and with the mace of
  Geb.
He took the rule of the two banks of the river, the
  white crown firm on his head.
The earth was reckoned to him to be his property.
Heaven and earth were under his supervision.
Mankind, common folk, gentle folk, and humanity were
  entrusted to him,
Egypt, the northern regions, and the circuit of the sun
  were under his counsels and also the north wind, the
  river, the flood, the trees of life, and all green
  plants. . . .
Everyone rejoices, hearts are pleased, hearts are filled
  with joy.
Everyone is happy, everyone worships his beauty.
How sweet is his love in our presence.
His grace traverses hearts and his love is great in
  every body, when they have rightly offered to the son
  of Isis.
His enemy has fallen because of his crime, and evil is
  done to the mischief-maker.
He who has done evil, his deed has returned to him.
The son of Isis has avenged his father so that he is
  satisfied and his name has become excellent. . . .
Let your heart be glad, Wennofer.
The son of Isis, he has assumed the crown,
the office of his father has been assigned to him in the
  hall of Geb.
(When) Re spoke and Thoth wrote, the court was
  pleased.
Your father, Geb, has given command for your benefit,
and it has been done according to that which he said.

Works Cited

1. TEXTS

ANET, *Ancient Near Eastern Texts,* edited by James B. Pritchard. 2nd edition. Princeton 1955 (The Egyptian Texts are translated by John A. Wilson).

James H. Breasted. *Ancient Records of Egypt,* Vols. I-IV. New York 1906.

E. A. Wallis Budge. *The Book of the Dead.* An English Translation with Introduction, Notes, etc. London 1898.

———. The Book of the Dead: The Papyrus of Ani. London 1895 (with translation).

Adolf Erman. *The Literature of the Ancient Egyptians,* translated by Ailward M. Blackman. London 1927 (the "Hymn to Osiris" on pp. 140-45).

Henri Frankfort. *The Cenotaph of Seti I at Abydos.* 39th Memoir of the Egypt Exploration Society. London 1933.

Samuel A. B. Mercer. *The Pyramid Texts in Translation and Commentary,* Vols. I-IV. New York 1952.

Mythological Papyri Texts. Translated with Introduction by Alexandre Piankoff. Edited with a chapter on the Symbolism of the Papyri by N. Rambova (Bollingen Series XL, Vol. 3). New York 1957.

Kurt Sethe. *Dramatische Texte zu altaegyptischen Mysterienspielen* (Untersuchungen zur Geschichte und Altertumskunde Aegyptens, Band 10). Leipzig 1928 (the text concerning the coronation of Sesostris I on p. 81 ff.).

The Shrines of Tut-ankh-Amon. Texts translated with Introductions by Alexandre Piankoff. Edited by N. Rambova (Bollingen Series XL, Vol. 2). New York 1955.

The abbreviations *Pyr., C.T.,* and *B.o.D.* refer to the hieroglyphic text editions of the Pyramid Texts, Coffin Texts, and Book of the Dead respectively. For translation see above the books of Budge and Mercer.

2. BOOKS OF REFERENCE, DISCUSSIONS, ETC.

Rudolf Anthes. "Egyptian Theology in the Third Millennium B.C.," *Journal of Near Eastern Studies,* Vol. 18 (1959), pp. 170-212.

Hans Bonnet. *Reallexikon der aegyptischen Religions-geschichte.* Berlin 1952.

Map of ancient Mesopotamia, showing the Purattu and Idiglat rivers.

Etienne Drioton. "Le papyrus dramatique du Ramesséum," *Annuaire du Collège de France,* 59e année (1959). Résumé des cours de 1958-59, pp. 373-83.

Etienne Drioton et Jacques Vandier. *L'Égypte.* Contains an extensive bibliography of mythology and religion with introductions, on pp. 107-28. Paris 1952.

Henri Frankfort. *Kingship and the Gods.* Chicago 1948.

Henri Frankfort et al. *The Intellectual Adventure of Ancient Man.* Chicago 1946. (Reprinted with the title, *Before Philosophy,* as a Pelican Book, 1951.)

Hugo Gressmann. *Tod und Auferstehung des Osiris nach Festbraeuchen und Umzuegen (Der Alte Orient,*

Band 23, Heft 3). Leipzig 1923.

Hermann Kees. *Der Goetterglaube im alten Aegypten.* 2. Auflage. Berlin 1956.

Alexandre Piankoff. "The Theology in Ancient Egypt," *Antiquity and Survival,* no. 6 (1956), pp. 488-500.

Siegfried Schott. "Mythen in den Pyramidentexten," in Samuel A. B. Mercer, *The Pyramid Texts,* Vol. IV, pp. 106-23.

C. Scott Littleton (essay date 1970)

SOURCE: "The 'Kingship in Heaven' Theme," in *Myth and Law Among the Indo-Europeans: Studies in Indo-European Comparative Mythology*, edited by Jaan Puhvel, University of California Press, 1970, pp. 83-121.

[*In the essay that follows, Littleton studies various versions of the widespread and pervasive motif of the divine king, and concludes that the theme does not have a single Indo-European origin.*]

Introduction

By all odds the most important single episode in Greek mythology is the one that begins with the emergence of Ouranos out of Chaos and ends with the final triumph of Zeus over Kronos and his fellow Titans; for on this account of how Zeus came to succeed to the "Kingship in Heaven" depend, directly or indirectly, almost all other Greek myths, sagas, and folktales, to say nothing of their associated rituals and ceremonies. It formed, in the Malinowskian sense, the "charter"[1] that legitimized the position of the Olympians relative to all other classes of natural and supernatural beings, and in so doing provided a firm foundation for the religious beliefs and practices of the ancient Greek-speaking community.

Yet, despite its fundamental importance to the whole structure of Greek myth and religion, the parenthood of these traditions relative to the "Kingship in Heaven" remains obscure. Through archaeological and linguistic research[2] it has become increasingly apparent that the "Kingship in Heaven" theme,[3] as it has come to be called, was in fact quite widely distributed and that it generally served a legitimizing function similar to that served by it among the Greeks. Its presence can be documented in the Hittite and Hurrian "Kumarbi" myths, in the Phoenician "Theogony" of Philo of Byblos, in the Iranian *Sh-n-meh* or "Book of Kings," as recorded by Firdausi, and, as I attempt to demonstrate, in two Bablyonian accounts of the Creation—the well-known *Enãma-Elish*[4] and the newly translated "Theogony of Dunnu"—and in the Norse traditions surrounding the ancestry and ascendance of Odin, as recorded in the *Edda*'s of Saemund and Snorri. In each instance a single pattern of events is present: an existing generation of gods was preceded by two (and in some cases three) earlier generations of supernatural beings, each succeeding generation being presided over by a "king in heaven" who has usurped (or at least assumed) the power of his predecessor. Moreover, there is generally a fourth figure, a monster of some sort, who, acting on behalf of the deposed "king" (in the Iranian and Babylonian versions, as we shall see, the monster became identified with the deposed "king" himself), presents a challenge to the final heavenly ruler and must be overcome before the latter can assert full and perpetual authority.

In considering the source of this "Kingship in Heaven" theme, one question necessarily looms large to the student of comparative Indo-European mythology: despite its apparent absence in the Indic, Balto-Slavic, Italic, and Celtic traditions (discussed later) and its occurrence in a variety of non-Indo-European speaking traditions, is there any possibility that the theme is ultimately derived from one that was present in the Indo-European *Urmythologie?* Perhaps the most ardent advocate of the Indo-European origin theory is the eminent Swedish Iranianist Stig Wikander,[5] who maintains that "l'histoire des Ouranides," as he terms it, reached the non-Indo-European peoples of Mesopotamia and Syria only *after* they had come into contact with the Hittites and Indo-Iranians who penetrated this region after 2000 B.C. This opinion is not shared, however, by most Orientalists. E. A. Speiser,[6] for example, although he suggests that the extant form of the *Enãma-Elish* seems to reflect an immediate Hittite or Hurrian origin, is nevertheless convinced that its roots lie deep in the early Babylonian and Sumerian traditions. A basically similar view has been advanced by the Hittitologist H. G. Güterbock,[7] who asserts that the Hittite version of the theme, from which the Phoenician and eventually the Greek versions appear to derive, is itself based upon Hurrian models, which in turn are probably derived from early Mesopotamian prototypes.

No one, however, has as yet attempted to resolve this question on the basis of a systematic, comparative survey of *all* the mythological materials relative to the "Kingship in Heaven."[8] The purposes of this paper[9] are thus (1) to put into evidence the salient points of similarity and difference between the several versions of the theme in question, among which I include two that heretofore have not generally been recognized as such, the Norse and Babylonian versions, and (2) to consider the question of Indo-European origin in light of the patterns revealed by this survey. I begin with the Greek version which, although it contains neither the oldest[10] nor necessarily the "purest" expression of the theme, is by far the most elaborate, best documented, and most familiar of the versions to be considered and thus can serve as a convenient point of departure.

The Greek Version

Inasmuch as the Homeric epics do not fully express the "Kingship in Heaven" theme and thus, for our purposes, cannot serve as primary sources, the earliest and most important Greek source of data concerning the theme under discussion is to be found in the Hesiodic poems, especially the *Theogony*. Composed during the later part of the eighth century B.C.,[11] the *Theogony* is concerned primarily with the events surrounding and preceding the ascension of Zeus as "king" in heaven. It served as the major source of information about cosmogonic and theogonic matters for most Greek (and Roman) poets, essayists, and dramatists. A second source is to be found in the *Bibliotheca* of Apollodorus, which was composed sometime during the first or second centuries B.C.[12] While drawing heavily upon Hesiod, Apollodorus also includes certain data that are at variance with those contained in the *Theogony,* and therefore, as it may reflect an ongoing popular tradition that was either overlooked by or inaccessible to Hesiod, the *Bibliotheca* must be considered a primary source not only for the Greek version of the "Kingship in Heaven" but for Greek mythological data in general. Our third source is the *Dionysiaca* of Nonnos which, despite its fifth century A.D. date,[13] includes some original materials relevant to the theme not found elsewhere among classical works on myth. Nonnos, as we shall see, is especially concerned with the combat between Zeus and Typhon, and his description of this struggle may reflect a popular tradition unknown to either Hesiod or Apollodorus.

According to both the *Theogony* and the *Bibliotheca*[14] the first "king" in heaven is Ouranos ("Heaven" or "Sky"). In the *Theogony,* Heaven is born of Gaia ("Earth"), who is apparently autochthonous, although she is preceded by the nonpersonified state or condition termed Chaos: "Verily at first Chaos came to be, but next wide bosomed Earth, the ever sure foundation of all. . . . " Earth or Gaia then gives birth to various beings (e.g., Hills; Pontos ["the Deep"]; *Theogony* 130) who are not specifically important to the theme under consideration. Next, she takes Heaven as a husband: "But afterwards she lay with Heaven . . ." (*Theogony* 135). Thus Hesiod defines the first generation.

In the *Bibliotheca,* these events are simplified: "Sky was the first who ruled over the whole world. And having wedded Earth . . ." (1.1.1). There is no hint of the incestuous situation described in the *Theogony*. To Apollodorus, both Sky and Earth appear to be autochthonous.

At any event, with the marriage of Ouranos and Gaia we may proceed to the second generation, which in-cludes the offspring of this primal pair, the youngest of whom is destined to become the second "king" in heaven. In the *Theogony* (135) Earth has intercourse with Heaven and brings forth first "Okeanos, Koios and Krios and Hyperion and Iapetos, Theia and Rhea, Themis and Mnemosyne . . . Phoibe and . . . Tethys." After these, she bears the so-called Hundred-handed: Kottos, Briareos, and Gyes, termed by Hesiod "presumptuous children" (*Theogony* 145). Then she bears the Cyclopes ("Orb-eyed"): Brontes, Steropes, and Arges;[15] finally, she bears Kronos.[16]

In the *Bibliotheca* these events are similarly reported (1.1.2-4). Here, Apollodorus introduces the terms "Titan" (male) and "Titanide" (female) to refer to these offspring, terms Hesiod uses at a later point (see below).

Ouranos was jealous of his offspring, especially the Cyclopes and the giant Hundred-handed, and "used to hide them all away in a secret place of Earth . . . [Tartaros] . . . so soon as each was born, and would not suffer them to come up into the light . . ." (*Theogony* 155). Apollodorus (1.1.2-4) gives us a similar picture, locating Tartaros as a "gloomy place in Hades as far from earth as earth is distant from the sky." Here he follows Hesiod, who, in a later context (*Theogony* 725) describes Tartaros as so far below the earth that "a brazen anvil falling from earth nine nights and days would reach Tartaros upon the tenth."

Gaia, incensed over the treatment of her children by Ouranos, exhorts them to "' . . . punish the vile outrage of your father; for he first thought of doing shameful things'" (*Theogony* 165). None but Kronos, however, has the courage to take action (*Theogony* 165), and he tells her: "' . . . I will undertake to do this deed, for I reverence not our father of evil name. . . . '" The deed consists of an emasculation of Ouranos, performed with an "element of grey flint" made into a "jagged sickle" (*Theogony* 170), which Apollodorus (1.1.4) terms an "adamantine sickle."[17] Kronos ambushes his father, cuts off the latter's "members," and casts them into the sea. The blood so spilled impregnates Earth, who gives birth to the Giants (*Theogony* 180) and to the Furies (*Bibliotheca* 1.1.4). The seaborne "members" ultimately reach Cyprus and give birth to Aphrodite.[18]

With the emasculation of Ouranos his power has gone, and Kronos becomes "king in heaven." It is worth noting here for later comparative purposes that Ouranos is *not* killed by Kronos, merely rendered powerless. Kronos is a rebel, but not a parricide.

As regards the nature of this rebellion there seems to be a divergence between the two main sources. Hesiod, as we have seen, gives the impression that it was all accomplished—through guile—by Kronos himself, whereas Apollodorus implies that Kronos was merely the leader of a general attack against the father, one in which all save one of those siblings not previously consigned to Tartaros took part (*Bibliotheca* 1.1.4): "And they, all but Ocean, attacked him . . . and having dethroned their father, they brought up their brethren who had been hurled down to Tartaros, and committed the sovereignty to Kronos." In any case, after his ascension to power Kronos reconsigns all(?) these siblings to Tartaros (*Bibliotheca* 1.1.5): "But he again bound and shut them up in Tartaros. . . . "

Kronos, now firmly seated on the heavenly throne, marries his sister Rhea (*Theogony* 455; *Bibliotheca* 1.1.5). The children produced by this union suffer an unhappy fate, for Kronos, hearing from Heaven and Earth a prophecy that he is destined to be overthrown by his own son (*Theogony* 410, *Bibliotheca* 1.1.5), swallows his offspring as fast as they are born. Here, too, we have an episode that may be used for later comparative purposes: the swallowing of one's offspring.

The swallowed children include first (*Bibliotheca* 1.1.5) Hestia, "then Demeter and Hera, and after them Pluto (Hades) and Poseidon." Finally, pregnant with Zeus, Rhea decides to foil Kronos. As to the birth of Zeus our sources differ slightly. Both Apollodorus and Hesiod claim that the event took place in Crete; just where in Crete has long been a matter of some debate.[19]

A great deal of attention is given to the events surrounding the birth and upbringing of this youngest of Kronos' sons, an attention directed neither to the births of Zeus's siblings nor to those of the preceding generations of gods (or Titans), and several of these events must be mentioned as they have analogues in the versions to be discussed shortly. After hiding her son in Crete, Rhea gives Kronos (*Theogony* 485) "a great stone wrapped in swaddling clothes. Then he took it in his hands and thrust it down into his belly. . . . " Thus is Kronos deceived by his wife, an event that seems to parallel the duplicity of Gaia in the castration of Ouranos. Apollodorus gives us some information concerning the childhood of Zeus which may also have some comparative value (*Bibliotheca* 1.1.7): "She [Rhea] gave him to the Kouretes and to the nymphs Adrasteia and Ida,[20] daughters of Melissues, to nurse. So these nymphs fed the child on the milk of Amalthea." This last is apparently either a goat or a cow.[21] We shall have occasion to observe two other cases of this sort, that is, suckling by a goat or a cow, in the Iranian and in the Norse traditions.

Thus, Zeus matures to manhood, being one of the few Greek gods (or Titans) to have a defined childhood.[22] Both Apollodorus (1.2.1) and Hesiod (*Theogony* 490) indicate that this childhood lasted for a fair number of years.

Upon reaching adulthood, Zeus returns to heaven and sets about the overthrow of his father. According to the *Bibliotheca* (1.2.1) he "took Metis, daughter of Ocean, to help him, and she gave Kronos a drug to swallow, which forced him to disgorge first the stone and then the children whom he had swallowed. . . . " In the *Theogony* (495) Zeus is aided by Earth, who, apparently realizing that her son is evil, beguiles Kronos with "deep suggestions" and causes him to vomit up her grandchildren. This time, however, the older generation does not give up without a fight, and there ensues the famous "War of the Titans and Gods," (the latter term now used by both Hesiod and Apollodorus to distinguish the third generation [i.e., that of Zeus, Poseidon, Hera, *et al.*] from the two that preceded it). The war lasts ten years (*Bibliotheca* 1.2.1). On the one side are ranged Kronos and his siblings (save those still bound in Tartaros), and on the other Zeus, his mother,[23] and his siblings. Zeus enlists the aid of the Hundred-handed and the Cyclopes, whom he delivers from their subterranean prison. The latter forge thunderbolts for use against their Titan brethren, and for this they later escape the punishment of Kronos and the rest of the Titans (*Bibliotheca* 1.2.2). It is in this connection that we first see Zeus associated with the sky and with meteorological phenomena, for Zeus's chief weapon is the thunderbolt.

Having defeated the Titans, Zeus now becomes the third and perpetual "king in heaven." As Apollodorus puts it (1.2.2), Zeus "overcame the Titans, shut them up in Tartaros, and appointed the Hundred-handed their guards.[24] According to the *Bibliotheca* (1.2.2), the gods cast lots for the sovereignty, and "Zeus was allotted the dominion of the sky, to Poseidon the dominion of the sea, and to Pluto the dominion in Hades." This lot-casting aspect is not included in the *Theogony;* apparently Hesiod merely assumed that Zeus succeeded to the position vacated by his father.

Thus the Olympians, a new breed of supernatural beings, have succeeded to power. But this power is not yet secure; it remains to be confirmed by the conflict between Zeus and a final challenger, the monster Typhon (or Typhoeus).[25]

According to Hesiod, "Typhoeus" is the youngest child of Earth, fathered by a personification of Tartaros at some point following the defeat of the Titans (*Theogony* 820). Apollodorus agrees as to the parentage of the monster, but locates his birth at a somewhat later point, that is, after a successful conclusion of the war of the Olympians against the Giants (offspring of Earth; see above). According to the *Bibliotheca* (1.4.2), "When the gods had overcome the giants, Earth, still more outraged, had intercourse with Tartaros and brought forth Typhon in Cilicia, a hybrid between man and beast." This reference to Cilicia has been used to claim an Oriental origin for the Typhon story; I return to this point shortly when I consider the Phoenician and Hittite traditions.

While there are some minor differences as to details, all three of our Greek sources agree upon one important aspect of Typhon's (or Typhoeus') physical appearance: snakes grow from his body. As Hesiod puts it (*Theogony* 823), "From his shoulders grew a hundred heads of a snake." This aspect of Typhon's appearance will be especially important when we turn to the Iranian version (cf. below, Firdausi's description of the monster Zohak). Also worthy of note here is Nonnos' description of Typhon advancing to battle (*Dionysiaca* 1.266-268), "There stood Typhon in the fish-giving sea, his feet firm on the weedy bottom, his belly in the air and (his head?) crushed in the clouds," which corresponds almost exactly to a similar description in the Hittite version (see below, the description of the monster Ullikummi before Mount Hazzi).

That Zeus defeats this monstrous challenger is agreed upon by all concerned. But between Hesiod and both Apollodorus and Nonnos there are some important divergences when it comes to the manner and location of this defeat. In the *Theogony* the defeat of Typhoeus is accomplished rapidly and apparently with little effort on Zeus's part; the latter merely "leaped from Olympus and struck him (i.e., Typhoeus), and burned all the marvelous heads of the monster about him." This accomplished, "Typhoeus was hurled down, a maimed wreck . . ."; finally, "in the bitterness of his anger Zeus cast him into wide Tartaros" (*Theogony* 850-869). Apollodorus, however, claims that Zeus uses an "adamantine sickle" to inflict a mortal wound upon Typhon, who flees to "Mount Kasios[26] which overhangs Syria." There, however, Typhon is able to wrest the sickle from Zeus and use it(?) to sever the sinews of the latter's hands and feet.[27] Then Typhon lifts Zeus to his shoulders (his power having briefly returned, apparently owing to Zeus's temporary physical incapacity) and carries him to the famous Corycian cave, again in Cilicia. Hiding the sinews, he leaves the "she-dragon Delphyne" to guard his prisoner. Hermes and Aigipan steal the sinews from their bearskin hiding place and, unobserved by the monster, fit them again to Zeus (*Bibliotheca* 1.3.2). There is also a tradition (Oppian, *Halicutica* 3.15-25) wherein Corycian Pan lures Typhon out of the cave with a fish meal. In any event, Zeus regains his power. He pursues Typhon across Thrace and finally to Sicily, where he administers the coup de grâce by burying the monster inside Mount Etna (*Bibliotheca* 1.3.3).

It is clear that this final battle between the chief of the Olympians and the last and most monstrous representative of the old order involves more than is usually involved in most mythological monster slayings. Nonnos underscores this: "No herds of cattle were the cause of that struggle, no flocks of sheep, this was no quarrel for a beautiful woman, no fray for a petty town: *heaven itself was the stake in the fight . . .*" (*Dionysiaca* 2.359-363; italics mine). Thus, having defeated Typhon, Zeus has firmly consolidated the position of his revolutionary Olympian regime. Henceforth, he will rule as perpetual and unchallenged "king" in heaven.

Before leaving the Typhon episode, I should perhaps mention in passing that some years ago F. Vian suggested that it presents a number of interesting parallels to the widespread and quite probably Indo-European tradition wherein a hero (or a triad of heroes) slays a three-headed monster that is menacing the peace and security of the community (cf. the Indian account of the conflict between Indra and the tricephalic son of Tvastar and the Roman legend of a fight between the three Horatii and the three Curiatii).[28] I shall have more to say about this later on in the context of a general discussion of the possibility that the idea of the divine kingship is Indo-European in origin.

The myths concerning the later exploits of Zeus, his brethren, and his offspring, as well as those that concern the affairs of gods and mortals in subsequent generations (e.g., the Oedipus cycle, the siege of Troy) are not specifically germane to the theme in question, and therefore the delineation of the Greek version is concluded at this point. If I have dwelt here overlong, it is only because in the Greek tradition relative to the "Kingship in Heaven" there is a "model," so to speak, which can be utilized in making comparative statements as I consider the evidence from Anatolia, Phoenicia, Iran, Scandinavia, and Mesopotamia.

The Hurrian-Hittite Version

Since the first study over thirty years ago[29] of the Hittite "Theogony" and the Hittite myth which H. G. Güterbock[30] has labeled the "Song of Ullikummi," there has been a renewed interest in the argument—originally based on the presence of a Phoenician version of the theme under consideration—that the Greek "Kingship in Heaven" tradition just delineated is actually composed of myths having their origin somewhere in the ancient Near East. Indeed, I use the term "Hittite-Hurrian" here because of the indisputable evidence[31] that the Hurrians, who were well established in northern Syria and Mesopotamia by the middle of the second millennium B.C., and whose language appears to have been neither Indo-European nor Semitic, also possessed versions of the myths discussed below.

The texts containing the Hittite and/or Hurrian myths in question date approximately from the thirteenth century B.C. and were translated from a series of cuneiform tablets[32] found at Hattusha, the ancient Hittite capital, the site of which is located near the modern Turkish village of Bogazköy. These tablets are not well preserved and countless interpolations have had to be made in order to arrive at anything like a coherent narrative.[33] That which Güterbock terms the "Theogony"—the Hittite title is unfortunately missing—deals specifically with the "Kingship in Heaven." In it we see four generations of gods. The first is called Alalu, who reigns in heaven nine "years."[34] His future successor, Anu, is described as he who "bows down to his [Alalu's] feet and puts the cups for drinking into his hand" (i.10-11).[35] Although Anu (whose name derives from the Akkadianized form of the Sumerian god An, or 'Sky'[36]) is not specifically identified as Alalu's son, the fact that a god Alala is listed in a Babylonian god list as a father of Anu[37] leaves no doubt as to the filial relationship here. In the ninth "year" of Alalu's reign Anu rebels against him and either drives or hurls him "down to the dark earth" (i.12), the latter expression apparently referring to a subterranean region.[38]

Thus, Anu becomes the second "king in heaven." But he, too, must cope with a rebellious offspring, the "mighty Kumarbi."[39] At first, Kumarbi is described as serving Anu in a manner identical to that in which the latter had served Alalu; however, like his father before him, Anu is only permitted to reign for nine "years," and in the ninth "year" Kumarbi rebels. This time the elder god flees, but Kumarbi "took Anu by the feet and pulled him down from heaven" (i.23-24). Then follows a most interesting passage in light of our Greek "model": "He [Kumarbi] bit his loins[40] [so that] his manhood was absorbed in Kumarbi's interior . . ." (i.25); compare Kronos' emasculation of Ouranos. Indeed, the striking correspondences[41] here between Anu and Ouranos and between Kumarbi and Kronos have been noted frequently (see above).

Subsequent to his deposition and emasculation, Anu informs Kumarbi that by "absorbing" his "manhood" he has been impregnated with five "heavy" divinities: the Weather-god (i.e., the Hurrian Teshub),[42] the river goddess Aranzah (i.e., Tigris),[43] Tashmishu,[44] who is destined to be the vizier of the gods, and two others whose names are not mentioned by Anu.[45] Having thus addressed his successor, Anu "went up to heaven" and, after a visit to Nippur, perhaps to consult its chief deity Enlil about his pregnancy, Kumarbi becomes the third to occupy the heavenly throne.

From here on the text is too fragmentary for a consecutive narrative. It appears that Kumarbi attempts to avoid bearing these unwelcome offspring by spitting out Anu's seed (end of col. i);[46] nevertheless, a fragmentary reference to Kumarbi's failure to count months and the phrase "the ninth month came" clearly indicate that he carried Teshub *et al.* within him for a full term. Güterbock[47] points out that the theme of the mutilated first part of column ii is childbirth and that two of the gods in Kumarbi's "interior," Marduk and KA.ZAL (see n. 45), discuss with him several ways in which they might be born. Especially miraculous is the birth

of the Weather-god or Teshub[48] (cf. the attention devoted by our Greek sources to the birth of Zeus,[49] to whom, as we shall see, Teshub corresponds in most respects). Then follows a passage that is especially interesting in view of the equivalence between Kumarbi and Kronos. In it someone (Kumarbi?) says "give me the child . . . I shall eat" (i.42); later there occurs the expression "Kumarbi begins to eat" (i.52), and prominent mention of the words "mouth" and "teeth" in connection with the Weather-god.

It seems that Teshub and his siblings are able to dethrone Kumarbi, for when we first meet the Weather-god he is already "king in heaven." Just how the rebellion is accomplished is not quite clear. Is it possible that Earth, like her Greek counterpart, conspired with her offspring (if indeed they were such) to bring about Kumarbi's downfall? Considering Earth's probable connection with the birth of Teshub and his siblings, this is quite likely; perhaps we have here a merging of Gaia and Rhea in the person of Earth.

The second Hittite myth relevant to the theme in question is entitled the "Song of Ullikummi" and contains many important parallels to the previously discussed Typhon story.[50] Kumarbi, having been dethroned, has intercourse with a rock; from this unnatural union is produced the Stone-monster[51] (also termed the Diorite after the substance of which the monster is composed), or Ullikummi. Conceived by his father in order to avenge the latter's overthrow, Ullikummi is destined to be a rebel against Teshub.[52] That Typhon was born with a similar purpose in life can be seen from a passage in the *Dionysiaca* (2.565-568) wherein Kronides (an epithet of Zeus), after wounding the monster sorely, chides him saying: "A fine ally has old Kronos found in you, Typhoeus! . . . A jolly champion of Titans!'"

The young Ullikummi is placed on a shoulder of the Atlas-like Upelluri and allowed to grow: "In one day one yard he grew, but in one month one furlong he grew . . . when the fifteenth day came the Stone had grown high. And in the sea on his knees like a blade he stood. Out of the water he stood, the Stone . . . , and the sea up to the place of the belt like a garment reached . . . ; he was lifted, the Stone, and up in Heaven the temples and the chamber he reached" (I.23-32). This can be compared to Nonnos' description of Typhon cited earlier, that is, feet in water and head "crushed" against the clouds.

The first of the gods to see Ullikummi is the Sun-god, who reports his terrified observations to Teshub. The latter goes to see for himself, and when he does so he weeps, for apparently he can see no way of overcoming this monster. His sister, Ishtar (Aranzah?) comforts him and tries to enchant Ullikummi by music (cf. Kadmos' charming of Typhoeus while recovering Zeus's sinews [*Dionysiaca* 1.409-534]). Here, however, we learn that the Stone is deaf and blind. So Teshub decides to fight him, but to no avail, for the monster is too powerful. The gods retreat from this battle, fought in the shadow of Mount Hazzi (i.e., Mount Kasios on the Syrian coast), and retire to Kummiya,[53] the city of Teshub. Ullikummi follows, endangering even Teshub's wife Hebat. At this point Tashmishu enters the picture. After climbing a tower to tell Hebat of her husband's defeat, he suggests to Teshub that they visit Ea,[54] the Babylonian god of wisdom and witchcraft (cf. the *Enū-ma-Elish,* shortly to be discussed, wherein Ea occupies a prominent position), and together they journey to the wise god's home in Apsuwa (the Babylonian Apsu).[55] Ea, willing to help, first ascertains that Upelluri has no knowledge of what is resting on his shoulder and then orders the "former gods" (i.e., those who ruled in heaven before Alalu, such as Enlil, the Sumerian storm-god) to produce the "ancient tool" (a sickle?) used at one time to separate Earth and Heaven. With this tool Ea cuts Ullikummi from Upelluri's shoulder and thus magically renders him powerless.[56] Here, too, we have a parallel to the Greek tradition, for Apollodorus, as we have seen, described the use of a cutting tool (i.e., the "adamantine sickle") by Zeus in his struggle with Typhon. The same tool, of course, was used against Ouranos by Kronos, and some authorities, both ancient and modern, have interpreted the castration of Ouranos as a symbolic separation of heaven and earth.[57] It is interesting that the Hittites preserve a tradition of a primeval cutting tool once used to separate heaven and earth, and which must later be used to defeat Ullikummi, although no specific tool is mentioned in the account of Anu's castration. Perhaps in the latter case the teeth of Kumarbi have been substituted for the stone "teeth" of a neolithic sickle (i.e., the "ancient cutting tool").

When word reaches the gods that Ullikummi has been rendered powerless, they join together under the leadership of Teshub and attack the monster. From here on the text is unreadable; however, we may assume with Güterbock[58] that Teshub and his fellows are ultimately victorious. For it appears that here, as in the Greek tradition, the new "king in heaven" must meet this final challenger so as to validate his position as perpetual ruler, and there is no doubt that Teshub, like Zeus, is able to accomplish this validation. It should be noted, though, that the conflict here is much more general than in the Greek tradition. Perhaps in the conflict between Teshub and Ullikummi we have a merger of the Titanomachia and the Typhon fight.

The Phoenician Version

In the *Phoenician History* of Herennios Philo of Byblos, known only through the works of Eusebius (*Praeparatio Evangelica*) and Porphyrius (*De Abstinentia*), is contained a version of the "Kingship in Heaven" which closely parallels the two just discussed, a version that has often been regarded as an intermediary between those of the Hittites and the Greeks. Philo's date is uncertain, although the best evidence leads me to believe that he wrote during the latter half of the first century A.D.; Clemen places his birth in the last years of the reign of the Emperor Claudius.[59] Claiming to have obtained his information from the works of a certain Sanchunjathon, a Phoenician scholar who, he asserts, "lived before the Trojan War," Philo attempts to reconstruct the "history" of his city and to trace the origins of its gods. He begins by outlining a four-generational sequence of "kings in heaven," all of whom are intimately associated with the city of Byblos and its environs.

According to Philo, the first "king in heaven" is named Eliun (or Hypsistos "Highest") (I.14),[60] who with his wife Bruth (i.e., Beirut) comes to live in Byblos. They give birth to a son called Ouranos and a daughter named Ge or Gaia. Ge and Ouranos marry and produce four sons: El (who is also referred to as Kronos), Baitylos, Dagon, and Atlas (I.16). A quarrel ensues between Ouranos and his wife, and El (or Kronos) and his siblings side with their mother. Ouranos then tries to destroy his rebellious offspring, but El, on the advice of Hermes, whom he has taken as a counselor, forges a sickle (or spear?) and with it drives out his father. El then becomes "king in heaven" (or at least in Byblos), but turns out to be a bad ruler, casting out his brother Atlas and murdering a son and a daughter. Meanwhile, Ouranos has fled unharmed. He sends Rhea, Astarte, and Dione, his young daughters, to plead his case before El. These three El takes to wife,[61] and by each he produces a number of children. The most important of these is Baal[62] (or Baaltis), who succeeds him.

Thirty-two years later, El lures his father back to Byblos, into an ambush, and castrates him (cf. *Theog.* 175). Thus, the castration theme is present, although it does not accompany the deposition of the "Heaven figure" as it does in the Greek and Hittite-Hurrian versions. Furthermore, what appears to me to be a crucial element is lacking here: the idea that castration is a necessary step in reducing the power of the Heaven figure. In Philo it seems but an afterthought. Castration figures again in Philo's account, although this time it is self-inflicted. For some obscure reason El mutilates himself thirty-two years after so altering his father.

Finally, the fourth generation (in the person of Baal) takes over the heavenly kingship. This transfer of power is apparently made without much conflict, an occurrence unique in the distribution of the theme. Typhon is mentioned by Philo along with the children of El, but there is no mention of a fight.[63] Moreover, the role of the "Zeus figure" (Baal) is minor when compared with that played by him in the Greek and Hittite-Hurrian versions, and in the Iranian, Norse, and Babylonian versions as well.

In view of its late date and the high probability that its author was thoroughly familiar with Hesiod, many scholars have been skeptical of this Phoenician "Theogony," labeling it a poor attempt at syncretism. The discovery of some Hurrian texts at Ras Shamra, however, wherein the double name El-Kumarbi occurs,[64] has thrown a new light on the matter. As El is clearly identified by Philo with Kronos, it is reasonable to infer that there was some sort of a Kronos-El-Kumarbi syncretism present in northern Syria, at least, as early as 1400 B.C. If this is correct, then it is also quite reasonable to infer with Güterbock that the Phoenician tradition here forms a link between the Hittite-Hurrian version and the later Greek version, and that what formerly appeared as rank syncretism on Philo's part can now be seen as antedating rather than reflecting the Hesiodic version of the theme.[65]

But there still remain other possibilities. That the Phoenicians undoubtedly received elements of the Kumarbi myth from the Hittites as the latter expanded their empire after 1500 B.C. is not questioned here; indeed, the Ras Shamra evidence renders it almost certain. What is questioned, however, is the assumption that the Phoenicians were necessarily the link in a chain of diffusion from northern Syria to Greece. There is always the possibility that the theme reached Hesiod and/or his immediate sources directly from the Hittite-Hurrian region. This alternative is enhanced somewhat by L. R. Palmer's assertion[66] that the Luvians, first cousins to the Hittites, invaded the Peloponnesus and Crete at the beginning of the second millennium B.C., and that the first speakers of Greek arrived several centuries later. If Palmer is correct in this assertion, and there is good reason to believe that he is, then it is remotely possible that the "Kingship in Heaven" theme was taken over by the Greeks along with other aspects of Luvian culture.[67] Another possibility, that the theme was borrowed directly from Babylonia during Mycenaean times, is discussed presently.

The Iranian Version

It was Stig Wikander who, in 1951,[68] first demonstrated the presence of the "Kingship in Heaven"—if indeed the term "heaven" is applicable in this instance—in the Iranian tradition. Bypassing the more ancient and mythological Avestan literature, Wikander pointed out that a threefold set of royal usurpers similar to those present in the Greek, Hittite-Hurrian, and Phoenician traditions occupies a prominent position in Firdausi's *Shānāmeh,* which was composed about A.D. 976. Despite its relatively recent date and the high probability that its author was familiar with Greek myth, the *Shāh-nāmeh* has long been recognized as a repository of popular traditions not elsewhere represented in Iranian literature. This would certainly appear to be true as far as the theme in question is concerned.

In any event, the three Iranian kings cited by Wikander as comparable with Ouranos, Kronos, Zeus, *et al.,* are Jamshid, Zohak, and Feridun, who occupy, respectively, positions four, five, and six in Firdausi's king list. Jamshid is preceded by three relatively indistinct figures, Kaiumers (equals Gayōmart in the *Avesta*), Husheng, and Tahumers. These three do not seem to be related to their successors in any important sense—Jamshid is made the son of Tahumers, but little else is said about the relationship between them. Thus it is Jamshid who occupies the Ouranos-like position, despite his lack of an autochthonous or truly divine origin.

Jamshid, whose name corresponds to that of Yima Xša-ēta[69] in the *Avesta,* is said to have ruled for some seven hundred years, and the early portion of this reign is described as a sort of Golden Age, when men were at peace with one another and the land was bountiful. But this state of affairs did not last. "Then it came about that the heart of Jamshid was uplifted with pride, and he forgot whence came his weal and the source of his blessings."[70] Wikander, in discussing the position of Jamshid, notes that he "règne d'abord sur une humanité heureuse, mais il commet ensuite le premier péché, ce qui amène la perte de la Gloire Royale et sa chute."[71] Wikander also remarks that some texts show Jamshid as having been deceived by "une figure féminine qui aurait inspiré ses transgressions et causé sa chute."[72] Thus, we have some indication that here, too, there is a Gaia-like figure somewhere in the background.[73]

Jamshid is eventually overthrown by Zohak (equals Aži Dahāka in the *Avesta*), who in terms of our model occupies an ambiguous position. He is at once Typhon and Kronos. Both in his physical appearance and in his relationship with the third member of the trio, Feridun, who occupies the position of Zeus figure, Zohak strongly resembles Typhon. Yet he enters the epic occupying the position of a Kronos figure. Like Typhon, his physical appearance is characterized by the presence of snakes growing from his shoulders;[74] yet he is the one who overthrows Jamshid and who commits the inevitable act of mutilation, although in this instance it is not castration but rather a sawing in half.[75]

There are two interesting parallels here to the Phoenician version. Like El, Zohak waits a hundred years before mutilating his deposed enemy: "in the hundredth year [after his overthrow] the impious shah [Jamshid] appeared one day beside the Sea of Chin. Zohak clutched him forthwith, gave him no respite, and, sawing him asunder, freed the world from him and the fear that he inspired."[76] A second parallel can be seen in the fact that Zohak, like El, marries two sisters who stand in close kinship to him—only in this instance they are sisters of the deposed first-generation ruler (Jamshid).

Wikander emphasizes the similarity between the saw that cut Jamshid in half and the sickle that castrated Ouranos. "Azdahak ou un autre ennemi le mutile avec une 'scie' . . . cette 'scie' est évidemment identique à la 'serpe aux dents aigues' d'Hésiode."[77] He also characterizes Zohak as the "neveu" of Jamshid, although nowhere in our reading of the epic is there any clear-cut statement as to the relationship, if any, between the two figures. Zohak is characterized simply as the son of an Arabian king[78] who is invited to come to Iran and replace Jamshid.

Zohak, in his turn, is overthrown by the grandson of Jamshid, Feridun (equals Thraētaona in the *Avesta*), who, like Zeus, has a marvelous childhood. Again we see the theme of the mother hiding away the child from the wrath of the father (in this case Zohak). Zohak, it seems, while having no offspring of his own, has an insatiable desire to consume human beings. Furthermore, the serpent-king dreams that Feridun will someday overcome him (cf. Kronos' fore-knowledge of Zeus's coming, and his subsequent swallowing of his offspring), and on the basis of this dream "bade the world be scoured for Feridun."[79] Feridun's mother first places him in the care of a wondrous cow, Purmaieh, who suckles the infant. Then, fearing that Zohak will find this hiding place, she removes him to the care of a shepherd "on the Mount Alberz" (i.e., the Elbruz?), who raises him to manhood. Here we can compare the hiding away of Zeus on Mount Ida (or Aigaion). Finally, Feridun grows to manhood and sets out to overcome his monstrous enemy. Instead of a cutting instrument, Feridun uses a club, the head of which is shaped like a cow—in memory of Purmaieh.[80] The combat between Feridun and Zohak is strongly reminiscent of the conflict between Zeus and Typhon. Again, it is a single-combat situation, not the type of group action which dethroned Kronos.

Feridun overpowers Zohak but does not actually kill him (a fusion, perhaps, of the Typhon and Kronos motifs); rather, he chains the monster to a rock[81] on Mount Demawend(?), and Zohak eventually dies of exposure. After this deed is accomplished, Feridun reigns as king, if not actually "in heaven," then certainly as a divine king in Iran.

While it is certain that the Avestan names Yima Xša-ēta, Aži Dahāka, and Thraētaona correspond, respectively, to Jamshid, Zohak, and Feridun, the only clear thematic parallels between the two sets of figures are that both Yima and Jamshid can be seen to be in one respect or another primordial (although both do actually have forebears), that both were "Golden Age" rulers who "sinned," that Aži Dahāka and his later namesake share draconic characteristics, and that both are rendered harmless, respectively, by Thraētaona and Feridun. Even in the latter instance there is an important difference. Thraētaona is characterized as the "smiter" of Aži Dahāka,[82] while Feridun, as we have seen, imprisons Zohak. Thus it can be safely asserted that the theme qua theme, despite some similarities, is not present in the *Avesta*.

Nor is it to be found in the Indic tradition. To be sure, there are some very general parallels, both thematic and philological, between the Avestan figures mentioned above and some of the dramatis personae of the Indic literature. For example, Avestan Yima parallels Vedic Yama; Aži Dahāka is equivalent to the three-headed monster Vrtra; Thraētaona bears a resemblance to Trita ptya, the slayer of Vrtra (also to Indra in this context); and the cow-headed weapon (*gurz*) used by Feridun is linguistically cognate to the thunderbolt *vajra* used in the slaying of Vrtra. But other than these isolated correspondences, together with one other possibility to be mentioned shortly in connection with the Norse version, there is no evidence for the presence of the theme in question in the *Veda's, Mahābhārata,* and so on.[83] This negative evidence, so to speak, is a most important matter when it comes to the question of possible Indo-European origins, and I return to it later on.

The Norse Version

All too often there is a tendency among students of comparative mythology to equate "Norse" with "Germanic," to assume that the materials contained in the *Edda's, Heimskringla, Gesta Danorum,* and the like, are a true reflection of common Germanic religious beliefs and practices. To make such an equation is, of course, an error; for it is abundantly clear that there were differences in religious outlook among the several branches of the Germanic-speaking peoples. One need only compare Tacitus with Saxo Grammaticus to see examples of these differences. While there are some common figures (e.g., *Tīwaz, probable prototype of Norse Týr, Anglo-Saxon Tiw, and perhaps the figure reflected in Tacitus' Tuisto),[84] any attempt to draw general conclusions about the nature of Germanic religion from any one region or era must be made cautiously.

Yet, when it comes to cosmogonic and theogonic matters we are necessarily limited to a single region and a single era: Scandinavia (primarily Iceland) in the eleventh and twelfth centuries A.D. Moreover, our chief sources,[85] the *Elder* or *Poetic Edda,* attributed to Saemund Siggfusson, and especially the *Younger,* or *Prose Edda* of Snorri Sturluson, were composed at a time when the old religion was fast giving way to Christianity (Snorri approaches his subject from an explicitly Christian standpoint), and the extent to which non-Norse materials were interwoven with the native tradition is still not wholly clear.

That Saemund and Snorri were aware—albeit dimly—of the mythic traditions of the eastern Mediterranean is entirely possible.[86] It is also possible that whatever parallels may exist between their accounts of the creation and those previously discussed in this paper are wholly or partially the result of independent invention. In any case, all the foregoing must be kept firmly in mind as we proceed to a brief examination of the Norse theogony to see if it contains materials relevant to the "Kingship in Heaven."

In the beginning was Ginnungagap (equivalent to the Greek Chaos), which can be loosely translated as "yawning void." Out of this yawning void were created initially two regions: Muspellheim on the south (i.e., a "Land of Fire") and Niflheim on the north (i.e., a "Land of Mist"). Ice crystals combined with sparks, and out of this combination there was created the first being, called Ymir. Ymir, defined as a giant of enormous proportions, lies down and sleeps. While he sleeps two things happen: first, a second autochthonous creature appears, a cow named Audhumla. While Ymir sleeps the cow nourishes him, at the same time she licks the salty ice and slowly uncovers first the hair, then the body of a third autochthon: Buri. Thus Audhumla serves as a link between these two generationally equivalent Jöntin, or "Giants" (occasionally rendered Etin). Meanwhile, in his sleep, Ymir androgynously gives birth to several offspring (*Lay of Vafthrudnir* 33): "The ice-*etin*'s [i.e., Ymir's] strong arms, beneath there grew both girl and boy, one with the other, the wise *etin*'s shanks begat a six-headed son." The latter is named Thrudgelmir. He, in turn, gives birth to the crafty Bergelmir. Thus, we have one three-generation line of descent from Ymir. As the *Lay of Vafthrudnir* (29) has it: "Ages before the earth was made, Bergelmir came to be. Thrudgelmir was that *thur*'s(?) father. But Aurgelmir [i.e., Örgelmir, or Ymir] oldest of all."

A second three-generation line descends from Buri, who, after emerging from the ice, produces a son: Bör. Bör marries a giantess named Bestla (one of Ymir's offspring?). They, in turn, produce three sons: Odin, Vili, and Vé (cf. Zeus, Poseidon, Hades). Odin and his siblings (who, unlike their Greek equivalents, become shadowy figures very quickly) are the first of the Aesir (or "Gods" as opposed to "Giants"). Their first act is to overthrow Ymir, and with him Thrudgelmir. Bergelmir they banish (or he escapes) to subterranean Jöntinheim (cf. Tartaros?).[87] Ymir they cut up (the tool involved is not mentioned), forming the world: "of Ymir's flesh the earth was shaped, of his blood the briny sea, of his hair, the trees, the hills of his bones, out of his skull the sky" (*Lay of Grimnir* 40).

There is a parallel to this in *Rig-Veda* 10.90, wherein Indra and others create the world from the flesh and bones of the giant Purusa. Another parallel can be seen in the Babylonian *Enūma-Elish,* in the use to which Marduk puts the body of the slain Tiamat. The simi-

larities here, however, may best be explained in terms of a common folkloristic motif which has nothing specifically to do with the theme under discussion. Yet the fact that Odin and his siblings *cut* the primeval figure is significant. It is this feature, rather than the subsequent use of his remains, that is relevant for our purposes.

In any event, it is only after the Jöntin have been defeated that Odin and his brothers create mankind.[88] This, of course, is paralleled in the Greek version (i.e., the human race is only created after the final defeat of the Titans; cf. *Bibliotheca* 1.4.1).

It is our contention that the events just described contain all the essential ingredients of the "Kingship in Heaven" theme: First, there is a three-generational line of descent (although bifurcated); second, there is the mutilation of the first-generation "king" (i.e., Odin's cutting up Ymir); third, there is the banishment of a descendant of this first-generation being by one who has usurped power from him (Bergelmir is the logical inheritor of Ymir); fourth, the final and perpetual holder of power (Odin) is, together with his siblings and offspring, defined as an altogether different sort of supernatural being (i.e., "Gods" or Aesir, as opposed to "Giants" or Jöntin; cf. the Greek distinction between "God" and "Titan"). And finally, there is a battle between these Aesir and the Giants, a battle that seems to be equivalent to that between the Olympians and the Titans[89] (or Giants, too, for that matter).

That the characteristic structure of the theme, as expressed in the Greek and Hittite-Hurrian tradition, is absent, must be admitted. Contained within a broad three-generational framework, however, most of the significant components of this structure are present. To put it another way, the same broad configuration is present in Norse mythology, yet the elements within this configuration are not for the most part structured as they are in the Greek tradition. Indeed, we have seen other cases, generally held to be part of the theme in question, which also deviate from this typological structure, yet which maintain the same broad configuration. We may cite here the Iranian version, wherein Zohak, who most clearly resembles Typhon, appears in the role of a Kronos figure. We may also cite the Phoenician case, wherein Baal does not have to fight his way to power, as is characteristic of the other versions—including the Norse.

It seems fair to assert that the Norse, like the Greeks, Hittites, Hurrians, Phoenicians, Iranians, and Babylonians, knew the "Kingship in Heaven" theme. Whether its presence here can best be explained in terms of diffusion or independent invention is still a moot point, although I believe that the former possibility is the more probable in view of the extremely late periods from which the primary sources date. There is, of course, the alternate possibility that the presence of the theme can be explained in terms of a common Indo-European heritage. Once again, let me defer consideration of this possibility—seemingly quite remote—until I look at the Babylonian versions.

The Babylonian Versions

Like the Norse version, the two Babylonian versions deviate in a number of important respects from that which for convenience sake I have labeled the typological version (i.e., that of the Greeks). Yet these two related accounts of how the gods came to be may well prove to be far closer to the source of the theme in question than any previously considered. Although no extant text of the *Enūma-Elish* is earlier than 1000 B.C., internal evidence alone indicates that its composition probably dates at least from the Old Babylonian period, that is, the early part of the second millennium B.C., and that its content may be considerably older.[90]

The *Enūma-Elish* begins with an account of the primeval state of things: "When on high the heaven had not been named,/Firm ground below had not been called by name,/Naught but primeval Apsu,[91] their begetter,/(And) Mummu-Tiamat,[92] she who bore them all,/Their waters commingling as a single body . . ." (i.1-4).[93] We see here the by now familiar pair of autochthons, in this instance defined as fresh and salt water. From this union several generations of divinities are born, including the figures (for our purposes obscure) Lahmu and Lahamu, Anshar and Kishar, and Anu. Finally, there appears the figure who, together with another shortly to be discussed, occupies the Kronos position, the "all-wise" Ea (or Nudimmud; cf. Sumerian Enki). Although the exact parentage and birth order of Ea are obscure, by all indications he is the youngest of the lot (who can, for our purposes, be reckoned as a single generation; that is, they band together and act as a generational unit).[94] If this interpretation is correct, then there is an interesting parallel here to the ultimogeniture pattern so clearly evident in the Greek version.

Under the apparent leadership of Ea, the gods of what we may term the second generation (see above) "disturbed Tiamat as they surged back and forth" (i.22). Apsu, too, is annoyed by "their hilarity in the Abode of Heaven" (i.24) and decides to do away with them. His decision is strengthened by the advice of the vizier Mummu,[95] but is opposed by Tiamat, who counsels forgiveness. Nevertheless, the gods discover Apsu's intentions. After putting Apsu to sleep with an incantation (cf. the "deep suggestions" with which Zeus beguiles Kronos[96]), Ea slays him, yet before doing so he tears off the former's tiara or halo (symbolic, perhaps, of sovereignty and the masculine vigor that accompanies it) and puts it on himself (i.60-69). Admittedly, I may be guilty of overinterpretation here, but it does occur to me that the act of tearing off Apsu's tiara is comparable with an act of castration. By so doing, Ea clearly renders his forbear powerless to resist, just as Kronos, Kumarbi, *et al.* render their progenitors powerless by dismembering or "biting" them. In any event, thus passes the first generation.

After having become "king in heaven" Ea[97] takes up residence upon the dead Apsu[98] and is joined by his wife Damkina. In time Damkina gives birth to the great Babylonian divinity Marduk, who is patently the Zeus figure in this version. Many lines follow describing Marduk's brilliance and prowess, for example, "He was the loftiest of the gods, surpassing was his stature,/His members were enormous, he was exceeding tall" (i.97-100). Meanwhile, Tiamat schemes in order to seek revenge for the slaying of her husband. She causes a heretofore unmentioned god, Ea's half-brother, Kingu, to be elevated to command of the Assembly of the Gods, apparently, though the text makes no mention of it, displacing Ea. She then sets about creating a host of monsters (cf. i.126). From this point on Ea fades into obscurity, and the threat presented by Tiamat and Kingu is met by Marduk. A great fight ensues. Marduk eventually slays Tiamat in single combat and destroys her host. He then captures the rebel Kingu and consigns him to Uggae, the god of the dead (iv. 119-120). Afterward, Marduk and Ea create heaven and earth from Tiamat's inflated body by splitting it in two[99] (cf. the fate of Ymir). Marduk now reigns perpetually as "king in heaven."[100] He has validated his claim to sovereignty by emerging victorious in the epic duel with Tiamat.

Taken as a whole, the *Enūma-Elish* presents some remarkable parallels to the other versions of the "Kingship in Heaven," although there are, of course, several important structural differences. For one thing, there is a bifurcation of the Kronos figure. Taken together, the careers of Ea *and* Kingu approximate closely that of the typical second generation "king": initially, in the person of Ea, we see him usurping the kingship through a ruse and (perhaps) performing an act of emasculation; later on, in the person of Kingu, we see him defeated by the Zeus figure and consigned to what would appear to be a Tartaros-like place. In the case of Tiamat we have not bifurcation but fusion. She is at once Gaia and Typhon (cf. Zohak, who is both Kronos and Typhon). It is in the latter role, however, that she appears most clearly, and the fight between her and Marduk is strikingly similar to that between Zeus and Typhon, Teshub and Ullikummi, and so on. The relationship between Tiamat and Kingu is, of course, the opposite of that between Kronos and Typhon or Kumarbi and Ullikummi: in the Babylonian account the "king" is a creature of the monster. Yet on balance it seems clear that the theogony contained in the *Enūma-Elish* is akin to those we have previously surveyed. And given its date, it is probably their prototype.

Until recently, the *Enūma-Elish* was the only known Babylonian creation myth that came anywhere near to approximating the idea of the divine kingship. In 1965, however, W. G. Lambert published (with A. R. Millard) and subsequently translated[101] a cuneiform text (BM 74329) which may be termed for convenience' sake the "Theogony of Dunnu."[102] In it we can see essentially the same course of events as described in the *Enūma-Elish,* although the locale and figures involved are for the most part quite distinct. The date of this new text is late. Lambert and Walcot assign it to the Late Babylonian period (i.e., between 635 and 330 B.C.), although it is suggested that it belongs to the earlier phase of this period and that, as in the case of the *Enūma-Elish,* it may contain materials originally composed perhaps as early as the beginning of the second millennium B.C.[103]

Here the action centers on the ancient city of Dunnu, an otherwise obscure place as far as the overall Babylonian tradition is concerned.[104] The text itself is far shorter and more literary than the one just discussed. In this instance the two autochthons are the figures Hain (unknown outside this text)[105] and Earth. Although the first three lines are incomplete, it appears that they give birth first to Sea (cf. Tiamat) by means of a plow, and then in an apparently more normal fashion to the male figure Amakandu (once again we encounter the ultimogeniture pattern). Amakandu is seduced by his mother: "[Earth] cast her eyes on Amakandu, her son,/'Come, let me make love to you' she said to him" (lines 8-9). After marrying his mother, Amakandu slays Hain and lays him to rest in the city of Dunnu, "which he loved" (line 12). He then assumes his father's overlordship of the city (line 13). Subsequently, Amakandu marries Sea (his sister: cf. Kronos and Rhea), who gives birth to a son called Lahar. Lahar in turn slays his father, marries his mother (i.e., Sea), and assumes the kingship. He, too, produces offspring: a daughter, River, and a son, whose first name is unreadable. The latter eventually kills both Lahar and Sea (his mother), marries River (his sister), and assumes power. At this point the text is somewhat obliterated, but the pattern seems to be carried out for at least two more generations. Sons slay their fathers and mothers, marry their sisters, and usurp the sovereignty. The female figures here whose names are readable include Ga'um and Ningeshtinna. There is no clear termination to the text, which is contained on the obverse and reverse of a single tablet, although the last readable line (40) indicates that the seat of power has been transferred to the city of Shupat [or Kupat].

In this "Theogony of Dunnu" can be seen in abbreviated and somewhat redundant form the essential outlines of the theme. The fact that there are five generations rather than three is not a crucial deterrent to putting the text into comparison with the other versions. It will be recalled that both the Hittite-Hurrian version and that of the Phoenicians, to say nothing of the version contained in the *Shāhnāmeh,* all describe one or more generations as existing prior to those upon whom attention is centered. In the present case the replication follows rather than precedes the principal sequence of events. To be sure, there is a major structural problem here in that in all other versions surveyed, including the *Enūma-Elish,* there is a denouement. One figure, be he Zeus, Teshub, Baal, Feridun, Odin, or Marduk, puts a seal on the succession. In the "Theogony of Dunnu," however, Lahar is in turn overthrown, and the series of usurpations is seemingly without end. Nor do we see here any indication of emasculation, although Lambert and Walcot, in comparing the text with Hesiod, suggest, perhaps leaning a bit too heavily upon Freud, that mother lust is equivalent to castration.[106] On this point I suggest that the very brevity and laconic nature of the text perhaps precluded the elaboration of such details as how the sovereignty was transferred (e.g., via emasculation or the "tearing off" of a tiara).

One interesting point of comparison between the Dunnu text and Hesiod's *Theogony* relates to the order in which Sea and River appear. According to Hesiod, the two figures associated with the sea, Pontos and Okeanos, emerge in succeeding generations. Pontos is essentially an autochthon, having emerged from Gaia without benefit of sexual intercourse, while Okeanos is born of Ouranos and Gaia. There is no doubt that Pontos is the sea proper, but Okeanos is more specifically defined as the 'father of rivers,'' the river that circles the earth (cf. *Theogony* 695-696). This order is paralleled in the "Theogony of Dunnu"; Sea is an autochthon, whereas River belongs to the third generation.[107] Lambert and Walcot also point out that there is a parallel to Hesiod in the marital relationships that obtain. The Titans regularly contract sibling marriages (cf. Kronos and Rhea), "but it is only Ouranos and Pontos who practice incest to the extent of mating with their own mother. . . . "[108] Again, in the "Theogony of Dunnu" both Sea and Earth are involved in such marriages, and matings between siblings abound.

These, then, are the Babylonian versions. So far no Sumerian counterpart has come to light, although several important Sumerian divinities are present in the texts just discussed, for example, Enki (Ea) and Anu. I do not mean to suggest that the Greek and other non-Babylonian versions of the "Kingship in Heaven" theme are necessarily based specifically upon the *Enūma-Elish* or the "Theogony of Dunnu." Rather, in one way or another all the previously discussed theogonies[109] may be based upon the immediate sources of these two Babylonian texts, sources that themselves would appear to have been Babylonian and perhaps even Sumerian. This suggestion is strengthened in that we now have two distinct versions of the theme, each dating from the early second millennium B.C., from two distinct centers of Babylonian culture, that is, Babylon proper and Dunnu. The fact that one of these was a minor center adds even more strength.

Conclusions

Most of the principal points of comparison among the several versions which have been noted are summed up in the table on the facing page. The question that remains is whether or not the "Kingship in Heaven" theme is Indo-European.

Wikander's assumption that the theme is part of the Indo-European mythological inheritance is based principally upon the concordances among the Greek, Hittite, and Iranian versions. These concordances are in fact present, and there is no doubt that the three versions are part of a single tradition. But the fact that these three Indo-European-speaking communities share a common theogonic theme does not in itself mean that such a theme is part of their common mythological inheritance. By the same token, it can be said that a fair number of Indo-European speaking communities today share a common belief in how the world was created: by a God whose principal attributes are omnipotence and an intense jealously of all other pretenders to divine status. There is, of course, no doubt whatsoever that this idea was borrowed from the Judaic tradition. We have a clear record of when and where the borrowing occurred. But suppose that we did not have such a record; suppose that a Martian scholar eons hence were to be confronted with this common tradition—present, albeit, among many non-Indo-European speakers as well. Would he not be tempted to view the relationships from a genetic standpoint? Would he not be tempted to reconstruct a common Indo-European cosmogony involving "the hand of God moving across the waters," and so on?

I suggest that those who argue for an Indo-European origin as far as the divine kingship is concerned have most likely fallen into the same trap as our hypothetical Martian. The problem here is that, unlike the spread of the Judaic cosmogony, the spread of the idea of divine kingship cannot be documented. There is no clear record of events to mark its spread from ancient Babylonia to Anatolia, Phoenicia, Iran, Greece, and ultimately, perhaps, to Scandinavia. There is nothing here comparable with the conversion of Clovis or the ministry of St. Patrick. Yet spread it did, from one religious system to another, the initial impetus being perhaps the prestige of the Babylonian tradition. By the time the theme reached Scandinavia (if indeed it did not evolve there independently), the Babylonian roots had long since become obscure, and the prestige would have been that of the Greco-Roman tradition, to which it had diffused perhaps two millennia earlier.

Two of the chief reasons for ruling out an Indo-European origin are the absence, previously noted, of the theme in the Indic tradition and its very late appearance in that of ancient Iran. Also important in this connection is its absence in the ancient Celtic tradition. Admittedly much of our knowledge of Celtic religion is confined to those elements of it that persisted in Ireland; yet even here, given the care taken by the medieval Irish monks to preserve their heritage, one would assume that if the theme had been present before the arrival of Christianity it would have carried over. But only by the most Procrustean of methods can one make a case for its presence in the traditions relating to the Túatha Dé Danann and their predecessors. It is simply not present.

Thus, that neither the *Veda*'s, the *Avesta,* nor the *Lebor Gabála* know the theme is highly significant. With the exception of the Norse, all known versions center upon Mesopotamia. Even Egypt does not seem to have known a clear version of the "Kingship in Heaven."[110] Its diffusion to Greece, usually thought to have been accomplished via Phoenicia,[111] may indeed have been much earlier than heretofore suspected. Lambert and Walcot suggest that the mythical conception of a divine kingship may have diffused directly from Mesopotamia to Greece during the Late Helladic period and cite recent archaeological evidence (e.g., the presence of Babylonian cylinder seals at Thebes) indicative of widespread Mycenaean-Mesopotamian contacts.[112] Its diffusion to the Hittites would probably have been accomplished via the Hurrians, who had come into close contact with the mainstream of Mesopotamian civilization by the middle of the second millennium B.C. Its late diffusion eastward to Iran may reflect more immediately the Hesiodic and/or Phoenician versions rather than the Babylonian versions themselves (cf. the very specific parallels between Zohak and Typhon). But whatever the course taken, its absence in at least three widely separated and important Indo-European traditions, coupled with the early dates of the Babylonian versions, would seem to give powerful support to my contention that it is of Babylonian[113] and perhaps even ultimately of Sumerian origin.

No discussion of Indo-European origins would be complete without reference to Professor Dumézil's theory of a common tripartite social and supernatural system, a system that is clearly evident in most of the ancient Indo-European speaking domain.[114] Dumézil himself has refrained from any attempt to apply the tripartite model to the idea of the "Kingship in Heaven," despite the fact that at first glance, at least, the three-generational sequences would seem to offer a fertile field in this regard. Even Wikander, in many ways Dumézil's most brilliant disciple, and, as we have seen, the chief proponent of the Indo-European origin theory, has refrained from attempting such an application.[115] The closest

Dumézil has come to the problem is the suggestion[116] that the proto-Indo-European mythology possibly included a tradition that Heaven was the last and only surviving offspring of a great water deity (probably female), who drowned all but one of her children as soon as they were born. His suggestion is based upon a comparison between the Norse god Heimdallr and the Vedic divinity Dyauh. Both are connected with water. Heimdallr is said to have had nine mothers, who were conceived as "sea waves"; Dyauh and his seven brothers (the *Vasus*) are linked with the river goddess Gaṅgā (Ganges), who drowns seven of the eight siblings, leaving only Dyauh to reach maturity (cf. *Mahābhārata* 1.3843-3963).

Certainly the personifications of sea and heaven play parts in both the Greek and the Babylonian versions of the divine kingship (cf. Pontos, Tiamat), but in neither case do we have any clear identification of the drowning of all but one of their offspring. Moreover, Heimdallr plays no part whatsoever in the Norse version, nor do any of the other traditions surrounding the rather otiose Dyauh come anywhere near to approximating the sort of divine succession so crucial to the presence of the theme in question. In short, it would seem to me that, even though Dumézil may well be correct in his suggestions as to the Indo-European roots of the traditions surrounding the births of Dyauh and Heimdallr, it would not be germane to the problem at hand. The presence of such a common Indo-European tradition would in no way alter my convictions as to the origin of the theme.

One of the most interesting suggestions yet made from a Dumézilian standpoint is that previously mentioned by F. Vian[117] relative to the Greek Typhon myth. As Vian sees it, Zeus's battle with the monster derives from an isolated story paralleling what Dumézil[118] and others have suggested is the typical Indo-European myth of a fight between a second-function or warrior figure and a tricephalic monster (cf. Indra versus the son of Tvastar, and the like). This story later fused with a widespread non-Indo-European dragon-slaying account (which had also diffused to the Hittites; cf. the Ullikummi and Illuyanka narratives)[119] that had been introduced into Greece by the Phoenicians in the early eighth century B.C. Thus, according to Vian, by the time of Hesiod the story as it is generally known in Greek mythology had fairly well crystallized. It is interesting that in later versions of the Typhon episode (i.e., those of Apollodorus and Nonnos) the details undergo progressive elaboration and become more and more similar to those of the Hurrian-Hittite version. As noted, the Hittite description of Ullikummi before Mount Hazzi is almost identical with Nonnos' description of Typhon.

If Vian is correct, then some intriguing possibilities present themselves. Perhaps the Hittites, too, grafted the dragon-slaying myth onto an inherited Indo-European three-headed monster tale and, like their Greek cousins a thousand years later, eventually fused this with the Babylonian account of the divine kingship. Thus there would be three distinct strata in both the Greek and Hittite versions: (1) the Indo-European account of the slaying of the tricephalus, (2) the dragon-slaying myth, and (3) the "Kingship in Heaven" theme proper. Of course, it is by no means clear that the monster-slaying episode is disassociated in its origins from the rest of the theme under discussion. It is just as easy to make a case for the presence of this figure in the person of Tiamat—although its presence in the "Theogony of Dunnu" is less clear.

In sum, while it presents some alternative possibilities of interpretation of certain specific episodes associated with the "Kingship in Heaven," I do not feel that Vian's arguments relative to Typhon add anything substantive to the argument favoring an Indo-European origin for the theme as a whole, and I must reiterate my conclusion that it is most probably rooted in the Babylonian tradition.

Notes

[1] According to B. Malinowski (*Magic, Science and Religion* [New York, 1955], p. 101), myth is " . . . a vital ingredient of human civilization; it is not an idle tale, but a hard-worked active force; it is not an intellectual explanation or an artistic imagery, but a pragmatic charter of primitive faith and moral wisdom."

[2] The first to recognize the basic similarity between the Hittite-Hurrian and Greek versions of the "Kingship in Heaven" theme seems to have been E. O. Forrer; cf. his "Eine Geschichte des Götterkönigtums aus dem Hatti-Reiche," in *Mélanges Franz Cumont, AlPhO* 4 (Brussels, 1936), pp. 687-713. A second pioneer work in this area is H. G. Güterbock's *Kumarbi, Mythen vom churritischen Kronos, aus den hethitischen Fragmenten zusammengestellt, übersetzt und erklärt* (Istanbul, 1946). The Phoenician version was first put into its proper perspective by C. Clemen (*Die phönikische Religion nach Philo von Byblos* [Leipzig, 1939]), and the Iranian version was discovered by S. Wikander, "Hethitiska myter hos greker och perser," *VSLA* (1951), pp. 35-56.

[3] Cf. Güterbock's "Königtum im Himmel"; E. Laroche's "Royauté au Ciel." By *theme* I mean an expression of an idea or set of related ideas rather than a specific type of narrative or tale; cf. S. Thompson's definition of "tale-type:" " . . . a traditional tale that has an independent existence" (*The Folktale* [New York, 1946], p. 415). It should be noted, however, that in perhaps the majority of instances cognate expressions of a given theme will involve similar patterns of events and consequently may reflect a single tale-type.

[4] Literally "When-on-High," from the opening words of the poem.

[5] *Op. cit.;* "Histoire des Ouranides," *CS* 36 (314):9-17 (1952).

[6] "An Intrusive Hurro-Hittite Myth," *JAOS* 62:98-102(1942).

[7] "The Hittite Version of the Hurrian Kumarbi Myths: Oriental Forerunners of Hesiod," *AJA* 42:123-134 (1948).

[8] Note should be taken of a doctoral dissertation by Gerd Steiner, *Der Sukzessionmythos in Hesiods 'Theogonie' und ihre orientalischen Parallelen* (University of Hamburg, 1958), as yet unpublished, in which the *Enūma-Elish* is held to be the ultimate source of the theme, although the author does not consider the relevant Norse and Iranian traditions.

[9] A shorter version of this paper, "Is the 'Kingship in Heaven' Theme Indo-European?", was delivered at the Third Indo-European Conference, held at the University of Pennsylvania on April 21-23, 1966, under the auspices of the American Council of Learned Societies, the National Science Foundation, and the University of Pennsylvania. It will appear in the proceedings (cf. p. 263, below). I should like to thank Professor Jaan Puhvel for his invaluable advice and encouragement not only as far as the present paper is concerned, but also throughout the entire course of the research upon which it is based. Special thanks are owing as well to Professor H. G. Güterbock of the Oriental Institute of the University of Chicago for his most helpful comments and suggestions.

[10] The Hittite-Hurrian version (*ca.* 1400 B.C.) antedates Hesiod by at least 700 years, and the Babylonian versions may well be of much greater antiquity.

[11] Cf. H. G. Evelyn-White, *Hesiod, The Homeric Hymns and Homerica* (London, 1914), p. xxvi.

[12] Cf. J. G. Frazer, *Apollodorus: The Library* (London, 1921), p. xvi.

[13] Cf. W. H. D. Rouse, *Nonnos: Dionysiaca* (London, 1939), p. vii.

[14] The numbers enclosed by parentheses refer to lines in the original texts of the *Theogony, Bibliotheca,* and *Dionysiaca;* the translations utilized are those, respectively, of H. G. Evelyn-White, J. G. Frazer, and W. H. D. Rouse.

[15] Called, respectively, "Thunderer," "Lightener," and "Vivid One" (cf. Evelyn-White, *op. cit.,* p. 89.).

[16] The etymology of Kronos [*Kronos*] is obscure (cf. H. Frisk, *Griechisches etymologisches Wörterbuch* [Heidelberg, 1961], II, 24-25; L. R. Farnell, *The Cults of the Greek States* [Oxford, 1896], I, 23). It has been suggested that the name was a variant form of Chronos ([*Chronos*] or 'Time'), though the shift from initial X to K would be difficult, if not impossible, to support philologically (cf. H. J. Rose, *A Handbook of Greek Mythology* [New York, 1959], p. 69). Another etymology has connected Kronos with [*Kraino*] and has rendered the meaning as 'ripener' or 'completer.' While both Frisk (*op. cit.*) and Rose (*op. cit.*) consider this equally impossible philologically, the fact that Kronos was inevitably equated with Saturnus by most Latin authors (cf. Vergil, Ovid, Plutarch, *et al.*) should not be overlooked. Saturnus appears originally to have been a harvest god, a god who "ripened" or "completed" crops, and the early and consistent equation of this Roman deity with Kronos may well indicate that the latter once served a similar function. Finally, S. Janez ("Kronos und der Walfisch," *Linguistica* 2:54-56 [Supplement of *Slavisti na Revija* 9, 1956] has proposed that the name Kronos be equated with Old English *hrān,* 'whale,' which, according to the first Germanic sound shift, would be philologically acceptable. He points out that the Greeks referred to Gibraltar as [*Kronov stelai*] and compares this to Old English *Hronesnaess* (Beowulf 2805, 3136). Janez suggests that certain "popular superstitions" concerning emasculation of the whale during the sex act may yield a clue to the relationship between Kronos and whales; indeed, in a number of late traditions, especially in the younger Orphic theogonies, Kronos is represented as having been castrated by Zeus (cf. Pauly-Wissowa, *Realencyclopädie der Klassischen Altertumswissenschaft,* vol. 11, p. 2009 [33]: "Zeus den Kronos mit Honig trunken macht und ihn dann im Schlaf fesselt und entmannt"; W. H. Roscher, *Ausführliches Lexicon der griechischen und römischen Mythologie* [Leipzig, 1890], II, 1470-1471). It appears likely, however, that these late traditions were the result of conscious attempts by theologians to harmonize Zeus's overthrow of Kronos with the latter's overthrow of Ouranos, and it seems to me that, if Janez's equation [*Kronos*] = *hrān* be correct, the mere fact that the whale is an obvious symbol of bigness (cf. the English expression "a whale of a . . .") may explain the relationship more efficiently; perhaps the name Kronos itself is but the survival of an epithet once applied to a being (a harvest god?) whose proper name had disappeared before Homer's time.

[17] Cf. M. P. Nilsson, "The Sickle of Kronos," *ABSA* 46:122-124 (1939). Like Kronos, Saturnus is also associated with a sickle, Greek [*harpe*]. This seems to be a proto-Indo-European term found also in Balto-Slavic (Lettish *sirpe,* Russian *serp*) and borrowed into Finno-Ugric (Finnish *sirppi,* 'sickle'). Perhaps the "adamantine" blade used by Kronos against Ouranos was origi-

nally a tool associated with an Indo-European harvest god ancestral to both Kronos and Saturnus (cf. n. 16, above).

[18] Cf. Rose, *op. cit.,* p. 22.

[19] Frazer (*op. cit.,* p. 6) sums up this controversy rather succinctly: "According to Hesiod, Rhea gave birth to Zeus in Crete, and the infant god was hidden away in a cave of Mount Aegeum (*Theogony* 468-480). Diodorus Siculus (5.70) mentions the legend that Zeus was born at Dicte in Crete, and that the god afterwards founded a city on the site. But according to Diodorus, or his authorities, the child was brought up in a cave on Mount Ida. . . . The wavering of tradition on this point is indicated by Apollodorus who, while he calls the mountain Dicte, names one of the gods Ida."

[20] Cf. *ibid.*

[21] Frazer (*ibid.,* p. 7) claims that "According to Callimachus, Amalthea was a goat. Aratus also reported, if he did not believe, the story that the supreme god had been suckled by a goat (Strabo, viii.7.5, p. 387). . . . "

[22] Cf. that of Hermes (*Homeric Hymn* 4.17-19): "At dawn he [Hermes] was born, by noon he was playing on the lyre, and that evening he stole the cattle of Apollo Fardarter. . . . "

[23] Although the extent to which Rhea is involved in the conspiracy to dislodge her offspring from Kronos' stomach is unclear, all accounts agree that she sides with Zeus in the ensuing struggle against her husband; cf. W. H. Roscher, "Rhea," in L. Preller, *Griechische Mythologie,* I (Berlin, 1894), 638 f.

[24] That Kronos and his fellow Titans escaped eternal punishment in Tartaros is reflected in a number of variant traditions, some of them quite early. In his *Works and Days* (169), Hesiod himself claims that Zeus gave Kronos and his fellows "a living and an abode apart from men, and made them dwell at the ends of the earth . . . untouched by sorrow in the islands of the blessed along the shore of deep swirling Ocean, happy heroes for whom the grain-giving earth bears honey and sweet fruit. . . . " Hesiod also claims (*ibid.*) that "Kronos rules over them; for the father of men and gods [i.e., Zeus] released him from his bonds." The idea that Kronos' ultimate fate is to rule over a group of western Elysian islands (i.e., the "islands of the blessed") is reflected in Pindar (*Olymp. Odes,* 2) and later in Plutarch (*De defectu oraculorum* 420), the latter claiming that Kronos, guarded by Briareos, sleeps peacefully on a sacred island near Britain. Vergil (*Aeneid* 8.319, 355-358) asserts that the defeated Titan fled by sea to Latium, where he founded a city, Saturnia, on the future site of Rome, and that the name of the

district stems from Kronos' (i.e., Saturnus') hiding (*latere*) in it (cf. Rose, *op. cit.,* p. 45). The association of Kronos with the West, especially Italy, in the minds of later Greek and Roman writers can be seen in the assertion by Dionysius of Halicarnassus (1.36.1) that the Golden Age, which preceded the ascension of Zeus as "king in heaven," was in Italy under Kronos. It should also be noted that the element of escape or banishment resulting in a sea voyage has an interesting counterpart in the Norse version to be considered presently; cf. the fate of the giant Bergelmir.

[25] Hesiod renders the monster's name as "Typhoeus"; Apollodorus and Nonnos render it as "Typhon."

[26] The modern Kel Dag or "Bald Mountain," located just south of the mouth of the Orontes River in what is now Turkey.

[27] Nonnos also mentions the sinew-cutting episode (*Dionysiaca* 1.482-512). Here Kadmos comes to Zeus's aid instead of Hermes. In a note to his translation of the *Dionysiaca* (*op. cit.,* pp. 40-41) Rouse points out that "the story is obscurely told, and probably Nonnos did not understand it; it is obviously old. By some device or by a well-aimed blow, Typhon had evidently cut the sinews out of Zeus's arms, thus disabling him; Cadmos now gets them back by pretending that he wants them for harp strings." In this version there is no mention of a sickle, adamantine or other.

[28] F. Vian, "Le mythe de Typhée et le problème de ses origines orientales", *Éléments orientaux dans la religion grecque ancienne* (Paris, 1960), pp. 17-37. For a discussion of the Indo-European character of the tricephalic monster, see G. Dumézil, *Horace et les Curiaces* (Paris, 1942) and elsewhere.

[29] By Forrer, *op. cit.*

[30] "The Hittite Version of the Hurrian Kumarbi Myths," p. 124.

[31] Primarily in the form of Hurrian god names; cf. *ibid.,* p. 123 and H. G. Güterbock, "Hittite Mythology," in S. N. Kramer, ed., *Mythologies of the Ancient World* (New York, 1961); abbr.: *MAW.*

[32] The texts are written in the Indo-European *Nesili* language, which was the official court language of the Hittite kingdom (cf. Güterbock, *MAW,* p. 142), but employ Akkadian cuneiform characters.

[33] Güterbock, "The Hittite Version of the Hurrian Kumarbi Myths," p. 124; A. Goetze in J. B. Pritchard, ed., *Ancient Near Eastern Texts Relating to the Old Testament* (Princeton, 1955), p. 121; abbr.: *ANET.*

[34] More likely "ages" or "eras" rather than calendar

years; cf. Güterbock, "The Hittite Version of the Hurrian Kumarbi Myths," p. 124 n. 11.

[35] The numbers enclosed by parentheses refer respectively to columns and lines in the original texts; cf. Güterbock, *Kumarbi,* pp. 6-10, 13-28.

[36] Güterbock, *MAW,* p. 160.

[37] *Ibid.*

[38] Cf. Goetze, *ANET,* p. 120; Güterbock, "The Hittite Version of the Hurrian Kumarbi Myths," p. 134.

[39] The name Kumarbi is apparently Hurrian; cf. Güterbock, *MAW,* p. 160, who points out that Kumarbi is frequently, although not consistently, equated with the great Sumero-Akkadian god Enlil.

[40] The approximate meaning "his loins" or "his thighs" seems to fit the reading *paršnuššuš* which various Hittite scholars, including Güterbock (personal communication, and *MAW,* p. 156), now prefer to the earlier emendational interpretation *genuššuš* "his knees" (cf. E. A. Hahn, *JAOS* 85:298-299 [1965]). In either case there is a euphemistic approximation for "male parts." On the widespread sexual connotations of the knee Professor Jaan Puhvel has contributed the following philological note:

Hittite *genu-* means both 'knee' and (secondarily) '[male] genitals' (sometimes combined in anatomical lists with *arraš* [= Old High German *ars*] 'anus'; cf. J. Friedrich, "Einige hethitische Namen von Körperteilen," *IF* 41:372-376 [1923]). This usage, however, is not a euphemism but has much more basic implications. Without having to delve deep into folkloristic and psychoanalytical records we find that "knee" is often an expression for sexual potency (cf., e.g., J. Laager, *Geburt und Kindheit des Gottes in der griechischen Mythologie* [Winterthur, 1957], p. 136). As random examples we may refer to the passage in the Old Norse *Flóamannasaga* where a man dreams of leeks (a well-known fertility symbol) growing from his knees (cf. W. P. Lehmann, *Germanic Review* 30:166 [1955]), and quote in translation these lines of Hesiod's *Works and Days* about the "dog days" (582-587; imitated in a drinking song of Alcaeus [*Oxford Book of Greek Verse,* p. 170]): "But when the artichoke blooms and the chirping grass-hopper sits in a tree and pours down his shrill song continually from under his wings in the season of wearisome heat, then goats are plumpest and wine sweetest; women are most wanton, but men are feeblest, because Sirius parches head and KNEES."

In various Semitic languages (e.g., Akkadian, Ethiopic) *b r k* (Akkadian *birku*) means both 'knee' and 'penis,' and then more widely 'strength,' 'family,' or 'tribe' (cf. M. Cohen, "Genou, famille, force dans le domaine chamito-sémitique," *Mémorial Henri Basset* [Paris, 1928], I, 203-210, and more generally W. Deonna, "Le genou, siège de force et de vie," *RA* 13:224-235 [1939]). 'Knee' in the sense of 'offspring,' 'family' is commonly found in Indo-European and Finno-Ugric languages: much as Akkadian *tarbit birkiya* means 'nursel-ing of my *birku*,' we have the synonymous Old Irish *glūn-daltae,* 'knee-nurseling' (cf. J. Loth, "Le mot désignant le genou au sens de génération chez les Celtes, les Germains, les Slaves, les Assyriens," *RC* 40:143-152 [1923]) and the Sogdian *z'nwk' z'tk,* 'knee-son' (see E. Benveniste, *BSL* 27:51-53 [1926]). Similarly Old English *cnéow,* Old Slavonic *koléno,* and Finnish *polvi,* 'knee,' also mean 'offspring, generation.'

Some have claimed a connection between IE * *genu,* 'knee,' and the root * *gen-*on the basis of ancient evidence for childbearing labor in a kneeling position (e.g., R. Back, "Medizinisch-Sprachliches," *IF* 40:162-167 [1922]; J. Klek, *IF* 44:79-80 [1927]; and S. Simonyi, "Knie und Geburt," *Zeitschrift für vergleichende Sprachforschung* 50:152-154 [1922]). Yet in spite of the Hittite *genzu,* 'lap,' 'female genitals,' metonymically 'love,' the root of Latin *genus, gignō,* Greek [*genos*], [*gennao*] means primarily 'beget,' while other words are used for 'bear' (Latin *pari* , Greek [*tikto*]). Others have argued that in patriarchal society formal recognition of a newborn child on the father's knee was the true means of legal affiliation or adoption, thus 'birth' in a juridical sense (cf., e.g., Old Norse *knēsetningr,* 'adopted son,' and Homeric and Roman practices, and see Benveniste, *op. cit.,* and M. Cahen, "'Genou', 'adoption', et 'parenté' en germanique," *BSL* 27:56-67 [1926]). In archaic Estonian the phrase *lapse põlvede peale tõstma,* 'lift a child on the knees,' is glossed with 'ein Kind gehörig zur Welt bringen' by F. Wiedemann, *Ehstnisch-deutsches Wörterbuch* (2d ed.; St. Petersburg, 1893), p. 864, and *põlwile sãma,* 'come on knees,' is rendered by 'geboren werden' (*ibid.*). Latin *genuīnus* was similarly connected with *genu,* 'knee,' by A. Meillet (*BSL* 27:54-55 [1926]), and IE *gnē -, 'know, recognize,' was brought into play, including the vexed question of its possible original affinity with *gen-, 'beget' (cf. [*gnesios*] 'genuine'). The semantic tangle was further aggravated by R. Meringer ("Spitze, Winkel, Knie im ursprünglichen Denken," *Wörter und Sachen* 11:118-123 [1928]) and H. Güntert (*ibid.,* pp. 124-142, esp. pp. 125-127), who tried to combine both Greek [*gonu*], 'knee,' and [*genus*], 'chin,' with [*gonia*], 'angle.'

Even without reference to such inconclusive root etymologies, however, we have unraveled the semantic ramifications of the notion of 'knee' in many languages as comprising 'genitals,' 'potency,' 'offspring,' 'family,' and 'filiation.'

[41] Although both Ouranos and Anu are connected with the sky, we refer here of course to functional rather than linguistic correspondences.

[42] Although the Hittite reading of the ideogram for weather-god is as yet unknown, it is highly probable that, given this and other contexts (cf. the Ullikummi texts), the Hittite deity in question can be none other than the Hurrian Weather- (or Storm-) god Teshub (cf. Goetze, *ANET*, p. 120; Güterbock, *Kumarbi*, p. 35; id., "The Hittite Version of the Hurrian Kumarbi Myths," p. 124 n. 14; id., *MAW*, p. 158); thus I follow Güterbock and call the Hittite Weather-god by his Hurrian name.

[43] Cf. Güterbock, "The Hittite Version of the Hurrian Kumarbi Myths," p. 124 n. 15.

[44] *Ibid.,* n. 16.

[45] From a reference in column ii it seems that these unmentioned divinities are Marduk (represented by a rare Sumerian name) and one whose name is written with the word sign KA.ZAL, 'lust'; cf. Güterbock, *MAW*, p. 158.

[46] Apparently Earth becomes pregnant thereby, although the names of the divinities she bears are unclear.

[47] *MAW*, pp. 157-158.

[48] *Ibid.,* p. 158.

[49] Cf. also the birth of Erichthonios: Hephaistos, desiring to wed a reluctant Athena, struggles with her, and in the course of this struggle his seed falls on the ground; Gaia is thus impregnated and in due time gives birth to Erichthonios (cf. Rose, *op. cit.,* p. 110).

[50] Text and translation published by Güterbock, *JCS* 5:135-161 (1951), 6:8-42 (1952).

[51] There is an interesting counterpart to this in Phrygian mythology; cf. Arnobius, *Adversus Nationes* 5.55, Pausanias 7.17.10-12. Papas, the Phrygian "Zeus," inseminates a rock called Agdos and begets Agdistis, an indolent hermaphrodite monster who, initially at least, is not unlike Ullikummi in some respects. The Phrygian monster, however, is castrated by the gods and thereby transformed into the mother-goddess figure Cybele. The blood produced by the castration causes a marvelous pomegranate or almond tree to spring up, and the fruit of this tree impregnates Nana, daughter of the river god Sangarios. Nana gives birth to Attis, who later castrates himself out of love for Cybele.

Agdistis' birth and early resemblance to Ullikummi may possibly indicate a relationship between the two traditions. Save for the castration motif, however, which might conceivably be implied in Ullikummi's loss of power after being cut from Upelluri's shoulder, the rest of the story does not have any clear Hittite parallels.

[52] Ullikummi is not the only rebel to oppose Teshub's power; there is also a text (Güterbock, *Kumarbi,* pp. 10-13, Text 1; *MAW*, pp. 161-164) which describes the rebellion of a god known to us only by the highly ambiguous word sign KAL (cf. Güterbock, *MAW*, p. 161, who claims that neither the reading Sumerian LAMA, Akkadian *LAMASSU*, nor the Hittite reading Inara [an Anatolian goddess; cf. the Illuyanka myth, *MAW*, p. 151] fits the context). This text presents some interesting, although not conclusive, parallels to the Greek myths concerning Prometheus and his defiance of Zeus. Unfortunately the KAL text (if indeed it is a separate text) is extremely fragmentary; the tablet is broken in such a way that we possess neither the beginning nor the final colophon that would indicate the name of the text and its exact relationship to the other two texts. Nevertheless, the events described almost certainly follow the ascension of Teshub; whether they precede or follow the Ullikummi affair is, however, much less certain.

Unlike Prometheus, KAL actually seems to have assumed the kingship for a time, for when we first meet him he is described as taking "the reins and [the whip] out of the Storm-God's [i.e., Teshub's] hands" (i.18-19). Like Prometheus, however, and unlike Typhon and/or Ullikummi, KAL eventually submits. Addressing the Weather-god as "my lord," he is subjected to some form of bodily punishment involving mutilation; cf. the fate of Prometheus bound to a rock (or mountain) and continually mutilated by an eagle (*Theogony* 521). There are other aspects of KAL's rebellion which also seem broadly similar to that of Prometheus. In the text, one of the chief objections raised against KAL is that he encourages mortals to be lax in their sacrificial duties: Ea, who apparently had appointed KAL to the kingship, later becomes dissatisfied with his protégé's conduct and claims that "'just as he [KAL] himself is rebellious, so he has made the countries rebellious, and no one any longer gives bread or drink offerings to the gods'" (iii.18,40); Prometheus, too, is accused of encouraging humans to withhold sacrificed food from the gods (cf. *Theogony* 535). While there seems to be no connection here between KAL and either the creation of mankind or man's knowledge of fire, the Hittite rebel can be seen to occupy a role broadly similar to that of Prometheus: a champion of mortals in their dealings with the gods. Furthermore, KAL's downfall, like that of Prometheus, is apparently the result of a plot hatched by the gods and implemented by the chief god's lieutenant (i.e., Teshub's vizier Ninurta [*MAW*, p. 164]; cf. the role played in Prometheus' punishment by Hephaistos [*Theogony* 520]).

[53] Apparently located in the mountains of southeast Anatolia; Güterbock suggests (*MAW*, p. 166) that the name Ullikummi itself simply means "Destroyer of Kummiya."

[54] Güterbock, "The Hittite Version of the Hurrian Kumarbi Myths," p. 129. In col. iii.19—22 there is the suggestion that Anu wants to make Ea king instead of Teshub; cf. P. Meriggi, "I miti di Kumarpi, il Kronos Currico," *Athenaeum* 31:101-157 (1953).

[55] Güterbock, *op. cit.*

[56] *Ibid.*

[57] W. Staudacher, *Die Trennung von Himmel und Erde* (Tübingen, 1942), pp. 61 f.

[58] Güterbock, *op. cit.,* p. 130.

[59] Clemen, *op. cit.,* p. 2.

[60] The numbers enclosed by parentheses refer to lines in the original text of the *Phoenician History;* the translation is by Clemen.

[61] There is a close parallel to this in the Iranian tradition wherein the "Kronos figure" Zohak marries two of Jamshid's sisters after deposing him. See Wikander, "Hethitiska myter hos greker och perser," p. 52.

[62] Cf. the relationship between El and Hadad, the god of thunder and lightning, as delineated in the Ras Shamra texts. The association of Baal and Hadad has long been recognized in the Caananitic tradition; cf. W. F. Albright, *Archaeology and the Religion of Israel* (Baltimore, 1946), pp. 72-74; S. H. Hooke, *Middle Eastern Mythology* (Harmondsworth, 1963), pp. 86-87.

[63] Clemen, *op. cit.,* p. 28.

[64] Güterbock, "The Hittite Version of the Hurrian Kumarbi Myths," p. 133.

[65] A further argument against interpreting Philo wholly in syncretistic terms is that he preserves a "pre-Ouranos" figure, i.e., Eliun; cf. the position of Alalu in the Hurrian-Hittite version.

[66] L. R. Palmer, *Mycenaeans and Minoans* (2d ed.; London, 1965).

[67] Palmer (*ibid.*) suggests that the name Parnassos is derived from a Luvian form meaning 'place of the temple' (Luvian *parna-,* 'temple,' plus the suffix *-ass-* denoting appurtenance).

[68] "Hethitiska myter hos greker och perser."

[69] Literally the "first man."

[70] Helen Zimmern, *The Epic of Kings* (New York, 1926), p. 4. For a more recent translation, see R. Levy, *The Epic of Kings, Shāh-nāma* (Chicago, 1967).

[71] "Histoire des Ouranides," p. 13.

[72] *Ibid.*

[73] Wikander, "Hethitiska myter hos greker och perser," p. 41.

[74] Cf. J. Atkinson. *The Shá Námeh of the Persian Poet Firdausi* (London, 1832), p. 34.

[75] Atkinson (*ibid.*) asserts that Jamshid was laid between two planks and sawed lengthwise; see also A. Warner and E. Warner, *The Shāh-nāma of Firdausi* (London, 1905), p. 140.

[76] *Ibid.*

[77] Wikander, "Histoire des Ouranides," p. 13.

[78] Warner and Warner, *op. cit.,* p. 142; cf. Wikander, "Histoire des Ouranides," p. 7, Levy, *op. cit.,* p. xvii.

[79] Zimmern, *op. cit.,* p. 8.

[80] *Ibid.,* p. 12.

[81] Or imprisons him in a cave; cf. Wikander, "Hethitiska myter hos greker och perser," p. 47.

[82] Warner and Warner, *op. cit.,* p. 171; the Warners suggest (p. 174) that Feridun is actually a coalescence of two Avestan figures, Thraētaona and Thrita (cf. *Yasna* 9.21-30).

[83] For a discussion of the possible Vedic parallels here, see Wikander, "Hethitiska myter hos greker och perser," esp. p. 46.

[84] Tuisto can be interpreted as meaning 'Twin'; cf. Ymir, possibly cognate with Yama, and Tacitus' Mannus, whom he combines with Tuisto and who belongs etymologically with Manu; for a discussion of Tuisto and Mannus see H. R. Ellis Davidson, *Gods and Myths of Northern Europe* (Harmondsworth, 1964), pp. 54-61, 196-199; E. O. G. Turville-Petre, *Myth and Religion of the North* (London, 1964), esp. p. 7.

[85] The translations utilized are by Lee M. Hollander, *The Poetic Edda* (Austin, 1928), and Jean Young, *The Prose Edda* (Cambridge, 1954).

[86] For a discussion of the extent to which Snorri, to say nothing of Saxo Grammaticus, was influenced by the *Aeneid,* see my paper "A Two-Dimensional Scheme for the Classification of Narratives," *JAF* 78:21-27, esp. pp. 24-25.

[87] In the *Gylfaginning* Snorri describes Bergelmir's flight as occurring in the context of a universal flood created from the blood that gushed from Ymir after his demise. As this is the only clear reference to a flood in Norse myth, it seems reasonable to infer that Snorri, as a Christian, felt the need of it. This is underscored by the etymology of the word *luðr,* used by him to refer to the "boat" in which Bergelmir and his wife survive the deluge. Although Snorri clearly uses the word in the context of "boat," earlier usages of the term (cf. *Lay of Vafthrudnir* 35) would seem to indicate that it meant 'coffin' or 'bier.' See E. O. G. Turville-Petre, "Prof. Dumézil and the Literature of Iceland," *Hommages à Georges Dumézil* (Brussels, 1960), pp. 211-212; see also H. Petersson, "Aisl. *luðr* 'Trog usw,'" *IF* 24:267-269 (1909), who asserts that the basic meaning here is 'hollowed tree trunk' and proposes a derivation from Indo-European **lu-tró-* (cf. Skt. *lunāti,* 'cut, clip').

[88] I.e., *askr,* 'ash,' and *embla,* 'elm,' respectively, the first man and woman.

[89] I am not the first to make such an observation. Well over a century ago Jakob Grimm, in his *Teutonic Mythology* (translated from the German by J. S. Stallybrass [London, 1883], II, 275), had occasion to observe that "As the Edda has a Buri and Börr before Odinn, so do Uranus and Kronus here come before Zeus; with Zeus and Odinn begins the race of gods proper, and Poseidon and Hades complete the fraternal trio, like Vili and Vé. The enmity of gods and titans is therefore that of ases [Aesir] and giants. . . ."

[90] E. A. Speiser, "Akkadian Myths and Epics," *ANET,* p. 60. It should be noted, however, that P. Walcot (*Hesiod and the Near East* [Cardiff, 1966], p. 33), suggests that the rise of Marduk to supremacy among the gods of Mesopotamia was quite late and that the *Enūma-Elish* as we know it was most likely composed around 1100 B.C. He thus concludes that "In terms of chronology, Enuma Elish now seems to stand between the Hattusas tablets and the Theogony. . . . " Nevertheless, this would not preclude earlier Babylonian and/or Sumerian prototypes wherein some other god played the part of Marduk.

[91] Sumerian Abzu; see S. N. Kramer, "Mythology of Sumer and Akkad," *MAW,* p. 120.

[92] I.e., "Mother" Tiamat; see Speiser, *op. cit.,* p. 61.

[93] The translation of the *Enūma-Elish* utilized here is that of Speiser, *ANET,* pp. 61-72.

[94] Cf. i.52, wherein Apsu plots "against the gods, his sons"; i.56, wherein Apsu's intentions are made known "unto the gods, their first-born."

[95] Not to be confused with the epithet of Tiamat; cf. i.4 and n. 92, above.

[96] See Walcot, *op. cit.,* p. 34.

[97] M. L. West, in the "Prolegomena" to *Hesiod: Theogony* (Oxford, 1966), p. 23, asserts that Ea's elder sibling (or grandfather) Anshar assumes the kingship. Nowhere in the text is this clearly evident. The only passage that may possibly reflect such a royal status is iii.I ff., wherein Anshar sends a message to Lahmu and Lahamu via "Gaga, his *vizir*" (italics mine). Otherwise, Anshar appears as but one of the siblings (or forebears) of Ea who plays a prominent albeit essentially supporting role in the deposition of Apsu and the subsequent conflict with Tiamat.

[98] There is some confusion here. Kramer suggests (*MAW,* p. 121) that Ea actually takes up residence upon Apsu's corpse. The text itself would seem to indicate that Ea names his place of residence (i.e., the location of his "cult hut"; cf. i.77) *after* his deceased parent.

[99] Cf. Kramer, *MAW,* p. 121.

[100] "He took from him [i.e., Kingu] the Tablets of Fate, not rightfully his, sealed [them] with a seal and fastened [them] on his breast" (iv.121-122).

[101] W. G. Lambert and P. Walcot, "A New Babylonian Theogony and Hesiod," *Kadmos* 4:64-72 (1965). It should be pointed out that Walcot is responsible for the appended "classical commentary" (pp. 68-72); the translation and accompanying commentary are by Lambert.

[102] I should emphasize that this is my term, not that of Lambert and Walcot.

[103] Lambert and Walcot, *op. cit.,* p. 64.

[104] *Ibid.,* pp. 67-68.

[105] Lambert and Walcot suggest that the two signs *ha-in* may have been miscopied from the one large sign used to write the name of the corn goddess Nisaba (*ibid.,* pp. 66-67).

[106] *Ibid.,* p. 72.

[107] *Ibid.,* pp. 66, 71.

[108] *Ibid.,* p. 72.

[109] The Norse version may be only indirectly derived from that which took shape in Babylonia some four thousand years ago; its immediate roots probably lie in the version best known to the Greco-Roman world, i.e., that of Hesiod *et al.*

[110] But Lambert and Walcot, *op. cit.,* p. 69, point out that there is an Egyptian tradition according to which Sky devoured her children, quarreled with her husband, Earth, and therefore they were separated; for the relevant text. see H. Frankfort, *The Cenotaph of Seti I at Abydos* (London, 1933), p. 83.

[111] Güterbock, "The Hittite Version of the Hurrian Kumarbi Myths," pp. 133-134.

[112] Lambert and Walcot, *op. cit.,* p. 72. Walcot, as we have seen (see n. 90), has since modified his views and is convinced that the theme most likely diffused to Greece only after sustained contact had been reestablished with the Near East in the eighth century, B.C. (*op. cit.,* p. 47).

[113] The historical relationships proposed here are generally congruent with those proposed by Steiner (*op. cit.,* p. 104), who sees the *Enūma-Elish* as the immediate source of two unattested versions of the theme which he labels "X" and "Y." The "Y" version, Steiner suggests, ultimately reached Greece and manifested itself in Hesiod's *Theogony.* The Hurrian-Hittite version reflects both the "X" and the "Y" versions, although the former would seem to be the most immediate source. He also suggests that the "X" version perhaps gave rise to a third unattested version, "Z," which, together with the Hesiodic version, is reflected in Philo's "history." If Steiner is correct, it might be suggested that his hypothetical "Z" version could have diffused to Iran as well as to Phoenicia (cf. the specific correspondences between Philo and Firdausi as noted in the table and elsewhere); the Hesiodic version would be the immediate source of that contained in Snorri's *Edda.*

[114] The most succinct statement of Dumézil's theory can be found in his *L'idéologie tripartie des Indo-européens* (Brussels, 1958). For a brief analysis of this theory see my article "The Comparative Indo-European Mythology of Georges Dumézil," *JFI* 1:147-166 (1964); for a more extended discussion of Dumézil's ideas see my *The New Comparative Mythology: An Anthropological Assessment of the Theories of Georges Dumézil* (Berkeley and Los Angeles, 1966).

[115] Cf. *ibid.,* pp. 63, 85.

[116] "Remarques comparatives sur le dieu scandinave Heimdallr," *EC* 8:263-283 (1959).

[117] *Op. cit.*

[118] *Horace et les Curiaces.*

[119] For a thorough discussion of the dragon-slaying myth, see J. Fontenrose, *Python: A Study of Delphic Myth and Its Origins* (Berkeley and Los Angeles, 1959).

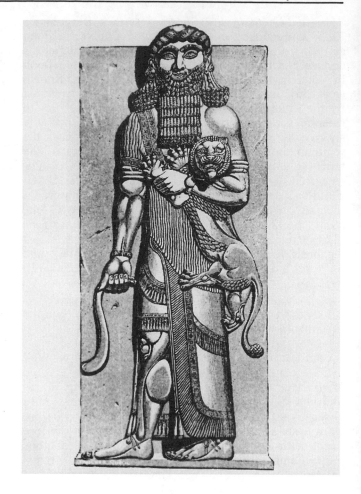

A depiction of Gilgamesh with a lion.

Alan R. Schulman (essay date 1989)

SOURCE: "Pharaoh Triumphant: The Royal Myths of Ancient Egypt," in *Ancient Economy in Mythology: East and West,* edited by Morris Silver, Rowman & Littlefield Publishers, Inc., 1991, pp. 163-86.

[*In the following essay, originally published in 1989, Schulman recounts the central theme of the divine king in Egyptian mythology and contends that scholars need to be more critical in their study of the information contained in ancient documents in order to ground historical speculation on more objective foundations.*]

Pharaonic Egyptian history lasted over two-and-a-half millennia, from ca. 3200 B.C.E. until 525 B.C.E. In this chapter, emphasis will be given to the second half of the second millennium B.C.E. when Imperial Egypt was one of the superpowers of the Ancient Near Eastern world. Like every other empire in antiquity, that of Egypt came into existence as a result of Egypt's victories in war. Actually there were two Egyptian empires, that of the Eighteenth Dynasty, which can best be compared with the post-World War II neocolonial empires in which the imperial power rules through satellites, surrogates, and puppets. When this form of empire collapsed at the end of the Eighteenth Dynasty, it was replaced by the more classical form in which the imperial power exercised control through both military garrisons and a colonial elite which provided the administration and the administrators. The rise and triumphs, though not the fall, of the Egyptian empire is seemingly attested by a plethora of sources, both written and visual, primarily of royal provenance, but occasionally of private, nonroyal origin. I have qualified this last sentence by the use of the adjective "seemingly" because, although we normally group these sources together under the rubric "historical sources," we must understand that the Egyptian sense of history was quite different from our own, and that when the Egyptians recorded an event that took place at a fixed time in the past, they did this for reasons that are far from those of preserving the memory of something that had transpired in the past for the benefit of the present or of the future (see Redford 1986, 1979; Verner 1975; Van Seters 1983).

Indeed, the aphorism that those who do not remember or learn from history are condemned to repeat it would have no meaning for or applicability to the pharaonic Egyptians. At the risk of sounding iconoclastic, I would assert that what passes for ancient Egyptian history today is mostly not history, but rather is historical speculation. Of course there is history and historical memory preserved in our documentation, but this, and particularly that of royal provenance, must first be carefully scrutinized and criticized in order to determine its bias, its credibility, and its reliability, before it can be used. Crucial to such an essay is an understanding of those myths that center on and around the persona of the Egyptian king and the royal myths of ancient Egypt (Wilson 1956). Two of these will be examined here, the myth of kingship and the myth of the triumphant king.

The myth of kingship is deceptively simple: The Egyptian king was, from the beginning of recorded Egyptian history until the triumph of Christianity, god. In theory this never changed. The basis of his power, authority, and rule lay solely in his divinity. He *was* a god (Wilson 1949, 80-96). This theoretical basis of kingship which, at the outset of Egyptian history, was virtually identical with its factual basis, is perhaps best seen in the king's titulary (Gardiner 1927, 71-76; Wilson 1949, 80-96). By the end of the First Dynasty the royal titulary consisted of four names, each of which identified the king with a pair of deities. Each name comprised two elements: the fixed and unvarying[1] identification of the pharaoh with certain deities; and the epithet that varied from monarch to monarch and which distinguished them from one another. The first of the four names, Horus Mighty Bull, equated the king with

the cosmic god. Horus, the most constantly observable phenomenon in the sky: by day the Sun, by night either the planet Venus or the Dog Star, (Anthes 1961, 34-36) and, probably by a paraphrasis of "Mighty Bull" with the most common epithet of "Min" (the Bull of his mother) with that of the cosmic fertility god from Africa (Badawy 1959). The second of the names, the Two Ladies, identified the king with the ancient titulary deities Nekhbet and Wadjit, the vulture and the cobra goddesses of the predynastic capitals of Nekhen and Pe. The third name, the so-called Golden Horus name because it is written with the Horus-falcon perched over the hieroglyph for "gold" (*nb*), and which can be understood as a sportive writing of "Horus who triumphs over the Nubtian (Seth)"[2] firmly equates the king with Horus, the son of Osiris, the king of the living who was proclaimed the right king by the assembly of the gods, and who became transfigured into Osiris, the king of the dead (Anthes 1961, 36-43; Wilson 1949, 83-84). The fourth name, which is conventionally translated as "king of Upper and Lower Egypt" and whose epithet is written within a cartouche, is again geographic and is literally rendered "he of the reed-plant, that is, Upper Egypt, and "he of the bee," that is, Lower Egypt. By the later Fourth Dynasty, however, a divergence of the theoretical concept of kingship from its actual basis can already be discerned with the occasional appearance of the name of the Sun god Rē ᶜ as an element of the king's fourth name.[3] By the advent of the Fifth Dynasty, although we still do not know the mechanics of how it came to be, there was a distinct revolution by the clergy of the Sungod Rē ᶜ (Wilson 1951, 87-89). Although the evidence is circumstantial, it is quite persuasive: The kings of the Fifth Dynasty each built his own pyramid complexes and, at the same time, each built a solar pyramid for the Sungod Rē ᶜ. In the course of the Dynasty, the royal pyramid became successively smaller while, simultaneously, the solar pyramid grew progressively larger until, by the end of the dynasty, the king's pyramid was diminutive and Rē ᶜ's pyramid dwarfed it.

A literary text, "The Story of Khufu and the Magicians" (Papyrus Westcar) records how the Fourth Dynasty king Khufu summons the most learned magician and soothsayer, Dedi, to learn the future. He is told that after the prosperous Fourth Dynasty comes to its end, Egypt is going to fall prey to chaos and all sorts of terrible things will happen. Nevertheless, Khufu should not despair, for:

[I]t is the wife of a priest of Rē ᶜ . . . who has conceived three children to Rē ᶜ . . . and he has said of them that they are to fill this beneficent office [of king] in this entire land and that the eldest of them is to be High Priest [of Rē ᶜ] in Heliopolis. [Wilson 1951, 88].

Even more telling than this propagandistic story are two other points. Starting with the first king of the

Dynasty, every king added a fifth name to his titulary, a name in which he acknowledged in the unvarying element that he was the physical and carnate son of the Sungod, Rē ᶜ, while, starting with the second king of the Dynasty, the majority of the kings who followed him incorporated the name of Rē ᶜ as an element of the epithet, which was enclosed by a cartouche in such a way as to leave no question about his relationship to Rē ᶜ, for example: Rē ᶜ is my protection (Sahurē ᶜ); beautiful is that which the *ka-soul* of Rē ᶜ does (Neferirkarē ᶜ); august is the *ka-soul* of Rē ᶜ (Shepseskar ᶜ); he belongs to the power of Rē ᶸ (Nyuserrē ᶜ); and stable is the *ka-soul* of Rē ᶜ (Djedkarē ᶜ). The significant point about the fifth name is that the king, still theoretically a god, now admits that another god is his father which, in the Near East, at least implies, if it does not actually indicate, a situation wherein he acknowledges dependence on and, consequently, inferiority to the latter (see Munn-Rankin 1956, 78-84).

When one thinks of Egypt, inevitably one thinks of mummies and of pyramids. Essentially the pyramid filled three functions: first of all it was the tomb, the "house of eternity" of the deceased and transfigured king; secondly it could be thought of as a launching pad from which the dead king could blast off whenever he wanted to visit with his fellow gods in heaven; and thirdly, although unintentionally, it served as a large *X* for any potential treasure hunter or tomb robber, telling him "dig here!" There was, of course, more than this to the pyramid and to what it signified. In the Predynastic periods of Egyptian history, everyone, to judge from the thousands of graves of the Nagada I-III periods (Baumgartel, 1955-1960), was assured of a life and/or a continuance in the afterworld, which the Egyptians conceived as a macrocosm of this world, save that everything was bigger and better. From the First Dynasty on, however, through the end of the Old Kingdom, it was only the king who was *guaranteed* life in the otherworld, or rather the king and those to whom he granted the boon of eternity, that they might continue to serve him until the end of time. These were the nobles and high magnates of the land. Until the end of the Fifth Dynasty, the nobles felt constrained to be buried as close as possible to their deceased master, in the shadow of his tomb, so to speak, with the provincial tomb being the rare exception, but by the Sixth Dynasty the provincial tomb *was* the rule and not the exception (Wilson 1951, 95). It is not only here that what was originally granted to the nobles as a privilege was then usurped by them as a right. By the end of the Fifth Dynasty the "Pyramid Texts" first appeared. These were a collection of spells, incantations, and rituals, some of them of great antiquity, which were designed to ensure for the king his proper place in the afterlife (Faulkner 1961-1971). In the Middle Kingdom, now with some deletions and some additions, they appeared on the coffins of the nobles, hence the name the "Coffin Texts" (Faulkner 1973-1978). Ulti-

mately, at the beginning of the Eighteenth Dynasty, and now known as the "Book of the Dead" (Faulkner 1972), with some additions and some deletions, these texts were written on rolls of papyrus and deposited in the tomb. Immortality was available to whosoever had the price to buy it. The royal tombs of the First and Second Dynasties are called *mastabas,* for they have the same rectangular shape as does the bench found outside of every Egyptian peasant's house. However, by the Third Dynasty the royal tomb began to assume a pyramidal or quasipyramidal shape, while the private tomb took the form of the *mastaba.*

The Egyptian designation for the tomb, royal or otherwise, the "house of eternity" is significant, for the tomb was exactly that and since the afterworld was conceived of as a macrocosm of this world, it was clear that the tomb owner needed to eat and drink, to be dressed in garments of fine linen, and to be anointed with ungents and perfumes until the end of eternity. This meant, in the case of the king, that large mortuary foundations were established and equipped with the finest fields, orchards, and fishponds in order to supply the wherewithal for the king's mortuary cult and this was their only raison d'être (Wilson 1951, 98-100). They were established in such a way that they could not be tampered with or diverted.

From the reign of Khufu in the Fourth Dynasty on, and probably even earlier, we may assume that these foundations were beginning to drain and deplete the king's resources and to diminish the factual basis of his kingship. It is to be noted that, again starting with Khufu, every king who constructed a pyramid built one somewhat smaller than that of his predecessor, a clear indication, I believe, of the lessening of his wealth and resources, and, consequently, of his power and authority. It is further to be noted that, unlike the Fifth Dynasty pyramids and solar temples, the second and third of the Giza pyramids each skip a generation before being built. Indeed, it is even possible that the occurrence of the name of Rē ᶜ as an element of their builders' names, Khafrē ᶜ and Menkaurē ᶜ, as well as in that of Khufu's immediate successor, Rē ᶜdjedef, may be taken as evidence that these kings, perhaps in financial difficulties, were already making overtures to the temple and clergy of Rē ᶜ for assistance and support, and that the Rē ᶜ revolution of the Fifth Dynasty was the ultimate outcome of this. One may even go so far as to say that the Rē ᶜ revolution, particularly the aspect of it that saw each king building both a pyramid for himself and a solar temple for Rē ᶜ and maintaining the cults and foundations of not only those which he had instigated, but also all of those which his predecessors had caused to be constructed and established, was ruinous to both the economy of Egypt and to the actual status of the king as opposed to his theoretical status. This can be seen in both the relatively modest Sixth Dynasty royal tombs and in the numerous provincial cemeteries.

For all practical purposes, the Sixth Dynasty came to an effectual end after the reign of Pepi II, who came to the throne when he was about four years old and whose highest regnal year was regnal year ninety-six. Obviously, in the earlier years of his reign and probably in its last decades he reigned but did not actually rule. This would have been left to his regents, who should have been the highest magnates in the land. They certainly, then, would have become accustomed to exercising power and making decisions, of course all theoretically in the king and god's name. Now a young child or an extremely old man trapped out in the regalia of kingship and godhood, particularly on ceremonial occasions, would have looked the role for the mass of his subjects. However, to the powers behind the throne, he was still a young child or a crotchety and, perhaps, senile old man. After all, no general is a hero to his valet. Shortly after the overlong reign of Pepi II had ended, night descended upon Egypt. The land split apart at its geographical seams and was drenched in blood through civil wars; the literary texts revile the king as the one responsible for the chaos (Wilson 1951, 115-16). Lo, how the mighty are fallen! When the chaos of this First Intermediate Period came to an end and Egypt again was unified in the Middle Kingdom, the factual basis for kingship was that the king was the most charismatic of his peers, the provincial governors. *Primus inter pares,* he needed their support to rule (Wilson 1951, 126-27), the *moreso* as in both the Old and Middle Kingdoms, a standing professional Egyptian army, did not yet exist (Faulkner 1953, 32-41). When the king went to war, his army was comprised of the local levies that each provincial governor could or would raise among *his* vassals (Gardiner 1961, 95-96). The impetus for the reestablishment of the centralized state of the Middle Kingdom came from the South, from the obscure city of Thebes. The first ruler of the Twelfth Dynasty, while still a loyal servant of the last Eleventh-Dynasty king (whose throne he ultimately usurped), was granted the signal honor of being permitted to erect a modest shrine on the East Bank of the Nile to his personal god, a minor deity named Amūn (the hidden one). Once in power he then moved the capital back to the North, to the area of Memphis. Thebes, the city of the Dynasty's origin, however, flourished, as did the shrine of Amūn, which eventually became the great temple of Amūn at Karnak, and Thebes became the city of Amūn, the No-Amon of the Bible whose fate the prophet Nahum recalled when he foresaw the forthcoming destruction of the Assyrian capitol, Nineveh (Nahum 3, 8-10).

The Middle Kingdom collapsed during the Thirteenth Dynasty, to be followed by the anarchy of the Second Intermediate Period. The unity of the state was again shattered. The Northland, the Delta, was ruled by Asiatics, the so-called Hyksos, but Thebes and the South remained independent. Indeed, it was Thebes that finally led the movement that germinated into the War of Liberation. The Hyksos were expelled and Egypt was reunited under the victorious guidance of the rulers of Thebes, who now became the kings of the New Kingdom Eighteenth Dynasty. The natural sequel to the expulsion of the Hyksos, moreover, was the establishment of the Egyptian empire. Nubia had already been conquered in the Middle Kingdom, lost during the Second Intermediate Period, and regained at the outset of the Eighteenth Dynasty. Consequently, Egypt's imperial ambitions turned mainly to the East, to West Asia. Theoretically, the Egyptian king ruled because he was a god; but in fact he ruled because he was, first and foremost, the visible commander of the victorious army, an army which, unlike any earlier armies Egypt had known, was a fully professional and standing army (Faulkner 1953, 41-47; Schulman 1964). The empire grew and Egypt prospered accordingly. The earliest kings of the Dynasty, however, rather than waging great wars of conquest, led great raids in force to both keep the Asiatics weak and off balance and, more important, to secure the riches of Asia as booty and loot. The king led the army to battle, but it was the god of Thebes, Amūn, who was the source of victory. This is best illustrated by a series of dramatic narrative reliefs from the mortuary temple of the Twentieth Dynasty pharaoh, Ramesses III, at Medinet Habu on the west of Thebes. In the first scene the king is conducted by two other deities into the presence of Amūn who confers upon him a sword and simultaneously tells him: "I give to you valour and victory" (Nelson 1930, pl. 13).

In the next scene the king is shown emerging from the temple, holding the sword, and about to mount his waiting chariot. In front of the royal vehicle is the chariot of Amūn, easily recognizable by the ram-headed standard of the god which it holds (Nelson 1930, pls. 14, 16; cf. Schulman 1986, 46-47). Next, preceded by the chariot of Amūn, the king, riding in his own vehicle, leads the army forth to battle (Nelson 1930, pls. 17, 31; 1932, pl. 59). Now the battle is joined and the king wreaks great slaughter among the already-defeated enemy (Nelson 1930, pls. 18-19, 37-39; 1932, pls. 68, 70, 72, 87-90, 94). The participation of the rest of the army is confined to mopping up among the corpses of the slain, to collecting hands and phalli to bring them to the military scribes to be recorded for the bodycount of the dead, and to offer them to the king on the battlefield as evidence of the victory (Nelson 1930, pls. 22-23, 42; 1932, pls. 74-75). After this the army is shown on the march back to Egypt, the king at its head, the prisoners in its train (Nelson 1930, pl. 24; 1932, pls. 77, 92, 98). Once home, the king gives thanks and dedicates the spoil to Amūn (Nelson 1930, pls. 26, 44; 1932, pls. 73, 93, 99), ultimately bashing out the brains of the captured enemy ruler(s) (Nelson 1932, pls. 101, 102, 120-22). Clearly this should be a historical narrative, although there certainly are unreal elements in it, namely the participation of the gods and also the instant victory at the king's epiphany on the battlefield. The king's divinity is expressed by having him appear larger than any of the humans in the scene. When he appears before or with other gods, he is of the same size as they. In view of this, one may ask if he does what he does on the battlefield as the king or as the god, the more so since it *is* Amūn who gives the victory to him. In gratitude for this, the king then thanks the god by giving him a large share of the booty (Gardiner 1952, 9-19) whereupon the god again grants victory to the king (Wilson 1951, 185). In short, what we have here is a situation of *do ut des ut dem ut des ut,* "I give that you may give that I may give that you may give that" (Federn 1958). Nevertheless, underneath this divine rationale for the king's wars and triumphs we should be dealing with a historical event or sequence of events. But are we?

The iconographic motif of the triumphant king executing a defeated enemy ruler, frequently in the presence of a god, has been familiar in Egyptian art since, at least, the onset of the First Dynasty (Schulman 1988; Schoske forthcoming; Hall 1986; Sliwa 1973, 1974; Seton 1971-1972; Schäfer 1957). It is found on the pylons, gateways, walls, columns, and pillars of the palaces of the kings and the temples of the gods. Wherever the armies of Egypt marched, against the Nubian, the Asiatic, or any other foe, they left this scene carved on the cliffsides of Egypt's frontier marches, both to mark the limits of the army's advance and to serve as a cold reminder of the power of Egypt, a warning of the doom that would be meted out to her enemies. The motif is found not only in royal, monumental art. It occurs on all kinds of objects, both royal and nonroyal: stelae, scarabs, pectorals, weapons, and even artists' sketches on ostraca. Wherever it is found, it normally functioned on at least two levels, as did every piece of Egyptian two-dimensional art: the abstract and the concrete. On the concrete level (and this applies especially to its occurrence on stelae and in narratives such as those just described), it clearly records an event that took place at a fixed point of time in the past, while on the abstract level it repeats this same event over and over until the end of eternity (Schulman 1984, 176-77; 1988, 196-97).

The Fifth Dynasty king, Sahurē ᶜ, left a scene in his temple at Abusir which shows the king slaughtering a Libyan ruler whose name is either not given or not preserved. Watching in horror are the Libyan's wife and two sons who *are* named by name. The wife is called "Khutyotes" and the sons "Usa" and "Uni." Herds of animals, cattle, donkeys, goats, and rams, with the specific numbers of each kind, presumably booty taken, are appended to the scene (Borchardt 1913, pl. 1). Obviously this should be a historical scene, picturing a real event that takes place during the reign of Sahurē ᶜ, the conquest and subsequent ceremonial execution of a Libyan ruler in the presence of his wife

and children. However, from the mortuary temple at Abusir of a later king of the Fifth Dynasty, Nyuserrē ᶜ, a group of fragmentary reliefs show the king, both in the form of a lion and in human shape, slaughtering several enemies. In each of these scenes of execution at least one of the doomed prisoners is a Libyan, and in five of them, facing the enemies who are being slaughtered by the Egyptian king, are two pairs of children's feet and one pair of adult's feet (Borchardt 1907, pls. 8-11).

In the temple complex of the Sixth Dynasty ruler Pepi I, at Sakkara, there is a fragment of relief which pictures the king grasping the hair of two prisoners (one of whom is a Libyan) to steady their heads as he prepares to bash out their brains, while two young boys and a woman watch, their hands raised in a gesture of horror. They are named by name and are Khutyotes (the woman), and Usa and Uni (the two boys) (Leclant 1980, 49-54). Likewise, toward the end of the Sixth Dynasty, Pepi II left a scene in his temple complex at Sakkara, in which, from the attitudes of the preserved portions of their feet, Pepi II is sacrificing a captured Libyan ruler while two boys, Usa and Uni (the names are preserved), and a woman, Khutyotes, watch. Another small fragment of this scene shows part of the animal booty taken by the king: a herd of donkeys (Jéquier 1938, pls. 8, 9, 11). And, finally, over two millennia later and deep in the Sudan, the Twenty-fifth Dynasty Kushite king, Taharka, had himself pictured in two analogous scenes on one wall of his temple of Kawa in each of which, in the form of a lion, he is shown killing three enemies. One of these is an anonymous Libyan, but once again, two boys named "Usa" and "Uni" and a woman named "Khutyotes" stand and watch in horror. A text accompanying one of the two scenes records that Taharka "has plundered the Libyans of their animals and of all of their herds of cattle," and over the text a herd of cattle is shown. In the parallel scene, only one of the boys, Usa, is named and a fragment of the captured animal booty is pictured, possibly a herd of goats (Macadam 1955, p. 19).

Taken by itself, without the slightest suspicion or awareness that the other versions of this scene existed, any one of these occurrences would have been accepted without question as the documentary evidence for and the pictorial/textual record of a real historical event that had taken place at some point in time during the reign of Sahurē ᶜ, Nyuserrē ᶜ, Pepi I, Pepi II, or Taharka—namely, the ceremonial sacrifice (at the conclusion of a triumphant campaign) of an unnamed, but nevertheless specific, captured Libyan ruler before the terror-stricken gaze of his wife, Khutyotes, and his two sons, Usa and Uni. However, if we *are* aware of the parallels, then this explanation implies that not only was it the doom of every Libyan ruler to be captured and executed before the eyes of his wife and two children, in every instance the wife was named Khutyotes and the sons Usa and Uri. This, obviously, is a patently ridiculous proposition. A different solution must be found for this seeming dilemma.

It is clear that the different versions of this same scene do not illustrate a real historical event from the reigns of these five kings, but rather picture another type of the royal myth. Certainly at some point in time an Egyptian king, possibly Sahurē ᶜ, but more probably some much earlier pharaoh, did conquer Libyans, capture great numbers of Libyan herds of goats, cattle, donkeys, and sheep, and execute the Libyan ruler in the presence of his wife, Khutyotes, and his children, Usa and Uni. During the course of time the Libyan's name was lost or forgotten, but for some reason unknown to us, the name of the wife and those of the two sons were remembered. This conquest must have been so significant, so important that it became a part of the Egyptian king's persona, so that every succeeding Egyptian ruler felt himself compelled to remember and celebrate this same triumph in every single detail, as if he himself had brought it to pass.[4] When understood from *this* perspective, then for all practical purposes the historical reality of the scene, particularly with regard to the later examples of it, is negated. Moreover, the historical reality of *every* such picture of this genre should be challenged, unless there is an unquestionable and valid context into which it can be fixed and which would confirm its historicity. In fact, these same criteria for historical reality and accuracy might be applied to *all* scenes of a royal provenance in which the acta and dicta of the king are illustrated, and not only to those that portray the ceremonial execution of a captured enemy ruler.

In both the Eastern and Western artistic traditions, beginning with the time of Classical Antiquity, when a piece of art that depicts a historical incident is studied, it is clearly understood that the intent of such a work was usually to register, within the artist's frame of reference, an event that had happened at a particular moment in time so that it would be preserved for all time. While abstract or symbolic notions may be present in such an illustration, it is, nevertheless, clear that the depiction was to function on its primary level to visually record what had happened. However, this understanding is not and was not applicable to Egyptian "historical" works of art. The Egyptian concept of history as something that happened once and then repeated itself timelessly was and is rather distinct from our concept of history. It does not portray what did happen, but rather what its instigator wanted portrayed as having happened. Before we can discern the reality or comprehend the rationale behind Egyptian "historical" art, we must first understand, if possible, the raison d'être of each individual piece of it, as well as the cultural and intellectual milieu that produced it.

It is a virtual platitude that the chief concern of the ancient Egyptian was the afterworld, which he conceived of as just as real or even more real than this world. His basic understanding of the afterworld was that existence there continued and repeated life in this world, that whatever had been done here would be forever repeated there. This, then, brings an element of timelessness to any Egyptian "historical" work of art, even though a specific happening *may* have been recorded. Indeed, in addition to the two levels on which Egyptian art always simultaneously functioned, we may add still another level which I would characterize as psychological or propagandistic. It is, clearly, most evident in "royal" art, which is intended to propagandize and transmit the royal myth for the glorification of the king. It is likewise present in Egyptian private art, which almost invariably pictures its subjects as eternally youthful and healthy, who always prosper on account of their excellence.

The propagandistic and psychological level was undoubtedly the most important level on which Egyptian "historical" art operated. The royal myths that emphasized the king, his divinity, and his inevitable success in whatsoever he attempted to do pervades all aspects of Egyptian life and thought. Royal art concentrates on two areas: religion and war, and the latter is of interest to us here. With respect to war, clearly the operative principle was *l'état c'est moi!* In those scenes that portray the battlefield, although the ordinary soldiers are pictured, it is the king who is the central dominating focus. It is he who wins the victory (Wreszinski 1925, pls. 50, 65, 77, 101, 109, 114, 122, 130, passim). All others are not important, only incidental to the scene and their absence would not have even been noticed (Gaballa 1976, 100).

What is true for the pictorial versions of the royal myths of pharaonic Egypt is equally true for the textual versions and, as in the case of the visual instances, is best evidenced in the military inscriptions of the New Kingdom. One such inscription is the outcome of the battle of Megiddo fought by the Eighteenth Dynasty pharaoh Thutmose III (often regarded as the "Napoleon of Egypt" [Wilson 1951, 177-84; Gardiner 1964, 189-98]), in his twenty-second regnal year, ca. 1468 B.C.E. During this battle he smashed a coalition of Syro-Palestinian princes in the plain of Jezreel, before the Canaanite city of Megiddo. Modern scholarship usually accords this victory the pride of place in the establishment of the Egyptian empire of the Eighteenth Dynasty (for example, Wilson 1951, 180). Megiddo is one of the few battles of ancient Near Eastern history, as well as the earliest known battle in history for which we have a long, detailed narrative description which, purportedly, contains enough specific information so as to enable us to reconstruct it step-by-step. A number of the inscriptions of Thutmose refer to the battle of Megiddo (*Urk.* IV, 645-67; 739-40; 757-60; 1227-243).

The primary and most complete account of this battle is recorded in the king's annals, which are preserved on the walls of the great temple of Amūn at Karnak (*Urk.* IV, 645-67). In this version, which is riddled with lacunae at the beginning and end of virtually every line, it is now recognized that the text is a potpourri of literary and nonliterary genres. The most important of these are the extracts from the day books and war diaries of the army, a nonliterary genre (Spalinger 1982, 136-42), which was blended with an artificial literary format, the socalled "Königsnovelle" (Spalinger 1982, 106), which is intended to glorify and magnify the brilliance, genius, and skill of the king's persona.

In this format the king is faced with an extremely difficult choice. His advisors counsel a prudent course of action, but the king rejects their advice and follows a course of action that is fraught with danger and which, if it miscarries, could lead to total disaster. But, of course, the king succeeds (Hermann 1938, Herrmann 1953). With regard to the battle of Megiddo, the events leading up to the confrontation on the battlefield are given in detail. The Egyptian army, led by the king in person, marches out of Egypt to Gaza and then continues north along the Canaanite coast as far as the entrance to the Aruna Pass through the Carmel Ridge (probably the Wadi Ara near modern Hadera, see Gauthier 1925, 136). A council of war is held in which Thutmose III is warned against going through the Aruna Pass because it is so narrow and dangerous. He is, rather, advised to take a much safer route much farther to the north of Haifa. He rejects this advice and takes the danger-laden crossing of the Carmel Ridge via the Aruna Pass, which will bring him and the army into the Plain of Jezreel just south of Megiddo. While no figures are given for the size of the Egyptian forces, it *is* clear from the text that it was comprised of both infantry and chariot-mounted troops.[5] After the army had successfully debouched into the Plain of Jezreel, it camped and prepared for battle. On the day of battle its dispositions are clearly and explicitly detailed. Then the good god, the king, made his epiphany on the battlefield. The enemy fled in great disorder and the battle was over. The victory was gained.

Since it is clear that the events of the battle are, to a great extent, viewed through the prisms of the *Königsnovelle,* we are entitled to ask whether they actually took place as they are described the text, or whether they have been compressed or distorted so as to fit into this artificial literary format. There are many factors we cannot confirm, such as the numerical strengths of the two armies, the composition and disposition of the enemy forces, the length of the battle, the weather on the day of battle, and the time of day when the fighting took place. There is, however, one factor which we *can* confirm, and this, fortunately, is a major topos in the account of the battle: the terrain and particularly the difficulties inherent in the Aruna

Pass. It was reported to be so narrow and twisting that the army would have had to traverse it strung out in a single file, man walking behind man, horse going behind horse (*Urk.* IV, 649-50; 652-53). The terrain has hardly changed since the time of Thutmose III. Sometime early in the twentieth century, probably during the British Mandate, a paved road was laid through the Wadi Ara. However, even without this modern improvement, the bulk of the length of the Wadi was quite straight and flat. The difficult ascent and descent into the Valley of Jezreel starting at the village of Musmus, is only a few kilometers long and it is not very narrow. In fact, during the Turkish Period, when the road was probably still a dirt track, it was still wide enough to allow a considerable frontage of infantry to traverse it with ease (Nelson 1913, 31-32; 37-39). Even today it is wide enough to allow a company front of fifteen to twenty-five men wide and/or several chariots to travel along it without being crowded. Thus, on the basis of the terrain, even discounting the rhetorical hyperbole the Egyptians loved, it is clear that some details of our text have been distorted. Moreover, one may well ask, if the Egyptian victory at Megiddo was as decisive as the amount of space devoted to it in comparison with that given over to Thutmose's subsequent wars in Asia seem to suggest, why, then, did Thutmose III continue to campaign in Asia virtually every year for the next twenty odd years? While it is clear that some of these "campaigns of victory" were probably little more than promenades to "show the flag" (Wilson 1951, 180; cf. Gardiner 1961, 193), there is no question but that some of these were hard-fought campaigns in which Thutmose attacked the same enemies and captured the same cities.

Perhaps even better known than the battle of Megiddo is the battle of Kadesh, which the Nineteenth Dynasty pharaoh Ramesses II (known to posterity as Ramesses the Great) fought against the Hittites in his fifth regnal year (*KRI* II, 2-147; Gardiner 1960). The Egyptian king was so proud of this battle that he had it celebrated in word and picture on the walls of the major temples of Egypt and Nubia. The majority of the textual and visual accounts of the battle are damaged, fragmentary, or otherwise incomplete, but together with the version preserved on the walls of the rock-cut temple of Abu Simbel in Nubia, which is intact (Noblecourt, Donadoni, and Edel 1971, pl. 4), they provide us with a complete and coherent account of the battle. As is to be expected, a good deal of the textual record is framed within the format of the *Königsnovelle* (Spalinger 1982, 109-10), while much of the visual record enshrines the myth of the omnitriumphant king. At Kadesh, Ramesses II, misled by disinformation emanating from the Hittites, blythely marched his army into an ambush. The Egyptians managed to hold their own and even to severely maul the Hittites. Nevertheless, the Egyptians lost the battle and Kadesh remained in Hittite hands. Of course, neither the textual nor the pictorial records of the battle even mention this. They dwell, rather, on the incredible heroism and extraordinary courage of Ramesses: While the rest of his army was either fleeing in panic or cowering in fear, unwilling to join in the fray, the king kept his wits about him and entered the fighting. With neither soldier of the infantry nor chariot-warrior of the chariotry to help him, he attacked the 2,500 chariots of the oncoming Hittites, wreaked great slaughter among them, and put them to flight, thereby saving his own army. He continued to hold the Hittites at a distance until the onset of darkness suspended the day's hostilities. Battle was resumed on the next day and again the Hittites suffered grievous losses, so severe that the Hittite king was appalled and immediately sued for a cessation of fighting. Ramesses graciously assented and the battle was over. The Egyptian documentation does not mention the fact that Ramesses lost the battle, but the Hittite sources do (Schulman 1981, 10 nn. 22-23). What the Egyptian material emphasizes is the bravery of the king.

The Abu Simbel visual record of the battle occupies one full wall of the first hall of the temple and shows details not found elsewhere, particularly the arrival of an enigmatic Egyptian military force, the *n‘rn,* which arrives on the field at the height of the Hittite attack and saves the day for Egypt (Schulman 1962, 1981; Noblecourt, Donadoni, and Edel 1971, pls. 20, 21, 4). This is also not mentioned in the two major textual accounts of the battle, the Poem and the Bulletin, but only in a caption to this scene. The main thrust in the *Königsnovelle* framework in which the textual accounts are set emphasizes the king's courage in saving his army, when he repelled, by himself, the attack of the 2,500 Hittite chariots.

The chariotry forces of any given state in the ancient Near East were not particularly large (Schulman 1979-1980, 135-40; 141-42). In order to have chariots, it is obvious that horses are required. Each chariot had a team of two horses to pull it and needed at least one reserve horse, possibly two, for replacements (Yadin 1963, 88-89). Consequently, unless we dismiss as rhetoric and hyperbole the statements that the Hittites deployed some 2,500 chariots for their ambush of Ramesses's army at Kadesh, then their equine requirements should have had to have been somewhere between 7,500 and 10,000 steeds. Such a number of horses would have presented logistical problems which, undoubtedly, would have been beyond the Hittites' capacity to solve, particularly since the Hittite army, like that of any other contemporary ancient Near Eastern army, normally had no supply train that we know of, but was, rather, expected to forage and live off the land (cf. Schulman 1964, 78 par. 197). Moreover, the costs of even assembling such a force of horses and chariots is mind-boggling. An Egyptian literary text of the Nineteenth Dynasty that deals with the hardships of the life of the chariot-warrior (Papyrus Anastasi III,

see Schulman 1964, 100-1 par. 96) records that a chariot, together with its pole, cost eight *deben* (about £1.6), probably in silver, which the Egyptians valued more than gold. The only other figure we have for the price of chriot-horses comes from the Bible, where it is explicitly stated that Solomon imported horses on a large scale and that the going rate for a chariot was 600 shekels (I Kings 10:26-29; II Chronicles 1:16-17), while that for a horse alone was 150 shekels of silver. Thus, since Solomon is supposed to have possessed 12,000 horsemen and 1,400 chariots (Schulman 1983, 121 n. 5; 1979-1980, 141-42), and since these would have had to have been imported, inasmuch as Solomon's kingdom had neither a tradition nor a topography for horse breeding, his horses and chariots would have cost several *tons* of silver. Even taking into account the storied riches of Solomon's kingdom, it seems highly unlikely that it really could have afforded or would have paid such an inordinate sum.

Additional pictorial and visual examples of the royal myths would only reinforce what has already been said. Therefore, we may briefly turn to yet another sector of Egyptian psychology where the royal myths had a discernible effect, namely in the vocabulary of conflict and the way it was written with Egyptian hieroglyphs. Usually, when an Egyptian king waged war, his excuse for doing so was because the particular enemy with whom he was fighting had been "plotting rebellion" or had actually "rebelled" against him (see Spalinger 1982, 60; 67-69). It was of no importance that this enemy may have been the sovereign ruler of a sovereign state that had never been subject to Egypt. In the Egyptian scheme of the world's order, every land in theory and all of their peoples were naturally subordinate to and ruled by Egypt (see Bleiberg 1984). Their kings were never styled *nśwt,* the usual Egyptian word for "king" (*Wb.* II, 325; 1-332; 7), although in cuneiform royal documents issuing from the Egyptian king to foreign rulers, both the Egyptian monarch and his foreign counterpart are designed by the same Akkadian term, *śarru* (king). In hieroglyphic documents, however, foreign rulers, at best, were addressed as *wr* (great one) (*Wb.* I, 328; 14-329; 20) in the sense that they were the greatest one of a region or of an office.

In all periods of Egyptian history, one of the commonest words used to indicate an "enemy" was *ḥrw,* literally "the overthrown one," "the fallen one" (*Wb.* III, 4; 321; 6-322) since, obviously, if anyone were rash enough to wage war against the Egyptian king, the outcome was a foregone conclusion: he would be overthrown and slain. In fact, the very ideographs used as the determinative for this word, its synonyms, and for related words like "rebel," "rebellion," and the like, were the hieroglyphs showing a man fallen down, his arms stretched out, a man falling, with blood spurting copiously from his head, or a man with his hands tied behind his back (Gardiner 1927, 436 nrs: A13-A15). This, after all, was the merited fate of the enemy and the rebel. Basically Egyptian has two words for "tribute", *b3kw* (*Wb.* I, 428; 6-14) and *inw* (ibid. 91; 12-16). The former, when used of Egyptians means "taxes," "imposts," and only when used of foreigners does it mean "tribute." The latter likewise means "tribute" when used of foreigners, but when used of Egyptians it means "gifts" (Gordon 1983). In the Annals of Thutmose III (*Urk.* IV, 668-756) and elsewhere, however, the two terms are used interchangeably and always with reference to foreigners. On one series of the large commemorative scarabs of Amūnhotpe III (*Urk.* IV, 1738) the king describes his marriage to Giluhepa, a princess of Mitanni, as if it were the payment of tribute to him, although we know from the Amarna Letters, the diplomatic correspondence of the Egyptian "Foreign Office" from his reign and that of his successor, Akhenaton, that this was a freely negotiated marriage between two great kings, theoretically two equals (Schulman 1979, 191-92).

A few concluding remarks are now in order. The royal myths of Egypt, centering as they do on the divinity of the Egyptian ruler, on his omnipotence and his omniscience are, in a way, rather unique and, to my knowledge, have no parallel in either the Ancient Near Eastern World or the Classical World. It is true that in many of the states of antiquity the king, technically, was divine, but in no way was their divinity like that of the Egyptian pharaoh. We have seen how the royal myths distort what *may* have happened into a kind of Potemkin village in a Potemkin world. In our own modern world there is, at least among sophisticates, intellectuals, and probably even among a moiety of the general public, there is a tendency to view what they read, see, or hear in the media with a modicum of suspicion. In other words, they are aware of the fact that there may be a credibility gap between what may have happened and the recording of it.

Yet these very same people tend to accept as the Gospel from Sinai, if I may mix my metaphors, the contents of an ancient document, simply because it is an ancient document and because, in antiquity, for some reason unbeknown to us, no one lied or distorted. Speaking now as a historian who is well aware that *pas des sources, pas d'histoire,* there is no question but that the historian must work with whatever source material is available. Nevertheless, he must not accept it blindly, but must, as stated at the outset of this paper, first critically examine it for its bias, its intent, its reliability, and its credibility. Only after this is done and both the nature and the purpose(s) of the individual document are determined, may the historian be free to use it. What may emerge from this kind of scrutiny may prompt the historian to ask new questions rather than the same old ones (which, unless there is new material, can only yield the same old answers). New questions may generate, then, new understandings and perceptions of the past and these, in turn, may be much closer to a historical reality than is the historical speculation which currently passes for history.

Notes

[1] There are, however, two exceptions among the latter kings of Dynasty.

A king Peribsen replaced his Horus name with a Set name, and one of his successors, Khasekhemwy altered both his Horus and his Two Ladies name to a) the Horus and Set Khasekhemwy and b) the Two Lords are at peace in him. Most scholars see this as a rebellion of the North under Peribsen, and the restoration of the South's dominance, with the duality of Horus and Set in the first two names of Khasekhemwy, (itself a dual) indicating this (Gardiner 1961, 416-18; Newberry 1922).

[2] There was a major cult center of Set at the city of Nub, the Greek Ombos. Therefore, if we read *nb* as a *nisbe*-adjective (Gardiner 1927, 61-62; par. 79) we may understand it as "he of Nub," "the Nubtian," i.e., Set. The hieroglyph for Horus is physically written over the gold sign. This being "over," "upon," "on top of" would be expressed in writing by the preposition *hr*. An Egyptian could easily read the two hieroglyphs and their physical arrangement as *Hr* (*hr*) *nb*(y). "Horus is over Set," i.e., "Horus who triumphs over Set."

[3] E.g., Rēᶜdjedef, Khafrē ᶜ, and Menkaurēᶜ.

[4] A fitting parallel is found in a passage in the Passover Haggadah:

In every generation each person is bound to regard himself as if he, *personally,* had gone forth from Egypt, for it is said: 'And you shall tell it to your son on that day, saying this is because of what Yahweh did for *me* when *I* went forth from Egypt.

[5] In the Eighteenth Dynasty, until the reign of Amūnhotpe III, only designations which had to do with the chariot are attested, not ranks and titles which pertain to the chariotry as a distinct and separate arm of the military. This then points to a major reorganization of the army into two arms, infantry and chariotry, each with their own organization and administration, sometime during the reign of Amūnhotpe III.

Works Cited

Anthes, R. 1961. Mythology in ancient Egypt. In S. N. Kramer (ed.), *Mythologies of the Ancient World.* Garden City, NY: Doubleday, 15-92.

Badawy, A. 1959. Min, the cosmic fertility god of Egypt. *Mitteilungen des Instituts für Orientforschung der Deutschen Akademie der Wissenschaften zu Berlin* 7: 163-79.

Baumgartel, E. J. 1955-1960. *The cultures of prehistoric Egypt.* 2 vols. Oxford: Oxford University Press.

Bleiberg, E. L. 1984. *Aspects of the political, religious, and economic basis of ancient Egyptian imperialism during the New Kingdom.* Unpublished Ph.D. dissertation. Canada: The University of Toronto.

Borchardt, L. 1907. *Das Grabdenkmal des Königs Neuser-re^c.* Leipzig: J. C. Hinrichs.

———. 1913. *Das Grabdenkmal des Königs S^ca3hu-Re^c. II. Die Wandbilder.* Leipzig: J. C. Hinrichs.

Faulkner, R. O. 1953. Ancient Egyptian Military Organization. *Journal of Egyptian Archaeology* 39: 32-47.

———. 1961-1971: *The Ancient Egyptian Pyramid Texts,* 2 vols. Oxford: Clarendon Press.

———. 1972. *The Book of the Dead. A Collection of Spells Edited and Translated from Papyri in the British Museum.* New York: The Limited Editions Club.

———. 1973-1978. *The Ancient Egyptian Coffin Texts.* 3 vols. Warminster: Aris and Phillips, Ltd.

Federn, W. 1958. *Htp (r)dj(w) (n) 'Inpw:* zum Verständnis der vor-osirianischen Opferformel. *Mitteilungen des deutschen archäologischen Instituts Abteilung Kairo* 16: 120-30.

Gaballa, G. A. 1976. *Narrative in Egyptian art.* Mainz: Von Zaubern.

Gardiner, A. H. 1927. *Egyptian grammar, being an introduction to the study of hieroglyphics.* Oxford: Clarendon Press.

———. 1952. Tuthmosis III returns thanks to Amūn. *Journal of Egyptian Archaeology* 38: 6-23.

———. 1960. *The Kadesh inscriptions of Ramesses II.* Oxford: The Griffith Institute.

———. 1961. *Egypt of the pharaohs.* Oxford: Oxford University Press.

Gauthier, H. 1925. *Dictionnaire des noms géographiques contenus les textes hiéroglyphiques.* Vol. 1. Cairo: Institut français d'archéologie orientale.

Gordon, A. H. 1983. The context and meaning of the ancient Egyptian word *inw* from the Proto-Dynastic Period to the end of the new kingdom. Unpublished

Ph.D. dissertation. Berkeley: The University of California.

Hall, E. S. 1986. *The pharaoh smites his enemies: A comparative study.* Munich: Deutscher Kunstverlag.

Hermann, A. 1938. *Die altägyptische Königsnovelle.* Glückstadt and Hamburg: J. J. Augustin.

Herrmann, S. 1953. Die Königsnovelle in Ägypten und in Israel. *Wissenschaftliche Zeitschrift der Karl Marx Universität, Leipzig.* Gesellschafts- und Sprachwissenschaftliche Reihe 55, 51-62.

Jéquier, G. 1938. *Le monument funéraire de Pepi II. II. Le* temple. Cairo: Institut français d'archéologie orientale.

Leclant, J. 1980. La familie libyenne au Temple Haut de Pepi Ier. In *Le Livre du Centenaire 1880-1890.* Cairo: Institut français d'archéologie orientale.

Macadam, M. F. L. 1955. *The temples of Kawa. II. History and archaeology of the site.* Oxford: Oxford University Press.

Munn-Rankin, M. J. 1956. Diplomacy in Western Asia in the early second millenium B.C. *Iraq* 18: 68-109.

Nelson, H. H. 1913. *The battle of Megiddo.* Ph.D. dissertation, the University of Chicago, private edition distributed by the University of Chicago Libraries.

———. (ed.) 1930. *Earlier historical records of Ramses III.* Chicago: The University of Chicago Press.

———. (ed.) 1932. *Later Historical Records of Ramses III.* Chicago: The University of Chicago Press.

Newberry, P. E. 1922. The Set Rebellion in the IInd Dynasty. *Ancient Egypt* 7: 40-46.

Noblecourt, C. D., S. Donadoni, and E. Edel. 1971. *Grand temple d'Abou Simbel: la bataille de Qadech.* Cairo: Centre de documentation et d'études sur l'Ancienne Égypte.

Redford, D. B. 1979. Egyptology and history. In K. Weeks (ed.), *Egyptology and the Social Sciences. Five Studies.* Cairo: American University Press, 1-20.

———. 1986. *Pharaonic king-lists, annals, and daybooks: A contribution to the study of the Egyptian sense of history.* Missassauga, Canada: Ben-ben.

Schäfer, H. 1957. Das Niederschlagen der Feinde. Zur Geschichte eines ägyptischen Sinnbildes. *Wiener Zeit-schrift für die Kunde des Morgenlandes* 54: 168-76.

The Isis Omnia of Egypt

Schoske, S. Forthcoming. *Die Siegreiche König. Bild-quellen zur altägyptischen Feindsymbolik.* Wies-baden: Harrasowitz.

Schulman, A. R. 1962. The *N^{c}rn* at the Battle of Kadesh. *Journal of the American Research Center in Egypt* 1, 47-52.

———. 1964. *Military rank, title, and organization in the Egyptian New Kingdom.* Berlin: Bruno Hessling.

———. 1979. Diplomatic marriage in the Egyptian New Kingdom. *Journal of Near Eastern Studies* 38: 177-93.

———. 1979-1980. Chariots, chariotry, and the Hyksos. *The SSEA Journal* 10: 105-53.

———. 1981. The *N^{c}rn* at Kadesh once again. *The SSEA Journal* 11: 7-19.

———. 1983. Kings, chronicles, and Egyptian mercenaries. *Bulletin of the Egyptological Seminar* 5: 117-33.

———. 1984. The Iconographic theme: "Opening of the mouth" on Stelae. *Journal of the American Research Center in Egypt* 21: 169-96.

———. 1986. The so-called poem on the king's chariot Revisited. *The SSEA Journal* 16: 19-35, 39-49.

———. 1988. *Ceremonial execution and public rewards. Some historical scenes on New Kingdom private stelae.* Freiburg, Switzerland: Universitätsverlag.

Seton, D. R. 1971-1972. *The king of Egypt annihilating his enemies: A study in the symbolism of ancient Monarchy.* Unpublished M.A. thesis. Birmingham, England: University of Birmingham.

Sliwa, J. 1973. The question of the representation of the victorious ruler in Egyptian art. *Prace Archeologizne* 1973: 7-22 (in Polish).

———. 1974. Some remarks concerning victorious ruler representations in Egyptian art. *Forschungen und Berichte* 16: 97-117.

Spalinger, A. J. 1982. *Aspects of the Military Documents of the Ancient Egyptians.* New Haven and London: Yale University Press.

Urk. IV = Sethe, K. (ed.). *Urkunden des ägyptischen Altertums, IV, Urkunden der 18. D nastie.* Hft. 1-16, Leipzig, J. C. Hinrichs, 1927-30; Helck, Wolfgang (ed.): *Urkunden des ägyptischen Altertums, IV, Urkunden der 18. Dynastie,* Hft. 17-22, Berlin, Akademie verlag, 1955-1958.

Van Seters, J. 1983. *In search of history. Historiography of the ancient world and the origins of biblical history.* New Haven, CT and London: Yale University Press.

Verner, M. 1975. Confrontation of man and time. In V. Soucek (ed.), *Aspects of ancient oriental historiography.* Prague: Charles University, 40-55.

Wilson, J. A. 1949. Egypt. In H. and H. A. Frankfurt, J. A. Wilson, and T. Jacobson, *Before philosophy: The intellectual adventure of ancient man.* Harmondsworth: Penguin Books.

———. 1951. *The burden of Egypt. An interpretation of ancient Egyptian culture.* Chicago: The University of Chicago Press.

———. 1956. The royal myth in ancient Egypt. *Proceedings of the American Philosophical Society* 100: 439-42.

Wb. = Erman, A., and H. Grapow (eds.). 1925. *Wörterbuch der ägyptische Spracheim Auftrage der deutschen Akademien.* 12 vols. Unveränderter Neudruck. Berlin, Akademie Verlag.

Wreszinski, W. (ed.) 1925. *Atlas zur altägyptischen Kulture-geschichte* 2. Leipzig: Hinrichs.

Yadin, Y. 1963. *The art of warfare in biblical lands.* New York: Toronto, and London: McGraw-Hill.

CROSS-CULTURAL PERSPECTIVE

W. Michael Kelsey (essay date 1981)

SOURCE: "Salvation of the Snake, the Snake of Salvation: Buddhist-Shinto Conflict and Resolution," in *Japanese Journal of Religious Studies*, Vol. 8, No. 1-2, March-June, 1981, pp. 83-113.

[*In the following essay, Kelsey examines the use of the snake figure in Buddhist and Shinto narratives of evil and redemption.*]

Introduction

Buddhism and Shinto have had a remarkably harmonious coexistence over the past fourteen centuries. This is most probably due to two factors: on the one hand, Shinto lacked a formal structure from which to organize resistance, and on the other, Buddhism had always assimilated the traditions native to the countries it entered. Even so, it is not realistic to maintain that the first period of contact between these two religions was completely free of strife. Indeed, one senses a sometimes violent conflict lurking beneath the surface of certain Japanese Buddhist stories.

This conflict which accompanied Buddhism's entry to the gates of the Japanese spirit also provided the basis for the Buddhist-Shinto syncretization that was to prove so remarkable in later years; what was first a minus was later to become a plus. This essay will examine Buddhist-Shinto relationships as seen in a single cluster of stories, namely, those having to do with snakes. In brief, my thesis is that we can find in these stories first conflict between Buddhism and Shinto, and then, as the relationships between the two settle down, a creative Buddhist use of those ancient Shinto deities that appeared as reptiles.

The malevolent reptilian deity existed in Japan before the introduction of Buddhism, and it is initially regarded by the Buddhists, as well as by other Japanese, as being an evil creature. As Buddhism took a deeper hold on the Japanese consciousness, however, the image of the violent snake—which never completely died out—came to be supplemented by that of a snake of salvation. The movement is from the image of a snake that terrorizes the populace at the one extreme to the image of a snake that is none other than a manifestation of Buddha at the other.

These two extremes are linked by a road which is far from straight. There are five images of the snake found in mythological (that is, pre-Buddhist) and early sources. These are:

1. The mythical snake.

2. The mythical snake as saved (defeated) by Buddhism.

3. The Buddhist snake.

4. The mytho-Buddhist hybrid.

5. The snake of salvation.

I will discuss each of these in turn, but first a word about my sources.

The mythological material has been drawn primarily from the various *fudoki,* or local histories compiled by Imperial order in the early eighth century, and from *Kojiki* (Record of ancient matters), compiled in 712. The Buddhist material is drawn from the short tale collections known as *setsuwa shū*, which flourished in the Heian and Kamakura periods and which reveal much about how Buddhism was understood and dis-siminated in its early stages in Japan. There is a large number of such collections extant and nearly all of them contain tales of snakes, but I have limited my references here to two. These are *Nihon ryū iki,* compiled in the early ninth century by the monk Kyōkai (also read Keikai), and *Konjaku monogatari-shū*, compiled about 1100 by an unknown Buddhist monk. *Ryōiki,* being the oldest extant *setsuwa* collection, is especially valuable for stories from the second of my five categories; in the pages of *Konjaku* one can find examples of tales from all of the categories.[1]

The Mythical Snake

Hostility to mortals. The mythical snake is characterized by its general hostility to mortals. It should not be considered an "evil" deity, however, since the reptilian form is only one of the manifestations of the water or thunder deity, a complex creature with both desirable and undesirable personality traits. The reptilian manifestation is generally associated with the undesirable personality traits, and rather than to speak of a "snake deity," it is more accurate to speak of deities who sometimes take the form of snakes. It must be remembered, though, that they do so in order to cause mischief, and the snake itself therefore has negative associations. The reptile is an outward manifestation of the violent spirit (*aramitama*) of the deity, a sort of public warning that the deity is in no mood to be bothered. A consideration of two related tales should clarify this aspect of the reptile.

The first story concerns the founding of the Kamo Shrine, and is located in *Yamashiro fudoki* (*Fudoki,* pp. 414-415). A young maiden playing alongside a river notices a red painted arrow float by, which she takes home and puts in her bedroom. Soon thereafter she becomes pregnant and gives birth to a son. Her father then gathers all of the deities for a feast and asks the boy to present a cup of *sake* to his father; the child promptly ascends to heaven, where he becomes a thunder deity.

The second story is from *Hitachi fudoki* (*Fudoki,* pp. 78-80), and relates a similar mysterious birth. In this case a woman called Nuka-bime lives with her brother, Nuka-biko. She is visited by a man she does not know, and after sleeping with him for only one night gives birth to a snake. She puts the snake-child in a bowl, and he grows so quickly that the following day she must put him in a larger bowl; this process is repeated each day until the woman runs out of bowls. She then tells the child she cannot keep him and that he should go to his father. When he hears this the child becomes angry and eventually kills his uncle, Nuka-biko. He unsuccessfully attempts to ascend to heaven, but is doomed to reside in the local mountains, where he is worshiped by the ancestors of Nuka-bime.

In each of these tales a woman has a strange visitor and is impregnated under unusual circumstances; in each, the child is the son of a deity; and in each, the child is associated with thunder (reptile) deities. However, the child in the Kamo Shrine origin tale is born in human form and does no harm to any mortal, while the son of Nuka-bime is a snake and kills his uncle. I will not enquire into the reasons that one child is born a mortal and the other a snake, but would like to stress one obvious fact: the deity in its reptilian form does harm to mortals while the deity in human form does not.

Two levels of harm. In his reptilian form the deity poses threats to mortals on two levels: first, as a general violent nature god especially harmful to agriculture, and second as a specific danger to mortal women. Snakes or reptilian deities are often depicted as raping and devouring mortal women. These two aspects of this deity are probably related, as we shall see.

To begin with a brief look at the communal threat posed by the deity in his reptilian form, we might note a story from *Hitachi fudoki* (*Fudoki,* p. 54), in which a snake deity called Yatsu no kami interferes with the efforts of a certain Yawazu no Matachi to clear a field for cultivation. Matachi dons the garb of a warrior and stands at the foot of a nearby mountain, where he draws a line in the ground with his staff, declaring that the area above the line will henceforth be reserved for the deity, but that everything below it will be used for agriculture. He pledges to build a shrine and worship

the deity if it leaves him alone, but to kill it if it attempts to interfere further with his farming. After this show of force Matachi has no further problems, and we are told that his descendants are still maintaining the shrine.

In a somewhat similar tale also in *Hitachi fudoki* (*Fudoki,* pp. 445-446) a thunder deity kills a woman working in a field. Her brother, seeking revenge, tracks the deity down and extracts a promise to cease such violent acts.

It is also interesting to note that Susa-no-wo no mikoto, the famous underworld storm deity, is said to have committed all eight of the "Eight Heavenly Sins" against rice farmers, and generally poses a threat to farmers because of his violence. He, too, is associated with snakes.[2]

Violence against women. The story from *Hitachi fudoki* noted above (*Fudoki,* pp. 445-446) involved, in addition to a deity who interfered in the cultivation of a rice field, a woman who was murdered by a deity. In most cases of deities claiming individual (as opposed to general) victims in Japanese mythology, that victim is a woman. These tales often take the form of a "one-night consort" (*hito-yo zuma*) tale, in which a woman is mated with a deity for one night, then killed and eaten by the deity. I will deal with this cycle in more detail in the following section, but it is worth noting here that these tales are very likely reflections of religious rites involving sacrifices, either actual or symbolic, of women to water deities (Matsumura III, pp. 212-213). In other words, the women may have been sacrificed in order to protect the community from the mischief of the violent deity.

Whatever their source, however, such "one-night consort" tales reveal a deity associated with aggressive and often deadly sexual appetites. In this respect, they resemble the dragon figures of the West; the British dragon, for example, is said to resemble a "large worm" and to be "avid for maidens."[3]

Salvation of The Snake

Harnassing thunder. Stories about snakes were extremely popular with the early Japanese Buddhists. *Nihon setsuwa bungaku sakuin* (pp. 894-897), for example, lists some eighty-two tales in twenty-two primarily Buddhist sources; if stories of related reptiles were to be included, the number would exceed one hundred tales. I will treat in this section only those tales in which the mythical snake is subjugated by the forces of Buddhism, and save the more purely Buddhist reptiles for the following section.

Let us begin with a consideration of the reptile in his guise as a general danger to the communal (agricultural) good. I wish to focus primarily on one tale, *Nihon ryōiki* I. 3, but in the course of this discussion we shall have occasion to introduce other stories as well. The story in question has been entitled "On the strength of the child born from the gratitude of the thunder deity" by *Ryōiki* compiler Kyōkai, and for the purposes of summation we can divide it into four parts:[4]

A. A farmer holds a metal rod in his hand during a shower that has come up while he is irrigating his fields; this causes the thunder deity to appear before him in the form of a small child and beg for mercy. The deity promises to repay his debt of gratitude to the farmer by granting the farmer a child. The child thus born has a snake coiled around its head.

B. This child has extraordinary physical strength and bests a prince famous for his own strength in a series of contests.

C. The child enters the temple Gangō-ji as an apprentice and singlehandedly kills a demon that has been devouring monks attempting to ring the temple bell.

D. The child, now a lay monk, puts on a display of power to intimidate certain princes who have been damming up the source of water to the temple's fields. The princes cease their interference and the hero is ordained a monk and called Dōjō.

As even a glance at the above summary will show, the story has obvious ties to Japanese myth. It is indeed thought by some scholars (Kurosawa 1976; Moriya 1978, esp. pp. 132-182) to have its immediate origins in myth. However, there is little evidence to establish any direct line of transmission from myth to *setsuwa,* and our time is better spent in tracing the ways in which the tale goes beyond its mythological base. It is in the gaps between the story's mythological parallels and Kyōkai's version that the tale's major interest lies. To state my conclusion concerning the relationship between this tale and Japanese myth at the outset, I am of the opinion that this tale expresses, in symbolic form, many of the problems and their resolutions connected with the introduction of Buddhism to Japan.

I would like to begin with a consideration of the myth patterns that can be found in the tale. The most obvious of these is that of the mortal gaining power over thunder. (More will be said of this below.) The encounter with the violent thunder deity and extracting a promise from him is reminiscent of the *Hitachi fudoki* tale discussed above in which the farmer threatens the deity in order to revenge his sister's death.

As to the motif of the mortal who is able to get control over the thunder deity, we have a clear instance of this in the first tale in *Nihon ryōiki,* "On catching thunder." This story is based on an account in *Nihon shoki* of the

exploits of one Chiisakobe no Sugaru, a retainer of the Emperor Yūraku. In the *Nihon shoki* account, Sugaru brings the thunder deity to the emperor in the form of a large snake, whereas in *Nihon ryōiki* there is no indication of his form. Further, the thunder deity in *Ryōiki* is portrayed as something of a bumbling fool humiliated by a mortal, an element lacking in *Nihon shoki,* where the deity is held in more awe. The hero of this tale, as his name Chiisako (literally, "small child") implies, is small of stature, but he also has extraordinary strength, both characteristics of the hero of *Ryōiki* I. 3.

Breaking myth patterns. The important thing about the Gangō -ji story, however, is not whether it is based on a myth pattern, but how it breaks that pattern to establish its own reality. With the above patterns in mind, then, let us consider how the tale goes beyond the myth.

It will be noted that the story begins and ends in the rice fields, with the problem of irrigation being central to both episodes A and D. The nature of the field has changed, however, shifting from a secular one in episode A to a sacred one (that is, one on Buddhist temple grounds) in episode D. This suggests a contrast between "secular" and "sacred" which is pivotal to the organization of the tale. This can be expressed as follows:

secular half
  A. Violent deity subdued.
  B. Prince defeated.

sacred half
    C. Violent deity subdued.
    D. Princes defeated.

The action in each half of this tale is essentially the same but takes place on a different plane from the corresponding action in the other half. We have first a mythological rendering of this action, then an "instant replay" from a Buddhist perspective.

In the mythological half of the tale, a violent deity is pacified and the child he bestows on the world proves extraordinary; but in the Buddhist half, the violent deity is one that *threatens Buddhism,* and the secular forces brought under control are similarly those *opposed to Buddhism.* Further the force which has made the world safe for Buddhism is not just any hero but one directly linked with the Shinto thunder deity, that erstwhile terrorist of the rice fields already shown (in *Ryōiki* I. 1) to have come under the dominance of the mortal world. To put things rather bluntly, a Shinto deity has not only been subdued, it has been converted to Buddhism and used to pave the way for the new religion. We might call this the "Buddhification" of a Japanese myth.

I will return shortly to the role of the small boy in this "Buddhification" process, but would like to introduce another tale, "About the construction of the original Gangō-ji during the reign of Empress Suiko" (*Konjaku monogatari-shū* XI. 22) at this point. In this tale we learn about the problems experienced with a large zelkova tree on the proposed site for the temple, Gangō-ji. The tree was the home of some local deities that were reported to have caused the deaths of the first people who tried to fell it. A clever Buddhist monk spends the night near the tree and overhears the deities discussing the Buddhists' efforts. In the course of their conversation the secret of cutting down the tree is revealed. The monk reports what he has discovered and the tree is felled successfully. The Emperor, however, feels compassion for the uprooted deities and has a shrine built for them.

Moriya (1978, p. 166) holds that the demon defeated by the monk Dōjō in episode C of *Ryōiki* I. 3 is one of these defeated deities who has been lingering about the temple to revenge his defeat. There is no direct evidence for this position in the story—the demon there is said to be the evil spirit of a former slave of the temple—but a consideration of the chronology involved sheds some interesting light on the matter.

The reign of Empress Suiko (593-629 according to *Nihon shoki*) saw a large number of Buddhist temples constructed and in general was a time of considerable Buddhist activity. The birth of Dōjō is placed by Kyōkai in the reign of the Emperor Bitatsu (572-586), which would put Dōjō somewhere between the ages of 10 and 24 when the temple was completed in 596, and from this we can deduce that the events related in *Ryōiki* I. 3 would have been seen by Kyōkai as having taken place at very nearly the same time as those related in *Konjaku* XI. 22. It certainly does not seem unreasonable to assume that the bell tower demon and the tree spirits are essentially the same creatures—Shinto deities who attempted to oppose the building of the temple on their native soil.

Going further back, however, the story seems even more closely related to the introduction of Buddhism. As noted, Dōjō was said to have been born during the reign of Emperor Bitatsu, the period during which Buddhism is said in *Nihon shoki* to have been introduced to Japan. Granted that the dates found in *Nihon shoki* are not always reliable to the modern scholar, it must be kept in mind that this document would have been Kyōkai's major source, and in this regard the accounts in *Nihon shoki* of conflicts between Buddhism and Shinto followers, and those between Prince Regent Shōtoku and various imperial princes take on considerable significance. That is to say, the fact that Kyōkai locates Dōjō during a time when there were (or were thought to be) actual conflicts between forces of Buddhism and Shinto gives Dōjō

even more significance as a mediating force between Buddhism and Shinto.

I do not think it wide of the mark to suggest that in this tale Dōjō symbolizes the conversion of the "spirit of Japan" to Buddhism, which in turn allowed the new religion to spread throughout the country.

Thunder reborn. According to Moriya, this Buddhist hero is not simply a child bestowed by a Shinto deity; he is the reincarnation of the deity himself. This interpretation of the nature of Dōjō is, it should be noted, based on a reading of the *Ryōiki* text that is not generally accepted, but the theory bears investigation nonetheless. The passage in question is the thunder deity's response to the farmer's question, "How will you repay your debt to me [if I do not kill you]?"

The deity replies: *"nanji ni yose ko wo haramashimete mukuimu."* This response is understood by the editors of the *Nihon koten bungaku taikei* edition of *Ryōiki* to mean, "I will use you as a vehicle to receive a child, and thus repay my debt" (p. 71), but Moriya argues that the insertion of the word *yose* (which he reads *yosete*) implies that the thunder deity intends to use the farmer as a vehicle through which he himself can be reborn (Moriya 1978, p. 140).

The matter is far from simple to resolve, but it does seem to me that Moriya's reading of the text appears plausible enough and in any event, that even if the child is not *the* reincarnation of the thunder deity he is certainly an aspect of that deity. His size is apparently smaller than average and his strength greater than average, and he has been born with a snake coiled around his head; all of these attributes are associated with the thunder deity.

The crucial element here is the *on,* or obligation, that the deity feels towards the farmer when the farmer spares his life. In mythological sources mortals are frequently able to get the better of deities (especially reptilian deities) if the mortals are angry enough to take violent steps of their own. The most they ever gain from these victories, however, is a promise that the deity will cease his anti-social, destructive behavior. In this case, though, things clearly go beyond the traditional limits. The deity not only ceases his undesirable behavior, he acknowledges his obligation to the farmer and repays it.

The idea of *on* is central to the Buddhist concept of humanity (Nakamura, pp. 62-63), and by embracing this precept the thunder deity is in effect embracing Buddhism. One might then argue that it is for this reason he is able to be reborn as a Buddhist hero. Kyōkai himself seems to follow this line of interpretation when he says at the end of the story, "It is clear, then—this strength was something accumulated by his acts of virtue in former lives. This is a miracle that took place *in Japan*" (italics added).

Thus, by accepting the idea of *on,* even the most "Japanese" of deities is able to gain salvation and become a Buddhist hero. To Kyōkai, whose foremost concern is to show that Buddhism has meaning in a Japanese context, such a story would have had a strong appeal, and it is not surprising that he takes particular pains to note that this was indeed a "Japanese" miracle.

Indeed, it is not insignificant that the first three tales in *Nihon ryōiki* deal with mortals' relationships with deities, while only in the fourth story do we move to "Buddhism proper," with the mandatory tale of Prince Regent Shōtoku, generally interpreted as the person who brought Buddhism to Japan.[5]

The sexual snake. The sexually dangerous reptilian deity makes a number of appearances in *setsuwa* collections, and we can note that the ideas of *on* and the initial dissemination of Buddhism in Japan prove important in the *Nihon ryōiki* treatment of this aspect of the mythological snake just as they did in the tale discussed above. Let us begin our consideration of this snake with a look at *Ryōiki* II. 33, "How a woman was eaten by an evil demon."

In this tale we are told of a beautiful maiden named Yorozu no Ko, who has refused all of her numerous suitors for reasons not mentioned. She is courted by a man who offers several expensive gifts and finally consents to become his bride. On the night of the consummation of the marriage her parents hear her cry out three times. "It hurts!"; thinking her to be merely sexually inexperienced they pay these cries no heed. When on the following morning she fails to come out of her room her mother goes to investigate and discovers that she has been devoured by her bridegroom, and only her head and one finger remain. In addition, the carts full of silk brought by the man have been transformed to old wood. Kyōkai tells us that this is an "unusual event," and says that some people called it the mysterious work of a deity, while others hold that it was done by a demon.

This tale fits into the mythological tradition of stories about women wed to a deity for one night (*hito-yo zuma*) who are killed and frequently eaten by their immortal bridegrooms. It is in many ways similar to a story found in *Hizen fudoki* (*Fudoki,* p. 396), in which a woman named Otohi-hime is visited by a man who resembles her husband even though her husband left some days before to participate in a military campaign. In this tale the woman is suspicious of her one-night lover and follows him to a mountain pond, where she finds a snake-like creature who recites a poem to the effect that he has had one night with her and will now take her "home"; he then pulls her into the pond. There

is enough similarity in the poem in this episode with a poem in the *Ryō iki* tale to cause Moriya to suspect the two tales are closely related (1974, pp. 165-168).

The *Fudoki* tale is clearly tied to some kind of religious ritual. Before the appearance of the demon lover the young woman goes to the top of a peak, where she waves her scarf to call back her departing husband. We are readily drawn to imagine a shamaness engaged in a ritual to summon her immortal lover in this scene. Although no such ritualistic overtones can be found in the *Ryōiki* tale, it is important to note the fact that the woman has refused a large number of suitors from good families, as though she were saving herself for this deity.

The *Ryōiki* story is linked only tenuously to Buddhism by Kyōkai, who informs us at the end that the fate of Yorozu no Ko was determined by her "past actions," although he does not elaborate. An examination of two similar tales from *Ryōiki,* however, will bring us to some understanding of why "past activities" might have lead the unfortunate Yorozu no Ko to her untimely end. The tales in question, II. 8 and II. 12, are quite similar but each contains unique elements important to our understanding of the tale cycle as a whole, and hence deserve to be treated separately.

In II. 8 we are told of a holy woman named Okisome no omi Taime, the daughter of a nun, who out of great devotion to Buddhism chose to remain a virgin and to go each day to the mountains to collect herbs for the holy man Gyōki (also read Gyōgi; 668-749). One day she sees a snake swallowing a frog and implores it to release its captive, promising to become its wife if it will do so. The snake assents to that promise and comes later to consummate the marriage but the woman is afraid and will not let it in her house. She goes to Gyōki for advice and he tells her to maintain her faith in Buddhism and honor her promise to the snake. After reaffirming this faith the woman meets a strange old man with a crab. She buys the crab from him, paying with her clothing, and sets it free in a Buddhist ceremony. That evening when the snake forces its way into her house through the roof the crab kills it to repay his debt of gratitude to the woman. The old man, Kyōkai informs us, was probably an incarnation of Buddha.

The situation is very similar in II. 12. Here the woman first releases eight crabs, then, when she encounters the snake, promises first to give it offerings, then to worship it as a deity, and finally to marry it. At this last promise the snake releases the frog. The heroine in this tale also goes to visit Gyōki, and is given the same advice as the heroine of II. 8. When the snake appears to claim his bride the eight crabs released by the woman earlier tear it to pieces.

That the snake in these stories has the status of a deity can be seen in the sequence of promises made by the heroine of II. 12. She promises first to make offerings, then to worship it, and finally to marry it, all of which is roughly parallel to the way violent deities were treated by their mortal victims. The female shrine attendant, or shamaness, was in charge of the worship of the deity and was also held to have a sexual relationship with it. The picture of the woman as sacrifice to the deity is clear in both II. 8 and II. 33, where Taime and Yorozu no Ko are said to be both beautiful and virginal; each has shunned sexual contact out of some sense of mission.

Taime, however, has dedicated her life to the service of Buddhism, while Yorozu no Ko seems more impressed by secular riches, and hence the fates of the two differ accordingly. This lack of accumulation of merit is doubtless what Kyōkai had in mind when he called Yorozu no Ko's fate the result of "past activities."

Role of Gyōki. The immediate salvation of the women in these tales is brought about by the *on* felt by the crabs they have released. This *on* has been triggered by the compassion shown by the woman involved, but it is not a simple case of repayment of *on,* for the holy monk Gyōki is brought into each story to refine the women's compassion into a more Buddhistic expression. Such a rhetorical strategy was not necessary in I. 3, in which the thunder deity repays his *on,* for there the object of salvation was the deity himself, and in this case the objects of salvation are the women whose actions have caused the feelings of *on* in the first place. By bringing in Gyōki and further defining the action of these two tales in Buddhist terms, Kyōkai is in effect taking no chances that the stories be understood as having taken place outside of a Buddhist context, which is, of course, the way the story is normally understood in its oral versions.

Gyōki was very popular with editors of *setsuwa* collections. There are seven tales about him in *Nihon ryōiki* alone, and numerous other stories in a variety of other collections. But these two *Ryōiki* stories are the only ones in which he is specifically associated with either snakes or the repayment of *on,* and some consideration of his special role here is undoubtedly necessary for a fuller understanding of the tales.

Best known for his efforts in popularizing Buddhism among the people, Gyōki was also associated with a variety of good works such as building bridges. His exalted stature was nearly equal to that of Prince Regent Shōtoku, and it is not surprising that Kyōkai finds in him the ideal person to serve as the Buddhist catalyst in the two tales under consideration. In both of them Gyōki makes his appearance *after* the woman has made her marriage pledge, and in both cases his

advice is the same: offer no physical resistance and renew faith in Buddhism.

The problem faced by the women in these tales is one created by the values of ancient (pre-Buddhist) Japan, but the solution counseled by Gyōki is a Buddhist one, radical for its time. The structure of II. 8 is particularly revealing in this sense. It may be capsulized as follows:

1. The woman (Taime) meets the problem;

2. she takes her problem to Gyōki;

3. she follows his advice and reaffirms her faith in Buddhism;

4. Buddha sends a messenger who at the same time is both a test of her compassion and the means of her salvation;

5. she passes this test and is saved from danger.

Had it been the frog initially saved by the woman that repaid its *on,* Gyōki's role would have disappeared and the story would have lost its Buddhist significance. We will, incidentally, encounter the "unlikely messenger" element in a later cycle of tales.

The enemy without. In these *Ryōiki* tales the evil or danger encountered by the characters originates *outside* of the characters, and the means of escape from the problem also come primarily from outside the characters, although there is an inner quality to the characters that enables the escape mechanism to come into play. Essentially the escape entails the accumulation of a reservoir of good, in the form of good works and a faith in Buddhism, and not in direct and active resistance to the danger.

In time, however, the perception of both the danger and the salvation changes, with both coming to be seen as *internal* rather than external matters. This new interpretation appears to be influenced by the advent of a more "Buddhist" serpent, one which seems to fall largely outside the patterns described above. It is to that serpent that I would like now to turn my attention.

The Buddhist snake

The snake and reincarnation. The Buddhist snake, which we can identify fairly confidently as belonging to a different tradition from those already discussed, is basically associated with reincarnation. Stories in this tradition tend to center around monks but women on occasion also assume the role of protagonists. The basic plot of such tales is simply that those who have placed too much attachment on things of this life are likely to find themselves as snakes in the life to come. Such tales are to be found in Japan from the earliest period—there is an example in *Nihon ryōiki*—but do not seem to have come completely of age until *Konjaku monogatari-shū* (ca. 1100) and later collections. They are closely associated with Amida and his Pure Land, and tend to emphasize the dangers for those who wish to be reborn in the Western Paradise of dwelling on things in this world.

In the sole example of this type of tale found in *Ryōiki* (II. 38; the story is also found in *Konjaku, XX. 24*), we read of a monk who tells his disciples not to open his door for three years after his death. However, forty-nine days after his death (seven days in *Konjaku*) a large snake appears near his door. His disciples realize that this is the reincarnation of their greedy master and open the door in spite of his dying command, where they find some money their master has hidden. They realize that the monk's attachment to this money is what has caused his having been reborn as a snake, so they use it to do Buddhist works in hopes of saving him. We are not told if their efforts were successful.

The *Konjaku* compiler, in words not used in *Ryōiki,* says that this monk practiced Buddhism diligently but was not enlightened, and calls the monk's attitude "stupid." There is no mention in the tale of the monk's aspirations for the life to come, nor any indication of whether he was successfully delivered from his reptilian existence by the works of his disciples.

In contrast to this monk the hero of *Konjaku XX. 23* (a story which seems to have been intended by the compiler of *Konjaku* to serve as a contrast to XX. 24) is very holy, a man who has earnestly prayed for rebirth in the Western Paradise of Amida but is reborn as a small snake in spite of his enlightenment and lifetime of devotion. The reason for his misfortune is that just before his death he noticed a small jar and wondered which of his disciples would get it after he was gone. A similar hero appears in *Konjaku XIV. 1*. In this case the monk had some money which he had decided to save for his disciples to use after his death, but because he forgot to tell them about it he was reborn as a snake coiled around the place in the roof where he had hidden it. Both of these monks are said to have shed their snake skins and to have achieved final rebirth in the Western Paradise because of the efforts exerted by those they left behind; these efforts amount to dedicating sutras in behalf of the dead monks.

Role of the Lotus Sutra. The sutra dedicated for this monks was the *Lotus Sutra* (*Hokkekyō*), which was seen as being especially effective in dealing with snakes. This is probably due in part at least to the influence of a mid-eleventh century *setsuwa* collection, *Dai-nihon hokke genki* [Japanese miracles wrought by the Lotus Sutra], which, as the name implies, was compiled to inspire faith in the *Lotus Sutra* and the

miracles with which it was associated in Japan. The compiler of the collection is generally taken to be the monk Chingen. Of its one hundred twenty-nine tales, eleven are concerned with snakes, all of which were also used by the compiler of the later *Konjaku monogatari-shū*. *Hokke genki,* however, is more concerned with recounting miracles than with stories of reincarnation, and there are thus only two tales in the collection which might be called examples of the Buddhist snake. In both, the heroes are saved from their snake existence by the power of the *Lotus Sutra* and the tales are best read as testimonies to the power of that sutra rather than as tales directly concerned with Pure Land belief.

The stories, as noted, come from a more purely Buddhist tradition, and do not seem directly linked to pre-Buddhist mythological stories about snakes, but there are some interesting points in common which are worth noting here. The first of these concerns the associations the snake has in the stories.

As we have seen, snakes in the mythological tradition tend to be associated with the land of the dead. This is, of course, also the case in the tales of the Buddhist snake recounted above, where an individual becomes a snake after death. Hence the stories are at least compatible with Japanese tradition in this regard.

There is one other area in which the stories maintain this compatibility, namely the habitat of the snake when it visits the land of the living. In *Konjaku XX. 23*, for example, the snake is reborn in a small jar, and in various other stories, most notably *Konjaku XIV. 1*, it is found in the roof. We have seen a *fudoki* tale in which the snake child of a mortal woman was kept in a series of jars; in the *Ryōiki* tales about women who are able to escape their snake bridegrooms the snake entered the house from the roof.

None of these points indicates "influence" from the mythological story patterns and in all probability the similarity is purely accidental. It is, however, interesting to note that even in these seemingly unrelated tales some effort has been made to put the stories in a context more readily appreciated by a contemporary audience. Further, these elements of containment and the entering the house through the roof (much as the spirits of the dead were thought to enter the houses of the living) prove to be important in later tales about snakes as well; in my opinion their presence here underscores the associations the snake has with the dead on the one hand, and the soul on the other. More will be said about this in later sections.

The Mytho-Buddhist Hybrid

The one-night consort revisited. What happens when the Buddhist snake meets its mythical counterpart head on? The tales dealing with such encounters are considerably more complex than those we have been discussing to this point, and they allow a far wider range of Buddhist interpretations.

As an example, let us consider *Konjaku monogatari-shū* XIV. 4, in which a woman, unnamed but said to be of great beauty, spends a single night with the Emperor Shōmu, who finds her charming and rewards her with money. Shortly after their night together both the Emperor and the woman die. The woman specifies that she is to be buried together with the money she received from the Emperor.

Thereafter, the story informs us, strange things start happening at a certain temple in the Nara area: "All who went to that temple died without returning, so that people stopped worshiping there. Everyone thought it extremely frightening." Hearing this, a certain famous governmental official visits the temple and recites spells during the night. He is visited by the spirit of the woman, who begs him for help. She has attempted to seek the aid of others who visited the temple, she says, but they all died of fright at her appearance. She wishes him to liberate her from her present suffering by digging up the money buried with her and using it to dedicate a sutra reading. The minister does as she requests and finds the cash in her grave, protected by a large snake. He commissions a dedication of the *Lotus Sutra* and the woman is reborn in a Buddhist paradise.

The woman in this tale seems rather closely related to the one-night consorts (*hito-yo zuma*) of the mythological stories we have discussed. She is beautiful and charming, is embraced by an extraordinary lover for one night and dies soon afterwards, just as many of these women do. However, the tale can also be read as a story of the Buddhist snake, for the woman is reborn as a snake because of the attachment she had for the money presented her by the Emperor.

On yet another level, her spirit is confined to appearances in a Buddhist temple, where—intentionally or unintentionally—it kills worshipers; in this sense the story is reminiscent of *Ryōiki* I. 3, in which the defeated Shinto deity interferes with worship at a Buddhist temple.

In short, the *Konjaku* compiler has taken most of the elements we have found in snake stories from other traditions and fused them into a new product, a true hybrid. It is worth noting that this is the fourth tale in volume XIV of *Konjaku* and that the preceding three tales have also featured serpents (we saw XIV. 1 above), so that it serves as a fitting climax to this series.

It is not only the fact that all the elements of snake stories we have seen thus far are included in this tale that makes it a true hybrid. The compiler here has set about reinterpreting the nature of the danger posed by the serpent. In the Buddhist renditions of tales about mythological snakes salvation is offered to the *victims* of the deities. In *Ryōiki* II. 8 and II. 12, for instance, the women are able to escape through their commitment to Buddhism, and in *Ryōiki* I. 3 the defeat of the demon at the temple means that monks will no longer have to die. In the Buddhist snake tales, on the other hand, salvation is offered to the *snake itself,* which is not pictured as a violent deity, but rather as the unfortunate victim of his worldly desires.

In this hybrid story, however, salvation is offered to *both* the victims (the minister recites Buddhist spells to protect himself from the spirit, and his pacification of it through Buddhism means that people will no longer have to die) and to the snake itself (after the *Lotus Sutra* is dedicated the woman is able to achieve rebirth in a Buddhist paradise). Further, the salvation is not effected by force, as was the case in the earlier stories, but by compassion and wisdom. The nature of the danger is also treated differently here: the minister's heroism reveals that what was perceived as a danger by the people of the world was actually harmless, and that the people who died, perished of their own fear, and not due to some external cause. While the violence involved is still shown to have originated external to the victims, it is not any external force that actually killed them.

Snakes, monks and caves. A similar story which brings us to an even more internally based perception of evil is *Konjaku* XIII. 17. This tale relates how a monk who specializes in the recitation of the *Lotus Sutra* spends the night in a cave on his way to a pilgrimage at Kumano (see also *Hokke genki* I. 14; the tale is virtually identical in both collections). Frightened by the cave, the man decides to recite the *Lotus Sutra* for protection. A large snake appears and seems about to devour him, but at the recitation of the sutra it disappears. After a pounding rain, a man comes to the cave and thanks the monk, telling him that the rain drops were really tears of repentance, and that he has now been released from his evil existence.

As in the mythical snake stories, the creature appears before the man in the form of a snake when he intends to do him harm. However, the snake is pacified by the power of the *Lotus Sutra* and makes a second appearance in the form of a human. Interestingly, this is a man whose features the monk cannot discern, which is a vagueness rather similar to the descriptions of the unknown males who visit women married to snake deities. This much of the story, in any event, is compatible with the mythological tales.

We may further note that this tale lacks any explanation of why the snake was in that particular location, or of why it was a snake, and in this sense the tale differs from that of the Emperor's consort, discussed above. There is no doubt that this snake—again unlike the spirit of the Emperor's consort—is truly evil. The man informs the monk: "I have been living in this cave for several years, taking lives and killing the people who came here, but now, because I have heard you recite the *Lotus Sutra,* I have given up this evil heart and will turn towards good." In this case Buddhism is able to save both the monster and its intended victim.

In *Konjaku* XIV. 4, the story of the Emperor's consort, the apparent evil proved not to be evil after all, but to be merely a misunderstood spirit, albeit one originating outside of its "victims." This story, by way of contrast, depicts evil which is indeed evil, but even here we cannot say with certainty that this is an evil which has originated outside of its intended victims. We will gain a deeper understanding of the story through a consideration of *Konjaku* XIV. 17, another tale of a monk whose main religious practice is the recitation of the *Lotus Sutra.*

The monk in *Konjaku* XIV. 17, never able to memorize the final two volumes of the sutra, in frustration closes himself up for ninety days and prays earnestly for enlightenment regarding his lapses of memory. He is told that in a previous existence he had been a snake and was on the point of devouring a monk, who for protection began reciting the *Lotus Sutra.* The snake listened to the recital and gave up his meal, but dawn broke before the monk had recited the final two volumes. As a result of the experience, the snake was reborn as a monk, but will never be able to learn the final two volumes, which he did not hear.

This tale is closely related to XIII. 17, and one is at once tempted to speculate that the monk in story XIV. 17 was indeed the snake in XIII. 17. While there is no direct evidence for such an assertation, there are certain elements in the two tales that bear a closer look. Primary among them is the idea of enclosure.

Frustrated at his inability to memorize the final two volumes of the *Lotus Sutra,* the hero of XIV. 17 practices enclosure (*komori*) for ninety days, reciting various spells and incantations. This he does in order to increase his spiritual power so that he might at least understand why he is unable to learn the sutra. He is rewarded for his devoted practice with an insight into his past (in this case, a past life); in other words, the result of his enclosure is greater self-awareness. He comes, as it were, face to face with his own former evils and is able to understand how they affected his current condition. The hero of XIII. 17, who meets a snake in a deserted cave during the course of a religious pilgrimage, has had an essentially similar experience.

So we must be prepared to interpret the experiences of the monk in the cave in *Konjaku* XIII. 17 as self-

revelatory. He is, it must be remembered, on his way to Kumano, the site of ascetic religious practices designed to accumulate spiritual power. In the course of this pilgrimage he crosses, in effect, into another world; the cave can be thought of as the entrance to the underworld. This new world is, according to the text, "a world far removed from people." There he recites a magic formula (the *Lotus Sutra*), and it is not surprising that he has this remarkable experience. His meeting with the snake can, I think, be thought of as a face to face encounter with his own past evil acts.

The monk resolves to place his faith totally in the *Lotus Sutra:* when the snake appears he says, "I am to lose my life suddenly here to this viper. However, I will not fall into an evil existence, but will be reborn in the Pure Land by the strength of the *Lotus Sutra.*" This act of devotion and complete faith cancels out his evil and the monk is elevated to a higher level of awareness. If the cave can be thought of as a womb, he has been reborn on a higher level of existence. While the evil in this tale apparently exists independently of the monk—there can be no doubt of the existence of the snake—it nonetheless must be thought of as evil which stemmed initially from the monk himself and had therefore to be subdued by him, with the aid of the *Lotus Sutra.*

In any event, all three of these tales depict both victim and aggressor as being saved through the forces of Buddhism. Moreover, it is not at all clear that victim and aggressor are to be taken as separate entities, especially in the stories of the monks. The snake has gone through a process of internalization, leading the way to the next logical step: if the snake is one aspect of the individual, then it can also be one aspect of the Buddha, and hence serve as the actual agent of salvation of the individual.

The snake of salvation

Dragons, demons and monks. Let us begin with a look at a tale that does not appear very "Buddhist," *Konjaku monogatari-shū* XX. 11. In this story a dragon is sunning himself near his home in the form of a small snake when he is suddenly attacked and captured by a *tengu,* or mountain demon. This dragon is unable to counter the attack because he lacks the water necessary to release his powers. The *tengu,* on the other hand, is unable to devour him on the spot because of the dragon-strength inherent in the snake, so it puts the snake-dragon in its lair—a mountain cave—and goes off to Mt. Hiei, returning presently with a monk he captured while the monk was washing his hands. In fact, the monk was taken so quickly that he is still clutching his water bowl, and there is a drop of water left in it. The dragon uses the water to assume the form of a small boy, and saves the monk. He then goes off to find the *tengu,* which has assumed the form of an itinerate monk and is begging on the road, and kicks it to death.

The *Konjaku* compiler notes here: "In truth, the dragon was able to prolong his life because of the virtue of the monk; and the monk was able to return to his mountain because of the strength of the dragon. This was all a matter of fate stemming from previous existences."

As noted, this tale does not seem at first reading to be very "Buddhist," mostly because there is no account of the power of the sutras. However, the compiler praises the monk's "virtue" (*toku,* which should be thought of as power accumulated by spiritual purity), and the implication is that an ordinary person—one without the special protection of Buddhism—would have been unable to achieve such a rescue.

The fact that events take place in a mountain cave, as was the case in *Konjaku* XIII. 17, provides a further point of comparison. And the snake's assumption of the form of a small boy in order to save the monk is consistent with what we have seen in previous tales about the interaction between mortals and snakes. Finally, it is significant that the *Konjaku* compiler explains the events in reference to former lives. The snake, as we have seen, has strong associations with reincarnated monks, and it must therefore follow that it cannot be a *totally* bad creature. But the important thing to keep in mind about this story is that both snake and monk are mutual victims of yet another outside danger, and that it is actually the snake who has saved the monk in this case, rather than the monk having saved the snake. (It is, of course, the monk's virtue which enables the snake to make the rescue.)

The snake in the vat. In another *Konjaku* tale a snake indirectly affects the salvation of a mortal. This is *Konjaku* XIX. 21, in which a monk uses temple rice to make himself some *sake.* When he looks in the vats to see if the *sake* is ready to drink, he finds a number of snakes crawling around inside and orders all the vats discarded in a field. Three men, notoriously heavy drinkers, happen to pass by, look in the vats and discover that they contain *sake.* They are somewhat worried about it—if the *sake* were good, why would it have been discarded, they ask themselves—but try it anyway. It is delicious, and they have a good long drunk with it. The monk hears about their experience and realizes that this was a warning to him. He takes it to heart, and his Buddhist faith increases. The *Konjaku* compiler informs us that this was clearly the work of Buddha.

In this tale the snakes appear only to the evil monk, and they have been sent by Buddha. It is unclear whether or not they are actually his incarnations, but there is no question that he has used them to advance the salvation of this monk. When the monk first sees

the snakes he does not recognize them as reflections of his misdeeds, but when he hears of the experiences of the three drunks, he understands their nature. Clearly the snake here is a tangible manifestation of wrong-doing, and contact with it actually helps the monk improve.

Kannon as a reptile. This use of the snake symbol finds consummate expression in *Konjaku monogatari-shū* XVI. 6, a story that was particularly popular with compilers of *setsuwa* collections, for reasons that I think will be obvious. It tells of a man who is gathering hawk chicks from the nest in precarious surroundings, with the intention of selling them later. A neighbor has assisted him by lowering him over a cliff in a basket to a spot where he can get out and gather up the chicks, which he then sends back up in the basket. Instead of then sending the basket back down, however, the neighbor simply leaves, abandoning the man to die on the narrow ledge of the cliff. The Bodhisattva Kannon, to whom the the unfortunate man had paid regular homage every month, takes pity on him and assumes the form of a snake to save his life. After his rescue the protagonist shaves his head and becomes a monk, giving up his evil ways.

Salvation is presented here in a dramatic form, and bears analyzing in some detail. Alone on the ledge and facing death, the man recognizes and confesses his own past wrong-doings:

> For years I have caught these hawk chicks just before they could fly and, binding their feet so they could not fly away, used them to catch fowl. It is because of this sin that I am now about to be punished with death. My wish is that the compassionate Kannon I have revered for these many years will, even though this life of mine has now come to its end, keep me from falling into Hell in the life to come, and greet me in the Western Paradise.

When he makes this confession and plea for mercy a snake emerges from the water below him and climbs up to him, apparently to devour him. The man decides, "I would rather die by falling into the ocean than be eaten by a snake," and drawing his sword he pierces the head of the snake. The snake then carries him up to the top of the cliff, where it disappears.

The story states explicitly that the snake is a manifestation of Kannon, who has taken this form out of compassion in order that the man might be saved. On first glance, this appears to be a rather unusual method of salvation indeed, particularly since the first thing the snake does is try to devour the man. If we consider the circumstances of the snake's appearance, however, the act becomes easier to understand.

The snake appears only *after* the man has acknowledged his past evil and begged for compassion in the life to come; this act of confession was necessary to move the Bodhisattva to this act of compassion. Further, when the snake appears the man runs it through, intending to kill it, thereby showing a willingness to abandon his attachments to life and his past evils. His words are remarkably similar to those of the monk who encounters the snake in the cave in *Konjaku* XIII. 17.

It is only when he has taken the two steps of confession and repudiation of past evils that he can be saved. It is significant that the man does not hold his neighbor responsible for his danger, even though the neighbor was the immediate cause of his problem. The man clearly recognizes that the neighbor is only an agent, and that the true source of his problem is not any outside element, but his own evil.

Here we have come full circle. The snake is, as is so often the case, a symbol of the man's attachments to life and his past misdeeds; it is also an immediate danger to his life. At the same time that it is a symbol of his past evils, though, it is also an incarnation of the Bodhisattva Kannon, thus demonstrating dramatically that there is good in evil and that the recognition and repudiation of that evil in the self can enable one to turn the evil around and make it work in one's own favor. "Evil" can either devour us or save us, depending on our own attitude towards it.

Conclusion

"We have met the enemy," says one of the characters created by the cartoonist Walt Kelly, "and it is us." Ultimately, this is what the tales of snakes we have examined in these pages have to say to us.

The early Shinto, or mythical snake, was basically a danger originating outside the individual, and needing to be dealt with as one would deal with other violent forces of nature. It posed a general threat to the agricultural community and a specific threat to human women, and was the manifestation of the violent aspect of those deities connected with thunder, water and the dead. In some ways, its existence must have had a comforting effect: it was the "enemy," but it was not "us."

The earliest Buddhist snake, on the other hand, was indeed "us," but it was not the "enemy." That is to say, it was a symbol of attachment to things of this world, and transformation into a snake was that which happened to individuals who valued such things too highly. But it posed no threat to innocent bystanders. It merely lurked behind the scenes as the symbol of the evil inside us all.

Interestingly, it was mostly Buddhist monks and women who needed to fear the snake within themselves. We

Osiris, symbol of resurrection, depicted with the insignia of rule.

have seen that women were associated with the mythical snake, as victims of its sexual appetites; monks, on the other hand, had been victims of the same serpent in its guise as the angry deity, disgruntled at its defeat by the superior forces of Buddhism.

The defeat of this snake—which, in the story of the temple Gangō-ji, amounted to its conversion to Buddhism—was significant in *Nihon ryōiki* for two main reasons. First, as we saw in the Gangō-ji tale, it gave the Buddhists a sort of hold over the spiritual forces of Shinto. The conversion of the thunder deity both established the Buddhists' claims to dominance over the native deities, and also allowed them to propagate their religion in freedom. Secondly, as we saw in the tales featuring Gyōki and the would-be brides of snakes, Buddhism offered mortals the means of escaping the dangers posed by the mythical snake.

But the Buddhist snake and the mythical snake are mated by enterprising compilers of tale collections and eventually give birth to a unique hybrid, one which is at the same time both "us" and the "enemy." Now violence is no longer seen as something impersonal, arising from somewhere outside the individual, but rather as something arising from within. This means that Buddhism was suddenly able to save not only the intended victim of violence, but its perpetrator as well, in a single stroke. This leads to a reassessment of the nature of violence.

Buddhist stories about *shukke* ("taking of the Buddhist vows") generally center around extraordinary experiences, for people do not enter Buddhism as a matter of daily course, but must be pushed into it by forces outside their normal control. This is the case with the snake tales, as well; encounters with the violence posed by the serpents lead to the salvation of the people involved because they are so frightened that they take unusual, direct action they would never have considered under normal circumstances. But if this the case, then we must reconsider the snake—if it has pushed us to enter Buddhism or attain a greater level of self awareness, it is difficult to say that it is completely "bad."

Indeed, as we saw in the tale of the man gathering hawk chicks, the snake might even be a direct manifestation of the Bodhisattva Kannon. If in the *Ryōiki* Gangō-ji story we can say that the snake *has been converted* to Buddhism, here we must say that the snake *has converted* the hero of the story to Buddhism. The snake, in this instance, has been sent by Buddha so that we might understand our misdeeds and be liberated from them. It is still the evil within us, but once we have developed the ability to actually see this evil, we are able to deal with it effectively.

Notes

[1] For a complete translation of *Nihon ryōiki*, see Nakamura 1973. All translations from Japanese sources in this essay are my own work. I would like to gratefully acknowledge the assistance of Professor Mori Masato of Aichi Kenritsu Daigaku, who went to the trouble of reading the entire manuscript and offering several helpful comments on both its contents and the translations. All errors, of course, are my own responsibilities.

[2] The sins are: breaking down ridges around rice paddies, filling up irrigation ponds, breaking sluices, double planting, putting stakes in others' fields, skinning alive, skinning backwards and defecation in fields. See *Kojiki-Norito*, p. 425; also Philippi, pp. 403-404.

[3] See Briggs 1976, p. 57. It is interesting that Blacker (p. 52) notes that snake deities in Japan have also been described as resembling earthworms.

[4] I owe the following four-part division of this tale to Moriya 1978. Moriya and Kurosawa, among others, have written extensively on this story, and I must acknowledge my debt to their scholarship even when I do not agree with their conclusions.

[5] Later *setsuwa* collections such as *Honchō ōjō gokuraku ki*, *Dai-nihon hokke genki* and *Konjaku monogatari-shū* begin with stories of Shōtoku, for example, and it is interesting to note that Kyōkai alone felt there was something of importance to deal with before the appearance of this historical Buddhist hero.

Works Cited

Blacker, Carmen

1975 *The caltalpa bow: A study of shamanistic practices in Japan*. London: George Allen and Unwin Ltd.

Briggs, Kathrine

1976 *An encyclopedia of fairies, hobgoblins, brownies, bogies, and other supernatural creatures*. New York.

Fudoki

1958 Akimoto Kichir , ed. *Nihon koten bungaku taikei*, Vol. 2. Tokyo: Iwanami Shoten.

Kojiki-Norito

1958 Kurano Kenji and Takeda Yūkichi, eds. *Nihon koten bungaku taikei*, Vol. 1. Tokyo: Iwanami Shoten.

Konjaku monogatari-shū

1962 Yamada Yoshio et. al., eds. *Nihon koten bungaku taikei*, Vols. 22-26. Tokyo: Iwanami Shoten.

Kurosawa Kōzō

1976 *Nihon kodai denshō bungaku no kenkyū* [Research on ancient Japanese oral literature]. Tokyo: Hanawa Shob .

Matsumura Takeo

1955 *Nihon shinwa no kenkyū* [Research on Japanese mythology], Vol. 3. Tokyo: Baif Kan.

Moriya Toshihiko

1974 *Nihon ryōiki no kenkyū* [Research on *Nihon ry iki*]. Tokyo: Miaisha.

1978 *Zoku Nihon ryōiki no kenkyū* [Further research on *Nihon ryōiki*]. Tokyo: Miaisha.

Nakamura, Kyoko Motomochi

1973 *Miraculous stories from the Japanese Buddhist tradition: The* Nihon ryōiki *of the monk Kyōkai.* Cambridge, Mass.: Harvard University Press.

Nihon ryōiki

1967 Endō Yoshimoto and Kasuga Kazuo, eds. *Nihon koten bungaku taikei,* Vol. 70. Tokyo: Iwanami Shoten.

Nihon setsuwa bungaku sakuin

1974 Sakaida Shirō and Wada Katsushi, eds., revised edition. Tokyo: Aobundō .

Philippi, Donald L., transl.

1969 *Kojiki.* Tokyo and Princeton, N.J.: Tokyo University Press and Princeton University Press.

K. D. Irani (essay date 1991)

SOURCE: "The Socioeconomic Implications of Conflict of Gods in Indo-Iranian Mythology," in *Ancient Economy in Mythology: East and West,* edited by Morris Silver, Rowman & Littlefield Publishers, Inc., 1991, pp. 59-71.

[*In the essay that follows, Irani contends that the central theme of conflict between gods in Indo-European mythology reflects a broad worldview linked to socioeconomic conditions.*]

In the mythology of many branches of the Indo-Europeans there appears a particular theme, that of conflict of gods. Whatever else this conflict may reflect, it certainly is what I consider to be a dramatic expression of a deep and pervasive conflict of ideologies, or socioeconomic systems associated with worldviews and ethical systems. This is what I shall present in the early part of this paper. In the latter part, I shall refer to some peculiar mythologic accounts of the termination of the conflict, which by their oddity incline us to look for some unusual reference. That reference, I suggest, is to metallurgical technology, an aspect not unrelated to the dominance of one of the ideologies.

The mythological theme of conflict of gods appears in its most prominent and clear form in the Eastern Indo-European tradition, that is, in the traditions of ancient India and Iran. It is particularly interesting since the conflict, though of the same character in both traditions, is resolved in opposite directions in India and Iran. An intermediate resolution is arrived at in the analogous conflict in ancient Scandinavian mythology. Thus we shall consider the theme of the conflict of gods in three traditions: the Indian conflict between the Asuras and the Devas; the Iranian conflict between

Ahura (Mazda) and the Daevas; and some aspects of the Nordic between the Aesir and the Vanir.

We shall first focus on the conflict appearing in the earliest stratum of the *Rig Veda.* This makes it very probably the earliest record of Indo-European material. It probably refers to the beliefs of the peoples in the Caucasus and around the Caspian Sea before they migrated south and separated into two groups, one crossing the Hindu-Kush Mountains and spreading to the Indus Valley (in present-day Pakistan) and eastward into the Indo-Gangetic Plain (in present-day India), the other moving in a westerly direction (in present-day Iran) and gradually southward (in present-day Afghanistan). The former came to be called the Hindus, the latter the Iranians.

The earliest set of myths recorded in the *Rig Veda* refer, as mentioned, to a period when the full separation between the Hindus and the Iranians had not taken place, as the same characters and concepts appear in both traditions. The version of the *Rig Veda* is of course part of the sacred lore of the Hindus. We may date this tradition as covering the third millennium B.C.E. into early second millennium B.C.E. when the migrations took place. The consolidation of these myths in the form in which we find them is of the middle and later part of the second millennium, as are the Iranian poems known as the *Gathas,* the composition of the Iranian prophet, Zarathushtra, from which we shall draw the Iranian version of the conflict.

The very early Indian mythic accounts deal with the conflict between two sets of gods: the Asuras, meaning lords, and the Devas, meaning the shining or the luminous ones. Chief among the Asuras are Varuna and Mitra, the sons of Aditi. These two gods very frequently appear jointly. They are gods of order. Varuna controls *Rta,* an abstract concept meaning order, but often taken to refer to the orderliness in nature, that is, nature as cosmos. Mitra is the lord of social order. He is primarily the divinity that preserves the sanctity of contract. However, he is protective of any social bond, whether it be a treaty between states, a contract between merchants, a bond of loyalty in a clan, a promise between two persons, or a bond of friendship.

The myth portrays them as the rulers of the universe. Varuna particularly is the ruler because his control of *Rta* gives him dominion over existence. This authority, however, is challenged by Indra. He is the chief of the Devas, and the one who most clearly typifies them. The Devas live as luminaries in the interspace between the remote heaven of the lords and the earth of human habitation. Indra is a war-god. He rides a chariot and carries a special mace, likened to a thunderbolt, with which he destroys his enemies. He is accompanied by an army of Maruts, young warriors, who are invincible. Both these sets of dieties are worshiped in the usual way of offerings laid in front of a fire and some poured into the fire. However, Indra receives the special offering of *soma,* a ritually prepared intoxicating drink that energizes him and makes his appearance highly threatening.

The conflict begins in the following way. Varuna is lord of the world by reason of the order he has generated, that is, *Rta,* through which life is properly maintained. This is the appropriate availability of the water, fields, pastures, and cattle. The appearance of water was especially vital to these peoples, who came from semiarid lands to the plains of India, where away from the river valleys, drought was always a frightening prospect. This is the issue of the conflict between the Asuras and the Devas. Varuna, the chief Asura, claims his lordship has provided the order through which satisfaction came. The incident from which Indra is inclined to claim his lordship is this. The monster dragon, Vratra, has coiled itself around the store of sky-water and thereby caused drought, starvation, and death. Indra decides to destroy this creature. After various episodes, and a crisis in resolve, Indra drinks enormous quantities of *soma,* eats great quantities of the sacrificial meat, and confronting Vratra hurls his supernaturally powerful mace and cracks its head. The waters are thereby released and life assured. Thus Indra having provided the life-giving waters claims the kingship of the world.

The interchange between the two dieties is presented in the *Rig Veda* (Hymn IV: 42). The first few verses are the speech of Varuna, these are followed by the speech of Indra in the next few verses. Here is the translation, with minor omissions (Zaehner 1962):

> I Varuna, am king. To me was the dignity of Asura first assigned. . . . I, Varuna, am Indra [too]. I, knowing the two wide, deep, firmly established areas of space in all their grandeur, [knowing] all creatures as their fashioner, I have set in motion both worlds and maintain them. I made the dripping waters swell forth. In the seat of the law did I establish the heavens. By virtue of the law is the son of Aditi, possessed of the law, and threefold has he extended the earth.

To this claim of the creation and maintenance of cosmic order, Indra responds by an appeal to sheer power:

> It is I whom heroes, rivalling each other in riding their goodly horses, invoke when they are surrounded in battle. I, Indra, the widely generous, stir up the battle. I, Indra, raise up the dust, I whose might is overwhelming. All this I have done; no power of the gods can restrain me, for I am invincible. Once soma and the hymns have made me drunk, then are both immeasurable worlds struck with terror.

Here is the conflict. But as we shall see, what is of importance is the set of reasons each offers, and the

ideologies underlying them that Vedic poets have so effectively disclosed. But to continue with our description of the conflict, we find that there is no resolution at this stage. The character of Indra becomes progressively more important, more exalted, and gradually incorporates the attributes of Varuna. At one point, he says, "I am Varuna too," the term "Varuna" having been transformed from a proper noun to an adjective. Nevertheless, Varuna's essential character as the father of "natural law" remains present to the Vedic mind as evidenced by the way Indra addresses Varuna in a later passage, when Indra says: "[A]ccept O King, who can *tell right from wrong,* the overlordship of my kingdom."

As time passed, the Devas were regarded as gods, and the Asuras, at first degraded, later came to be regarded as demons. The final discomfiture of the new demons is given in a very curious account in the *Satapatha Brahmana.* There the demons attempt to learn a ritual that will give them Truth, but fail and lose hope of power completely. The resolution of the conflict and the mythic account of the loss of power of the Asuras is something I shall discuss in detail later. At this point I turn to the interpretation of the conflict.

I shall call the ideology associated with the Asuras, the *"order ideology";* and the ideology associated with the Devas, the *"conquest ideology"*—however, in its early stages, it might more appropriately be called "aggrandisement ideology." Each ideology represents a way of life, a concept of social existence. The order ideology rests its confidence in the orderliness of natural phenomena, for example, seasonal changes and climatic regularities; and it demands from its adherents reliable patterns of behavior for the balancing of social interests. The conquest ideology applies to a social structure functioning to support a military organization, or at least a constantly available raiding-group. Such a society keeps replenishing itself, if not completely living upon the gains made by forcible acquisition from neighboring or remote groups and villages.

In each case, the social stratification, mode of work, kind of technology and the set of beliefs about their existence were unified in the unformed and undeclared ideology which found expression in the only general form of articulation available to them—their mythology. These were not residuary myths established in bygone days. These myths used some traditional theological concepts to give significance and provide justification for their ways of life in the only way they could, that is, to make their lives a reflection of the wishes and injunctions of their divinities.

When the Indo-Iranian peoples moved into the lands east and south of the Caspian Sea, they gradually changed from a nomadic existence to pastoral settlements. The two ways of life embedded in the two ideologies were found there. The order ideology supported the establishment and contractual control of clearly identified villages and counties. The conquest ideology, at this time perhaps better called "aggrandisement ideology," promoted the practice of predatory raids and acquisition of wealth by violence. The obvious thievery involved was redescribed in the language of heroism, as long as the activity was in imitation of, and dedicated to, the divinity.

When the tribes moved into the plains of India, climactic guarantees were less on their minds than the problem of overcoming the native residents. Conquest now became the preeminent guarantee of success. In this stage of Indian consciousness, Indra was viewed as the conquering god, and the ideology shifted from the earlier aggrandisement form to that of imperial conquest. In the earlier form, the raiding-group of a chief and his accompanying warriors captured their neighbors' herds and cattle and brought the booty home. This is Indra with the Maruts on their thunderous raids. Such situations were common before the tribes made permanent settlements in India, and was typically the case in Iran. But after they settled in India, they conquered and occupied the lands. Indra changed from being a raiding war god to a conquering overlord. It is at this stage that his status became incompatible with that of Varuna's.

We have a reflection of this sociocultural transformation of Indra in the *Rig Veda*. Commonly, Indra has the Maruts as his companions. The Maruts are described as having Indra as their leader in the *Rig Veda* (Hymn VI: 51, 15). But when Indra confronts Vratra, they are nowhere to be found and so Indra abandons them. "Who can count upon your friendship?" asks Indra of the Maruts in the *Rig Veda* (Hymn VIII: 7, 13). This is the mythologic change in the character of Indra reflecting the ideologic shift from the aggrandisement ideology to conquest ideology (Perry 1880).

In this mythic account there is a critical question that has been left unanswered: what led to the resolution of the conflict between Varuna and Indra in favor of Indra? The answer, entirely in mythic terms, appears in Hymn X: 124. The god of fire, Angi, the necessary agent of the sacrifice, transfers his allegiance to Indra, and thereby causes the shift of ultimate sovereignty from his erstwhile Asura (that is, Varuna) associates to his new master. The following are sections from verses 2 to 4 in Zaehner's translation (Zaehner 1962) Agni:

> Secretly and hidden do I, a god, depart from him who is no longer a god, forseeing immortality. If I, [now] inauspicious [to him], leave him who was auspicious, so do I go from an old comradeship to a strange stock. . . . To the father Asura I say a kindly word: from having no part in the sacrifice I go to enjoy my share in the sacrifice. Many years did I pass with him. Choosing Indra I leave the father.

This is the resolution of the conflict seen as the location of power in an ideological group. However, philosophically speaking, the values of the understanding of the natural order and the maintenance of the social order, in other words, of truth and morals, which were the special characteristics of the Asuras, do not seem to be part of the mythology of the Devas. No religious tradition can flourish ignoring these fundamental values for long. We shall see how this was handled in the *Satapatha Brahmana,* a work of later date than the *Rig Veda.* But at this point we shall close our discussion of the Indian tradition and start discussion of the Iranian.

Let us recall that Iranians and Indians shared the same East Indo-European culture for centuries before the groups separated. The conflict between Asuras and Devas of the India pantheon appears in the Iranian. In the Gathic language (the language of the *Gathas*—the hymns of Zarathushtra), sometimes called the Old Avestan, "Asura" becomes "Ahura," and "Deva" becomes "Daeva." This conflict is resolved in the religious reform introduced by Zarathushtra, sometime in the latter part of the second millennium B.C.E. The relation of Zarathushtra's theology to the Indo-Iranian inherited belief system is quite complex (Boyce 1975). We shall focus on Zarathushtra's treatment of the conflict and the theology in which it is embedded.

In this theology there is one divinity, Ahura Mazda (the Wise Lord). He creates six spiritual abstract entities that later become immanent in the material world and affect existence. Of these we shall be concerned with two. The first entity is Asha, the Gathic equivalent of *Rta,* which is to be interpreted as both the Truth and the Right. Second is Vohumana (the Good Mind). This is not only an abstract concept, it is also a capacity inherent in all rational beings. This is a capacity to do two distinct things, to recognize situations for what they are in our experience, and to grasp abstract concepts.

Now let us consider Zarathushtra's mythology of creation: Ahura Mazda envisioned a scheme of perfect creation, Asha. He created the material world to unfold according to Asha. However, within creation there arose a spirit of opposition to Asha. Thus in the world we are in there is a conflict of two spirits, or fundamental moral attitudes, that which promotes Asha, the Truth, and that which violates it, Druj, the Falsehood. The latter also came to be known as the Deceiver, or the Liar. It is crucial for this theology that this conflict be seen not just as a cosmological or metaphysical one, but also as a moral one. For the Truth is indeed the Right, and Falsehood is Evil.

The ethics that emerges from this myth of creation is the following: Every human being endowed with the Good Mind (that is, Vohumana), upon looking at the world, is able to distinguish the appropriate state of things from the flawed, maladjusted, or deficient state, and is also able to grasp what the ideal state of things should be, that is, to grasp the Right, Asha. From this the proper course of action is immediately determinable: to act so as to restore and/or promote Asha. This is the vindication of truth, and the righteousness of one's conduct. Hence the ideology preached in this tradition is an order ideology, explicitly so. But that is not all.

The mythology of this tradition views existence as an unrelenting conflict between two metaphysical and moral forces. The good ultimately coming from Ahura Mazda, the evil being the work of the spirit of falsehood and destruction—the Daevas.

Thus the warrior gods of the Indians (Devas) become the destructive demons of the Iranians (Daevas). And the degraded and demonized Asuras of the Indians become the exalted divinity, Ahura Mazda, of the Iranians. The conflict that Iranian theology is concerned with is not the one between the tribe and its enemies; it is between stable, civilized existence as a mode of life, and the culture of raiders led by warrior heroes. The victory would have come not through the shedding of blood and the destruction of villages, but by the ever brightening good mind recognizing the power of truth.

This theological and moral stance is quite explicit in Zarathushtra's hymns, of which I cite a few examples in the translation by D. J. Irani (Irani 1924).

From *Yasna* 31, verse 22:

> Clear is this to all, to the man of wisdom
>   as to the one who thinks with care.
> He who upholds the Truth with all the might of
>   his power,
> He who upholds Truth the utmost in his word and
>   deed,
> He indeed is Thy most valued helper, O Mazda
>   Ahura!

From *Yasna* 45, verse 9:

> Him with our good-mind we seek to propitiate
> Who through His discernment maketh weal and woe.
> May the Lord in his wise authority prosper our
>   peasantry, our workmen and our herds,
> Through the good-mind according to the holy law
>   of Truth!

From *Yasna* 31, verse 15:

> This I ask Thee, Ahura,
> What is the recompense ordained for one who seeks
>   to achieve sovereignty for the Liar,
> For one of violent deeds who seeks not his living

> without harm to the flock of the shepherd,
> And of the good who listen to the voice of Untruth?

From *Yasna* 32, verse 10

> . . . He who leads the good to wickedness
> He who makes the meadows waterless and the
>   pastures desolate,
> He who lets fly his weapon against the innocent,
> A destroyer of Thy principles is he!

The sociocultural demand of the tribes moving into Iran was stability, settlement, and resulting fair recompense. The order ideology, which enshrines this demand, is embedded in the religiomythic system of Zoroastrianism. At that time, the tribes moving into India were engaged in conquest and expansion supported by the appropriate conquest ideology we have examined. Of course, neither the historical circumstances nor the ideological commitments of the two traditions remained unchanged. Later Indian religious thought developed a highly sophisticated order ideology under the concept of *dharma*. But by that time the theme of the conflict of gods was replaced by that of human conflict within the family and the clan. As Iran, after centuries of minor wars, became an imperial power, it developed a conquest ideology by making the enemy an agent of evil.

From the sociopolitical interpretation of myths about the conflicts of the gods, what can we say about the economic systems related to them? The order ideology, *Rta,* or its equivalent, Asha, required fair exchange and just recompense. We have no historical evidence of how this worked in practice. Economic activities were associated with religious festivities related to Mitra and Varuna with appropriate religious functions (Dumézil 1988) applicable to particular vocations. We can assert this by extrapolating back from practices in India some centuries later. In the earliest times, before the constructions of temples, established markets were probably not in existence. But by the end of the second millennium B.C.E., economic exchange with market foci varying in place and time were present in the Indian tradition. We know this from the fact that cheating and fraud in exchange and labor transactions were identified as offenses against Varuna, and promise breaking or breach of contract, offenses against Mitra.

In Iran the establishment of markets was a very ancient practice. Their character can only be gleaned from extrapolation back from historic times. In the Achemenian period from the sixth century B.C.E., the state and its institutions were explicitly constructed according to Asha. Markets were established at important points on highways. The use of standard weights and measures was imposed, and a standard imperial coinage was introduced. It is interesting to note that though there was no official price fixing, and buyers

Osiris, from the fifth century B.C.

and sellers were free to contract with each other, bargaining was looked down upon and discouraged on the grounds that it promoted lying and deception.

The socioeconomic stability of Iran in practice reflected the ideological stability of Iranian culture. This does not mean that over the span of centuries Iran was free of military conflict. In Iran, warfare, though common enough, never received the kind of Indraic theological-ideological justification it did in India. The rationale of Iranian wars was invariably greed, hatred, or vengeance, with only vengeance being viewed as proper justification. This is very different from the intrinsic exaltation of the use of power and heroic aggrandisement as justification in conquest ideology.

When the warrior groups in the Indo-Gangetic Plains acquired territory and became small kingdoms with a military social structure and an elaborate Indraic religious system, their economy reflected their ideology. The ritual, mythic, and legendary material centered on kingly power and heroic exploits. Social productive life was geared to supporting the warriors. The war-

riors in their turn brought booty for distribution among the populace. Distribution was dominated by the bonds of loyalty and the largesse of the powerful. The non-warrior population engaged in producing anything above subsistence necessities produced military goods. The superiority of military production, as always, determined success. And military production meant arms, armor, and military vehicles. The impact of military production upon the culture came most significantly with the shift from the use of bronze to the use of steel.

Metallurgy, though a technology, was in its early days associated with sacred lore and the invocation of occult forces. Its techniques, particularly the manufacture of steel arms, were for obvious reasons protected by shrouds of secrecy. Some of the technology, requiring the use of furnaces, became the speciality of fire-priests in temples that maintained fire-altars—particularly the techniques of generating fires of varying intensities.

One might now look for some reflection of this close relation between the warrior divinities and the metallurgy of arms. It is this exploration into mythology we shall be concerned with later. But first we should have a short description of the process whose mythologization we will later examine.

The process of making steel in ancient times consisted of three steps, that is, three separate firings in the furnace. The first heating of the ore produced what is sometimes called the bloom, a mixture of metal and slag. This was cleaned and heated a second time when the barely melted metal was agitated with a dry stick, which often caught fire. This shining metal was later heated a third time when it was hammered into shape. Thereafter it was tempered, its edges were honed, and sharp points were made on the anvil. Such weapons were indeed associated with Indra. Of course Indra's weapon was the thunderbolt, but notice its properties: it was shining, brazen, golden, multiedged, multipointed and required honing (Perry 1880).

There are two accounts of the resolution of conflict of gods, one in an Indian source written after the *Rig Veda,* the other in the Nordic poem, *Voluspa.*

The Indian account appears in the *Satapatha Brahmana;* IX "Kanda," 5 "Adhyaya," 1 "Brahmana" 12-27 (Eggeling 1897). Being a *Brahmana,* it is concerned with giving a quasihistorical explanation of ritual in mythic form. The account harks back to the establishment of the Devas under Indra and the degrading of the Asuras. But the Devas ruled by force, not through truth, which was originally in the possession of the Asuras. However, the Devas at this point seemed to possess it. How did this happen? This is what is being explained in the sections we are considering. It is a long account, which I shall render in abbreviated form. Both the Asuras and Devas were offspring of Prajapati, hence they had the power of speech, both truth and untruth. The Devas abandoned untruth and held on to truth, while the Asuras abandoned truth and held on to untruth. (Note the reversal of the position of the *Rig Veda.*) The Devas spoke only the truth; as a result, they suffered and became impoverished, but in the end they prospered. The Asuras spoke only falsehood; as a result they flourished, but in the end they came to naught. However, the Devas had not consolidated their hold on truth, so they decided to achieve that by the performance of a sacrifice! They started their operations by spreading out the sacrifice, at which time the Asuras came believing that the truth was being spread out to pick up their share. The Devas snatched up the sacrifice, hid it and pretended to be doing something else. The Asuras, seeing that the Devas were doing something else, went away. The Devas then prepared the opening offering, whereupon the Asuras turned up again; but they were misled a second time in the same way and they left. This happened a third time. After the Asuras had left the third time, the Devas performed the concluding part, having in this sacrifice recited only the kindling-verses.

This episode is recast in a slightly different repetitive form, after which we are told that over the course of two days, the operation was complete and the Devas "obtained the whole truth." Thus "the Devas prevailed and the Asuras came to naught. And he who knows this prevails and his spiteful enemy comes to naught."

What shall we make of this account? The first part can be understood in part as a reaction to the Iranian order ideology, where truth was the central concept. Also it is an attempt to rehabilitate Truth with the Devas—with some moral wisdom interestingly incorporated. But the ritual story is extremely odd, even by mythological standards. Consider these elements of the account: Truth to be gained by sacrifice; Truth spread out such that it could be stolen; a ritual sacrifice that must be secretive; a ceremony interrupted three times with very little done in between and then rapidly completed by singing some verses to the fire; and the ritual ends with the granting of power over enemies. This is sufficiently bizarre to incline us to think that some unknown event or institution is being metaphorically captured.

There are various conflicts that appear in Nordic mythology, especially between the gods and the giants, but there is only one presentation of the conflict between the Aesir and Vanir gods, and that is in the poem, *Voluspa,* verses 21-24. As suggested by Turville-Petre (1964) the narrative makes more sense if verse 24 is placed before verse 23. The account of this is markedly vague. There seem to be problems between the two sets of gods, the Aesir and the Vanir. Gullveig,

who is in, or has been brought into, the hall of Odin (an Aesir) is riddled with spears hurled by the Aesir, perhaps including Odin, whereupon she is burnt. However, she revives. The situation is repeated twice, hence Gullveig is burnt and revives thrice. Then they call her "Heid," and she becomes a prophetess, casts spells, and becomes the joy of evil women. This becomes the cause of a great conflagration. Odin hurls his spear at the enemy, and the Vanir destroy the castle of the Aesir with magic. Thereafter the Aesir and the Vanir gather in a council to settle the conflict and decide who should pay what tribute to whom.

This is another odd story. We do not know much about the characters, nor their motivations; the focus is upon a conflict and some peculiar incidents. Who is Gullveig? She does not appear anywhere else. Examining her name, the first part means "gold" or perhaps, "metal"; "veig" may most probably mean "power" or "strength." The character into which she is reborn is "Heid" and that is derived from the adjective "heidr," which means shining (Turville-Petre 1964). The striking peculiarities are, however, the fact that being riddled with spears causes burning; also that the burnt ash revives; and finally, that it is repeated three times. None of these items has any relevance to the rest of the narrative. Their detailed description indicates that this material was imported from elsewhere. If we look at the last two myths (the conflict between the Devas and Asuras, and that between the Aesir and Vanir, we find the stories entirely different, nonetheless some episodic elements are related. The warrior gods (the Devas and the Aesir) get something—truth; and Gullveig is transformed into Heid. Each precious object is burned three times. The Devas make the appropriate payment after the sacrifice; the Aesir are in negotiations to settle accounts. There is another item of information, external to the stories, but relevant; it is that the god of fire, in both cases, changes sides. Agni, originally an Asura, joins the Devas; and Loki, originally associated with the Vanir, serves the Aesir.

The speculative hypothesis I am suggesting is that these two mythological accounts refer to the metallurgy of steel. Though the stories have different narrative contents, the structural elements of the metallurgical operation are accurately preserved. It is the warrior gods who are associated with this technology, and seem to acquire power thereby. One should be very circumspect in suggesting such farfetched interpretations unless one is forced, or at least strongly induced, by two factors acting jointly: the intrinsic oddity or inappropriateness of the myth and a reasonable matching of the mythic elements when given the analogic interpretation. When such interpretations are made, the question naturally arises as to why these myths were formed in the first place. Why could they not have described the operations in a commonsensical way as we do today?

The answer lies in the fact that the framework of thought in the period we are talking about is essentially mythic. Significant events in human existence could have been comprehended only as supernatural interactions. Human life, if it was to be lived successfully, was taken to be sustained through a series of transnatural interactions, in which we influence the supernatural through ritual, and the supernatural influences us through all that we would otherwise call chance. Though this may explain why technology, and much else, becomes mythologized ritual, it cannot tell us why it takes a specific mythological, narrative form. These forms are determined by the specific historic, religious, and literary circumstances of the times. For this reason the interpreter is forced to use the imagination as much as analysis to make an interpretation. That is of course not a way to validate interpretations. Interpretations are at best plausible, but they have a right to be considered seriously until other better interpretations emerge.

Works Cited

Boyce, M. 1975. *A History of Zoroastrianism.* Vol. I. Leiden: E. J. Brill.

Dumézil, G. 1988. *Mitra-Varuna.* Tr. into English by D. Coltman. New York: Zone Books.

Eggeling, J. 1897. *Sacred books of the East.* Vol. 43, Ed. by F. Max Muller. Oxford.

Irani, D. J. 1924. *The divine songs of Zarathushtra.* London: George Allen & Unwin.

Perry, E. D. 1880. Indra in the Rig-Veda. *Journal of the American Oriental Society* 11:16-91.

Turville-Petre, E.O.G. 1964. *Myth and religion of the North.* New York: Holt, Rinehart & Winston.

Zaehner, R. C. 1962. *Hinduism.* London: Oxford University Press.

RELATIONS TO HISTORY AND SOCIETY

C. J. Gadd (essay date 1933)

SOURCE: "Babylonian Myth and Ritual," in *Myth and Ritual: Essays on the Myth and Ritual of the Hebrews in Relation to the Culture Pattern of the Ancient East,* edited by S. H. Hooke, Oxford University Press, 1933, pp. 40-67.

[*In the following essay, Gadd explores the network of Babylonian rituals centering around the motif of renewal and suggests that it reflects existential concerns.*]

It is tedious to read in a first sentence the familiar complaint that the material to be studied in the following essay is sadly deficient. Those who are concerned about the affairs of remote antiquity must accustom themselves to being constantly in this situation, and I should not, therefore, consider it worthy of remark that the remains of Babylonian ritual, and partly also of myth, are scanty and almost wholly preserved in late documents were there not a special and interesting reason for this. The Babylonian priesthood was, by a practice that only after very many centuries deteriorated into a mere theory, a closed corporation with strictly hereditary functions. Father instructed son in the complicated mystery and learning of his office, and during a number of centuries which is indeed extraordinary there was no need, and certainly no desire, to divulge the treasured secrets of priestcraft. A serious breach had indeed been made in this tradition at the time when a Semitic language definitely ousted from daily use the old Sumerian in which all religion was enshrined, and this was at a comparatively early period. Henceforth many of the ritual chants were at least committed to writing, though it would be exaggeration to speak of them as published, for they still circulated only among priests, and were somewhat intelligible only to those who had plied their Sumerian phrase and word books. But what the priest had to do in his daily or special services about the temple still remained the absolute domain of tradition, as it was reputed to have been delivered first by the age-old Enmeduranki, king of Sippar before the Flood, and so remained to be observed even by so late an author as Diodorus. It can hardly be doubted that what finally led to the necessity of adding the 'prayer book' to the 'hymn-book' (if such language may be permitted) was the ever-increasing traffic in priestly functions and their attached perquisites, which reached its maximum in the Hellenistic period, to which most of our extant ritual-texts belong.

The importance of the material goods in question is amply illustrated, as an incidental, by the ritual which I propose to consider first, not indeed as evidence of any commercial arrangements, but as representing a type somewhat sharply distinguished from the second which will engage our attention. As, however, it has no direct connexion with myth, it will be sufficient to pass somewhat rapidly over its main features, but it should not be neglected, because it is very characteristic of one important aspect of Babylonian religion.

Though there was probably no complete uniformity in the daily service of the gods throughout the temples of all the land, the ritual of the daily offerings to the gods of Erech may fairly be assumed as typical for the cult in general. The text[1] in which this is preserved was written in the Seleucid period, but it is expressly stated that it was copied from one which Nabopolassar had removed from Erech in the seventh century; this archetype therefore was no doubt of somewhat earlier date than that. The one tablet we have is but one of many which altogether, we are told, comprised the 'rites of the prerogative of Anu, the holy offices, the ceremonies of kingship, the divine offices of the Bit-resh, Esh-gal, E-anna, and the temples of Tir-anna, the proceedings of the enchanters, the conjurers, the singers, and the craftsmen, all who are in the company of the foreman, not counting all that pertains to the students of divination'.

Of this formidable corpus of ritual, only the directions for the daily meals of the gods are preserved, and the text is more an enumeration of quantities than a direction for the service of the divine tables. The quantities are very impressive, and though Anu and his wife Antu, as the principal gods, are the principal recipients, provision in ample measure is also made for the goddesses Ishtar and Nana and for all the other gods, who, according to the general usage, had accommodation in the temples of other cities than their own. The main points to be observed are these: the gods took four meals each day, called the great and little meals of the morning and the same of the evening, and at each of these drink, bread, oil, dates and fruit, and a great quantity of mutton and beef was provided. The totals are considerable, for example, 50 sheep, 2 oxen, a calf, and 8 lambs, about 250 loaves, 18 cups of drink for the principal god, 14 for his wife, and 22 for two other goddesses. All this is in addition to special oblations on certain occasions such as the days of 'opening the doors', of 'clothing' the images, of celebrating the 'nightly festivals', and the extraordinary offerings of the king.

Of more interest than this rather soulless inventory are the occasional glimpses of true ritual. The eighteen cups before Anu are set out on his table, seven to his right containing only two kinds of beer, and seven to his left, with a variety of beverages, then four of wine in front of him. From these vessels the priest takes five of assorted contents and pours libations from them. The miller is charged to deliver flour for the loaves to the appropriate priest, and must chant over his mill an incantation beginning 'The astral Ploughman has yoked in the plain (of Heaven) the seed-sowing Plough', and likewise the baker has to say over his bread 'Nisaba, luxuriant plenty, pure food', and the butcher, as he slaughters the beasts, exclaims 'The son of Shamash, lord of cattle, has created fodder in the plain'. Lastly there is a list of prohibitions; in the Sun-god's house sheep are not to be offered to the god of cattle, in the Moon-god's house oxen are not to be offered to a god of oxen who seems to be his son, birds are forbidden before the 'Lady of the Plain', and both birds and beef to the goddess of the underworld; we recollect that Odysseus was instructed by Circe that sheep were the acceptable offering to the shades and their rulers.

Having already described this particular text as mostly a soulless inventory I shall not pause longer upon it, except to characterize it. The colophon translated above shows this to be but one chapter of a comprehensive liturgy which would have embraced the whole of the ordinary and special offices, including, no doubt, the god's toilet in some such form as the Egyptian ritual described in the preceding essay. In this chapter itself there is one feature not as yet remarked upon, the presence of astral elements; the two principal deities receive daily and monthly offerings in their astral form, and offerings are also prescribed for the seven planets, to be rendered in the shrine at the top of the ziggurrat. This astral character the text has in common with the other rituals which are to be described later, but in other respects it is distinct from them. First, and most important from the point of view of this essay, this daily observance has no visible connexion with myth, and here it differs also from its Egyptian parallel. It is merely the ordering of the god's household, and its main pre-supposition is civilized and town-dwelling life, an idea by no means due to the late date of the text as we have it, but characteristic of early Sumerian views, which had always regarded two things as requisite to civilization—city life and kingship. The reproach that they 'had no king' or 'knew not a city' had been used against ancient invaders with the plain implication that they were barbarians, and in the inscriptions of the celebrated Gudea,[2] not much after the middle of the third millennium, we get a sketch of the city god's household which proves that the same highly civilized needs and organization of service already prevailed. It is not necessary to dwell longer upon this, and we may leave the daily ritual with our minds directed upon its character as a priestly institution, little in touch with the needs and thoughts of the people.

Despite the urban conditions and ideas of Babylonian culture, it was, like that of all ancient peoples, in very close touch with the soil, and depended for its maintenance almost wholly upon agriculture. Whatever more artificial elements therefore may enter into Babylonian religion, we may be sure that nature-worship was the religion of the people, and thereby powerful, though not all-powerful, in the official cults. In the early documents of accountancy certain months have, in different cities, names indicating that particular feasts were held in them, or that certain foods were then eaten. Unfortunately we have little or no information about these celebrations, what was done at the feasts, what stories were told of the divine being whose festival they were, or how a connexion was established between the thing done and the story told. Anthropology has now learned to recognize that a certain broad similarity prevails in the basic religious conceptions of agricultural peoples, the preoccupation with the due recurrence of times and their increase, and that this preoccupation finds widespread expression in their rituals and myths. All such observances in Babylonia centred about the figure of

Dumu-zi, that is Tammuz, and there seems no doubt that his worship was, in the practice of the people, of unique importance. This being so, it is very surprising how little is to be learnt about him from the literature. Almost all that we have is a copious supply of lamentations imagined as uttered by his sister-wife Ishtar, or whatever name she passed under at particular times or places, even as Tammuz himself generally appears with quite other names. These lamentations[3] are very disappointing as sources of information, being empty and incoherent, telling neither at all clearly what was the history and fate of Tammuz nor what was done to represent or repair the disaster of his death. Indeed, very little would be known about him at all but for the famous Syrian traditions of Adonis,[4] which represent, as we need not doubt, the ideas concerning Dumu-zi, the 'true son', which first arose in Sumer.

The nearest approach we get in Sumerian to an account of the death of Tammuz are a few hints that he was drowned in the river, i.e. the Tigris or Euphrates, and, as this was held to have happened in the month called Tammuz after him, at midsummer, we may suppose that his death and the death of the plants was symbolized in the falling of the life-spreading rivers. The Syrian river Adonis which

> from his native rock
> Ran purple to the sea, suppos'd with blood
> Of Thammuz yearly wounded

may be taken as a counterpart of this, though the blood of Adonis was of course shed by a boar. In the various Syrian stories about Tammuz or Adonis, some of which seem, oddly enough, to have been transferred to St. George, there is a complete revelation of his character as a god of grain, particularly in the repeated deaths which were inflicted upon him by persecuting kings or emperors, from all of which he recovered until the oppressor ground his bones or drove over him in a crushing chariot; here too comes in the ancient familiar song of Sir John Barleycorn who was ploughed into the ground, cut down with scythes, pierced with pitch-forks, and at last ended by being ground betwixt two stones.

Remembering that the seasonal god, who may pass under the general name of Tammuz for convenience, yet had many other names, and that certain of these may have been peculiar to one city or another, we can now proceed to consider the circumstances in which this story is better known to us in Babylonia. We shall so far anticipate as to say at once that this occasion is the festival called *akitu* celebrated in certain cities according to our evidence, and almost certainly in all, though the evidence happens to be missing. It would help greatly if we could tell, to begin with, what the word *akitu* means, but philologically that still seems impossible. It is applied even more frequently to a

building outside the city, to which the god journeyed in a ceremonious procession, than to the festival itself. At Babylon, and in some other cities the festival was held in the first days of the month of Nisan, but at Erech and Ur there were two celebrations, the first in Nisan and the second in Tisri, i.e. in the first and seventh months, at the beginning of each half of the year. Despite the difficulty caused by the holding of two such festivals there is ample evidence to prove that, even if the word *akitu* has nothing to do with seasons, the *akitu* Festival was the New Year Festival, at the opening of spring. Any attempt to explain the double celebration at both Ur and Erech could only be conjectural, and would have to rest upon the hypothesis that, for certain purposes at any rate, the beginning of the second half of the year was reckoned a new beginning.

At Babylon the course of the New Year celebrations is partly revealed to us by a number of texts all of the late period,[5] and to these there is added a most important section of the accompanying mythology in the celebrated Epic of Creation,[6] as now called, or 'When above' (*enuma elish*) as known to the Babylonians. It must be said at once that this long poem, now almost completely recovered, is very far from conveying the whole of the story of Marduk, the god of Babylon and hero of the story; what is known of the ritual, and still more what is obscurely conveyed in certain explanatory texts, make this very evident. We know that the Creation Epic was recited from beginning to end by the high-priest late in the evening on the fourth day of the festival before the image of Marduk, while the emblems of Anu and Enlil stood covered. After this we have the ritual for the fifth day, but up to this time nothing is indicated as happening which could be paralleled with the story of the Epic. Therefore, if the Epic can be taken (as it certainly can) for part of the myth connected with the festival, it must refer to happenings which found their place between the sixth and eleventh (the last) day, for all of which days the ritual is lost. Hence the myth and the ritual do not in this case mutually illustrate each other to the extent we might have expected.

Let us now see, in as brief summary as possible, what was done in the course of the festival, which occupied in all the first eleven days of the year. Chance has determined that the first day's observances are lost. Our texts begin with the second day of Nisan. Two hours before sunrise the *urigallu,* or high-priest, rose, washed himself in river-water, entered in before the statue of Marduk, put on a linen robe, and recited a long prayer, mostly a series of praises, but containing references to the god's victory over the enemies of the great gods, and his restoring their well-being, obvious references to his championship of the gods against Tiamat and the monsters of Chaos. It ended with a prayer for Bel-Marduk's favour towards Babylon, Esagil his temple, and the people of the city. This first long prayer was of special efficacy, because it was forbidden to any but the high-priest. After its recitation, however, the throng of other priests including the singers was admitted by the doors being opened, and each set about his daily ministration before Marduk and his wife Sarpanitu. Meanwhile the high-priest, after certain other ceremonies, had to repeat three times another prayer, very ill preserved, which appears to invoke especially the aid of Marduk against all enemies, both natural and supernatural, no doubt, who might set themselves against Babylon.

After a fairly long gap, which has deprived us of the remainder of the second day's ritual, the text goes on to the 3rd of Nisan. It began similarly to the day before, with an early rising of the high-priest, and a long prayer recited by him before Bel, then again the doors were opened and the priests and choir proceeded to their daily functions. Three hours after sunrise a notable ceremony began. The chief priest summoned a metal-worker, a wood-carver, and a jeweller, and delivered to them a supply of wood, gold, and gems so that they might make two figures, which were to be richly ornamented, and clothed in red with a fabric specially made by a weaver. Certain quarters of a victim were appointed to each of these workmen as reward. The figures were to be prepared for use on the sixth day; they were to be seven finger-breadths high, one made of cedar, the other of tamarisk-wood, and ornamented with a shekel of gold and some precious stones. One of them held in his left hand a serpent, and held out his right hand so as to point to the god Nebo, when he came in. The other was similarly disposed, but he held a scorpion in his right hand. We are told that on the sixth day, when Nebo arrived in the temple from his own seat in the neighbouring city of Borsippa, he came into the chapel called 'House of the Mountain of Life', and found these statuettes standing before him. A swordsman at once, upon Nebo's entering, struck off their heads, a fire was lit before the god, and the figures were cast into the midst of it. What the meaning of this act was we are left to conjecture, for the ritual of the sixth day is lost, but it is most likely that the two figures were embodiments of evil in some way, and represented forces which were to seek to hurt Bel and so must be overcome by his son Nebo. The making of these figures, in any case, is the last thing we hear of as being done on the third day.

On the 4th of Nisan the chief priest rose still earlier (exactly 3 hours and 20 minutes before sunrise), washed, put on his linen garment, and went now before Bel and his wife Beltis or Beltia, and recited before Bel what was called a 'prayer of the raising of the hand'. In this he first introduced himself as 'the high-priest of E-umush-a, who blesses thee', and went on once more to solicit the god's indulgence and blessing upon the city. Next followed a prayer to Beltia, the goddess, praise and intercession for her favour, and

the petition that she would plead with Marduk (as we so often see the goddess represented as doing on the cylinder-seals) for the life and prosperity of the king and the Babylonians, and would take by the hand, to lead him before the god, 'the servant who blesses thee';

> In need and danger take his hands, in sickness and lamentation grant him life, that he may walk ever in joy and gladness, and proclaim thy excellent acts to all the world.'

After this he went out into the courtyard, where the stars were still bright above him, turned to the north and waited until the 'Acre'-star,[7] that is, apparently the Ram, became visible, for at that time it was the Ram which came to its heliacal rising in the first days of Nisan, and was thus the sign which proclaimed the spring. We might remember another spring time, how the Canterbury pilgrims were heartened by the season to set forth when

> the yonge sonne
> Hath in the Ram his halfe cours yronne.

Probably because it rose just before sunrise at this important time the 'Acre'-star, or Ram, was the constellation of Babylon. To this star, then, in that hour of dawn, the chief-priest turned, and three times recited the prayer or incantation 'Acre-Star, E-sagil, counterpart(s) of heaven and earth'—only the opening line is quoted. After this the daily service went forward as usual, until the evening when the special observance was, as said before, that the Creation Epic, 'When above', was recited by the chief-priest from beginning to end, after the 'little meal' at the end of the day.

This Creation Epic[8] is, of course, with one possible exception, the masterpiece of Babylonian literature, and so well known that I hope I may consult the space at my disposal by giving only the barest outline of its contents. It begins with a vivid picture:

> 'When the heavens above were yet unnamed'

and nothing existed at all but primeval waters, out of which sprang the generations of the ancient gods. A division at length arose between the hoary deities Apsu, Mummu, and Tiamat and their descendants. In this strife the god Ea, representative of the younger generation, overcame Apsu and Mummu, leaving only the female monster Tiamat or the chaos of waters. Meantime the wondrous child Marduk was born as son of Ea, and his form and surpassing power are described. Tiamat, resolved to be avenged on the gods for the slaying of her husband Apsu, spawned a hideous brood of devils and monsters to be her host in the coming battle, and entrusted their leadership to her lover, a being called Kingu, upon whom she also bestowed the 'tablet of destiny'. At the report of these preparations incredible panic seized on the gods, and they sought among themselves in vain for a champion: even Ea was powerless against the frightful fiend and her crew. But he bethought him of his son Marduk, and found him willing to fight the dragon, but only on the condition that he should be invested with the supreme charge of destiny, and that the gods should ratify whatever proceeded out of his mouth. So immense was the relief with which the gods thus found a defender that they hastened not merely to grant everything that he demanded, but entered at once into their assembly chamber, ate bread, drank beer, and forgot their recent cares in drunkenness. Marduk prepared for the battle, took bow and arrow, a thunderbolt, a net and certain amulets, and advanced with seven winds that he had prepared behind him. He overcame the dragon by catching her in his net and causing his winds to enter in by her open jaws and finally by shooting an arrow into her inward parts. He then split the gigantic body into two halves and made of them heaven and earth. In heaven he made the sun, moon, and stars and ordered their courses, on earth he created finally, and by a separate inspiration, man, whom Ea fashioned out of the blood of Kingu, who thus paid the penalty for his rebellion. Man was created to serve the gods, and his ministration was designed to free them from every kind of toil. In further reward for the services of Marduk, the other gods now desired to bestow some lasting gift, and therefore at his desire they built Babylon and the temple E-sagil. The poem ends with praises of Marduk, and particularly with enumeration of his fifty good names, which are expanded and expounded with the pedantic learning dear to the ancient scribes.

Such is the story of the Creation Epic, which must for the moment be left without comment while we continue what remains of the New Year Festival. The Creation Epic was recited as the last act in the evening of the fourth day; on the fifth, four hours before sunrise, the high-priest arose as before, washed himself in water of the Euphrates and Tigris, and began again two long litanies of praise before Marduk and Sarpanit, which identify them in particular with the heavenly bodies. After this the priests again set about their daily duties, but to-day there was a special purification ceremony carried out by an enchanter or priest of incantation. To avoid accidental defilement the high-priest was not to be present at this ceremony. The enchanter aspersed the temple with water of the rivers, smeared the door-posts with cedar-oil, and burned incense. Then followed a strange rite; the enchanter called a butcher to cut off the head of a sheep. With the body he then went round smearing (the word is *kuppuru*[9]) the walls of the temple while the butcher waited with the head. The two then went down to the river, turned their faces to the west, the way of the desert and the way of death, and hurled the body and head of the sheep into the river, while they themselves fled into the desert from

which they were forbidden to return before the 12th of Nisan, when the festival was over. The object of all this is, of course, plain enough: the impurity, whatever there may have been in the temple, was ceremonially wiped off on to the corpse of the sheep, and the whole carcass then cast into the river which bore it away with the defilement. As for those who had touched the unclean body, they themselves shared the stigma, and must keep away from the city altogether during the holy season, for fear of bringing anything unclean back with them. The ceremony is of course similar in purport to the sending out of the scapegoat.

To pursue the events of the fifth day of the festival—after the foregoing rites, craftsmen began to cover the chapel of Nebo in E-sagil with the canopy called the 'golden sky', and when it was in place all recited an incantation calling upon various deities, principally Marduk himself, to cast out all malignant influences from the place which Nebo was to occupy on the following day, when he arrived from Borsippa.

But the rites of the fifth day were as yet far from being done. A meal was set out before Marduk, a prayer was recited craving the god's favour for 'him who takes thy hand', i.e. the king who was to lead Marduk out in procession, and then the table and all were taken away to Nebo's chapel, so that (we are told) the viands might be offered to Nebo when he arrived the next day. An episode of great strangeness and interest followed. The king now entered for the first time. Escorted in by priests he was immediately left alone before the statue. Soon the high-priest appeared and took away from him his regalia, his sceptre, ring, and crooked weapon, and his crown, which he placed upon a stool before Marduk. Next he struck the king a blow on the cheek, pulled his ears, and forced him to kneel before the god. In this humiliation the king had to recite a sort of 'negative confession',

> I have not sinned; O Lord of the lands, I have not been unregardful of thy godhead,
> I have not destroyed Babylon, I have not commanded her ruin,
> I have not shaken E-sagil, her rites have I not forgotten,
> I have not smitten the cheek of the people in my charge
> . . . nor caused their humiliation.
> I take thought for Babylon, I have not beaten down her walls.

To this the chief-priest replied with a message of comfort and blessing from the god; he would hear his prayer, increase his majesty, and strike down his enemies. Hearing these words, the king might now reassume his sovereign bearing, and at once received back from the god, by the priest's hands, his insignia of royalty. Once more, however, the priest was to strike him upon the cheek and that not softly, for a sign was to follow—if tears came into his eyes, Bel was gracious, if not, Bel was wroth; the enemy would arise and work his ruin.

One more ceremony at the end of the day; the priest bound a bundle of forty whole reeds with a palm-branch, laid them in a trench dug in the courtyard, and had a white bull brought out and stood beside the trench, and the king, who was again with him, set fire to the reeds with a torch. King and priest then joined in a prayer which began

> 'Divine Bull, glorious light which lightens the darkness'.

In this rite there seems certainly to be an astrological reference to the constellation of the Bull, the fire of reeds imitating the brightness of the stars. Modern scholars have pointed out that religious conservatism has herein preserved an anachronism, for in the late period to which the text that we possess belongs the Sun was no longer in the sign of the Bull at the opening of spring; for this must be the significance of the rite.

With this end of the fifth day of Nisan ends the ritual that has been preserved. But the festival went on until the eleventh day, and it was in these later days that, as we can tell, the most interesting and significant episodes were staged. Fortunately there are enough scattered references in other places, and inferences to be drawn from rituals in other cities to restore a good deal of the subsequent acts.

The most important event of the sixth day was the arrival of the god's son Nebo from his own temple at Borsippa to the part of the temple at Babylon which had already been, as we have seen, purified and bedecked for him. Upon his arrival the two figures, ornamented with gold and gems, which had been made upon the third day, were taken by a swordsman and had their heads cut off and were cast into a fire before the face of Nebo. The meaning of this is far from clear, but they evidently represented some malignant power such as the primeval gods who are overcome by Ea and Marduk himself in the Creation Epic.

Nebo, however, was not the only arrival, for we hear that all the gods, even including such great figures as Anu from Erech and Enlil from Nippur, arrived at Babylon on the 6th, 'to take the hands of the great lord Marduk', and go forth with him to the Festival House. On their arrival the gods were arranged in a carefully-regulated order of precedence, and were supposed to glorify Marduk. But the real purpose of their meeting was to 'fix the fates' of the coming year, and this they did on two separate occasions, the eighth and the eleventh days. This ceremony took place in an apartment called the 'Assembly-room' situated in the part of the temple dedicated to Nebo, whose particular function, as the scribe of the gods, was to write down upon the tablets of destiny the good and evil fates which the gods had decreed for the coming year. It is very notable that in the Creation Epic there is a double 'fixing of the fates'; first by the gods for Marduk, when he is appointed their champion against Tiamat, and secondly, in E-sagil itself, which the Anunnaki had built for Marduk after the creation of mankind. Here the connexion between the poem and the ritual is especially manifest; every year at Babylon a new 'fate' of supremacy was decreed by the gods to Marduk, and by a parallel acceptation no doubt to the king of Babylon as his earthly vicegerent.

The preceding rites are almost all that can be related in order of the New Year Festival; as already observed, the texts relating to the later and most important of the eleven days have not yet been found. Yet room has still to be found for at least three most significant events, which are, the ritual marriage of the god, the procession to the Festival House outside the city, and the dramatic representations which were so characteristic of the course of the festival. Upon all of these essential matters our knowledge is rather scanty, yet it is enough to show that they were of profound significance in the purport of the whole observance.

About the ritual marriage we have almost no information at all, and yet are assured not merely that it took place, but that it was symbolically of the utmost importance, being in fact the cult-act of the old agricultural religion upon which the fruitfulness of the year depended. By an odd chance there has survived much more about this matter from the Sumerian period than from the late Babylonian times to which the New Year texts in their present form belong. There is native and ancient evidence to confirm the statements of Herodotus about the god's bridal chamber on the top of the stage-tower, and we know something of the ceremonious arrival of the goddess-bride, the giving of wedding presents, and the beneficial effects which the divine union was thought to produce, particularly the rise of the waters which irrigated the land and brought forth its fruits. Omitting much in the way of description for which there is no space here, it is essential to point out that the very multiplicity and varying age of the sources from which our knowledge of this act is derived, show conclusively that the New Year celebrations at Babylon were, in one aspect at least, simply one local version of a rite practised in every one of the old cities, in each case with the local god and goddess, and also the local ruler, as the chief participants. This is, of course, amply attested, and the connecting link is the Tammuz and Ishtar conception, the course of nature dramatized and enacted for magical purposes. Whatever other ideas may have taken their part in this festival (and I will try to mention some later) no doubt this was the most fundamental.

Concerning the celebrated procession from E-sagil to the Festival House outside the city we are rather curiously informed. Thanks not only to the elaborate building-inscriptions of Nebuchadrezzar, but even more to the German excavations at Babylon, a great deal is known about the actual course and guise of the procession. We are now familiar with the Sacred Way at Babylon, its fine stone paving and its wonderful walls of enamelled and moulded bricks, and the splendid Ishtar Gate through which it led, with the figures of bulls and dragons in relief. We know also how the king 'took the hand of Bel' to lead him out, and a good deal about the wagon on which the god's statue travelled, the barge to which it was transferred to pass over the canals, and even of the Festival House itself we can form some idea from descriptions and from the remains of another such that was discovered at Ashur. About the hymns and the interesting subsidiary accompaniments of the procession much has been recovered, especially the anxious and superstitious watch that was kept for the appearance of small untoward accidents about the statue or its escorters, from which unfavourable omens might be deduced. All these things we know, but what we do not hear anything at all about is, what Marduk and his divine companions did all the three days (the 8th-11th) in which they were at the Festival House. We are not entirely reduced to guessing, however, for we know that on the doors of this house at Ashur was represented the combat between the hero-god and the monster Tiamat, one of the central episodes in the Creation Epic. It can hardly be doubted, therefore, that this ritual combat took place there between the eighth and eleventh days.

How it resulted we know, but do we know all? This question leads directly to the matter of Bel's death and resurrection, obviously one of the principal features of the ritual, yet one of peculiar obscurity. There is, for example, no hint of it in the Creation Epic, the purposes of which evidently required that this event should be completely ignored. Yet there can be no reasonable doubt that Bel did die and rise again; the course of the Tammuz-story requires it, the stage-tower at Babylon was undoubtedly regarded for some purposes as 'the grave of Bel', most positively of all it is attested by the fragments of a commentary which purports to reveal the inner meaning of certain dramatic acts which were performed in the course of the New Year Festival.

Some of these acts can be traced in the commentary, though obscurely, with many gaps, and without adequate note of time. I cannot pause to describe them, except in the most hasty summary: Bel was imprisoned in the mountain, or realm of the dead; he was smitten, wounded, and his clothing taken from him. With him a certain 'sinner' was led away and put to death. After Bel's disappearance the city fell into strife, but he was finally brought back by the intercession of his wife, who stood at the door of the tomb bewailing

him and beseeching the help of the gods who at last bored a hole in the door and released him. Such are the barest facts, so far as they can be gathered from a broken text, amid many accompanying ceremonies, often unintelligible, and a running commentary on their esoteric significance. Much has been written upon the various aspects of this singular drama which cannot be alluded to here, but the main point of interest is that Bel, presumably at the Festival House, and some time during the eighth to the eleventh days of Nisan, met the monster Tiamat in battle and, as we certainly know, vanquished her in the end. But how then came he by his death? As we have seen there is nothing of this in the Creation Epic, but in a text[10] very recently published there is actually a hint of Tiamat's victory over Marduk, which is somewhat the happening we might suspect to account for the death of Marduk. If this did occur, it would merely be the parallel to the work of a monster which brings about the god's death in the other Tammuz-stories. Admittedly it is at present little more than a possibility, but we may have to reckon with the existence of another part of the 'Bel and the Dragon' story in which the Dragon, not Bel, was at first victorious.

This leads naturally to a general consideration of the motives of human concern which underlay the New Year ritual and its accompanying myth. Enough perhaps has already been said about the primitive conception of the year-god, of which widespread class Marduk was certainly a member. It is, however, surely wrong to speak, as some authors have done, of the character of Tammuz, or of the year-god in general, having been abusively foisted upon the local god of Babylon by the political ambition of his priesthood. On the contrary, all that we know of the local city-gods in general suggests that this was a regular part of their character, though by no means all of it; for it represents the agricultural interests and necessities upon which the cities were well aware that their whole life and prosperity depended—it is only an intense industrial development which can even partly obscure this perception. In one place of the Creation Epic, the description of Marduk at his birth, there is a direct reference to him as a son of the Sun-god, and this is perhaps only a natural development of the idea of a year-god, who is normally likened to the waxing sun of the new year after the winter solstice; but there is no more than this in our texts, and the character of Marduk as a sun-god has perhaps been overstressed. We may remember that the lamentations for Tammuz took place at midsummer, when the sun had reached its height and was only at the point of declining. In the climate of Babylonia the sun is far from being, as in Europe, the fosterer of crops.

Of the astrological element which is so very strong in the Creation Epic it is difficult to speak with certainty, whether it is original or the result of speculation. There are at least no astrological references in the dramatic performances so far as we possess them, and in the Epic the astrological element is brought in at the time of the Creation, that is, after Bel's victory over chaos, out of which he made the firmament. To this extent the astrology may be original in the story, but the elaborate cosmology of the Fifth Book seems to belong rather to the academic spirit which is responsible for the obscure learning of the Seventh, and also, one might add, for the highly artificial literary form of the whole poem, for which I might take, as a crowning example, a line of the Fourth Book—

nahlapti apluhti pulhati halipma

where in addition to the ordinar rhythmical structure we shall be only in the appropriate pedantic vein if we detect also the figures of paronomasia and chiasmus.

There is, however, a department in which the New Year myth and ritual has an interest which has not been much concerned—I refer to its political significance. It is often said, and, in a sense with truth, that the position of Marduk as king of all the gods is but a reflection of the late political ascendancy of Babylon. We see how his place was taken by Ashur among the Assyrians, and so also was it in all other cities, the local god was the hero of a similar story, and was attended by a court of the other principal gods though subordinate cities no doubt had to use their own images of the remaining gods, and were not able to command the presence of the actual statues from other cities as Babylon seems to have done in the period of her supremacy. But we cannot assume that a man of Ur or Erech would ever have acknowledged as a point of faith that Marduk was superior to Sin or Anu respectively.

It is, however, a different matter that I wish to mention now. From very ancient times the Sumerians had regarded the earthly king as no more than the shadow, or 'tenant' as they called it, of the divine king, i.e. the local god, as whose representative he ruled. As things were in heaven so on earth, but the converse is more significant—as on earth, so in heaven. On earth there comes a time when the king grows old and feeble, no longer fit to govern, and it is hardly too much to presume that originally, at any rate, when such a time came and the king, on the 5th of Nisan, surrendered his regalia to the city-god, and was humbled before him, he may not have received them back with the divine blessing, but may have been dismissed in favour of his son.

Now in the Creation Epic there is a plain instance of this kind of thing: Ea, who in his time was able to cope with and vanquish Apsu and Mummu, was powerless to deal with their new avenger Tiamat, against whom he was forced to rely upon the fresh strength of

Isis holding Horus, god of the sun.

his son Marduk. We find, however, that Marduk himself had a son, Nebo, who played a part in the New Year ritual which has always been difficult to understand. It is evident from the drama that Nebo came from Borsippa in some way as the helper and rescuer of Marduk when he was held imprisoned in the 'mountain', and it has been observed that Nebo seems partly to duplicate the part of his father as a champion against the powers of evil; may we say he is an embryo champion? Of course it could never have been admitted in theology that Marduk might pass in his turn, and his kingdom be taken by his son Nebo, but at least there was a point in the ritual when the earthly counterparts of these gods, namely the king and his son, could formally accomplish, or could once have accomplished, the acts of abdication and accession. It must, however, be insisted upon that we have no direct evidence for this, but it is quite according to Babylonian ideas that the natural succession of son to father should be sanctified by imagining and even representing the same process at work in the kingdom of the heavens. How the institution of a kind of Saturnalia, which is also with some reason thought to have been held at Babylon during the festival, was connected with this might be the subject of some speculation for which this is hardly the place.

What was the purpose of the Creation Epic? It was not composed merely as *belles lettres,* of that we may be certain. It was to be recited as part of the New Year ritual, but even this is not a sufficient account of it. What was it to do, what was the use of it?—a question which is never out of place in considering any aspect of early civilization. The answer we shall give is, that it was to have a magical virtue, the recitation of the triumphs of Bel was to bring about those triumphs and the annual benefits for which they stood. One detail of this is actually found in the commentary on the ritual— '*enuma elish* which they recite before Bel, and sing in the month of Nisan: that is because he was taken captive . . . '. The epic then was part of the means employed to release him from that captivity. The explanation is quite in accord with what we know of other Babylonian myths: the 'bilingual' Creation story is simply the prelude of an incantation, a third Creation poem which began 'When Anu, Enlil, and Ea created Heaven and Earth' was chanted at the re-founding of a temple, the myth of the siege laid by the Seven Devils against the Moon-god occurs in the great series of incantations against those fiends, and as a last example, the miniature myth, as we might call it, of Marduk seeking advice from his father Ea was so indispensable an ingredient of all incantations against sickness that it is sometimes indicated in the texts merely by mnemonic signs. It is probably not too bold to affirm that all Babylonian mythology is magical in purpose, and directly or indirectly forms an efficient part of some incantation. The proof of this would be far and perhaps elusive to seek—what, to take a crowning example, is to be done with the Gilgamesh epic?—but it would not be a hopeless quest.

The preceding suggestion leads on to the concluding section of our study, which must be greatly curtailed owing to the full treatment given to the New Year Festival. The greatest part of Babylonian ritual, and a fair share of the surviving myths, are included in the disciplines of the three principal classes of priests— the diviners, enchanters, and hymners. The functions of these may be described in the broadest terms as apotropaic and curative; the rituals consist of elaborate directions for all kinds of cult-ceremonies, and the sovereign prescription is the incantation, which was, of course, the province of the second class of priests called *ashipu.* It would be useless to attempt even an outline of these rituals, directed as they are to the most varied circumstances of life, ranging from supreme concerns of state to the quieting of a baby that will not stop crying and let its parents sleep. But it may be more possible and profitable to state briefly the ideas upon which they were founded, the concep-

tion of the nature of those evils which they were designed to remedy.

In this province we move less in the familiar company of the great gods than in the underworld of demonology. Evil occurs to mankind not by the direct infliction of the great gods so much as by their sufferance, by the withdrawal of their protecting favour, which gives opportunity to the infernal hosts. Deliverance from evil can only be effected by winning back the favour of a god, and this in turn is only to be secured by the proper use of the proper incantation, which will simultaneously lame the crafts and malignity of the devils. As prevention is better than cure, there is a whole science of prophylaxis under which is included the interesting rituals of making and animating for their work the whole array of apotropaic figures, from the great stone winged bulls to the humble little clay models of divinities, animals, and monsters, and the cult-objects such as the copper drum covered with a bull's hide, the re-covering of which is fully described in one of this large class of ritual texts. The figures were to fight against intruding demons and repel them, the drum was to dismay them with its thundering sound.

But most rituals of this class are better described as curative; the cult-acts, concluding with an incantation, are to remedy evils that have occurred or are directly threatened. This is the real core of Babylonian medicine, to which the use of drugs and treatment, even when tolerably efficient according to modern notions, is quite subsidiary. But this system extended its supposed efficacy far beyond the bounds of bodily or even mental sickness, and was as trustingly employed in almost every conceivable need and employment of human life.

However vain these conceptions they were held as part of a logical whole, of which it may be worth a few words to examine the other, and preceding, part. This is, the belief in, and practice of, divination. Omens were discernible to the expert eye of the seer, in almost everything that passed in heaven and earth, in sickness and sacrifice, in sleeping and waking. Many, perhaps most, of these were of unfavourable boding, and when such occurred it was necessary to guard against their effect at once by use of the ordinary kind of curative ritual and incantation—the proper specimen is regularly appended to the tablets of omens and their foreseen consequences. The ideas involved seem to have been logical, even if based upon false presuppositions: an evil omen is the sign that there is something amiss in the order of the universe (to put it in the broadest way) just as a symptom of sickness is the sign that something is amiss in the body. What is amiss is, that a god, being angered by some sin, or neglect, or defect in his service, has averted his gaze and allowed the forces of evil for a moment to prevail. And the ritual with its incantation is, we have already observed, the recognized and only means to bring round the favourable countenance of the god to contemplate the world and his servants and thus to foil the aggressors.

Mythology, often in small fragments, is rather commonly embedded in incantations of this kind. The purpose of it seems, in general, to give an explanation of how a certain ill condition came about, and also how it was remedied—demons and gods playing their characteristic parts. The most elaborate of these myths is the account of how the Seven Devils caused an eclipse of the moon by besetting the Moon-god with their evil powers. Enlil had appointed Sin, Shamash, and Ishtar to guide the heavens aright, but the Seven set upon the Moon-god and surrounded him. Thus an eclipse was brought about, amid the consternation of the gods. Enlil saw the distress of Sin and sent his messenger Nusku to bring the alarming news to the god Ea, whom we already know as the master of incantation. When Ea heard this in the Ocean his mouth was filled with lamentation and he bit his lip. Then follows the conventional scene which is reproduced in so many incantations—Ea sends his son Marduk to see the evil that has been wrought, or the ill from which a sick man is suffering; Marduk returns with a report and asks the advice of his father, who after repeating a polite formula signifying that Marduk already possesses all knowledge, details the magical means that are to be used for the remedy of the ill disposition. A regular ingredient in the incantations is the identifying of the priest with Ea, so that his words and actions become symbolically those of the god himself.

We may conclude with the Legend of the Worm, in which we shall see once again the use of a miniature myth, as it were, for magical purposes, to account for the cause of toothache, and describe its cure: 'When Anu made heaven, heaven made earth, earth made the rivers, rivers made the ditches, the ditches made the marsh, and the marsh made the worm. The worm came weeping before the Sun-god, before Ea his tears flowed down. "What givest thou me for my meat and drink?" "I give thee a ripe fig and a sweet pomegranate." "What have I to do with a ripe fig and a sweet pomegranate? Lift me up and let me dwell between teeth and jaw. I will suck the blood of the teeth, and will devour the roots in the jaw." ' The story ends with the priest's curse: 'Because thou hast said this, O Worm, may Ea smite thee with his mighty hand!'

I have tried to set forth in the space allowed a summary of the principal kinds of Babylonian ritual and myth, not labouring to draw every conclusion and to stress every possibility. But since Babylonia was at once the creator of one of the world's oldest civilizations, and the general mentor of Western Asia, both in religion and in the arts, it is only natural that its influence upon the Hebrews, both before and particularly

after the Exile, would be the most distinguishable of all. In the special province with which these essays are concerned there is, of course, no need to look far in Babylonia for the 'ritual-pattern' which Professor Hooke has traced, for here it is with all its particulars developed in the New Year Festival at Babylon which the foregoing pages have described. In the Old Testament it is far less easily discernible, and the succeeding essays are to show how many of its lineaments may be picked out here and there, partly obliterated by other religious prepossessions.

Yet it is right to point out that even in Babylonia, despite the precision with which the 'ritual-pattern' fits the most important festival, there were not merely the other kinds of ritual—temple-service and curative—described above, but also the most important of the myths, which seem to have little or no relation to it. The reason for this is, of course, that the 'ritual-pattern' is concerned only with renewal, which could cover only a part of the 'unpredictable element' in human affairs. Beyond it is all the effort of mankind to escape from, or at least make tolerable, an environment which the thoughtful Babylonian felt, as poignantly as any modern, was ordered without any reference either to his happiness or to his moral notions.

Notes

[1] See Thureau-Dangin, *Rituels accadiens,* 1921, pp. 80 ff.

[2] 'Cylinder B', see Thureau-Dangin, *Sumerische und akkadische Königsinschriften,* 1907, pp. 122 ff.

[3] See various specimens translated in Langdon, *Semitic Mythology,* 1931, pp. 342 ff.

[4] Some account of what is now being revealed by the Phoenician tablets of Ras Shamra is given in the fourth essay of this volume.

[5] Thureau-Dangin, *Rituels accadiens,* 1921, pp. 127 ff., and H. Zimmern, *Zum babylonischen Neujahrsfest,* 1. und 2. Beiträge, 1906, 1918.

[6] A convenient account and translation is given in the British Museum brochure *The Babylonian Legends of the Creation,* 1931. For the text in transcription, with commentary and references, see Langdon, *The Babylonian Epic of Creation,* 1923.

[7] This picturesque name was given to a group of stars fancifully regarded by the Babylonians as a plot of land in heaven, which was cultivated by the neighbouring constellation of 'the Labourer'. It has been identified with the 'square' of Pegasus, or with part of Aries and Cetus.

[8] See [note 6].

[9] Which appears in Hebrew in the form *kipper* and in the word *kapporeth.* For the Babylonian use, see Schrank, *Babylonische Sühnriten,* 1908, pp. 81 ff., and for the Hebrew G. Buchanan Gray, op. cit., pp. 67 ff.

[10] E. Ebeling, *Tod und Leben,* 1931, pp. 24 ff.

Jaan Puhvel (essay date 1987)

SOURCE: "Epic India," in *Comparative Mythology,* The Johns Hopkins University Press, 1987, pp. 68-93.

[*In the essay that follows, Puhvel discusses the ancient epics of India—the* Ramayana *and the* Mahabharata*—considering in particular the intermingling of myth and history in these complex narratives.*]

The five-century time span of roughly 800 to 300 B.C.E. effects the transition from Vedic to classical culture. Its early stages fit such tags as "later Vedic" or "post-Vedic," and the latter centuries qualify as "pre-classical" or "early classical." It is punctuated by a series of crucial cultural events. About the sixth century B.C.E. India becomes literate. By 500 Gautama Siddhārtha preaches in Magadha and has launched Buddhism, in considerable measure beholden to post-Vedic Sāmkhya and Yoga philosophies and thus presupposing the earlier rise of the latter. About 400 the activity of grammarians (notably Pānini) starts the codification of Sanskrit, which in the course of the next few centuries renders it both "classical" and literary or "dead," in favor of the varieties of folk speech (Prākrits, 'natural' or 'common' languages, vs. *sāmskārt* 'done over, contrived, refined'); among the Prākrits, Pāli was preferred by the lower-class missionary zeal of southern Buddhism. By 300, finally, India has entered history with the coming of the Greek ambassador to the Maurya court in Magadha. During the third century the Maurya emperor Aśoka extends his Buddhist rule over much of the subcontinent, leaving his edicts on rocks and pillars all over the realm (mostly in Prākrit; but even a Greek-Aramaic bilingual version has been found in Afghanistan).

Those centuries also mark the rise of the great epics. Although the *Mahābhārata* and the *Rāmāyana* may not have reached their full-blown preserved shapes and scopes before the early centuries of our common era, the staging of their action and their basic creation antedate the middle of the first millennium B.C.E., as do the pre-Pāninean linguistic traits of Epic Sanskrit. The locales differ: the *Mahābhārata* takes place in the North Indian plains between the Yamun and the Ganges, whereas the *Rāmāyana* is centered farther to the east and is symptomatic of more advanced Indo-Aryan penetration of the subcontinent, with the action reaching all the way to Lank (Ceylon). The *Mahābhārata* is more specifically "national" ("Great Bhārata", the latter an ancestral designation; cf. *Bhārat,* the Hindi name of India), while the *Rāmāyana* has the kind of universal folkloristic appeal that has made it a staple of narrative, pictorial, and theatrical art all over Southeast Asia (but much of the *Mahābhārata,* too, was translated into Old Javanese about 1000 C.E.). Certain broad parallels can be drawn to the character of the *Iliad* versus the *Odyssey,* as a war epic centered on a showdown event in contrast to the far-flung and fantastic adventures of a name-hero. But the differences predominate, for the *Mahābhārata* in particular is always something more, something larger and more diffuse than any one definition can encompass.

It is the largest epic known to world literature, comprising anywhere from 78,000 to more than 100,000 couplets (depending on recension), mostly *ślokas* of thirty-two syllables (the Greek hexameter normally has fourteen to seventeen syllables, and the *Iliad* and the *Odyssey* have about 27,800 hexameters between them; hence the size ratio is about 6.5:1). Its eighteen *parvans* or "books" (plus the appendix *Harivamsa*) are of very unequal length, with some of the later ones verging on sketchiness. The climactic central event, the great battle of Kuruksetra, with its preparations and cleanup operations, accounts for books 5-11, but even here there is room for lengthy excrescences, such as the *Bhagavadgītā,* which is a dialogue fitted into book 6. Book 3 is for the most part a vast collection of tales (including a mini-*Rāmāyana*), and books 12-13 are an agglomeration of assorted encyclopedic advice and wisdom from the mouth of a slowly dying battlefield hero. Otherwise books 1-4 deal with the prelude of the main action and books 14-18 with its aftermath, ranging pretty nearly from Creation to posthumous paradise. The whole is cast within frame stories and narrated by various speakers, with overall authorship attributed to Krsna Dvaipāyana, called Vyāsa 'Compiler' (on whom the Vedas are also foisted for good measure), himself paradoxically a figure in the epic. Thus we hear the entire battle sequence as described to the sidelined blind old king by his "eyes" Samjaya, who is preternaturally equipped with wide-angle, zoom, and infrared vision as well as long-range eavesdropping and recording devices, so that he can convey panoramic vistas, close-up detail, nighttime accounts of battlefield happenings, and long verbatim dialogues between distant participants.

What is the relevance of this monstrosity to mythology in general and comparative mythology in particular? In the most general terms, granted the encyclopedic nature of books 3, 12, and 13, it is bound to incorporate incidental matter of relevance. Unlike the Vedas it is secular in genre, which does not preclude the inclusion of a Vīsānuite minibible, the *Bhagavadgītā.* All together it is a repository of enough ancient para-Vedic material to have earned in Indic antiquity the nickname

"Fifth Veda". . . . Along with the earlier *Brāhānas* and the later *Purānas,* the *Mahābhārata* is an important link in the post-Vedic preservation, transmission, and elaboration of Indic mythical lore.

But even as we strip away all the padding, it remains to be determined where the main line of characters and story should be pegged on the scale of myth versus history. The setting is "real" enough, centered on the tribal kingdom of the Kurus in the northern plains of the "Indic Mesopotamia," the riverine interspace formed by the Ganges and Yamun as they flow nearly parallel south from the Himālaya ('Abode of Snow'), subsequently turn southeast, and ultimately converge into an enlarged Ganges; downstream (east) from the confluence lay Kāśi (present-day Banaras), and farther down was the land of Magadha, scene of the Buddha and Megasthenes alike. To the south of Kuru country were the Vrsnis or Yadus (with their stronghold of Mathurā on the Yamunā), west of them across the Yamunā the Matsyas, east of them on both banks of the Ganges were the Pañcālas, and farther south, beyond the now east-flowing Yamunā, lay the kingdom of Cedi.

Although the locale is firm, the "Book of Beginnings" (*Ādiparvan*) typically takes its time getting the protagonists into place and the action going. The authors of the *Mahābhārata* did little to deserve Horace's praise of Homer for plunging right in (*in medias res*) and not starting the *Iliad* from the 'twin egg' (*gemino ab ovo,* i.e., the birth of Helen and the Dioskouroi from Leda and the Swan back in Sparta). The *Mahābhārata* dawdles for well over a hundred pages of preface matter, summary descriptions of content, little previews, and frame stories with their own incrustations of legend, before getting down to the ancestral tales, tracing the line of the protagonists through the ages. This middle third of the *Ādiparvan* is a sort of self-contained chronicle-epic, where generations and happenings are lined up on a time axis rather than all being spread out in a vast synchronic tableau of events; thus the great action epic incorporates into its boundlessness even a specimen of the other genre, the chronicle type that we shall meet in Iran, Italy, Ireland, Scandinavia, and Russia.

But even here the narration proceeds jerkily, not as a true chronicle but spaced by the contrived queries of the frame story, at times in speedy summation, then again in detailed and leisurely episodic fashion, studed with repetitions and not in strict chronological order. With typical measurelessness we are provided comprehensive theogonies, demonogonies, and anthropogonies of Brahmanism, a host of incarnations, and a plethora of semidivine or miraculous births of the ancestors, down to the contemporaries of the main action of the *Mahābhārata.*

In the cradle of transmigration (*samsāra*) that is classical India, the device of incarnation assumed a life of its own, far beyond any Vedic inheritance. It was a convenient theological (and by extension literary) device for projecting divinity onto an earthly plane, individualizing a piece of godhead for its "human interest" value, causing avatars (literally 'descents') that mesh with mortality and yet retain their immanence and transcendence for repeated revelation. Thus the great god Visnu was incarnated either theriomorphically (fish, tortoise, boar) or as a freakish (man-lion [Narasimha], dwarf) or relatively normal human being (Para ur ma, Rāma, Krsna), and a mighty demon might go through several careers as an earthly evildoer (e.g., Hiranyaka-   śipu, Rāvana, and Śiśupāla, killed by Narasimha, Rāma, and Krsna respectively). Such avatars are wholly apart from the folkloristic animal or human disguises gods occasionally don, usually for purposes of sexual coupling (Vivasvat or Poseidon turning into a stallion, Indra or Zeus impersonating the husband of Ahalyā or Alkmene). The incarnations provide important figures of the *Mahābhārata* (e.g., Bhīsma, Krsna, Draupad), but the dynasty itself is explained on the whole as being merely of ultimate divine descent (not unlike Roman or "Holy Roman" emperors of other climes), liberally interspersed with additional lateral infusions of divine genes through the generations, usually on the male side (as in Greece), but with occasional childbearing by goddesses (e.g., Urvaśī with Purūravas, like Aphrodite with Anchises).

The line descends from Manu (son of Vivasvat and Savarnā) via his daughter/son Ilā, 'Libation', claimed to be both mother and father of Purūravas, whose ultimately unhappy union with his fairy bride Urvaśī . . . produced six sons, notably Āyus who begot Nahusa who begot Yayāti. Here the story expands into an elaborate body of legendry surrounding King Yayāti, his turbulent marriages to Devayānī (daughter of Kāvya Uśanas, sorcerer in service of the demons) and Śarmisthā (daughter of the demon-king Vrsaparvan), his five sons, the youngest of whom, Pūru, shoulders his father's old age for a millennium and thereafter, restored to youth, succeeds Yayāti, Yayāti's subsequent posthumous fall from heaven into the company of his four grandsons, and his restoration to salvation by their pooled virtues. How he came by those grandsons, who were born to his here-unmentioned virgin daughter Mādhavī, is explained later in an incidental tale of book 5, a story of wide ramifications for the mythoepical underpinnings of Indo-European kingship (see chap. 14). There was clearly a wide body of folklore around Yayāti, ultimately of mythic origin, centering on the notion of a primeval sovereign who fell because of pride (hints of hybris attach also to Purūravas and, in the garbled tale of Indra's sinnings in book 5, involve Yayāti's father Nahusa as well).

After the eponymous Pūru, his Paurava line descends through a dozen or so gap-filling "begats" to Duhsanta, and here the epic expands once more into the tale of Duhsanta and Śakuntalā, anachronistically placed just ahead of Yayti's chapter by the makers of the *Mahābhārata*. Duhsanta is described as an ideal ruler of the earth in an idyllic era. During a hunt he comes upon the forest hermitage of the renowned ascetic Kanva, in whose absence he is received by a young girl who introduces herself as Kanva's daughter. Duhsanta challenges her, because he is certain that the holy man "has never spilled his seed." The girl then recounts the true story of her parentage, which she had once overheard as Kanva told a fellow hermit. It epitomizes an ever-recurring theme of the *Mahābhārata* and classical India, the place and nature of brahmin asceticism in the total culture. Unlike Western monasticism, the stress is not on continence and mortification per se, but on a kind of creative tension. Indic ascetics are true athletes of austerity; they store up *tapas* 'heat' amounting to an accumulation of spiritual power that can even threaten the gods. But they stockpile sexual energy as well, and this pent-up force can on proper stimulation explode into gross eroticism and sensuality. Sex-crazed ascetics impregnating young girls are stock characters in this culture. Conversely, there is arrogant pride in abstinence; the same Prime Minister Desai who disclosed urine drinking as his recipe for longevity also boasted of not having had sex for many decades. Here is the girl's account: Viśvāmitra, an upwardly mobile ascetic (he was one of the rare men ever to be promoted from ksatriya to brahmin), performs such awesome austerities that Indra himself feels threatened and sends the Apsaras Menakā to take him down a peg by seducing him. The nymph feels intimidated by the terrible-tempered holy man but finally agrees to perform a wind-assisted striptease in front of the sage. In no time the "bull among brahmins" lusts for the "good-assed nymph," as this "strictest of seers" sees her nude and clutching at her skirt. And so he begets a girl, whom the Apsaras abandons on a riverbank, where the saintly Kanva finds her. He names the foundling Śakuntalā and raises her at the hermitage.

King Duhsanta is overjoyed to hear all this, for the girl is by male bloodline a ksatriya like himself, and he is hence eligible to marry her. He offers to do so on the spot and, when akuntal temporizes for Kanva's return, delivers a lecture on various types of wedlock, informing her that marriage by free consent of the couple without the presence of a third party is legal for ksatriyas. She consents, being promised that any son born will be Duhsanta's heir, they consummate the marriage, he leaves, and the returning, all-knowing Kanva blesses the match as proper. At the end of a protracted pregnancy of three years Bharata is born at the hermitage, and after assorted troubles he ultimately gains acceptance by Duhsanta and the right to royal succession. The freewill marriage of akuntal points back all the way to Indo-European antiquity on the one hand (cf. the Old Roman marriage practices discussed

in chap. 9), and her story has also become renowned in subsequent Indic literature (as in Kālidāsa's drama). Here, however, it points the dynasty forward via the eponymous Bharata. Several gap-filling Bhārata generations lead down to Samvarana, who marries Vivasvat's daughter Tapat (another side-infusion of divinity, right back to the beginnings!) and sires another eponym, Kuru. Thereupon half a dozen Kauravas bring the line to Śamtanu.

Here the lineage is approaching "contemporaneity" and gets more complicated. Śamtanu's father arranges for him to meet and marry the river goddess Gangā (= Ganges), on condition that he not question her identity or actions. Gangā had earlier promised Dyaus and seven other Vasu deities, who had been cursed by the wronged sage Vasistha (Varuna's son) to become incarnated as men, that she would bear them in her womb and then promptly drown their incarnations in her own waters, thus expeditiously shortening their humiliation. Gangā duly killed her sons by Śamtanu, but relented with the eighth (or, as a variant, bore a ninth), thus giving Śamtanu the son Devavrata, who came to be known as Bhīsma. It was all foreordained: Gangā had so contracted with the Vasus, and it was contingent on Vasistha's curse itself, for he had doomed Dyaus alone as the chief culprit to undergo a lengthy incarnation as a man, yet without siring human offspring. Thus long-lived Bhīsma, the old wise warrior of the *Mahābhārata*, is the explicit incarnation of the old sky-god Dyaus (see chap. 4).

After this intermezzo, Old Girl River just kept on flowing along, and Śamtanu turned toward the parallel stream of Yamunā for his sexual needs. On the Yamunā he smelled an overpowering perfume, and thereby hang other tales. The source of the fragrance was Satyavatī, with a history of her own. Her father was Vasu Uparicara, whose story is told earlier in book I. He was not some Vasu divinity but a hero of the Paurava line, who with Indra's help had become king of Cedi. When he showed ascetic tendencies and retired to the forest, the gods worried about the potential power of his *tapas*. Rather than sending him a seductive Apsaras, however, Indra personally negotiated his return to worldliness with a set of divine gifts; besides a fadeproof lotus garland and a bamboo pole as talismanic ritualistic tokens of Indra's trust, he was given an airborne crystal chariot that he put to good use (hence the nickname Uparicara 'High-Flyer'). The rest of his life story casts him as a "universal monarch" (*samrāj*) who parallels Yayāti in several respects (five sons whom he spreads around other kingdoms and especially, as told in books 12, 13, and 14, his later sinning and fall from grace, not however from pride but rather for having truck with untruth, and not posthumously from heaven to earth but rather from his aeronautic conveyance into the ground; he too is saved, not however by any grandsons but by Visnu). The story of Vasu, like that of Yayāti, is important for the reconstruction of a coherent Indo-Iranian *Yamá-,* as will be seen in chapter 6.

Here, however, we catch Vasu at an early stage of his career, as the young king of Cedi. His wife is Girikā, born of Vasu's hometown river, who had been raped by a nearby mountain. Once, when he is about to cohabit with Girikā, his apparitional ancestors interrupt him and inconsiderately order him to go hunting. (The dead are hungry!) He complies, but he ejaculates during the hunt and collects his semen on a leaf. An obliging kite is to fly it back home to Girikā but is attacked by another en route, and the leaf drops into the Yamunā, where it is swallowed by a curse-ridden Apsaras in fish form. She conveniently conceives, for only by bearing twins can she be freed from her pisciform predicament. Ten months later she is caught and opened up by fishermen, who find a boy and a girl and present them to the king. The Apsaras is off the hook, literally and figuratively, and Vasu unknowingly takes in his own brood. The son Matsya 'Fish' will become the eponymous founder of the Matsya tribe to the west, but the beautiful girl smells so fishy that she has to be turned back to fisherfolk. As a nubile oarswoman she is seen on the river by the saintly ascetic Parāśara, who is touring the local hermitages. He imperiously desires her; like Poseidon in Homer he creates a misty boudoir for their privacy, vows to restore her virginity (lest father find out), promises to deodorize her, and has his way. As he departs for his next devotional appointment, she is left perfumed and pregnant and gives birth the same day to Vyāsa, the great Compiler who is to become the maker of the *Mahābhārata.* It is after this incident that Śamtanu smells the fragrance and tracks down its source. Satyavatī's fisher-father will consent to a marriage only if Satyavatī's son will have exclusive rights to royal succession. Śamtanu cannot do this to his son Devavrata and grieves instead, whereupon the son himself magnanimously negotiates the match, not only forgoing his primogeniture but vowing to remain without offspring who might later challenge the succession (not knowing that the pact of Gangā and the Vasus had barred him from having progeny anyway). For these superhuman renunciations he is dubbed Bhīsma 'Awesome', and Śamtanu grants him the boon of dying only by an act of his own will, something that Bhīsma makes good (ab)use of later in the *Mahābhārata.*

Śamtanu and Satyavatī, at the ancestral seat of Hastinapura on the Ganges, had two sons, Citrāngada and Vicitravīrya. Both died young and childless, but Vicitravīrya left two widows. Under the rules of the levirate a dead man's brother could beget children in his name. The paternal half-brother Bhīsma having taken a vow of celibacy, Satyavat enlisted the maternal one, her son Vyāsa. Before the great ascetic could compose the *Mahābhārata,* he had to buckle down to siring its protagonists! He was glad to oblige, but the two widows were aghast at their hairy and smelly partner: one shut her eyes and the other blanched during the enforced insemination. In the true tradition of old wives' pregnancy lore, one bore the blind son Dhrtarāstra and the other the pale-faced Pāndu, 'Pallid'. When mother-in-law Satyavat tried to breed the first widow a second time, she stealthily substituted as proxy a śūdra girl who bore the half-breed Vidura. The three half-brothers were accordingly not dynastic mainliners at all, being descended from the Pauravas only through their paternal grandmother Satyavatī, the daughter of Vasu Uparicara, whose sperm had landed inside on ichthyomorph Apsaras. They were brought up by Bhīsma as regent. Pāndu excelled in archery, Dhrtarāstra in physical strength, and Vidura in law and sagacity. Pāndu was designated to become king, the others being disqualified by blindness and by half-caste status.

Consulting with Vidura, who early on acquired a reputation as a wise and discreet adviser in general and marriage consultant in particular, Bhīsma set out to find wives for the other brothers. For Dhrtarāstra he negotiated the princess Gāndhārī, who resolved always to wear a blindfold out of sympathy for her husband's disability. She had been endowed with the boon of bearing a hundred sons. Pāndu first married the Yadu chieftain's daughter Prthā, better known as Kuntī. Her story is told repeatedly, first in book 1 and later at length in book 3. As a young girl she had well pleased an "awesome and dreadful brahmin of strict vows," who in appreciation supplied her with a spell for summoning up gods at will to beget children on her. Out of girlish curiosity she had called upon the sun-god Sūrya, who had come in all his splendor and, despite her terrified second thoughts, gotten her with child. A son was born with a miraculous gleaming breastplate and earrings, to be known as Karna, 'Ear'. Kuntī disconsolately floated the baby downriver in a basket, whence it was rescued by a coachman's wife, to grow up around Dhrtarāstra's court as a foundling of unknown (hence suspect) parentage. Despite this youthful indiscretion, Kuntī now became Pāndu's virginal bride, her maidenhead having been restored by Sūrya. Bhīsma also bought Pāndu a second wife, Mādrī. After a series of punitive military expeditions Pāndu retired to an idyllic life as a woodsman in the company of his two wives, running his kingdom by remote control. Gāndhārī, meanwhile, after a two-year pregnancy, aborted a huge blob of flesh that was divided into one hundred pieces and hatched in individual pots. Thus were born the hundred sons of Dhrtarāstra, notably Duryodhana and Duhśāsana, the archvillains of the plot to follow (many of their names have the pejorative prefix *Dus-,* antonymic to the usual *Su-* 'good, well'). Bad omens attended Duryodhana's birth, and sages advised doing away with the child, but Dhrtarāstra, with an irresolution that was to become characteristic, demurred. Pāndu, meanwhile, had shot a buck in the act of copulation, who turned out to be a mighty ascetic in theriomorphic disguise; with his dying breath he condemned Pāndu himself to perish if he ever engaged in sex. Thus reduced to impotence on pain of death, Pāndu had to find other means of perpetuating his dynasty. Here Kuntī's spell came in handy; in close consultation with her husband she conceived Yudhisthira 'Steady in Battle' by the god Dharma, Bhīma 'Terrible' by Vāyu, and Arjuna 'Shiny, White' by Indra. She then lent her mantra to her cowife Mādrī, who invoked the Aśvins to father the twins Nakula and Sahadeva. Pāndu thus put together a happy family, but one spring day in the woods he was overcome with lust for Mādrī, forgot himself, forcibly penetrated her, and fell dead. Mādrī dutifully committed suttee on his funeral pyre.

With the five Pāndavas and the hundred Kauravas now in place, the action proper of the epic begins, starting with the boyhood stories of the two sets of cousins as they are brought up together by Dhrtarāstra, who now rules despite his blindness with the help of the ageless Bhīsma. Childish horseplay soon takes vicious turns, as Duryodhana tries to drown and poison Bhīma. Great tutors are engaged for the unruly boys—Krpa and Drona, whose birth tales continue the litany of lecherous holy men ejaculating at the sight of heavenly nymphs. The Pāndavas make good athletic progress—notably Bhīma in wrestling and Arjuna in archery—but animosities increase, and Arjuna and Karna have a tense showdown during a tournament after Bhīma insults Karna about his supposed low-class origin, as Indra and Sūrya shower rain and sunshine on their jousting sons in a supernatural show of paternal support. The Pāndavas are clear popular favorites, but Duryodhana engineers their temporary sojourn away from the seat of power and even plots to cremate them and their mother Kunt in combustible lodgings. Saved by Vidura's providential warnings, they escape to the woods. A minor "forest book" is intercalated here, comprising encounters with demons and retrospective tales (Tapatī, Vasistha), until our heroes make their way, in brahmin disguise, to the "self-choice" (*svayamvara*, i.e., husband selection) of the Pañcalas princess Draupadī. Arjuna alone of the assembled wooers passes the crucial bow-shooting test and, after an incognito run-in with Karna, walks off with the bride, who becomes the joint wife of the five Pāndavas (with daily renewable virginity). A weak folkloristic explanation (inadvertent and misspoken but binding words by Mother Kuntī) is given for such *anārya* polyandry. The brothers also make the acquaintance of the Yadu (or Yādava) princes Krsna and Balarāma, sons of Kuntī's brother Vasudeva. After the wedding in Drupada's kingdom word gets out that the Pāndavas are well and are maritally allied to the Pancālas. Duryodhana and Karna are frantic, and the weak-willed weathervane Dhrtarāstra is as wishy-washy as ever, but Bhīsma, Drona, and Vidura advocate recall and

conciliation. The Pāndavas return and are awarded half the kingdom, where they found Indraprastha, the future Delhi, on the banks of the Yamunā, some sixty miles southwest of Hastinapura. Yudhisthira rules, while Arjuna has assorted forest adventures and ends up marrying (on top of his 20 percent share of Draupad) Krsna's sister Subhadrā, on whom he sires Abhimanyu. Book 1 ends with a kind of theomachy, in which Arjuna and Krsna confront gods and demons in the frame of a great forest fire.

Book 2 is much shorter and more schematic. Yudhisthira constructs a great palace at Indraprastha and plans a royal consecration (*rājasūya*). Krsna advises him that one more threat exists to his sovereignty, King Jarāsamdha of Magadha, who with the help of his marshal Śiśupāla, has become *samrāj* and has in fact captured and imprisoned a large number of lesser kings, intending them as human sacrifices to his divine patron Śiva. An expedition is mounted, Bhīma kills Jarāsamdha in an extended wrestling match, the kings are freed, and Yudhisthira's path to world sovereignty is open. His four brothers secure the allegiance of the four corners of the earth, and all kings are summoned to the consecration. The laws of hospitality require the designation of a guest of honor, and on Bhīsma's nomination the award goes to Krsna, whom Bhīsma knows to be Visnu incarnate. At this Śiśupāla of Cedi, who was born with the marks of Śiva, demurs vehemently, because Krsna is not even a king, and escalates the quarrel to a point of no return, until Krsna (alias Visnu) decapitates him with his discus and, as Universal God, absorbs his essence into his own being. These extraordinary traditions about Jarāsamdha + Śiśupāla reflect transmuted ancient Indo-European warrāior myths attested also in Greece and Scandinavia, in the figures of Herakles and Strakaðr in their dealings with gods (see chap. 13). After this incident the ceremony goes off as scheduled. Back home the envious Duryodhana, abetted by a crooked gambler friend, prevails on his ever-vacillating father to invite the Pāndavas for a "friendly" visit. Once there, the "Law-King" (Dharmarāja) Yudhisthira succumbs to his one tragic flaw, the gambling urge that was one of the cardinal vices of ancient India (starting with the "Gambler's Lament," *RV* 10.34). As the dice game proceeds, the king successively loses his wealth, his kingdom, his brothers, and in the end Draupadī, whereupon Duhśāsana drags her by the hair into the hall, despite her protestations that she is having her period. He rips off her garment, which is magically replaced, shielding her nakedness, while Bhīma vows that he will drink Duh Śāsana's blood. Upset by the brutality, Dhrtarāstra has a momentary fit of willpower and declares the crooked game void, allowing the guests to depart. Yet still bitten by the gambling bug, Yudhisthira heeds a later repeat invitation and loses on lesser stakes: twelve years' exile and one further incognito year. Amid portents of disasters to come, the Pāndavas depart for a forest on the river Sarasvat.

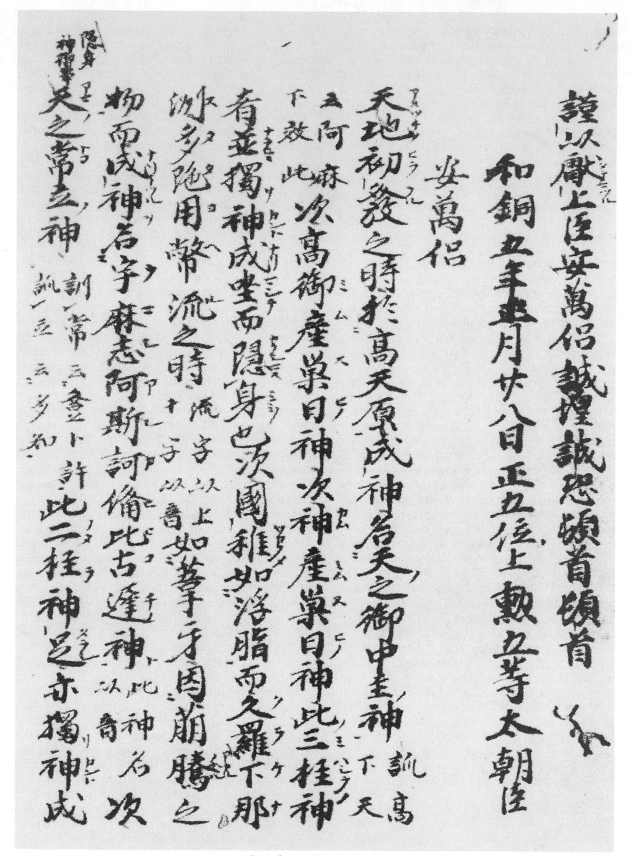

Page from a 1522 copy of the Kojiki.

In book 3 (*Vanaparvan*, 'Forest Book'), despite its length (about 17,500 couplets), there is hardly any action (except for a brief abduction of Draupadī), the twelve-year exile being filled with assorted excuses for story telling such as the tales of the lovers Nala and Damayantī, of the great sage Agastya (already in *RV* 1.179; a match for Viśvāmitra and Vasistha) with his unique digestive capabilities, of Ŕśyaśrnga (a precursor of the unicorn legend), of Cyavana and Sukanyā (mentioned in chap. 4), and of the Fish, the Flood, and Manu, and of Rāma and Sītā.

For their year of disguise (book 4) the brothers choose the court of the Matsya king Virāta, where they pass themselves off as itinerant, unemployed sometime household staff of the Pāndavas. The king engages Yudhisthira as a brahmin gamester, Bhīma as butcher-cook and athlete, Arjuna as a transvestite dance teacher, and Nakula and Sahadeva as horse groom and cattleman respectively; Draupad becomes maidservant to the queen. They manage to get by well as humble folk, supplementing their wages by secondhand dealings in food and clothing. Virāta's marshal and brother-in-law Kīcaka importunes Draupadī but is wrestled and killed by the mayhem specialist Bhīma, who pushes his limbs into his trunk, which leads to assorted unpleasantness involving Kīcaka's kinsmen. Soon the Matsya country suffers two invasions, the second by the cattle-raiding Kauravas themselves, and the P ndavas (still in disguise) mount a valiant defense of their master Virāta in a battle scenario that is a kind of abbreviated dress rehearsal for the big event to come, especially pitting Arjuna successively against Krpa, Drona's son Aśvatth man, Karna, Bhīsma, and Duryodhana. When it is over, the victorious Pāndavas shed their disguises, and the grateful Virāta offers Arjuna his daughter Uttarā, whom Arjuna reserves as bride for his son Abhimanyu.

Book 5 is heavily laced with incidental tales (such as those of Yayāti and Mādhavī and of Indra's misdeeds, mentioned earlier) but also lays the groundwork for the showdown. The Pāndavas lay claim to their erstwhile holdings while starting war preparations. Krsna joins them as a noncombatant, and they can count on the Pañcālas and the Matsyas, on Cedi and Magadha, among others. The more remote easterly, northerly, and westerly tribes side with the Kauravas. There follow protracted negotiations, with embassies back and forth, interspersed with lengthy soul-searchings and consultations by the troubled and weak-willed Dhrtarāstra, since he and the moderate party (Vidura, Bhīsma, Drona) are up against the increasingly maniacal intransigence of Duryodhana and Karna. Krsna as the Pāndavas' ambassador conducts a final climactic peace mission to Hastinapura, complete with pleadings, threats, and even an awesome vision of himself as the avatar of the Universal God, but Duryodhana's terminal fatuity stays unshakable. With the help of Kuntī, Krsna tries to sway Karna by revealing his true origin

as a half-brother of the Pāndavas, but the stubborn solar son merely promises his mother to fight only Arjuna, while sparing her other Pāndava sons. Krsna then reports back that war is inevitable. Bhīsma is installed as Kaurava supreme commander, while Yudhisthira appoints Draupadī's brother, the Pañcāla Dhrstadyumna. The book ends with Bhīsma's declared resolve not to fight the strange figure of Śikhandin (a woman transformed into a man), the complex tale that has brought him to this tabuistic refusal, and the marching of the vast armies toward the battlefield of Kuruksetra.

Books 6-10 describe the eighteen-day battle, as reported to the blind Dhrtarātra by his confidant Samjaya. For all its ferocity, it remains a gentleman's war, observing banker's hours of combat and with considerable civility during the intervals. Even before the start, Arjuna turns fainthearted in the face of this intrafamily massacre, and it takes his charioteer Krsna's lengthy sermon of the *Bhagavadgītā* "Blessed's Song" to restore his resolve, including a terrifying vision of Krsna-Visnu as "like unto a thousand suns" and as "death, ripe to bring ruin to the world." Ten days under Bh sma's command end when the ageless one himself spills to Yudhisthira the secret of Śikhandin, after which he is cut down by a shower of arrows. He thus makes use of his privilege to die on his own terms, and emphatically so, for he is not yet through: propped up on the arrows that penetrate his body, he watches the rest of the battle like a reclining Saint Sebastian and waits for his turn to fill up books 12-13 with his interminable Mirror for Royalty; compared with this longest deathbed sermon on record, Homer's long-winded old man Nestor was a paragon of laconism.

Drona assumes command in book 7 but, disconsolate over faked news of the death of his son Aśvatth man, drops his guard and is killed by Dhrstadyumna. Karna takes over in book 8 and is slain after a great duel with Arjuna. Mādrī's brother Śalya succeeds but is killed in book 9, after which Bhīma confronts Duryodhana and fulfills his earlier vow to crush his thighs, having also had the satisfaction of clubbing down Duhśāsana, cutting open his chest, and drinking his blood. With this the Pāndavas have triumphed.

But not quite. In book 10 three surviving enemy warriors, led by Drona's son Aśvatth man, who is inspired by and practically an incarnation of Śiva, invade the Pāndava camp accompanied by a host of phantasmagoric monsters and butcher the sleeping warriors, including Dhrstadyumna and the five sons of the Pāndavas by Draupadī. The Pāndavas themselves and Krsna escape by being elsewhere. After reporting his success to the dying Duryodhana, Aśvatthāman is confronted in the forest by our surviving heroes and neutralized in the course of a showdown that pits the beneficent might of Krsna-Visnu against the malevolence of Aśvatthāman-Śiva.

In the remaining books, Dhrtar stra and the Pāndavas are reconciled, the dead are buried, and Yudhisthira is persuaded to reign at Hastinapura, is subjected to the dying Bhīsma's endless sermons, and celebrates the great horse sacrifice (*avamedha*) that is one ritual form of regal consolidation. After helping him for many years, the old uncles Vidura and Dhrtarāstra, along with the latter's wife Gāndhāri and Queen Mother Kuntī, retire to the forest. Vidura, dying, transfuses his being into Yudhisthira (a mystical operation that would hary raise an eyebrow in India), while the others perish in a forest fire. Krsna (who had been cursed by Gāndhārī at the close of the war) and his Yadu tribe also fall on evil days, with internecine killings topped off by Krsna's being shot in the woods by the hunter Jarā 'Old Age'. When Yudhisthira himself is ready to retire, he installs as ruler Arjuna's grandson (Abhimanyu's son) Par ksit and sets out with his brothers and Draupad on a long march beyond the Himālaya, toward the mythical Mount Meru and Heaven (*svarga*). Draupadī, Nakula, Sahadeva, Arjuna, and Bh ma successively collapse en route, but Yudhisthira makes it, accompanied by a faithful dog who turns out to be his father Dharma in disguise. Posthumous recognition scenes and celestial bliss conclude the epic. Parīksit's son Janamejaya is instrumental to the frame story within which the *Mahābhārata* is recited by the sage Vaiśampāyana, who had learned it from Vyāsa.

After this summary of the main line of the story we can better assess its mythological significance, both in the ancestral tales and in the action epic proper. We have clearly glimpsed ancient, embedded myth of Indo-European or Indo-Iranian relevance in and around such figures as Yayāti, Duhsanta, Vasu Uparicara, Bhīsma, and Jarāsamdha. We have also been exposed to an inordinate number of miraculous boons, amorous ascetics, recyclable virgins, metamorphoses of all sorts, in short, the stock-in-trade of India's imaginative folklore. The somewhat cozy, even symbiotic Vedic opposition of gods and demons has passed from the stage of live religion, being replaced by a sectarian Vaisnava: Śaiva antagonism. The *Mahābhārata* is in the main a Visnuite work, and hence the only truly religious incarnation is that of Krsna or, in a negative vein, of ivaistic badmen such as Śiśupāla or Aśvatthāman. The other explicit incarnations like Bhīsma, the many "sons of deities," and the superannuated gods themselves such as their "king" Indra are part of an epic, not a religious apparatus. But what is the genesis of this "epic apparatus"? Is it a historical tale of early dynasts in the Ganges-Yamunāriverland, overlaid with generous helpings of folklore, encrusted with a secularized divine setup in the manner of Homer, and further complicated by the omnipresence of avatars and incarnations in classical India? If it were so, any mythological interest would be late and secondary. Such a historicist approach has long been and is still prevalent but is worthless for the student of myth. While it is perfectly valid to study the *Mahābhārata* synchronically, as a self-contained expression of a certain period of Indic culture, diachronic historicism seems delusionary. Instead the *Mahābhārata* as a whole, in its genealogical structure, its protagonists, and its main action, points back to a mythic inheritance of Vedic, para-Vedic, pre-Vedic, Indo-Iranian, and ultimately Indo-European provenance.

The basic structure of the Pāndavas bears this out. Though they themselves are "historically" ksatriyas, their roster of divine fathers—Dharma, Vāyu, Indra, and the Aśvins—recalls the Vedic god lists of the three varnas (e.g., *RV* 5.51.10, dityas, Indrā-Vāyū, Vasus) and thus comprehensively covers the Vedic pantheon (with the substitution of the classical abstraction Dharma for the obsolete Mitra). There is even a hint of pre-Vedic archaism in the placing of Vāyu over Indra, which is supported by Iranian data; Indra's ascendancy at the expense of V yu was a Vedic phenomenon that did not affect this para-Vedic structural relic of Indo-Iranian date. Here alone is proof that the *Mahābhārata* preserves mythical petrifacts that cannot be secondary incrustations, for later mythologizers would not have imposed obsolete structures that eluded them. A second blow to the historicist view is administered by the "scandalous" polyandry of Draupadī. A "sociological" interpretation invoking Dravidian influence is ruled out by the epic tradition itself, which found it intrinsically incomprehensible and resorted either to accidental sanction through word tabu or to convoluted theological explanations via the "sins of Indra" (the P ndavas were born of the shattered pieces of Indra's total glory,[1] which were deposited in several gods and reinvested in the wombs of Kuntī and Mādrī; thus they were piecemeal incarnations of the one Indra, and there was no real polyandry in Draupadī's [herself an incarnation of either Śrī 'Lady Luck' or of Mrs. Indra] marrying them jointly). The real explanation is again via theology of Indo-Iranian and Indo-European date, where the transfunctional goddess whom Draupadī reflects . . . spans the whole range of the compartmentalized male deities. Thus we have in reality an old pantheonic structure transposed to the level of heroic saga through the device of divine fatherhood. This is simply an Indic way of transposition through time, alternative to outright incarnation, unlike, for example, Greek heroes who may have divine fathers (Herakles) or be heroicized divine sons (Dioskouroi) but who do not serve as allonymous vessels for the epic transfusion of their divine originators.

Once this principle is established, it is possible to investigate figures and plot alike for the mythic prototypes of character and action, and optimally even to reconstruct elements of these prototypes back to the mythical level.

Yudhisthira's right-minded self-control and "saintliness," the clubwielding Bhīma's near-mindless brutality, the archer Arjuna's adventurous high-mindedness, the good looks and modest helpfulness of Nakula and Sahadeva all point to type concepts rather than individualized personalities. They are bundles of Vedic (or pre- or para-Vedic) theologems about the spheres of Mitra, Vāyu, Indra, and the Aśvins, secularized and epicized in a later milieu and fitted into the literary frame of a changed culture. They are ksatriya brothers who act out roles ancestral to the brahmin and vaiśya classes as well, with all the tensions inherent in such cross-cutting (brahmin: ksatriya rivalries, but also their basic solidarity as against the "lower class," seen in the maternity of Kuntī [marriage by *svayamvara*] vs. Mādrī [bartered wife in *vaiśya* fashion], and in the deferential attitude of the twins toward the older brothers). In their year-long masquerade at Virāta's court the brothers actually "sort out" their intrinsic natures in some degree: Yudhisthira readily chooses the disguise of a brahmin, while the twins easily dress up as vaiśyas; Bhīma and Arjuna must also hide their inherent ksatriya nature, but they choose vocations that are only travesties of their true caste characteristics: "butcher" is after all a fit sobriquet for a brutal warrior, and Arjuna has merely exchanged his military finery, which harks back to his Vedic father Indra and his prancing Maruts, for the fancy drag of a eunuch dance master. Episodes of transvestism occur with other warrior figures as well, for example, the Greek Herakles at Omphale's court, Achilles on Skyros, and the Norse Thor dressing up as "bride" of the giant Thrymr.

It was noted in chapter 4 that the peculiar hymnic style of the *Rig-Veda* tended to invoke the Aśvins jointly and without differentiation, with only scant and allusive reference to their separate characteristics. The *Mahābhārata,* on the other hand, provides in its discursiveness data on the individualities of Nakula and Sahadeva that are not novelistic "character development" but reflect traits matched elsewhere (Iran, Greece) by the Indo-European Divine Twins. Nakula hires on as a horse specialist (just as the Greek Kastor was *hippódamos* 'horse tamer'), whereas Sahadeva is cattle oriented (even as Polydeukes was the sole victor in the twins' Arcadian cattle raid). When differentiation is in order Nakula is better looking, more warlike, more ksatriya oriented, while Sahadeva is gentle, wise, and benevolent—in short, a kind of lower-echelon understudy of Yudhisthira himself (already *RV* 1.181.4 called one Aśvin [the original Horseman!] "victorious," while the other, the son of Dyaus, rated the epithet *subhága-* 'fortunate, blessed'). In such instances the evidence of the *Mahābhārata* either supplements or skirts Vedic information and points back to more remote Indo-Iranian and Indo-European vistas.

We glimpsed above snatches of the story of Karna— his miraculous birth as son of the youthful Kuntī by the sun-god Sūrya, his childhood as a foundling, his early antagonisms with the Pāndavas and with Arjuna in particular ripening into mature hatred on the side of Duryodhana, hatred that neither Krsna's nor Kuntī's representations could deflect, and his death at the hands of Arjuna in the great duel of book 8. He is an overt son of the sun, born wearing the stigmata of his sire (golden earrings and breastplate) and rendering him frequent and open homage. Sūrya beams down on him in his initial youthful joust with Arjuna, even as Indra showers rainy refreshment on his opponent. In short, Karna is the epicized transposition product of Sūrya. Sūrya, however, for all the solarity that permeates parts of the Vedic pantheon, is curiously deficient in myth. Just about the only item is the allusion to the hostilities of Indra and Sūrya mentioned in chapter 4, how Indra "stole" a wheel of Sūrya's chariot (*RV* 1.175.4, 4.30.4), how he "tore forward one wheel" and "made the other free to run" (*RV* 5.29.10), and how he "pressed down" the wheel (*RV* 4.28.2), all in the course of helping his heroic client Kutsa Ārjuneya. Similarly, in the climactic showdown between Karna and Arjuna in book 8, after many vicissitudes and the deployment of miraculous panoplies, after Arjuna shoots a magic arrow at Karna's chariot, Death (Kāla) announces that "the earth swallows the wheel," whereupon the left wheel falls into the ground and cripples the chariot. Karna exits, tries in vain to wrench the wheel loose, confronts Arjuna on foot, and is decapitated by another arrow. His death scene is bathed in the poetic imagery of the setting sun. This accordance is a splendid instance not only of mythic characters but also of actions transferred into epic narrative. Whether other traits of Karna reflect further lost Sūrya myths is less clear, but in his dual maternity there may lurk (under the typical Raglan type of hero legend) a hint of the joint motherhood of Sūrya by Night and Dawn (see chap. 4). Karna's epic character traits include stubbornness, boastfulness, and above all a boundless generosity, in itself a reflection of the sun that shines on the good and evil alike. In one episode, when Indra asks for his golden earrings and breastplate as alms, he unhesitatingly tears off these live parts of his anatomy and hands over the bloody specimens, thereby robbing himself of vital battlefield protection against Arjuna. Such matter may well be mythic reminiscence rather than epic invention.

In the explicit divine "paternity cases" or outright incarnations considered so far the Vedic Ādityas are notably absent (except for Dharma as reflecting Mitra), no doubt as a result of the swift decline of these abstractions in post-Vedic theology and tradition (Varuna had become a sea-god of little account). But it is still possible to discern transpositions, without the benefit of name tags. Thus Pāndu reflects Varuna by his punitive inflictions, his remote-control government, his pallor, and his impotence (compare Varuna's vindictiveness, far-off cosmic abstractness, and ritual allusions to pallor and impotence alike, the latter probably afflictions symbolic of a shamanistic magician figure).

Pāndu is succeeded by the "Law King" Yudhisthira, even as in other chronicle-epics to be studied later (e.g., Roman, Russian) the peacemaker (Numa, Oleg) follows upon the turbulent Magic Sovereign (Romulus, Rurik); thus in epicization the Varuna-Mitra pair is projected onto a diachronic dynastic plane.

Vidura, that specialist in interpersonal relations whom Bh sma consults early on about his brothers' marriages, who tries long and hard to mediate the quarrels of the cousins and to avert war, and who serves as a kind of minister of social harmony in Yudhisthira's postwar government, is an equally evident epic projection of Aryaman, the personification of Aryan family solidarity. When he finally fuses himself into Yudhisthira, piece by piece, this Yogic miracle is a mystic affirmation of an old truth of Vedic and pre-Vedic theology: Aryaman was a "satellite," a spin-off of Mitra, a "minor" Āditya hypostasized from the "major" one, and what was spun off can in the fullness of time be spun back into the Whole. Vidura is said to be an incarnation of Dharma;[2] since Dharma as a new abstraction (and father of Yudhisthira) replaced Mitra and his "satellites," this identification of Uncle Vidura is merely old wine in a new bottle.

Symmetry (Vidura: Aryaman as Dhrtarāstra: x) would now indicate an identification of Dhrtarāstra with the "minor" Āditya Bhaga, and the data bear this out. Bhaga the Vedic "Apportioner" is reflected in the preconflict and postwar role of Dhrtarāstra when he serves as a sort of chief disburser of handouts and honoraria under Pāndu and Yudhisthira respectively. In para- and post-Vedic tradition, however, Bhaga was something more sinister than the divine paymaster of the Vedas; he was blind, thus Blind Fortune, the personification of inexorable fate and random chance alike, either evil, indifferent, or too weak to act. This aspect of Bhaga's theology is reflected in Dhrtarāstra's demeanor in crisis, when he pathetically vacillates between wrong and right, summons up an occasional modicum of willpower, but for the most part lets Duryodhana have his way and laments the tyranny of fate. This concept also paves the way for his rehabilitation after the debacle of Kuruksetra and his reconciliation with the P ndavas, since in the last analysis it is futile to thwart the workings of Fate, incarnate or otherwise.

We saw above that Bhīsma incarnates Dyaus, that Vedic *deus otiosus* who has a barely ancestral role but behind whom lurks the important Indo-European figure of the sky-god (see chap. 4). The strange story of Bhīsma—birth from a great water deity, primordial avuncular role through three generations as procreation manager, guardian, and counselor rather than king or father, curious detachment in the great battle, despite being enemy commander, to the point of disclosing to Yudhisthira the means of killing him, voluntarily suspended death for observation and disclosure—all this bespeaks mythic matter presumably original to a para-

and pre-Vedic Dyaus who had not yet been stripped of his mythical patrimony in the Rig-Vedic manner. The mythologems involved are in fact of Indo-European age, judging from their Germanic parallels involving the Norse god Heimdalr (see chap. 11). Thus the *Mahābhārata*'s epic matter can in given instances bypass the silence of the Vedas and tie in directly with other Indo-European mythic traditions.

The central plot of the *Mahābhārata* also has clear implications that transcend dynastic squabbles of early kingdoms. The enmity between the essentially noble Pāndavas and their demonically infused Kaurava cousins has features of Vaisnava-Śaiva sectarian strife, epitomized in the last-resort magical showdown between Krsna and Aśvatthāman as Visnu and Śiva incarnate in book 10, where they contend over the future embryos, and thus the very perpetuation, of the Pāndava line. One is the preemptive Destroyer, the other emerges as the Savior who shall reanimate Arjuna's stillborn grandson Parīksit. Aśvatth man bears the marks of the classical Śiva, while Krsna, for all his Vaisnava trappings, is older and more basic than merely the latest avatar of Visnu: in the services he renders Indra's son Arjuna as the latter's charioteer there are echoes of the *Indrā-Visnū* duality of the *Rig-Veda,* where the wide-striding Visnu is the helpmate of Indra (see chap. 4). On a synchronic level, however, it is safe to say that the central plot is an epic transposition of he classical doctrine of the *yugas* or world ages, and especially of the eschatological turning point of their nadir, the *Kāliyuga,* whose horrors cry out for cyclical annihilation and regeneration. But since, as we saw, various main actors (especially the Pāndavas, Krsna, and Bhīsma) have clear preclassical mythical pedigrees, it is plausible to search for earlier roots of the showdown as well.

Vedic tradition is silent on eschatology. But there is good reason to push beyond India by the para-Vedic route and to view the climactic battle of Kuruksetra as a transposition of an Indo-European myth of the final confrontation of the gods and their evil counterparts, an epicized equivalent of what appears in full cataclysmic authenticity elsewhere, in the Old Iranian one-to-one end struggle between divine and demonic entities, when the world is purified and transfigured in molten metal (see chap. 6), and in the Old Norse world-end story of Ragnarök (chap. 11). The latter resembles the *Mahābhārata* in protagonists, plot, and outcome. It is significant that two crucial divine actors of the Ragnarök-drama, Vīðarr and Heimdalr, were singled out above as the specific comparands of the Vedic Visnu (incarnated as the Epic Krsna) on the one hand (see chap. 4) and of the Epic Bhīsma (as reflecting the para-and pre-Vedic Dyaus) on the other.

The structured similarities between the *Mabābhārata* and Old Norse traditions extend even further, involving the story of the battle of Brāvellir as told in Icelandic sagas and especially in books 7 and 8 of Saxo's *Gesta Danorum.* The accordances intimate not merely that mythical battle material was capable of separate epicizations in India and Scandinavia (while also surviving as world-end myth in Iran and Iceland), but that saga-epics had existed already in Indo-European times, complete with genealogical and action-related patterns, prehistoric common denominators handed down independently via Indo-Iranian and Germanic traditions. Of this kind are the warrior legends relating to Jarāsamdha + Śiśup la (*Mahābhārata,* book 2, mentioned above), compared with the saga of Starkaðr in Saxo and Icelandic sources (see chap. 13). Such also are the complex, parallel three-generational tangles that precede and include the battles of Brāvellir (Swedish Bråvalla, allegedly fought between Swedes and Danes ca. 700 C.E.) and of Kuruksetra:

Gesta Danorum: Drot was the mother of Hildiger by Gunnar and of the bastard Haldan by Borkar. Hildiger died. The princess Gurith had to perpetuate the Danish dynasty. She first rejected the ugly Haldan with his chronic ulcerated facial sore, but ultimately she married him. They had a son Harald.

Mahābhārata: Satyavat was the mother of (Citrāngada and) Vicitravīrya by Śamtanu, having earlier given birth to the bastard Vyāsa, fathered by Parāśara. Vicitravīrya (like his brother) died. His two widows had to perpetuate the Kaurava dynasty. They were aghast at their hirsute and ugly partner Vyāsa but submitted to the insemination. Each bore a son, Dhrtarāstra and Pāndu.

Gesta Danorum: Harald rebuilt Danish might, but in blind old age he had the great showdown of Bråvalla against his nephew (sister's son) Ring of Sweden. Great marshaling of forces and allies. Cataclysmic, apocalyptic battle description ("one might have thought that the whole of creation was in turmoil and had returned to ancient chaos . . ."). On the Danish side the great Frisian champion Ubbi was riddled with 144 arrows. Harald's retainer Bruni (Odin in mortal disguise) forsook him, swung the battle luck to Ring, and clubbed Harald to death with his own mace.

Mahābhārata: Pāndu conquered widely but died, leaving blind old Dhrtar stra to a great conflict with his nephews the Pāndavas. Monstrous levies and battle sequences even beyond the call of martial hyperbole. On the Kaurava side, the great champion Bhīsma was cut down and left suspended by a shower of arrows.

Battle luck deserted Dhrtarāstra (himself the helpless embodiment of blind fate), and his two principal sons were clubbed down by the mace-wielding Bhīma, son of the god Vāyu.

Apart from a palpable Indic tendency to duplicate and proliferate characters, as opposed to the spareness of the Scandinavian framework, and various nonessential details, the only significant difference in the two accounts relates to the role of Odin at the end. This trait is anchored in Germanic martial theology, where Odin was the fickle and underhanded dispenser of war, as opposed to the more fatalistic "luck would have it" approach of the *Mahābhārata.* It thus seems that the ultimate sources of Indic epic take us back to rarefied, prehistoric Indo-European levels, where plots capable of independent survival were current as early as the fourth millennium B.C.E.

Tracing the descent of the *Mahābhārata* to an Indo-European past may seem somewhat like tracking the course of the river Ganges back to the heavens. But nothing is too fanciful in India, and the Ganges legend actually gets told in book 1 of the *Rāmāyana.* Compared with the mind-boggling scope of the *Mahābhārata,* the *Rāmāyana* is far more compact and cohesive, a mere 24,000 lokas in seven books, attributed to the sage Vālmīki. Its somewhat more easterly locale (the Iksvāku tribe living in Kośala with its capital Ayodhy east and north of the Ganges, and Videha even farther east) and "international" ramifications stretching down to Ceylon do not preclude rough contemporaneity with the *Mahābhārata,* and as a self-contained entity it may have been rounded out earlier; as I said above, the agglomerated *Vanaparvan* (book 3) of the *Mahābhārata* actually incorporates a summary, rather divergent Rāma epic. At least the nucleus comprising books 2-6 of the *Rāmāyana* constitutes an ancient unit by itself, while the first and last books are somewhat awkward pre- and postfixes that stamp the work in the Vaisnava mold and launch Rāma on his subsequent career as an important avatar of Visnu. While there is, as we have seen, some evidence that Krsna's identification with Visnu is anchored in theology of the Vedic period and that he may hence have been an epic avatar of Visnu before waxing great under the new theology, there is none for Rāma. His mythical background before "Visnuization" was different. The name itself is commonplace: just like the frequent *Krsná-* (cf., e.g., Krsna Dvaipāyana, the real name of Vyāsa the Compiler), *Rāmá-* meant 'Black' and was the name of various heroes (we met above Paraśurāma, Visnu's avatar before Rāma, and Krsna's brother Bala-rāma), though perhaps equated with the adjective *rāma-* 'pleasing, charming' in folk-etymological association.

The beginnings of the *Rāmāyana* are expectably laced with Visnuite legendry, such as the tale, known also from various Purānic sources, of how Visnu in his earlier dwarf avatar tricked a demon who had taken over the universe into allowing him a mere three steps and then instantly reinflated himself to retake the "three worlds" by his famous three strides. The cast of preliminary characters includes those two awesome ascetics mentioned earlier, Vasistha and Viśvāmitra; we are treated first to the story of their early conflict, also told repeatedly in the *Mahābhārata,* how King Viśvāmitra offended Vasistha by trying to rob him of his wonder cow, and how by mighty millennial austerities he ultimately won promotion to brahmindom and made his peace with Vasistha. Vasistha's eugenic ministrations relieve the barrenness of King Daśaratha's three wives Kaikeyī, Kausalyā, and Sumitrā, so that the sons Bharata, Rāma, and Laksmana + Śatrughna are born respectively. Rāma and Laksmana quickly hit it off, and they are entrusted by the king to Viśvāmitra, at whose hermitage Rāma first wins his spurs in demon slaying and is invested by the sage with hereditary weapons that go back to a legendary Krśāśva 'Lean Horse' (son-in-law of the creator figure Prajāpati), obscure but significant as the validator of the Indo-Iranian origin of the important Old Iranian hero Krsāspa. . . . Under Viśvāmitra's tutelage Rāma attends the *svayamvara* of the Videha princess *Sītā* 'Furrow', who had been born to King Janaka from the earth in the wake of his plow, and wins her in a bow-stringing contest (shades of Arjuna and Draupadī). Back home Rāma is designated heir apparent, only to see his hopes dashed on the eve of his consecration as a result of harem intrigue, when conqueen Kaikeyī retires to the "anger chamber" and by her sulking forces weak old Daśaratha to cancel the ceremony. On the basis of some old promise, Kaikeyī's son Bharata is to succeed instead, and Rāma gets fourteen years of exile (a baker's dozen compared with the P ndavas' twelve or thirteen). Ever the perfect Boy Scout, Rāma says "Yes, Father" and starts packing. Accompanied by Sītā and Laksmana, he moves to the demon-infested Dandaka forest, while back home Daśaratha grieves and dies, and Bharata, nobly refusing the succession but unable to induce Rāma's premature return from exile, places Rāma's shoes on the empty throne and rules as regent in his brother's name.

Back in the forest Rāma gears up for some serious demon hunting, after assembling an arsenal from Indra on the advice of Agastya, the great austere digestion champion chronicled in the *Vanaparvan.* His mass exterminations, and finally the indignities visited on a demoness named Śūrpanakhá, at length attract the attention of the latter's brother Rāvana, the powerful archdemon of Lankā whose lecherous character sees possibilities in an abduction of Sītā. Rāvana devises and executes a scheme to draw Rāma and Laksmana away from the hermitage, gain access to Sītā in confidence-inspiring disguise, and spirit her off to Lankā in his airborne conveyance. The grieving Rāma now concludes a pact of assistance with the monkey-king

Sugrīva and helps him vanquish his usurper-brother Vālin by shooting Vālin in the back. Sugrīva's henchman Hanuman carries out aerial surveillance of Lankā, and in the course of much extravagant folkloristic derring-do even manages a clandestine interview with Sītā. Bounding back to the mainland he briefs Rāma, who resolves to build a causeway to the island and attack Rāvana head-on. There follows an extended free-for-all, less majestic than the ponderous goings-on at Kuruksetra but even more bathed in the magic aura of martial fairy tales. In the finish Rāma kills Rāvana at the end of a twenty-four-hour duel and recovers Sītā. Instead of a happy reunion, however, the priggish paragon finds her stained by her demonic surroundings, questions her fidelity, and pompously rejects her; such selfish cruelty resembles the treatment that Śakuntalā, the mother of Bharata, suffered at the hands of Duhsanta in book 1 of the *Mahābhārata.* The heartbroken Sītā, solemnly proclaiming her fidelity by an "act of truth," is vindicated by a fire ordeal; Agni himself certifies she is untainted, and the gods hail Rāma as Visnu incarnate who has delivered them from Rāvana. Rāma takes Sītā back, they pilot Rāvana's airship to Ayodhyā, and Rāma is consecrated by Vasistha and reigns happily ever after.

Or almost. The final, tacked-on book 7 indulges in assorted flashbacks and irrelevancies involving Rāvana and also spins on about Rāma and Sītā. Sītā has become pregnant, Rāma's pathological suspicions return, and he dismisses her once more. In a kind of frame story she bears twins at the hermitage of Vālmīki, who teaches the boys the *Rāmāyana,* which they subsequently recite at a public ceremony. Rāma learns their identity and is about to put Sītā through a second public ordeal, when by another desperate "act of truth" she induces the ground to part and disappears in the arms of her mother the earth-goddess. (The Furrow returns to the soil!) Rāma, too, winds up his earthly career and reverts to the godhead of the all-encompassing Visnu.

The self-righteous, humorless Rāma in all his virtue and purity resembles not a little the *pius Aeneas* of another clime and epic. The *Rāmāyana* has made a great literary and artistic fortune in and beyond India, with innumerable spin-offs in the arts throughout Southeast Asia. It combines to perfection outlandish exotic appeal with the homely satisfaction of seeing the dragon get his due from an upright and noble paragon.

But what does it mean to the mythologist? I said above that the Vaisnava trappings are a secondary gloss. A historicist would see in Rāma, as in Krsna, another quasi-real tribal hero encrusted with legend. In fact, however, the personalities and the story of the *Rāmāyana* are closely analogous to the Vedic myths of Indra. Rāma's closeness to Indra is even superficially palpable, for example, in Indra's magic weapons that Rāma stockpiles and in the war chariot he gets from Indra at a crucial juncture of the duel with Rāvana. Rāma's underhanded, behind-the-back slaying of Vālin and his killing of Rāvana are reminiscent of Indra's sneaky assault on Namuci and his murder of Triśiras. In Rāma's unchivalrous treatment of Śūrpanakh and in his disgraceful repudiation of Sītā there are echoes of sexual villainy as well, thus completing the triple-sinner pattern. Hardly coincidentally, at Sītā's *svayamvara* Rāma stumbles over a rock that turns out to be Ahalyā, whom her husband Gautama had thus petrified for her adultery with Indra, and whom Rāma's kick liberates (see chap. 4). Rāma seems to be a folk version of Indra in a post-Vedic, agricultural milieu, unlike the patron of the Vedic pastoralists. Sītā appears in the *Rig-Veda* as the deified Furrow, and in later Vedic texts she is the genius of the plowed field, wife of Indra or Parjanya. Rāvana matches Vrtra or Triśiras (Rāma actually kills a three-headed Triśiras in the poem), and significantly his son is called Indraśatru 'Indra Challenger', which is also an epithet of Vrtra. Rāvana's abduction and confinement of Sītā the Furrow are agriculturalist analogues to Vrtra's and the Panis' rustling and sequestering of cattle. The high-flying and far-bounding Hanuman is called Māruti, being the son of the wind-god, an ally of Indra. Even as in the *Rig-Veda* Indra's emissary Saram crosses the river Rasā to track down the hoard of the Panis, Hanuman crosses the sea to Lankā to find Sītā.' All together, it appears that the prosopographic and topical models of the *Rāmāyana* are transmuted replications of Vedic Indra myths, and that its primary relevance to Vedic and by extension Indo-Iranian mythology is hence without question.

As we have seen, post-Vedic India, particularly in its epic dimension, is just as crucial for comparative mythology as is the chronologically earlier and more archaic Vedic period. Vedic data provide the oldest theology, but the epics supply the narrative. The unique significance of Old India for comparative mythology lies in the triple preservation of myth, ritual, and saga as much as in its anchor position at one end of the Indo-European continuum. . . .

Notes

[1] According to the *Mārkandeya-Purāna* (chap. 5) Indra lost his *tejas* 'sheen' for killing Triśiras, his *bala* 'strength' for treacherously slaying Vrtra, and his *rūpa* 'looks' for impersonating Gautama in his seduction of Ahalyā. This triple set of transfunctional boons resembles such brahmin-inspired stock lists for the three varnas as *dharma* 'law', *kāma* 'love', *artha* 'wealth', or *sattvam* 'truth', *rajas* 'passion', *tamas* 'dullness'.

[2] The story parallels Vasistha's curse on Dyaus to take mortal shape as Bhīsma. The great ascetic Māndavya, framed by criminals and unable to defend himself because of his vow of silence, was impaled by royal authority but stayed alive by might of austerity. Freed at length by the impressed king, he hied to Dharma and asked what karma or past act had caused his suffering. Informed that as a child he had stuck stalks up the rectums of locusts and in retribution had now himself suffered impalement by the anus, the outraged holy man cursed Dharma to a half-breed incarnation and legislated religious immunity from karma for childish misbehavior.

FURTHER READING

Clark, R. T. Rundle. *Myth and Symbol in Ancient Egypt.* London: Thames & Hudson, 1959, 292 p.
   Surveys the major themes and figures of Egyptian mythology.

Cooper, W. R. *An Archaic Dictionary: Biographical, Historical, and Mythological.* London: Samuel Bagster and Sons, 1876, 295 p.
   An index of names from a wide range of cultural tradition; includes not only mythological heroes, gods, and creatures, but geographical and historical references.

Fergusson, James. *Tree and Serpent Worship: Illustrations of Mythology and Art in India in the First and Fourth Centuries after Christ.* Delhi: Oriental Publishers, 1971, 247 p.
   Presents and discusses the significance and scope of tree and serpent worship in ancient India.

Griffiths, J. Gwyn. *The Conflict of Horus and Seth from Egyptian and Classical Sources.* Liverpool: Liverpool University Press, 1960, 182 p.
   Studies the primal conflict between Horus and Seth in Egyptian mythology and chronicles the portrayal of this conflict in ancient and medieval European scholarship.

Kirk, G. S. *Myth: Its Meaning and Functions in Ancient and Other Cultures.* Berkeley and Los Angeles: University of California Press, 1970, 299 p.
   Traces the relationship between myth and the larger cultural contexts of history, ritual and social institutions, particularly in ancient Near Eastern civilizations.

Kramer, Samuel Noah. *Sumerian Mythology: A Study of Spiritual and Literary Achievement in the Third Millenium B.C.* rev. ed. Westport, Conn.: Greenwood Press, 1972, 130 p.
   Reviews the primary myths of Sumerian culture, with particular focus on origin myths.

Piatigorsky, Alexander. *Mythological Deliberations: Lectures on the Phenomenology of Myth.* London: University of London Press, 1993, 218 p.
   Investigates the relation between myth and philosophy,

and the significance of myth as a component of cultural heritage.

Poolthupya, Srisurang. "Thai Customs and Social Values in the *Ramakien.*" In *Nation and Mythology*, edited by Wolfram Eberhard, Krzystof Gawlikowski, and Carl-Albrecht Seyschab, pp. 97-119. Bremen, West Germany: Simon & Magiera Publishers, 1983.

Contrasts the norms and values expressed in the eighteenth-century Thai epic *Ramakien* with those of the ancient Indian *Ramayana*.

Wilson, J. V. Kinnier. "Stories of the Heroic Age," pp. 77-91. In *The Rebel Lands: An Investigation into the Origins of Early Mesopotamian Mythology.* Cam-bridge University Press, 1979.

Investigates the historical grounding of the Gilgmesh and Lugalbanda narratives from Sumerian mythology and explains the importance of natural phenomena in these myths.

Greek Mythology

INTRODUCTION

Greek mythology has been variously interpreted and analyzed almost since its beginnings, and its origins have been as widely debated as the myths themselves have been interpreted. The difficulty in identifying the origins of Greek myths stems from the fact that, until the time of the Greek poets Hesiod and Homer (both of whom flourished around the eighth century B.C.), the transmission of myths was primarily an oral affair. Hesiod's *Theogony* and *Works and Days,* in addition to Homer's *Iliad* and *Odyssey,* are the oldest extant written sources of Greek mythology, and most scholars agree that certain mythological elements in each can be dated to a much earlier period. Many scholars also concede that certain elements of these works have definite Near Eastern parallels, but the extent to which such parallels indicate that Near Eastern myths served as a source for Greek myths remains an issue of critical debate. In addition to studying the age and origins of Greek mythology, modern scholars have also examined such topics as the relationship between myth and history, the themes and motifs of Greek myths, and the treatment of women in Greek mythology.

In searching for the origins of Greek mythology, Martin P. Nilsson first makes a distinction between the myths dealing with heroes and those concerned with divinity and cosmogony, stressing that it is erroneous to assume that "the hero myths were derived from the same source as the myths concerning the gods." Nilsson contends that while divinity myths may indeed have "pre-Greek" origins, the heroic myth cycles as found in Greek epics can be dated back to the epoch known as the Mycenaean Age (1950 to 1100 B.C.) in Greece. Such critics as Richard Caldwell and Robert Mondi are more concerned with the Near Eastern origins of Greek creation myths. Mondi examines this issue by focussing not on the textual transmission of myths, but on the diffusion of "mythic ideas" or motifs. Such ideas include the "cosmic separation of earth and sky," the hierarchical organization of the cosmos, and the "cosmic struggle" by which divine kingship is attained. Mondi concludes by stating that elements in Greek myths are "derived from contact with the considerably more advanced cultures to the East and South."

The analysis of the historical aspects of mythology, specifically the heroic myths, is another way mythology is studied. H. J. Rose begins his study of mythology by noting that "it is very clear that we cannot take [myths], as they stand, as historically true, or even as slightly idealized or exaggerated history." Rose then goes on to review (and invalidate) other approaches to mythology, including attempts to view myths allegorically, rationally, and "euhemeristically" (euhemerism being a school of thought in which mythical gods are viewed as deified human men). Carlo Brillante, on the other hand, examines the ways the ancient Greeks viewed mythology, and argues that mythical heroes were regarded as historical figures by the Greeks. Brillante contends that the Greeks distinguished heroic myths as being situated in "a well-defined past," as a part of the human world, and as separate from those myths which focus on the "age of the gods." He then considers whether an historical approach, similar to that taken by the ancient Greeks, is "adequate" today, and outlines the drawbacks and benefits of various types of historical analyses.

G. S. Kirk breaks down the traditional groupings of gods and heroes sketched by earlier critics even further. For Kirk, divinity myths include those that deal with the creation of the universe (cosmogony); with the development of the Olympian gods; and with the creation of men, man's place in the world, and his relationship with the gods. Kirk divides hero myths into three categories as well: those that deal with older heroes (in myths set in a "timeless past," long before the Trojan War); with younger heroes (in myths set in a time close to or during the Trojan War); and later "inventions" based on "definitely historical figures." In his study of the divinity myths, Richard Buxton identifies several characteristics of Greek gods as well as the prevalent themes of these types of myths. Buxton notes that Greek gods appear as neither good nor evil, but simply as powerful, and that conflict arises between gods and mortals when imbalances of power occur or when mortals overstep their boundaries. The most common themes of these myths include violence, deception, negotiation, reciprocity, and honor. Edward F. Edinger takes another approach in his analysis of the cosmogonical myths; he examines them from a psychological standpoint, noting what the myths appear to demonstrate about the nature of the conscious and unconscious mind. Edinger argues that in these myths, whenever a being is brought from an unconscious state into a conscious one, a split into opposites occurs, and that conflict invariably results; unity is only present in the unconscious state.

In analyzing the hero myths, Kirk details the exploits of some of the more prominent Greek heroes, including Perseus, Theseus, Oedipus, and Odysseus. He notes that many elements in these myths were added on to older motifs over time. Some of the common folktale motifs Kirk identifies, for example, in the Perseus myths, include: escaping danger as a baby, defending one's mother against a seducer, a quest that is meant to be fatal but is not, magical devices used during the quest, the rescuing of a princess, and the accidental killing of a relative. Kirk uses various motifs to attempt to date some elements in these myths, contending that the hero myths demonstrate greater narrative complexity than divinity myths. While the heroic figures Kirk studies are all male, Deborah Lyons argues for the recognition of female heroes, such as Helen, Semele, and Iphigeneia, demonstrating how these meet the typical criteria established for male heroes. Additionally, Lyons cites a number of sources from which evidence of mythical heroines and cults of heroines may be deduced.

Just as Lyons asserts the case for the acknowledgment and study of heroines, Charlene Spretnak champions the cause of early Greek goddesses. Spretnak argues that prior to the establishment of the patriarchal Olympic mythological tradition, which developed after early Greece was invaded by the Ionians, the Achaeans, and later by the Dorians, who took up residence from about 2500 to 1000 B.C., there existed an oral tradition "firmly rooted" in "Goddess worship." The goddesses of these matriarchal pre-Hellenic myths were both powerful and compassionate, but Spretnak notes that when they were incorporated into the Olympian myths, they were transformed into jealous, disagreeable, sexual objects. Robert Emmet Meagher also examines how early myths depicting women as birth goddesses and creators were subverted by the later mythological system and by the poet Hesiod into beings created by male gods for the purpose of bringing misery and death to human males as a punishment. In a different approach to the role of women in Greek mythology, C. Kerényi studies the nature of the Kore, or maiden goddess, in Greek myth. Kerényi discusses both the subjugation of the maiden goddess, as in the rape of Persephone, and the power of the bond between mother and daughter, as demonstrated by Demeter's descent into the Underworld to recover her daughter, Persephone.

The scholars who study Greek mythology appear to agree on little with regard to the origin and early developments of myth, except perhaps that parallels between Greek myths and Near Eastern myths exist. As far as interpretation goes, clearly no one can say with any confidence what a given myth "means." Rather, scholars can only suggest ways to approach myth, suggesting that it be analyzed allegorically, historically, or psychologically, for example. Whatever their approach, scholars and students alike continue to find in these ancient tales an endless source of inspiration, analysis, and discussion.

OVERVIEWS

H. J. Rose (essay date 1928)

SOURCE: Introduction to *A Handbook of Greek Mythology*, Methuen & Co. Ltd., 1928, pp. 1-16.

[*In the following essay, Rose reviews the various approaches that have been taken to interpret Greek mythology. He also distinguishes between several types of myth, including "myth proper," saga, and* märchen *(folktales).*]

We use the word mythology to signify the study of certain products of the imagination of a people, which take the form of tales. These tales the Greeks called [mythoi], or myths, an expression which originally meant simply 'words'. The purpose of this book is to set forth what stories were produced by the active imagination of those peoples whom we collectively know as Greek, and by the narrow and sluggish imagination of the ancient inhabitants of Italy. It is well to begin by inquiring what manner of tales they were; for it is very clear that we cannot take them, as they stand, as historically true, or even as slightly idealized or exaggerated history. Full as they are of impossible events, it needs no argument to prove that they differ widely from Thucydides' account of the Peloponnesian War, or Hippokrates' discussions of the effect of diet on a patient. We may disbelieve some of Thucydides' statements, and we have come to consider many of Hippokrates' methods erroneous; but obviously both are trying to state facts and draw reasonable conclusions therefrom. What are we to say of the tellers of these quite unbelievable, although picturesque, legends, and of those who heard and more or less credited them? It is here that opinions differ most widely, and have differed in the past.[1]

I. *The Allegorical Theory.* One of the most ancient explanations is that these tales of wonder are allegories, concealing some deep and edifying meaning, which the wisdom of primeval sages prompted them to hide in this manner, either to prevent great truths passing into the hands of persons too ignorant or too impious to use them aright, or to attract by stories those who would not listen to a dry and formal discussion. As an example, I will cite the interpretation given of a well-known myth, the Judgment of Paris, by the so-called Sallustius.[2] As he tells the story, the gods were at a banquet, when Eris (Strife, Emulation) cast among them a golden apple, inscribed 'For the Fairest'. Three goddesses, Hera, Athena and Aphrodite, having all claimed it, the decision was referred by Zeus to Paris, son of Priam of Troy. Aphrodite having bribed him with the promise of the loveliest of mortal women as his wife, he decided in her favour. 'Here,' says our author, 'the banquet signifies the supramundane powers of the gods, and that is why they are together; the golden apple signifies the universe, which, as it is made of opposites, is rightly said to be thrown by Strife, and as the various gods give various gifts to the universe they are thought to vie with one another for the possession of the apple; further, the soul that lives in accordance with sense-perception (for that is Paris), seeing beauty alone and not the other powers in the universe, says that the apple is Aphrodite's.'

It needs no great amount of argument to show that such a view as this is wrong. It assumes that these early Greeks among whom the story of Paris originated possessed a systematic philosophy concerning the powers, both visible and invisible, of the universe, and also the moral duties of man. Now we know enough of their early history to be able to say that neither they nor any other people in a similar stage of development ever had any such philosophy, which is the product of ages of civilized thought. Had any system of the kind existed in the days before Homer, we may be very certain that the long series of brilliant intellects to whom the organized thought of Greece, and ultimately of modern Europe, is due, would not have had to begin at the very beginning and discover for themselves the elements of physics, of ethics, and of logic. The myth cannot be an allegory, because its originators had little or nothing to allegorize.

Still, we can see how the idea originated. In the first place, the Greeks, like most peoples, had great respect for their ancestors, and were apt to credit them with much that later generations had produced. Hence came a tendency to try to find deep wisdom in anything they were reported to have said or done. Secondly, allegory is really very old in Greece; we shall find examples in Homer and Hesiod, for instance.[3] Moreover, one of the oldest forms of religious composition, the metrical answers given at oracular shrines, affected a dark and allegorical language. Hence it is no wonder that this theory, although false, gained popularity, was widely used by orthodox pagans to explain away certain features in the stories told of their gods and heroes which seemed inconsistent with a divine or exalted nature, and was in turn eagerly adopted by Jewish and Christian commentators to read sublime meanings into puzzling passages of the Old Testament.

2. *The Symbolic Theory.* After lasting in various forms through the Middle Ages, this view appeared in a modified form as late as the nineteenth century. Friedrich Creuzer (1771-1858), in a very learned but very cloudy and uncritical work,[4] set forth a theory which may be interpreted as follows. The ancestors of the ancient nations whose history we know,—Egyptians, Indians, Greeks, Romans and others,—possessed, not indeed a complete philosophy, but a dim and at the same time grandiose conception of certain fundamen-

tal religious truths, and in particular of monotheism. These truths their priests set forth in a series of symbols, which remained much the same for all peoples, but were hopelessly misunderstood in later times. To recover the oldest ideas, according to him, we shall do well to take those myths which seem absurdest, and try to interpret them. For myths are not the result of the artistic activity of poets, but something far older. One specimen of his methods will be enough.[5] Thus, it is stated that Talos' name meant 'sun' in Cretan. His legend, says Creuzer, signifies that the Cretans set forth the beneficent powers of the sunlight under the form of a divine guardian of their island; they also, like the Phoenicians with their Moloch, symbolized his destructive power, perhaps by a human sacrifice by burning; but also they gave a moral aspect to his nature, for is it not stated that Talos was in reality a man, who went about with bronze tablets containing the laws of Minos, whose observance he enforced?

All this is very ingenious, but falls to pieces at a touch of criticism. To begin with, there is the old difficulty which beset the allegorical theory in its cruder form; we have no right to suppose either that the early Cretans had an elaborate solar philosophy or that, if they had had one, they would have expressed it in allegories. Moreover, his account of Talos is a mere jumble, made up of tags from various late or lateish authors, which Creuzer has put together into a composite picture of what never existed in the Cretan imagination or any other, save his own. He goes on to make the jumble worse by adducing further supposed parallels with which the story of Talos has in reality nothing to do. And if we look at other interpretations of myths scattered up and down his work, or similar works by his followers and predecessors, we shall find many instances of just this uncritical handling of a myth, *i.e.,* this mixture of older and newer forms, combined with absence of any clear recognition of how stories of this sort really do originate.

But for all his absurdities, Creuzer was right on one point. Schiller, to whom he owed much, had said that Art breaks up the white light of Truth into the prismatic colours; and the imagination works in a somewhat similar way, not setting forth facts clearly and sharply, as the reason does, but dealing in pictures. In a sense, myths are symbolic, though not as Creuzer supposed them to be.

Besides this truth which he recognized, and which entitles him to a not dishonourable place in the history of Mythology, there is another and a worse reason why symbolism continues here and there to have a certain popularity, and that is the childish fascination which anything mysterious has for certain minds. A story, or anything else, which is supposed to have a hidden meaning attracts some adults, just as a secret society with pass-words and so forth attracts children;

and so there are to this day half-educated persons who read all manner of extraordinary meanings of their own invention into details of pictures by great artists, obscure passages in such documents as the Book of Daniel, or the measurements of ancient monuments, particularly, for some reason, the Great Pyramid of Gizeh. I have even come across one ingenious theorist who had found abstruse secrets hidden in the letter H and in one or two buildings the ground plan of which suggested that letter.

3. *Rationalism*. There is a type of mind, which also existed in antiquity, which is utterly incapable of realizing how simple people think. To such a mind, certain facts of experience are so self-evident that every one except a fool must always have recognized them. It follows therefore that no one who thought at all can ever have believed, for instance, that a monster half-horse and half-man could exist, or that a woman was turned into a stone or a tree. If therefore stories of this sort are told, they must be the result of misunderstanding or trickery. There have come to us from antiquity several treatises which put this theory into operation, for instance a little work *On incredible tales*[6], which bears the name of Palaiphatos. The author, after proving elaborately that there are no such things as Centaurs, gives the following reconstruction of the legend. When Ixion was King of Thessaly, the country was much plagued by herds of wild cattle. On his offering a reward for their destruction, certain enterprising archers from a village called Nephele went out on horseback and shot them down. Hence arose the tale that Ixion was the father by Nephele (the Cloud) of a race of beings called Kentauroi (prickers of bulls) who were a mixture of man and horse.

One example is enough of this sort of nonsense, which hardly needs to be refuted. It supposes such a state of mind as never existed or will exist in this world. People so blind to facts as to make a tale of wonder out of a commonplace event like the shooting by mounted archers of some wild cattle would have believed easily enough in all sorts of marvels, and freely invented them without any motor to set their imaginations at work. For savages and barbarians (and it is to be remembered that the origins of Greek and other myths go back to barbarism or savagery)[7] have but a small range of experience, and therefore have generally no standard by which to try whether a tale is incredible or not; and even among civilized men there are to be found plenty who will believe almost any wonder if only it is far enough off in space or in time. But even the lowest savages are not as a rule so densely stupid as to misunderstand what is clearly visible to them, or simple statements in their own tongue about things happening to their neighbours; and Palaiphatos supposes the tale of the shape and parentage of the Centaurs to have arisen from a remark that 'the Bull-stickers from Nephele . . . ; the phrase might be taken to

mean "born of the Cloud") are raiding', and the supposedly novel sight of horses with men on their backs. Nevertheless, this feeble and irrational 'rationalism' still persists.

I have seen a children's book containing the story of Dick Whittington, which solemnly stated in its introduction that Whittington really laid the foundation of his fortune by a successful venture in a ship called *The Cat*. Among other things, this explanation neglects the fact that in Whittington's own day the story of the cat was at least two centuries old, for he died in 1423 and the story is to be found in the *Annals* of Albert von Stade, who died in 1264. Who first told it we do not know. Naturally the old story had been attached to the historical Whittington, as such tales often are to a well-known and popular man.

This miserable theory has not even the grain of truth which is to be found in the first two. Such origins of stories as it imagines simply do not exist. The nearest approach to the supposed process is that, as we shall see presently, legendary details are often enough added to historical facts.

4. *Euhemerism*. Somewhat less absurd is the theory called after Euhemeros, a writer who lived not long after Alexander the Great,[8] although it existed in a less systematic form before him. His ideas were couched in the shape of a romance, in which he claimed to have discovered evidence that the gods of popular tradition were simply men deified by those whom they had ruled or benefited. Thus Zeus became an ancient king of Crete, who rebelled against and overthrew his father Kronos, the former king, and similar biographies of the remaining deities were offered. Omitting the absurdities in detail,—for the events in these alleged lives of the gods were arrived at simply by rationalizing the current legends,—we may look for a moment at the kernel of the theory, namely that popular gods are nothing but deified men. Here at least we have a fact alleged as a cause, for there is abundant evidence that some men have been deified, from flattery or gratitude, in Greece and out of it. But to make a dead man into a god, one must believe already in gods of some sort; hence this theory will not do as an explanation of the origin of either religion or mythology. Even in its modified form, that the cult of gods arose from fear of ghosts, a view put forward by Herbert Spencer and others, it is unsatisfactory. However, in a book of this sort we are chiefly concerned to note, first, that it will not explain more than a small fraction of the existing mythical tales; second, that there is an element of truth in it, since no very sharp line of cleavage can be drawn between legends of heroes and myths concerning gods.

In antiquity the theory of Euhemeros had a great vogue. In particular, Christian apologists seized joyfully on a statement coming from pagan sources that the best-known pagan gods were nothing but men, for by that time the sense of historical reality was grown too faint for the absurdities of Euhemeros to be noticed, and apart from this particular development, numerous writers tried to discover in these venerable tales some reminiscence of early history, a proceeding which, however mistaken in its methods, was not irrational in itself.

5. *Theory of Nature-myths.* We may distinguish here an older and simpler form of the theory from a later and more sophisticated one; but they are fundamentally the same, and both alike possess both truth and falsehood. It is admitted on all sides that the gods of Greek religion and of most if not all others are supposed to be able to control the forces of nature. It seems therefore a suggestion at least worth considering that the gods are these natural forces and nothing else, at least originally. Thus Zeus would be the sky, or the celestial phenomena; Hera, the ancients suggested, using an etymology which was hardly more than a bad pun, was the air, *aër;* Aphrodite was the moist principle in nature, Hephaistos the element of fire, and so forth, while in later times there was a decided tendency to make all gods into personifications of the sun⁹. Into these supposed personifications were read, of course, whatever physical theory the interpreter might happen to hold.

Obviously, the idea that gods are personifications cannot stand, for a personification is a kind of allegory, and therefore open to all the objections urged against the allegorical and symbolic theories. When Spenser personifies the virtue of chastity under the lovely figure of Una, or holiness as the Red-Cross Knight, he is merely putting into poetical form what he could have expressed in prose, namely a current theory, derived from Aristotle, of the virtues and vices, and adorning it with the flowers of his inexhaustible fancy. Had no ethical doctrine then existed, the *Faerie Queene* could never have been written; and in like manner, personified physical forces are unthinkable among a people who were not to learn for centuries that any such forces existed.

But it remains possible to suppose the gods, or some of them, to be the result, not of allegorizing known and understood physical forces, but of a sort of imaginative speculation about unknown ones. In this sense we may say, for instance, that a river-god (usually imagined, in Greece, under the form of a bull-headed man) is simply the river itself, the noise of whose waters is naïvely accounted for by envisaging it as a powerful, noisy beast. The early Greeks, we might conjecture, observed the apparent daily motion of the sun and were sharp-witted enough to see that it must move very fast, in order to get over so much ground in a day. They therefore fancied it as a charioteer, since a chariot drawn by swift horses was the fastest mode of locomo-

tion they knew. The difficulty is, that there seems no very cogent reason why they should worship forces thus explained, and especially why, as appears on careful investigation of their religion, they gave so little worship to the most impressive of them, as the sun, the moon, earthquakes, thunder and lightning, and so forth. It is far more consistent with what we can see of their thoughts and what we know of the ideas of peoples still in the myth-making stage or very near it to suppose that they worshipped the gods whom they supposed to control these forces,—Zeus, who lived in the sky, and not the sky or its thunder and lightning; Poseidon, who lived in the sea, and not the actual seawater, and so forth. The problem of how the idea of divine beings really originated is very complex and far from being fully solved as yet; fortunately it is not necessary to solve it in order to discuss the myths concerning them.

The most famous exponent of the doctrine that mythology springs from imaginative treatment of physical forces is in modern times the great Sanskritist F. Max Müller. His theory was briefly this. Primitive man was filled with a vague feeling of awe and reverence, leading to ideas of divinity, to which, in his hesitating and imperfect speech, he tried to give expression. Of course, his effort to voice the ineffable was hopeless from the first, and the words he used were sadly lacking in precision, ambiguous and metaphorical. Thus, trying to find a name for the divine Being whose existence he dimly conjectured, he hit upon the word 'sky' as the least inadequate he could think of; but some at least of those who heard him could not understand his metaphor, and hence imagined that the literal sky was either the abode of God or God Himself.

Müller further imagined that he had come fairly near to this primitive stage of religion by studying the earliest Sanskrit documents, the Vedas, which undoubtedly are of venerable antiquity. Analysing these and comparing them with what he knew of the mythology of other peoples, he believed that he could trace back a number of names, and consequently the legends containing them, to the sort of primeval metaphors which he postulated. In particular, he held that numerous deities, indeed almost all of them, owed their being originally to the metaphorical use of language concerning the sun. Thus to him Athena, born from the head of Zeus, is the sky's daughter, Dawn, whose birth is helped by the young Sun (Hephaistos). She is called virgin, because her light is pure; golden from its colour; Promachos (Champion) because she does battle with the darkness, and so forth.¹⁰

It is not necessary to dwell nowadays on the many weak links in this chain, such as the true character of the Indian literature, which although old is very far from primitive, the badness of many of Max Müller's etymologies, his imperfect knowledge of Greek religion and mythology, and so forth. It is enough to remind ourselves that, firstly, Müller's picture of the primitive theologian is about as unlike that practical person, the savage, as possible; that examination of savage traditions and beliefs indicates that savages are but little impressed by such regular phenomena as sunrise, seldom worship the sun, and have not many legends about it; further, that their tales seem to deal with a very wide variety of subjects, which makes it highly unlikely that the ancestors of the Greeks confined themselves to imaginative and metaphorical talk about the weather; and also that the earliest and most primitive languages we know have a large vocabulary but are extremely poor in general terms capable of a confusing variety of senses, which makes it unlikely that the 'disease of language', as it has been unkindly called, postulated by Müller, was ever a reality. In particular, the more we study the different Wiro languages[11], the more evident it becomes, firstly, that the peoples who speak them have many legends and beliefs which they share with their non-Wiro neighbours, and secondly, that the number of traditions provably common to all Wiros is very small; so that even if Müller's theories were proved up to the hilt for India, they would throw but little light on the state of things in early Greece. Incidentally, it seems now to be recognized by the best students of the subject that the supposed preponderance of sun-myths in the Vedic literature is the result rather of the theories of later commentators than of the true nature of the legends themselves.[12]

6. *Modern methods.* The failure of so many theories may well make us hesitate before adopting another; and indeed, the best modern mythologists are as a rule none too eager to put forward a complete theory of the origin and primary meaning of any myth. There are, however, four things which we may do:

(*a*) We begin by carefully examining the source of the tale, and determining its date. This is not so easy as it sounds, for it is not enough to discover, for example, that one form of a story is found in Sophokles and another in Plutarch. We must find out, if we can, where Sophokles and Plutarch got the story, and it may turn out that the earlier writer invented a good deal of what he says, while the later one drew upon some very early source now lost. The first modern writer to lay emphasis, consistently and thoroughly, on this point was the most notable of the opponents of Creuzer, C. A. Lobeck (1781-1860; principal work, *Aglaophamus,* 1829).

(*b*) We may now try to determine, if we can, to what section of the very mixed population of Greece the story is due, *i.e.,* whether it is Achaian, Dorian, Ionian, or belongs to some other Greek people, or whether it is pre-Greek, or a later importation from Asia or Thrace. A great pioneer in this work was K. O. Müller (1797-1840).

(*c*) Next we may ask to what class the legend in question belongs, *i.e.,* whether it is myth proper, saga, or *märchen.* This, as will be explained presently, may throw light on its ultimate origin. The distinction cannot be attributed to any one researcher, but its existence has become recognized largely through the work of the folklorists and investigators of medieval European and other non-classical legends during the nineteenth century, prominent among whom were the indefatigable brothers, Jakob and Wilhelm Grimm (1785-1863 and 1786-1859).

(*d*) Lastly, when we have constructed a theory of the origin and continuance of a story, we shall do well to compare it with those tales which we can study in an early and undeveloped form,—the legends of savages and, to a less degree, of peasants. In a word, we may apply the Comparative Method, but with due caution, for nothing is more misleading than a false but plausible analogy. That this method is now part of the equipment of most scholars is due above all (if we leave out of account men still living) to one of the most learned and honest researchers Germany ever produced, J. W. E. Mannhardt, 1831-80, and one of the most brilliant and versatile of British writers, the late Andrew Lang.

7 *Psychological analysis.* Since legends are the work, not of memory (as historical traditions largely are) or of the reason, but of the imagination, it is obvious that all mythologists must wish well to those who study the imagination, that is, to psychologists. Hence it is interesting to note that the school of psychological thought now most in fashion, that associated with the names of Freud and Jung, devotes considerable attention to myths and tries to explain their genesis. Thus far one can approve; but beyond general approval of endeavour in what may be a fruitful field I for one cannot go. Hitherto, even allowing the truth of the main positions taken up by the psycho-analytic school with regard to the composition of the human mind, I have failed to find in its writings a single explanation of any myth, or any detail of any myth, which seemed even remotely possible or capable of accounting for the development of the story as we have it. I therefore content myself with mentioning their methods, without going into a full account of them.[13]

We may divide legends, in a fashion which by now is almost traditional, into three classes. We have first the myth proper, concerning which a word of explanation is necessary. Man, brought face to face with the world about him, cannot help reacting to his environment in some way. Besides bodily actions, whether practically useful, such as chipping flints, ploughing fields, and making locomotives, or those meant to be practically useful, such as the various operations of magic, he has two mental processes open to him; he may reason about the world and the objects in it, or he may let his imagination play upon them. Speaking very roughly and very broadly, the more civilized he is, the more apt he is either to reason or, if not, at least to realize when he is not reasoning but imagining. Let us take as an example the phenomenon of rain. A man may busy himself collecting rain-water in a cistern or tank: he may construct a rain-gauge and observe the amount of rain that has fallen, and the season of year at which it falls most abundantly, and from these and other observations theorize about the cause of rain. These proceedings we may call applied and pure science respectively. Also, especially if he is a savage, he may work magic intended to make the rain fall abundantly, or to stop altogether. This, being in intention practical, is a sort of bastard sister of applied science. But there is a third set of activities possible. A poet or other artist may let the rain inspire him to production, and so give the world an ode, good or bad, to the rain, a picture such as Turner's *Rain, Steam and Speed,* or a pretty fantasy concerning the refreshment brought to the earth by a shower. But the imagination of the artist has also a half-sister, namely the less controlled but equally lively imagination of the myth-maker. He does not try to reason out the causes of rain, nor is he particularly concerned to make an artistic picture of it; he attempts rather to visualize the whole process, for the imagination of course works in pictures, or, if we like to use a favourite word of psychologists, in symbols. The result of this visualizing may be some such mental picture as of a being, or beings, who pour water out of a reservoir upon the earth. The nature of these beings and of their reservoir will vary enormously, and the myth may be anything from very grotesque and absurd to very beautiful, just as the picture made by the civilized painter might be good or bad; but an imaginative picture of some kind it will certainly be.

But now the myth touches upon science, for it offers a sort of cause for the rain-shower. Asked why it rains, scientist and myth-maker alike can give an answer. The former answers 'Because of such-and-such atmospheric conditions', and can give proofs of his statements, more or less cogent according as he is a better or a worse scientist. The myth-maker can reply, 'Because Zeus is pouring down water out of heaven', 'because Yahweh has opened the windows in the firmament', 'because the angels have poured water into a great tub in the sky which has holes in its bottom'. To any one who has dealt with inquisitive children it must be obvious that in many cases this kind of answer would be satisfactory; it gives *a* reason, and the hearers' minds are not developed enough for them to inquire whether it is *the* reason.

We see therefore that myths, in the proper sense, are a somewhat primitive form of those mental processes which, further developed, give us both art and science. Of the two sides, the more active is what we may term the artistic or imaginative and visualizing process. This

consideration enables us largely to dispose of a question which often arises, namely, Did the myth-makers, in Greece for instance, believe in their myths? The absurdity of this will be evident if we transfer it to a higher sphere and ask, Did Michael Angelo believe in his Moses, or Swinburne in his *Atalanta in Calydon?* No doubt Michael Angelo believed that there had been a man called Moses, who had done the things recorded of him in the Pentateuch; Swinburne doubtless believed that one of the districts of classical Greece was called Kalydon, and probably did not believe that there had ever been a virgin huntress called Atalanta; but these are intellectual processes, and had nothing to do with the statue or the poem. So with the man who first thought of thunder and lightning as caused by Zeus hurling a celestial dart; it probably would be far truer to say that he imagined it than that he either believed or disbelieved it. It is, however, no doubt true that many people accepted his imagination as a sufficient reason for thunder-storms, while others in time grew doubtful, that is, set their reason, as well as their imagination, to work, perceived that there were other possible causes, and found grounds for preferring one or another of them.[14]

We may then define a myth proper as *the result of the working of naïve imagination upon the facts of experience.* As a large proportion of these facts are natural phenomena, it follows that the nature-myth is a common kind; and as the imagination is commonly set going by an object which appears wonderful or puzzling, it follows that a very large proportion indeed of myths is of the kind known as *aetiological,* concerned, that is, with the causes of all manner of things from the apparent movement of the heavenly bodies to the shape of a neighbouring hill or the origin of a local custom. In the last case, the myth often tells what purports to be a history, and this brings us to the next form of legend.

The name *saga* (in origin, simply the Scandinavian word for 'tale, story') is commonly given to those legends which deal with historical events. To take common instances from the modern countryside: if a folk-tale attributes the formation of a peculiarly-shaped hill to the devil, that is myth pure and simple; but if an ancient earthwork is said to have been built by Julius Caesar, that, if not due to some local antiquary, is rather saga, and may contain a germ of historical fact. That is, the earthwork may really be part of a Roman camp, and we have but to substitute for 'Julius Caesar' the words 'some unknown Roman officer'. Excavation may enable us to find, if not the name of the officer and his force, at least their date, and so we pass from saga into history. There are instances of fragments of real history being preserved for an extraordinary length of time in legends of the peasantry.[15]

Few are so well-trained as to be able to see any event quite as it is without reading into it something which exists only in their own fancy; and this applies much more strongly to events which are not seen but remembered, and most strongly of all to those which are not remembered but told by another. A story handed down from father to son is rapidly altered in two ways; real details are forgotten and unreal ones are added. These additions, being imaginary, are almost invariably of a picturesque kind, attractive to the teller or the hearer, or both; and the omissions are especially of details which teller and hearer alike find dry, such as dates, geographical minutiae (except those of a well-known locality, which are generally found interesting), exact figures of all kinds, economic facts, and the doings and sayings of commonplace people. The Homeric account of the Trojan War is one of the best possible examples. The war was a perfectly real one, very likely caused by trade rivalries; it seems to have consisted in a blockade by the Achaians of the fortress of Ilion, be it Hissarlik or not, interrupting the Trojan communications with the neighbouring country; and it was apparently decided by the exhaustion, economic and military, of the Trojans, which led to the subjugation of the cities allied with them and at last to the fall of Ilion itself. In Homer, the cause of the war is the abduction of Helen by Paris, and the decisive factors are the personal intervention of various gods, together with the surpassing prowess of numerous heroic chieftains, the most prominent of whom is Achilles. Of trade jealousy we hear nothing at all, of the wearing down of the Trojan resources only a few casual remarks, and of the details of the tactics and strategy of both armies practically nothing whatsoever. The result is, at some cost to history, the greatest and most fascinating epic poem ever written, the *Iliad,* which is the product of a first-class genius finding a good saga ready to his hand.

There remains one form of legend, the *märchen.* This German word fits it better than the nearest English equivalent, 'fairy-tale', because it does not always deal with fairies or supernatural beings of any kind. It differs from the last two in an important particular. They both are intended to command, if not exactly belief, at least imaginative assent, and their aim is often to find or record a truth: but the *märchen* aims rather at amusement. It accounts for the cause of nothing, it records no historical or semi-historical event; it need not fit the hearers' notions of probability. It is a story pure and simple, and makes no pretence to being anything else.

This brief outline of the classification of legends must suffice. It is, however, to be noted that any given story may well combine two of these forms, or even all three. For instance, the tale of Herakles probably started as a saga, an imaginative telling of the adventures of a real man. But it combined at an early date with elements of aetiological myth; thus, the presence of certain hot springs was explained by the myth that they had sprung from the ground to provide Herakles with a hot bath after some of his labours, and a certain

ancient sacrifice on Mt. Oite was declared to commemorate the death of the hero. Also, an element of *märchen* intruded here and there; for instance Herakles, like many other adventurers, goes forth to look for the pot of gold at the end of the rainbow, represented in his case by the golden apples of the Hesperides.

Another and a more important point to be remembered in the case of Greek myths is the way in which they reflect the national character. The Greeks at their best were sane, high-spirited, clear-headed, beauty-loving optimists, and not in the least other-worldly. Hence their legends are almost without exception free from the cloudiness, the wild grotesques, and the horrible features which beset the popular traditions of less gifted and happy peoples. Even their monsters are not very ugly or uncouth, nor their ghosts and demons paralysingly dreadful. Their heroes, as a rule, may sorrow, but are not broken-hearted; on occasion they are struck down by adverse fate, but not weakly overwhelmed; they meet with extraordinary adventures, but there is a certain tone of reasonableness running through their most improbable exploits. As for the gods and other supernatural characters, they are glorified men and women, who remain extremely human, and on the whole neither irrational nor grossly unfair in their dealings. Such tales as contain savage and repulsive elements tend to drop into the background or be modified. In short, the handling of the myths, even, it would appear, by unlettered Greeks, shows the spirit expressed in two famous sayings of famous poets:

'Winsomeness, by which are wrought all lovely things for mankind, lends its lustre to make even the incredible seem credible full often.'

'If I deal in falsehood, let it be such as may persuade the ears of the listener.'[16]

Notes

(*For the full titles of books cited, see General Bibliography.*)

[1] See, for a history of the subject from the end of antiquity to the year 1913, Gruppe 1921. Nilsson, *GgR,* i, 3 *sqq.*

[2] Nock 1926, pp. 6, 7; Murray 1925, p. 245. See Chapter V, p. 106.

[3] *Iliad,* XIX, 91 foll.—a passage very likely interpolated into the original poem by a later hand, but nevertheless old—may serve as an example.

[4] See General Bibliography.

[5] *Symbolik,* I, p. 37 foll. For Talos, see Chapter VIII, p. 204.

[6] *De incredibilibus,* I. The work we have is not that of Palaiphatos himself, who lived in the time of Aristotle, but a later epitome.

[7] I have discussed the problem how much of their savage ancestry the historical Greeks retained in *Primitive Culture in Greece.*

[8] For Euhemeros, see Jacoby in Pauly-Wissowa VI, col. 952 foll.

[9] The Stoics were particularly fond of explanations of this kind, see, for instance, *R.P.*[8], 503, but it was by no means confined to them, see, for example, Plato, *Cratylus,* 397 C, and for many such explanations, Athenagoras, *legat. pro Christ.* 22. For the theory that all gods were in some way the sun, see Macrobius, *Saturn.,* I, 17, 2 foll. See, in general, Frazer, *W.N.* J. Tate in *C.Q.,* xxiii, 41-5; 142-54; xxviii, 105-14.

[10] See *Lectures on the Origin of Religion* (1882), Lecture IV; *Introduction to the Science of Religion* (new edition, 1882), pp. 49, 197.

[11] By Wiro I mean the group of languages otherwise called Aryan, Indo-European, or Indo-Germanic, to which Latin, Greek, Sanskrit, etc., belong. By Wiros I mean the people or peoples who spoke the language from which all these tongues are supposedly derived. The word in the latter sense is due to Dr. Giles.

[12] See Sten Konow in Chantepie de la Saussaye,[4] II, p. 23 foll.

[13] See, for instance, Jung, *Psychology of the Unconscious* (trans. B. M. Hinkle, London, 1922), Chapter VI.

[14] For a deliciously funny sketch of the type of mind which is hungry for a reason and content with whatever is offered it, see Aristophanes, *Clouds,* 366 foll.

[15] Excellent examples are given by van Gennep, 1910, p. 155 foll.

[16] Pindar, *Olymp.,* I, 32; Kallimachos, *Hymn.,* I, 65.

Additional Note

For full accounts of the ancient authors quoted, the reader is referred to the many good manuals of Greek literature in English, French and German. It may, however, be mentioned that our sources in Greek are firstly the poets, of all dates from Homer and Hesiod down; and of these, especially those up to and including the great Attic dramatists of the fifth century B.C. Next in importance to these are the Alexandrian poets, such as Kallimachos, from the fourth century onwards, who often give us curious information not to be had elsewhere, but who must be used with caution, as they often of set purpose confine themselves to very out-of-the-way stories, not forming part of what may be called the normal mythology of Greece; moreover, they not infrequently re-shape the legends or invent new ones, to suit their own purposes, a fault, from the modern mythologist's point of view, of which the older writers also are sometimes guilty. Next come the earlier historical writers, such as Pherekydes, who unfortunately are known to us only in fragments and excerpts; these, in dealing with early history, treated also of legends, which were indeed often their only source for events of other than recent date, and later compilers, such as Diodoros of Sicily, drew freely upon them. Finally, a great deal is due to the mythological handbooks, for these contain much of the learning of the Alexandrian critics, although in an epitomized form. Of these, one of the best is the so-called Apollodoros, whose work (first century A.D.?) contains much good old material. With these may be reckoned the scholiasts, or ancient commentators on classical authors, such as Pindar and above all Homer, and on Alexandrian poets such as Apollonios of Rhodes. As regards the Latins, even their earliest poets draw upon the Alexandrians, and may for our purposes be counted as late Greek authors. Here again, notably in the case of Ovid, the writers' own fancy is the source of not a little. Roman scholarship also is often of value; we have, for example, the so-called Hyginus, whose *fabulae,* although but an epitomized, mutilated, and very ill-copied treatise, yet often preserves in a not too garbled form some story otherwise lost, as told in a vanished work of Euripides or some other classical writer. Much can also be gleaned from Latin scholiasts, notably that commentator on Vergil who is conventionally called Servius. But there is hardly a writer in either language who does not somewhere mention a myth or saga, and on whom therefore we cannot now and then draw for information. This applies to the Christian writers, for they often, in order to show what absurd and immoral stories the pagans told, relate these stories at considerable length, thus preserving for us the erudition of sundry mythologists whose works have not come down, or of poets now lost.

Bibliography

A. CLASSICAL AUTHORS

A few editions and abbreviations are given here. . . .

RP[8]. *Historia Philosophiae Graecae.* Testimonia auctorum conlegerunt notisque instruxerunt H. Ritter et L. Preller. Editio octaua, quam curauit Eduardus Wellmann. Gothae, 1898. . . .

B. MODERN WORKS

The following is a brief list of some of the books which the author has found particularly useful. A few more are named in the notes

Chantepie de la Saussaye. *Lehrbuch der Religionsgeschichte, begründet von Chantepie de la Saussaye.* Vierte, vollständig neubearbeitete Auflage . . . herausgegeben von Alfred Bertholet und Edvard Lehmann. Tübingen, 1925 (2 vols.). . . .

Creuzer. Friedrich Creuzer, *Symbolik und Mythologie der alten Völker, besonders der Griechen.* Dritte, verbesserte Ausgabe. Leipzig und Darmstadt, 1836-42 (4 vols.). . . .

Frazer, *W.N.* Sir J. G. Frazer, *The Worship of Nature.* Vol. I, London, 1926.

van Gennep 1910. A. van Gennep, *La Formation des Legendes.* Paris, 1910. . . .

Gruppe 1921. Otto Gruppe, *Geschichte der klassischen Mythologie und Religionsgeschichte.* Supplement zu Roschers Lexikon. Leipzig, 1921. . . .

Murray 1925. Gilbert A. Murray, *Five Stages of Greek Religion* Oxford, 1925. . . .

Nilsson, *GgR.* M. P. Nilsson, *Geschichte der griechischen Religion,* 2 vols. Munich, 1955 (ed. 2, I²), 1955. . . .

Nock 1926. *Sallustius, Concerning the Gods and the Universe.* Edited with Prolegomena and Translation by Arthur Darby Nock. Cambridge, 1926. . . .

Pauly-Wissowa. *Paulys Realencyclopädie der classischen Altertumswissenschaft.* Neue Bearbeitung begonnen von Georg Wissowa (etc.). Stuttgart, 1894— . . .

Rose, *P.C.G.* H. J. Rose, *Primitive Culture in Greece.* London (Methuen), 1925. . . .

William F. Hansen (essay date 1983)

SOURCE: "Greek Mythology and the Study of the Ancient Greek Oral Story," in *Journal of Folklore Research,* Vol. 20, Nos. 2 & 3, June-December, 1983, pp. 101-12.

[*In the following essay, Hansen examines Rose's inclusion of* märchen *in his study of Greek mythology and argues that Rose fails to adequately treat the category of folktales. Hansen suggests that the idea that mythology encompasses "all Greek traditional stories" has not been fully explored.*]

The late Professor Cedric Whitman of Harvard University told of an old sailor with whom, many years earlier, he had shared a ride on a train going to New York.

> He was reading a comic book and I was reading *Paradise Lost.* Presently he began to read over my shoulder, then nudged me and asked: 'Hey, you like dat stuff?' I said I did, and a conversation began. I asked how long he had been in the Navy, and he said something like twenty-five years. I remarked that he must have liked it to have stayed in it so long. His answer was: 'Look, when I get out of dis Navy, I'm gonna put an oar on my shoulder and walk inland; and when somebody says, "Where'd'ya find a shovel like dat?" dat's where I'm gonna build my house.' He made no mention of a sacrifice to Poseidon; he was shamelessly secular about it all, but clearly the inland journey spelled release from, and forgetfulness of, the hardships of the sea, peace at last. I didn't ask him if he'd read the *Odyssey,* but I doubt it; he had not read *Paradise Lost.* He seemed, in fact, pretty nearly illiterate—perhaps a bard? Anyway, that's all I remember, except that the experience gave me a pleasantly creepy feeling that I was talking to One Who Was More Than He Seemed.[1]

Whitman had in mind of course the curious passage in Homer's *Odyssey* (11.121-137) in which Odysseus is told that after he reaches Ithaka he must walk inland with an oar upon his shoulder until he comes upon a man who mistakes it for a winnowing-shovel. There Odysseus is to plant the oar in the ground and make his peace with Poseidon, that is, with the Sea.[2]

The conversation of the classics professor and the sailor illustrates the impressive fact that many motifs and stories known from modern oral tradition were already in oral circulation in ancient Greece. Correspondence between modern oral narratives and their ancient Greek counterparts began to attract attention around the middle of the last century. In 1816 Jacob Grimm made the observation that the Greeks too had their Märchen, and in 1857 Wilhelm Grimm published "Die Sage von Polyphem," in which he compared Homer's Cyclops narrative with nine folktale texts of essentially the same plot (AT 1137) gathered from more recent tradition.[3] Other scholars followed these two leads, especially as the subsequent collecting of oral tales made comparative materials more abundant.[4] Accordingly, following Jacob Grimm, there have been quests for evidence of ancient Greek folktales, springing (at least in part) from a desire to demonstrate that the folktale as a genre existed side by side with the familiar Greek myths and legends. Consider Ludwig Radermacher's survey of traditional narratives in Homer's *Odyssey,* Wolf Aly's study of folktales and legends in Herodotos, Thaddaeus Zieliński's quest for folktales in Attic comedy, Otto Crusius's discussion of allusions to folktales in ancient Greek proverbs, Georgios Megas's study of Aesopic fables with modern Greek analogues, and, of course, the ancient Greek materials collected in the fourth volume of Bolte and Polívka's commentary on the tales of the Brothers Grimm.[5] And, following Wilhelm Grimm, there have appeared comparative studies of individual Greek oral stories of any genre whatsoever for which analogues exist in modern oral tradition, such as Albin Lesky's study of the Alcestis story (AT 899) and, among more recent work, Justin Glenn's article on the Polyphemos tale (AT 1137), Lowell Edmunds's monograph on the Oedipus story (AT 931), Alex Scobie's article on the story of the Pygmies and the cranes, and my own investigation of the story of Odysseus and the oar.[6] These are not the only kinds of studies that have been produced, but they show that the discovery of the folktale in the nineteenth century has made an impact upon Greek studies.

Where, then, has the folktale come to fit into Greek studies? To which subfield do traditional oral stories and oral storytelling belong? Histories of Greek religion inevitably do pay some attention to myth and legend, and Nilsson's history even devotes some space to a discussion of Märchen, but the interest in oral stories is not systematic, and such narratives clearly have not been central to the study of ancient Greek religion.[7]

Nor will one find much on the subject in the surveys of Greek literature. Lesky's *History of Greek Literature,* which is 900 pages long in its English translation, has no section devoted specifically to myth, legend, or the oral story in general. It does have a section devoted to the folktale, but the treatment is only four pages long and concerns itself mostly with Greek animal fables.[8] Clearly, Lesky does not attempt any real treatment of the Greek folktale, let alone the Greek traditional oral story more generally. As a rule, historians of Greek literature do not include traditional stories in the category of literature, and so treat them only incidentally. An oral story is, after all, not necessarily also a written story, and literary histories are perhaps by definition concerned with written, not oral, literature.

That being so, the subfield to which these narratives belong must surely be Greek mythology, for *it* unquestionably takes as its subject Greek traditional stories. If, however, one scrutinizes the familiar lexica, handbooks, and other retellings of Greek (or classical) mythology, both scholarly and popular, one soon finds that not all genres of traditional narrative are included. The standard surveys of mythology, with the notable exception of Rose's *Handbook of Greek Mythology,* typically offer a selection of Greek myths and hero legends and, if one is lucky, the tale of Cupid and Psyche or the tale of Hero and Leander or the like. The four volumes of Ludwig Preller's and Carl Robert's *Griechische Mythologie,* for example, are devoted exclusively to the myths of the gods and the legends of the great heroes. Similarly, Mark Morford's and Rob-

ert Lenardon's college textbook. *Classical Mythology,* covers myths of the gods (in the course of which the story of Cupid and Psyche is told) and legends of the heroes, together with a chapter on Greek "local legends" (which paraphrases a variety of stories, including the romantic stories of Akontios and Kydippe, Hero and Leander, and Pyramus and Thisbe).[9] In practice, then, Greek mythology means only certain kinds of oral stories, primarily fabulous stories of allegedly historical content, or, more precisely, the traditional oral history of the Greek world from its beginning through the generations of the heroes, with the optional inclusion of a handful of other well-known stories.[10] One cannot count on finding the folktale here.

If Greek traditional stories are not classified as literature because they are oral, and if they only in part qualify as mythology, which does not embrace all genres of story, where *does* one look for a systematic treatment of the folktale or of the traditional story in general? The answer is that one looks in no single place, because there is none. If it is a myth one wants, or a hero legend, one consults the mythologists. If it is an Aesopic fable, one must consult the literature on the fable. If it is an anecdote about Plato or Aristotle, one looks in the scholarship on ancient philosophy.[11] And so on. Oral narratives are not seen as the scattered materials of a single branch of study, for the prevailing view of the Greek oral story is not holistic; rather, myths and hero legends belong to the subfield of mythology, and the other hundreds of traditional oral stories, representing other genres of essentially the same phenomenon, mostly belong to the authors in whose works they are found.

Is it, then, worthwhile for us to continue to retain the ancient categories that we have inherited and preserved.[12] or should we, for our own scholarly ends, devise our own categories? For without the benefit of a unified concept of the traditional oral story and of a single locus in the discipline, there is little exchange of ideas among the scholars of the various subdisciplines: mythologists study their own materials, Homerists study Homer, historians study Herodotos, fable scholars study the fable.[13] No shared concepts have arisen; no common terminology has been developed; no general body of knowledge on the subject exists.[14] If we desire to understand Greek storytelling, we must develop a more comprehensive view of the ancient Greek oral story.

There is another good reason for not retaining the ancient categories. Since a given story can be told in one place or time as a legend and in another as a tale, in many instances there are historical links between stories usually included in the category of mythology and those that are not. This phenomenon particularly affects the study of Greek mythology, since stories found in ancient Greek sources as myths or legends often appear in modern European collections as folktales. The legend of Odysseus and Polyphemos and the folktale of the blinding of the ogre (AT 1137) are examples at hand. Little is gained and much is lost as a result of our not having a general concept of the Greek oral story. We need not wholly give up all sensitivity to the ancient categories; we need only relate them to an all-encompassing notion of oral narrative.

Perhaps the simplest solution would be to modify what we already have, enlarging the familiar and closely-related category of Greek mythology to include *all* Greek traditional stories. In other words, let the well-established category of mythology accommodate the more recent category of the folktale. This idea is not wholly new. Its classical roots go back over one hundred years, when George Cox included Herodotos' famous story of the treasury of Rhampsinitos (AT 950) in his *Tales of Ancient Greece* in order to show "the existence of a common popular mythology relating neither to gods nor heroes."[15] He also included several other traditional stories from Herodotos, as well as a retelling of the epic parody, *The Battle of the Frogs and the Mice,* a literary work that does contain a traditional animal tale (AT 278). The impulse to include these stories evidently came from Cox's acquaintance with contemporary collections of tales and legends, for he specifically mentions Scandinavian, German, and Arabic relatives of the Rhampsinitos story, and his phrase "popular mythology" is reminiscent of "popular antiquities" and other folkloric terms commonly employed in the last century.[16] What is significant is Cox's slight stretching of the inherited parameters of Greek mythology by introducing stories that are realistic (Rhampsinitos) or make no claim to historicity (animal tales), so that he moved, however modestly, toward a holistic concept of the Greek traditional oral story.

In 1928, H. J. Rose, who was well acquainted with contemporary folk-narrative scholarship, published his *Handbook of Greek Mythology.* When he introduced the work with a division of Greek mythology into myth, saga, and Märchen, and even devoted an entire chapter of the book to Märchen, it was certainly revolutionary.[17] The relatively young category of the folktale appears here to have been adopted into the established category of Greek mythology, which then became the corpus of all Greek traditional stories. And indeed, since the publication of Rose's *Handbook,* which is as close to being the standard survey of the subject in English as any work is, it has become common (but by no means universal) for the folktale to be acknowledged *in some way* in works devoted to Greek mythology, both scholarly and popular.[18] As a result, classical scholars, like folklorists, sometimes employ or at least imply a tripartite classification of their materials, dividing the stories into three broad classes, or genres, usually named myth, legend (or saga), and folktale (or fairy tale or Märchen).[19] Traditional cosmogonies and most of the traditional stories that are set in the early

days of the cosmos or that feature gods as principal characters, or both, are usually classified as myths. By legends classical mythologists usually mean the traditional stories of the great heroes, such as Perseus, Oedipus, Jason, Achilleus, Meleager, Odysseus, and Herakles, or other traditional stories set in the heroic age. These two classes of story, according to Rose, are intended to command belief, or something like it, whereas "the Märchen aims rather at amusement. It accounts for the cause of nothing, it records no historical or semi-historical event. . . . It is a story pure and simple, and makes no pretense to being anything else."[20]

So we seem to have witnessed a happy marriage of the traditional mythological genres and the folktale. Is this not in fact the comprehensive category that I have argued is needed? Unfortunately, it is not, because nowhere can one find the notion realized, not even in Rose's own book.[21]

What exactly does Rose offer in his survey of the ancient folktale? We do not find tales that aim at amusement rather than at belief, tales that record no historical event, stories pure and simple. In other words, we do not find Greek jests, comic tales, fables, and the rest; rather, we find a collection of ancient stories of various genres few of them being Märchen by Rose's own definition. What they have in common is merely that all of them have analogues in modern oral tradition. For example. Rose lists the story (p. 294), told by Pausanias (10.33.9-10), about the city of Ophiteia. A certain man of Phocis once saw a serpent near his infant son, and, thinking that the serpent intended to attack the child, threw his javelin, killing both animal and baby. He then learned that the serpent had in fact been protecting the child from a wolf. In gratitude he buried them together. The city of Ophiteia was named after this very serpent (Greek *ophis* = "serpent"). The story does not fit Rose's criteria for Märchen because, first, it is clearly a belief-story rather than a tale of pure amusement, and, second, it concludes with an etiology for the name of the city of Ophiteia and so does in fact account for something. This same story is known in modern oral tradition (AT 178A).

Elsewhere in his chapter (p. 288) Rose informs us that the story of Odysseus's return in time to prevent the remarriage of Penelope is in fact a Märchen, not a saga, although (Rose says) Odysseus himself is a figure of saga. But the story of Odysseus and Penelope is not obviously less historical and more amusing than the stories of other Greek heroes and heroines. Again, Rose's classification is not in harmony with his own definition of Märchen; rather, what is significant for Rose is that the story of the returning husband and his faithful wife can be heard *today* as a folktale (AT 974). Rose promises us ancient folktales but he gives us ancient analogues of modern folktales and legends. The real loss in Rose's handbook is not that some stories are mislabelled as Märchen but that ancient folktales as such—Märchen in the sense defined by Rose in his introduction—find little place in Rose's book, just as they generally find little or no place in other surveys of Greek oral stories. Rose proposed to include folktales as a major branch of Greek mythology, but he did not really succeed in doing so. He was deceived by the variability of genre.

From Rose's own definition we might classify as folktales Greek jests, such as those found in the collection from late antiquity known as *Philogelos;* and the comic tales of extraordinary fools such as those told of Margites, who would not sleep with his wife for fear that she would tell her mother; and those told of extraordinarily lazy or sensitive folk, such as the cycle of tales about the Sybarites. And we can include many of the fables compiled by the ancient Greek fabulists. (We can include them all if Rose's criterion of "amusement" can be expanded to embrace also rhetorical and other functions.) We can probably include most of the oral stories often called novelle, such as the story alluded to by Aristophanes (*Thesmophoriazusae* 499-501) and known also from modern tradition (AT 1419C) of the woman who covered up her husband's eye or eyes with a garment and thereby allowed her lover to slip away. And we can also include the supposed Greek prototype of Apuleius's tale of Cupid and Psyche (AT 425A), as an example of the magic tale (German *Zaubermärchen*). The term folktale in fact must refer not to a single kind of tale but to a rather large class that actually comprises many different kinds of tale: jests, comic tales, fables, novelle, magic tales, etc.[22] Rose does not include all these kinds of tale or even most of them, and neither does any other writer on Greek mythology. He does mention, in his chapter on Märchen, the tale of Cupid and Psyche (pp. 286-87), and he once states, without explanation, that "this work does not deal with fables" (p. 298), before discussing the single fable mentioned in the book. On the whole it is clear that he does not deliver what his own definition of the Märchen promises. His definition is larger than its application, and as a result many kinds of oral story are nowhere acknowledged.

Even if the category of folktale should be better appreciated than it has been, it does not follow that Greek traditional oral stories can be efficiently divided into three broad classes. That is, adopting the folktale as the third in a tripartition of mythology may not work. What, for example, are we to do with a story such as the report of the death of the god Pan, recounted by Plutarch (*De defectu orac.* 17)? A mysterious voice from an island told a voyager that when he passed by a certain island, he should announce that great Pan was dead. The voyager did so, upon which there was instantly heard from the island a great chorus of lamentation. The international nature of this story is proved by the fact that essentially the same story, told of other

characters, is familiar in modern oral tradition, especially in northern Europe.[23] It was evidently told to Plutarch, as it has usually been told to others in modern times, as a report of an actual event that occurred in the recent past; that is, it is told as a belief-story, not as a light tale of pure amusement in which the factor of belief or disbelief is unimportant. Clearly this story does not qualify as a legend (or saga) in the usage given above, where legend means hero legend, since it neither features a hero nor is it set in the age of heroes. Nor can it be classified as a Märchen, since it is reported as a wondrous but true event to which distinguished men, including the Emperor Tiberius, allegedly gave credence, and not as a mere piece of entertainment. In short, here is an excellent and famous Greek oral story which the usual categories of classification exclude.

What, moreover, shall we do with the familiar exemplum of the Spartan mother who instructed her son to come back from war either with his shield or upon it?[24] Was this a belief-story, and thus properly classified as a kind of legend, or was it taken as ideal, and thus more akin to the Aesopic fable? And how are we to classify the apothegms and other anecdotes of famous men and women that ancient literature offers in such abundance? Are they minor legends? amusing fictions? both? neither? And, in a different vein, what about the traditional cautionary tales or bogy tales that were told to Greek children, such as those about Lamia and other ogresses?[25] Who believed them? Who, if anyone, was amused by them?

I shall not draw out this list. The point is that many important Greek traditional stories do not fit into the familiar classificatory schemes that have evolved. In particular, it may be that a triadic classification, no matter how we define its parts, will never contain the data usefully, and that it reflects more our cultural fondness for tripartition than our need for useful analytic categories.

In sum, we have inherited from late antiquity a category of story-compilation which in time acquired the label mythology, and we have maintained this category both in scholarly publications and in popular handbooks. We publish and study the other traditional stories of Greek antiquity by genre, just as before us the ancients published fables in one place and jests in another. The Greeks did not abstract from all these kinds of traditional narratives a general concept of traditional oral story, and modern scholars of Greek studies have followed suit. When in the nineteenth century, interest in living oral stories became widespread among scholars, and studies on the folktale and its analogues were published, the notion eventually arose that all these stories were simply different genres of oral story, so that some scholars, with good intuition, added the folktale to the familiar category of mythology. And so the notion of Greek mythology as the class of all Greek traditional stories came into being; but the full implications of this idea have never been explored. It is time for Hellenists—as well as for scholars in other disciplines that have borrowed these categories from the Greeks—to free ourselves from this fragmentary view of oral story and to operate with one inclusive category of the oral story, whether we wish to call it mythology or something else, and however we may wish to divide it up into genres.

Notes

1 Personal letter (October 13, 1975).

2 On the ancient story and its modern counterparts, see Wm. F. Hansen, "The Story of the Sailor Who Went Inland," in *Folklore Today: A Festschrift for Richard M. Dorson,* ed. Linda Dégh, Henry Glassie, and Felix Oinas (Bloomington: Research Center for Language and Semiotic Studies, Indiana University, 1976), pp. 221-30; idem, "Odysseus' Last Journey," *Quaderni Urbinati di Cultura Classica* 21 (1977): 27-48; and Dietz-Rüdiger Moser, "Die Homerische Frage und das Problem der mündlichen Überlieferung aus volkskundlicher Sicht," *Fabula* 20 (1979): 116-36.

3 Jacob Grimm, in his preface to Liebrecht's translation of the *Pentamerone* (1846), cited by Wolf Aly, "Märchen," in Pauly-Wissowa 14:254. Wilhelm Grimm, "Die Sage von Polyphem," *Abhandlungen der königl. Akad. der Wiss. zu Berlin, phil.-hist. Kl.* (1857): 1-30.

4 For Greece, see Georgios A. Megas, "Märchensammlung und Märchenforschung in Griechenland seit dem Jahre 1864," *Deutsches Jahrbuch für Volkskunde* 8 (1962): 153-59, and, for the context, Michael Herzfeld, *Ours Once More: Folklore, Ideology, and the Making of Modern Greece* (Austin: University of Texas Press, 1982).

5 Ludwig Radermacher, "Die Erzählungen der Odyssee," *Sitzungsb. der Akad. der Wiss in Wien, phil.-hist. Kl.* 178 (1915), Abh. 1 (despite the promise of its title, Denys Page's recent work, *Folktales in Homer's Odyssey* [Cambridge: Harvard University Press, 1973], does not survey the tales of the *Odyssey*). Wolf Aly, *Volksmärchen, Sage, und Novelle bei Herodot und seinen Zeitgenossen,* 2nd ed. (Göttingen: Vandenhoeck & Ruprecht, 1969. Th. Zieliński, "Die Märchenkomödie in Athen," *Iresione* 1, *Eos* suppl. 2 (Leopoli, 1931): 8-75. Otto Crusius, "Märchen-reminiscenzen im antiken Sprichwort," *Verhandlungen der 40. Philologenversammlung deutscher Schulmänner und Philologen* (Nuremberg and Leipzig, 1890): 31-47. Georgios A. Megas, "Some Oral Parallels to Aesop's Fables," in *Humaniora: Essays in Literature, Folklore, Bibliography, Honoring Archer Taylor on his Seventieth Birthday,* ed. Wayland D. Hand and Gustave O. Arlt (Locust Valley N.Y.: J. J. Augustin, 1960), pp. 195-207

(see also Bengt Holbek, *Æsops Levned og Fabler,* vol. 2 [Copenhagen: J. H. Schultz, 1962]). Johannes Bolte and Georg Polívka, *Anmerkungen zu den Kinder- und Hausmärchen der Brüder Grimm,* 2nd ed. (Hildesheim: Georg Olm, 1963 [orig. ed. 1930]), 4:41-44, 108-22.

6 Albin Lesky, "Alkestis: der Mythus und das Drama," *Sitzungsb. der Akad. der Wiss. in Wien, phil.-hist. Kl.* 203 (1925), Abh. 2. Justin Glenn. "The Polyphemus Folktale and Homer's *Kyklôpeia,*" *Transactions of the American Philological Association* 102 (1971): 133-81. Lowell Edmunds. *The Sphinx in the Oedipus Legend,* Beiträge zur klassischen Philologie 127 (Königstein Ts.: Hain, 1981). Alex Scobie, "The Battle of the Pygmies and the Cranes in Chinese, Arab, and North American Indian Sources," *Folklore* 86 (1975): 122-32. For the story of the sailor and the oar, see above, note 2. The present paper focuses upon ancient Greek stories, so that references to Roman narratives are usually not given; but the problems are essentially the same.

7 Martin Nilsson, *Geschichte der Griechischen Religion* (Munich: C. H. Beck, 1967), 1:17-23.

8 Albin Lesky, *A History of Greek Literature,* trans. James Willis and Cornelis de Heer (New York: Thomas Y. Crowell, 1966), pp. 154-57.

9 Ludwig Preller, *Griechische Mythologie,* 4th ed., 3 vols., bearbeitet von Carl Robert (Berlin: Weidmannsche Buchhandlung, 1891-1926). Mark P. O. Morford and Robert J. Lenardon, *Classical Mythology,* 2nd ed. (New York: Longman, 1977).

10 The modern collections of Greek mythology, with their severely limited range, do in fact possess an old pedigree. In ancient compilations of traditional stories, we find basically two different principles of selection, which could be called the *generic* and the *historical.* The former collections select for a particular genre of story, such as the anecdote or the jest on the fable. The historical compilations, on the other hand, focus on the traditional stories concerning the early history of the world and of the Hellenic people, selecting primarily for myths of the gods and for legends of the great families of Greece in early times. Thus, the *Bibliothêkê* ("Library") of Pseudo-Apollodoros (first century A.D.?) recounts Greek traditional oral history, starting with a mythical cosmogony and continuing to the end of the heroes. The *Genealogiae,* or *Fabulae,* attributed to Hyginus (second century A.D.?), likewise includes scarcely any stories that we would not ordinarily classify either as myths or as legends of the heroic age. In short, these two works are collections of what we today should label Greek mythology. Taken together, they show most of the features that are familiar in modern compilations. The former is recounted as a continuous narrative, like a universal history, and is

ancestor to those compilations, such as Preller-Robert's *Griechische Mythologie* and Rose's *Handbook,* which opt for the panorama, whereas the latter consists of stories told briefly and discontinuously, the prototype of the mythological dictionary, such as Herbert Hunger, *Lexikon der Griechischen und Römischen Mythologie,* 6th ed. (Vienna: Verlag Brüder Hollinek, 1969), Pierre Grimal, *Dictionnaire de la Mythologie Grecque et Romaine,* 4th ed. (Paris: Presses Universitaires de France, 1969), Edward Tripp, *The Meridian Handbook of Classical Mythology* (New York: New American Library, 1974), and W. H. Roscher, ed., *Ausführliches Lexikon der Griechischen und Römischen Mythologie,* 7 vols. (Leipzig: B. G. Teubner, 1884-1893). By the time of Fulgentius (ca. 467-532 A.D.), if not before, this kind of compilation receives the label mythology, or, as Fulgentius has it, "mythologies." His *Mythologiae* also contains the story of Hero and Leander and the story of Cupid and Psyche, the latter retold from Apuleius, so that it is perhaps due ultimately to the influence of this work that these two romantic stories are often admitted into the company of Greek myth and family legend. The striking similarity of content in ancient and modern mythological compilations is presumably a consequence of the continuous tradition of Greek mythological compilation, stretching from antiquity to the present day, in which, without much fresh thought, compilers select again and again the same stories for inclusion. On the ancient compilations, see Carl Wendel, "Mythographie," in Pauly-Wissowa 16:1352-74; on Renaissance handbooks of classical mythology, see Jean Seznec, *The Survival of the Pagan Gods,* trans. Barbara Sessions (New York: Harper Torchbooks, 1961). See also note 21, below.

[11] Ingemar Düring, *Aristotle in the Ancient Biographical Tradition,* Acta Universitatis Gothoburgensis, Göteborgs Universitets Arsskrift, vol. 63 (Gothenburg, 1957). Alice Swift Riginos, *Platonica: The Anecdotes Concerning the Life and Writings of Plato* (Leiden: E. J. Brill, 1976).

[12] See above, note 10.

[13] The fragmented study of Greek traditional stories is in turn a microcosm of the fragmented study of mythology in academia in general; for a discussion, see Burton Feldman and Robert D. Richardson, *The Rise of Modern Mythology 1680-1860* (Bloomington: Indiana University Press, 1972), pp. xix-xxii.

[14] Nor do things seem to be appreciably better outside of Greek studics. When, for example, folklorists glance back at ancient Greece, they tend to see only those stories and motifs that are reminiscent of more recent tradition, and to ignore the rest; for the truth of this, pick up almost any modern survey of the folktale or the legend, and read the several pages devoted to classical antiquity. This view is just as partial as that promulgated by classicists.

[15] George W. Cox, *Tales of Ancient Greece* (London and Toronto: J. M. Dent; New York: E. P. Dutton, 1915), p. 31. This extremely popular work has been issued in one edition after another since the first edition of 1868. I have been able to consult only two editions, one dated 1915, the other undated; both have the line quoted here, and both have the stories mentioned, gathered at the end in a section entitled "Miscellaneous Tales."

[16] Cox's comparative notes are not wholly accurate by modern standards, but that is beside the point here. See further, Richard M. Dorson, "The Eclipse of Solar Mythology," in *Myth: A Symposium,* ed. Thomas Sebeok (Bloomington: Indiana University Press, 1958), p. 42.

[17] H. J. Rose, *A Handbook of Greek Mythology* (London: Methuen, 1928). "We use the word mythology to signify the study of certain products of the imagination of a people, which take the form of tales" (p. 1). "We may divide legends, in a fashion which by now is almost traditional, into three classes" (p. 10), which prove to be myth, saga, and Märchen (pp. 10-14). Rose refers to the tripartite division as "almost traditional," but it was not so in classical studies, and Rose no doubt borrowed it from folklorists. His immedite source was probably Charlotte Burnes's *Handbook of Folklore,* which Rose once mentions in passing (p. 286). Burnes introduces her chapter on stories as follows: "Traditional stories may be roughly classified as Myths, Legends (including Hero-Tales and Sagas), and *Märchen* or Folk-tales, with which last may be reckoned the minor varieties of Beast-tales, Drolls, Cumulative tales, and Apologues." See Charlotte S. Burnes, *The Handbook of Folklore* (London: Publications of the Folk-lore Society 73, 1913), p. 261.

[18] Joseph Fontenrose, *The Ritual Theory of Myth,* University of California Publications in Folklore Studies 18 (Berkeley and Los Angeles, 1966), pp. 54-56. G. S. Kirk, *The Nature of Greek Myths* (Harmondsworth: Penguin, 1974), pp. 30-37. Walter Burkert, *Structure and History in Greek Mythology and Ritual* (Berkeley and Los Angeles: University of California Press, 1979), pp. 1-2, 33. Michael Grant, *Myths of the Greeks and Romans* (New York: New American Library, 1964), pp. 72-76, 362-66. Cf. Michael Grant, *Roman Myths* (New York: Charles Scribner's Sons, 1971), pp. 262-63, note 27. Morford and Lenardon (see above, note 9), pp. 1-3.

[19] Fontenrose, pp. 54-56. Kirk, p. 31. Morford and Lenardon, pp. 1-3 (notice also their comment on p. 2: "The definitions set forth by Rose in his invaluable handbook have deservedly won wide acceptance").

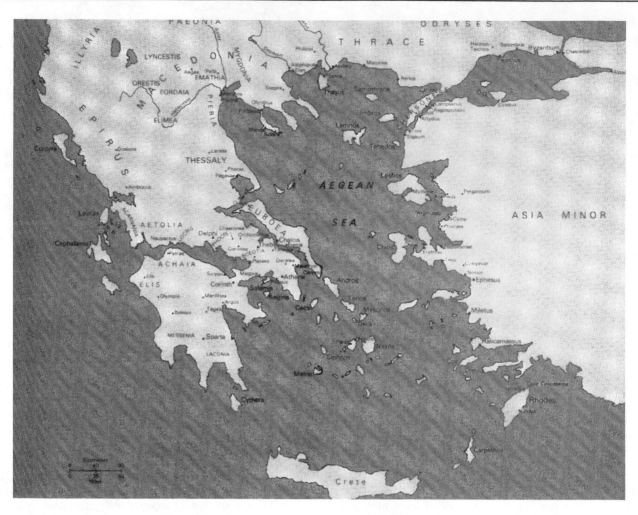

A map of Asia Minor in Homer's time.

William Bascom, "The Forms of Folklore: Prose Narratives," *Journal of American Folklore* 78 (1965): 3-20.

[20] Rose, *Handbook,* p. 14.

[21] Fontenrose, *Ritual Theory,* is a near exception here. He suggests grouping together myths, legends, and folktales under the term mythology, but *only if* they contain supernatural elements; accordingly, realistic tales are deliberately excluded (p. 55). While Fontenrose's definition succinctly expresses approximately what the ancient Greeks meant by *mythologia,* his concept (though larger than Greek mythology in its current usage) is smaller than the class of *all* Greek traditional stories, as he intends it to be.

The modern usage of the term "mythology" does not precisely continue the ancient Greek usage of the noun *mythologia* and its verb *mythologein. Mythologia* means a fabulous or fictional story, or the telling of such stories, and *mythologein* means to tell a (fabulous) story.

See Liddell-Scott-Jones, *A Greek-English Lexicon,* 9th ed. (Oxford: Clarendon Press, 1940), s. vv. These words could be employed in reference to any fabulous story, including the Aesopic fable. *Mythologies* occurs in titles of collections of fabulous stories as early as Alexandrian times, as, for example, in Deinarchos's *Mythologiai peri Krêtên* ("Fabulous Stories about Crete"): see Carl Wendel, "Mythographie," in Pauly-Wissowa 16:1356.

[22] Cf. Bengt Holbek, "Tacit Assumptions," *Folklore Forum* 14 (1981): 125-26.

[23] Reidar Th. Christiansen, *The Migratory Legends,* FFC No. 175 (Helsinki: Academia Scientiarum Fennica, 1958), Type 6070A, "Fairies Send a Message."

[24] For the story, see Mason Hammond, "A Famous *Exemplum* of Spartan Toughness," *Classical Journal* 75 (1979-80): 97-109. The mother means that her son should either return alive and honorably (= carrying his shield) or dead and honorably (= carried upon his shield) but not alive and dishonorably (= without his

shield, which a warrior might cast away in order to disencumber his flight from the enemy).

[25] See Alex Scobie, "Storytellers, Storytelling, and the Novel in Graeco-Roman Antiquity," *Rheinisches Museum für Philologie,* N.F. 122 (1979): 245-50, and John Winkler, "Akko," *Classical Philology* 77 (1982): 137-38.

ORIGINS AND DEVELOPMENT OF GREEK MYTHOLOGY

Martin P. Nilsson (essay date 1932)

SOURCE: "How Old Is Greek Mythology?," in *The Mycenaean Origin of Greek Mythology*, University of California Press, 1932, pp. 1-34.

[*In the following essay, Nilsson argues that Greek epics and the heroic myth cycles they include (rather than elements or motifs found in individual myths) can be dated to the Mycenaean age (1950 to 1100 B.C.).*]

The question: *How old is Greek mythology?* may at first sight seem idle, for Greek mythology is obviously of many different ages. For example, many genealogies and eponymous heroes created for political purposes are late, such inventions having been made through the whole historical age of Greece; yet most of them are earlier than the very late myths like the campaigns of Dionysus, or the great mass of the metamorphoses, especially the catasterisms, which were invented in the Hellenistic age. The great tragic poets reshaped the myths and left their imprint upon them, so that the forms in which the myths are commonly known nowadays often have been given them by tragedy. Similarly, before the tragic poets, the choric lyric poets reshaped them. The cyclical epics also are thought to have exercised a profound influence upon the remodeling of the myths. In Homer we find many well-known myths, often in forms differing, however, from those in which they are related later. Finally, it cannot be doubted that myths existed before Homer.

Our question concerns, however, not the reshaping and remodeling of myths, which often consists only of an imitation of current patterns, but the real creation of myths, especially the creation of the great cycles of myths. From this standpoint, the Hellenistic and many earlier myths may be put to one side. The tragic poets hardly invent new myths but do reshape old ones, often in a very thorough fashion, and the same is to be said of the choric lyric poets. For the glory and fame of ancient poets depended not, like that of modern poets, on their invention of something quite new and original, but rather on their presentation of the old traditional material in new and original fashion.

Consequently our question concerns the old stock of mythology after all secondary inventions have been discarded and is really not so idle as may appear at first glance. In fact various attempts have been made to give an answer, although the question has not been put so simply and straightforwardly as it is here, but has been enveloped in inquiries and reasonings having other purposes. The point, however, which I wish to emphasize is the importance of the principles which underlie our research and determine our procedure.

I pass over comparative mythology very lightly, because it began to lose favor in my youth, thirty years ago or more, and nowadays is very little reckoned with in scientific discussion. But I should like to draw attention to one point of some interest in this connection. Comparative mythology was so called because it compared Greek myths with those of other Aryan peoples and by this means tried to discover the original myths and religion of the Aryan people from whom the peoples of Europe and some peoples of Asia are descended, just as comparative philology discovered by similar means that the languages of these peoples were derived from the language once spoken by the old Aryans. The underlying supposition was clearly that the Greek myths were pre-Greek in the sense that the Greeks had taken them over from the Aryans and brought them with them when they immigrated into Greece. Comparative mythology overlooked, however, the very important distinction between divine and heroic mythology and thought erroneously that the heroic myths were derived from the same source as the myths concerning the gods. This source it found in the phenomena of nature. If the view of comparative mythology were right, these lectures would really be pointless, for then it must needs be admitted that Greek mythology existed not only in the pre-Homeric age but also before the Greeks immigrated into Greece. But since the seventies of the last century the whole problem has been extraordinarily deepened and complicated. We have learned to distinguish between religion and mythology and we have learned to know a new epoch of Greece which cannot be considered as wholly prehistoric in the usual sense of the word—the Mycenaean age.

Max Müller and his followers condemned Euhemerism, but this theory has come to the fore again in recent years. In my opinion the reaction is just but goes too far. Certain English scholars take mythology as reproducing actual historical facts, just as the logographers did when they brought the myths into a historical system. They do not, of course, overlook the fabulous elements of the myths but think that the mythical persons and such exploits as are not of a fabulous character are good history, and they go so far as to accept without question the mythical genealogies and the mythical chronology. I am unable to do this. I know and appreciate the tenacity of folk memory, but I know also how popular tradition is preserved—and confused and remodeled. The remodeling affects especially the chronological relations of the personages, which are changed freely.[1] In so far as epical tradition is concerned, the right analogy is not the traditions which have an historical aspect but the Nibelungenlied and the Beowulf and similar epical traditions which I shall characterize later. We know how badly historical connections fared in them, how history was confused and mixed up with fabulous elements. If good historical tradition is to be preserved, an undisturbed life both in regard to settling and to civilization is an absolute condition, but the downfall of the Mycenaean civilization was a most stormy and turbulent age, and its turmoils, which mixed up the Greek tribes and changed their places of settlement, mixed up and confused their traditions, too. The historical aspect of Greek mythology and especially the mythical chronology are products of the systematizing of the myths by the poets of cyclical epics and still more the product of rationalization and historification by the logographers.[2]

A very different standpoint is taken by German scholars, whose preoccupation is a historical treatment of the myths; in opposition to the theories of comparative mythology, this school is called the historical school. The answer given by this school is not so simple as that proposed by nature mythology. I must therefore try to clear up the underlying principles to the best of my ability, although the numerous works of the school often are contradictory in details and it is very difficult to do full justice in a short analysis of principles.

The historical school acknowledges that elements of myths existed in an early period, before the development of epic poetry, but supposes that these rather simple elements were brought into connection with one another and composed so as to form more complex myths through the agency of poetry. From this process a very deep-going reshaping and even creation of myths resulted. The poetry to which this creative expanding of mythology is ascribed is the epic poetry; viz., the Homeric and post-Homeric epics, the cyclical epics, and many lost epics of which we have only a scanty and fragmentary knowledge. Further, it is reasonably inferred that epics existed also before Homer and were used in composing the extant Homeric poems.

The historical school assumes not only a remodeling and reshaping of myths but indeed a creation of cycles of myths—and that is what concerns us here—for it is supposed that the mythical cycles came into being through the union of various simple mythical elements. If this process were ascribed to the Mycenaean age, I should have little to say against it; but as it is ascribed

to the Homeric and the immediately preceding and following periods, I must disagree. I shall use a few examples to illustrate the methods of the historical school and the discrepancies to which they lead.

Several years ago Professor Friedländer tried to trace the development of the Heracles cycle.[3] According to his theory, the fundamental fact is the belief of the Tirynthians in their helpful hero. From the Peloponnese, Heracles emigrated to the island of Rhodes and here new adventures were added to those which had been brought from the Peloponnese. Thus the cycle of the twelve adventures was developed and formed on Rhodes.

The most comprehensive and significant example, however, is Professor Bethe's attempt to explain the origin and development of the Trojan cycle.[4] He finds the old kernels of this cycle in the duels between heroes who, according to him, were originally localized on the mainland of Greece. These simple and unconnected myths were brought to Aeolia by the different tribes to which the heroes belonged when these tribes immigrated to northwest Asia Minor shortly before or in the seventh century B. C. The Aeolians brought their Achilles, the Locrians their Aias, the Arcadians Aeneas, and the Troes, who originally were a tribe living in the mother country, the name of the Troes (Trojans), etc. The various myths of the various immigrant tribes met and were fused in Aeolia and were attached to the ruins of the city of Ilion. In this manner the Trojan cycle was created. The destruction of the sixth city of Troy is ascribed to barbarians immigrating from the north. If this view of the development of Homeric poetry were right, it would of course imply not a reshaping but an actual creation of myths, for the fundamental idea of the Trojan cycle would be due to the epic poets of the seventh century B. C. Although space forbids my entering upon a criticism, I cannot but point to the improbability involved in assuming three different waves of immigration into Aeolia about which tradition is absolutely silent. They are invented only in order to suit a hypothesis which is very artificial and has not succeeded in gaining approval.

Another great scholar, Professor Wilamowitz, differs from Professor Bethe in the analysis of the poems but takes the same point of view in regard to the development of the myths. In a recent paper[5] he states briefly that Phthiotians and Magnesians who emigrated from Thessaly to Aeolia brought Achilles with them; that the house of Agamemnon originated at Cyme and in Lesbos, whilst his appearing as king on the mainland of Greece is due to epic poetry; and that Ionians, in whose towns descendants of Glaucus and Sarpedon were rulers, introduced these heroes into the epos. But, and in this he differs essentially from Professor Bethe, who takes the Trojan war to be an invention of the seventh century B. C., he gives voice to the opinion that the historical fact underlying the Homeric story of the Trojan war was an old one, a vain attempt of the Greeks to gain a foothold in the Scamander Valley.

The underlying presumption is an echo of the tribal mythology of K. O. Müller, the founder of the historical school. The leading idea is that the myths were transferred to other regions with the wanderings of the tribes and that, as the tribes met and mixed, their myths met and were fused. If this leading principle were applied to Teutonic epics, we must needs date the Scandinavian invasion of England two or three centuries earlier than it actually took place, for Beowulf tells only of Danes, Swedes, and Geatas, nothing of the English. And we must needs assume an immigration of Teutonic tribes from the Continent to Scandinavia before the ninth or tenth century A. D. in order to explain the fact that the myth of Sigurd appears in the Edda songs. I omit the Russian *bylinas* and their wanderings. I cannot but think that in regard to the wanderings of myths and songs, conditions in Greece were not altogether dissimilar to those in other countries. Consequently I cannot but suppose that even in Greece myths and songs wandered independently of the wanderings of the tribes. As soon as we know anything of the minstrels, we find that they are wandering people. The localizations of cults and heroes must be regarded with a critical eye and must not be used as arguments unless their reliability is tested, for they are often due to the influence of epics. The localizations of Agamemnon are illuminating examples to which I shall recur in another place.[6]

All that we know of other epics tends to show that the fundamental principle, the doctrine that the wanderings and the amalgamating of the myths depend on the wanderings and the amalgamating of the tribes, is erroneous. With this presumption another is connected which, according to my view, is the fundamental error of the method; namely, that two things are identified which must be distinguished—the development of the myths and the development of epic poetry. Moreover, epic poetry is taken into account only to the extent to which it can be reached through an analysis of the extant poems and fragments. It has very often been said that a lost epos of Heracles created the cycle of Heracles, and this may seem not improbable in this case where we do not have the epos but are free to reconstruct it according to our fancy. The attempt to carry through the same idea in regard to the Trojan cycle proved to be a failure and showed the frailty of the principle, for in this case we have the epos and can use it as a control. To take another instance, Professor Wilamowitz contends that the bravery of Diomedes is the oldest song of the Iliad and an imitation of the Thebais.[7] If this is true, it is extremely remarkable that the Theban myths in Homer and Hesiod differ so markedly from the common version.[8] The unavoidable conclusion would be that the Thebais, supposed to be

earlier than Homer, has not been able to impress its version either upon Homer or upon Hesiod. Wild shoots of the myth have lived in spite of epical cultivation.

The fundamental but hardly expressed principle underlying the work of the historical school is that a mythological cycle is created and developed through the agency of and contemporaneously with the development of epic poetry; and furthermore, only that epic poetry is taken into account of which we have some knowledge through literary sources. But this principle does not stand the test. The opposite alternative also must be considered; namely, that a cycle of myths existed in its chief outlines and was the store from which the Homeric poets drew, of course not without remodeling the material, in composing their chants. If this view is accepted, the epic poets followed the same line as the choric lyric and the tragic poets, who took over and utilized the old store of myths, remodeling them, sometimes profoundly. This is the case with epic poetry in countries where our knowledge of its development is fuller than is our knowledge of the development of the Greek epics. Neither of the two alternatives is strictly demonstrable, but it ought to be evident that both are to be taken into consideration.

The view of the development of mythology which I have tried to characterize here is, however, closely bound up with the methods of Homeric research prevailing among the scholars who have adopted it; namely, with the literary analysis of the poems. In England and America this method is now little heeded, and Homeric research follows different lines. I think in fact that full justice has hardly been done to this method and the many works produced by its adherents. In spite of the apparent discrepancies in their results, they have brought about a profounder apprehension of Homer and Homeric problems and have obtained important results. But literary analysis is not the last word in the Homeric question. To shut our eyes to a further development than that which can be traced through literary analysis leads us astray, if the earlier development is regarded as irrelevant because it is hard to unravel. Such a standpoint is unjustifiable, but it is in fact taken up by those who ascribe the development of the mythical cycles to the Homeric and post-Homeric periods, neglecting what may have happened in an earlier age of which no literary records are preserved. The Homeric question must be widened so as to be the epic question. The proverb says: *vixere etiam ante Agamemnona fortes viri;* I think: *vixere etiam ante Homerum poetae.* Homeric poetry is an issue of countless generations. That is recognized, generally speaking, but we must try to work out in earnest the implications of this thesis.

The gap is apparent if the two following questions are put side by side: *How far can literary analysis be carried back?* and *How old are the oldest elements in Homeric poetry which can be dated with certainty?*

Literary analysis discovers earlier poems which the Homeric poets utilized and partly took over in composing their poems. Not even the most zealous unitarians deny that such poems may have existed. Nobody will of course believe that these earlier poems were written down, so that they could have been preserved for a long time. But if they were preserved by the memory of the minstrels and handed down by oral tradition, it is difficult to imagine that they survived more than two or at most three generations. However, I have nothing against granting them a life of four or five generations, although that they survived so long seems extremely unlikely. The unavoidable conclusion is that the earliest poems incorporated in the Homeric poems and utilized in their composition cannot be more than a century or a little more older than the Homeric poems themselves. That is the limit which literary analysis cannot transgress.

Archaeology affords means of dating certain elements appearing in Homeric poetry. The latest of these elements belong to the Orientalizing period; here we are concerned with the oldest. These go back to the Mycenaean age and moreover, what is most remarkable, many of them to its earliest phase.[9] At this point a few hints concerning this important subject must suffice. Homeric arms have given rise to a vast literature, and Nestor's cup is often mentioned; yet the body shield was already superseded by the small shield in late Mycenaean times—the attempts to vindicate it for later periods are proved by archaeology to be futile. Nestor's cup was found in the fourth shaft-grave at Mycenae, one of the earlier group. To this another most remarkable observation is to be added; namely, that these Mycenaean elements appear not only in the earliest and earlier parts of the Homeric poems but in the latest and later parts also. For example, the boars' tusk helmet which we had been unable to understand until aided by the Mycenaean finds is described in one of the very latest parts, the lay of Dolon.

Archaeology is, however, not the sole means of dating some elements of Homeric poetry; there are also references to conditions of history and civilization which may serve the same end. When we meet the Phoenicians as masters of the sea and traders who bring the most appreciated and valuable articles to Greece, we recognize of course the end of the Geometric and the beginning of the Orientalizing period. On the other hand, Homer hardly mentions the Dorians although at his time they had already long inhabited the Peloponnese. The king of Mycenae is the overlord of the Greeks, and the other heroes are his vassals. Mycenae rich in gold is the foremost city of Greece and its king the mightiest monarch of Greece. The attempt to derogate these facts[10] is vain, for it is inconceivable that an Ionian minstrel of the seventh century B. C. should have happened on the idea of ascribing such a position to the town and the king of Mycenae, which at that time was in fact a rotten borough. Nor has Agamemnon any real existence except in the Trojan cycle, although the contrary often is asserted.[11] Attempts to deny these facts can only lead us into error and to the erection of frail hypotheses. Here we ought also to speak of the really kingly power of Agamemnon, but as this is not so evident I shall recur to it in a later place.

In regard to these elements in Homer, derived from widely differing times and civilizations, scholars have divided themselves into two parties engaging in a tug of war. One party tries to put as much as possible in a time as late as possible; namely, into the developed Geometric and the Orientalizing periods, and to treat the elements which it is impossible to fit into this scheme as irrelevant survivals. The other party treats the elements which undoubtedly belong to a late age as irrelevant additions and takes Homer on the whole to be Mycenaean. It appears that neither of these two methods is the right one. We have to concede without circumlocutions that Homer contains elements from very differing periods and to try to comprehend and explain this state of things, not to obliterate it and get rid of it through artificial interpretations.

The gap between the earliest and the latest elements in Homer comes nearer to a whole millenium than to a half-millenium. Literary analysis of the extant poems can reach only the time immediately preceding the latest elements and so can cover only a very small part of this gap, say a century or at most a little more. Some scholars who think that we cannot attain a well founded opinion of the stages preceding the literary evidence have confined themselves to literary analysis. The unitarians by principle are still less interested in the preceding stages. But this voluntary restriction makes them shut their eyes to more far-reaching vistas and vitiates the fundamental problem. The epic question has been unduly limited to the Homeric question. The extant Homeric poems are, however, the final achievement of a lengthy development—*fuere etiam ante Homerum poetae;* the epic question, i.e., the problem of the origin and development of Greek epics from their beginnings, cannot be put on one side.

It can be understood why some scholars have done so, for they are of the opinion that all means are wanting for attacking a problem which goes so far back into an unknown age. That is not literally true; for there is a method which may be utilized. Since, however, it is neither strictly philological nor strictly historical but is comparative in a general sense, it is viewed with undue diffidence by many who know it only from the outside.

Many years ago Professor Steinthal tried to introduce a comparative study of epics, but his attempt had no decided success, chiefly because he was hampered by the romantic presumption of collective popular poetry. A comprehensive study of this vast subject has never been taken up, only hints and minor attempts have been made. Professor von Pöhlmann drew attention to living epic poetry and pointed to the failure of Homeric research in not taking this into account,[12] but in vain. Professor Drerup gave a survey of various popular epics[13] but seems to have been forgotten, perhaps because these materials were not utilized by him in their true bearing upon Greek epics. English works are one-sided, and that is true not only of Professor Andrew Lang's more cursory comparison of Homeric epics with the *chansons de geste*[14] but also of Professor Chadwick's important book, in which he institutes a detailed comparison between Greek and Teutonic epics.[15] It is self-evident that a comparison ought to be instituted on the largest possible basis, and that everything which is accidental and not essential ought to be discarded.[16]

It is impossible here to give an account of the numerous instances of popular epics. I simply enumerate them. We have, in the first place, Teutonic epics in their branches: old German, Anglo-Saxon, and Scandinavian epics. Their off-shoots are, at least in part, Finnish-Esthonian, Russian, and even old French epics (*bylinas* and *chansons de geste*). In Serbia popular epics are still living; in Asia we find epics among several tribes, the Kara-Kirgizes and the Abakan Tartars in Siberia and the Atchinese on Sumatra. The historical incidents underlying Greek mediaeval epics (Digenis Akritas) are too little known. From a comparative study of these epics the following statements may be deduced. Epics do not originate in collective popular poetry but are the creation of a heroic age, a fact which Professor Wundt stated and Professor Chadwick developed at length. They originate in an aristocratic or even feudal society, praising the deeds of living men and describing contemporary events, but mythical traits and folk-tale elements may be attributed even to living men. The exaggerated praise of heroes and the still undeveloped intellectualism of the age, from the very beginning, open the doors for the supernatural. Epic poetry is composed not by the people in general but by certain gifted individuals, who live as minstrels and often as court minstrels in the *entourage* of some great man. But there is no intellectual cleavage between persons of higher and of lower standing; the lower classes share the warlike spirit and the admiration of valorous deeds and take up epics enthusiastically.

This is the original stage, which usually is short-lived. It is impossible to confine the subsequent development within a scheme, as Professor Chadwick has attempted, but two alternatives are to be considered. The heroic age may continue; epics chant ever fresh materials which change according to circumstances. Or the heroic age may come to an end and the people settle down to a less eventful life. But the interest in great deeds and the zeal for epic poetry do not die out immediately. Epic poetry is preserved but it sings now of the deeds of a past age and shows a tendency to limit itself to one cycle or to very few cycles of adventures, from which the minstrels choose their subjects, although fresh songs are invented, additions made, and changes devised. Under such conditions epics may be still more popular than before and may spread among the common people but they are in a certain sense stagnant.

This state of things may be interrupted by a new heroic age and by new epics dealing with contemporary men and events, but the stagnant conditions may also continue until epics are abandoned for other kinds of literature or obliterated by a higher culture. The epics may also wander far abroad and be received by people who lead a monotonous life on a low cultural plane but love poetry and preserve the epic chants. Of course epic poetry will undergo many and varied changes under such varying conditions.

Epic poetry is a floating mass confined within certain limits. This it is essential to know and to understand, and to this end the art and technique of composition must be considered; they seem to be similar everywhere. The art of singing is always exercised by certain gifted persons; but talents vary, and the most gifted become craftsmen, minstrels who chant in the courts or to the people according to circumstances. Everyone learns through hearing, consequently family tradition is important. Families, even schools, of minstrels appear.

The art of singing and of composing epic poetry is learned, and hence a question of fundamental importance is, how this art is learned. First, it is to be stated that every one learns through hearing; but that a poem is never learned and repeated word by word, even if a minstrel takes over and repeats a chant, as occurs frequently. In fact the forms of a poem are just as many as its recitals. The variability differs considerably, however, according to time, individuals, and other conditions.

For that which is learned is essentially not single poems, even though a successful chant may be learned and repeated by others, but is the epical technique, the poetical art by which the material is formed; the subject may be taken from the usual store or a new one may be chosen. Every chant is in its form more or less an improvisation, so that the minstrels may claim divine inspiration as Phemius does in the Odyssey. Such an art of singing is possible because the minstrel through lengthy practice possesses a language which puts words and phrases on his lips.

In the epical language of all peoples occurs a store of stock expressions, constantly recurring phrases, half and whole verses and even verse complexes; and repetitions are characteristic of the epic style. E.g., when a message is delivered it is repeated word for word. Of the 27,853 verses in Homer, 2,118 verses occur two or more times making a total of 5,162 repeated verses, or one-fifth of Homer. Furthermore, typical descriptions are characteristic of all epics. Though they are not repeated in identical words, they are substantially identical. These are the elements which the epical technique delivers ready for use to the minstrel forming his chant. What is said of the Kara Kirgiz minstrels is applicable to all: The singer has a large store of poetical parts ready, and his art consists in coordinating these parts according to the course of events and connecting them by the aid of new-made verses. A skilled poet is able to improvise a poem on every subject.[17]

If we consider the effect of this traditional technique, we understand why epics which sing of by-gone days always archaize both in contents and in language. The stock expressions and typical descriptions preserve the old elements, even if they are no longer understood, and introduce them into even the latest chants. The old background of events is kept because the singer is conscious of chanting the past and not his own time, but with the naïveté characteristic of his cultural stage the minstrel mixes up the old elements with new taken from his own time.

These general statements agree completely with what Greek epics themselves, especially the Odyssey, say as to the art and manner of the recital of Greek mistrels, and we may surmise with certainty that it was not otherwise in the pre-Homeric age. The fact that the stock expressions often are philologically very old-fashioned and that their meaning was no longer understood by the minstrels themselves proves a great antiquity in the epical technique and in the epics themselves. If this high degree of antiquity of epical tradition is considered earnestly, a natural explanation ensues of the fact that Homer contains elements which differ in age by more than half a millenium, in fact by nearly a whole millenium. This long lapse of time is not amazing though it may seem so; Russian epics vegetated nearly a millenium, preserving reminiscences of the empire of Kieff and the age of the Vikings.

To this view that the origins of Greek epics must be carried back into the Mycenaean age a serious objection may be made. For the Mycenaean civilization is essentially Minoan, and it is an acknowledged fact that the Minoan civilization sprang from a non-Greek and not Aryan people at all. Consequently Sir Arthur Evans himself and many scholars take the Mycenaeans to be Minoans who have established themselves on the mainland of Greece and subjugated the indigenous population. He admits the view that epics go back into the Mycenaean age and supposes consequently that they were at first chanted in the Minoan language and after-

wards, in a bilingual society, transferred into Greek.[18] A similar process took place elsewhere, but the result was in reality new epics, and such a process would of course invalidate the above reasoning concerning the preservation of old elements through the epical technique.

Like epics, mythology, too, would consequently originate among the Minoan people. But this seems to be disproved through the fact that almost all mythical names are clearly Greek; those which are certainly Minoan are extremely few. One would of course expect a considerable number of Minoan mythical names if the epos descended from the Minoans. In spite of the great authority of the scholar I have mentioned, I am firmly convinced that the Mycenaeans were immigrated Greeks who took over the Minoan civilization. It would take too long to set forth my reasons and I refer the reader to previous writings in which I have dwelt upon this question.[19] This view is prevailing nowadays. Younger archaeologists are prone to throw back the commencement of the Greek immigration to the end of the Early Helladic age or earlier, whilst I find it probable that it began at the end of the following Middle Helladic age. Thus I take it for granted that the Mycenaeans were Greeks, and I hope that the following exposition will corroborate this view.

Epics praise heroes and originate in a heroic age. They belong to a social milieu in which certain persons become prominent through power, wealth, or deeds, and desire to be praised and chanted. Such an age was the Mycenaean age; for although opinions differ, it was admittedly an age of great wanderings of tribes and peoples, and its wealth and power are proved by the treasures of the shaft-graves of Mycenae, and of the bee-hive tombs at Dendra, Vaphio, etc., not to mention the bee-hive tombs themselves, the palaces, and the mighty walls of the cities. To this age the oldest elements in Homer go back, and I hesitate not the least in stating that in this age Greek epics originated. The minstrels chanted their songs at first to the princes and their retainers, but the people, who shared this admiration for valorous deeds, took over the epics and preserved them.

The stormy Mycenaean age came to an end and the subsequent transitional period between the Mycenaean and the Geometric ages is the poorest and darkest in all Greek history and pre-history. Conditions were poor and straitened; people were attached to the soil; and Greece was split up into a great number of cantons without much intercommunication, as the marked local varieties of Geometric ceramics prove as contrasted with the uniformity of Mycenaean pottery. Moreover, the Phoenicians became masters of the sea. It seems unthinkable that epics originated in such a time, but epics which already existed may very well have been preserved, stagnant and vegetating, just as they were, e.g., in Russia or Finland. The subjects were limited to one or two cycles, to the Trojan and perhaps even the Theban cycle. Why these were preferred to others is just as difficult to say as why the unimportant skirmish of Roncevaux was put into the foreground of French epics. How epics were transmitted we have already seen. The elements were at hand and they were repeatedly composed anew and mixed up with new elements.

In the ninth and the following centuries a fresh life cropped up in Greece; wealth commenced to increase; the Greeks began again to sail the sea and to make expeditions on a large scale; the period of colonization began, which in a certain sense is another heroic age; but aristocracy preserved still its social and political privileges. Thus the ground was prepared for a renascence of epics, but the old tradition was so vigorous that the old cycle was kept and the new elements incorporated with it. The really new creation is the Odyssey, which does not deny the stamp of the age of colonization which it glorifies. The salient point was, however, the appearance of a great poet, whom I should like to call Homer. He infused new life and vigor into epic poetry, putting the psychology of his heroes into the foreground and planning a comprehensive composition under this aspect.

I may seem to have given an only too dogmatic exposition of my opinions of the Homeric question instead of entering upon the subject of the Mycenaean origin of Greek mythology. But this exposition could not be passed over, because some scholars neglect the previous stages of Homeric poetry, and others adhere to the opinion that before the time which on an average may be called the Homeric age only single and disconnected myths existed and that these myth elements were composed into cycles of myths by the poets whose chief representative is Homer. If this were right, my thesis that the cycles of myths go back into the Mycenaean age would evidently be wrong.

In opposition to this view I have tried to prove two things: The first is that the development of epics lasted much longer and that epics go back into an early period of the Mycenaean age, a fact which is proved by the Mycenaean elements imbedded in the epos. It is clear that this first point must be still more valid for mythology than for archaeological objects or for elements of civilization and social life, because both the latter are much more liable to be altered and changed through assimilation to the conditions prevailing at the time when the poems were composed. Thus we have a great general probability that the myths occurring in Homer go back into the Mycenaean age, though nothing is proved in detail for specific myths.

Secondly, it appears that the background of the Greek epos, i.e., the Trojan cycle in its chief features, the power of Mycenae, and the kingship of Mycenae, can-

not possibly have come into existence through the joining together of minor chants and myths, but that it existed beforehand, being the cycle from which the minstrels took their subjects. A cycle of events with certain chief personages invariably appears in all the epic poetry of which we have a more definite knowledge than we have of Greek epics as the background from which episodes are taken and to which episodes are joined; it is a premiss of epics, not their ultimate result. I refer to the tale of the Nibelungen in German epics, to that of Roland in old French epics, to the narratives of Vladimir the Great and his men in the *bylinas,* of Marko Kraljevitch and the battle on the Throstle Field in Servian epics, of the Islamic prince Manas and the heathen prince Joloi in the Kara Kirgiz epics, etc. In the same manner the background of the Homeric epos—the story of the war of Troy between the Trojans and the Greek heroes under Agamemnon's leadership, or, in other words, the chief features of the Trojan cycle—must be the primary fact and originate in the Mycenaean age. From this the minstrels chose and to this they added episodes. It is of course in detail uncertain and questionable what is of ancient origin and what is added later; here we are concerned with the fundamental idea, which we call the Trojan cycle, and we have tried to prove that this idea originated in the same age as the epos, the Mycenaean age.

I have drawn attention to the fact that the minstrels limited their choice to one or two cycles of myths. Other myths may have been chanted at an earlier age and have gone out of fashion. It may not be inferred that other cycles did not exist or were quite forgotten. We have to take account not only of epics but also of plain tales told in prose and preserving a great number of myths which lyric and tragic poets made famous in a later age. Such prose epics are not unparalleled. The cycle of the Nartes, heroes of the Ossetes and other peoples of the Caucasus, is told in prose.[20]

It can be demonstrated that numerous other myths and cycles of myths go back into the Mycenaean age. I begin by referring to an acute philological observation which proves that a number of mythical heroes must go back to an age much earlier than that of Homer. Professor Kretschmer drew attention to the fundamental difference between two series of heroic names.[21] The names of the older series have the ending -*eus* and are generally abbreviated forms; the names of the sons of these mythical personages are on the contrary chiefly common compound names; e.g., Peleus, Achilleus, as compared with Neoptolemus; Odysseus—Telemachus; Atreus—Agamemnon, Menelaus; Tydeus—Diomedes; Neleus—Nestor; Oeneus—Meleager, etc. The names of the older series are often difficult to explain etymologically; those of the younger series are clear and explicable. It is evident that the heroes whose names belong to the series ending in -*eus* go back to earlier times than the heroes with common names, and to this philological fact corresponds the mythological fact that the latter are said to be sons and descendants of the former. But the latter are quite current in Homeric poetry; their ancestors must consequently go back to much earlier, pre-Homeric times. That this time is the Mycenaean age is of course not demonstrable through philology solely, but the span of time necessary for the development of this difference must be supposed so great that these heroes are thrown back some centuries and very probably into the Mycenaean age. And if the names are so old, the myths attached to them must also be so to a certain extent.

It may be rightly objected that hereby only the great antiquity of isolated myths is demonstrated, but it can also be proved that the great mythical cycles are very much older than Homer, that, in fact, they go back to the Mycenaean age. I have briefly given the proof of this in earlier writings[22] and a detailed discussion will be the chief content of my subsequent lectures; here I dwell only on the question of principles. We know that mythology was the guide which led to the discovery of the Mycenaean and Minoan sites; it conducted Mr. Schliemann to Troy and Mycenae and Sir Arthur Evans to Cnossus. In these cases myths served as a heuristic means and the success of the investigations thus induced proved a connection between mythological centers and Mycenaean centers. My proof is nothing but a consequent application of this principle, a thorough-going comparison of the cities to which mythological cycles are attached with the cities where finds from the Mycenaean age have been made. If the correlation is constant; i.e., if we find that the cities to which the mythological cycles are attached were the centers of the Mycenaean civilization also, this constant correlation cannot be considered as accidental; it will prove the connection between the mythological cycles and the Mycenaean civilization; i.e., that the mythological cycles in their chief outlines go back into the Mycenaean age.

The proof however goes much further. For a close inspection shows that the mythical importance of a site closely corresponds to its importance in Mycenaean civilization. The mythical importance of a city is, to use a mathematical term, a function of its importance in Mycenaean civilization. This close and constant correspondence precludes any thought of casual coincidence. There are additional proofs also, elements inherent in certain myths which are of Mycenaean origin, but as these are less frequent and sometimes doubtful, they must be discussed separately.

To the application and elaboration of this principle of the close relationship between mythology and Mycenaean sites the following exposition will be devoted. But I am well aware of the difficulties and pitfalls of the detailed discussion and therefore it will be to the purpose to add some methodological remarks.

In regard to the Mycenaean remains, it may be objected that they are known only incompletely and that they have not been methodically explored all over Greece.[23] That is true, for every year new discoveries are made. In time their distribution will certainly be much better known than now, but on the other hand it seems not likely that the picture will be changed essentially. The primacy of Argolis and next to it of Boeotia will remain. And so much is already known concerning other provinces that it is hardly to be expected that new discoveries will greatly change their relative importance. The map of Mycenaean sites and civilization will be completed, not turned upside down nor even substantially altered. Certain irregularities exist which will be treated in due course.[24]

In regard to mythology, certain points ought to be emphasized. We have noted that myths were remodeled in late and even in very late times. The science of mythography sets forth the development of the myths as far as it can be traced with the aid of literary and monumental evidence. As mythographic research is concerned with the historical period of the development of the myths, we have here only to accept its results, when it proves that certain forms of myths are developed or added in historical times. Far-reaching deductions concerning the development of the myths have often been connected with the reconstructions of lost epics or of those preserved only in fragments, but these reconstructions are very hypothetical and conflicting and must be regarded with a certain diffidence. The form in which a myth appears in Homer is often treated with a certain disesteem; nevertheless it must be considered thoroughly because it is the oldest recorded form, although of course not always the oldest form which has existed.

Further, a distinction is to be made between myths of different kinds and especially between divine and heroic mythology. The divine mythology consists of myths concerning the gods, and cult myths. I cannot dwell here upon this important distinction; we are little concerned with divine mythology and only casually with cult myths. Nor are we concerned with the many minor and isolated myths which crop up everywhere. For every town had its heroes or made them, and eponymous heroes were created freely. We are chiefly concerned with the cycles of heroic mythology and our aim is to test to what extent their distribution and varying importance correspond to the Mycenaean remains.

Well marked differences appear even in heroic mythology, since it incorporated very different elements, beginning with folk-tales and ending with incidents having a rather historical appearance. Motifs of the folk-tale are, e.g., prominent in the myths of Perseus and of Achilles, whilst on the contrary the Pylian myths seem very little mythical, but rather almost historical.

This is intelligible in view of the lengthy development of myths and of epics. The Pylian cycle is a late creation referring to the deeds of princes who were very little mythologized, whilst Perseus and Achilles are older and more popular heroes. The Oedipus myth is in its kernel a folk-tale, but the War of the Seven is an historical myth and the same seems to be true of the Minyans of Orchomenus.

I am quite aware of the difficulty of the subject and I am prepared to be met with objections. It will perhaps be said that I resuscitate the old and justly condemned method of eliciting history from myths. There are certainly historical facts underlying heroic myths to a certain extent, but mythology can never be converted into history, and we can never attain a knowledge of these historical facts if there is not an independent historical tradition as there is, e.g., in the case of the Nibelungenlied. For myths are always myths and largely fiction; the underlying facts have been reshaped and confused by fiction. For Greek myths no historical tradition exists which can serve as a control. There is only archaeology, and control by archaeology does not suffice for proving historical events but serves at most to present the cultural milieu. This cultural background, however, carries weight. If details in my reasoning may be contradicted or proved to be erroneous, this does not ruin the whole. The historical background of Greek heroic mythology is amply proved by its close correspondence to the geographical distribution of Mycenaean civilization.

That the thesis of the Mycenaean origin of Greek mythology has not been set forth and recognized earlier is due to some peculiar circumstances. Although numerous works of art and various sculptural or pictorial representations from the Mycenaean age have been discovered, mythical scenes seemed to be wanting in these works. They have been eagerly sought for, but those representations which until lately were claimed to have mythical contents are very doubtful. One is the so-called Scylla of a Cretan seal impression depicting a man in a boat who seems to fight with a marine monster rising up from the sea. The monster is not like Scylla and it is very doubtful whether a mythical incident is here represented.[25] The second instance is a gold ring from a find near Tiryns, the engravings on which represent a ship and two couples, each consisting of a man and a woman. The scene is called the abduction of Helen, but this interpretation has never been taken in earnest; it is quite arbitrary; the scene may as well be a scene of salutation or of congée. It belongs probably to the scenes of daily life which sometimes occur in Mycenaean art.[26] I prefer to pass over the famous treasure from Thisbe in silence.[27]

In the light of these facts one must needs reason as follows: the Minoan art, which had no mythical but only cultual representations, was taken over wholly and without change by the Mycenaeans. It is practically certain that Minoan artists worked for the Mycenaean sires; as mythical representations were absent from their art, Mycenaean myths were not depicted although they were related. Even elsewhere Mycenaean characteristics were ousted by Minoan art and appear only rarely and hesitatingly. It seems, however, somewhat astonishing that the Mycenaeans had a rich supply of myths but did not depict them in spite of their high standard of art, although such a fact would not be inconceivable. The same thing occurs in Geometric art, which loves to depict men, women, horses, and ships but does not represent mythical scenes—though there are one or two exceptions belonging to its late phase. But the Geometric period is the Homeric age, which had plenty of myths.

Quite recently, however, a new discovery has put it beyond doubt that myths were represented occasionally even in Mycenaean art. Among the very rich and beautiful contents of the bee-hive tomb at Dendra, near old Mideia, which was excavated in 1926 by Professor Persson, were eight plaques of blue glass, evidently made in a mold, for they are identical. They show a woman sitting on the back of a big bull.[28] The representation is very similar to that of the well-known metope from Selinus, and if it had belonged to classical times everybody would have immediately recognized Europa on the back of the bull. I am unable to see why we should not accept this identification, even if the object is Mycenaean.

Among the same finds there are also another glass plaque and fragments of two others which represent a big standing lion and before it a man.[29] From the back of the lion a head seems to grow up; the lion's tail is very long. The plaques are in a bad state of preservation so that details are uncertain, but it cannot reasonably be doubted that this is another mythical representation, the Chimaera and Bellerophon. It may seem astonishing that of the two myths illustrated the scenes of both are laid in foreign countries—I shall recur to this topic later.[30] A third representation referring to a Greek myth is that of two centaurs, each with a dagger in his hand, on a steatite gem found by Dr. Blegen in a Late Mycenaean tomb during his excavations at the Argive Heraeum.[31] Here I wish only to stress the fact that Mycenaean representations of Greek myths actually have come to light. If it is proved that the myths of Europa, of Bellerophon, and of the Centaurs go back into the Mycenaean age, the view will be still more justified that the great mythical cycles also which are attached to the Mycenaean centers go back into the Mycenaean age.

Notes

[1] See my article "Ueber die Glaubwürdigkeit der Volksüberlieferung bes. in Bezug auf die alte Geschichte" in the Italian periodical *Scientia,* 1930, pp. 319 *et seq.*

[2] The lectures of one of my predecessors in the Sather professorship, Professor Myres, came into my hands through the kindness of the author after my lectures had already been written down. Professor Myres thinks that heroic genealogy makes up a fairly reliable chronological scheme. My different standpoint I hope to justify in the following pages. I have tried to take justly into account the circumstances of time, of popular tradition, and of the transmission of epic poetry.

[3] P. Friedländer, "Herakles," *Philologische Untersuchungen,* H. XIX (1907).

[4] E. Bethe, *Homer,* I-III (1914-27; Vol. II, ed. 2, with only slight additions, 1929).

[5] U. v. Wilamowitz-Moellendorff, "Die griechische Heldensage, II," *Sitzungsberichte der preussischen Akademie der Wissenschaften,* 1925, p. 241.

[6] Below pp. 148 *et seq.*

[7] U. v. Wilamowitz-Moellendorff, *Die Ilias und Homer* (1916), p. 339.

[8] *Il.* xxiii, v. 676 *et seq.;* Hesiod, *Erga,* v. 161 *et seq.*

[9] H. L. Lorimer, "Defensive Armour in Homer," *Liverpool Annals of Archaeology and Anthropology,* XV (1928), pp. 89 *et seq.;* and "Homer's Use of the Past," *Journal of Hellenic Studies,* XLIX (1929), pp. 145 *et seq.*

[10] Bethe, *loc. cit.;* cp. below p. 45.

[11] *Vide* below, pp. 46 *et seq.*

[12] R. v. Pöhlmann, "Zur geschichtlichen Beurteilung Homers," *Sybel's historische Zeitschrift,* LXXIII (1894), pp. 385 *et seq.;* reprinted in his "Gesammelte Abhandlungen," *Aus Altertum und Gegenwart,* I., pp. 56 *et seq.* What he says, p. 59, is true to this day: "Es ist ein wesentlicher Mangel der modernen Homer-Forschung, dass sie dieses gerade für die geschichtliche Seite der homerischen Frage so überaus wichtige Material bei weitem noch nicht in dem Umfang herangezogen und verwertet hat, in welchem es uns jetzt vorliegt."

[13] E. Drerup, "Homerische Poetik," I., *Das Homerproblem in der Gegenwart* (1921), pp. 27 *et seq.* Cp. the brief survey by John Meier, *Werden und Leben des Volksepos* (1909).

[14] A. Lang, *Homer and his Age* (1906), pp. 297 *et seq.*

[15] H. M. Chadwick, *The Heroic Age* (1912).

[16] I hope to be able to give a fuller exposition of this subject in a forthcoming book with the title *Homer and Mycenae,* the basis of which is a series of lectures delivered in the University of London in 1929.

[17] W. Radloff, "Die Sprachen der nördlichen Türkstämme," V, *Der Dialekt der Kara-Kirgizen* (1885), p. xvi.

[18] A. J. Evans, *Journal of Hellenic Studies,* XXXII (1912), pp. 387 *et seq.*

[19] In my *Minoan-Mycenaean Religion,* pp. 11 *et seq.*

[20] G. Dumézil, *Légendes sur les Nartes* (1930).

[21] P. Kretschmer, in the periodical *Glotta,* X (1920), pp. 305 *et seq.*

[22] See my article, "Der mykenische Ursprung der griechischen Mythologie," '[*Antidōron*] *Festschrift für J. Wackernagel* (1924), pp. 137, *et seq.* and my *History of Greek Religion,* pp. 38 *et seq.*

[23] A good but very summary review of the prehistoric sites and find-places is given by Dr. Fimmen in his book, *Die kretisch-mykenische Kultur* (1921). The second edition (1924) is merely a reprint with very slight additions. In particular, a better map is needed than the rather poor one which has been added; moreover, the Mycenaean sites ought to be sharply distinguished from the pre-Mycenaean sites. A summary of the reports on excavations and finds with very rich illustrative material is given by the late Professor O. Montelius in his work, *La Grèce préclassique,* I, II:2 (1924-28). It is to be regretted that this posthumous work has not been brought up to date.

[24] Cp. below pp. 128 and 182.

[25] British School at Athens, *Annual,* IX, p. 58, fig. 36; the latest treatment by S. Marinatos . . .

[26] See e.g. my *Minoan-Mycenaean Religion,* p. 44, n. 3.

[27] A. J. Evans, "The Ring of Nestor, etc.", *Journal of Hellenic Studies,* XL (1925), pp. 1 *et seq.* The genuineness of this most amazing find is vigorously contested; I have given some objections in my *Minoan-Mycenaean Religion,* pp. 304 *et seq.*

[28] A. W. Persson, *Kungagraven i Dendra* (1928), p. 123; cp. below p. 38, n. 6.

[29] *Loc. cit.,* p. 125.

[30] Below pp. 53 *et seq.*

[31] Dr. Blegen has kindly shown me a design of this

gem, which will be published in his forthcoming work, *Prosymna,* and has given me his permission to mention it.

Richard Caldwell (essay date 1989)

SOURCE: "Texts and Contexts," in *The Origin of the Gods: A Psychoanalytic Study of Greek Theogonic Myth*, Oxford University Press, 1989, pp. 71-93.

[*In the following essay, Caldwell reviews early Greek history to Hesiod and examines similarities between Greek and Near Eastern creation myths.*]

Before Hesiod

Shortly before the end of the eighth century B.C., a Boiotian Greek named Hesiod wrote or dictated a poem of some one thousand lines on the beginning of the world, the emergence of the first gods, and the conflicts between generations, which resulted finally in the permanent seizure of power by Zeus, ruler of the world and king over gods and men.[1] We do not know what name, if any, Hesiod gave to his poem, but it has always been known as the *Theogony,* the "Origin of the Gods" (the Greek word is *theogonia,* from *theos,* "god," and *gone,* "birth" or "offspring" or "generation"). The *Theogony* is also literally a cosmogony, an account of the beginning of the world (from *kosmos,* "world"), but since in Greek myth as in many creation myths the component parts of the universe as it gradually came into existence were also gods and goddesses, the two terms are here synonymous.

Hesiod and his contemporary Homer stand at one of the great dividing points in Greek history, as authors of the earliest surviving works of Greek literature. Although most modern scholars regard Homer as somewhat earlier than Hesiod, this is not certain; the earliest ancient authorities seemed to think that Hesiod was earlier than Homer, and they may be correct. The very fact that priority is disputable shows that there is no incontrovertible evidence that either Homer or Hesiod knew the works of the other. What similarities exist between the two poets should not be taken as borrowings or references, but rather as signs they both were composing within a long-established tradition of oral poetry, which now, for the first time, could be preserved in writing.

Hesiod and Homer invented neither writing nor literature, but their works were the first committed to writing in the alphabetic script the Greeks borrowed from Phoenicia, probably during the eight century.[2] Once before the Greeks had possessed a method of writing, the syllabic script known as Linear B, which the Myceneans adopted from Minoan Crete. The use of Linear B, however, seems to have ended with the destruction of Mycenean civilization 500 years before Hesiod, and in any case the surviving Linear B material contains nothing literary or mythological except for the names of a few gods, some of them familiar.

It is not only literature that began to receive definite form at the time of Hesiod; Greek history itself can be said to have begun during the eighth century. Everything before this time, despite the brief presence of Mycenean writing, is prehistoric in the sense that virtually all we know about the way people lived, including their religious beliefs and myths, is based on the physical remains studied by archaeologists and not on written records. For this reason almost everything said in the following survey of Greek prehistory is probable at best; the present state of our knowledge does not allow certainty in most matters, and in some of the most important does not even guarantee probability. This is not true, at least to the same extent, of the ancient Near East, where written records and literature existed long before the arrival of the first Greek-speaking people in Greece, starting at the end of the third millennium. Nevertheless the question of influence and exchange between Greece and the East during the prehistoric period is still largely a mystery.

The Greek language is Indo-European; that is, it belongs to the large family of languages derived from a single language spoken by a hypothetical people who lived in northeast Europe or northwest Asia during the Neolithic period. In irregular waves of migration from the beginning of the third millennium to the middle of the second, descendants of this people spread throughout Europe and into central Asia as far east as India. One branch of these Indo-European nomads, who spoke an early form of the language we now know as Greek, entered the mainland of Greece around the beginning of the second millennium. They presumably brought with them both poetry and a polytheistic religion in which the chief god was associated with fatherhood and the sky, since these are elements of the general Indo-European tradition. In Greece they met, probably conquered, and merged with a native people, the early Helladic culture of the beginning of the Greek Bronze Age; before the coming of the Greeks, metallurgy had been introduced into Helladic Greece from the east, just as argiculture, the domestication of animals, and the painting of pottery had come earlier to Greece from Mesopotamia through Asia Minor. We know hardly anything about Helladic religion, of which only a few figurines have survived; whether it may have resembled the religion of nearby Minoan Crete remains a guess.

When the first Greeks entered Greece, one of the great civilizations of the ancient world was already flourishing on the island of Crete to the south. This culture, known as Minoan after Minos, the mythical king of Crete, had been in contact with the Near East and Egypt during the third millennium; thanks to these contacts (which were to increase greatly during the second millennium), a favorable climate, and a protected location, the Minoans had developed a prosperous civilization with large unfortified cities, great royal palaces, and spectacular refinements in art and architecture. The Minoans also possessed writing in the form of a pictographic or hieroglyphic script, which developed later into Linear A, the syllabary that the Myceanean Greeks adopted to write Greek. Since neither Minoan scripts have been deciphered, all our evidence for Minoan religion is pictorial and conjectural. A goddess (or probably goddesses, who may yet represent different aspects of one goddess), presumably associated with the earth and fertility, seems to be the dominant figure; male figures who may be gods appear, and later myths such as Hesiod's story of the infancy of Zeus on Crete (*Theogony* 468-84) may point to a Minoan myth of a son or consort (or both) of a goddess.

Within a few centuries of their arrival, the Greek rulers of the mainland came squarely under the influence of the Minoans. The power and cultural sophistication of the mainland increased rapidly through the Middle Helladic period and reached its height during the late Helladic period, the sixteenth through the thirteenth centuries. Meanwhile the Minoan civilization, at its greatest during the seventeenth and sixteenth centuries, went into decline after the destruction of the palaces, caused perhaps by the eruption of the volcanic island Thera around 1450.

The Late Helladic period, the final phase of the Bronze Age on the Greek mainland, is most commonly named the Mycenean period, since the city of Mycenae in the Peloponnese seems to have been the most important Myceanean center (an assumption strengthened by the pre-eminence of Mycenae and its king Agamemnon in the myths of the Trojan War). The chief Mycenean cities—Mycenae, Tiryns, and Argos in the Argolis, Pylos in Messenia, Thebes and Orchomenos in Boiotia, Iolkos (modern Volos) in Thessaly, Eleusis and Athens in Attika, as well as Knossos on Crete, which was taken over by the Myceneans during this period—all play a significant role in later myth, and it is this period that provides the setting for much of Greek myth as it was later known to Hesiod and Homer.

Minoan influence on Mycenean civilization is so extensive that the few exceptions stand out clearly. There is nothing in Crete like the battle scenes in Mycenean art, or the enormous Cyclopean fortifications that protect the Mycenean citadels (the archaeological term is derived from myths crediting the one-eyed giants called Kyklopes with building these walls; post-Mycenean Greeks did not believe that ordinary mortals could have lifted the great stone blocks). Mycenean frescoes, jewelry, pottery painting and shapes, and architecture (with such exceptions as the distinctive Helladic room-style called the *megaron*) imitated Minoan models so closely that it is often difficult to tell them apart. Whether the same assimilation applied to religion and myth is impossible to say; the iconographic evidence shows great similarity, but the absence of literary records makes these pictorial data difficult to interpret. The figure of a bull, for example, appears everywhere in the Minoan remains—on buildings, frescoes, pottery, and jewelry and in sacrificial, ritual, and athletic contexts—and the bull is very prominent in later Greek myths concerning Crete, but the exact connection between artifacts and myth is impossible to establish. In the case of Mycenean culture we have the advantage of written records in a known language, but since the Linear B tablets are almost entirely inventories and accounting records of the religious and political bureaucracy, all they can tell us are the names of some deities and the facts that sacrificial cults existed and that the religious system was highly organized.

Names on the Linear B tablets that correspond with gods and goddesses in later Greek religion include Zeus, Hera, Poseidon, Hermes, Enyalios (a double of Ares), Paiaon (an epithet of Apollo), Erinys (an epithet of Demeter, as well as the singular form of the three Erinyes or Furies), Eleuthia, and perhaps Athena, Artemis, Ares, Dione, and Dionysos. In addition, there is a goddess, or many goddesses, called Potnia ("lady" or "mistress"), a name occurring usually but not always with some qualification: Potnia of horses, Potnia of grain, Potnia of the labyrinth, and so forth. Finally there are several deities whose names do not appear later, such as Manasa, Drimios the son of Zeus, and Posidaija (a feminine form of Poseidon). The tablets, on a few of which these names appear, were found in great number at Knossos and Pylos and in smaller quantities at Mycenae and Thebes; they were preserved by the fires that accompanied the destruction of these sites during the fourteenth through twelfth centuries.

The end of Mycenean civilization coincided with general disruption in the eastern Mediterranean area and may be due, at least partially, to the raids of the mysterious Sea Peoples, who appear most prominently in Egyptian records. A major role may also have been played by the movement into central Greece and the Peloponnese of new groups of Greek-speaking peoples from the northwest, the Dorian invasion. Only Athens and its surrounding area, and a few isolated places in the Peloponnese, escaped destruction. Most survivors of this turbulent period probably remained in Greece under the new Dorian regime, but the level of culture changed radically; writing, building in stone, and representational art disappeared, and cultural depression and poverty were widespread, especially in the century or two immediately following the Mycenean collapse. A Mycenean group fled to the island of Cyprus soon after the Dorian invasion; they were followed, toward the end of the second millennium, by large-scale migrations from the Greek mainland to the eastern Aegean islands and the coast of Asia Minor. Aiolians from Boiotia and Thessaly moved into the northern part of this area, Ionians (a mixed group chiefly from Attika and Euboia, but perhaps including temporary refugees in Athens from other parts of Greece) occupied the central section, and Dorians settled in the south, including Crete. A cultural revival began in Athens around 1050, marked by a distinctive pottery style called Proto-Geometric, and gradually spread throughout the Greek world. Other than changes in the Geometric pottery series and a great increase in the use of iron during the eleventh century, however, there is little we can say about Greek higher culture during the period 1200 to 800, appropriately called the "Dark Age" of Greece.

The Question of Influence

The poetic tradition in which Hesiod wrote has obvious connections not only with the Minoan-Mycenean world but also with the Near East and western Asia. The end of the Dark Age and the beginning of the Archaic period is marked by an increase in population and prosperity after an extended period of relative calm and stability. Prosperity both brought and benefited from rapidly expanding trade relations with the Near East, especially Syria and Phoenicia. A wealth of new ideas poured into Greece, including the Orientalizing style in pottery and, of course, the alphabet. But this is not the first time that Greece came into contact with the great civilizations to the east. The Minoan and Mycenean civilizations both traded actively in the eastern Mediterranean, the Minoans especially with Egypt and the Myceneans especially with the Ugaritic cities of Syria and the Hittite empire in north Syria and the interior of Asia Minor. The island of Cyprus, located much nearer to Syria than to Greece, must have been a favorable place for the exchange of goods and ideas; after early contacts with Asia Minor and Syria, it was colonized by Myceneans from the fifteenth century through the massive migrations of the thirteenth and twelfth centuries, and seems to have received Syrian and Phoenician colonists during the ninth century.

These are merely the most obvious times and places for Greek acquaintance with the Near East. In fact, there is no time throughout and even before the entire Bronze Age and early Iron Age at which such contact can be absolutely ruled out. Furthermore, a still more complex network of diffusion and transmission existed within the Near East itself. The situation is summarized by Kirk:

> The Near East and western Asia in the third and second millennia . . . were a cauldron of customs and ideas that passed from Mesopotamia to Egypt and occasionally back again, to Syria and Asia Minor and into the Aegean, to Cyprus and Crete and the Greek mainland. Semitic tribes absorbed concepts from Indo-Iranian ones and vice versa. Indo-European-speaking Hittites derived their theology from the non-Indo-European Hurrians, the Semitic Akkadians from the non-Semitic Sumerians. The Aegean peoples were in contact during the second millennium with Trojans and Hittites in Asia Minor, with Egypt through casual trade and mercenaries, with the Levant through Cyprus and trading posts in Syria and Palestine.[3]

West notes that "Ugarit [or Ras Shamra, the most important city of Canaanite Syria from 1450 to 1350] was an extremely important center of trade—no less than seven languages are represented on the tablets found there."[4] Nor was Ugarit unique in its cosmopolitan connections; a similar situation and the same number of languages existed at the contemporary Hittite capital of Hattusas, where tablets have been recovered written in Hittite, Akkadian, Sumerian, Hurrian, Hattite, Luwian, and Palaic.

No other subject has attracted the attention of scholars working on the *Theogony* as much as the question of how, and how much, his subject was influenced by the myths of the Near East. There are several instances in which it is clear that the Hesiodic theogony is derived from Near Eastern sources, and many for which such derivation is claimed by some and denied by others. In order to demonstrate derivation, it is not enough to point out separate characters, functions, and ideas in Hesiod that have identical or rather similar parallels in Asiatic literature, and then to select the most probable means by which these concepts traveled from East to West. If this approach were valid, little in Hesiod could be regarded as a Greek original, since an Asiatic parallel could be cited for most single and separate elements. Kirk attributes "the apearance in different places of vaguely similar or very general ideas (like those of a mother goddess, a storm god or the moulding of mankind out of clay)" to the continual and widespread diffusion of customs and ideas throughout the eastern Mediterranean and western Asia; the direct influence, however, of one culture upon another cannot be demonstrated by parallels such as these, but "only when a rather complex and specific motif occurs in two distinct places and not elsewhere."[5] Kirk's argument that derivation can be shown only by the similarity of complicated patterns instead of isolated elements is quite true (despite the facts that single elements can be and certainly were transmitted from one people to another, and that, as Kirk admits, the determination of how much complexity is sufficient to prove derivation is always a subjective judgment). A similar argument could be made by comparing Greek myths with those of cultures the Greeks could not have known directly or indirectly. Parallels can be found outside of Europe, Asia, and north Africa for many of the elements in Hesiod; to take Kirk's three examples, the notions of a mother-goddess, a storm-god, and creation from clay appear regularly in the myths of Africa, Australia, and the Americas (as well as the ideas of an original void, the theft of fire, and many others), and there simply were not enough intercontinental land bridges around in the prehistoric era to explain all these parallels as the result of diffusion and influence.

The Enuma Elish

Two Eastern myths are most frequently cited as examples of Hesiod's dependence on non-Greek sources. First is the Akkadian-Babylonian creation epic, called the *Enuma Elish* (the first two words of the poem), a ritual text that was recited annually to the god Marduk on the fourth day of the New Year's festival. Although no texts written earlier than the end of the second millennium are known, the epic was once generally regarded as having been composed during the Amorite or Old Babylonian dynasty (nineteenth-seventeenth centuries), the age of the famous law-giver Hammurabi. More recent opinion, however, has tended to reject this early dating and to place the composition of the epic during the Kassite period (the four centuries following the Old Babylonian period) or even later.[6] Precise dating is not as important in regard to possible influence on Greece as some have thought; even if a late date is correct, the epic is based on earlier Akkadian and Sumerian material, and presumably the theogonic material at the beginning of the poem would be oldest and least resistant to change, as opposed to the detailed accounts of Marduk's new dispensation. The epic is written in the Akkadian dialect and, like most Babylonian mythological texts, is greatly dependent on Sumerian myths.

The Sumerians, whose language was neither Indo-European nor Semitic, were the first great civilization of Mesopotamia. They dominated the area throughout the third millennium, except for two centuries (about 2340-2150) during which Mesopotamia was ruled by the Semitic kingdom founded by the legendary Sargon, king of Akkad. The Sumerians regained dominance during the Third Dynasty of Ur (2125-2000), but disappeared as a separate people after another defeat by Semitic armies. The Sumerian language was no longer spoken, but continued to be written as an official language of some religious, political, and literary documents. Sumerian achievements in religion, literature, architecture, law, astronomy, and economic organization were adopted by succeeding Semitic peoples, and Sumerian culture remained the leading influence on the civilizations of Mesopotamia. When the Old Babylonian empire, perhaps Hammurabi himself, set out to validate their rule and that of their god Marduk, the Summerian creation myth was rewritten to make Marduk the ultimate ruler of all the gods and the *Enuma Elish,* or an earlier version, was composed.

The *Enuma Elish*[7] begins with the union of primal waters, Apsu and Mummu-Tiamat; Apsu is male fresh

waters and Tiamat is female sea waters (the epithet Mummu probably means "mother"). Within their waters were born the first gods: Lahmu and Lahamu, then Anshar and Kishar, then their son Anu (Sky) and Anu's son Ea, chief of the gods. The new gods disturbed Apsu and Tiamat by their "loathsome" and "unsavory" behavior within the body of Tiamat, and Apsu decided to destroy the gods. Tiamat protested, but Apsu persisted with his plan. Then Ea, the "all-wise," learned of Apsu's intention, cast a spell upon him, and killed him. Ea now married Damkina and their son was Marduk, a giant with four eyes and four ears.

Some of the gods complained to Tiamat about Marduk and persuaded her to avenge Apsu. With the help of "Mother Hubur" (perhaps the earth goddess), who produced eleven monstrous children, Tiamat appointed Kingu, one of the "older gods," as commander, gave him the "Tablet of Destinies," and prepared for battle. Ea went to Anshar for help and Anshar sent Anu to confront Tiamat, but Anu (like Ea before him) turned back in fear. Anshar then sent for Marduk, who agreed to fight Tiamat if the assembled gods proclaimed him as supreme ruler. They granted Marduk his wish and, armed with a bow, mace, lightning, a net, eleven winds, and a storm-chariot, he went to face Tiamat. At first sight of the "inside of Tiamat" and "Kingu, her consort," Marduk and his followers were temporarily confused and alarmed, but he quickly recovered and engaged Tiamat in single combat; first, however, he accused her of having caused a situation in which "sons reject their own fathers," of having given to Kingu the rightful position of Anu, of plotting evil against Anshar, and of not loving those whom she should.

In the combat Marduk snared Tiamat in his net; when she opened her mouth to swallow him, he sent in winds to hold her mouth open and her stomach distended, then shot in an arrow and killed her. All her helpers, including Kingu and the monsters, were captured and imprisoned, and Marduk cut Tiamat's body in half to create the sky and the earth. He then gave to the great gods (Anu, Ea, and Enlil) their proper places, arranged the weather and the heavenly bodies, and created the features of the earth from parts of Tiamat's body. Finally Ea created mankind from the blood of the rebel Kingu, for the express purpose of serving the gods. The epic ends with the building of a great temple in Babylon for Marduk, where a banquet is held at which the grateful gods recite the fifty honorific names of Marduk.

There are clear similarities between the Babylonian and Greek theogonies, and there are also many differences. Both begin with a primal couple (Apsu and Tiamat/Ouranos and Gaia) from whom the other gods are descended; children remain within the body of the first mother and are hated by their father; a solution is found by a clever god (Ea/Kronos) who defeats the father; the son (Marduk, who replaced Sumerian Enlil/Zeus) of the clever god then becomes king, but first must defeat monstrous enemies (the older gods and the monsters produced by Hubur, who seems functionally equivalent to Gaia and Rhea/the Titans, the Giants, and Typhoeus, all of whom are children of Gaia); mankind is created either by the clever god or during his reign.

Differences between the two epics, however, are more obvious than similarities, as a few examples will show. The first Babylonian couple are both water-gods, while the first Greek couple are Gaia (Earth) and Ouranos (Sky); the clever god Ea overthrows Apsu (Fresh Waters), not his father Anu (Sky), while Kronos overthrows his father Ouranos—in fact, the Babylonian Sky and his son (Anu and Ea) are allies against their common enemy Apsu; likewise Zeus overthrows his father Kronos and Kronos' brothers, while Marduk succeeds his great-grandfather Anshar, who is called "king of the gods," and defeats neither his father Ea nor Anshar, but is their champion against Tiamat.

It is unnecessary to extend the comparison, since it is clear that both myths share the same very general pattern, and that there is not much correspondence in details, especially the family relationships of characters to one another. Another recently discovered Babylonian theogony also displays a pattern similar to the Greek succession myth, but with characters different from either Hesiod or the *Enuma Elish*.[8] In it the first couple are Hain and Earth; Earth commands her son Amakandu to marry her, which he does and kills his father Hain; Amakandu then marries his sister Sea and their son Lahar kills his father and marries his mother; the unnamed son of Lahar and Sea kills both his parents and marries his sister River; their son kills his parents and marries his sister Ga'um; their son kills his parents and marries his sister Ningeshtinna; at this point the tablet becomes unreadable, although the same cyclic pattern of violence and incest seems to continue. While this theogony can hardly be a model for the Hesiodic version, it is nonetheless closer to it than the *Enuma Elish* in its insistence on father-son conflict and incest (both mother-son and brother-sister) as primary motives. On the other hand, incest is found (and is often logically necessary) in creation myths from around the world; this is especially true of the earliest cosmogonic myths of India, although it should be remembered that Hindu myth is Indo-European and therefore shares a common background with Greek myth.

Walcott has made an elaborate and impressive attempt to derive Hesiod's *Theogony* primarily from the *Enuma Elish* and other Babylonian material with which the Greeks became familiar at the beginning of the Archaic period, but his views have not met general acceptance.[9] It is probably best to say that the *Enuma Elish,* whatever its date (Walcott would put it around

1100), represents a common theogonic pattern in the Near East during the second millennium, which regularly was subject to local adaptation (as Marduk could replace Enlil, his Sumerian equivalent, or the Assyrian god Ashur could replace Marduk), and that the Greeks could have learned of this pattern at any time, the most probable guess being during the Minoan-Mycenean era.

"Kingship in Heaven"

Our second example, regarded by most as the closest Near Eastern parallel to Hesiod, is the Hurrian-Hittite myth called "Kingship in Heaven" with its sequel, the "Song of Ullikummi." The Hurrians were a non-Indo-European, non-Semitic people (as were also the Sumerians) who moved south into Assyria at the beginning of the second millennium and eventually migrated across northern Mesopotamia into Syria. They adopted many aspects of Mesopotamian culture, and it may be through Hurrian versions for the most part that the Greeks came to know Sumerian and Babylonian myths. The Hittites were an Indo-European tribe who appeared in Asia Minor about 1800; by the fourteenth century they had won control of Syria, and during the New Kingdom (about 1450-1200) they were one of the great powers of the Near East. The Hittites were approximate contemporaries of the Myceneans, and their two languages are our earliest examples of a written Indo-European language (in both cases in a borrowed script—the Myceneans used the Minoan syllabary and the Hittites used the Babylonian cuneiform). Some of the more than 10,000 texts found at the Hittite capital Hattusas are mythological and religious, and most of these are Hittite versions of Hurrian myths, which had themselves been influenced by Mesopotamian precedents.

"Kingship in Heaven"[10] begins with the reign of Alalu in heaven; after nine years, he was overthrown by Anu (Sky) and went down to the "dark earth"; Anu ruled for nine years and then was attacked by Kumarbi and fled to the sky; Kumarbi pursued, seized Anu by the feet, and then bit off and swallowed Anu's genitals; when Kumarbi began to laugh, Anu told him that because of what he had swallowed he was now pregnant with three gods: the Storm-God Heshub (the chief god of the Hurrians and Hittites), the river Aranzaha (the Tigris), and Tasmisu (an attendant of the Storm-God); Anu now hid in the sky and Kumarbi spat out what he could (later Aranzaha and Tasmisu will be born from the earth), but the Storm-God remained inside him; Anu now spoke to the Storm-God and the two had a long debate about how the Storm-God should escape from Kumarbi's body; Kumarbi became dizzy and asked Aya (Ea) for something to eat; he ate something (variously read as "stone" or "son"), but it hurt his mouth; finally the Storm-God, after being warned not to exit through other orifices, especially the anus, came out through Kumarbi's "good place," evidently his penis;[11] at this point the text becomes unreadable, but the Storm-God must defeat Kumarbi and become king.

In the "Song of Ullikummi" Kumarbi plots revenge; he had intercourse repeatedly with a huge female rock, who gave birth to a stone child, Ullikummi; the child was hidden from the Storm-God and placed on the right shoulder of Ubelluri (the Hurrian Atlas), where he grew at the rate of an acre per month; the first battle between the Storm-God and Ullikummi, who was now 9000 leagues high, ended with the Storm-God's defeat; the gods were upset and threatened by Ullikummi, and Ea ordered the "old gods" to bring out the ancient copper "cutter" with which heaven and earth had been separated, and to use this to cut through the feet of Ullikummi; the Storm-God again came to fight Ullikummi (and must defeat him, although the final lines cannot be read).

The parallels between the Hurrian and Hesiodic myths are clear once we eliminate the reign of Alalu: Anu is equivalent to Ouranos, Kumarbi to Kronos, and the Storm-God to Zeus; Anu and Ouranos are both castrated and various gods are born from their severed genitals; Kumarbi and Kronos castrate their fathers and have children inside themselves; the Storm-God and Zeus win the kingship of the gods, then must win a second victory over an enormous monster (Ullikummi/Typhoeus).

The parallels cannot be pressed too far. For example, is the Storm-God the son of Kumarbi, from whom he is born, or of Anu, whose genitals make Kumarbi pregnant, or of both, with Anu as father and Kumarbi as mother? Also, Zeus, unlike the Storm-God, never shares his siblings' fate of being inside Kronos but is rescued by the trickery of Rhea and Gaia. As for the similarity between the monsters Ullikummi and Typhoeus, the Hurrian myth seems closer to the much later version of Apollodoros (1.6.3) than to Hesiod's (but according to Apollodoros it is Zeus, not the monster, whose feet are cut through).[12]

Kirk's use of a structuralist model to show that the Hurrian and Hesiodic versions are independent of one another is no more plausible than his discovery on the basis of this model that the underlying message of Hesiod's succession myth is a combination of "an eye for an eye" and "crime doesn't pay."[13] Nevertheless Kirk's conclusion that "the Greek version may be ultimately derived from a pre-Hurrian *koine* account"[14] is as likely a conjecture as the limited evidence available to us will allow and coincides with West's suggestion that the Greek and Hurrian myths "represent common descendants of a version itself derived from Mesopotamia."[15] Where the Babylonian *Enuma Elish* would appear in this line of derivation would depend on its early or late dating, and in any case is not as important as the recognition that the Greek *Theogony*

occupies a relatively late position in a complex, widespread, and interrelated theogonic tradition encompassing western Asia and the Mediterranean.

Fire and Water

The project of identifying or refuting lines of connection between myths of successive or separate cultures, by far the major occupation of scholars who have studied Hesiod cross-culturally, takes on a much different (in fact, almost diametrically opposed) aspect when the subject is approached from a psychoanalytic viewpoint. The accusation of "reductionism" so often made against psychoanalytic studies would seem more applicable to an approach that reduces the explanation of cross-cultural similarities in myth to one of two possibilities: culture A copied X from culture B, or culture A did not copy X from culture B (in which case the similarity is explained by a suspiciously Jungian reference to "general" or even "universal" concepts). Chinese and Americans both enjoy Chinese food, but to show how America learned of Chinese cuisine is not the same thing as explaining why it was adopted or why it is enjoyed.

The proposition that one (perhaps the most important) reason why myths are invented, borrowed, and retained is their success in responding to the emotional needs of a culture leads to certain conclusions:

1. The similarity of isolated elements in the myths of different cultures is potentially as significant as the repetition of complex patterns. Either case is as likely to reveal a common response to a common need.

2. The complexity of similar patterns in different cultures is a major determinant of the possibility of transmission from one to the other, but transmission only occurs *freely* (that is, without compulsion) when the transmitted myth responds to the needs of its adoptive culture better than other alternatives. This may help explain why a conquering people so often assumes the myths of the conquered.

3. The appearance of similar elements or patterns in cases where transmission is impossible does not happen by chance (nor because of a "collective unconscious"), but may result from the existence of independent but similar psychocultural situations. This is one reason why theogonic elements similar to Hesiod's version appear in such distant areas as subsaharan Africa, Polynesia, and the Orient.

4. That there is more similarity than difference in myths worldwide follows from the fact that there is more similarity than difference in virtually all cultures in regard to the conditions of growing up in a family with acknowledged parents and of attempting to establish satisfactory relationships with other persons within the cultural framework.

5. Like the apparently insignificant detail in a manifest dream that clarifies or reveals the latent meaning, an element, motif, or pattern in the myths of one culture may throw unexpected light on the meaning of myths in another culture. This is not a license for the Jungian attribution of any meaning to any concept anywhere— cultures *are* different, and even if the primary emotional concerns embodied in myth are similar for all humans, the modalities in which they are expressed are largely culture-specific—but cross-cultural reference is valuable when it supplies a missing link to, or verifies or illuminates, an argument already probable on the basis of internal considerations.

An interesting example of the occurrence of a similar mythic pattern in two cultures that share a common background is found in the comparison of Greek and Hindu concepts of *ambrosia,* a special food eaten by the gods and providing them with immortality. Both cultures are Indo-European and the original idea of a magical food of the gods must be derived from an early common source; the concept is ubiquitous in Indo-European cultures, and the Greek word *ambrosia* is cognate with Sanskrit *amrta* (the literal meaning of both words is "immortality"). Nevertheless it is unthinkable that the complexity and force of these concepts as they developed independently can be explained by derivation or influence.

There are actually two Sanskrit words for ambrosia, *amrta* and *soma.* Soma is the name of the moon and of a god, but both of these usages are derived from its two primary meanings: the name of a plant whose juice is offered (and sometimes drunk) during the Vedic oblation ritual, and the name of the elixir that provides immortality.[16] What men offer in sacrifice is carried to the gods by fire and smoke and becomes what gods eat; amrta and soma are usually synonymous, but if a distinction is made between them it is that amrta is soma after the sacrificial transformation has occurred. Amrta and soma are thus, respectively, the narrow and broad definitions of the same thing. It might be said that amrta represents a particular form of soma, but this is probably too limiting; the two words share certain extended meanings and associations (for example, with milk or rain).

The god principally associated with soma is Agni, the Hindu god of fire. As the fire that consumes the sacrifice, whether liquid or solid, Agni is called the "Oblation-Eater," and as the "Oblation-Bearer" he is the smoke rising from the sacrifice to feed the gods and give them immortality. But in addition to carrying the sacrificial offerings up to heaven, he also makes the journey from heaven to earth, sometimes in the form of a bird, carrying fire or soma in his beak or in a hollow reed.

The elemental opposition of fire and water that appears in the oblation sacrifice is conspicuous through-out the myths of Agni and soma. Agni seems most at home in water, as in the many myths in which he flees from the gods and hides in water, often in order to dictate to the gods a redistribution of the sacrificial portions. The notion of fire-in-liquid is balanced by that of liquid-in-fire, especially the soma sacrifice, which must pass through fire to reach the gods but retains its liquid nature so that it can be drunk by them (but not by mortals). In the several versions of the "submarine mare" myth we find liquid-in-fire-in-liquid: when a great fire threatened to destroy the universe, Brahma put the fire in the body of a mare with fiery ambrosia in her mouth and then put the mare in the ocean to be kept until the final flood. Soma itself is first created from the ocean, when all the gods and demons churn its waters with the uprooted mountain Mandara; a huge fire caused by friction from the churning burned the herbs on the mountain, and their juices (called "liquid gold") flowed into the ocean which, mixed with the soma juice, turned first to milk, then to clarified butter (the two usual oblation liquids), and finally produced for the gods a white bowl of ambrosia.

The underlying meaning of fire/water and ambrosia is its analogy with semen, an equivalence that appears explicitly on many occasions, especially in the earliest Hindu myths (written versions of the Rg Veda, Brahmanas, and Upanishads are generally dated 1200-700). In a Rg Veda creation myth, with Sky as father and Earth as mother, Agni makes the semen of the creator god. In the Brahmanas, the semen of Prajapati, lord of creatures, is cast into the sacrificial fire in place of the usual liquid oblation (or, conversely, Prajapati produces milk and clarified butter and fire through manipulating his own body by "rubbing" or "churning"); in another variant, found in the Jaiminiya Brahmana, Tvastr throws soma into the sacrificial fire and Vrtra is born. The most explicit statement occurs in the Brhadaranyaka Upanishad: "Now, whatever is moist he [Brahma, the Creator] created from semen, and that is soma. All this universe is food and the eater of food [i.e., soma and fire]. For soma is food, and Agni is the eater of food."[17]

Semen is the combination of fire and water, a liquid that contains the spark of life.[18] The semen of the gods is always fiery: in the Kalika Purana, the earth conceives from the "fiery semen" of Vishnu; in the Shiva Purana the burning semen of Shiva is passed from Agni to the gods, the wives of six of the Seven Sages, the mountain Himalaya, and the river Ganges, none of whom can bear its "feverish burning" until finally the son of Shiva is born.

Tantalos and Prometheus

Even this brief sketch of the Hindu concept recalls many Greek parallels. Most obvious is the function of

Zeus' rain and lightning, water and fire, as the two means by which the sky god impregnates the earth goddess.[19] Or the nine years' sojourn of Hephaistos, the Greek Agni, in the cavern of Thetis under the ocean.[20] But we should begin with the actual occurrence in Greek myth of ambrosia, the equivalent of amrta and soma.

The key Greek myth concerning ambrosia is the story of Tantalos, who lived in that early time (perhaps the golden age) when men lived and dined together. Tantalos wanted to prove himself equal or superior to the gods, and the close relations then of gods and men provided him with the opportunity for a great crime, as a result of which he was punished with eternal hunger and thirst in Tartaros. He is said to have revealed the gods' secrets, or to have served his cooked son Pelops to the gods when they came to his house for dinner, or to have stolen ambrosia. The usual explanation of these crimes is quite general and obvious: men who want to be like gods, men who overstep the boundaries between men and gods, are guilty of *hybris,* and so the crimes of Tartaros are variant violations of the Delphic prescription "nothing in excess."

We can be more specific, however, about this "infringement of Zeus' prerogative."[21] From a psychoanalytic viewpoint, the crimes of Tantalos are oedipal transgressions,[22] similar to the offenses of the other three sexual criminals who receive special punishment in Tartaros. Sisyphos also was guilty of revealing the gods' secrets, and in his case the sexual and voyeuristic nature of the crime is clear, while Ixion and Tityos each tried to have a sexual relationship with one of Zeus' wives, either Hera or Leto. The second crime of Tantalos is both oedipal and counter-oedipal; like Ouranos and Kronos, he tries to kill his potential successor and furthermore he does this in order to prove his superiority over Zeus,[23] who, we should remember, is the real (as well as symbolic) father of Tantalos.

Tantalos' third crime, the theft of ambrosia, fits this general pattern, as an hybristic and oedipal attack on the prerogative of his father Zeus. At this point it would seem both appropriate and justifiable to introduce the Hindu analogy; soma and ambrosia, the food of the gods and the source of their immortality, are also symbolic manifestations of paternal sexuality, as the Hindu myths explicitly state. What Tantalos wants, when he steals ambrosia (and in his other crimes as well), is to acquire the sexual power and freedom of his father Zeus.

This interpretation can be argued by a Greek analogy as well as by comparison to the Hindu myths. The other great example in Greek myth of the usurpation of a divine (that is, paternal) prerogative is the theft of fire from Zeus by the Titan Prometheus. We would already expect, from the Hindu parallels, that the di-

vine fire signifies paternal sexuality, and this meaning is repeatedly confirmed in Greek philosophy and myth (to cite just one example, when Zeus is deceived into making love to Semele in his true form, the hapless girl is consumed in the god's fiery sexuality).[24] The theft of fire is a sexual crime, and therefore Prometheus receives virtually the same punishment as the giant Tityos received for his attempted rape of Zeus' wife; both are bound in chains while birds (an eagle or two vultures) eat their livers. Thus the sexual nature of Prometheus' crime, like the overtly sexual crimes of the other sufferers in Tartaros, confirms the sexual nature of Tantalos' crime, and the Hindu associations of soma and fire with semen and with each other further strengthen this interpretation.

The similarities between Tantalos and Prometheus extend beyond the obvious connection between ambrosia and fire, and supplement their roles as oedipal pretenders. In Hesiod's account (*Theogony* 507-616), the quarrel between Zeus and Prometheus began at Mekone, where gods and men met to make a decision concerning the distribution of sacrifices. Prometheus cut up a sacrificed ox and placed before men the meat covered by the skin and stomach, while before Zeus he put the bones "rightly arranged and covered with shining fat" (541). Although Hesiod says that Zeus "recognized the trick" (551) but acted as if he did not, commentators agree that in the original version Zeus really was deceived and that the Hesiodic account is an attempt to rescue Zeus from the charge of being duped.[25] In his anger Zeus took back from men the gift of fire, but Prometheus again deceived him by stealing fire and carrying it to men in a hollow reed. As a result Zeus punished mankind by the creation of Pandora, the first woman, and condemned Prometheus to be tortured by the eagle eternally.

The meeting at Mekone, as West notes, "must be the one that took place at the end of the period when men and gods lived and ate together."[26] Kirk agrees that men and gods "met at Mekone for the last time," adding "Their decision to separate must have been caused by the end of the golden age, the displacement of Kronos and the new rule of Zeus," and he also connects the meeting at Mekone with the dinner of Tantalos (along with the weddings of Peleus and Thetis and Kadmos and Harmonia) as examples of the relationship between men and gods in a golden age.[27] All three of Tantalos' crimes could only occur in the hypothetical conditions of a golden age if, as Kirk indicates, one of the characteristics of this era was the intimate association of gods with men. The same is true of the criminal Ixion, who conceived his passion for Hera during his frequent visits to Olympos.

Neither Kirk nor West notices, however, the similarity that exists between the deceptions employed by Prometheus and Tantalos. Each of them chooses the communal meal for his crime, and each conceals something beneath the surface of the food in an ambiguously successful attempt to deceive the gods; Zeus may recognize Prometheus' trick but chooses the wrong portion anyway, while the other gods recognize Tantalos' trick except for Demeter, who eats a shoulder of Pelops.

The myths of Prometheus and Tantalos, then, are virtual doubles of one another; each of them is punished for having stolen the sexual possession of the gods and also for having deceived the gods by a meal with hidden contents. The difference between them lies in the permanent punishment of the mortal Tantalos and the eventual victory of the god Prometheus, a victory, moreover, that consists precisely in reminding Zeus that only by a limitation of his sexual activity (in fact, by giving up a desired female to another male) will he avoid being overthrown by an oedipal rival, the son who is destined to be greater than his father.[28]

At this point we could once more turn to the Hindu myths for comparison. The theft of fire from the gods, as we have seen, is often accompanied by a dispute concerning the distribution of the parts of a sacrifice; a Rg Veda version in which Agni claims for himself the "nourishing part of the offering"[29] is particularly reminiscent of the Promethean division. The punishments of both Prometheus and mankind also have Hindu parallels. Although the conception of the liver as the organ of desire does not appear in Greek literature until 200 years after Hesiod, this does not mean that it did not exist before Aeschylus; if it did, the particular torment of Prometheus may be compared to Agni, who appears "tortured with desire" in the *Mahabharata* and is punished with "feverish burning" of a clearly sexual nature for having stolen the semen of Shiva in the *Shiva Purana.* Mortal men, on the other hand, are punished by Zeus through the creation of Pandora, the first woman and the source of all evils for men; similarly we read in the *Mahabharata* that "there is nothing more evil than women" and that God "created women by a magic ritual in order to delude mankind."[30]

There is, of course, not much in those sections of Greek myth concerned principally with the gods that cannot find a parallel somewhere in the interminable Hindu myth cycles. Still I cannot resist mentioning one more, in connection with Hesiod's account of the birth of Aphrodite from the severed phallus of Ouranos, which Kronos threw into the ocean. Aphrodite's name means "born from foam," and the phallus of Ouranos is surrounded by foam; as West notes, "Aphrodite is formed in foam to explain her name."[31] Association of the goddess of desire with the phallus is not difficult to understand, but why the connection with foam? Hesiod may put Aphrodite in foam because he found foam in her name, but how is foam connected with Aphrodite in the first place? The association must result, I would

think, from a prior connection with the phallus and consequently from a visual similarity between semen and the foam excreted by the sea.

Again in the *Mahabharata,* soma, a mythic counterpart of semen, is created by the gods in the form of the foam produced by churning the ocean with an uprooted mountain; the sexual symbolism of this cosmic penetration is obvious. The Sanskrit verb that means "churn" is *manth,* a word that embodies many of the associations we have been discussing. Its primary reference is "vigorous backwards and forwards motion of any sort"; it also refers to the production of fire from fire sticks, sexual activity, and stealing (especially the theft of soma), it is related to the name Mandara (the mountain used for churning soma), and it is cognate with the Greek Prometheus.[32] In addition, the name "Prometheus" could be related to the Hindu culture-hero Prthu, who steals the cow of immortality from the gods to help a mortal, and "restores food and establishes civilization."[33]

The derivation of both Greek and Hindu myths from a common Indo-European tradition in neolithic times helps to explain some of the striking similarities of symbolic patterns in the two cultural systems. However, the lapse of more than two millennia between the neolithic period and the early Iron Age, when the first written versions of these myths appeared in both India and Greece, makes it impossible to trace either the descent of separate traditions or connections between different traditions. Mesopotamian influence certainly affected both Greek and Hindu myth, and the pre-Aryan Harappa culture of the Indus valley must have influenced Hindu myth in much the same way as Minoan/Mediterranean myths were incorporated into Greek myth, but any specific certainty about these matters cannot be attained.

Worth noting, however, is a non-Greek, non-Indian myth that seems to predate Hesiod and has striking associations with the mythic configuration we have been discussing. A. Olrik collected and analyzed myths from the region of the Caucasus that tell of the punishment of an impious giant, chained to a mountain while a vulture eats his "bowels."[34] His crime is an attempt to steal the "water of life" (that is, immortality), and in his punishment this water flows just beyond his reach (like the punishment of Tantalos) or is swallowed by him but then removed from his bowels by the vulture. A connection with the myths of Tantalos, Tityos, and Prometheus is clear, but there are also similarities with the myths of Agni and soma. The water of life is equivalent to Tantalos' ambrosia, Prometheus' fire, and the soma/semen of Hindu myth; the bird who removes the swallowed "semen" is comparable to Agni, who frequently swallows the "seed of the gods" or, in the form of a bird, steals the semen swallowed or produced by others. Also the giant of the Caucasus, if ever freed from his punishment, will destroy the whole world in his rage, and a cosmic cataclysm by fire or flood figures importantly in Hindu, Norse, and Near Eastern myth and, in a muted form, in Greek myth. If Olrik is correct about the dating and precedence of the Caucasus myth, we may possibly see here a point of intersection in the mysterious journey of an involved mythic pattern.

At the level of psychological significance, it is of course unnecessary to demonstrate diffusion or dependence; the same emotional concerns appear in the myths of Japan and New Guinea as well as in Greece or India. It is the similarity in the specific modality of these appearances, in the mythic circumstances that embody these concerns, that we may attribute, at least in part, to the influence of one group upon another. Yet even in cases of elaborate similarity in myths we cannot leave out of account the possible impact of cultural similarity between groups—not only societal and familial universals and similarity in the current level of cultural development, but also similarity in the vicissitudes of past history.

The Theogony *of Hesiod*

Although Hesiod's *Theogony* may be the oldest *written* Greek literature we possess, there was probably a theogonic tradition in Greek myth as old as the myths themselves. Striking similarities between the *Theogony* and various earlier Near Eastern theogonies suggest that Hesiod's version goes back in some parts at least half a millennium, to contacts between the Minoan-Mycenean world and eastern cultures, and in some cases the ultimate source may lie even earlier, in the largely uncharted migrations of the Indo-Europeans. Other theogonic poems almost certainly existed in Greece before Hesiod's, but these were oral literature and we know next to nothing about them.

Other Greek theogonies may still have existed at the time of Hesiod, but we cannot know whether the story of the world's beginning told in the *Theogony* represents the usual view held at the time, or whether it was merely one of several competing views. The scant hints we do have of a genuine mythic alternative to Hesiod's version amount to only a few scattered lines and passages, particularly in the *Iliad*. Whether the theogonic tradition before Hesiod was fluid or relatively fixed, and whatever the competition may have been like, the *Theogony* became for almost all later Greeks the true story of how the world and the gods began. The theogonic summary found at the beginning of the *Library* of Apollodoros, for example, differs from the *Theogony* in only a few details, although it was probably written almost a thousand years after Hesiod.

Notes

[1] The indebtedness of Sections 1-4 of this chapter to the summary of Greek prehistory in Burkert (1985) and to the discussion of Hesiod's relationship to Near Eastern myth by both West (1966) and Kirk (1970, 1974) will be obvious.

[2] Although it has been argued, on the basis of comparative letter-shapes in Semitic and Greek alphabets, that the Greeks adopted an alphabet as early as the eleventh century, no examples of alphabetic writing in Greece earlier than the eighth century have survived.

[3] Kirk (1974) 255.

[4] West (1966) 30.

[5] Kirk (1974) 255.

[6] Pritchard (1969) 501.

[7] Pritchard (1969) 60-72, 501-3.

[8] Pritchard (1969) 517-18.

[9] Walcot (1966).

[10] Pritchard (1969) 120-25.

[11] Kirk (1970) 216.

[12] See Walcot (1966) 12-18 and Ch. 3, p. 124.

[13] Kirk (1970) 218 and Ch. 1, pp. 4-5.

[14] Kirk (1970) 215-16.

[15] West (1966) 30.

[16] O'Flaherty (1975) 15.

[17] O'Flaherty (1975) 15.

[18] LaBarre (1980) 110.

[19] See Ch. 4, pp. 138-139.

[20] See Ch. 4, pp. 171, 184.

[21] Guthrie (1950) 121.

[22] LaBarre (1970) 447-48, 472 n. 58.

[23] See Ch. 4, p. 137.

[24] See Ch. 4, pp. 138-39.

[25] See West (1966) 321.

[26] West (1966) 318.

[27] Kirk (1970) 228, 197.

[28] See Ch. 4, pp. 169-70.

[29] O'Flaherty (1975) 99.

[30] O'Flaherty (1975) 36, 37.

[31] West (1966) 212.

[32] O'Flaherty (1980) 333, citing Adalbert Kuhn, *Mythologische Studien,* vol. 1 (Guetersloh, Germany, 1886) 15-17, 218-23.

[33] O'Flaherty (1980) 330, 332.

[34] Olrik's research is summarized with approval by West (1966) 314-15.

[35] The translation follows the Oxford edition of West (1966). Bracketed passages are, in West's view, later interpolations.

[36] The translation follows the Loeb edition of Frazer (1921).

Bibliography

Burkert, Walter (1985). *Greek Religion.* Trans. J. Raffan. Cambridge, Mass.

Guthrie, W. K. (1950). *The Greeks and their Gods.* Boston.

Kirk, G. S. (1970). *Myth: Its Meaning and Functions in Ancient and Other Cultures.* Berkeley.

Kirk, G. S. (1974). *The Nature of Greek Myths.* New York.

LaBarre, Weston (1970). *The Ghost Dance: Origins of Religion.* New York.

LaBarre, Weston (1980). *Culture in Context: Selected Writings.* Durham, N.C.

O'Flaherty, Wendy (1975). *Hindu Myths.* Baltimore.

O'Flaherty, Wendy (1980). *The Origins of Evil in Hindu Mythology.* Berkeley.

Pritchard, James, ed. (1969) *Ancient Near Eastern Texts Relating to the Old Testament,* with Supplement. 3d ed., Princeton.

Walcot, P. (1966). *Hesiod and the Near East.* Cardiff, UK.

COSMOGONIES AND DIVINITIES IN GREEK MYTHOLOGY

G. S. Kirk (essay date 1974)

SOURCE: "The Mythos of the Gods and the Early History of Men," in *The Nature of Greek Myths*, Penguin Books, 1974, pp. 113-44.

[*In the following essay, Kirk identifies three categories of myths about Greek divinities: those dealing with the origins of the universe; those that concern the development of the Olympian gods; and those that deal with the creation of men, their place in the world, and their relationship with the gods. Kirk reviews the content, themes, and folktale-type motifs found in these types of myths.*]

In considering Greek myths in detail my plan is not to attempt a complete survey, but rather to divide the myths into six categories and examine some outstanding instances in each. The first three categories are included [here]. . . .

The categories are as follows: first the cosmogonical myths, secondly those that describe the development of the Olympian gods. These are the divine myths as a whole. Thirdly, myths concerned with the early history of men and the fixing of their place in the world, especially in relation to the gods. The fourth category contains tales of the older heroes—the heroic myths in the fullest sense; the fifth has tales of the younger and more imitative heroes, including those of legend and the great Panhellenic sagas. These are the heroic myths as a whole. Finally, the sixth category contains later inventions of the historical period.

First come *the cosmogonical myths* about the formation of the world; they concern the initial separation of sky from earth and the replacement of the older gods of nature by Zeus and his contemporaries. Ouranos, it will be remembered, will not separate from Gaia, Earth, until the young Kronos castrates him. Kronos becomes king, but continues swallowing his own children by his sister Rhea until the infant Zeus is saved by a trick and displaces him in his turn. These events are incomparably described by Hesiod, who is also our oldest source for tales to which Homer has occasion to make only the briefest allusion. Hesiod's account in the *Theogony* is as follows:

> All that were produced by Gaia and Ouranos—most dreadful of children—were hated from the beginning by their own begetter. He hid them all away, just as soon as any came into being, in an inward place of Gaia, and did not let them into the light; and Ouranos rejoiced in his evil deed. Huge Gaia groaned within, for she was crowded out, and contrived a crafty and evil device. Without delay she created the element of grey adamant and wrought a great sickle; then she addressed her dear children in encouraging tones,

though troubled in her heart: 'Children of mine and of a reckless father, if you consent to do what I say, we could avenge your father's outrageous treatment; for it was he that first devised shameful deeds.' These were her words, but the children were all possessed by fear, and none of them uttered until great Kronos of crooked counsels after a while addressed his noble mother thus: 'Mother, I shall give you my promise and accomplish the deed, since I care nothing for my father of evil name; for it was he that first devised shameful deeds.' These were his words, and huge Gaia rejoiced greatly in her heart. She sent him into a hidden place of ambush, put in his hands a jagged-toothed sickle and instructed him in the whole deceit. Great Ouranos came, bringing on Night; desiring love he stretched himself on Gaia and spread all over her. And his son from his place of ambush stretched out with his left hand, and with his right hand he grasped the monstrous sickle, long and jagged-toothed, and swiftly reaped off the genitals of his dear father, and flung them behind him to be carried away. They did not escape his hand in vain, for all the bloody drops that flowed out were received by Gaia, and with the turning seasons she gave birth to the strong Furies and great Giants, gleaming in their armour and with long spears in their hands, and the Nymphs they call Ash-tree Nymphs over the boundless earth. And the genitals, once he had cut them off with the adamant, he flung away from the land into the turbulent deep; and so they were borne for a long while through the sea, and white foam rose up from the immortal flesh. In it a girl was nurtured, and first came close to sacred Cythera, then to sea-girt Cyprus . . . (154 ff.)

This, we learn was Aphrodite, and it is a typical aetiological and etymological detail, since her name can be interpreted in Greek as meaning 'she who came out of the foam' and both Cythera and Cyprus laid claim to be the centre of her worship. Similarly Hesiod goes on to say that Ouranos called his children 'Titans' because they stretched or strove (Greek *titainein*) to do the deed.

After the birth of sundry other beings the poet returns to Kronos, now full-grown:

> Rhea was subjected to Kronos and bore him glorious children: Hestia, Demeter, Hera with golden sandals, strong Hades who dwells with unrelenting heart in his halls under the earth, the loud-roaring Earthshaker [that is, Poseidon] and Zeus wise in counsel, father of gods and men, under whose thunder the broad earth quivers. These were swallowed by great Kronos as each of them came toward her knees from out of their holy mother's womb; his intention was that no other proud descendant of Ouranos should have kingly honour among the immortals. For he had learnt from Gaia and starry Ouranos that he was fated, strong as he was, to be subdued by his own son through the will of great Zeus. Therefore he kept no idle watch, but

keenly observing them he swallowed down his children, and Rhea was possessed by unforgettable grief. But when she was about to give birth to Zeus, father of gods and men, then she besought her own dear parents, Gaia and starry Ouranos, to devise a plan whereby she might bear her child in secret, and repay the avenging furies of her father and of the children great crooked-counselled Kronos kept swallowing. They listened carefully to their dear daughter and did as she asked; they told her all that was fated to happen with king Kronos and his strong-hearted son. They despatched her to Lyktos, into the rich community of Crete, as she was about to give birth to her youngest child, great Zeus; and huge Gaia agreed to nurture and tend him in broad Crete. Then Rhea brought him through the swift, dark night to Lyktos first; she took him in her hands and hid him in a steep cave under the recesses of sacred earth, on thickly-wooded Mount Aigaion. To Kronos, great lord and son of Ouranos, former king of the gods, she presented a great stone that she had wrapped in swaddling-clothes. He took it in his hands and deposited it in his belly, the villain, and did not notice how his son was left behind, unconquered and carefree, in place of the stone—his son who was soon to subdue him with the might of his hands and drive him from his honoured position and reign among the immortals himself. Swiftly then did the strength and shining limbs of that lord grow, and with the turning seasons, deceived by the wise biddings of Gaia, great Kronos of crooked counsels brought up again his offspring, defeated by his son's arts and strength. First he vomited up the stone, the last to be swallowed, and Zeus set it in the broad-wayed earth in fair Pytho, under the hollows of Parnassus, to be a sign in later times, a wonder for mortal men. And he released his father's brothers, children of Ouranos, from the destructive bonds with which their father had bound them in his infatuation; and they were grateful to him for his kindness, and gave him thunder and the smoky thunderbolt and lightning—huge Gaia had hidden them before; trusting in these he rules over mortals and immortals. (453 ff.)

A few points in both passages need explanation. In the first part of the myth, where exactly is Kronos' imagined physical position? Probably within Gaia's vagina and not just sandwiched between earth and sky. Then, even before his enforced separation, Ouranos 'brings on Night', which suggests that he is already separate. Lastly it is not clear how Zeus makes Kronos vomit up the children. Some such areas of vagueness or inconsistency reflect the combination of different versions, others the unreal fantasy that fills the two episodes. Several folktale-type motifs can be detected: the son destined to replace his father, the father's attempts to destroy him; the youngest is the bravest (Zeus has it both ways, since when his brothers and sisters are reborn he becomes the senior); swallowing a stone destroys a monster. The blood or seed of gods, if it falls on the ground, is nearly always fertile; Aphrodite's name, and the foamy appearance of both sperm and spume, suggest her as the product here, and her derivation from Mesopotamian Inanna or Ishtar, the 'Queen of Heaven', makes Ouranos or Sky the obvious male parent. Crete is suitably remote, but Zeus' removal there is mainly due to his relatively late identification with a Cretan dying-and-reborn god as well as to the prominence of Cretan cave cults. As for his uncles at the end, these are the Cyclopes and Hundred-handed Giants, and they are mentioned because they are needed as allies in his decisive fight against the Titans.

More important, this whole myth has a close Near-Eastern parallel, known from a Hittite version of a Hurrian tale of the mid-second millennium B.C.—the Hurrians being a non-Indo-European people spread across western Asia at this time.[1] Kumarbi deposes the sky god Anu by biting off his phallus; he swallows it and becomes pregnant with the all-powerful storm god, parallel to the sky and weather god Zeus. The storm god is born in an unnatural way, then in a last fling Kumarbi generates the monster Ullikummi, parallel to Greek Typhoeus, who is eventually defeated. The details are so closely similar that the Greek and Hurrian versions must be related, probably by derivation from a common west-Asiatic model. Kumarbi bites off Anu's phallus, while Kronos cuts off his father's; in both cases the blood and seed fertilize earth and produce minor gods (Aphrodite being a special detail); both Kumarbi and Kronos end up with gods inside them (the former by becoming pregnant, the latter by swallowing); these are born in peculiar ways (through the phallus, perhaps, and by vomiting); Kumarbi generates Ullikummi by copulating with a rock, while Typhoeus is born from Gaia—but according to one version Kronos smears two eggs with his seed and places them underground.

A structural analysis, emphasizing relationships rather than surface details, increases the neatness of the whole pattern as well as the similarity of the two versions. There is an unnatural retention of children within a parent, in Greek sources in the mother's womb, in Hurrian in the father's belly; they are released by violent and unnatural means, castration in the one case and pseudo-abortion in the other. In the one case sexual excess leads to castration, in the other castration leads to sexual abnormality (the male mother, the unnatural birth). Swallowing is important in both versions, but in the one case it is the fertile member, in the other living children and the sterile stone that are swallowed.

Whether these balancing relationships imply a Lévi-Straussian mediation between contradictions (for example between sexual excess and deficiency) is not clear; some kind of interest in sexual norms and functions certainly lurks beneath the surface. Freudians find the castration of the father significant, of course—but then is Kronos swallowing his children a symbol not of penis- but of uterus-envy? We must remember that

the continuing sexual theme originated in the analogy between rain fertilizing the earth and a male parent fertilizing a female. Once Ouranos and Gaia are so far personified, castration becomes a plausible means of usurpation. That still leaves Ouranos' refusal to separate as a curious feature, but herein must lie a reminiscence of other and less physiological versions in which earth and sky were originally conjoined. In any case the degree of nature allegory is limited, and only extends to earth and sky and the implication of rain as seed. Zeus is a weather god, but that does not emerge naturally from the progress of the myth, for Kronos, who has no clear association with cosmology, intervenes.

Kronos (as mentioned earlier) seems to have had agrarian functions, and perhaps these mediated between sky/earth and Zeus. Otherwise his role is rather mysterious, as indeed is that of his brothers and sisters the Titans. In Hesiod's listing they include pure nonentities as well as Okeanos, the freshwater river surrounding the circular earth, and abstract ladies like Themis, Custom, and Mnemosyne, Memory. These earlier gods may be related to Asiatic 'older gods', both Hittite and Akkadian. In the Babylonian Creation Epic there is war between the older gods, led by Apsu and Tiamat (salt and sweet primeval water), and their offspring who were disturbing them, led by Ea the developed water god and by Enlil 'lord of air', later replaced by the Babylonian city god Marduk.[2] Here the younger gods irritated the older ones by behaving so rowdily that Apsu, encouraged by his vizier Mummu, planned an otherwise unprovoked attack. But these 'older gods' have clear associations with the elements, whereas most of the Greek Titans, and of course Kronos himself, do not. Possibly the Titans are unfavourably depicted in the Hesiodic version precisely because of the example of the Asiatic 'older gods'; and yet there is a strong tradition, followed by Hesiod himself in the myth of the Five Races, that Kronos was king during the Golden Age. There is undoubtedly some confusion of different mythical *schemata* at this point. Zeus is king of the gods in the present epoch, and has imposed justice and hard work upon men. Any Golden Age must have been before his time, and therefore in the reign of Kronos, for that of Ouranos was too primeval for there to be men or heroes. Kronos' association with agrarian festivals would not be inconsistent with this idea, since corn without labour was part of the Golden Age vision. From a completely different point of view, however, Zeus had to win his way to power by a struggle, and so his predecessor was also seen as an enemy of justice.

These cosmogonical myths, which certainly include themes of high antiquity, remain uneven in detail and rather mysterious. Unlike other Greek myths they have clearly withstood much of the long process of organizing and expurgation. *The other divine tales,* which form our second category, were not so fortunate. They touch mostly on the actual birth of the developed gods and goddesses and on the way they acquired their special functions and prerogatives. Apart from this they are rather thin in distinctive episodes, except where gods intervene in the actions of heroes, and even there their role tends to be secondary. The thematic variety of the heroic tales is one of the particular marks of Greek myths as a whole, and it seems plausible that in the course of development many themes originally attached to gods (for example the founding of cities and festivals, or the disposal of monsters) were displaced on to heroes. The gods, as a result, were left in majestic inactivity, comparatively speaking; nevertheless many of the tales of their birth and development are memorable enough to foster the inaccurate impression that there is a wide range of divine myths.

Zeus has defeated the Titans and established his rule among the gods, and he now embarks on a series of marriages of which the clearest account is once again Hesiod's:

> Zeus, king of the gods, made Metis his first wife, she who is most knowledgeable of gods and mortal men. But when she was about to give birth to owl-eyed goddess Athena, then he deceived Metis with a trick, and through crooked words deposited her in his belly, following the advice of Gaia and starry Ouranos. This was the advice they gave him, so that no one apart from Zeus should have kingship over the everlasting gods. From Metis, they said, it was fated that children of surpassing intelligence should be born—first the Triton-born owl-eyed maiden [that is, Athena], equalling her father in power and careful counsel, but then a child that was to be king of gods and men. But Zeus, before that could happen, deposited her in his belly . . . (924) And out of his own head he gave birth to the owl-eyed Triton-born . . . (*Theogony*, 886 ff.)

'Metis' means 'counsel', and this part of the myth is allegorical and presumably not particularly ancient: Zeus becomes wise by swallowing wisdom. But the motif also corresponds closely to that of Kronos swallowing his children. Zeus in his turn is threatened by the problem of a powerful son destined to overthrow him, and he meets it, in a repetition that is unimaginative rather than structurally significant, by swallowing the mother and so preventing the child from ever being born. Inconsistently the other child, Athena, is born from Zeus himself—not from his phallus, as Hurrian Kumarbi probably bore the storm god, but respectably and allegorically (for Athena, like Metis, is clever) from his head. The craftsman god Hephaestus is shown in many vase paintings splitting Zeus' skull with an axe to allow the fully-armed goddess to emerge; it was a famous pictorial motif. Again there is a smack of sophistication and scholarship about this piece of theogony. In fact Athena was probably a Mycenaean

house-and palace-goddess, and was earlier felt to be a permanent dweller in her city of Athens; she had not been 'born' at all. Perhaps that made her available for Zeus' head; incidentally yet another god, Dionysus, was born from Zeus—snatched out of Semele's womb, when Zeus was forced to blast her with lightning, and sewed in Zeus' own thigh until the proper time for his birth.

After Metis, Zeus marries Themis, another personified quality ('custom' or 'law'), who gives birth to the Seasons and the Fates. Next he marries Eurynome, one of the many daughters of Okeanos, who bears the Graces; then, in a return to older and more concrete material, he takes his sister Demeter to his bed and she bears Persephone. Mnemosyne, 'Memory', bears him the Muses (transparent allegory here), Leto bears Apollo and Artemis, and last of all he weds Hera, who remains as his often-deceived wife from then until, presumably, eternity. These are his divine consorts; there is a long list of human mistresses too, from Semele mother of Dionysus, and Alcmena mother of Heracles, to Danaë mother of Perseus, and Europa mother of King Minos of Crete and his brother Rhadamanthys.

Zeus' daughter Athena, as protector of the royal household, became associated with the fortunes of the city as a whole, in her case Athens, which either gave her its name or derived its name from her. When Homer listed the various Achaean contingents in the second book of the *Iliad* the Athenians were described as

> those who possessed Athens, the well-founded city, the community of great-hearted Erechtheus, whom once Zeus' daughter Athena reared and to whom the life-giving earth gave birth; and she set him down in Athens in her own rich temple, and there the young men of the Achaeans propitiate him with bulls and with sheep as the seasons come round . . . (*Iliad* 2, 546 ff.)

Erechtheus was one of the early legendary kings of Athens, he is 'born from the soil' because the Athenians claimed to be autochthonous, not immigrants, and Athena's temple is virtually the same as his palace on the Acropolis. That we learn from an allusion in the *Odyssey* (7, 80 f.) in which Athena left the island of Phaeacia 'and came to Marathon and broad-wayed Athens, and slipped into the compact house of Erechtheus'; it is her own home too, because in a Mycenaean city the shrine of the god or goddess is set within the palace itself. Here, then, is Late Bronze Age religious realism as well as Athenian local patriotism. The tale of Athena's contest with Poseidon, in which she offers the city olive-trees and so wins its possession, elaborates the general theme. It is as Polias and Poliouchos, 'Holder of the City', that she comes to be associated with its warriors and craftsmen, especially potters and metal-workers; her protection of spinning and weaving, on the other hand, goes back to her function as goddess of the *oikos,* the household. The two contradictory sides of her are shown in the *Hymn to Aphrodite,* where she is one of those over whom the love goddess has no control:

> For the works of golden Aphrodite do not please her, but rather wars and the works of Areas . . . it was she that first taught mortal joiners to make carts and chariots thick with bronze, and she too who taught shining works to the soft-skinned maidens in their halls . . . (9 ff.)

She has no consort and is not interested in love, she is Parthenos, the maiden. With Hera she was defeated by Aphrodite in the Judgement of Paris, and in a sense she is Aphrodite's antithesis, rather like Artemis in Euripides' *Hippolytus.* There is an element of reasoned symbolism here, since marriage (Hera) and the maintenance of the household (Athena) are inconsistent with love as a luxury (Aphrodite) and with countryside pursuits like hunting (Artemis). It is important to notice that, by the time this valuation originated, problems of fertility were already subordinate to those of advanced social organization.

Athena is not just an impersonal household and city goddess; from Homer onward, and probably much earlier too, she is a protector of individual heroes and intervenes in many of their pursuits. She helps Perseus, for example, to overcome the Gorgons, but it is Odysseus in the *Odyssey* that is her most obvious protégé. She meets him in disguise when he is set ashore in Ithaca by the Phaeacians:

> Owl-eyed goddess Athena smiled at his words and stroked him with her hand; she was in the likeness of a woman fair and tall and accomplished in glorious works, and she spoke winged words to him and addressed him: 'He would be cunning and deceitful who could surpass you in all kinds of trickery, even if a god should come up against you. Wretch, cunning one, insatiably crafty, you were not going to desist from deceits and the lying words you love so deeply, even in your own land! But come, let us talk of this no longer. We both know how to get the better of others, since you are by far the best of mortals at giving advice and making speeches, and I am renowned among all the gods by reason of my intelligence and craftiness. Yet you did not recognize me as Pallas Athena, daughter of Zeus, who always stands by your side and guards you in every toil, and made you dear to all the Phaeacians.' (13, 287 ff.)

In this intimate scene Athena exaggerates her own reputation for cunning (which is not, usually, one of her most conspicuous qualities) in order to identify herself with Odysseus, for whom she seems to feel an almost lover-like sympathy. Odysseus in return is not above a mildly malicious ingratitude:

> 'It is hard, goddess, for a mortal who meets you to recognize you, even if he knows you well, because you take on all sorts of likenesses. But of this I am well aware, that in former times you were kind to me, when we sons of the Achaeans were fighting in the land of Troy; but when we had sacked Priam's steep city and were departing in our ships, and a god scattered the Achaeans, then I did not see you, daughter of Zeus, and did not notice you setting foot on my ship to keep grief away from me.' (*Odyssey* 13, 312 ff.)

I have quoted from this context not only to illustrate Athena's role as a personal protector of heroes but also to show the unusual subtlety that Homer can impose on a mythical scene. Odysseus may be a half-legendary figure, and Athena here may be doing little more than encourage him and act as informant. It is not a particularly memorable episode in narrative terms, but the description, which is leisurely and detailed and not merely allusive in the manner of so much later poetry, gives an extraordinary sense of divine epiphany and the ambivalent relationship between god and man. It is in the literary handling of mythical ideas, rather than the imaginative variety of narrative themes as such, that the Greeks as we know them were unique.

Other revealing examples of divine myths of birth and function relate to Apollo and then Dionysus, whom Nietzsche saw as symbols of opposing aspects—classical and romantic, controlled and ecstatic—of the Greek spirit. Apollo's birth on Delos is a favourite literary theme. Delos is a fascinating but arid little island, and the Greeks were evidently puzzled as to why such an important cult should have become established there in prehistoric times. The *Hymn to Apollo* is a relatively early (seventh century B.C.), if artificial, exercise in the Homeric style, compounded of two parts. The first relates how all other lands had refused to be the birthplace of the god; the second describes the foundation of his other great cult centre at Pytho (Delphi). Leto is pregnant by Zeus and has reached Delos:

> When Eileithyia, goddess of the pangs of birth, set foot on Delos, then travail seized Leto and she longed to give birth. She cast her arms around the palm-tree and pressed her knees on the soft meadow, and the earth smiled beneath; and he leapt forth into the light, and all the goddesses shrieked in triumph. Then, divine Phoebus, the goddesses washed you with fair water, cleanly and purely, and wrapped you in a fine white newly woven cloth, and set a golden swaddling-band around you. His mother did not give suck to Apollo of the golden sword, but Themis with immortal hands gave him a first offering of nectar and lovely ambrosia, and Leto rejoiced at the birth of her strong archer son. (115 ff.)

The foundation of the oracle at Delphi is no less miraculous, for Apollo in the form of a dolphin leaps aboard a Cretan ship and diverts it to the bay of Crisa, where at last he reveals himself:

> Strangers who dwell around many-treed Knossos— or did so formerly, but now you shall never again return to your lovely city and each to his fair home and dear wife, but here shall possess my rich temple honoured among many men: I declare to you that I am the son of Zeus; I am Apollo. I brought you here over the great gulf of the sea with no evil intent, but you shall possess here my rich temple held in much honour among all men, and shall know the counsels of the immortals and by their help be continually honoured for all your days. (475 ff.)

The Cretans are worried about their means of livelihood on this barren hillside, but the god assures them that they will be able to live off their share of the sheep that worshippers will bring for sacrifice. This mundane detail reminds us that the *Hymn,* in spite of its lyrical touches, is a priestly affair, clumsily aetiological in tone. Apollo Delphinios had an ancient cult in Crete—therefore let his priests at Delphi be of Cretan origin, and let Apollo appear to them as a dolphin. This kind of mythical detail does not appear very old, and probably developed as part of the established worship of Apollo at Delphi and Delos in historical and post-Mycenaean times.

For less cult-ridden attributes we can turn to a later source, Pindar, who for his royal patrons in the rich African colony of Cyrene sang of the nymph Cyrene and her wooing by Apollo on Mount Pelion. The god sees her wrestling with a lion and asks the Centaur Cheiron, in his nearby cave, who she is and whether he should make love to her. Cheiron replies with fitting humour and caution:

> Your gentle temper has inclined you (for whom it is not lawful to touch untruth) to speak this word obliquely. You ask, lord, of the girl's family? You who know the proper end of all things, and every path? The number of leaves the earth sends forth in spring, of grains of sand in sea and rivers whirled by waves and rushing winds, and what shall come to be and whence—all this you clearly discern! But if I must contend even against one that is wise, this is my answer. You came to this glade to be her husband, and you intend to carry her overseas to the incomparable garden of Zeus; there you shall make her ruler of a city [that is, Cyrene], and shall gather an island people round her to the hill among the plains. (*Pythians* 9, 42 ff.)

Elsewhere Pindar lists the god's main functions:

> It is he that assigns to men and women cures of harsh diseases; he brings them the lyre, and grants the Muse to whom he wishes, implanting in their minds a harmonious disposition that rules out warfare; and it is he that controls the oracle's hidden shrine. (*Pythians* 5, 63 ff.)

Apollo is god of prophecy and divination, of all kinds of inspiration, of poetry and music; from his oracle at Delphi he sponsors colonies like Cyrene itself. He is not always so unwarlike as Pindar implies, and in the *Iliad* is depicted as eager to defend Troy. As for his powers of healing, they probably depend on his identification with a local Cretan god called Paian. There is a shrine of Apollo Paian at Epidaurus, and a tale, again in Pindar's words, that Asclepius is really his son:

> She (Coronis) had consented to another marriage, secretly from her father, when she had already lain with Phoebus of the unshorn hair and carried the god's pure seed . . . for she slept in the bed of a stranger who came from Arcadia, and did not escape the god's watching . . . and he knew then of her lying with the stranger, Ischys son of Elatus, and of her unlawful deceit, and sent his sister [that is, Artemis], rushing with irresistible might, to Lakereia . . . And many of Coronis' neighbours shared her fate and were destroyed with her . . . but when her kinsmen had placed the maid within the pyre's wooden boundary, and the fierce gleam of Hephaestus [that is, fire] ran all round, then spoke Apollo: 'I shall not, after all, endure in my heart the destruction of my own progeny by a pitiable death, at the same time as his mother's doom.' So he spoke, and with a single stride he reached the child and snatched him from the corpse, as the burning pyre made a way clear for him; and he brought the child and gave him to the Magnesian Centaur [that is, Cheiron] to be taught how to cure men's painful diseases. (*Pythians* 3, 12 ff.)

The gods do not normally tolerate the later adulteration of their seed within a mortal woman; if they do, there are twins, of which the elder is the semi-divine offspring (as Heracles was), the younger the mortal one. Apollo snatches the infant from his dead mother's body just as Zeus snatched Dionysus out of Semele, and in both cases, too, the woman is killed by the god himself. Apollo's son Asclepius grew up to be a great healer, and was worshipped both as god and hero; but he went too far (like his mother) and tried to raise a man from the dead—an impious act that earned a thunderbolt from Zeus. Apollo was annoyed at this high-handed act and took revenge, not of course on Zeus himself, but on the Cyclopes who supplied the thunderbolt.

One cannot help admiring Pindar's mythological learning and the instant recognition he expects in his audience. Allusiveness and scholarship were to become a disease in the poetry of the Alexandrian age; for the moment, given Pindar's genuine feeling for religion, they actively enrich the power of his narrative core.

All the same one does not feel that the main thematic structure of these Apollo myths is necessarily very ancient. The god's omniscience, the nymph Cyrene, the Arcadian stranger Ischys, even the snatching of Asclepius from the pyre, may well be comparatively recent elaborations, marking one stage in the constant process of mythical extension. What is assuredly old is Apollo's association with healing, as Paian, and with oracles in his Pythian aspect; also of course his birth in Delos and his kinship to Artemis. There are other episodes that I have not mentioned: he shot down the giant Aloadae that threatened to attack the gods by piling Pelion on Ossa; together with Artemis he killed the giant Tityus who tried to rape their mother Leto, and slaughtered Niobe and her children because of a foolish boast; he was servant for a year to a mortal, King Admetus, for killing the Cyclopes (the motif is similar to Heracles serving Queen Omphale to purge his killing of his own children). He had a habit of loving, but failing to win, mortal women, notably Cassandra daughter of Priam and Marpessa who preferred Idas; he was more successful with Hyakinthos at Amyclae near Sparta, but actually the beautiful boy must have been, with that name, a pre-Hellenic god whom Apollo merely absorbed into his own worship. When H. J. Rose writes that Apollo has an 'extensive mythology', this is the kind of narrative range that is actually meant; not so extensive after all, and much of it dependent on the elaboration of themes used elsewhere.

Finally Dionysus, the god who came down into Greece through Thrace, ultimately from Phrygia in Asia Minor, and became the focus of an ecstatic religion. His myths are often tales of obduracy. The Thebans refused his worship and were driven to madness and murder, and so were the daughters of King Minyas of Orchomenus and King Proetus of Argos, even perhaps Orpheus himself. Some interpreters have been tempted to take these as reflections of actual historical resistance to his cult (which reached Greece comparatively late, perhaps after 1000 B.C.), and that could be so. The myth of Pentheus at Thebes, after all, depicts a whole city at odds with the god in various ways. But there is also an individual, psychological level of meaning. Dionysus represents the irrational element in man, and his myths the conflict between reason and social convention on one side, emotion on the other. That comes out in the tale of Pentheus, to be described shortly. Homer pays little attention to Dionysus—not at all a god fit for heroes—but refers briefly to his birth from Semele and his arranging to have Ariadne killed by Artemis in Naxos once he had finished with her. His fullest reference is to another tale of resistance, one of several mythical instances of the unwisdom of opposing a god:

> Nor did the son of Dryas, strong Lycurgus, last for long, because he strove against the heavenly gods.

Once on a time he chased the nurses of raving Dionysus over holy Mount Nysa; and they all together cast their sacred rods on the ground, under the blows of manslaying Lycurgus' ox-goad, and Dionysus took to flight and sank into the waves of the salt sea, and Thetis received him terrified in her bosom, for strong trembling possessed him when the man threatened him. With Lycurgus the easy-living gods were afterwards enraged, and the son of Kronos made him blind; nor did he last for long once he became the enemy of all the immortal gods. (*Iliad* 6, 130 ff.)

This Lycurgus is a Thracian, and it is interesting that the opposition tales range from Thrace, in the very north-east of Greece, through Thebes and Orchomenus in its centre, to Argos in the Peloponnese. Here Dionysus is represented as a child, although his 'nurses' are also his female votaries, his Bacchants, and the rods they cast on the ground are the *thyrsi,* fennel staves with ivy bunched at the tip, that were the special implements of Dionysiac worship and ecstasy.

A number of tales show the impact of Dionysus on various Greek cities. The most famous is the tale brilliantly retold by Euripides in his *Bacchae* about the fate that befell King Pentheus of Thebes when he opposed the cult of Dionysus and his worshippers. First he tried to throw the god, disguised as a beautiful young stranger, into prison. Here is how Dionysus reports the incident to his Bacchants:

> This was just the ignominy I subjected him to, that he thought he was binding me, but neither touched nor laid hands on me, but fed on empty hopes. He found a bull by the stalls where he had taken me and locked me up, and round *his* knees and hooves he cast his nooses, panting out his rage, dripping sweat from his body, setting his teeth to his lips. But close by I was peacefully sitting and watching. (*Bacchae,* 616 ff.)

No less powerful than the miracles (the palace of Pentheus was shaken by earthquake soon afterwards) are the songs sung by the chorus of Bacchants about the god they adore. They see themselves as bringing him from their native Asia Minor to Greece, and recall his miraculous birth:

> Onward Bacchants, onward Bacchants,
> bringing Dionysus,
> Bromios, god and child of a god,
> down from the Phrygian mountains
> into Hellas' spacious streets,
> Bromios the roaring one!
>
> Bearing him within her, in forced
> pangs of childbirth
> when Zeus' lightning flew
> his mother thrust him premature

from the womb, and left her life
at the lightning's stroke.
Instantly into chambers of birth
Zeus son of Kronos received him,
and hiding him in his thigh
confined him with golden
pins, secret from Hera.

He brought to birth, when the Fates
accomplished the time, a bull-horned god
and crowned him with garlands
of snakes; for this reason the maenads
twine in their tresses
the beast-reared prey.

(Bacchae, 83 ff.)

Dionysus is here 'the roaring one', a 'bull-horned god', because he so often manifests himself as a bull, rampant with fertility and power—which is why the deluded Pentheus had tied up a bull in mistake for the god himself. Dionysus' mother Semele, it will be remembered, was loved by Zeus and asked him to appear to her in his true form, which he did as lightning; he took the embryo from her womb as she died. The extract ends with a piece of minor cultic aetiology.

The god persuades Pentheus to dress as a Bacchant and spy on the crowds of infatuated women on Mount Cithaeron; he is instantly recognized and torn to pieces by his own mother and aunts. This is how the chorus exult, allusively as always:

Let us dance to the Bacchic god,
shout aloud the disaster
of the dragon's descendant, Pentheus;
who took female raiment
and the fennel-rod, Hades' pledge,
in its thyrsus-shape
with a bull to lead him into disaster.

(Bacchae, 1153 ff.)

Pentheus is 'the dragon's descendant' because he is descended from the Sown Men, the armed warriors who grew from the ground when Cadmus had killed the dragon that guarded the site of Thebes, and sown its teeth. The bull, again, is Dionysus himself. The disaster Pentheus suffered was a literal tearing apart, which is what the Bacchants regularly did to any young animal that fell into their hands during their crazy dances across the mountains.

The myths of Dionysus are part of his religion, and their power is derived as much from an exotic and thrilling form of worship as from their narrative themes as such. In that respect they may be unusual—although even those of Apollo, apparently more firmly rooted in Greek culture, are seen to depend for much of their apparent richness on the elaboration and nostalgic fervour of poets like Pindar.

The third category of myths is no longer divine, although it remains closely in touch with the life of the gods. It comprises tales that describe *the emergence of human beings* and the complicated acts by which their role, and in particular their exact relation to the gods, is established. Essentially it contains the myths about the Golden Age, Prometheus and the Fall of men. Hesiod once again is our main and for much of the time our only source, although the details he records (with the exception of the Five Races myth which is idiosyncratic in places) were probably familiar to many Greeks of his era.

The Greek conception of a Golden Age is rather imprecise, because it contains two separate ideas that were gradually conflated and then further complicated by later eschatologies from Italy and Sicily. The two ideas are as follows. First, there was a period in the past, often associated with the time Kronos was king of the gods, when a 'golden' race of men lived without toil and died as though in sleep after a happy life. Second, there is a distant land, called either Elysium or the Islands of the Blest, where divinely favoured humans live on instead of dying—especially the sons and daughters of one divine parent, like Peleus, Cadmus, Menelaus, Helen. They go there instead of Hades and live an eternal life of bliss, free from toil.

The first concept is represented by the golden race in Hesiod's schematic account (not an ordinary myth because it has no obvious story) of the Five Races of men:

First the immortals who have their homes on Olympus made a golden race of men; they lived in the time of Kronos, and he was king of heaven. They lived like gods with a spirit free from care, far from toils and grief; neither did vile old age come upon them, but with unwithering limbs they rejoiced in festivity, away from all evils, and died as though subdued by sleep. All good things were theirs; the life-giving earth bore its fruit freely and in abundance, and in contentment and peace they lived off their lands in prosperity. But when the earth covered this race, through the will of great Zeus they have become good daemons on earth, guardians of mortal men. (*Works and Days,* 109 f.)

The same kind of life is ascribed by Pindar to the Hyperboreans, a people especially favoured by Apollo and imagined as dwelling, as their name suggests, 'beyond the North Wind':

Everywhere are girls dancing and the noise of lyres and the shrill whirlings of flutes; with their hair bound with golden bay they feast in joyfulness. Maladies and destructive old age have no part in that sacred race, but they dwell without toils or battles, free from severe Nemesis. (*Pythians* 10, 38 ff.)

The second concept, of Elysium or the Isles of the Blest, is clearly described by Hesiod and applied to his fourth race, the race of heroes. They were killed off in the great expeditions against Thebes and Troy, and

> then some of them did the end of death enclose, but to the others father Zeus, son of Kronos, gave a life and abode apart from men, and settled them at the limits of the earth; and they dwell with carefree spirit in the Isles of the Blest by the side of deep-swirling Okeanos—blissful heroes, for whom the life-giving earth thrice yearly bears its rich honey-sweet fruit. (*Works and Days,* 166 ff.)

At this point some probably non-Hesiodic verses were appended in antiquity; they claim that Kronos was king of these blessed heroes, and that Zeus had brought him up from imprisonment in Tartarus for the purpose. Obviously this is designed to reconcile the two different concepts. Pindar, too, associates Kronos with a development of the Isles-of-the-Blest conception when he takes over the traditional picture of the blessed life, laces it with 'Orphic' and Pythagorean ideas from Italy and Sicily about the rebirth of the soul, and presents the result as a reward for those who have completed just lives on earth:

> But all who have endured, while remaining in each world, to keep their soul three times apart from injustice pass over the road of Zeus to the tower of Kronos, where breezes born of Okeanos blow around the Isles of the Blest, and golden flowers blaze out, some on land from glorious trees, others nurtured by the water; and they weave necklaces and wreaths from them under the just rule of Rhadamanthys, whom the great father [that is, Kronos], husband of Rhea of the all-lofty throne, keeps ever seated by his side. (*Olympians* 2, 68 ff.)

Here (Pindar goes on to say) are Peleus and Cadmus and Achilles—one more detail that belongs to the strict conception of the Isles as a kind of Valhalla for semi-divine heroes.

So we can now distinguish *three* distinct but related ideas, each of which tends to give rise to similar language (the earth bringing forth its fruits without toil, and so forth). First, there was a stage in the past when all men lived in Golden Age conditions. Second, a few privileged members of the age of heroes survive death, in similar conditions, in Elysium or the Isles of the Blest. Third, such a life is still possible for the souls of the just, as a reward after death and after judgement in Hades. The third view is certainly a later adaptation of the second, the second possibly a later adaptation of the first. Curiously, Kronos tends to be associated with all three, and at one stage Greek myths must have had far more to say about him than they do now, or at least than Hesiod chooses to reveal.

A more specific idea of a Golden Age is implied in occasional mythical allusions to men having banqueted with the gods either regularly or on certain special occasions, in particular at the marriages of mortals to immortals. It was the marriage of Peleus, father of Achilles, to the sea-nymph Thetis, and of Cadmus, founder of Thebes, to Harmonia the daughter of Ares and Aphrodite, that made the strongest mark in art and literature. Pindar uses both heroes to illustrate a moralism:

> Neither Peleus son of Aeacus nor godlike Cadmus had a life without difficulties; yet they are said to have possessed the highest blessedness of mortals, for they heard the Muses with diadems of gold singing on Mount Pelion and in seven-gated Thebes, when the one married ox-eyed Harmonia and the other Thetis, renowned daughter of Nereus the good counsellor. (*Pythians* 3, 86 ff.)

Among others who were intimate with the gods was Tantalus, the father of Pelops who later defeated King Oenomaus of Pisa for the hand of his daughter and gave his name to the Peloponnese. Pindar refuses to believe the common form of the tale, which was that Tantalus invited the gods to dinner and served up his own son Pelops, freshly cooked, to see if they could tell the difference. Demeter, still distracted by grief because of Persephone, absent-mindedly ate a shoulder, but the rest of the gods immediately detected the crime. Poseidon brought Pelops to life, gave him a beautiful ivory shoulder and was later overcome by his charms. Pindar, however, protests that 'It is impossible for me to call any of the blessed gods a glutton; I stand apart!' and implies a different reason for Tantalus' disgrace (which resulted in his being eternally tantalized by food and water that lay just out of reach). Yet the important thing at present is that Tantalus

> invited the gods to the most orderly of banquets in his own dear Sipylon, offering them a return for the dinners they had given him. (*Olympians* 1, 37 ff.)

King Lykaon of Arcadia, in a thematically overlapping tale (see p. 238 ff.), invited Zeus to dine with him on Mount Lykaion and offered him human flesh. Again it is the idea of gods and mortals dining together—not always with such lurid menus—that interests us here, indicating as it does an era when gods and men were not so stringently separated as they were even in the developed age of heroes.

Somehow that era came to an end. The precise cause is not clear from the myths, and could have been the supplanting of Kronos by Zeus, or the crimes of Tantalus and Lykaon, or the general increase in impiety and bloodshed implied by Empedocles and the Orphics, of which more later. Somewhere here the flood must be fitted in . . . ; it was sent by Zeus to punish mankind, and only Deucalion and his wife Pyrrha survived it. That is the commonest version, although others talk of King Ogygus as responsible, or connect the flood with the human sacrifice initiated by Lykaon or his sons. Deucalion and Pyrrha, at any rate, recreate the human race on purely etymological principles; they do so by throwing stones over their shoulders, and the stones turn into people—but that is because the Greek word for stone (*laas*) is similar to that for people (*laos*). From such trivial ideas are myths sometimes made, more generally in Egypt and Mesopotamia than in Greece (see p. 58 f.).

At some indeterminate period after the end of the Golden Age men were poor, defenceless and weak, and a great protector came on the scene in the person of Prometheus. Prometheus was a minor god, his parents the Titan Iapetus and the Oceanid Clymene. For everything that concerns him—and he is of the highest importance for this whole third group of myths—Hesiod is once again our prime authority. This is how he describes his birth and ultimate salvation:

> Iapetus led away the fair-ankled maid Clymene, daughter of Okeanos, and shared his bed with her; and she bore stubborn Atlas as her son, also renowned Menoetius and subtle Prometheus of cunning counsel and foolish Epimetheus, who from the beginning was a disaster to industrious humans; for it was he that first received the fabricated maiden from Zeus. Wide-seeing Zeus sent insolent Menoetius down into Erebus by striking him with smoky lightning . . . Atlas holds the broad sky at the ends of the earth through strong necessity . . . and Zeus bound subtle-counselled Prometheus with harsh inescapable bonds, driving them through the midst of a pillar, and sent a long-winged eagle upon him; and it used to eat his immortal liver, which grew back to its full size during the night, as much as the long-winged bird might eat during the whole day. The strong son of fair-ankled Alcmena, Heracles, slew it, and warded off cruel pain from Iapetus' son and released him from his grief, not without the will of Olympian Zeus who reigns on high . . . (*Theogony*, 507 ff.)

Menoetius is rather obscure; Atlas is well-known because he was envisaged as holding up the sky (a probably archaic concept parallel to the Egyptian idea of a sky supported on pillars); Epimetheus ('Afterthought', invented to match Prometheus which seems to mean 'Forethought') is known simply for his presumably lustful folly in receiving the first woman as a gift; but it is Prometheus who is the key figure. His imprisonment by Zeus, in the Caucasus mountains as we learn elsewhere, comes as climax to a series of clashes between the two, Prometheus begins the quarrel by trying to cheat Zeus over the division of sacrificial meats once the era of dining together had come to an end:

> For when the gods and mortal men were making a settlement at Mecone, then Prometheus with eager

spirit divided up a great ox and set it before him, trying to delude the mind of Zeus. For in the one lot he placed the flesh and guts, rich with fat, inside mere skin, covering them with the ox's stomach; in the other he placed the ox's white bones by an artful trick, putting them in order and covering them with shining fat. Then did the father of gods and men address him: 'Son of Iapetus, most famous of all the lords, how one-sidedly, my dear fellow, have you divided out the portions!' Thus spoke Zeus of undying cunning in rebuke, but crooked-counselled Prometheus addressed him in reply, gently smiling and not forgetting his crafts of deceit: 'Most glorious Zeus, greatest of the eternal gods, take whichever of these your heart and mind bid you.' He spoke with deceitful intent, and Zeus of undying cunning recognized and did not overlook the trick, and he devised evils in his heart for mortal men, that were destined to be fulfilled. Then with both hands he took up the white fat; he was enraged in his mind, and anger possessed his spirit, when he saw the ox's white bones as a result of the artful trick. Because of this the races of men on earth burn white bones to the immortals on their fragrant altars. Then in great wrath cloud-gathering Zeus addressed him: 'Son of Iapetus, cunning above all others, so you did not yet, my dear fellow, forget your art of deceit!' Thus did Zeus of undying cunning speak, and from this time forth, always remembering the trick, he withheld from the ash-trees the power of unwearying fire for mortal men who dwell upon earth. But the good son of Iapetus deceived him by stealing the far-seen gleam of unwearying fire in a hollow fennel-stalk, and he angered high-thundering Zeus in the depths of his spirit, and Zeus was enraged in his heart when he saw among men the far-seen gleam of fire. Immediately he made an evil for men in return for fire; for the famous cripple [that is, Hephaestus] moulded out of earth the likeness of a reverent maiden through the will of Zeus. The owl-eyed goddess Athena girded her and adorned her with a silver robe, and with her hands she hung down from her head an embroidered veil, a marvel to see . . . (*Theogony*, 535-75)

I consider first the deceit over the sacrifices and the theft of fire, and continue with the creation of woman. The story of the division at Mecone (said to be near ancient Sicyon, not far from Corinth) is of fundamental importance, both because it treats a crucial question of the relation between men and gods and because it shows, more clearly than any other Greek instance, a myth that is working towards the resolution of a real problem. To say that it is simply aetiological in the most superficial sense, that it offers a pretty story to divert men's attention from the apparent anomaly that the gods are given the worst bits at a sacrifice, is the reaction of most people and is, I am afraid, rather inadequate. It does that, as Hesiod indicates, but it also goes deeper. The deceptive choice offered by a god to a mortal or vice versa is a widespread folktale motif often used to account for the fact of death: man was offered a choice between death and life, as in the

Akkadian tale of Adapa, and through trickery or misinformation he made the wrong choice. The Prometheus tale is more complex. It is the mortal, or rather the defender of mortals, that offers the choice to the supreme god, not the other way round. Whether the god is fully conscious of the deceit remains doubtful; Hesiod's account vacillates and suggests the conflation of different versions. Not the least interesting implication of the myth is that the practice of making sacrifices is itself a relic of a Golden Age when gods and privileged mortals dined together.

Sacrifice was a crucial act of social and religious life, but men simply had to retain the flesh and the most edible parts. Meat was even rarer and more expensive than in Greece today, and sacrifice was in one sense a by-product of the profession of butchery. It was essential for the Greeks to offer *some* of their meat to the gods, but it had to be a token. Actually it was a perfectly logical one, since the only part that could pass from the sacrificial burning up into the sky, where the gods could receive it, was the smoke and savour, and that emanated best from the fat and not the flesh. From another but no less important point of view what was symbolically offered to the gods was the *whole animal;* this too was best represented by the bones, especially if they were 'put in good order' as Hesiod says near the beginning of the text last quoted—the intention being to reconstruct the animal symbolically.

On this occasion, then, the mythical justification of an apparent contradiction (that the gods are given the worst bits rather than the best) is rather inept; indeed a better defence of the practice could have been made in rational and quasiphilosophical terms. And yet such a defence might not in the end have been emotionally satisfying. It could easily fail to remove the guilt men felt over keeping the best parts of the animal for themselves. Guilt is a cardinal feeling, and much of the lifetime of ordinary mortals is consumed in suppressing it by one means or another. Some such feeling demanded that men should be made to pay for the offending practice, and that is where the myth came in. First, Zeus withdrew fire itself, which was thought to reside above all in ash trees, a reference to kindling from special kinds of wood. Its withdrawal was a cunning move, directly related to the practice of sacrifice, as though Zeus had said 'All right, if you're not going to give us gods the share of the burnt meats we deserve, there shall be no burning at all. *We* shall be no worse off, but *you* will have to eat your appetizing portion of flesh and innards all raw. Just try that!'

In the later tradition Prometheus developed into a general technological benefactor, one who brought men the arts not only of healing, mathematics, medicine, navigation and divination, but also of mining and working metals; that view of him is best seen in Aeschylus' *Prometheus Vinctus,* 436-506. No doubt

his recovery of fire was part of the same conception, but in all probability this extension of his functions is not much older than the sixth century B.C., when interest in the evolution of men from a crude and savage state—an idea that directly contradicts the mythical scheme of a decline from the Golden Age—first became prominent.

The Hesiodic account continues with Zeus' second act of revenge, the creation by various gods and goddesses of the first woman. Incidentally the Greeks seem to have had no commonly accepted myth about the creation of *man,* who undoubtedly came first. This was credited in later sources, as one might expect, to Prometheus himself, who became patron of the potters in Athens and no doubt elsewhere, and was envisaged as making men, after a common Mesopotamian pattern, out of clay. At Panopeus in central Greece visitors were shown lumps left over from the work.[3] . . . Even the creation of woman exists in two versions, and Hesiod gives both, one in the *Theogony* and the other in *Works and Days.* In the former, Hephaestus completes his creation . . . , and leads her before gods and men:

> from her are the destructive race and tribes of women, who dwell as a great misery among mortal men, as suitable companions not of deadly poverty but of surfeit. (*Theogony,* 591-3)

The theme of women's extravagance and ill-nature is developed in what follows. It is widespread all over the world, and its unfairness is one of the less feeble testimonies to the idea of a male conspiracy against womankind. But Hesiod, who was no fool, could see beyond the one-sided viewpoint of folktale motifs, for he added that Zeus established a complementary evil, namely that the man who refuses to marry has a dismal old age with no one to look after him and no family to inherit his possessions; while the man who happens to get a good wife (and it is eventually conceded that this is possible) has at least a mixture of good and evil.

The *Works and Days* version, on the other hand, gives a different and more familiar story. After a similar process of manufacture Hermes filled the woman with deceit,

> and placed in her a voice, and named this woman Pandora (because all that have their halls on Olympus gave her a gift), a misery to industrious men. But when he had brought to perfection this drastic and irremediable deceit, the father sent the glorious slayer of Argos [that is, Hermes], swift messenger of the gods, to Epimetheus, bringing her as a gift; and Epimetheus failed to remember that Prometheus had told him never to accept a gift from Olympian Zeus, but to send it back lest it should turn out to be some evil for mortals, but accepted her and recognized the evil only when it was his.

For, before that, the tribes of man lived on earth far removed from evils and hard toil and harsh diseases that bring doom to men. But the woman with her hands took the great lid from the jar and scattered them, and contrived baneful cares for mankind. Only Hope remained there in its unbreakable dwelling-place, under the lip of the jar, and did not fly out; before that could happen she replaced the lid of the jar by the will of aegis-bearing cloud-gathering Zeus. But ten thousand other banes wander among men; for the earth is full of evils, and full the sea, and diseases come upon men by day, and others of their own accord by night, bringing ills to mortals in silence, since Zeus took away their voice. (*Works and Days,* 80-104)

The aetiological details (the etymology of Pandora, literally 'all-gifts' or 'all-giving', and the silent diseases that arrive unnoticed during the night) and the rather self-conscious allegory about Hope may be relatively new embroideries, but the jar looks like a great Mycenaean or Minoan affair, and the tale as a whole is old. Once again it probably relies on an essentially folktale theme that Hesiod has suppressed, for presumably what made Pandora take the lid off was meddling curiosity. At this point the poet is even more cursory and allusive than usual. The jar is not explained, but is simply assumed to be familiar to his audience—an assumption that aided its transformation into Pandora's *box* in the Renaissance tradition.

Immediately after the myth and its moralizing conclusion that 'thus it is in no way possible to escape the intention of Zeus' comes the semi-mythical account of the Five Races, beginning with the men of the golden race . . . who were still free of all the diseases Pandora released. So Hesiod presents in his two poems an overlapping, quite complex and ultimately rather subtle picture of the Fall of Man from a condition of divine privilege and sodality to his present one of misery, disease, family trouble and old age. Some parts of the organization and a few of the details probably belong to Hesiod or his immediate sources, but most of the mythical complex, and certainly its main tendencies, seem traditional. In the end it transpires that the apparently avoidable aspects of man's condition—not death itself, for that is inevitable, but disease, painful old age, poverty and the need for unremitting toil—are the indirect result of the first quarrel between Zeus and Prometheus. The quarrel arose out of the division of the sacrifices, and that may be held to symbolize, in a way, the whole dilemma of the relation between men and gods. Ultimately it is something myths cannot explain: what they do is to suggest that things were once all right, but that men were too demanding. If they had shown self-restraint, or if Prometheus and Epimetheus had done so on their behalf, the quarrel with the gods would never have begun and women could have been accepted in a less extreme form.

Even that is pressing the myths too hard. Women are a fact of life, the human race could never have started without them. What seems to be happening is that a dilemma at the folktale level (involving the conflict between the peasant's princess-dream and his brutal assessment of actual wives by their economic value) became connected with a more basic contradiction in the human condition, that between men's immortal longings and the harsh facts of human existence. Something similar seems to have happened with the theme of the quarrel over sacrifices, since that too must once have existed independently. Yet its relevance to the question of the decline was obvious, and it became woven into the mythical texture in a way that gave a deeper and more complex meaning to the whole. Indeed the entire sequence of myths in Hesiod— Prometheus, the sacrifice, the theft of fire, the creation of women, the punishment of Prometheus, the five races of men—might be said to leave one with a feeling that things are not quite so unfair as they were, that evil is more equable than it seemed, that old age and disease are in some ways our own fault, even that things might improve if only we learned to behave better. Prometheus remains mysterious. Why he champions men is never made clear; probably he dropped into the role by the accident of being a trickster figure, one suitable to undertake the futile but engaging contest of wits with Zeus. In the end he matches Zeus—that too makes one feel that fate is not necessarily relentless, for (as we learn from Aeschylus) he knows something that Zeus does not, namely that whoever marries Thetis will have a son greater than his father. Zeus and Poseidon were both, as it happens, competing for the honour at the time, and Prometheus' secret had to be bought at the price of his release by Heracles. Even the gods have to temper the wind on occasion.

In the end it was Peleus who married the dangerous Thetis. Like all sea deities she changed her shape to avoid capture, but he ultimately caught her and their son was Achilles, greater than his father but no danger to the gods. Even this tale has its underlying relevance to the Hesiodic group, because Peleus grew old while his divine wife remained eternally young. Eventually she left him, and he ended, after much sorrow, in the Isles of the Blest. Another mortal lover, Tithonus, was not so fortunate, as the *Hymn to Aphrodite* (composed probably in the sixth century B.C.) relates:

> So too golden-throned Eos [that is, Dawn] ravished god-like Tithonus of the Trojan race; and she went to ask the black-clouded son of Kronos that he should be immortal and live for all the sum of days, and Zeus nodded in approval and accomplished her prayer. Yet she was foolish, for Lady Eos did not think in her heart of asking for youth and of stripping off destructive old age. As long as lovely youth possessed him, he dwelt by the streams of Okeanos at the limits of the earth, rejoicing in early-born golden-throned Eos; but when the first grey hairs

poured down from his fair head and noble chin, then did Lady Eos keep away from his bed, but cherished him still in her halls with food and ambrosia, and gave him fair raiment. But when finally hateful old age overpowered him, and he was unable to move his limbs or lift them up, this seemed to her in her heart to be the best plan: she placed him in a chamber and closed the shining doors upon him. His voice flows on unceasing, yet there is no strength in his bent limbs such as once there was. (218-38)

The Greeks were sensible about old age, passionately though they resented it, just as they were about emulating the gods or trying to become immortal. Odysseus, who rejected the chance of living on with the nymphs Circe and Calypso and insisted on returning to the admirable but ageing Penelope, was the counter-paradigm to Tithonus. The myths not only reflected that attitude to age, they even helped to define it—particularly those among them that bore directly on the relations between men and gods. It is for such reasons that I have spent so much time on them, despite Hesiod's verbose and often clumsy style. For it is here, in this relatively early but still literary form, that Greek myths come closest to the pointed functionality of their oral predecessors, a functionality that responds at times to the aetiological, structural and psychological interpretations discussed in earlier chapters. Even more important, perhaps, it is here that we are left with the strongest sense of myths as a part of life itself.

Notes

[1] H. G. Güterbock in *Mythologies,* 155 ff.; *Myth,* 214 ff.

[2] *ANET,* 60 ff.; *Mythologies,* 120 f.; *Religions,* 69-71

[3] Pausanias 10: 4, 4

Edward F. Edinger (essay date 1994)

SOURCE: "Cosmogony," in *The Eternal Drama: The Inner Meaning of Greek Mythology*, edited by Deborah A. Wesley, Shambhala Publications, Inc., 1994, pp. 1-17.

[*In the following essay, Edinger offers a psychological reading of the Greek creation myths, noting the prevalence of the idea that when a being is brought into consciousness, a split into opposites results, followed by conflict between those opposites.*]

A consideration of Greek mythology must start with at least a brief look at the myths of creation or cosmogony. There are several versions of how the cosmos came into existence. The simplest is that first there was Chaos, and out of Chaos earth, or Gaia, emerged. Gaia gave birth to the sky, or Uranus, and then Gaia and Uranus produced a great progeny. So from Chaos a pair of world parents emerged and separated, who then created all the rest that exists.

What would that mean psychologically? For one thing it is an image of how the personality or the prefigurations of the ego (we can't speak of the ego yet) first begin. One can also think of it as representing how each new bit of psyche is created. After all, it is a creation myth, and it does fit our psychological experience that the creative act itself involves exposure to chaos. Creation means that something new comes into the world that did not previously exist. And if so, from whence does it come? The only place it can come from is the void region of nonbeing characterized in the myth as Chaos. That is the womb, the unbegotten womb of all things yet to be, and hence the experience of creativity commonly has as a forerunner or an accompaniment the experience of chaos. Nothing new can emerge unless one is willing to dip into chaos and pull it out.

Once it is out, it promptly splits into two, into earth and sky in terms of the myth. This is something we see whenever something is coming into awareness: the very process of achieving consciousness involves a split into opposites. Things can remain in their state of oneness only as long as they are unconscious. When they reach consciousness, they must divide into opposites and then we have the experience of conflict. When things are seen in twos in dreams, there is the suggestion that they are achieving a conscious status for the first time.

The myths tell us that Uranus and Gaia were the first king and queen in the divine kingdom. There were wars for the kingship, and a series of dethronements took place in this very early mythology. The king did not want to let anything survive that was threatening to him, so he took certain repressive measures, which then called forth counteractions. These early dethronements, can be thought of psychologically. Humankind had not yet appeared at this stage of the story; hence, if we take the human being to signify the ego, the ego did not really exist. These ancient deities can be seen as prefigurations of the ego or as the primordial Self in conjunction with the ego germ. They were undergoing a certain transformative evolution, signified by the early dethronements.

Uranus got into trouble because he imprisoned certain of his children. The two major branches of his offspring were the Titans on the one hand, and the Cyclopes on the other. The Cyclopes, giants that had a central round eye—the word means "wheel eye" literally—were confined in the earth. Upset at Uranus' imprisonment of them, the mother, always the more merciful of the two parents, stirred up her son Kronos to revolt against Uranus. Kronos lay in wait for him and castrated him; the drops of blood that fell on the earth generated the Erinyes, the Furies, and the genitals fell into the sea and are said to have given rise to Aphrodite. One could say that the Cyclopes, since they were characterized primarily by their one round eye, represent a psychic aspect that has not split into doubleness. The roundness suggests a certain primordial wholeness that was being repressed by Uranus. The consequences of Uranus' castration might be thought of as the birth of desire (Aphrodite) and the birth of punishment (the Erinyes).

The castration of Uranus was taken by Freud as a mythological example of the castration complex, the son wanting to supplant the father and in effect castrate him but fearing like treatment from the father. The episode can also be thought of in a more general sense. In the case of both Uranus and Kronos, a principle that is in power seeks to perpetuate itself and to eliminate all threats to its authority. This is an image of what can happen within the psyche: an old principle must die if development is to proceed, and it has to be overcome by the emerging new principle itself. That was the case with Uranus, and it happened as well when Kronos, who succeeded him, behaved no better. It was prophesied that Kronos might be deposed by one of his offspring; he reacted by swallowing all his children—a primordial version of the devouring parent, an image universally encountered. Ultimately Kronos, a Titan, was cast out in a war between the gods and the Titans and was replaced by Zeus, who belonged to the race of the gods. A whole dynasty of psychic authorities was being overthrown and replaced by a new one. There was a real *Götterdämmerung* in the ancient Pantheon.

The Titans who were vanquished served some very useful purposes. Two outstanding ones were Atlas and Prometheus. Atlas' punishment for losing the war, so to speak, was to be condemned to hold up the earth, which he has been doing ever since. In a certain sense, the Titans became sacrifices for humankind's well-being. The archetypal contents that they represent went into the service of the ego.

The primary example of this is the story of Prometheus. Even though the Titans had lost the war, Prometheus was still present and still against the gods, and at that stage opposing the gods meant being on the side of humanity. Prometheus' story begins when he was assigned to supervise the separation of the sacrificial meat to determine which part went to the gods and which to humankind. Previously, gods and humans had eaten together, but now they were to eat apart, signifying a separation of the ego from its archetypal origins. Prometheus deceived the gods by wrapping up bones and skin for them in a very enticing package and leaving all the nourishing meat for humankind. In punishment for this, Zeus deprived humanity of fire.

Prometheus proceeded to steal it for the benefit of humankind, and for that crime he was chained in the Caucasus Mountains. There, his liver was eaten away each day by a vulture, but the wound would heal each night. In this way, the process repeated endlessly.

Prometheus' story gives us profound images of the nature of emerging consciousness. First there is the process of separation, which determines what belongs to the gods and what belongs to humankind, the ego gaining increments of meat, or energy, for itself. Then humanity is provided with fire, one could say with light and energy: consciousness and the effective energy of will to carry out conscious intention are created. However, there was a fearful price for this, because the acquisition of consciousness was a crime, as described in the myth, and its consequence was to generate in Prometheus an unhealing wound, the wound inflicted by the vulture by day—during the time of light and consciousness. This particular detail indicates that consciousness itself is the vulture, the wound-producer. Prometheus pays for the consciousness of humanity with his suffering, much like Christ. As a Titan, he belongs to the divine realm; he is not human but an archetypal or non-ego factor, which so loved humankind that it put itself in humanity's service, that is, in the service of the ego, in order to promote its development.

The image of Prometheus has fascinated the poets and led them to identify with him—a dangerous identification. Goethe was one. He declared, "The fable of Prometheus came alive in me. I cut the old Titan rope to my own size." Shelley and Byron were both preoccupied with the image of Prometheus. Longfellow has some lines in his poem "Prometheus" that express a quite widespread feeling about the Promethean quality in the creative artist:

> First the deed of noble daring,
> Born of heavenward aspiration,
> Then the fire with mortals sharing,
> Then the vulture—the despairing
> Cry of pain on crags Caucasian.
>
> All is but a symbol painted
> Of the Poet, Prophet, Seer;
> Only those are crowned and sainted
> Who with grief have been acquainted,
> Making nations nobler, freer.
>
> In their feverish exultations,
> In their triumph and their yearning,
> In their passionate pulsations,
> In their words among the nations,
> The Promethean fire is burning. . . .
>
> Though to all there be not given
> Strength for such sublime endeavor,

Thus to scale the walls of heaven,
And to leaven with fiery leaven,
All the hearts of men forever;

Yet all bards, whose hearts unblighted
Honor and believe the presage,
Hold aloft their torches lighted,
Gleaming through the realms benighted,
As they onward bear the message![1]

Another consequence of Prometheus' acts was the punishment meted out to his brother Epimetheus, who can be thought of as a variant of Prometheus. He received the gift of Pandora. In a certain sense we could say that Pandora and fire are equivalent. Fire is energy and one of the aspects of energy is desire: Pandora, the beautiful woman, is the object of desire. As the ego is given the powers of desire and will and longing, it also receives the contents of Pandora's box, the sufferings of human life. This is a very close parallel with the myth of Adam and Eve. Both signify the painful aspect of being born into egohood. As these myths describe it, the unconscious state is paradise and the birth of the ego is paid for by suffering.

Aeschylus' *Prometheus Bound* pictures how Prometheus was regarded by the Greeks of the fifth century BC. He was a culture hero and hence we can say he was the incarnation of the consciousness-bringing principle itself. In Aeschylus' play, Prometheus says:

[L]isten to the sad story of mankind, who like children lived until I gave them understanding and a portion of reason; yet not in disparagement of men I speak, but meaning to set forth the greatness of my charity. For seeing they saw not, and hearing they understood not, but like as shapes in a dream they wrought all the days of their life in confusion. No houses of brick raised in the warmth of the sun they had, nor fabrics of wood, but like the little ants they dwelt underground in the sunless depths of caverns. No certain sign of approaching winter they knew, no harbinger of flowering spring or fruitful summer; ever they labored at random, till I taught them to discern the seasons by the rising and the obscure setting of the stars. Numbers I invented for them, the chiefest of all discoveries; I taught them the grouping of letters, to be a memorial and record of the past, the mistress of the arts and mother of the Muses. I first brought under the yoke beasts of burden, who by draft and carrying relieved men of their hardest labors; I yoked the proud horse to the chariot, teaching him obedience to the reins, to be the adornment of wealth and luxury. I too contrived for sailors sea-faring vessels with their flaxen wings. . . .

If sickness visited them, they had no healing drug, no salve or soothing potion, but wasted away for want of remedies, and this way my greatest boon; for I revealed to them the mingling of bland medicaments for the banishing of all diseases. And many modes of divination I appointed: from dreams I first taught them to judge what should befall in waking state; I found the subtle interpretation of words half heard or heard by chance, and of meetings by the way; and the flight of taloned birds with their promise of fortune or failure I clearly denoted, their various modes of life, their mutual feuds, their friendships and consortings; . . . And the secret treasures of the earth, all benefits to men, copper, iron, silver, gold—who but I could boast of their discovery? . . . Nay, hear the whole matter in a word—all human arts are from Prometheus.[2]

He was the bringer of consciousness. Although many figures carry this quality, Prometheus must have been profoundly meaningful to the ancient Greeks, to be described in this way by their chief dramatist.

The parallel to Christ is obvious. There are also similarities to the Biblical "suffering servant" passage in Isaiah, except that Prometheus is defiant, where the suffering servant is described as meek. We read in Isaiah this description of the suffering servant of God:

He grew up before the Lord like a young
    plant
whose roots are in parched ground;
he had no beauty, no majesty to draw our
    eyes,
no grace to make us delight in him;
his form, disfigured, lost all the likeness of a
    man,
his beauty changed beyond human semblance.
He was despised, he shrank from the sight of
    men,
tormented and humbled by suffering;
we despised him, we held him of no account,
a thing from which men turn away their eyes.
Yet on himself he bore our sufferings,
our torments he endured,
while we counted him smitten by God,
struck down by disease and misery;
but he was pierced for our transgressions,
tortured for our iniquities;
the chastisement he bore is health for us
and by his scourging we are healed.
We had all strayed like sheep,
each of us had gone his own way;
but the Lord laid upon him
the guilt of us all.[3]

This clearly echoes the story of Prometheus. Surely it is significant that a basically similar figure appears in each of our three major scriptural sources, the Greek, Hebrew, and Christian. The psychological meaning is difficult to encompass, but two aspects seem clear. One is that consciousness is accompanied by suffering, and the other is that the ego does not have to do all the suffering. There is an archetypal advocate or benefactor that supports and assists the ego. Whether we call him the suffering servant of Isaiah or Prometheus or Christ, there is an advocate in the archetypal realm. Prometheus is perhaps the first and one of the finest expressions of this archetypal fact.

Notes

[1] Henry Wadsworth Longfellow, "Prometheus," lines 11-25, 56-65.

[2] Aeschylus, *Prometheus Bound,* trans. E. D. A. Morshead, in *The Complete Greek Drama I,* ed. W. J. Oates and Eugene O'Neill (New York: Random House, 1950), lines 437-504.

[3] Isa. 53:2-6 (New English Bible).

Bibliography

Aeschylus. *Prometheus Bound,* trans. Paul Elmer More, in *The Complete Greek Drama I,* ed. W. J. Oates and Eugene O'Neill. New York: Random House, 1950.

Richard Buxton (essay date 1994)

SOURCE: *Imaginary Greece: The Contexts of Mythology,* Cambridge University Press, 1994, 250 p.

[*In the following essay, Buxton examines the characteristics of Greek divinity and discusses such prevailing themes of the divine myths as violence, deception, negotiation, power, and honor.*]

Relating the landscape and the family of the Greek *imaginaire* to the world behind and beyond them involves . . . considerable methodological complexities. When we focus on narratives about gods, matters become more problematic still, since the world which the stories transform may be seen as either (1) the whole fabric of social life, or (2) the practices of ritual, or (3) 'ordinary' beliefs about divinities. Later I shall have a little to say about (2)—a subject which has exercised a perhaps excessive dominance over recent scholarship—and rather more to say about (3), which has, by comparison, been neglected. But I begin by recalling some general features of the Greeks' narratives about gods, in order to raise certain issues relevant to (1).

The nature of divinity

The first general characteristic of the divinities of Greek mythology is that they are neither good nor evil, but powerful.[1] Their powers range over the entire field of experience: whatever a human being is doing—being born, fighting, stealing, sleeping, getting married, committing adultery, dying—his or her activity is related to a structure mapped out at the divine level.[2] Even

Ares and the Furies, for whom it is quite possible to express hatred or revulsion, represent activities which are part, perhaps even a necessary part, of human experience: brutal warfare, and vengeance upon kin-murderers.[3] The second characteristic is that divine activities, interrelationships and behaviour towards mortals are to some extent modelled on the institutions and customs of Greek society. But only to some extent: *some* divine activity is, as we shall see, beyond human comprehension, incommensurate with any pattern of real intra-human behaviour.

The presentation varies, of course, according to context. The most detailed picture appears in epic, since it was a convention of the genre that the action unfolded on two levels, to both of which the narrator claimed to have access. As a first illustration we may take the *Iliad,* not because it was typical, but because it was uniquely authoritative.

Relations between the Iliadic Olympians are based on a combination of violence, deception, negotiation and reciprocity. The violence is evident already in Book 1, when Hephaistos ruefully reminds his mother Hera that

> It is too hard to fight against the Olympian.
> There was a time once before now I was minded to help you,
> and he caught me by the foot and threw me from the magic threshold,
> and all day long I dropped helpless, and about sunset
> I landed in Lemnos, and there was not much life left in me.
>
> (1.589-93)

But there are more ways than one of cooking a goose. The use of trickery is famously exemplified in Book 14, when Zeus's wife outwits him 'with deceitful purpose' (300), aided by the irresistible power of Aphrodite. More subtle still is the situation at the beginning of Book 4. Hera wants to enforce the sacking of Troy, a city hateful to her. Acquiescing, Zeus nevertheless retorts that, if ever there is a city which *he* wants to sack, Hera is not to stand in his way. Hera's reply is complex:

> Of all cities there are three that are dearest to my own heart:
> Argos and Sparta and Mycenae of the wide ways. All these,
> whenever they become hateful to your heart, sack utterly.
> I will not stand up for these against you, nor yet begrudge you.
> Yet if even so I bear malice and would not have you destroy them,
> in malice I will accomplish nothing, since you

are far stronger . . .
Come then, in this thing let us both give way
  to each other,
I to you, you to me, and so the rest of the
  immortal
gods will follow.

                      (4.51-64)

Within the general framework of the imbalance of power in Zeus's favour, there is room for movement. Even one of the humblest figures in the divine power-hierarchy, Thetis, can rely on the mighty argument of reciprocity to support her case:

Father Zeus, if ever before in word or action
I did you favour among the immortals, now
  grant what I ask for.

                      (1.503-4)

Again, although Zeus is the most powerful, each divinity has a sphere which the others may not infringe:

[Hera] went into her chamber, which her
  beloved son Hephaistos
had built for her, and closed the leaves in the
  door-posts snugly
with a secret door-bar, *and no other of the
  gods could open it.*

                      (14.166-8)[4]

In relationships between Iliadic gods and mortals, imbalance of power is always the decisive factor. The mortals sweat, bleed and die, but Athene can protect Menelaos from an arrow 'as lightly as when a mother brushes a fly away from her child who is lying in sweet sleep' (4.130-1). This is not to say that the gap is unbridgeable. The gods can be emotionally involved in the mortals' actions, as when Zeus weeps tears of blood over Sarpedon, whom he is—Hera has convinced him—powerless to save from death (16.459); and Thetis' tenderness for Achilles frames the poem.[5] Yet in other contexts the relationship is more dispassionate, as with the distancing image of Zeus's two urns, from which derives mankind's fate (either a mixture of good and evil, or unrelieved evil) (24.527ff.). This oscillation between divine involvement and divine aloofness constitutes the uncomfortable and unpredictable setting within which Iliadic heroes act. If a god's protégé is insulted, intervention will follow, as with the priest of Apollo in Book 1. If the gods' honours are skimped, there will be consequences: the Greeks' walled ditch, constructed without proper sacrifices, was not to stand for very long (12.8-9). Yet at the crucial moment, mankind may be alone (22.208-13). In the end divine power asserts itself by re-emphasising the boundary with mortality. Although Diomedes is given temporary permission to see the difference between gods and men, and even to wound Aphrodite, his attempt to go too far is rebuked:

Take care, give back, son of Tydeus, and
  strive no longer
to make yourself like the gods in mind, since
  never the same is
the breed of gods, who are immortal, and men
  who walk groundling.

                      (5.440-2)

When the horses which the gods had given to Peleus, and which had seen the death of Patroklos, weep for their dead master, Zeus remarks conclusively:

  Poor wretches,
why then did we ever give you to the lord
  Peleus,
a mortal man, and you yourselves are
  immortal and ageless?

                      (17.442-4)

Features of the Iliadic picture recur throughout Greek mythology in respect both of god/god and god/mortal relations. As to the former, relationships continue to operate at a variety of points on the scale which leads from violence to negotiation. The use of force in the constitution of the universe is a central theme of Hesiod's *Theogony;* in the same poem, the mode by which wily Prometheus chooses to circumvent Zeus is deception. But negotiation was another option. An amicable arrangement is reached in the *Homeric Hymn to Hermes,* where the honour-dispute between Apollo and Hermes is resolved through Zeus's authoritative arbitration; in Aischylos' *Eumenides* the differences between Apollo and the Furies are settled without violence—though Athene has the keys of Zeus's thunderbolt if her persuasion fails (827-8). A more bitter boundary-dispute forms the plot of Euripides' *Hippolytos.* Artemis maintains (1328-30) that on principle the gods avoid confrontations with each other (which has indeed been true of Artemis and Aphrodite in this play). The balance will simply be restored by the wronged divinity taking it out on a human favourite of the wronger (1420-2). As usual, cookery varies with context. In Pindar, when Helios is accidentally omitted from an apportionment of lots, Zeus helpfully offers to hold the draw again, though Helios gets what he wants anyway (*Ol.* 7). Even violent Ares warms his heart to Apollo's lovely music, and conflict is resolved in the harmony of choral song (*Pyth.* 1.10-12).

The immortal/mortal boundary, so fundamental to the *Iliad,* is explored elsewhere in a variety of ways (though never with greater poignancy than in that work). A typically Pindaric version of the relevant similarity and difference is set out at the beginning of *Nemean* 6:

There is one
race of men, one race of gods; both have
  breath

of life from a single mother. But sundered
   power
holds us divided, so that the one is nothing,
   while for the other the brazen sky is
   established
their sure citadel for ever. Yet we have some
   likeness in great
intelligence, or strength, to the immortals,
though we know not what the day will bring,
   what course
after nightfall
destiny has written that we must run to the
   end.

Herakles gained Olympos after hard effort; Asklepios raised the dead, and was thunderbolted; Cheiron was agonisingly wounded and wanted to die, but could not unless he found someone (Prometheus) willing to take over his immortality; Tithonos, blessed with immortality but not with immortal youth, shrivelled up beside his eternally young bride: myths about heroes explore the perilous interface between mortality and immortality.

An important area in which this is true is that of reciprocity. Humans nowadays owe the gods certain things; the implications of these debts are examined through myths. One thing humans owe is sacrifice. The reason why Hera supported the expedition of the *Argo* was that Pelias, Jason's foe, forgot her when making offerings to the gods; when Admetos failed to sacrifice to Artemis on the occasion of his marriage, the bridal chamber turned out to be full of coiled snakes.[6] A related debt concerns giving the gods due honour and respect. In Euripides' *Trojan Women,* Athene's wrath towards the Greeks derives from Ajax's crime of dragging Kassandra from her temple in Troy; she urges Poseidon to wreck their fleet 'so that in future the Achaeans will learn to respect my power and to worship the other gods' (85-6). At an earlier stage in the history of Troy, King Laomedon failed to pay the wages of Apollo and Poseidon, who had fortified his city for him; he got a plague and a sea-monster for his reward.[7] Another kind of respect is due acknowledgement of superiority. Here again, heroic myths narrate what happens when proper distances are elided: Thamyras, Arachne, Marsyas and a host of others fail to appreciate the riskiness of competing with those who are, by definition, *hors de concours.*[8]

Many of the themes noted above—power, violence, deception, negotiation, reciprocity, conflicts over interests and honour—have obvious echoes and models in the human sphere. Yet there are striking differences. One has been highlighted by John Gould in a paper which stresses the alien, uncanny and horrific dimension of divinity.[9] This is exemplified in the narrative in Euripides' *Hippolytos* in which the messenger relates the overthrow of Hippolytos on the appearance of the

monstrous bull from the sea, despatched against him by Poseidon in response to the curse invoked by Theseus. The gods here exceed all human analogy, inhabiting a territory which can best be indicated through the Greek word *deinon,* 'terrible', 'awesome'.

Another quality shared by many mythical narratives is their laying bare of motives and explanations which in the superficial traffic of everyday life remain hidden. What mortal could know as much about the causation operative in his or her existence as the Homeric narrator claims to know about his subject matter? What human being could see with the clear eyes of the gods in Euripidean prologues? Once more, we can see myth as a device for making explicit, for highlighting what is behind life. But, paradoxically, one of the aspects of the world made explicit in myths is the *incompleteness* of human understanding of the world, and the *insufficiency* of human models of behaviour for comprehending divinity. This is above all true of tragedy, in which certain key episodes and scenes are simply inexplicable, certain divine actions baffling, because the drama either provides too few clues to reconstruct a coherent pattern of motivation, or incorporates too much, because conflicting, information. A classic example of the former is the notorious question of why, in the version of the tale given in Aischylos' *Agamemnon,* Artemis grew angry at Aulis before the departure of the Greek expedition to Troy. While explanations of her wrath are easy to find in other versions, this particular account shrouds the matter in mystery. On the other hand, Euripides' *Herakles* positively overflows with explanations for the reason for the downfall of the great hero, to such an extent that, here too, providing a coherent account involves disregarding some information at the expense of the rest.[10] The purposes of the gods are sometimes opaque, their voices silent or beyond interpretation.

Telling and acting

In twentieth-century scholarship, the aspect of Greek social behaviour which has most frequently been juxtaposed with myth is ritual. The history of myth-and-ritual approaches is complicated, not least because it is inseparable from the larger question of the shifting relationships between the disciplines of anthropology and classics.[11] But from Jane Harrison to Walter Burkert a golden key to unlock the meanings of 'what is said' has been found in the investigation of 'what is done'. The terms of the enquiry have varied enormously, as have conclusions about, especially, the priority of one of these modes of symbolic expression over the other. There has even been an attempt (by C. Calame) to undermine the polarity altogether by calling into doubt the conceptual identity not just of myth but also of ritual, both being seen as products of western anthropological thought.[12] However, collapsing both into a general category of *énonciations de la pensée symbolique*[13] would seem to leave us with an excessively blunt analytical tool, and in the brief remarks which follow I have, along with virtually all scholars, kept ritual as a potentially useful concept.

That the narration of a Greek myth might actually form part of a ritual is certain. At the mysteries of the Mother Goddess, observes Pausanias *à propos* of a bronze near Corinth representing Hermes with a ram, a story was told: 'I know it, but will not relate it' (2.3.4). Circumstantial details are often lacking, as here; usually we have to make do with suggestive parallels between myths and 'their' festivals, rather than with fully documented accounts which would enable us to describe in proper contextual detail the nature of the integration between the two. Even suggestive parallels have their fascination, however, and they can sometimes generate plausible guesses about a close symbiosis between myth and festival. The inhabitants of Lemnos celebrated a rite of New Fire, when for a nine-day period all fires on the island were extinguished, to be relit afterwards by fire brought from over the sea.[14] Corresponding to this is a myth, according to which the women of the island incur the wrath of Aphrodite: they are afflicted with a bad smell which drives away their husbands and puts a stop to normal conjugal relations.[15] The motif of the disruption of the everyday repeats itself in even more emphatic form when the husbands, who have consoled themselves with some Thracian slavegirls, are murdered by their wives. But eventually life begins again, as—from across the sea—Jason and the Argonauts sail in to rekindle that which had been extinguished.[16] The structure of the mythical narrative corresponds to the rhythm of the festival, and confirms the observation of one ancient source that the fire was extinguished *epi tōi ergōi,* 'in consequence of the [murderous, Lemnian] deed'.[17] Story and festival go together, even if we are not aware of any role which *narration* of the myth might have played in the ritual.

In cases where correspondences between narrative and ritual make it reasonable to talk of symbiosis, we can frequently observe the now familiar process of clarification and making-explicit, whereby mythology expresses openly or in extreme form that which in ritual remains hidden or disguised. Jan Bremmer has argued convincingly that, in rites enacting the expulsion of a scapegoat, the victim, typically a person of low status who becomes temporarily the focus of attention, is chased alive out of the city; in the corresponding myths the victim is a person of *high* status who is *killed*.[18] Myth translates ritual: to leave one's city is—if you spell it out—to die. Again, the women who worship Dionysos at the *oreibasia* return to their normal lives after the conclusion of the rites. By contrast, the corresponding myths express the disruption of family life in *irreversible* terms, as in the tale of Agaue's murder and dismembering of her son Pentheus. Temporary, ritual disruption of the family is translated mythically into permanence.

If the women who took part in the *oreibasia* had actually killed their kin as opposed to merely abandoning them temporarily, they would have been committing, in addition to murder, an unforgivable category-mistake. It did occasionally happen, or was said to have done; with predictable results.

> They say that the daughters of Minyas, Leukippe and Arsinoe and Alkathoe, became frenzied and craved for human flesh, and drew lots about their children. The lot fell upon Leukippe and she gave her son Hippasos to be torn in pieces . . . And up to the present time the people of Orchomenos give this name to the women of the family descended from them. And once a year at the Agrionia festival there takes place a flight and pursuit of them by the priest of Dionysos holding a sword. And when he catches one of them he may kill her. *And in our own time Zoilos the priest did indeed kill one of them. But this resulted in no good for the people; for Zoilos fell sick of a chance ulcerous wound, and after it had long festered, he died.*[19]

The myth recounts cannibalism and the catastrophic destruction of a family. The corresponding ritual *should* dramatise a symbolic pursuit of women escapers, which should in turn lead to a return to normality after the ritual. By a mischance, the behaviour appropriate to myth has invaded ritual, bringing death upon the agent responsible as well as upon his innocent victim—innocent, because only in the symbolism of the ritual was she guilty. The return to normality has been blocked, the essential temporariness of ritual cancelled.

A further, related difference between mythology and its festival context is worth introducing here. Rituals are designed to fulfil their objectives.[20] They set up dramatic situations, enact them, and at the end return participants and observers to undramatised reality: from *Fest* to *Alltag.* Sacrifice, for example, is a procedure by means of which proper relations with the gods and solidarity between humans are achieved through correct apportioning of cooked meat. The rules of the game are carefully prescribed; if they are followed, the ritual, by definition, works. But myths are, or may be, rather different. They *may* reach an 'end', as with the finale to Aischylos' *Oresteia,* or the eventual arrival of the Argonauts at Lemnos in order to ensure a future. But they may also draw attention to the open-endedness and ambiguity of action, to dilemmas without solution and wounds without healing. In tragedy, above all, we regularly find that the shapes into which myths cast experience are baffling and contradictory. Rituals set themselves achievable goals; some myths remind their hearers that any hope of tailoring reality to suit human desires is bound to fail.

We spoke earlier of the symbiosis which can exist between myth and festival. But this is not the only possible relationship between the two. Some deities worshipped in cult are unimportant or even absent from extant mythology.[21] Again, many myths, while drawing on ritual, are not tied to one kind of ceremony, let alone to a particular cult at a particular time and place. Neither epics nor victory songs nor tragic dramas can be reduced to the status of libretti for ritual action, although the festival context undeniably affects the narrative perspectives adopted in those genres. The *Odyssey,* with its complex structure and its remarkable exploration of Greekness as contrasted with the behaviour of the diverse peoples visited by Odysseus, cannot be boiled down to a ritual pattern; yet its recitation at the Panathenaia must have lent it a special resonance, given the narrative's persistent opposing of Athene to Poseidon—the two rivals for the patronage of Athens.[22] No more can Pindar's odes, rich and intricate and full of subtle allusion, be explained away as mere reflections of ritual action; yet the prevalence in the poetry of agonistic imagery and of myths about returning demonstrates a significant link between context and content. Nor, finally, have attempts to shoehorn tragedy into a ritual pattern won lasting assent. As the Greeks' phrase 'nothing to do with Dionysos' should not mislead us into ignoring the link between this god of changing identities and the masked drama put on to honour him, no more should we mistake the regular *exploitation of ritual themes* in drama (supplication, laments for the dead, sacrifice) for some hypothetically all-pervading ritual structure.

Believing in myths

Paul Veyne's short book *Les Grecs ont-ils cru à leurs mythes?* was published in 1983; several translations soon followed, including one in English.[23] Having achieved the status of *savant,* Veyne declaims from beyond the Flannel Barrier; but, if you persevere through the style, you are rewarded. The argument is in two parts. Only one is directly relevant here; I confine discussion of the other to an extended footnote.

The first part of the case can be stated simply: believing in Greek myths, indeed believing *tout court,* is essentially plural. This is already implicit in the Preface, where Veyne cites Dan Sperber's *Rethinking Symbolism.* The Dorzé of Ethiopia believe that leopards, being Christians, observe the fasts of the Coptic church on Wednesdays and Fridays. However, a Dorzé protects his livestock on *all* days of the week, including Wednesdays and Fridays. 'Leopards are dangerous every day; this he knows from experience. They are also Christians; this is guaranteed by tradition.'[24] Beliefs, that is, are plural: persons and communities may hold, without strain, apparently incompatible beliefs. Veyne's Christmas parallel (stockings are filled *both* by Mum and Dad *and* by Santa) is perhaps too close for comfort to the Tylorian equation of the primitive with the childlike; a better example is Veyne's reference to his own views about ghosts: 'For my part, I

hold ghosts to be simple fictions but . . . I am almost neurotically afraid of them.'[25]

More relevant for us are Veyne's discussions of plurality of belief in relation to Greek stories; or rather, plurality in *expressions* of belief. He is more concerned with the Hellenistic and Roman periods than with the Archaic and Classical, and cites telling examples from Galen and Pausanias. When Galen has a philosophical hat on, he refers at one point (siding with Plato in order to pour scorn on Stoic attempts to make sense of mythology by rationalising it) to 'Hippocentaurs' and the Chimaira; 'and a multitude of such shapes comes flooding in, Gorgons and Pegasuses and an absurd crowd of other impossible and fabulous natures'.[26] But elsewhere, when seeking to persuade, to proselytise, to give an account of medicine within a more generally accepted framework, Galen mentions, with no explicit statement of incredulity, such traditional figures in the early history of medicine as 'the Centaur Cheiron and the heroes of whom he was the teacher', and Asklepios.[27] So belief can figure differently in different works by the same author. But more than that: Pausanias, within one and the same work, refuses to give credence to the myth of Medusa, yet accepts the authenticity of the tale about the werewolf Lykaon: ' . . . I believe this legend, which has been told in Arkadia from ancient times and has likelihood on its side'.[28]

Emphasis on the problems involved in deciphering Greek expressions of belief is by no means original to Veyne. In a beautiful article written in 1976, Tom Stinton showed how expressions of *dis*belief can function as 'signifiers' whose 'signifieds' are by no means what they seem.[29] For instance, Herodotos tells a story about men living beyond the Scythians who are bald from birth; beyond them are mountains inhabited, according to the bald men, by a goat-footed race, 'though I do not regard this as credible'; and beyond *them* are men who hibernate for six months: 'but this I *totally* refuse to accept' (4.23-5). The effect is both to convince us of Herodotos' *general* trustworthiness (for he is *so* sensitive to gradations of likelihood) and to encourage the reader to accept the existence of the bald men as going without saying—or with saying.[30] Knowing how to take expressions of belief depends on our assessment of the context and of the strategy of the writer; since Stinton, assumptions about Euripides' famous scepticism have needed very careful handling. Veyne is stylistically a million miles from Stinton, but he too leads us to recognise just how intractable some of the apparently straightforward evidence about belief actually is.[31]

Let us turn to some of this evidence. Scholars sometimes tend to operate, half-unconsciously, with a model which goes like this. Archaic Greeks, with the exception of odd-balls like the Presocratic philosopher

Xenophanes, on the whole believed in myths. In the fifth century, more sceptical voices were raised, for example by Euripides. In Hellenistic times a still greater distance opened up between myths and belief. And as for the ultra-knowing Ovid . . . This model cannot, I believe, be dismissed as a straw one. Oswyn Murray was perhaps being over-optimistic when he alluded to 'one of the most dubious and insidious of all *nineteenth-century* postulates, [namely] the idea of social development from the primitive and religious towards the complex and secular'.[32]

What do we do with this model? First, we have to distinguish between belief in myths, that is in *stories,* and belief in gods. It is quite possible to disbelieve in certain *stories* about Artemis while still believing in her existence. This may seem to be merely a trivial debating point, but it is in fact of considerable relevance when we think about what might count as evidence for belief. Whether belief is conceived of as a mental occurrence or a disposition, and whether we are concerned with believing *in* or believing *that,* establishing the nature of a belief held by someone else often entails making inferences from actions as well as utterances.[33] If we want to establish whether X believes in socialism, Y in free love, or Z that charity begins at home, we shall need to canvass their actions as well as what they profess. Of course, there is a potential gap between the two: people may *fail* to act upon their beliefs, or be obliged to act *against* their beliefs; but their actions will still count at least as relevant evidence. Now religion would seem to be one area where actions ought to be taken into account in assessing the extent and strength of beliefs: it is a matter of *ex votos* as well as *credos.* So when Robin Osborne points to the rapid spread of the cult of Pan in Attica after 500 BC as evidence for a changing perception of the countryside, we may well be tempted to describe this process as a development in religious *belief.*[34] Indeed, this is the more so because of the nature of Greek religion. Jean Rudhardt, and more recently Marcel Detienne, have argued that to 'believe' in the Greek gods just *is* to honour them in cult: to sacrifice to them, pray to them, sing and walk in procession for them: these are *ta nomizomena* (things 'thought', things 'customary').[35]

But assessing belief in *stories* is a rather different matter, since in many cases it is not clear what kind of action could count as evidence for or against the presence of a particular belief—say, the belief that the madness of Herakles followed his Labours. In such cases we have characteristically to rely on the evidence of utterances—the fact, for example, that a narrator opts for this version of a tale rather than that. The bulk of our evidence, that is, will consist of explicit statements about, or expressions of, belief, together with mythical narratives from which belief-states have to be inferred. Of course, it would be absurd to deny

all relevance to what we might inelegantly call the worship-situation: this would, presumably, figure in *some* way in the account we would want to give of a twentieth-century opera which included, say, Dionysos as a character. But in practice, in an ancient Greek context, we rarely find ourselves well enough informed about the extent or absence of relevant practised religion to limit our uncertainties about belief in myths.

So: utterances: texts in contexts. And the plurals should be emphasised; because the crucial element in the situation is contextual plurality.

Age and gender could be thought of as factors shaping attitudes to the stories. A passage from Plato's *Laws* makes the point in relation to the young:

> ' . . . yet it proved easy to persuade men of the Sidonian story [= the myth of Kadmos], incredible though it was, and of numberless others.'

> 'What tales?'

> 'The tale of the teeth that were sown, and how armed men sprang out of them. Here, indeed, the lawgiver has a notable example of how one can, if one tries, persuade the souls of the young of anything.'[36]

Old men too are sometimes seen as subject to an intensification of belief. I quote two voices. The first is that of Kephalos, a very old man with whom the Platonic Sokrates likes (he says) to converse. Asked about how life is when one is so near the brink, Kephalos relates how he and other old men often meet together, and talk. They chin-wag about the past, of course, some regretting it, others bidding it good riddance. They speculate too about the future:

> . . . when a man begins to realise that he is going to die, he is filled with apprehensions and concern about matters that before did not occur to him. The tales that are told of the world below and how men who have done wrong here must pay the penalty there, though he may have laughed them down hitherto, then begin to torture his soul with the doubt that there may be some truth in them.[37]

The second voice belongs to the lyric poet Anakreon.

> My temples are already grey,
> my head is white,
> delicious youth is here no more;
> my teeth are old, and I no longer
> have much time of sweet life left.
> So I sob, often, in fear of Tartaros.
> For Hades' house is terrible:
> the way down is hard, and once you follow it,
> there is no return.[38]

True reflections of talk in the *leschē?* Perhaps. But we should remember that Plato is the greatest ironist of antiquity, while Anakreon is another Ovid for self-mockery.

Women are presented as another credulous group. According to Polybios, they are characterised by a love of the marvellous (12.24-5). Not only are they *tellers* of old wives' tales: they are also said to be particularly susceptible to them. Referring to the myth of Theseus' abandonment of Ariadne on Naxos, Philostratos observes that '[nurses] are skilled in telling such tales, *and they weep over them whenever they will'.*[39] It goes without saying that these ascriptions of degrees and kinds of credulity need not correspond to anything which an ancient opinion survey amongst children, the elderly or women might have come up with: we have the familiar problem of evaluating utterances—and it is (to say the least) no easier to evaluate a 'they believe' than an 'I believe'.

If age and gender constituted two kinds of relevant plurality, a third concerned a different sort of social division. We may take Martin Nilsson's views as representing a strong form of this approach. For Nilsson, the Greek 'folk' was one thing, the urban sophisticates, especially atypical intellectuals who might go so far as to embrace atheism, quite another.[40] This is an important point to make, in particular in relation to the Hellenistic period—it is easy to forget that the Kallimachean attitude to tradition is contemporary with a huge proliferation of popular recitation and festival performance, at which myths were also retold. Yet at the same time Nilsson's dichotomy has to be subjected to massive refinement in relation to varying historical contexts. It is evident that analysis of the difference between 'the people' and 'the sophisticates' is going to look very different depending on whether we are dealing with Alkman's Sparta or Lykophron's Alexandria.

But there is another and more interesting kind of plurality which needs to be confronted: plurality of context for a single individual at any one time. Take the case of an Athenian adult male living at the end of the fifth century. His recent experience of mythology includes: looking at temple friezes, vases and coins; being present at a rhapsodic recital which presented excerpts from the *Odyssey;* singing one of Alkaios' hymns at a *symposion;* attending performances of the *Bakchai* and the *Frogs;* and holding those vague, basic, unfocused, lowest-common-denominator views about divine intervention and the afterlife which Jon Mikalson discusses in *Athenian Popular Religion.*[41] Mikalson's essay is like a breath of fresh air in a room usually filled with methodological perfumes that are pungent, contrasting and not always expensive. But it does, quite deliberately, base its conclusions about Athenian belief on a very restricted type of evidence: oratory, inscriptions,

Xenophon. And matters are perhaps not quite so clear-cut as Mikalson implies when he maintains that 'in the study of popular religion the need now is for some descriptive work; a theoretical bias would only impede this work'.[42] On the contrary, the really taxing question seems to me to be precisely: how were such lowest-common-denominator attitudes (taking 'little interest in the bleak and uncertain prospect of the afterlife'; having views about *daimones* that were 'quite vague and imprecise')[43]—how were such attitudes integrated with those implicit in the artistic-performance contexts? Or *were* they integrated? For I suggest that we have no idea how, or whether, most people reconciled the perspectives implied by the various ways in which they might confront mythology. Few Greeks will have felt the need to work out for themselves, in the manner of a Plato, an explicit reconciliation between or hierarchisation of the alternative modes of access to the sacred. They will simply have accepted as normal the fact that different ways of imagining the gods were appropriate to different contexts. To ask which constituted their real belief is to miss the point.[44]

All this does not mean that we must rule out entirely the possibility of making generalisations about Greek belief in myths: for example, it would seem that no ancient author denies the *existence* of, say, Theseus, Meleager, or Agamemnon. Nor, needless to say, should we minimise the importance of relating the different kinds of myth-telling that we find in Pindar, Euripides or Kallimachos to the societies for which they composed, or of noting developments in attitudes towards the mythological tradition implicit in their works. The point is, rather, that to describe those changes in terms of strength or weakness in belief, or of the size of the credulity supply in circulation at any one time, needs at the very least to take account of the complicating factors just mentioned.

But there is another way out of the belief maze. For to ask about the extent of *belief* in stories is in fact to ask one of the least rewarding questions about them. Let us return to four images of mythical women which we discussed earlier: Penelope before her web; Polyneikes persuading Eriphyle; Tekmessa tending the dead Ajax; the abduction of Hippodameia by Pelops. These are paradigms, types, models of behaviour—sometimes extremely ambiguous models—from which human conduct may diverge or to which it may correspond. The question of the extent of *belief* in such powerful, persistent images seems not just unverifiable, but irrelevant. It might be argued that the belief issue becomes more pressing in relation to verbal narratives in the past tense: 'Zeus hid fire'; 'Oidipous solved the riddle'. But even in such cases the crucial point in relation to functional importance is that the stories are told, retold, and gradually stop being told, to be replaced by other narratives.

A potentially fruitful analogy here is that between myths and proverbial expressions.[45] The analogy might seem flawed from the outset, since myths are narratives, while proverbs are not. However, in a Greek context at least, proverbs very often *depend* on narratives, which have to be supplied if the force of the proverb is to be understood. Moreover, many of these implied narratives are mythical. A few minutes' browsing in the standard collection of ancient maxims yields references to the nemesis of Adrastos (applied to those formerly happy but later unfortunate), the fiery robe (sent by Deianeira to Herakles; refers to those who inflame quarrels), the cap of Hades (which conferred invisibility on the wearer; said of those who practise concealment), the laughter of Ajax (manic laughter, recalling that of the crazed hero), the glare of Atreus (a baleful look like that on the face of the betrayed husband plotting a ghoulish revenge), the sleep of Endymion (applied to sleepy-heads: Endymion slept for eternity), the sufferings of Io (woe upon woe), not to mention a Kadmeian victory, a Troy of troubles, 'not without Theseus', the madness of Thamyris, Bellerophon's letters, and plenty of others.[46] Such expressions provided a ready-made way of 'locating' certain aspects of behaviour, by implicitly making generalisations about them. But these generalisations do not aspire to the status of *universal* truths: while a given maxim may work in one context, its opposite may be more relevant in another. That too many cooks spoil the broth does not mean that many hands don't make light work: what convinces in one context need not be required to convince in another. So too with myths, whose force, like that of proverbs, is essentially context-bound. (To repeat: myths are not *the same as* proverbs; they are, however, in one important respect *analogous* to them.) Hence the problem of 'reconciling', to which we referred earlier, is really not so intractable, since what are apparently contradictory propositions can happily coexist *provided they are embedded in different contexts.* Nor is the analogy with proverbs irrelevant to belief. If someone asks you how you can *really believe* that too many cooks spoil the broth, while at the same time *really believing* that many hands make light work, you may reasonably retort that they are barking up the wrong tree.

Greek myths were retold because they were authoritative: partly in virtue of the various authorities conferred on tellers by the context (women in the house, bards at the feast, poets at archon-sanctioned, *polis*-organised dramatic performances); partly because of the authority which tellers created for themselves, thanks to the content of the tale and the manner of its telling; partly because the telling of similar tales in a variety of contexts and at all ages (from nursery stories to adolescent choirs to the old men's *leschē*) can hardly have failed to produce a reinforcing effect. But the authority of myths did not go without saying, in spite of the fact—perhaps even because of the fact—that

tellers regularly claimed to be reporting the truth. An audience hears a poet maintain that he is inspired by the Muse; they find his song convincing. But they do so in the knowledge, not only that he is distancing himself from previous tale-tellers (as with Pindar in *Olympian* 1, where stories involving the gods in cannibalism are indignantly rejected), but also that the *next* poet in the tradition will tell his *own* tale, again inspired, again claiming the truth. Greek myths constitute a corpus of plausible, telling tales which aim, within their contexts, at achieving *peithō*, persuasion. . . .

Notes

[1] This applies even to Zeus. Cf. Nilsson 1951-60, on the inconclusiveness of connections between Zeus and justice: 'Zeus war der einzige Gott, der, abgesehen von blutlosen Personifikationen, sich der Gerechtigkeit annehmen konnte, sie war aber nicht in seinem Wesen begründet, und schwer wog es, dass die Mythen viele ungerechte Taten von ihm erzählten' (p. 315).

[2] The analysis of the structured division of divine power seems to me to be the aspect of the work of J.-P. Vernant and M. Detienne which is most likely—and most justifiably—to endure.

[3] Hatred of Ares: Hom. *Il.* 5.890 (expressed by Zeus himself), S. *OT* 190ff. Revolting Furies: A. *Eum.* 52-4.

[4] Cf. *Od.* 8.280-1: Hephaistos' workmanship is so fine that its products are imperceptible even to the other gods.

[5] On the general capacity of Greek myths about immortal beings to be *moving,* one may note the remark of Rudhardt 1958, p. 76: 'La légende toutefois oublie l'immortalité des dieux en traitant un épisode limité de leur histoire; elle les soumet à la durée, à l'intérieur de l'épisode, et, dans cette limite, à la souffrance et au changement; elle achève ainsi de les humaniser.'

[6] Pelias: A. R. 1.13-14. Admetos: Apollod. 1.9.15.

[7] Apollod. 2.5.9.

[8] See Weiler 1974.

[9] Gould 1985.

[10] Cf. Buxton 1988.

[11] The best *mise au point* is Versnel in Edmunds 1990, pp. 25-90; see also Bremmer 1992.

[12] See ch. 1 of Calame 1990b.

[13] Calame 1990b, p. 50.

[14] Philostr. *Her.* 207 (Teubner edn).

[15] For the myth and the ritual, see the classic account in Burkert 1970.

[16] Myrsilos of Lesbos records a custom on Lemnos according to which on one day in the year the women kept their menfolk at a distance 'because of their bad smell': the link between myth and rite is reinforced (*FGrH* 477 1a; cf. Burkert 1970, p. 7).

[17] Philostr., *loc. cit.* in n. 14.

[18] Bremmer 1983a.

[19] From no. 38 of Plutarch's *Greek Questions* (= *Mor.* 299e-f, trans. slightly adapted from that by W. R. Halliday; my italics).

[20] Cf. Burkert 1985, p. 264: 'Ritual creates situations of anxiety in order to overcome them . . . '

[21] Cf. Rudhardt 1958, pp. 82-5.

[22] Panathenaia: Pl. *Hipparch.* 228b, Lyc. *Leocr.* 102.

[23] Veyne 1988.

[24] Sperber 1975, p. 95.

[25] Veyne 1988, p. 87.

[26] *De placitis Hippocratis et Platonis* 3.8.33 (Kühn v, p. 357; de Lacy p. 231). Trans. by P. de Lacy.

[27] *Introductio seu medicus* I (Kühn XIV, pp. 674-5); cf. Veyne 1988, p. 55.

[28] Medusa: 2.21.6-7. Lykaon: 8.2.4 (trans. P. Levi). Cf. Veyne 1988, pp. 96 and 99.

[29] Reprinted in Stinton 1990, pp. 236-64. The Saussurian terms are not Stinton's, but seem appropriate to his argument.

[30] Stinton 1990, p. 237.

[31] At this point I include some comments about the second stage in Veyne's argument. This consists in holding that we must talk, not just of a plurality of beliefs, but of a plurality of truths, or of criteria for truth (p. 113). 'The *Iliad* and *Alice in Wonderland*', declares Veyne, 'are no less true than Fustel de Coulanges' (p. xi). (What shall we say? Finley's *Ancient Economy?* Hammond's *History of Greece?*) Now the nature of this plurality of truths is, intriguingly, itself multiple, or at least dual. At times it seems to be a matter of chronological succession, of one Kuhnian paradigm being replaced by another ('Once one is in one of these fishbowls, it takes

genius to get out of it and innovate' (p. 118).) But at other times Veyne writes as if at all times a range of strategies—but, as far as one can see, the *same* range of strategies—has existed towards belief (scepticism, total credulity, rationalisation, etc.)—a view in apparent contradiction with the fishbowl approach. These and other inconsistencies have been highlighted in Méheust 1990. (To add another paradox, this time an authorial one, when I telephoned M. Veyne to ask him what *he* recommended that one should read about his work in general and *Les Grecs ont-ils cru* in particular, he immediately cited Méheust's rather critical article.)

If we *are* to assign a consistent view on the truth question to Veyne here, I think it should be done in the terms expressed by C. Brillante (in Edmunds 1990, pp. 116-17), who maintains that for Veyne 'any reflection, whether qualified as mythic or rational, is shown to be the creation of an *imagination constituante,* that is, of a reason that need not account for its own affirmations, except to itself. If Brillante is right, this is a road down which I have no wish to follow Veyne. However, in the light of recent notorious attempts to deny the genocide practised by the Nazis during the Second World War, it is important to note this observation: 'It is clear that the existence or the nonexistence of Theseus and gas chambers in one point in space and time has a material reality that owes nothing to our imagination . . . [However] the materiality of gas chambers does not automatically lead to the knowledge one can have about them' (Veyne 1988, p. 107). Even the most pachydermatous of epistemological relativists must (fortunately) think twice before espousing views compatible with a denial of that particular historical reality. (Parenthetically, we may observe that those who do follow an extreme 'no closure of historical interpretation' line risk getting into bed with some pretty dubious company.)

[32] In O. Murray and Price 1990, p. 6; my emphasis.

[33] See H. H. Price 1969, for a philosophical analysis of belief.

[34] Osborne 1987, p. 192.

[35] Rudhardt 1958, p. 142; Detienne and Sissa 1989, pp. 191-2.

[36] 663e-664a (trans. adapted from that by R. G. Bury, Loeb edn).

[37] *R.* 330d-e (trans. P. Shorey, Loeb edn).

[38] *PMG* 395 (my translation).

[39] *Imag.* 1.15.1.

[40] E.g. Nilsson 1940.

[41] Mikalson 1983.

[42] Mikalson 1983, p. 7.

[43] Mikalson 1983, pp. 82 and 65.

[44] Mikalson himself has subsequently attempted to integrate the evidence of tragedy with that of popular religion (Mikalson 1991), but with only mixed success; cf. the review by H. Yunis in *CR* NS 43 (1993), pp. 70-2.

[45] *Muthoi* as similar to yet distinct from proverbs: Pl. *Lg.* 913b9-c3; cf. Brisson 1982, p. 124, Detienne 1986, p. 95.

[46] Leutsch and Schneidewin 1839-51.

Acknowledgements

. . . Passages from Homer are usually cited in the translations by Richmond Lattimore (*The Iliad:* University of Chicago Press, 1951 by The University of Chicago; *The Odyssey:* Harper & Row, 1965, 1967 by Richmond Lattimore). For Pindar, I have drawn on the versions by (p. 118) C. M. Bowra (Penguin Books, C. M. Bowra 1969), and, again (pp. 149 and 176), Richmond Lattimore (University of Chicago Press, 1947 by the University of Chicago Press). For other authors, in cases where I have taken over or adapted existing translations, I have tried always to acknowledge the fact. Otherwise, the version given is my own. . . .

Abbreviations

CQ: Classical Quarterly

CR: Classical Review

FGrH: Die Fragmente der griechischen Historiker, ed. F. Jacoby, Berlin, 1923—

HSCP: Harvard Studies in Classical Philology

PMG: Poetae Melici Graeci, ed. D. L. Page, Oxford, 1962

Bibliography

Bremmer, J. N., 1983a: 'Scapegoat rituals in ancient Greece', *HSCP* 87: 299-320.

————, 1992: 'Mythe en rite in het oude Griekenland: Een overzicht van recente ontwikkelingen', *Nederlands Theologisch Tijdschrift* 46: 265-76.

Brisson, L., 1982: *Platon, les mots et les mythes.* Paris: Maspero.

Burkert, W., 1970: 'Jason, Hypsipyle, and New Fire at Lemnos', *CQ* NS 20, 1-16.

————, 1985: *Greek Religion: Archaic and Classical* (trans. of *Griechische Religion der archaischen und klassischen Epoche,* 1977). Oxford: Blackwell.

Buxton, R. G. A., 1988: 'Bafflement in Greek tragedy', *Métis* 3: 41-51.

Calame, C., 1990b: *Thésée et l'imaginaire athénien.* Lausanne: Payot.

Detienne, M., 1986: *The Creation of Mythology* (trans. of *L'Invention de la mythologie,* 1981). Chicago University Press.

Detienne, M., and Sissa, G., 1989: *La Vie quotidienne des dieux grecs.* Paris: Hachette.

Edmunds, L., ed., 1990: *Approaches to Greek Myth.* Baltimore: Johns Hopkins University Press.

Gould, J., 1985: 'On making sense of Greek religion', in P. E. Easterling and J. V. Muir, eds., *Greek Religion and Society* (Cambridge University Press) 1-33.

Halliday, W. R., 1913: *Greek Divination.* London: Macmillan.

Hammond, N. G. L., 1986: *A History of Greece*[3]. Oxford: Clarendon Press.

Leutsch, E. L., and Schneidewin, F. G., eds., 1839-51: *Paroemiographi graeci.* Göttingen: Vandenhoeck and Ruprecht.

Méheust, B., 1990: 'Les Occidentaux du XXe siècle ont-ils cru à leurs mythes?', *Communications* 52: 337-56.

Mikalson, J. D., 1983: *Athenian Popular Religion.* Chapel Hill: University of North Carolina Press.

————, 1991: *Honor thy gods.* Chapel Hill: University of North Carolina Press.

Murray, O., and Price, S., eds., 1990: *The Greek City from Homer to Alexander.* Oxford: Clarendon Press.

[Nilsson, M. P.,] 1940: *Greek Folk Religion.* New York: Columbia University Press.

————, 1951-60: 'Die Griechengötter und die Gerechtigkeit', *Opuscula selecta* (Lund: Gleerup) vol. III, 303-21.

Osborne, R., 1987: *Classical Landscape with Figures.* London: Philip.

Price, H. H., 1969: *Belief.* London: Allen and Unwin.

City of Troy beside the sea.

Rudhardt, J., 1958: *Notions fondamentales de la pensée religieuse et actes constitutifs du culte dans la Grèce classique.* Geneva: Droz.

Sperber, D., 1975: *Rethinking Symbolism.* Cambridge University Press. (A near-equivalent French version came out in 1974.)

Stinton, T. C. W., 1990: *Collected Papers on Greek Tragedy.* Oxford: Clarendon Press.

Veyne, P., 1988: *Did the Greeks believe in their Myths?* (trans. of *Les Grecs ont-ils cru à leurs mythes?*, 1983). Chicago University Press.

Weiler, I., 1974: *Der Agon im Mythos.* Darmstadt: Wissenschaftliche Buchgesellschaft.

HEROES AND HEROINES IN GREEK MYTHOLOGY

G. S. Kirk (essay date 1974)

SOURCE: "The Heroes," in *The Nature of Greek Myths*, Penguin Books, 1974, pp. 145-75.

[*In the following essay, Kirk asserts that the narrative complexity of hero myths is much greater than that of the divine myths. He then classifies hero myths as those related to older heroes (in myths set in a "timeless past long before the Trojan War"), those related to younger heroes (in myths set at a time close to or during the Trojan War), and those concerned with "definitely historical figures."*]

Powerful as some of the divine myths are, it is the hero myths that constitute the most prominent and varied side of Greek traditional tales as a whole. Many other ethnic collections, perhaps most, are virtually confined to divine tales and contain few heroic ones. Ancient Mesopotamia and Egypt exemplify the tendency. The Mesopotamian tales of Gilgamesh are admittedly imaginative, and important from many points of view; Egyptian heroes, on the other hand, are both few in number and predominantly legendary and realistic in character. Yet in Greece there are innumerable heroes, and they are involved in a wide variety of actions. Standard situations proliferate, but even so the total narrative complexity far outweighs that of the divine myths.

The heroes fall into an older or a younger type, according to whether their main activity is set in a timeless past long before the Trojan War, or close to the

war itself. Later inventions based on definitely historical figures form another and subsidiary kind. . . . The
first two types, whose nature will become plainer as
the chapter proceeds, are at some points hard to separate. Some of the 'older' heroes possess certain later
characteristics, since the myths were undergoing continuous development; conversely a few of the younger
and quasi-legendary ones have important older associations. Theseus is involved in historicizing and relatively recent actions, but the tale of the Labyrinth makes
it eccentric not to treat him as a member of the primary group. Agamemnon on the other hand is connected through Menelaus with Helen, who seems to be
descended from an ancient tree goddess; yet the story
of the House of Atreus belongs for the most part to the
more historicizing and younger set. Jason presents similar difficulties, but I have placed him among the older
group in the first instance.

Philologists have sometimes thought that heroic names
themselves may give a clue to the age of the heroes
and their myths. Those ending in *-eus,* especially if
they have a non-Greek stem, are thought to be among
the earliest. That works well for a few less prominent
heroes like Tydeus, Neleus, Salmoneus, and perhaps
Orpheus. Theseus and Oineus, with Greek stems, might
then be secondary developments, but Achilleus
(Latinized as Achilles) would be one of the older group
and not, as appears from his mythical context, a younger
quasi-legendary type. His father Peleus is neutral, since
his name is based on that of Mount Pelion, itself probably pre-Greek. Many of the *-eus* heroes turn out to
have sons with specifically Greek compound names;
for instance Aga-memnon is son of Atreus, and Neoptolemus of Achilleus. Several of these belong to the
younger group of heroes, whereas those with names
that are neither Greek nor end in *-eus,* like Kadmos
(Cadmus), Bellerophon(tes) or Tantalos, tend to belong to the older. Yet on the whole this is a speculative
and inadequate criterion, especially since some names,
like Oedipus, Perseus, Caeneus, Jason (Iason in Greek),
could be either Greek or foreign in derivation. The
whole matter has been complicated by the relization
that Greek was spoken in the peninsula as early as
around 2100 B.C., that the Mycenaeans were thoroughly
Greek, and that the Linear B tablets suggest that names
of all these types were in use towards the end of the
Bronze Age. Finally Heracles is beyond dispute an
older hero, yet his name is completely Greek in form
and means 'glory of Hera' or something similar.

Only a selection of heroes, in any case, can be discussed here. From *the older heroes* I have chosen
Perseus, Bellerophon, Theseus, Cadmus and Jason, in
that order, not only because they are (or used to be)
household names, but also because they illustrate several different tendencies of heroic myths. Heracles is
reserved for special treatment in Chapter 8 [of *The
Nature of Greek Myths*].

This is how Apollodorus (the best of the
extantmythographers, even though he wrote no earlier
than the second century A.D.) tells of the birth and
youth of Perseus:

> When Acrisius consulted the oracle about begetting
> male children, the god said his daughter would have
> a son who would kill him. As a precaution, Acrisius
> built a brazen underground chamber and kept Danaë
> under guard there. But Proetus, as some say, seduced
> her, and that was the cause of their quarrel. Others
> say that Zeus changed into gold which poured into
> Danaë's lap through the roof, and so had intercourse
> with her. Acrisius, on learning later that the child
> Perseus had been born from her, refused to believe
> that Zeus was her seducer, and so cast his daughter
> with her child into a chest and hurled it into the
> sea. The chest was carried to Seriphos, and Dictys
> took it up and brought up the boy. Dictys' brother
> Polydectes, who was king of Seriphos, fell in love
> with Danaë . . . (2.4, 1 ff.)

Acrisius, as well as being brother of Proetus, was king
of Argos, and it is there that Danaus had taken refuge
from Egypt with his daughters, as described by
Aeschylus in his *Suppliant Women.* That may reflect a
memory of conflict between Mycenaeans and Egyptians, and Danaë too, with her similar name ('Danaans'
is one of Homer's names for the Greeks), is probably
a Bronze Age character. Yet the motif of the oracle
must be later. It is common in Greek myths, but all the
foundation legends of the great oracles (Delphi,
Dodona, Didyma, and so on) point to the early Iron
Age, after 1100 B.C., as their time of origin. Curiously
enough there was a tale, preserved only by Aelian in
the Roman period, that the mother of Sumerian
Gilgamesh had been locked up for similar reasons, and
that the illicit baby, thrown from her lofty prison, had
been caught and rescued by an eagle. This tends to
confirm that the idea of keeping one's daughter a virgin by locking her up, quite apart from the overthrow-
by-grandson motif, was an ancient one; it has, of course,
a marked folktale appearance. Gilgamesh's birth was
said to be due to a man getting in; the Greek version
is more exotic and poetical ('the son of Danaë, who
we say was born from gold that flowed of its own
accord' as Pindar put it—the gold being Zeus, although
later rationalizers typically reduced it to a bribe given
to her jailers). Two other odd details are the underground brazen house and the launching on the sea in
a chest, both with parallels in other Greek myths. The
house reminds one of the bronze jar that is a place of
refuge for Eurystheus or imprisonment for Ares,
whereas the chest is an almost traditional way of disposing of unwanted relatives or babies (for example
Tenes and his sister Hemithea). It is tempting, but not
especially plausible, to think of underground grain-si-
los or huge 'beehive' tombs as precedents for the idea
of the brazen house. The floating-chest idea is less
susceptible of facile interpretation, and since it is loosely

paralleled in Moses and the bulrushes it seems preferable to think of it as a widely-diffused folktale idea (rather than, for instance, a Freudian memory of the embryo).

King Polydectes (his name means 'much-receiving' and resembles a title given to Hades, who receives innumerable dead into his kingdom) sent Perseus, now grown up, to get the Gorgon's head, hoping to be rid of him once and for all and so seduce Danaë without further interference. But with Athena's help the hero forced the Graiai, the old grey women, by stealing the single eye and tooth they shared between them, to tell him the way to certain nymphs. These then gave him winged sandals, the cap of invisibility and a special wallet for the Gorgon's head. Actually there were three Gorgons, Medusa being the mortal one; they were sisters of the two Graiai, and their parents were Phorcys (an old-man-of-the-sea type) and the female sea-monster Ceto. Athena guided Perseus so that he could see Medusa's reflection in his shield and so decapitate her without being turned to stone. Pindar has a pretty tale that Athena imitated the Gorgon's shrieks by playing on the flute the so-called 'many-headed tune':

> . . . the art that Pallas Athena invented when she wove together the deadly dirge of the reckless Gorgons. Perseus heard it flowing in bitter agony from the monstrous snake-heads of the maidens when he put an end to one of the three sisters, bringing doom for Seriphos and its island people. Yes, he annihilated the prodigious offspring of Phorcus, and made a bitter contribution to Polydectes' feast . . . (*Pythians* 12, 6 ff.)

On the way back from the Gorgons, who lived at the ends of the earth across the stream of Okeanos, Perseus went northward to visit the Hyperboreans, and also as far south as Ethiopia or Joppa. In one of these the Andromeda adventure took place. She was daughter of King Cepheus and his silly wife Cassiopeia—silly because she boasted that she was prettier than the Nereids. The inevitable consequences followed, this time both a flood and a sea-monster. An oracle said the monster could only be sent away if given Andromeda to devour, but Perseus rescued her just in time on the promise of her hand in marriage. Cepheus' brother Phineus tried to make trouble on the grounds that Andromeda was pledged to him, but the Gorgon's head dealt with him soon enough. Then Perseus returned to Seriphos, petrified Polydectes and his supporters, left for the mainland and accidentally killed Acrisius with a discus, thus fulfilling the original oracle. He finally became king of Tiryns and founder, with Andromeda, of the Perseid dynasty.

It has long been recognized that the Perseus complex is more than usually dependent on folktale-type motifs: the escape as a baby, defending one's mother from a seducer, the meant-to-be-fatal quest, the ingenious devices (tooth-and-eye, magical gadgets for flying and invisibility, avoiding a lethal gaze), rescuing the princess, killing a relative by accident. It also exemplifies an interest in exotic lands (Ethiopia, the Hyperboreans) that is typical of test-and-quest tales. Yet this does not mean that the myth is not substantially an ancient one. Obviously it has been elaborated, as any traditional tale must be—perhaps in respect of the oracle, some of the details of Athena's help, and the magical implements; possibly in respect of the whole Andromeda episode (which must however have had a certain independent status) and some of the events after Perseus' return to Argos and Tiryns. But the birth from Danaë, the Seriphos connection and the decapitation of the Gorgon form a substantial nucleus with no special mark of later date. Homer alludes to Zeus' love of Danaë and to Perseus himself, and Hesiod adds that Chrysaor and the horse Pegasus sprang from Medusa's body as Perseus cut off her head; also that Poseidon had slept with Medusa. The location in Seriphos, an utterly unimportant island, is at first strange, but is probably aetiological in a simple way. Seriphos is notable for its rock pinnacles jutting up from the hills, and these were identified with the people turned to stone. Of serious implications there are few signs. The tale is remarkable in its own right, and the death-gazing Medusa, not to speak of the fertile golden shower, a powerful conception. There is a faint possibility, however, that underneath lies a primitive tale of an attack (by Perseus meaning 'destroyer'?) on death itself; for the Gorgons are death-dealing, and they are sisters of the Graiai who represent old age. The possible associations of Polydectes with Hades are also relevant.

Next, Bellerophon, who is connected with the preceding tale not only through Pegasus but also through Proetus the brother of Acrisius. Bellerophon is associated with Tiryns, but also with Ephyra which probably denotes Corinth. I mentioned earlier . . . Homer's account of his feats against the Chimaera, the Solymi and the Amazons. He first found himself in Lycia because of his innocent involvement with Proetus' voracious wife, and at the end of his successful quests was granted the daughter of the Lycian king (Iobates, according to a lost play by Sophocles) and a share of the kingdom. But then he decides to put Pegasus—first tamed with the help of a magic bridle supplied by Athena, an incident that recalls her part in procuring magical aids for Perseus—to an impious use, no longer to rid the earth of menaces but to carry his rider to the very halls of the gods:

> If a man sets his eye on things afar, he is not tall enough to reach the brazen-floored home of the gods. Winged Pegasus threw his master, Bellerophontes, when he wished to come to the abodes of heaven and the companions of Zeus; a bitter ending awaits

pleasure that lies beyond what is right. (*Isthmians* 7, 43 ff.)

Apparently Bellerophon was not killed outright, since Homer says that

> when at last he became hated by all the gods, he wandered alone over the Plain of Wandering, eating out his spirit, avoiding the steps of men. (*Iliad* 6, 200 ff.)

Bellerophon's move to Lycia may not have been a particularly early detail. It is integral to the Homeric account, but there are indications that the Chimaera may once have carried out its depredations in the region of Corinth itself. The embroilment with Proetus' wife, too, need not be organic. Like other elements in the Bellerophon complex (the magic bridle, the cryptic message that could not be understood by its bearer, the tasks designed to be fatal, the attempt at ambush, the hand of the princess as reward) it is a familiar folktale motif. In this respect, as well as in several other details, Bellerophon's deeds resemble those of his close countryman Perseus. Even the connection with Corinth may have been primarily intended to relate him to Sisyphus, whose grandson he was shown to be; Sisyphus had tried to outwit the gods by avoiding death, and that, on the most probable interpretation, is what Bellerophon was trying to do in his last ride on Pegasus. Neither in this nor in the Perseus myth are there signs of charter, political or historical overtones. On the other hand there may be an implied association between magic flight and superhuman aspiration, and the hero's eventual fate, vague but sinister, gives the myth in its developed form a distinct moral flavour.

Theseus, by contrast, owes much of his mythical *persona* to the desire of Athenians, and especially the tyrant Peisistratus in the sixth century B.C., to make of him a great national hero. They did so in two ways: by associating him as closely as possible with Heracles, the *beau idéal,* and by ascribing to him various political and benevolent acts that were held to be the beginning of Athenian democracy. There can be no question that the myths about Theseus were enormously elaborated at a relatively recent date, particularly during the sixth and fifth centuries B.C., not only by Peisistratus and his sons, but also by the anonymous authors of more than one *Theseis,* or sub-epic poem about Theseus, and various writers of Athenian local history in the fifth century and after. Yet parts of the Theseus cycle are clearly much older, and the difficulty for the modern critic is to draw the dividing line with reasonable accuracy.

He was born at Trozen, down the coast from Athens and its ancient ally. His mother was Aethra and his father her secret lover, the Athenian King Aegeus, or even Aegeus' patron-god Poseidon himself. Aegeus left a sword and sandals under a rock as tokens, with instructions that when the boy was big enough to shift the rock he should bring them to Athens. At sixteen he did so; but instead of coming the safe way inland he took the coast road in order to dispose of several dangerous brigands—congratulating himself, it is said, that Heracles at the time was under servitude to Queen Omphale and so had left this particular bunch of villains unmolested. The lyric poet Bacchylides imagines Aegeus giving an account of these deeds:

> A herald has just arrived after traversing the long road from the Isthmus, and reports the wonderful deeds of a mighty man. He has killed the lawless Sinis, strongest of mortals, child of Kronos' son the Earthshaker; he has slaughtered the man-slaying sow in the glades of Cremmyon, and insolent Sciron too; he has gained possession of Cercyon's wrestling-place; and Procoptes, meeting a better man than himself, has thrown away Polypemon's strong hammer. (18, 16 ff.)

Bacchylides did not need to tell his audience that Sinis tied his victims to pine-trees bent together and then released; that the Cremmyonian sow was notorious for its savagery; that Sciron made travellers wash his feet and then kicked them off the cliffs into the sea, where they were finished off by a giant turtle; that Cercyon lived near Eleusis and made passers-by wrestle with him until he killed them; and that Procoptes, better known as Procrustes, 'The Smasher', caught them on the borders of Athens and by stretching or pruning made them an exact fit to his lethal bed.

Aegeus and his wife Medea, whom he married when she was thrown out by Jason, were suspicious of the stranger and tried to be rid of him by sending him after the Marathonian bull, perhaps the one that Heracles had caught in Crete and brought to the mainland. Theseus returned successful to Athens, and this time Aegeus thwarted Medea's attempt to poison his son and dismissed her. Soon afterwards Theseus disposed of the sons of Pallas, who welcomed a new heir no more than Medea had, but perhaps before that he had already engaged in his most famous exploit, the killing of the Minotaur, the 'Minos-bull'.

King Minos of Crete, in revenge for the death in Attica of his son Androgeos, had begun to exact a three-yearly tribute consisting of seven Athenian boys and seven girls; they were offered to the Minotaur, half man and half bull, offspring of Pasiphaë's union with the Cretan Bull, a union made possible by one of Daedalus' mechanical devices. This unnatural beast lives in the Labyrinth, a maze usually identified with the intricate Minoan palace at Knossos. Theseus enters the maze and kills its occupant; Minos' daughter

Ariadne helps him escape, either with the famous clew or with a magic crown of light that enables him to see in the dark. The tribute is now ended.

The tale is elaborated at its beginning by a contest (also described by Bacchylides) in which Theseus dives down and visits the goddess Amphitrite in the depths of the sea, to prove his divine descent from Poseidon and so match Minos' claim to be son of Zeus. And on the way home from Crete he stops at Naxos, and there, somehow, his mistress Ariadne is left behind. Either he abandons her for another girl, or he is divinely made to forget her, or the god Dionysus desires her and takes her over, or Artemis slays her there at his behest. Theseus next calls at Delos, where he and his companions dance a special 'crane-dance' that reproduces the sinuosities of the Labyrinth. Then, as he approaches Athens he forgets to replace the black sail with the white one that was to announce a successful outcome, and his father Aegeus casts himself from the Acropolis in despair.

Theseus is now king. He wins the friendship of Peirithous King of the Lapiths, and helps defeat the lecherous Centaurs at Peirithous' wedding. Peirithous helps him in his turn in an expedition against the Amazons, modelled closely on one of Heracles' adventures, and also in repelling them when they later attack Athens to regain their queen Antiope, another victim of Theseus' manly charms. For the hero has another side to him, best represented in the curious tale of how he and Peirithous abducted Helen from Sparta when she was only twelve, to keep her in the countryside until ripe for marriage; but her brothers the Dioscuri rescued her. Later he has to help Peirithous win *his* ideal girl, no less than Persephone herself, from the underworld. They get no further than the Styx in some versions, and are then trapped in magic stone seats—although usually Theseus, but not Peirithous, is later rescued by Heracles. He returns to Athens, unifies the rural communities and performs other politic acts, then is displaced by Menestheus and takes refuge with King Lycomedes of Scyros, who treacherously throws him over the cliffs; and that (though without the turtle) is the end of Theseus.

It's a curious hotch-potch, ranging from the solemn and mysterious (the Labyrinth and Ariadne, 'Very Holy', who seems once to have been a goddess of vegetation not unlike Persephone herself) to the trivial and derivative (Helen, and especially the episode in the underworld). The politically-minded parts, with Theseus as the great democrat, are barely mythical, and the involvement with the Amazon queen, together with the subsidiary tale of his second wife Phaedra and his son Hippolytus, looks like a romantic development. The adventures modelled on Heracles, the disposal of robbers as well as the Amazon expedition as a whole, seem from the literary and artistic evidence to be sub-

stantially the creation of the seventh or sixth centuries B.C. The association with the Lapiths is unlikely to be much older, and could be the creation of the tyrant Peisistratus who had Thessalian allies. Several other points are folktale-type elements of almost any date, particularly the tale of the black and white sails on his return from Crete.

The Cretan adventure itself, however, goes back at least to the time of Homer and Hesiod and probably earlier. Indeed the later Bronze Age is plausibly reflected not only in the palace-Labyrinth (*labyrinthos* being a pre-Greek word based apparently on the term for 'double-axe', a symbol carved on several of the surviving stones of the palace) but also in the bull itself—for bull-worship and bull-games were a prominent part of Minoan culture—and in the idea of Athens as tributary to Crete, which makes sense for the Late Bronze Age but for no subsequent period. It is now known that the Achaean Greeks gained control of Crete around 1500 B.C., and the myth may reflect that, although with special emphasis on Athens. At least the island of Ceos off the Attic coast (home, incidentally, of Bacchylides) was once a Minoan colony, and conceivably parts of Attica too had come for a time under Minoan control.

Curiously enough the rape of Helen and the attempt on Persephone are not particularly recent elements, since they figure on works of art (the throne at Amyclae and the chest of Cypselus at Olympia) described by the traveller Pausanias and belonging to the late seventh or early sixth century B.C.[1] They must already have been traditional by that date. I doubt, all the same, whether they go back as far as the Mycenaean era, although it is strange that they were not suppressed in the process of making Theseus into an august founder of the state, and this suggests an almost sacrosanct traditionality. Peirithous, too, is an ambivalent figure. He is the son of Ixion, a famous sinner who tried to rape Hera herself, and his efforts with Persephone may therefore be a narrative doublet. Yet he is traditionally associated with the Centaurs, and that part of his myth is probably quite old.

The myths of Theseus seem almost too complex for a brief treatment, yet one conclusion would remain unchanged even after a longer examination: that their main development took place during the literary period. Only the quest against Crete looks undeniably ancient, and it is rightly accepted as one of the most powerful narrative themes in Greek myths. Interestingly enough it seems to reflect, and perhaps to justify, some dimly-remembered historical event, and so provide a model for the political elaborations to which many other parts of the Theseus story owe their existence.

The fourth of our older heroes is Cadmus, an example of a mythical founder figure. Like Pelops, founder of the Pelopid dynasty at Mycenae, he came to Greece from the Near East—not, like Pelops, from Lydia, but from Phoenicia where he was one of the sons of Agenor. He and his brothers were dispatched by their father to look for their sister Europa who had disappeared; actually she had been carried off to Crete for amatory purposes by Zeus in the form of a bull, and so a Cretan bull appears indirectly in this myth as well as in those of Theseus and Heracles. Cadmus arrived in Greece and was directed by the Delphic oracle to follow a cow(!) until it lay down, and there to found the city of Thebes. Euripides tells the tale, allusively as usual, in a choral ode from his great pageant of Theban history, *The Phoenician Women:*

> Cadmus of Tyre came to this land, for whom the four-legged calf sank to the ground of its own accord, so fulfilling the oracle destined to be accomplished where the divine decree announced that Cadmus should settle in the wheat-bearing plains that were to be his home, where too the fair river's moisture spreads over the lands of Dirce . . . There was the murderous serpent of Ares, a savage guardian, watching the watery rivers and fertile streams with ever-wandering glances. Cadmus as he came for lustral water slew it with a rock, striking the murderous head of the deadly beast with his arm's full throw, and through the counsels of the divine unmothered goddess [that is, Athena] cast its teeth on the ground, into the deep-seeded earth; then the earth sent up a vision of men in full armour that towered over the farthest borders of the land. Iron-hearted murder joined them again with the earth that gave them birth . . . (638-73)

In short, there was a spring where the cow lay down, but it was guarded by a dragon sacred to Ares; Cadmus killed it and sowed its teeth, which produced a crop of armed warriors. By throwing a stone among them he turned them against each other, but the five that stayed alive became ancestors of the chief clans of Thebes.

After a period of expiation Cadmus was allowed to marry Ares' child Harmonia, and they had four daughters: Agaue, Autonoë, Ino and Semele. They were an unfortunate group, in their lifetimes at least. Agaue tore her son Pentheus to pieces, and Autonoë, who also joined in, had a son Actaeon who had already been devoured by his own hounds. Ino was driven mad for plotting against her step-children and threw herself into the sea, whereas Semele spoiled her good fortune as Zeus' mistress by demanding that he come to her in his true shape, and being incinerated as a consequence. Cadmus and Harmonia themselves had a curious later history, predicted to Cadmus by his quasi-grandson Dionysus:

> You shall be turned into a serpent, and your wife shall change into the savage form of a snake— Harmonia, Ares' daughter, whom you won though

yourself a mortal. With your wife, as the oracle of Zeus declares, you shall drive an ox-cart at the head of foreigners. Many are the cities you shall overthrow with your numberless hordes; when they have ravaged the oracle of Loxias [that is, Apollo] they shall have a miserable return home, but Ares will rescue you and Harmonia and transplant your life to the land of the blessed. (Euripides, *Bacchae,* 1330 ff.)

Euripides, who had strong aetiological interests, seems to combine a number of curious legends, none of them perhaps very early except for the ultimate resort to the Isles of the Blest: that Cadmus and his wife became leaders of a people in the west of Greece called the *Encheleis* or Eels, that they themselves turned into snakes, that Delphi was destined to be sacked by foreigners. Perhaps the snake-transformation reflected Cadmus' essential connection with the soil of Thebes (rather than with the underworld, another possible association), for the 'house-snake' was a symbol of stability and possession; the birth from the dragon's teeth of the 'Sown Men' who became ancestors of the Thebans likewise stresses their autochthonous nature. If so, this is a good example of a charter myth that is doing its best to confirm a politically desirable but historically dubious idea; for if there is anything we know about the Thebans, it is that they were subject from early times to displacement and migration. As for the foundation itself: its association with the oracle, and the use of the standard theme of founding a city where an animal performs a certain action, are presumably not earlier than the ninth or tenth century B.C., and the fight with the guardian monster, closely parallel with Apollo's fight against the Python-snake at Delphi, need be no older. The sowing of the teeth is reproduced in the story of how Jason dealt with the monster that guarded the Golden Fleece, but the Theban tale seems the earlier of the two.

What is left, then, to suggest that Cadmus goes back even so far as the Late Bronze Age? Partly that Thebes was indeed an important Mycenaean city, its inhabitants known in Homer as 'Cadmeians'; partly the association with the tale of Europa and Zeus, which is related to Bronze Age Crete; partly the mythical connections of his daughters, especially Semele and Ino. (The myth of Ino and Athamas is particularly well established, and is connected in turn with that of Phrixus and the Fleece.) There is also the cleavage between Cadmus and the later history of Thebes (from Labdacus through Laius to Oedipus and his sons), which suggests an archaic element that could not be completely integrated; and finally his Phoenician origins. These last have been doubted. Admittedly he is credited with the introduction of 'Phoenician writing' into Greece, but it is uncertain whether this connotes a Linear-B-type script or the alphabet, the latter a certainly Phoenician invention. Some scholars have thought the term 'Phoinix' to imply Cretan rather than Phoenician in this connection. Yet that seems unlikely, and we know that there were close cultural contacts between Late Bronze Age Greece and the eastern Mediterranean: for instance Ugarit (modern Ras Shamra) on the Syrian coast had a Mycenaean trading-quarter in the fourteenth century B.C.

It would be unwise to press these speculations too hard. The story of Cadmus is a particularly good example of a complex Greek myth that has attracted details from many sources and different eras: folktale motifs, miscellaneous historical details, charter-type elaborations, and so on. Modern scholarship has attacked the problem with all its power, and the result has been confusion and indecision as great as any in the ancient sources. One difficulty is that it is only with Euripides that our evidence becomes at all full for the early part of the Theban cycle. Sporadic earlier references exist, together with sixth-century artistic representations of favourite details like the marriage of Cadmus and Harmonia, but there is little else to guide us through the variants that proliferated by the time Hellanicus and Pherecydes brought their confident but crude scholarship to bear during the classical era.

The last of the selection of older heroes must undoubtedly be Jason. His myth, too, was much embroidered, but he too surely goes back into the Bronze Age. Much of the detail of the voyage of the Argo to Colchis at the eastern end of the Black Sea (the Euxine or 'Hospitable' sea as the Greeks called it to disguise or assuage its terrors) probably belongs to the age of colonization that began around 1000 B.C.; but the voyage itself is older. Iolcus, the Thessalian coastal city from which it started, was important in Mycenaean times but not later (at least, until the third century B.C.); Homer, in his single brief but apparently traditional allusion to the Argo, calls it 'well-known to all'. Hesiod, on the other hand, summarizes the union of Jason and Medea in a list of mixed marriages appended to the *Theogony:*

> Aison's son [that is, Jason] led away Zeus-reared King Aietes' daughter by the will of the eternal gods, after accomplishing the many grievous tasks enjoined on him by the arrogant great king, insolent Pelias, wicked and violent. He accomplished these and came to Iolcus, after suffering much, bringing the slant-eyed maid on his swift ship . . . (*Theogony,* 992 ff.)

Unfortunately the poet is richer in epithets than in hard information. Of our fuller sources, Pindar in his fourth *Pythian* describes part of the Argo's journey quite brilliantly, but at too great length for quotation here, whereas Apollonius of Rhodes, who wrote an epic poem on the theme in the third century B.C., is both too prolix and too infected by Alexandrianism to be of great value for our purposes. Apollodorus depends heavily on Apollonius and is even more prosaic than usual. Even Pindar gives up half-way through the tale and claims that 'time constricts me, and I know a short cut' (*Pythians* 4, 247 f.); this is to give a rapid summary, and on this occasion I follow suit.

Aison has been cheated of the throne of Iolcus by Pelias, who is warned by the Delphic oracle that he will be deposed by a one-sandalled man. This turns out to be Aison's son Jason, who has been educated by the Centaur Cheiron and arrives in town wearing only one sandal. He is promptly persuaded to set off and recover the golden fleece belonging to King Aietes of Colchis—the one from the ram that had rescued Phrixus and Helle from the wrath of their stepmother Ino. Naturally the mission is meant to be fatal. Jason gathers all the young noblemen of the region for the expedition, and Phrixus' son Argos is commissioned to build a ship. As the myth grew in popularity the expedition became a Panhellenic affair; practically everyone who was anyone joined in, including Orpheus and Heracles. The Argo's distinguished crew sail north-eastward through the Dardanelles and meet various adventures, including a preliminary dalliance with the women of Lemnos. . . . In the Propontis they kill King Cyzicus by mistake in a night landing and leave Heracles ashore searching for his beloved Hylas; then blind Phineus, in return for the routing of the greedy bird-women called Harpies, tells them how to pass between the Clashing Rocks in safety. The Argonauts seem to be in the Black Sea by now, but probably these rocks are based on a navigator's memory of the dangerous passage through the Bosporus or even the Dardanelles.

Finally they reach the river Phasis and the land of Aietes, whose father is the Sun and whose daughter is Medea skilled in magic. Athena sees to it that she falls in love with Jason, and gives him an ointment that protects him against fire or metal. This enables him to yoke the fire-breathing brazen-footed bulls that Aietes produces as a preliminary test. He then kills the dragon that guards the fleece, sows its teeth and disposes of the armed men that grow out of the ground by throwing a stone among them, exactly as Cadmus did. He rushes back to the Argo with the fleece, Medea, and her young brother Apsyrtus; Aietes pursues, and drops behind only when Medea has the good idea of cutting up Apsyrtus and throwing the bits overboard for his father to gather. Jason is purified from the crime, and they return to Iolcus by devious routes about which the tradition was flexible: usually round the stream of Okeanos somehow, or up the Danube, into the North Sea and then through Libya. Back in Iolcus, Pelias is removed when Medea persuades him to be 'rejuvenated' by being boiled in a cauldron, a process she has just made work with an old sheep. She and Jason are expelled for the murder and find their way to Corinth, where eventually Jason acquires a proper Greek wife.

Medea murders her children in revenge, at least according to Euripides' *Medea,* and finds refuge for a time with Theseus at Athens; Jason dies when a bit of the now rotting Argo falls on his head.

Plainly the tale as a whole is an amalgam of diverse elements. Folktale motifs are the most prominent: recognition by token (the sandal), disposing of an enemy by sending him on a dangerous quest (both Pelias and Aietes try this), killing a friend by mistake (Cyzicus), the barbarian enchantress, love-charms and magical gadgets, tricks to make enemies fight each other, delaying pursuit by scattering objects that have to be collected (Atalanta had done so more humanely, with golden apples), killing someone under pretence of doing him a favour. Next there is a strong geographical interest, no doubt in response to explorations in and rumours about the Black Sea and Danube. It has been suggested that Miletus on the Asia Minor coast played a part in forming the myth; it was populated by Greeks, including 'Minyans' from Orchomenus near Iolcus, after 1100 B.C., and took a prominent part in the exploration of the Euxine. Finally great care has obviously been taken to connect the myth with as many others as possible, not only through the heterogeneous crew (the Dioscuri and the sons of Boreas the North Wind, as well as Peleus, Orpheus and Heracles), but also through Pelias at Iolcus, the relation of Jason to Cheiron, the fleece connected with Phrixus and so with the Ino-Athamas myth, and through Jason at Corinth and Medea at Athens.

Most of the details of Jason's adventures fail to mark him with any particular clarity as an 'older hero', yet such, at heart, he undoubtedly must be. His name 'Iason', 'Healer', suggests an originally rather different role. He is clearly not on a level with younger legendary heroes like Agamemnon or Achilles, yet in a sense his diversity is typical of the difficulty in distinguishing older and younger traits in the subjects of heavily elaborated myth complexes. Ultimately we have to take the tale of the Argonauts as we find it in our sources: complex in detail but straightforward, almost ordinary, as narrative. It contains few significant overtones (except for those added by specifically literary sources like Apollonius, for example, that Jason is indecisive and unheroic by comparison with Heracles), and the myth as a whole does not respond easily to special interpretations: no charter aspects, no aetiology beyond feeble explanations of place-names in the Propontis and Black Sea, no creative evocation, heavily muted fantasy. It is enthralling but bland, even superficial; and that, in the end, may be a fault in varying degrees of most of the heroic myths as they survive in the literary sources.

The 'younger' heroes must be treated no less selectively. As examples I take Oedipus, Agamemnon, Orestes, Odysseus and Orpheus; they suffice to make certain additional distinctions clear as well as to stress the difference between historicizing and non-historicizing myths.

Oedipus is one of the best-known and most powerful figures of Greek myths, and it may be disconcerting to see him labelled as a 'younger hero'; indeed I do not deny that in some respects his origins may go back into the Bronze Age. Yet his 'real' mythical essence is contained in Sophocles' plays: his murder and marriage, his self-discovery, his agony and blinding, his miraculous assumption in the grove of Colonus near Athens. Most of this is likely to be comparatively recent in anything like that form. Homer knows about his killing his father and marrying his mother (although he gives her name as Epicaste not Iocaste), but differs over the aftermath. Here is Odysseus describing the figures he saw in the underworld:

> And I saw the mother of Oedipus, fair Epicaste, who committed a dreadful deed in the ignorance of her mind by marrying her own son; and he married her after slaying his own father—deeds the gods immediately made notorious among men. But he in grief ruled over the Cadmeians in lovely Thebes through the destructive counsels of the gods, whereas she went to the narrow-gated strong house of Hades, tying a steep noose from the lofty hall, possessed by her own grief . . . (*Odyssey* 11, 271 ff.)

Here is no self-blinding, no immediate and self-imposed exile from Thebes. A passage in the *Iliad* (23, 679 f.) confirms that Oedipus died not in exile at Colonus but at Thebes itself, and that funeral games were given for him as a still-established monarch. Indeed the whole Theban saga (as one may rightly call it, since it obviously has a legendary and quasi-historical basis) was the subject of considerable elaboration between the time of Homer and the fifth century B.C.

Oedipus does not fit well with the early history of Thebes or the descendants of Cadmus and the Sown Men. His grandfather, who had started a fresh dynasty, is called Labdacus, a curious name which, if it is indeed related to the Phoenician letter *labda* (Greek *lamda*), is not particularly old, since the Phoenician alphabet did not reach Greece till around 900 B.C. and had been formed in Phoenicia itself not more than three centuries before that. Oedipus' father Laius incurs a family curse for abducting the beautiful boy Chrysippus—the curse theme was applied to the house of Atreus also, and was an effective device for interrelating tales about different generations. Oedipus himself has a bizarre name redolent of folktale, if indeed it means 'swollen-foot'; his exposure by his parents, his rescue by a shepherd, his winning the kingship of Thebes by solving the Sphinx's riddle—all these, too, are folktale elements. These, rather than the dramatic and deeply evocative tale developed by

Sophocles (whose main point is the idea of a man relentlessly exploring his true situation at the risk of his own destruction), are the most traditional elements in Oedipus. He is a mixed figure, therefore, but one who unlike Perseus, Heracles and the rest only became an important hero of myth after the end of the Bronze Age.

There is a similar distinction of dynasties at Mycenae. Atreus is founder of the Atreid dynasty, and his famous son is Agamemnon. Beyond Atreus, but seemingly in a different landscape, stands Pelops, brought to southern Greece from Asia Minor by his father Tantalus, himself a shadowy figure associated with the gods; and behind Tantalus, as one of the earliest kings of Mycenae or its near neighbour Tiryns, is Perseus. Atreus quarrels with his brother Thyestes; the theme of the quarrelling brothers is a folktale one, but is similarly applied to quasi-historical dynastic problems through Proetus and Acrisius as well as Eteocles and Polyneices. Thyestes seduces Atreus' wife Aerope and gets the kingdom by a trick, then Atreus regains it after serving up Thyestes' own children for him to eat. These are the highly indirect consequences of a curse once laid on Pelops by Oenomaus' charioteer Myrtilus. Agamemnon inherits the curse, which is why he has to sacrifice his daughter Iphigeneia on the way to Troy, why he is slain by his wife Clytaemnestra on his triumphant return, and why his son Orestes has to kill his own mother Clytaemnestra and her lover Aegisthus. This all forms the material of Aeschylus' great trilogy, the *Oresteia*. The curse is finally ended after Orestes, driven mad and so punished for the crime of matricide, is set free by the Furies on the Areopagus (the Hill of Ares in Athens). This is an aetiological and validatory myth of the foundation of the Athenian High Court of historical times. It is obvious that Athens is here appropriating an Argive myth and turning it to her own greater glory, much as she did with Oedipus at Colonus in Sophocles' play, or less effectively with Medea.

Here we have fifth-century developments of the myth, powerful but undeniably recent. Yet Agamemnon himself is a considerably older figure, established as leader of the Achaean forces in Homer's *Iliad* and indeed as one of the key figures of the Trojan War. Why then should he be classified as a 'younger' hero? The answer is that the Agamemnon of the *Iliad* is predominantly a realistic character, a historical picture of a man. His actions there are legendary and not mythical in the stricter sense. His direct connection with the era of the older heroes is mainly through his brother Menelaus who married Helen, and superficially by the political inheritance stressed by Homer:

> Strong Agamemnon rose, and stood holding the sceptre made by Hephaestus. Hephaestus had given it to Lord Zeus, son of Kronos, and then Zeus gave it to the Messenger [that is, Hermes] . . . and Lord

Hermes gave it to Pelops, whipper of horses, and Pelops again to Atreus, shepherd of the people. Atreus when he died left it for Thyestes rich in sheep, and Thyestes again left it to be carried by Agamemnon, to rule over all Argos and many islands. (*Iliad* 2, 100 ff.)

But here Homer is trying to bolster Agamemnon's position as a 'Zeus-born' king by tracing his staff of office back to Zeus, and the untraditional nature of the attempt is strongly suggested by his omitting Perseus and ignoring Thyestes' quarrel with Atreus.

With Orestes the case becomes clearer, mainly because he is an explicitly post-Trojan-War figure. *His* relations to the distant Pelops are not stressed; he is an entirely realistic character whose one fantastic experience, being driven mad by the Furies for his pious matricide, is little more than a pathological interlude. Homer reduces the killing of Aegisthus and Clytaemnestra to a precise and pseudo-realistic chronology:

> For seven years Aegisthus ruled over Mycenae rich in gold after killing the son of Atreus, and the people were subjected to him. But in the eighth year Prince Orestes came back as a bane to him from Athens, and slew the murderer of his father . . . After slaying him he gave a funeral feast to the Argives for hateful Clytaemnestra and cowardly Aegisthus, and on the same day Menelaus came . . . (*Odyssey* 3, 304 ff.)

Orestes draws Agamemnon with him, as it were, away from the Bronze-age past, from Pelops and Helen and the Dioscuri, into the historical period that is initiated by the Trojan War itself and develops with the emergence of Athens in the eleventh, tenth and ninth centuries B.C. Homer, around 700, knows that Orestes comes *from Athens* to take vengeance on Aegisthus; could that detail have formed part of the tradition for long?

One of the difficulties of drawing a distinction between 'older' and 'younger' heroes is that even those suggested by historical associations as belonging to the latter class tend to be involved in folktale-type actions from time to time. For Martin Nilsson that was a sign of great antiquity. I am sceptical. The use of standard motifs, some of them of the kind we associate with folktales, was so deeply rooted in the Greek mythical tradition from its earliest known phases to its latest ones that I doubt whether we can take it as a sure sign of age. Admittedly, where a myth is almost wholly composed of folk-tale motifs, like that of Perseus, we can suspect a highly traditional quality; but Atreus is not necessarily made an ancient figure by cooking his nephews, any more than Oedipus by accidentally killing his father. Conversely a detail about an oracle does not turn the whole of its surrounding myth into a recent creation.

With Odysseus we become involved in a different and rather special situation. He obviously goes back at least as far as the first versions of the *Odyssey*—and that means, in the light of the long and cumulative oral epic tradition, close to the time of the Trojan War. Yet he is a 'younger' hero in comparison with Perseus and others, since none of his affiliations take him beyond that point by more than a generation or so. He is simply not involved in the elaborate network of mythical events outside the range of Troy. His father Laertes is otherwise devoid of myths, and so to all intents and purposes is his mother Anticleia; his maternal grandfather Autolycus is something of a trickster and lives near Mount Parnassus, but again is not integrated into the general heroic pattern. Odysseus takes full part in the events at Troy and its aftermath; his son Telemachus is incorporated into the later fictional tradition and is even married off to Circe in one unhappy version. But we cannot take Odysseus' feats at Troy as 'mythical' in the same sense as those of Cadmus at Thebes. Admittedly he is represented as being under the special protection of Athena . . . , and the intervention of gods is something that gives the whole Trojan *geste* a touch of mythical glamour. But it is no more than a touch, except in the specifically divine parts of the poems, and most of the actions of Odysseus and his fellow-fighters are a mixture of realism and ordinary non-mythical fiction, no doubt with a dash of genuine historical memory.

What makes Odysseus a special case is his involvement in the well-known folktale adventures that he describes to the Phaeacians in the ninth to the twelfth books of the *Odyssey*. The Lotus-eaters, Polyphemus the Cyclops, Aeolus king of the winds, the huge Laestrygonians, Circe, the journey to the underworld, Scylla and Charybdis, the cattle of the Sun, Calypso's island, the Phaeacians themselves—it would be pleasant to recount these tales once again, but they are too extensive and too familiar for that, and in any case Homer's version is best. Now this *is* genuinely mythical material. It includes many folktale themes, of disguise and ingenuity and the rest, but they have been formed into homogeneous narratives that are both fantastic and other-worldly. They have a quite different appearance from the automatic and rather tired look of many later mythical complexes, in which quests are accomplished almost as easily as proposed, heiresses are offered by the handful and the air hums with errant discuses fulfilling highly predictable oracles. Yet most critics would agree, I believe, that Odysseus' sea adventures (which begin when a storm blows up soon after he leaves Troy and end when he is set ashore in Ithaca by the semi-divine Phaeacians) are for the most part not only independent from but older than Odysseus himself, or mythical Troy, or Ithaca.

Admittedly these adventures include different strata. Scholars have demonstrated, for instance, that north-eastern details from the exploration of the Euxine have been added to events envisaged as belonging to the western seas. The Homeric poets undoubtedly carried out certain elaborations in this and other respects, and we should not be dealing with oral traditions if it were not so. But these accretions were added to a substantial nucleus that can claim to be far more ancient than the war at Troy. There are folktale elements, too, in the tale of Odysseus' return to Penelope and Ithaca: the theme of the faithful wife, or how to keep one's suitors guessing, or the husband in disguise. But in his more realistic actions, which vastly predominate, Odysseus is based on the conception of a real if provincial chieftain from north-western Greece. The association with the folktale adventures and a powerful vengeance-plot made him a mythical figure in his own right—one that developed into an object of sporadic cult, or a continuing symbol of deviousness in Sophocles' *Philoctetes* and the post-classical tradition, but one that is not in itself particularly ancient.

One of the most familiar figures of Greek myths is Orpheus, yet he is not even mentioned in Homer or Hesiod. The first surviving reference comes in a two-word fragment of the sixth-century B.C. lyric poet Ibycus: 'famous Orpheus'. Perhaps his omission from the poetry of the late eighth and seventh centuries is accidental, or due to his being a semi-barbarian, a Thracian from across the northern borders of Greece. When he enters literature it is mainly because of his wonderful power of drawing to him birds, beasts, fishes, even stones, by his singing and lyre-playing. Simonides, in the second surviving literary reference, of around 500 B.C., writes:

> Over his head fly innumerable birds, and the fishes leap straight up from the dark water at his fair song. (frag. 62 in D. L. Page's edition)

Aeschylus said something similar, as did Euripides, but in his lost play *The Bassarids* Aeschylus gave a quite different emphasis: that Orpheus resisted the worship of Dionysus and was torn to pieces by the god's female worshippers, the Bacchants. That he died at the hands of women, at least, is a common part of his legend. Roman poetry in particular liked recounting how his scattered limbs were thrown into the sea and his head floated to the island of Lemnos, where it was taken ashore and buried, and thereafter gave oracular responses. A curious connection, this, between the gentle singer and the victim of human prejudice and savagery, and one that seems less than startling only to those familiar with the tale of Jesus Christ.

Apart from the power of Orpheus' music, it is his love for Eurydice that is best known. Yet Eurydice is hardly mentioned in the whole of surviving Greek literature, and her story is told at length only by a Roman poet, Virgil, in his fourth *Georgic*. Admittedly it is indirectly alluded to by Euripides in *Alcestis,* produced in 438 B.C., for there the odious Admetus tells his wife, about to die on his behalf:

> If I had Orpheus' tongue and song, so that I could bring you back from Hades by charming Demeter's daughter [that is, Persephone] or her husband with my strains, I should have gone down there; and neither Pluto's dog [that is, Cerberus] nor Charon at his oar, the ferryman of souls, would keep me back, until I had set you living once more into the light of day. (*Alcestis,* 357 ff.)

The tale that becomes clear in subsequent sources is that Orpheus' wife, the nymph Eurydice, dies soon after her wedding as a result of a snake-bite, according to Virgil because Aristaeus, son of Apollo and Cyrene and protector of flocks and bees, had tried to assault her. Orpheus is heart-broken and makes his way down to the underworld, where by the power of his music he persuades King Hades and his consort Persephone to release her. One condition is set: that he shall go ahead of her, and shall not address or look back at her until they reach the world of the living. He almost succeeds, but at the last moment gives in either to love or to fear (because he can see no shadow beside him) and looks round. She departs for ever; he, inconsolable, moves towards his mortal fate at the hands of the women, who are incensed, according to late versions, either because he refuses to join their Bacchic revels, or because he spurns their love in mourning for Eurydice, or because he introduces the practice of homosexuality. We need not bother about these maundering speculations, so typical of the fervent yet arid imaginations of Hellenistic and Roman mythographers. What matters more is that the whole Eurydice tale made so little impression on Greeks of the classical age, and that Aristaeus is neither seen nor heard of in this paradoxical role (since he is usually the placid and benevolent bee-keeper and protector of flocks) until the time of Virgil. This element of the tale is unlikely to be older than the Hellenistic age.

In short, Orpheus is quite definitely a 'younger' hero in the terms I am using. The idea of a singer who could charm birds and animals might go back to the Mycenaean age; some have quixotically professed to see in a fresco from Pylos, depicting a bird *flying away from* a man with a lyre, a prototype of Orpheus himself.[2] But the silence of Homer, Hesiod and the entire epic tradition is suspicious. Other aspects of Orpheus, which do not fit well with this peaceable conception, could be Dionysiac—but then Dionysus himself came comparatively late on the scene. Eurydice appeals to the romantic imagination, but made only a passing impression on classical Greeks. A completely different kind of evidence is provided by the 'Orphics', a mystical sect that as early as the sixth century B.C. propounded a form of immortality under the auspices of

the sweet singer, who was already being classed with Homer and Hesiod as the source of anonymous (and usually bad) epic verses.[3] That, once again, takes us back a little way in time; but the central fact remains that the Thracian Orpheus, with his barbarically-named father Oeagrus, has no connection with the regular framework of Greek myths, heroic or divine, at least until the time when he was signed on among the crew of the Argo. His quasi-magical powers, his extreme devotion to his wife and his pathetic ill-fortune make him, for us, a powerful and evocative symbol. The Romans felt the same, but the Greeks seem to have been less impressed.

The last category of heroic myths, *the later inventions,* is a subsidiary one, but is revealing for the way in which a myth-making tradition can persist in fully literate surroundings. Herodotus has already been cited in this respect in Chapter 5 [of *The Nature of Greek Myths*], and I now offer two further examples of how a historical personage could be turned into a mythical hero. The first of them is the great Croesus of Lydia, the second the boxer Cleomedes from the insignificant Aegean island of Astypalaea.

Croesus was the last king of the Lydian empire, in Asia Minor, that collapsed with the capture of Sardis by Cyrus of Persia in 546 B.C. He made a powerful impression on the Greeks, for after seizing their cities on the Aegean coast he had behaved quite mildly and even made rich offerings at Apollo's shrine in Delphi. Pindar refers to his 'kindly excellence', and the story of his miraculous escape from death was well known, not only to Herodotus and Ctesias but also to the poet Bacchylides:

> . . . when Sardis was captured by the army of the Persians, Apollo of the golden sword protected Croesus, who encountered a day he never expected, and, refusing to wait for tearful slavery, built a pyre in front of his palace with its brazen walls. He mounted it together with his virtuous wife and his daughters with their beautiful hair, who wept most miserably; lifting his hands to steep heaven he cried out: 'Almighty god, where is the divine favour? Where the lord that is son of Leto? The house of Alyattes goes down in ruin . . . Pactolus with its golden eddies is reddened with blood, the women are shamefully taken from their well-built halls. What was hateful before, now becomes desirable: the sweetest thing is to die!' So saying he bade a soft-stepping servant kindle his wooden abode. The girls shrieked and cast their dear arms round their mother, for the death one can see coming is the most hateful for mortals; but when the terrible fire's bright strength darted through, Zeus set overhead a black cloud and quenched the orange flame. Nothing that the care of the gods creates is beyond belief, for then Apollo, Delos-born, carried the old man with his slim-ankled daughters to the Hyperboreans, and set them to dwell there on account of Croesus'

piety, because he had sent to holy Pytho the greatest gifts of all men. (3, 25 ff.)

Bacchylides wrote this in 468 B.C., only two or three generations after the event he celebrates. One might think it a mere poetical exaggeration, the assignment of a mythical fate and a typical folktale reversal as a light-hearted compliment; but Herodotus, too, tells the tale, which was taken quite seriously by many Greeks of the classical age (although Croesus may, in fact, have been killed by Cyrus). There was disagreement about whether he mounted the pyre of his own will, as Bacchylides asserts, or under compulsion from Cyrus. Herodotus also differs in saying that Cyrus decided to spare him and then, when he could not extinguish the pyre, Apollo intervened; and there were of course rationalists like Xenophon who simply made Cyrus pardon Croesus at the last moment and without divine intervention. It is the idea of Croesus going to the land of the Hyperboreans . . . that is most remarkable in all this. He was accorded no cult by the Greeks—that would have been going too far for a barbarian monarch, however generous—but in other respects seems to have attained a status not far removed from that of a Theseus, an Oedipus or a Menelaus.

From the remote but famous monarch to a more specific and humbler character. The boxing finals at Olympia in 492 B.C. ended with Cleomedes killing his opponent and being deprived of the prize. This is how Pausanias, our only source, continues the story:

> . . . he went out of his mind through grief and returned to Astypalaea. There he attacked a school of about sixty children and overturned the column that held up the roof. The roof fell on the children; he was stoned by the townsfolk and took refuge in Athena's sanctuary, climbed into a chest that lay there and pulled down the lid. The Astypalaeans toiled in vain in their efforts to open the chest; in the end they broke open its planks but found no Cleomedes there, either living or dead, so they sent men to Delphi to ask what had happened to him. This, they say, was the Pythian priestess's oracular reply: 'Cleomedes of Astypalaea is the last of the heroes; honour him with sacrifices, since he is no longer mortal.' So from that time on the Astypalaeans paid honours to him as a hero. (6. 9, 6 ff.)

Admittedly Pausanias is writing some six hundred years later, which is testimony to the myth's persistence if not to its total accuracy. Credulous villagers will believe almost anything, especially a strange event like an apparently inexplicable disappearance. What is especially interesting is that Cleomedes shares some of the characteristics of Heracles himself—his madness, his brute strength and his disappearance from a lethal situation. It is curious, too, that another boxer, who won at Olympia only twelve years later, likewise

achieved heroic status. He was Euthymus from Locri, a Greek colony in southern Italy, and he rescued and married one of the maidens offered each year to an unpleasant ghost called simply 'the Hero'.[4] Euthymus escaped death, departing 'in some other way', and came to be regarded as the son not of a mortal father but of the local river. He had no cult, but these other typically heroic appurtenances emphasize his Perseus-like performance. And yet he was a real man in origin, a well-known competitor at Olympia who like Cleomedes became involved in an argument over an umpire's decision there.

These later inventions are important not so much because their heroes are strongly imaginative in conception, but because they show how history can be made mythical at almost any stage. They suggest, too, that the tendency to raise certain humans to the status of demi-gods became something of a habit with the Greeks, despite their obsession with the distinction between mortal and immortal. That tells us a little about the formation of the other heroes, too. . . .

Notes

[1] Pausanias 3: 18, 6 to 19, 5 (Amyclae); 5: 17, 5 to 19, 10 (Cypselus)

[2] T. B. L. Webster, *from Mycenae to Homer,* 1958, p. 47 and fig. 9; cf. Mabel Lang, *The Palace of Nestor* II, Princeton, 1969, pl. 126.

[3] I. M. Linforth, *The Arts of Orpheus,* Berkeley, 1941, 167 ff.

[4] Pausanias 6: 6, 4 ff.

Deborah Lyons (essay date 1997)

SOURCE: *Gender and Immortality: Heroines in Ancient Greek Myth and Cult,* Princeton University Press, 1997, 269 p.

[*In the following essay, Lyons argues that archaic texts, including the works of Homer and Hesiod, include a feminine form of the idea of the "hero." Lyons reviews the traditional criteria used to identify heroes in texts, applies the same criteria to heroines, and identifies several heroines that satisfy those qualifications.*]

> "Hero" has no feminine gender in the age of heroes.
>
>   —M. I. Finley

What, If Anything, Is a Heroine?

The daunting judgment of a distinguished ancient historian that "'hero' has no feminine gender in the age of heroes" might appear to call into question the very phenomenon I propose to study here: heroines in ancient Greek myth and cult.[1] If there is no word for the female counterpart to the hero in the earliest times, how can we speak of the myths and cults of heroines without being anachronistic? How can we speak coherently of heroines at all?

Based on his observation that no word for *heroine* is attested in archaic Greek, Finley concludes that there is no female counterpart to the hero, that heroism, for the Greeks of the archaic period, is impossible for a woman. He makes this observation within the context of Homeric epic, where it is perhaps true. We must not allow this to deter us, however, given that the object of our study is not only *heroism* but rather the entire range of cultural meanings and practices associated with the *myths and cults of heroines*. I will argue, furthermore, that the "feminine gender" of *hero* is recoverable, if not in Homer, then in other archaic texts.

Homeric epic is famous for its silence on the topic of hero cult, but even so it can be made to yield some evidence. The opinion of earlier scholars such as Wilamowitz, Rohde, and Farnell, that hero cult was unknown to Homer or irreconcilable with the worldview of the poems, has been effectively challenged.[2] The most explicit references to cult are in the *Catalogue of Ships* in the *Iliad,* which mentions the tomb of Aipytos (2.604) and offerings to Erechtheus in the temple of Athena (2.546-51), but hints of cult may be found in other passages.[3] Nagy finds traces of hero cult in the treatment of the dead warrior Sarpedon in *Iliad* 16, suggesting that the tradition preserves knowledge even of practices that cannot be made explicit.[4] It has recently been argued that Homeric epic was directly responsible for the diffusion of hero cult, but this claim has not been universally accepted.[5] The generic requirements of epic limit its usefulness for an archaeology of hero cult, but it has a few things to tell us, not only about heroes, but about heroines as well. Other archaic texts are fortunately more forthcoming, and archaeological evidence shows that heroines are included in some of the earliest manifestations of hero cult.[6] The shrines of Pelops and Hippodameia at Olympia may be of great antiquity, early hero-reliefs show hero and heroine pairs, and a dedication to Helen is perhaps the earliest known Laconian inscription, dating from the second quarter of the seventh century.[7]

The difficulties posed by these kinds of early evidence must be confronted, insofar as they call into question the category of heroine as the female equivalent of hero. In the absence of a word for *heroine* in the earliest texts, we are forced to extrapolate, looking on the one hand toward figures, such as the famous women (called "wives and daughters of the best men") whom Odysseus meets in the Underworld in *Odyssey* 11, and on the other hand to some of the more powerful female figures of myth, who in fact share many characteristics with male heroes. But "wives and daughters of the best men" may seem to be less than heroes, while figures like Ino-Leukothea, or Helen, for whom we have some of the earliest evidence, are at times worshipped as goddesses (*theoi*) and hence seem to be more than heroines.[8] The category of heroine as female counterpart to the hero, poised neatly between mortal and immortal beings, seems threatened.

Despite Homeric reluctance to speak of hero cult, there are clear epic references to heroes who transcend their heroic status. The *Odyssey* refers to one of the most famous of all heroes, Herakles, in a way that emphasizes not his status as a heroized mortal, but his apotheosis.[9] . . .

> And after him I saw the powerful Herakles,
> or rather, his phantom; he himself among the
>   immortal gods
> enjoys the feast, and has as his wife lovely-
>   ankled Hebe,
> child of great Zeus and golden-sandled Hera.
>   (*Odyssey* 11.601-4)

Strikingly similar treatment is accorded Leukothea, the divine apotheosis of the heroine Ino: . . .

> But then Kadmos' daughter, slender-ankled
>   Ino, saw him—
> Luekothea, who once was a mortal endowed
>   with human speech
> but now deep in the sea, has a share of honor
>   among the gods.
>   (*Odyssey* 5.333-35)

Although the reference to Herakles' phantom has been treated by some as an interpolation, no one has ever challenged the authenticity of the lines about Ino. We can conclude from this that Homeric epic (or at least the *Odyssey*) has no objection to speaking of heroes— once they have become gods, admittedly a rather exclusive company. The other conclusion to be drawn is that the poet of the *Odyssey* is at least as willing to speak of divinized *heroines,* and to speak of them in a way that leaves no doubt about their originally human status. By the same token, the cults of heroines are not likely to have been any more foreign to the Homeric tradition than the cults of heroes.

The phrase "wives and daughters of the best men (*aristoi*)," which introduces the catalogue of heroines in the *Nekyia* (Underworld) section of the *Odyssey* (11.227), provides another clue. The women, who include Alkmene, wife of Amphitryon (266), and Ariadne, daughter of Minos (321-2), are identified by their male relatives, not only husbands and fathers, but also sons (e.g., Herakles 267-68). What is more, all of these male relations—fathers, husbands, sons—are heroes of myth and cult. As Nagy has shown, being "the best" is not merely a characteristic of heroes, but their defining feature. The heroes are the *aristoi,* the best, and *aristos* is the functional equivalent of *hērōs.*[10] To see the relevance of this to our elusive heroines, we may now turn to that other more extensive, although fragmentary, catalogue of female mythic figures, the Hesiodic *Catalogue of Heroines.* . . .

> Now sing about the race of women, sweet-
>   voiced
> Olympian Muses, daughters of aegis-bearing
>   Zeus,
> sing of those who were the best of their time
> who loosened their girdles,
> mingling in union with the gods
>   (frg. 1 Merkelbach-West)[11]

The poet begins by asking the muses to sing of the *gunaikōn phulon,* the "tribe of women." In the fragmentary lines that follow, these *gunaikes* are described as "the best of their time" (*hai tot' aristai*) who "had intercourse with the gods" (*misgomenai theosin*). In other words, they are not ordinary women, but the same wives and daughters (and mothers) of heroes encountered by Odysseus in the *Nekyia,* along with others of similar mettle.[12] The poet of the *Catalogue,* however, in referring to them as *aristai,* has given these figures an appellation that clarifies their heroic status. The word *aristai* shows that they are the counterparts of the heroic *aristoi* of the Homeric poems. A more complete examination of the linguistic field shows that Finley did not look far enough. Here, then, is the "feminine gender" of hero in the age of heroes.

The troublesome indeterminacy found in the earliest texts gives way by the early fifth century. By the time of Pindar at the latest, *heroine* is clearly a recognizable category. Pindar's use of the word *hērōis* . . . , in an ode written for Thrasydaios of Thebes, is generally taken to be the earliest extant example of a female equivalent of *hērōs.* . . . Thrasydaios, according to the scholia, won two victories, one in the boy's foot-race of 474, and one twenty years later. Most commentators assign this ode to the earlier victory. The word *hērōis* . . . is unlikely to be a Pindaric invention, especially as it appears in an invocation, generally a conservative element in Greek poetry. A fragment of the Boiotian poet Corinna (*PMG* 664b = Campbell 664b) proclaims her subject as the "merits (or valor) of heroes and heroines." . . . [13] If she was indeed a contemporary of Pindar, as the ancient tradition has it, this is further evidence for the diffusion of a female form of *hērōs* (at least in Boiotia) by the first quarter of the fifth century.[14] Indeed, the fragment from Corinna may be even older than the Pindaric ode, even if we do not accept the later date for the victory of Thrasydaios which it celebrates.

We may also approach the problem of the heroine by examining the criteria for establishing the status of male heroes. For a male hero, in the absence of archaeological evidence such as a named dedicatory inscription, we rely on textual evidence for myth or cult. Heroes are generally considered to be those who have one or more of the following attributes: heroic or divine parentage; a close relationship—erotic, hieratic, or antagonistic—with a divinity in myth; ritual connection with a divinity, such as a place in the sanctuary or a role in the cult; a tradition or evidence of a *hērōon* (hero-shrine) or tomb, sacrificial offerings, or other ritual observance. If we consider those figures generally numbered among male heroes, we will find these criteria to cover most instances. The next step is to see whether we can apply the same criteria to heroines.

As a test, let us consider some figures for whom we have the kind of archaeological evidence we spoke of above, and see whether the other criteria apply. Both Herakles and Helen have divine parentage, and both have ample evidence of cult.[15] Hyakinthos and Semele are united erotically in myth with divinities, and in each case there is the requisite cult evidence.[16] These two figures could fit equally well into our third category, that of ritual connection with a god, but we can supply other examples, such as Hippolytos and Iphigeneia.[17] This demonstrates the degree to which the various features of heroic myth and cult coincide, regardless of the gender of the heroized figure. Other heroes and heroines languish in comparative obscurity, and in these instances we do not have the evidence on which to base firm conclusions. We can, nonetheless, learn something about heroines by extrapolating even in circumstances in which we have less than complete documentation.

If "heroine" is clearly a recognized category by the early fifth century, it is also true that the category "hero" is an extremely expansive and inclusive one, which changes through time. The term *hērōs,* ostensibly more stable and tangible by virtue of its impeccable Homeric lineage, proves scarcely easier to define than its linguistically more elusive female counterpart. To put our problem in perspective, let us examine attempts by several scholars, all of whom have made considerable contributions to the field, to define *hero.* For Brelich, the hero is "a being venerated in cult and remembered in the myths of the ancient Greeks."[18] That he felt it necessary to defend this definition, stressing the essentially religious character of myth, was a reaction to prevailing tendencies in the study of Greek religion at the time. Kirk offers a more hesitant definition: heroes are "men who had a god or goddess as one parent or who at least walked the earth when such figures existed."[19] With time, the balance has shifted. Unlike Brelich, who is concerned to restore myth to its rightful place in the study of religion,

Kirk, writing more than a decade later, takes the importance of myth for granted but is somewhat apologetic about cult, and about the fact that many of the heroes have only the most tangential relation to it.[20] Burkert recognizes two separate senses of "hero," the first being a character in epic, and the second, "a deceased person who exerts from his grave a power for good or evil and who demands appropriate honour."[21] This two-part definition corresponds to the two parts of Brelich's formulation, but the substitution of "epic" for the broader category of "myth" is surprising, given the importance of myth in Burkert's own work.

If heroines, while retaining the right to be called by that name, deviate in various ways from standards of male heroism, it is also true that heroes themselves frequently do so. If female heroized figures frequently slip across the border into divinity, male heroes occasionally do so as well. In other words, although the mass of heroines act or react in ways that deviate from the male heroic norm, nothing they do—allowing for biological difference—is outside the range of possible behavior for heroes.

In what follows, I adopt a flexible definition of "heroine," which corresponds to Brelich's two-tiered definition of "hero." While I insist on the integrity of the category of *hero/ine* as a distinct religious and mythic phenomenon, I do not consider it to be a privileged one, and in this I follow the usage of the ancient Greeks themselves. While for the purposes of my study, I will admit to finding those heroines who figure in both cult and myth the most interesting, we do not always know who they are. For this reason, the operating definition must be the more inclusive one of "female figure in epic, myth, or cult." As we saw in attempting to bring the heroes of Homer into relation with the practice of hero cult, there is some overlap, and there would likely be more if both archaeological data and literary sources were more complete. Since there is no way of knowing what we are missing, it seems unwise to exclude anything that might allow patterns to emerge. To prevent this inclusivity from becoming imprecision, I will indicate the limits of available evidence for each heroine, signaling those places where conjecture has been allowed to exceed it.

. . . . .

Ancient Sources for Heroines

Where does one go to look for evidence of heroines? The sources consist of material remains—inscriptions, vase paintings, archaeological finds—as well as a great variety of literary sources. These writings range in date from the late eighth or early seventh century B.C.E. to the sixth century C.E. and include the disparate genres of epic, tragedy, guidebook, and lexicon. Not only is our evidence varied in kind, but it also concerns two partly separate matters: the stories told about heroines and heroes, and the cult practices enacted in their honor. The definition of myth and its relation to cult are difficult problems of long standing, which this study does not pretend to solve. In the material at hand, which deals with both myth and cult, the two will frequently be seen to be inextricably entwined. Nonetheless, there is a distinction to be made.

One way of expressing this distinction would be to borrow the terms applied by Jane Harrison to the Eleusinian mysteries, *legomena,* "things said," and *drōmena,* "things done."[34] Inscriptions tell us something about the *drōmena,* as do archaeological sites, when we know how to read them. Our written sources generally concentrate on the *legomena,* the stories told about gods and heroic figures, which constitute the corpus of Greek myth. It is important to keep in mind, however, that much of what we know about ancient Greek cults and cultic practice comes from written texts, and that in these texts the distinction between myth and cult is frequently pushed to its limits. Here, in the grey area between myths of heroic exploits and descriptions of contemporary cultic practice, we find foundation myths attributing the establishment of these very cults to the heroes and heroines themselves. Thus we have not only myth that may or may not be the reflex of cultic practice, but also myth *about* that cultic practice, which strives to place it within the heroic context. In this way the hero acts as a pivotal figure, at times being heroized as a direct result of a role in the founding of a divine cult (as was the tragedian Sophocles).[35]

Sources for the myths of heroines range over many centuries, creating considerable difficulties of interpretation. Most important for this study are Homeric epic and the Homeric Hymns; the Hesiodic corpus, especially the *Theogony* and the *Catalogue of Women;* lyric poetry, especially Stesichorus and Pindar; tragedy, especially Euripides; Plutarch; Pausanias; Apollodorus; and Antoninus Liberalis. Ancient commentaries known as scholia provide much useful information. Some valuable citations come also from Byzantine and Alexandrian reference works from the fifth to the twelfth centuries C.E.[36] The earliest of these texts, by virtue of their antiquity, may be presumed to provide us with early versions, but the converse is not necessarily true, that later texts must give us only late versions.[37] Pindar, for example, frequently uses unfamiliar versions of myths, but these apparent innovations often turn out on further investigation to be earlier traditions he has chosen to revive.[38] Euripides, a known innovator, may play fast and loose with the plot but usually seems to conform to contemporary practices when he places an aetiology in the mouth of the deus ex machina at the end of so many of his plays.[39] A source like Pausanias reports both on the monuments he sees and on the local traditions and cult practices surrounding them, both the *legomena* and the *drōmena.* That he is in fact a reliable witness about what he has seen has by now been well established.[40] From this, and from the care he takes to detail his own and other peoples' disagreement with these traditions, we can assume that he is equally reliable about what he has heard.

As the ancient myths and cults become more a focus of antiquarian interest than of piety, authorial emphases change. Later sources are less likely to manipulate the material for political or moral propaganda, although there are some exceptions. (Plutarch is as much a moralist as Pindar.) On the other hand they are more likely to shape it to suit the generic requirements of the project at hand. For example, a compiler of *katasterismoi* will obviously prefer versions of myths in which the heroine is transformed into a star, even when there may be other traditions of greater antiquity. Such a writer may have rewritten myths to fit his requirements, on the analogy of others he knows, but even this does not render a source useless.[41] The late Byzantine commentators and lexicographers are closer in years to our own time than to Homer, but they have nonetheless the benefit of a continuous tradition. Moreover, the genres of commentary and lexicon are inherently conservative, designed as they are to elucidate ancient data. Used with care, they can be illuminating.

The following discussions of specific sources and genres are intended both to provide a brief introduction to some texts that may not be familiar to all readers, and also to indicate my assumptions about the usefulness of these texts for the study of heroines. It includes some works used primarily as sources for the catalogue of heroines at the conclusion of this work.

Catalogue Poetry

The largest archaic source for heroines is certainly the Hesiodic *Catalogue of Women,* also known as the *Ehoiai,* from the repeated phrase . . . "such a one [was] . . ." which introduces many of the heroines.[42] This long (albeit fragmentary) genealogical poem, although in a class by itself, may be compared to other shorter pieces of catalogue poetry in the Homeric corpus, which are also fruitful sources.[43] One of these is the catalogue of gods who mate with mortals at the end of the *Theogony,* long recognized as a bridge to the *Ehoiai.*[44] The possibly interpolated, but certainly archaic, catalogue of heroines in the *Nekyia* (Underworld) episode of the *Odyssey* (11.225-332) is also of great interest, together with the scholia containing commentary by the fifth-century mythographer Pherecydes.[45] In this passage Persephone sends forth the "wives and daughters of the best men" (. . . 227) to meet Odysseus. These women are not explicitly called heroines, but neither are their male connections called heroes. Moreover, the use of the key term *aristoi* has its counterpart

in the use of *aristai* (frg. 1 M-W), as discussed above. Most of their stories involve an encounter with a god, and the inevitable birth of a child. In a short space, Odysseus sees fourteen or fifteen women.[46] The passage reflects obvious delight in the stories for their own sake, as one might expect, considering that the narrator is none other than Odysseus himself.

Other comparable passages show a more purely genealogical interest, such as the brief catalogue of Zeus' erotic adventures in *Iliad* 14, or the *Catalogue of Ships* in *Iliad* 2, with its interest in dynastic information.[47] In this passage the spheres of men and women in the heroic age achieve their greatest point of contact. The role of women is to produce the sons who will be warriors. The woman's moment of crisis in childbirth is the logical precondition of the hero's moment of crisis on the battlefield. Later in the poem, the pain of a wound suffered by Agamemnon is compared to the pain of childbirth.[48] In these texts sons and fathers are important, while heroines are treated quite summarily. Nonetheless, the archaic catalogues are helpful in trying to reconstruct the "prehistory" of the heroine.

From these early examples, it is clear that women have a place in heroic poetry as far back as that tradition is accessible to us. These wives and daughters of heroes are important for dynastic reasons, since they provide access to the divine lineage desired by any noble family. Here "biographies" of heroines are stripped to their essentials. In the few lines allotted each woman are the kernels of the more developed myths of seduction, concealment, and disaster that will be represented on vases, staged by tragedians, and eventually collected by the writers of mythological handbooks.

Drama

A look at the titles not only of extant tragedies, but also of lost ones shows how important a role was played by the myths of heroines. Figures like Iphigeneia, Medea, Elektra, Helen, and others are the eponymous protagonists of familiar tragedies. Among the lost works of the tragedians are numerous plays bearing the names of heroines.[49] Heroines also play an important role in plays named for the chorus or a male protagonist (*e.g.,* Deianeira in Sophocles' *Trachiniai,* Phaidra in Euripides' *Hippolytos*). Sometimes doubt about the actual name of a lost play makes it unclear whether it was named after a female protagonist, a male protagonist, or the chorus: Aeschylus' *Semele* is also referred to as the *Hydrophoroi,* and Sophocles' *Hippodameia* may actually have been called the *Oinomaos.*[50] These uncertainties point nonetheless to the importance of heroines in almost all tragedies, regardless of title. In fact, only one extant tragedy, the *Philoktetes* of Sophocles, has no female characters, and in many tragedies they are central.

While a general treatment of female characters in the Greek tragedians lies beyond the scope of this study, the female protagonists of tragedy are of interest to us insofar as they are representations of figures of myth and cult. That Greek tragedy deals almost exclusively with the myths of a few important heroic houses is well known. For our purposes, then, these works are valuable as instantiations of the myths. No myth exists in "pure form," but only in its versions—individual attempts to present, and of necessity to interpret, the themes at hand. The more innovative the poet, the farther away we may find ourselves from early mythic material. Poetic license in the plots of tragedy is not uncommon. Familiar examples are the Sophoclean *Antigone,* radically different from any earlier version, or Euripides' *Medea,* for the first time a deliberate murderer of her children.[51] Neither of these mythic innovations can, however, be assigned with complete confidence to the particular tragedian, who may not have been the first to present the myth in this form. Tragic poets may also, like Pindar, choose at times to exploit an old but less-known variant of the myth in question. Still, tragedians are rarely the sources of first resort for early versions. This is not, however, to dismiss the tragic texts as of no interest for this study. One feature of tragedy that is invaluable for the study of heroine cult, and of Greek religious practice in general, is the frequent use of an *aition,* a brief narrative establishing some religious rite or custom, to achieve closure. These *aitia* are usually put in the mouth of the deus ex machina, whose function it is to resolve the tragic conflict, to predict the future, and to establish cult.[52]

As I have said above, even for a poet like Euripides, whose use of the mythic inheritance is often inventive, the treatment of cultic practice is quite another matter. These cults are in some sense the common property of all Athenians (or all Greeks, where Panhellenic cult is concerned), and a fair degree of accuracy would be demanded by the audience.[53] Although Euripides uses the device of deus ex machina and cult aetiology more consistently than any other tragic poet, he is not the only one to do so.[54] The ending of Aeschylys' *Eumenides* provides the earliest extant example of cult aetiology in tragedy, and Sophocles uses the same technique at the end of the *Oidipous at Kolonos,* to predict the establishment of the hero cult there. The *aition* most important for us is the one at the end of the *Iphigeneia among the Taurians,* which specifies dedications to Iphigeneia at Brauron. Other *aitia* of particular significance are those that close the *Helen,* concerning the burial of Klytemnestra and the divinity of Helen.

While other dramatic forms also drew on the myths of heroines, too little has survived for these to be valuable sources here. The satyr-play at the end of a trilogy often burlesqued the same myths used in the tragedies that preceded it. Aeschylus' lost *Amymone,* for example, was a satyr-play. Comedy as well made use of this material, although often as a parody of a particular tragedy. Aristophanes wrote a play called the *Danaids,* while another practitioner of Old Comedy, Plato, wrote the *Europe, Io,* and *Nux Makra* ("The Long Night," a play about Zeus' encounter with Alkmene). We also have suggestive titles by other dramatists, but the use of mythological themes is more a characteristic feature of Middle Comedy, which exists only in fragments.[55] Philemon, a writer of New Comedy, seems to have continued the use of mythological themes with his *Neaira* and *Nux,* but the practice was on the wane. For visual evidence of this tradition, we can point to a comic scene of the birth of Helen on a fourth-century South Italian vase . . .[56]

Pausanias

The second century C.E. travel writer, and a major source of information for ancient cult-sites and religious customs, has a great deal to say about heroines and their role in religious tradition and practice. I have already commented on his reliability, but since he is so frequently cited throughout this study, it is worth saying more about the nature of his contribution. In writing his *Description of Greece,* he is mainly interested in recording monuments and other sites of interest, and the local traditions about them. (He is only interested in Greek antiquities and does not even record contemporary Roman monuments.) As he travels around, he picks up not only many local versions of myths about known figures, but also traditions about local ritual observances. These traditions typically connect a familiar myth to some feature of the local landscape or history. In his chapter on Messenia, for example, Pausanias describes "a place on the coast regarded as sacred to Ino. For they say that she came up from the sea at this point" (4.34.4).[57] The pattern is to "bring the myth home" in some way, and then to use this point of contact as the aetiology for a local monument or observance.

Pausanias faithfully records local claims to the grave of a particular heroine along with the inhabitants' testimony about how she came to be buried there. At times he dissents from the local tradition, usually because he finds an opposing local tradition more plausible:

> [The Megarians] say that there is also a hero-shrine of Iphigeneia; for she too according to them died in Megara. Now I have heard another account of Iphigeneia that is given by the Arcadians, and I know that Hesiod, in his poem *A Catalogue of Women,* says that Iphigeneia did not die, but by the will of Artemis is Hecate . . . [58] (1.43.1)

The insistence on finding the correct location befits a guidebook, but it also emphasizes a central feature of hero cult, its necessarily local, place-bound quality. The efficacy of the heroine or hero as helper emanates directly from the physical remains. The most explicit example in Pausanias concerns the dispute about where to bury the bones of Alkmene (1.41.1), which brings to mind Herodotus' accounts of struggles over the bones of the heroes Orestes (1.67-8), or Adrastos and Melanippos (5.67).[59]

As in the passage cited above, Pausanias often bases his judgments about the authenticity of local tradition on something he has read. The works he cites most in this connection are Hesiod, Homer, Pindar, Stesichorus, and other lyric poets. He also makes extensive use of otherwise unknown local writers, both poets and historians. Thanks to his reading habits, Pausanias is a major source for modern reconstructions of both the *Catalogue of Women* (*Ehoiai*) and the Great Catalogue (*Megalai Ehoiai*) attributed to Hesiod.[60]

Pausanias frequently speaks of the tombs of mythic women, but only occasionally mentions cult observances connected with them, and it is hard to say if they are in fact hero-shrines (*hērōa*). Pausanias uses the word only occasionally, in most cases preferring the word *mnēma,* or "memorial," with its overtone of commemoration.[61] He frequently uses the word *taphos* (tomb or burial) interchangeably with *mnēma,* to avoid repetition, which he is at greater pains to do than classical Greek authors. He also uses these two terms in alternation (presumably to preclude the idea of a joint burial), when he describes the graves of those who, hostile to each other in life, are nonetheless buried in close proximity.[62] In fact, we know very little about the form of hero-shrines, and particularly about heroines' shrines. A recent work on three temples to Artemis in Attica argues against the notion of an architectural feature common to all, an inner room that has been called the *adyton,* with a common function in honor of the heroine Iphigeneia. Even in this case, in which there is some archaeological evidence, interpretation is difficult.[63]

In Pausanias, mention of heroines is not limited to burial but may include dedications and offerings to them, or the dedications or festivals they themselves established in honor of the gods. Occasionally, the object Pausanias discusses is not only a monument but itself a carrier of mythic information. There are two works of art of particular relevance for heroines, each of which he describes at length. These are the "Kypselos chest" in the temple of Hera at Olympia (5.17.5-5.19.10), and Polygnotos' paintings of the *Ilioupersis* (Sack of Troy) and the *Nekyia* (Odysseus' visit to the Underworld) at Delphi (10.25-31), great pictorial summaries of myths of gods and heroes which we know only from his descriptions. Several mythic scenes are also shown on the throne at Amyklai (3.18.9-16). Pausanias only rarely uses works of visual art to support his arguments, tending rather to see them as objects requiring interpretation, although he is at great pains to record the information they contain.[64]

Pausanias' descriptions are accompanied by a great deal of mythological commentary, which is almost always concretely bound to the physical context. His goal is to describe a landscape, and it is a landscape marked by the works of mortals. But it is also a landscape inhabited by gods and heroes, and most of the human monuments he describes are attempts at communication with the divine, part of the dialogue between mortal and immortal which is an essential feature of Greek religion. Given a general tendency to translate female mythic figures into natural phenomena (e.g., the Pleiades) or features of the landscape (e.g., Niobe), it is instructive to note that for Pausanias they are also firmly embedded in a physical space that is decidedly human in origin.[65]

Other Graeco-Roman Sources

Sources from the Hellenistic period and beyond fall in general into two main categories: works that are primarily antiquarian in character, like that of Pausanias, and those that deal exclusively with mythology. Among the antiquarian writings, the works of Plutarch, dating from the end of the first to the beginning of the second centuries C.E., are particularly important. Especially valuable for our purposes are the *Quaestiones Graecae* (Greek Questions), and some of the lives, particularly those of mythic figures, like the *Life of Theseus*. Innumerable valuable citations from ancient texts otherwise lost are preserved for us by Athenaeus, whose collection of table talk, the *Deipnosophistai* (Sophists at Dinner), dates to the end of the second century C.E.

Notable among the mythological works is the *Bibliothēkē* (Library), which bears the name of Apollodorus. Apparently compiled in the second century C.E., it is a compendium of familiar myths along with some unusual variations. The considerably more erratic and idiosyncratic *Fabulae* of Hyginus (2nd c. C.E.) provide intriguing variants, but one is often hard-pressed to know what to make of them. This work shows the Alexandrian influence in its organization into headings such as *Qui filios in epulis consumpserunt* (Those who ate their children for supper), and the unfortunately missing *Quae immortales cum mortalibus concubuerunt* (Goddesses who slept with mortals). The Hellenistic interest in collecting and codifying myth also led to the development of specialized genres, among which the two most useful for the study of heroines are the books of *Katasterismoi* and Metamorphoses. The former genre, accounts of catasterism, i.e., transformation into constellations, goes back at least as far as Eratosthenes (3rd c. B.C.E.), although the fragments that survive under his name are apparently not genuine. The Metamorphosis tradition can be traced at least as far as the second-century poet Nicander, although this part of his work does not survive. Ovid takes off from this tradition in his *Metamorphoses,* although his poem transcends the dry nature of the genre. More typical is the work of the same name by Antoninus Liberalis, a writer of the second or third century C.E. who frequently cites Boios or Nicander as his source.[66]

We have alluded above to the problems inherent in the use of these materials for our study. Works centered around metamorphosis or catasterism naturally tend to emphasize the most dramatic aspects of heroic mythology, those involving crises in the mortal sphere which can only be resolved by drastic divine intervention, usually resulting in the translation to another sphere. In such contexts the solution to the problem of mortality is translation into the animal or vegetable world, with species-continuity replacing the continuing life of the individual, or transformation into astronomical phenomena whose enduring nature is obvious.

These specific interests act to narrow the range of action available to a mythic figure. Female figures are especially prone to this kind of presentation, perhaps because of their limited sphere of action in the world outside of myth.[67] Orion becomes a constellation, but this is only a small part of his very rich mythic tradition. By contrast, many heroines, deprived of the ability to defend themselves, can hope for nothing better than a transformation as a way out of present difficulties. For those who would interpret mythic treatment of the heroine, such material is especially problematic. That heroines are frequently transformed in this manner is a point to which I will return.[68] On the other hand, once books of metamorphoses become popular, these transformations of heroines may take on a certain decorative nature that obscures the degree to which we are in the presence of authentic mythic material.

Categories of Hero and Heroine

For many scholars of Greek religion, the starting point for understanding hero cult is the proper categorization of heroes. There has been no more enthusiastic or influential proponent of this approach than Farnell. In *Greek Hero Cults and Ideas of Immortality,* he offers the following categories: 1) heroes and heroines of divine origin or hieratic type, with ritual legends or associated with vegetation ritual; 2) sacral heroes and heroines; 3) heroes of epic and saga; 4) cults of mythic ancestors, eponymous heroes, and mythic oecists [city-founders]; 5) functional and culture-heroes; 6) cults of real and historic persons.[69]

The list of categories, some based on origin and some on function, recalls Borges' Chinese Encyclopedia, in which the classifications "animals belonging to the Emperor" and "animals which from a distance resemble flies" are given equal weight, and the frame of refer-

ence constantly shifts.[70] It is nonetheless of great interest as an attempt to describe hero cult and a potential source of information about heroines, compiled by a scholar of profound learning. Unfortunately, the conclusions one can draw from Farnell's work are somewhat limited by the incompleteness of his data. Several of Farnell's categories overlap, and the arbitrary assignment of a figure to one group or another is often unsatisfying, while some heroines whom we would expect to find are excluded. In almost every category, heroes outnumber heroines by a significant margin, as might be expected. Only in the first group, "heroes and heroines of divine origin or hieratic type, etc.," is this trend reversed. Here female figures outnumber male, approximately two to one. Although this finding is suggestive, certain features of Farnell's organization seriously limit the value of his categories. Why, for example, is Helen placed among the "heroes of epic and saga" when she might equally well be considered a hero of divine origin? Why does Penelope appear neither among heroes of epic and saga, nor anywhere else? For that matter, why is Klytemnestra omitted? Hippodameia, here among the ancestors, eponymous heroes, and oecists, could also be placed among sacral heroines as founder of the *Heraia* (for it is in this category that Farnell has placed Physkoa, whom Pausanias mentions almost in the same breath). And where is Aithra, whose role in the cult of Athena Apatouria ought to give her a place? Many eponymous heroines mentioned by Pausanias are omitted from the list of ancestors, eponymous heroes, and oecists. The task of classification is a difficult one, and one can only regret that Farnell did not make explicit his principles of inclusion.

The problem lies partly in the necessity of integrating information that, leaving aside tremendous variations in antiquity and reliability, simply does not always answer the same questions. How are we to harmonize myth or saga recounting the adventures of heroes and heroines as living beings, with local tradition about the acts of these figures in religious contexts, as founders of cults and festivals, as well as the evidence of honors accorded these figures after their death? This information may take the form of aetiologies of the classical period, or of local traditions recounted by Graeco-Roman antiquarians, or it may come to us from the realia—inscriptions, temples, or other dedications. A heroine of epic like Helen may be the recipient of both heroic and divine cult honors, as we know from a combination of extant inscriptions and local traditions from different parts of the Greek world. Choosing an original version or meaning is futile, and it is therefore usually impossible to assign a single "value" to any heroic figure.

The least ambiguous of Farnell's categories is that of "real and historical persons." While the individual figures, for the most part, fall outside the scope of this study, some useful inferences can be drawn. This list contains 93 heroized individuals, of whom 13 are female. This ratio certainly corresponds to our expectations, given the restricted role of women in the Greek world. Accordingly, the heroines in this list are mainly Hellenistic queens and hetairai. The exception is the poet Sappho, who like other poets of the archaic and classical periods, received heroic honors.[71]

Pfister, writing a decade before Farnell, makes less of an attempt to categorize types of heroes. His interest is in the cult of relics of heroes (and its similarity to the cults of Christian saints), and so he concentrates on the nature of the remains, and their location. He does list graves of eponymous heroes, but it is interesting to note that none of the heroines in the list appears in Farnell's list of eponymous figures. His larger list of hero-shrines accompanied by a tomb includes figures from four of Farnell's six categories, as well as some, like Penelope, whom Farnell omits entirely. His most inclusive list of heroes' graves includes those of 80 heroines, of whom only 23 coincide with Farnell's 52 nonhistorical heroines.[72]

The approach of Brelich, instead of seeking to establish the "essential nature" of the hero, examines roles and functions, recognizing that they may be multiple and overlapping. He considers heroes in their relation to a number of mythic and religious themes, both as figures in myth or epic taking part in a variety of relationships—social, familial, and religious—and as the focal points for cults embodying many of the diverse aspects of Greek ritual practice. In considering the relation of a particular hero to healing, to choose one example, he discusses in turn the hero as a healer in myth, and the role of healing in the cult of that hero. His approach stresses both the importance of the distinction and the necessity of bringing together the two kinds of evidence.[73] This is an especially important point for the study of heroines, as will become clear if we look at two areas of heroic activity—invention and city-founding. The prestige of both these kinds of activities derives from the special honor accorded to those who did something for the first time.[74] So pervasive was the interest in "being the first," that it has been said that in Greek culture, "everything had to have an 'inventor.'"[75]

The range of action permitted heroines in myth is perhaps not as restricted as the actual scope of women's lives in the archaic and classic periods.[76] It is, however, more limited than that allowed male heroes. Let us start with the example of city-founding. Founders of cities, as we know, are often honored with burial in the agora and other observances. These honors, also given to mythic and historical ancestors and legislators, were the most notable exception to the general Greek prohibition against burial within the city, and one that lasted until the end of Greek antiquity.[77] The

sacral aspect of city-founding is reflected in myth and in religious practice.[78] It is also the case that glorious enterprises could be made more glorious by the imprimatur of a heroic name, in which case the foundation of a city becomes just another deed easily inserted into the hero's busy program. For these reasons it is difficult to decide if one becomes a hero by founding a city, or if one founds a city because one is a hero and that is what heroes do. When all we have is the name of an eponymous hero, of whom we have heard nothing before, it is tempting to assume that the hero has been trumped up for the occasion.[79]

This indeterminancy has particular consequences for our interpretation of eponymous heroines. Given the unlikelihood of a woman having led a colonial expedition, we do not expect to find many heroines as city-founders, nor do we. The inscription in honor of the "Founder Heroines" (*Hērōissai Ktistai,* mentioned above) is suggestive, but relatively late in date, and its use of the plural may also signal a symbolic collectivity rather than any specific historical figures. The degree of women's participation in Greek colonization is a matter of debate.[80] Pausanias has two examples of female oecists: Leprea, founder of Lepreus (5.5.5), and Antinoe, daughter of Kepheus (8.8.4), who in obedience to an oracle and guided by a snake, moves the city of Ptolis to a new site. Antinoe, by virtue of not being eponymous, may appear the more convincing of the two. Her foundation story, moreover, is carefully buttressed by sacral and mystical details that would make female participation more palatable. What is more, Pausanias' account suggests that she may have received heroic honors for her role, as he tells us that her tomb was to be found among other famous graves near the theater in Mantineia (8.9.5).

Pausanias provides other examples of eponymous heroines, particularly in Boiotia, where the cities are more often named for women than men (9.1.1), but he gives them no explicit role in foundation.[81] He also considers somewhat critically the tradition of an eponymous Mykene (2.16.3-4), citing both "Homer in the *Odyssey,*" i.e., the *Nekyia* in book 11, and the *Great Ehoiai* as sources, and rejects the idea of a male eponym Mykeneus son of Sparton, on the grounds that although the Laconians have a statue of Sparte, they would be very surprised to hear of a Sparton. Here we have a chance to see the material evaluated not by modern notions of plausibility, but by local, more or less ancient ones. From Pausanias' discussion we see that while female founders of cities, mythic or not, may have been rare, the idea of an eponymous heroine caused no trouble. Indeed, in instances such as this, a female eponym could be more credible than a male one, if the sources concurred.[82]

Perhaps our best evidence for the political and religious importance of an eponymous heroine comes again from Pausanias, in his account of the founding of Messene in 369 B.C.E. after the liberation of Messenia by Epaminondas. The importance of Messene the daughter of Triopas for the community called by her name is both religious and political. She, together with Polykaon, was supposed to have consecrated the precinct of Zeus on Mt. Ithome and for this reason was given heroic honors (4.3.9). While the role of cult-founder is a more frequent one for heroines than that of city-founder, Messene was also given at least a symbolic role in the refoundation of the Messenian polity.[83]

As Pausanias describes the ritual surrounding the foundation of the city, it is here that Messene assumes preeminence. When the Messenians summoned the heroes to return to their midst, Messene was first and foremost, and only the hero Aristomenes was summoned with greater enthusiasm (4.27.6). Pausanias also records among the sights of Messenia the temple of Messene and her image of gold and Parian marble (4.31.11).

Few if any heroine-inventors are recorded. I have found only three. According to a certain Agallis, a learned Corcyraean woman, Nausikaa invented ball-playing (Athenaeus 1.14d). This is a perfect example of Robertson's dictum: as the first to appear playing ball in Greek literature (*Odyssey* 6.100), she must be its inventor. The other examples are rather obscure. Boudeia is associated with the invention of the plough (schol. *Iliad* 16.572). She is also known as Bouzuge, a talking name (Ox-Yoke) apparently related to this invention (schol. AR. 1.185), but the exact nature of her contribution is unclear. The third example, Phemonoe, is doubly important as the first Pythia and the inventor of hexameter (Paus. 10.5.7). But as with city-founding, myths of invention may attract heroines even if only as passive participants. One such tradition links a heroine to the invention of writing. According to Skamon in his fourth-century book on inventions, the alphabet was named by its inventor, Aktaion king of Attica, in honor of his daughter Phoinike who died young.[84] In this instance, the letters gain prestige from the name of the princess, while in turn giving honor to her.

In our investigation of the nature of heroes and heroines, two questions alternately claim our attention: "What do heroes do?" and "What does one do to become a hero?" The relationship between these two questions is complicated by the fact that we are dealing with a phenomenon that is already old at the time of our first sources, and that continues to be vigorous into the late Hellenistic period. This means not only that the old traditions about heroes are being maintained, and that observance continues, but that new heroes are still being made throughout the period in which many of our sources were written. It is difficult

to say exactly when hero cult ceased in antiquity, especially since it can be seen to reappear in the form of emperor cult in certain parts of the Greek east.[85] There are those who would even see its survival in the Christian cult of saints.[86]

It seems likely that the Greeks were generally comfortable with a flexible notion of what heroes were and did, and that this notion allowed a certain amount of revision and reevaluation backward and forward in time. The earliest and most venerable source of information about heroes was the *Iliad,* perhaps supplemented by other epics and especially the Hesiodic Catalogues, and it was easy to extrapolate the behavior of later heroes on the basis of these poems. If the Greeks knew their city-founders as the inhabitants of heroic tombs in the agora, then obviously founding cities was something heroes did. Some of this flexibility comes from the fact that, although in the historical period people could only be heroized after their death, the earliest traditions about heroes concerned people who were very much alive.

The prestige offered by a heroic ancestor or antecedent is clear, but when an invention or other "first" is ascribed to a hero the prestige is in some sense reciprocal, as with the *Phoinikeia grammata.* The same holds true for the establishment of a religious institution: on the one hand, the heroine is magnified by her role in founding a festival or dedicating a temple, and on the other, so important an undertaking as temple-foundation must, of necessity, have been carried out by an important personage. There is little to be gained by trying to establish the order of these events, but taken together they give us a very clear idea of what the Greeks expected of their heroes once they had made them.

Notes

[1] M. I. Finley, *The World of Odysseus,* 2d rev. ed. (New York, 1978) 33. The title of this section calls for apologies to Stephen Jay Gould, "What, If Anything, Is a Zebra?" in *Hen's Teeth and Horses' Toes* (New York, 1983) 355-65.

[2] Ulrich v. Wilamowitz, *Homerische Untersuchungen* (Berlin, 1884); Erwin Rohde, *Psyche* (London, 1950 [Freiburg, 1898]); L. R. Farnell, *Greek Hero Cults and Ideas of Immortality* (Oxford, 1921). An early attack on these views can be found in R. K. Hack, "Homer and the Cult of Heroes," *TAPA* 60 (1929) 57-74.

[3] Erechtheus is also mentioned in *Odyssey* 7.80-81, where Athena is said to enter his *pukinon domon* (well-built house). The relationship with the goddess is clear, but the passage does not explicitly refer to cult honors.

[4] G. Nagy, *The Best of the Achaeans* (Baltimore, 1979), and "On the Death of Sarpedon," in *Approaches to*

Homer, ed. Rubino and Shelmerdine (Austin, 1983) 189-217, now reprinted in different form in G. Nagy, *Greek Mythology and Poetics* (Ithaca, 1990) 122-42.

[5] The debate can be followed in A. Snodgrass, *The Dark Age of Greece* (Edinburgh, 1971) and *Archaic Greece* (Berkeley, 1980); T. Hadzisteliou Price, "Hero-Cult and Homer," *Historia* 22 (1973) 129-44 and "Hero Cult in the 'Age of Homer' and Earlier," in *Arktouros*, ed. G. Bowersock et al. (Berlin, 1979); J. N. Coldstream, "Hero-Cults in the Age of Homer," *JHS* 96 (1976) 8-17, and *Geometric Greece* (London, 1977).

[6] For an important reconsideration of early evidence for hero cult, see C. Antonaccio, *An Archaeology of Ancestors: Tomb Cult and Hero Cult in Early Greece* (Lanham, Md., 1995).

[7] Hadzisteliou Price (1979) 223-24 considers the Pelopeion at Olympia the "earliest reasonably well-attested heroon," along with the nearby Hippodameion (Paus. 6.20.7). Antonaccio (1995) 176 comes to a more negative conclusion. For the shrine of Helen and Menelaos at Therapne and its dedications, see H. W. Catling and H. Cavanagh, "Two Inscribed Bronzes from the Melenaion, Sparta," *Kadmos* 15.2 (1976) 145-57 and Antonaccio (1995) 155-66. For hero-reliefs, see below, p. 47.

[8] As Isocrates says about Helen and Menelaos, they are worshipped not as heroes, but as gods (. . . , *Praise of Helen* 10.63).

[9] Lines 602-4 were rejected by ancient critics as an interpolation, and many modern critics have held the same opinion. See F. Solmsen, "The Sacrifice of Agamemnon's Daughter in Hesiod's 'EHOEAE,'" *AJP* 102 (1981) 355nn. 6 and 7. Mark Griffith, "Contest and Contradiction in Early Greek Poetry," in *Cabinet of the Muses: Essays on Classical and Comparative Literature in Honor of Thomas G. Rosenmeyer*, ed. M. Griffith and D. J. Mastronarde (Atlanta, 1990) 206n. 48 remarks that it hardly matters if the passage was interpolated, since "in either case, the effect of the existing text on the reader/listener is the same."

[10] Nagy (1979) esp. 26-41.

[11] The Greek text cited is that of R. Merkelbach and M. L. West, *Fragmenta Hesiodea* (Oxford, 1967). Brackets indicate missing text or conjectural readings.

[12] Another text that brings together male and female figures in an epic setting is *Hom. Hymn* 3 (Apollo) 160, in which the Delian maidens delight their audience by singing a hymn about the women and men of long ago. . . .

[13] The dialect form used by Corinna. . . .

[14] Sources for Corinna: Plutarch *Glor. Athen.* 4, 347f-348a; Aelian *Varia Historia* 113.25; Paus. 9.22.3. See J. M. Snyder, *The Woman and the Lyre* (Carbondale, 1989) 41-54 and M. Lefkowitz, *The Lives of the Greek Poets* (London, 1981) 64-65.

[15] For Herakles, see Chapter 2, n. 93; For Helen, see n. 7 above and Appendix. Also L. Clader, *Helen: The Evolution from Divine to Heroic in Greek Epic Tradition* (Leiden, 1976) 63ff.

[16] For Hyakinthos, see S. Eitrem, *RE* 9.1 (1914) 4-16. For Semele's *abaton:* Paus. 9.12.3; her tomb: Paus. 9.16.7. There is only late inscriptional evidence (3rd c. C.E.) for observances at her tomb (*SEG* 19.379 Delphi), but sacrifices are recorded for her in the ritual calendar of Erchia (*SEG* 21.541) discussed below.

[17] Hippolytos: Eur. *Hipp.* 1423ff.; Paus. 3.12.9—*hērōon;* 1.22.1—grave at Athens. Iphigeneia: Eur. *I.T.* 1462ff.; Paus. 1.33.1; 2.35.1; 7.26.5; Chapter 5 below.

[18] "Un essere venerato nel culto e ricordato nei miti degli antichi greci," *Heros: Il Culto greco degli eroi e il problema degli esseri semi-divini* (Rome, 1958b) 14.

[19] G. S. Kirk, *Myth: Its Meaning and Function in Ancient and Other Cultures* (London, 1970) 175.

[20] "The truth seems to be that cultic association and semi-divine ancestry were felt more and more, from the time of Homer and Hesiod on, to be the hallmark of important heroes; but that many heroic figures of myth, and not only in the developed literary forms of the *Iliad* and *Odyssey,* just belonged to aristocratic families that traced their ultimate genesis to a god or goddess. Such heroes would normally have no individual cult, but were nevertheless conceived as belonging to a generation that still enjoyed the protection of the gods and shared, to a varying extent, their supernatural capabilities, in favoured cases their very blood." Kirk (1970) 176.

[21] Walter Burkert, *Greek Religion,* trans. J. Raffan (Cambridge, Mass., 1985) 203. . . .

[34] See *Themis: A Study of the Social Origins of Greek Religion* (Cambridge, 1927) 42, 329. . . .

[35] He was honored as the *Hērōs Dexiōn* (the receiving hero) for giving house-room to the cult of Asklepios before a temple was built in Athens (*Etym. Mag.* 256.6). On his role see H. W. Parke, *Festivals of the Athenians* (Ithaca, 1977) 135.

[36] Hesychios' *Lexicon* was written in Alexandria in the fifth or sixth century. From Byzantium come the writings of Stephanus Byzantinus, a sixth-century grammarian; Photius' reading notes from the ninth century

(known as the "Library"); the *Suda,* a tenth-century lexicon; the twelfth-century *Etymologicum Magnum;* and Eustathius' commentaries on Homer from the same period.

[37] See Brelich, *Gli eroi greci* (Rome, 1958) 23-77 for a detailed discussion of the many problems attendant on the use of ancient sources for myth.

[38] See G. Nagy, "Pindar's *Olympian* I and the Aetiology of the Olympic Games." *TAPA* 116 (1986) 71-88 and Nagy (1979) 71 on Pindar's conservatism.

[39] For the debate on this point, see below n. 53.

[40] C. Habicht, *Pausanias' Guide to Ancient Greece* (Princeton, 1985) uses recent archaeological excavations to corroborate Pausanias' assertions. Brelich (1958) 45ff. also considers Pausanias a reliable witness for local traditions.

[41] See P. M. C. Forbes Irving, *Metamorphosis in Greek Myths* (Oxford, 1990) 19-32 for a concurring view. He remarks (32), on the subject of one Hellenistic author, "Everything we have considered so far suggests that if Nicander is innovating he is at least doing it according to the rules and in a framework that does not belong just to his own times, and that therefore even his innovations would be a valuable source for the study of Greek myths."

[42] Merkelbach and West's edition (1967) has now been supplemented by the third edition of West's *Hesiodi Opera* (Oxford, 1990). See also West (1985) for discussion of the character of the work, its structure, and origins.

[43] G. McLeod, *Virtue and Venom: Catalogues of Women from Antiquity to the Renaissance* (Ann Arbor, 1991) 9, aims to analyze "all catalogues as attempts to express or critique cultural attitudes towards women." Unfortunately, despite this interesting approach, the sections on ancient Greek poetry contain inaccuracies that limit their usefulness.

[44] Although the *Catalogue* was traditionally considered the work of Hesiod, West (1985) believes that it cannot be the work of the poet of the *Theogony* (127). He argues for a sixth-century, Attic origin (130-36; 164-71). For a view of the Hesiodic corpus as emerging from a tradition of oral composition, see R. Lamberton, *Hesiod* (New Haven, 1988) 11-27.

[45] See West (1985) 127-30 on the connection between the *Theogony* and the *Catalogue of Women.* He also notes the similarity of the *Nekyia* passage with these texts (32 with n. 7).

[46] Tyro (235-59); Antiope (260-65); Alkmene (266-68); Megara (269-70); Epikaste (271-80); Chloris (281-97); possibly Pero, Chloris' daughter (whose story begins at line 287); Leda (298-304); Iphimedeia (305-20); Phaidra, Prokris, and Ariadne (321-25); Maira, Klymene, and Eriphyle (326-27).

[47] The heroines mentioned in *Iliad* 14 (discussed at length in Chapter 3) are Dia (317-18), Danae (319-20), Europe (321-22), Semele and Alkmene (323-25). In the *Catalogue of Ships,* we find the heroines Astyoche (513-15), Astyocheia (658-60), Aglaia (672), Alkestis (714-15), and Hippodameia (742-44). On the relation of the *Iliad*'s "little catalogues" to larger free-standing ones, see R. Hope Simpson and J. F. Lazenby, *The Catalogue of the Ships in Homer's Iliad* (Oxford, 1970) 166.

[48] *Iliad* 11.268-72. This comparison is given a different emphasis by Euripides' Medea, who says, "I would rather stand three times in the front lines than give birth once." (. . . *Medea* 250-51). See N. Loraux, "Le Lit, la guerre," *L'Homme* 21.1 (1981) 37-67, now translated as "Bed and War" in *The Experiences of Tiresias,* trans. Paula Wissing (Princeton, 1995) 23-43. For a contemporary feminist analysis of this theme, see N. Huston, "The Matrix of War: Mothers and Heroes," in *The Female Body in Western Culture,* ed. S. Rubin Suleiman (Cambridge, 1985) 119-36, esp. 130-31.

[49] Known titles of plays by Aeschylus contain the names Alkmene, Atalanta, Europe, Helen (three titles), Hypsipyle, Iphigeneia, Kallisto, Penelope, and Niobe; Sophocles: Andromache, Andromeda, Danae, Erigone, Eriphyle, Hermione, Hippodameia, Iphigeneia, Kreousa, Nausikaa, Niobe, Polyxene, Prokris, Tyro, Phaidra, and possibly others; Euripides: Andromeda, Antiope, Hypsipyle, Ino, Melanippe (two titles), and Stheneboia.

[50] See *Tragicorum Graecorum Fragmenta,* 2d ed., ed. A. Nauck with suppl. by B. Snell (Hildesheim, 1964).

[51] Sophocles' tragedy is the first extant text in which Antigone dies for the crime of burying her brother. *Iliad* 4.394, where Maion is said to be the son of Haimon, may reflect an earlier tradition in which they live to marry. For Medea, it is impossible to be certain that Euripides was indeed the innovator. See R. Seaford, "Dionysos as Destroyer of the Household: Homer, Tragedy, and the Polis," in *Masks of Dionysos,* ed. Carpenter and Faraone (Ithaca, 1993) 123n.38.

[52] See B. M. W. Knox, "The *Medea* of Euripides," *YCS* 25 (1977) 206. Nagy (1979) 279n.2 stressing the important distinction between explanation and motivation, defines an *aition* as "a myth that traditionally motivates an institution, such as a ritual."

[53] The argument over the reliability of Euripides' descriptions of ritual continues. See R. Eisner, "Euripides'

Use of Myth," *Arethusa* 12 (1979) 153-74 and Christian Wolff, "Euripides' *Iphigeneia among the Taurians:* Aetiology, Ritual, and Myth," *CA* 11 (1992) 308-34. Francis M. Dunn, "Euripides and the Rites of Hera Akraia," *GRBS* 35 (1994) 103-15 takes a particularly sceptical view, concluding that Euripides rewrites "not only character and legend but the 'real world' of cultural practice and belief." I am more in sympathy with Richard Seaford's cautions against underestimating Euripides' traditionalism, *Reciprocity and Ritual: Homer and Tragedy in the Developing City-State* (Oxford, 1994) 285n.21.

54 W. S. Barrett, ed. *Hippolytos* (Oxford, 1964) 412 notes that every Euripidean play for which we possess a satisfactory ending, except the *Trojan Women,* ends with an *aition.*

55 Some known titles for Old Comedy: Epicharmos' *Atalantai* and *Medea* (possibly by Deinolochos), Strattis' *Atalante* and *Medea,* and Theopompos' *Althaia* and *Penelope;* Middle Comedy: Alexis of Thurii's *Anteia* (possibly by Antiphanes), *Galateia, Helen, Hesione;* Antiphanes' *Alkestis, Anteia* (possibly by Alexis), *Omphale;* Euboulos' *Antiope, Auge, Europe, Laconians* or *Leda, Medea, Nausikaa, Prokris* (known to be a parody of a tragedy), *Semele* or *Dionysos;* Nikostratos' *Pandrosos;* Philetairos' *Atalanta;* Timokles' *Neaira.*

56 *LIMC* s.v. "Helene" 5. See A. D. Trendall, *Phylax Vases,* 2d ed. (*BICS* suppl. 19) 1967, 27-28.

57 Trans. W. H. S. Jones and H. A. Ormerod, *Pausanias' Description of Greece,* vol. 2 (Cambridge, Mass., 1920). Pausanias himself reports a conflicting tradition at 1.42.7, where the Megarians claim that it was on *their* shores that Ino was washed up. See Gregory Nagy, "Theognis and Megara: A Poet's Vision of His City," in Thomas J. Figueira and G. Nagy, *Theognis of Megara: Poetry and the Polis* (Baltimore, 1985) 79-80 on this variant tradition.

58 Translation adapted from Jones.

59 See D. Boedeker, "Hero Cult and Politics in Herodotos: The Bones of Orestes," in C. Dougherty and L. Kurke, eds., *Cultural Poetics in Archaic Greece: Cult, Performance, Politics* (Cambridge, 1993) 164-77.

60 See Habicht (1985) 132-34, 142-44, on Pausanias' literary tastes and sources of information.

61 In Pausanias only the following heroines are explicitly said to have a *hērōon:* Andromache (1.11.2), Ino (1.42.7), Iphigeneia (1.43.1), Hyrnetho (2.28.7), Kyniska (3.15.1), and Plataea (9.2.7).

62 For example, he speaks of the tomb (*taphos*) of Phaidra, located near the monument (*mnēma*) of Hippolytos (2.32.4). In the same way, at 2.21.7, he distinguishes the grave (*mnēma*) of Gorgo from that (*taphos*) of Gorgophone, who, as the daughter of Perseus, is presumably opposed to her by reasons of etymology as well as lineage. (Her name, "Gorgonslayer," commemorates her father's most famous exploit and calls ironic attention to their proximate burial.)

63 See M. B. Hollinshead, "Against Iphigeneia's Adyton in Three Mainland Temples," *AJA* 89 (1985) 419-40.

64 For a reconstruction of Kypselos' chest, see K. Schefold, *Myth and Legend in Early Greek Art,* trans. A. Hicks (New York, [1966]) 72-73. See also H. A. Shapiro, "Old and New Heroes: Narrative, Composition, and Subject in Attic Black-Figure," *CA* 9 (1990) 138-40. On Polygnotos, see M. D. Stansbury-O'Donnell, "Polygnotos' *Iliupersis:* A New Reconstruction," *AJA* 93 (1989) 203-15.

65 F. Pfister, *Der Reliquienkult im Altertum* (Giessen, 1909) 1:328-65, lists natural phenomena connected with heroes. These are for the most part not the results of actual transformations but are landmarks connected with and occasionally created by the heroes themselves. Heroines are frequently associated with springs, which they create either deliberately, like Atalante striking her spear against the rock (Paus. 3.24.2), or inadvertently, like the weeping Niobe (Pherec. in schol. T *Iliad* 24.167). For Niobe herself as a rocky outcropping, see Paus. 1.21.3. See Forbes Irving (1990) passim.

66 For a discussion of this tradition, see Forbes Irving (1990) 19-36.

67 F. I. Zeitlin, "Configurations of Rape in Greek Myth," in *Rape,* ed. S. Tomaselli and R. Porter (Oxford, 1986) 122-51, 261-64 (notes) explicitly connects metamorphosis with the woman's flight from sexual violence (123).

68 See Chapter 3, below, pp. 96, 101.

69 Farnell (1921). See discussion throughout, and the lists on pp. 403-26.

70 Jorge Luis Borges, *Other Inquisitions,* trans. Ruth L. C. Simms (New York, 1968) 103.

71 See Farnell (1921) 367 on the cult of Sappho on Lesbos. For poets as heroes, see Brelich (1958) 320-22 and Nagy (1979) especially 279-308. Other female poets who might have received cult honors are Telesilla and Corinna, who are not mentioned here. See Paus. 2.20.8-9 for the bravery of Telesilla, and the relief commemorating it, and 9.22.3 for the tomb of Corinna.

[72] Pfister's list of heroes' graves seems to include every instance in which Pausanias records a *mnēma* or a *taphos* (two words he uses almost interchangeably for "grave"). Farnell applies a more complicated, and at times elusive, standard. For eponymous heroes and heroines, see Pfister (1909) 1:279-89; for hero-shrines with tomb, Pfister (1912) 2:450-55; for graves of heroes and heroines, 2:627-40.

[73] See Brelich (1958) 79 for elucidation of this principle; 113-18 for its application to healing. See also Deborah Lyons, "Manto and *Manteia:* Prophecy in the Myths and Cults of Heroines," in *Sibille e linguaggi oracolari,* ed. I. Chirassi Colombo and T. Seppilli (Pisa, forthcoming).

[74] See Brelich (1958) 27 for the importance of the first time; 166-77 for the hero as *protōs heuretēs,* "inventor" or "originator."

[75] Robertson, "Adopting an Approach I," in *Looking at Greek Vases,* ed. T. Rasmussen and N. Spivey (Cambridge, 1991) 4.

[76] The topic of the position of women in archaic and classical Greece lies for the most part outside the scope of this study. For an account of the debate on seclusion, see I. Savalli, *La Donna nella società della Grecia antica* (Bologna, 1983), and M. Arthur, "Review Essay: Classics," in *Signs* 2.2 (1976) 382-403. Overviews of women's economic and legal status include D. M. Schaps, *Economic Rights of Women in Ancient Greece* (Edinburgh, 1979); R. Just, *Women in Athenian Law and Life* (London, 1989); and R. Sealey, *Women and Law in Classical Greece* (Chapel Hill, 1990).

[77] Roland Martin, *Recherches sur l'agora grecque* (Paris, 1951) 194-95. F. de Polignac, *La Naissance de la cité grecque* (Paris, 1984) 132, argues that these founder-tombs need not all have been new installations. Some may have been ancient burials rediscovered and attributed to hero-founders. See Antonaccio (1995).

[78] See Marcel Detienne in the *Annuaire. Ecole pratique des Hautes Etudes* 94 (1985-86) 371-80, on Apollo as the city-founding god. For the role of Delphi in colonization, see H. W. Parke and D. E. W. Wormell, *The Delphic Oracle* (Oxford, 1956) 1:49-81; Joseph Fontenrose, *The Delphic Oracle* (Berkeley, 1978) passim; Carol Dougherty, *The Poetics of Colonization: From City to Text in Archaic Greece* (New York, 1993).

[79] According to Martin (1951) 195, the eponymous hero is "le produit d'une réfection de la tradition religieuse" (the product of a remaking of the religious tradition) in response to internal political events or major external ones. De Polignac (1984) 132ff. also suggests that sometimes it was necessary to invent the mythic founder.

[80] See A. J. Graham, "Religion, Women and Greek Colonization," in *Religione e città nel mondo antico* (Rome, 1984) 293-314.

[81] Heroines who give their names to cities include Abia, Alalkomenia, Amphissa, Andania, Araithyrea, Arene, Arne, Boura, Dyme, Eirene, Ephyre, Harpina, Helike, Hyrmina, Ismene (?), Kombe, Kyrbia, Kyrene, Lampsake, Larisa, Larymna, Messene, Mothone, Mykene, Myrine, Nemea, Nonakris, Oichalia, Oinoe, Physkoa, Psothis, Side, Sparte, Tanagra, Thebe, Therapne, Thespia, Thisbe, Thyia (2), Triteia. Others are said to give their names to demes (Aglauros, Hekale, Melite), tribes (Hyrnetho, Milye), and the gates of Thebes (Elektra). On the eponymous heroines of demes, see E. Kearns, *The Heroes of Attica. BICS* suppl. 57 (1989) 101-2.

[82] Pfister (1912) 2:279-89, lists about 60 examples of graves of eponymous heroes, 10 of whom are actually heroines.

[83] The subject of heroines as cult-founders is discussed in Chapter 5 (with appendix). See Carolyn Dewald, "Women and Culture in Herodotus' *Histories*" in *Reflections of Women in Antiquity,* ed. Foley (New York, 1981) 91-125, especially p. 110-12; 122.

[84] *FGrH* 476 F 3 = Photius and *Suda* s.v. . . . See J. Svenbro, *Phrasikleia: An Anthropology of Reading in Ancient Greece,* trans. J. Lloyd (Ithaca, 1993 [Paris, 1988]) 8-9, 82-86.

[85] On cults of emperors, see S. R. F. Price, *Rituals and Power: The Roman Imperial Cult in Asia Minor* (Cambridge, 1984).

[86] Pfister, for example, follows pagan examples with Christian ones throughout his study of *Reliquienkult.* It is precisely in the matter of relics that the comparison is most tempting. See P. Brown, *The Cult of the Saints* (Chicago, 1981) 5-6 for a critique of this idea.

Abbreviations

Journals and Compilations

AC: *L'Antiquité Classique*

AJA: *American Journal of Archaeology*

AJP: *American Journal of Philology*

AK: *Antike Kunst*

AW: *Antike Welt*

BCH: Bulletin de Correspondence Hellénique

BICS: Bulletin of the Institute of Classical Studies

CA: Classical Antiquity

CIG: Corpus Inscriptionum Graecarum

CJ: Classical Journal

CQ: Classical Quarterly

CR: Classical Review

CW: Classical World

FGrH: Die Fragmente der griechischen Historiker ed. F. Jacoby (Berlin/Leiden, 1923-64)

FHG: Fragmenta Historicorum Graecorum ed. C. Muller and T. Muller (Paris, 1841-51)

GRBS: Greek, Roman, and Byzantine Studies

HSCP: Harvard Studies in Classical Philology

HThR: Harvard Theological Review

IG: Inscriptiones Graecae

JHS: Journal of Hellenic Studies

LIMC: Lexicon Iconographicum Mythologiae Classicae

M-W: Fragmenta Hesiodea ed. R. Merkelbach and M. L. West (Oxford, 1967)

PMG: Poetae Melici Graeci ed. D. L. Page (Oxford, 1962)

PP: Parola del Passato

QUCC: Quaderni Urbinati di Cultura Classica

RE: Realencyclopädie der classischen Altertumswissenschaft

REA: Revue des études anciennes

REG: Revue des études grecques

RM: Rheinisches Museum

SEG: Supplementum Epigraphicum Graecum

SMSR: Studi e Materiali di Storia delle Religioni

TAPA: Transactions and Proceedings of the American Philological Association

YCS: Yale Classical Studies

ZPE: Zeitschrift für Papyrologie und Epigrafik

Ancient Authors Frequently Cited

Aesch.: Aeschylus

Alc.: Alcman

Ant. Lib.: Antoninus Liberalis

Apollod.: Apollodorus

AR.: Apollonius of Rhodes

Aristoph.: Aristophanes

Athen.: Athenaeus

Callim.: Callimachus

Cert. Hom. et Hes.: The Contest between Homer and Hesiod

Diod.: Diodorus Siculus

Eur.: Euripides

Hdt.: Herodotus

Hes.: Hesiod

Cat.: Catalogue of Women attributed to Hesiod

Theog.: Theogony

WD: Works and Days

Hesych.: Hesychius

Hom. Hymn: Homeric Hymns

Hyg. *Fab.:* Hyginus *Fabulae*

Lycoph.: Lycophron

Paus.: Pausanias

Plut.: Plutarch (see below for individual titles)

schol.: scholia (ancient commentaries)

Soph.: Sophocles

Theocr.: Theocritus

Thuc.: Thucydides

All others may be found in the *Oxford Classical Dictionary* or *A Greek-English Lexicon,* ed. Liddell, Scott, and Jones.

Plutarch Moralia: *Titles of Individual Works*

Amat. narr.: Love Stories

Apotheg. Lac.: Sayings of Spartans

De def. orac.: On the Obsolescence of Oracles

De frat. am.: On Brotherly Love

De gen. Socr.: On the Sign of Socrates

De Herodot. malig.: On the Malignity of Herodotus

De mul. virt.: On the Bravery of Women

Glor. Athen.: On the Fame of Athens

Parall.: Parallel Stories

Praec. coniug.: Advice to Bride and Groom

Quaest. conviv.: Table-Talk

Quaest. Gr.: Greek Questions

Quaest. R.: Roman Questions

Sept. sap. conviv.: Dinner of the Seven Wise Men

Plutarch Lives: *Titles of Individual Works*

Alcib.: Alcibiades

Arist.: Aristides

Rom.: Romulus

Them.: Themistocles

Thes.: Theseus

WOMEN IN GREEK MYTHOLOGY

C. Kerényi (essay date 1949)

SOURCE: "Kore," in *Essays on a Science of Mythology: The Myth of the Divine Child and The Mysteries of Eleusis,* by C. G. Jung and C. Kerényi, translated by R. F. C. Hull, Bollingen Series, XXII, Princeton University Press, 1969, pp. 101-55.

[In the following excerpt, from an essay originally published in 1949, Kerényi analyzes the nature of "maiden goddesses" and their role and function in Greek mythology. Kerényi describes the Kore, or maiden goddess, as a paradox, in that she represents both mother and maiden, both "begetter and begotten."]

How can a man know what a woman's life is? A woman's life is quite different from a man's. God has ordered it so. A man is the same from the time of his circumcision to the time of his withering. He is the same before he has sought out a woman for the first time, and afterwards. But the day when a woman enjoys her first love cuts her in two. She becomes another woman on that day. The man is the same after his first love as he was before. The woman is from the day of her first love another. That continues so all through life. The man spends a night by a woman and goes away. His life and body are always the same. The woman conceives. As a mother she is another person than the woman without child. She carries the fruit of the night for nine months in her body. Something grows. Something grows into her life that never again departs from it. She is a mother. She is and remains a mother even though her child die, though all her children die. For at one time she carried the child under her heart. And it does not go out of her heart ever again. Not even when it is dead. All this the man does not know; he knows nothing. He does not know the difference before love and after love, before motherhood and after motherhood. He can know nothing. Only a woman can know that and speak of that. That is why we won't be told what to do by our husbands. A woman can only do one thing. She can respect herself. She can keep herself decent. She must always be as her nature is. She must always be maiden and always be mother. Before every love she is a maiden, after every love she is a mother. In this you can see whether she is a good woman or not.

Let these words of a noble Abyssinian woman, quoted by Frobenius in one of his finest books, *Der Kopf als Schicksal* (p. 88), stand as a motto in preparation and confirmation of what is said in the sequel. I did not know them when I wrote my study of the Kore. They are meant at the same time to stand in remembrance of a great man, whose life's work is an abiding stimulus to all those concerned with anthropology and mythology.

Anadyomene

The Florentine Renaissance came to love the Homeric hymns even more than the two great epics. Marsilius Ficinus, the translator of Plato, began by translating the Homeric and Orphic hymns. We know that he also sang them in the antique manner to the accompaniment of a lute. Angelo Poliziano, another leading spirit of Florentine humanism, paraphrased a hymn to

Aphrodite—neither the greatest nor the least of those ascribed to Homer—in his own verses. We could say that he painted it in the style of the Quattrocento were it not for the painter who actually did so, with Poliziano's poetic assistance: Botticelli.[1] *The Birth of Venus* is not a good name for this picture. It is rather Aphrodite's arrival in Cyprus according to the Homeric hymn, or, in accordance with the significance of this masterpiece and the rôle it has played in our civilization, Aphrodite's arrival among *us*. Botticelli's picture contains at least as much living mythology as the Homeric hymn.[2]

Aphrodite's *birth* is different: brutal and violent, and departing from the style of Homeric poetry in just as archaic a manner as from the style of Botticelli. In both cases the mutilation of Uranos, the casting of his manhood into the sea, the whole terrible foregoing history, the titanic mythology of the world's beginnings—all this was swept aside. The unity of that mythological moment when begetter and begotten were one in the womb of the water[3] had been broken up even in Hesiod and become a historical process. In Hesiod, too, we hear of Aphrodite drifting, drifting on the waves, as Maui did in the myth of the Polynesians.[4] At last the white foam gave birth to the girl who took her name from it: [aphros] is foam and Aphrodite the goddess. This ancient etymology, accepted by Hesiod, derived its credibility from a grand mythological vision that must be still older: from the picture of Anadyomene, the goddess risen from the waves. Representations of Aphrodite's *arrival* are later. The mild breeze carries the great goddess, already born, to one of her sacred islands, or, in Botticelli's picture, to firm ground.

The soft foam that cushions Aphrodite is a symbol of her birth, and fits in with the Homeric style just as the mussel-shell does with Botticelli's. In the Roman poets we read that Venus was born of a mussel-shell, or that she journeyed in a mussel-shell over the sea. Ancient representations show her as if growing out of a mussel. We need not surmise with H. Usener, the eminent philologist, that the growth of the pearl was at the bottom of the symbol.[5] Later, this image was blended with the archaic foam-image. Originally yet another kind of mussel, by no means so noble, was the creature sacred to Aphrodite in Cnidos.[6] The mussel in general constitutes a most graphic example and expression, appealing at once to the senses, of the aphrodisian properties of the "humid element." The Homeric poem was too spiritual to employ this symbol. Poliziano was too sensual to be able to forget it. Venus steps out of her mussel-shell in Botticelli in such a way that you can see immediately: it belongs to the goddess, yet she is leaving it behind her as she leaves behind the whole of primitive mythology, which Poliziano nevertheless relates according to Hesiod.

From the high sea, stepping out of a mussel-shell, borne along by the wind and received by the gaily clad goddess of earth, Aphrodite Anadyomene arrives. She is an aspect of the primordial maiden, Protogonos Kore. Botticelli's picture helps us, as modern men, to conjure up the vision of Anadyomene. And she must be conjured up if we want to understand the goddesses of the Greeks. She is the closest to the origins.

The Paradox of the Mythological Idea

To the religious-minded man of the Greek world, his divinities had always appeared in classical perfection since the time of Homer. And undoubtedly they appeared not as the fictions or creations of art but as living deities who could be believed in. They can best be understood as eternal *forms*, the great world-realities. "The reason for the mightiness of all these figures lies in their truth."[7] As psychologists we may stress the fact that this truth is always a *psychic reality;* as historians we may add that the psychic reality of such a truth, as indeed of all truth, *changes with time;*[8] as biologists we may call the alteration of the power that so moves us *natural decay,* but the essentially convincing inner structure of the classical Greek divinities remains unshakable for all time.

We have a handy comparison in the kind of formula that gives us a clear picture of the balance of tremendous cosmic forces, that catches the world in each of its aspects as though in a *border-line situation* and presents it to the mind as though the least disturbance of that balance would bring about a universal collapse. Every natural law is just such a balanced aspect of the world and is immediately intelligible as the mathematical formulation of a border-line situation.

So it is with the figures of gods. In *Apollo* sublimest clarity and the darkness of death face one another, perfectly poised and equal, on a border-line;[9] in *Dionysus,* life and death;[10] in *Zeus,* might and right[11]—to name only the three greatest. In relation to the cosmos as a whole, these divinities are merely certain aspects of it; in themselves they are wholes,[12] "worlds" which have aspects in their turn, and contradictory aspects for the very reason that their structure combines contradictions in perfect equilibrium.

Such gods can only be understood *as spiritual ideas;* in other words, they can only be known by immediate revelation.[13] They cannot emerge step by step from something quite different. And conversely, we cannot imagine or believe in a god who did not appear to the *spirit,* who was not an immediate spiritual revelation. The very possibility of the Greek divinities, the reason for their credibility, consists in the fact that they are *ideal.*

If the historian ventures to adopt an attitude in accord with this knowledge; if he is bold enough to take the things of the spirit spiritually, and religion religiously, he immediately lights on a paradox. He can easily go so far back into the prehistory of the Greek gods that the balance we have spoken of dissolves before his eyes and all certain outlines vanish. *Artemis,* for instance, is to be found in the untamedness of young animals and equally in the terrors of birth. In the classical figure of this goddess, the wildness and the terrors meet at a border-line: they are in equilibrium.[14] The further we penetrate into her prehistory, the more the outlines connected with the name of "Artemis" evaporate. The border-line situation widens into a border-*region* midway between motherhood and maidenhood, *joie de vivre* and lust for murder, fecundity and animality. The more we realize that the divinity of the gods can only be experienced spiritually, in the illumination of an *idea,* by direct revelation, the more we sense a difficulty. The majority of investigators shrink from recognizing *ideal* figures in the gods, thinking of much that is the reverse of ideal in the early history of Greek religion so far as known.

It is a paradox, but nothing impossible, that we meet here: the revelation of something that is dark in comparison with an idea, but ideal in comparison with blind feeling—the revelation of something *still unopened, like a bud.* All the most ancient mythological ideas are buds of this sort. Above all, the idea of genesis and origin—an idea which every living thing experiences in its own genesis and, to that extent, realizes in fact. Mythologically, the idea is embodied in miraculous "primal beings," either in such a way that in them father and child, prime begetter and prime begotten, are one and the same, or that the fate of the woman becomes the symbol and expression of all genesis and origination. Zeus, Apollo, Dionysus, Hermes, Asklepios, Heracles—all may be regarded as having evolved out of a mythological *primordial child,* who originally comprised both begetter and begotten.[15] The same idea, seen as the woman's fate, presented itself to the Greeks in equally budlike form. The budlike quality of it is expressed in the name often given to its personification: *Kore,* which is simply the goddess "Maiden."

The Kore-goddess throws light on the old mythological idea in its budlike capacity to unfold and yet to contain a whole compact world in itself. The idea can also be likened to a nucleus. We have to understand, as it were, the structure hidden in the "abyss of the nucleus." In so doing, we must not forget the figure of Anadyomene. We shall have an assurance that our understanding is true to life if this ideal structure, as we conceive it, remains compatible with her image.

Maiden-Goddesses

Maiden-goddesses are far more typical of Greek reli-

gion than boy-gods or even, perhaps, divine youths. Divine maidens are in fact so typical of this religion that it cannot be called either a "Father religion" or a "Mother religion," or yet a combination of both. It is as though the Olympian order had thrust the great Mother Goddesses of olden time into the background for the sole purpose of throwing the divine Korai into sharper relief. In the innermost circle of the hierarchy of Greek gods—both on Olympus and in the lesser world of many a Greek city—it was not *Hera,* Zeus' spouse, who shared dominion with him so much as the androgynous figure of Pallas Athene.

In the Peloponnese she was also adored as "Mother Athene,"[16] and to the Athenians she was very much the "Mother."[17] Nevertheless, this designation does not affect her essence, which cannot be better expressed than by the word "Kore." She was called by this more often than by the other name for virgin—*parthenos.* The very coins that bore her image were known as *korai* in Athenian parlance.[18] Her "maidenhood," however, was not thought of in connection with the mother whose daughter she might have been. The goddess Metis, who might have been her mother, vanished in Zeus, and Pallas Athene sprang from her father.[19] Still less was her "maidenhood" understood in connection with a man, for whom she might have been intended or to whom she might have fallen like any other maiden. The Greek idea of divinity seems first to have freed itself from sexuality in the maidenhood of Athene, without, however, forfeiting a characteristic otherwise peculiar to male divinities like Zeus and Apollo, namely intellectual and spiritual power.[20]

In the outer circle of the Olympian hierarchy there reigns yet another maiden—Artemis. She too is both Kore and Parthenos. But *her* maidenhood expresses something different from Athene's.[21] Her world is the wide world of Nature, and the brute realities balanced in her—unsubdued virginity and the terrors of birth— have their dominion in a *purely naturalistic, feminine world.* Athene's maidenhood excluded the very possibility of her succumbing to a man; with Artemis, on the other hand, her maidenhood presupposes this possibility. The connection between Artemis the Kore and her mother is looser than between the Kore Persephone and Demeter. Yet Leto is not forgotten when we evoke a vision of Artemis: she is there, enjoying the spectacle of Artemis dancing.[22] The great mythological poets of antiquity, like Aeschylus,[23] and the experts on old mythologems, like Callimachus,[24] ventured to hint that it was a question of only one Kore and one mother, namely Demeter's daughter, be she called Artemis or Persephone.

Persephone, generally called Kore or Pais . . . by the Greeks, differs from Athene in the same way as Artemis. She is a Kore not because she is above all feminine connections—with mother or husband—but because she embodies these connections as two forms of being each carried to extremes and balanced against one another. One of the forms (daughter with mother) appears as life; the other (young girl with husband) as death. Mother and daughter form a living unity in a border-line situation—a natural unit which, equally naturally, carries within it the seeds of its own destruction. As a maiden, Persephone is an Artemisian figure. She might well have been one of the companions of Artemis who were untrue to their maidenhood and thus paid the penalty of death. This is what in fact happens (though she herself is guiltless) because it is in her nature to happen.

Athene and Artemis as the playmates of Persephone, who were present at her rape[25]—thus the myth unites the three variations on the theme of the Kore in a single incident. Artemis and Persephone are like two sides of the same reality. Artemis is the active one. She carries death in herself in the form of murder; according to Homer she was a lioness to women,[26] and in Arcady and Attica she was a bear.[27] Persephone is completely passive. She was picking flowers when she was raped by the Lord of the Dead. They were heavily scented flowers, stupefying flowers like the narcissus.[28] Poets have never failed to catch the significance of this scene. For one of them[29] the flowers were "hell-hounds on her heels"; for another[30] it was a case of "Persephone gathering flowers, herself a fairer flower." The Kore is a creature destined to a flower-like existence which cannot be better described than by one of the poets mentioned:[31]

> . . . a little torrent of life
> leaps up to the summit of the stem, gleams, turns
> over round the bend
> of the parabola of curved flight,
> sinks, and is gone, like a comet curving into
>   the invisible.

Such would seem to be the essence of Persephone: a lingering on the borders of Hades, a fleeting moment of climax, no sooner here than gone. This Kore would be a perfectly *ideal* figure, a poetic image as clear and pure as a mathematical formula, if it were all nothing but an allegory. An allegory of woman's fate: the borders of Hades an allegory of the border-line between maidenhood and the "other" life, and the seducer, King of the Underworld, an allegory of the earthly bridegroom and husband. But it is not so. As the relics of the Persephone cult show, the meaning is the other way about. She was worshipped in the most serious manner as the *Queen of the Dead*, and the rape of the bride was an allegory of death. Lost maidenhood and the crossing of the borders of Hades are allegorical equivalents—the one can stand for the other equally well.

This kind of equivalence only exists in a given sphere, in an immediately recognizable spiritual connection that can combine very different things, such as marriage and death, in one *comprehensive idea.* Mythological ideas are like the compact buds of such connections. They always contain *more* than the non-mythological mind could conceive. This is also true of the Kore, whom we have so far been considering only in her most *human* form. Here, then, is our Persephone: a creature standing unsubdued on a pinnacle of life and there meeting her fate—a fate that means death in fulfilment and dominion in death.

Hecate

The oldest account of the rape of the Kore is at the beginning of the Homeric hymn to Demeter. The unknown poet sets out to sing of Demeter, the great Mother Goddess, "of her and her daughter." The "two goddesses" . . . , so they were called at Eleusis, the sacred place whose fame the hymn declares. They are to be thought of as a *double figure,* one half of which is the ideal complement of the other. Persephone is, above all, her *mother's* Kore: without her, Demeter would not be a *Meter*.

Persephone appears in just as ideal a light in another connection as well—as the half of another double figure, the Rulers of the Underworld. Here, as *her bridegroom's Kore,* she belongs (much as the equivalent Thessalian figure was called "Admetus' Kore")[32] to her husband, Hades, to whom she was given by Zeus. The triad consisting of Mother, Kore, and Seducer has a clear and natural place in Zeus' world-order. Clarity and naturalness and a well-defined place in Zeus' world are characteristic of the Homeric style of the hymn.

But a third goddess has a notable part to play beside mother and daughter. According to the hymn, Persephone was raped somewhere in the distance, on the flat ground near the mythological Mount Nyssa, where she was playing with the daughters of Oceanus. The scene, however, is still of our world, the world in which our sun shines, to whom Demeter can appeal as the surest eye-witness of the rape. Like the sun, this third goddess appears to belong to the Demeter-Persephone world: *Hecate.* She is in her cave when the sun sees the seduction. All she hears are the cries of the seduced. She is often held to be the representative of the moon, particularly as she is closely related to this heavenly body in other ways.[33]

On the other hand she would seem to be the *double of Demeter herself.* She hears the victim's voice, just as Demeter hears it. She meets Demeter "with a light in her hand" and asks about the seducer in words which, according to an Orphic version of the hymn, are Demeter's own. Then, the poet says, they both go to seek the sun, the eye-witness. There are, however, two versions of the mythologem, one of which leads Demeter,[34] the other Hecate,[35] to the Underworld in search of Persephone. After mother and daughter are reunited, Hecate once more appears in the hymn in order to receive the Kore and remain her companion always: Hecate and Persephone are as inseparable as Persephone and Demeter. *Gaia,* the Earth Mother, has no connection whatever with Demeter in the hymn; she is the seducer's accomplice. So Hecate's close relationship with the double figure of Demeter and the Kore is all the more striking.

A compact group, a triad of unmistakable individuals, this is how the hymn shows the three goddesses: Mother, Daughter, and the moon-goddess Hecate. They are easily confused on sacred monuments, because the torch appears to be the attribute of each of them. This emblem accords with the epithet *phosphoros,* which is applied to Hecate more than once.[36] She is thus explicitly called the "bringer of light." The torch she carries is described in the hymn as . . . "light," but not as a means of purification, which is how many moderns are inclined to take this palpable symbol. "Light-bringing" is no doubt an essential part of the goddess's nature, but the torch is characteristic not only of Hecate, it also plays an important part in the Demeter and Persephone cult. One torch, two torches held by the same goddess, three torches in a row,[37] or the "crossed torch" with four lights, all these occur as attributes of both Demeter and Persephone;[38] and this variety of forms proves that we are dealing with some sort of expression rather than an application; a symbol, not a means to a practical end. In the hymn itself Demeter appears with two burning torches.[39] Further investigation outside the confines of the strictly Homeric Zeus-world convinces us that we are not far wrong in our surmise that Hecate is a second Demeter.

As Greek religion developed, there appeared, even in places where the overlordship of Zeus so characteristic of the Homeric religion was of long standing, certain divinities who, on the fringes of the Hellenic cultural world, had retained all their pre-Homeric, pristine freshness. Thus the great goddess of the town of Pherai in Thessaly—*Pheraia*—came to Athens as a "foreign" divinity. In this torch-bearing goddess the Athenians recognized their own Hecate,[40] whereas in her Thessalian home Pheraia was none other than Demeter herself.[41] Pheraia's daughter was also known as Hecate, a different Hecate from the great goddess of Pherai, though obviously resembling her mother.[42] Demeter and her daughter display, in a more primitive form than the Homeric and Attic one, features that permit both of them to appear as Hecate. Or, looking at it from the other point of view, we could say: the Greeks attached the name "Hecate" to a goddess who united in herself affinities with the moon, a Demetrian nature, and Kore-like characteristics—not only those of Persephone but

of *Artemis* as well. She was invoked as the daughter of Demeter and the daughter of Leto.[43] Hecate and Artemis, Trivia and Diana are used so often as equivalent names in ancient literature that we cannot regard this as wholly groundless, any more than we can the familiar equation of Persephone with the moon[44] and Diana with Luna.[45]

The budlike idea of the connection between three aspects of the world—maiden, mother, and moon—hovers at the back of the triad of goddesses in the Homeric hymn. Hecate has a subordinate part to play in keeping with her position on the fringes of the Zeus-world. And yet she still retains, even under Zeus' rule, the characteristics of that archaic figure who preceded the historical Hecate. One such characteristic, and the chief among them, is the *triple form* which appears relatively late in artistic representations of the goddess,[46] but is indirectly confirmed by Hesiod. The poet of the *Theogony* acclaims her as the mighty Mistress of *three* realms—earth, heaven, and sea.[47] He also says that the goddess already had this dominion in the time of the Titans, before Zeus and his order. The new ruler of the world honoured her by leaving her in her former majesty.

The classical figure of Hecate stands stiff and strange in the Greek world, built up on a triangle, and with faces turned in three directions. They tried to get rid of the stiffness of these Hecate statues by breaking up the triune goddess into three dancing maidens. Later times were to stick more rigidly to the characteristic number 3 than did the classical age of Hesiod. The fact that *Hecateia* were set up at the crossing of three roads and that these places were held especially sacred to Hecate does not militate against the Hesiodic or cosmic conception of the number 3: all crossings of three roads point clearly and obviously enough to the possibility of dividing the world into three parts. At the same time Hecate, as Mistress of the Spirits, warned the Greeks that a threefold division would necessarily leave, side by side with the ordered world of Zeus, a chaotic region in which the amorphousness of the primitive world could live on as the Underworld. The Greeks took Hecate's triplicity as something underworldly.

But in earlier times, before Hecate's three faces had petrified into the well-known *Hecateia,* these three aspects, it seems, were so many aspects or realms of the world, so many possible developments of one and the same compact, budlike idea. Hence we see the inner connection between Demeter, the Kore, and Hecate—and thus the profoundest idea of the mythologem as unfolded in the hymn—in the figure of what is *apparently* the least of the goddesses, the most subordinate of the three.

Besides her Kore quality, her affinity with the moon and with a primitive world of ghosts, a sort of motherliness also pertains to the idea of Hecate. Like Artemis or Mother Earth herself, she was . . . *nurse and nourisher* of all those born after her.[48] In the hymn it is Demeter that appears in this role, as nurse of the king's youngest son in Eleusis. And it is to *her* figure that our concern with Hecate now leads us. In her as well those elements are contained which, besides those already mentioned, constitute the fundamental idea of the hymn. We must not forget for an instant that it is not the idea of the classical or still later Hecate that comes closest to this fundamental idea, but of an original *Demeter and Hecate in one person*.

Demeter

The sphere of human realities, such as maidenhood and motherhood, is enlarged in the Demeter hymn insofar as it now, thanks to Hecate, suggests a relationship to the moon. At the same time Demeter herself seems to lead us back to something purely human. "La déesse mère vouée à l'éternel regret de sa fille disparue" is how a historian of Greek sculpture describes the celebrated seated statue of her found in Cnidos.[49] These words might also characterize the Demeter of the hymn. The poet describes Persephone's rape at the beginning of the poem, and from then on it is full of her divine mother's pain and grief. Even in their reunion there is still a portion of bitterness, for Persephone has eaten, while with her husband, of the pomegranate and has to spend a third of every year with him.[50] The mother never quite succeeds in getting her daughter back again.

Human sorrow, yet not *merely* human. For the goddess lets no crops grow during her daughter's absence, and by means of the earth's unfruitfulness she compels the gods to restore her daughter. And she it is who, appeased, lets fruit and flowers grow once more. She "lets" all this "come up,"[51] she who is adored as Anesidora, Chloe ("the Green One"), and Karpophoros ("Bringer of Fruit"). As Horephoros she also brings the favourable season. Science is in the greatest doubt whether she should be identified with the earth or with the grain, or should be regarded as a subterranean power. There are adherents to all three views among the learned. In order to decide for one or the other we must have a clear understanding of the Homeric poet's point of view.

Demeter describes herself in the hymn as being "of the greatest use and the greatest joy to gods and men."[52] There is not a word about her having *taught* men the use of agriculture and the joys of the grain. She could have done—and, according to other sources, did—this just as Aphrodite taught *her* particular "works"—love—had she felt any special desire to do so. Aphrodite is all love, the great goddess who is the cosmic principle and ideal illustration of her works, which she alone makes possible. Once Aphrodite has become a psychic

reality, love is the unavoidable and obvious thing. Equally obviously, the idea of Demeter includes, for the Homeric poet, the idea of agriculture, and her fate the fate of the grain.

Neither does the goddess *show* men what has to be done with the grain. What she does show, after the earth has yielded up its fruit, are the *mysteries of Eleusis*. The mythical king of that place and his sons learn from her the secret usages of the cult, which the poet may not disclose. He who has seen the unutterable works of Demeter is fortunate: the uninitiate will enjoy no such lot in the darkness of death.[53]

So much we learn from the Homeric poet. For him, grain is the self-evident gift of the goddess. What Demeter shows to mortals over and above this is something worthy of note but not to be named. . . . The hymn is completely unthinkable without this allusion to the mysterious, supreme gift of the goddess. But we do not need to write a poem just to say something self-evident and already tacitly assumed, as is this connection between Demeter and the grain.[54] It is no less fundamental to the hymn than the other connections we have mentioned, between marriage and death and maiden and moon. On this self-evident foundation rests the special thing that the goddess does and shows. One of the symbols that was displayed in the Eleusinian mysteries on Demeter's instructions was a single ear of grain.[55] So the *self-evident* gift of the goddess serves to express what was revealed only to the *initiate*. The core of the Demetrian idea has *grain and motherhood* as its natural sheath and disguise. All three aspects—Mother Goddess, Corn Goddess, and Goddess of esoteric mysteries—belong to the figure of Demeter; none of them can be thought away, and the latter two in particular are closely connected in the hymn.

The strange conduct of Demeter as a nurse seems, in the hymn, to rest likewise on these two aspects. When, still unknown, the goddess came to Eleusis she offered her services as nurse to the friendly daughters of the king. These gave her the king's youngest son, Demophoön, to look after. Every night she laid him secretly in the fire—a singular method of obtaining immortality for her charge! The Homeric poet likens the child so placed to a flaming brand or torch. . . . He may have been thinking of the great part the torch played in the nocturnal celebrations at Eleusis. The mythological picture of the child in the fire[56] is in accord with the fact that in the mysteries the birth of a divine child was celebrated with the shining of a great light. Caught in her strange and awful act, the goddess speaks, in words of mystic revelation, of the *ignorance* of men.[57] Had they understanding of good and evil, she says, they would also understand the significance of that apparently deadly deed.

The meaning of it—good concealed in evil—is *immortality*. There can be no doubt of that. It is scarcely necessary to point out that Demeter's behaviour is not "anthropomorphic." To be laid in the fire and yet to remain alive, indeed to win immortality—that is no human fate. Does the goddess, perhaps, overstep the bounds of the humanly possible by reason of her sovereignty in that other domain of hers, which includes the *fate of the grain?* And not only by reason of her *power,* but because of her *form?* It would seem so, when we consider that the Demetrian fruit is perfected for human nourishment *in the fire.* Whether it is parched or baked as bread, death by fire is the fate of the grain. Nevertheless, every sort of grain is eternal. "I am not dead"—so sings the Maize God of the Cora Indians of Mexico after he is given over to the fire.[58] "My younger brothers (mankind) appear but once. Do they not die forever? But I never die; I appear continually. . . . " Among another tribe of Mexican Indians, the Tahumares, new-born boys undergo, on the third day, a rite very similar to what the Cora Indians do to the cobs that signify the Maize God: they make a great fire out of the stalks and carry the child three times through the smoke in all four directions. They do this, so runs the explanation today, in order that the child may thrive and be successful in life, i.e., in "raising corn."[59]

Of all the analogies that have been collected[60] this seems to fit best. Demeter treats Demophoön as though he were grain. Not, however, in order to make a successful farmer out of him. The Demophoön incident points as clearly as does the whole hymn to the fact that immortality is one of Demeter's gifts and that this immortality is akin to that of the grain. Old questions at once arise: Is Demeter's motherhood to be understood metaphorically? Was not the goddess, before she became completely anthropomorphic, a "Corn Mother," the ripe corn being taken as a maternal entity? And consequently, is not her daughter only apparently a maiden, but in reality a kind of plant? In late antiquity the word [*korē*] was explained as the feminine form of [*koros*] (sprout).[61] Another old interpretation is in the same spirit, which saw in Demeter's ravished daughter the grain for sowing.[62] The disappearance of both as though in death and their resurrection-like return said much in favour of this view. Yet even in antiquity such interpretations were merely rationalistic explanations which reversed the religious meaning: for the religious-minded man the *grain* expressed an inexpressible divine reality rather than that the goddess, Demeter's daughter, expressed the grain. The Kore figure of Persephone may have been the allegorical equivalent of the grain, but they are so equivalent that each can stand for the other. Both allude only to that unutterable thing hinted at in the very name of this Kore— . . . the Maiden not to be named.[63]

Mother divided from daughter, and the mown ear, are two symbols of something unspeakably painful that is hidden in the Demeter-aspect of the world; but also of something very consoling. Demeter contains this consolation in herself and reveals it in Eleusis. Seen as a whole, the Demetrian idea is not confined to purely human forms and relations, nor is it exhausted in the great reality of the grain. But in this non-human reality the idea is more comprehensive than it is in its purely human forms. The grain-figure is essentially the figure of both origin and end, of mother and daughter; and just because of that it points beyond the individual to the universal and eternal. It is always *the grain* that sinks to earth and returns, always the grain that is mown down in golden fullness and yet, as fat and healthy seed, remains whole, mother and daughter in one.

The symbolical value of the grain in the Demeter religion is vouched for in every way. The mown ear in Eleusis, five beautiful stalks of wheat in a little temple depicted on a vase[64]—there is evidence enough. The two great goddesses . . . [65] are not diminished in their aspect as grain; on the contrary they become greater, more comprehensive, more cosmic. Herein lies the real religious value of everything in the fate of the grain that reminded the Greeks of the fate of Persephone. And what did not remind them of it? There was hardly anything that did not do so. The only thing that is impossible is to reduce the whole mythologem of mother and daughter, and the innumerable associations that unfold in it like a bud, *merely* to the fate of the grain and to understand it purely allegorically. The mythological idea does not keep strictly to any natural process; it is enriched by them and enriches them in turn. It takes from nature but gives back again, and this is the sense in which we are to think of the relationship between the Persephone myth and the fate of the grain.

In Attica, besides the lesser mysteries in Agrai and the great mysteries in Eleusis, there were various other festivals connected with Persephone. Two of them fell at the time of the sowing: the Eleusinian mysteries and a women's festival, the Thesmophoria, from which men were excluded. Both involved fasting, following the example of Demeter's fast; and thus both were in some way connected with the disappearance of the Kore, which occasioned the fasting. Hence it was the sowing of the grain that reminded the Greeks of the Kore's rape.

The link between sowing the grain and vanishing in the underworld is confirmed by a further correspondence of myth and cult. The Orphic variants of the mythologem relegated the events in the Homeric hymn to a very primitive setting.[66] A swineherd comes in, with the name of *Eubuleus* (a name also of Hades); he is the witness of the rape, because his pigs were swallowed up by the earth along with Persephone. This story is borne out—as the sources themselves show[67]— by the fact that *young pigs* were cast into pits in honour of the two goddesses. We learn this in connection with the Thesmophoria; but it would be clear enough in any case that an analogy existed between the cavalier treatment of pigs and the sowing of the grain.

The pig is Demeter's sacrificial animal. In one connection, where it is dedicated to the Eleusinian mysteries, it is called . . . [68] the "uterine animal" of the earth, just as the dolphin was the "uterine animal" of the sea.[69] It was customary for Demeter to receive a gravid sow as a sacrificial offering.[70] The mother animal is a fit offering to the Mother Goddess, the pig in the pit a fit offering to her vanished daughter. As symbols of the goddesses, *pig* and *grain* are perfect parallels. Even the decomposed bodies of the pigs were drawn into the cult: the noisome remains were fetched up again, put on the altar, and used to make the sowing more fruitful.[71] If, then, the pig-and-grain parallel lays stress on corruption, it will no doubt remind us that the grain *decays* under the earth and thus, in this state of fruitful death, hints at the Kore dwelling in the realm of the dead.

So the Demeter idea is not lacking in the element of corruption coupled with the Kore's subterranean abode. Seen in terms of the Persephone myth, the fruitful death of the grain, religiously emphasized by the particulars of the pig-sacrifice, acquires a symbolic value, just as it is used as a parable for another idea: "Verily I say unto you, except a corn of wheat fall into the ground and die, it abideth alone: but if it die, it bringeth forth much fruit."[72] The corn and the pig buried in earth and left to decay point to a mythological happening and, interpreted accordingly, become transparently clear and hallowed.

The happenings of the natural process and the development of the mythological idea coincide thus far and no further. Persephone spends a *third* of every year in the underworld. Does the "fruitful death" of the grain last that long? The new crop sprouts much earlier;[73] and Demeter, the mother proud of her daughter (the ripened grain), appears much later in her golden garment of ears. According to the myth, the ripened wheat grains would have to fall to earth, the scene of their death and resurrection, immediately after their separation from the "mother." Under the original conditions, when grain grew wild, this was in fact the case. The corresponding mythologem is probably just as old and is closer to the natural process than to the artificial process. True, even in early antiquity the grain was kept in storage chambers and containers almost as in a tomb, the seed-corn generally for four months;[74] but it was preserved *from* decay and coming to life again. This has nothing to do with the myth. The grain in the vaults of Eleusis was part of the *temple treasure* of Demeter and meant to keep for a long time.

Hence the third of the year cannot be explained as a mere allegory of the agricultural process. The three-fold division is inextricably bound up with the primitive form of the goddess Demeter, who was also Hecate, and Hecate could claim to be mistress of the three realms. In addition, her relations to the moon, the grain, and the realm of the dead are three fundamental traits in her nature. The goddess's sacred number is the special number of the underworld: 3 dominates the chthonic cults of antiquity.[75] The division of the year into three in the Persephone myth corresponds not to a natural process but to a mythological idea.

Persephone

A divinity with a number of aspects is very apt to appear only in the *one* aspect under which he or she is being regarded at the moment. So it is with the primary goddess, who could equally well be called Hecate. In her Persephone aspect she exemplifies the Greek idea of *non-being;*[76] in her Demeter aspect she is a Hellenic form of the idea of the All-Mother. Those of us who are inclined to regard the Greek divinities as unmixed types must, in this case, accustom themselves to a duality of fundamentally different goddesses. But they must also realize that the idea of non-being in Greek religion forms the root-aspect of being.[77] This realization will enable them to understand the deeprooted identity of those two different and yet so closely related figures. Those, on the other hand, who do not incline to this view are tempted to assume a superficial and subsequent merging of two originally independent goddesses.

For this subsequent merging there is of course no evidence whatever, and the connection between the goddesses is anything but superficial. In the very place where, according to modern assumptions, this "superficial" connection is supposed to have been made, namely Eleusis, we see how intimately the Kore and Demeter are in fact connected. The daughter as a goddess originally quite independent of her mother is unthinkable; but what *is* thinkable, as we shall see, is the original *identity* of mother and daughter. Persephone's whole being is summed up in an incident that is at once the story of Demeter's own sufferings. The daughter's being is revealed like a flash in her mother's, only to be snuffed out the next moment:

> turns over round the bend
> of the parabola of curved flight,
> sinks, and is gone. . . .

The Kore who appears with Demeter is comparable with the *Hebe* who appears with the great goddess *Hera*. In ancient Arcadia[78] Hera had three forms: maiden . . . , fulfilled woman . . . , and woman of sorrows. . . . As [fulfilled woman] she has in Hebe *her own maiden self* . . . , for constant companion.[79] That is the static or plastic way of putting what is told in dynamic mythological form in the story of Hera emerging from her bath in the spring Kanathos ever again as a virgin.[80] As Hebe's mother she always has Hebe in herself; and as [woman of sorrows] she is endowed with characteristics that remind us of the grieving and recriminatory Demeter.

The comparison with Hera and her daughter may be allowed to stand as a mere analogy, and the question of whether they are both to be regarded as developments of the same mythological idea may be left undiscussed. Archaic Demeter figures are vivid proof that they always contain their own maiden form. Arcadia was familiar with two such Demeters, or rather with one that had two names: a dark, age-old goddess whose bitter rancour makes her kin both to the [Maiden self] and to the sorrowful Eleusinian mother.[81] In Phigalia she was called the Black One . . . in Thelpusa, Demeter Erinys. Both places had the same legend about her, a legend that expresses the deep-rooted identity of the original Demeter and the original Kore mythologically, but none the less clearly.

This is the mythologem of the marriage of the reluctant goddess, and the best-known variation of it came at the beginning of the cyclical epic, *Cypria*.[82] Here the bride—the original Kore—was called *Nemesis;* the bridegroom and seducer, *Zeus.* Pursued by the god's desire, the goddess transforms herself into various beasts of the earth, sea, and air. In this last mutation, as wild birds of the primeval swamp—she as a goose, he as a swan—the two divinities celebrate their marriage by rape. For this marriage was and remained a rape. The goddess was not to be softened by love; she succumbed to violence and therefore became the eternal avenger—Nemesis. The Kore to whom she gave birth was called *Helen.* The daughter had Artemisian traits from her Artemisian mother, Zeus' unwilling bride; and Aphrodisiac traits that were the reason for her being continually ravished. But in her ravishment and revenge, to which so many mortals fell victim, her mother's nature was only repeating itself. Helen is the eternally youthful Nemesis, spoiling for a rape and always wreaking her vengeance afterwards.

A similar story was told in Arcadia of the Demeter whose cognomen *Erinys* is the same as Nemesis. She, too, was pursued by a god—Poseidon, whose name simply means that he became Demeter's spouse.[83] She, too, transformed herself into the shape of an animal in order to escape from her seducer. Our source only speaks of her transformation into a mare, in which shape she was overpowered by Poseidon the *horse.* Her image in the Phigalian cave, however, was distinguished not only by a horse's head with "snakes and other animals growing out of it," but by a dolphin and a bird as well, apparently a dove. An aquatic animal and a creature of the air would therefore seem to indicate the two other realms in which, apart from the earth, the pursued goddess might have undergone trans-

formations. The Kore who was born of this Nemesis-like marriage was called "Mistress" . . . in Phigalia—that is, with one of Persephone's ritual names. Our source further remarks that in Phigalia the daughter was *not* a horse, that in Thelpusa she was a being "not to be named" before the uninitiate, and that she had a brother there who was the horse *Areion.* So the original Demeter seems to have been reborn in her mysterious daughter with the horse-brother just as Nemesis was in Helen.

Strangest of all is the explanation of the goddess's dark Erinys aspect. She is wroth because of the rape of her daughter and *at the same time* because of the marriage by rape which she herself had to undergo. In the legend that has come down to us, it is said that she was overpowered by Poseidon while she was looking for her ravished daughter. This mythological elaboration *doubles* the rape, for the goddess experienced the rape in *herself,* as Kore, and not in a separate girl. A daughter with the name of "Mistress" or "She who is not to be named" was born of this rape. The goddess becomes a mother, rages and grieves over the Kore who was ravished *in her own being,* the Kore whom she immediately recovers, and in whom she gives birth to *herself* again. The idea of the original Mother-Daughter goddess, at root a single entity, is at the same time the idea of *rebirth.*

To enter into the figure of Demeter means to be pursued, to be robbed, raped, to fail to understand, to rage and grieve, but then to get everything back and be born again. And what does all this mean, save to realize the universal principle of life, the fate of everything mortal? What, then, is left over for the figure of Persephone? Beyond question, that which constitutes the structure of the living creature *apart from* this endlessly repeated drama of coming-to-be and passing-away, namely the *uniqueness* of the individual and its *enthralment to non-being.* Uniqueness and non-being understood not philosophically but envisaged corporeally in figures, or rather as these are envisaged in the formless, unsubstantial realm of Hades. There Persephone reigns, the eternally unique one who is no more. Her uniqueness, so we could put it philosophically, forms the [ti]—that something in regard to which even non-being *is.* . . . [84] Had that uniqueness not been, had nothing ever stirred and started up in non-being, then the realm of Hades would not exist; in relation to pure nothing it would not be at all, not even an aspect of the past.

Homer conceives the realm of Hades as amorphously as it was possible for a Greek—that is to say, as poor in form and without any contours, with no connecting lines. He has no use for the method employed in archaic art to express the dead and the deadly: the creation of terrifying monsters and hybrids. Apparitions of this kind are as little suited to his style as to his conception of the shadowy realm. It is no awful shape that prevents the soul of Patroclus from passing through the gate of Hades and across its river. (The gate of Hades, the river, and even the House of Hades in which Patroclus' soul wanders, are all fluid, not marked off from one another; only in comparison with the realm of the living are they something wholly different.) Instead of a single terrifying shape, the whole kingdom of the dead rises up to oppose the entry of the soul of one not yet buried—the shadowy, amorphous kingdom seen as the congregation of all the souls. . . . [85]

Taken individually, the souls are not amorphous: they are the *images of the departed* . . . , but not corpselike images. They have nothing of the "living corpse" about them[86] which figures in the ghost stories of so many peoples. The soul of Patroclus still has the lovely eyes of the hero, though in the corpse these have long since decayed.[87] The [images] in the realm of the dead represent as it were the *minimum conceivable amount of form;* they are the image with which the deceased individual, through his uniqueness, has enriched the world.[88] Over the countless "images" of all that has once been, now heaped together and merged into an indeterminate featureless mass, there reigns *Persephone*—the eternally unique.

Whenever she is mentioned in the Iliad, she receives the title of . . . ("awful"), which implies praise and fear of her in equal measure; and she is indissolubly linked to the ruler of the dead. Her husband is sometimes called Hades, sometimes the *Zeus of the Underworld.* The wife of this Zeus undoubtedly counts as a great goddess, to whom all mortals are subject just as they are to that other Zeus—the ruler of the world seen in his deadly aspect. She has dominion over the manifold powers of death. Here we have the terrible aspects of Persephone, which are merely hinted at in Homeric poetry and are only associated with her—or with her and her husband as an indivisible pair—by implication. The association does not give rise to the firm outlines of a concrete figure, a monstrous figure, say, like the Black Demeter in Phigalia. Homer does not draw any frightening apparition for us, but he brings out the association all the more clearly. In the ninth book of the Iliad it is unmistakable. On one occasion the *Erinyes* are invoked in the plural. The curse, however, is heard and fulfilled not by a vague throng of vengeful spirits but by the underworldly Zeus and Persephone.[89] The second time the curse is addressed to the rulers of the Underworld. The utterer of the curse beats the earth with her hands. She is heard by Erinys, the mist-wandering goddess who dwells in the gloomy nether regions of Erebos.[90]

There are two ways of considering connections like this between Erinys and the rulers of the Underworld. One way begins with the dispersed state of the various aspects of the gods and believes in a *subsequent* mythological combination of them, with the result that mythology is understood at best as a co-ordinating and embellishing activity of the mind. Our way is opposed to this. It begins with the mythological ideas, which are easily recognized by their pristine *richness and many-sidedness.* Mythology is then understood as the mind's *creation* of gods in the sense that something real and valid is brought into the world.[91] Realities that disclose themselves to the mind are timeless. The *forms* in which they disclose themselves are stages in a process of (budlike) unfolding, and every unfolding tends ultimately towards dissolution. The primary thing for us is not this final state, not the Erinyes as spirits of vengeance, or Demeter and Persephone existing independently side by side, but the historical *Demeter Erinys* who contains in herself her own Kore figure—Persephone.

The Odyssey furnishes proof that the deadly powers associated with the Homeric Underworld may be regarded as allusions to this goddess. One such power, the power to terrify, to petrify with fright, to *turn to stone,* is possessed by the *Gorgon's head.* Odysseus is thinking of this when he sees the countless host of the dead approaching him: perhaps Persephone has sent the Gorgon's head from Hades![92] The mass of shades and the frightful apparition are respectively the *indefinite* and the *definite* manifestation of the realm of the dead. Though this realm is the domain of Persephone and her husband, the definite form of it points to the original Demeter.

Gorgon-like features are in fact displayed by the Black Demeter, who had a legend in common with Demeter Erinys. The horse-headed goddess was further characterized by having "snakes and other animals growing out of her head." The Gorgon's head in conjunction with a horse's body can be seen in an archaic representation of the killing of Medusa.[93] The Gorgon-headed Medusa was, like Demeter, Poseidon's bride. Like her, she gave birth to a horse—Pegasus—and to a mysterious son with the name of Chrysaor, the cognomen of Demeter Chrysaor. Closer scrutiny shows that the most important features in the fate of Persephone are also common to Medusa: she too was the only member of a divine triad—the trinity of Gorgons—to succumb to death *by violence.*[94]

The Kore's rape and the killing of Medusa are further connected by the name of the killer. Persephone (in Homer, "Persephoneia," Attic "Perrephatta") may well be a pre-Hellenic word that has been given Greek form; it is most probably connected with the name of Medusa's killer *Perseus,*[95] and can be understood in Greek as "she who was killed by Perseus."[96] Perseus has various things in common with Hades; for one thing he wore Hades' cap that made him invisible, and in Lerna he was actually identical with Hades. He immersed Dionysus in the waters, which in this case probably signified the Underworld.[97] The similarity between the fates of Dionysus and Persephone does not rest on this alone. We shall not pursue it further here, but shall keep to one aspect of the Medusa-killing.

The Gorgon's head was cut off with a *sickle,* an ancient mythological weapon with which Uranos was mutilated by Kronos.[98] If anything can throw light on the *meaning* of the use of this instrument and no other, it is the simple fact that from the remotest times this moon-shaped instrument has been used for the cutting of that which *bears the seed,* i.e., the standing corn. It is almost as if something *lunar* were fated to die by something *moon-shaped.* At any rate, certain features in Medusa's fate transparently connect this goddess with the bride, grain, and death aspects of Persephone.

Or, looking at it the other way round, we could say that through the figure of Persephone, the stately Queen of Hades, we glimpse the Gorgon. What we conceive philosophically as the element of *non-being* in Persephone's nature appears, mythologically, as the hideous Gorgon's head, which the goddess sends forth from the Underworld and which she herself bore in her archaic form. It is not, of course, *pure* non-being, rather the sort of non-being from which the living shrink as from something *with a negative sign:* a monstrosity that has usurped the place of the unimaginably beautiful, the nocturnal aspect of what by day is the most desirable of all things.

If we wanted to answer the question of the origin of this symbol, we should have to go more deeply into the antecedents of the other two great Kore figures, Artemis and Athene. There, too, we would meet with the Gorgon's head. Athene wears it on her breast, and Medusa appears on archaic monuments as a primitive form of Artemis, the mistress of wild animals.[99] She also has the wings of Nemesis. In her most ancient aspect as Medusa and Nemesis, Artemis proves to be identical with the original Demeter and thus with Persephone. The picture of the killing of Medusa—the most ancient form of Persephone's fate—on the pediment of the archaic temple to Artemis in Corfu commemorates this primitive mythological state.[100]

From it, the classical figure of Persephone rises up pure and beautiful, Artemisian and Aphrodisiac at once, another Helen, herself the daughter of Nemesis. Her Gorgonesque features remain in the background. On the wonderful little votive tablet in a temple to Persephone in Lower Italy[101] the Kore's departure is depicted as well as her rape. It is worthy of Aphrodite herself: winged cupids draw the chariot of the goddess. One would think that it was not Persephone celebrating her triumph, but Aphrodite. And indeed reference could be made to *Aphrodite Epitymbidia* or *Tymborychos,*[102] goddess of the tombs and the dead. In Persephone the sublimest beauty as well as the most hideous ugliness has its foundation. Non-being can put on an alluring face, and the goddess of the dead can appear in the form of an hetaera. Such were the sirens, Circe and Calypso, but not the Grecian Persephone. The foundation of her aphrodisiac beauty lies in what we have called her *uniqueness.*

In a world of living and dying, that is, in the world of Demeter and Persephone, there is an intimate connection between uniqueness and beauty. We can regard it from the point of view of beauty alone, as Winckelmann did, thinking unconsciously of Persephone when he said: "Strictly speaking, a beautiful person is beautiful for a moment only." Or we can regard it from the point of view of that instant after which non-being comes, like a dark abyss. At such moments the beautiful shines out in all its supreme radiance, and even a mortal maiden—Antigone advancing towards her bridal chamber, the grave—is then in the likeness of "beautiful Persephone."[103] . . .

Notes

[1] Details in A. Warburg, *Die Erneuerung der heidnischen Antike,* pp. 6ff.

[2] "Mythology" in the sense defined in the Prolegomena, supra.

[3] Cf. supra, p. 56.

[4] Cf. supra, p. 47.

[5] Cf. Usener, *Vorträge und Aufsätze* (pp. 119ff.) for the classical references.

[6] Pliny, *Historia naturalis,* IX, 80.

[7] W. F. Otto, *Der europäische Geist und die Weisheit des Ostens* (1931), p. 21.

[8] Kerényi, *Apollon* (1941), pp. 15ff.; *La Religione antica,* pp. 1ff.; *Die antike Religion,* p. 45.

[9] *Apollon,* pp. 37ff.

[10] W. F. Otto, *Dionysos* (1933), p. 186.

[11] *Die antike Religion,* pp. 78f.

[12] Otto, *The Homeric Gods,* p. 241.

[13] Otto, *Dionysos,* p. 29; Kerényi, *Die antike Religion,* p. 3.

[14] *Apollon,* p. 72.

[15] Cf. supra, the sections (6-9, in I) on the first four divinities.

[16] Pausanias, V, 3, 3.

[17] Euripides, *Heraclidae*, 771.

[18] Hyperides, in Pollux, IX, 74.

[19] Hesiod, *Theogony*, 886ff.

[20] Cf. Otto, *The Homeric Gods*, pp. 54f.

[21] Ibid., pp. 89f.

[22] *Odyssey*, VI, 106.

[23] Herodotus, II, 156; Wilamowitz, *Hellenistische Dichtung*, II, p. 48.

[24] Schneider, *Callimachea*, II, pp. 197ff.

[25] Homeric Hymn to Demeter, 424. Parallels in Allen and Sikes, *The Homeric Hymns;* cf. also L. Malten, "Altorphische Demetersage," pp. 422ff.

[26] *Iliad*, XXI, 483.

[27] L. R. Farnell, *The Cults of the Greek States*, II, pp. 435 ff.

[28] Hymn to Demeter, 7; Preller, *Griechische Mythologie*, I, p. 760.

[29] D. H. Lawrence, "Purple Anemones."

[30] Milton, quoted in Allen and Sikes, verse 17.

[31] D. H. Lawrence, "Fidelity," in his book *Pansies.*

[32] Hesychius, s.v.

[33] Cf. Farnell, II, 598 f.

[34] Kerényi, "Zum Vorständnis von Vergilius Aeneis B. VI," p. 422, confirmed by a fragment from the poet Philikos; cf. A. Körte, *Hermes*, pp. 450f.

[35] Callimachus in Scholium to Theocritus, II, 12; Schneider, p. 691.

[36] Scholium to Theocritus, II, 12; Euripides, *Helen*, 569 (fr. 959).

[37] Picture of a sacrifice to Persephone in an Attic vase-painting, L. Deubner, *Attische Feste*, fig. 2.

[38] Kerényi, "[ANODOS]-Darstellung in Brindisi," p. 279.

[39] Line 48. Similarly Hecate in a *relievo* in Thasos, cf. Farnell, II, Pl. XXXIX a.

[40] Hesychius, s.v.

[41] Eckhel, *Doctrina Nummorum Veterum*, II, p. 147; cf. Lobeck, *Aglaophamus*, II, p. 1213. Cf. also P. Philippson, *Thessalische Mythologic*, pp. 69ff.

[42] Scholium to Lycophron, *Alexandra*, 1180.

[43] Euripides, *Ion*, 1048; *Phoenissae*, 108.

[44] Kerényi, *Pythagoras und Orpheus*, pp. 47ff.

[45] P. Kretschmer, "Dyaus, [Zeus], Diespiter und die Abstrakta im Indogermanischen," pp. 111ff.

[46] Farnell, II, pp. 449ff.

[47] Hesiod, *Theogony*, 411ff.

[48] Hesiod, *Theogony*, 45off., scholium to Aristophanes, *Wasps*, 804.

[49] Collignon, *Histoire de la sculpture grecque*, II, p. 362.

[50] According to later tradition (Ovid and Hyginus), *half* the year. We are not concerned with this easily understandable version here, since it is obviously not the primary one.

[51] Hymn to Demeter, 471. . . .

[52] Ibid., 268f.

[53] Ibid., 473-480.

[54] Because of this, the analysis put forward by Wilamowitz (*Der Glaube der Hellenen*, II, pp. 47ff.) falls to the ground.

[55] Hippolytus, *Elenchos*, V, 8, 39.

[56] Cf. supra, pp. 35ff., Kullervo; and Kerényi, *Niobe*, pp. 75f., 259.

[57] Hymn to Demeter, 256f. The words used here by Demeter are taken up in the Orphic version (fr. 49, 95f.), in a later Orphic poem (fr. 233), and in the *Carmen aureum Pythagorae*, 54f.

[58] K. T. Preuss, *Der religiöse Gehalt der Mythem*, p. 8.

[59] C. Lumholtz, *Unknown Mexico*, I, p. 272.

[60] Frazer, in his edition of Apollodorus (1921), II, pp. 311f.

[61] Porphyry, in Eusebius, *Praeparatio Evangelica*, III, 11, 7, 9.

[62] Cicero, *De natura deorum*, II, 66.

[63] Euripides, *Helen*, 1307 (fr. 63); Carcinus in Diodorus Siculus, V, 5, 1; cf. [*aphrastos*] in Hesychius, s.v., and [*Hekatē Aphrastos*] *Jahrbuch für Phil.*, Suppl., XXVII (1900), 111.

[64] Farnell, III, Pl. 111b, with Lenormant's explanation in Daremberg and Saglio, *Dictionnaire des antiquités grecques et romaines*, I, p. 1066.

[65] Nilsson, "Die eleusinischen Gottheiten," p. 87.

[66] Cf. Malten, pp. 429ff.

[67] Clement of Alexandria, *Protrepicus*, II, 17, 1; Rabe, scholium to Lucian, p. 275.

[68] Epicharmus, fr. 100.

[69] Cf. supra, p. 50.

[70] Farnell, pp. 330, 91; 365, 246.

[71] Scholium to Lucian, loc. cit.

[72] John, 12:24.

[73] This objection comes from Nilsson, p. 107.

[74] Here, with Cornford, Nilsson (op. cit., p. 108) finds the explanation of the Persephone myth.

[75] H. Diels, *Sibyllinische Blätter*, p. 40.

[76] Kerényi, *Die antike Religion*, pp. 220ff.

[77] Kerényi, *Dionysos und das Tragische in der Antigone*, p. 10.

[78] In Stymphalis; Pausanias, VIII, 22.

[79] Or, from Hebe's point of view: "It is as though Hebe had separated herself only gradually from the goddess to become her daughter and an independent divinity, as though in the beginning she had been a manifestation of Hera herself." P. Philippson, *Griechische Gottheiten in ihren Landschaften* (*Symbolae Osloenses*, suppl. fasc. IX, 1939), p. 48.

[80] Pausanias, II, 38, 2.

[81] Pausanias, VIII, 25 and 42, our source for what follows. The credibility of Pausanias' description of the Demeter statue in Phigalia is vouched for by the mythologem and art relics as against Wilamowitz, *Der*

Glaube der Hellenen I, pp. 402f.

[82] Kerényi, *Die Geburt der Helena*, pp. 9ff.

[83] Kretschmer, "Zur Geschichte der grechischen Dialekte," pp. 28ff.

[84] The Platonic expression is here used in the same sense as in *Die antike Religion*, p. 234.

[85] *Iliad*, XXIII, 72.

[86] Nor anything of the "corpse spiritualized or dematerialized in some mysterious way," as W. F. Otto (*Die Manen*, p. 37) expresses the idea that, in his view, best corresponds to the Homeric "shade."

[87] Compare with this the terrible state Hector was in when his spirit appeared to Aeneas in Virgil, *Aeneid*, II, 270ff. As F. Altheim once observed to me, it is as though the Romans clung even in death to the *historical* figure, the Greeks to the *ideal* one.

[88] According to the Pythagoreans, the image of the unique mixture of elements that produced the individual passes to the moon, never to be replaced (Kerényi, *Pythagoras und Orpheus*, 2nd edn.: p. 59). Every individual being is accordingly preserved not only in the *past* of a world temporally conceived (consisting of what *has been* and *is*), but in a definite portion of the spatial universe as well. Another such storage-place is the House of Hades, the *thesaurus Orci* of the Romans.

[89] *Iliad*, IX, 454-457.

[90] Ibid., 569-572.

[91] Kerényi, *Apollon*, 120; *Die antike Religion*, p. 65.

[92] *Odyssey*, XI, 634f.

[93] Boeotian wine-jar in relief in Paris, cf. R. Hampe, *Frühe griechische Sagenbilder in Böotien*, Pls. 36 and 38.

[94] Hesiod, *Theogony*, 276-282; Apollodorus, *Bibliotheca*, II, 4, 2.

[95] Wilamowitz, *Der Glaube der Hellenen*, I, pp. 108f.; further details in Altheim, "Persona," pp. 45f.

[96] Like [*theopompos*] in the connotation "he who is sent by God."

[97] C. Robert, *Die griechische Heldensage*, I, p. 243.

[98] Hesiod, *Theogony*, 174-181.

[99] Kerényi, *Die Geburt der Helena,* p. 19; cf. *Journal of Hellenic Studies,* 1885, Pl. LIX.

[100] The inscriptions mention Artemis; cf. Kaiser Wilhelm II's *Erinnerungen an Korfu,* p. 105.

[101] Lokroi Epizephyroi, cf. Quagliati, "Rilievi votivi arcaici," p. 188.

[102] Plutarch, *Quaestiones Romanae,* XXIII; Clement of Alexandria, *Protrepicus,* XXXVIII.

[103] Kerényi, *Dionysos und das Tragische in der Antigone,* pp. 12ff.; *Die antike Religion,* p. 239. Virgil (*Aeneid,* VI, 142) calls Persephone *pulchra Proserpina; . . .* cf. Preller, *Griechische Mythologie,* p. 301, n. 3. . . .

References Cited

Abbreviations: *ArchRW = Archiv für Religionswissenschaft* (Freiburg i. B.). AV = Albae Vigiliae. BS = Bollingen Series. CWJ = Collected Works of C. G. Jung (New York/Princeton and London).

Allen, Thomas William, and Edward Ernest Sikes (eds.). *The Homeric Hymns.* London, 1904; 2nd edn., Oxford, 1936.

Collignon, Léon Maxime. *Histoire de la sculpture grecque.* Paris 1892-97. 2 vols.

Deubner, Ludwig. *Attische Feste.* Berlin, 1932.

Diels, Hermann. *Sibyllinische Blätter,* Berlin, 1890.

Eckhel, Joseph. *Doctrina Nummorum Veterum,* II. Vindobonae [Vienna], 1792-1839. 8 vols.

Farnell, L. R. *The Cults of the Greek States.* Oxford, 1896-1909. 5 vols.

Hampe, Roland. *Frühe griechische Sagenbilder in Böotien.* (Deutsches Archäologisches Institut.) Athens, 1936.

Kerényi, C. [*or* Karl]. "[*ANODOS*]-Darstellung in Brindisi, mit einem Zodiakus von II Zeichen," *ArchRW,* XXX (1933), 271-307.

———. *Die antike Religion: eine Grundlegung.* Amsterdam, 1942 [3rd edn., Düsseldorf, 1952]. (Cf. *The Religion of the Greeks and Romans* and *La Religione Antica,* qq. v.)

———. *Apollon: Studien über antike Religion und Humanität.* 2nd edn., Amsterdam and Leipzig, 1941; [3rd edn., Düsseldorf, 1953].

———. *Dionysos und das Tragische in der "Antigone."* (Frankfurter Studien zur Religion und Kultur der Antike, XIII.) Frankfurt a. M., 1935. (Translation in preparation.)

———. "Die Geburt der Helena: eine mythologische Studie dis manibus Leonis Frobenii." *Mnemosyne: Bibliotheca classica batava* (Lugduni [Leyden]), N.S. 3, III (1939), 161-79.

———. *Niobe: Neue Studien über antike Religion und Humanität.* Zurich, 1949.

———. *La Religione antica.* Bologna, 1940. (Tr. from *Die antike Religion,* q.v.; cf. *The Religion of the Greeks and Romans.*)

———. "Zum Verständnis von Vergilius Aeneis B. VI: Randbemerkungen zu Nordens Kommentar," *Hermes,* LXVI (1931), 413-41.

Körte, Alfred. "Der Demeter-Hymnos des Philkos," *Hermes,* LXVI (1931), 442-54.

Kretschmer, Paul. "Dyaus, [*Zeus*], Diespiter und die Abstrakta im Indogermanischen," *Glotta* (Göttingen), XIII (1924), 101-14.

———. "Zur Geschichte der griechischen Dialekte: 1. Ionier und Achäer, 2. Die Apokope in den griechischen Dialekten," *ibid.,* I (1909), 9-59.

Lawrence, D. H. "Fidelity." In: *Pansies.* [London?, 1929.]

———. "Purple Anemones." In: *The Collected Poems of D. H. Lawrence.* London, 1928. 2 vols. (Vol. II, pp. 163-65.)

Lenormant, F. "Ceres, [*Demeter*]" In: Charles Daremberg and Edmond Saglio. *Dictionnaire des antiquités grecques et romaines.* Paris, 1877-1919. 5 vols. in 10. (Vol. I, pp. 1021-78.)

Lobeck, Christian August. *Aglaophamus; sive, de theologiae mysticae Graecorum causis libri tres . . . idemque Poetarum Orphicorum dispersas reliquias collegit.* Regiomontii Prussorum (Königsberg = Kaliningrad), 1829. 2 vols.

Lumholtz, Carl. *Unknown Mexico: A Record of Five Years' Exploration among the Tribes of the Western Sierra Madre in the 'tierra caliente' of Tepic and Jalisco and among the Tarascos of Michoacan.* New York, 1903.

Malten, L. "Altorphische Demetersage," *ArchRW,* XII (1909), 417-46.

Nilsson, Martin P. "Die eleusinischen Gottheiten," *Archrw*, XXXII (1935), 79-141.

Otto, Walter F. *Dionysos: Mythos und Kultus.* (Frankfurter Studien zur Religion und Kultur der Antike, IV.) 2nd edn., Frankfurt a. M., 1933.

———. *Der europäische Geist und die Weisheit des Ostens: Gedanken über das Erbe Homers.* Frankfurt a. M., 1931.

———. *The Homeric Gods: the Spiritual Significance of Greek Religion.* Translated by Moses Hadas. New York, 1954; London, 1955.

———. *Die Manen, oder Von den Urformen des Totenglaubens.* Berlin, 1923.

Philippson, Paula. *Thessalische Mythologie.* Zurich, 1944.

Preller, Ludwig. *Griechische Mythologie.* Edited by Carl Robert. 4th edn., Berlin, 1887-1926. 2 vols. in 6 parts.

Preuss, Konrad Theodor. *Der religiöse Gehalt der Mythen.* Tübingen, 1933.

Quagliati, Q. "Rilievi votivi arcaici in terracotta di Lokroi Epizephyroi," *Ausonia* (Rome), III (1908), 136-234.

Robert, Carl. *Die griechische Heldensage.* Berlin, 1920-26. 3 parts. (In: Ludwig Preller. *Griechische Mythologie,* q.v., II.)

Schneider, Otto (ed.) *Callimachea.* Leipzig, 1870-73. 2 vols.

Usener, Hermann. *Vorträge und Aufsätze.* Leipzig, 1914.

Warburg, Aby Moritz. *Die Erneuerung der heidnischen Antike: Kulturwissenschaftliche Beiträge zur Geschichte der europäischen Renaissance.* Leipzig, 1932. 2 vols. in 4.

Wilamowitz-Moellendorf, Ulrich Von. *Hellenistische Dichtung in der Zeit des kallimachos.* Berlin, 1924. 2 vols.

Charlene Spretnak (essay date 1992)

SOURCE: Introduction to *Lost Goddesses of Early Greece: A Collection of Pre-Hellenic Myths*, Beacon Press, 1992, pp. 17-38.

[*In the following essay, Spretnak discusses the early, pre-Hellenic Greek goddesses and argues that follow-ing Greece's invasions by the Ionians, Achaeans, and Dorians, the native oral tradition which embraced matriarchal mythology was incorporated into the patriarchal, Olympic tradition of mythology. Under this system, the once-powerful and compassionate pre-Hellenic goddesses were transformed into jealous, disagreeable, troublesome beings.*]

Gaia created the world, Pandora gave bountiful gifts, Artemis led Her worshippers in ecstatic dances, Hera rewarded the girls who ran the first Olympic races, and Athena peacefully protected the home. These Goddesses are among the earliest deities known in Greece, but the original mythology surrounding them has been lost. We know their names only through the relatively late myths of the classical period.

Yet for thousands of years before the classical myths took form and then were written down by Hesiod and Homer in the seventh century B.C., a rich oral tradition of mythmaking had existed. Strains of the earlier tradition are evident in the later myths, which reflect the cultural amalgamation of three waves of barbarian invaders, the Ionians, the Achaeans, and finally the Dorians, who moved into Greece from 2500 to 1000 B.C. These invaders brought with them a patriarchal social order and their thunderbolt God, Zeus. What they found when they entered Greece was a firmly rooted religion of Goddess worship. In various regions of the mainland and the islands, a Goddess was held sacred and was associated with order, wisdom, protection, and the life-giving processes (e.g., seasonal change, fertility of womb and field). Among the Goddesses we know to have preceded the Olympian system are Gaia, Themis, Rhea, Pandora, Aphrodite, Artemis, Leto, Britomaris, Diktynna, Selene, Hecate, Hera, Athena, Demeter, and Persephone.

The invaders' new Gods, the Olympians, differ in many ways from the earlier Goddesses. The pre-Hellenic Goddesses are enmeshed with people's daily experiencing of the energy forces in life; Olympian Gods are distant, removed, "up there." Unlike the flowing, protective love of a Mother-Goddess, the character of the Olympian Gods is judgmental. Olympian Gods are much more warlike than their predecessors and are often involved in strife. The pre-Hellenic Goddesses are powerful and compassionate, yet those whom the Greeks incorporated into the new order were transformed severely. The great Hera was made into a disagreeable, jealous wife; Athena was made into a cold, masculine daughter; Aphrodite was made into a frivolous sexual creature; Artemis was made into the quite forgettable sister of Apollo; and Pandora was made into the troublesome, treacherous source of human woes. These prototypes later evolved into the wicked witch, the cruel stepmother, the passive princess, etc., of our fairy tales. Of all the great Mother-Goddesses, only Demeter survives intact. However, she is not included in the main group on Mount Olympus, in spite of the fact that she is a very old deity and was well known on both the islands and the mainland.

Although the pre-Hellenic Goddesses pre-date considerably the Greek Gods, these Goddesses are relatively late derivatives of the Great Goddess, the supreme deity for millennia in many parts of the world. Her worship seems to have evolved from the awe experienced by our early ancestors as they regularly observed woman's body as the source of life. Paleolithic statues celebrate the mysteries of the female: Woman's body bled painlessly in rhythm with the moon, and her body miraculously *made people,* then provided food for the young by making milk. (In a primitive culture, copulation is not usually associated with the miracle of new life; paternity was not recognized for a long while.) A further mystery to our ancestors was that woman could draw from her body women and men.

Perhaps the earliest Paleolithic statues, dating from 25,000 B.C., are expressions of the female body as living microcosm of the larger experiences of cyclic change, birth, renewal, and nurture. In time these energies became embodied in the sacred presence of the Great Goddess, the encompassing matrix of female power. On her surface she produced food, into her womb she received the dead. Rituals in her honor took place in womb-like caves, often with vulva-like entrances and long, slippery corridors; both the cave entrances and grave sites were often painted with blood-like red ochre, a clay used as pigment. As society evolved, so did the powers of the Goddess. She was revered as the source of life, death and rebirth; as the giver of the arts, divine wisdom, and just law; and as the protector of peace and the nurturer of growth. She was all forces, active and passive, creative and destructive, fierce and gentle.

The Great Goddess was known by many names in many cultures. At various sites of her worship, certain attributes were stressed. Because the traits that were emphasized came to be associated with the local name for the Goddess—and may have been inspired by a particular woman—many derivative forms evolved. The seeming multiplicity of deities is misleading since each was a facet of the one, omnipotent Goddess. Eventually, some of the Goddesses reproduced, always parthenogenetically in prepatriarchal mythology. If the child was a daughter, she joined her mother in administering supernatural powers. If the child was a son, he became his mother's lover and held a subordinate role in the mythology. In graphic representations the son/lover is always pictured as being smaller than the Goddess and is usually in the background. The original perception of the Goddess as the parthenogenetic source of life was still held sacred long after certain biological facts were recognized among her worshippers.

Reclaiming Pre-Hellenic Mythology

The Greek myths of the classical period have long been considered *the* Greek myths. The classicist Jane Ellen Harrison was among the first to recognize that those myths are actually a late development in a long mythic tradition: "Beneath this splendid surface [of Homer's Olympian myths] lies a stratum . . . at once more primitive and more permanent." Drawing from various sources of evidence, Harrison delineated the strong contrasts between the matrifocal, pre-Hellenic body of mythology and the patriarchal, Olympian system that later evolved.

As successful conquerors, the invaders blended certain aspects of pre-Hellenic religion, i.e., principally the Goddesses' names, with their own patriarchal Gods and themes. For example, Hera had long been associated with the "sacred marriage"—the merging of the lunar cow and the solar bull. However, "sacred marriage" is used in Olympian mythology to refer to Hera's marriage to Zeus. The fact that their union was always a stormy one is thought by many classicists to be a historical reference to the forced merging of the two cultures: Hera is the powerful native queen who is coerced but never subdued by the alien conqueror.

There are a number of reasons why this chapter of our cultural history has been "lost." The most obvious is that the pre-Hellenic myths are the religion of a conquered people, so they were co-opted and replaced for political reasons. Second, pre-Hellenic mythology was an oral tradition, and many of the clues to its nature have been lost over the past 3500 years. Third, a culturally imposed bias among many Victorian and contemporary scholars prevented them from accepting the evidence that deity was originally perceived as female in most areas of the world. In the literature, one never reads of "the religion of Artemis" and "the cult of Jesus"; it is always the other way around. One of the most renowned living mythologists wrote a few years ago that although "paleolithic deposits in Asia and Europe have yielded a great many bone statuettes representing a nude Goddess . . . we cannot deduce from the *presence* of the paleolithic female statuettes, the *non-existence* of the worship of a divine masculine Being" [his italics]. Similarly, another scholar theorized that the reason numerous Goddess statues are the sole trace of deity during the early Neolithic period on Crete is that the actual supreme deity was probably a male God whose representation was forbidden! If these researchers had dug up numerous statues of male Gods on a remote island, it is extremely unlikely that they would deduce the existence of an unrepresented, supreme "divine feminine Being."

Fortunately for posterity, a number of open-minded classicists and archaeologists have labored to uncover the realities of our pre-Hellenic past. Jane Ellen

Harrison, Marija Gimbutas, Lewis Farnell, Robert Graves, E. O. James, Carl Kerenyi, Martin Nilsson, George Thompson, and R. F. Willetts are among those who have made extensive contributions to our understanding of pre-Hellenic culture and consciousness. Still, much information has been lost concerning pre-Hellenic religion. In order to reconstruct the myths, fragments must be assembled from various sources. One area of evidence is archaeological discoveries. Very early statues, shrines, picture-seals on rings, and labelled figures on ceramic vessels all point to the deeds and rituals associated with various Goddesses. A second area is the writings from the classical period. Homer, Hesiod, Pausanius, Herodotus, Strabo, and others sometimes mentioned, and occasionally recorded rather fully, very old observances of Goddess worship that still took place at certain sites in Greece. A third area is the oral tradition. Many of the stories were preserved among the rustic people; at Ephesus in Anatolia, for instance, the worship of Artemis was kept alive well into the Christian era. . . .

The charge can be leveled against the pre-Hellenic myths that they have less plot design, intrigue, and dramatic tension than does Olympian mythology. This is true. Since pre-Hellenic religion flourished and then was crushed before the era of extensive written records, we can hardly do more than piece together portraits of the Goddesses. However, our knowledge of the pre-Hellenic myths, even if incomplete, reveals a compelling alternative to patriarchal cosmology and metaphysics—a more integrated view of life on Earth. . . .

In addition, the pre-Hellenic myths depict a view of life that is quite different from that expressed in the Olympian myths. Even if we had encyclopedic records of the earlier mythology, it seems highly unlikely, judging by what *has* survived, that themes of deceit, treachery, alienation, and brutality informed the pre-Hellenic sacred stories. If such Olympian themes had been embraced by the pre-Hellenic peoples as well, they would have been expressed in the many artifacts and fragments of script. They are not. The pre-Hellenic myths, instead, tell of harmonious bonds among humans, animals, and nature. They express respect for and celebration of the mysteries of body and spirit.

The latest edition of the voluminous *Cambridge Ancient History* deftly notes that various aspects of the pre-Hellenic religion are "under lively discussion." Quite so. It is important that the evidence be aired, that connections be made, that particulars be debated. Yet the essence of these prehistoric myths will be grasped only if we can let go of a protective, supposedly detached pose and enter into the body of myths with openness. If we can succeed in reading these spiritual stories with spiritual perceptions, a sense of continuity with our past may result.

Implications for Patriarchal Religion and Culture

When compared to the religions of the Goddess in Europe and elsewhere, the Judeo-Christian tradition was "born yesterday." In fact, the very notion of supreme deity, i.e., ultimate power, being male is a relatively recent invention. Zeus first appeared around 2500 B.C., and Abraham, the first patriarch of the Old Testament, is dated by Biblical scholars at 1800 B.C.; in contrast, some of the Goddess statues are dated at 25,000 B.C. Therefore, what we see around us, that is, patriarchal religion and social order, is not "the natural order" for all humankind since Day One based on "the Natural Law."

The new, patriarchal religion co-opted the older mythic symbols and inverted their meaning: The female, Eve, was now weak-willed and treacherous; the sacred bough was now forbidden; and the serpent, symbol of regeneration and renewal with its shedding skins, was now the embodiment of evil. The Goddess religion and its "pagan" worshippers were brutally destroyed in the Biblical lands, just as they had been conquered, co-opted, and destroyed in Old Europe, the Middle East, and India by Indo-European invaders. The Old Testament is the military and cultural record (albeit considerably laundered) of a massive political coup. It is important to note that we did not emerge into patriarchal religion from a dark, chaotic, immature period of primitivism; Goddess-centered cultures, including Minoan Crete, were highly evolved. (See *When God Was A Woman* by Merlin Stone and *The Language of the Goddess* and *The Civilization of the Goddess* by Marija Gimbutas.)

In the Christian tradition, the Virgin Mary is clearly rooted in the older Goddess religion because she produces her child parthenogenetically (And Jesus himself is true to the older pattern of the Goddess' son/lover dying at the Spring Equinox and being reborn at the Winter Solstice.) The church co-opted Mary in order to make converts. She is not included in the core symbols, i.e., the trinity, but the church fathers discovered they could not attract followers in the heavily Goddess-oriented Mediterranean and Celtic cultures, which then stretched from the Balkans to the British Isles, without a Goddess on their banners: Mary, Mother of God, formerly God herself. Far from "elevating the feminine," the church demoted her, stripped her of her power, and rendered her docile and sexless.

The Judeo-Christian tradition has long sought to eradicate all traces of Goddess religion. The Old Testament is full of references to slaughtering the pagans and destroying their shrines, yet their presence continued through every Biblical era. On the other side of the Mediterranean, her worshippers were equally steadfast. Long into the Christian age, the women of Greece and Anatolia (Turkey) insisted on praying to Artemis in time of childbirth, and the church forcibly closed the last Goddess temple as late as 500 A.D. Many of the Goddess' sacred sites, such as the Parthenon of the Acropolis, were converted into Christian churches. During the Middle Ages, the widespread witch-burnings, a patriarchally approved campaign of mass murder, were largely designed to eliminate independent women who still followed the Old Religion, i.e., worshipped the Goddess in some form, observed nature's holy days (solstices and equinoxes), and practiced herbal healing, abortion, and contraception. In the medieval legends of St. George (the church) slaying the dragon (the huge snake-like symbol of the Old Religion), the dragon's head often grows back. Today a similar wave of rebellion is challenging patriarchal religion. (See *The Spiral Dance: A Rebirth of the Ancient Religion of the Great Goddess* by Starhawk and *Drawing Down the Moon* by Margot Adler.)

Problems with Jungian Uses of Greek Goddess Mythology

There are almost as many interpretations of myth as there are mythologists. Two poles of the spectrum are represented by Robert Graves and Carl Jung. Graves maintains, "Greek mythology was no more mysterious in content than are modern election cartoons."[1] In his two-volume study, *The Greek Myths,* Graves' extensive annotations are a treasury of information on the interplay of matriarchal and patriarchal politics. Jung, in contrast, wrote, "We can hardly suppose that myth and mystery were invented for any conscious purpose; it seems much more likely that they were the involuntary revelation of a psychic, but unconscious, pre-condition."[2] With regard to pre-Olympian mythology specifically, both of these perspectives are valid.

Certainly there are a number of political references in classical mythology to the trauma of occupation by the barbarian invaders. Just as Hera's turbulent marriage to Zeus is thought to be a historical reference, so classicists have proposed that the rape of Persephone reflects the rape of the pre-Hellenic culture and does not seem to have been part of her mythology before the invasions. (In Jungian terms, the rape would be seen as an intrusion of patriarchal consciousness into the earlier matriarchal mode.)

Another example supporting Graves' view is the myth of the rivalry between Athena and Poseidon, which bears clues to a massive societal shift away from pre-Hellenic customs. In a vote by the citizens of Athens, the men voted for Poseidon and the women for Athena. Since the women outnumbered the men by one, Athena won. To appease the wrath of Poseidon, the men inflicted upon the women a triple punishment: They were to lose their vote, their children were no longer to be called by their mothers' name; and they themselves were no longer to be called Athenians after their Goddess.

On the other hand, both pre-Hellenic and classical mythology also abound with references to the psyche. Jung was aware, of course, of the matriarchal stratum of our cultural history. He warned that most myth reflects archetypes only indirectly because the mythological traditions that have survived through long periods of time have "received a specific stamp," have been "submitted to conscious elaboration," and have evolved as a "historical formula."[3] Jung knew that the classical Greek myths, for instance, had been "elaborated" extensively, and he once referred to them as "the hackneyed *chronique scandaleuse* of Olympus."[4] However, he never made a clear, consistent distinction between the two bodies of Greek mythology. In 1954 Jung wrote, " . . . in Greek mythology matriarchal and patriarchal elements are about equally mixed."[5] This is an accurate statement only if one specifies that pre-Hellenic mythology is matriarchal and classical mythology is largely patriarchal. We have seen that the nature of the deities in each of these traditions varies so markedly that it is misleading to speak simply of *the* Greek myths. When Jungian psychologists purport to cite from mythology original "revelations" of the female psyche and then go back only as far as the patriarchal, revisionist portraits of the Goddesses, they are looking in the wrong place.

In addition to the character traits and deeds of the pre-Hellenic Goddesses, their symbols were radically transformed. To gloss over this transformation is to present misinformation. In a discussion of the mother archetype in mythology, Jung wrote, "Evil symbols are the witch, the dragon (or any devouring or entwining animal, such as a large fish or serpent) . . . This list is not, of course, complete; it presents only the most important features of the mother archetype."[6] Does it? Or does it present only features of the *patriarchal* archetype of the mother? Witches, serpents, and dragons were never "evil symbols" in the traditon of the Goddess.

When Jung spoke of archetypes and their symbols, he was reaching for "collective unconscious contents . . . primordial types, that is, with universal images that have existed since the remotest times."[7] In view of patriarchy's "managing of information" for the past 3500 years, their traditions of mythology and religion do not allow us full views of our earliest archetypal images. Therefore, it would seem more accurate to speak of "patriarchal archetypes," rather than "archetypes," when discussing psychological developments in patriarchal cultures such as our own.

The concept of elucidating the nature of the modern female psyche by drawing on expressions of the female in myth is a creative and potentially profound approach. Dozens of books and scores of articles have been written by Jungians who seek such answers in Greek mythology. Unfortunately, almost none of them conveys an understanding of the two radically different systems therein. Nearly always they turn to the classical myths, composed in seventh century B.C. and even later. These are a very limited source of data on the female psyche; they are clearly tales with a point of view.

Somewhere near the beginning of Jungian treatises on this topic is usually a disclaimer about interest in any historical or social framework of the mythology: The myths are studied purely for their expressions of the unconscious. However, continual references are made to the antiquity of the myths, so as to place them far back in history. The problem is that this is almost never done specifically. For example, throughout *Women's Mysteries,* Esther Harding refers to "the ancients."[8] Does this mean our ancestors from the Neolithic, matrifocal period of culture—or the later patriarchal stage? The adjective *antique* is equally nebulous. Maria-Louise von Franz refers simply to "the antique mother-goddesses."[9] Does she mean the wise, powerful, autonomous Goddesses of the pre-Olympian era—or the petty, jealous, victimized Goddesses of the classical era? Like most of her colleagues, she would have it both ways: She states, " . . . the mother-goddesses depict absolutely unreflecting femininity," which is exemplified by "a terrible scene" about jealousy, for instance. Then von Franz observes "the mother-goddess always behaved like that."[10] In patriarchal mythology, that is! The Goddesses are portrayed so differently in the two traditions that there is almost nothing that "always" applies in both their pre-Hellenic and their classical versions.

Another problem is that the Great Goddess may be too large a concept for the Jungian constructs of "the feminine." Jungian analysts speak of the Goddess as being synonymous with "the feminine principle, Eros"[11] or with "feminine nature."[12] True, the Goddess was the ultimate expression of female being, but her nature was all-encompassing, e.g., giver of divine law, fierce protector, gentle nurturer. If she were a pure expression of the Jungian notion of "the feminine consciousness," these traits would not be possible. They would have to be explained via "animus energies," which would be impossible in an embodiment of pure "femininity." The Great Goddess was supreme power and was all. (For a discussion of the patriarchal biases involved in the Jungian theory of anima/animus, see *Changing of the Gods* by Naomi Goldenberg.)

An exception to most Jungian treatments of Greek Goddess mythology is "Hera: Bound and Unbound" by Murray Stein.[13] Drawing on the work of classicists, principally Kerenyi, Stein does acknowledge the difference between the pre-Hellenic and the Olympian portrayals of Hera. However, he asserts that her classical role as the archetypal wife had also been her pre-Hellenic role and that "'wifehood' was her essential

mode of being."[14] Stein maintains that Hera's central goal was always "perfection in marriage."[15] This is quite impossible. Hera was a very ancient pre-Hellenic deity who was probably worshipped long before the relatively late discovery of paternity and certainly long before the invention of patriarchal marriage. She had always been associated with mating and fecundity, but this is quite different from formalized marriage. As Elizabeth Fisher pointed out in *Woman's Creation,* human history's first and longest reigning social unit was the mother and child, not the husband and wife.

A more typical example of Jungian treatments of Greek mythology as being revelatory of the modern female psyche is Robert A. Johnson's popular *She: Understanding Feminine Psychology,* subtitled *An Interpretation Based on the Myth of Amor and Psyche and Using Jungian Psychological Concepts.* Johnson opens by explaining, "the story of Amor and Psyche is one of the best elucidations available of the psychology of the feminine personality. It is an ancient, pre-Christian myth, first recorded in classical Greek times, having enjoyed a long oral tradition before that . . ."[16] Not *very* long. The tale of Amor and Psyche became part of the Latin novel *The Golden Ass,* which was written in the second century A.D. by Apuleius. No doubt it was told before then, but its patriarchal aspects date the myth firmly in the classical era. Johnson further explains that "when we want to study the basic patterns of human behavior and personality, it is instructive to go to the earliest sources."[17] Absolutely right. But patriarchal myths are not they.

A principal theme of Johnson's exegesis is that every woman naturally contains "the Aphrodite nature" within her. This sounds quite plausible; after all Aphrodite was the powerful procreative energy that ensured the survival of the race. However, this original nature of Aphrodite is not what Johnson has in mind. Rather, he paints an ultra-patriarchal picture of Aphrodite that almost outdoes Apuleius: She is called "primitive femininity," with "her chief characteristics being vanity, conniving, lust, fertility, and tyranny when she is crossed."[18] (Some might find Johnson's inclusion of "fertility" among a string of negative adjectives to be clinically interesting.) In case readers may have missed the point, Johnson then labels Aphrodite "a thorough bitch" and illustrates her existence in modern females with several examples that are pregnant with woman-hating.[19] But the mental health of one individual author is not the issue. The central question raised by this approach is *What is the effect of telling a woman that much of her true nature is that of "a thorough bitch"— and that this is "proved" by "the earliest sources" of mythology?*

More than any other Jungian writer, Erich Neumann recognized the powerful implications of the long era of matrifocal mythology. He did so, however, within the boundaries of Jungian theory and so viewed "matriarchal consciousness" as an immature stage "in which the independence of the ego system is not yet fully developed."[20] Having spent years compiling the matrifocal research that became *The Great Mother*, Neumann brought to his interpretation of Amor and Psyche a comprehension of the matrifocal fragments that had survived into the patriarchal myth. Whereas Johnson sees Psyche's sisters only as "the serpent in her paradise" (an ironic metaphor on his part, to be sure) and as evil forces who are intensely jealous and who "devise a venomous plan,"[21] Neumann recognizes them as messengers of matrifocal consciousness. Their agitations correspond to a current in Psyche of "matriarchal protest" whereby she begins to question the "unconsciousness of her situation" with Eros (Amor) and her "seemingly total abandonment of her individual consciousness."[22] Neumann concludes that it is the conflict between matriarchal and patriarchal psychology that makes the myth of Amor and Psyche intelligible.[23]

As the search continues for an understanding of archetypal images, Jung would probably have us remember that an archetype is "a hypothetical model, something like the 'pattern of behavior' in biology."[24] The portraits of the Goddesses in patriarchal mythology are, indeed, patterns of behavior: They are stories told by men of how women react under patriarchy. As such, they are two steps removed from being natural expressions of the female mode of being. Even when women go back to matriarchal mythology to search for valid expressions, these are not easily captured. Their implications nearly overwhelm us. We dance deftly around their power. And we remember Jung's warning about attempting to fully explain and interpret myths and archetypes: *"The most we can do is to dream the myth onwards and give it a modern dress."*[25]

Mythology as a Path in the Spiritual Quest

Today we are experiencing and creating a spiritual awakening. Many people are exploring "new" paths of inner growth; the Judeo-Christian myths and symbols no longer resonate for some of us, if they ever did. Freud believed that the Judeo-Christian tradition "keeps people stupid" because it hands them everything and denies, even forbids, them the individual quest that results in true growth and wisdom. Jung agreed but insisted, "Only religion can replace religion," and encouraged his patients to seek their own means of spiritual exploration and integration. The prepatriarchal Goddess tradition is a rich source from which women and men may draw. Yahweh/God the Father is not the omnipotent deity of all humankind, but is merely a figure in one of the many mythological/religious systems from which people may select personally meaningful aspects. In a world where spiritual expressions are valued for nurturing integration, growth, and a sense of our embeddedness in nature—rather than for pro-

viding lockstep control over a populace—diversity and evolutionary *process* are honored. Such are the values of pre- and postpatriarchal spirituality.

Notes

[1] Robert Graves, *The Greek Myths,* Vol. 1, Middlesex, England: Penguin Books, 1960 (1955), p. 22.

[2] C. G. Jung, *Collected Works,* Vol. 9, Princeton: Princeton University Press, Bollingen Series 20, 1969 (1959), part i, par. 316.

[3] *Ibid.,* par. 6.

[4] *Ibid.,* par. 26.

[5] Jung, *Collected Works,* Vol. 11, par. 711.

[6] Jung, *Collected Works,* Vol. 9, part i, par. 157.

[7] *Ibid.,* par. 316.

[8] M. Esther Harding, *Women's Mysteries, Ancient and Modern,* London: Rider & Company, 1971 (1955), p. 103.

[9] Marie-Louise von Franz, *The Feminine in Fairytales,* Irving, Texas: Spring Publications, 1972, p. 22.

[10] *Ibid.*

[11] Harding, p. 34.

[12] von Franz, p. 28.

[13] Murray Stein, "Hera: Bound and Unbound," *Spring,* 1977, pp. 105-119.

[14] *Ibid.,* pp. 106-107.

[15] *Ibid.,* p. 114.

[16] Robert A. Johnson, *She: Understanding Feminine Psychology,* New York: Harper & Row, 1977, p. 1.

[17] *Ibid.*

[18] *Ibid.,* p. 6.

[19] *Ibid.,* p. 7.

[20] Erich Neumann, *The Great Mother: An Analysis of the Archetype,* Princeton: Princeton University Press, Bollingen Series 47, 1963 (1955), p. 78.

[21] Johnson, pp. 18-19.

[22] Erich Neumann, *Amor and Psyche: The Psychic*

Development of the Feminine, Princeton: Princeton University Press, Bollingen Series 54, 1956, p. 76.

[23] *Ibid.,* p. 146.

[24] Jung, *Collected Works,* Vol. 9, part i, par. 5n.

[25] *Ibid.,* par. 271.

Robert Emmet Meagher (essay date 1995)

SOURCE: "The Duality of Helen," in *Helen: Myth, Legend, and the Culture of Misogyny*, Continuum, 1995, pp. 49-69.

[*In the following essay, Meagher examines the depiction of women as both goddesses and humans in Greek mythology, specifically in Hesiod's* Theogony *and* Works and Days. *Meagher notes the ways in which Hesiod subverts earlier oral traditions, in which women were birth goddesses and creators rather than (as in Olympian myths) created by male gods to bring misery and death to human men.*]

The many facets and faces of Helen have come down to two. The one is bright, provoking desire and joy. The other is dark, provoking hatred and grief. The relationship and balance between these two, however, remains to be examined. To minds like the Greeks', noted for critical reasoning, committed to ratio and proportion, unresolved dualism is no better than an unanswered question. Besides, the poetic and political traditions of archaic and classical Greece make it manifestly clear that men were at peace neither with Helen in particular nor with women in general.[1]

Indeed, outside the artistic *temenos* of those poems and pots in which Helen's bared face or breasts made warriors drop their swords and surrender to her loveliness, Helen's spectacular beauty provided her with little or no protection against the insults of centuries. Helen-bashing was an accepted poetic pastime. However desirous Helen was renowned to be, she was mostly an object of contempt. Add to this phenomenon the demonstrably profound and rarely denied misogyny of the Greek tradition, and it is a short leap to some rather disturbing conclusions regarding male ambivalence, or the lack thereof, toward Helen and her countless, more ordinary images, the women of Greece. We will avoid that leap for now, however, and take instead what may appear to be an unwarranted detour. We will consider the figure of Pandora, the first woman of Hesiod; and from her we will find our way back—a short distance—to Helen. Our own eventual and peculiar defense of Helen will be seen to depend on what we discover from Pandora and on the relevance of those discoveries to Helen's case. For now all that is needed is the benefit of whatever doubt this detour might instill.

The composition of the *Theogony* and of *Works and Days,* attributed to a supposed Boeotian farmer-poet by the name of Hesiod, is commonly assigned to the late eighth or early seventh century.[2] To confine these works, however, to the pen or stylus of a single man and to a narrow chink of all but lost time is to overlook several salient realities. The works of Hesiod, like those of Homer, represent both the terminus of a vast oral tradition and the source of a vast written tradition. Their debts to the past as well as their authority over the future are incalculable. Since we are unable to hear a past we cannot read, the words of Homer and Hesiod appear to have emerged from a silent void resembling that of the first verses of Genesis. Indeed, what we know as Greek literature was first conjured into existence by the voices of Homer and Hesiod. We cannot afford to forget, however, those countless other anonymous voices of uncertain origin and age, who like underground rivers fed the first visible streams of archaic Greek poetry.[3] They are the true Muses to whom both Homer and Hesiod were so outspokenly grateful.

All this is to say that when we read Hesiod we cannot really know whose voice we hear nor precisely whence it comes. The alphabet, like a cloak thrown over a ghost, makes merely spoken words visible; yet we cannot see through that cloak, behind the written word, to the oral past which is lost in its own preservation. The more we learn about that past from other sources, however, the older and more vast it becomes, a fact that we will soon confront in the figure of Pandora.

The *Theogony* is an account of origins, preeminently the origins of those divine beings who compose and preside over the cosmos. It is also a narrative of divine history, tracing the succession of regimes seen to have culminated in the reign of Olympian Zeus. The narrative of Zeus's rise to power and of the consolidation of his regime is doubtless rooted in an earlier array of succession myths, which circulated throughout the ancient Near East. The proportion of Hesiod's debt owed to each tradition and the itinerary of each transmission are matters of wide and likely irresolvable disagreement. The likeliest principal influences on Hesiod's account of the succession from Ouranos to Kronos to Zeus, together with Zeus's collateral struggles with the Titans, with Prometheus, and with Typhoeus, would seem to be the Hittite versions of the Hurrian Kumarbi[4] and Ullikummi[5] myths as well as the Babylonian *Enuma Elish.*[6] M. L. West suggests that a hellenized version of such Oriental material reached Hesiod via Crete and Delphi, whereas P. Walcot traces its transmission, particularly that of the *Enuma Elish,* from Al Mina in northern Syria to Euboea, and from there to Boeotia, the reputed homeland of Hesiod and a center of cultural influence in the archaic period.[7]

The *Theogony,* like most theological works, is no example of sublimely unbiased metaphysics. Instead, it is highly political. In it, the regime of Zeus and the reign of Olympian justice are celebrated as the achievement of the aeons, the arrival of celestial civilization. It is, one might say, Hesiod's version of "how the West was won." In the *Theogony,* Hesiod, a poet with "a burning passion for Zeus," offers "not just the story of the beginnings of the universe and the history of the gods" but "even more a resounding hymn of praise in honor of Zeus . . . relating the exploits of the king of the gods, as just as he is terrible."[8] It is most like the hymns to Yahweh attributed to David or the *Enuma Elish,* which sings the praises of the divine warrior-king Marduk. In each instance, there is a fusion of absolute authority, martial glory, and what promises to be justice. In each instance, too, there is the clear subordination of female to male, presented as an evolution from the old order to the new, and from savage, even theriomorphic, ways to resplendent anthropomorphism.[9] When the divine becomes so transparent to the human, it is little wonder that the human is seen to resemble the divine.

The *Theogony* may be the oldest Greek literature we possess; in any event, it addresses the oldest of times and of concerns, human concerns. For while humanity may appear quite peripheral to the *Theogony,* the opposite is the case. Indeed, "Hesiod's cosmos is human—or at least protohuman—before it is a cosmos, and the *Theogony* is the story of its progressive humanization."[10] In other words, Hesiod's account of origins traces the development of a world that becomes progressively familiar with time, progressively human and progressively Greek.

The origin of peculiar immediate interest to us, in our defense of Helen, is not surprisingly the origin of women, the first woman, who is called the *"kalon kakon."*[11] In fact, it is this very name that draws us to the *Theogony.* Comprised of two adjectives—*kalon* meaning "beautiful" and *kakon* meaning "evil"—it is essentially dualistic. Paradigmatic Woman, which we may assume this first woman to be, is, it seems, a living oxymoron, a living contradiction, which is precisely what we have already found Helen to be. Perhaps the faithless Helen has been faithful at least to her origins as a woman; and it would appear that Hesiod has provided, in *kalon kakon,* her definitive epithet. The truth is that he has provided much more.

Out of any context, *kalon kakon* would be irresolvably ambiguous. It could mean "beautiful evil" or "evil beauty" or "beauty-evil." We would have no clear indication as to which of woman's elements is substantive and which only modifying. We could not know whether woman, in being called *kalon kakon,* was being called: (a) essentially beautiful though qualifiedly evil; or (b) essentially evil though qualifiedly beautiful; or (c) essentially both evil and beautiful. In this tangle of

words there lie profound differences, which Hesiod for his own purposes sorts out for us. When he is through, there is no ambiguity left. In the context provided by Hesiod, it is *kakon* that defines the substance or essence of woman. Repeatedly, *kakon* is made to stand alone, stripped of *kalon.* The truth of woman is stripped of pretense, and woman is revealed as unambiguously evil: "Thunderous Zeus made women to be a *kakon* for mortal men";[12] "he fashioned this *kakon* for men to make them pay for the theft of fire."[13] What then, has become of the *kalon,* the beauty of woman?

Before responding to this question directly, we must consider the fuller context within which the story of the *kalon kakon* occurs. Woman, as stated above, is made and presented to man in retaliation for the theft of fire; but that theft by Prometheus, son of Iapetos, was provoked by Zeus's withdrawal of fire from mankind in retaliation for Prometheus's earlier theft of the finest sacrificial portions. In the perpetration of both thefts, Prometheus proved himself more clever than Zeus, using his *doliē technē,*[14] his "deceptive skill," to outwit the king of the gods. In the first instance, Prometheus wrapped the meat and fatty portions of the sacrificial ox in the victim's inedible hide and stomach and then wrapped the bare bones in glistening fat, knowing that Zeus would mistakenly insist on the latter as his prerogative. In the second instance, Prometheus concealed living embers in a hollow fennel stalk, enabling him to elude Zeus's embargo and to return fire to mankind. The theme is unmistakable. Skill or craft (*technē*) is set to work in creating a ruse (*dolon*) which even a reputedly intelligent godhead would fall for. Poetic justice, much less Olympian justice, requires, however, that the tables be turned. In falling twice for the same *dolon,* Zeus has to have learned, or remembered, something. Enter woman; but not yet.

The words *technē, doliē,* and *dolon* occur repeatedly in Hesiod's account of Prometheus's twin offenses, which lead up to Zeus's retaliation in kind.[15] But these are not their first appearances in the *Theogony.* There is an older and equally significant Hesiodic history to these words and the deeds they describe. When the hate of Kronos for his father peaked and Kronos plotted with his mother Gaia against Ouranos, she thought up for the two of them an "evil deception" (*doliēn . . . kakēn . . . technēn*),[16] which West translates "a nasty trick,"[17] an understatement to be sure. Later, when Kronos learned from Gaia and Ouranos that he too would be undone by his own child and began to swallow methodically his wife's children as they dropped from her womb, further *technē*[18] did the trick. Zeus was hidden away in a rock cave; and a massive rock was wrapped in swaddling clothes. Kronos, of course, went for the *dolon* and swallowed the rock-baby, just as Zeus in due course would swallow the bundle of bones, and as man, the last in a line of dupes, would take woman home with him.

It is this same word—*dolon*—that resolves the ambiguity of woman and puts her seeming contradictions in perspective; for woman, once she is properly adorned, veiled, and crowned, is called a *dolon,*[19] a "trick," a "baited trap." It is eminently true of woman, as fashioned and fitted out by the gods, that what you see is not what you get, which makes her a fitting rebuttal for the glistening bag of bones foisted upon Zeus. The difference between woman's beauty and her evil is the difference between appearance and reality.[20] Robed in silver, modestly veiled, garlanded with flowers, and crowned with gold, woman is a *thauma,*[21] a "wonder to behold." Gods and men, mortals and immortals, are filled with awe at the sight of her. Unlike the gods, however, men are defenseless against her charms. Woman is a "lure" before which men are "without resistance."[22] She is, in short, the irresistible bride whom men will be unable not to take home with them. But when they do, when they remove the veils, the robes, the flowers, all the cosmetic evasions given her by the gods, when they rapidly exhaust her superficial charms, then men will find out that they have taken into their homes and their lives a *pēma mega,*[23] a great misery, a great pit into which all of their toilsome efforts will be quite futilely poured.

Before considering this woman, man's *pēma mega,* in still further detail, we would do well once again to open wide the scope of our considerations to encompass the history within which this moment, the moment of woman's creation and man's ruin, occurs. More precisely, the moment I have in mind begins with the sacrifice gone wrong at Mekone and ends with humanity's, even Prometheus's, consequent misery. Brief insubordination results in lasting subordination, with a vengeance to be remembered. This moment is framed by two statements: first,

> It was just as men and gods were in crisis (*ekrinonto*) at Mekone that he [Prometheus] cunningly cut up a great ox, apportioning it in such a way as to seduce Zeus into making a big mistake;[24]

and second,

> Thus it is impossible to mislead or to elude the mind of Zeus.[25]

The issue here is clearly sovereignty. What has happened before, one would imagine, could happen again. In a line of ultimately unstable regimes, the stability of Zeus's regime is theoretically and practically open to question. That there is indeed a crisis, something remaining to be decided, is made evident by the two stunning challenges to Zeus's wit and rule soon offered by Prometheus in the name of humankind. In fact, all four sons of Iapetos and Klymene—Atlas, Menoitios, Prometheus, and Epimetheus—are minor trouble from the start. Coeval with Zeus, they represent a rival line of descent from Ouranos and Gaia, which, if allied with unruly mankind, could spell major trouble. Indeed, their very names—"the Endurer," "the Endeavorer," "the Forethinker" (one with creative imagination, seeing things before they exist or happen), and "the Afterthinker" (one who sees things only after they exist or happen)—suggest that these figures represent larger-than-life human paradigms, magic mirrors, in which men may see themselves and their possibilities blown large. Most troublesome is Prometheus, who seems determined to bring Zeus down and to elevate the status of humankind by giving them creative imagination, defiant wit, and divine fire, in short all that is needed to make them like gods.[26] With Prometheus as a model[27] and benefactor, humankind may embrace ambitions which they have yet to imagine, much less act on.

Apparently, at Mekone in Sikyon, all this—the imminent contest between humankind and Zeus—was to be decided. In the act of animal sacrifice,[28] the central ritual act of Greek religion, the essential order of the cosmos would be affirmed and entrenched. The primacy of gods over men and of men over beasts would be made ritually visible and politically secure. The cornerstone of Greek piety and Olympian politics would be laid. For all this to be, however, the sacrifice must be duly performed, which was what Prometheus neither had in mind nor did. The humiliating failure of the *krisis,* the critical test of Zeus's sovereignty, prompted Zeus to take the more extreme measure of withholding from men any access to divine firepower or transformative force, without which men would soon be virtual animals, shivering in caves and eating their meat raw. Then, thwarted a second time, Zeus devised his final solution: woman. Woman would guarantee that man, with or without fire, had offered his last threat to the sovereignty of Zeus. She would be living testimony to the truth that "it is impossible to mislead or to elude the mind of Zeus." As an added bonus, she would make man suffer for ever having imagined otherwise.

Essentially the same account of the First Woman, man's *pēma mega,* the exquisitely tied fly—momentary splendor and then all hook—is to be found in Hesiod's *Works and Days.* The context for that account is, however, a good deal more mundane than the framework of the *Theogony.* While in the *Theogony* the human story was only beginning, humankind is mostly old history in *Works and Days.* Four ages of man have come and gone, each a good deal worse than the one before;[29] and Hesiod finds himself in the fifth, wishing he were anywhere else. Strife defines every relationship; virtue is rewarded with misery, and so is everything else. Yet it was not always so. Men once lived without toil and without pain. Like fruit they ripened in the sun of the god's blessings; and then, when full, they dropped from life, as from a tree, quietly in their sleep. Hesiod's account of the fall of man begs the question Why? Why and from where so much misery? The answer is again woman, the source of all of man's woes.[30]

Although in *Works and Days* the First Woman has a name, a name of great significance (*Pandōra*), she is presented in very much the same terms as in the *Theogony*. She is bait set by the gods for men, who with pounding enthusiasm throw themselves upon her, expecting to embrace bliss and discovering, in retrospect, that they have swallowed their doom. It is no wonder that her first husband is named Epimetheus, that is, "Afterthought"—one who learns the truth, the essential evil of woman, only later, on the morning after. She is given the awesome exterior of a goddess;[31] the *ēthos* or inner character of a sneak thief; and the *noos,* the heart and mind, of a *kyōn,* a dog, a predatory scavenger who waits for men to fall and then picks clean their bones.[32] Her face, the focus of her appearance, is immortal, provoking immortal thoughts; her soul, invisible at first yet revealed implacably in all she does, is the deadly handiwork of Argos-slaying Hermes, the guide of souls lost to the world below.[33] Woman is like a gleaming gold cup brimming with poison, with honey smeared around its lip: lovely to behold, sweet to the lips, and lethal to the last drop.

Woman, adorned by the gods with every beauty and grace, burdens man with all that is hideous and devouring in his new condition. Woman, the recipient of all that is bright, is the giver of all that is dark. Indeed, both of these claims are conveyed in her name, *Pandōra,* which means at the same time both the "All-gifted" and the "All-giver." Like her other, impersonal name, *kalon kakon,* this new name suggests an essential ambiguity which Hesiod is quick to interpret and so to resolve. Hesiod's comment on the naming of woman tells the whole story. She is called Pandora, he informs us, because "all those who dwell on Olympos gave each one to her a gift, a grief for men who strive and toil."[34] Pandora, "all-gifted" with every *kalon* is the "all-giver" of every *kakon.* All of the divine largesse which she embodies has only one purpose: human misery.

Pandora, then, is indeed the recipient of the gifts of all the gods. She is not, however, their final recipient; for these gifts are intended ultimately and primarily for men, to provide for their endless torment. First there are the cosmetic gifts, Pandora's various charms and adornments, which serve to ensnare men; then there are the dark contents of Pandora's jar, released forever among men when Pandora removes its lid. Toil, disease, pain, care, old age—all of the *myria lygra,*[35] the innumerable miseries that make up man's condition—pour from the jar of Pandora the "All-giver," the giver of all grief.

The transparent meaning of this text has been obscured over recent centuries by the substitution of "box" for

"jar," a decisive change of image attributed to the sixteenth-century monk Erasmus, who mistranslated the original Greek word *pithos* with Latin *pyxis.*[36] A *pithos* is an often huge earthenware jar used to store and to preserve wine or oil or other foodstuffs.[37] Womb-like in shape, it is also a symbol for the earth, the mother of all. In early Helladic burials, the pithos frequently served as a coffin.[38] After the corpse was folded into fetal position and inserted into the pithos, honey was often poured over the dead as a preservative;[39] and then the lid was sealed in place. The womb-like shape of the pithos, the fetal position of the corpse, and the sweet nourishing fluid surrounding it all suggest birth as well as death—in other words, the presence of hope, the hope of regeneration, which like the hope in Pandora's jar remains in the pithos until the end of time.

In this context we may recall the story of Glaukos, who as a child fell into a pithos full of honey and disappeared.[40] When Polyeidus, commanded by Minos to find the boy, descended into the labyrinthine palace and came upon an owl,[41] he knew the boy to be dead and soon found him head down in a pithos of honey. Minos's next demand was for the regeneration of his son from the pithos, which Polyeidus was enabled to accomplish through the magical properties of an herb, which a serpent[42] happened to be carrying in its mouth to its own dead mate.[43] While this story contains multiple images integral to our concerns here, our present focus is upon the pithos, the symbol and locus of both death and rebirth.

The implications of the pithos for the story of Pandora are immediately clear and telling. Pandora's gifts are released not from some box she holds but from her own womb. Her fault lies not in her curiosity but in her being. She is constitutionally deceptive and essentially lethal; for when she opens the lid of the pithos and gives birth, she brings death as well. Death, Hesiod makes clear, comes soon and miserably, after a toilsome life. The lid of Pandora's pithos is opened first in the act of love, to which men are drawn by her irresistible charms; and then the lid is opened again to give birth either to men who will live out short miserable lives or to her own unique progeny, the separate race of women, who will extend the human plague indefinitely. At the end of the day, as it were, the lid is opened a last time to receive the dead, exhausted by life.[44]

Pandora herself, it would appear, *is* the pithos, from which dismal, prolific mankind issues forth and to which men return, either to bury their desires for a moment or to be buried forever. This image of woman as pithos is very old indeed, the inheritance and not the creation of Hesiod.[45] From the Neolithic period onward, over four thousand years before Hesiod, earthenware vessels—some large and wide-mouthed for storage and others in a range of shapes for a variety of uses—were frequently shaped or painted to suggest their identity with woman or womb. In addition to bearing the face, the breasts, the vagina, and other anatomical features, these pots were commonly painted or inscribed with emblems, images, and what may be interpreted as a symbolic script, all together making unmistakable the intimate association of woman with life, death, and regeneration.[46]

It is also true that Pandora *is not* the pithos, which Hesiod mentions as an object apparently separate from Pandora herself, the woman. Imaginatively one, they are literally two, disconnected, estranged. What is more, a profound, pervasive estrangement may be discerned within the entire account of Pandora, from her creation to her deployment. Like her pithos, assuming for the moment its earthenware composition, Pandora is fashioned from clay, moistened with water.[47] Commissioned by Zeus, she is the handiwork of Hephaestos. Her beginning, then, is uniquely unnatural. She is the work not of nature (*physis*) but of craft (*technē*). Although the entire race of women and, from this day forth, all men are to issue from a womb, either hers or that of one of her daughters, Pandora herself comes into being not from the belly of a woman but from the hands of a man.[48]

There is a double humiliation and reversal here: first, that woman, the womb of all humankind, should be fashioned from clay, literally like a pot; and second, that the potter should be a man. In Hesiod's account, man has somehow come into being long before and without woman; it is woman who is the afterthought, derivative and secondary. At the very least, this violates unmolested common sense. Admittedly, the emergence of the first human being presents a challenge to any imagination, ancient or modern; but already with the second and the third human being, a clear pattern presents itself. Nothing is observed more universally than that every human being comes from woman. The existence of women before men is a mystery, while the existence of men before women is a contradiction, which is precisely what Hesiod intends.

The inseparable bond between woman and the unfolding of life is embedded in the word *physis,* a word encompassing the entire order of nature and yet referring quite specifically to the female *genitalia,*[49] the lips of Pandora's jar. In Hesiod, what spills from these lips is not so much joy and life as misery and death.[50] Sex, something apparently new and overwhelming to Epimetheus, disrupts the harmonious order of things. Woman, herself a contrivance, overturns nature, irrevocably. Because of her, men can no longer appear and disappear inexplicably, like flowers. Instead, they must be born and must die. No thought, if we enter Hesiod's imagination, is to him stranger and more unsettling. We are mistaken, however, if we suppose

his imagination to be innocent and primitive, the product of clueless wonder. He knows what he is doing, and why. His is not the original account of such matters; rather, his is a conscious denial of that account, an effort to articulate its demise. He is a man not with a silly idea but with a powerful ideology, which at the same time happens to be silly.

Hesiod is not alone, of course, in his overturning of the self-evident order of things in which woman and womb are the natural—that is, genital—source of man. In the J, or Yahwist, account of creation, composed during the reign of Solomon and thus the older of the two creation accounts in Genesis, man is created first to a deathless, god-like existence; and woman is the afterthought, a by-product of man.[51] Soon, almost inevitably it seems, she brings sex, laborious birth from the womb, a life of labor, and certain death. Similarly, Enkidu, Adam's Mesopotamian counterpart, is torn from idyllic nature by woman, the seductress, whose irresistible charms leave him weakened and marked for death, a death whose universal claim Gilgamesh sees reflected in his dying friend's eyes. Amidst the diverse complexity of these and other ancient accounts of the first man and woman, we may perceive a common thread in the assertion that it is woman, an unwitting interloper into the original scheme of things, who disturbs the natural order, bringing sex, strife, suffering, and death.

The second form of humiliation and reversal inflicted upon woman by Hesiod is related to the first. She is made to be the one fashioned from clay and not the fashioner—the pot, as it were, and not the potter. Contrary to Hesiod's account, however, woman seems to have been the first to work with clay, whether as creatrix or as simple potter. "The art of pottery," writes Robert Briffault, "is a feminine invention; the original potter was a woman. Among all primitive peoples the ceramic art is found in the hands of woman, and only under the influence of advanced culture does it become a man's occupation."[52] This original association of woman with pottery is reflected in those early creation myths wherein it is woman who fashions man from clay. In perhaps the earliest of these,[53] already current in the third millennium, the birth-goddess Nammu, the primeval sea, "the mother who gave birth to all the gods," mixes the first mortal clay and, together with Earth-mother Ninmah and the goddesses of birth, fashions the first human beings. Compared with these goddesses, the likes of Greek Hephaestos and Egyptian Khnum are newcomers to the art of pottery, much less to the fashioning of human life.

A striking feature of these myths of female creativity is the conflation of nature and craft, sexuality and ceramics, in the fashioning of humankind. The potters are birth-and-womb-goddesses, mothers all. Thus, in *Atrahasis,* the first mortals—nips of clay fashioned into human form by birth-goddesses—step forth nine months later from a "womb." Womb and kiln, it seems, are one, as are flesh and clay. To say with the same breath that all life comes from earth and that all life comes from woman is not yet a contradiction but a truth, reflected in the art and imagery of clay, softened with water and impregnated with form. In a world of images, pithos, woman, womb, and earth are one.

Hesiod works with these same images, disfiguring them until they reflect only shame. The poet too is a potter of sorts; and it is, after all, Hesiod who shapes Pandora and her pithos on his poetic wheel. His Pandora, the mother of all living, is not only less than divine but less than human. Prehistoric and ancient potters and artists, in their creation of female figurines and "pot-ladies,". . . commonly emphasized woman's genitals and breasts, her mysterious fonts of life and nurture; and, when they gave the lower torso exaggerated proportions, it was to provide space for the fullness of life contained therein. Hesiod, on the other hand, in his depiction of Pandora and of the separate race of women who are her daughters, is all but obsessed with the female *gastēr,* the belly.[54] For him, it might be said, the belly is the *physis* of woman.

Zeus's preoccupation with "bellies" is not surprising in context; for bellies have been a theme and a problem in the *Theogony* long before the appearance of woman. In fact, the succession myth in which Zeus takes the ultimate place involves a succession of "bellies." When the offspring of Gaia and Ouranos prove frightful and loathsome to their father, he hides them away at birth in Gaia's *keuthmōn*[55] her "hiding place" or "hole," the chthonic equivalent of a *gastēr*. Later, when Kronos has filled his father's shoes and begins doing away with his own children, he takes no chances. He swallows them himself, which works well until he consumes an indigestible boulder wrapped in swaddling clothes. We remember the scheme; but now we sharpen our focus on two words crucial to the account of it. While the stone-baby passes into the *nēdys*[56] (meaning any of the body's cavities: belly, bowels, or womb) of Kronos, the flesh-and-ichor baby Zeus passes into a dark cave deep within the sacred *keuthos*[57] (the same word as *keuthmōn*), or "hiding place," of Gaia or Earth, wherein Ouranos once upon a time confined his unwanted progeny. The womb of Earth, once a place of peril, has become, it seems, a place of refuge. The next relevant belly is Zeus's own, which he hopes to fill with the sacrificial feast at Mekone. Clearly his outrage over being given a bag of bones wrapped in slabs of fat and his ensuing outburst have to do not only with wounded pride but also with an empty stomach, which brings us back to the belly of woman, created as a curse to repay man in kind for a spoiled feast and for stolen fire.

Ever since the revenge of Zeus, men's days are long and hard, full of labor. Meanwhile, like bees, or bellies with heads, women stay at home in their hives, waiting to consume the fruit of others'—namely, men's—labors.[58] Woman is reduced by Hesiod to her belly; and the belly, the *gastēr,* is seen as a symbol of lazy, insensitive, insatiable demand.[59] Like a living, bottomless pithos, woman swallows the labors and the very life of her mate. On the other hand, the full force of the synecdoche by which woman is her belly, as well as its close connection with the pithos of Pandora, are lost unless we recall that *gastēr* means not only "belly" but also "womb." Women's demands are not confined to food. Her sexual demands, and their consequences, are likewise consuming. Defined by compulsive desire, woman hungers for both food and sex; and, in return, she produces only more hungry mouths and wombs and, admittedly, male offspring—her sole justification—who will in turn and all too soon inherit the misery of their fathers. In short, Epimetheus and every man after him, to use a familiar colloquialism, can say legitimately of his spouse that "she will be the death of me."

The ultimately lethal and bottomless *gastēr* or pithos that is woman is, admittedly, only an image of and a prelude to that all-consuming chasm or hole, the dark *keuthmōn* of goddess Earth, certain to swallow from first to last every child of woman. Pandora, the first mortal woman, is but an image and agent of Gaia, the first divine woman. Thus, when Pandora removes the lid from her pithos, we may imagine her opening the gates of Tartaros, "a place of decay, at the end of the vast earth."[60] Indeed, Hesiod, in his description of Tartaros[61] in the *Theogony,* seems to think of it as a great storage jar.[62] This same thought clearly guided the painter of a fifth-century *lekythos* or funerary vase on which Hermes *psychopompos,* guide to the world below, is depicted standing next to a giant pithos, half-buried in the earth, from which come forth in flight the winged spirits of the dead.[63]

Pandora is not, then, the first female to be reduced to and indentified with her all-consuming "hole." Nor is she the first female to be the living source of misery and grief. In the beginning, according to the *Theogony,* there was Chaos, which in Greek means dark "Abyss" or "Chasm" without any connotation of confusion or disarray;[64] and there was Gaia, the "Mother of All,"[65] the first Pandora or "All-giver," the foundation of all.[66] These two, Gaia and Chaos, simply come to be—like the primordial hillock emerging from the waters of chaos in Egyptian myth[67]—and from them proceeds all that ever is; but this line of descent and its early products prove mostly unacceptable in poetic retrospect. Besides, nothing about mortal men—their origins and history—is revealed in this account, a matter to which Hesiod turns in *Works and Days.* There, before presenting his own version of man's story, however, he alludes to an account of divine and human origins quite different from his own and makes the following offer:

> If you like, I will summarize another tale
> for you, well and skillfully—mind you take
> it in—telling how gods and mortal men have
> come from the same starting-point.[68]

Possibly he has no takers. For whatever reason, Hesiod says no more here of this common source of all divine and human being, perhaps because he has already told that tale in the *Theogony.*

That Earth, emergent from watery Chaos, is the common source of all beings—human, divine, and otherwise—is confirmed on the golden diadem fashioned by Hephaestos for the first woman. On this wondrous object, we are told, there are wrought many images presenting to the eye "all the awesome creatures spawned by sea and earth."[69] There is telling irony in this crown's being placed on the head of woman, from whose fertile depths shall pour out *myria lygra,* all the innumerable ills of humankind. Queen of grief, woman shall repeat within time what took place before time, before Kronos, before the erotic lineage that led to Zeus. At first, we recall, Chaos brought forth Erebos, the darkness of the world below, and black Nyx, night. From feminine Nyx came forth an ominous brood[70] including Death, Pain, the Fates, the Destinies, Nemesis, hateful Age, and Eris or strife. Daughter Eris, in turn, spawned progeny[71] every bit as dark as those of her mother Night, progeny that include Quarrels, Labor, Famine, Lies, Murder, Wars, Anarchy, and Ruin. All of these, we know, have found their way into the pithos, the belly-womb, of Pandora, the mortal image of that dark, primeval chasm from which everything we know and dread has come.

At the same time, Gaia produced her own firstborn, Sky, "as an equal to herself,"[72] and soon, under the novel influence of Eros, the "limb-weakener,"[73] Earth and Sky mated and produced Kronos and his siblings, all so monstrous and hateful to Ouranos that he refused them entry into the light, keeping them hidden away in Gaia's "secret hole." Groaning with distress, Gaia schemed with her son to release her brood from the tyranny of Ouranos. Their scheme and its outcome are already familiar to us; yet it is well to have certain details fresh before our eyes. According to plan, as Ouranos, quickened with desire, spread himself over Gaia, Kronos, with a jagged flint sickle, sliced away his father's genitals, hurling them into the sea. The fertile blood of Ouranos sprayed Gaia with the seed of Giants and of the Furies, while the sea boiled up and from its foam there emerged the goddess Cypris or Aphrodite, accompanied by Eros and *Himeros,* or Desire. When,

after the act, the hated sons were released into the light, Ouranos named them Titans and said that vengeance would follow them, a vengeance whose trail led all the way to Pandora.

There are quite evidently too many distinct fibers here to weave now into our account of woman and of the feminine origin of evil. With only a few in place, however, the pattern of the whole becomes clear. Long before Pandora releases from her womb the full plague of toil and pain and death, which humans know as their condition, Gaia and Nyx, female Earth and Night, have released into the cosmos the paradigms, as it were, of Pandora's "gifts." From the "hole," the dark, mysterious cavity, the *gastēr,* the belly-womb of woman, divine and human, imagined as a great pithos or jar, pour out all those bitter realities under which the divine and human orders, the cosmos and the polis, languish. Not until the female *gastēr* is replaced by its male counterpart will the pollution of woman be lifted from the family of the gods and from the race of men. The last great birth of the *Theogony,* the birth of Athena from Zeus marks precisely that event in the divine order. In fact, the entire movement of the *Theogony,* the narrative of the origin of the gods, may be seen as a progression, a triumphal ascent as Hesiod would have it, from the female womb of Gaia to the male womb of Zeus, and so from savage nature to Olympian civility.

After Zeus has proved himself supreme in cosmic combat, he becomes king and lord of the gods. Hesiod's one-sentence account of this moment provides all we need to assess the dynamics of the scene.[74] Like Marduk of Babylon and Yahweh of Israel, but unlike several other divine warrior-kings who "win some and lose some," Zeus has swept the field of rivals.[75] His power is incontestable. Gaia, who has retained her realism if little else, knows that hers and anyone else's independent claims to primacy are memories now, nothing more. Zeus, we are told, is elevated into place by acclamation, but not spontaneously; for Hesiod adds the intriguing detail that behind the proclamation of Zeus's sovereignty by the divine assembly lie Gaia's *phradmosynēsin,* her "cunning maneuvers."[76] She is not so far behind the scenes or the times to escape his notice. If nothing else, she is a survivor.

Conquest alone does not make kings. Proper sovereignty requires not only prowess in battle but preeminence in the council of the gods.[77] The arts of war must be complemented by the arts of peace. For a king to rule both in time of peace and in time of war, his word must prevail as surely as does his sword. In the *Enuma Elish,* the warrior king Marduk, triumphant in battle, is confirmed in his kingship by the full pantheon.[78] Having slain Tiamat, Marduk forms the ordered cosmos from her chaotic matter;

and, in response, the other gods bestow upon him the "Fifty Names," encompassing all of their own proper powers and prerogatives. He is now not only the one who "performed miracles in the battle with Tiamat," but is "profound in wisdom, skilled in understanding."[79] His sovereignty is whole and complete.[80]

We find this very same pattern replicated in the *Theogony.* After the last of his dynastic battles, Zeus, triumphant over Ouranos, Titans, and Typhoeus, restores order to the cosmos; but his will not be a lasting order unless he can complete his sovereignty with wit, cunning, and wisdom. This he accomplishes with the "swallowing" of Metis, the goddess of cunning and wise counsel, "who among all gods and mortals is wisest."[81] In short, he metabolizes all of her powers. Initially, of course, he makes her his wife, his first wife; but he seems to be aware that we are what we eat, not what we marry. Both his father and his grandfather were outwitted by their wives because they had failed to realize this. As a result, they married too soon and swallowed too late; mistakes he does not repeat.

Zeus, with timely advice from Ouranos and Gaia, works a unique variation on the succession and swallowing themes, appropriating his own eminently clever wife's powers and plots before it is too late not to succumb to them. "By marrying, mastering, and swallowing Metis," write Marcel Detienne and Jean-Pierre Vernant, "he becomes more than simply a monarch: he becomes Sovereignty itself."[82] Then, after putting away mother and daughter, pregnant Metis and unborn Athena, deep within his *nēdys*[83] (meaning any bodily cavity: mouth, belly, or womb) Zeus takes, as his second wife, Themis. Like Egyptian *Maat* or the Mesopotamian *mes,* Themis is the embodiment of all that is right and just in the societies of mortals and immortals. Unlike Metis, Themis, it seems, need not be swallowed in order to be at his disposal. It is enough for her to be at his side. Of all the gods, surely she is the one who can be trusted. Their six daughters—the *Horai* (the "Watchful Ones": Order, Justice, and Peace) and the *Moirai* (the "Fates": the Spinner, the Allotter, and the Unyielding One)—take after their mother and serve their father, perfectly complementing his inhuman force and his unprincipled cunning. Now the reign of Zeus promises to be both secure and just, unable either to be overthrown from without or to be corrupted from within.

Zeus, in swallowing Metis, not only reverses the succession of unwitting, unstable regimes beginning with Ouranos, but reverses as well the primacy of female fecundity beginning with Gaia. Hesiod's insistence that Zeus does so with the advice and consent of both Ouranos and Gaia[84] may resemble the

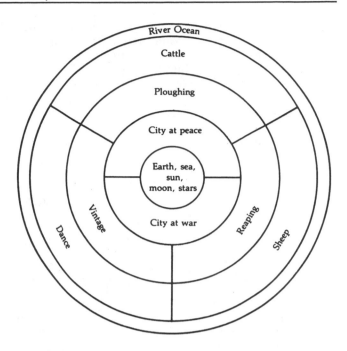

Descriptive drawing of the shield of Achilles.

charade in which consent is elicited from sacrificial animals just prior to their demise. Regardless, their apparent concurrence in this most radical of overturnings confers upon it both a certain legitimacy and a seeming continuity with the past, neither of which it could claim for itself.

Already first in "firepower," now—with Themis at his side, Metis in his head, and Athena in his "womb"—Zeus has consolidated in himself every essential power and prerogative in the universe. For the moment, we focus on fecundity; for this is perhaps his most strange and radical acquisition. Nothing, it was suggested earlier, is observed more universally than that every human being, and for that matter every anthropomorphic divine being, comes from woman. Zeus, by absorbing pregnant Metis, fetus and all, and taking the unborn Athena into his own male womb, from which she will soon be born, overturns the most inalienable claim of woman and severs her defining bond with nature and with life. With the parthenogenetic birth of Athena from the head of Zeus, history has a new beginning, in which woman plays no essential role. Not only is she powerless in the formulation of *nomos* (custom and law), but now she is irrelevant to the unfolding of *physis,* or nature. Like *Pandora,* every woman is an afterthought—and an unfortunate one at that.

There are, as one might expect, alternative accounts of Athena's origins.[85] One such account, preserved iconically, is found on a pithos dating from approximately 700 B.C.E., whose neck is "decorated with a picture of a winged goddess, who sits with outstretched arms on a throne; from her head there springs another winged figure, armed with a helmet, a spear, and perhaps a thunderbolt."[86] Walcot argues that there is only one possible interpretation of this scene: the birth of Athena from a goddess, presumably Metis. There is indeed a tradition according to which Metis not only conceived Athena but gave birth to her as well.[87] Regardless, by any account the female womb did not go out of service. Even Hesiod's Zeus continued to employ the wombs of his wives and of other women. In giving birth himself, he apparently intended to establish a principle, not a practice.

In the human order, men have been, so far, unsuccessful in finding a male replacement for Pandora and her womb. In the Greek world, this failure was not for lack of will or desire. Indeed, "the dream of a purely paternal heredity never ceased to haunt the Greek imagination."[88] Greek poetry is resonant with the voices of men who long for a world exorcised of women, a world in which men by themselves are capable of producing their own sons. Insofar as the divine order, as imagined by men, reflects the human order, as experienced by men, Zeus's two parthenogenetic successes, that is, Athena born from his head and Dionysos born from his fatty thigh, may reflect directly the failures of men at the same endeavor. Here, misogyny may be seen to conspire with the love of men for men; for when men make love to men, their seed often finds its way to the head and to the thighs, the would-be "wombs" of Zeus. Fantasy, likewise, finds its way to poetry and to being born as myth.

Apart from these moments of fantasy, Gaia and Pandora, Earth and Woman, remain the mothers of all that lives. Pandora is to the human order and the race of men what Gaia is to the divine order and the race of gods. Pandora is "Gaia in human form,"[89] "a kind of Gaia reborn, symbol of the power of the female, displaced from the divine onto the human realm."[90] The power of Gaia and Pandora, focused on the *gastēr,* is in Hesiod's revisionist mythology, however, no longer primarily the power of fecundity and life, but rather the power of hunger and death. The homology between Gaia and Pandora (and, by extension, between Helen and Gaia) is indeed close and complex. In fact, the virtual identity of Gaia and Pandora has long been widely accepted and rarely questioned.[91] The remaining question for us here concerns the bond, if any, between Helen and Pandora and, by extension, between Helen and Gaia.

The most obvious, indisputable bond between Helen and Pandora lies in the fact that Pandora is the first woman, the mother of the separate *genos* or race of women, and Helen is thereby her distant daughter.

When we consider that Hesiod describes that race as *oloion,*[92] which means at the same time both "deadly" and "lost," we may go further and propose that Helen is the most notorious of Pandora's daughters. Helen, then, may be seen as Pandora's avatar or emanantion, her image, which in turn recalls Helen's relationship with Aphrodite, and appropriately so; for Aphrodite is as close to the figure of Pandora as she is to the figure of Helen. After all, Pandora and Helen possess in common the divinely compelling *charis,* the outward loveliness or simply "charm," of Aphrodite. It is Aphrodite's gift to them both. Furthermore, in *Works and Days,* Pandora is accompanied by *Potnia Peitho,* mistress Persuasion, who, as we have already seen, is the virtual "double"[93] of Aphrodite, perhaps even a designation for Aphrodite herself.[94] This same Peitho, whom Sappho regards as a "cheat" and as "Aphrodite's daughter,"[95] is at the same time a frequent "vase-companion" of Helen. In fact, in ancient iconography, it is frequently Aphrodite and Peitho together who accompany Helen to ensure either Helen's elopement with Paris or her reconciliation with Menelaos.[96] Additionally, two other cosmetic benefactors of Pandora, Hephaestos and Athena, have equally close associations, respectively, with Helen, the weaver of tapestries, and with Aphrodite, the heartthrob of Hephaestos.

What is most telling, however, is that in the Greek poetic tradition Pandora and Helen manifest the same profound duality and suffer the same resolution of that duality in the consistent disfavor in which they find themselves. Pandora and Helen are virtually defined by the contradiction between their outward loveliness and their inward perversity, the disparity between their apparent charm and their essential fatality. Both are misleading and mischievous, not by virtue of anything they say or do but by virtue of what they are: in a word, "women"; and, in the words of the seventh-century iambic poet Semonides, women represent "the greatest *kakon* or evil Zeus has made."[97] Woman's *noos* or mind and heart, the seat of her perversity, was made by Zeus "apart" and "in the beginning."[98] Zeus creates woman from the inside out, while men discover woman from the outside in. In other words, Zeus begins with the essential reality, while men start with the appearances. The intended and actual result is that women—Pandora, Helen, and "all the other tribes of women"[99]—are desired by men, briefly, and then forever hated. In no more time than it takes for men to pass from illusion to reality, women pass from being objects of desire to being objects of loathing.

> Yes, women are the greatest evil Zeus has made.
> If someone who has a woman imagines her useful
> To him, she will prove all the more evil.

A man's good spirits never last a whole day
When the day includes a woman . . .
Yes, women are the greatest evil Zeus has
  made,
And men are bound to them, hand and foot,
With impossible knots tied by god.
It is no wonder that Hades waits at the door
For men at each others' throats
Over women.[100]

The only reason, presumably, why Pandora was not fought over was that she had, for all we know, only two possible suitors, Prometheus and Epimetheus, and one of them could see beyond the *prima nox.*

The consortium of Helen, Pandora, and Gaia is, at root, the timeless consortium of women. If Pandora is Gaia in human form, then Helen is Pandora in person. And all three are familiar with golden Aphrodite, who in the *Theogony,* alone among all the deities eventually composing the Olympian household of Zeus, spans the aeons separating the regime of Zeus from the regime of Ouranos. Thus, in Greek chronology, Aphrodite links the time of origins with the present; for although she belongs to the first generation of gods, Aphrodite finds her way into the Olympic pantheon and to Helen's side. And Helen—the living image of Gaia, Aphrodite, and Pandora—is, at least potentially, all women.

Lineage among images and emanations is, admittedly, a tenuous reality traced in leaps as often as in close, careful steps. Some would find any movement now from Helen to Gaia to be a leap, while others would consider it a modest, even obvious, step. Perhaps, once again, Aphrodite provides a common bond and a bit of light here. Aphrodite's communality with Pandora and with Helen is already clear; and her bond with Gaia should become, momentarily, a shade more evident.

According to Herodotus, the very oldest temple of Aphrodite was her temple in Ascalon, Syria.[101] It was from there, he said, that her cult was carried to Cyprus and to Cythera, which coincides with what has been said already of her Near Eastern roots. What is more, Aphrodite's cult name in the temple of Ascalon was *Ourania,* "Queen of Heaven," a name and a cult denounced in the prophetic writings of Jeremiah[102] and possibly her earliest title among the Greeks, a title suggesting her association with Ouranos. The cult of Aphrodite *Ourania* is widely attested among Hellenic communities, and her most illustrious cult image was carved of ivory and gold for her by Pheidias for her shrine at Olympia. How close the name *Ourania* brings Aphrodite to Gaia, who mothered, mated with, and helped to unman Ouranos, is surely a matter for speculation and debate; but at the least it is one more gesture back to the earliest times, to the time of origin. The name *Ourania* is for us a heuristic clue to the meaning of Aphrodite, Pandora, and Helen, the meaning of Woman. It points us in the direction of, if not directly to, Gaia, the Mother of All.

The worship of Gaia, Earth, was aboriginal to the earliest Hellenic tribes. To her belonged the mysterious powers of life and of death and of regeneration, of dreams and of prophecies. Incarnate as a serpent, she brought healing, vision, and rebirth. Hesiod, we know, lamented the steady decline in the status and condition of men from the first to the fifth age, wherein he found himself, full of complaints; but we also know that his complaints, though legitimate, overlook the far more drastic decline of women, human and divine. Gaia, the first woman, the first mother, shared the denigration of her human daughters. Even so, in the *Oresteia* of Aeschylus, which heralds the final Olympian eclipse of the feminine, celebrating male ascendancy in cosmos and polis alike, Gaia is not forgotten. At the earth's navel, in the holy precinct of Delphi, the Pythia, the serpent-priestess, pays Gaia peculiar deference. "Of all the gods," she says in the opening lines of the *Eumenides,* "I pray to Gaia first."[103]

Aphrodite, Pandora, and Helen, as well as their myriad imaginative counterparts such as Demeter,[104] Ariadne, and Korē, like emanations from a single source, point us back to the first woman, the first mother, the first *pithos,* the first font of life and of death and of regeneration. They point us to a time beyond the specific traditions of Greece, before the familiar voices of Greek poetry construe Mother Earth and the mortal mothers who imitate her[105] as devouring and deceitful beings, loved too soon and loathed too late. We may catch a glimpse of that first feminine power and presence, the true mother of Helen, in the *Hymn to Gaia:*

> The Mother of us all,
>   the oldest of all,
> hard,
>   splendid as rock
>
> Whatever there is of the land
>   it is she
>   who nourishes it,
>   it is the Earth [Gaia]
>   that I sing
>
> Whoever you are,
> howsoever you come
>   across her sacred ground
>   you of the sea,
>   you that fly,
>   it is she
>   who nourishes you

she,
  out of her treasures
   Beautiful children
   beautiful harvests
    are achieved from you
   The giving of life itself,
    the taking of it back
    to or from
     any man
     are yours. . . . [106]

Here too, unless I am mistaken, we glimpse the reality of Helen, a reality that Euripides too must have glimpsed; for, . . . he sought eventually to disclose it.

Notes

[1] Robert Lamberton, in his work on Hesiod, finds the "echoes" of Hesiod's virulent sexism to be "omnipresent in Greek literature and in the sphere of its influence. The exclusion of the female from the world of discourse in Hesiod, constitutes, along with the degradation of the female into a series of bestial grotesques in the poetry of Semonides of Amorgos, the principal archaic manifestation of a hostility that is one of the most problematic aspects of the subsequent tradition" (*Hesiod* [New Haven: Yale University Press, 1988], p. 103).

[2] P. Walcot argues that the *floruit* of Hesiod was approximately 730 B.C.E. and that the *Theogony* preceded *Works and Days* (*Hesiod and the Near East* [Cardiff: University of Wales, 1966], pp. 109, 81). Chester G. Starr, however, who argues for different authors for the above works, places the *Theogony* in the early or mid-seventh century, which is in general agreement with G. S. Kirk's linguistic comparisons of the *Theogony* with the *Iliad* and the *Homeric Hymns*. See Chester G. Starr, *The Origins of Greek Civilization* (New York: Knopf, 1961), pp. 268, 270-71; G. S. Kirk, *Hesiode et son Influence,* Entretiens sur l'antiquité classique 7 (Geneva, 1962), pp. 63-64.

[3] Many of the arguable "sources" of Homeric and Hesiodic poetry are not altogether invisible, of course; for the emergence of written from oral traditions occurred much earlier in Egypt and the Near East than on the Greek mainland.

[4] See Hans G. Güterbock, *Kumarbi,* in *The American Journal of Archaeology* 52 (1948): 123-34. H. W. F. Saggs suggests that the ultimate source for both the Greek and the Hurrian/Hittite succession myths may be the Babylonian Myth of Harab (*Civilization Before Greece and Rome* [New Haven: Yale University Press, 1989], p. 294). See also Thorkild Jacobsen, "The Harab Myth," in *Sources from the Ancient Near East* (Malibu, Calif.: Undena, 1984), vol. 2, fasc. 3, pp. 6-26.

[5] See Hans G. Güterbock, *The Song of Ullikummi* (New Haven: Yale University Press, 1952).

[6] See *The Epic of Creation,* in *Myths from Mesopotamia,* translated by Stephanie Dalley (New York: Oxford University Press, 1989), pp. 228-77.

[7] See Hesiod, *Theogony & Works and Days,* translated by M. L. West (New York: Oxford University Press, 1988), Introduction, p. xii; Walcot, *Hesiod and the Near East,* pp. 121-23. Walcot suggests, as well, that the same route may have been taken by the Phoenician alphabet, brought home by Greeks who had been resident in northern Syria.

See also Roland Hampe, *Frühe griechische Sagenbilder in Böotien* (Athens: Athen. Dt. Arch. Inst., 1936), p. 55; Pierre Guillon, *La Béotie antique* (Paris: Belles Lettres, 1948), p. 27.

[8] Walcot, *Hesiod and the Near East,* pp. 30, 32, 129.

[9] For a discussion of the influence of Babylonian materials, most specifically the *Enuma Elish,* on Hesiod, see Walcot, *Hesiod and the Near East,* pp. 27-54. Concerning the origins and development of the cult of Yahweh in ancient Israel, see Mark S. Smith, *The Early History of God* (New York: Harper & Row, 1987). And for a comparison of the Hebrew and Babylonian materials regarding the origins of the cosmos and of humanity, as well as the ascendancies of Marduk and of Yahweh, see Alexander Heidel, *The Babylonian Genesis* (Chicago: University of Chicago Press, 1951). Gerda Lerner considers all three traditions, though most substantially those of Mesopotamia and Israel, in *The Creation of Patriarchy* (New York: Oxford University Press, 1986).

[10] Lamberton, *Hesiod,* p. 77.

[11] Hesiod, *Theogony* (Oxford), 585, translation mine.

[12] Ibid., 600-601.

[13] Ibid., 570. A further, admittedly remote, though possible, connection between Pandora and stolen fire may be glimpsed in legends recounting how woman once kept fire in her vagina. See Mircea Eliade, *The Forge and the Crucible* (New York: Harper & Brothers, 1962), p. 80.

[14] Ibid., 560.

[15] See ibid., 540, 547, 550, 555, 560, 562.

[16] Ibid., 160; see 175.

[17] Hesiod, *Theogony & Works and Days,* trans. West, p. 8.

¹⁸ Hesiod, *Theogony* (Oxford), 496.

¹⁹ Ibid., 589.

²⁰ I use the categories "appearance" and "reality" advisedly here, where one might be tempted to use, instead, "form" and "matter" (particularly as Hesiod refers to woman as a likeness or form); for the latter more technical categories are quite volatile and prone to change. In the metaphysics of Plato and Aristotle, form—not matter—is the more real of the two; and Aristotle explicitly contrasts the sexes by likening man to form and woman to matter.

²¹ Hesiod, *Theogony* (Oxford), 581.

²² Ibid., 589.

²³ Ibid., 592.

²⁴ Ibid., 535-37.

²⁵ Ibid., 613.

²⁶ For a fuller discussion of what the figure of Prometheus represents, see Jean-Pierre Vernant, "The Myth of Prometheus in Hesiod," in *Myth and Society in Ancient Greece* (New York: Zone, 1980), pp. 183-201; and Robert Emmet Meagher, (*"Technē,"* in *Perspecta 24, The Yale Architectural Journal* (New York: Rizzoli, 1988), pp. 159-64. If, indeed, the threat posed by Prometheus, in concert with humankind, is that men might become like gods, it may be of interest to note that a similar promise is presented to Adam and Eve by the serpent who tells Eve that if she and her mate will eat of the forbidden tree they "will be like divine beings" (*Tanakh* [Philadelphia: Jewish Publication Society, 1988], Genesis 3:5). At the outset of this encounter, the serpent is described as "the shrewdest of all the wild beasts" (2:25), while Adam and Eve are depicted as naked but as yet feeling no shame (3:1). What is obvious only in the original Hebrew is that the author of this account has created a pun here. The serpent is "shrewd" (*'arum*) and the first humans are "naked" (*'arom*), words written alike but vocalized differently. Soon Adam and Eve, in seeking to be shrewd like the serpent realize their nakedness, knowing desire and shame in the same instant. This same convergence of nakedness, desire, and would-be resemblance to the gods is suggested in the *Gilgamesh,* wherein the temple prostitute "exposes her sex" to the primordial man Enkidu, and six days later, we are told, "he drew himself up,"

> for his understanding had broadened.
> Turning around, he sat down at the harlot's feet,
> gazing into her face,
> his ears attentive as the harlot spoke.

The harlot said to Enkidu:
> "You are beautiful, Enkidu,
> you are become like a god."

(*The Epic of Gilgamesh,* translated by Maureen Gallery Kovacs [Stanford: Stanford University Press, 1985], p. 9, lines 183-88).

The correspondence of these earlier Near Eastern stories with that of Prometheus and Pandora is evident. Aided and abetted by Prometheus, men will soon be as shrewd as Zeus, and possibly more so. God-like cleverness combined with divine force is all the provocation Zeus needs to act. He will give to man, in the person of Epimetheus, a woman to consume him and his desires. Man will know nakedness, the secrets of woman, not the secrets of god. Intimacy with woman will spell estrangement from god, as it does in Genesis and *Gilgamesh.* See David Damrosch, *The Narrative Covenant: Transformations of Genre in the Growth of Biblical Literature* (New York: Harper & Row, 1987), chapter 3, "Gilgamesh and Genesis," pp. 88-143, esp. pp. 138-43.

²⁷ Particularly when this account is conflated with its synopsis in *Works and Days* (47-58), Prometheus emerges as the First Man, or precisely as the most threatening of the several aspects of original man reflected in the sons of Iapetos and Klymene. This is made clear when Zeus tells him that the First Woman, whose creation he is about to commission, will be a *pēma mega* for Prometheus himself and "for future men" (*andrasin essomenoisin,* 56).

²⁸ In the slaughtering of a willing beast, both the fellowship and the divide between men and animals is made evident; and in the meat feast that follows, wherein the choice portions are raised to the gods and the lesser portions are shared among men, both the fellowship and the divide between men and gods is made evident. In the sacrificial ritual, duly performed, the hierarchical ordering of god, man, and beast is articulated and enacted. For a further and fuller consideration of animal sacrifice, see Walter Burkert, *Homo Necans, The Anthropology of Ancient Greek Sacrificial Ritual and Myth* (Berkeley: University of California Press, 1983), *passim,* and *Greek Religion* (Cambridge, Mass.: Harvard University Press, 1985), pp. 55-68. See also Jean-Pierre Vernant, *Mortals and Immortals: Collected Essays,* edited by Froma I. Zeitlin (Princeton: Princeton University Press, 1991), chapter 17, "A General Theory of Sacrifice and the Slaying of the Victims in the Greek *Thusia,"* pp. 290-302; and Robert Emmet Meagher, *Mortal Vision, the Wisdom of Euripides* (New York: St. Martin's, 1989), pp. 64-65. For a more specific discussion of the Athenian Buphonia, the slaying of an ox for "Zeus of the City," see Burkert, *Homo Necans,* pp. 136-43.

²⁹ Actually, this simplified schema is complicated and contradicted by Hesiod's insertion of a fifth race of heroes between the brazen and the iron races. The delineation of world ages in steady decline and their association with specific metals of diminishing value may be traced to Babylonian materials. See A. Jeremias, "Ages of the World (Babylonian)," *Encyclopedia of Religion and Ethics* (New York: Charles Scribner's Sons, 1908), 1:183-87. The same idea is found in other traditions as well, such as the Persian *Avesta* and the Hebrew *Book of Daniel,* wherein Daniel interprets for the Babylonian king Nebuchadnezzar his dream of a brilliant and dreadful statue with a gold head, silver chest and arms, bronze belly and thighs, iron legs, and feet of both iron and clay, a statue that fell apart into tiny pieces before the king's eyes. Daniel takes it all to mean the rise and fall of five kingdoms to be succeeded by the never-ending kingdom of the God of heaven (2:31-45).

³⁰ Pietro Pucci provides an illuminating schematization of the differences between life before woman and life with woman. In the oppositions listed below, which Pucci calls "the *edifying* intentions of the text," Hesiod's original man and original woman are neatly distilled for us:

Godlike man	Woman resembling the goddesses
Identity	Imitation, copy
Symmetry	Addition, excess, loss
Natural birth from earth	Manufacture with earth and water
No reproduction, unicity	Sexuality, reproduction
Spontaneity	Artifice, art, toil
Truth	Falsity
Natural sleep	Diseases, death

See Pietro Pucci, *Hesiod and the Language of Poetry* (Baltimore: Johns Hopkins University Press, 1977), p. 106.

³¹ The dressing and adorning of Pandora in *Works and Days* (72-76), together with the corresponding account in the *Theogony* (573-89), find a close parallel in the second Homeric *Hymn to Aphrodite,* wherein Aphrodite, when she emerges newborn from the sea at Cyprus, is enrobed and crowned by the Horai, the daughters of Zeus and Themis, whereupon she is brought before the immortals, who wonder at her. Although the first woman, fashioned from moistened clay, may be said to emerge from the earth, she is crowned at once with a golden diadem, wrought by Hephaestos, on which were worked images of "all the myriad creatures spawned by the solid land and the sea" (*Theogony,* 582). Like Aphrodite, who steps from the sea onto dry land to be welcomed, adorned, and gazed upon, so the first woman is at once associated with both earth and sea.

Walcot, on the other hand, emphasizes the likeness between the Hesiodic scenes of the First Woman's being robed, adorned, crowned, admired, and named and similar scenes of the Egyptian queen Hatshepsut's birth and coronation presented in a series of reliefs and inscriptions on a colonnade of her memorial temple at Deir el-Bahari in West Thebes. In order to explain the possible influence of these scenes from fifteenth-century Egypt on eighth-century Greek poetry, Walcot cites evidence of direct Mycenaean contact with Egypt in the period after approximately 1570 B.C.E. and the resulting Egyptian influences discernible in Mycenaean ideas and images of sacred kingship. Finally, he endeavors to trace those same influences still further into archaic Greek poetry and concludes that "there is nothing improbable after all in the theory that Hesiod's description of the preparation of Pandora may be traced back to the Mycenaean period, and that, when we start to look for its origins, we must go beyond the confines of the Greek world" (Walcot, *Hesiod,* pp. 65-74). See also Edouard Henri Naville, *The Temple of Deir el Bahari* (London: Egypt Exploration Fund), Part II (1897), pp. 12-18 and plates 46-55; Part III (1898), pp. 1-9 and plates 56-64; James H. Breasted, *Ancient Records of Egypt II* (Chicago: University of Chicago Press, 1906), pp. 75-100; H. Brunner, *Die Geburt des Göttkonigs,* Ägyptologische Abhandlungen 10 (Wiesbaden: O. Harrassowitz, 1964).

³² See Hesiod, *Works and Days* (Oxford), 60-68.

³³ See ibid., 68, 77

³⁴ Ibid., 81-82, translation mine. M. L. West (*Theogony & Works and Days* [New York: Oxford University Press, 1988], p. 39) translates this line as follows: "and he named this woman Pandora, Allgift, because all the dwellers on Olympus made her their gift—a calamity for men who live by bread." Presumably, "Allgift" is intended to mean both "recipient" and "source," both "all-gifted" and "all-giving," while emphasizing that Pandora is from the outset intended and "gifted" by the gods as a deadly "gift" to men. In short, the gift (*dōron*) of woman comes down to grief (*pēma*).

³⁵ See Hesiod, *Works and Days* (Oxford), 100.

³⁶ See Dora and Erwin Panofsky, *Pandora's Box: The Changing Aspects of a Mythical Symbol,* Bollingen Series 52 (Princeton: Princeton University Press, 1962), pp. 17-20, for a discussion of Erasmus's possible reasons for what must have been a conscious substitution of *pyxis* for *dolium,* which surely the learned Erasmus knew to be the Latin equivalent for the Greek *pithos.* The Latin word *pyxis,* on the other hand, properly translates its exact phonetic equivalent in Greek.

[37] Walcot has argued that Pandora's *pithos* or jar referred to in *Works and Days* is a magic cauldron or pot, made of metal, most probably bronze ("Pandora's Jar, *Erga* 83-105," *Hermes,* 89 [1961]: 250). Concerning the magical properties of bronze, see G. Germain, *Essai sur les origines de certains thèmes odysséens et sur la genèse de l'Odyssée* (Paris: Thèse Fac. des Lettres Paris Presses Universitaires, 1954), pp. 153 ff. Walcot suggests elsewhere that the Homeric counterpart to Hesiod's jar, a place of imprisonment and not merely storage, is the bronze cauldron in which Ares was chained for thirteen months by the sons of Aloeus, until, nearly dead from his long ordeal, he was rescued at last by Hermes, presumably in his capacity as *psychopompos,* guide of souls lost to the light (*Hesiod and the Near East,* p. 61). See also Homer, *Iliad* (Loeb), 5.385-91. The idea that bronze might be an appropriate material for Pandora's jar finds support in the Old Anatolian myth entitled "The Disappearance of Telipinu," the son of the great storm god, in which we read:

> Down in the Dark Earth stand great *pahli*-vessels.
>
> Their lids are of lead. Their latches are of iron.
>
> That which goes into them doesn't come up again;
>
> it perishes therein. So may they seize Telipinu's
>
> anger, wrath, sin, and sullenness, and may they not
>
> come back (here).

Bronze *pahli*-vessels, were wide-mouthed storage pots with lids, essentially bronze *pithoi.* An identical account of these vessels and their function appears in the corresponding myth of "The Disappearance of Hannahanna," the Hurrian-Hittite Mother Goddess frequently associated with myths of vanishing gods. See Harry A. Hoffner, Jr., trans., and Gary M. Beckman, ed., *Hittite Myths* (Atlanta: Scholars Press, 1990), pp. 17, 28.

[38] Long before this, as early as 3500 B.C.E., burial in large earthenware jars may be traced to Asia Minor. Also very early and quite widespread was the use of honey in the cult of the dead. See Erich Neumann, *The Great Mother,* Bollingen Series 47 (Princeton: Princeton University Press, 1963), pp. 264-67; and A. W. Persson, *The Religion of Greece in Prehistoric Times,* Sather Classical Lectures 17 (Berkeley: University of California Press, 1942), pp. 13-18. In fact, burial in fetal position within egg-shaped earthenware pots is documented throughout southern and southeastern Europe from the Neolithic period onward, which practice clearly expresses "the idea of burial in the mother's womb. Burial in the womb is analogous to a seed being planted in the earth, and it was therefore natural to

expect new life to emerge from the old" (Marija Gimbutas, *The Language of the Goddess* [New York: Harper & Row, 1989], p. 151).

[39] The *choe,* drink offerings poured out from large vessels over the earth to the dead and to chthonic deities, may include honey, milk, water, oil, and wine. See Burkert, *Greek Religion,* pp. 70-72. Thus Odysseus, in preparation for his visit to the land of the dead, digs a pit and pours into it three cups for the dead and the gods below to drink: the first of honey mixed with milk, the second of sweet wine, and the third of water. See Homer, *Odyssey* (Loeb), 10.517-20. See also Aeschylus, *Persians* (Oxford), 607-22 and *Libation Bearers* (Oxford), 84-164; Sophocles, *Oedipus at Colonus* (Oxford), 466-92; Euripides, *Iphigenia in Tauris* (Oxford), 157-66.

[40] From the Geometric period onwards, simple pot burials were regularly given to infants and children, a practice that persisted in the classical period. See Robert Garland, *The Greek Way of Death* (Ithaca: Cornell University Press, 1985), p. 78. For a full discussion of the myth of Glaukos, see Persson, *Religion of Greece in Prehistoric Times,* pp. 9-24.

The expression "to fall into a jar of honey" means simply and euphemistically "to die." See Persson, *Religion of Greece in Prehistoric Times,* p. 12. Curiously, there is one preserved instance of a child's having "fallen" not only into honey but into the honeycomb itself. In the museum at Vrana near Marathon, there are kept the local remains of a child buried in two beehives, placed end to end to make his coffin. It is perhaps mistaken to suggest, however, as Garland does, that these two hives provided merely a "cheap" form of makeshift burial. "In the light of this evidence"—namely, the evidence for burying children in simple pots and even beehives—Garland concludes, "it is difficult to resist the impression that any serviceable container was acceptable for the body of a child" (*Greek Way of Death,* pp. 78, 81). Yet it may be that we would do well to resist just this impression in the additional light shed by the central significance of honey and of bees in the cult of the dead. See Gimbutas, *Language of the Goddess,* pp. 270-75, and *The Gods and Goddesses of Old Europe* (Berkeley: University of California Press, 1989), pp. 181-85. See also E. Richards-Mantzoulinou, "Melissa Potnia," *Athens Annals of Archaeology* 12 (1980): 1.72-92; and Anne Baring and Jules Cashford, *The Myth of the Goddess* (London: Arcana/Penguin, 1993), pp. 118-20.

In this context, it is interesting to recall that the infant Zeus, born in a Cretan cave inhabited by bees, was said to have been nourished by them. The fact that this Zeus was a year-child, dying and being reborn annually, would suggest that the bees and their nourishment may have played a role in his rebirth. See Martin P.

Nilsson, *The Minoan-Mycenaean Religion and its Survival in Greek Religion* (Lund: Gleerup, 1950), pp. 542-43.

Also, Gorgons, who can draw out one's very life-breath and turn living flesh to stone, sometimes have the heads of bees, as depicted on a proto-Attic vase found at Eleusis and dated ca. 675-650. See G. M. A. Richter, *A Handbook of Greek Art* (London: Phaidon Press, 1959), p. 286, fig. 405.

Finally, we may note that in the Old Anatolian myths of vanishing gods, it is the bee, "holding honey in its heart," that is sent repeatedly to search for the lost god, perished in the land of no return. It is the bee that stings him back to consciousness, soothes him with the sweet balm of its wax, and brings him home. See Hoffner and Beckman, *Hittite Myths,* pp. 13-16, 18, 21, 29, 30, 32-33, 36.

[41] The owl, an early symbol for the uterus, commonly presides over the cult of the dead. The figure of the owl served for the Egyptians as the hieroglyph for death. The Burney plaque, from the late Sumerian period (2300 B.C.E.), depicts a winged demon, flanked by owls. She is commonly identified with the Hebrew Lilith, hag of the night and of the dark realms, whose name means "screech owl." See B. Johnson, *Lady of the Beasts* (New York: Harper & Row, 1988), p. 82; and Isaiah 34:14. Lilith appears in Sumerian myth as *Lillake,* a demon inhabiting, along with the *Anzu*-bird and the serpent, the *huluppu*-tree (possibly a willow), planted and tended by the goddess Inanna. See Samuel Noah Kramer, *Sumerian Mythology* (Philadelphia: University of Pennsylvania Press, 1961), p. 33. Eventually, according to a Sumerian tablet from Ur, the hero Gilgamesh strikes the serpent, smashes the home of Lillake, sending her off like the *Anzu*-bird to live in the wild, and carves from Inanna's holy tree a throne and a bed. See Diane Wolkstein and Samuel Noah Kramer, *Inanna: Queen of Heaven and Earth, Her Stories and Hymns from Sumer* (New York: Harper & Row, 1983), pp. 3-9, 178-80. Lilith was later said to have been the first wife of Adam, rejected for her refusal to lie beneath him in a posture of submission, and sent off to the wilderness, like her Sumerian counterpart, to live in the company of animals. See Robert Graves and Raphael Patai, *Hebrew Myths: The Book of Genesis* (New York: Doubleday, 1964), pp. 12, 65-69, 101. Interestingly, in a story dating from sixteenth-century Palestine, Helen of Troy is closely associated with Lilith. See H. Schwartz, *Lilith's Cave* (New York: Oxford University Press, 1988), pp. 40-51. For a full discussion of the archaeological evidence linking the owl with death both in Greece and beyond, see Gimbutas, *Language of the Goddess,* pp. 185, 187, 189, 190-95, 207, 319, 321.

[42] Mysteriously emerging from and returning to earth and water, and residing in the tree of life, the serpent is commonly associated both with death and with life, with the world above and the world below. See Gimbutas, *Language of the Goddess,* pp. 121, 133, 135, 207. The observed fact that the serpent sloughs its dry, dead skin and thereby rejuvenates itself makes it a powerful symbol of rebirth. So embedded was this phenomenon in the Greek imagination that the same word, *gēras,* means both old age and the slough of the serpent. Frequently, in the mythologies of the ancient Near East, the serpent is associated not only with death but also with regeneration. Thus, in the epic of *Gilgamesh,* when the wife of Utanapishtim, the Sumerian Noah, persuades her husband to share with Gilgamesh the gift of immortality granted them by the gods, this gift comes in the form of a plant. This plant, pulled up from the *Apsu,* the fresh, sweet waters below the earth, restores youth each time it is eaten. (The *Apzu,* the waters of Enki, god of the abyss, like semen and amniotic fluid, are alive with engendering power. Enki presides over all three: the sweet waters that impregnate the earth, the semen that impregnates the mother, and the "birth water" that issues forth from the womb. The Sumerian language makes no distinctions here. So, when Gilgamesh plunges into the Apzu in search of rejuvenation, he is returning to the fecund earth and its fertile waters, to the womb of all life. See Thorkild Jacobsen, *The Treasures of Darkness: A History of Mesopotamian Religion* [New Haven: Yale University Press, 1976], p. 111; and Sylvia Brinton Perera, *Descent to the Goddess* [Toronto: Inner City, 1981], p. 67).

Gilgamesh, however, does not eat the magical plant at once. Instead, exhausted by his efforts to secure the plant, he decides to rest; and, while he is sleeping, a serpent slithers up, eats the plant, and sloughs its skin as it slithers off again. When he awakes, Gilgamesh weeps not only for himself but for all of humankind; for this was the last chance not to die, one by one, forever. See *The Epic of Gilgamesh,* trans. Kovacs, pp. 106-7, lines 266-309.

The serpent in Genesis, of course, requires no introduction. There too, through the intervention of the serpent, the tree of life is lost and, with it, immortal youth.

Finally, a possible and intriguing link between Helen and the cultic elements preserved in the Glaukos myth is suggested by Nilsson when he states: "From the archaic age onwards the symbols of the Dioscuri are two amphoras, and reliefs and coins show one or both of the amphoras entwined with snakes, or snakes approaching the amphoras" (*The Minoan-Mycenaean Religion and its Survival in Greek Religion,* p. 320). Like the snake in the Glaukos myth, the Dioskouroi are here understood as house gods, who appear as snakes and receive offerings left for them in earthenware vessels.

[43] See Robert Graves, *The Greek Myths* (Mt. Kisco: Moyer Bell, 1960), 90: d, e.

[44] Hope, which remains in the pithos to greet those who reenter it in death, is accorded little if any significance in Hesiod. The *Works and Days* presents what no one I know would call a hopeful picture. The timeless hope that the earth, the womb of all life, is a place from which anyone is born a second time seems to have left the kind of impression in Hesiod that plants leave in stones: the silent trace of life in the lifeless. *Elpis* or hope is nothing but a fossil from a forgotten time when the womb of woman and of the Mother Earth was the source not only of life but of its endless renewal.

[45] Erich Neumann holds the central archetypal symbol of woman as vessel to be "the essence of the feminine." "The basic symbolic equation woman = body = vessel corresponds," by his account, "to what is perhaps mankind's—man's as well as woman's—most elementary experience of the Feminine" (*Great Mother*, p. 39). Interestingly, the Old Egyptian hieroglyph for woman is a pot. See Robert Briffault, *The Mothers* (New York: Johnson Reprint, 1969), 3:473-74.

[46] See Gimbutas, *Language of the Goddess, passim,* particularly pp. 7, 21, 22, 37. Frequently, these vessels took the form of a bird-woman, surrounded by symbols indicating the presence of water and/or trees, the primeval waters and the tree of life. Clearly, both Aphrodite's and Helen's close association with fertility, death, trees, birds, and water suggest that we may find in these oldest pots their faint reflection. Indeed, the claim was made in ancient times that the very first bowl was shaped by using Helen's breast as a mold. See Briffault, *The Mothers,* 1:473.

Commenting on the identification of woman and pot, Erich Neumann points out: "The vessel character of the Feminine is often emphasized by a duplication of the jar: the woman represented as a jar carries a second jar" (*Great Mother,* p.121). In this same context, B. Johnson writes: "A figure from the Hisarlik site of Troy furnishes a curious duplication: The Pot Mother holds a jar on her head; at the same time she carries in her hands a small vessel connected to her larger pot body. The pot, in turn, represents the inexhaustible womb of the Bird Goddess, the primeval deep" (*Lady of the Beasts,* p. 49; see also pp. 38-50).

[47] See Hesiod, *Theogony* (Oxford), 571; *Works and Days* (Oxford), 60-62. P. Walcot finds a possible model for this episode in a scene depicted in the already mentioned reliefs on the funerary temple of Hatshepsut at Deir el-Bahari. In a series of these reliefs, the ram-god Khnum is ordered by the high god Amon to fashion Hatshepsut and her *ka,* her life-force, which he proceeds to do on what appears to be a potter's wheel (*Hesiod and the Near East,* p. 67). See also Brunner, *Die Geburt des Göttkonigs,* p. 68.

[48] In referring here and in the following discussion to Hephaestos as a "man," I am underlining his anthropomorphic masculinity. If it were not unduly awkward, I might refer to him as a "man-god" or "he-god" in the same way that we speak of a "she-witch" or a "she-goat."

[49] See John J. Winkler, *The Constraints of Desire: The Anthropology of Sex and Gender in Ancient Greece* (New York: Routledge, 1990), Appendix 2, "*Phusis* and *Natura* Meaning 'Genitals,'" pp. 217-20.

[50] According to Robert Lamberton, the unspoken claim of Hesiod is that "the female genitals are the source of all evil" (*Hesiod,* p. 102).

[51] The name given to the first woman by Adam, after the Fall, is Eve or *hāwwa,* the "mother of all the living" (Genesis 3:20). Quite another interpretation of Eve's name, however, is suggested by the fact that in Aramaic it means "serpent." See Stephen Langdon, *The Sumerian Epic of Paradise, the Flood and the Fall of Man,* University Museum Publications of the Babylonian Section, vol. 10, no. 1 (Philadelphia: University of Pennsylvania Press, 1915), pp. 36-37.

The prior and more essentially definitive name given to the first woman by God Yahweh at her creation is *'issā,* the one "taken from man" (*'īs,* Genesis 2:23). Here, she appears to be the source neither of all living things as they were meant to be, nor of Adam, original "man." Her only brood is fallen human beings, who were never meant to be and must wrest their livelihood from nature. They must take everything they get from the earth's withholding grasp until it holds them in its grasp forever.

Eve's organic derivation from Adam in the J text is indeed curious. There are myriad interpretations of Eve's origination from Adam's rib, which mostly come down to her inferiority, dependence, and consequent subservience. An interesting alternative is suggested by a Sumerian poem, which Kramer entitles "Enki and Ninhursag: The Affairs of the Water-God." Its two central characters are Enki and Ninhursag, who, under the name of Nintu, may have once been identical with Earth. In this poem, Enki is cursed by Ninhursag for having eaten eight plants, sprouts from Uttu herself, great-granddaughter of Ninhursag and goddess of plants. Eventually, Ninhursag withdraws her curses from the ailing Enki, who hurts all over. For each of his many pains, Ninhursag gives birth to a healing deity. The most relevant section reads as follows:

> *Ninhursag:* "My brother, what hurts thee?"
> *Enki:* "My rib hurts me."
> *Ninhursag:* "To the goddess Ninti I gave
>   birth for thee."
>   (Kramer, *Sumerian Mythology,* pp. 54-59).

Gerda Lerner, in commenting on this same passage, adds the salient fact that "in Sumerian, the word 'Ninti' has a double meaning, namely 'female ruler of the rib' and 'female ruler of life,' a meaning so close to the meaning of Hebrew *hāwwa,* that "there may be a fusion of the Sumerian Ninti with the Biblical Eve" (*Creation of Patriarchy,* p. 185).

[52] Briffault, *The Mothers,* 1:466.

[53] See Kramer's discussion of the myth of *Enki and Ninmah,* the Sumerian forerunner to *Atrahasis* (*Sumerian Mythology,* pp. 68-72). In the Old Babylonian version of *Atrahasis,* Nintu, "birthlady"—also called Mami, identical with Ninhursag, whose epithets include "womb-goddess," "mother of the gods," and "mother of all children"—entered the "room of fate" where "the womb-goddesses were assembled." There she pinched off fourteen pieces of clay, which she gave to the womb-goddesses, who created seven males and seven females. See *Atrahasis I,* in *Myths from Mesopotamia,* trans. Dalley, p. 14. In the *Gilgamesh,* it is this same goddess, under the name of Aruru, who pinches off a piece of clay and fashions Enkidu. See *Gilgamesh,* in *Myths from Mesopotamia,* trans. Dalley, pp. 52-53; and Jeffrey H. Tigay, *The Evolution of the Gilgamesh Epic* (Philadelphia: University of Pennsylvania Press, 1982), chapter 10, "The Creation of Enkidu," pp. 192-97. For a discussion of similarities between the creation of Enkidu and the creation of Adam and Eve, see Morris Jastrow, "Adam and Eve in Babylonian Literature," *American Journal of Semitic Languages and Literatures* 15 (1899): 193-214; and *The Religion of Babylonia and Assyria* (Boston: Ginn, 1898), chapter 23. See also Alexander Heidel, *The Babylonian Genesis* (Chicago: University of Chicago Press, 1942).

[54] See Marilyn B. Arthur, "Cultural Strategies in Hesiod's *Theogony:* Law, Family, Society," *Arethusa* 15 (1982): 74-79, and "The Dream of a World without Women: Poetics and Circles of Order in the Theogony Prooemium," *Arethusa* 16 (1983): 102-4, for a consideration of the meaning of *gast r* in Hesiod and Homer.

[55] Hesiod, *Theogony* (Oxford), 158.

[56] Ibid., 487.

[57] Ibid., 483.

[58] See ibid., 596-99.

[59] M. B. Arthur lists a number of epithets attached to the *gastēr* in the *Odyssey:* "hateful" (*stygerē*), "deadly" (*oulomenēs*), "greedy" (*analton*), "insistent" (*memauian*), "dismal" (*lygrēs*), "unappeasable" (*margēi*), "evildoing" (*kakoergos*), and a cause for reproach (*oneidizōn*) ("The Dream of a World without Women," p. 102). See Homer, *Odyssey,* 7.216, 15.344, 17.228 = 18.364, 17.286, 17.473, 18.2, 18.53, 18.380.

[60] Hesiod, *Theogony & Works and Days,* trans. West, p. 25, line 731.

[61] See *Theogony* (Oxford), 721-33.

[62] See Hesiod, *Theogony & Works and Days,* trans. West, p. 70, note to line 727; and Walcot, *Hesiod and the Near East,* p. 61. The *pithos* imagined by Hesiod in his description of Tartaros is made not of clay but of bronze, like the jar in which Ares was confined and from which he was delivered by Hermes. See Homer, *Iliad* (Loeb), 385-91. Whether made of bronze or of clay, however, the pithos was widely understood as a symbol of the underworld. "It is of interest to note," comments Persson, "that one of the meanings of the word pithos during the classical period was 'the kingdom of the dead,' Hades. The frequent, often humorous stories which are connected with the the pithos or storage vessel in later mythology show how widespread this idea must have been at one time (cf. Gruppe, *Griechische Mythologie,* p. 816)" (*Religion of Greece in Prehistoric Times,* p. 17).

That the Romans too envisioned the underworld as a kind of pot is argued by H. Wagenvoort, *Studies in Roman Literature, Culture and Religion* (Leiden: E. J. Brill, 1956), pp. 102-31.

[63] See Garland, *Greek Way of Death,* p. 54, on whose description of this vase I rely in my account. The scene on this vase would appear to confirm the identification of Ares' "*pithos*-prison," discussed above, as indeed Tartaros.

[64] See Hesiod, *Theogony & Works and Days,* trans. West, p. 64, note to line 116 of the *Theogony.*

[65] Hesiod, *Works and Days* (Oxford), 563.

[66] See Hesiod, *Theogony* (Oxford), 116-17.

67 Among the several prominent Egyptian myths of creation, the Heliopolitan, which may be traced to the second and third dynasties in the Old Kingdom, came to be the most widely accepted. This myth was centered in On, or Heliopolis (its Greek name), the eminent center of the Egyptian cult of the sun. It was here (six miles northeast of modern Cairo), at the apex of the Nile delta, that the annual floodwaters of the Nile would first begin to recede, revealing the rich earth buried below. This yearly sight was, for the Egyptians, an image of the first emergence of earth, on which the creation of the world took place. The sun-temple of On was itself said to have been built over that primeval hill on which creation began.

In the Hermapolitan myth, referred to in Pyramid texts, that same primeval hill was envisioned as an island—the Isle of Flames—circled by the waters of chaos and death. This island, before the drama of creation began, rose from the dark chaotic waters and provided a place of appearance for the Ogdoad, the eight deities—four male and four female—who created an egg from which broke forth the sun who fashioned humankind and ordered the world. In a variant version, the sun was born on this same hill from a lotus flower, while from the primordial egg there came the first sacred goose. For texts and commentary, see James B. Pritchard, *The Ancient Near East* (Princeton: Princeton University Press, 1958), 1:1-3; H. Frankfort, H. A. Frankfort, J. A. Wilson, Thorkild Jacobsen, and W. A. Irwin, *The Intellectual Adventure of Ancient Man* (Chicago: University of Chicago Press, 1946), pp. 50-61; Henri Frankfort, *Ancient Egyptian Religion* (New York: Harper & Row, 1948), pp. 20-22, 154.

68 Hesiod, *Theogony & Works and Days,* trans. West, p. 40, lines 106-8. See also fragment 1.6 in Merkelbach-West, *Fragmenta Hesiodea* (Oxford: Oxford University Press, 1967), pp. 3ff. For a discussion of this passage and of counterinterpretations to that one suggested here, see Pucci, *Hesiod and the Language of Poetry,* pp. 88-89, and n. 14, p. 117-18.

69 Hesiod, *Theogony* (Oxford), 582, translation mine. The word for earth here is *ēpeiros,* "solid land," as opposed to sea. Specifically in Egypt, this word was used to name that land rising above the floodwaters, suggesting a clear link to the primeval hillock of creation. See Liddell and Scott, revised by Jones with McKenzie, *A Greek-English Lexicon* (Oxford: Clarendon, 1968), p. 7776, s.v. *ēpeiros.*

70 See Hesiod, *Theogony* (Oxford), 211-25.

71 See ibid., 226-33.

72 Ibid., 126.

73 Ibid., 120.

74 Ibid., 881-85.

75 Marduk of Babylon, Assur of Assyria, Yahweh of Israel, and Zeus of Greece represent a new breed, as it were, of Iron Age "strongmen," who are marked by militarism and absolute power. See Mark S. Smith, *Early History of God,* p. 56. Two other Near Eastern storm-gods, Baal and Teshub, in their respective myth cycles, know defeat as well as victory, and even when victorious are not always single-handedly so. See Walcot, *Hesiod and the Near East,* p. 25. Many of Baal's enemies, for example, are defeated not by him but by Anat. A mythic cycle with perhaps even closer links to the *Theogony* is the Hurrian Kumarbi Cycle, in which the central contest for kingship among the gods is between Teshub and Kumarbi. Ea, the Mesopotamian god of wisdom, who in the *Song of Kumarbi* is the foe of Teshub and the ally of Kumarbi, eventually changes sides and, in the *Song of Ullikummi,* becomes altogether crucial to Teshub's final success. See Hoffner and Beckman, *Hittite Myths,* II. "Hurrian Myths," pp. 38-61, especially Nos. 14 and 18. Then too, there is the cosmic and dynastic combat of Seth and Horus (see E. A. Wallis Budge, *The Gods of the Egyptians* [New York: Dover, 1969], 2:241-60) in which the victory of Horus is neither unassisted nor total, as indicated by the fact that in the reliefs depicting Queen Hatshepsut's coronation, the twin crowns of upper and lower Egypt are placed on her head not by Horus alone but by both Horus and Seth together (see Henri Frankfort, *Kingship and the Gods* [Chicago: University of Chicago Press, 1972], pp. 106-7).

76 Hesiod, *Theogony* (Oxford), 884.

77 In books 1 and 2 of the *Iliad,* this issue informs and even defines the contest between Agamemnon and Achilles over who is the "Best of the Achaeans." It is at root a contest between the scepter, which Agamemnon carries and claims to be traceable to Zeus, and the spear, in the use of which Achilles is peerless. These two symbols, the scepter and the spear, represent the two essential elements of divine kingship: authority and force. Both are ultimately divine. Clearly, Zeus possesses both and rules accordingly. When his word is questioned, his fire decides the matter (see Homer, *Iliad* [Loeb], 1.580-81; 8.5-27). On earth, in cities, among men, there is rarely if ever the convergence of wisdom and power. Homer knew this as well as did Plato. The question this raises is whether the Olympian paradigm—the perfect coincidence of authority and power—can ever be replicated in the human realm. Then, if the answer is no, if we must choose between brute force

Ajax, in battle dress, thrusts his lance into a fallen Trojan.

and right counsel, the question becomes whether we choose to be governed by only one element of the divine paradigm or find, instead, another paradigm altogether for the formation and governance of human community. Homer, I believe, sought the latter path and with it a new definition of "the Best of the Achaeans."

[78] See *Myths from Mesopotamia,* trans. Dalley, *The Epic of Creation,* tablet VII, pp. 267-74.

[79] Ibid., p. 272.

[80] Ibid., p. 273: "With fifty epithets the great gods called his fifty names, making his way supreme."

[81] Hesiod, *Theogony* (Oxford), 886.

[82] Marcel Detienne and Jean-Pierre Vernant, *Cunning Intelligence in Greek Culture and Society* (Chicago: University of Chicago Press, 1991), p. 109. From this they go on to explain: "Because all the *mētis* in the world, all the unexpected possibilities which cunning time conceals are now within Zeus, sovereignty ceases to be the stake played for in a series of indefinitely repeated conflicts and becomes, instead, a stable and permanent state. At this point the king of the gods can celebrate his marriage to Themis and beget fine chil-

dren for her: the Seasons and the Fates. His irrevocable decisions have fixed the succession of future events as it has [*sic*] the hierarchy of the different functions, ranks and honours. He has settled them by ordinance once and for all. Whatever comes to pass in the future has, for all time, already been foreseen and determined in the head of Zeus."

[83] Hesiod, *Theogony* (Oxford), 899.

[84] Ibid., 891. The reaction of Gaia to the birth of Athena, as recorded in the first Homeric *Hymn to Athena,* seems a bit more authentic. When she, we are told, together with the rest of the immortals, saw Athena "jump suddenly out of his [Zeus's] sacred head shaking her sharp spear . . . the earth groaned awfully" (*The Homeric Hymns,* translated by Charles Boer [Chicago: Swallow, 1970], p. 137).

[85] See Jane Ellen Harrison, *Prolegomena to the Study of Greek Religion* (Princeton: Princeton University Press, 1991), pp. 300-307.

[86] Walcot, *Hesiod and the Near East,* pp. 113-14.

[87] See F. Brommer, "Die Geburt der Athena," *Jahrbuch Römisch-Germanisches Zentralmuseum* 8 (1961): 72-73.

[88] Jean-Pierre Vernant, "Hestia Hermès: Sur l'expression religieuse de l'espace et du mouvement chez les Grecs," in *Mythe et pensée chez les Grecs* (Paris: F. Maspero, 1965), p. 124; see Arthur, "The Dream of a World without Women," p. 97.

[89] Christine Downing, *The Goddess* (New York: Crossroad, 1987), p. 154.

[90] Arthur, "Cultural Strategies in Hesiod's *Theogony*," p. 75.

[91] See L. R. Farnell, *The Cults of the Greek States* (Oxford: Clarendon, 1896-1909), 3:25.

[92] Hesiod, *Theogony* (Oxford), 591.

[93] Walter F. Otto, *The Homeric Gods: The Spiritual Significance of Greek Religion* (Boston: Beacon Press, 1954), p. 102. Pucci points out that "Aphrodite does not appear, but sends in her place some of her occasional helpers to beautify Pandora. The goddess is, then," he concludes, "*vicariously* represented by the Charities, Peitho, and the Horai, all of whom may bespeak her, but none of whom is a univocal 'sign' of Aphrodite" (*Hesiod and the Language of Poetry,* p. 96).

[94] See Farnell, *Cults of the Greek States,* 5:624.

[95] *Sappho,* translated by Mary Barnard (Berkeley: University of California Press, 1958), #65.

[96] Again, for a thorough presentation and discussion of the ancient iconographic tradition depicting the varied abductions and retrievals of Helen and its relationship to the poetic tradition's treatment of the same theme, see Lilly B. Ghali-Kahil, *Les enlèvements et le retour d'Hélène, dans les textes et les documents figurés,* École Francaise D'Athènes, Travaux et Mémoires (Paris: E. de Boccard, 1955).

[97] Semonides, 96,115, translation mine. For Greek text, commentary, and a complete translation, see Hugh Lloyd-Jones, *Female of the Species* (London: Duckworth, 1975).

[98] Ibid., 1-2.

[99] Ibid., 94-95.

[100] Ibid., 96-100, 115-18, as above, translation mine.

[101] See Herodotus, *The History* (Loeb), 1.105.

[102] See Jeremiah 7:17; 44:18.

[103] Aeschylus, *Eumenides* (Loeb), 1.

[104] Farnell speaks of Demeter as "the brightest of all Gaia's emanations," and states that "her individuality was rooted in the primitive and less developed personality of Gaia" (*Cults of the Greek States,* 3:28; 3:30).

[105] See Plato, *Menexenus* (Loeb), 238a.

[106] *Homeric Hymns,* trans. Boer, p. 5.

FURTHER READING

Bremmer, Jan, ed. *Interpretations of Greek Mythology.* Totowa, N.J.: Barnes & Noble Books, 1986, 294 p.

Collection of essays focusing on a variety of issues related to Greek mythology and its interpretation, including essays on the origins and historical aspects of Greek myth, as well as discussions of particular myths and types of myths.

Brillante, Carlo. "History and Historical Interpretation of Myth," pp. 91-140. In *Approaches to Greek Myth,* edited by Lowell Edmunds. Baltimore: The Johns Hopkins University Press, 1990.

Studies the relationship between myth and history, examining in particular the way ancient Greeks viewed myth as a means of transmitting historical events. Brillante notes that they distinguished between heroic myths and divinity myths.

Burkert, Walter, ed. *Structure and History in Greek Mythology and Ritual.* Berkeley: University of California Press, 1979, 226 p.

Series of lectures designed to approach the study of myth from a variety of disciplines. Examines how myths are organized, the relationship between myth and ritual, and discusses several groups of myths.

Cook, Arthur Bernard. *Zeus: A Study in Ancient Religion, Volume I: Zeus, God of the Bright Sky.* New York: Biblo and Tannen, 1964, 885 p.

Analyzes the myths related to "Bright Zeus" as god of the "Upper Sky" and the Hellenistic efforts to associate him with the sun, moon, and stars as well. Subsequent volumes study the myths related to "Dark Zeus" as god of thunder, lightning, earthquakes, clouds, wind, dew, rain, and meteorites.

Dowden, Ken. *The Uses of Greek Mythology.* London: Routledge, 1992, 204 p.

Studies the nature and diversity of Greek myth and the ways in which Greeks understood and employed their mythology.

Finley, M. I. "Myth, Memory, and History." In *The Use and Abuse of History*, pp. 11-33. New York: The Viking Press 1971.

Examines the idea of pitting history against poetry, arguing that among the ancients "everyone accepted the epic tradition as grounded in hard fact," but that, in reality, "whatever else it may have been, the epic was *not history*."

Gordon, R. L., ed. *Myth, Religion, and Society*. Cambridge: Cambridge University Press, 1981, 306 p.

Collection of essays concerned with the treatment in myth of divinity, the human condition, social order, and disorder and deviance. The essays are introduced by Richard Buxton, who characterizes the approach taken by the essayists (M. Detienne, L. Gernet, J.-P. Vernant, P. Vidal-Naquet) as structuralist.

Mondi, Robert. "Greek Mythic Thought in the Light of the Near East," pp. 141-98. In *Approaches to Greek Myth*, edited by Lowell Edmunds. Baltimore: The Johns Hopkins University Press, 1990.

Explores the diffusion of "mythic ideas" or folklore motifs (as contrasted with the diffusion of texts and philological influences of one text on another) and discusses the parallels between Greek and Near Eastern myths.

Nilsson, Martin P. "Myths and Politics." In *Cults, Myths, Oracles, and Politics in Ancient Greece*, pp. 4-80. Lund: C. W. K. Gleerup, 1951.

Explores the political purposes for which Greeks appropriated mythology. Nilsson explains that myths helped to "justify the possession of a country or a district, they served to assert claims on some territory which a city wanted to win, and to impress the righteousness of these claims upon public opinion."

Penglase, Charles. *Greek Myths and Mesopotamia: Parallels and Influence in the Homeric Hymns and Hesiod*. London: Routledge, 1994, 278 p.

Uses the works of Hesiod and Homer to identify ideas and motifs which figure prominently in Mesopotamian myths. Penglase notes that one of the most common, prominent parallel ideas is that of a journey used to assert "the god's acquisition and demonstration of power in the journey."

Sergent, Bernard. *Homosexualtiy in Greek Myth*, translated by Arthur Goldhammer. Boston: Beacon Press, 1984, 344 p.

Offers an examination of various Greek myths which contain examples of homosexual behavior, following a discussion of the historical facts related to homosexuality in Greece and other early non-Christian societies.

Vernant, Jean-Pierre. *Myth and Thought among the Greeks*. London: Routledge & Kegan Paul, 1965, 382 p.

Uses Greek myths to examine, from a perspective of "historical psychology" a variety of aspects of Greek life and culture. Vernant covers such topics as religion, philosophy, science, art, social institutions, and economic data, considering all of these issues "as having been created by the human mind."

Norse Mythology

INTRODUCTION

The stories that have come down to us as Norse myths developed throughout Northern Europe as part of an oral tradition dating from the eighth to the eleventh centuries. The forms of the tales we have today come from the earliest extant manuscripts, dating to the thirteenth century. Encompassing both mythological tales of the gods and heroic tales of warriors and leaders, the Norse mythological tradition offers insights into both the religious beliefs and the history of the cultures of Northern Europe between the fall of the Roman Empire and the birth of early modern national cultures. Its primary myths treat themes common to most cultures: the creation of the world, the nature of good and evil, and the cycles of life, death and regeneration. The heroic tales present glimpses of the daily life and thought, as well as of the significant historical figures and moments of the Northern tribal peoples. The *Poetic Edda* stands as one of the most significant literary works of the middle ages, and the Eddic tradition as a whole remains valuable not only for research into mythology and literary history, but also for the study of folklore, medieval history, and Scandinavian, Germanic, and Old English culture.

Norse myths have their roots in tales told by a variety of Indo-European peoples who populated much of north and central Europe from as early as 600 B. C. These groups moved steadily south from Scandinavia, through what is now central and eastern Europe, toward the ever-expanding border of the Roman Empire. After the fall of Rome, Indo-European peoples migrated further into former Roman territory, and the Angles and Saxons settled in England. Latin culture remained dominant and the fall of the Roman Empire did not stop the spread of Christianity. By the seventh century, Christianity had spread widely throughout the British Isles and Western Europe. It would not arrive in Scandinavia for another three hundred years. It was during these years that the northernmost of the old Indo-European tribes began to move south into England and Western Europe, and as far west as Iceland and the North American continent, in the relentless Viking raids. It is these people, known as the "Northmen," who told and preserved the stories of the old gods and inspired many of the heroic legends that form the basis of Norse mythology.

These stories were part of an oral tradition in a pagan culture, but the written versions that have come down to us were written centuries later, in Christianized cultures. Thus, dating the works and separating out differing cultural influences is a difficult, if not impossible, task.

The primary literary sources are the *Snorra Edda*, the *Saemander Edda*, and the Skaldic poems. Saxo Grammaticus's *History of the Danes*, Old Icelandic sagas, primarily family histories and genealogies, and other historical accounts round out the picture. The most well known sources are the *Eddas*. The word *Edda* is of uncertain and somewhat debated origin; it is most often interpreted as a form of the place name "Oddi," which is associated with both the main compiler and the main commentator on the Eddic tradition. Other accounts treat it as stemming from a variant of the Norse word for poetry, or poetics, or from the term for great-grandmother. One recent interpretation connects it to the Latin word *edere*, meaning to write or publish.

The *Snorra Edda*, or *Prose Edda*, is a kind of Norse "poetics," written by Snorri Sturluson, one of the most learned and influential Icelanders of his day. It explicates the art of poetry for the Skalds (poets), bards who told tales in praise of their Viking lords. Sturluson (1178-1241) was chief judge and president of the legislative assembly as well as a writer and scholar. His *Edda* is a three-part work with a loosely Christian preface. The first part provides an account of the major Norse gods and goddesses, with extended quotations from the oral poems that make up the *Poetic Edda*. This mythological tradition was referred to by the Skaldic poems and is implicit in much of their meaning. The second section analyzes the poetry of the Skalds, offering both advice on composition and excerpts from exemplary work. The final section follows on this with a detailed explanation of the meters Skaldic poets used in composing their poems. Snorri's other major work was the *Heimskringla*, a compilation of sagas about the Norse kings.

The *Poetic Edda* was discovered in 1642, in a manuscript dating to 1300 that contained twenty-nine poems. It has been attributed to Saemund, an Icelandic priest and collector of poetry who died in 1133. Later, other poems found in old manuscripts were added to the collection. Scholars believe that Saemund may or may not have been the collector of the poems, but that he did not write them. They represent the work of many authors over several centuries, most likely dating back to anywhere from 850 to 1000. These are the oldest and most authentic accounts of the Norse mythological tradition, antedating the widespread establishment of Christianity. Perhaps the most important and striking of these tales is *Voluspa*, addressed to Odin by a seeress. It is a long and comprehensive account of the origin of the cosmos, the gods, and their rise and fall. Other stories, such as *Grimnismal* and *Vafprudnismal*, offer encyclopedic retellings of important events. *Grimnismal* is Odin's fireside account to a king and his sons; *Vafprudnismal* is written in the form of a dialogue between Odin and the giant Vafprudnir. All of the poems are written in characteristic meters derived from the practices of oral storytelling. They are strongly alliterative, with the accent on the first syllable of each word. Lines are broken in half, with a noticeable caesura (or pause) in the middle, and there are three consistent verse forms: a story meter (for narrative exposition), a speech meter (for dialogue or monologue), and a song meter.

The Skaldic poems, primarily elegies and eulogies, derive from a similar time period, though in general, they are later. Both the Eddic and the Skaldic poems assume an audience with a deep knowledge of the stories of the Norse gods. The oldest Eddic poems are in dialogue format, with little or no narrative exposition; the assumption was that the listeners knew the main outlines of a tale as well as the characteristics of the primary actors. The art of telling lay in the variation of interpreting and the dramatic rendering of the events. Skaldic poetry could be even more elliptical, since the main focus was on the lord being praised. Mythological details enter in metaphors or in descriptive verbal formulas commonly used in the oral tradition. Poems about the gods and elegies to heroes often share a similar structure: there is a challenge, battle, and death, followed by renewal or "resurrection" in the warriors' pantheon of Valhall. Interaction or mingling between the gods and humans are at best a small part of any of the poems.

Because the tales come from many sources over centuries, a considerable variety has developed in the stories told and the beliefs described in them. Thus, while there is a tendency to speak of a uniform Norse tradition, in fact, the written record we have represents fragments and discontinuous elements of the literatures of many related but decentralized peoples. Notwithstanding this variability, there are broad common outlines to the Norse pantheon and cosmology. The cosmos of Norse mythology is divided into three levels, corresponding loosely to the realm of the gods, the realm of humans, and an underworld. These realms are subdivided into nine worlds, peopled variously by gods, slain warriors, elves, humans, dwarves, giants, and the dead. In the creation myth, the giants preceded the gods, who emerged from them to create the rest of the world. The giants and the gods were enemies and much of the drama of the myths centers around their conflicts and, more generally, conflicts resulting from contact between disparate worlds. After the initial emergence of the gods and the creation of the tripartite cosmos, there was a brief golden age which was soon disrupted by conflict and battles, especially between the gods and the giants. The gods won the largest battle, instigated by the trickster Loki, but suffered significant losses, most notably the death of Baldur. Conflict continued until Ragnavok, the final "battle of all," which resulted in the end of the world and the gods, and the dawn of a new cycle of time.

The main characters in the stories are the gods; dwarves and giants tend to be generic and usually remain unnamed. Descriptions of the Norse pantheon vary somewhat from account to account, but the most important figures are constant. Odin is the "all-father," the oldest and highest of the gods. He is the creator and is associated with poetry, charms, battle, and the dead. Thor, the most popular god, represents strength, stability, and order. With his association with thunder and lightning, which bring rain for crops, he is also linked with fertility, as is Frey, the god of plenty, fertility, prosperity, and the weather. The masculine Frey may have become Freya, a fertility goddess. Freya, in her turn is often associated with Frigg (or Frigga), the wife of Odin. Baldur, the most pure god, was slain in one of the conflicts that led inexorably to the final battle and the destruction of the world; some later accounts interpret Baldur as a Christ figure. His death was instigated by Loki, who is not properly a god. A giant, he became foster brother to Odin's sons, and is a classic trickster figure, begetting monsters, changing sex and appearance, and bringing chaos and conflict.

As a whole, the works of Norse mythology provide valuable insights into the literary and religious thought of the pre-Christian peoples of Northern Europe and offer impressive examples of poetic imagination. Their tales and figures have also had a lasting influence on many European languages and cultures, lingering in place names, the days of the week, and in the characters and landscapes of folk and fairy tales.

HISTORY AND MYTHOLOGICAL TRADITION

Brian Branston (1955)

SOURCE: "Historical Introduction," in *Gods of the North*, Thames and Hudson, 1955, pp. 1-46.

[*In the following excerpt, Branston provides the historical context and description of the Norse people and culture, particularly in Iceland.*]

Mythology is every man's business; whether it be of the private kind called psychology or the collective kind which manifests itself in stories of the gods.

A myth is like a dream; it is a direct expression of the unconscious mind, and the events of a myth, its characters and symbols are to the human race as the events, characters and symbols of his dream are to the individual. Like a dream the myth may ignore the conventional logic of space and time relationships, of events following one after another in a causal sequence. Nevertheless, a dream has a meaning which can be made plain; and so has a myth. It is not easy to interpret the myths of our own race, for our near ancestors—those of a thousand odd years ago—were persuaded to forget them or to relegate their broken remnants to the nursery. The Gods of the North were once upon a time the gods of our forefathers. The fossilized remains of these deities survive in place-names for instance, as Wansdyke, Wednesbury, Wensley, Tuesley and Thundersley; in the names of the days of the week, as Sunday, Monday, Tuesday, Wednesday, Thursday and Friday; in folklore and fairy tale with their stories of Wayland Smith, witches on broomsticks and the Wild Rider. Such remains are, on their own, largely useless as an aid to reconstructing the mythology of our forefathers; if we want to do that we can call in archaeology and philology but mainly we must rely on a literature which grew, first orally and then in manuscript, in Iceland. How we should have such close links with the men of Iceland asks for an explanation.

1

Northmen

The basic written authority for early English history is the *Old English* or *Anglo-Saxon Chronicle,* a sort of national diary. This diary begins with a summary of history in Britain from before the invasion by Julius Caesar down to the year A.D. 1 when it records *Octavianus reigned 56 years and in the 42nd year of his reign Christ was born.* Scanty annals follow up to the year A.D. 449 when the coming of the Angles, Saxons and Jutes to Britain is recorded. From then on the entries become (in general) more detailed and longer. Today there exist seven known manuscripts of the *Old English Chronicle.* All are derived as far as the year A.D. 891 from a set of annals written (in the English language of the time) in the reign of Alfred the Great (*d.* 26 Oct. 899). Soon after 891 the *Chronicles* begin to differ from one another, presumably because they were sent out to different churches for their continuation. Still, up to the year 915 the *Chronicles* have much material in common. After the Norman Conquest they begin to peter out.

The entry in the *Old English Chronicle* for the year A.D. 787 runs:

This year Beorhtric took to wife Eadburg daughter of King Offa. It was during Beorhtric's days that three ships of the *Northmen* first came here from Hörðaland. The reeve galloped to meet them, intending to drive them to the king's town (Dorchester) for he did not know who or what they were. They killed him.

These were the first ships of the *Danes* ever to seek England.

The filibustering crews of these three clinker-built longships shouted and splashed ashore in Weymouth Bay,

Dorset. It is instructive to note what the *Chronicle* calls them: it says they were "Northmen", "Danes" and that they came from "Hörðaland", a district on the west coast of Norway. The name Hörðaland is equivalent to "Lancashire", "Yorkshire" or any other of the English counties with a coastline. No doubt the invaded English fishermen and farmers recognized their assailants in general as coming from Scandinavia or Denmark, but for them to remember and for their clerks in holy orders to put on record the actual name of the district whence the pirates came argues two things: first, that the speech of both peoples was near enough for them to understand each other and second, that some of the Dorset men asked the raiders where they came from and were told in reply "Hörðaland".

Can we picture the scene when (round about A.D. 787) the three keels ran up on to Weymouth sands? It is reasonable to suppose that the blond-haired, bewhiskered crews (some 30 to 40 in each boat) had dropped their single sails of black and yellow vertical stripes hanging from a single yard and a single mast. And to suppose that they lifted their round shields in readiness from the gunn'ls, and keeping their swords and iron axes out of the salt water, waded ashore. Were they attacked or did they themselves attack at once? Neither, it would seem. A certain amount of inquisitive chat must have gone on between them and the locals while word was sent up to Dorchester ten miles away of the arrival of strangers. King Beorhtric of Wessex's representative in Dorchester was his reeve Beaduheard. The reeve, "with a few men", trotted out of Dorchester town for the last time: he passed (probably without a thought) the monuments of former peoples, the grass-grown Romano-British amphitheatre on his left, the long hog-back of the Stone Age earthwork Maiden Castle on his right. He passed them, cantering down from the heights to the sea with the Stone Age round barrows pimpling the skyline behind him, and he little realized that he was to be one of the first eye witnesses of the scouts of a new invasion. Beaduheard saw the blue sea, the three ships, their canting masts, the knot of skin-bleached men with their conical helmets and round shields; it is said that he thought "the newcomers were merchants rather then enemies. He addressed them in a commanding tone and ordered them to be brought to the king's vill. But he was killed there and then, and those that were with him."[1]

If these sailormen actually came from Hörðaland on the west coast of Norway then the *Chronicle* is right to call them "Northmen" but wrong to refer to them as "Danes". Is there any meaning behind this confusion? Perhaps we can get further light from another entry, the annal for the year A.D. 793:

This year awful forewarnings (which terrified the wretched people) were witnessed throughout Northumberland: first there were continuous lightning storms and next, fiery dragons were seen flapping across the sky. A mighty famine quickly followed these portents and shortly after, on 8th June of this same year, the Heathens grievously harried and destroyed God's church on Lindisfarne in order to plunder and slay.[2]

This new designation "heathen" emphasizes two points: at this time and for many years to come the invaders *were* heathen, while the invaded had for many years been Christian. "Northmen", "Danes", "heathen"—the *Chronicle* employs these terms imprecisely without taking much account of whether the invaders were Norwegians, Danes or Swedes. Another frequent *Chronicle* term for this thorn in the flesh was the Old English word *here* meaning "army" or "host", particularly an "enemy host". A word found in Old English glossaries dating from the eighth century is *wīcingsceaða;* the first part of this word is related to Old Norse *víkingr;* but the word "viking", which has been in fashion for only a century and a half, came into vogue with the Victorians.[3] "Viking" really refers to a way of life lived by some members of all four of the countries Denmark, Sweden, Norway and Iceland between the years 700-1100 A.D.

The historical Norse saga writers (e.g. Snorri Sturluson in *Heimskringla*) use the term "Northmen" (O.N. *Norð(r)menn*) when alluding to natives of Denmark, Sweden, Norway and Iceland; this is equivalent to the *O.E. Chronicle's Norðmenn,* and to the monks' medieval Latin *North(o)manni.* It must be admitted that O.N. *Norð(r)menn* can bear the restricted meaning "Norwegians", but this is hardly ever the case with O.E. *Norðmenn* and med. Lat. *North(o)manni* where the general meaning is "men from the north". "Northmen" then is the blanket term which will be employed in this book, except where "viking" may be used to indicate a Northman of the raiding, trading, colonizing years 700-1100 A.D., and except where it is necessary to indicate Icelander, Norwegian, Swede or Dane.

. . . . .

6

The Vikings: Settlement of Iceland

Through the world of their time the vikings spread like a terrible tide: England, the coasts of Wales, Scotland, Ireland, Frisia, France, Spain, Italy and America. Northmen colonized the Faroes, Iceland, Greenland; gained a foothold on the Wendish and Prussian coasts, gave their name to, and became lords of Russia, harried north Persia and formed the Greek Emperor's bodyguard at Constantinople. But like the tide that spreads over a porous land and, except for isolated pools, disappears, so disappeared the Northmen, or seemed to do so as they merged into the peoples they had briefly dominated. Only the pools remained—the Faroes, Iceland and for a time Greenland.

Of these three places, Iceland is most important, for Iceland became the cradle of the written records of the traditions concerning the Gods of the North. These traditions are mainly contained in the two *Eddas;* the *Verse Edda* being a collection of ancient poems by unknown authors, and the *Prose Edda* a later combined account of Norse myth and poet's handbook by a famous Icelander, Snorri Sturluson (*d.* 1241).

Apparently the Northmen first discovered Iceland by chance: a Norwegian called Naddoð was driven by contrary winds on to the coast; Garðar a Swede drifted there from the Pentland Firth. Flóki, another Norwegian, attempted to settle in Iceland but neglected to make hay to over-winter his cattle. He was forced to leave. Before he did so, he climbed a mountain and saw a fiord filled with pack ice: he called the country Iceland. These visits to Iceland took place around A.D. 860, five years before the "Great Army" (see page 20) descended on East Anglia and began the foundation of the Danelaw in England. Some ten or twenty years later a significant and famous battle took place at Hafrsfjörðr[10] in Norway when Harold Fairhair (son of king Halfdan the Black) after fifteen years of fighting broke the resistance of the West Norwegians and made himself king of all Norway. It seems that the threatened loss of independence drove many of Harold's defeated enemies to emigrate (another reason for the flitting "west-over-sea") and most of them went to Iceland, the first settler being one Ingolfr. According to Ari Thorgilsson, writing between 1122-1133, Ingolfr:

> settled in the south, in Reykjavik. He first touched land at the spot called Ingolfr's Head east of Minþakseyrr; and he laid claim for ever to Ingolfr's Fell west of Ölfossa. At that time Iceland was well wooded between the fells and the sea shore. (*Libellus Islandorum*).

Ari Thorgilsson goes on to say:

> There were living in Iceland then those Christian folk whom the Northmen called *papishers.*[11] But they afterwards went away, not liking to remain here with heathens though they left behind them Irish books, bells and croziers: and this was sufficient evidence of their being Irish monks. After that there was a great flitting of people from Norway out here until king Harold [Fairhair] put a stop to it for fear of depopulating the homeland. (*Libellus Islandorum.*)

Ingolfr settled at Reykjavik (now the capital) about the year 874; Ari Thorgilsson says it took another fifty years to colonize the island completely. A traveller of a later day has left us a description of the topography of Iceland:

> Imagine to yourself an island, which from one end to the other presents to your view only barren mountains, whose summits are covered with eternal snow, and between them fields divided by vitrified cliffs, whose

high and sharp points seem to vie with each other to deprive you of the sight of a little grass which scantily springs up among them. . . . Rivers and fresh-water lakes abound; the latter of very considerable extent and well supplied with fish; the former . . . much obstructed by rocks and shallows.[12]

The traveller who wrote this, William Jackson Hooker, describes the barren moors, morasses, volcanoes, sulphur springs and boiling fountains; he mentions what the main items of the native diet were, and there is little reason to suppose these items had changed a great deal since Ingolfr's days—fish and butter. The fish was eaten mostly dry and uncooked, and the butter made without salt and with all the whey and superfluous moisture pressed out (so that if necessary it could keep indefinitely—ideal provender for long sea voyages). Milk was converted into *syra* or sour whey preserved in casks until it fermented. This mixed with water was called *blanda.* Then there was *striugar,* whey boiled to the consistency of curd; *skiur,* which was *striugar* with the moisture squeezed out. The flesh of sheep and bullocks could be eaten only by the well-to-do.

It is important to remember that not all the first colonists of Iceland came from Norway, Denmark and Sweden. Many emigrated from the colonies of Northmen in the British Isles, especially from the settlements in the Hebrides and Ireland. Even if these Northmen themselves had no Celtic blood in their veins, many of their descendants had, for their fathers married or entered into concubinage with Celtic women; and a childhood spent at a Celtic knee meant for the child an absorption of Celtic lore and culture. Evidence of links between Iceland and the Celtic countries can be seen in the names borne by famous Icelanders of the tenth century, Njáll, Kormákr, Kjartan; and by such stories as that of Helgi the Lean who settled in Iceland and whose mother was Rafarta (Irish *Rafertach*) daughter of an Irish king, Kjarvalr, said to be Cearbhall, king of Ossory who died in 887. Many of the Icelandic thralls obviously came from Ireland or the Hebrides: they have such names as Dufan and Melkólfr, while the Vestmannaeyjar to this day bear witness as a group of islands where thralls from Ireland set up a brief republic. A fair sprinkling of Icelandic places have names of Irish origin, and how are they to be explained except as the abodes of Celts or Northmen with Celtic links? Examples of such place-names are Papey, Pappabýli, Patreksfjörðr, Minþakseyrr (near Ingolfr's first landing place), Brjánslœkr and Dufgusdalr. As regards Irish loan words in Old Icelandic, examples are to be found in *slavak,* chickweed (<Ir. *sleabhac*), *súst,* a flail (<Ir. *súiste*), *tarfr,* a bull (<Ir. *tarbh*). This evidence of Celtic links is important when one comes to consider whether or not the Old Icelandic eddaic verse holds notions deriving from Christianity through the Christian Irish.

Still, the bulk of emigrants to Iceland came from Norway bringing with them, besides their pots and pans, a fierce spirit of independence, a love of adventure and a superb seamanship to back it up. They brought, too, long memories and to assist those memories a strong mould of genealogy and another strong mould of alliterative verse both of which gave and kept shape to their oral tales and unwritten ballads. Ten centuries later a visitor to Iceland was struck forcibly by the tough fibre of this oral tradition:

> Scarcely a man in Iceland bears the same surname as his father. Only a few householders have a family name and they are all recent arrivals. A man whose name is Eric Sigurdsson may have his son baptized Olaf, and this child will all his life bear the name of Olaf Ericsson. If, in turn, Olaf gives the Christian name of Hankur to his son, that fellow will have, as his full name Hankur Olafsson. . . .

> This would be a shiftless arrangement were it not for the genealogical interest which each man takes in his forefolk. They can all tell you their ancestors' names for the last thousand years, and are thus conscious of living, not in the current generation but a river of personal life. "I am the thirty-fourth generation since the immigration," one will tell you. The immigration is the year 874, when the first of them landed on their empty island.[13]

The strength of tradition (and the Icelander's respect for it) is contained in that sentence *They can tell you their ancestors' names for the last thousand years;* and there is not the slightest doubt but that that tradition was just as strong and just as respected for those first immigrants themselves.

At first, none of the traditions was warped or transmuted (according to the way you look at it) by Christianity, for the settlement of Iceland as an outpost of heathendom continued for over a century. Then, at a famous meeting of the Council of the country, the *Althing,* in A.D. 1000 it was decided officially to accept Christianity.

The Althing was set up about 930 after the Icelandic *góðar* or chiefs-cum-religious leaders had appointed one of their number, Ulfljót, to draw up a code of laws which he did after spending three years as an observer in Norway. A president over the Althing, the Lawspeaker (*lögsögumaðr*) was appointed for a term of years, and one of his duties was to recite the laws (or part of them) at the yearly meeting. This meeting always took place on the Thingvellir in the summer time. Few details of the ancient laws remain, but enough to show they were given some force by heathen oath and ritual.

The Althing played an important part in the conversion of the country. To all intents and purposes Iceland remained pagan from its first colonization by the Northmen in 874 down to the year 1000. Some of the earlier settlers were indeed Christianized emigrants from Ireland or the

Hebrides such as Helgi the Lean (already mentioned) and Aud the Deepminded, widow of Olaf the White, viking king of Dublin (page 18). Helgi made the best of both worlds: he believed in Christ and called his estate in Iceland *Kristnes* (*Christ's Headland*), its name to this day; but in any tight corner or when he was at sea he always invoked the help of Thor. Aud, on the other hand, was a devout Christian who set up crosses near her home at the spot which thenceforward to the present has been called *Krosshólar* (*Cross Mounds*). Aud's nephew, Ketill, was nicknamed "the Fool" by his heathen neighbours because of his Christian religious practices; but Helgi the Lean's descendants returned to paganism. So, though at first some settlers were Christian and some others were influenced by Christianity, it would seem that after a generation the pagan gods reclaimed their own and throughout the ninth century heathenism was general in Iceland.

How far the Icelanders of these early years could be called practising pagans is something of a puzzle. Probably (and I speak without irony) with as much truth as one could call the population of Great Britain practising Christians today. The pagan religion (in contrast to Christianity) had no dogma and appears to have made few moral or ethical demands on its subscribers. The poem *Völuspá* does indeed speak of oathbreakers, murderers and possibly adulterers as persons who must tread the Helway. But in general, the pagan ritual of Iceland seems to have called mainly for propitiation of the gods by prayer and sacrifice. The centre of organized religion was the temple, a simple rectangular building. Remains at Hofstadir near Mývatn in the north of Iceland show a building oriented north-south with two rooms, a main one and a smaller one at the north end where (it seems likely) were set up wooden figures representing the god or gods. Round the walls of the main room there were benches for the participants. In *Eyrbyggjar Saga* there is a description of furniture used in a temple dedicated to Thor and built by Thórólfr, a settler in the Broadfirth region who had come there from Norway. In the middle of the small room, standing on the floor, was a pedestal (like an altar) on which lay a great arm ring "without join". This ring weighed twenty ounces and all oaths had to be sworn on it. At public gatherings the temple priest had to wear the ring on his arm. Animals were sacrificed and their blood caught in a bowl which also stood on the pedestal; in the bowl was a sacrificial twig like the aspergillus used in the Roman Church to sprinkle holy water over the congregation: but the twig spattered blood. This blood was called *blaut;* and according to *Eyrbyggjar saga* the effigies of the gods stood around the altar-like pedestal.

Even as late as A.D. 1013, Wulfstan, Archbishop of York, bears witness to heathen customs which he must have observed in the Danelaw or heard of being used in the northern countries; he says in the course of the sermon already quoted from on page 25:

> Among the heathen Danes no man dare withhold one jot or tittle laid down for the honouring of their idols:

but we everywhere far too frequently fail to render God His lawful dues. Nor among the heathen dare men desecrate inside or out the offerings or sacrifices laid before their graven images: but we have stripped clean God's Church of every due, out and in. Everywhere (or nearly so) the servants of God are deprived of the respect and reverence which is their right: yet men say among the heathen nobody dare as much as offer to hurt their priests. . . .

Of course, we have to remember that Wulfstan was very likely exaggerating his contrasts for effect; and he shows no evidence of understanding the peculiar position of the heathen priest as a temporal as well as a spiritual leader.

The gods who were actively worshipped in Iceland appear to have been few in number. The favourite (if personal and place-names are anything to go by) was Thor: Thor was a favourite in Norway and the preponderance of his devotees in Iceland is another indication that the majority of settlers came there from Norway. Frey was the favourite in Sweden; in Iceland he was commemorated in place-names, had temples dedicated to him and was patron of a famous *góði* called Hrafnkell (nicknamed *Freysgóði*) and of a family called *Freysgyðlingar.* Njörðr is remembered in such place-names as *Njarðvík;* and there is slight evidence of a cult of Týr and Balder.

Perhaps the first regular attempts to convert Icelanders to Christianity were made shortly after A.D. 980. An account of such attempts is given in *Kristni saga* (*Saga of Christianity*) and *Þorvalds Þáttr Víðförla* (*Story of Thorwald the Wanderer*). Both date from the thirteenth century and while unreliable as connected historical accounts they probably have a basis of truth. If one person could be called responsible for the conversion of Iceland, that person must be Olaf Tryggvason, a very famous Norwegian viking who made himself king of Norway in 995. In the five years of his reign, Olaf Tryggvason is said to have made Christians of six nations (according to *Agríp*), namely the peoples of Norway, Iceland, Greenland, Faroe, Shetland and Orkney. It is told how Olaf while harrying in England played a similar sort of trick on a Christian hermit as Charles the Dauphin and Gilles de Rais are said to have played on Joan of Arc. Olaf's disguise was spotted at once and the hermit (to give good measure) foretold happenings which took place in the next few days and convinced Olaf of the genuineness of the new religion. He is said to have been baptized. At all events, Olaf Tryggvason appears in English records accompanied by Swain Forkbeard in an attack on London (8th September 994). King Ethelred the Redeless bought his peace by the pound (16,000 pounds of silver) and stood sponsor for Olaf to be confirmed into the Christian religion. When Olaf Tryggvason returned to Norway the next year, 995, and made himself king, he took with him a bishop (sometimes called Jón, sometimes Sigurd) and a number of other priests. There can be little doubt but that Olaf preached Christianity in Norway with fire and sword wherever he met opposition: he himself went out like a light, dowsed in the waters of the Baltic when his ship the *Long Serpent* was ambushed by one Eirík. Fifteen years after Olaf's death, the interior of Norway was completely pagan while the people of the coastal districts, although baptized, knew little of Christian teaching. It was left to St. Olaf, king of Norway, who worked on much the same lines as Olaf Tryggvason, to complete the conversion before he was killed at the battle of Stiklastaðir A.D. 1030.

As to Iceland, one of the six countries claimed as proselytized by Olaf Tryggvason, conversion dates from the year 1000. At the June meeting of the Althing that year the pagan party and Christian party declared each other outlaws and each elected its own Lawspeaker. But moderation prevented bloodshed and finally the parties agreed to abide by the decision of the pagan Lawspeaker, a man of recognized integrity called Thorgeir. Thorgeir retired into his booth and pulled a cloak over his head; he spoke to nobody for a day and a night. He then came out of his tent and ascending the Lawrock announced his decision: all Icelanders were to be Christian in name and to be baptized, but at the same time, those who desired were to be allowed to observe their pagan rites in private. It was some years before these heathen observances were forbidden.

It is instructive to compare the tolerance meted out to paganism in Iceland with the intolerance it received in Norway. Although paganism as a religion lived on longer in Norway, when it came to be dealt with it was fanatically and fiercely burnt and cut out: that treatment effectively suppressed pre-Christian religious traditions in Norway. But in Iceland those traditions lived on, at first orally, then to this day in written edda and saga.

Notes

[1] According to Ethelweard, aldorman of West Wessex telling the story some 200 years later. *v. Monumenta Historica Britannica,* ed. H. Petrie and T. Sharpe (1848).

[2] The *Chronicle* says "January" not "June". A scribal error: the Northmen's boats were unsuitable for winter expeditions.

[3] *N.E.D.* gives 1807 as first appearance of "vikingr" (noun) and 1847 "viking" (adjective). . . .

[10] Ari Thorgilsson writing in the twelfth century fixed the date of the battle of Hafrsfjörðr at *c.* 872. Vigfusson and Powell argued that Harold Fairhair's reign was much later, i.e. 900-945. Modern opinion tends to split the difference and dates Hafrsfjörðr *c.* 884.

[11] O.N. *papar,* Irish *pab(b)a,* Lat. *papa.* This word meant in Irish a monk or anchorite.

[12] William Jackson Hooker, F.L.S., *Journal of a Tour in Iceland in the summer of 1809,* printed by J. Keymer (King St., Yarmouth) 1811, ("Not published").

[13] Alastair M. Dunnett, *Land of Promise* in the *Sunday Times,* 27th Sept., 1953.

John Arnott MacCulloch (1964)

SOURCE: "The Other World," in *The Mythology of All Races,* Cooper Square Publishers, Inc., 1964, pp. 303-47.

[In this excerpt, MacCulloch summarizes the Eddic creation myths and the conception of the Heavens and Earth.]

The Eddic picture of the origin of the universe goes back to a time when neither gods nor men, Heaven nor earth, existed. There was a great abyss, Ginnunga-gap, 'Yawning chasm,' a conception probably due to popular belief in an abyss outside the ocean surrounding the earth. North of it had been made (by whom?) Niflheim, a frost and mist region, within which was the well Hvergelmir, 'Cauldron-rushing,' from which flowed several rivers. To the south was Muspell, light and glowing, ruled over by Surt. The streams or Elivagar from Niflheim, as they flowed, became ice, which spread into Ginnunga-gap. There the ice met warm airs from Muspell or Muspellheim and began to melt. Life was quickened in this by the power of that which sent the heat (whose was this power? there is perhaps a Christian influence here), and took form as a giant Ymir. From him came the Frost-giants.

From the dripping rime there sprang the cow Audhumla (explained as 'the rich, polled cow,' *audr,* 'riches,' i.e., its milk, and *humla,* 'polled'). Streams of milk from its udders nourished Ymir, and the cow was nourished by licking the salty iceblocks. As she licked there came forth from the ice Buri, who was father of Borr. Borr married Bestla, a daughter of the giant race. They had three sons, Odin, Vili, and Ve.

Thus the giant race preceded the gods, as Saxo also indicates, and gods and giants were opposed to each other.

The sons of Borr slew Ymir, and his blood drowned all the Frost-giants save Bergelmir with his wife and household. The three brothers bore Ymir's body into Ginnunga-gap and made of it the earth. Sea and waters came from his blood; gravel and stones from his teeth and such bones as were broken; rocks from his bones. The sea was placed as a ring round the earth. His skull became the sky, set up over the earth and upheld by four dwarfs. The earth is ring-shaped, and on its coasts the gods gave lands to the giants. Within the earth they erected a wall against the giants, made of Ymir's eyebrows. This they called

Midgard. Of Ymir's brain, thrown into the air, they made the clouds. The glowing embers and sparks from Muspellheim were set in the Heaven, above and beneath, to illumine Heaven and earth. The gods assigned places to all, even to such as were wandering free.[1]

This is Snorri's account, based partly on sources now lost, partly on stanzas of *Voluspa, Grimnismal,* and *Vafthrudnismal. Voluspa* says:

> In time's morning lived Ymir,
> Then was no sand, sea, nor cool waves;
> No earth was there, nor Heaven above,
> Only a yawning chasm, nor grass anywhere.
>
> Then Borr's sons upheaved the earth
> And shaped the beautiful Midgard;
> From the south the sun shone on earth's stones,
> And from the ground sprang green leeks.[2]

The first verse seems to contain the myth of Ymir formed in Ginnunga-gap. The second gives a myth of earth raised out of an existing ocean, not made from Ymir's flesh. The sun shone on it and growth began. Whether both verses come from one hand or, as Boer holds, the second alone belongs to an earlier form of the poem, is immaterial. The myth of earth raised out of ocean is found in other mythologies.[3] The next verses tell how sun, moon, and stars were allotted their places, and how the gods gave names to night, new and full moon, etc.

In *Vafthrudnismal* the giant in response to Odin's question, tells how earth and sky arose, but does not speak of them as a work of the gods.

> Out of Ymir's flesh was shaped the earth,
> The mountains out of his bones,
> The Heaven from the ice-cold giant's skull,
> Out of his blood the boisterous sea.

This is succeeded by an account of the giants, the first of whom is said to have been made out of the venom from Elivagar. No mention is made of fire and heat, only of frost and ice.[4]

Grimnismal speaks of the origin of earth from Ymir's flesh, ocean from his blood, Heaven from his skull, the hills from his bones, and it adds that trees were formed from his hair, Midgard from his eyebrows, made by the gods for men, and out of his brain the clouds.[5]

In *Voluspa* three gods lift earth out of ocean, but the other poems merely mention gods, without specifying the number or saying how they came into existence. Snorri says that from Odin and Frigg came the kindred known as the Æsir, a divine race.[6] In an earlier passage he speaks of All-father or Odin living through all ages and fashioning Heaven, earth, and all things in them.[7] The latter is probably a reflexion from Christian views of Creation.

The conception underlying Snorri's main account is that giants, gods, and all things may be traced back to the union of water (ice and mist) and fire. The ice contains salt, and this plays an important part in the myth of Audhumla. An interesting comparison is found in Tacitus, who, speaking of the sacred salt springs near the Saale, says that the waters were made to evaporate on red-hot coals, and salt was thus obtained from two opposite elements, fire and water. This may point to an old Germanic cosmogonic myth with fire, water, and salt as elements.[8] Skaldic kennings illustrate the Eddic myth of Ymir. Heaven is 'skull of Ymir' or 'burden of the dwarfs'; earth is 'flesh of Ymir'; the sea is 'blood of Ymir'; the hills are 'Ymir's bones.'[9]

Grimm cites passages from medieval ecclesiastical documents dating from the tenth century onwards, in which man is said to have been created out of different materials. One of these says that Adam's bones were made from stone, his flesh from earth, his blood from water, his heart from wind, his thought from clouds, his sweat from dew, his hair from grass, his eyes from the sun. The four documents differ in details, but there is a curious inverse parallel with the Eddic account, which 'uses the microcosm as material for the macrocosm, and the other inversely makes the universe contribute to the formation of man.'[10]

Voluspa goes on to tell that the gods met at Ithavoll in the midst of Asgard and built temples and altars, made forges to work gold, wrought tongs and fashioned tools. This was during their golden age. Then the creation of dwarfs is described.[11] Snorri amplifies this. All-father gave counsel about the town in the midst of Ithavall. A temple was made with twelve seats and a thirteenth for All-father. It is all of gold and is called Gladsheim. A second house was built for the goddesses, called Vingolf. Houses were made for workshops; and tools, anvils, hammers, and tongs were fashioned. The Æsir worked in metals, stone, and wood, and fashioned their household wares of gold. Hence that time is called the Age of Gold. Then follows the creation of the dwarfs.[12]

Voluspa next gives the myth of human origins. Odin, Hœnir, and Lodur came forth to the land and found Ask and Embla (Ash and Elm) unprovided with fate and without strength, soul, breath, movement, heat, or colour. Odin gave them soul, Hœnir sense, Lodur heat and goodly colour.[13] Snorri says that Odin, Vili, and Ve, walking on the shore, found two trees, which they shaped into human beings. Odin gave them soul, Vili life, Ve hearing and sight. They named the male Ask and the female Embla, and of them mankind was begotten.[14] In an earlier passage, where biblical influence may be seen, Snorri says that All-father made man, giving him spirit which shall never die, though the flesh-frame rot or burn to ashes.[15] The shaping of human beings out of trees may have been suggested by wooden images, such as those which the speaker in *Havamal* says that he found and on which he put clothes. Now they regarded themselves as champions. Such images, called *tremadr*, are mentioned in other documents.[16] In *Rigsthula* the different classes of men were begotten by Rig. The account given by Tacitus of the founders of the Germanic race is interesting by way of comparison. The Germans celebrate in ancient hymns a god Tuisto, issued from the earth, and his son Mannus, as the originators of their race. Mannus had three sons, progenitors of the Ingvæones, Herminones, and Istævones. Some, however, think that the god had other sons, progenitors of other tribes.[17] Mannus is thus the first man, born of a god who comes out of the earth, perhaps regarded as spouse of a Heaven-god. His sons were eponymous ancestors of three chief German groups. If Tuisto was thought to be produced by earth alone, and himself alone produced sons, he would resemble Ymir, who begat giants without a female (p. 275).

Separate cosmogonic myths occur here and there. A river, Van, is formed from the slaver out of the mouth of the Fenris-wolf. Stars were made of the eyes of Thjazi or Aurvandill's toe; a well from the footprint of Balder's horse, etc.[18]

For the Eddic conception of the universe we begin with the earth, the middle of things, a general Teutonic conception—Gothic *midjungards,* OS *middelgard,* AS *middangeard,* OHG *mittigart,* ON *midgard,* literally 'boundary-wall,' i.e., the mountains by which the giants were shut out from the habitable earth, then the earth as the dwelling-place of man, or, as Snorri conceived it, a citadel. Thor is 'Midgard's warder' (*veorr*) against the giants.[19] Earth is a vast disc, surrounded by the ocean or floating upon it, and in this ocean is the Midgard-serpent, lying about the land and surrounding it, his tail in his mouth, 'the girdle of all lands.' Around the shores of earth are mountains, rocks, wastes, and caves, and these are the dwelling of giants, Jötunheim or Utgard, though Utgard was also regarded as being beyond the ocean.[20]

According to one passage of Snorri, Asgard, the abode of the gods, is a city which men call Troy, in the midst of Midgard. It is the new Asgard, in place of the elder Asgard in Asia.[21] This conception of Asgard is due to Snorri's euhemerism and the desire to connect the Scandinavian people and deities with ancient Greece. The earlier pagan view of Asgard made it a heavenly abode, or possibly it was on the top of a lofty central mountain, which would give a link with Snorri's view of Asgard on earth.

Above all was Heaven, overarching and resting on earth. Between Heaven and earth was the bridge Bifrost or Bilrost, which the gods had made, the Ásbru or 'bridge of the Æsir.' It is the rainbow, of three colours. It is very strong and made with greater craft than any other structure. The red colour is fire, which keeps the Hill-giants off. Over this best of bridges the gods ride daily to their tribunal at Urd's well. Another name of the bridge is Vindhjalmsbru, 'Wind-helmet's (the sky) bridge.' At the

Doom of the gods the sons of Muspell will cross it and break it down. Meanwhile Heimdall is its guardian.[22]

Valhall is Odin's hall in Asgard, where are also Gladsheim and Vingolf, but *Grimnismal* places Valhall in Gladsheim, 'the Place of joy.'

Separate dwellings of gods and others are enumerated in *Grimnismal* and by Snorri, and these appear mainly to be in Heaven. The chief of them are Alfheim, abode of the Alfar and Frey; Breidablik, Balder's abode; Valaskjalf, 'Seat of the fallen,' possessed by Odin and thatched with silver, in it is Hlidskjalf, 'Gate-seat,' whence Odin surveys all worlds. Valaskjalf may be Valhall. Thrudvangir, with its hall Bilskirnir, is Thor's abode.

Much speculation has been indulged in regarding the 'nine worlds,' spoken of in *Voluspa* and *Vafthrudnismal,* as well as in an interpolated stanza in *Alvissmal* where the dwarf says: 'Oft have I fared in the nine worlds all, and wide is my wisdom in each.' In *Voluspa* the Volva says that she knows 'nine worlds, nine rooms of the mighty World-tree.' The giant in *Vafthrudnismal* says that he has been in every world, the nine worlds, even to Niflheim.[23] In all three passages the idea is that of comprehensive knowledge on the part of the speaker—dwarf, seeress, giant. This knowledge is possessed by different kinds of beings dwelling in different regions. Alviss knows the names given to various things by several orders of beings dwelling in earth, Heaven, Alfheim, etc. 'Nine worlds' would thus be more a figurative phrase than one expressing local geography or cosmology. In *Voluspa* these worlds are connected with the World-tree, itself a comprehensive symbol.

Regarded as different regions, the nine worlds may be—1. Asgard, 2. Vanaheim, 3. Alfheim (though this is one of the dwellings in Heaven), 4. Midgard, 5. Jötunheim, 6. Muspellheim, 7. Svartalfheim, 8. Hel or Niflhel. The ninth is uncertain. It may be obtained by dividing Hel from Niflhel or, preferably, by including a Water-world.[24] Undoubtedly the numbering of nine worlds is connected with the sacredness and importance of the number nine in religion, myth, folk-belief, and poetry.[25]

Below Midgard is Svartalfheim, the region of the dwarfs. Hel or Niflhel is also a subterranean abode. While Snorri speaks of Niflhel in this sense, he also speaks in error of Niflheim, apparently another form of the name, as a region in the North, the cold region of mist, whence streams flowed into Ginnunga-gap. In Niflheim Snorri places the well Hvergelmir, whence spring certain rivers, among them Gjoll, which is near Hel-gates. It is under the root of Yggdrasil which stands over Niflheim. In *Grimnismal,* the site of Hvergelmir is not given, but it is said that from the horns of the hart which eats the branches of Lærad, a stream drips into Hvergelmir and thence all the rivers run.[26]

The Ash Yggdrasil

To the seeress of *Voluspa* the World-tree with its nine divisions or worlds, is 'the mighty Fate-tree (or 'well-planned tree,' *mjotvithr*), deep in the earth.' The nine worlds are contained in the tree or symbolized by its divisions. In later passages the Volva speaks of an ash called Yggdrasil, reaching high aloft, wet with white water, thence come the dews that fall in the dales. It stands by Urd's well, and the three Norns dwell in a hall under it.[27] This reference to the three Norns may be interpolated, enlarging on Urd's connexion with the tree. Heimdall's horn is hidden under the tree, and a mighty stream pours from Odin's pledge (which is in Mimir's well) on the tree. At the Doom of the gods the tree shakes and its leaves rustle.[28]

The picture of the tree in *Svipdagsmal* is similar. Mimameith ('Mimir's tree'?) stretches its branches over all lands. No one knows what roots are beneath it. Few can guess what shall fell it, not fire and not iron. Then follows a piece of folklore. The fruit of the tree placed in fire is good for women in childbirth. What was within then comes out, such might has the tree for men. Gering points out that in Icelandic belief a hard legumen borne to Iceland by the Gulf Stream is used for the same purpose. On the highest bough stands the cock Vithofnir, glittering like gold, shining like lightning, ever-watchful, the terror of Surt and Sinmora.[29] If this bird is the same as Gollinkambi, who wakes the heroes in Valhall, the top of the tree must be in Asgard. The bird's watchfulness is a terror to the enemies of the gods.

These two passages give a picture of a wonderful world-tree, its roots on or under the earth, beside it Mimir's well—probably the older conception—or Urd's well. As we shall see, Snorri puts these two wells beside two separate roots of the tree.

A more elaborate picture is given in *Grimnismal*. The ash Yggdrasil is 'best of trees.' Beneath one of its three roots is Hel; the Frost-giants beneath the second; mankind are beneath the third. A lost stanza may have spoken of the wise eagle that sits on the top of the tree, for the next stanza speaks of the squirrel Ratatosk which carries the eagle's words to the dragon Nidhogg below. Four harts nibble the uppermost twigs, perhaps a later amplification of the single hart of a succeeding stanza. Numerous serpents lie beneath the tree and gnaw its branches. Thus the tree suffers, for the hart bites its top; its trunk is rotting; and Nidhogg gnaws its roots. Meanwhile the gods ride daily to give judgments at the tree. Thor walks there.[30]

Snorri combines this information, but gives varying details. Of the three roots, one is among the Æsir, one among the Frost-giants, and one over Niflheim. Beneath each is a well or stream. As the Æsir are in Heaven, a root cannot be there, unless we assume that Snorri still regards Asgard as on earth. But later he says that the root

is in Heaven, and underneath it is Urd's well. Mimir's well is underneath the root among the Frost-giants. The third root, over Niflheim, is gnawed by Nidhogg. The eagle in the tree knows many things. Between his eyes sits the hawk Vedrfolnir. Ratatosk bears envious words between the eagle and Nidhogg.[31]

Snorri thus upsets the whole conception of Yggdrasil by placing one of its roots in Heaven, with Urd's well there, and by setting Mimir's well among the Frost-giants.

Most of the details in *Grimnismal* may be no more than decorative *motifs,* perhaps derived from the presence of birds or other animals in sacred trees or groves, or, as R. M. Meyer supposes, from sculptured representations of trees with conventional animals.[32] Bugge thought that the poet had seen monuments in the north of England with ornamentation like that on the Bewcastle cross in Cumberland, if not that cross itself. On such crosses was carved a tree, in the foliage of which sat an eagle or hawk, squirrels and serpents, and ate of its fruits.[33] If the tree or the animals had any mythic significance, the key to it is lost, in spite of the ingenious conjectures of modern mythologizers.

The ash Yggdrasil has many prototypes. It recalls sacred trees beside sacred wells from which oracles were obtained. It is linked to the Vårträd or 'Ward-tree' growing beside Swedish houses, which, if cut down, brings the prosperity of the house to an end—a significant fact when we remember that the gradual destruction of Yggdrasil denotes the approach of the Doom of the gods. It may thus have once been a mythic heavenly Vårträd, growing beside the hall of the gods. Such a tree is spoken of in a stanza quoted by Snorri—Glasir growing by the doors of Valhall, its leafage of red gold, the fairest tree known among gods and men.[34] *Grimnismal* also speaks of a tree, Lærad, growing beside Odin's hall. From the horns of the hart which bites its branches a stream falls into Hvergelmir, whence all the rivers flow. This also resembles a Vårträd, and both trees may be forms of Yggdrasil.[35] When *Grimnismal* speaks of the gods riding to judgment beneath Yggdrasil, this may be reminiscent of actual processions to judgment beneath a Vårträd or a temple tree.[36]

Yggdrasil also resembles the sacred tree growing beside a temple, like that one described by the scholiast to Adam of Bremen. Beside the temple at Upsala was a great tree with spreading branches, always green, even in winter. Its origin was known to none. Near it was a spring used for sacrifices.[37] The branches of Yggdrasil were also far-spreading; it was always green; beside it was a spring; no one knew its fate or its roots. The Old Prussian holy oak at the sanctuary called Romove also offers an analogy to Yggdrasil. It had three divisions, each sacred to a god, and an image of each stood in each section. Before the god Perkuna of one division burned perpetual fire; before Potrimpo was the snake fed by the priests and priestesses; before Patollo the heads of a man, horse, and cow. This tree was also evergreen.[38]

The full name of the Eddic tree was Askr Yggdrasils, 'the Ash which is Ygg's (Odin's) Steed,' or 'the Ash of Odin's Horse.' Yggdrasil was a kenning for Odin's horse Sleipnir. The name may be due to the fact that victims sacrificed to Odin were hung on sacred trees, riding the tree, gallows, or horse sacred to him. Other explanations are given. It is the tree in which is Odin's steed, the wind. Or Odin tethered his horse to the tree, or, less likely, it is the tree on which Odin hung, hence his gallows or steed.[39] In the same way the gallows was called 'the ice-cold steed of Signy's husband' in a skaldic poem.[40] But, as Chadwick points out, there is 'not a single reference to the World-tree having served as Odin's gallows,' while 'the name Yggdrasil may have been applied to the earthly Vårträd, and transferred together with the conception of the tree to its heavenly copy.'[41]

The mythic Yggdrasil was almost certainly a tree growing on earth before it was transferred to the Other World and the region of myth.

This tree is also connected with wide-spread myths of a World-tree growing on a mountain or in the centre of the earth, and reaching to Heaven. Such a tree also resembles the mythic World-pillars supporting Heaven. Both trees and pillars are many-storied. The roots of the tree go down into the Underworld, its topmost branches pierce the sky, and it stands by a spring, lake, or sea, or in the sea itself. As in a Yakut tale, a goddess dwells at the root of the tree and foretells the future, like Urd or Mimir. Tree or pillar is often the tethering-post of deities, especially of the Over-god, as in the Yakut tale, and this throws light on Yggdrasil as connected with Odin. Such mythical pillars and trees are known all over Northern Asia, and can be traced in India, Iran, Mesopotamia, and Egypt. The eagle Garuda or Garide is believed to dwell in the tree. At its roots is a dragon or snake at which the eagle pecks.[42] In some of these myths a spring flows from the tree or from its sap, and, as in Iranian belief, all the rivers of earth have their source in it.[43] So out of Yggdrasil flows dew, called by men honey-dew, on which bees are nourished, and the source of rivers is connected with the tree Lærad.[44]

Such mythic trees would be suggested by lofty forest-trees on which the sky seemed to rest, and, as in some Polynesian myths, which separated earth and Heaven. Then, as the sky seemed to recede into a remoter distance, arose the fable of one lofty tree reaching from earth to Heaven.[45] Myths of a Heaven-supporting tree are numerous, and they survive in tales of 'Jack and the Beanstalk.'[46] The resemblances of the Scandinavian tree to such mythic trees are numerous, and its origin need not therefore be sought in medieval Christian legends of the Cross as a World-tree, which, in fact, carry on the tradition of these mythical trees.

The myth of the sky as a tent-roof supported on a pillar or post occurs among the Lapps, Finns, and North Asiatic tribes, Japanese, and ancient Egyptians.[47] The Asiatic pillar is seven-storied, representing the seven Heavens, and it is the tethering-post of the stars or of the horses of the gods.[48] Posts with seven branches, on which sacrificial victims are hung, symbolize the mythical post. The Lapps also had such sacrificial pillars, representing the heavenly pillar supporting the world, with an iron nail at the top, a symbol of the World-nail which fixed the sky in place. The nail of the sky is the Pole Star, round which the Heavens are thought to revolve. This belief of the Lapps may have been borrowed from the Scandinavians.[49] Similar beliefs were entertained by the Celts and in ancient India.[50] The symbolism of the seven Heavens in tree or pillar, like the three divisions of the Romove tree, recalls the nine worlds or divisions of the Eddic tree.

This helps us to understand the Irminsul of the Saxons, a word denoting 'sanctuary,' 'image,' or 'pillar,' such as was destroyed by Charlemagne,[51] but its general significance was that of a pillar or tree-stump. Rudolf of Fulda says that the Saxons venerate leafy trees and springs, and worship a huge tree-trunk called Irminsul, which means *universalis columna,* as if it sustained all things.[52] The Irminsul must have been a symbol of a mythic World-pillar, and connected with the cult of a god Irmin. The nail of the sky may also have been known in Scandinavia, as its name, *veraldarnagli,* occurs in Icelandic folk-poetry.[53] The mythic World-mountain may be seen in the Himinbjorg, or 'Heaven-mountain,' situated at the end of Bifrost.

These various conceptions show that, whatever details may be due to Christian influences, the Eddic World-tree was a native conception. The theory that it was copied from the medieval legend of the Cross was advanced by Bugge, E. H. Meyer, and Golther, though Bugge admitted the existence in Scandinavian belief of a wonderful holy tree, which, under Christian influence, was transformed into a World-tree. In the medieval legend the Cross was a tree linked to the Tree of Life in Paradise. Its end, set in the earth, reached down to the Underworld, the top reached to Heaven, the two arms spread over the world. The Cross was our Lord's steed, according to medieval poetic usage, and 'steed' was a metaphor for 'gallows,' the victim being the Rider. The *point d'appui* here is the explanation of Yggdrasil as Odin's gallows, because he hung on it. As we have seen there is no evidence that the tree on which he hung was Yggdrasil. The dragon Nidhogg is the serpent of Eden, associated with the Tree from which the Cross was derived.[54] Be this as it may, the Yggdrasil conception is not entirely, if at all, due to such legends as these.

The Doom of the Gods

A phrase used in the Poetic *Edda* is *ragna rok,* 'fate or doom of the gods' (*ragna* being genitive plural of *regen,* 'powers,' 'gods'). It resembles the phrase *aldar rok,* 'destruction of the world,' used in *Vafthrudnismal.* Another phrase, with which it is often confused, is *ragna rokr,* 'the darkness of the gods,' which occurs in *Lokasenna* and is used by Snorri.[55] Used mistakenly as a proper noun, Ragnarok, the phrase is often rendered 'Twilight of the gods.'

This Doom of the gods, the central incident of a wider myth of the destruction of the world, is the subject of a great part of *Voluspa,* and shows that, as the gods are not eternal *a parte ante,* so their life at last comes to an end. In view of that Doom, Valhall must be filled with heroes, and even now Thor fights with the enemies of the gods.

The *Voluspa* poet connects the Doom with the coming of the three giant-maids, the Norns, which brought the Golden Age of the gods to an end. Now the gods are brought under the power of fate. The Doom is also linked to the first war, when gods fought the Vanir, and, more immediately, with the death of Balder.[56]

The verses describing these events do not all belong to the original poem, and may have been interpolated by a moralizing poet. The dualism which results in the conquest of gods by demoniac beings, who are themselves annihilated, is the foundation of the myth. This is bound up with fate, stronger than the gods, but the verse regarding this (the coming of the Norns) is isolated and is followed by interpolated verses about the dwarfs, which may have ousted stanzas continuing the subject.

Then follows an outrage perpetrated by the gods—a wild kind of justice, described in two interpolated stanzas. This is 'the first war in the world,' and concerns the slaying of Gullveig by the gods. She must have had some evil design in coming to the gods' world: hence they slew her, yet she ever lives. This may be connected with the war between Æsir and Vanir, if Gullveig was Freyja, a Vanir goddess. This war is also called the first war. During the contest with the Vanir, the wall of the gods' citadel was broken down. A moralized sign of the end is now introduced—a reference (intelligible only from Snorri's account of the myth) to the breaking of oaths made by the gods to the giant artificer, whom Thor slew. The gods have perjured themselves. Balder's death is the next step to the Doom. The working of demoniac might through Loki against the gods has begun. Loki is put in bonds, but greater woes are coming, and 'Frigg weeps sore for Valhall's need.' The coming Doom was almost certainly the subject whispered by Odin into the dead Balder's ear.[57] As a consequence of the gods' violence and treachery, evils abound among men—oath-breaking and revenge, and these are punished in the Underworld.[58]

That the final destruction and Doom of the gods is a genuine Teutonic myth, we take for granted. There seem, however, to be different myths of the manner in which this would happen, and these are more or less combined in *Voluspa.*

1. A destruction of the world by its sinking into the sea, from which it had emerged, according to one cosmogonic myth.

> The sun becomes black, earth sinks into the sea,
> From Heaven fall the bright stars.

This is also described in *Hyndluljod:*

> The sea ascends in storm to Heaven,
> It swallows the earth, the air becomes sterile.

To this may be linked the swallowing of the sun by a monster—an eclipse myth used to heighten the effect of the myth of the world's destruction.[59] This myth of the sinking of the earth into the sea is perhaps connected with the daily apparent sinking of the sun into the sea, as seen by dwellers on the coast.

2. The world ends with a mighty winter, *fimbul-vetr.* In *Vafthrudnismal* Odin asks what of mankind shall survive the mighty winter. Vafthrudnir answers that Lif and Lifthrasir, hid in Hoddmimir's wood, will survive it. In Snorri's account they survive the destructive fires of Surt. *Hyndluljod* speaks of snows and furious winds which follow the sinking of earth in the sea, and in *Voluspa* mighty storms come in summer. Snorri says that this winter will precede the Doom. Snow will drive from all quarters, with sharp frost and wind; the sun will be without power. Three such winters will follow in succession with no summer between. Over the earth are mighty battles. Brothers will slay each other for greed's sake: none spares father or mother in murder and incest. He then cites a stanza of *Voluspa* which refers to these evils:

> Brothers shall fight and slay each other,
> Sisters' sons break kinship's bonds;
> Hard is it on earth, with much unchasteness,
> Axe-age, sword-age,
> Shields are cloven,
> Wind-age, wolf-age, ere sinks the world;
> No man will ever another spare.[60]

3. A third myth is that of the destruction of the world by fire. *Voluspa* tells how Surt comes from the South with 'the scourge of branches,' i.e., fire. In the stanza which describes earth sinking into the sea, it is said that steam rages and the preserver of life (fire); fire shoots high to Heaven itself. The fires of Surt are also mentioned in *Vafthrudnismal* as occurring at the end of the world. The possible destruction of the world by fire, viz., by the sun, is spoken of in *Grimnismal.* If it were not for the shield in front of the sun, mountains and seas would be set in flames. Snorri often refers to this final fire, and says that Surt will cast fire and burn the world. The sons of Muspell ride forth, Surt at their head, before him and after him burning fire. His sword is very good, from it shines a light brighter than the sun. As they ride over Bifrost, the bridge breaks down. In an earlier notice, Surt is said to

sit at the world's end by Muspellheim. At the last he will go forth and harry, overcome the gods, and burn the world with fire.[61] Fire and heat were sources of life: now they are its destruction.

These separate myths, or at least the first and second, are combined in *Voluspa,* together with the myth of the freedom gained by chained monsters, the Fenris-wolf, Loki, and Garm, and all three appear in Snorri's account of the Doom, in which he quotes freely from the poem.

The doom begins with moral evils on earth.[62] The sons of Mim (the waters or spirits of the waters) are in motion.[63] The Gjallar-horn sounds the note of Doom as Heimdall blows it. All the Hel-ways are in fear. Yggdrasil shakes; its leaves rustle, for the giant, the Fenris-wolf, is free. Odin consults the head of Mim, but the wolf will slay him soon. Then comes an impressive stanza:

> How fare the gods? How fare the Alfar?
> All Jötunheim roars; the gods take counsel.
> The dwarfs stand groaning before their rock-doors,
> The lords of the rock-walls. Would ye know yet more?

From the East comes Hrym, leader of the giants. The Midgard-serpent writhes in giant-fury. The eagle Hræsvelg screams aloud, gnawing corpses. The ship Naglfar is loose, steered, as Snorri says, by the giant Hrym and carrying the giants.[64] Another ship sails from the North with the people of Hel, steered by Loki. Wild hosts[65] follow the Wolf. With them is Byleipt's brother (Loki). From the South comes Surt with fire. The hills are shattered; the giantesses fall; the dead crowd Hel-way; Heaven is cloven.

To Frigg comes yet another grief: she sees Odin die by the Wolf. Frey seeks out Surt, Vidarr pierces the Wolf with his sword, avenging Odin. Thor advances against the Midgard-serpent, and strikes a death-blow, but himself falls dead, suffocated by the venom. Now the sun turns black; earth sinks into the sea, stream and flame grow in fierceness, and fire leaps up to Heaven itself. It is the end.

Snorri's account of the advance of the gods and the fighting is vivid. The Wolf rushes forward, mouth gaping, the upper jaw touching Heaven, the lower the earth, fire blazing from eyes and nostrils. The Midgard-serpent by its side blows venom. Heaven is cloven, and Muspell's sons, led by Surt, ride forth, fire preceding and following them. They ride to a field Vigrid, and there come also the Fenris-wolf, the Midgard-serpent, Loki, Hrym, and the Frost-giants. The people of Hel follow Loki. Heimdall blows his horn. Odin rides to Mimir's well to take counsel with him. Yggdrasil trembles: all in Heaven and earth are in fear. The Æsir arm themselves and ride to the field, with all the Einherjar from Valhall. Odin is in front, with golden helmet, birnie, and spear. Thor is beside him, but cannot aid him against the Fenris-wolf, as he must encounter the Midgard-serpent. The watch-dog of Hel, Garm, is loose, doing battle with Tyr, each slaying the other. Thor slays the Serpent, strides away nine paces, and falls dead, overcome by its venom. Frey fights with Surt and falls, for he lacks his sword, having given it to Skirnir. The Wolf swallows Odin, but Vidarr sets one foot on its lower jaw, and with his hand seizes the upper jaw, and tears them in two. Loki fights with Heimdall, and each slays the other. Surt then throws fire over the earth and burns it up.[66]

Snorri gives details not in *Voluspa,* e.g., Tyr's fight with Garm, and Heimdall's with Loki. He incorporates some incidents from *Vafthrudnismal* which also contains some notices of the Doom, viz., the field Vigrid, Njord's return to the Vanir before the end, the mighty winter which Lif and Lifthrasir survive, the swallowing of the sun, the fires of Surt, Odin's death by the Wolf, its slaying by Vidarr, and Thor's end.[67]

In spite of the large muster of forces, only a few are described as actual combatants—on one side Odin, Thor, Tyr, Heimdall, Frey, and Vidarr; on the other the Wolf, the Serpent, Garm, Loki, and Surt. No account of the participation of other gods or of the Einherjar is given. Some of these pairs of opponents are found in hostility to each other in non-eschatological myths—Thor and the Serpent, Heimdall and Loki.

The Doom is known to the poets who wrote *Baldrs Draumar* and *Grimnismal.* In the former the sibyl tells Odin that none shall seek her till Loki is free from his bonds and the destroyers come to the Doom of the gods. In the latter Thor is to dwell in Thrudheim 'till the gods are destroyed'—a phrase used also in *Vafthrudnismal.*[68] Some of the skaldic poems also refer to it. In *Eiriksmal* Odin speaks of the time not being known when the grey Wolf shall come upon the seat of the gods. In *Hakonarmal* are the words: 'the Fenris-wolf shall be let loose on mankind ere such a good king as Hakon shall arise.' Verses by Kormak (*c.* 935 A.D.) say: 'the earth shall sink, the mountains drop into the sea' before such a fair woman as Steingud shall be born. Arnor Iarlaskald (*c.* 1065 A.D.) wrote: 'the bright sun shall turn black, the earth sink into the dark sea, the dwarfs' burden (Heaven) shall be rent, the sea rush up over the hills, ere such a one as Thorfinn shall be born.' These references are in conformity with the Eddic account. In the story of the Hjadnings' battle, it is said that the fight will continue till the Doom of the gods; and when the maiden saw the dead Helgi and his men riding to their barrow, she cried: 'Is this the Doom of the gods, that dead men ride?'[69]

How far Christian influences have coloured or moulded the ideas and incidents of the world catastrophe is problematical. Different critics assume more or less of such influence. While here and there echoes of Scriptural language and incidents may be found, the conception as a whole seems original, or at least based on native folk-lore and eschatological myths. Parallels from other mythologies exist, but it does not follow that there was borrowing from these. The swallowing of the sun by a monster is a wide-spread myth. Iranian mythology has a parallel to the mighty winter in its eschatology—the devastation caused by the rain of Malkōsh, when most of mankind die of excessive cold, snow, and famine. Rydberg and others regard the Iranian and Eddic myths as examples of an old Indo-Germanic belief.[70] The belief in the world's destruction by water and fire existed among the Celts, apart from Christian influence. There are classical references to this belief among the Celts, and it exists in native Irish documents. The prophecy of the War-goddess Badb about evils to come and the end of the world, and that of Fercertne in *The Colloquy of the Two Sages* have a certain likeness to the prophecy of Doom in *Voluspa*.[71]

One point requires further elucidation. Snorri says that the sons of Muspell ride with Surt at their head over Bifrost bridge. At the end of the conflict the fires of Surt consume the world. He has already spoken of the southern region of fire, Muspell or Muspellheim, at whose frontiers sits Surt waiting to go forth against the gods and destroy the world with fire. Muspell has the largest ship, Naglfar. From the sparks flowing out of Muspell, the gods made the chariot of the sun and the lights of Heaven.[72]

Two passages only of the Poetic *Edda* mention Muspell. Loki told Frey that when the sons of Muspell ride through Myrkwood he will be weaponless. In *Voluspa* the manuscripts have the reading 'the people of Muspell,' which is corrected by critics to 'the people of Hel.'[73] Bifrost is spoken of twice. In *Fafnismal* the gods assemble at Oskopnir ('the not yet created,' perhaps another name for Vigrid) to meet Surt, and Bifrost breaks down as they cross it. Elsewhere it is the hosts of Surt who break it down. A stanza in *Grimnismal* speaks of Thor wading through rivers, for Bifrost burns in flame. This may either refer to the time of Doom or express a myth of the sun's reappearance after thunder when the rainbow-bridge seems to be on fire.[74]

Is Muspell a word originating from pagan or from Christian conceptions? Grimm says that in it 'we find another striking proof of the prevalence of Old Norse conceptions all over Teutondom.'[75] The word occurs in the Saxon *Heliand*: 'the power of *mûdspelli* fares over men,' and '*mûdspelli* comes in dark night as a thief.' The reference is to the Day of Judgment; and a Bavarian poem says of the fire which burns up the world: 'no friend can help another for the *mûspilli*.'[76] Thus the word refers to a world conflagration as in the *Eddas*. Did it first betoken the fire as a Christian conception, or was it originally applied to a similar pagan conception? Opinions are sharply divided here, as also on the root-meaning of the

word. Grimm takes it to mean 'fire,' its component parts being *mud, mu,* 'earth,' 'wood,' 'tree,' and *spilli,* cognate with ON *spilla,* 'destroy': hence the word is an epithet of fire. Others connect *spilli* with OHG and AS *spell,* 'prophecy,' and regard *mud* as a Latin loan-word from *mundus*—hence 'a prophecy of the world,' viz., of its end. In this sense the word, originating from Christian preaching about the end of the world by fire, took root in Teutonic thought and passed to Scandinavia.[77] Other derivations have been suggested and there is a copious literature on the subject.[78]

There is every likelihood that the destruction of the world by fire was a native conception, as in other mythologies, though Christian influences may have worked upon it. The Poetic *Edda* personifies the agents of destruction as 'Muspell's sons,' i.e., spirits of fire of Fire-giants. Fire may have been personified as a giant called 'Muspellr.'[79] Snorri then gives the conception of a southern region of fire, Muspell or Muspellheim, whether this originated with him or not. The destruction of the world by fire was a Celtic conception, as has been seen, and this may have passed from Celts to Teutons or have been a belief common to both.

Why a myth of the destruction of the gods should have originated in Scandinavia is uncertain. It does not appear to signify the defeat of Norse gods by the Christian religion, for there is no trace of such a conception in the sources. We cannot even say that it arose out of a weakening of the old religion among the people. They were still firmly attached to it when Christianity appeared in the North. The best parallel to it is found in Scandinavian mythology itself (as in Greek)—the destruction of the older race of giants by the gods.

The Renewal of The World

The gods are gone, men destroyed, the earth sunk in the sea or burned, but now appears a new world. This is the theme of the final stanzas of *Voluspa:*

> Now I see for a second time
> Earth in fresh green rise from the sea;
> The cataracts fall, the eagle flies,
> He catches fish from the rocks.
>
> The Æsir assemble on Ithavoll,
> They speak of the mighty earth-engirdler,
> They recall the mighty events of the past,
> And the ancient-runes of Fimbul-tyr.
>
> Then once more will the wonderful
> Golden tables be found in the grass,
> Which once in old time the gods possessed.
>
> On fields unsown will fruits spring forth,
> All evils vanish; Balder comes back.

Hod and Balder dwell in Hropt's battle-hall,
The hall of the mighty Battle-gods.

Then can Hœnir choose the prophetic wand.
The sons of the brothers of Tveggi abide
In spacious Vindheim. Would ye know yet
   more?

A hall I see, brighter than the sun,
O'erlaid with gold, on Gimle stand;
There dwell for ever the righteous hosts,
Enjoying delights eternally.

From on high comes a Mighty One
To the great judgment, ruling all.
From below the dark dragon flies,
The glistening snake from Nithafjoll;
On his wings bears Nidhogg, flying o'er the
   plain,
The corpses of men. Now must I sink.[80]

There is thus a new earth without ills, where fruits unsown ripen—a typical Elysian or Golden Age world. Some of the gods return—those who were not destroyed, Balder, Hod, Hœnir, the sons of Tveggi's ('the Twofold,' Odin) brothers, of whom nothing is known. They speak of the things of the past, of the Midgard-serpent, of Odin's runes (Fimbul-tyr, 'the mighty god'). They find the golden tables on which the gods had once played a kind of draughts in the Golden Age (cf. v. 8: 'In their home at peace they played at tables'). The mysterious 'Mighty One' is almost certainly a borrowing from Christianity, just as the hall on Gimle is a reflexion of the Christian Heaven. The final stanza about Nidhogg is apparently not in its right place. Its last words, however, belong to the end of the poem, and refer to the Volva, who, having delivered her prophecy, sinks back whence she came. Some have taken the verse as meaning that the dragon tries to rise, but is defeated and sinks for ever. This is unlikely, and 'she must sink' = 'I must sink') refers to the seeress.

Hyndluljod also speaks of the High God to come:

There comes another, a Mightier,
   Yet dare I never his name forthtell;
Few are they who can further see
Than when Odin shall meet the Wolf.[81]

The new world, as well as other details, is known to the poet of *Vafthrudnismal.* During the mighty winter Lif and Lifthrasir survive. The sun (Alfrodull) will bear a daughter ere the Wolf swallows her, and this daughter will follow her mother's ways when the Powers fall. Odin then enquires about the maidens who shall fare over the sea. Vafthrudnir's reply shows that three throngs of maidens descend over Mogthrasir's dwelling-place. They will be guardian spirits to men, though they come of giant stock. These are perhaps kindly Norns. The giant then tells Odin that, after Surt's fires have sunk, Vidarr and

Vali shall dwell in the realm of the gods, and Modi and Magni, sons of Thor, shall have his hammer Mjollnir.[82] In this forecast of the new world, there is a further conception. Lif and Lifthrasir ('Life' and 'Vitality'), progenitors of a new race of men, are hidden in Mimir's grove, possibly Yggdrasil if Mimameid, 'Mimir's tree,' mentioned in *Svipdagsmal,* is the World-tree. This corresponds to the Iranian myth of the *vara* or 'enclosure' of Yima, the first mortal, whose reign is a Golden Age. He was commanded to make this *vara* and fill it with happy mortals, who will repeople the earth after the devastating winter has passed.[83] There will be a new sun, and certain gods will reappear, their names differing from those in *Voluspa.* The giant maidens who act as guardian spirits, presumably to the dwellers on the new earth, descend over Mogthrasir's 'thorp' or dwelling-place; and, as Boer suggests, Mogthrasir, 'he who desires sons,' may be the same as Lif, progenitor of the new race.[84]

Snorri combines the *Voluspa* and *Vafthrudnismal* passages in his account of the new world. But he adds a description of places of bliss and punishment, and here, as we have seen, he seems to have misunderstood his sources.[85]

Apart from the reference to Gimle, which appears to be for the righteous dead, the poems say nothing about the lot of the dead in the renewed world.

Notes

[1] *Gylfaginning,* cc. 4 ff.

[2] *Voluspa,* 3 ff.

[3] Boer, *in loc.,* Holmberg, *Siberian Mythology,* in this Series, Chapter II; Alexander, *North American Mythology,* p. 279.

[4] *Vafthrudnismal,* 20 f.

[5] *Grimnismal,* 40 f.

[6] *Gylf.,* c. 9.

[7] ib., c. 3.

[8] Tacitus, *Annals,* xiii. 57.

[9] *Skaldskaparmal,* cc. 23 ff.; *Corpus Poeticum Boreale* i. 277, ii. 55, 194.

[10] Grimm [a], ii. 563 ff.; Kemble, i. 408.

[11] *Vol.,* 7, 9 ff.

[12] *Gylf.,* c. 14.

[13] *Vol.,* 17, 18.

[14] *Gylf.,* c. 9.

[15] ib., c. 3.

[16] See Clarke, p. 107 and note.

[17] Tacitus, *Germ.,* c. 2.

[18] *Gylf.,* c. 34; *Bragaraedur,* c. 1; *Skaldsk.,* cc. 17, 23; *Harb.,* 19; cf. *CPB* ii. 9.

[19] *Vol.,* 56.

[20] *Gylf.,* cc. 35, 45, 47; *Hym.,* 23; *Vol.,* 50.

[21] *Gylf.,* cc. 9, 14. Asgard is mentioned twice in the Poetic *Edda.* Loki tells Thor that, if his hammer is not recovered, the giants will dwell in Asgard, *Thrymskvitha,* 17. Thor and Tyr go from Asgard to get the giant Hrym's kettle, *Hym.,* 7.

[22] *Gylf.,* cc. 13, 15, 27, 51; *Grim.,* 29, 44; *Fafnismal,* 15; *Helgakvitha Hundingsbana,* ii. 48.

[23] *Vol.,* 2; *Vaf.,* 43; *Alvissmal,* see Sijmons and Gering, i. 152.

[24] So Gering, *Edda,* note to *Vaf.,* 43, p. 66.

[25] Mogk, 'Neunzahl,' in Hoops, iii. 312.

[26] *Gylf.,* c. 4 and see Gering's note, p. 300; cc. 5, 34, 42; *Baldrs Draumar,* 2; *Vaf.,* 43; *Grim.,* 26.

[27] *Vol.,* 2, 19 f.

[28] ib., 27, 47; *Svipdagsmal,* 29 f.

[29] Gering, *Edda,* p. 132.

[30] *Grim.,* 31 f.

[31] *Gylf.,* cc. 15 f.

[32] R. M. Meyer, p. 477.

[33] Bugge, [b], Introd., p. xxiv.

[34] *Skaldsk.,* c. 34.

[35] *Grim.,* 25 f.

[36] Chadwick [b], p. 78.

[37] ib., p. 75 f.; Müllenhoff [a], v. 103 f.

[38] E. Welsford, 'Old Prussians,' *Encyclopaedia of Religion and Ethics* ix. 489.

[39] Cf. Gering, *Edda,* p. 105.

[40] *CPB* i. 246.

[41] Chadwick [b], p. 75.

[42] Cf. U. Holmberg, *Der Baum des Lebens,* Helsinki, 1922, pp. 67, 68.

[43] ib., p. 75 and *passim;* cf. also *Siberian Mythology* in this Series, pp. 349 ff.

[44] *Gylf.,* c. 16; *Grim.,* 26.

[45] MacCulloch [c], pp. 442-3.

[46] ib., Chapter XVI.

[47] ib., p. 441; Holmberg, *Finno-Ugric and Siberian Mythology,* pp. 222, 333 ff.

[48] Holmberg, p. 337.

[49] ib., pp. 221-2; *Der Baum des Lebens,* p. 17 f.

[50] ib., *Der Baum,* p. 19; MacCulloch [a], pp. 228, 232.

[51] Grimm [a], i. 116.

[52] *Monumenta Germ. Hist., Scriptores,* iii. 423.

[53] A. Olrik, 'Irminsul og Gudestøtter,' *Maal og Minne,* 1910, p. 4 f.; Holmberg, *Der Baum,* p. 10.

[54] E. H. Meyer [b], §112; Golther, p. 530; Bugge, *Studien,* pp. 421 ff.

[55] *Vol.,* 44, 49, 58; *Vaf.,* 55; *BDr.,* 14; *HH* ii. 39; *Atlamal,* 21, 38, 42. Cf. *Vaf.,* 38, 39, 42, *tiva rok* (*tivar,* 'gods'). *Lokasenna,* 39.

[56] *Vol.,* 8, 21 f., 32; cf. Mogk, *ERE* iv. 845, 'the golden age of the gods came to an end when the Norns came into being.'

[57] *Vol.,* 25 f.

[58] ib., 39.

[59] ib., 57, cf. 45, 'the world falls'; *Hyndluljod,* 44; *Vaf.,* 46 f. and *Vol.,* 40. Cf. p. 199. *Gylf.,* c. 51, speaks of the wolf swallowing the sun, and the other wolf swallowing the moon. The stars vanish from the Heavens. This follows the passage in *Grim.,* 39, and Snorri's own earlier narrative in c. 12. For Eclipse myths see MacCulloch [a], p. 178; A. Lang, *Myth, Ritual, and Religion,*[2] London, 1906, i. 132 f.; Grimm [a], i. 244, ii. 705; *ERE* x. 368. Swedish, Danish, and Norse folk-lore knows the sun-wolf. In Iceland an eclipse is 'Ulfakreppa.' Golther, p. 524.

[60] *Vaf.,* 44 f.; *Gylf.,* c. 53; *Hynd.,* 44; *Vol.,* 41, 45, cf. *Gylf.,* c. 51.

[61] *Vol.,* 52, 57; *Vaf.,* 50 f.; *Grim.,* 38; *Gylf.,* cc. 4, 17, 51.

[62] In *Gylf.,* c. 51, the mighty winter precedes or is contemporary with these evils.

[63] Perhaps Mimir's sons are giants, if Mimir is to be regarded as a giant, cf. Boer, ii. 22. Hence Heimdall blows his horn, because the giants are in motion.

[64] After the account of the mighty winter Snorri here inserts the swallowing of the sun and moon; the trembling of earth and breaking of all fetters; the advance of the Wolf; the sea rushing over the land because the Serpent is stirring in giant fury; the ship Naglfar loose and floating on the flood, steered by Hrym. In *Vol.,* 50, Hrym comes from the East; the Midgard-serpent and the Eagle seem to be with him. The stanza ends with 'Naglfar is loose.' Does this mean that they are on board it? Or should this line go with the next stanza, which tells of a vessel coming from the North steered by Loki, with the people of Hel. Is this vessel Naglfar? If the people of Hel are the dead, not giants, Naglfar would be a ship of the dead, and, by a false etymology, the ship made of dead men's nails. But why should the dead attack the gods? Snorri elsewhere assigns Naglfar to the sons of Muspell, *Gylf.,* c. 43. In c. 51 Snorri says that this ship is made of dead men's nails, wherefore men should be warned that if a man die with uncut nails he is adding material to this ship, which gods and men would fain see unfinished.

[65] The 'wild hosts,' *fifl-meger,* are perhaps the people of *fifl,* a giant or monster, or 'the nameless host who follow without knowing why.'

[66] *Gylf.,* c. 51.

[67] *Vaf.,* 18, 39, 41 f.

[68] *BDr.,* 14; *Grim.,* 4; *Vaf.,* 52.

[69] *CPB* i. 261, 265, ii. 65, 197; *Skaldsk.,* c. 49; *HH* ii. 39.

[70] E. W. West, *Pahlavi Texts,* in *Sacred Books of the East,* xviii. 109 f.; N. Söderblom, *La vie future d'après Mazdéisme,* Paris, 1901, p. 179 f.; Rydberg, pp. 256 ff.; L. H. Grey, *ERE* ii. 703; A. J. Carnoy, *Iranian Mythology,* in this Series, p. 307.

[71] See MacCulloch [a], p. 232, [b], p. 34.

[72] *Gylf.,* c. 51, cf. cc. 4, 5, 8, 11, 13, 37, 43, 51.

[73] *Lok.,* 42; *Vol.,* 51.

[74] *Faf.,* 15; *Grim.,* 29.

[75] Grimm [a], ii. 808.

[76] ib.; *Heliand,* 2591, 4358.

[77] Golther, p. 541.

[78] See these in W. Braune, *Althochdeutsche Lesebuch,*[7] p. 190 f.

[79] Mogk, in Hoops, iii. 288.

[80] *Vol.,* 59 ff.

[81] *Hynd.,* 45.

[82] *Vaf.,* 44 ff.

[83] *Svip.,* 30; *ERE* ii. 702 f.

[84] Boer, ii. 58 f.

[85] *Gylf.,* c. 52. See p. 318.

Kevin Crossley-Holland (1980)

SOURCE: Introduction to *The Norse Myths,* Pantheon Books, 1980, pp. xiv-xli.

[*In this excerpt, Crossley-Holland describes the Norse pantheon and the primary sources for the Norse mythological tradition.*]

The Pantheon

Snorri Sturluson, writing in Iceland in the thirteenth century, says that, excluding Odin and his wife Frigg, 'The divine gods are twelve in number . . . The goddesses [who number thirteen] are no less sacred and no less powerful.' This section introduces the four principal deities, Odin, Thor, Freyr and Freyja, in some detail, and points to the principal attributes of the others; they, and other protagonists, are discussed further in the notes where appropriate.

Odin is often called Allfather: this means he was not only the actual father of many of the gods and (with his two brothers) created the first man and woman, but that he was also foremost of the gods. Snorri Sturluson is quite clear on this point:

> Odin is the highest and oldest of the gods. He rules all things and, no matter how mighty the other gods may be, they all serve him as children do their father . . . He lives for ever and ever, and rules over the whole of his kingdom and governs all things great and small. He created heaven and earth and sky and all that in them is.

Germanic pre-Christian Europe was fraught with conflict between family and family, tribe and tribe, country and country. A culture finds the gods it needs and the Norse world needed a god to justify the violence that is one of its hallmarks. Odin appears to have inherited the characteristics of the earliest Germanic war gods, Wodan and Tîwaz, and is seen above all as the God of Battle. Terrible, arrogant and capricious, he inspired victory and determined defeat; in his hall, Valhalla, he entertained slain warriors, chosen and conducted there by the Valkyries, who were to fight with him at Ragnarok; and he required propitiation with human and animal sacrifice.

The same inspiration that enabled one man to win a battle enabled another to compose poetry. Thus Odin, the God of War, travelled to Jotunheim to win the mead of poetry for the gods (Myth 6), and one reason why he is so prominent in the eddaic poems may be that he was the patron of the poets who composed them!

Odin was not only the God of Battle and the God of Poetry; he could also act as a seer. Like a shaman, he could send out his spirit, sometimes riding on his eight-legged steed Sleipnir, sometimes in another shape, on journeys between worlds; like a shaman, he could win wisdom from the dead. In the eddaic poem *Voluspa,* and in his voluntary sacrifice on the world ash Yggdrasill (Myth 4), we see him as the God of the Dead.

Odin is a formidable presence. He has only one eye and wears a wide-brimmed hat to escape instant recognition; he always wears a blue cloak and carries the magic spear Gungnir; on his shoulders sit the ravens Huginn (Thought) and Muninn (Memory), birds of battle symbolic also of flights in search of wisdom; and from the high seat of Hlidskjalf, in his hall Valaskjalf, he could survey all that happened in the nine worlds. He is a terrifying god: maybe a god to be respected, but not a god to be loved.

Thor, son of Odin and Earth, was second in the pantheon and it is clear from the terms in which he is described by the eddaic poets, Snorri Sturluson and the saga writers, and from the large number of place names embodying his name, that he was the most loved and respected of the gods. While Odin stood for violence and war, Thor represented order. With his hammer Mjollnir, he kept the giants at bay and was physically strong enough to grapple with the world serpent, Jormungand. Men invoked him in the name of law and stability.

Odin championed the nobly born—kings, warriors, poets; Thor championed the farming freemen (Myth 22) who constituted the majority of the population. His physical image fits this role well; he was huge, red-bearded, possessed of a vast appetite, quick to lose his temper and quick to regain it, a bit slow in the uptake, but immensely strong and dependable. The eddaic poets (and Snorri Sturluson in their wake) may have exaggerated Odin's significance; according to the eleventh-century historian Adam of Bremen, Thor was the greatest of the Norse gods and, in the great temple at Uppsala, his statue occupied the central position between Odin and Freyr.

The second myth in this collection which forms a complete cycle, beginning with the creation and ending with the destruction of the nine worlds, describes a war between the warrior gods, the Aesir, and the fertility gods, the Vanir. This conflict appears to embody the memory of a time when two cults struggled for the possession of men's minds and, as invariably happens when one religion replaces another, were ultimately fused. Thor thus took on characteristics associated with fertility and made them his own. The hammer Mjollnir, for instance, was not only an instrument of aggression but also of fertility (see Note 10). Likewise, Thor was the cause of thunder (the noise made by the wheels of his chariot) and lightning (fragments of a whetstone were lodged in his head) and, in the words of Adam of Bremen, Thor was held to control 'the winds and showers, the fair weather and fruits of the earth'.

The most important of the fertility gods, however, was Freyr, God of Plenty. Freyr appears to have been a descendant (who somehow changed sex) of Nerthus, the Earth Mother whom Tacitus described as having been worshipped in Denmark in the first century AD. And Snorri Sturluson writes: 'Freyr is an exceedingly famous god; he decides when the sun shall shine or the rain come down, and along with that the fruitfulness of the earth, and he is good to invoke for peace and plenty. He also brings about the prosperity of men.' The idol of Freyr at Uppsala had a gigantic phallus and Freyr was clearly invoked not only for the increase of the earth but also for human increase. Freyr's principal possessions, the ship Skidbladnir and the boar Gullinbursti, are both ancient fertility symbols, and the one surviving myth directly concerned with him (Myth 11) is a celebration of all that he stands for.

Freyr's father was Njord and his sister was Freyja . . . and all three were involved in the exchange of leaders when the Aesir and Vanir made a truce (Myth 2). Njord, the senior god of the Vanir, governed the sea and the winds and guarded ships and seafarers. His hall was called Noatun or shipyard. Njord married the frost giantess Skadi and his son the frost giantess Gerd in myths which both symbolise the union of opposites (see Notes 9 and 11).

There are a bewildering number of theories about another of the leading gods, Heimdall, but he, too, was probably originally one of the Vanir. He was associated with the sea and was the son of nine maidens (perhaps nine waves). According to Snorri, 'He needs less sleep than a bird, and can see a hundred leagues in front of him as well by night as by day. He can hear the grass growing on the earth and the wool on sheep, and everything that makes more noise.' His stamina and acutely developed senses made Heimdall the ideal watchman for the gods. His hall Himinbjorg (Cliffs of Heaven) stood near the rainbow Bifrost, and he owned the horn Gjall whose blast could be heard throughout the nine worlds. Heimdall is also identified in the prose preface to the *Rigsthula* as the progenitor of the races of men (Myth 5); we do not know enough about his origins to be sure why he and not Odin (who, with his brothers, actually created the first man and woman) appears in this context.

Another leading god, Tyr, was a son of Odin, although one source (Myth 17) makes him the son of the giant Hymir. Like Odin, he inherited characteristics from earlier Germanic gods of battle, and his origins are discussed in Note 7. He is the bravest of the Aesir and only he is prepared to sacrifice a hand so that the wolf Fenrir can be bound (Myth 7), thereby ensuring the safety of the gods until Ragnarok.

Ragnarok is precipitated by the death of Balder, the gentle and beloved son of Odin and Frigg, who is felled by a mistletoe dart thrown by his own brother Hod, a blind god whose aim is guided by the evil Loki. Balder's character is discussed in detail in Note 29; in the inimitable words of Snorri Sturluson:

> There is nothing but good to be told of him. He is the best of them and everyone sings his praises. He is so fair of face and bright that a splendour radiates from him, and there is one flower so white that it is likened to Balder's brow; it is the whitest of all flowers. From that you can tell how beautiful his body is, and how bright his hair. He is the wisest of the gods, and the sweetest-spoken, and the most merciful, but it is a characteristic of his that once he has pronounced a judgement it can never be altered.

None of the remainder of the twelve 'leading' gods feature significantly in the surviving myths. Forseti, the son of Balder and Nanna, was god of justice; Bragi, son of Odin, was god of poetry and eloquence; Ull was particularly concerned with archery and skiing, and was invoked in duels; Vali, son of Odin and his mistress Rind, who avenged Balder's death by killing his unwitting murderer, and Vidar, son of Odin and the giantess Grid, who will avenge Odin's death, both survive Ragnarok.

Apart from the twelve principal gods three other male inhabitants of Asgard must be mentioned. Honir (Myths 2, 8 and 26) was involved in the exchange of leaders between the Aesir and Vanir. His most pronounced characteristic appears to have been his indecisiveness and he was associated with Odin and Loki on several occasions. It seems that after Ragnarok he will be Odin's successor as first among the gods. Secondly, Hermod, a son of Odin, makes one significant appearance: his name implies resolve and it is he who journeys to the underworld of Hel in an attempt to recover his dead brother Balder. And, finally, there is Loki.

The son of two giants and yet the foster-brother of Odin, Loki embodies the ambiguous and darkening relationship between the gods and the giants. He is dynamic and unpredictable and because of that he is both the catalyst in many of the myths and the most fascinating character in the entire mythology. Without the exciting, unstable, flawed figure of Loki, there could be no change in the fixed order of things, no quickening pulse, and no Ragnarok.

Snorri Sturluson says that Loki

> is handsome and fair of face, but has an evil disposition and is very changeable of mood. He excelled all men in the art of cunning, and he always cheats. He was continually involving the Aesir in great difficulties and he often helped them out again by guile.

This is a very fair description of the Loki of the earlier myths: he is responsible for a wager with a giant which imperils Freyja (Myth 3) but by changing both shape and sex, characteristics he has in common with Odin, he bails out Freyja and the gods; his shearing of Sif's hair is more mischievous than evil, and he makes handsome amends in the end (Myth 10); and although his deceit leads to the loss of the golden apples of youth (Myth 8), he retrieves them again.

Loki's origins are particularly complex and he has been compared to a number of figures in European and other mythologies; it is now generally accepted, though, that he was no late invention of the Norse poets but an ancient figure, and one descended from a common Indo-European prototype. Noting this turn and turnabout quality in Loki's make-up, H. R. Ellis Davidson has also tellingly compared him to the Trickster of American Indian mythology:

> The trickster is greedy, selfish, and treacherous; he takes on animal form; he appears in comic and often disgusting situations, and yet he may be regarded as a kind of culture hero, who provides mankind with benefits like sunlight and fire. At times he even appears as a creator. He can take on both male and female form, and can give birth to children. He is, in fact, a kind of semi-comic shaman, half way between god and hero, yet with a strong dash of the jester element, foreign to both, thrown in.

But, as time goes on, the playful Loki gives way to the cruel predator, hostile to the gods. He not only guides the mistletoe dart that kills Balder but stands in the way of Balder's return from Hel; his accusations against the gods at Aegir's feast (Myth 30) are vicious and unbridled; even when fettered, he remains an agent of destruction, causer of earthquakes. And when he breaks loose at Ragnarok, Loki reveals his true colours: he is no less evil than his three appalling children, the serpent Jormungand, the wolf Fenrir and the half-alive, half-dead Hel (Myth 7), and he leads the giants and monsters into battle against the gods and heroes.

We hear far less about the goddesses in the myths; and since Snorri Sturluson asserts their equality with the gods, we can only assume a disproportionate number of stories concerning them have been lost. Freyja is the only 'divine' goddess to have survived as a fully rounded and commanding figure. With her father Njord and brother Freyr she came to represent the Vanir when they exchanged leaders with the Aesir. Her husband was called Od (sometimes equated with Odin) and Freyja is often described weeping for this shadowy figure who had for some reason left her. Freyja was invoked by pre-Christian Scandinavians as goddess of love, and is portrayed in the myths as sexually attractive and free with her favours: on two occasions, giants lusted after her; she sold herself to four dwarfs (Myth 13) in exchange for the Necklace of the Brisings—the most striking symbol of her fertility; and the giantess Hyndla roundly censured her for riding on her human lover Ottar (Myth 18) and for leaping around at night like a nanny goat.

Freyja was also associated with war. She rode to battle in a chariot drawn by two cats and the eddaic poem *Grimnismal* says that she divided the slain with Odin; half went to Valhalla and half to her hall, Sessrumnir, on Folkvang (Field of Folk). The end of Myth 13 displays this warlike face of Freyja, while it is noteworthy that in Myth 17 the alias of Freyja's lover Ottar is Hildisvini, which means 'battle-boar'.

War and death stand shoulder to shoulder and, like Odin, Freyja had connexions with the world of the dead. She was said to have been mistress of magic and witchcraft (Myth 2) and owned a falcon skin which enabled her spirit to take the form of a bird, travel to the underworld, and come back with prophecies and knowledge of destinies. But although a great deal about the practice of shamanism in pre-Christian Scandinavia (and Freyja's association with it) can be adduced from contemporary sources, no myth survives that displays Freyja as seer or *volva*.

Of the other twelve 'divine' goddesses, Gefion was also counted among the Vanir, and the story of how she tricked Gylfi, the King of Sweden (Myth 21), establishes her connexion with agriculture in general and ploughing in particular. Eir was goddess of healing; Sjofn and Lofn were concerned with firing human love and bringing together those 'for whom marriage was forbidden or banned', while Var heard the marriage oath and punished those who strayed from it; Vor was a goddess from whom nothing could be hidden and watchful Syn was invoked by defendants at trials; Snotra was wise and gentle and knew the value of self-discipline; Saga was distinguished only for drinking each day with Odin in her hall Sokkvabekk; and Lin, Fulla and Gna appear to have been no more than handmaidens to Odin's wife, Frigg.

It is a pity that we do not know more about Frigg herself, who shared with Odin a knowledge of men's destinies. Like Freyr, she must have had her origin in the image of the Earth Mother: she was the daughter of Fjorgyn, the Goddess of Earth; she was invoked by women in labour; and her maternal qualities are evident in her mourning for the loss of her son Balder. H. R. Ellis Davidson has written of the likely connexion between Freyja and Frigg:

> The two main goddesses of Asgard indeed suggest two aspects of the same divinity, and this is paralleled by the twofold aspect of the fertility goddess in the Near East, appearing as mother and as lover. Sometimes both roles may be combined in the person of one goddess, but it is more usual for the different aspects to be personified under different names. It is even possible to recognise a triad of goddesses, such as Asherah, Astarte, and Anat of Syria, or Hera, Aphrodite, and Artemis of Greece. Here the three main aspects of womanhood appear side by side as wife and mother, lover and mistress, chaste and beautiful virgin. Frigg and Freyja in northern mythology could figure as the first two of such a trio, while the dim figure of Skadi the huntress might once have occupied the vacant place.

We know rather more about other female inhabitants of Asgard than about some of the 'divine' goddesses. Idun, the wife of Bragi, was custodian of the apples of youth, and the myth of how she was tricked by Loki into leaving Asgard and then kidnapped by the giant Thiazi is one of the most haunting in the cycle (Myth and Note 8). Like Idun, Sif, the wife of Thor, must have been a fertility goddess; she had incomparable golden hair and its loss is the starting point for Myth 10. Nanna was Balder's loyal wife; her heart broke at the sight of him lying dead on the ship Ringhorn and she was cremated with him and accompanied him to Hel. And Sigyn was no less loyal to her husband Loki; when he was bound by the gods, she stood beside him and with a bowl caught the deadly venom that dripped from a snake's fangs on to his face.

The gods and goddesses symbolise specific beliefs and many of them have highly distinctive personalities. Giants and dwarfs, on the other hand, appear as a genera. There is little to choose between one giant and another, one dwarf and the next. The giants largely represent the forces of chaos, attempting through physical force, trickery and magic to upset the order of the universe. They range from the blunt and brutal Geirrod and Hrungnir, both disposed of by Thor, to the wily and evil Utgard-Loki, who sees Thor off the premises. But the distinction between gods and giants is far from absolute. Some gods have bad qualities, some giants have good; and the gods and giants do not only fight one another, but form friendships and embark on love relationships. Perhaps it is legitimate, indeed, to see the gods and giants not as polarised opposites but rather as opposing aspects of one character—warring, making peace, warring again and, in the end, mutually destructive.

The ugly, misshapen dwarfs, meanwhile, represent greed; they do nothing that is not in their own interests. Mastersmiths and magicians, quick to show malice, they lust after fair women, after power and, above all, after gold. Light elves and dark elves and the inhabitants of Niflheim are mentioned in the myths from time to time, but they do not have an active part to play in them. Of the five myths (5, 12, 20, 21 and 25) involving humans, I will have more to say. . . .

Sources

The greater part of this magnificent mythology, Indo-European in origin, took shape in Germanic Europe between 1000 BC and the birth of Christ. The survival of Bronze Age rock carvings, however, some of them featuring religious symbols, indicates that certain elements in the myths were current in Scandinavia in the previous millennium. But not until Tacitus's *Germania,* written at the end of the first century AD, do we have a written record of ancient Germanic religious beliefs, and our chief sources are much later still, dating from thirteenth-century Christian Iceland, when the old beliefs were largely discredited. We have to rely on poets and antiquarians 'out on the end of an event, waving goodbye'.

There are six primary literary sources (some single, some plural) fundamental to a study of Norse mythology. The notes at the end of the book discuss in some detail the source(s) for each myth and also refer to mythological parallels, literary analogues and archaeological finds.

In 1643 the Bishop of Skalholt in Iceland discovered a manuscript, *Codex Regius,* now thought to have been written in about 1270, consisting of twenty-nine mythical and heroic poems. Confusion over its authorship led to its being called *Saemund's Edda* (the term 'edda' is thought to derive from the Old Norse oðr meaning poem or poetry). A few other poems of the same type were subsequently discovered, notably a group of six in the *Arnamagnaean Codex* of which five appear in the *Codex Regius* and one (*Baldrs Draumar*) does not. The *Elder Edda* or *Poetic Edda* was adopted as the umbrella title for these poems, thirty-four in all, unified by subject matter and form. They appear to have been composed by poets who believed in the old gods, many of them are unique sources for individual myths, and many are highly accomplished poems in their own right. The *Elder Edda,* moreover, possesses in *Voluspa* (The Sibyl's Prophecy) a poem that is by common consent one of the greatest literary achievements of the Germanic world— a powerful and moving account of how the world was created, how it moved from a Golden Age to an age of strife, and how it had to end in total destruction before there could be a new innocence and a new cycle of time.

Although the majority of its poems were probably composed in the tenth century, the *Elder Edda* is actually an anthology of different poets from different places and times; this accounts for the contradictions and many chronological inconsistencies (detailed in the notes)

within the myths they recount. There is, of course, no 'right' order or version for the myths (pre-Christian Germanic Europeans were no more uniform in their religious beliefs than any other people) and in retelling the cycle, I have simply attempted to find a psychologically satisfying sequence that reduced difficulties of this kind to a minimum.

Scaldic poems—eulogies and elegies by known poets celebrating their contemporaries—are the other major poetic source for the myths. Their intricate form, which includes syllabics, alliteration, internal rhyme and consonance, resists the most stout-hearted attempts to render them in an acceptable modern poetic translation, but the rich allusive detail they contain is invaluable. The 'shield poems', as a few of them are known, describe mythical scenes painted on the quarters of a shield presented to some king or local chieftain; the poem came along as, so to speak, an ancillary present. These are important sources for a number of the myths, but the greatest pertinence of the scaldic poems lies in the countless kennings, or condensed metaphors, that comprise part of their diction. Many of the kennings are rooted in myths with which the poem's original audience was clearly familiar. So, for instance, four of the kennings for gold are 'Freyja's tears', 'Sif's hair', 'Otter's ransom' and 'Aegir's fire'. As readers of these myths will discover, this is because Freyja wept tears of gold; because when the goddess Sif's hair was cropped by Loki, it was replaced by spun gold; because three gods had to pay a ransom for killing Otter by covering his pelt with gold; and because the sea god Aegir's hall was illumined only by gold that shone like fire. Many of the kennings, then, endorse those myths that have survived and give us tantalising glimpses of those that have not.

The finest man of letters that Iceland has ever produced was Snorri Sturluson (1179-1241). An important political leader and landowner, he was also a great poet, sagaman, historian and critic. His poems include *Hattatal,* a scaldic eulogy for King Hakon and Duke Skuli; his sagas include the brilliantly vivid *Egil's Saga,* while the *Heimskringla* is nothing less than a survey of the whole of Norwegian history from its legendary origins up to his own time. But by far Snorri's most significant work for the student of Norse mythology is his *Prose Edda.*

Iceland had democratically adopted Christianity in 1000 AD, and the accompanying exposure to new European literary modes was eroding both the use of the old scaldic technique and familiarity with the kennings. Snorri's reaction was to write a handbook to encourage poets to compose in the scaldic style—a kind of North European equivalent of Aristotle's *Poetics.* The *Prose Edda,* written in about 1220, includes rules of poetic diction, quotes extensively from scaldic poems that would otherwise be lost to us, displays familiarity with almost all the poems in the *Elder Edda* and retells in full many of the myths that lie behind the kennings in scaldic poetry. One section in particular, 'Gylfaginning', consists exclusively of retellings from the myths.

Snorri Sturluson was writing here both as a Christian and an antiquarian, and we must keep this in mind in using and assessing his work. It would be wrong to suppose that, writing in thirteenth-century Iceland, Snorri Sturluson gives a thoroughly reliable and authentic firsthand view of ancient beliefs. His material fascinated and at times amused or misled him, but above all it fired the storyteller and poet in him (see Note 17 for the complete version of Thor's visit to Hymir). Absorbed by the drama of, and interplay between the nine worlds, he took material from existing sources and, with his own imaginative touch, created in 'Gylfaginning' a superb and delightful work of art— pages that tell many of the myths better than they have been told before or since.

In about 1215, just twenty years before Snorri Sturluson completed *Heimskringla,* a Dane called Saxo, nicknamed Grammaticus, wrote the last words of his sixteen-volume Latin history of the Danes, *Gesta Danorum.* Like *Heimskringla,* this work began with prehistoric times, and the first nine books are a confused medley of myth, legend and religious practice. Saxo Grammaticus knew and used variant versions of many of the myths recorded by Snorri, but his approach is markedly different. Snorri does not sermonise about the gods but lets them stand or fall by their own actions. But, as E. O. G. Turville-Petre writes:

> For Saxo, as for the medieval Icelanders, the gods were not gods, but crafty men of old. With superior cunning they had overcome the primeval giants; they had deluded men into believing that they were divine. But Saxo carried euhumerism further than the Icelanders did. Saxo's gods play a more intimate part in the affairs of men. . . . Saxo differs from the Icelandic writers chiefly in his bitter contempt of the gods and all they stood for. Snorri sometimes poked fun at them, but it was a good-humoured fun, of a kind which had no place in Saxo's mind.

Nevertheless, *Gesta Danorum* is still the primary source for the Danish and West Norse traditions, just as Snorri Sturluson represents Icelandic tradition. The note to 'The Death of Balder' (Myth 29) includes a detailed comparison of the versions offered by Snorri and Saxo.

The great Icelandic sagas (there are no fewer than seven hundred) together constitute the most surprising and one of the most distinguished achievements in European literature. Written in the thirteenth century by known and unknown hands, some are historical and revolve around the lives and deeds of kings and saintly bishops, some celebrate legendary heroes such as Sigurd the Volsung, some describe the Norsemen's insatiable appetite for exploration and settlement; and perhaps

the greatest are the racy, ice-bright family sagas that tell of the lives, loyalties, dilemmas and feuds of individuals and families in Iceland's Heroic Age around 1000 AD.

Inevitably the sagas reflect the religious beliefs and attitudes of their protagonists, and they make available to us a great deal of information about pre-Christian belief and practice—much of which appears to have persisted well into the Christian period in Iceland. In the *Eyrbyggja Saga,* for example, one Thorolf decides to migrate to Iceland. In order to decide where to disembark

> Thorolf threw overboard the high-seat pillars from the temple—the figure of Thor was carved on one of them—and declared that he'd settle at any spot in Iceland where Thor chose to send the pillars ashore.

Thorolf did just that and the saga then describes in detail the building of a temple to Thor, the function of the temple priest, and the use of the temple and its surrounds:

> Thorolf used to hold all his courts on the point of the headland where Thor had come ashore, and that's where he started the district assembly. This place was so holy that he wouldn't let anybody desecrate it either with bloodshed or with excrement; and for privy purposes they used a special rock in the sea which they called Dritsker [Dirt Skerry].

In the last category are actual historians and their histories. As mentioned above, Tacitus was the first to write about the religions of the Germanic tribes within the Roman Empire. In the tenth century, the Arab diplomat Ibn Fadlan wrote a detailed record of his prolonged contact with the Norsemen, including a horrifying account of a ship burial in Russia; in the eleventh century, Adam of Bremen offered a sustained description of Swedish paganism and left a very vivid and detailed picture of the greatest of the heathen temples, dedicated to Odin, Thor and Freyr, at Uppsala. The thirteenth-century *Landnamabok* (Book of Settlements), which is a survey of Iceland man by man and inch by inch, contains a significant amount of religious history, including the Icelandic heathen law concerning sacerdotal functions, sacrifices, oath swearing, and so forth. These and many other historical sources, some no less significant than those cited, help us to build up a picture of pre-Christian Scandinavia.

Our principal sources stand only half-way between us and the people who accepted the myths as truths. The filters of literary artifice, fragmented manuscripts, prejudice and contempt occasioned by conflicting religious belief, and hindsight, all obscure our picture. However much we may know, there is far more that we can never know; we are rather like searchers using glow worms to guide us through the darkness.

The Literary Structure of the Myths

The majority of the myths are vigorous dramatic narratives. They are also episodes in a slowly developing, panoptic story.

First Odin and his brothers create the worlds and their inhabitants, and then follows a time of peace. Snorri Sturluson characterises this as the Golden Age, metaphorically because it is pure and untarnished and literally because the god's halls and sanctuaries and implements and utensils were made of gold.

This Golden Age ends with a war between the Aesir and the Vanir, the first war in the world. When it becomes clear that neither side will prevail, a truce is called and leaders are exchanged. But no sooner have the Aesir and the Vanir learned to live side by side than, in the third myth in the cycle, the recurring motifs of the myths announce themselves: the antagonism of gods and giants, and the ambivalence of Loki.

A giant masquerading as a mason visits Asgard. He tricks the gods into a wager involving Freyja, the sun and the moon, but Loki's cunning prevails. And the citadel's walls, shattered in the war between the Aesir and the Vanir, are restored into the bargain.

There now follow a number of myths ranging between the worlds in which the gods and giants flex their muscles against one another. Initially worsted (sometimes because of Loki's double dealing), the gods invariably come off better in the end (sometimes because Loki, under pressure, rights the situation). Odin journeys to the world of the giants, Jotunheim, to win the sacred mead of poetry; Loki follows in his footsteps to retrieve Idun and the apples of youth; and in a hilarious burlesque, Thor and Loki travel to Jotunheim together, disguised as bride and bridesmaid, to recover Thor's stolen hammer. In all three myths, the gods achieve their aims and the giants are killed.

But during this time the gods sustain losses too; the wise Kvasir is murdered by two dwarfs and his blood is the basic ingredient of the mead of poetry; in order to fetter the wolf Fenrir, Odin's son Tyr is obliged to sacrifice one hand; and in what is the longest and most picaresque of the myths, superbly told by Snorri Sturluson, Thor suffers very considerable loss of face in the course of a visit to the court of the magical Utgard-Loki. We see here that illusion is not only the tool of the gods but of the giants too.

Running parallel to this motif of antagonism is one of love and friendship. Two gods, Njord and Freyr, marry giantesses, and both Odin and Thor have a number of giant mistresses. The giantess Grid lends Thor her iron gloves, her belt of strength and her staff which enable him to dispose of the giant Geirrod and his two daughters. As already suggested the conflict between gods and giants is all the more tragic because they are also drawn to one another and, in many respects, resemble one another; because, in a sense, they are fighting a civil war in which both sides are inevitably the losers.

The theme of sexual attraction between inhabitants of different worlds persists throughout the cycle: four dwarfs buy the body of the goddess Freyja for four nights; in an intricate and passionate myth, the human Svipdag searches for and wins Menglad, a figure with one foot in Asgard, one in Jotunheim; Odin, so quick to boast of his conquests, is frustrated by a human girl, Billing's daughter; and the dwarf Alvis's journey to claim Thrud, Thor's daughter, as his bride ends when the sun rises and he is turned into a block of stone.

There are elements of playfulness and genial humour in many of the myths in the early part of the cycle. But the time of prodigious contests, of thefts and retrievals, and unexpected love matches, comes to an end with the myth of Thor's visit to the giant Geirrod (Myth 24); here, once again, the giants are bent on destroying Thor and unseating the gods, but here it is also apparent that the greatest threat to the gods is not the giants but one of their own number—Loki.

In the most famous of the myths, certainly one of the world's great tragic stories as it is told by Snorri Sturluson, the beautiful and innocent god Balder is killed by a mistletoe dart—and his return from the world of the dead is prevented by one cynical goddess, Thokk, who refuses to weep for him. Loki's is the hand that guides the dart and Loki is the giantess. From this moment on, it is clear that the world is approaching its end. Loki subjects gods and goddesses to vitriolic abuse; he is pursued and fettered. But the forces of evil cannot long be contained. Odin has already learned the future; he knows it is the destiny of gods, giants, men, dwarfs, and all creation to fight and destroy one another at Ragnarok.

But a shaft of light penetrates the final darkness of this most fatalistic mythology. Odin has also learned that a new cycle of time and of life will begin after Ragnarok. Balder, several other gods, and two humans will survive and return to Asgard and Midgard to repeople the world. The end will contain a beginning.

Interspersed with these colourful and often racy narrative tales are a number of myths whose form is quite different. They are pauses in the development of the cycle somewhat like arias in opera; their function is to reveal mythical knowledge. They are taxing to read in that, although they may have a skeletal narrative framework, they are actually litanies—condensations of a great number of names and facts into the minimum number of words. Three of these myths reflect Odin's unceasing search for, and acquisition of, wisdom. In 'Lord of the Gallows', Odin voluntarily sacrifices himself on Yggdrasill and, as he

Depiction of the Norse God Thor.

says, learns nine magic songs and eighteen highly potent charms; we learn what effects they have. In 'The Lay of Vafthrudnir', Odin successfully pits his knowledge against a giant, and in 'The Lay of Grimnir', he reveals a plethora of facts to the boy prince Agnar about both the layout and inhabitants of the mythical universe; both these myths were extensively used by Snorri Sturluson and are unique sources for much information about the cosmology, protagonists and other constituents of the myths.

Two 'flyting' poems—contests of abuse—also furnish many valuable details about the gods. In 'The Lay of Harbard', Odin, disguised as a ferryman, and Thor, anxious to get home, fling taunts at one another across a deep river; and in 'Loki's Flyting', Loki savages one god after another with injurious disclosures and gratuitous insults.

Five myths tell specifically of traditions in Midgard, the world of men. 'The Song of Rig' describes the social structure of the Norse world, 'The Lay of Loddfafnir' lays down a number of rules for social conduct, and 'The Lay of Alvis' is effectively a list of synonyms, an aide-mémoire for poets (put into the mouths of a god and a dwarf); 'Gylfi and Gefion' describes how Sweden and Denmark were given their present shape and 'Hyndla's Poem' is a catalogue of many legendary heroes known to the Norseman. From these myths especially, much information can be elicited about day to day life in the Norse

world, the people who believed or half-believed in the gods and who composed, in the tenth century, most of the surviving poems about them.

EDDIC POETRY

Lee M. Hollander (1927)

SOURCE: "Were the Mythological Poems of the Edda Composed in the Pre-Christian Era?," in *The Journal of English and Germanic Philology*, Vol. XXVI, 1927, pp. 96-105.

[*In the following essay, Hollander examines the problem of dating the Eddic poems and considers their relation to paganism and Christianity.*]

"Concerning the mythological poems of the Edda, it follows from their very contents and their relation to paganism that they were composed in heathen times. Precisely this fact is an excellent point of departure for dating them."

I quote this assertion from Finnur Jónsson's (shorter) 'History of Icelandic Literature';[1] but with more or fewer reservations this is, indeed, the sentiment of practically all scholars who have ventured opinions on this vexed question of the date and provenience of the Eddic lays.[2]

So far, neither the study of metre, of language, of legendary form, nor of specific references, or any other philological method known to us, has rewarded scholars with tangible criteria acceptable to all, or even a majority, of scholars. Under such conditions the only good chronological hold for approximately dating at least a few lays has seemed—and the above quoted remark illustrates this faith—has seemed the conversion of Western Scandinavia accomplished about the end of the tenth century.

To be sure, the having to rely solely on this all too broad fact only tends to converge our attention on its precariousness and the dubiousness of the results gained therefrom.

With this in mind I shall here bring together the evidence available, and also offer some general considerations, with the professed intention to demonstrate the unreliableness of this criterion.

The Scandinavians were the last of the Germanic tribes to be Christianized. Their first contact with the new faith was had in Viking expeditions—increasingly from the eighth century down—along the shorelands, both of the Carolingian empire and of the British Isles, where the rich churches and cloisters lured them with expectations of booty. After the establishment of Scandinavian kingdoms in the littorals and archipelagoes of the West, intermarriage with natives—all Christians by this time—is frequent, and generally followed by the conversion of the conquerors or their settled offspring. It has been doubted[3] whether the effects of this process ever made themselves distinctly felt in the homeland—with small reason, I believe. For the fact remains that many returned, bringing news from these parts. From the West came King Hákon the Good, fosterchild of Æthelstan, who made a valiant but unsuccessful attempt (936) to convert his Norwegians. The failure was due no doubt quite as much to the active political opposition of the nobles as to a general unreadiness to absorb the new ideas. Thanks, possibly, to fear of missionary endeavor on the part of the sons of Eiríkr, who had also been subjected to Christian influences while in England, Earl Hákon Sigurðsson, a crafty, uxorious tyrant zealous for the old faith, succeeds to the royal power, if not title. He is overthrown by Ólaf Tryggvason (995) who, in an hour of defeat had been converted in the West and who now in a surprisingly short time, "with the energy of a Viking and the fanaticism of a recent convert," manages to Christianize Norway, however superficially.

However, all in all, a more solid influence, both by continued political and spiritual pressure, was exercised on Norway from the South, by way of Denmark which had been Christianized some two generations earlier, under Harold Bluetooth. It is of him the Large Jællinge Runestone boasts that "he made the Danes Christians." And for all the apostasy of his son, Svein Forkbeard, the ground won there was never wholly lost. Most of the missionaries and emissaries of the Hamburg-Bremen archiepiscopate take their way to the farther North through Denmark; and we may safely assume that most of the new cultural and religious thoughts of the time percolated to the North through the medium of its closest racial and geographical neighbor; just as, centuries before, the Cult of Othin had thus come.[4]

Obviously, with such century-long and multifarious contacts on two sides, it would be strange if West Scandinavian lays that came into being during, say, the tenth, or even the ninth, centuries, showed no influence of the new religion. It is to be observed, nevertheless, that the number of indubitable references to Christianity in the Edda is exiguous. There certainly are none in the mythological lays, barring the *Grógaldr;* and very few in the heroic lays. Is it safe, herefrom to infer, as has been done,[5] that the bulk of these lays originated in pre-Christian times?

Let us examine the cases of certain or possible references first.

The only direct occurrence of the word Christian in the entire Eddic corpus is to be found in *Grógaldr,* stanza 13, in the eighth 'galdr,' or magic spell, communicated by the *volva* to Svipdag:

> *þann gelk þér átta   ef þik úti nemr*
> *natt á niflvegi:*

at því miðr megi   þér til meins gørva
Kristin dauþ kona.

(This eighth heed thou,   if without find thee
a misty night on the moors:
lest ill o'ertake thee,   or untowardness,
from the wraith of a Christian
wretch!)

The poem is found only in Paper MSS. But all agreeing, there is no call for violently emending the reading *kristin dauþ kona* to *kynstr* ('magic'; this is a word occurring only in prose) *dauþrar konu,* or *kynstrdjorf* ('strong in magic') *kona,* as Gering proposed; or, still worse, to *kveldriþur koma,* as did Vigfússon. Finnur Jónsson, while admitting that the lay is not particularly old, infers from this reference that the poem must date from the very last times of paganism, or else the very first times after the introduction of Christianity;[6] and similarly Mogk.[7] But already in 1893 Falk[8] convincingly argued that the reference appears, rather, the attempt of a much later age—the 13th century—to stamp Gróa a heathen witch; a view which is further supported by the great dependence of this lay on other Eddic poems in point of vocabulary, and also by the evident sophistication and polish indicating conscious and recent authorship.

Few are, at present, inclined to deny a Christian tinge in the preparations for. Atli's burial in the Greenlandish *Atlamol.* But then, this lay shares with *Gripisspo* the distinction of having practical unanimity as to provenience and date.

All other occurrences are at best doubtful if not wholly negative.

At first blush, *Guthrúnarkvitha III* would seem to be a clear case of Christian influence: Guthrun, Atli's wife, clears herself of the suspicion of adultery with Thiothrek by successfully undergoing the ordeal of boiling water. We know that the *ketiltak* was introduced into Norway by Olaf the Saint. Unfortunately, however, this nevertheless does not furnish the eleventh century as the date *a quo.* On the one hand, as was pointed out by Maurer,[9] the ordeal is in the poem itself implied to be foreign, or still imperfectly known in the North, since it is still best managed by 'Saxi, the Southron lord,' stanza 7.[10] On the other, Guthrun declares herself ready 'to swear all oaths' as to her innocence 'by the white, holy stone'; by which, not improbably, is meant one of the phallic symbols so frequently encountered in the North. Still more rankly heathen would this reference be if we adopt Th. Petersen's recent suggestion[11] that the *jarknasteinar* which she fetches up from the bottom of the kettle (stanza 9) are identical with the phallic symbols of marriage by which she has just sworn. Nor need this naive mixing of Christian and heathen rites surprise us in early Christian times. Also, the punishment of the calumniatrix Herkja—she is cast into a foul swamp—certainly harks back to an age-old Pan-Germanic custom which supposedly disappeared with heathendom.[12]

However, we would be mistaken for these reasons to attribute the lay to the end of the heathen period, with Finnur Jónsson;[13] for it has all the ear-marks of a much later time. Not only is the spirit of Guthrun unbelievably conciliatory for an earlier period—she is deeply concerned about Atli's despondency although she lays her brothers' death at his door; and Atli is unfeignedly overjoyed at her cleansing herself of suspicion—but the very presence of Thiothrek at Atli's court is sufficient to establish late origin. On the other hand it is true that the mere fact of the lay not being made use of by Snorri or in the *Volsunga saga* should not be taken as evidence for very late origin. Its legendary form is so much at variance with the other lays treating of Guthrun and Atli that later authors may have chosen to disregard it.

Among the mythological poems, *Voluspa* is by some scholars supposed to be profoundly influenced by Christian ideas, whether directly or, as a whole, conceived as a counterblast against them; others as stoutly maintaining that its basic conception is purely heathen. In another connection[14] I have thrown out the suggestion that even this noble poem was, conceivably, didactic in purpose. Pondering deeply on the origin of all things, the past and future of the world, the poet wove together the shreds and wisps of cosmogonic and eschatological conceptions fluttering about from of old in myths and magic lore into a coherent whole which need not shun comparison with the Hebrew and Vedic accounts of Creation. He may have added a touch, he may have colored it with his own views of life, he may have contributed figures from his own mythopoetic, austere imagination—with what view in mind, no one will ever know for certain. Whether or no the apocalypse is dependent on Christian lore is purely a matter of opinion. At any rate, and that is the point here, it will never yield any chronological hold.

No doubt, a number of interpolations were made in his work and are plainly discernible as such; but I look with distrust on the vaticinations of Müllenhoff and Boer who, with enviable self-assurance, have shown us how to take the thing apart. I go still further in calling in question the wisdom of the greater number of editors who calmly omit the supplementary lines of the Paper MSS. in stanze 65 (*kømr enn ríki* etc.):

> semr hann dóma   ok sakar leggr,
> véskop setr   þaus vesa skulu.

> (he settles strife,   sits in judgment,
> and lays down laws   which shall last alway.)

because, forsooth, they do not agree with their *a priori* views as to non-Christian origin. And yet it is quite conceivable that *Voluspa* was composed a century or two after the introduction of Christianity.

In the case of *Havamal,* however, I readily grant that much of it may be classed among the oldest intellectual possessions of the North whose ethnic and ethical idea conceptions it bodies forth so admirably. As to stanzas 139, 140, few will at present be inclined to follow S. Bugge in his contention[15] that the conception of Othin as the "hanged god" (hangatýr) necessarily is dependent directly on the Crucifixion; especially since Sir James Frazer has shown the deceptiveness of such similarities.[16]

My reasons for thinking *Vafþrúþnismal* and *Grimnismal*—both generally, assigned to the tenth century—and especially *Alvíssmal,* considerably later, in fact, productions of the Icelandic Renaissance, I have set forth elsewhere.[17] The argument that the eschatological speculations such as fill the minds of these poets, as well as that of the *Voluspa* poet, betray the period of approaching Christianity and are meant to demonstrate the power and wisdom of the gods,[18] is of course worth considering, but far from compelling.

That *Skírnismal* cannot belong to the oldest lays seems evident from the fact pointed out by Mogk,[19] though not by him made use of sufficiently, that the ring Draupnir mentioned in a passage above suspicion of interpolation, belongs distinctly to later Baldr myths. Neither can the *vafrlogi,* vaguely referred to as established around a maiden of giant kin, be accounted old. It may be also pertinent to remember Neckel's observation[20] that the peculiarly erotic nature of the Gerth motif singles it out as foreign to the North.

The *Hárbarþsljóð* yield no definite hold whatever; for the suffixed article found in them sporadically, and supposedly indicating late origin, might easily have been added by the late copyist or the collector, no firm metrical structure interposing. If Finnur Jónsson[21] asserts considerable age for this lay because of its masterly dialogue and characterization, and finds corroboration for this view in the (supposedly) many accretions added in the course of time, this is in consonance with his general, distinctly Romantic, attitude of, like wine, "the older, the better," and *vice versa.* The present case aptly demonstrates the possibilities of this *in circulo* reasoning. Mogk's observation[22] on the poem: "Dass man die Götter zum Gegenstand solcher mannjafnaðr macht, zeigt, dass der alte Glaube in Verfall geraten. . . . " is by all means a *non sequitur;* for it postulates for Germanic antiquity a rigid orthodoxy and implied reverence such as is true of no polytheistic religion. If the analogy of Lucian be thought of who pours scorn on the old gods, certain Homeric episodes come to mind, too, which immediately destroy its force. In *þrymskviða,* regarded as unquestionably heathen, certainly no reverence is shown to Thor, dressed up in woman's weeds![23] In other words, there is no cogency in this reasoning, either way.

Very nearly the same is true of the argument afforded by *Lokasenna* which Finnur Jónsson[24] insists was composed during times when the old faith in the gods was as yet unshaken. According to him, the poet wished to depict the demoralization and irreligiosity of his own times—personified in that enemy of the gods, Loki—about to destroy the good old faith and morals. . . . wished to show that all this wickedness would in the end subside; that the disbelief of the times would give way to the truths of the old faith etc. etc." "In Christian times," he says in another place, "the composition of such a poem would be simply unthinkable, unless there was the express purpose to ridicule the old gods and heathen beliefs." "On the other hand, (still quoting), if the poem had a Christian author, then the conclusion would needs be altogether different—Thor, too, would then have been made to come off second-best, instead of saving the situation." But, as was pointed out by Sijmons,[25] it is hard to believe that so witty a poet would allow sheer physical force, represented by Thor, to have the last word against the superior vituperative powers of Loki. Nor does he, in fact: in the end, after all, the whole company of gods, including Thor, sit there shamed and sullied, even though Loki has been shown the door. The lay is a *jeu d'esprit,* a *chronique scandaleuse* of the Northern Olympos, irresponsible and bitter, and written with an abandon such as one is not accustomed to seek under the grey skies of the far North, but which yet is by no means without parallels there. Witness, not only the Gallic Kielland (and many others) of the nineteenth century, but the superbly Heinesque *Skíþaríma* of the fifteenth.

As to the two lays celebrating Thor's exploits, *Þrymskviða* and *Hymiskviða,* I confess to a feeling that they, too, are conscious art to a far greater degree than is generally thought to be the case; though a considerable difference in their relative age is to be admitted. Concerning their relation to the new faith, about the same holds true as of those already discussed: from their complete silence about it nothing can be safely inferred.

Neither *Baldrs draumar* nor *Hyndluljóð* will alter our conclusion that in no mythological poem can the mere absence of direct or indirect reference to Christianity be sufficient proof of pre-Christian origin.

And now, to view the problem from another angle: does silence about the new faith necessarily imply unacquaintance with it? By all means the possibility is to be reckoned with that the entirely 'heathen' viewpoint of various lays may be due, not to unadulterated paganism, but to the fact that Christianity was already regarded as a matter of course, a thing no longer debatable; or at least as a condition of affairs which may be reasonably assumed and does not need to be particularly mentioned, in a lay.

Just as we should expect, there is plentiful and significant blending of heathen and Christian elements in the poems of the skalds who were contemporary with the great upheaval.[26] Thus the talented Hallfrøðr

vandræðaskáld, the faithful follower of Ólaf Tryggvason, specifically mentions his regret at having to exchange Othin for the White Christ—Othin who yet has given him his gift of song![27] In other skalds, such as Eilífr Goðrúnarson, there is an odd mixture of Christian and pagan elements in the kennings. He and others plainly show the confusion, and at times, mental anguish, attendant on the great change. A century or so later, and the Icelander had no more squeamishness about composing on purely heathen themes than, say, a Christian Esthonian or Finnish runo singer in the nineteenth century about inditing a new song to Väinamöinen.

Specifically, we have to recall, in this connection, the singularly apathetic or tolerant, almost enlightened, attitude of the Icelandic community as a whole with regard to adherence to the 'older manner.' They kept their convictions in fairly separate compartments—much as we do. At one and the same time, clerics penned the *Postola sogur,* the *Maríu sogur,* and both clergymen and laymen amused themselves with the *Fornaldarsogur*—some of which reflect or, better, resuscitate, the spirit of the Viking Age with remarkable fidelity; and skalds composed not only spiritual lays like *Harmsal* and *Placitúsdrápa,* but also others which, like *Krakumal* and the poems in the *Orvarodd saga* and *Hervarar saga,* vie with the Helgi lays of the Edda in glorifying the slaughterous deeds of sea-kings. If we were wholly dependent on internal evidence we should class some of these as typical productions of the Viking Age. In *Krakumal,* e.g., neither language nor versification nor kennings would prevent assumption of, say, late tenth century origin.[28] As Finnur Jónsson himself says concerning the last stanza of that fine lay: "Than the author of these lines, none has expressed more tersely, more clearly, and more truthfully, the essentials of the old heathen conception of life and of death and of the life after death in Valholl with the god of war."[29] Would it be safe to infer that, hence, these lays are pre-Christian?

Again, the whole literary activity of men like Ari, Snorri, Saxo, and the many unnamed authors of sagas and Eddica minora, when dealing with subjects of the mythical age shows that they were able to project themselves with remarkable success into the spirit of heathen antiquity. In fact, most of them exhibit a decided lack of interest in Christian lore, but all the more in native myth and ancient history.[30] In other words, however slender this movement in extent, in scholarship, in great works, we are bound to class it properly as a Renaissance movement; and its products as, culturally, equivalent to those of the Renaissance proper and of eighteenth century Classicism. Like them it was essentially reminiscent, an upper class movement in ideals and presuppositions.

Granted that Goethe's *'Iphigenie,'* Racine's *'Phèdre,'* Thorvaldsen's *'Jason'* are not true Greek art: Yet are they, considered purely as works of art, fully equal, and probably superior, to many genuine works of antiquity unthinkingly vaunted to the skies. With respect to Old Norse lays we lack, as stated, the certain criteria to distinguish work of the Renaissance period from that of earlier times—lays of the ninth and tenth centuries, handed down by word of mouth, from poems of the twelfth and thirteenth centuries directly committed to parchment. It is not a detraction from any merit they may possess to surmise that a number of Eddic poems belong to the later date: they may be good though not old.

However, I do not wish to be understood to imply that all of the Eddic poems mentioned are late; only, that the nimbus of antiquity must be dispelled from poems that are, supposedly, "pagan in spirit."

Notes

[1] *Den Islandske Litteraturs Historie,* 1907, 35; no such categorical expression is given it in his comprehensive *'Den Oldnorske og Oldislandske Litteraturs Historie'* but the viewpoint is the same. Cf. especially pp. 37-54. In the following I quote from the second edition (1920 f).

[2] For the literature, see Sijmons, *Einleitung,* CCVI ff. Nothing of incisive value on the point here mooted has since appeared.

[3] Strongest, by Finnur Jónsson, *Norsk-Islandske Kultur- og Sprogforhold i 9. og 10. Århundrede,* chap. 1-5, who dwells too exclusively on the negative evidence of language.

[4] Cf. Chadwick, *the Cult of Othin,* chap. 3.

[5] E.g. Sijmons, *loc. cit.,* CCLXII.

[6] *Lit. Hist.* I, 220.

[7] *Grundriss,* 53 (607).

[8] *Arkiv f. n. Fil.* IX, 357.

[9] *Z. f. d. phil.* II, 443.

[10] Again, the abolishment of the ordeal by Hákon Hákonsson in 1247 is hardly a safe date *ad quem* because the very news of this act may have stimulated interest in it on the part of an Icelander.

[11] *Festschrift für Mogk,* 496 f.

[12] Cf. Detter-Heinzel, *Anmerkungen,* 510; *Hálfs saga,* ed. A. LeRoy Andrews, note p. 89.

[13] *Loc. cit.,* 220.

[14] *The Germanic Review,* I, 85.

[15] *Studier over de Norrœne Gudesagns Oprindelse,* p. 291 ff.

[16] The Golden Bough, Pt. IV, vol. 1, chap. V.

[17] *Loc. cit.* 74.

[18] Boer, *Die Edda,* II, 59; Finnur Jónsson, *Lit. Hist.* I, 44.

[19] *Loc. cit.,* 46 (600).

[20] *Die Überlieferungen vom Gotte Baldr,* 138.

[21] *Loc. cit.* I, 154.

[22] *Loc. cit.* 37 (591); cf. also Finnur Jónsson, *Lit. Hist.* I, 83 ff.

[23] Cf. Neckel, *Beiträge zur Eddaforschung,* 49.

[24] *Loc. cit.* I, 186 f.

[25] *Loc. cit.* CCCXLV.

[26] Cf. Kahle, *Das Christentum in der altwestnordischen Dichtung,* Ark. f. n. Fil. 1901, p. 3 ff.

[27] *Lausavisa* 7. (Finnur Jónsson, *Den norsk-islandske Skjaldedigtning, B.* 158.)

[28] The single suspicious kenning *odda messa* = 'the mass, or song, of the swords,' i.e. 'battle' would not militate seriously against comparatively early origin.

[29] *Loc. cit.* II, 152.

[30] This was observed by R. Keyser, *Efterladte Skrifter, Nordmændenes Yidenskabelighed* etc., I, 531.

Peter H. Salus and Paul B. Taylor (1967)

SOURCE: Introduction to *The Elder Edda: A Selection,* translated by Paul B. Taylor & W. H. Auden, Random House, 1967, pp. 13-32.

[*The following excerpt gives an overview of the Icelandic poetic tradition, with a description of the forms and meters used.*]

The Old Icelandic Poetic Tradition

Icelandic traditional poetry finds its origin in oral composition long before the art of writing was known or used in Scandinavia to record poetic texts. The poetry is traditional in the sense that it was transmitted by oral performance, and survived for centuries, passed from generation to generation, by oral transmission. There is no question of authorship, for the poet (*fornskáld*) was a performer rather than an originator. He recounted familiar material and his performance of a particular story differed from other performances in metrical and lexical interpretation. Two versions of the story of Atli's death (Attila the Hun) appear in the heroic poems of the *Edda,* one told economically, the other with an abundance of detail. Not until poetry was recorded in manuscript, most likely during the thirteenth century, was there a sense of a unique copy or of an 'authentic' version.

On the other hand, alongside eddaic, or traditional poetry, there existed a poetic tradition formal in character and individual in composition. This tradition is known as skaldic poetry, after the Icelandic word for poet—*skáld.* While the meter and diction of eddaic poetry are relatively simple, skaldic verse is composed in a variety of complex forms and employs a larger number of involved metaphors, or *kenningar.*

Old Icelandic traditional poetry appears to have derived from the same common Germanic stock as Old High German, Old English, and Old Saxon poetry. It shares the same verse line, known generally as the long alliterative line. It shares, apparently, the same lexical inventory, the same stereotyped diction. For example, the formula *firar i fólki* 'warriors among the folk', which appears in 'The Treachery of Asmund', occurs in the Old High German *Hildebrandslied* (*fireo in folche*) and in the Old English riddles (*firum on folce*), although the forms in which these poems appear suggest that their dates of composition span half a millennium. The similarity of meter and repetition of diction throughout the Germanic poetic traditions are evidences of the striking stability of traditional poetry, even before writing 'fixed' such forms.

The materials of the Germanic traditions are also comparable. The heroes of Icelandic heroic legends participate in the same events and belong to the same historical milieu as the heroes of Old High German and Old English heroic poetry. Old Icelandic poetry is unique, however, in the manner in which it treats traditional Germanic gods. There are only scant references and allusions to the Germanic pagan pantheon in Old English Chronicles and genealogies. Possibly the early arrival of Christianity in England—first with the converted Romans during the last years of the Empire's occupation, and then with the Celtic monasteries, and finally with the proselytizing Roman Catholic Church during the sixth century A.D.—seems to have inhibited the continuation of whatever poetic tradition might have existed about the older gods. Both Old English and Old High German traditional poetry successfully adapted their techniques to the incorporation of Christian materials, while the Old Icelandic tradition seems never to have been able to incorporate the new materials, except in a few isolated later literary imitations of the traditional form. The reason for this difference in development lies undoubtedly with the late arrival of Christianity in Scandinavia A.D. 1000), and the paucity of foreign clergy in Iceland before the four-

teenth century. Traditional myths appear to have been very popular in Iceland for three centuries after the conversion, while comparable poetry was being forcibly suppressed on the Continent and in the British Isles. Further, poetry as entertainment was obviously tolerated and encouraged in Iceland at a time when arts in Christian Europe were directed toward revelation of Scripture and declaration of Church doctrine. Of course, the lack of a substantial number of foreign clergy in Iceland prevented the literate decay—or corruption—of the Icelandic language that would have resulted from competition with the more acceptable language of Christian culture—Latin. The vernacular remained a rich means of literary expression and developed to a greater extent than elsewhere in Europe, with the possible exception of England under the enlightened King Alfred. Into Icelandic were translated French romances and Latin Chronicles. The thirteenth-century Icelander could read in his own language the romances of *Le Chevalier au Lion,* the legends of Merlin and Arthur, and the history of Charlemagne.

Icelandic traditional poetry differs from the other Germanic traditions in several other respects as well. First, the poetry falls syntactically into stanzas, or strophes, while the rest of Germanic traditional verse, with very few exceptions, is stichic; that is, without strophic division and with a considerable amount of emjambment, which is absent in the Icelandic. Second, eddaic poetry uses dialogue to a larger extent than either Old English or Old High German poetry. There is, proportionally, little poetic narrative in the Old Icelandic corpus. However, in place of narrative description there are frequently prose narrative links at the head or the foot of poems and even interpolated between strophes. These suggest either degeneration of older poetic narrative passages or a late editor's attempt to make clear a dramatic situation obscured by the economy of the verse. One must remember, however, that the intended audience of the poetry was familiar with the poet's material. No traditional performer would dream of trying to be 'original' in selecting material. His audience expected the old 'true' stories, and not 'made-up' ones, but awaited the skáld's personal inventions in dialogue. The mythological allusions which to the modern reader seem obscure and remote, must have been suggestive to the audience and readers of the thirteenth century. So the poetic performance could afford to be economical. It suggested rather than described the details of incidents.

Performance of traditional poems did not depend on dramatic suspense, since the audience was expected to know the outcome of the story anyway. The poet could, however, play on his audience's anticipation of the manner in which the inevitable was to come about. So, for example, in the heroic poems three different versions of the manner of Sigurd's death are offered in three separate poems. The fact of Sigurd's death could not be altered, but one could vary the details of *how* death comes.

Traditional Icelandic poetry also contains a good deal of what may be called 'courtesy-book' materials; that is, instruction relating to domestic and heroic rituals of everyday life. The same sort of materials appear in the Old English poetic *Maxims,* and in the Finnish *Kalevala.* Such an interest is evidence of how close these poetic traditions were to the priestly tradition of moral instruction from which these aphoristic guides to a good life probably derive.

Prosody

A reader brought up on English poetry since Chaucer—or, for that matter, on Greek and Latin poetry—may at first have some difficulty in 'hearing' Icelandic verse, for he will find nothing he can recognize as a metrical foot, that is to say, a syllabic unit containing a fixed number of syllables with a fixed structure of either (as in English) stressed and unstressed syllables or (as in Greek and Latin) long and short syllables.

In English verse, lines are metrically equivalent only if they contain both the same kind of feet, and the same number of syllables. But in Icelandic verse, as in Anglo-Saxon, all lines are metrically equivalent which contain the same number of stressed syllables: the unstressed syllables preceding or succeeding these may vary between none and three (occasionally more).

The principal meters in Icelandic poetry are two: Epic Meter (*fornyrðislag:* 'old verse') and Chant Meter (*ljóðaháttr*).

Epic Meter

This is essentially the same as the meter of *Beowulf.* Each line contains four stresses and is divided by a strongly marked caesura into two half-lines with two stresses each. (In printing Icelandic verse, the convention has been to leave a gap between the two half-lines: in our translations we have printed the whole line as it is normally printed in an English poem.)

The two half-lines are linked by alliteration. The first stressed syllable of the second half-line must alliterate with either or both of the stressed syllables in the first: its second stressed syllable must not alliterate.

All vowels are considered to alliterate with each other. In the case of syllables beginning with s, sc (sk) can only alliterate with sc, sh with sh, and st with st etc.: similarly, voiced and unvoiced *th* can only alliterate with themselves.

In Icelandic poetry, unlike Anglo-Saxon, the lines are nearly always end-stopped without enjambment, and are grouped into strophes varying in length from two to six or seven lines, the commonest strophe having four.

Depárt! You sháll not páss through
My táll gátes of tówering stóne:
It befíts a wífe to wínd yárn,
Nót to knów anóther's húsband.

Chant Meter

The unit is a couplet, the first of which is identical with the standard line of Epic Meter: the second contains three stresses instead of four (some hold that it only contains two), two of which must be linked by alliteration.

If you knów a fáithful fríend you can trúst,
    Gó óften to his hóuse:
Gráss and brámbles grów quíckly
    Upón an untródden tráck.

Speech Meter and Incantation Meter

Though these are officially classified as separate meters, they are better thought of as variations on Epic Meter and Chant Meter respectively. There is no case of a poem written entirely in either, nor even of a long sustained passage within a poem.

In Speech Meter (*málaháttr*), each half-line contains an extra stress, making six in all.

Líttle it ís to dený, lóng it ís to trável

In Incantation Meter (*kviðuháttr*), two couplets of Chant Meter are followed by a fifth line of three stresses, which is a verbal variation on the fourth line.

I know a tenth: if troublesome ghosts
    Ride the rafters aloft,
I can work it so they wander astray,
    Unable to find their *forms,*
    Unable to find their *homes.*

Quantity

In Icelandic verse, vowel length plays a role, though by no means as important a one as in Greek and Latin. For example, if a line ends in a single stressed syllable (a masculine ending), this may be either short or long: but if it ends in a disyllable, the first of which is stressed (a feminine ending), the stressed syllable must be short. For example, *Ever* would be permissible: *Evil* would not.

Icelandic, like Greek and Latin, is an inflected language: modern English has lost nearly all its inflections. This means that, in modern English, vowels which are short in themselves are always becoming long by position, since, more often than not, they will be followed by more than one consonant. For example, in the line

Of Man's first disobedience, and the fruit

there is, if it is scanned quantitatively, only one short syllable, *dis*.

Quantitative verse, as Robert Bridges has demonstrated, *can* be written in English, but only as a virtuoso feat. In our translations, therefore, we have ignored quantity. Also now and again, though actually very seldom, we have ignored the strong caesura between the two half-lines, when it seemed more natural to do so.

The Kenning

The kennings so common in Icelandic poetry are, like the epithets in Homer, metrical formulae but, unlike the latter, their meaning is not self-evident. *Diomedes of the loud war-cry* is a straightforward description, but no reader can guess that *Grani's Road* means the river Rhine, unless he already knows the Volsung legend in which Grani is the name of Sigurd's horse. The kenning may be exemplified by such usages as 'Meiti's plain' for the sea or 'Meiti's slopes' for the waves: Meiti was one of the sea-gods and thus stands in the same relationship to the sea as other gods stand to the land or the mountains. Other kennings are based on allusion to a mythological event: Odin was once hanged himself—see the 'Words of the High One'—he is therefore the 'gallow's load'; the Nibelung's treasure was submerged in the Rhine and all gold glitters, therefore gold can be called 'Rhine fire, or 'Rhine gravel'. In later verse the kennings become most complicated. For example, falconry caused 'hawk's land' to become a kenning for 'arm'. The wearing of arm-rings of gold caused 'gold' to be called 'arm-fire'. These were then combined so that 'hawk's land's flame' means 'gold', etc.

The Riddles and Charms

Poetic composition of riddles was principally an exercise of scholastic wit throughout the Middle Ages. Hundreds of Latin riddles in poetic form have survived. In general they are puzzles in which some object or phenomenon is described; the reader or listener is expected to 'solve' the puzzle and state the object. Riddle-making was equally popular in the vernacular. In Old English, for example, almost a hundred survive.

The lack of a Latin-educated clergy in Iceland accounts for the non-existence of such a tradition there, but a similar type of riddle does appear in Old Icelandic poetry. In the *Heidreks saga,* Odin disguises himself as Gestumblindi and challenges the king to guess his riddles, all of which are elaborate metaphors for common things. Since Odin knows the answers himself, the whole affair is a sport, a rather elaborate parlor game. But, when Gestumblindi tires of the sport he asks a question of Heidrek, the answer to which no one can know except Odin: 'What said Odin in the ear of Baldur before he was carried to the fire?' The same question ends his battle of wits with Vafthruthnir, and the loser of such a challenge

has usually wagered his head. A sort of riddle occurs in the *Halfs saga* poem 'The Treachery of Asmund' in the dreams of Innstein. Half fails to guess the true portent of the dreams (or, more likely, is too bold to be prudent even though he suspects ill of his host), and is subsequently killed. The riddles of Gestumblindi and the dreams of Innstein are puzzles demanding a correct interpretation. They appeal to a process of thought rather than to an inventory of knowledge.

The riddles in the mythological poems of the *Edda* are of a different character and appear to serve a different function. The questions Thor poses of Alvis, and Alvis' subsequent replies, make up a textbook of poetic diction for common things in each world. The purpose of the inquisition, outside of the immediate dramatic situation in which Thor guards a goddess by keeping a dwarf at bay, is mnemonic. The poetic structure preserves, and makes memorable, poetic synonyms for important vocabulary items. Such emphasis on the *mot juste* for a thing, according to the speaker is an example of Germanic name-magic, associated with the primitive belief that knowledge of the proper name for a thing gives the knower the ability to evoke the object, or its power. There is a saga incident in which several Icelanders, floundering in a small boat at sea, want to pray for deliverance from their peril, but they have to seek someone who knows the name of God. Once he is found, they are saved.

'The Lay of Vafthrudnir' is also mnemonic, but an exposition of myth rather than a lexicon. The riddles, or questions, in the poem, however, are pertinent to the dramatic situation as well. Challenging an opponent with riddles is a means whereby Odin can coerce giants and the dead to reveal more of their wisdom than they would wish to, especially if they knew who their inquisitor was. Odin must disguise himself so that the challenge will be accepted. Odin searches for knowledge of the fate of the gods, so his questioning leads toward revelation of the future, though it begins with asking for exposition of the past. Proper questioning—that is, ritual questioning—functions like a charm. It compels response unless the questioned person does not know the answer, in which case the inquisition ends. This is, in a sense, Odin's security, for he can end the challenge at any point by asking the unanswerable question.

Riddles also suggest the Nordic fascination with the apparent relationship between the structure of language and the structure of the cosmos. For the Scandinavians the wisest man—he who knows most of the structure of the cosmos—is also the most skilful poet. It is, hence, appropriate that the god who is compelled to search out the facts of the cosmogonic scheme is the god of poetry. Before Odin, the giants possessed the mead of poetry, and the giants still have knowledge unknown to the gods. They can, for example, remember a time when the gods did not yet exist, and they must, therefore, have been present at the birth of language. Knowing the name of something and knowing the events of the past imply some control over the future. There is in the Nordic mind a subtle relationship, and a necessary one, between an event and the language with which it is described or anticipated. Questions and answers, then, seek to put into a harmonious relationship man's thought and the facts of the world about him which he cannot fully comprehend or control.

Charms, as T. S. Eliot so nicely puts it in *The Music of Poetry,* 'are very practical formulae designed to produce definite results, such as getting a cow out of a bog'. Charms derive from priestly incantations which solicited gods and forces of nature to fulfil their roles in turning the wheel of seasons. By the time priestly incantation transformed into poetry, and poetry found a means of being recorded in manuscript, charms had developed into ritual accompaniment for the warrior on the battlefield as well as domestic tool in the home. Charms render weapons more efficient and a hero's courage more resolute. Charms are the healer's accompaniment in the fabrication and application of remedies for wounds and disease.

The Old Icelandic word for charm is *galdr,* associated with the verb *gala* 'to sing, to chant'. They are extant in Old High German (*galtar*) and Old English (*galdor*), but references to charms are more plentiful in the literature of Iceland and Finland, where magic continued to influence domestic life and thought for centuries after the arrival of the Christian Church. Charms in Ireland and Wales seem to have degenerated into curses and insults after the arrival of Christianity and there are comparable curses and insults in the flyting episodes of Old Icelandic heroic poetry, where exchange of words between antagonists before a battle seems to have lost its character of evoking divine assistance in favour of heaping imprecations.

Charms exist intact in Icelandic only in runes—the pre-Christian Germanic form of writing. Runes ('mysteries, secrets') are magic signs whose individual shape, or *stafr* (English *stave*), represents an incantation—that is, a charm itself. Runes are not a practical form of writing, but priestly inscription for divination or sortilege. Odin learns effective charms in the form of runes in 'The Words of the High One', and each rune (there are normally sixteen runes in the Scandinavian runic 'alphabet') is associated intrinsically with a particular charm. Odin's first charm, for example, is a 'Help' charm, and Help-charms may be associated with the N-rune, which represents the word *Nauðr* 'Need'. If one scratched this rune . . . on a fingernail, it should evoke aid for a particular distress. N-rune charms seem to have been used especially for delayed child-birth.

For Odin, it appears, achieving knowledge of charms consists merely in learning runes, rather than in learning the incantations associated with each rune. Incantations are still extant in Old English and Old High German but they no longer exist in Old Icelandic poetry. Runic inscriptions, however, survive in great numbers in Scandinavia, usually as inscriptions on stone grave-markers (there are over two thousand in Sweden alone). These are evidence of a traditional association between runic charms and an intent to protect the dead. The Christian Church officially disapproved of the use of runes because of their suggestion of pagan religious practices. Runes were outlawed for some time in Iceland and their practitioners were punished as witches. Some grave-markers have both roman and runic letters, as if the inscriber was assuring success by appealing to both pagan and Christian powers.

The function of runic charms in Old Icelandic poetry varies. Some charms, probably older than the others in origin, directly solicit forces of nature. Charms for delayed birth, for example, demand nature to fulfil itself. Odin's ninth charm calms waves and winds so that seamen may return safely to shore. His second charm, for healers, seeks to improve the body's resistance to infection and pain. These may be classified as domestic charms, and their lineal descendants seem to be popular medicinal recipes.

Odin also knows charms for the battlefield, such as those which protect against the weapons of others. Odin's third charm blunts his enemies' weapons, and his fourth gives him power to escape fetters. His seventh protects his companions from the fires of opponents (burning others within a hall or house was considered the worst of heroic behavior, and is the cruel culmination of the feuds involving the family of Njal in *Njals saga.* Asmund fires the hall in which his guests sleep in 'The Treachery of Asmund'). Such charms are often anti-charms, for swords, if made of iron, were already considered charmed.

Besides these beneficial charms, Odin knowns another kind of magic, *seid* 'sorcery, magic', which is used to bring misfortune upon another. His tenth charm, which keeps spirits from their proper resting place, is an example. His sixteenth charm, a form of love-magic to deceive a desirable girl, is undoubtedly a form of *seid* as well.

Evocation of the dead involves still another kind of magic, known as *ergi,* 'unnaturalness, filth'. This power can be used to transform oneself (and Odin is a notorious shape-changer) or to bring about unnatural behavior in another, such as cowardice or homosexuality. Odin's twelfth charm, reviving the dead which hang from the gallows, seems to be *ergi* (a filth-rune). Skirnir, in 'Skirnir's Ride', threatens Gerd with *ergi* if she will not submit herself to Frey. Though other threats have failed, this one frightens her into submission, for she knows that *ergi* can transform her so that she will ever be loathsome to men, or so that her lust for men will be unnatural.

Edgar C. Polomé (1969)

SOURCE: "Some Comments on Voluspá, Stanzas 17-18," in *Old Norse Literature and Mythology: A Symposium*, edited by Edgar C. Polomé, University of Texas Press, 1969, pp. 265-90.

[*In the following essay, Polomé analyzes an important creation episode in the* Voluspá, *one of the greatest Eddic poems.*]

Among the controversial problems of Eddic cosmology, the identification of the Scandinavian trinity that presides over the creation of man is certainly one of the most disputed. This creation episode is related in two stanzas of the *Voluspá* ("The Seeress' Prophecy"), whose wording reads as follows in Dr. Hollander's rhythmical translation:[1]

> To the coast then came,   kind and mighty,
> from the gathered gods   three great Æsir;
> on the land they found,   of little strength,
> Ask and Embla,   unfated yet.
>
> Sense they possessed not,   soul they had not,
> being nor bearing,   nor blooming hue,
> soul gave Óthin,   sense gave Hœnir,
> being, Lóthur,   and blooming hue.

In like manner, Snorri Sturluson[2] gives this account in the *Gylfaginning* ("Beguiling of Gylfi"): "While the sons of Borr[3] were walking along the shore, they discovered two tree trunks, took them up, and made men out of them; the first gave them breath and life, the second wit and movement, and the third appearance, speech, hearing and vision." Here, the gods are not explicitly mentioned by name, but the structural similarity of the two versions of the creation myth is obvious.

Several attempts have been made to find parallels to this myth, without great success, however. Thus, it is quite striking to notice that Hesiod, in his *Works and Days,* reports that "Zeus created a . . . race of men . . . from the ash-trees"[4] since the Eddic name of the first man, *Askr,* is precisely the Germanic word for 'ash-tree,' although the parallelism of the two traditions does not go any further. Friedrich von der Leyen[5] compared the Eddic account to an Indian tale in which a sculptor, a goldsmith, a weaver, and a priest are seen traveling together. After cutting a piece of sandalwood into the effigy of a pretty woman, the sculptor successively hands it over to the weaver, who dresses it, and to the goldsmith, who adorns it with jewels. Then, the priest succeeds through his incantations in breathing life into it, after which the problem arises as to who will get the pretty creature as his wife.

If the point of departure is apparently the same—a human being fashioned out of a piece of wood—the elaboration upon the theme is obviously totally different. The Hindu tale is a curious apologue intended to throw light upon a problem of casuistry; it describes step by step the shaping of a human being who is endowed with life only in the final stage, as the crowning act of a long process. In the Scandinavian tradition, on the contrary, there is no trace of a similar process: the triad of gods creates the primordial *couple* straight away. We witness a *creative act,* performed through *direct divine intervention;* through it, the pieces of wood immediately acquire the fullness of life.[6] In other words, the characteristic feature of the Eddic account is the *unity* of the creative act in spite of the *distribution of the human attributes by three different gods.* This has evidently been the understanding of the exegetes of the *Voluspá* stanzas who have also tried to reduce the triad of gods to one by considering Lóðurr and Hœnir merely as poetic creations due to Christian influence[7] or as hypostases of Othin.[8] Without drawing such far-reaching conclusions, we cannot fail to notice with surprise that, whereas the attribution of vital breath to the human being normally falls within Othin's province, this is not also the case with the inspired cerebral activity which Hœnir's gift implies.

Let us reexamine the facts, text in hand.[9] From Othin, man receives *ond,* in which everyone agrees to recognize the 'breath of life' (it would, indeed be rather imprudent to translate it as 'soul,' considering the Christian implications of this term, which the Old Norse substantive acquired only at a later date; literally, *ond* means 'breath'). Such a gift is quite in keeping with the very nature of Othin as the sovereign god meting out *life-giving* power. Besides, it should be remembered that his name in Proto-Germanic, **Wōðanaz,* is ultimately derived from an Indo-European theme **awē-,* meaning 'to blow,' whose participial form, **wē-nt-,* supplied the Indo-European word for 'wind.' Further analysis of this theme led George van Langenhove to posit a root **H₂éw-,* which would designate the 'life-giving power.'[10] But the name of Othin, **Wōðanaz,* is more directly connected with the Western Indo-European stem **wāt-,* which appears in Lat. *vātes,* 'soothsayer,' OIr. *fáith,* 'seer, prophet,' and Ger. *Wut,* 'rage'; Adam of Bremen himself considered the name of Othin as synonymous with *furor.* Actually, Othin is the inspired god, the prince of poets, the magician *par excellence,* the master of divinatory runes—attributes which agree perfectly with the meaning of his name, of which the stem denotes inspired cerebral activity and the suffix possession and mastery.[11]

The same meaning, 'inspired cerebral activity,' should also be ascribed to ON *óðr,* which is usually translated 'mind,' 'reason (understanding),' or 'sense' in the context of the *Voluspá* stanza, where it appears as Hœnir's gift to man. The noun *óðr* can indeed hardly be dissociated from the adjective *óðr,* which means 'mad, frantic' or 'furious, vehement' or 'eager, impatient,' meanings which point either to strong emotional stress or to lack of control of the power of reasoning. This is in keeping with the fact that the inspired mental activity expressed by Germanic *wōð- can verge on ecstasy, as shown by the name of the poetic mead stimulating inspiration: óðrœrir, literally 'rousing to the point of ecstasy.'[12] That ON óðr denotes an 'inspired mental activity,' and not merely 'intelligence,' conceived as the faculty of reasoning, is further confirmed by its second meaning, 'poetry,' especially in the skaldic phrase designating the poet as óðar smiðr, 'smith of inspired thought.'[13] Actually, the only context in which the meaning 'intelligence, mind, reason' is assumed for óðr is in stanza 18 of the *Voluspá,* and in modern Norwegian the noun continued to exist as a neuter under the form od, besides a feminine oda, with the meaning 'strong desire' (sterk lyst).[14] The current interpretation of óðr as 'mind, intelligence, reason' in the Eddic passage under reference is ascribable to the parallel text of Snorri, where the second god participating in the creation of man endows him with vit ok hrœring, usually translated 'wit and movement,' with special focus on vit, because the association of 'movement' with 'intelligence' sounds rather awkward. However, hrœring does not necessarily apply to a physical movement: in the compound hugarhrœring, as well as in numerous contexts and phrases like geðs hrœringar, it indicates emotion and may therefore, better than vit, reflect the connotations of the Eddic noun óðr, which Leiv Heggstad glosses more adequately hugrørsla (movements of the mind).[15] It is consequently legitimate to question Georges Dumézil's statement:

> la répartition des tâches est claire: le premier dieu fait le grand miracle, il anime, donne aux deux planches cette force vitale qui est commune à l'homme, aux animaux et aux plantes; le second leur donne ce qui est le propre de l'homme, l'esprit, l'intelligence ou la raison; le troisième leur donne les moyens de s'exprimer, la parole et l'apparence ou les "belles couleurs,"

because it implies that:

> sous le grand dieu Odhinn, qui fait le don primordial et la plus général (la vie), Hœnir patronne donc la partie profonde, invisible de l'intelligence, "l'intelligence en soi", tandis que Lôdhurr patronne l'intelligence incarnée dans le "système de relation", dans les organes, accrochée aux sens, au gosier, à la peau, comme une araignée à sa toile.[16]

Dumézil's assumption that Hœnir is the god of careful thought is the basis of this interpretation, which would confirm the ingenious etymology of the name *Hœnir* proposed by George van Langenhove, namely its derivation from a Germanic prototype *hōnija-, reflecting Indo-European *kōniyo-, derived from the root *kō-, 'make keen, sharpen,' Hœnir being the 'sharpener'[17]—the god who sharpens the wit.

This view is based mainly on the interpretation of Hœnir's attitude on two occasions: (a) when Þjazi, in the shape of an eagle, requests of him a full share of the gods' meal,

Hœnir does not answer, but cannot help breathing heavily with anger;[18] (b) whenever he attends the þing as chief of the Vanir and fails to get Mímir's advice, he does not take a stand but merely says: ráði aðrir (Let others decide).[19] Dumézil considers Hœnir's refusal as the only wise attitude under the circumstances and contrasts it with Loki's rash decision, which turns to disaster for him when he tries to beat Þjazi with a stick after snatching four pieces of beef away from the sacred table to feed him. Hœnir knows the giant is not supposed to receive any of the food of the gods, but since he can do nothing about it, he remains passive, though not without emotion.

In the case of his refusal to make decisions in the absence of Mímir, Dumézil offers an ingenious explanation:

> Le binôme Hœnir-Mîmir . . . , réuni, fait un chef parfait et . . . , séparé, ne vaut plus rien. . . . [It constitutes] une juste image du mécanisme de nos meilleures pensées: devant une question, une difficulté, nous suspendons d'abord notre réaction et notre jugement, nous savons d'abord ne pas agir et nous taire, ce qui est déjà une grande chose; et puis nous écoutons la voix de l'inspiration, le verdict qui nous vient de notre savoir et de notre expérience antérieurs ou de l'expérience héréditaire de l'espèce humaine ou de plus loin encore, cette parole intérieure qui, comme la Raison des philosophes ou la "conscience collective" des durkheimiens, est à la fois en nous et plus que nous, autre que nous. Mîmir, près de Hœnir . . . représente cette partie mystérieuse, intime et objective, de la sagesse, dont Hœnir représente la partie extérieure, individuelle, l'attitude conditionnante. Hœnir a l'air d'un sot? Il pourvoit seulement au vide, à l'attente que remplira Mîmir.[20]

For all the brilliant style of the French scholar, one cannot help wondering whether he has not begged the question. All the texts show is that Hœnir is incapable of acting on his own. If this does not make him weak in wits, as has often been assumed,[21] it hardly points him out as the "dieu de la pensée réfléchie"; he is much rather the instrument of godly inspiration, the one who utters the message conveyed by outside wisdom. Therefore, he remains mute in the discussions of the þing of the Vanir when this inspiration, embodied by Mímir, fails him; therefore, he is described as the most fearful of the Æsir in the *Sogubrot,*[22] since he cannot act without being advised; therefore, also, he appears in a sacerdotal function after Ragnarok, when he will hlautvið kjósa, that is, consult the oracles according to the age-old practice of picking up sticks marked with divinatory symbols.[23] Here, again, interpreting the signs given by an outside Power, he is the vehicle of divine inspiration. It is also in this capacity that he is instrumental in endowing man with 'inspired mental activity' (óðr).[24]

But, to return to the third component of the divine triad, what do we actually know about Lóðurr? Very little indeed. Aside from the reference to him in the stanza under consideration, he appears only in a poetic paraphrase designating Othin by the name of 'friend of Lóðurr,'[25] a phrase which tells us nothing new, since the association of this divine personage with the majestic sovereign god of the *Edda* is already known. Besides, in a considerable number of parallel kennings Othin is associated with the most diverse gods.[26] In short, Lóðurr is practically unknown to us except by the role he plays in the creation of man according to Scandinavian mythology.

This has not prevented exegetes from indulging in numerous conjectures concerning Lóðurr. Numerous are those who, relying upon the parallel association between Othin, Hœnir, and Loki in Snorri's prose *Edda,* wish to compare Lóðurr with Loki, but one would seek in vain for any cogent argument backing up this hypothesis. Proceeding from the idea that Loki was a god of fire, these authors merely resort to etymology in endeavoring to associate the two names more closely. Because the nature assigned to Loki is most debatable[27] and because, on the other hand, Lóðurr has apparently not the least connection with fire, it is superfluous to analyze the multiple etymological reconstructions advanced in order to justify this parallel.[28] In an important study devoted to Loki, E. J. Gras[29] has, however, attempted to bring new elements into the debate by comparing the name *Lóðurr* with the name *logapore,* which appears beside *wigiponar* and *wodan* in the runic inscription of the Nordenhof brooch, and with the name of the Brabantine demon *Lodder.*

This hypothesis is based on three postulates, which Jan de Vries[30] has seriously questioned:

1. the identification between Loki, Lóðurr, and the demon Lodder, also known by the name *Loeke;*

2. the interpretation of runic *logapore* as a divine name, related to ON *logi* 'fire';

3. the survival in the Lodder-Loeke of Brabant of an ancient Germanic divinity.

The idea that Loki, Lóðurr, and Lodder belong to the same religious sphere had already been expressed by H. Grüner-Nielsen and Axel Olrik in 1912.[31] By describing Lodder as a definite, facetious, nocturnal creature, most frequently a kind of will-o'-the-wisp ("et eller andet natligt gækkende væsen, snarest af lygtemandsartig art"), they manage to associate the Brabantine demon rather plausibly with the Lokke of Scandinavian folklore, which appears especially in connection with certain natural phenomena such as the vibration of the air as a result of heat or the sulfurous odor following a flash of lightning, with certain sacrificial ceremonies on the family hearth, with certain weeds and vermin (particularly spiders), as well as in phrases referring to lying and deceit.[32] However, this association remains superficial, because the

Brabantine Lodder is somewhere halfway between a werewolf and a fiery ghost,[33] and he definitely appears to be very remote from the Scandinavian conception of the demon of the hearth, to say nothing of the possibility of comparing him to the Eddic god Loki. Several years ago, I suggested[34] considering him as a 'wanderer'—a sort of *terrā vagans*—a hypothesis which is confirmed by the use of the term *lodder* to designate a vagrant in Middle Dutch and by the clear etymological parallel of Russ. *lytá*, 'to wander,' and I see no reason to reconsider this opinion. Nothing, indeed, justifies the assertion that the Lodder of Brabant is a distant reminiscence of any Germanic god. On these grounds the third postulate of Miss Gras's hypothesis can be safely dismissed. Indeed, if Lodder is only a local variant of the *kludde,* a demonic horse which hurls into the water the drunken peasant who thinks to be dealing with one of his own animals that has not been taken back to the stable,[35] one can hardly see what such an equine and aquatic demon would have in common with the god Loki: To be sure, it could be objected that Othin's horse, Sleipnir, was born to Loki, transformed into a mare, after intercourse with Svaðilfœri, stallion of the giant builder of the stronghold of the gods, as is told in Chapter 42 of *Gylfaginning.* But, enlarging upon a suggestion of Jan de Vries, Georges Dumézil[36] has clearly shown that the bringing forth of Sleipnir is a merely episodic event in the life of the Scandinavian god: "si Loki se transforme ici en jument, c'est que, seul des dieux scandinaves, il a une faculté illimitée de métamorphoses animales." This is not the only case in which Loki has functioned as a female in order to give birth to some monstrous creature. The short *Voluspá,* inserted in the *Hyndluljóð,* gives another example of it in stanza 43: "with child he grew from the guileful woman. Thence are on earth all ogres sprung."[37] His association with the horse is accordingly rather fortuitous: it just happened to be necessary to deprive the master-builder of the stronghold of the Æsir of the aid of his horse Svaðilfœri in order to provide the gods with an excuse for not meeting their obligations to him; hence, the *ad hoc* metamorphosis of Loki to distract the stallion from his duty. Furthermore, the superficiality of possible resemblances disregarded, there is a matter of principle involved. Lodder is a strictly localized demon of little importance. Nowhere in the region where Lodder appears do we find any trace of Loki. The latter does not appear anywhere in pagan tradition as an aquatic and equine demon; if the Lokke of Scandinavian folklore is actually a distant survival of Loki,[38] there is a gap between these traditions and those to which the Brabantine Lodder was supposed to go back. How can one, in this case, reasonably conclude in favor of the identity of Lodder, Lokke, and Loki?

What about Lóðurr? It is hard to see what would make his association with Lodder possible, except for a vague etymological possibility of considering the Dutch term as derived from a Germanic stem *lōðr-.*[39] It would then be necessary to show that this god, associated with Othin in the work of creation, could have degenerated into an aquatic spirit—or should it be assumed that the role assigned to Lóðurr results from a promotion of a secondary demonic being, similar to the modern Lodder or Lokke? All of this is, indeed, too hypothetical.[40]

As for Miss Gras's second point, if *logaþore* is assumed to be identifiable with Lóðurr—which would entail the identification of Hœnir with Donar, the triads Oðinn-Lóðurr-Hœnir and Wodan-Logaþore-Wigiþonar being interchangeable[41]—the same problems as with Lóðurr arise: how to explain his importance with regard to the ghostlike nature of the Brabantine Lodder in view of his association with such gods as Donar and Wodan in Old High German in the seventh century?

But is it really justifiable to associate Logaþore with Lóðurr? While admitting that the term *logaþore* is rather difficult to interpret, Wolfgang Krause, in the first edition of his *Runeninschriften im älteren Futhark*,[42] subscribed to the hypothesis of Friedrich von der Leyen and W. von Unwerth, who consider *logaþore* an alternate form, under the conditions of Verner's Law, of Gmc. **lohaþoraz,* from which Lóðurr would have developed. It would originally mean 'der mit Feuer Andringende,' the second element being related to the Old Norse verb *þora,* 'have the courage to do something'. But the only argument which Krause presented in favor of this interpretation was the fact that one of the two gifts Lóðurr grants to man in the eighteenth stanza of *Voluspá* is *lá,* that is, 'vital warmth,' as the Old Norse term is usually translated.[43] Upon closer examination, the grounds on which the translation of ON *lá* by 'vital warmth' was based, however, appear to be most questionable. First of all, this meaning is not confirmed by any parallel passage; it merely results from a rather disputable etymological comparison of a conjectural Germanic prototype **wlahō* with Lat. **volca,* contained in *Volcanus,* and with Skt. *ulkā,* 'heat of the fire.'[44] However, the name *Volcanus* is presumably a borrowing from the pre-Italic Mediterranean culture, like the fire-god who bears it,[45] whereas the Old-Indic term *ulk* means in fact 'meteor, fiery appearance in the sky' and is related to Gk. [*awlax*] [*lamprōs*] (Hesychios), [*ēlektōr*], 'bright sun.'[46] Accordingly, the interpretation of ON *lá* as 'vital warmth' remains unfounded, and this line of argument for relating Logaþore to Lóðurr has to be abandoned. One would then be tempted to subscribe to de Vries's stern judgment about Logaþore: "Die oft versuchte Gleichsetzung mit dem altnordischen Gott Lóðurr ist nur eine etymologische Spielerei und ist auch sachlich unbedingt abzulehnen."[47] But historians of Germanic religion find it difficult to give up the tempting identification Lóðurr = Logaþore = Loki, and if Karl Helm considers the identification Logaþore = Lóðurr only as "quite possible,"[48] interpreting Logaþore as a "Feuerdämon," his disciple Ernst A. Philippson endeavors to save the whole set of correlations of divinities through the expedient of an ingenious etymology. Pointing out that Loki is handsome and attractive in appear-ance, but evil in conscience,[49] Philippson asserts that Loki's beauty evokes the gift of a 'beautiful complexion' (*lito góða*), attributed to Lóðurr, while Lóðurr's name suggests the wiliness of Loki. According to him, *Lóðurr* and *logaþore* are, indeed, closely related with OE *logðor, logeðer,* which Joseph Bosworth and T. Northcole Toller[50] translate 'plotting mischief, wily, crafty'—epithets perfectly fitting the essential trait of Loki's personality.[51] Furthermore, his name could be merely a hypocoristic of the appellative contained in *logaþore.*

Without endeavoring to discuss in detail the cogency of this etymology, first proposed by Willy Krogmann[52] and now adopted by various runologists,[53] it must be recognized that the argument set forth in order to connect *Lóðurr* to these terms is hardly convincing. The mere possibility of an etymological explanation of the name *Lóðurr* by comparison with *logaþore* and an Old English term meaning 'cunning', and the rather vague statement that the attribution of a beautiful complexion to man by *Lóðurr* evokes the purely external beauty of Loki,[54] is not enough to legitimately justify the conclusion that *Lóðurr* is just another name for *Loki* in the divine triad involved in the creation of man in Scandinavian cosmogony.

But who, then, is Lóðurr? Attempts have also been made to identify him with Lotherus, the son of Dan, the eponymous hero of the Danes, and of a Teutonic noblewoman, Grytha. According to the account of Saxo Grammaticus,[55] Lotherus dethroned his brother Humblus and was then killed by the people. But this identification is erroneous because this tale is related to the epic tradition of the struggle between the Huns and the Goths, and Saxo's Lotherus is to be identified with Hloðr, appearing in the *Hervarar saga.* The Danish chronicler has obviously related this name to the Norse poetic epithet *hløðir,* 'destroyer, vanquisher,' when, in fact, it came by metathesis from *Hrøþil,* the Old Norse form of the Old English personal name *Hréþel* of the king of the Geats in *Beowulf.*[56] Thus, no more than Humblus ultimately goes back to the same origin as Gaulish (Mars) Camulus[57] is Lotherus identifiable with Lóðurr.

It would be rather futile to enumerate all the attempts to explain this term through etymology. Those who wanted at all costs to compare Lóðurr with Loki sought by ingenious parallels to attribute to his name an original meaning in keeping with the assumed essential traits of Loki's personality. Thus, Lóðurr is the 'seducer' (*der Verführer*) for Hugo Gering,[58] who compares MHG *luoder,* 'bait.' F. Holthausen[59] is thinking of Loki's perfidy when he relates *Lóðurr* to ON *lómr,* 'treachery,' mainly preserved in compounds. Such constructions, which usually neglect to analyze in detail the formation of the Scandinavian divine name, can hardly be taken very seriously—no more, actually, than the hypothesis of George van Langenhove[60] which derives *Lóðurr* from IE **lāturo-,* from the root **lā(t)-,* 'to be concealed,' attested by . . . Lat. *lateo,* and so on, with the primary meaning 'he who conceals, makes invisible,' or 'he who is concealed, the invisible one.' None of these interpretations, indeed, shows any direct relation with the text of the only Eddic stanza in which the name they pretend to explain occurs. In the absence of any other positive element related to Lóðurr, would it not seem obvious to look first for the basis of a plausible explanation in the context in which he appears? And rather than overemphasize his association with Othin and Hœnir in the creational work by taking *Lóðurr* for a hypothetical surname of Loki merely because Loki forms, in other circumstances, a triad with the two aforementioned gods, isn't it preferable to examine more closely the attributes with which he endows man?

Before Lóðurr's intervention, man was without that which the Norse text calls *lá, læti,* and *lito góða.* What is to be understood by these terms?

The last of these attributes—in the Old Norse nominative plural *litir góðir,* literally 'good colors'—is the indication of good health. The Old Norse term *litr,* 'complexion,' corresponds to OE *wlite,* which designates physical beauty, a sign of noble ancestry with the Anglo-Saxons as with the Germanic peoples in general. It will be remembered that Beowulf differs from his companions by his handsome appearance, which the poet describes with the term *wlite* and *ænlic ansȳn,* 'peerless appearance.'[61] In this connection it is worth noticing that in the *Gylfaginning* Snorri uses precisely the Old Norse term *ásjóna* 'appearance,' corresponding with OE *ansȳn,* in order to designate the attribute indicated by the phrase *lito góða* in *Voluspá.*

The second trait characterizing Lóðurr's intervention in the creation of man is *læti,* but the text of the Eddic stanza hardly insists on it, since it is only cited among the things man is deprived of and is not repeated, like the other two, among the attributes the various gods confer upon him. Its interpretation does not present much of a problem: ON *læti* is a well-attested term, with the meanings 'noise, voice,' 'gestures, attitude.' It corresponds to MHG *gelæze,* 'behavior, conduct,' and is closely related to ON *lát,* 'manners.'[62] This is probably also the meaning that should be ascribed to it in the Eddic stanza, as Gering does,[63] in view of the parallelism with the first line of stanza 39 of *Grípisspá—lit hefir þú Gunnars ok læti hans* ("thou hast the appearance and the manners of Gunnar")—where *læti* is contrasted with *mælska,* 'way of speaking,' in the following line. Nevertheless, it should also be pointed out that Snorri mentions speech (*malit*) specifically among the gifts of the third divinity creating man, but in association with sight (*sjón*) and hearing (*heyrn*). In addition to external appearance (*ásjóna*), Snorri actually attributes to the divinity the principal sensory perceptions, which is apparently not the case in the corresponding Eddic stanza.

But the third attribute is presumably the key to the whole problem. What does *lá* designate? It has been pointed out

that the meaning 'vital warmth,' most often ascribed to it, is hardly plausible, What of other interpretations?

The translation 'blood' has also been proposed[64] by a rather audacious interpretation of the Old Norse substantive *lá,* 'sea, wave, shoal water along the shore.'[65] It has been attempted to make the implied shift more plausible by referring to the kenning for 'blood': *oddlo,* appearing in the fifth line of the eighth stanza of the *Hákonarmál* of Eyvindr skáldaspillir.[66] However, the verb *ymia,* 'resound,' of which this term is the subject in this context, only applies to sounds, and the compound *oddlo* is strictly parallel to the Old Norse kenning for 'combat': *oddregn,* literally 'rain of shafts.' This is why Jöran Sahlgren is justified in ruling out the translation of *oddlo* as 'blood.' The simile indicates that the tips of the shafts (*oddar*) resound upon the shields, weapons, and breastplates as the waves (*láar*) driven by the storm boom upon the shore.[67]

Quite different, however, must be the meaning of *lá* in a stanza of the skald Kormákr ogmundarson,[68] in which the term appears associated with the adjective *solr.* This is the only attestation of *solr* in Old Norse poetry, although the term survives in dialectal Norwegian in the form *sal* in Røldal.[69] Old Norse *solr* means 'pale' and is related to OE *salu,* 'dusky, dark' (surviving in Modern English *sallow,* applying to the complexion), to OHG *salo,* 'turbid, dull' (from which the French word *sale* 'dirty' is derived), and to MDu. *salu(w),* 'yellowish, dirty.' Obviously, the association of such an adjective with a noun meaning 'blood' would be rather unexpected; therefore, the phrase *lásolva* in line 4 of the stanza under reference is usually translated 'sallow-complexioned.'[70] Why, then, could not *lá* simply mean 'look, mien, face'?

In this case, a plausible etymology would be available for the Old Norse term. There is, indeed, in the Tocharian texts, a noun *lek,* meaning 'appearance, mien,'[71] for which, to the best of my knowledge, no satisfactory etymology has as yet been supplied.[72] This word can reflect an Indo-European prototype *lēk-,* whose reduced grade would yield Gmc. *lah-;* the *-ō* theme derived from this root[73] would, indeed, normally be reflected by *lá* in Old Norse. This interpretation, furthermore, fits perfectly into the context of the Eddic stanza: "Lóðurr has given man his mien and fair complexion." *Lá* and *lito góða* would then be associated into a kind of hendiadys to designate the physical aspect of the newly created human being, both indications of his external appearance being summarized by Snorri's *ásjóna,* which means altogether 'face,' 'mien,' 'countenance,' and 'look.'

But this interpretation remains dependent upon the correctness of an always disputable etymology.[74] One can, accordingly, wonder whether the poetic meaning of 'hair,' which *lá* also shows,[75] cannot, after all, supply an acceptable interpretation for the term in the text of *Voluspá.* Adolph Noreen[76] once suggested it, but Hugo Gering[77] utterly rejected such an interpretation. Nevertheless, it rests upon an etymologically flawless explanation: *lá, lo* reflect a Germanic prototype **lawō,* meaning literally 'cutting,' derived from a root **lu-,* attested in another connection by OHG *lō,* 'tan,' ON *logg,* 'croze,' and by Lith. *lóva,* 'bedstead,' Russ. *láva,* 'bench, board.' The transition from the idea of 'cutting' to that of 'hair' (i.e., 'that which one cuts') is also illustrated by OInd. *lava-,* 'cutting, wool, hair,' and Alb. *léš,* 'wool, hair,' derived from the same Indo-European root. As for the importance of the hair in the creation of man, one could refer to the numerous passages in the sagas where it appears as the most significant element of human appearance. The hair was sacred for the ancient German; freely growing hair hanging on the shoulders was characteristic of priests, kings, and women; hair was the vehicle of the *hamingja,* of the soul, of happiness.[78] In support of this, it might be relevant to cite paragraph 35 of Salic law, in which the act of cutting the hair of a young girl without the permission of her parents is taxed forty-five shillings, whereas one pays only thirty for having seduced a female servant of the king.[79] Important also are Tacitus' notes[80] on Germanic manners of wearing the hair, in which he describes the Suevian chiefs and deals with the Chatti warriors' custom of cutting their beards and hair only after killing an enemy. The cutting of the hair is also a rite of passage, which marks the accession of the adolescent to manhood.[81] Furthermore, descriptions in the sagas closely associate complexion and hair to suggest the fine presence of their heroes, and a particular shade of hair color is never dissociated from a definite hue of the face.[82] Would it be surprising, then, that features so essential to the noble bearing of the Norsemen be put directly under the patronage of Lóðurr in the Eddic line "Lóðurr gave hair and fair complexion to man"?

Thus, a choice between two interpretations of *lá* is offered. Without trying to settle the question of which is the more plausible, it should be pointed out that both emphasize, like *litir góðir,* the physical aspect of man, whereas the qualities bestowed upon him by Hœnir and Othin are essentially spiritual. Accordingly, it is likely that the divinity responsible for these purely external features of man is a god governing the physical aspect of living beings, a god closer to nature than the Æsir—the majestic sovereigns—were. In a word, a god of the Vanic group of the ancient Germanic fertility cult.

These are the kind of considerations that led F. Detter and R. Heinzel[83] to identify Lóðurr with Freyr, without, however, being able to give any more support to such an identification than the derivation of the name *Lóðurr* from the stem contained in ON *lóð,* 'produce of the land.' Since such an etymology can hardly be considered as a sufficient argument to interpret *Lóðurr* as a mere surname of Freyr, the god *par excellence* of agricultural production, this hypothesis has been abandoned. In my opinion, the principle of interpretation which motivated it was, however, correct. This is why, in his *Altgermanische Reli-*

gions-geschichte,[84] Jan de Vries gave preference to the explanation of Jöran Sahlgren,[85] which proceeds from the same principle. Having recognized the zero grade of the Indo-European root **leudh-* 'grow,' in the first component, *lud-* of a series of Swedish toponyms,[86] Sahlgren identifies the deity *Ludhgodha,* attested by place-names, as one of the Germanic hypostases of the Great Goddess of fertility. Because, in the parishname *Locknevi* (1378: *Lodkonuvi*), this deity also appears under the name *Loþkona,* whose second component is ON *kona,* 'woman,' corresponding to Goth. *qino* and OE *cwene,* Sahlgren interprets Lóðurr as her male counterpart, deriving the name from an original **Loþverr,* whose second component would be ON *verr,* 'man, husband,' akin to Goth. *wair,* Lat. *vir,* and so on. The long -ō- of *Lóðurr,* required by Eddic metrics, would then be of secondary origin, since it would replace the short -o- of **Loþverr*—long by position in the line *lá gaf *loþverr*—when this term became *Lóðurr* by reduction of the unstressed syllable of the second component. The *Edda* manuscript merely shows *loðvR* without indication of quantity, but the length of -ō-, implied by the meter, is confirmed by the skaldic kenning *Lóðurs vinr,* 'Lóðurr's friend,' for Othin.[87] On the other hand, parallels like *onundr* from *onvondr,* adduced by Sahlgren, show that the loss of the vowel of the second component does not necessarily entail compensatory lengthening of the vowel of the first component. Unless lengthening for metrical purposes may be admitted, there remains, accordingly, an unsolved phonological difficulty connected with Sahlgren's interpretation.[88]

Should it, therefore, be abandoned? I think not, for various reasons. First of all, the interpretation of Lóðurr as a male counterpart of the goddess of agrarian fertility fits in neatly with the purely physiological qualities he grants man—the more so since the root to which **Loþverr* is linked is that of Goth. *liudan,* 'grow,' whose Old Norse correspondent occurs only in the past participle *loðinn,* meaning 'hairy, shaggy, woolly, covered with thick grass'[89]; in Old Swedish *ludhin* means 'hairy, shaggy' (as *luden* still does in Modern Swedish), and in the Swedish dialects, a word *lå* occurs, meaning 'hair of animal, spring fleece.'[90] The meaning of these terms obviously brings to mind the interpretation of ON *lá* as 'hair,' whereas the meanings of related Germanic terms—Goth. *ludja.* [*prosōpon*] (Matt. 6:17), *laudi* (marginal gloss for [*morphē*]); OS *lud,* 'figure' (*Heliand,* vs. 154);[91] OHG *antlutti,* 'face'[92]—correspond to those of *ásjóna,* which replaces *lá* and *litir góðir* in Snorri. Furthermore, it should be remembered that the root whose zero grade occurs in **Loþverr* is the same as appears in the Germanic term for 'people' (ON *ljóðr,* OE *lēode,* OHG *liuti*) in the meaning of 'full-fledged members of the ethnic community,' which points to its close semantic link with Lat. *līber* and Gk. [*eleutheros*]. Also derived from the same root is the name of the Italic god *Liber,* the deity of Eddic *loðvR,* applying to a divinity of generation and growth, as, cluded the protection of the popular commu-.

nity.[93] Sahlgren's hypothesis accordingly shows far-reaching implications, not even surmised by its author, and the minor objection concerning the vocalism of *Lóðurr* can easily be dismissed if one takes into consideration the semantic field to which he belongs. Indeed, two West Norse terms, at least, could promote the lengthening, required by the meter, of the short -*o*- of Eddic *loðvR,* applying to a divinity of generation and growth, as, for example, ON *lóð,* 'produce of the land' (which belongs etymologically with Gk. [*latron*], 'pay, hire,'[94] and Icelandic *lóða,* 'in heat' (applying to a bitch), which Evald Lidén has compared with MIr. *lāth,* 'rut' (of a sow).[95] If these arguments are cogent, *Lóðurr,* bestower of beautiful complexion and hair, appears in the Germanic North as the counterpart of the Italic Liber, just as the Scandinavian Viðarr corresponds to the Illyrian Vidasus[96]—a new element in the rich set of common features between Germanic and Italic culture and religion.[97]

Notes

[1] Lee M. Hollander (trans.), *The Poetic Edda* (2nd ed.; Austin: University of Texas Press, 1962), p. 3.

[2] Anne Holtsmark and Jón Helgason (eds.), *Snorri Sturluson Edda, Gylfaginning og Prosafortellingene av Skáldskaparmál* (Copenhagen: Ejnar Munksgaard, 1950), p. 10: *þá er þeir Bors synir gengu með sævarstrondu, fundu þeir tré tvau ok tóku upp tréin ok skopuðu af menn, gaf hinn frysti ond ok lif, annarr vit ok hrœring, .iii. ásiónu, málit ok heyrn ok sión . . .*

[3] Name of the father of Othin as well as of *Vili* (lit., 'strong will' [if its first *i* is originally short]) and of *Vé* (lit., 'religious feeling'). The name appears as *burr* in the manuscripts and is undoubtedly identical with ON *burr,* 'son' (Sveinbjörn Egilsson, *Lexicon Poeticum Antiquae Linguae Septentrionalis,* ed. Finnur Jónsson [2nd ed.; Copenhagen: S.L. Møller, 1931], p. 57).

[4] Lines 143-145: [*Zeus de patēr . . . genos meropōn anthrōpōn polēs . . . ek meliān*] (A. Rzach [ed.], *Hesiodi Carmina* [Stuttgart: B. G. Teubner, 1958], p. 62). The meaning of [*meropos*] remains obscure ('articulate'? 'mortal'? see Hjalmar Frisk, *Griechisches etymologisches Wörterbuch,* [Heidelberg: Carl Winter, 1963], II, 211-212). Ancient *scholia* already identified [*meliān*] with the [*Meliai*] Nymphs mentioned in line 187 of the *Theogony* (see Agostino Pertusi, *Scholia Vetera in Hesiodi Opera et Dies* [Milano: Vita e Pensiero, s.a.], p. 59), but this presumably reflects a cosmogonic tale in which Ash-nymphs were the mothers of the human race (Paul Mazon, *Hésiode* [Paris: Les Belles Lettres, 1947], p. 37 n. 1). The translation '(ashen) spears' (Hugh G. Evelyn-White, *Hesiod: The Homeric Hymns and Homerica* [London: W. Heinemann, 1936], p. 13; Richmond Lattimore, *Hesiod* [Ann Arbor: University of Michigan Press, 1959], p. 35) has little to commend itself in this context (cf. [*meliēgenēs*] [Apollonius Rhodius],

'ashborn'). On Hesiod's myth of the generations of men, cf. the collection of articles by F. Bamberger, R. Roth, E. Meyer, R. Reitzenstein, A. Heubeck, A. Lesky, and Th. G. Rosenmeyer in Ernst Heitsch (ed.), *Hesiod* (Darmstadt: Wissenschaftliche Buchgesellschaft, 1966), pp. 439-648.

[5] Quoted by Jan de Vries, *The Problem of Loki* (Helsinki: Suomalainen Tiedeakatemia, 1933), pp. 34-35; for a complete translation of the tale, see Johannes Hertel, *Indische Märchen* (Düsseldorf: Diederichs, s.a.), pp. 182-183: "Die belebte Puppe." Von der Leyen's comparison appears in *Das Märchen in den Göttersagen der Edda* (Berlin: Reimer, 1889), p. 12:

Derselbe glaube findet sich auch in dem folgenden indischen belebungsmärchen (vgl. meine 'Indische Märchen,' s. 145 f.): Ein jüngling schnitzt ein mädchen aus holz, ein zweiter bemalt sie, ein dritter verbessert sie und macht sie einen frauenzimmer ähnlich, ein vierter beseelt sie und sie wird ein schönes weib. Alle vier streiten sich um sie: wem soll sie gehören?—Von diesem punkt an ist der verlauf der geschichte ein doppelter; in ihrer türkischen fassung, die wie ich glaube, auf der älteren indischen beruht, wird schliesslich ein gottesurteil angerufen, da tut sich ein baum auf, an dem das mädchen gelehnt und nimmt es wieder zu sich (Rosen, *Tuti Nameh* I, 151).

To this he adds the following comments:

In diesen beiden berichten also, dem nordischen und dem indischen, wird die schöpfung, hier eines menschenpaares, dort eines menschen, von verschiedenen wesen vollzogen. Im nordischen werden die lebenskräfte verteilt, während sich im indischen die beseelung in einem akt vollzieht, die herrichtung des baumes dagegen, bis er einem menschen äusserlich ähnlich wird, den erzähler hauptsächlich beschäftigt. Demgemäss ist es den mythologen bis auf den heutigen tag unklar, wie man sich Ask und Embla vor ihrer belebung zu denken habe: ob als baumhölzer (Mogk, s. 378) oder ob als menschen in baumgestalt (Golther, s. 526). Vgl. auch Mannhardt, W[ald- und] F[eld]k[ulte], s. 8.

Man darf hier auch auf Hygin, fabula CCXX verweisen: Cura, cum quendam fluvium transiret, vidit cretosum lutum, sustulit cogitabunda et cœpit fingere hominem. Dum deliberat secum, quidnam fecisset, intervenit Jovis. Rogat eum Cura, ut ei daret spiritum; quod facile ab Jovē impetravit. Cui cum vellet Cura nomen suum imponere, Jovis prohibuit, suumque nomen ei dandum esse dixit. Dum de nomine Cura et Jovis disceptarent, surrexit et Tellus, suumque nomen ei imponi debere dicebat, quandoquidem corpus praebuisset. Sumpserunt Saturnum judicem, quibus Saturnus secus videtur judicasse: "Tu Jovis quoniam spiritum dedisti, corpus recipito. Cura, quoniam prima eum finxit, quamdiu vixerit, Cura eum possideat. Sed quoniam de nomine ejus controversia est, homo vocetur, quoniam ex humo videtur esse factus."

[6] Friedrich von der Leyen, *Die Welt des Märchen,* (Düsseldorf: Diederichs, 1953), I, 205-206.

[7] Elard Hugo Meyer, *Mythologie der Germanen* (Strasbourg: K. Trübner, 1903), pp. 411, 449-450.

[8] Friedrich von der Leyen, *Die Götter der Germanen* (München: C. H. Beck, 1938), p. 268.

[9] The edition used here is Gustav Neckel, *Edda. Lieder des Codex Regius nebst verwandten Denkmälern,* ed. H. Kuhn (3rd ed.; Heidelberg: Carl Winter, 1962), I, 4-5:

(17) Unz þrír qvómo   ór þrí liði,
     oflgir oc ástgir,   æsir, at húsi;
     fundo á landi,   lítt megandi,
     Asc oc Emblo,   ørloglausa.
(18) Ond þau né átto,   óð þau né
                          hofðo,
     lá né læti   né lito góða;
     ond gaf Óðinn,   óð gaf Hœnir,
     lá gaf Lóðurr   oc lito góða.

[10] *Linguistische Studiën. II: Essais de linguistique indoeuropéenne* (Antwerp: De Sikkel, 1939). p. 46-47.

[11] See my "L'étymologie du terme germanique *ansuz* 'dieu souverain'," *Études Germaniques,* VIII (1953), 39.

[12] Jan de Vries, "Über das Verhältnis von Óðr und Óðinn," *Zeitschrift für deutsche Philologie,* LXXIII (1954), 344.

[13] In a line in *Egils saga* (cf. Rudolf Meissner, *Die Kenningar der Skalden* [Bonn and Leipzig: Kurt Schroeder, 1921], p. 364).

[14] Leiv Heggstad, *Gamalnorsk Ordbok* (Oslo: Det Norske Samlaget, 1930), p. 501.

[15] *Ibid.* See also de Vries, "Über das Verhältnis von Óðr und Óðinn," *Zeitschrift für deutsche Philologie,* p. 345. In this article (pp. 340-343), de Vries also discusses Dr. Hollander's interpretation of the god Óðr in his relationship with Freyja as a Scandinavian reflex of the myth of Cupid and Psyche ("The Old Norse God *Óðr,*" *Journal of English and Germanic Philology,* XLIX [1950], 307-308.) In view of the semantic content of ON *óðr,* it is undoubtedly disputable that "*Óðr* . . . as closely as possible translates [*psyché*] 'animus, spirit'."

[16] Dumézil, *Loki* (Paris: G. P. Maisonneuve, 1948), p. 283; German edition (Darmstadt: Wissenschaftliche Buchgesellschaft, 1959), p. 232-233.

[17] *Linguistische Studiën,* II, p. 70-72.

[18] *Haustlong,* st. 4: *hlaut . . . hrafnásar vinr blása.* On the interpretation of this line, cf. Ernst A. Koch, *Notationes Norrœnœ* (Lund: C. W. K. Gleerup, 1926), Part 7, sec. 1016, p. 18-19). Anne Holtsmark ("Myten om Idun og Tjatse i Tjodolvs Haustlong," *Arkiv för nordisk Filologi,* LXIV [1950], 17), however, thinks that Loki is meant, to continue the comic effect of the preceding stanza, but Dumézil (*Loki* [1948], p. 275 n. 7, 276; [1959], p. 226 n. 94) is presumably right in claiming that the described reaction would hardly fit with the subsequent readiness of Loki to parcel out the meat to Þiazi. In the parallel tale in the *Snorra Edda (Skáldskaparmál,* Chap. 1), Hœnir is not even mentioned in this connection.

[19] *Heimskringla: Ynglinga saga,* Chap. 4. This is the only context in which a specific description of Hœnir is given: "*kolloðu hann allvel til hofðingja fallinn; hann var mikill maðr ok inn vænsti*" (they [i.e. the Æsir] said he was very worthy, indeed, to be a chief; he was a big man, and a very beautiful one). The only additional information is from kennings, which characterize him as 'the rapid Ás' or as 'long-legged'—a feature which may also account for his designation as 'pace-Meili' (*fet-Meili*) in the fourth stanza of *Haustlong* (cf. A. Holtsmark, "Myten om Idun og Tjatse," *Arkiv,* p. 46). No further clue can be derived from the kenning for Loki: *Hœnis hugreynandi* (*Haustlong,* st. 12), literally 'Hœnir's mind-assayer.'

[20] Dumézil, *Loki* (1948), p. 278; (1959), pp. 228-229.

[21] See, e.g., Wolfgang Golther, *Handbuch der germanischen Mythologie* (Leipzig: S. Hirzel, 1895), p. 398-399: "Hönir [ist] zwar schön und stattlich, aber schwachim Geiste und unselbständig im Urteil. Er braucht stets Mimirs Beirat, sonst weiss er sich nicht zu helfen." That Hœnir should grant *óðr* to man "is surprising when we remember how witless Hœnir appeared to be when Snorri described him in the *Ynglinga Saga*" (E. O. G. Turville-Petre, *Myth and Religion of the North* [London: Weidenfeld and Nicolson, 1964], p. 142). Following R. M. Meyer (*Altgermanische Religionsgeschichte* [Leipzig: Quelle and Meyer, 1910], p. 370), where the exchange of Kvasir against Mímir and Hœnir is considered as "später Mythologenwitz," Jan de Vries wrote in the first edition of his *Altgermanische Religionsgeschichte* ([Berlin and Leipzig: W. de Gruyter, 1937], II, 309-310): "Die Geschichte ist sehr sonderbar; wenn sie nicht ganz für den Roman des Skaldenmetes, den Snorri in seiner Edda aufgenommen hat, erdichtet worden ist, so ist sie doch wohl bei der Einarbeitung so start umgemodelt worden, dass wir die ursprüngliche Form and Bedeutung nicht mehr herausfinden können." In the second edition ([1957], II, 270), however, he no longer questions the authenticity of the tale and follows Dumézil in stating: "eine schweigende Rolle . . . braucht aber . . . dennoch nicht die Rolle des Unverstandes zu sein."

[22] *Sogubrot af fornkonungum,* Chap. 3: *er brœddastr var ása.*

²³ *Voluspá*, st. 63. This practice of divination is described by Tacitus (*Germania*, Chap. 10; see the comment of Rudolf Much, *Die Germania des Tacitus* [Heidelberg: Carl Winter, 1937], pp. 130-132). On its relation with the Scandinavian sacrifice, see de Vries, *Altgermanische Religionsgeschichte*, (2nd ed.; 1956), I, 417, 432-433.

²⁴ This does not, by far, solve the problem of Hœnir. His interpretation as a vehicle of divine inspiration has recently been illustrated from a different angle: reexamining Elof Hellquist's derivation of the name *Hœnir* from Gmc. **hōnya-*, 'belonging to the rooster,' "a *vrddhi*-formation from *hani*," Anne Holtsmark ("Mythen om Idun og Tjatse," *Arkiv*, pp. 48-53) considers Hœnir as an emanation of Othin in the shape of a rooster, whose part is played by a priestly performer imitating the rooster's step in a cultual drama. Folke Ström (*Loki. Ein mythologisches Problem* [Göteborgs Universitets Årsskrift, LXII, No. 8 (1956)], pp. 56-58; "Une divinité-oiseau dans la mythologie scandinave," *Ethnos*, XXI, [1956], 73-84; "Guden Hœnir och odensvalan," *Arv*, XII, [1956], 41-68), while dismissing the poorly documented hypothesis of the cultural drama, confirms the view that Hœnir must be a hypostasis of Othin in bird-shape: names like *aurkonungr*, translated 'king of the silt,' or phrases like *inn langi fótr*, 'the long-legged,' currently designating Hœnir in skaldic poetry, seem to point to a stilt, and Ström ultimately identifies Hœnir with the black stork, also called *odensvala*, 'Othin's swallow.' E. O. G. Turville-Petre, however, argues that, if Hœnir's name is derived from a bird-name, he must be Othin's bird, i.e., a raven: "When divorced from their master, Óðinn's ravens could have little wit, for it was his wit which they incorporated. When separated from Mímir, Hœnir had no wits, and was no better than a barnyard cock" (*Myth and Religion of the North*, p. 142).

²⁵ *Lóðurs vinr* (Eyvindr skáldaspillir, *Háleygjatal*, 10.7: *vinar Lóðurs;* Haukr Valdísarson, *Íslendingadrápa*, 1.2: *Lóðurs vinar;* cf. Ernst A. Kock [ed.], *Den norskisländska Skaldediktningen* [Lund: C. W. K. Gleerup, 1946], I, 38, 261); cf. Rudolf Meissner, *Die Kenningar der Skalden*, p. 252.

²⁶ Meissner, *Die Kenningar der Skalden*, p. 252; Jan de Vries, *De Skaldenkenningen met mythologischen inhoud* (Haarlem: H. D. Tjeenk Willink, 1934), p. 19; the parallel kenning *Lopts vinr*, 'friend of Loptr (i.e., Loki)' in Einarr skálaglamm, *Vellekla*, 12.2 (tenth century), is assumed to have served as a model for the twelfth century *Lóðurs vinr*.

²⁷ On the challenging study of Dumézil, *Loki*, see mainly the comments of de Vries, *Altgermanische Religionsgeschichte* (1957), II, 265-267, and Turville-Petre, *Myth and Religion of the North*, pp. 144-146. Recent efforts to interpret Loki, including Folke Ström, *Loki*, and Anna Birgitta Rooth, *Loki in Scandinavian Mythology* (Skrifter utgivna av Kungl. Humanistiska

Vetenskapssamfundet i Lund, Vol. LXI [Lund: C. W. K. Gleerup, 1961]), are discussed by Anne Holtsmark in "Loki—en omstridt skikkelse i nordisk Mytologi," in *Maal og Minne*, 1962, pp. 81-89.

²⁸ They are briefly analyzed by Jan de Vries, *The Problem of Loki*, pp. 50-51.

²⁹ *De Noordse Loki-Mythen in hun onderling verband* (Haarlem: H. D. Tjeenk Willink, 1931), pp. 9-11.

³⁰ *The Problem of Loki*, pp. 53-55.

³¹ "Efterslæt til Loke-myterne. I. Loeke, Lodder i flamsk folktro," in *Danske Studier*, 1912, pp. 87-90.

³² De Vries, *The Problem of Loki*, pp. 225-227 (summarizing the extensive collection of popular traditions by Axel Olrik); Dumézil, *Loki* (1948), pp. 71-79, (1959), pp. 45-52; Rooth, *Loki in Scandinavian Mythology*, pp. 196-202.

³³ Jos. Schrijnen, *Nederlandsche Volkskunde*, (2nd ed.; Zutphen: W. J. Thieme, 1930), I, 97-98.

³⁴ Marcel Renard, "Les figurines d'Asse-Elewijt et le culte d'Epona," in *Latomus*, X (1951), 182 n. 2.

³⁵ Cf. Schrijnen, *Nederlandsche Volkskunde*, I, 97-98. On the alleged relationship of this *kludde* with the Celtic goddess Epona, see Renard, "Les figurines," *Latomus*, pp. 181-187.

³⁶ *Loki* (1948), pp. 116-120; (1959), pp. 80-83 (see also de Vries, *The Problem of Loki*, pp. 74-78).

³⁷ Hollander, *The Poetic Edda*, p. 139 ("The Short Seeress' Prophecy," st. 14). Loki, called *Loptr* in this context, had eaten a woman's heart which he found half-roasted. Hollander's translation of ON *flagð* by 'ogre' is presumably too specific; as Turville-Petre points out (*Myth and Religion of the North*, p. 129), "the poet probably expresses an ancient tradition, when he says that every female monster (*flagð hvert*) on earth comes from Loki's brood."

³⁸ On the basis of the meaning 'spider' of the appellative *locke* and on the basis of the spider's role as a trickster in other cultures, Rooth has tried in her study on *Loki in Scandinavian Mythology* (1961) to correlate some constitutive elements of the Old Norse myths, like Loki's invention of the net, with modern folklore material, but her argumentation fails to convince. See, e.g., Willy Krogmann, "Neue Untersuchungen zur germanischen und keltischen Mythologie. I. Loki in der germanischen Mythologie," in *Zeitschrift für Religions- und Geistesgeschichte*, XV (1963), 361-363.

³⁹ E. J. Gras, *De Noordse Loki-Mythen*, p. 10, follows H.

Grüner-Nielsen and A. Olrik in considering Brabantine *Loeke* (which appears sporadically instead of *Lodder*) as hypocoristic to *Lóðurr*. This implies a prototype with long *ō. Consequently, in *Lodder*, the voiced dental must have been "geminated" before *r* with shortening of the preceding vowel. It is, however, more plausible to derive the Dutch dialectal word from Germanic *luðar- (= OHG [Gl.] *lotara* vana, inania), with "expressive gemination" as in OE *loddere*, 'beggar' (cf. André Martinet, *La gémination consonantique d'origine expressive dans les langues germaniques* [Copenhagen: Levin and Munksgaard, 1937], p. 179).

[40] Cf. de Vries, *The Problem of Loki,* pp. 54-55.

[41] *Ibid.,* p. 55 n. 1. But one can hardly conceive of Donar bestowing man with "inspired mental activity" (*óðr*)!

[42] Halle/Saale: Max Niemeyer, 1937, p. 204-205 (Schriften der Königsberger Gelehrten Gesellschaft, XIII, 626-627).

[43] This interpretation is based on Hugo Gering, *Kommentar zu den Liedern der Edda,* Vol. I: *Götterlieder* (Halle/Saale: Buchhandlung des Waisenhauses, 1927), p. 21. Cf., e.g., Jan de Vries, *Edda* (Amsterdam: Elsevier, 1944), p. 25 ('warmte'); C. A. Mastrelli, *L'Edda. Carmi Norreni* (Firenze: Sansoni, 1951), p. 3 ('calore'); E. A. Philippson, *Die Genealogie der Götter in germanischer Religion, Mythologie und Theologie* (Urbana: University of Illinois Press, 1953), p. 42 ('Lebenswärme'). F. Genzmer, *Die Edda,* Vol. II: *Götterdichtung und Spruchdichtung* (Iena: Eugen Diederichs, 1934), p. 76, translates it first by 'Lebenswärme' and, then, simply by 'Leben,' and Hollander, *The Poetic Edda,* p. 3, merely uses the rather vague term 'being.'

[44] Adolf Noreen, *Tidskrift for philologi og pædagogik,* N.R., IV, 31 ff. (quoted from H. Gering, *Kommentar zu den Liedern der Edda,* cf. also Sigurður Nordal, *Völuspá. Vølvens spådom* [Copenhagen: H. Aschehoug, 1927], p. 46). Karl Schneider, *Die germanischen Runennamen* (Meisenheim am Glan: Anton Hain, 1956), pp. 318-321, goes a step further. He derives both ON *Lóðurr* and Runic *logaþore* from Germanic alternating forms *wlōhaþuraz ~ *wlōyaþuraz, reflecting IE *wlōkāturos, assuming a lengthened grade *wlōk- to *wlok- in *wlokā, 'brightness, > Gmc. *wlahō > ON *lá, lo,* 'blooming hue,' reconstructing an alliterative line: *vlá gaf *Vlóðurr ok *vlito góða. He does not pay enough attention to the implied chronological problem: the loss of initial *w-* before -*l-* is assumed to have taken place between 650-850, whereas *Voluspá* is usually considered to have been composed after 950. Furthermore, the assimilation of Lóðurr with the 'sky-god' Tyr on the basis of this etymology is unwarranted.

[45] In his *Griechische Götter im alten Rom* (Giessen: Alfred Töpelmann, 1930), pp. 172-208, Franz Altheim made a strong case for the Etruscan origin of *Volcanus,* pointing out Etruscan names to which it bears resemblance. His argumentation on such premises has, however, been strongly criticized (cf., e.g., J. L. M. de Lepper, *De Godsdienst der Romeinen* [Roermond and Maaseik: J. J. Romen and Zonen, 1950], pp. 27-28). Furthermore, Rætic *velχanu* (on the Caslir situla; *Prae-Italic Dialects of Italy,* Vol. 2, ed. J. Whatmough [Cambridge, Massachusetts: Harvard University Press], No. 215, pp. 26-29) and Cretan [*welchanos*] have also been connected with Lat. *Volcanus.* Leaving aside the obscure Rætic form, the Cretan [*welchanos*], who appears on coins from Phaistos as a young man sitting in a tree with a rooster in his lap, can hardly be closely identified with the fire-god Volcanus, though the latter's association with Zeus may be a rather late phenomenon (Margherita Guarducci, "Velchanos-Volcanus," in *Scrilti in onore di B. Nogara* [1937], p. 183 ff., quoted by Martin P. Nilsson, *Geschichte der griechischen Religion,* Vol. I [Münich: C. H. Beck, 1941], p. 300 n. 2; 2nd ed. [1955], p. 323 n. 2). It remains preferable to keep them apart, in spite of the efforts to correlate the widely divergent functions of [*welchanos*] and Volcanus (Guarducci, "Velchanos-Volcanus"; Paul Kretschmer, in *Glotta,* XXVIII (1939), 109-110; Albert Grenier, *Les Religions étrusque et romaine* [Paris: Presses Universitaires de France, 1948], pp. 44-45). Nevertheless, Volcanus' name is "certainly not Latin" (H. J. Rose, "Volcanus," in *The Oxford Classical Dictionary* [Oxford: The Clarendon Press, 1949], p. 953), and [*welchanos*] is "offenbar vorgriechisch" (Hjalmar Frisk, *Griechisches etymologisches Wörterbuch,* I, 503-504). Perhaps Kurt Latte (*Römische Religionsgeschichte* [Münich: C. H. Beck, 1960], p. 130 n. 3) is right when he suggests: "Es könnte sich nur um einen Gott der Mittelmeerkultur handeln, dem die italischen Einwanderer eine andere Bedeutung unterlegten"—presumably by divinizing the 'third aspect of fire,' the 'hungry' fire on the lurk for evil spirits, corresponding to the *daksināgni* of Old Indic liturgy (cf. Georges Dumézil, *La religion romaine archaïque* [Paris: Payot, 1966], p. 315). If, however, this should be the original function of Volcanus, as Dumézil claims ("Quaestiunculae Indo-Italicae. 2. Les *pisciculi* des Volcanalia," in *Revue des Etudes Latines* XXXVI (1958), 121-130), his suggestion that Lat. *Volco-* would be related to Skt. *várcas-,* Avest. *varačah-,* 'brilliance' (*ibid.,* p. 123 n. 4) would deserve further consideration. Further relation with Hittite [d]GUL-*aššeš* (read *Valhannaššeš* by E. Forrer) is improbable (see Alois Walde and J. B. Hofmann, *Lateinisches etymologisches Wörterbuch,* [3rd ed.; Heidelberg: Carl Winter, 1954], II, 825-826; on the nature of the [d]GUL-*aššeš* deities, whose Hittite name remains unknown, see Emmanuel Laroche, *Recherches sur les noms des dieux hittites* [Paris: C. P. Maisonneuve, 1947], p. 99).

[46] Although approved without reservation by Manfred Mayrhofer, (*A Concise Etymological Sanskrit Dictionary,* [Heidelberg: Carl Winter, 1954], I, 112) and by J.

B. Hofmann (*Etymologisches Wörterbuch des Griechischen* [München: R. Oldenbourg, 1950], p. 106), this etymology is considered as unacceptable, without further comment, by Hjalmar Frisk (*Griechisches etymologisches Wörterbuch,* I, 629), who considers Gk. [*ēlektōr*] unexplained.

[47] *Germanische Religionsgeschichte,* (Berlin and Leipzig: Walter de Gruyter, 1935), I, 234; see also Vol. II (2nd ed., 1957), pp. 271-272.

[48] *Altgermanische Religionsgeschichte,* Vol. II: *Die nachrömische Zeit. 2. Die Westgermanen* (Heidelberg: Carl Winter, 1954), pp. 276-277.

[49] *Gylfaginning,* Chap. 33: *Loki er fríðr ok fagr sýnum, illr í skaplyndi.*

[50] *An Anglo-Saxon Dictionary* (London: Oxford University Press, 1898), p. 646. The Old English adjective is glossed *cacomicanus* (from Gk. [*kakomēchanos*], 'mischief-plotting') or *marsius* (Middle Latin derivation from the name of the Marsi, who were celebrated as magicians and snake-charmers).

[51] According to Ernst Alfred Philippson, *Die Genealogie der Götter in Germanischer Religion,* pp. 45-48, this etymology "betont das Dämonisch-Böse in Loki," but he does not succeed in establishing that this "Arglist" is indeed Loki's fundamental feature, as he fails to take fully into account the complexity of the dossier assembled by Dumézil. This was briefly attempted by Friedrich von der Leyen in his study "Zur grösseren Nordendorfer Spange" (*Beiträge zur Geschichte der deutschen Sprache und Literatur,* LXXX [Western ed.; 1958], 210-213). Pointing out that Loki appears as a god of all shapes ("Keiner beherrscht wie er die Künste der Verwandlung"), von der Leyen suggests that, in a later, Christian context, the evil side of his complex personality was strongly emphasized, whereas, in Logaþora and Lóðurr, his creativeness prevailed ("das Schöpferische blieb das Überwiegende"). In those two cases, the ethical approach is different: for the pagan, there is no such strong moral censure for his "kluge Überlistungen" and "frechen und übermütigen Betrug." However, von der Leyen concedes that his suggestions are purely tentative and rejects Krogmann's etymology as "sprachgeschichtlich zu künstlich und inhaltlich ein Fehlgriff."

[52] "Loki," *Acta Philologica Scandinavica,* XII (1938), 67-69. The etymology was suggested independently by Siegfried Gutenbrunner to Helmut Arntz and Hans Zeiss in *Die einheimischen Runendenkmäler des Festlandes* (Leipzig: Otto Harrassowitz, 1939), p. 297.

[53] E.g., Lucien Musset, *Introduction à la Runologie* (Paris: Aubier, 1965), p. 371; Wolfgang Krause and Herbert Jankuhn, *Die Runeninschriften im älteren Futhark,* Vol. I: *Text* (Göttingen: Vandenhoeck and Ruprecht, 1966), p. 293. Cf., however, the negative comment of de Vries, *Altgermanische Religions geschichte* (1956), I, 310-311.

[54] Obviously, in this context, the *deceitful* outward appearance is meant to contrast with the evil disposition of Loki.

[55] *Gesta Danorum,* ed. J. Olrik and H. Ræder (Copenhagen: Levin and Munksgaard, 1931), I, 10-11; see de Vries, *Altgermanische Religionsgeschichte* (1957), II, 271.

[56] Cf. Kemp Malone, "Humblus and Lotherus," *Acta Philologica Scandinavica,* XIII (1939), 200-214, esp. 213-214.

[57] Against this identification, see my remarks in "Notes critiques sur les concordances germano-celtiques," *Ogam,* VI (1954), 157-158.

[58] *Kommentar zu den Liedern der Edda,* I: *Götterlieder,* p. 23.

[59] *Vergleichendes und etymologisches Wörterbuch des Altwestnordischen* (Göttingen: Vandenhoeck and Ruprecht, 1948), p. 184-185; on the meaning of ON *lómr,* see Stefán Einarsson, *Acta Philologica Scandinavica,* IX (1934), 94-5.

[60] *Linguistische Studiën,* II, 67-70.

[61] Cf. *Beowulf,* ll. 247-251, where the Danish coast guard immediately recognizes Beowulf as a nobleman because of his impressive stature and fine presence: "Never did I see a bigger man among the warriors on earth . . . ; he is no mere retainer . . . unless his countenance [*wlite*], his peerless appearance [*ænlīc ansȳn*] deceives . . ." (see Willi Gramm, *Die Körperpflege der Angelsachsen* [Heidelberg: Carl Winter, 1938], p. 8).

[62] Swedish *later* (plural to the obsolete *laat* [Stiernhielm]) and Danish *lader* (plural to *lade,* O. Dan. *ladh(æ)*) are late loan words from Middle Low German (*lāt(e),* 'Benehmen,' Gebärde,' *gelāt,* 'Aussehen, Gebärde, äusseres Benehmen'). See Elof Hellqvist, *Svensk etymologisk ordbok* (3rd ed.; Lund: C. W. K. Gleerup, 1948), I, 563; Niels Åge Nielsen, *Dansk etymologisk Ordbog* (Copenhagen: Gyldendal, 1966), p. 221.

[63] *Kommentar zu den Liedern der Edda,* I: *Götterlieder,* p. 22.

[64] Cf., e.g., Johan Palmér, "Till Voluspá," *Studier tillägnade Axel Kock* (Lund: C. W. K. Gleerup, 1929), p. 100; Egilsson, *Lexicon poeticum,* ed. Jónsson, p. 390; Heggstad, *Gamalnorsk Ordbok,* p. 397; Johan Fritzner, *Ordbog over Det gamle norske Sprog* (reprint of 1891 ed.; Oslo: Tryggve Juul Møller, 1954), II, 391.

[65] Cf., e.g., Richard Cleasby and Gudbrand Vigfusson, *An Icelandic English Dictionary*, ed. William A. Craigie (2nd ed.; Oxford: The Clarendon Press, 1957), p. 376. In this meaning, it corresponds to MLG *lā*, 'boggy water, spring,' and reflects a Gmc. prototype *lahō*, akin to Lat. *lacus*, 'lake'; it survives in Norw. *laa*, 'boggy water (esp. reddish with iron ore).' See, e.g., Jan de Vries, *Altnordisches etymologisches Wörterbuch* (Leiden: E. J. Brill, 1961), p. 343.

[66] *Umðu oddláar í Óðins veðri* (Kock, *Den norsk-isländska Skaldediktningen*, I, 36). "the . . . resounded in the fight (literally: 'Othin's weather')." On the translation of the kenning by 'blood,' see, e.g., Meissner, *Die Kenningar der Skalden*, p. 205; Egilsson, *Lexicon poeticum*, ed. Jónsson, p. 434; Heggstad, *Gamalnorsk Ordbok*, p. 501.

[67] *Eddica et Scaldica. Fornvästnordiska Studier*, Vol. I (Lund: C. W. K. Gleerup, 1927), pp. 69-71, 122.

[68] 'Visor,' st. 6 (Kock, *Den norsk-isländska Skaldediktningen*, p. 43):

> Svort augu berk sveiga
> snyrti-Grund til fundar
> -þykkik erma Ilmi
> allfolr - ok la solva.

[69] Heggstad, *Gamalnorsk Ordbok*, p. 487; see also Egilsson, *Lexicon poeticum*, ed. Jónsson, p. 561.

[70] Cf. e.g., Egilsson, *Lexicon poeticum*, ed. Jónsson, p. 390, where it appears in association with the translation of *lá* in *Voluspá* by 'blood,' but as reflecting a particular semantic development: the phrase *sol lo* means 'pallor' ('blegt udseende, lød'), as is confirmed by its relation with *allfolr* in the context of the stanza ("With black eyes and a pallid countenance, I betake myself to a meeting with the elegant lady with the snoods—very pale do I seem to be to the lady" [literally: 'the *Ilmr* of the sleeves']).

[71] Wilhelm Schulze, Emil Sieg, and Wilhelm Siegling, *Tocharische Grammatik* (Göttingen: Vandenhoeck and Ruprecht, 1931), p. 49 (etwa 'Aussehen, Geste'); Pavel Poucha, *Institutiones Linguae Tocharicae*, Vol. I: *Thesaurus Linguae Tocharicae Dialecti A* (Prague: Státní Pedagogické Nakladatelství, 1955), p. 271 ('aspectus, gestus'). It appears frequently in a phrase with *pikār* in the meaning 'appearance and gestures,' e.g., *k„uleñci wanke lek pikār* (55b4) 'weibliches Geschwätz, Miene und Gebärde.'

[72] A. J. van Windekens, *Lexique étymologique des dialectes tokhariens* (Louvain: Muséon, 1941), p. 56, derives it from IE *wlek-*, 'shine,' and compares Skt. *ulkā*, 'meteor'; since this is semantically rather unconvincing, Vittore Pisani (*Glottica Parerga. 5. Etimologie tocariche*

[Milan: Ulrico Hoepli, 1942-1943], p. 26) prefers to compare OCS *lice. [prosōpon]*, Russ. *lic*, 'face' (about which, see Max Vasmer, *Russisches etymologisches Wörterbuch*, [Heidelberg: Carl Winter, 1953], II, 41), but he must admit that Toch. B *e*, instead of *ai*, hardly agrees with the Indo-European prototype *leyk-* implied by the Slavonic terms. In genuine Tocharian words, A B *e* is, indeed, deemed to reflect IE *ē* (cf. Walter Couvreur, *Hoofdzaken van de Tochaarse Klank- en Vormleer* [Louvain: Philologische Studiën, 1947], p. 10; Wolfgang Krause and Werner Thomas, *Tocharisches Elementarbuch* [Heidelberg: Carl Winter, 1960], p. 56).

[73] With initial stress like Gmc. *lahœ*, 'water,' in ON *lá, la* (see Charles Clyde Barber, *Die vorgeschichtliche Betonung der germanischen Substantiva und Adjektiva* [Heidelberg: Carl Winter, 1932], p. 44).

[74] "Wörter mit -e- im Ost- und Westtoch, sind selten und sämtlich etymologisch dunkel, soweit es sich nicht um Lehnwörter handelt" (Wolfgang Krause, in a personal communication). Though Krause considers *lek* as "echt tocharisch" (*Tocharisches Elementarbuch*, p. 55), one may therefore wonder whether the term is not borrowed from a common source in the two dialects? Because of the -e- vocalism, the possibility of a Bactrian origin might be taken into consideration (see Werner Winter's paper "Bactrian Loanwords in Tocharian," read before the American Oriental Society meeting at New Haven, Connecticut, on March 22, 1967).

[75] *Skáldskaparmál* Chap. 69: *Hár heitir lá.*

[76] *Tidskrift for philologi og pædagogik*, N.R., IV, 31 ff.

[77] *Kommentar zu den Liedern der Edda*, I: *Götterlieder*, p. 21.

[78] F. de Tollenaere, *De schildering van den mensch in de Oudijslandsche familiesaga* (Louvain: De Vlaamsche Drukkerij, 1942), p. 67; with reference to Vilhelm Grønbech, *Vor Folkeœt*, III, 157 ff. (= *The Culture of the Teutons*, [London: Oxford University Press/ Copenhagen: Jespersen and Pios, 1931], II, 123-125, with further bibliographical data, III, p. 100-101) and to Åke Ohlmarks, *Heimdalls Horn und Odins Auge* (Lund: C.W.K. Gleerup/Copenhagen: Levin and Munksgaard, 1937), p. 362 (in Saxo's narrative the priest of Svantovit has long hair and a long beard, in contrast with current fashion). See also Wolfgang Krause, *Die Frau in der Sprache der Altisländischen Familiengeschichten* (Göttingen: Vandenhoeck and Ruprecht, 1926), p. 82; Willi Gramm, *Die Körperpflege der Angelsachsen*, pp. 9, 13-16, 70-79 (to which should be added the remarks of Valtýr Guðmundsson on "Haarpflege" and "Haartracht" in Johannes Hoops, *Reallexikon der Germanischen Altertumskunde*, [Strasbourg: Karl J. Trübner, 1914], II, 345-347). On the concept of *hamingja*, see, e.g., de

Vries, *Altgermanische Religionsgeschichte,* (1937), II, 348-351; (1956), I, pp. 222-224.

⁷⁹ Karl August Eckhardt (ed.), *Lex Salica: 100 Titel-Text* (Weimar: Hermann Böhlau, 1953), pp. 148-149 (XXXV.2, XXXVI.2).

⁸⁰ *Germanica,* Chap. 38 (*Suebi*); see Much, *Die Germania des Tacitus* pp. 332-337. Whether the description *muliebri ornatu* of the Naharvalian priests (Chap. 43) also implies long hair is more doubtful; if the Vandalic (H)astingi are to be closely associated with the Naharvali, as Karl Müllenhoff claims, their name (Gmc. **Hazdingōz,* derived from **hazdaz,* 'woman's hair' [ON *haddr,* OE *heord*], would point in that direction (see Much, *Die Germania des Tacitus,* p. 380; Georges Dumézil, *La Saga de Hadingus* [Paris: Presses Universitaires de France, 1953], pp. 126-127).

⁸¹ Tacitus, *Germania,* Chap. 31; cf. V. Grønbech, *The Culture of the Teutons,* II, 123; Much, *Die Germania des Tacitus,* pp. 291-298.

⁸² Cf. de Tollenaere, *De schildering van den mensch,* pp. 100-101.

⁸³ *Beiträge zur Geschichte der deutschen Sprache und Literatur* XVIII (1894), 560.

⁸⁴ (1937), II, 312; (1957), II, 272.

⁸⁵ "Förbjudna namn. V. Luggude, Ludgo och Luggavi," *Namn och Bygd,* VI (1918), 28-40.

⁸⁶ E.g., *Luggude* (Skåne, thirteenth century: *Lyuthgudhæret;* on the secondary insertion of *-j-,* see Sahlgren, "Förbjudna namn," *Namn och Bygd,* pp. 36-37. *Ludgo* (1293: *Liuthguthuwi*); *Luggavi* (1310: *Ludhgudwi;* the second component is OSwed. *gudha,* 'goddess,' [see Sahlgren, "Förbjudna namn," p. 32]).

⁸⁷ Hugo Gering (*Kommentar zu den Liedern der Edda,* I: *Götterlieder,* p. 23) considers that the "völlig gesicherte länge des wurzelvokals (*Lóþors* steht in der Isl[endinga] dr[ápa] in aðalhending mit *glópa*)" excludes Sahlgren's hypothesis; to this, de Vries (*The Problem of Loki,* p. 53) comments: "The objection of Gering . . . is of no value, for Haukr Valdísarson, who lived in the 12th century has borrowed the kenning *Lóþurs vinr* for Othin from Eyvindr's Háleygjatal, where the vowel may be short as well as long. In fact, the Voluspá proves the length of the vowel, as in the line of st. 18 lo gaf *Lóðurr* no other quantity is possible." Willy Krogmann ("Loki," *Acta Philologica Scandinavica,* p. 61) however, objects: "Wir haben gar keinen Grund anzunehmen, dass *Lóðurr* sein ō erst dem Verfasser der Íslendinga drápa verdanke, ganz abgesehen davon, dass schon wegen des Unterschiedes zwischen *lið Lóðurs vinar* und *gnýr vinar Lóðurs* nicht an eine unmittelbare Uebernahme aus Eyvindrs Háleygjatal

zu denken ist." Actually, de Vries does not assume that the length of ō only developed in the twelfth century, since he states: "Sahlgren has aptly suggested that the long *ó* may be the consequence of the fact that in course of time the name Loðverr (where the first syllable is by position long) was changed into Loðurr and then the syllable *Loð-,* used in the same line, had to lengthen its vowel." However, as Krogmann pointed out ("Loki," p. 61), Sahlgren merely said: "Det metriska skemat fordrar hos *loðvR* lång första stavelse. Man har därfor i normaliserade texter insatt *Lóðurr.* Detta är enligt min mening fullständigt oriktigt. Sättes i stället in *Loþverr* blir stavelsen fortfarande lång och ett begripligt fonem erhålles."

⁸⁸ The basic difference between personal names like *Onundr* and *Lóðurr* is that the former reflect the loss of *-v-* with a change of *o* to *u* (see Adolf Noreen, *Altnordische Grammatik. I. Altisländische Grammatik* [4th ed.; Halle/Saale: Max Niemeyer, 1923], pp. 127-128, sec. 148), whereas a syncope of *-e-* in the second syllable seems to be involved in **Loþverr.* At any rate, at the time of the reduction of *Loþverr to *Loðurr (which must be posterior to the composition of *Voluspá,* i.e., after 950), the use of the term was confined to verse reflecting mythological tradition, in which the metrical length of *o* in *Loþverr had to be preserved.

⁸⁹ See, e.g., Alexander Jóhannesson, *Isländisches etymologisches Wörterbuch* (Bern: A. Francke, 1954), p. 746; Jan de Vries, *Altnordisches etymologisches Wörterbuch,* p. 363.

⁹⁰ J. Sahlgren, "Förbjudna namn," *Namn och Bygd,* pp. 34-35.

⁹¹ *is unca lud giliðen, lîk gidrusnod* (Otto Behaghel, *Heliand und Genesis* [4th ed.; Halle/Saale: Max Niemeyer, 1933], p. 9. OS *lud* is translated by German 'Gestalt' by Edward H. Sehrt (*Vollständiges Wörterbuch zum Heliand und zur altsächsischen Genesis* [Göttingen: Vandenhoeck and Ruprecht, 1925], p. 352) and by Ferdinand Holthausen (*Altsächsisches Wörterbuch* [Münster and Köln: Böhlau, 1954], p. 48). Heinrich Wagner, however, translates 'Lebenskraft' and compares MIr. *lúth,* 'Kraft' (*Zeitschrift für celtische Philologie,* XXIV [1953], 92).

⁹² Sigmund Feist, *Vergleichendes Wörterbuch der gotischen Sprache* (Leiden: E. J. Brill, 1939), p. 323, 337; Jóhannesson, *Isländisches etymologisches Wörterbuch,* p. 146.

⁹³ Cf. my comments on Adrien Bruhl's *Liber Pater* (Paris: E. de Boccard, 1953), in *Latomus,* XIII (1954), 295-296.

⁹⁴ Jóhannesson, *Isländisches etymologisches Wörterbuch,* p. 732; de Vries, *Altnordisches etymologisches Wörterbuch* (1959), p. 343; see also Frisk, *Griechisches*

Depiction of the Norse Goddess Frigga.

etymologisches Wörterbuch, pp. 89-90.

[95] "Wortgeschichtliches. 3," in *Mélanges linguistiques offerts à M. Holger Pedersen* (Aarhus: Universitetsforlaget, 1937), pp. 41-42. Ferdinand Holthausen (*Vergleichendes und etymologisches Wörterbuch des Altwestnordischen-Altnorwegisch-isländischen* [Göttingen: Vandenhoeck and Ruprecht, 1948], p. 365) considers *Lóðurr* as possibly derived from this etymon.

[96] "Die illyrischen Götter *Vidasus* und *Thana*," in *Glotta,* XXXI (1951), 238-243. For a different interpretation of *Viðarr,* see Dumézil, "Le dieu scandinave Viðarr," *Revue d'Histoire des Religions,* CLXVIII (1965), 1-13, and *La religion romaine archaïque,* p. 331.

[97] A brief oral presentation of some of the ideas discussed in this paper was given at the March 1955 meeting of the *Société pour le Progrès des Etudes philologiques et historiques* (Brussels, Belgium); see *Revue Belge de Philologie et d'Histoire,* XXXIII (1955), 493-494. Further research for this paper was made possible through a University of Texas Research Council grant (no. R O 45). Not all the problems connected with the Eddic myth of the creation of man have been tackled here; further research would have to focus, for example, on the etymology of the name *Embla* (see Sigurður Nordal, *Völuspá,* p. 44-45; de Vries, *Altgermanische Religionsgeschichte* (1957) II, pp. 371-372.

Joseph Harris (1985)

SOURCE: "Eddic Poetry," in *Old Norse Icelandic Literature: A Critical Guide,* edited by Carol J. Clover and John Lindow, Cornell University Press, 1985, pp. 68-156.

[*In the following excerpt, Harris discusses critical debates about the oral nature of Eddic poetry.*]

Eddic Poetry as Oral Poetry

[The] study of the oral nature of eddic poetry—to the extent that this is its nature—bears on almost every branch of research on the poems and, I would argue, changes some of the terms under which we must understand them. In a sense eddic scholars have always "known" that eddic poetry was oral poetry, but that knowledge was mostly an unspoken assumption based on the age of the verse and the introduction of writing to the north. This is still our basic assumption: eddic poetry flourished in a milieu in which writing did not play a major role in the conception, creation, performance, preservation, and transmission of poetry. But this assumption by the older scholarship only gradually acquired form, becoming a consciously held "idea." Heusler distinguished early between the oral (heroic) lay, with its brevity and characteristic narrative style, and the West Germanic *Buchepik* (*Beowulf, Heliand,* and others), which cultivated the enjambed style and depended on writing (Andreas Heusler, *Die altgermanische Dichtung,* 2d ed.; also 13:1905). But the notion of oral poetry gained clarity as it was foregrounded in the comparative studies of H. M. and N. K. Chadwick (15:1932) and problematicized in the work of Milman Parry (15:1971), Albert Lord (15:1960), and Francis P. Magoun (15:1953). From an unanalyzable assumption we had a new idea, orality, but with the heirs of Parry the idea had been overrefined into an equation of one type of oral poetry—the improvised formulaic narrative typified in the South Slavic heroic epics—with the entire phenomenon. Since the mid-1970s several scholars, most notably Ruth Finnegan (15:1976, 1977), have tried to reclaim the notion of "oral poetry" for something like the common-sense definition implied above. In the following pages I will use "oral poetry" (when not otherwise qualified) to mean simply poetry "before and outside of" writing.

The tremendous international and interdisciplinary interest in all manner of studies that build on or touch on the contrast of "oral" and "literate" has already been often enough chronicled (e.g., 15 Foley 1981). In addition to the philologically oriented line started by Parry, there are anthropological and philosophical orientations. Closer to our subject there is a mass of work on Old English poetry and C. M. Bowra's classic book on heroic poetry worldwide (15:1952). Communications theory, in its more or less exotic manifestations, builds on the contrast of oral and literate cultures, and exotic or not, the history of literacy is obviously not irrelevant to the history of literature (e.g., 15 Bäuml 1980). In this would-be inter-disciplinary age current students of eddic poetry should be able to make use of the work in these neighboring fields, and in particular it seems to me a mistake to ig-nore the oral formulaic theory (or more recently simply the "Oral Theory") of Lord, for we owe particularly to Lord the fresh formulation of the problems of oral po-etry. The study of an oral poetry should not be overly influenced by Lord's brilliant analysis of the South Slavic tradition, and a major task is to determine the specific nature of each tradition. But it would be shortsighted as well as false not to admit that we are asking these ques-tions at all not out of the assumptions of the mainstream of eddic studies but because of the stimulus from the oral studies in other areas. The international interest in oral literature has been received coolly by students of Norse literature, and its positive accomplishments here are so far meager. As one of the earliest eddic scholars to take an interest in the Oral Theory, Robert Kellogg worked its principles into the preface to his concordance (5:1958), and Paul Beekman Taylor (15:1961; 45:1963) applied Lord's model briefly to eddic poetry without try-ing to come to grips with the many problems. These are also the assumptions and limitations of *The Nature of Narrative* (15 Scholes/Kellogg 1966). Another early reference to the Oral Theory as background is W. P. Lehmann's brief appreciation of the structure and unity of *Lokasenna* and *Volundarkviða* (15:1963). Lehmann approves of the Oral Theory but shows an awareness of some of the differences between eddic poetry and "oral epic," and some of his conclusions about the two poems would now seem to speak more strongly against a straight-forward "application" of the Oral Theory than he realized. Still, in the early 1960's Einar Ól. Sveinsson offered a severe and unsubtle rejection of the application of Oral Theory to eddic poetry (15:1965); one has to wonder at whom this not very well-informed blast is aimed since so little had then been written. Presumably it was a preemp-tive strike (cf. 3 Einar Ól. Sveinsson 1962:150). More recently von See has taken as a theme the pillorying of forms of thought that work with oral stages, orality in any sense, or—bête noire—the Oral Theory itself (13 von See 1978, 1981). These criticisms add nothing posi-tive to our subject. I can, however, think of two possible reasons for not pursuing the study of eddic poetry as oral poetry.

The first would deny that it is oral at all, either in the sense of improvised or in the sense I defined above: not written. Different traditions of poetry whether oral or written entail different audiences and modes of produc-tion: in certain Chinese poetry, I understand, calligraphy is part of the art; John Donne's sugared sonnets circu-lated in a few manuscripts among his courtly friends; in much modern poetry the *Schriftbild* is at least as impor-tant as the sound or sense; medieval Latin and the Renais-sance vernaculars exhibit acrostics and figure poems (al-

tars, wings); there are the marketplace minstrel, Bellman in his pubs, Chaucer reading to the court, Dickens writing for serial publication, and so on. Where within this col-orful picture do the eddic poems fit? In the thirteenth century there must have been some sort of reading audi-ence to account for the preservation in manuscripts, but to my knowledge there is almost no evidence to support a claim that the original audiences and poets depended on writing. (The relevant publications of Gutenbrunner and Klingenberg are discussed below.) It is true that Bugge thought that "the old Norse poems which arose in the British Isles were carried . . . to Iceland,—and certainly in written form" (14 Bugge 1899:xviii). One reason for Bugge's claim is surely that he had developed many argu-ments for the derivation of particular Norse phrases from Old English poetry, derivations that often depended on misunderstandings of written forms or on scribal corrup-tions; but Bugge did not explain what happened to the hypothetical Viking Age manuscripts in Iceland, and in general no modern scholar takes this idea seriously.

Björn M. Ólsen accorded a large role to runes in the preservation of Icelandic literature (15:1883), and Jón Steffenson, in an interesting recent essay on why the eddic collection was preserved, returns to the theory of runic preservation (15 Jón Steffensen 1968). There is some evidence in the sagas for the idea that even longer poems (most conspicuously *Sonatorrek*) might have been pre-served on wooden rune-staves; Einar Ól. Sveinsson re-views this evidence and the entire question, submitting Björn M. Ólsen's arguments to a point-by-point critique, and concludes in the negative: "Considering all this, it must be the case that runic texts were hardly sources for the old, written literature; and written literature did not come into being before the adoption of the Latin alpha-bet" (3:1962:59-62). There are, however, several actual cases of surviving runic inscriptions in verse (as Einar Ól. Sveinsson notes), and in very recent times new finds, especially of wooden rune-staves, suggest that runes were indeed more widely used than previously thought for just such purposes. The finds from Bergen also show that during the twelfth to fourteenth centuries verse of the eddic type (as defined by meter and diction, if not by subject matter) lived on in Norway, and Aslak Liestøl reveals a few strikingly close relations to passages in the Poetic Edda (15:1964, 1974; see also 1968, 1971). Liestøl's results show clearly that runes could be "a means of communication and . . . of documentation—an aid to failing memory" (15:1974:33). He concludes that it is time for a revision of the received opinion that runes were not used to record poetry. (See also 15 Nielsen 1970, Holm 1975.) It is, however, worthwhile making a distinction between the possible recording of an oral poem in runes (as Þorgerðr offers to do in *Egils saga*) and a composition in runes. The one famous case of Old Ice-landic verse composed to be carved in runes—the still amazing demonstration by Magnus Olsen that Egill's *níð* verses were probably so intended (15:1916)—seems an exception that proves the rule, but the charms and spells of the newly discovered *rúnakefli* or rune-staves may have more than accidental runic-written character too.

If the possible written character of (some?) eddic poetry seems no more than a mild caveat at this point in the history of eddic research, the second objection I imagine could be formidable. If we exclude the strict Lordian model, as I think we must, for Old Norse, have we robbed the distinction between written and oral, and therefore the sense of the inquiry, of all meaning? I think not. An Oral Theory revisionist such as Finnegan knows that the sharp and total contrast between oral and written literature does not stand up to the empirical tests of her fieldwork in Africa. We have to reckon with "transitional texts," mutual influences and parallel traditions of written and oral literature, and a wide range of possible modes within oral poetry. It is reasonable to assume that different modes of performance (with "performance" including technologies such as manuscripts or movable type and the audience and occasion of poetry) will have some reflection in the structure of literature, but even with this assumption we should be careful not to beg the question: a "criterion of immediate rhetorical effect," such as is proposed for *Beowulf* by Michael D. Cherniss (15:1970) would seem likely in any oral poetry, but an episode in *Gísla saga* tells how the hero's sister unraveled a fatal stanza only after mulling it over for some time: the situation is purely oral, but the dark language, like the Provençal *trobar clus,* is not easily understandable. Our task is not to apply grand generalizations borrowed from other fields but simply to use the categories and hypotheses of Lord and others, in fact any suitable concepts that come to hand, to work out the special characteristics of the types of oral poetry in Old Norse. There is much to be done, as the following review of scholarship will show.

The performance of oral poetry necessarily has a dramatic dimension that is missing or replaced by "persona" in poetry for private reading. Bertha S. Phillpotts (15:1920) long ago recognized this essential nature, although her emphasis was, of course, on the ritual portion of the idea of "ritual drama." Lönnroth's sequence of publications on the "drama" of performance seem to me to constitute the most interesting and solid achievements of the new focus (15:1971, 1978, 1979). Heusler had already noted that vocabulary points to a clear distinction between composition (*yrkja* 'to make a poem') and performance (*flytja, færa fram* 'to deliver a poem') (Heusler, p. 20); Lönnroth discusses this contrast with the Oral Theory (15:1971), and I attempted to systematize the possibilities (15 Harris 1983). The slight anecdotal evidence about the presentation of eddic verse is also discussed by Lönnroth; the major text, *Norna-Gests þáttr,* shows a wandering poet performing before a king and his followers. Various traditions are at work in this thirteenth- or fourteenth-century *þáttr,* but there is no reason to dismiss its picture of an oral performance as without a typical value; and the author was careful enough to incorporate a realistic detail about the audience's reception of Gestr's poetry (13 Harris 1976).

Lönnroth's later article and book focus on one interesting aspect of performance; when a performer renders a scene comparable to the actual setting of the performance there is an effect like the play within the play—a moment Lönnroth calls the "double scene." Lönnroth's reading of Orvar-Oddr's drinking contest (including "man-matching" or *mannjafnaðr* verses) in terms of audience expectations and identification is very illuminating. Of course, we cannot know these audiences except through their texts (cf. 15 Foley 1977), and the dramatic approach to eddic poetry can go completely awry as in Gutenbrunner's fanciful directions for the "staging" of *Voluspá* (46:1958).

Most comments on performance have focused on the performing poet or simply on the poet instead of the audience. The older literature particularly looked to the term *þulr* for enlightenment about the history of the institution of poetry (15 Vogt 1927-28), and the *þyle* has been rediscovered by recent Old English scholars (e.g., 15 Baird 1970). Old English and West Germanic in general preserve more information about the performance of older Germanic verse, and this subject has been extensively studied (15 Anderson 1903, Werlich 1964, 1967). Jeff Opland's recent book-length survey of the external evidence about poets and poetry in Anglo-Saxon England (15:1980) and his many articles (e.g., 15:1975) take the Oral Theory and his own fieldwork among the Xhosa praise-poets in South Africa as a background. Stefán Einarsson and Tauno Mustanoja looked to Finnish parallels to fill out the scanty picture from Germanic Scandinavia rather than to West Germanic (or African) analogues (15 Stefán Einarsson 1951a; 1951b, 1962, 1963, 1965, Mustanoja 1959). The general Finnish connections are impressive (including shamanism, of course), especially when further emphasized by Otto Andersson's close coupling of the *Kalevala* meter with *fornyrðislag* (12:1937), but the Germanic evidence for recital by twos on the Finnish pattern is thin and mainly limited to "spook" verses. The exceptions are the pairs of (praise) poets mentioned at Attila's court, in *Widsith* (if Scilling is indeed a fellow poet, as seems probable to me), and in the twelfth-century English-Latin *Life of Ethelbert,* a king of East Anglia killed in 794 (15 Moisl 1981:238-39). We might possibly be entitled to add to this list of pairs of praise-poets the memorable scene of competition before a prince between Hrafn and Gunnlaugr in *Gunnlaugs saga ormstungu.* Other references to pairs of poets do not rule out competition, and it is explicit in *Deor* (in which the hero is displaced by a rival singer), in comic form in the Old Icelandic story of Sneglu-Halli, and perhaps in a poem on the coronation of King Athelstan in 925, preserved in a twelfth-century source ("Ille strepit cithara, decertat plausibus iste" [15 Opland 1980:176]). But if the competition of two praise-poets is the subject of (some of) these references, the dual runo singers of Stefán Einarsson clearly represent a different tradition.

Most scholars agree with Heusler that eddic poetry was not sung to music (e.g., 15 Lehmann 1963), and Finnur

Jónsson's collection of material suggested that there was very little knowledge of the harp (or lyre) in the North in early times (15 Finnur Jónsson 1907). Most recently a few more traces of the harp in Scandinavia have appeared (46 Nesheim 1967; 15 Lawson 1978), and of course there is good evidence for at least some use of the lyre in performance of the nearly related Old English verse (15 Bessinger 1967, Bruce-Mitford 1974, E. R. Anderson 1977). The *rímur,* those long Icelandic narrative poems that flourished from the late thirteenth century on and seem to resemble no foreign genre very closely, were sung without instrumental accompaniment, and their melodies and mode of singing are known (15 Róbert Abraham Ottósson 1969; Stefán Einarsson 1950). Thus eddic poetry, if it was unaccompanied and not sung, stands alone, geographically and chronologically bordered by sung narrative verse. This might seem unlikely except for the unmusical support of skaldic verse, the wide range of possibilities within "singing," and the likelihood that Continental heroic poetry, too, was only recited, chanted, or given in recitative (*Sprechstimme*). See the examination of all these questions and the actual music by the philologist Dietrich Hofmann and the musicologist Ewald Jammers (15 Hofmann 1963, Jammers 1964, Hofmann/ Jammers 1965). There is a melody from the eighteenth century which is supposed to belong to *Voluspá* and some other bits of old music from Iceland, but Jón Helgason throws doubt on the authenticity of these melodies or, more precisely, on the outward circumstances of their association with the medieval texts (15 Jón Helgason 1972). The Icelandic historian of music Hallgrímur Helgason, however, states confidently that eddic heroic poems were presented in "a kind of half-singing as is still done in Icelandic *rímur*-poetry and South Slavic narrative song" and that the tune printed in Paris in 1780 is "ancient" (15 Hallgrímur Helgason 1975:285). The questions about the connections of eddic verse with music seem to be still open.

The Yugoslavian singers do not memorize their texts but compose as they sing. (Lord discourages the use of the word "improvise," but his phrase "orally compose" seems to level all "oral poets" to the model of improvising *guslar* [15 Harris 1983:232, n. 5]). But Norse vocabulary offers *nema* for 'learn (a poem, etc.),' and many hints speak for a "memorial" tradition in the North. Perhaps the most important conclusion of Lönnroth's many-sided earlier article is that eddic tradition is more memorial than improvisational, and he suggests that when parallel texts diverge they often reveal formulaic patching as if formulas were used to help a lapse of memory (15:1971). An article of mine (written in 1975 but in press until 1983) pursues this question of textual stability with similar methods (15:1983). I agree generally with Lönnroth's picture but am more inclined to see variations between parallel passages as attributable to "conscious revisers" but impeccably oral revisers (cf. 15 Friedman 1961). My article also tried to characterize the work of some of the conscious oral revisers as "skaldic revision" and to claim

the basic shape of composition in longer skaldic poems, the "deliberative" composition of such anecdotes as the origin of *Hofuðlausn,* as models for eddic tradition. This skaldic model (which is not the only picture given for the composition of skaldic poetry) has a limited applicability, and the word *skáld* is apparently applied only once to eddic verse (15 Harris 1983:229-31). Further work on the overlap of the two Northern poetic traditions would be useful. Even the etymologies of *skáld* and *scop* are not settled to the satisfaction of all scholars; but both words probably indicate the poet's connection with satire, the obverse of praise (cf. 15 von See 1964).

After *Norna-Gests þáttr,* there are at least three or four passages in historical writings that seem to throw external light on the uses and occasions of oral poetry. The Icelandic wedding at Reykjahólar in 1119 included single stanzas and a longer poem probably in the late eddic style proper to the type of saga recited, although it is called by the skaldic term *flokkr.* The primary function of this oral literature was named as entertainment by the author of *Þorgils saga ok Hafliða;* however, we moderns like to find other, more profound functions for even the most trivial entertainment, and we might well fasten on the genealogical component of these stories in the context of the social sanctioning of the propagation of families precisely at a wedding. In any case, the apparently trivial entertainment was hotly debated for its "truth."[18] The Danish historian Saxo Grammaticus (writing about 1200) tells how a singer, in the year 1131, attempted to warn Knud Lavard of an ambush without breaking his loyalty to the attackers, who were led by a cousin of Knud. The singer, whom Saxo identifies as a Saxon, sang for Knud the lay of "the very famous perfidy of Grimhild against her brothers" (XIII:6:7; cf. 13 Andersson 1974). This seems to be the same *Guðrúnarbrogð in fornu* that Norna-Gestr presented for the first time before a Norwegian court, an event imagined for the period 995-1000 (13 Harris 1976), but in Saxo's account the German version of the Sigurd story in the mouth of a Saxon singer was supposed to be an indirect warning to the doomed prince. Some of the eddic poems in direct speech could, especially in their "double scenes," also function as "a kind of indirect exhortation of their audience," according to Lönnroth (15:1971:8).

Saxo also mentions, among other incidents preceding a battle of 1157, how "a minstrel [*cantor*] rode between the ranks rehearsing Sveno's murderous treachery in a famous song [*parricidalem Suenonis perfidiam famoso carmine prosequendo*], and he excited the warriors of Waldemarus to battle by appealing to them loudly for revenge."[19]

The weightiest member of this series of passages is the famous singing of the *Bjarkamál* by the Icelandic skald Þormóðr on the morning of the battle at Stiklarstaðir (ÍF, 27:361-62; ÍF, 6:261-63). Lönnroth (15:1971:7, n. 25) and others had already noted the "interesting parallel" with the recitation of the *Song of Roland* before the battle of Hastings, but von See (15:1976, 1981) has devoted two challenging articles to showing that the Norwegian incident is borrowed, probably in some twelfth-century predecessor of the preserved accounts, ultimately from William of Malmsbury's Anglo-Latin version of the early twelfth century. I cannot do the entire argument justice here, but the strongest point seems to me to be that another incident in St. Olaf's life is indeed borrowed in just this way. But I can see no reason why the Þormóðr incident should not be historically true or at least an independent development of the common ideas we have seen in the series of passages just cited, especially the idea of the "applied heroic poem." William's account is itself perhaps more likely to be partly fictional (cf. 15 von See 1976:5-7), as the Bédier school claimed, because the *Song of Roland,* at least in the long form we know, is not well suited to such an occasion. The *Bjarkamál* fits the occasion almost too well, and if we are to be suspicious of the historicity of the Norse anecdote, this fit seems to me a better reason than William's similar scene. Von See suggests that the *Bjarkamál* was inappropriate because it would have meant singing a Danish poem at a moment when St. Olaf was going to meet his Danish enemy (15:1981); but I think this argument stands the situation on its head: the enemy was primarily the Trøndelag farmers, and only secondarily their ally Knútr; in 1030 nationality would not have been so significant in a song that was known as "the ancient" since all the older heroic songs were international; but later, in the late twelfth or early thirteenth centuries—a period that produced stories such as *Tóka þáttr Tókasonar* that clearly projected Danish-Norwegian rivalry back into heroic times—it would have seemed strange to invent, as von See supposes, the Norwegian performance of a Danish song. (At that period an author might have been expected to substitute the similar verse from *Hálfs saga ok Hálfsrekka;* cf. the comparison in *Tóka þáttr.*)

At another point von See, noting in passing that the recitation of the *Bjarkamál* is the "only evidence in Old Norse literature of the performance of a heroic poem," argues: "If such a performance is mentioned this one time, the deduction is probable that the stimulus for it came from abroad, for it obviously did not belong to the canon of things worth telling in Scandinavian literary tradition to mention the recitation of heroic poems (which will have happened in the military camps and other places)" (15:1976:2). Clearly I disagree about the uniqueness of the occasion and would relate the *Bjarkamál* to a tradition of applied poetry that would include the heroic. But even if the Stiklarstaðir incident were isolated, it is hard to see how the rest follows. Von See seems to mean that the recital of poems under such conditions was in real life so common that it did not belong to the canon of things worth telling until promoted by the foreign influence; but without the historical Þormóðr incident we would not be entitled (according to von See) to believe any heroic poems were performed at all. Whatever else

it is, this reasoning is not justification for the rejection of the Stiklarstaðir performance. Another of von See's points is that both William and the Norse accounts have a Christian tinge (but that belongs to the period) that takes the specific form of prayers on the night before battle. But prayers on the night before battle must have been a literary and real-life commonplace at least through Shakespeare's portrayal of Bosworth Field; in any case the details are not similar (15:1976:2).

Certainly there is more to say about the two passages, but in brief I see no reason not to believe that somewhat similar real events, involving verse before battle—Haraldr harðráði (Harald Hardrule) before Stamford bridge is another instance—and going back to common Norwegian-Norman customs, lie behind both reports. From that point William could have elaborated with the introduction of the name of a currently fashionable poem. But nothing about the Stiklarstaðir passage need belong to a late period of elaboration, and everything could be historically true. It is also possible, though, that the Stiklarstaðir anecdote achieved its elaborate shape in Norwegian oral tradition in the century or so after the battle; but if so, the events would still be true to an understandable type of real-life event.

The biggest task ahead in the study of eddic poetry as oral poetry would seem to be the analysis of the "poetic grammar" of the genre in comparison with that of other oral poetry. Chiefly this means its use of language and a coming to terms with the concept of formula. The subject of the formula is old in the study of Germanic verse (11 Heinzel 1875, Meyer 1889, 15 Arndt 1877, Sievers 1875) and has recently been chronicled and put into a large context by Teresa Pàroli (15:1974, 1975). A more modern collection of formulas is by H. M. Heinrichs (15:1954), and some contemporary scholars combine the idea of formula with other types of repetition and variation (15 Sonderegger 1969, Andersson 1941, 1963, Kuusi 1952). Outside the Old Norse field such repetition and variation, including formulas, have been interpreted in terms of communications theory (15 Lindow 1974, Wittig 1973), and metrical templates or formulas have come in for attention by Old English scholars (e.g., 12 Cable 1975). Little of this activity is specifically directed to Old Norse. Pàroli has devoted about forty pages of her Italian book on the inquit formulas in Germanic poetry entirely to the Poetic Edda (15:1974:19-61). Her description and categorization are extremely thorough (cf. the only extensive review: 15 Curschmann 1978). The book is nothing if not complete, but the inquits are notoriously repetitive and are not representative of the language of the poems as a whole. A very interesting study of a single formula is Lönnroth's treatment of *jorð ok upphiminn* (15:1981), and in his 1971 article Lönnroth made good suggestions about the use of formulas in the verse in general.

Much remains to be done. Since formulas cannot now be taken as proof of improvisation, we need a new theory of the language of eddic poetry and a new definition of the units of its poetic grammar. But whatever a formula is (or will be defined as), it has to do with repetition, and to determine the degree of repetition the new eddic concordance will be extremely important. (The older comments on this subject lack statistical evidence.) To begin with, it would be helpful to have a computer-based study of repetition such as Joseph Duggan produced for the *Roland* (15:1973).

Formulas and formulaic systems are the lowest level in Lord's poetic grammar, and mediating between formulaic language and the whole song he recognized repeated narrative units called themes. Another "middle-level" unit, adopted from Homeric studies, is the "type scene," and the two have been neatly defined by Fry (15:1968) in terms intended to be suitable for the analysis of Old English verse. Does eddic poetry have themes or type scenes? Probably the question should be put in terms of a complete theory of oral eddic poetry: what are the structural patterns between those of the language itself and the genres and subgenres? Only the beginnings of an answer are to be found in my suggestion that privileged speech events became oral genres that could be realized as middle-level building blocks or as poem types (15 Harris 1983; 36:1979). But there is very little analogy between such units as the *senna* in eddic poetry and the South Slavic heroic poems almost wholly composed of themes and type scenes.

A fuller recognition of the oral nature of eddic poetry is bound to have far-reaching effects on the way we conceive intertextual relations in the tradition and, in turn, the history of the genre. Lord's model, in effect, provides for no intertextual relations except through the competence of singers since texts exist only as instantly consumed products of the generative device, the "grammar" of extemporized poetic language in the particular tradition. No literary history is possible except as a history of individual singers or, perhaps, as evolution of the generative device, the tradition. In practice, the South Slavic model encourages a synchronic, purely descriptive approach. But the historical dimension has always seemed of primary importance to eddic scholars, and an enormous philological literature has accumulated that argues "borrowings" among specific poems or from literature of one type or area to another.

One scholar's treatment of one poem can be taken as an example. In the first Helgi poem, with its fifty-six stanzas averaging four lines, Jan de Vries recognizes borrowings from *Voluspá,* some lost Sigurd poetry, the preserved *Reginsmál* and *Fáfnismál* complexes (to wit the reconstructed sources known as *Vaterrachelied, Hortlied,* and *Vogelweissagung*), also from *Haraldskvæði* and *Glymdrápa* by Þorbjorn hornklofi and the anonymous *Eiríksmál* (three tenth-century praise poems), and from various poems by the mid-eleventh-century skalds Þormóðr Kolbrúnarskáld, Þjóðólfr and Bolverkr

Arnórssynir, and Þórarinn loftunga (de Vries, 1:304-9). To these twelve or more still extant sources one must add the main source of the poem, the partly preserved *Volsunga kviða in forna.* There have been no attempts (comparable to those for Old High German and medieval English) to estimate the extent of the "lost literature" of medieval Scandinavia, but it would be safe to say that much has been lost. If a larger corpus of verse were preserved and the same principles of determining borrowings applied, would not *Helgakviða Hundingsbana I* appear to be a veritable cento of quotations? The principles by which borrowings are recognized have never been analyzed, and the practice and implicit principles differ from practitioner to practitioner, but a method such as that exemplified here by de Vries obviously presupposes a very different model of oral poetry from that that can be derived from Lord's work, a model in which texts have reality and permanence and direct intertextual relations are to be expected. The dramatic clash of assumptions between traditional eddic scholarship and the claims of the orthodox Oral Theory is captured in brief compass by F. P. Magoun (15:1958).

A reexamination of intertextual relations in eddic poetry in the light of, but not distorted by, the standard Oral Theory would be an important but formidable project. It would have to be, in part, an analysis of the unspoken assumptions of past scholars, but such an examination of methodology might have a practical consequence in giving us standards for approving this and rejecting that proposed borrowing. It should also have significance for eddic poetics by establishing a set of intertextual categories. We might, for example, find that two texts can relate through Indo-European formulas in Germanic; Common Germanic formulas; Common Germanic genres and their traditional diction; the diction of later specific generic traditions, with their chronological and geographical limits; borrowings from a specific poem or from a genre (a group) with its diction pool; allusions to a single poem or to a genre; and imitations, including parodies, of a single poem or a genre. I do not underestimate the difficulty of trying to make such distinctions in practical cases, but it must be clear that our sense of the date of a poem and its place in literary history is closely bound up with these judgments about intertextual relations. In Lord's model any text is as old as its most recent singing, but in Old Norse and, I think, in early Germanic in general we have reason to believe in relatively fixed texts that undergo the complex processes of *zersingen* but also undergo complete renovations and less extensive revisions. A date probably should be understood as the date of the latest or dominant renovation.

So far few scholars have attempted to apply assumptions like these to the question of intertextuality. Lönnroth cataloged the different forms of the "earth and up-heaven" formula as it appears in the Old Germanic languages, developing schemata to describe the formula's three uses (in creation contexts, in contexts of world destruction, and in magic contexts), and explored the relationships of the three uses. Along the way Lönnroth sets out his assumptions about the intertextual relations of the works in which the formula occurs (15:1981:esp.317). When he speaks of forces in the traditional poetics that generate the formula "in several unrelated texts" and in the same breath affirms that the formula is proof that the texts are "historically related," Lönnroth captures something of the difficulty of conceptualizing "relationship" among the surviving texts of oral eddic poetry. Yet it seems overstated to reject, as Lönnroth seems to, any evidence of the use of one text by the author of another: "The fragmentary nature of our texts simply makes it impossible to advance genetic theories on such a specified level. Theories of this kind [he has been discussing a few specific "borrowings"] should be avoided also because they tend to conceal the basic fact that all texts are dependent on *oral tradition,* not on literary imitation" (p. 323). But a formula could obviously be borrowed by an illiterate poet as well as by a writer (as may be the case in *Njáls saga,* ch. 125 [15 Lönnroth 1981:323]), and if we pursue the ideas of formula pools and poetic traditions far enough, we must logically come to individual poets' reactions to individual texts. The distance at which we stand makes these details invisible, but even in Lönnroth's own material it is easy to see that we must conceive a closer relationship between the two instances in which "earth and up-heaven" are combined with "Saint Mary" in a prayer formula. The sharp distinctions between literary and oral tradition voiced by Lönnroth and Weber (in 15 Lönnroth 1981) seem to me without foundation (cf. 15 Finnegan 1977).

In contrast to the views just outlined, two recent scholars make the claim that certain eddic poems are in no sense oral but products of scriptoria. Gutenbrunner, who asserts a written origin for three poems regarded by all students of the subject as relatively late, mounts general arguments concerned with literary presentation and legendary development, not borrowing, in assigning *Grípisspá* to a scriptorium (15:1955). His section on *Helreið Brynhildar* works with similar general arguments and five supposed borrowings, four of which rest on latinisms. For example, behind stanza 6 "Lét hami vára hugfullr konungr, / átta systra, *und eic* borit" and its variant in *Norna-Gests þáttr* ("Lét mik af harmi hugfullr konungr, / Atla systor, *undir eic* búa"), Gutenbrunner scents misunderstood Latin, something like: "sustulit vestes eoque *robor* rex fortissimus et octo sorores secum duxit." This exercise is embarrassing to report and, needless to say, unconvincing.[20] Gutenbrunner's derivation for *Guðrúnarkviða III* imagines that "an Icelander in a scriptorium which maintained a lively intercourse with Norway heard about Erka's warning [to Attila not to marry Guðrún] and fragments of an egging-ballad [supposedly the core of stanzas 5 and 8 of the preserved poem] or a poem based on it and out of all that made the third Guðrún poem, stimulated by the fact that he had also been entrusted with the writing down of heroic poems" (p. 262).

The evidence of age is based on legendary development, Mohr's study, a couple of putative latinisms, and one more intriguing Latin parallel. When the evidence produced is sifted for believability, what is left (in my opinion) are the arguments for legendary development and general cultural features. These place the three poems "late" relative to, for example, the five old heroic poems but by no means demonstrate specifically written composition. In fact, Gutenbrunner rather assumes than argues this point, although the latinisms, if acceptable, would tend to establish a written origin.

At two points Gutenbrunner seems close to bringing forward an important argument for written origin of any piece: its composition for a special place in a particular book (pp. 253, 256). It is Klingenberg, however, who gets full value out of this argument. As we have seen, he asserts that *Helgakviða Hundingsbana I* is a late poem written precisely for its place in the Codex Regius, interpreting along the way all textual parallels as borrowings on the part of the poet of the first Helgi poem (10:1974). He does entertain the possibility that the "collector" only selected *Helgakviða Hundingsbana I* for its place, but he clearly perfers to imagine the collector's composing (writing) or commissioning it for its place (p. 116). I have already raised the objection that the poem does not perfectly fit its place, as would be expected if it were written to go there, but it does seem that a work which is composed for a specific place in a specific book must fairly be considered part of a written literary tradition, even if it imitates an oral genre. The distinction between selection, or even selection and modification, of a piece for a place in a manuscript and composition for that place seems crucial. *Voluspá* and *Hamðismál* were selected; many have suspected that *Grípisspá* was composed to introduce a Sigurd-pamphlet, but the contradiction it causes in the matter of the acquisition of Grani makes it more likely that it too was later selected for its position. Most of the borrowings laid at the door of the poet of *Helgakviða Hundingsgbana I* are debatable, but the crucial ones are the supposed borrowings from the Prose Edda (10 Klingenberg 1974:67-71), which would furnish a *terminus a quo* of 1230. The main evidence comes down to the fact that the poem uses a wealth of words for "prince," which appear also in the genealogy of Hálfdan inn gamli (Halfdan the Old) in Snorri's *Edda,* though the two lists do not completely agree. Obviously other explanations than textual dependence in the usual sense are likely here. On the other hand, two possible traces of the influence of *Helgakviða Hundingsbana I* on manuscripts of the *Snorra Edda* might just as well belong to Snorri's original and thus provide a *terminus ad quem* of 1223-30 (10 Klingenberg 1974:96-97, 115-16). Neither late date nor written origin has been demonstrated for *Helgakviða Hundingsbana I.*

Old Norse scholars have used textual loans to prove historical relationships but have not stopped to ask how to prove a textual loan. Drastically different conclusions are drawn from the same "borrowing" evidence. This could be demonstrated by arraying in tabular form the relationships proposed for the elegies and *Sigurðarkviða in skamma* (cf. Andersson's account in 13:1980), but a less complex example is the debate between von See (25:1977) and Franz Rolf Schröder (25:1976) on the priority of *Hamðismál* or *Guðrúnarhvot.* What was already an unsolved problem is made crucial by the realization that, even without invoking the Oral Theory, a recognition of the oral nature of eddic poetry entails reckoning with a world of unrecorded texts in a traditional poetic language. Against this background apparent similarities in surviving texts would seem to have less significance than in a culture of fairly well-preserved written literature.

Borrowings from verse to prose might be expected to be more reliably recognizable than from verse to verse; but when Willy Dahl (29:1960) proposed influences from *Hávamál* in *Konungs Skuggsjá* (the mid-thirteenth-century Norwegian prose *King's Mirror*), not everyone was convinced. To my mind these parallels are not without interest but are too general to build on (as Dahl does on p. 55). Ludvig Holm-Olsen (29:1969) puts *Konungs Skuggsjá*'s poetic borrowings in a more comprehensive framework, but how can we decide on an objective, "scientific" basis whether these are indeed reminiscences of extant verse? Scholars usually seem to decide on a partipris basis when constructing historical arguments of their own or simply to maintain a passive, skeptical stance. Occasionally there have been attempts to prove borrowings by reference to Latin sources which can be safely taken as primary. We have already considered such arguments from Gutenbrunner and von See (and less exact ones from Hagman and Singer). In a similar vein Andersson reasons that we can date *Grípisspá* by reference to that poem's relationship to the monk Gunnlaugr Leifsson's *Merlínússpá* and through it to its Latin source in Geoffrey of Monmouth (13:1980:105-6). Previously these similarities had been explained as influence of the eddic *Grípisspá* on the later *Merlínússpá*, but "it seems more likely that the poet of *Grípisspá* borrowed from Gunnlaugr's poem than vice versa. The phrases in question are taken over by Gunnlaugr from Geoffrey's Latin and need not be sought out in Eddic models" (p. 106). The passages cited in evidence, however, hardly support this interpretation; here is one of the two passages cited:

> Geoffrey: In ore populorum celebrabitur: et actus ejus cibus erit narrantibus.

> *Grp.* 10: sérðu Sigurðar snor brogð fyrir, / þau er hæst fara und himinscautom?

> *Merl.,* II, 27: Hann munu tígna tungur lýða, / sá mun gramr vera gummum tíðastr; / ey mun uppi oðlings frami / ok hans hróðr fara með himinskautum.

There is a real similarity here between the Norse poems: both say that someone's "[fame/deeds] will spread under/

through the heavens" (i.e., to the ends of the earth). But the Latin does not say this; it uses a different image, which Andersson rightly translates as "his deeds will be food for storytellers." Thus *Merlínússpá* has departed from its source. Why? The older explanation, as in the similar case of the parallels between *Hávamál, Hugsvinnsmál,* and *Disticha Catonis,* is that it was influenced by the eddic poem. This may be right, but it is possible that the passages are related only more distantly, through the diction pool from which a formula was fished. For in Norse verse we also find two other closely comparable instances of the formula (one emended, however), three more fairly similar uses, and a wider "system," and in Old English there are what seem to be elements of the same "system" or "systems."[21]

Another example of Latin-based borrowing is proposed by Ulrike Sprenger (15:1982). Here the theme of "swimming in blood" in *Sigurðarkviða in skamma* 24 is derived from a Latin prose miracle of the Virgin. The argument, which I will not pause to recapitulate, is more complicated and diffuse than those of Andersson, von See, and Gutenbrunner, and it is generally farfetched.

"Oralists'" objections seem generally to have a dampening effect on the sharp historical outlines that can be achieved without reference to orality. These objections, often justified, were, however, badly misplaced in the oralist reception of Andersson's book on the Brynhild legend (13 Andersson 1980; 15 Bäuml 1982; 15 Haymes 1982). In a review that evinces several misconceptions about Old Norse, Franz Bäuml criticizes Andersson's faith in the real existence of lost poems—an objection that shows no understanding of the fact that the original manuscript of the Poetic Edda contained a quire that has since been lost and that a version of the complete manuscript was the direct, ink-and-parchment source of the writer of *Volsunga saga,* who not only paraphrased it but quoted a few stanzas in verse. The problems of reconstruction and evaluation of such a partially lost source are still considerable. For example, Andersson parts with Heusler (13:1902) in interpreting all the paraphrased material as having belonged to just three poems: the end of *Sigrdrífumál,* all of *Meiri,* and the beginning of *Brot.* His arguments for seeing the material belonging to Heusler's separate *Traumlied* and *Falkenlied* as part of *Meiri* are debatable,[22] but Bäuml is badly mistaken in treating the enterprise as "hypothetical" in the sense he means or in thinking that any conclusions about oral literature are relevant here.

Even the sciences have their traditional rhetoric, and in surveys of progress one might expect to meet the modesty topos wherein our generation stands like dwarves on the shoulders of giants, seeing further only by virtue of that position. From my survey of some two and a half decades of eddic studies it will be apparent that our subject does not constitute science. Certainly there have been giants abroad, and some few still stalk the pages of our field every year. Reviewing this weighty scholarship may make us feel thoroughly dwarfed—as if, by an apt reversal of the cliché, the giants were standing on us. But the older scholarship does show a kind of progress, and its sheer bulk and difficulty, though at first they seem a hindrance to further progress, ought not to cow a new generation of students of eddic poetry—a generation which, as it accumulates new tools and new questions, will inevitably contribute work of value, both in the old forms and in forms the giants will not have foreseen.

Notes

. . . [18] *Þorgils saga ok Haflida,* ed. Ursula Brown [Dronke] (London: Oxford Univ. Press, 1952); Peter Foote, "Sagnaskemtan: Reykjahólar 1119," *SBVS,* 14 (1955-56), 226-39.

[19] *Saxo Grammaticus, Danorum Regum Heroumque Historia, Books X-XVI,* ed. and tr. Eric Christiansen, BAR International Series 118(i) (Oxford: BAR, 1981), II:414 (Book XIV, chap. XIX, par. 13, 11:24-27); cf. III:792, n. 198. Another Saxo passage (Book XIV, chap. XL, par. 9, 11:27-34), concerning the ill-educated Englishman Lucas, probably belongs with these passages but does not certainly mention verse (II:514; III:850).

[20] There is a close parallel to *undir eic (borit/búa)* in the Old English *Wife's Lament* (lines 28, 36) that would seem to support the eddic reading if support were necessary.

[21] In addition to *Grípisspá* 10 and *Merlínússpá* II:27, there are *Hyndluljóð* 14 ("hvarfla þótto hans verc með himins scautom") and Óttarr svarti's lausavísa 2 ("Svá skal kveðja / konung Dana, / Íra of Engla / ok Eybúa, / at hans fari / með himinskautum / londum ollum / lof víðara"). All four passages use the formula about the spread of fame and could be schematized: *lof/verk/brogð/hróðr fara/hvarfla með/und himinskautum.* The *Hyndluljóð* passage is from a very old part of the poem, but the Ottarr passage incorporates Finnur Jónsson's emendation of *himinkraptum* to *himinskautum.* Snorri's *Háttatal,* st. 95, uses *und himins skautum* to mean "anywhere" in a context of fame. A stanza in the late *Hjálmþérs saga* has *undir heims skauti* for "anywhere in the world" and continues in the next clause "ferr þín frægð" (your fame spreads). Two occurrences of *skaut* with words for land or sea are probably parts of the same system (see 5 Finnur Jónsson 1913-16). Old English combines *sceat* with words for earth (e.g., *under foldan sceat*) but not with *heofon* (cf. *under heofunhrofe* and *eorþan sceatas ond uprodor*); one line from *Widsith,* however, is comparable to the four Norse passages about fame: "hafað under heofonum heahfæstne dom" (143).

[22] The fact that both Eis (13:1956) and Schröder (13:1956) have a "hawk" seems to support the existence of a separate *Falkenlied.*

NORSE MYTHOLOGY AND OTHER TRADITIONS

Henning K. Sehmsdorf (1974)

SOURCE: "Archetypal Structures in Scandinavian Mythology," in *Facets of Scandinavian Literature,* edited by A. Wayne Wonderley, APRAP Press, 1974, pp. 53-67.

[*In this essay, Sehmsdorf analyzes the Icelandic mythological tradition in terms of Jungian psychology.*]

The title of my paper is "Archetypal Structures in Scandinavian Mythology." In the few minutes allotted to me, I want to give a rough sketch of an interpretation of the nordic mythological system along the lines of Jungian psychology. As source material I will rely almost exclusively on the *Poetic Edda* and the *Prose Edda* of Snorre Sturluson.

According to C. G. Jung, the archetypes are universal forms of the unconscious manifesting themselves in dreams, fantasies, art, fairytales, myths, and other expressions. As the archetypal images are received by the conscious mind, they initiate a process of reaction and assimilation. In the gradual development of psychological maturation, a person thus experiences and re-experiences the archetypes in ever new relationships and configurations. On the basis of clinical observation and studies in myth, moreover, Jungians have concluded that the gradual transformation of archetypes in the maturation process develops according to a recognizable and practically invariable pattern. Erich Neumann has defined this pattern in terms of three specific phases or cycles which, he has labelled, mythologically speaking: 1. the creation myth, 2. the hero myth, and 3. the transformation myth.[1]

In the first phase, the cycle of creation, the world and the unconscious are represented as one. The major motif of this stage is the motif of unity and the major form or metaphor is that of the maternal womb to which mythologists have given the name *uroboros* (from the Greek, meaning "perfect round"). In the two Eddas, the uroboros is symbolized by the image of Ginnungagap which Jan deVries has interpreted as "primordial space filled with magic power."[2] In this cosmic space or womb, suffused with life giving power, there are two primordial regions, one a region of icy rivers (Niflheim), the other a region of fire (Muspelheim). Effusions from the two regions mysteriously meet in the center of Ginnungagap, fire and ice merge and grow into the likeness of a human being. This description makes it quite clear that there is no outside father who implants the fructifying seed in the maternal womb; both biological principles, the masculine as well as the feminine, are contained in Ginnun-gagap.

The first being thus to emerge in Ginnungagap, is called Ymir ("The Bellower"). He is neither a god nor human, but a primitive, androgynous giant. Like an infant's, Ymir's primary form of existence is sleep. In that state he unconsciously brings forth offspring which grows from the sweat under his armpit and from the sexual union of his two legs. These are the ancestors of the frost giants.

Ymir, as we said, is bi-sexual; but the second being to emerge from the ice is specifically female, namely a cow by the name of Authumla. She nourishes the sleeping giant with her milk. After Authumla there appears a third group of beings and they are specifically male. Here the cow plays the role of midwife. As she licks the ice in Ginnungagap, there appears a man called Buri; Buri has a son by the name of Bor who marries Bestla, the daughter of a giant. From their union, the first heterosexual union in cosmic history, are born three sons: Othin, Vili, and Ve. These are the first of the shaper gods.

At this point a decisive change occurs in the development of the cosmos. The processes of creation as gradual emergence are superseded by processes of violent struggle, building and shaping. The three gods, Othin, Vili, and Ve, turn upon the primordial being and slay it; separating the feminine element from the masculine, they create a new world which is governed not by the principle of unity, but by the principle of opposites or polarity. Psychologically speaking, this act signifies the beginning struggle of consciousness to separate itself from unconsciousness. Now the Good Mother, originally represented by the life-giving womb and the life-sustaining cow, is transformed into Terrible Mother, the destroyer and devouring monster, symbolizing the tendency of the unconscious to resist assimilation by the conscious system. Thus mythology enters the second stage, the cycle of the hero. I should inject here that Jungian psychologists always hasten to add that the identification of the unconscious with the feminine principle must not be construed to mean that women are or represent the unconscious, while men by implication represent the conscious system. On the contrary, all human beings, male and female, are psychological hybrids, carrying both the feminine and the masculine in them. The processes described here refer to the development of the individual in a trans-personal and trans-sexual sense. However, in mythology the conscious is invariabley represented by masculine symbols, and the unconscious, by feminine symbols. The reason for this is the original identity of body and psyche in the alimentary uroboros of early infancy. The child recognizes father and mother as separate people only secondarily, thus separating the two principles at the same time it becomes conscious of itself as separate from the world.[3]

The hero slays the androgynous being and creates a new world. Scandinavian mythology has provided two models for this new cosmic structure. One is the image of the world as a series of concentric or superimposed circles or discs. The skull of Ymir becomes the arching vault of the sky, his body the round of the earth, his blood the encircling sea. The gods settle the center of the earth; around this divine center human beings have their abode, while the outermost rim, the mountains, is inhabited by the survivors of the primordial giants. Surrounding the entire world, biting its own tail, the great Midgard Serpent swims in the ocean. As circular snake, the serpent is another transformation of the primordial uroboros, the self-fructifying and perfect womb of nature. But consistent with the thematic shift in the heroic phase, the serpent is now invariably represented as a monster, the implacable enemy of gods and men.[4]

The second model of the universe is the World Tree. If we hold that the circular shape of the first model suggests the womb or maternal principle, we may well interpret the world tree as a representation of the paternal principle, the phallus.[5] In any case it is, as Mircea Eliade put it, a "Cosmic Tree *par excellence,* the image of polar opposition as well as interdependence.[6] In the top branches of the Tree sits an eagle and between his eyes a hawk, a double symbol of consciousness and both personifications of Othin. But while the tree as "erect phallus" topped by the symbol of Othin (the eye, the swift-flying bird), may thus be said to represent the hero's struggle toward the emancipation of consciousness, the myth leaves no doubt that the Tree is and remains rooted in the chtonic earth, the maternal unconscious. There are three roots: one reaches into the land of the giants in Ginnungagap, in other words, it connects the present to the beginnings. The spring of Mimir is found under this root; Othin's journey to this well and his voluntary sacrifice of one eye for a drink, may thus be interpreted as an acknowledgement of the wisdom buried in the primordial unconscious. Another root of the Tree reaches into the land of the dead, Niflheim; at the entrance lies a huge, man-eating dragon, Nidhøgg, a personification of the mother ogress in her most terrifying form. Nidhøgg, the arch-enemy of the eagle in the sky, gnaws at the Tree from below, trying to destroy it. The third root, however, paradoxically reaches up into the sky, the abode of the shaper gods. Under this root, too, there is a spring, and at this spring there live three women, the Mothers of Destiny, called the Norns. Their names (Urd, Verdandi, and Skuld) indicate that they represent Past, Present, and Future. They water the Tree from the sacred spring so that its branches shall not wither or decay. They also determine the fate of the universe; like the Greek Parces, or like Maya, the eternal spinner of Hindu mythology, they spin the web of existence for gods and men alike, determining the destiny both of the individual and of the entire cosmos. To this spring the gods ride daily and there they hold their council and court of justice, thus expressing clearly the interdependence of the maternal and paternal powers: fate spun out by the Norns (the Mothers), is actualized by the shaper gods (the Fathers).

The new cosmic order imposed by the gods of the sky is also carried through on the social level; Othin appoints twelve male gods to rule the world, as well as establishes a religious cult. But most poignantly the new order is expressed by the creation of the human being. Ymir had created his primitive offspring unconsciously; in his story, the power of life was associated with bodily secretions such as sweat and semen. The creation of the human being, by contrast, is a conscious act and here the power of life is preeminently associated with the breath as the representation of spirit. The three creator gods, Othin, Vili, and Ve, find two trees on the shores of the ocean and into these Ve infuses the spark of physical life, Vili the power of reason and will (Jung would identify this power with the ego, the subject of our conscious acts), while Othin gives breath or spirit. The significance of Othin's gift is the most difficult to understand, but here the etymology of his name can help us. Othin's name (related to oðr, meaning "raging") suggests that he represents the raging, dynamic force of nature, the furious, destructive storm as well as the creative, swift moving wind. The notion of divine creativity in the form of wind is known from many mythologies, including the classical and the Christian. Jung defines the creative wind-spirit as the dynamic principle in the human psyche which moves, fires and inspires us and thus forms the very antithesis of the stasis and inertia of our material being.[7] Jung says further that archaic man apprehended this spiritual factor as an invisible, breathlike presence, and, equally important, that in dreams, myths, legends, and fairytales spirit is mostly symbolized by two related figures, namely the figure of the Wise Old Man, or its negative aspect, the Terrible Hunter. Both of these descriptions fit Othin. In various heroic legends Othin is depicted as a one-eyed, bearded old man who appears precisely at the moment when the hero finds himself in a critical situation of mortal danger or choice, or when he is in need of special knowledge or inspiration. Othin may give him counsel or maybe a weapon which only the hero, the "inspired individual," is able to wield. Psychologically speaking, the Wise Old Man thus represents an archetypal and autonomous content of the unconscious presenting itself to the conscious mind as personified thought. But, as we said, the Wise Old Man can also appear as his own opposite, as a death-dealer as well as a life-dealer. Then he manifests himself as the wicked magician, a deceiver and evil-doer, or as the terrible hunter riding through the air on a magic horse to come swiftly and unexpectedly strike down the same hero he has supported with counsel and gifts. Again this description fits Othin, who is also called Ygg, The Terrible One. Othin may himself appear on the battlefield and kill his chosen hero, as he did in the case of Harald War-Tooth, or break the hero's weapon and leave him defenseless, as he did with Sigmund, the son of Volsung; or he may send his valkyries who ride on their flying horses and bring death to the best of warriors in the name of the raging god. The heroes are carried to Valhall, the great hall of Othin where they will fight and feast until the end of the cosmic eon. The warrior's death is thus a kind of rebirth into a higher, more perfect form of life; but it remains nonetheless a deeply ambiguous experience robbing the hero of victory and life on earth.

These examples indicate that Othin is an equivocal figure and, further, that he by no means represents only conscious contents of the psyche but also aspects of the unconscious. We will return to this presently, but first I want to take a look at other major sky gods, namely Tyr, Thor, and Frey. These gods are much simpler in their structure and play clearly identifiable roles in the confrontation of opposites. Tyr, the oldest of the Scandinavian pantheon, is remembered chiefly by the sacrifice of his weapon hand for the purpose of binding the monster of the underworld, the Fenris Wolf. Inasmuch as the hand, together with the head and the eye, is a major symbol of consciousness or the masculine principle, Tyr's loss may be interpreted as a form of propitiatory castration. To be sure, by castration in this context, mythologists do not mean actual loss of the male genitilia, but a symbolic castration typical of the hostility of the unconscious to the ego and to consciousness. Tyr's loss thus parallels Othin's payment of one eye for a drink from Mimir. However, it should be pointed out that in both cases the sacrifice was voluntary; Tyr submits to castration in order to contain or control the unconscious, Othin in order to partake of its knowledge; in both cases the act implies a positive, active offering up of consciousness for an important purpose.

Thor, too, is subject to symbolic castration, but his loss is not voluntary. Thor's hammer personifies the bolt of lightning followed by thunder and rain and thus is a bringer of fertility; moreover, like the lightning bolt of Zeus and Indra, the hammer represents the power of the sky pitted against the primordial powers of earth and sea. But once a giant had stolen the hammer and would give it up only if he received Freyja for a wife. This would mean, however, that the power of human productivity would pass out of the hands of the gods, back into the control of the primordial personfications of the earth. To prevent this disastrous possibility, the gods devise a ruse that is not without comedy; they dress the huge, big-bellied and red-bearded Thor in women's clothes, a grotesque image which expresses Thor's temporary emasculation very well. In this guise Thor journeys to the giant, is received by the happy bridegroom who places the hammer in the lap of the blushing bride to make her fruitful, and Thor forthwith slays the giant and all his kin.

A further variation of the symbolic complex of castration can be observed in the story of Frey who gave up his sword to possess Gerth, another personification of the maternal earth. Frey, of course, is a phallic divinity, the chief god of fertility. But here a distinction must be made between his function as the fecundator of the earth and his function as a representative of the masculine sky. From archeological and historical sources we know that during the late Stone Age and the Bronze Age, the chief divinity worshipped was female, the Great Mother Earth. Even during the Roman period the feminine divinities seem to have been in dominance. In Viking mythology, by contrast, we notice a progressive masculinization of the divine and a corresponding suppression of the feminine. Nerthus, the *terra mater,* whose fertility cult Tacitus had described in detail, appears as a male god Njord in the Scandinavian pantheon.[9] The war between the Wanir (the earth divinities) and the Æsir (the powers of the sky) suggests a clash between the two cults which was resolved by the absorption of the fertility gods into the tribe of the shaper gods.[10] It is characteristic that none of the Vanir contribute to the restructuring of the cosmic order in the heroic cycle. We notice, too, that none of the goddesses, of which there are at least as many as male gods, are included in the government of the world; nor do they have a seat in the high temple, or contribute to the making of the material culture or the making of tools. In the light of this overall trend, Frey's loss of his sword takes on added significance. His troubles begin when he presumes to sit in the highseat of Othin, the supreme sky god, and thus momentarily acquires the world penetrating vision of the All-Father. For in looking out over the world, Frey sees the beauty of the earth personified in the giant maiden Gerth and is possessed by such sexual passion that he gives up his sword, symbol of his higher masculinity or consciousness, for the sake of possessing the maiden. We are told that this is a momentous loss and will eventually cause Frey's death, because he will be defenseless in the great battle at the end of time when the powers of the underworld destroy the cosmos created by the sky gods.

What, then, is the function of the goddesses? By and large, the female divinities associated with the sky are projections of the Great Mother in her positive and beneficent aspects. Among these goddesses we count Frigg, the prophetic wife of Othin; Sif, the golden haired wife of Thor; Ithun, the keeper of the apples of youth; and Freyja, the patroness of human sexuality. Freyja is also called the sow, the bitch, the she-goat, and it is said of her that she lures all men indiscriminately. Thus she represents what mythologists call the "sacred prostitute," or vessel of fertility.[11] But Freyja, like Isis of ancient Egypt, has also some negative aspects. She lays claim to half the warriors that fall on the battlefield, for instance, a direct reminder that she represents not only the life-giving, but also the devouring, womb. Most of the truly monstrous qualities of the Terrible Mother, however, have been separated from Freyja and are projected into another figure, the ogress of disease, hunger and death, called Hel. Hel is one of the three monsters born of a giantess and fathered by Loki, a strange figure who claims to be a blood brother of Othin, but actually reveals himself to be an enemy of the sky gods.

The relationship of Loki to Othin is a paradox that has many parallels in world mythology. As Neumann points out: "The structure of the father, whether personal or trans-personal, is two-sided like that of the mother. In mythology there stands beside the creative, positive father, the destructive and negative father."[12] We have already talked about the split of Othin, the father figure,

into the Wise Old Man and the Terrible Hunter. Now we encounter a parallel split of Othin into the World-Creator on one hand and Othin, the World-Destroyer, on the other. The latter aspect, however, as an expression of absolute evil associated with supreme divinity, has been carefully masked. It is expressed and yet hidden through its projection into a separate figure closely linked with Othin, namely Loki, who is also called Father-of-Lies. Loki enjoyed no cult; he was not worshipped. But as the major representation of the negative power associated with the shaper gods, Loki is always involved whenever the gods find themselves in a major difficulty. One of Loki's disastrous deeds is to father the monsters representing the greatest dangers the gods ever have to face and which eventually conquer them. Psychologically, these monsters symbolize the disintegrative power of the unconscious, "its rending, destroying, devouring and castrating character."[13] As devouring forces, the children of Loki are closely associated with the uroboric womb; but just as that womb contained both principles in itself, the monsters of the unconscious can take on either feminine or masculine form. Thus we interpreted Hel, the ogress, as a direct representation of the Terrible Mother. But the second child of Loki, the Fenris-Wolf, a monster so huge that his upper jaw brushes against the sky while his lower jaw scrapes against the earth, appears as a representation of the Terrible Father. Loki's third child, however, the World Serpent called Jormungand, appears to be both. When the gods fling the phallic serpent into the ocean, it winds itself around the world in the shape of a circle, thus representing the womb that both sustains and threatens its offspring. Thor, the defender of the world, is repeatedly pitted against the great serpent. Once he nearly killed it with his hammer, another time he almost lifted it bodily out of the primordial ocean. But ultimately even Thor can defeat Jormungand only at the price of his own death. In the great battle at the end of time Thor slays the monster, but is himself killed by its poisonous breath.

The cataclysmic destruction of the world order is the most awe inspiring chapter in cosmic history written by the Fate and, again, Loki plays a major role in it. The first warnings of approaching disaster are the foreboding dreams of Balder, the young and innocent son of Othin. Psychologically and mythologically, the figure of the divine child or youthful hero is well known. Commenting on the child archetype, Jung says that one of its essential features is its futurity. The child paves the way for a future change of personality, anticipating "the synthesis of conscious and unconscious elements in the personality. It is therefore a symbol which unites the opposites," a symbol of wholeness transcending consciousness which Jung has called the "Self."[14] On the divine level, the child hero personifies the collective unconscious which is not yet integrated into the human being. Among the major motifs surrounding this god figure Jung mentions that "he can cope with the greatest perils, yet, in the end, something quite insignificant is his undoing."[15] To give an example, Jung refers to the story of Balder who is killed by the seemingly harmless mistletoe. Now Frazer, the author of *The Golden Bough,* has tried to show that the mistletoe, as a tree parasite, represents the "soul" of the World Tree; so that the myth of Balder's slaying should be interpreted as a scenario for a ritual in which the mistletoe was carved from the tree and the tree itself felled and burned in the expectation that it would renew itself and all of nature in the coming season.[16] Without committing ourselves to this particular ritual interpretation, it is of course suggestive to see Balder in relation to the World Tree, and his death as the failure of consciousness seeking to transcend itself and reach for the whole, integrated personality. Consciousness is doomed to defeat in the heroic cycle of cosmic time. The nascent "Self" must die.

Othin's role as a cause of this failure is again masked, with Loki acting in his stead. When Balder dreamed that his life was threatened, his mother (Frigg) elicited a promise from all things in the universe that they would not harm her beloved child. The only thing excluded from this promise was the mistletoe which Frigg thought too young and innocent to do harm. Loki, however, in the disguise of an old woman, found out this secret from Frigg herself, and when all the gods were gleefully throwing weapons at the invulnerable Balder, Loki placed the mistletoe in the hand of the blind god Høð, Høð threw it, and killed Balder. The blindness of Høð, a son of Othin, is another obvious expression of lacking consciousness; he is the "castrated" god who kills from ignorance. It should be mentioned, too, that stabbing with the spear was a preferred mode of sacrificing a human being to Othin. In a sense, then, Balder should go to Valhall, but this would necessitate an open admission of the role of the All-Father in the murder of his own son. No, Balder, though dying by the spear, is the one hero belonging to Hel, the devouring womb of the deep. While he yet sails on his funeral ship across the maternal ocean and into the realm of the dead, Othin sends another son, Hermod the Bold, to find out whether Hel would release Balder for a ransom. Hel answers that Balder may return if all living and dead things in the universe would weep for him. Everything did weep, except for Loki. The Father-of-Lies again took on a woman's shape and, disguised as the giantess Thøkk, he refused to shed a single tear. Thus Loki, the projection of the Terrible Father, but in the shape of woman and giantess, in other words, simultaneously as the projection of the Terrible Mother, once more acts as the demonic agent and representative of the unconscious in destroying the developing "Self." With Balder's death the social and spiritual and finally also the physical, form the shaper gods have wrought on the world, collapses in ruin. Ragnarok, the Doom or Fate of the Gods, has been fulfilled.

Yet eventually there rises a new world from the sea, still more beautiful than the old and cleansed of monsters and terror. A new sun illumines the sky. The Serpent and the Wolf are but memories of the past, while the Eagle, sym-

bol of the god of the sky, again flies high over the mountains. And two human beings have survived, a woman by the name of Lif (meaning "Life"), and a man by the name of Lifthrasir (meaning "The One who clings to Life"); they had hidden in a branch of the World Tree which, apparently, had been shaken in the universal cataclysm but not destroyed. And finally a younger generation of gods, the children of the old, return and take over the government of the world together with Balder who is resurrected from the realm of Hel.

The question presents itself whether this story of the death and resurrection of Balder does not give clear indication that Scandinavian mythology had reached the third cycle, the cycle of transformation? We should probably answer, both yes, and no. The description of the new world arising from the eternal womb, the ocean, is a transformed world, a world without monsters; in other words, it suggests a form of existence in which the unconscious is no longer a threat to consciousness, but rather an assimilated part of the self. However, as Neumann points out in his discussion of the death and resurrection of the Egyptian god Osiris, as long as "rebirth is passively experienced by one already dead," we cannot speak of this restoration to life as self-transformation.[17] And it seems, indeed, that in the case of Balder both death and resurrection are passive experiences expressing primarily the law of the life cycle, individual and cosmic, spun out by the maternal Fates and enacted by the sky gods. The hero myth is fulfilled and merges into the myth of transformation only when the hero experiences his death as a voluntary act and, simultaneously, as an act of self-regeneration. Only then has the hero overcome the enmity of opposite principles; only then is the twofold human being reborn as the whole and complete human being. The myth of Balder does not fulfill these conditions.

We should, however, take another look at some of the myths describing Othin's journeys to the realm of the maternal powers. For, in these stories, the unconscious appears not exclusively as projections of the Good or the Terrible Mother, but also as the feminine transformative principle, the soul guide, which Jung referred to as the anima. Besides the journey to the spring of wisdom (Mimir), Othin travelled to the realm of the unconscious twice more. Next to wisdom and knowledge, the major gift of the All-Father to mankind is inspiration, the creative power represented by the intoxicating beverage of the gods, the mead. In the paradoxical language of myth, the sources tell us that the mead originated with the gods but also with the primordial giants. When the two races of the gods, the Æsir and the Vanir, made peace between them, they spat into a crock and from this liquid they made a man called Kvasir who became renowned for his judgment. But Kvasir was killed by the dwellers of the underworld, who drained his blood into three vessels and mixed it with honey so that it fermented and became the precious mead of inspiration. This story suggests that the gods' contribution to inspiration is thought, while the fermenting, transformative power comes from the unconscious represented by the earth dwellers. The mead was then placed in the safekeeping of a giantess by the name of Gunnlød. Othin came to her abode, a mountain, drilled a hole through the wall and penetrated in the form of a snake. Once inside, he slept with Gunnlød for three nights and for each night he received one draught from each of the three kettles. On the third morning he escaped in the shape of a falcon. The sexual symbolism of Othin's quest for the mead is obvious. The god penetrates the primordial womb represented by the mountain with the phallus represented by the snake. He has intercourse with the keeper of the mead and for this he is rewarded with the treasured liquid itself. This act represents the creative union with the anima in the *hieros gamos,* the sacred marriage of the opposite principles.

Othin's third descent is yet more dramatic and involves his special relationship to the World Tree. The name of the World Tree is Yggdrasil which means "The Horse of the Terrible One," in other words, Othin. Now, there is an expression in Scandinavia, "to ride the gallows," which means to be hung by the neck. Sacrifice to Othin was performed this way, as well as by stabbing with the spear. The purpose of offering up a human victim was to ensure the help of the god in battle, to win his protection and counsel, and ultimately to achieve afterlife in Valhall. In a remarkable passage in the *Poetic Edda* (Havamal), however, the victim offered to Othin is Othin himself. By voluntary self sacrifice Othin thus achieves the *summa bonum,* the highest good, which is the conquest of death itself and self regeneration. For he experiences the moment of death as the very moment of rebirth, both physically and spiritually. In other words, Othin has successfully assimilated the prime creative force represented by the womb into himself. He rises back out of the underworld below the World Tree to the world of earth and sky, taking with him the magic runes which give him power over the dead and the living and over nature's elements.

We should note, too, that Othin's journeys to the spring of Mimir and to the giant maiden who guarded the mead are both included in this passage, in other words that these quests are seen as analogues to Othin's self sacrifice, or even as part of that sacrificial experience.

Othin's achievement is thus the high point in the development of Scandinavian myth as depicted in the two Eddas. The chief god, representing the dynamic and spiritual principle identified with the sun and sky, has opened up channels of creative communication with the unconscious depth, the primordial darkness from which all life takes its issue. He has travelled into the labyrinth of the psyche under the leadership of the soul guide, the transforming feminine anima. —And yet, his achievement is contradicted by the myth of Balder. The reconciliation of opposite principles has been begun on the level of the individual divinity, but it eludes the gods on the universal, all embracing level. In other words, the complete integration of the self, the total personality, has not yet been achieved.

Notes

[1] *The Origins and History of Consciousness* (Bollingen Series XLII), Princeton, N.J., Princeton U. Press, 1971, passim.

[2] *Altgermanische Religionsgeschichte.* Berlin, Walter deGruyter, 1970, II, 362.

[3] Neumann, op. cit., 27-29, 290-293.

[4] On snake symbolism, the phallic and the ring snake, see Neumann, ibid, 48-49.

[5] Jere Fleck ("Othin's Self Sacrifice—A New Interpretation, II: The Ritual Landscape," *Scandinavian Studies* 43/4 (1971), 400) takes an extreme position on Yggdrasil as cosmic model, interpreting the "connecting axis between a masculine heaven and a feminine earth (as) supremely phallic in nature," and the waters nourishing the world as well as the poet's mead, as Othin's sperm; Neumann (*The Great Mother. An Analysis of the Archetype* (Bollingen Series XLVII). Princeton, N.J., Princeton U. Press, 1972, 251) takes the opposite view, emphasizing the feminine aspect of the tree that is rooted in the maternal waters of destiny.

[6] *Patterns in Comparative Religion.* Cleveland and New York, World Publ. Co., 1963, 276-277.

[7] *The Collected Works of C. G. Jung* (Bollingen Series XX). New York, Pantheon Books, 1959, IX, part 1, 210.

[8] Neumann, *Origins,* 53-54 (note).

[9] Scholars have argued that the cult of Nerthus may have involved a male god who was her brother and consort, the same way that Njord is said to have a sister who is also his wife. One plausible explanation for the change of sex would then be that Tacitus neglected the male divinity because at the time the feminine was the dominant partner; in Viking mythology, by contrast, the dominance has been reversed. See: Folke Strøm. *Nordisk hedendom. Tro och sed i førkristen tid.* Gøteborg, Akademiførlaget, 1967, 41.

[10] An alternative and widely accepted interpretation of this war has been suggested by George Dumezil, who reads the conflict as a struggle between the agricultural and warrior classes. His "structuralist theory," based on an analogy with the class system of India, appears "exotic" (to quote Folke Strøm, op. cit., 105) when applied to the nordic context, where peasant and warrior were usually the same people and no priestly class ever developed as a separate group.

[11] Neumann, *The Great Mother,* 94.

[12] Neumann, *Origins,* 170-171.

[13] Ibid, 170.

[14] Works, IX, part 1, 164.

[15] Ibid, 167.

[16] Sir James G. Frazer, *The Golden Bough. A Study in Magic and Religion.* I Volume, Abridged Edition. New York, Macmillan Co., 1951, 703ff.

[17] Neumann, *Origins,* 254.

Gísli Sigurdsson (1988)

SOURCE: "Mythology," in *Gaelic Influence in Iceland: Historical and Literary Contacts*, Bókaûtgáfa Menningarsjóds, 1988, pp. 73-82.

[*In the following excerpt, Sigurdsson identifies and analyzes links between Gaelic folktales and Icelandic mythology.*]

Scandinavian Background

Old Norse/Icelandic mythology as it has been preserved, mainly in *Snorra-Edda* and the Eddaic poems, mostly written in Iceland in the 13th century, has its origins, at least partly, in pagan times. It can be assumed that the general framework of ideas concerning the gods was brought to Iceland as it existed at the time of the settlement. The ties with Scandinavia never broke so that myths which were later attached to Scandinavian gods could travel back and forth and be told on both sides of the Atlantic, in Iceland and Scandinavia alike. But these were scattered stories and linked up with poems about the gods. Knowledge of these, however, was fundamental for scaldic poets and their audience in order to understand kennings and the poetic vocabulary, much of which is based on the mythology.

The status of the gods was established by the Scandinavians themselves, who composed poems and told stories about them.

The Gaels who were faced with this tradition in Iceland could not have affected its roots or its general background. It is another matter how faithfully our sources reflect Old Norse mythology and pagan beliefs, or how much influence Christianity had on the tradition during the centuries. Such questions need not concern us here. Because of the nature of the material in pagan times, lack of an authoritative collection of myths related to the gods and a lack of any institution which decided on what was genuine tradition and what was not, the stories were open

to additions and variations. New stories could be told about the gods and fitted into what had been told of them before. It is in this manner that the Gaelic material could become a part of Old Norse/Icelandic mythology without changing its basic assumptions.

One may therefore suggest that Gaelic influence in Old Icelandic myths would be likely to be limited to single motifs and episodes, a few of which will now be discussed.

Single Gaelic Motifs

The Sons of Tuireann and Loki

From Ireland comes a story, called *The Fate of the Children of Tuireann* (see esp. pp. 188-89 and 196-97). The text dates from the 18th century but references to its contents are found as early as in *The Book of Leinster* (1160)[1] and A. B. Rooth[2] has argued that it might reflect an even older story.

The sons of Tuireann get the task of fetching the apples of life. They fly off as hawks, take the apples but are pursued by fire-vomiting ladies in the form of griffins. The sons—as hawks—catch fire, change again into swans, dart down into the sea and complete their mission.

In *Haustlong* (a poem dated to the 9th century) and *Snorra-Edda* we find a story of how Loki saves his life from the giant Þjazi (who is in the form of an eagle) by promising to bring him Iðunn and her apples of youth. This he does and when the Æsir find out they send Loki off to fetch them back. Loki transforms himself into a hawk, fulfils his task but is pursued by Þjazi, again in eagle guise, into Ásgarður. There, at the right moment, the gods light a fire into which Þjazi flies and is killed.

S. Bugge[3] has claimed that the Irish story depends on classical sources (this is deduced from the number of tasks involved, similar to those of Hercules, and the occurence of the name "Hisbe" which supposedly goes back to Latin "Hesperus/Hisperus") whereas *Haustlong* and *Snorra-Edda* are derived from the Irish.

In a more recent study, A. B. Rooth has accepted Bugge's argument, saying that:

> The tale of the sons of Turen agrees with regard to the order of motifs and details with the myth of Þjazi, for example the chasing in eagle guise; griffins chase hawks (the sons of Turen); fire, breathed out by the griffins, singes the hawks so that they fall into the sea; [. . .] it would seem that the motif of the burned hawks has been transformed into the motif of Þjazi burned by the fire of the Ása gods.[4]

Rooth further argues that apart from this the author of *Haustlong* was acquainted with material from the British

Isles as well as classical authors. She concludes, however, that the apples did not come into the poem from classical authors directly, but "probably through an intermediary British source such as the tale of the Sons of Turen."[5]

This story, however, would need to be subjected to more detailed research, and further comparison with other areas must be made before any final conclusions can be drawn.

Táin Bó Fraích and Þórr's Visit to Geirröðr

The Irish story *Táin Bó Fraích* has been suggested as a source for Þórr's visit to Geirröðr (in *Þórsdrápa* and *Snorra-Edda,* Skáldskaparmál, ch. 27)[6]

In *Táin Bó Fraích* the king, Ailill, lures Fróech to swim in a pool in which, he tells him, he knows of no danger. Fróech has to take off his belt and swims without a weapon, across the pond to fetch a branch of rowan. He is attacked by a water-monster which clings to him. Fróech receives a sword from Ailill's daughter, Findabair, whereupon Ailill throws a spear at Fróech which he catches in the air and throws back. He misses Ailill but the spear goes through his mantle and shirt. Then Fróech kills the monster with the sword, gets out of the pool and is taken away by a host of otherworld women to recover.

Loki lures Þórr to go to Geirröðr and tells him that the road is without dangers so Þórr leaves without his weapons but accompanied by Loki/or Þjálfi. Þórr obtains a magic belt, staff and iron gloves from a certain Gríðr with whom they stay overnight. On the way they have to pass a river and Þórr uses the staff from Gríðr to support himself, wading through the water with Loki/Þjálfi clinging to his belt. The river starts to rise and looking around him, Þórr sees the cause of this sudden rise: a giantess (or two, Geirröðr's daughters) standing with her legs spread, further up and producing large quantities of liquid. Þórr then grabs a stone and throws it at her, saying that a river should be stemmed at its mouth. Climbing out of the river he seizes a rowan tree for support. Þórr continues to the otherworld where Geirröðr resides and kills his daughters with the staff. Geirröðr throws a glowing metal lump/bar at Þórr which he catches with the gloves from Gríðr and throws back at Geirröðr. The bar goes first through a pillar, then through Geirröðr and finally through the wall, and into the ground.

Rooth has drawn attention to the following parallels[7]: 1) The monster clings on to Fróech "in the same way as Þjálfi (Loki) hung on to Þórr." (72) 2) Þórr and Fróech are both fooled into leaving their weapons behind them. 3) The river in Þórr's story is parallelled by the pond in *Táin Bó Fraích.* 4) The rowan tree appears in both stories but with a different function. 5) They receive a weapon (staff/sword) from a woman. 6) They both catch a spear/iron bar which is thrown at them and send it back. Fróech's

cast is harmless but Þórr, who never misses, does not miss this time either.

Rooth concludes that these parallels are "too numerous and too peculiar to be explained as "natural" in their contexts or as spontaneously originated parallel phenomena."[8] And since *Táin Bó Fraích* appears to be older than our oldest Icelandic source (*Þórsdrápa*) the receiver is deemed to be the Icelandic/Scandinavian tradition.

Death of Fergus—Death of Baldr

Similar conclusions are drawn in Rooth's work with regard to the relationship between the Old Irish *Aided Fergusa* and the story of Baldr's death, mainly found in *Snorra-Edda* (Gylfaginning, ch. 33-35, but references to it are also in *Völuspá, Baldrs draumar,* and Saxo).[9]

In *Aided Fergusa,* Ailill gets the blind fosterbrother of Fergus, Lugaid, to throw a spear at Fergus where he is playing joyfully with Medb, Ailill's wife, in a lake. Ailill tells Lugaid that these are a hart and a doe in the lake. Another version in *Silva Gadelica*[10] tells of how Ael (Ailill) kills Ferchis (Fergus) by throwing a spear of "hardened holly" at him, pretending to be aiming at a stag.

In *Snorra-Edda,* Loki fools Baldr's blind brother, Hoðr, into throwing a sprig of mistletoe at him and thus join in a favourite entertainment of the gods, namely, throwing objects at Baldr. This was a harmless game since all things had sworn to spare Baldr—except the mistletoe which was considered "too young" to swear. The mistletoe proves fatal and Baldr dies.

Comparing the Baldr myth with classical, Christian and Oriental motifs, Rooth concludes that these are too different from the Scandinavian version which agrees in details with traditions from the British Isles. "This indicates that the Baldr myth [Parts 1-2] has come to Scandinavia direct from, or has been influenced by the tradition in, the British Isles."[11]

The dialogue between Loki and Hoðr is parallelled by the dialogue between Ailill and Lugaid. In the Irish however, Lugaid's blindness is essential "whereas in the Scandinavian tradition it gives the impression of having been clumsily combined with the *mistletoe* as the only effective weapon."[12] It may also be noted that the motif of a plant in this connection is known in Ireland. The idea of a blind figure involuntarily killing his fosterbrother/brother is of course the same.

These examples from Rooth's study will suffice to show the nature of the relationship as argued for by her. Surprisingly, Rooth does not compare Bricriu, the troublemaker in Irish tradition, with his counterpart in the north, Loki. Turville-Petre[13] discussed this resemblance, referring to Dumézil, and claimed that Bricriu bore "a distinct resemblance to Loki"[14] without elaborating on that likeness in any detail.

The Masterbuilder

C. W. von Sydow has tried to establish a connection between stories in the Irish Finn cycle about a masterbuilder and *Snorra-Edda* (Gylfaginning, ch.25) where a giant builds Ásgarðr for the gods with the assistance of his horse, Svaðilfari. A similar story is also told about a certain Finn (according to von Sydow the name itself suggests a connection with the Irish) who builds the cathedral in Trondhjem. The story has spread in Scandinavia and been attached to other church buildings.[15].

This motif is widespread in the Finn-cycle. The masterbuilder offers to take on a project with his horse and complete it within a certain period. In *Snorra-Edda* the builder asks for Freyja as a reward as well as the sun and the moon. The last mentioned objects are used by von Sydow as an indication that the story originated in Ireland. He feels that this is too much to ask for as a reward and besides, it is not within the gods' power to give the sun and moon away. This, he claims, could be based on a misunderstanding of an Irish idiom:

> "do-bheirim grian agus éasga", ordgrant översatt: "jag ger sol och måne", men dess verkliga betydelse är: "jag svär vid sol och måne" eller helt enkelt: "Jag försäkrar dyrt och heligt". Det ligger nära till hands att en sådan formel skall missförstås av en person som ej är förtrogen med iriskans alla egendomliga idiom, översättas ordgrant och uppfattas som ett lönevillkor, i stället för vad det är, en bekräftelseformel. Men då är det också tydligt at det är nordborna som här varit låntagare.[16]

The problem has been discussed by numerous scholars, some of whom have held views irreconcilable to that of von Sydow. The motif is widespread in Scandinavia and whether its origins lie in Ireland or not is of no vital importance for the present discussion. If it is Irish, it may have reached Scandinavia relatively late, possibly via the Orkneys (see p. 47). Its popularity, though, might be seen as an argument against such late foreign influence.[17]

Þórr's Visit to Útgarða-Loki

A much more detailed study was carried out by von Sydow[18] on Þórr's visit to Útgarða-Loki (in *Snorra-Edda*, Gylfaginning ch. 26-31) in which he argued for Irish origins of the story. He was later criticized by Finnur Jónsson[19] which led to lively debate on this particular story, methodology and the Irish question in general in *Folkminnen och Folktankar* the year after.[20] This debate shows, among other things, how entirely correct von Sydow was when he earlier wrote in 1920:

> A andra sidan verkar än i dag blotta misstanken om lån från kelterna på germanisterna som ett rödt kläde på en tjur. Knappast någon germanist har underkastat

> sig mödan att lära sig det utomordentlig svåra gaeliska språket, och kännedomen om keltisk tradition har sålunda ej kunnat framtvinga en undersökning om sammanhanget.[21]

Ever since, scholars have been expressing their respective opinions on the possible Irish origins of Þórr's visit, most recently R. Power,[22] where references to earlier works may be found.

All this effort, however, has not led us to the ultimate goal, i.e. to prove beyond doubt where the story originated. Power's conclusions still leave us with questions to be answered even though it is hardly reasonable to call for more detailed research than that which has already gone into this particular story.

> Although it remains a possibility that 'Þórr's Visit' is independent of the Irish tale, the similarities are so great as to suggest some connection. In the absence of any evidence of a common source it is reasonable to assume that this is one case in which an Irish tale reached Iceland.[23]

We are always faced with the same results. We have to judge for ourselves which is the most likely interpretation of the evidence, basing our judgement on what can be learned from other sources. Individual elements tell us but little until they have been accumulated and thus give support to each other.

Talking Heads

Talking Heads appear in Old Icelandic sources, the most famous example of which is Mímir's head, which Óðinn prevents from rotting by smearing it with herbs. The head then speaks to him, tells of various tidings and hidden matters.[24]

A. Ross[25] has looked at the nature of severed heads in Celtic cultures. Of particular interest to us in this connection is the association of heads with wells. Ross[26] discusses this aspect of the beliefs and points out the similarities with Mímir's head and well. Óðinn's herbal treatment, she says, is "in the manner of the Celts, who preserved the heads of their enemies with oil and herbs"[27] and further:

> Thus we have, in a Norse context, a group of motifs which, untypical as they are of Norse tradition, are completely familiar from Celtic sources. The decapitation of the head, its preservation, its association with a well, and its powers of prophecy and other-worlds knowledge are all features which recur in Celtic tradition and belief. All the evidence suggests that this episode in Norse mythology, if not a direct borrowing from a Celtic source, at least owes its presence in the Norse tradition to a detailed knowledge on the part of the story-teller of such beliefs amongst the Celts.[28]

Elaborating on this possibility, J. Simpson[29] has considered the myth of Mímir with the idea in mind that he was essentially the Head and can be traced to "Celtic" material. Thus "Celtic" origins for this belief can explain what in Icelandic sources alone appears to be confusing and contradictory.

Rígsþula

Irish influence on *Rígsþula* seems to be well established and generally accepted.[30] The poem tells of the origins of three classes in society. Rígr (identified with Heimdallr in a prose introduction to the poem) travels from one married couple to another and sleeps with the woman in each place he visits, thus begetting the forefathers of slaves, free workmen ("karla ættir") and earls. A favourite problem of Old Norse philologists, the age of the poem, will not be dealt with here. Both the early 10th and the 13th centuries have been suggested. What concerns us is, first, the name of the poem. The *Ríg-* is taken to be derived from the Old Irish genitive singular, *ríg* of *rí,* meaning king.

Einar Ólafur Sveinsson[31] has summarized several parallels between the poem and Irish material. He compares the god Rígr with the Irish Dagda who is called Ollathaer—"the great father"—and begets a son, Mac Óc[32] ("young boy", similar to Konr ungr ("ungr" means "young") in *Rígsþula*) on another man's wife. The custom that a noble visitor is entitled to sleep with his host's wife is known from Ireland but not in Scandinavia.[33] Konr ungr also masters some power over birds which reminds us of Cú Chulainn[34] and his son, Conlae.[35]

Rígsþula is unique among the Eddaic poems in its realistic and detailed descriptions of domestic matters and different classes. In this it resembles an Old Irish law text where similarly detailed descriptions of different social orders, their possessions, dress and eating habits, may be found.[36]

Einar Ólafur Sveinsson thinks that the poem was probably composed in the tenth century by a person who was familiar with the British Isles.

In her study of *Rígsþula,* Young[37] drew attention to Heimdallr's popularity in the British Isles as is reflected on sculptured crosses with images identified as Heimdallr. She then proceeded to show affinities between a tale in the *Rennes Dindsenchas* (p. 294-95), explaining the river name Inber n-Ailbine, and references to Heimdallr in *Völuspá in skamma* (st. 7) and in the lost *Heimdallargaldr,* quotations from which are preserved in *Snorra-Edda* (Gylfaginning, ch. 15 and Skáldskaparmál, ch. 16).

> In both the central figure is a son born of nine mothers and in both there is an allusion to the use of a human head as a missile. The resemblance becomes the more

striking when we remember that *Völuspá in skamma* states that Heimdall's mothers were sea maidens and that he was nourished on the ice cold sea. The only serious discrepancy between the Heimdall myth and the legend preserved in the *Rennes Dinnsenchas* is that in the former case the offspring of the nine mothers is slain by a head used as a missile whereas in the latter this same person's own head is used as a weapon. This latter legend however recalls Snorri's kenning for a sword,—Heimdall's head.[38]

Young suggests that the poem may have been composed around the year 1000 and is a result of contacts in the British Isles between Scandinavians and Gaels; contacts which allowed for friendly cultural exchange by that time.

N. K. Chadwick[39] compared Manannán mac Lír, who is associated with the Hebrides and the Isle of Man, and Heimdallr, and pointed out similarities in their association with the sea, shape changing and their function as begetters of children. From this she postulated that the Hebrides were "the centre of distribution of the whole mythological and literary nucleus"[40] connected with these two figures.

There is no apparent reason why one should doubt the presence of Gaelic elements in *Rígsþula,* elements which can explain why the poem is different from other Old Icelandic poetry. But as the commentators have argued, the poem represents an example of later cultural contacts. It has had no radical, deep-felt influence in Iceland on the mythological tradition as a whole and can therefore hardly be a product of the "melting pot" there.

The general conclusions which may be drawn from looking at Gaelic influence in Old Norse/Icelandic mythology are therefore in line with what was said earlier. It neither formed the tradition nor changed its basic characteristics.

Notes

[1] See E. O'Curry (1862) 394-97.

[2] (1961) 20.

[3] (1889).

[4] A. B. Rooth (1961) 19. See 18-21 for her discussion.

[5] Ibid, 21.

[6] A. B. Rooth (1961) 72-75.

[7] (1961) 72-73.

[8] Ibid, 73.

[9] See A. B. Rooth (1961) 110-114.

[10] P. 119 and p. 129 in translation.

[11] A. B. Rooth (1961) 110.

[12] Ibid, 113.

[13] (1964) 145.

[14] Ibid.

[15] C. W. von Sydow (1907) (1908); and (1920) 26-27.

[16] Ibid (1920) 27. (""do-bheirim grian agus éasga", literally translated: "I give sun and moon", but its real meaning is: "I swear by sun and moon" or simply: "I declare by everything I hold dear and holy." It is easy to see how such a formulaic expression could be misunderstood by a person who was not familiar with all the local idioms of the Irish language, and then translated literally and regarded as a promise of reward, instead of what it is, a formula of assurance. If so, it is also clear that it is the Norsemen who have been the borrowers.").

[17] Apart from von Sydow's articles, see for example W. Liungman (1942); M. Fossenias (1943); I. M. Boberg (1955). M. Chesnutt commented on this whole discussion, saying: "It must be said, in justice to von Sydow, that none of his critics have accounted satisfactorily for the form of the Irish variants." ((1968) 126fn. See there for further references).

[18] (1910).

[19] (1921) 104-13.

[20] C. W. von Sydow (1922); Finnur Jónsson (1922).

[21] P. 22 ("On the other hand, the mere suspicion of a borrowing from the Celts affects the Germanists as a red rag affects a bull. Hardly any Germanist has undertaken the task of learning the extremely difficult Gaelic language, and a knowledge of Celtic tradition has thus not been able to promote an investigation of the connection.").

[22] (1985).

[23] R. Power (1985) 260-61.

[24] *Ynglinga saga,* chs. 4, 7. References to Mímir's head are in *Snorra-Edda* (Gylfaginning ch.38), *Völuspá,* st. 46 and *Sigrdrífumál,* st. 13. Apart from this, talking heads in Old Icelandic material are to be found in *Eyrbyggja saga,* ch. 43 and *Þorsteins þáttr bœjarmagns,* ch. 9 (see p. 58). Severed heads of enemies appear in *Orkneyinga saga,* ch. 5 (see pp. 45-6), *Grettis saga,* ch. 82, *Bjarnar saga Hítdœlakappa,* ch. 32, *Fóstbrœðra saga,* ch. 18, and *Ljósvetninga saga,* (Þórarins þáttr). Finally, supernatural qualities are attached to heads in *Ólafs saga Tryggvasonar,* ch. 28/19, *Eyrbyggja saga,* ch. 27, and

Njáls saga, ch. 157 (i.e. the head of King Brjánn). See also Þorvaldur Friðriksson (1985).

[25] (1959) (1962); see also her book (1967) 61-126.

[26] (1962).

[27] Ibid, 41.

[28] Ibid, 41.

[29] (1965).

[30] Einar Ólafur Sveinsson (1962) 251-53, 287-91.

[31] (1962) esp. 252-53.

[32] This is Óengus in *Aislinge Óenguso.*

[33] See J. I. Young (1933) 102 and references there.

[34] In *The Táin* Recension I, 1 781ff. Also in *Serglige Con Culainn.*

[35] In *Aided Óenfir Aife.*

[36] Apart from Einar Ólafur Sveinsson, see J. I. Young (1933) 100-01, who says: "In its minute description of the appearance, dress and food characteristics of the three classes of society *Rígsþula* exhibits Irish affinities." (100) Young also draws attention to the description of Mother in *Rígsþula* where "the poet heightens his description and employs synonymous adjectives in a typically Irish manner." (101) In *Rígsþula,* st. 28-29, the description of Mother reads: "hugði at ormu*m,* / strauk of ripti, st*erti ermar. // Keisti falld, / Kinga var a bringu, / siðar slæður, / serk blafaan; / brun biartari, / briost liosara, / hals hvitari / hrein*ni miollu." ("The lady sat, at her arms she looked, / She smoothed the cloth, and fitted the sleeves; / Gay was her cap, on her breast were clasps, / Broad was her train, of blue was her gown, / Her brows were bright, her breast was shining, / Whiter her neck than new-fallen snow." Transl. by H. A. Bellows (1968) 210-11 (st. 28)). This, she says, may be compared with a description in *The Táin* (Recension I, ll 32-37) of Feidelm, the poetess of Connact: "Agad fochóel forlethan. Díbroí duba dorchaidi. Abrait duib dáin co mbentáis foscod i mmedón a dá grúaide. [. . .] Teóra trillsi fuirri .i. dí thriliss immo cend súas, trilis tara haiss síar co mbenad a dá colphta inna díaid." ("Her eyebrows were dark and black. Her beautiful black eyelashes cast a shadow on to the middle of her cheeks. [. . .] She had three plaits of hair: two plaits wound around her head, the third hanging down her back, touching her calves behind.").

[37] (1933) 102ff.

[38] Ibid, 104-05.

[39] (1955) 111-15.

[40] Ibid, 115.

FURTHER READING

Adalsteinsson, Jon Hnefill. "Gods and Giants in Norse Mythology." *Tenemos* 26 (1990): 7-22.

> Discussion of the relations between gods and giants as depicted in Eddic and Skaldic literary traditions, and in the context of Old Norse religious beliefs.

Bayerschmidt, Carl F. and Friis, Erik J. *Scandinavian Studies*. Seattle: University of Washington Press, 1965, 458 p.

> Omnibus collection of essays on Scandinavian literature and history with sections on mythology and sagas.

Clover, Carol J. and Lindow, John. *Old Norse-Icelandic Literature: A Critical Guide*. Ithaca: Cornell University Press, 1985, 387 p.

> Extended essays covering the major genres of Norse literature, including myths, Eddas, Skaldic poetry, sagas and romances; includes a lengthy scholarly bibliography.

Davidson, H. R. Ellis. *Gods and Myths of Northern Europe*. Baltimore: Penguin, 1964, 251 p.

> Summary and survey of the Norse pantheon, cosmology, and creation myths.

Dronke, Ursula. "Marx, Engels, and Norse Mythology." *Leeds Studies in English* 20 (1989): 29-47.

> Examines mythological themes in the political philosophy of Karl Marx and Friedrich Engels, with specific analysis of Eddic poems.

Glendinning, R. J. and Bessason, Haraldur. *Edda: A Collection of Essays*. Winnipeg: University of Manitoba Press, 1983, 332 p.

> A collection of critical essays on the Eddic poems.

Heyman, Harald E. *Studies on the Havelok-Tale*. Upsala: Wretmans Tryckeri, 1903, 153 p.

> Collection of essays on the Havelok Tale in Old English and French sources, with discussion of the Norse origins of the story.

Niles, John and Amodio, Mark, eds. *Scandinavian Studies* 59, No.3 (Summer 1987).

> Special issue on Anglo-Scandinavian England with several articles on Norse mythology in Northumbria and Skaldic poetic techniques and influences in England.

Polomé, Edgar C., ed. *Old Norse Literature and Mythology: A Symposium*. Austin: University of Texas Press, 1969, 347 p.

> Collection of essays examining the linguistic, literary, historical, and cultural contexts of Old Norse literature, including the *Eddas* and Skaldic poetry.

Reiss, Edmund. "*Havelok the Dane* and Norse Mythology." *Modern Language Quarterly* 27, No.2 (June 1966): 115-24.

> Analysis of the sources of the Havelok Tale, arguing that it has roots in pre-Christian Scandinavian myths.

CLASSICAL AND MEDIEVAL LITERATURE CRITICISM

INDEXES

Literary Criticism Series
Cumulative Author Index

Literary Criticism Series
Cumulative Topic Index

CMLC Cumulative Nationality Index

CMLC Cumulative Title Index

CMLC Cumulative Critic Index

How to Use This Index

The main references

Calvino, Italo
1923-1985.....CLC 5, 8, 11, 22, 33, 39, 73; SSC 3

list all author entries in the following Gale Literary Criticism series:

BLC = Black Literature Criticism
CLC = Contemporary Literary Criticism
CLR = Children's Literature Review
CMLC = Classical and Medieval Literature Criticism
DA = DISCovering Authors
DAB = DISCovering Authors: British
DAC = DISCovering Authors: Canadian
DAM = DISCovering Authors Modules
   DRAM: Dramatists module
   MST: Most-studied authors module
   MULT: Multicultural authors module
   NOV: Novelists module
   POET: Poets module
   POP: Popular/genre writers module

DC = Drama Criticism
HLC = Hispanic Literature Criticism
LC = Literature Criticism from 1400 to 1800
NCLC = Nineteenth-Century Literature Criticism
PC = Poetry Criticism
SSC = Short Story Criticism
TCLC = Twentieth-Century Literary Criticism
WLC = World Literature Criticism, 1500 to the Present

The cross-references

See also CANR 23; CA 85-88;
obituary CA 116

list all author entries in the following Gale biographical and literary sources:

AAYA = Authors & Artists for Young Adults
AITN = Authors in the News
BEST = Bestsellers
BW = Black Writers
CA = Contemporary Authors
CAAS = Contemporary Authors Autobiography Series
CABS = Contemporary Authors Bibliographical Series
CANR = Contemporary Authors New Revision Series
CAP = Contemporary Authors Permanent Series
CDALB = Concise Dictionary of American Literary Biography
CDBLB = Concise Dictionary of British Literary Biography

DLB = Dictionary of Literary Biography
DLBD = Dictionary of Literary Biography Documentary Series
DLBY = Dictionary of Literary Biography Yearbook
HW = Hispanic Writers
JRDA = Junior DISCovering Authors
MAICYA = Major Authors and Illustrators for Children and Young Adults
MTCW = Major 20th-Century Writers
NNAL = Native North American Literature
SAAS = Something about the Author Autobiography Series
SATA = Something about the Author
YABC = Yesterday's Authors of Books for Children

Literary Criticism Series
Cumulative Author Index

See Ai
Anthony, John
See Ciardi, John (Anthony)
Anthony, Peter
See Shaffer, Anthony (Joshua); Shaffer, Peter (Levin)
Anthony, Piers 1934- .... **CLC 35; DAM POP**
See also AAYA 11; CA 21-24R; CANR 28, 56; DLB 8; MTCW; SAAS 22; SATA 84
Antoine, Marc
See Proust, (Valentin-Louis-George-Eugene-) Marcel
Antoninus, Brother
See Everson, William (Oliver)
Antonioni, Michelangelo 1912- .... **CLC 20**
See also CA 73-76; CANR 45
Antschel, Paul 1920-1970
See Celan, Paul
See also CA 85-88; CANR 33, 61; MTCW
Anwar, Chairil 1922-1949 .... **TCLC 22**
See also CA 121
Apollinaire, Guillaume 1880-1918 **TCLC 3, 8, 51; DAM POET; PC 7**
See also Kostrowitzki, Wilhelm Apollinaris de
See also CA 152
Appelfeld, Aharon 1932- .... **CLC 23, 47**
See also CA 112; 133
Apple, Max (Isaac) 1941- .... **CLC 9, 33**
See also CA 81-84; CANR 19, 54; DLB 130
Appleman, Philip (Dean) 1926- .... **CLC 51**
See also CA 13-16R; CAAS 18; CANR 6, 29, 56
Appleton, Lawrence
See Lovecraft, H(oward) P(hillips)
Apteryx
See Eliot, T(homas) S(tearns)
Apuleius, (Lucius Madaurensis) 125(?)-175(?) **CMLC 1**
Aquin, Hubert 1929-1977 .... **CLC 15**
See also CA 105; DLB 53
Aragon, Louis 1897-1982 **CLC 3, 22; DAM NOV, POET**
See also CA 69-72; 108; CANR 28; DLB 72; MTCW
Arany, Janos 1817-1882 .... **NCLC 34**
Arbuthnot, John 1667-1735 .... **LC 1**
See also DLB 101
Archer, Herbert Winslow
See Mencken, H(enry) L(ouis)
Archer, Jeffrey (Howard) 1940- . **CLC 28; DAM POP**
See also AAYA 16; BEST 89:3; CA 77-80; CANR 22, 52; INT CANR-22
Archer, Jules 1915- .... **CLC 12**
See also CA 9-12R; CANR 6; SAAS 5; SATA 4, 85
Archer, Lee
See Ellison, Harlan (Jay)
Arden, John 1930- **CLC 6, 13, 15; DAM DRAM**
See also CA 13-16R; CAAS 4; CANR 31; DLB 13; MTCW
Arenas, Reinaldo 1943-1990 **CLC 41; DAM MULT; HLC**
See also CA 124; 128; 133; DLB 145; HW
Arendt, Hannah 1906-1975 .... **CLC 66, 98**
See also CA 17-20R; 61-64; CANR 26, 60; MTCW
Aretino, Pietro 1492-1556 .... **LC 12**
Arghezi, Tudor .... **CLC 80**
See also Theodorescu, Ion N.
Arguedas, Jose Maria 1911-1969 .... **CLC 10, 18**
See also CA 89-92; DLB 113; HW
Argueta, Manlio 1936- .... **CLC 31**
See also CA 131; DLB 145; HW
Ariosto, Ludovico 1474-1533 .... **LC 6**

Aristides
See Epstein, Joseph
Aristophanes 450B.C.-385B.C. .... **CMLC 4; DA; DAB; DAC; DAM DRAM, MST; DC 2; WLCS**
See also DLB 176
Arlt, Roberto (Godofredo Christophersen) 1900-1942 .... **TCLC 29; DAM MULT; HLC**
See also CA 123; 131; HW
Armah, Ayi Kwei 1939- . **CLC 5, 33; BLC; DAM MULT, POET**
See also BW 1; CA 61-64; CANR 21, 64; DLB 117; MTCW
Armatrading, Joan 1950- .... **CLC 17**
See also CA 114
Arnette, Robert
See Silverberg, Robert
Arnim, Achim von (Ludwig Joachim von Arnim) 1781-1831 .... **NCLC 5; SSC 29**
See also DLB 90
Arnim, Bettina von 1785-1859 .... **NCLC 38**
See also DLB 90
Arnold, Matthew 1822-1888 .... **NCLC 6, 29; DA; DAB; DAC; DAM MST, POET; PC 5; WLC**
See also CDBLB 1832-1890; DLB 32, 57
Arnold, Thomas 1795-1842 .... **NCLC 18**
See also DLB 55
Arnow, Harriette (Louisa) Simpson 1908-1986 **CLC 2, 7, 18**
See also CA 9-12R; 118; CANR 14; DLB 6; MTCW; SATA 42; SATA-Obit 47
Arp, Hans
See Arp, Jean
Arp, Jean 1887-1966 .... **CLC 5**
See also CA 81-84; 25-28R; CANR 42
Arrabal
See Arrabal, Fernando
Arrabal, Fernando 1932- .... **CLC 2, 9, 18, 58**
See also CA 9-12R; CANR 15
Arrick, Fran .... **CLC 30**
See also Gaberman, Judie Angell
Artaud, Antonin (Marie Joseph) 1896-1948 **TCLC 3, 36; DAM DRAM**
See also CA 104; 149
Arthur, Ruth M(abel) 1905-1979 .... **CLC 12**
See also CA 9-12R; 85-88; CANR 4; SATA 7, 26
Artsybashev, Mikhail (Petrovich) 1878-1927 **TCLC 31**
Arundel, Honor (Morfydd) 1919-1973 ... **CLC 17**
See also CA 21-22; 41-44R; CAP 2; CLR 35; SATA 4; SATA-Obit 24
Arzner, Dorothy 1897-1979 .... **CLC 98**
Asch, Sholem 1880-1957 .... **TCLC 3**
See also CA 105
Ash, Shalom
See Asch, Sholem
Ashbery, John (Lawrence) 1927- **CLC 2, 3, 4, 6, 9, 13, 15, 25, 41, 77; DAM POET**
See also CA 5-8R; CANR 9, 37; DLB 5, 165; DLBY 81; INT CANR-9; MTCW
Ashdown, Clifford
See Freeman, R(ichard) Austin
Ashe, Gordon
See Creasey, John
Ashton-Warner, Sylvia (Constance) 1908-1984 **CLC 19**
See also CA 69-72; 112; CANR 29; MTCW
Asimov, Isaac 1920-1992 **CLC 1, 3, 9, 19, 26, 76, 92; DAM POP**
See also AAYA 13; BEST 90:2; CA 1-4R; 137; CANR 2, 19, 36, 60; CLR 12; DLB 8; DLBY 92; INT CANR-19; JRDA; MAICYA; MTCW; SATA 1, 26, 74
Assis, Joaquim Maria Machado de

See Machado de Assis, Joaquim Maria
Astley, Thea (Beatrice May) 1925- .... **CLC 41**
See also CA 65-68; CANR 11, 43
Aston, James
See White, T(erence) H(anbury)
Asturias, Miguel Angel 1899-1974 **CLC 3, 8, 13; DAM MULT, NOV; HLC**
See also CA 25-28; 49-52; CANR 32; CAP 2; DLB 113; HW; MTCW
Atares, Carlos Saura
See Saura (Atares), Carlos
Atheling, William
See Pound, Ezra (Weston Loomis)
Atheling, William, Jr.
See Blish, James (Benjamin)
Atherton, Gertrude (Franklin Horn) 1857-1948 **TCLC 2**
See also CA 104; 155; DLB 9, 78, 186
Atherton, Lucius
See Masters, Edgar Lee
Atkins, Jack
See Harris, Mark
Atkinson, Kate .... **CLC 99**
Attaway, William (Alexander) 1911-1986 **CLC 92; BLC; DAM MULT**
See also BW 2; CA 143; DLB 76
Atticus
See Fleming, Ian (Lancaster)
Atwood, Margaret (Eleanor) 1939- **CLC 2, 3, 4, 8, 13, 15, 25, 44, 84; DA; DAB; DAC; DAM MST, NOV, POET; PC 8; SSC 2; WLC**
See also AAYA 12; BEST 89:2; CA 49-52; CANR 3, 24, 33, 59; DLB 53; INT CANR-24; MTCW; SATA 50
Aubigny, Pierre d'
See Mencken, H(enry) L(ouis)
Aubin, Penelope 1685-1731(?) .... **LC 9**
See also DLB 39
Auchincloss, Louis (Stanton) 1917- **CLC 4, 6, 9, 18, 45; DAM NOV; SSC 22**
See also CA 1-4R; CANR 6, 29, 55; DLB 2; DLBY 80; INT CANR-29; MTCW
Auden, W(ystan) H(ugh) 1907-1973 **CLC 1, 2, 3, 4, 6, 9, 11, 14, 43; DA; DAB; DAC; DAM DRAM, MST, POET; PC 1; WLC**
See also AAYA 18; CA 9-12R; 45-48; CANR 5, 61; CDBLB 1914-1945; DLB 10, 20; MTCW
Audiberti, Jacques 1900-1965 .... **CLC 38; DAM DRAM**
See also CA 25-28R
Audubon, John James 1785-1851 .... **NCLC 47**
Auel, Jean M(arie) 1936- **CLC 31, 107; DAM POP**
See also AAYA 7; BEST 90:4; CA 103; CANR 21, 64; INT CANR-21; SATA 91
Auerbach, Erich 1892-1957 .... **TCLC 43**
See also CA 118; 155
Augier, Emile 1820-1889 .... **NCLC 31**
August, John
See De Voto, Bernard (Augustine)
Augustine, St. 354-430 .... **CMLC 6; DAB**
Aurelius
See Bourne, Randolph S(illiman)
Aurobindo, Sri 1872-1950 .... **TCLC 63**
Austen, Jane 1775-1817 **NCLC 1, 13, 19, 33, 51; DA; DAB; DAC; DAM MST, NOV; WLC**
See also AAYA 19; CDBLB 1789-1832; DLB 116
Auster, Paul 1947- .... **CLC 47**
See also CA 69-72; CANR 23, 52
Austin, Frank
See Faust, Frederick (Schiller)
Austin, Mary (Hunter) 1868-1934 .... **TCLC 25**
See also CA 109; DLB 9, 78
Autran Dourado, Waldomiro

See Dourado, (Waldomiro Freitas) Autran
Averroes 1126-1198 .... **CMLC 7**
See also DLB 115
Avicenna 980-1037 .... **CMLC 16**
See also DLB 115
Avison, Margaret 1918-**CLC 2, 4, 97; DAC; DAM POET**
See also CA 17-20R; DLB 53; MTCW
Axton, David
See Koontz, Dean R(ay)
Ayckbourn, Alan 1939-**CLC 5, 8, 18, 33, 74; DAB; DAM DRAM**
See also CA 21-24R; CANR 31, 59; DLB 13; MTCW
Aydy, Catherine
See Tennant, Emma (Christina)
Ayme, Marcel (Andre) 1902-1967 .... **CLC 11**
See also CA 89-92; CLR 25; DLB 72; SATA 91
Ayrton, Michael 1921-1975 .... **CLC 7**
See also CA 5-8R; 61-64; CANR 9, 21
Azorin .... **CLC 11**
See also Martinez Ruiz, Jose
Azuela, Mariano 1873-1952**TCLC 3; DAM MULT; HLC**
See also CA 104; 131; HW; MTCW
Baastad, Babbis Friis
See Friis-Baastad, Babbis Ellinor
Bab
See Gilbert, W(illiam) S(chwenck)
Babbis, Eleanor
See Friis-Baastad, Babbis Ellinor
Babel, Isaac
See Babel, Isaak (Emmanuilovich)
Babel, Isaak (Emmanuilovich) 1894-1941(?) **TCLC 2, 13; SSC 16**
See also CA 104; 155
Babits, Mihaly 1883-1941 .... **TCLC 14**
See also CA 114
Babur 1483-1530 .... **LC 18**
Bacchelli, Riccardo 1891-1985 .... **CLC 19**
See also CA 29-32R; 117
Bach, Richard (David) 1936-**CLC 14; DAM NOV, POP**
See also AITN 1; BEST 89:2; CA 9-12R; CANR 18; MTCW; SATA 13
Bachman, Richard
See King, Stephen (Edwin)
Bachmann, Ingeborg 1926-1973 .... **CLC 69**
See also CA 93-96; 45-48; DLB 85
Bacon, Francis 1561-1626 .... **LC 18, 32**
See also CDBLB Before 1660; DLB 151
Bacon, Roger 1214(?)-1292 .... **CMLC 14**
See also DLB 115
Bacovia, George .... **TCLC 24**
See also Vasiliu, Gheorghe
Badanes, Jerome 1937- .... **CLC 59**
Bagehot, Walter 1826-1877 .... **NCLC 10**
See also DLB 55
Bagnold, Enid 1889-1981 **CLC 25; DAM DRAM**
See also CA 5-8R; 103; CANR 5, 40; DLB 13, 160; MAICYA; SATA 1, 25
Bagritsky, Eduard 1895-1934 .... **TCLC 60**
Bagrjana, Elisaveta
See Belcheva, Elisaveta
Bagryana, Elisaveta .... **CLC 10**
See also Belcheva, Elisaveta
See also DLB 147
Bailey, Paul 1937- .... **CLC 45**
See also CA 21-24R; CANR 16, 62; DLB 14
Baillie, Joanna 1762-1851 .... **NCLC 2**
See also DLB 93
Bainbridge, Beryl (Margaret) 1933-**CLC 4, 5, 8, 10, 14, 18, 22, 62; DAM NOV**

See also CA 21-24R; CANR 24, 55; DLB 14; MTCW
Baker, Elliott 1922- .... **CLC 8**
See also CA 45-48; CANR 2, 63
Baker, Jean H. .... **TCLC 3, 10**
See also Russell, George William
Baker, Nicholson 1957- ..... **CLC 61; DAM POP**
See also CA 135; CANR 63
Baker, Ray Stannard 1870-1946 .... **TCLC 47**
See also CA 118
Baker, Russell (Wayne) 1925- .... **CLC 31**
See also BEST 89:4; CA 57-60; CANR 11, 41, 59; MTCW
Bakhtin, M.
See Bakhtin, Mikhail Mikhailovich
Bakhtin, M. M.
See Bakhtin, Mikhail Mikhailovich
Bakhtin, Mikhail
See Bakhtin, Mikhail Mikhailovich
Bakhtin, Mikhail Mikhailovich 1895-1975 **C L C 83**
See also CA 128; 113
Bakshi, Ralph 1938(?)- .... **CLC 26**
See also CA 112; 138
Bakunin, Mikhail (Alexandrovich) 1814-1876 **NCLC 25, 58**
Baldwin, James (Arthur) 1924-1987 **CLC 1, 2, 3, 4, 5, 8, 13, 15, 17, 42, 50, 67, 90; BLC; DA; DAB; DAC; DAM MST, MULT, NOV, POP; DC 1; SSC 10; WLC**
See also AAYA 4; BW 1; CA 1-4R; 124; CABS 1; CANR 3, 24; CDALB 1941-1968; DLB 2, 7, 33; DLBY 87; MTCW; SATA 9; SATA-Obit 54
Ballard, J(ames) G(raham) 1930- **CLC 3, 6, 14, 36; DAM NOV, POP; SSC 1**
See also AAYA 3; CA 5-8R; CANR 15, 39; DLB 14; MTCW; SATA 93
Balmont, Konstantin (Dmitriyevich) 1867-1943 **TCLC 11**
See also CA 109; 155
Balzac, Honore de 1799-1850**NCLC 5, 35, 53; DA; DAB; DAC; DAM MST, NOV; SSC 5; WLC**
See also DLB 119
Bambara, Toni Cade 1939-1995**CLC 19, 88; BLC; DA; DAC; DAM MST, MULT; WLCS**
See also AAYA 5; BW 2; CA 29-32R; 150; CANR 24, 49; DLB 38; MTCW
Bamdad, A.
See Shamlu, Ahmad
Banat, D. R.
See Bradbury, Ray (Douglas)
Bancroft, Laura
See Baum, L(yman) Frank
Banim, John 1798-1842 .... **NCLC 13**
See also DLB 116, 158, 159
Banim, Michael 1796-1874 .... **NCLC 13**
See also DLB 158, 159
Banjo, The
See Paterson, A(ndrew) B(arton)
Banks, Iain
See Banks, Iain M(enzies)
Banks, Iain M(enzies) 1954- .... **CLC 34**
See also CA 123; 128; CANR 61; INT 128
Banks, Lynne Reid .... **CLC 23**
See also Reid Banks, Lynne
See also AAYA 6
Banks, Russell 1940- .... **CLC 37, 72**
See also CA 65-68; CAAS 15; CANR 19, 52; DLB 130
Banville, John 1945- .... **CLC 46**
See also CA 117; 128; DLB 14; INT 128
Banville, Theodore (Faullain) de 1832-1891**NCLC 9**

Baraka, Amiri 1934- **CLC 1, 2, 3, 5, 10, 14, 33; BLC; DA; DAC; DAM MST, MULT, POET, POP; DC 6; PC 4; WLCS**
See also Jones, LeRoi
See also BW 2; CA 21-24R; CABS 3; CANR 27, 38, 61; CDALB 1941-1968; DLB 5, 7, 16, 38; DLBD 8; MTCW
Barbauld, Anna Laetitia 1743-1825 .... **NCLC 50**
See also DLB 107, 109, 142, 158
Barbellion, W. N. P. .... **TCLC 24**
See also Cummings, Bruce F(rederick)
Barbera, Jack (Vincent) 1945- .... **CLC 44**
See also CA 110; CANR 45
Barbey d'Aurevilly, Jules Amedee 1808-1889 **NCLC 1; SSC 17**
See also DLB 119
Barbusse, Henri 1873-1935 .... **TCLC 5**
See also CA 105; 154; DLB 65
Barclay, Bill
See Moorcock, Michael (John)
Barclay, William Ewert
See Moorcock, Michael (John)
Barea, Arturo 1897-1957 .... **TCLC 14**
See also CA 111
Barfoot, Joan 1946- .... **CLC 18**
See also CA 105
Baring, Maurice 1874-1945 .... **TCLC 8**
See also CA 105; DLB 34
Barker, Clive 1952- .... **CLC 52; DAM POP**
See also AAYA 10; BEST 90:3; CA 121; 129; INT 129; MTCW
Barker, George Granville 1913-1991 **CLC 8, 48; DAM POET**
See also CA 9-12R; 135; CANR 7, 38; DLB 20; MTCW
Barker, Harley Granville
See Granville-Barker, Harley
See also DLB 10
Barker, Howard 1946- .... **CLC 37**
See also CA 102; DLB 13
Barker, Pat(ricia) 1943- .... **CLC 32, 94**
See also CA 117; 122; CANR 50; INT 122
Barlow, Joel 1754-1812 .... **NCLC 23**
See also DLB 37
Barnard, Mary (Ethel) 1909- .... **CLC 48**
See also CA 21-22; CAP 2
Barnes, Djuna 1892-1982**CLC 3, 4, 8, 11, 29; SSC 3**
See also CA 9-12R; 107; CANR 16, 55; DLB 4, 9, 45; MTCW
Barnes, Julian (Patrick) 1946- .. **CLC 42; DAB**
See also CA 102; CANR 19, 54; DLBY 93
Barnes, Peter 1931- .... **CLC 5, 56**
See also CA 65-68; CAAS 12; CANR 33, 34, 64; DLB 13; MTCW
Baroja (y Nessi), Pio 1872-1956 .. **TCLC 8; HLC**
See also CA 104
Baron, David
See Pinter, Harold
Baron Corvo
See Rolfe, Frederick (William Serafino Austin Lewis Mary)
Barondess, Sue K(aufman) 1926-1977 .... **CLC 8**
See also Kaufman, Sue
See also CA 1-4R; 69-72; CANR 1
Baron de Teive
See Pessoa, Fernando (Antonio Nogueira)
Barres, Maurice 1862-1923 .... **TCLC 47**
See also DLB 123
Barreto, Afonso Henrique de Lima
See Lima Barreto, Afonso Henrique de
Barrett, (Roger) Syd 1946- .... **CLC 35**
Barrett, William (Christopher) 1913-1992 **C L C**

27
See also CA 13-16R; 139; CANR 11; INT CANR-11

Barrie, J(ames) M(atthew) 1860-1937 .. **TCLC 2; DAB; DAM DRAM**
See also CA 104; 136; CDBLB 1890-1914; CLR 16; DLB 10, 141, 156; MAICYA; YABC 1

Barrington, Michael
See Moorcock, Michael (John)

Barrol, Grady
See Bograd, Larry

Barry, Mike
See Malzberg, Barry N(athaniel)

Barry, Philip 1896-1949 .... **TCLC 11**
See also CA 109; DLB 7

Bart, Andre Schwarz
See Schwarz-Bart, Andre

Barth, John (Simmons) 1930-**CLC 1, 2, 3, 5, 7, 9, 10, 14, 27, 51, 89; DAM NOV; SSC 10**
See also AITN 1, 2; CA 1-4R; CABS 1; CANR 5, 23, 49, 64; DLB 2; MTCW

Barthelme, Donald 1931-1989**CLC 1, 2, 3, 5, 6, 8, 13, 23, 46, 59; DAM NOV; SSC 2**
See also CA 21-24R; 129; CANR 20, 58; DLB 2; DLBY 80, 89; MTCW; SATA 7; SATA-Obit 62

Barthelme, Frederick 1943- .... **CLC 36**
See also CA 114; 122; DLBY 85; INT 122

Barthes, Roland (Gerard) 1915-1980**CLC 24, 83**
See also CA 130; 97-100; MTCW

Barzun, Jacques (Martin) 1907- .... **CLC 51**
See also CA 61-64; CANR 22

Bashevis, Isaac
See Singer, Isaac Bashevis

Bashkirtseff, Marie 1859-1884 .... **NCLC 27**

Basho
See Matsuo Basho

Bass, Kingsley B., Jr.
See Bullins, Ed

Bass, Rick 1958- .... **CLC 79**
See also CA 126; CANR 53

Bassani, Giorgio 1916- .... **CLC 9**
See also CA 65-68; CANR 33; DLB 128, 177; MTCW

Bastos, Augusto (Antonio) Roa
See Roa Bastos, Augusto (Antonio)

Bataille, Georges 1897-1962 .... **CLC 29**
See also CA 101; 89-92

Bates, H(erbert) E(rnest) 1905-1974 .... **CLC 46; DAB; DAM POP; SSC 10**
See also CA 93-96; 45-48; CANR 34; DLB 162; MTCW

Bauchart
See Camus, Albert

Baudelaire, Charles 1821-1867 **NCLC 6, 29, 55; DA; DAB; DAC; DAM MST, POET; PC 1; SSC 18; WLC**

Baudrillard, Jean 1929- .... **CLC 60**

Baum, L(yman) Frank 1856-1919 .... **TCLC 7**
See also CA 108; 133; CLR 15; DLB 22; JRDA; MAICYA; MTCW; SATA 18

Baum, Louis F.
See Baum, L(yman) Frank

Baumbach, Jonathan 1933- .... **CLC 6, 23**
See also CA 13-16R; CAAS 5; CANR 12; DLBY 80; INT CANR-12; MTCW

Bausch, Richard (Carl) 1945-............... **CLC 51**
See also CA 101; CAAS 14; CANR 43, 61; DLB 130

Baxter, Charles (Morley) 1947-**CLC 45, 78; DAM POP**
See also CA 57-60; CANR 40, 64; DLB 130

Baxter, George Owen

See Faust, Frederick (Schiller)

Baxter, James K(eir) 1926-1972 .... **CLC 14**
See also CA 77-80

Baxter, John
See Hunt, E(verette) Howard, (Jr.)

Bayer, Sylvia
See Glassco, John

Baynton, Barbara 1857-1929 .... **TCLC 57**

Beagle, Peter S(oyer) 1939- .... **CLC 7, 104**
See also CA 9-12R; CANR 4, 51; DLBY 80; INT CANR-4; SATA 60

Bean, Normal
See Burroughs, Edgar Rice

Beard, Charles A(ustin) 1874-1948 .... **TCLC 15**
See also CA 115; DLB 17; SATA 18

Beardsley, Aubrey 1872-1898 .... **NCLC 6**

Beattie, Ann 1947- **CLC 8, 13, 18, 40, 63; DAM NOV; POP; SSC 11**
See also BEST 90:2; CA 81-84; CANR 53; DLBY 82; MTCW

Beattie, James 1735-1803 .... **NCLC 25**
See also DLB 109

Beauchamp, Kathleen Mansfield 1888-1923
See Mansfield, Katherine
See also CA 104; 134; DA; DAC; DAM MST

Beaumarchais, Pierre-Augustin Caron de 1732-1799 .... **DC 4**
See also DAM DRAM

Beaumont, Francis 1584(?)-1616 .. **LC 33; DC 6**
See also CDBLB Before 1660; DLB 58, 121

Beauvoir, Simone (Lucie Ernestine Marie Bertrand) de 1908-1986 **CLC 1, 2, 4, 8, 14, 31, 44, 50, 71; DA; DAB; DAC; DAM MST, NOV; WLC**
See also CA 9-12R; 118; CANR 28, 61; DLB 72; DLBY 86; MTCW

Becker, Carl (Lotus) 1873-1945 .... **TCLC 63**
See also CA 157; DLB 17

Becker, Jurek 1937-1997 .... **CLC 7, 19**
See also CA 85-88; 157; CANR 60; DLB 75

Becker, Walter 1950- .... **CLC 26**

Beckett, Samuel (Barclay) 1906-1989**CLC 1, 2, 3, 4, 6, 9, 10, 11, 14, 18, 29, 57, 59, 83; DA; DAB; DAC; DAM DRAM, MST, NOV; SSC 16; WLC**
See also CA 5-8R; 130; CANR 33, 61; CDBLB 1945-1960; DLB 13, 15; DLBY 90; MTCW

Beckford, William 1760-1844 .... **NCLC 16**
See also DLB 39

Beckman, Gunnel 1910- .... **CLC 26**
See also CA 33-36R; CANR 15; CLR 25; MAICYA; SAAS 9; SATA 6

Becque, Henri 1837-1899 .... **NCLC 3**

Beddoes, Thomas Lovell 1803-1849 ...... **NCLC 3**
See also DLB 96

Bede c. 673-735 .... **CMLC 20**
See also DLB 146

Bedford, Donald F.
See Fearing, Kenneth (Flexner)

Beecher, Catharine Esther 1800-1878 **NCLC 30**
See also DLB 1

Beecher, John 1904-1980 .... **CLC 6**
See also AITN 1; CA 5-8R; 105; CANR 8

Beer, Johann 1655-1700 .... **LC 5**
See also DLB 168

Beer, Patricia 1924- .... **CLC 58**
See also CA 61-64; CANR 13, 46; DLB 40

Beerbohm, Max
See Beerbohm, (Henry) Max(imilian)

Beerbohm, (Henry) Max(imilian) 1872-1956 **TCLC 1, 24**
See also CA 104; 154; DLB 34, 100

Beer-Hofmann, Richard 1866-1945 ..... **TCLC 60**

See also CA 160; DLB 81

Begiebing, Robert J(ohn) 1946- .... **CLC 70**
See also CA 122; CANR 40

Behan, Brendan 1923-1964**CLC 1, 8, 11, 15, 79; DAM DRAM**
See also CA 73-76; CANR 33; CDBLB 1945-1960; DLB 13; MTCW

Behn, Aphra 1640(?)-1689 . **LC 1, 30; DA; DAB; DAC; DAM DRAM, MST, NOV, POET; DC 4; PC 13; WLC**
See also DLB 39, 80, 131

Behrman, S(amuel) N(athaniel) 1893-1973 **C L C 40**
See also CA 13-16; 45-48; CAP 1; DLB 7, 44

Belasco, David 1853-1931 .... **TCLC 3**
See also CA 104; DLB 7

Belcheva, Elisaveta 1893- .... **CLC 10**
See also Bagryana, Elisaveta

Beldone, Phil "Cheech"
See Ellison, Harlan (Jay)

Beleno
See Azuela, Mariano

Belinski, Vissarion Grigoryevich 1811-1848 **NCLC 5**

Belitt, Ben 1911- .... **CLC 22**
See also CA 13-16R; CAAS 4; CANR 7; DLB 5

Bell, Gertrude 1868-1926 .... **TCLC 67**
See also DLB 174

Bell, James Madison 1826-1902**TCLC 43; BLC; DAM MULT**
See also BW 1; CA 122; 124; DLB 50

Bell, Madison Smartt 1957- .... **CLC 41, 102**
See also CA 111; CANR 28, 54

Bell, Marvin (Hartley) 1937- .. **CLC 8, 31; DAM POET**
See also CA 21-24R; CAAS 14; CANR 59; DLB 5; MTCW

Bell, W. L. D.
See Mencken, H(enry) L(ouis)

Bellamy, Atwood C.
See Mencken, H(enry) L(ouis)

Bellamy, Edward 1850-1898 .... **NCLC 4**
See also DLB 12

Bellin, Edward J.
See Kuttner, Henry

Belloc, (Joseph) Hilaire (Pierre Sebastien Rene Swanton) 1870-1953**TCLC 7, 18; DAM POET**
See also CA 106; 152; DLB 19, 100, 141, 174; YABC 1

Belloc, Joseph Peter Rene Hilaire
See Belloc, (Joseph) Hilaire (Pierre Sebastien Rene Swanton)

Belloc, Joseph Pierre Hilaire
See Belloc, (Joseph) Hilaire (Pierre Sebastien Rene Swanton)

Belloc, M. A.
See Lowndes, Marie Adelaide (Belloc)

Bellow, Saul 1915-**CLC 1, 2, 3, 6, 8, 10, 13, 15, 25, 33, 34, 63, 79; DA; DAB; DAC; DAM MST, NOV, POP; SSC 14; WLC**
See also AITN 2; BEST 89:3; CA 5-8R; CABS 1; CANR 29, 53; CDALB 1941-1968; DLB 2, 28; DLBD 3; DLBY 82; MTCW

Belser, Reimond Karel Maria de 1929-
See Ruyslinck, Ward
See also CA 152

Bely, Andrey .... **TCLC 7; PC 11**
See also Bugayev, Boris Nikolayevich

Benary, Margot
See Benary-Isbert, Margot

Benary-Isbert, Margot 1889-1979 .... **CLC 12**
See also CA 5-8R; 89-92; CANR 4; CLR 12; MAICYA; SATA 2; SATA-Obit 21

DLBY 81
Black Elk 1863-1950 ..... **TCLC 33; DAM MULT**
See also CA 144; NNAL
Black Hobart
See Sanders, (James) Ed(ward)
Blacklin, Malcolm
See Chambers, Aidan
Blackmore, R(ichard) D(oddridge) 1825-1900 **TCLC 27**
See also CA 120; DLB 18
Blackmur, R(ichard) P(almer) 1904-1965 **CLC 2, 24**
See also CA 11-12; 25-28R; CAP 1; DLB 63
Black Tarantula
See Acker, Kathy
Blackwood, Algernon (Henry) 1869-1951 **TCLC 5**
See also CA 105; 150; DLB 153, 156, 178
Blackwood, Caroline 1931-1996 .. **CLC 6, 9, 100**
See also CA 85-88; 151; CANR 32, 61; DLB 14; MTCW
Blade, Alexander
See Hamilton, Edmond; Silverberg, Robert
Blaga, Lucian 1895-1961 .... **CLC 75**
Blair, Eric (Arthur) 1903-1950
See Orwell, George
See also CA 104; 132; DA; DAB; DAC; DAM MST, NOV; MTCW; SATA 29
Blais, Marie-Claire 1939- .. **CLC 2, 4, 6, 13, 22; DAC; DAM MST**
See also CA 21-24R; CAAS 4; CANR 38; DLB 53; MTCW
Blaise, Clark 1940- .... **CLC 29**
See also AITN 2; CA 53-56; CAAS 3; CANR 5; DLB 53
Blake, Fairley
See De Voto, Bernard (Augustine)
Blake, Nicholas
See Day Lewis, C(ecil)
See also DLB 77
Blake, William 1757-1827 **NCLC 13, 37, 57; DA; DAB; DAC; DAM MST, POET; PC 12; WLC**
See also CDBLB 1789-1832; DLB 93, 163; MAICYA; SATA 30
Blasco Ibanez, Vicente 1867-1928 **TCLC 12; DAM NOV**
See also CA 110; 131; HW; MTCW
Blatty, William Peter 1928- . **CLC 2; DAM POP**
See also CA 5-8R; CANR 9
Bleeck, Oliver
See Thomas, Ross (Elmore)
Blessing, Lee 1949- .... **CLC 54**
Blish, James (Benjamin) 1921-1975 ..... **CLC 14**
See also CA 1-4R; 57-60; CANR 3; DLB 8; MTCW; SATA 66
Bliss, Reginald
See Wells, H(erbert) G(eorge)
Blixen, Karen (Christentze Dinesen) 1885-1962
See Dinesen, Isak
See also CA 25-28; CANR 22, 50; CAP 2; MTCW; SATA 44
Bloch, Robert (Albert) 1917-1994 .... **CLC 33**
See also CA 5-8R; 146; CAAS 20; CANR 5; DLB 44; INT CANR-5; SATA 12; SATA-Obit 82
Blok, Alexander (Alexandrovich) 1880-1921 **TCLC 5; PC 21**
See also CA 104
Blom, Jan
See Breytenbach, Breyten
Bloom, Harold 1930- .... **CLC 24, 103**
See also CA 13-16R; CANR 39; DLB 67
Bloomfield, Aurelius
See Bourne, Randolph S(illiman)
Blount, Roy (Alton), Jr. 1941- .... **CLC 38**

See also CA 53-56; CANR 10, 28, 61; INT CANR-28; MTCW
Bloy, Leon 1846-1917 .... **TCLC 22**
See also CA 121; DLB 123
Blume, Judy (Sussman) 1938- **CLC 12, 30; DAM NOV, POP**
See also AAYA 3; CA 29-32R; CANR 13, 37; CLR 2, 15; DLB 52; JRDA; MAICYA; MTCW; SATA 2, 31, 79
Blunden, Edmund (Charles) 1896-1974 **CLC 2, 56**
See also CA 17-18; 45-48; CANR 54; CAP 2; DLB 20, 100, 155; MTCW
Bly, Robert (Elwood) 1926- **CLC 1, 2, 5, 10, 15, 38; DAM POET**
See also CA 5-8R; CANR 41; DLB 5; MTCW
Boas, Franz 1858-1942 .... **TCLC 56**
See also CA 115
Bobette
See Simenon, Georges (Jacques Christian)
Boccaccio, Giovanni 1313-1375 **CMLC 13; SSC 10**
Bochco, Steven 1943- .... **CLC 35**
See also AAYA 11; CA 124; 138
Bodenheim, Maxwell 1892-1954 .... **TCLC 44**
See also CA 110; DLB 9, 45
Bodker, Cecil 1927- .... **CLC 21**
See also CA 73-76; CANR 13, 44; CLR 23; MAICYA; SATA 14
Boell, Heinrich (Theodor) 1917-1985 **CLC 2, 3, 6, 9, 11, 15, 27, 32, 72; DA; DAB; DAC; DAM MST, NOV; SSC 23; WLC**
See also CA 21-24R; 116; CANR 24; DLB 69; DLBY 85; MTCW
Boerne, Alfred
See Doeblin, Alfred
Boethius 480(?)-524(?) .... **CMLC 15**
See also DLB 115
Bogan, Louise 1897-1970 **CLC 4, 39, 46, 93; DAM POET; PC 12**
See also CA 73-76; 25-28R; CANR 33; DLB 45, 169; MTCW
Bogarde, Dirk .... **CLC 19**
See also Van Den Bogarde, Derek Jules Gaspard Ulric Niven
See also DLB 14
Bogosian, Eric 1953- .... **CLC 45**
See also CA 138
Bograd, Larry 1953- .... **CLC 35**
See also CA 93-96; CANR 57; SAAS 21; SATA 33, 89
Boiardo, Matteo Maria 1441-1494 .... **LC 6**
Boileau-Despreaux, Nicolas 1636-1711 ..... **LC 3**
Bojer, Johan 1872-1959 .... **TCLC 64**
Boland, Eavan (Aisling) 1944- **CLC 40, 67; DAM POET**
See also CA 143; CANR 61; DLB 40
Bolt, Lee
See Faust, Frederick (Schiller)
Bolt, Robert (Oxton) 1924-1995 . **CLC 14; DAM DRAM**
See also CA 17-20R; 147; CANR 35; DLB 13; MTCW
Bombet, Louis-Alexandre-Cesar
See Stendhal
Bomkauf
See Kaufman, Bob (Garnell)
Bonaventura .... **NCLC 35**
See also DLB 90
Bond, Edward 1934- **CLC 4, 6, 13, 23; DAM DRAM**
See also CA 25-28R; CANR 38; DLB 13; MTCW
Bonham, Frank 1914-1989 .... **CLC 12**
See also AAYA 1; CA 9-12R; CANR 4, 36; JRDA; MAICYA; SAAS 3; SATA 1, 49; SATA-Obit 62

Bonnefoy, Yves 1923- **CLC 9, 15, 58; DAM MST, POET**
See also CA 85-88; CANR 33; MTCW
Bontemps, Arna(ud Wendell) 1902-1973 **CLC 1, 18; BLC; DAM MULT, NOV, POET**
See also BW 1; CA 1-4R; 41-44R; CANR 4, 35; CLR 6; DLB 48, 51; JRDA; MAICYA; MTCW; SATA 2, 44; SATA-Obit 24
Booth, Martin 1944- .... **CLC 13**
See also CA 93-96; CAAS 2
Booth, Philip 1925- .... **CLC 23**
See also CA 5-8R; CANR 5; DLBY 82
Booth, Wayne C(layson) 1921- .... **CLC 24**
See also CA 1-4R; CAAS 5; CANR 3, 43; DLB 67
Borchert, Wolfgang 1921-1947 .... **TCLC 5**
See also CA 104; DLB 69, 124
Borel, Petrus 1809-1859 .... **NCLC 41**
Borges, Jorge Luis 1899-1986 **CLC 1, 2, 3, 4, 6, 8, 9, 10, 13, 19, 44, 48, 83; DA; DAB; DAC; DAM MST, MULT; HLC; SSC 4; WLC**
See also AAYA 19; CA 21-24R; CANR 19, 33; DLB 113; DLBY 86; HW; MTCW
Borowski, Tadeusz 1922-1951 .... **TCLC 9**
See also CA 106; 154
Borrow, George (Henry) 1803-1881 ..... **NCLC 9**
See also DLB 21, 55, 166
Bosman, Herman Charles 1905-1951 . **TCLC 49**
See also Malan, Herman
See also CA 160
Bosschere, Jean de 1878(?)-1953 .... **TCLC 19**
See also CA 115
Boswell, James 1740-1795 **LC 4; DA; DAB; DAC; DAM MST; WLC**
See also CDBLB 1660-1789; DLB 104, 142
Bottoms, David 1949- .... **CLC 53**
See also CA 105; CANR 22; DLB 120; DLBY 83
Boucicault, Dion 1820-1890 .... **NCLC 41**
Boucolon, Maryse 1937(?)-
See Conde, Maryse
See also CA 110; CANR 30, 53
Bourget, Paul (Charles Joseph) 1852-1935 **TCLC 12**
See also CA 107; DLB 123
Bourjaily, Vance (Nye) 1922- .... **CLC 8, 62**
See also CA 1-4R; CAAS 1; CANR 2; DLB 2, 143
Bourne, Randolph S(illiman) 1886-1918 **TCLC 16**
See also CA 117; 155; DLB 63
Bova, Ben(jamin William) 1932- .... **CLC 45**
See also AAYA 16; CA 5-8R; CAAS 18; CANR 11, 56; CLR 3; DLBY 81; INT CANR-11; MAICYA; MTCW; SATA 6, 68
Bowen, Elizabeth (Dorothea Cole) 1899-1973 **CLC 1, 3, 6, 11, 15, 22; DAM NOV; SSC 3, 28**
See also CA 17-18; 41-44R; CANR 35; CAP 2; CDBLB 1945-1960; DLB 15, 162; MTCW
Bowering, George 1935- .... **CLC 15, 47**
See also CA 21-24R; CAAS 16; CANR 10; DLB 53
Bowering, Marilyn R(uthe) 1949- .... **CLC 32**
See also CA 101; CANR 49
Bowers, Edgar 1924- .... **CLC 9**
See also CA 5-8R; CANR 24; DLB 5
Bowie, David .... **CLC 17**
See also Jones, David Robert
Bowles, Jane (Sydney) 1917-1973 ..... **CLC 3, 68**
See also CA 19-20; 41-44R; CAP 2
Bowles, Paul (Frederick) 1910-1986 **CLC 1, 2, 19, 53; SSC 3**
See also CA 1-4R; CAAS 1; CANR 1, 19, 50; DLB 5, 6; MTCW
Box, Edgar
See Vidal, Gore
Boyd, Nancy

See Millay, Edna St. Vincent
Boyd, William 1952- .... **CLC 28, 53, 70**
See also CA 114; 120; CANR 51
Boyle, Kay 1902-1992 .. **CLC 1, 5, 19, 58; SSC 5**
See also CA 13-16R; 140; CAAS 1; CANR 29, 61;
DLB 4, 9, 48, 86; DLBY 93; MTCW
Boyle, Mark
See Kienzle, William X(avier)
Boyle, Patrick 1905-1982 .... **CLC 19**
See also CA 127
Boyle, T. C. 1948-
See Boyle, T(homas) Coraghessan
Boyle, T(homas) Coraghessan 1948-**CLC 36, 55,**
90; DAM POP; SSC 16
See also BEST 90:4; CA 120; CANR 44; DLBY 86
Boz
See Dickens, Charles (John Huffam)
Brackenridge, Hugh Henry 1748-1816 **NCLC 7**
See also DLB 11, 37
Bradbury, Edward P.
See Moorcock, Michael (John)
Bradbury, Malcolm (Stanley) 1932- **CLC 32, 61;**
DAM NOV
See also CA 1-4R; CANR 1, 33; DLB 14; MTCW
Bradbury, Ray (Douglas) 1920-**CLC 1, 3, 10, 15,**
42, 98; DA; DAB; DAC; DAM MST, NOV,
POP; SSC 29; WLC
See also AAYA 15; AITN 1, 2; CA 1-4R; CANR
2, 30; CDALB 1968-1988; DLB 2, 8; MTCW;
SATA 11, 64
Bradford, Gamaliel 1863-1932 .... **TCLC 36**
See also CA 160; DLB 17
Bradley, David (Henry, Jr.) 1950- **CLC 23; BLC;**
DAM MULT
See also BW 1; CA 104; CANR 26; DLB 33
Bradley, John Ed(mund, Jr.) 1958- .... **CLC 55**
See also CA 139
Bradley, Marion Zimmer 1930- . **CLC 30; DAM**
POP
See also AAYA 9; CA 57-60; CAAS 10; CANR 7,
31, 51; DLB 8; MTCW; SATA 90
Bradstreet, Anne 1612(?)-1672 ... **LC 4, 30; DA;**
DAC; DAM MST, POET; PC 10
See also CDALB 1640-1865; DLB 24
Brady, Joan 1939- .... **CLC 86**
See also CA 141
Bragg, Melvyn 1939- .... **CLC 10**
See also BEST 89:3; CA 57-60; CANR 10, 48;
DLB 14
Braine, John (Gerard) 1922-1986 . **CLC 1, 3, 41**
See also CA 1-4R; 120; CANR 1, 33; CDBLB 1945-
1960; DLB 15; DLBY 86; MTCW
Bramah, Ernest 1868-1942 .... **TCLC 72**
See also CA 156; DLB 70
Brammer, William 1930(?)-1978 .... **CLC 31**
See also CA 77-80
Brancati, Vitaliano 1907-1954 .... **TCLC 12**
See also CA 109
Brancato, Robin F(idler) 1936- .... **CLC 35**
See also AAYA 9; CA 69-72; CANR 11, 45; CLR
32; JRDA; SAAS 9; SATA 23
Brand, Max
See Faust, Frederick (Schiller)
Brand, Millen 1906-1980 .... **CLC 7**
See also CA 21-24R; 97-100
Branden, Barbara .... **CLC 44**
See also CA 148
Brandes, Georg (Morris Cohen) 1842-1927**TCLC**
10
See also CA 105
Brandys, Kazimierz 1916- .... **CLC 62**
Branley, Franklyn M(ansfield) 1915- ... **CLC 21**
See also CA 33-36R; CANR 14, 39; CLR 13;

MAICYA; SAAS 16; SATA 4, 68
Brathwaite, Edward Kamau 1930- **CLC 11; DAM**
POET
See also BW 2; CA 25-28R; CANR 11, 26, 47;
DLB 125
Brautigan, Richard (Gary) 1935-1984**CLC 1, 3, 5,**
9, 12, 34, 42; DAM NOV
See also CA 53-56; 113; CANR 34; DLB 2, 5;
DLBY 80, 84; MTCW; SATA 56
Brave Bird, Mary 1953-
See Crow Dog, Mary (Ellen)
See also NNAL
Braverman, Kate 1950- .... **CLC 67**
See also CA 89-92
Brecht, (Eugen) Bertolt (Friedrich) 1898-1956
TCLC 1, 6, 13, 35; DA; DAB; DAC; DAM
DRAM, MST; DC 3; WLC
See also CA 104; 133; CANR 62; DLB 56, 124;
MTCW
Brecht, Eugen Berthold Friedrich
See Brecht, (Eugen) Bertolt (Friedrich)
Bremer, Fredrika 1801-1865 .... **NCLC 11**
Brennan, Christopher John 1870-1932**TCLC 17**
See also CA 117
Brennan, Maeve 1917- .... **CLC 5**
See also CA 81-84
Brent, Linda
See Jacobs, Harriet
Brentano, Clemens (Maria) 1778-1842 **NCLC 1**
See also DLB 90
Brent of Bin Bin
See Franklin, (Stella Maraia Sarah) Miles
Brenton, Howard 1942- .... **CLC 31**
See also CA 69-72; CANR 33; DLB 13; MTCW
Breslin, James 1930-1996
See Breslin, Jimmy
See also CA 73-76; CANR 31; DAM NOV;
MTCW
Breslin, Jimmy .... **CLC 4, 43**
See also Breslin, James
See also AITN 1
Bresson, Robert 1901- .... **CLC 16**
See also CA 110; CANR 49
Breton, Andre 1896-1966**CLC 2, 9, 15, 54; PC 15**
See also CA 19-20; 25-28R; CANR 40, 60; CAP 2;
DLB 65; MTCW
Breytenbach, Breyten 1939(?)-**CLC 23, 37; DAM**
POET
See also CA 113; 129; CANR 61
Bridgers, Sue Ellen 1942- .... **CLC 26**
See also AAYA 8; CA 65-68; CANR 11, 36; CLR
18; DLB 52; JRDA; MAICYA; SAAS 1; SATA
22, 90
Bridges, Robert (Seymour) 1844-1930 . **TCLC 1;**
DAM POET
See also CA 104; 152; CDBLB 1890-1914; DLB
19, 98
Bridie, James .... **TCLC 3**
See also Mavor, Osborne Henry
See also DLB 10
Brin, David 1950- .... **CLC 34**
See also AAYA 21; CA 102; CANR 24; INT
CANR-24; SATA 65
Brink, Andre (Philippus) 1935-**CLC 18, 36, 106**
See also CA 104; CANR 39, 62; INT 103; MTCW
Brinsmead, H(esba) F(ay) 1922- .... **CLC 21**
See also CA 21-24R; CANR 10; CLR 47;
MAICYA; SAAS 5; SATA 18, 78
Brittain, Vera (Mary) 1893(?)-1970 ...... **CLC 23**
See also CA 13-16; 25-28R; CANR 58; CAP 1;
MTCW
Broch, Hermann 1886-1951 .... **TCLC 20**
See also CA 117; DLB 85, 124

Brock, Rose
See Hansen, Joseph
Brodkey, Harold (Roy) 1930-1996 .... **CLC 56**
See also CA 111; 151; DLB 130
Brodsky, Iosif Alexandrovich 1940-1996
See Brodsky, Joseph
See also AITN 1; CA 41-44R; 151; CANR 37;
DAM POET; MTCW
Brodsky, Joseph 1940-1996**CLC 4, 6, 13, 36, 100;**
PC 9
See also Brodsky, Iosif Alexandrovich
Brodsky, Michael (Mark) 1948- .... **CLC 19**
See also CA 102; CANR 18, 41, 58
Bromell, Henry 1947- .... **CLC 5**
See also CA 53-56; CANR 9
Bromfield, Louis (Brucker) 1896-1956**TCLC 11**
See also CA 107; 155; DLB 4, 9, 86
Broner, E(sther) M(asserman) 1930- ... **CLC 19**
See also CA 17-20R; CANR 8, 25; DLB 28
Bronk, William 1918- .... **CLC 10**
See also CA 89-92; CANR 23; DLB 165
Bronstein, Lev Davidovich
See Trotsky, Leon
Bronte, Anne 1820-1849 .... **NCLC 4**
See also DLB 21
Bronte, Charlotte 1816-1855 **NCLC 3, 8, 33, 58;**
DA; DAB; DAC; DAM MST, NOV; WLC
See also AAYA 17; CDBLB 1832-1890; DLB 21,
159
Bronte, Emily (Jane) 1818-1848**NCLC 16, 35; DA;**
DAB; DAC; DAM MST, NOV, POET; PC 8;
WLC
See also AAYA 17; CDBLB 1832-1890; DLB 21,
32
Brooke, Frances 1724-1789 .... **LC 6**
See also DLB 39, 99
Brooke, Henry 1703(?)-1783 .... **LC 1**
See also DLB 39
Brooke, Rupert (Chawner) 1887-1915**TCLC 2, 7;**
DA; DAB; DAC; DAM MST, POET; WLC
See also CA 104; 132; CANR 61; CDBLB 1914-
1945; DLB 19; MTCW
Brooke-Haven, P.
See Wodehouse, P(elham) G(renville)
Brooke-Rose, Christine 1926(?)- .... **CLC 40**
See also CA 13-16R; CANR 58; DLB 14
Brookner, Anita 1928- ... **CLC 32, 34, 51; DAB;**
DAM POP
See also CA 114; 120; CANR 37, 56; DLBY 87;
MTCW
Brooks, Cleanth 1906-1994 .... **CLC 24, 86**
See also CA 17-20R; 145; CANR 33, 35; DLB 63;
DLBY 94; INT CANR-35; MTCW
Brooks, George
See Baum, L(yman) Frank
Brooks, Gwendolyn 1917-**CLC 1, 2, 4, 5, 15, 49;**
BLC; DA; DAC; DAM MST, MULT, POET;
PC 7; WLC
See also AAYA 20; AITN 1; BW 2; CA 1-4R;
CANR 1, 27, 52; CDALB 1941-1968; CLR 27;
DLB 5, 76, 165; MTCW; SATA 6
Brooks, Mel .... **CLC 12**
See also Kaminsky, Melvin
See also AAYA 13; DLB 26
Brooks, Peter 1938- .... **CLC 34**
See also CA 45-48; CANR 1
Brooks, Van Wyck 1886-1963 .... **CLC 29**
See also CA 1-4R; CANR 6; DLB 45, 63, 103
Brophy, Brigid (Antonia) 1929-1995 . **CLC 6, 11,**
29, 105
See also CA 5-8R; 149; CAAS 4; CANR 25, 53;
DLB 14; MTCW
Brosman, Catharine Savage 1934- .... **CLC 9**

See also CA 61-64; CANR 21, 46
Brother Antoninus
See Everson, William (Oliver)
The Brothers Quay
See Quay, Stephen; Quay, Timothy
Broughton, T(homas) Alan 1936- .... **CLC 19**
See also CA 45-48; CANR 2, 23, 48
Broumas, Olga 1949- .... **CLC 10, 73**
See also CA 85-88; CANR 20
Brown, Alan 1951- .... **CLC 99**
Brown, Charles Brockden 1771-1810 **NCLC 22**
See also CDALB 1640-1865; DLB 37, 59, 73
Brown, Christy 1932-1981 .... **CLC 63**
See also CA 105; 104; DLB 14
Brown, Claude 1937-**CLC 30; BLC; DAM MULT**
See also AAYA 7; BW 1; CA 73-76
Brown, Dee (Alexander) 1908-**CLC 18, 47; DAM POP**
See also CA 13-16R; CAAS 6; CANR 11, 45, 60; DLBY 80; MTCW; SATA 5
Brown, George
See Wertmueller, Lina
Brown, George Douglas 1869-1902 ..... **TCLC 28**
See also CA 162
Brown, George Mackay 1921-1996**CLC 5, 48, 100**
See also CA 21-24R; 151; CAAS 6; CANR 12, 37, 62; DLB 14, 27, 139; MTCW; SATA 35
Brown, (William) Larry 1951- .... **CLC 73**
See also CA 130; 134; INT 133
Brown, Moses
See Barrett, William (Christopher)
Brown, Rita Mae 1944- .. **CLC 18, 43, 79; DAM NOV, POP**
See also CA 45-48; CANR 2, 11, 35, 62; INT CANR-11; MTCW
Brown, Roderick (Langmere) Haig-
See Haig-Brown, Roderick (Langmere)
Brown, Rosellen 1939- .... **CLC 32**
See also CA 77-80; CAAS 10; CANR 14, 44
Brown, Sterling Allen 1901-1989**CLC 1, 23, 59; BLC; DAM MULT, POET**
See also BW 1; CA 85-88; 127; CANR 26; DLB 48, 51, 63; MTCW
Brown, Will
See Ainsworth, William Harrison
Brown, William Wells 1813-1884**NCLC 2; BLC; DAM MULT; DC 1**
See also DLB 3, 50
Browne, (Clyde) Jackson 1948(?)- .... **CLC 21**
See also CA 120
Browning, Elizabeth Barrett 1806-1861**NCLC 1, 16, 61, 66; DA; DAB; DAC; DAM MST, POET; PC 6; WLC**
See also CDBLB 1832-1890; DLB 32
Browning, Robert 1812-1889**NCLC 19; DA; DAB; DAC; DAM MST, POET; PC 2; WLCS**
See also CDBLB 1832-1890; DLB 32, 163; YABC 1
Browning, Tod 1882-1962 .... **CLC 16**
See also CA 141; 117
Brownson, Orestes (Augustus) 1803-1876**NCLC 50**
Bruccoli, Matthew J(oseph) 1931- .... **CLC 34**
See also CA 9-12R; CANR 7; DLB 103
Bruce, Lenny .... **CLC 21**
See also Schneider, Leonard Alfred
Bruin, John
See Brutus, Dennis
Brulard, Henri
See Stendhal
Brulls, Christian
See Simenon, Georges (Jacques Christian)
Brunner, John (Kilian Houston) 1934-1995 **C L C**

8, 10; DAM POP
See also CA 1-4R; 149; CAAS 8; CANR 2, 37; MTCW
Bruno, Giordano 1548-1600 .... **LC 27**
Brutus, Dennis 1924-**CLC 43; BLC; DAM MULT, POET**
See also BW 2; CA 49-52; CAAS 14; CANR 2, 27, 42; DLB 117
Bryan, C(ourtlandt) D(ixon) B(arnes) 1936-**CLC 29**
See also CA 73-76; CANR 13; INT CANR-13
Bryan, Michael
See Moore, Brian
Bryant, William Cullen 1794-1878 **NCLC 6, 46; DA; DAB; DAC; DAM MST, POET; PC 20**
See also CDALB 1640-1865; DLB 3, 43, 59
Bryusov, Valery Yakovlevich 1873-1924**TCLC 10**
See also CA 107; 155
Buchan, John 1875-1940 **TCLC 41; DAB; DAM POP**
See also CA 108; 145; DLB 34, 70, 156; YABC 2
Buchanan, George 1506-1582 .... **LC 4**
Buchheim, Lothar-Guenther 1918- .... **CLC 6**
See also CA 85-88
Buchner, (Karl) Georg 1813-1837 ...... **NCLC 26**
Buchwald, Art(hur) 1925- .... **CLC 33**
See also AITN 1; CA 5-8R; CANR 21; MTCW; SATA 10
Buck, Pearl S(ydenstricker) 1892-1973 **CLC 7, 11, 18; DA; DAB; DAC; DAM MST, NOV**
See also AITN 1; CA 1-4R; 41-44R; CANR 1, 34; DLB 9, 102; MTCW; SATA 1, 25
Buckler, Ernest 1908-1984 **CLC 13; DAC; DAM MST**
See also CA 11-12; 114; CAP 1; DLB 68; SATA 47
Buckley, Vincent (Thomas) 1925-1988 . **CLC 57**
See also CA 101
Buckley, William F(rank), Jr. 1925- **CLC 7, 18, 37; DAM POP**
See also AITN 1; CA 1-4R; CANR 1, 24, 53; DLB 137; DLBY 80; INT CANR-24; MTCW
Buechner, (Carl) Frederick 1926-**CLC 2, 4, 6, 9; DAM NOV**
See also CA 13-16R; CANR 11, 39, 64; DLBY 80; INT CANR-11; MTCW
Buell, John (Edward) 1927- .... **CLC 10**
See also CA 1-4R; DLB 53
Buero Vallejo, Antonio 1916- .... **CLC 15, 46**
See also CA 106; CANR 24, 49; HW; MTCW
Bufalino, Gesualdo 1920(?)- .... **CLC 74**
Bugayev, Boris Nikolayevich 1880-1934
See Bely, Andrey
See also CA 104
Bukowski, Charles 1920-1994**CLC 2, 5, 9, 41, 82, 108; DAM NOV, POET; PC 18**
See also CA 17-20R; 144; CANR 40, 62; DLB 5, 130, 169; MTCW
Bulgakov, Mikhail (Afanas'evich) 1891-1940 **TCLC 2, 16; DAM DRAM, NOV; SSC 18**
See also CA 105; 152
Bulgya, Alexander Alexandrovich 1901-1956 **TCLC 53**
See also Fadeyev, Alexander
See also CA 117
Bullins, Ed 1935-**CLC 1, 5, 7; BLC; DAM DRAM, MULT; DC 6**
See also BW 2; CA 49-52; CAAS 16; CANR 24, 46; DLB 7, 38; MTCW
Bulwer-Lytton, Edward (George Earle Lytton) 1803-1873 .... **NCLC 1, 45**
See also DLB 21
Bunin, Ivan Alexeyevich 1870-1953**TCLC 6; SSC**

5
See also CA 104
Bunting, Basil 1900-1985 **CLC 10, 39, 47; DAM POET**
See also CA 53-56; 115; CANR 7; DLB 20
Bunuel, Luis 1900-1983**CLC 16, 80; DAM MULT; HLC**
See also CA 101; 110; CANR 32; HW
Bunyan, John 1628-1688 **LC 4; DA; DAB; DAC; DAM MST; WLC**
See also CDBLB 1660-1789; DLB 39
Burckhardt, Jacob (Christoph) 1818-1897**NCLC 49**
Burford, Eleanor
See Hibbert, Eleanor Alice Burford
Burgess, Anthony**CLC 1, 2, 4, 5, 8, 10, 13, 15, 22, 40, 62, 81, 94; DAB**
See also Wilson, John (Anthony) Burgess
See also AITN 1; CDBLB 1960 to Present; DLB 14
Burke, Edmund 1729(?)-1797**LC 7, 36; DA; DAB; DAC; DAM MST; WLC**
See also DLB 104
Burke, Kenneth (Duva) 1897-1993 .... **CLC 2, 24**
See also CA 5-8R; 143; CANR 39; DLB 45, 63; MTCW
Burke, Leda
See Garnett, David
Burke, Ralph
See Silverberg, Robert
Burke, Thomas 1886-1945 .... **TCLC 63**
See also CA 113; 155
Burney, Fanny 1752-1840 .... **NCLC 12, 54**
See also DLB 39
Burns, Robert 1759-1796 .... **PC 6**
See also CDBLB 1789-1832; DA; DAB; DAC; DAM MST, POET; DLB 109; WLC
Burns, Tex
See L'Amour, Louis (Dearborn)
Burnshaw, Stanley 1906- .... **CLC 3, 13, 44**
See also CA 9-12R; DLB 48
Burr, Anne 1937- .... **CLC 6**
See also CA 25-28R
Burroughs, Edgar Rice 1875-1950 **TCLC 2, 32; DAM NOV**
See also AAYA 11; CA 104; 132; DLB 8; MTCW; SATA 41
Burroughs, William S(eward) 1914-1997**CLC 1, 2, 5, 15, 22, 42, 75; DA; DAB; DAC; DAM MST, NOV, POP; WLC**
See also AITN 2; CA 9-12R; 160; CANR 20, 52; DLB 2, 8, 16, 152; DLBY 81; MTCW
Burton, Richard F. 1821-1890 .... **NCLC 42**
See also DLB 55, 184
Busch, Frederick 1941- .... **CLC 7, 10, 18, 47**
See also CA 33-36R; CAAS 1; CANR 45; DLB 6
Bush, Ronald 1946- .... **CLC 34**
See also CA 136
Bustos, F(rancisco)
See Borges, Jorge Luis
Bustos Domecq, H(onorio)
See Bioy Casares, Adolfo; Borges, Jorge Luis
Butler, Octavia E(stelle) 1947-... **CLC 38; DAM MULT, POP**
See also AAYA 18; BW 2; CA 73-76; CANR 12, 24, 38; DLB 33; MTCW; SATA 84
Butler, Robert Olen (Jr.) 1945- . **CLC 81; DAM POP**
See also CA 112; DLB 173; INT 112
Butler, Samuel 1612-1680 .... **LC 16**
See also DLB 101, 126
Butler, Samuel 1835-1902**TCLC 1, 33; DA; DAB; DAC; DAM MST, NOV; WLC**

See also CA 143; CDBLB 1890-1914; DLB 18, 57, 174

Butler, Walter C.
See Faust, Frederick (Schiller)

Butor, Michel (Marie Francois) 1926- CLC **1, 3, 8, 11, 15**
See also CA 9-12R; CANR 33; DLB 83; MTCW

Butts, Mary 1892(?)-1937 .... TCLC **77**
See also CA 148

Buzo, Alexander (John) 1944- .... CLC **61**
See also CA 97-100; CANR 17, 39

Buzzati, Dino 1906-1972 .... CLC **36**
See also CA 160; 33-36R; DLB 177

Byars, Betsy (Cromer) 1928- .... CLC **35**
See also AAYA 19; CA 33-36R; CANR 18, 36, 57; CLR 1, 16; DLB 52; INT CANR-18; JRDA; MAICYA; MTCW; SAAS 1; SATA 4, 46, 80

Byatt, A(ntonia) S(usan Drabble) 1936- CLC **19, 65; DAM NOV, POP**
See also CA 13-16R; CANR 13, 33, 50; DLB 14; MTCW

Byrne, David 1952- .... CLC **26**
See also CA 127

Byrne, John Keyes 1926-
See Leonard, Hugh
See also CA 102; INT 102

Byron, George Gordon (Noel) 1788-1824 NCLC **2, 12; DA; DAB; DAC; DAM MST, POET; PC 16; WLC**
See also CDBLB 1789-1832; DLB 96, 110

Byron, Robert 1905-1941 .... TCLC **67**
See also CA 160

C. 3. 3.
See Wilde, Oscar (Fingal O'Flahertie Wills)

Caballero, Fernan 1796-1877 .... NCLC **10**

Cabell, Branch
See Cabell, James Branch

Cabell, James Branch 1879-1958 .... TCLC **6**
See also CA 105; 152; DLB 9, 78

Cable, George Washington 1844-1925 . TCLC **4; SSC 4**
See also CA 104; 155; DLB 12, 74; DLBD 13

Cabral de Melo Neto, Joao 1920- CLC **76; DAM MULT**
See also CA 151

Cabrera Infante, G(uillermo) 1929-. CLC **5, 25, 45; DAM MULT; HLC**
See also CA 85-88; CANR 29; DLB 113; HW; MTCW

Cade, Toni
See Bambara, Toni Cade

Cadmus and Harmonia
See Buchan, John

Caedmon fl. 658-680 .... CMLC **7**
See also DLB 146

Caeiro, Alberto
See Pessoa, Fernando (Antonio Nogueira)

Cage, John (Milton, Jr.) 1912- .... CLC **41**
See also CA 13-16R; CANR 9; INT CANR-9

Cahan, Abraham 1860-1951 .... TCLC **71**
See also CA 108; 154; DLB 9, 25, 28

Cain, G.
See Cabrera Infante, G(uillermo)

Cain, Guillermo
See Cabrera Infante, G(uillermo)

Cain, James M(allahan) 1892-1977 CLC **3, 11, 28**
See also AITN 1; CA 17-20R; 73-76; CANR 8, 34, 61; MTCW

Caine, Mark
See Raphael, Frederic (Michael)

Calasso, Roberto 1941- .... CLC **81**
See also CA 143

Calderon de la Barca, Pedro 1600-1681 .. LC **23;**

DC **3**

Caldwell, Erskine (Preston) 1903-1987 CLC **1, 8, 14, 50, 60; DAM NOV; SSC 19**
See also AITN 1; CA 1-4R; 121; CAAS 1; CANR 2, 33; DLB 9, 86; MTCW

Caldwell, (Janet Miriam) Taylor (Holland) 1900-1985 .... CLC **2, 28, 39; DAM NOV, POP**
See also CA 5-8R; 116; CANR 5

Calhoun, John Caldwell 1782-1850 .... NCLC **15**
See also DLB 3

Calisher, Hortense 1911- CLC **2, 4, 8, 38; DAM NOV; SSC 15**
See also CA 1-4R; CANR 1, 22; DLB 2; INT CANR-22; MTCW

Callaghan, Morley Edward 1903-1990 CLC **3, 14, 41, 65; DAC; DAM MST**
See also CA 9-12R; 132; CANR 33; DLB 68; MTCW

Callimachus c. 305B.C.-c. 240B.C. ..... CMLC **18**
See also DLB 176

Calvin, John 1509-1564 .... LC **37**

Calvino, Italo 1923-1985 CLC **5, 8, 11, 22, 33, 39, 73; DAM NOV; SSC 3**
See also CA 85-88; 116; CANR 23, 61; MTCW

Cameron, Carey 1952- .... CLC **59**
See also CA 135

Cameron, Peter 1959- .... CLC **44**
See also CA 125; CANR 50

Campana, Dino 1885-1932 .... TCLC **20**
See also CA 117; DLB 114

Campanella, Tommaso 1568-1639 .... LC **32**

Campbell, John W(ood, Jr.) 1910-1971 .. CLC **32**
See also CA 21-22; 29-32R; CANR 34; CAP 2; DLB 8; MTCW

Campbell, Joseph 1904-1987 .... CLC **69**
See also AAYA 3; BEST 89:2; CA 1-4R; 124; CANR 3, 28, 61; MTCW

Campbell, Maria 1940- .... CLC **85; DAC**
See also CA 102; CANR 54; NNAL

Campbell, (John) Ramsey 1946- CLC **42; SSC 19**
See also CA 57-60; CANR 7; INT CANR-7

Campbell, (Ignatius) Roy (Dunnachie) 1901-1957 TCLC **5**
See also CA 104; 155; DLB 20

Campbell, Thomas 1777-1844 .... NCLC **19**
See also DLB 93; 144

Campbell, Wilfred .... TCLC **9**
See also Campbell, William

Campbell, William 1858(?)-1918
See Campbell, Wilfred
See also CA 106; DLB 92

Campion, Jane .... CLC **95**
See also CA 138

Campos, Alvaro de
See Pessoa, Fernando (Antonio Nogueira)

Camus, Albert 1913-1960 CLC **1, 2, 4, 9, 11, 14, 32, 63, 69; DA; DAB; DAC; DAM DRAM, MST, NOV; DC 2; SSC 9; WLC**
See also CA 89-92; DLB 72; MTCW

Canby, Vincent 1924- .... CLC **13**
See also CA 81-84

Cancale
See Desnos, Robert

Canetti, Elias 1905-1994 .. CLC **3, 14, 25, 75, 86**
See also CA 21-24R; 146; CANR 23, 61; DLB 85, 124; MTCW

Canin, Ethan 1960- .... CLC **55**
See also CA 131; 135

Cannon, Curt
See Hunter, Evan

Cape, Judith
See Page, P(atricia) K(athleen)

Capek, Karel 1890-1938 TCLC **6, 37; DA; DAB;**

DAC; DAM DRAM, MST, NOV; DC 1; WLC
See also CA 104; 140

Capote, Truman 1924-1984 CLC **1, 3, 8, 13, 19, 34, 38, 58; DA; DAB; DAC; DAM MST, NOV, POP; SSC 2; WLC**
See also CA 5-8R; 113; CANR 18, 62; CDALB 1941-1968; DLB 2; DLBY 80, 84; MTCW; SATA 91

Capra, Frank 1897-1991 .... CLC **16**
See also CA 61-64; 135

Caputo, Philip 1941- .... CLC **32**
See also CA 73-76; CANR 40

Caragiale, Ion Luca 1852-1912 .... TCLC **76**
See also CA 157

Card, Orson Scott 1951- CLC **44, 47, 50; DAM POP**
See also AAYA 11; CA 102; CANR 27, 47; INT CANR-27; MTCW; SATA 83

Cardenal, Ernesto 1925- . CLC **31; DAM MULT, POET; HLC**
See also CA 49-52; CANR 2, 32; HW; MTCW

Cardozo, Benjamin N(athan) 1870-1938 TCLC **65**
See also CA 117

Carducci, Giosue (Alessandro Giuseppe) 1835-1907 .... TCLC **32**

Carew, Thomas 1595(?)-1640 .... LC **13**
See also DLB 126

Carey, Ernestine Gilbreth 1908- .... CLC **17**
See also CA 5-8R; SATA 2

Carey, Peter 1943- .... CLC **40, 55, 96**
See also CA 123; 127; CANR 53; INT 127; MTCW; SATA 94

Carleton, William 1794-1869 .... NCLC **3**
See also DLB 159

Carlisle, Henry (Coffin) 1926- .... CLC **33**
See also CA 13-16R; CANR 15

Carlsen, Chris
See Holdstock, Robert P.

Carlson, Ron(ald F.) 1947- .... CLC **54**
See also CA 105; CANR 27

Carlyle, Thomas 1795-1881 NCLC **22; DA; DAB; DAC; DAM MST**
See also CDBLB 1789-1832; DLB 55; 144

Carman, (William) Bliss 1861-1929 TCLC **7; DAC**
See also CA 104; 152; DLB 92

Carnegie, Dale 1888-1955 .... TCLC **53**

Carossa, Hans 1878-1956 .... TCLC **48**
See also DLB 66

Carpenter, Don(ald Richard) 1931-1995 CLC **41**
See also CA 45-48; 149; CANR 1

Carpentier (y Valmont), Alejo 1904-1980 CLC **8, 11, 38; DAM MULT; HLC**
See also CA 65-68; 97-100; CANR 11; DLB 113; HW

Carr, Caleb 1955(?)- .... CLC **86**
See also CA 147

Carr, Emily 1871-1945 .... TCLC **32**
See also CA 159; DLB 68

Carr, John Dickson 1906-1977 .... CLC **3**
See also Fairbairn, Roger
See also CA 49-52; 69-72; CANR 3, 33, 60; MTCW

Carr, Philippa
See Hibbert, Eleanor Alice Burford

Carr, Virginia Spencer 1929- .... CLC **34**
See also CA 61-64; DLB 111

Carrere, Emmanuel 1957- .... CLC **89**

Carrier, Roch 1937- ... CLC **13, 78; DAC; DAM MST**
See also CA 130; CANR 61; DLB 53

Carroll, James P. 1943(?)- .... CLC **38**
See also CA 81-84

Carroll, Jim 1951- .... CLC **35**
See also AAYA 17; CA 45-48; CANR 42

CHAYEFSKY

CUMULATIVE AUTHOR INDEX

See also DLB 7, 44; DLBY 81

Chayefsky, Sidney 1923-1981
See Chayefsky, Paddy
See also CA 9-12R; 104; CANR 18; DAM DRAM

Chedid, Andree 1920- .... **CLC 47**
See also CA 145

Cheever, John 1912-1982CLC 3, 7, 8, 11, 15, 25, 64; DA; DAB; DAC; DAM MST, NOV, POP; SSC 1; WLC
See also CA 5-8R; 106; CABS 1; CANR 5, 27; CDALB 1941-1968; DLB 2, 102; DLBY 80, 82; INT CANR-5; MTCW

Cheever, Susan 1943- .... **CLC 18, 48**
See also CA 103; CANR 27, 51; DLBY 82; INT CANR-27

Chekhonte, Antosha
See Chekhov, Anton (Pavlovich)

Chekhov, Anton (Pavlovich) 1860-1904 **TCLC 3, 10, 31, 55; DA; DAB; DAC; DAM DRAM, MST; SSC 2, 28; WLC**
See also CA 104; 124; SATA 90

Chernyshevsky, Nikolay Gavrilovich 1828-1889 **NCLC 1**

Cherry, Carolyn Janice 1942-
See Cherryh, C. J.
See also CA 65-68; CANR 10

Cherryh, C. J. .... **CLC 35**
See also Cherry, Carolyn Janice
See also DLBY 80; SATA 93

Chesnutt, Charles W(addell) 1858-1932TCLC 5, 39; BLC; DAM MULT; SSC 7
See also BW 1; CA 106; 125; DLB 12, 50, 78; MTCW

Chester, Alfred 1929(?)-1971 .... **CLC 49**
See also CA 33-36R; DLB 130

Chesterton, G(ilbert) K(eith) 1874-1936TCLC 1, 6, 64; DAM NOV, POET; SSC 1
See also CA 104; 132; CDBLB 1914-1945; DLB 10, 19, 34, 70, 98, 149, 178; MTCW; SATA 27

Chiang Pin-chin 1904-1986
See Ding Ling
See also CA 118

Ch'ien Chung-shu 1910- .... **CLC 22**
See also CA 130; MTCW

Child, L. Maria
See Child, Lydia Maria

Child, Lydia Maria 1802-1880 .... **NCLC 6**
See also DLB 1, 74; SATA 67

Child, Mrs.
See Child, Lydia Maria

Child, Philip 1898-1978 .... **CLC 19, 68**
See also CA 13-14; CAP 1; SATA 47

Childers, (Robert) Erskine 1870-1922 **TCLC 65**
See also CA 113; 153; DLB 70

Childress, Alice 1920-1994 **CLC 12, 15, 86, 96; BLC; DAM DRAM, MULT, NOV; DC 4**
See also AAYA 8; BW 2; CA 45-48; 146; CANR 3, 27, 50; CLR 14; DLB 7, 38; JRDA; MAICYA; MTCW; SATA 7, 48, 81

Chin, Frank (Chew, Jr.) 1940- .... **DC 7**
See also CA 33-36R; DAM MULT

Chislett, (Margaret) Anne 1943- .... **CLC 34**
See also CA 151

Chitty, Thomas Willes 1926- .... **CLC 11**
See also Hinde, Thomas
See also CA 5-8R

Chivers, Thomas Holley 1809-1858 .... **NCLC 49**
See also DLB 3

Chomette, Rene Lucien 1898-1981
See Clair, Rene
See also CA 103

Chopin, KateTCLC 5, 14; DA; DAB; SSC 8; WLCS
See also Chopin, Katherine

See also CDALB 1865-1917; DLB 12, 78

Chopin, Katherine 1851-1904
See Chopin, Kate
See also CA 104; 122; DAC; DAM MST, NOV

Chretien de Troyes c. 12th cent. - ...... **CMLC 10**

Christie
See Ichikawa, Kon

Christie, Agatha (Mary Clarissa) 1890-1976CLC 1, 6, 8, 12, 39, 48; DAB; DAC; DAM NOV
See also AAYA 9; AITN 1, 2; CA 17-20R; 61-64; CANR 10, 37; CDBLB 1914-1945; DLB 13, 77; MTCW; SATA 36

Christie, (Ann) Philippa
See Pearce, Philippa
See also CA 5-8R; CANR 4

Christine de Pizan 1365(?)-1431(?) .... **LC 9**

Chubb, Elmer
See Masters, Edgar Lee

Chulkov, Mikhail Dmitrievich 1743-1792 .. **LC 2**
See also DLB 150

Churchill, Caryl 1938- .... **CLC 31, 55; DC 5**
See also CA 102; CANR 22, 46; DLB 13; MTCW

Churchill, Charles 1731-1764 .... **LC 3**
See also DLB 109

Chute, Carolyn 1947- .... **CLC 39**
See also CA 123

Ciardi, John (Anthony) 1916-1986 . **CLC 10, 40, 44; DAM POET**
See also CA 5-8R; 118; CAAS 2; CANR 5, 33; CLR 19; DLB 5; DLBY 86; INT CANR-5; MAICYA; MTCW; SATA 1, 65; SATA-Obit 46

Cicero, Marcus Tullius 106B.C.-43B.C. **CMLC 3**

Cimino, Michael 1943- .... **CLC 16**
See also CA 105

Cioran, E(mil) M. 1911-1995 .... **CLC 64**
See also CA 25-28R; 149

Cisneros, Sandra 1954- . **CLC 69; DAM MULT; HLC**
See also AAYA 9; CA 131; CANR 64; DLB 122, 152; HW

Cixous, Helene 1937- .... **CLC 92**
See also CA 126; CANR 55; DLB 83; MTCW

Clair, Rene .... **CLC 20**
See also Chomette, Rene Lucien

Clampitt, Amy 1920-1994 .... **CLC 32; PC 19**
See also CA 110; 146; CANR 29; DLB 105

Clancy, Thomas L., Jr. 1947-
See Clancy, Tom
See also CA 125; 131; CANR 62; INT 131; MTCW

Clancy, Tom .... **CLC 45; DAM NOV, POP**
See also Clancy, Thomas L., Jr.
See also AAYA 9; BEST 89:1, 90:1

Clare, John 1793-1864NCLC 9; DAB; DAM POET
See also DLB 55, 96

Clarin
See Alas (y Urena), Leopoldo (Enrique Garcia)

Clark, Al C.
See Goines, Donald

Clark, (Robert) Brian 1932- .... **CLC 29**
See also CA 41-44R

Clark, Curt
See Westlake, Donald E(dwin)

Clark, Eleanor 1913-1996 .... **CLC 5, 19**
See also CA 9-12R; 151; CANR 41; DLB 6

Clark, J. P.
See Clark, John Pepper
See also DLB 117

Clark, John Pepper 1935- **CLC 38; BLC; DAM DRAM, MULT; DC 5**
See also Clark, J. P.
See also BW 1; CA 65-68; CANR 16

Clark, M. R.

See Clark, Mavis Thorpe

Clark, Mavis Thorpe 1909- .... **CLC 12**
See also CA 57-60; CANR 8, 37; CLR 30; MAICYA; SAAS 5; SATA 8, 74

Clark, Walter Van Tilburg 1909-1971 .. **CLC 28**
See also CA 9-12R; 33-36R; CANR 63; DLB 9; SATA 8

Clarke, Arthur C(harles) 1917-CLC 1, 4, 13, 18, 35; DAM POP; SSC 3
See also AAYA 4; CA 1-4R; CANR 2, 28, 55; JRDA; MAICYA; MTCW; SATA 13, 70

Clarke, Austin 1896-1974CLC 6, 9; DAM POET
See also CA 29-32; 49-52; CAP 2; DLB 10, 20

Clarke, Austin C(hesterfield) 1934- **CLC 8, 53; BLC; DAC; DAM MULT**
See also BW 1; CA 25-28R; CAAS 16; CANR 14, 32; DLB 53, 125

Clarke, Gillian 1937- .... **CLC 61**
See also CA 106; DLB 40

Clarke, Marcus (Andrew Hislop) 1846-1881 **NCLC 19**

Clarke, Shirley 1925- .... **CLC 16**

Clash, The
See Headon, (Nicky) Topper; Jones, Mick; Simonon, Paul; Strummer, Joe

Claudel, Paul (Louis Charles Marie) 1868-1955 **TCLC 2, 10**
See also CA 104

Clavell, James (duMaresq) 1925-1994CLC 6, 25, 87; DAM NOV, POP
See also CA 25-28R; 146; CANR 26, 48; MTCW

Cleaver, (Leroy) Eldridge 1935- . **CLC 30; BLC; DAM MULT**
See also BW 1; CA 21-24R; CANR 16

Cleese, John (Marwood) 1939- .... **CLC 21**
See also Monty Python
See also CA 112; 116; CANR 35; MTCW

Cleishbotham, Jebediah
See Scott, Walter

Cleland, John 1710-1789 .... **LC 2**
See also DLB 39

Clemens, Samuel Langhorne 1835-1910
See Twain, Mark
See also CA 104; 135; CDALB 1865-1917; DA; DAB; DAC; DAM MST, NOV; DLB 11, 12, 23, 64, 74, 186; JRDA; MAICYA; YABC 2

Cleophil
See Congreve, William

Clerihew, E.
See Bentley, E(dmund) C(lerihew)

Clerk, N. W.
See Lewis, C(live) S(taples)

Cliff, Jimmy .... **CLC 21**
See also Chambers, James

Clifton, (Thelma) Lucille 1936-CLC 19, 66; BLC; DAM MULT, POET; PC 17
See also BW 2; CA 49-52; CANR 2, 24, 42; CLR 5; DLB 5, 41; MAICYA; MTCW; SATA 20, 69

Clinton, Dirk
See Silverberg, Robert

Clough, Arthur Hugh 1819-1861 .... **NCLC 27**
See also DLB 32

Clutha, Janet Paterson Frame 1924-
See Frame, Janet
See also CA 1-4R; CANR 2, 36; MTCW

Clyne, Terence
See Blatty, William Peter

Cobalt, Martin
See Mayne, William (James Carter)

Cobb, Irvin S. 1876-1944 .... **TCLC 77**
See also DLB 11, 25, 86

Cobbett, William 1763-1835 .... **NCLC 49**
See also DLB 43, 107, 158

400

Author Index

See Agnon, S(hmuel) Y(osef Halevi)

Dabrowska, Maria (Szumska) 1889-1965CLC 15
   See also CA 106

Dabydeen, David 1955- .... **CLC 34**
   See also BW 1; CA 125; CANR 56

Dacey, Philip 1939- .... **CLC 51**
   See also CA 37-40R; CAAS 17; CANR 14, 32, 64;
   DLB 105

Dagerman, Stig (Halvard) 1923-1954 .. **TCLC 17**
   See also CA 117; 155

Dahl, Roald 1916-1990 .. **CLC 1, 6, 18, 79; DAB;
   DAC; DAM MST, NOV, POP**
   See also AAYA 15; CA 1-4R; 133; CANR 6, 32,
   37, 62; CLR 1, 7, 41; DLB 139; JRDA;
   MAICYA; MTCW; SATA 1, 26, 73; SATA-
   Obit 65

Dahlberg, Edward 1900-1977 .... **CLC 1, 7, 14**
   See also CA 9-12R; 69-72; CANR 31, 62; DLB 48;
   MTCW

Daitch, Susan 1954- .... **CLC 103**
   See also CA 161

Dale, Colin .... **TCLC 18**
   See also Lawrence, T(homas) E(dward)

Dale, George E.
   See Asimov, Isaac

Daly, Elizabeth 1878-1967 .... **CLC 52**
   See also CA 23-24; 25-28R; CANR 60; CAP 2

Daly, Maureen 1921- .... **CLC 17**
   See also AAYA 5; CANR 37; JRDA; MAICYA;
   SAAS 1; SATA 2

Damas, Leon-Gontran 1912-1978 .... **CLC 84**
   See also BW 1; CA 125; 73-76

Dana, Richard Henry Sr. 1787-1879 .. **NCLC 53**

Daniel, Samuel 1562(?)-1619 .... **LC 24**
   See also DLB 62

Daniels, Brett
   See Adler, Renata

Dannay, Frederic 1905-1982 **CLC 11; DAM POP**
   See also Queen, Ellery
   See also CA 1-4R; 107; CANR 1, 39; DLB 137;
   MTCW

D'Annunzio, Gabriele 1863-1938 .... **TCLC 6, 40**
   See also CA 104; 155

Danois, N. le
   See Gourmont, Remy (-Marie-Charles) de

Dante 1265-1321 **CMLC 3, 18; DA; DAB; DAC;
   DAM MST, POET; PC 21; WLCS**

d'Antibes, Germain
   See Simenon, Georges (Jacques Christian)

Danticat, Edwidge 1969- .... **CLC 94**
   See also CA 152

Danvers, Dennis 1947- .... **CLC 70**

Danziger, Paula 1944- .... **CLC 21**
   See also AAYA 4; CA 112; 115; CANR 37; CLR
   20; JRDA; MAICYA; SATA 36, 63; SATA-
   Brief 30

Da Ponte, Lorenzo 1749-1838 .... **NCLC 50**

Dario, Ruben 1867-1916 . **TCLC 4; DAM MULT;
   HLC; PC 15**
   See also CA 131; HW; MTCW

Darley, George 1795-1846 .... **NCLC 2**
   See also DLB 96

Darwin, Charles 1809-1882 .... **NCLC 57**
   See also DLB 57, 166

Daryush, Elizabeth 1887-1977 .... **CLC 6, 19**
   See also CA 49-52; CANR 3; DLB 20

Dashwood, Edmee Elizabeth Monica de la Pasture
   1890-1943
   See Delafield, E. M.
   See also CA 119; 154

Daudet, (Louis Marie) Alphonse 1840-1897NCLC
   1
   See also DLB 123

Daumal, Rene 1908-1944 .... **TCLC 14**
   See also CA 114

Davenport, Guy (Mattison, Jr.) 1927- **CLC 6, 14,
   38; SSC 16**
   See also CA 33-36R; CANR 23; DLB 130

Davidson, Avram 1923-
   See Queen, Ellery
   See also CA 101; CANR 26; DLB 8

Davidson, Donald (Grady) 1893-1968 **CLC 2, 13,
   19**
   See also CA 5-8R; 25-28R; CANR 4; DLB 45

Davidson, Hugh
   See Hamilton, Edmond

Davidson, John 1857-1909 .... **TCLC 24**
   See also CA 118; DLB 19

Davidson, Sara 1943- .... **CLC 9**
   See also CA 81-84; CANR 44

Davie, Donald (Alfred) 1922-1995CLC 5, 8, 10, 31
   See also CA 1-4R; 149; CAAS 3; CANR 1, 44;
   DLB 27; MTCW

Davies, Ray(mond Douglas) 1944- .... **CLC 21**
   See also CA 116; 146

Davies, Rhys 1903-1978 .... **CLC 23**
   See also CA 9-12R; 81-84; CANR 4; DLB 139

Davies, (William) Robertson 1913-1995CLC 2, 7,
   13, 25, 42, 75, 91; DA; DAB; DAC; DAM
   MST, NOV, POP; WLC
   See also BEST 89:2; CA 33-36R; 150; CANR 17,
   42; DLB 68; INT CANR-17; MTCW

Davies, W(illiam) H(enry) 1871-1940 .... **TCLC 5**
   See also CA 104; DLB 19, 174

Davies, Walter C.
   See Kornbluth, C(yril) M.

Davis, Angela (Yvonne) 1944- .... **CLC 77; DAM
   MULT**
   See also BW 2; CA 57-60; CANR 10

Davis, B. Lynch
   See Bioy Casares, Adolfo; Borges, Jorge Luis

Davis, Gordon
   See Hunt, E(verette) Howard, (Jr.)

Davis, Harold Lenoir 1896-1960 .... **CLC 49**
   See also CA 89-92; DLB 9

Davis, Rebecca (Blaine) Harding 1831-1910
   TCLC 6
   See also CA 104; DLB 74

Davis, Richard Harding 1864-1916 ..... **TCLC 24**
   See also CA 114; DLB 12, 23, 78, 79; DLBD 13

Davison, Frank Dalby 1893-1970 .... **CLC 15**
   See also CA 116

Davison, Lawrence H.
   See Lawrence, D(avid) H(erbert Richards)

Davison, Peter (Hubert) 1928- .... **CLC 28**
   See also CA 9-12R; CAAS 4; CANR 3, 43; DLB 5

Davys, Mary 1674-1732 .... **LC 1**
   See also DLB 39

Dawson, Fielding 1930- .... **CLC 6**
   See also CA 85-88; DLB 130

Dawson, Peter
   See Faust, Frederick (Schiller)

Day, Clarence (Shepard, Jr.) 1874-1935TCLC 25
   See also CA 108; DLB 11

Day, Thomas 1748-1789 .... **LC 1**
   See also DLB 39; YABC 1

Day Lewis, C(ecil) 1904-1972CLC 1, 6, 10; DAM
   POET; PC 11
   See also Blake, Nicholas
   See also CA 13-16; 33-36R; CANR 34; CAP 1;
   DLB 15, 20; MTCW

Dazai, Osamu .... **TCLC 11**
   See also Tsushima, Shuji
   See also DLB 182

de Andrade, Carlos Drummond
   See Drummond de Andrade, Carlos

Deane, Norman
   See Creasey, John

**de Beauvoir, Simone (Lucie Ernestine Marie
   Bertrand)**
   See Beauvoir, Simone (Lucie Ernestine Marie
   Bertrand) de

de Beer, P.
   See Bosman, Herman Charles

de Brissac, Malcolm
   See Dickinson, Peter (Malcolm)

de Chardin, Pierre Teilhard
   See Teilhard de Chardin, (Marie Joseph) Pierre

Dee, John 1527-1608 .... **LC 20**

Deer, Sandra 1940- .... **CLC 45**

De Ferrari, Gabriella 1941- .... **CLC 65**
   See also CA 146

Defoe, Daniel 1660(?)-1731LC 1; DA; DAB; DAC;
   DAM MST, NOV; WLC
   See also CDBLB 1660-1789; DLB 39, 95, 101;
   JRDA; MAICYA; SATA 22

de Gourmont, Remy(-Marie-Charles)
   See Gourmont, Remy (-Marie-Charles) de

de Hartog, Jan 1914- .... **CLC 19**
   See also CA 1-4R; CANR 1

de Hostos, E. M.
   See Hostos (y Bonilla), Eugenio Maria de

de Hostos, Eugenio M.
   See Hostos (y Bonilla), Eugenio Maria de

Deighton, Len .... **CLC 4, 7, 22, 46**
   See also Deighton, Leonard Cyril
   See also AAYA 6; BEST 89:2; CDBLB 1960 to
   Present; DLB 87

Deighton, Leonard Cyril 1929-
   See Deighton, Len
   See also CA 9-12R; CANR 19, 33; DAM NOV,
   POP; MTCW

Dekker, Thomas 1572(?)-1632 ...... **LC 22; DAM
   DRAM**
   See also CDBLB Before 1660; DLB 62, 172

Delafield, E. M. 1890-1943 .... **TCLC 61**
   See also Dashwood, Edmee Elizabeth Monica de
   la Pasture
   See also DLB 34

de la Mare, Walter (John) 1873-1956TCLC 4, 53;
   DAB; DAC; DAM MST, POET; SSC 14;
   WLC
   See also CDBLB 1914-1945; CLR 23; DLB 162;
   SATA 16

Delaney, Franey
   See O'Hara, John (Henry)

Delaney, Shelagh 1939-.. **CLC 29; DAM DRAM**
   See also CA 17-20R; CANR 30; CDBLB 1960 to
   Present; DLB 13; MTCW

Delany, Mary (Granville Pendarves) 1700-1788
   LC 12

Delany, Samuel R(ay, Jr.) 1942- . **CLC 8, 14, 38;
   BLC; DAM MULT**
   See also BW 2; CA 81-84; CANR 27, 43; DLB 8,
   33; MTCW

De La Ramee, (Marie) Louise 1839-1908
   See Ouida
   See also SATA 20

de la Roche, Mazo 1879-1961 .... **CLC 14**
   See also CA 85-88; CANR 30; DLB 68; SATA 64

De La Salle, Innocent
   See Hartmann, Sadakichi

Delbanco, Nicholas (Franklin) 1942- **CLC 6, 13**
   See also CA 17-20R; CAAS 2; CANR 29, 55; DLB
   6

del Castillo, Michel 1933- .... **CLC 38**
   See also CA 109

Deledda, Grazia (Cosima) 1875(?)-1936TCLC 23
   See also CA 123

Delibes, Miguel .... CLC 8, 18
   See also Delibes Setien, Miguel
Delibes Setien, Miguel 1920-
   See Delibes, Miguel
   See also CA 45-48; CANR 1, 32; HW; MTCW
DeLillo, Don 1936-CLC 8, 10, 13, 27, 39, 54, 76;
   DAM NOV, POP
   See also BEST 89:1; CA 81-84; CANR 21; DLB 6,
   173; MTCW
de Lisser, H. G.
   See De Lisser, H(erbert) G(eorge)
   See also DLB 117
De Lisser, H(erbert) G(eorge) 1878-1944 TCLC
   12
   See also de Lisser, H. G.
   See also BW 2; CA 109; 152
Deloney, Thomas 1560-1600 .... LC 41
Deloria, Vine (Victor), Jr. 1933- CLC 21; DAM
   MULT
   See also CA 53-56; CANR 5, 20, 48; DLB 175;
   MTCW; NNAL; SATA 21
Del Vecchio, John M(ichael) 1947- .... CLC 29
   See also CA 110; DLBD 9
de Man, Paul (Adolph Michel) 1919-1983CLC 55
   See also CA 128; 111; CANR 61; DLB 67; MTCW
De Marinis, Rick 1934- .... CLC 54
   See also CA 57-60; CAAS 24; CANR 9, 25, 50
Dembry, R. Emmet
   See Murfree, Mary Noailles
Demby, William 1922-CLC 53; BLC; DAM MULT
   See also BW 1; CA 81-84; DLB 33
de Menton, Francisco
   See Chin, Frank (Chew, Jr.)
Demijohn, Thom
   See Disch, Thomas M(ichael)
de Montherlant, Henry (Milon)
   See Montherlant, Henry (Milon) de
Demosthenes 384B.C.-322B.C. .... CMLC 13
   See also DLB 176
de Natale, Francine
   See Malzberg, Barry N(athaniel)
Denby, Edwin (Orr) 1903-1983 .... CLC 48
   See also CA 138; 110
Denis, Julio
   See Cortazar, Julio
Denmark, Harrison
   See Zelazny, Roger (Joseph)
Dennis, John 1658-1734 .... LC 11
   See also DLB 101
Dennis, Nigel (Forbes) 1912-1989 .... CLC 8
   See also CA 25-28R; 129; DLB 13, 15; MTCW
Dent, Lester 1904(?)-1959 .... TCLC 72
   See also CA 112; 161
De Palma, Brian (Russell) 1940- .... CLC 20
   See also CA 109
De Quincey, Thomas 1785-1859 .... NCLC 4
   See also CDBLB 1789-1832; DLB 110; 144
Deren, Eleanora 1908(?)-1961
   See Deren, Maya
   See also CA 111
Deren, Maya 1917-1961 .... CLC 16, 102
   See also Deren, Eleanora
Derleth, August (William) 1909-1971 .. CLC 31
   See also CA 1-4R; 29-32R; CANR 4; DLB 9; SATA
   5
Der Nister 1884-1950 .... TCLC 56
de Routisie, Albert
   See Aragon, Louis
Derrida, Jacques 1930- .... CLC 24, 87
   See also CA 124; 127
Derry Down Derry
   See Lear, Edward
Dersonnes, Jacques

   See Simenon, Georges (Jacques Christian)
Desai, Anita 1937- CLC 19, 37, 97; DAB; DAM
   NOV
   See also CA 81-84; CANR 33, 53; MTCW; SATA
   63
de Saint-Luc, Jean
   See Glassco, John
de Saint Roman, Arnaud
   See Aragon, Louis
Descartes, Rene 1596-1650 .... LC 20, 35
De Sica, Vittorio 1901(?)-1974 .... CLC 20
   See also CA 117
Desnos, Robert 1900-1945 .... TCLC 22
   See also CA 121; 151
Destouches, Louis-Ferdinand 1894-1961 CLC 9,
   15
   See also Celine, Louis-Ferdinand
   See also CA 85-88; CANR 28; MTCW
de Tolignac, Gaston
   See Griffith, D(avid Lewelyn) W(ark)
Deutsch, Babette 1895-1982 .... CLC 18
   See also CA 1-4R; 108; CANR 4; DLB 45; SATA
   1; SATA-Obit 33
Devenant, William 1606-1649 .... LC 13
Devkota, Laxmiprasad 1909-1959 .... TCLC 23
   See also CA 123
De Voto, Bernard (Augustine) 1897-1955 TCLC
   29
   See also CA 113; 160; DLB 9
De Vries, Peter 1910-1993CLC 1, 2, 3, 7, 10, 28,
   46; DAM NOV
   See also CA 17-20R; 142; CANR 41; DLB 6; DLBY
   82; MTCW
Dexter, John
   See Bradley, Marion Zimmer
Dexter, Martin
   See Faust, Frederick (Schiller)
Dexter, Pete 1943- .... CLC 34, 55; DAM POP
   See also BEST 89:2; CA 127; 131; INT 131;
   MTCW
Diamano, Silmang
   See Senghor, Leopold Sedar
Diamond, Neil 1941- .... CLC 30
   See also CA 108
Diaz del Castillo, Bernal 1496-1584 .... LC 31
di Bassetto, Corno
   See Shaw, George Bernard
Dick, Philip K(indred) 1928-1982CLC 10, 30, 72;
   DAM NOV, POP
   See also CA 49-52; 106; CANR 2, 16; DLB 8;
   MTCW
Dickens, Charles (John Huffam) 1812-1870
   NCLC 3, 8, 18, 26, 37, 50; DA; DAB; DAC;
   DAM MST, NOV; SSC 17; WLC
   See also CDBLB 1832-1890; DLB 21, 55, 70, 159,
   166; JRDA; MAICYA; SATA 15
Dickey, James (Lafayette) 1923-1997CLC 1, 2, 4,
   7, 10, 15, 47; DAM NOV, POET, POP
   See also AITN 1, 2; CA 9-12R; 156; CABS 2;
   CANR 10, 48, 61; CDALB 1968-1988; DLB 5;
   DLBD 7; DLBY 82, 93, 96; INT CANR-10;
   MTCW
Dickey, William 1928-1994 .... CLC 3, 28
   See also CA 9-12R; 145; CANR 24; DLB 5
Dickinson, Charles 1951- .... CLC 49
   See also CA 128
Dickinson, Emily (Elizabeth) 1830-1886 .. NCLC
   21; DA; DAB; DAC; DAM MST, POET; PC
   1; WLC
   See also AAYA 22; CDALB 1865-1917; DLB 1;
   SATA 29
Dickinson, Peter (Malcolm) 1927- . CLC 12, 35
   See also AAYA 9; CA 41-44R; CANR 31, 58; CLR

   29; DLB 87, 161; JRDA; MAICYA; SATA 5,
   62, 95
Dickson, Carr
   See Carr, John Dickson
Dickson, Carter
   See Carr, John Dickson
Diderot, Denis 1713-1784 .... LC 26
Didion, Joan 1934-CLC 1, 3, 8, 14, 32; DAM NOV
   See also AITN 1; CA 5-8R; CANR 14, 52; CDALB
   1968-1988; DLB 2, 173; DLBY 81, 86; MTCW
Dietrich, Robert
   See Hunt, E(verette) Howard, (Jr.)
Dillard, Annie 1945- ..... CLC 9, 60; DAM NOV
   See also AAYA 6; CA 49-52; CANR 3, 43, 62;
   DLBY 80; MTCW; SATA 10
Dillard, R(ichard) H(enry) W(ilde) 1937- CLC 5
   See also CA 21-24R; CAAS 7; CANR 10; DLB 5
Dillon, Eilis 1920-1994 .... CLC 17
   See also CA 9-12R; 147; CAAS 3; CANR 4, 38;
   CLR 26; MAICYA; SATA 2, 74; SATA-Obit
   83
Dimont, Penelope
   See Mortimer, Penelope (Ruth)
Dinesen, Isak .... CLC 10, 29, 95; SSC 7
   See also Blixen, Karen (Christentze Dinesen)
Ding Ling .... CLC 68
   See also Chiang Pin-chin
Disch, Thomas M(ichael) 1940- .... CLC 7, 36
   See also AAYA 17; CA 21-24R; CAAS 4; CANR
   17, 36, 54; CLR 18; DLB 8; MAICYA; MTCW;
   SAAS 15; SATA 92
Disch, Tom
   See Disch, Thomas M(ichael)
d'Isly, Georges
   See Simenon, Georges (Jacques Christian)
Disraeli, Benjamin 1804-1881 .... NCLC 2, 39
   See also DLB 21, 55
Ditcum, Steve
   See Crumb, R(obert)
Dixon, Paige
   See Corcoran, Barbara
Dixon, Stephen 1936- .... CLC 52; SSC 16
   See also CA 89-92; CANR 17, 40, 54; DLB 130
Doak, Annie
   See Dillard, Annie
Dobell, Sydney Thompson 1824-1874 . NCLC 43
   See also DLB 32
Doblin, Alfred .... TCLC 13
   See also Doeblin, Alfred
Dobrolyubov, Nikolai Alexandrovich 1836-1861
   NCLC 5
Dobson, Austin 1840-1921 .... TCLC 79
   See also DLB 35; 144
Dobyns, Stephen 1941- .... CLC 37
   See also CA 45-48; CANR 2, 18
Doctorow, E(dgar) L(aurence) 1931- . CLC 6, 11,
   15, 18, 37, 44, 65; DAM NOV, POP
   See also AAYA 22; AITN 2; BEST 89:3; CA 45-
   48; CANR 2, 33, 51; CDALB 1968-1988; DLB
   2, 28, 173; DLBY 80; MTCW
Dodgson, Charles Lutwidge 1832-1898
   See Carroll, Lewis
   See also CLR 2; DA; DAB; DAC; DAM MST,
   NOV, POET; MAICYA; YABC 2
Dodson, Owen (Vincent) 1914-1983CLC 79; BLC;
   DAM MULT
   See also BW 1; CA 65-68; 110; CANR 24; DLB
   76
Doeblin, Alfred 1878-1957 .... TCLC 13
   See also Doblin, Alfred
   See also CA 110; 141; DLB 66
Doerr, Harriet 1910- .... CLC 34
   See also CA 117; 122; CANR 47; INT 122

Domecq, H(onorio) Bustos
　See Bioy Casares, Adolfo; Borges, Jorge Luis
Domini, Rey
　See Lorde, Audre (Geraldine)
Dominique
　See Proust, (Valentin-Louis-George-Eugene-) Marcel
Don, A
　See Stephen, Leslie
Donaldson, Stephen R. 1947-CLC 46; DAM POP
　See also CA 89-92; CANR 13, 55; INT CANR-13
Donleavy, J(ames) P(atrick) 1926- . CLC 1, 4, 6, 10, 45
　See also AITN 2; CA 9-12R; CANR 24, 49, 62; DLB 6, 173; INT CANR-24; MTCW
Donne, John 1572-1631 ... LC 10, 24; DA; DAB; DAC; DAM MST, POET; PC 1
　See also CDBLB Before 1660; DLB 121, 151
Donnell, David 1939(?)- .... CLC 34
Donoghue, P. S.
　See Hunt, E(verette) Howard, (Jr.)
Donoso (Yanez), Jose 1924-1996CLC 4, 8, 11, 32, 99; DAM MULT; HLC
　See also CA 81-84; 155; CANR 32; DLB 113; HW; MTCW
Donovan, John 1928-1992 .... CLC 35
　See also AAYA 20; CA 97-100; 137; CLR 3; MAICYA; SATA 72; SATA-Brief 29
Don Roberto
　See Cunninghame Graham, R(obert) B(ontine)
Doolittle, Hilda 1886-1961CLC 3, 8, 14, 31, 34, 73; DA; DAC; DAM MST, POET; PC 5; WLC
　See also H. D.
　See also CA 97-100; CANR 35; DLB 4, 45; MTCW
Dorfman, Ariel 1942- CLC 48, 77; DAM MULT; HLC
　See also CA 124; 130; HW; INT 130
Dorn, Edward (Merton) 1929- .... CLC 10, 18
　See also CA 93-96; CANR 42; DLB 5; INT 93-96
Dorsan, Luc
　See Simenon, Georges (Jacques Christian)
Dorsange, Jean
　See Simenon, Georges (Jacques Christian)
Dos Passos, John (Roderigo) 1896-1970CLC 1, 4, 8, 11, 15, 25, 34, 82; DA; DAB; DAC; DAM MST, NOV; WLC
　See also CA 1-4R; 29-32R; CANR 3; CDALB 1929-1941; DLB 4, 9; DLBD 1, 15; DLBY 96; MTCW
Dossage, Jean
　See Simenon, Georges (Jacques Christian)
Dostoevsky, Fedor Mikhailovich 1821-1881NCLC 2, 7, 21, 33, 43; DA; DAB; DAC; DAM MST, NOV; SSC 2; WLC
Doughty, Charles M(ontagu) 1843-1926TCLC 27
　See also CA 115; DLB 19, 57, 174
Douglas, Ellen .... CLC 73
　See also Haxton, Josephine Ayres; Williamson, Ellen Douglas
Douglas, Gavin 1475(?)-1522 .... LC 20
Douglas, George
　See Brown, George Douglas
Douglas, Keith (Castellain) 1920-1944 TCLC 40
　See also CA 160; DLB 27
Douglas, Leonard
　See Bradbury, Ray (Douglas)
Douglas, Michael
　See Crichton, (John) Michael
Douglas, Norman 1868-1952 .... TCLC 68
Douglas, William
　See Brown, George Douglas
Douglass, Frederick 1817(?)-1895 NCLC 7, 55; BLC; DA; DAC; DAM MST, MULT; WLC
　See also CDALB 1640-1865; DLB 1, 43, 50, 79;

SATA 29
Dourado, (Waldomiro Freitas) Autran 1926-CLC 23, 60
　See also CA 25-28R; CANR 34
Dourado, Waldomiro Autran
　See Dourado, (Waldomiro Freitas) Autran
Dove, Rita (Frances) 1952-... CLC 50, 81; DAM MULT, POET; PC6
　See also BW 2; CA 109; CAAS 19; CANR 27, 42; DLB 120
Dowell, Coleman 1925-1985 .... CLC 60
　See also CA 25-28R; 117; CANR 10; DLB 130
Dowson, Ernest (Christopher) 1867-1900TCLC 4
　See also CA 105; 150; DLB 19, 135
Doyle, A. Conan
　See Doyle, Arthur Conan
Doyle, Arthur Conan 1859-1930 ... TCLC 7; DA; DAB; DAC; DAM MST, NOV; SSC 12; WLC
　See also AAYA 14; CA 104; 122; CDBLB 1890-1914; DLB 18, 70, 156, 178; MTCW; SATA 24
Doyle, Conan
　See Doyle, Arthur Conan
Doyle, John
　See Graves, Robert (von Ranke)
Doyle, Roddy 1958(?)- .... CLC 81
　See also AAYA 14; CA 143
Doyle, Sir A. Conan
　See Doyle, Arthur Conan
Doyle, Sir Arthur Conan
　See Doyle, Arthur Conan
Dr. A
　See Asimov, Isaac; Silverstein, Alvin
Drabble, Margaret 1939- CLC 2, 3, 5, 8, 10, 22, 53; DAB; DAC; DAM MST, NOV, POP
　See also CA 13-16R; CANR 18, 35, 63; CDBLB 1960 to Present; DLB 14, 155; MTCW; SATA 48
Drapier, M. B.
　See Swift, Jonathan
Drayham, James
　See Mencken, H(enry) L(ouis)
Drayton, Michael 1563-1631 .... LC 8
Dreadstone, Carl
　See Campbell, (John) Ramsey
Dreiser, Theodore (Herman Albert) 1871-1945 TCLC 10, 18, 35; DA; DAC; DAM MST, NOV; WLC
　See also CA 106; 132; CDALB 1865-1917; DLB 9, 12, 102, 137; DLBD 1; MTCW
Drexler, Rosalyn 1926- .... CLC 2, 6
　See also CA 81-84
Dreyer, Carl Theodor 1889-1968 .... CLC 16
　See also CA 116
Drieu la Rochelle, Pierre(-Eugene) 1893-1945 TCLC 21
　See also CA 117; DLB 72
Drinkwater, John 1882-1937 .... TCLC 57
　See also CA 109; 149; DLB 10, 19, 149
Drop Shot
　See Cable, George Washington
Droste-Hulshoff, Annette Freiin von 1797-1848 NCLC 3
　See also DLB 133
Drummond, Walter
　See Silverberg, Robert
Drummond, William Henry 1854-1907 TCLC 25
　See also CA 160; DLB 92
Drummond de Andrade, Carlos 1902-1987 CLC 18
　See also Andrade, Carlos Drummond de
　See also CA 132; 123
Drury, Allen (Stuart) 1918- .... CLC 37
　See also CA 57-60; CANR 18, 52; INT CANR-18

Dryden, John 1631-1700 .... LC 3, 21; DA; DAB; DAC; DAM DRAM, MST, POET; DC 3; WLC
　See also CDBLB 1660-1789; DLB 80, 101, 131
Duberman, Martin (Bauml) 1930- .... CLC 8
　See also CA 1-4R; CANR 2, 63
Dubie, Norman (Evans) 1945- .... CLC 36
　See also CA 69-72; CANR 12; DLB 120
Du Bois, W(illiam) E(dward) B(urghardt) 1868-1963 CLC 1, 2, 13, 64, 96; BLC; DA; DAC; DAM MST, MULT, NOV; WLC
　See also BW 1; CA 85-88; CANR 34; CDALB 1865-1917; DLB 47, 50, 91; MTCW; SATA 42
Dubus, Andre 1936- ... CLC 13, 36, 97; SSC 15
　See also CA 21-24R; CANR 17; DLB 130; INT CANR-17
Duca Minimo
　See D'Annunzio, Gabriele
Ducharme, Rejean 1941- .... CLC 74
　See also DLB 60
Duclos, Charles Pinot 1704-1772 .... LC 1
Dudek, Louis 1918- .... CLC 11, 19
　See also CA 45-48; CAAS 14; CANR 1; DLB 88
Duerrenmatt, Friedrich 1921-1990 . CLC 1, 4, 8, 11, 15, 43, 102; DAM DRAM
　See also CA 17-20R; CANR 33; DLB 69, 124; MTCW
Duffy, Bruce (?)- .... CLC 50
Duffy, Maureen 1933- .... CLC 37
　See also CA 25-28R; CANR 33; DLB 14; MTCW
Dugan, Alan 1923- .... CLC 2, 6
　See also CA 81-84; DLB 5
du Gard, Roger Martin
　See Martin du Gard, Roger
Duhamel, Georges 1884-1966 .... CLC 8
　See also CA 81-84; 25-28R; CANR 35; DLB 65; MTCW
Dujardin, Edouard (Emile Louis) 1861-1949 TCLC 13
　See also CA 109; DLB 123
Dulles, John Foster 1888-1959 .... TCLC 72
　See also CA 115; 149
Dumas, Alexandre (Davy de la Pailleterie) 1802-1870NCLC 11; DA; DAB; DAC; DAM MST, NOV; WLC
　See also DLB 119; SATA 18
Dumas, Alexandre 1824-1895 ..... NCLC 9; DC 1
　See also AAYA 22
Dumas, Claudine
　See Malzberg, Barry N(athaniel)
Dumas, Henry L. 1934-1968 .... CLC 6, 62
　See also BW 1; CA 85-88; DLB 41
du Maurier, Daphne 1907-1989 .. CLC 6, 11, 59; DAB; DAC; DAM MST, POP; SSC 18
　See also CA 5-8R; 128; CANR 6, 55; MTCW; SATA 27; SATA-Obit 60
Dunbar, Paul Laurence 1872-1906 . TCLC 2, 12; BLC; DA; DAC; DAM MST, MULT, POET; PC 5; SSC 8; WLC
　See also BW 1; CA 104; 124; CDALB 1865-1917; DLB 50, 54, 78; SATA 34
Dunbar, William 1460(?)-1530(?) .... LC 20
　See also DLB 132, 146
Duncan, Dora Angela
　See Duncan, Isadora
Duncan, Isadora 1877(?)-1927 .... TCLC 68
　See also CA 118; 149
Duncan, Lois 1934- .... CLC 26
　See also AAYA 4; CA 1-4R; CANR 2, 23, 36; CLR 29; JRDA; MAICYA; SAAS 2; SATA 1, 36, 75
Duncan, Robert (Edward) 1919-1988 CLC 1, 2, 4, 7, 15, 41, 55; DAM POET; PC 2
　See also CA 9-12R; 124; CANR 28, 62; DLB 5, 16;

MTCW

Duncan, Sara Jeannette 1861-1922 ..... **TCLC 60**
See also CA 157; DLB 92

Dunlap, William 1766-1839 .... **NCLC 2**
See also DLB 30, 37, 59

Dunn, Douglas (Eaglesham) 1942- ... **CLC 6, 40**
See also CA 45-48; CANR 2, 33; DLB 40; MTCW

Dunn, Katherine (Karen) 1945- .... **CLC 71**
See also CA 33-36R

Dunn, Stephen 1939- .... **CLC 36**
See also CA 33-36R; CANR 12, 48, 53; DLB 105

Dunne, Finley Peter 1867-1936 .... **TCLC 28**
See also CA 108; DLB 11, 23

Dunne, John Gregory 1932- .... **CLC 28**
See also CA 25-28R; CANR 14, 50; DLBY 80

Dunsany, Edward John Moreton Drax Plunkett
1878-1957
See Dunsany, Lord
See also CA 104; 148; DLB 10

Dunsany, Lord .... **TCLC 2, 59**
See also Dunsany, Edward John Moreton Drax Plunkett
See also DLB 77, 153, 156

du Perry, Jean
See Simenon, Georges (Jacques Christian)

Durang, Christopher (Ferdinand) 1949-**CLC 27, 38**
See also CA 105; CANR 50

Duras, Marguerite 1914-1996**CLC 3, 6, 11, 20, 34, 40, 68, 100**
See also CA 25-28R; 151; CANR 50; DLB 83; MTCW

Durban, (Rosa) Pam 1947- .... **CLC 39**
See also CA 123

Durcan, Paul 1944- .... **CLC 43, 70; DAM POET**
See also CA 134

Durkheim, Emile 1858-1917 .... **TCLC 55**

Durrell, Lawrence (George) 1912-1990**CLC 1, 4, 6, 8, 13, 27, 41; DAM NOV**
See also CA 9-12R; 132; CANR 40; CDBLB 1945-1960; DLB 15, 27; DLBY 90; MTCW

Durrenmatt, Friedrich
See Duerrenmatt, Friedrich

Dutt, Toru 1856-1877 .... **NCLC 29**

Dwight, Timothy 1752-1817 .... **NCLC 13**
See also DLB 37

Dworkin, Andrea 1946- .... **CLC 43**
See also CA 77-80; CAAS 21; CANR 16, 39; INT CANR-16; MTCW

Dwyer, Deanna
See Koontz, Dean R(ay)

Dwyer, K. R.
See Koontz, Dean R(ay)

Dye, Richard
See De Voto, Bernard (Augustine)

Dylan, Bob 1941- .... **CLC 3, 4, 6, 12, 77**
See also CA 41-44R; DLB 16

Eagleton, Terence (Francis) 1943-
See Eagleton, Terry
See also CA 57-60; CANR 7, 23; MTCW

Eagleton, Terry .... **CLC 63**
See also Eagleton, Terence (Francis)

Early, Jack
See Scoppettone, Sandra

East, Michael
See West, Morris L(anglo)

Eastaway, Edward
See Thomas, (Philip) Edward

Eastlake, William (Derry) 1917-1997 ..... **CLC 8**
See also CA 5-8R; 158; CAAS 1; CANR 5, 63; DLB 6; INT CANR-5

Eastman, Charles A(lexander) 1858-1939 **TCLC 55; DAM MULT**

See also DLB 175; NNAL; YABC 1

Eberhart, Richard (Ghormley) 1904- **CLC 3, 11, 19, 56; DAM POET**
See also CA 1-4R; CANR 2; CDALB 1941-1968; DLB 48; MTCW

Eberstadt, Fernanda 1960- .... **CLC 39**
See also CA 136

Echegaray (y Eizaguirre), Jose (Maria Waldo)
1832-1916 .... **TCLC 4**
See also CA 104; CANR 32; HW; MTCW

Echeverria, (Jose) Esteban (Antonino) 1805-1851
NCLC 18

Echo
See Proust, (Valentin-Louis-George-Eugene-) Marcel

Eckert, Allan W. 1931- .... **CLC 17**
See also AAYA 18; CA 13-16R; CANR 14, 45; INT CANR-14; SAAS 21; SATA 29, 91; SATA-Brief 27

Eckhart, Meister 1260(?)-1328(?) .... **CMLC 9**
See also DLB 115

Eckmar, F. R.
See de Hartog, Jan

Eco, Umberto 1932-**CLC 28, 60; DAM NOV, POP**
See also BEST 90:1; CA 77-80; CANR 12, 33, 55; MTCW

Eddison, E(ric) R(ucker) 1882-1945 .... **TCLC 15**
See also CA 109; 156

Eddy, Mary (Morse) Baker 1821-1910 . **TCLC 71**
See also CA 113

Edel, (Joseph) Leon 1907-1997 .... **CLC 29, 34**
See also CA 1-4R; 161; CANR 1, 22; DLB 103; INT CANR-22

Eden, Emily 1797-1869 .... **NCLC 10**

Edgar, David 1948- .... **CLC 42; DAM DRAM**
See also CA 57-60; CANR 12, 61; DLB 13; MTCW

Edgerton, Clyde (Carlyle) 1944- .... **CLC 39**
See also AAYA 17; CA 118; 134; CANR 64; INT 134

Edgeworth, Maria 1768-1849 .... **NCLC 1, 51**
See also DLB 116, 159, 163; SATA 21

Edmonds, Paul
See Kuttner, Henry

Edmonds, Walter D(umaux) 1903- .... **CLC 35**
See also CA 5-8R; CANR 2; DLB 9; MAICYA; SAAS 4; SATA 1, 27

Edmondson, Wallace
See Ellison, Harlan (Jay)

Edson, Russell .... **CLC 13**
See also CA 33-36R

Edwards, Bronwen Elizabeth
See Rose, Wendy

Edwards, G(erald) B(asil) 1899-1976 ..... **CLC 25**
See also CA 110

Edwards, Gus 1939- .... **CLC 43**
See also CA 108; INT 108

Edwards, Jonathan 1703-1758 . **LC 7; DA; DAC; DAM MST**
See also DLB 24

Efron, Marina Ivanovna Tsvetaeva
See Tsvetaeva (Efron), Marina (Ivanovna)

Ehle, John (Marsden, Jr.) 1925- .... **CLC 27**
See also CA 9-12R

Ehrenbourg, Ilya (Grigoryevich)
See Ehrenburg, Ilya (Grigoryevich)

Ehrenburg, Ilya (Grigoryevich) 1891-1967 **C L C 18, 34, 62**
See also CA 102; 25-28R

Ehrenburg, Ilyo (Grigoryevich)
See Ehrenburg, Ilya (Grigoryevich)

Eich, Guenter 1907-1972 .... **CLC 15**
See also CA 111; 93-96; DLB 69, 124

Eichendorff, Joseph Freiherr von 1788-1857
NCLC 8
See also DLB 90

Eigner, Larry .... **CLC 9**
See also Eigner, Laurence (Joel)
See also CAAS 23; DLB 5

Eigner, Laurence (Joel) 1927-1996
See Eigner, Larry
See also CA 9-12R; 151; CANR 6

Einstein, Albert 1879-1955 .... **TCLC 65**
See also CA 121; 133; MTCW

Eiseley, Loren Corey 1907-1977 .... **CLC 7**
See also AAYA 5; CA 1-4R; 73-76; CANR 6

Eisenstadt, Jill 1963- .... **CLC 50**
See also CA 140

Eisenstein, Sergei (Mikhailovich) 1898-1948
TCLC 57
See also CA 114; 149

Eisner, Simon
See Kornbluth, C(yril) M.

Ekeloef, (Bengt) Gunnar 1907-1968 ..... **CLC 27; DAM POET**
See also CA 123; 25-28R

Ekelof, (Bengt) Gunnar
See Ekeloef, (Bengt) Gunnar

Ekelund, Vilhelm 1880-1949 .... **TCLC 75**

Ekwensi, C. O. D.
See Ekwensi, Cyprian (Odiatu Duaka)

Ekwensi, Cyprian (Odiatu Duaka) 1921- **CLC 4; BLC; DAM MULT**
See also BW 2; CA 29-32R; CANR 18, 42; DLB 117; MTCW; SATA 66

Elaine .... **TCLC 18**
See also Leverson, Ada

El Crummo
See Crumb, R(obert)

Elder, Lonne III 1931-1996 .... **DC 8**
See also BLC; BW 1; CA 81-84; 152; CANR 25; DAM MULT; DLB 7, 38, 44

Elia
See Lamb, Charles

Eliade, Mircea 1907-1986 .... **CLC 19**
See also CA 65-68; 119; CANR 30, 62; MTCW

Eliot, A. D.
See Jewett, (Theodora) Sarah Orne

Eliot, Alice
See Jewett, (Theodora) Sarah Orne

Eliot, Dan
See Silverberg, Robert

Eliot, George 1819-1880**NCLC 4, 13, 23, 41, 49; DA; DAB; DAC; DAM MST, NOV; PC 20; WLC**
See also CDBLB 1832-1890; DLB 21, 35, 55

Eliot, John 1604-1690 .... **LC 5**
See also DLB 24

Eliot, T(homas) S(tearns) 1888-1965**CLC 1, 2, 3, 6, 9, 10, 13, 15, 24, 34, 41, 55, 57; DA; DAB; DAC; DAM DRAM, MST, POET; PC 5; WLC 2**
See also CA 5-8R; 25-28R; CANR 41; CDALB 1929-1941; DLB 7, 10, 45, 63; DLBY 88; MTCW

Elizabeth 1866-1941 .... **TCLC 41**

Elkin, Stanley L(awrence) 1930-1995**CLC 4, 6, 9, 14, 27, 51, 91; DAM NOV, POP; SSC 12**
See also CA 9-12R; 148; CANR 8, 46; DLB 2, 28; DLBY 80; INT CANR-8; MTCW

Elledge, Scott .... **CLC 34**

Elliot, Don
See Silverberg, Robert

Elliott, Don
See Silverberg, Robert

Elliott, George P(aul) 1918-1980 .... **CLC 2**
See also CA 1-4R; 97-100; CANR 2

Frye, (Herman) Northrop 1912-1991 **CLC 24, 70**
  See also CA 5-8R; 133; CANR 8, 37; DLB 67, 68;
    MTCW
Fuchs, Daniel 1909-1993 .... **CLC 8, 22**
  See also CA 81-84; 142; CAAS 5; CANR 40; DLB
    9, 26, 28; DLBY 93
Fuchs, Daniel 1934- .... **CLC 34**
  See also CA 37-40R; CANR 14, 48
Fuentes, Carlos 1928-**CLC 3, 8, 10, 13, 22, 41, 60;**
    DA; DAB; DAC; DAM MST, MULT, NOV;
    HLC; SSC 24; WLC
  See also AAYA 4; AITN 2; CA 69-72; CANR 10,
    32; DLB 113; HW; MTCW
Fuentes, Gregorio Lopez y
  See Lopez y Fuentes, Gregorio
Fugard, (Harold) Athol 1932-**CLC 5, 9, 14, 25, 40,**
    80; DAM DRAM; DC 3
  See also AAYA 17; CA 85-88; CANR 32, 54;
    MTCW
Fugard, Sheila 1932- .... **CLC 48**
  See also CA 125
Fuller, Charles (H., Jr.) 1939-.... **CLC 25; BLC;**
    DAM DRAM, MULT; DC 1
  See also BW 2; CA 108; 112; DLB 38; INT 112;
    MTCW
Fuller, John (Leopold) 1937- .... **CLC 62**
  See also CA 21-24R; CANR 9, 44; DLB 40
Fuller, Margaret .... **NCLC 5, 50**
  See also Ossoli, Sarah Margaret (Fuller marchesa
    d')
Fuller, Roy (Broadbent) 1912-1991 ... **CLC 4, 28**
  See also CA 5-8R; 135; CAAS 10; CANR 53; DLB
    15, 20; SATA 87
Fulton, Alice 1952-................................ **CLC 52**
  See also CA 116; CANR 57
Furphy, Joseph 1843-1912 .... **TCLC 25**
Fussell, Paul 1924- .... **CLC 74**
  See also BEST 90:1; CA 17-20R; CANR 8, 21, 35;
    INT CANR-21; MTCW
Futabatei, Shimei 1864-1909 .... **TCLC 44**
  See also CA 162; DLB 180
Futrelle, Jacques 1875-1912 .... **TCLC 19**
  See also CA 113; 155
Gaboriau, Emile 1835-1873 .... **NCLC 14**
Gadda, Carlo Emilio 1893-1973 .... **CLC 11**
  See also CA 89-92; DLB 177
Gaddis, William 1922-**CLC 1, 3, 6, 8, 10, 19, 43,**
    86
  See also CA 17-20R; CANR 21, 48; DLB 2;
    MTCW
Gage, Walter
  See Inge, William (Motter)
Gaines, Ernest J(ames) 1933-**CLC 3, 11, 18, 86;**
    BLC; DAM MULT
  See also AAYA 18; AITN 1; BW 2; CA 9-12R;
    CANR 6, 24, 42; CDALB 1968-1988; DLB 2,
    33, 152; DLBY 80; MTCW; SATA 86
Gaitskill, Mary 1954- .... **CLC 69**
  See also CA 128; CANR 61
Galdos, Benito Perez
  See Perez Galdos, Benito
Gale, Zona 1874-1938 ..... **TCLC 7; DAM DRAM**
  See also CA 105; 153; DLB 9, 78
Galeano, Eduardo (Hughes) 1940- .... **CLC 72**
  See also CA 29-32R; CANR 13, 32; HW
Galiano, Juan Valera y Alcala
  See Valera y Alcala-Galiano, Juan
Gallagher, Tess 1943-**CLC 18, 63; DAM POET;**
    PC 9
  See also CA 106; DLB 120
Gallant, Mavis 1922-**CLC 7, 18, 38; DAC; DAM**
    MST; SSC 5
  See also CA 69-72; CANR 29; DLB 53; MTCW

Gallant, Roy A(rthur) 1924- .... **CLC 17**
  See also CA 5-8R; CANR 4, 29, 54; CLR 30;
    MAICYA; SATA 4, 68
Gallico, Paul (William) 1897-1976 .... **CLC 2**
  See also AITN 1; CA 5-8R; 69-72; CANR 23; DLB
    9, 171; MAICYA; SATA 13
Gallo, Max Louis 1932- .... **CLC 95**
  See also CA 85-88
Gallois, Lucien
  See Desnos, Robert
Gallup, Ralph
  See Whitemore, Hugh (John)
Galsworthy, John 1867-1933 .. **TCLC 1, 45; DA;**
    DAB; DAC; DAM DRAM, MST, NOV; SSC
    22; WLC 2
  See also CA 104; 141; CDBLB 1890-1914; DLB
    10, 34, 98, 162; DLBD 16
Galt, John 1779-1839 .... **NCLC 1**
  See also DLB 99, 116, 159
Galvin, James 1951- .... **CLC 38**
  See also CA 108; CANR 26
Gamboa, Federico 1864-1939 .... **TCLC 36**
Gandhi, M. K.
  See Gandhi, Mohandas Karamchand
Gandhi, Mahatma
  See Gandhi, Mohandas Karamchand
Gandhi, Mohandas Karamchand 1869-1948**TCLC**
    59; DAM MULT
  See also CA 121; 132; MTCW
Gann, Ernest Kellogg 1910-1991 .... **CLC 23**
  See also AITN 1; CA 1-4R; 136; CANR 1
Garcia, Cristina 1958- .... **CLC 76**
  See also CA 141
Garcia Lorca, Federico 1898-1936**TCLC 1, 7, 49;**
    DA; DAB; DAC; DAM DRAM, MST, MULT,
    POET; DC 2; HLC; PC 3; WLC
  See also CA 104; 131; DLB 108; HW; MTCW
Garcia Marquez, Gabriel (Jose) 1928- **CLC 2, 3,**
    8, 10, 15, 27, 47, 55, 68; DA; DAB; DAC;
    DAM MST, MULT, NOV, POP; HLC; SSC 8;
    WLC
  See also AAYA 3; BEST 89:1, 90:4; CA 33-36R;
    CANR 10, 28, 50; DLB 113; HW; MTCW
Gard, Janice
  See Latham, Jean Lee
Gard, Roger Martin du
  See Martin du Gard, Roger
Gardam, Jane 1928- .... **CLC 43**
  See also CA 49-52; CANR 2, 18, 33, 54; CLR 12;
    DLB 14, 161; MAICYA; MTCW; SAAS 9;
    SATA 39, 76; SATA-Brief 28
Gardner, Herb(ert) 1934- .... **CLC 44**
  See also CA 149
Gardner, John (Champlin), Jr. 1933-1982**CLC 2,**
    3, 5, 7, 8, 10, 18, 28, 34; DAM NOV, POP;
    SSC 7
  See also AITN 1; CA 65-68; 107; CANR 33; DLB
    2; DLBY 82; MTCW; SATA 40; SATA-Obit
    31
Gardner, John (Edmund) 1926- .. **CLC 30; DAM**
    POP
  See also CA 103; CANR 15; MTCW
Gardner, Miriam
  See Bradley, Marion Zimmer
Gardner, Noel
  See Kuttner, Henry
Gardons, S. S.
  See Snodgrass, W(illiam) D(e Witt)
Garfield, Leon 1921-1996 .... **CLC 12**
  See also AAYA 8; CA 17-20R; 152; CANR 38,
    41; CLR 21; DLB 161; JRDA; MAICYA; SATA
    1, 32, 76; SATA-Obit 90
Garland, (Hannibal) Hamlin 1860-1940 **TCLC 3;**

    SSC 18
  See also CA 104; DLB 12, 71, 78
Garneau, (Hector de) Saint-Denys 1912-1943
    TCLC 13
  See also CA 111; DLB 88
Garner, Alan 1934- .. **CLC 17; DAB; DAM POP**
  See also AAYA 18; CA 73-76; CANR 15, 64; CLR
    20; DLB 161; MAICYA; MTCW; SATA 18, 69
Garner, Hugh 1913-1979 .... **CLC 13**
  See also CA 69-72; CANR 31; DLB 68
Garnett, David 1892-1981 .... **CLC 3**
  See also CA 5-8R; 103; CANR 17; DLB 34
Garos, Stephanie
  See Katz, Steve
Garrett, George (Palmer) 1929- . **CLC 3, 11, 51**
  See also CA 1-4R; CAAS 5; CANR 1, 42; DLB 2,
    5, 130, 152; DLBY 83
Garrick, David 1717-1779 . **LC 15; DAM DRAM**
  See also DLB 84
Garrigue, Jean 1914-1972 .... **CLC 2, 8**
  See also CA 5-8R; 37-40R; CANR 20
Garrison, Frederick
  See Sinclair, Upton (Beall)
Garth, Will
  See Hamilton, Edmond; Kuttner, Henry
Garvey, Marcus (Moziah, Jr.) 1887-1940 . **TCLC**
    41; BLC; DAM MULT
  See also BW 1; CA 120; 124
Gary, Romain .... **CLC 25**
  See also Kacew, Romain
  See also DLB 83
Gascar, Pierre .... **CLC 11**
  See also Fournier, Pierre
Gascoyne, David (Emery) 1916- .... **CLC 45**
  See also CA 65-68; CANR 10, 28, 54; DLB 20;
    MTCW
Gaskell, Elizabeth Cleghorn 1810-1865**NCLC 5;**
    DAB; DAM MST; SSC 25
  See also CDBLB 1832-1890; DLB 21, 144, 159
Gass, William H(oward) 1924-**CLC 1, 2, 8, 11, 15,**
    39; SSC 12
  See also CA 17-20R; CANR 30; DLB 2; MTCW
Gasset, Jose Ortega y
  See Ortega y Gasset, Jose
Gates, Henry Louis, Jr. 1950- .... **CLC 65; DAM**
    MULT
  See also BW 2; CA 109; CANR 25, 53; DLB 67
Gautier, Theophile 1811-1872**NCLC 1, 59; DAM**
    POET; PC 18; SSC 20
  See also DLB 119
Gawsworth, John
  See Bates, H(erbert) E(rnest)
Gay, Oliver
  See Gogarty, Oliver St. John
Gaye, Marvin (Penze) 1939-1984 .... **CLC 26**
  See also CA 112
Gebler, Carlo (Ernest) 1954- .... **CLC 39**
  See also CA 119; 133
Gee, Maggie (Mary) 1948- .... **CLC 57**
  See also CA 130
Gee, Maurice (Gough) 1931- .... **CLC 29**
  See also CA 97-100; SATA 46
Gelbart, Larry (Simon) 1923- .... **CLC 21, 61**
  See also CA 73-76; CANR 45
Gelber, Jack 1932- .... **CLC 1, 6, 14, 79**
  See also CA 1-4R; CANR 2; DLB 7
Gellhorn, Martha (Ellis) 1908- .... **CLC 14, 60**
  See also CA 77-80; CANR 44; DLBY 82
Genet, Jean 1910-1986**CLC 1, 2, 5, 10, 14, 44, 46;**
    DAM DRAM
  See also CA 13-16R; CANR 18; DLB 72; DLBY
    86; MTCW
Gent, Peter 1942- .... **CLC 29**

Goldsberry, Steven 1949- .... CLC 34
  See also CA 131
Goldsmith, Oliver 1728-1774 ... LC 2; DA; DAB;
  DAC; DAM DRAM, MST, NOV, POET; DC
  8; WLC
  See also CDBLB 1660-1789; DLB 39, 89, 104, 109,
  142; SATA 26
Goldsmith, Peter
  See Priestley, J(ohn) B(oynton)
Gombrowicz, Witold 1904-1969CLC 4, 7, 11, 49;
  DAM DRAM
  See also CA 19-20; 25-28R; CAP 2
Gomez de la Serna, Ramon 1888-1963 .... CLC 9
  See also CA 153; 116; HW
Goncharov, Ivan Alexandrovich 1812-1891 N C L C
  1, 63
Goncourt, Edmond (Louis Antoine Huot) de 1822-
  1896 .... NCLC 7
  See also DLB 123
Goncourt, Jules (Alfred Huot) de 1830-1870
  NCLC 7
  See also DLB 123
Gontier, Fernande 19(?)- .... CLC 50
Gonzalez Martinez, Enrique 1871-1952TCLC 72
  See also HW
Goodman, Paul 1911-1972 .... CLC 1, 2, 4, 7
  See also CA 19-20; 37-40R; CANR 34; CAP 2;
  DLB 130; MTCW
Gordimer, Nadine 1923- CLC 3, 5, 7, 10, 18, 33,
  51, 70; DA; DAB; DAC; DAM MST, NOV;
  SSC 17; WLCS
  See also CA 5-8R; CANR 3, 28, 56; INT CANR-
  28; MTCW
Gordon, Adam Lindsay 1833-1870 ...... NCLC 21
Gordon, Caroline 1895-1981 CLC 6, 13, 29, 83;
  SSC 15
  See also CA 11-12; 103; CANR 36; CAP 1; DLB
  4, 9, 102; DLBY 81; MTCW
Gordon, Charles William 1860-1937
  See Connor, Ralph
  See also CA 109
Gordon, Mary (Catherine) 1949- .... CLC 13, 22
  See also CA 102; CANR 44; DLB 6; DLBY 81;
  INT 102; MTCW
Gordon, N. J.
  See Bosman, Herman Charles
Gordon, Sol 1923- .... CLC 26
  See also CA 53-56; CANR 4; SATA 11
Gordone, Charles 1925-1995 .... CLC 1, 4; DAM
  DRAM; DC 8
  See also BW 1; CA 93-96; 150; CANR 55; DLB 7;
  INT 93-96; MTCW
Gore, Catherine 1800-1861 .... NCLC 65
  See also DLB 116
Gorenko, Anna Andreevna
  See Akhmatova, Anna
Gorky, Maxim 1868-1936TCLC 8; DAB; SSC 28;
  WLC
  See also Peshkov, Alexei Maximovich
Goryan, Sirak
  See Saroyan, William
Gosse, Edmund (William) 1849-1928 .. TCLC 28
  See also CA 117; DLB 57, 144, 184
Gotlieb, Phyllis Fay (Bloom) 1926- .... CLC 18
  See also CA 13-16R; CANR 7; DLB 88
Gottesman, S. D.
  See Kornbluth, C(yril) M.; Pohl, Frederik
Gottfried von Strassburg fl. c. 1210- .. CMLC 10
  See also DLB 138
Gould, Lois .... CLC 4, 10
  See also CA 77-80; CANR 29; MTCW
Gourmont, Remy (-Marie-Charles) de 1858-1915
  TCLC 17

See also CA 109; 150
Govier, Katherine 1948- .... CLC 51
  See also CA 101; CANR 18, 40
Goyen, (Charles) William 1915-1983 . CLC 5, 8,
  14, 40
  See also AITN 2; CA 5-8R; 110; CANR 6; DLB 2;
  DLBY 83; INT CANR-6
Goytisolo, Juan 1931-CLC 5, 10, 23; DAM MULT;
  HLC
  See also CA 85-88; CANR 32, 61; HW; MTCW
Gozzano, Guido 1883-1916 .... PC 10
  See also CA 154; DLB 114
Gozzi, (Conte) Carlo 1720-1806 .... NCLC 23
Grabbe, Christian Dietrich 1801-1836 . NCLC 2
  See also DLB 133
Grace, Patricia 1937- .... CLC 56
Gracian y Morales, Baltasar 1601-1658 .. LC 15
Gracq, Julien .... CLC 11, 48
  See also Poirier, Louis
  See also DLB 83
Grade, Chaim 1910-1982 .... CLC 10
  See also CA 93-96; 107
Graduate of Oxford, A
  See Ruskin, John
Grafton, Garth
  See Duncan, Sara Jeannette
Graham, John
  See Phillips, David Graham
Graham, Jorie 1951- .... CLC 48
  See also CA 111; CANR 63; DLB 120
Graham, R(obert) B(ontine) Cunninghame
  See Cunninghame Graham, R(obert) B(ontine)
  See also DLB 98, 135, 174
Graham, Robert
  See Haldeman, Joe (William)
Graham, Tom
  See Lewis, (Harry) Sinclair
Graham, W(illiam) S(ydney) 1918-1986 CLC 29
  See also CA 73-76; 118; DLB 20
Graham, Winston (Mawdsley) 1910- ..... CLC 23
  See also CA 49-52; CANR 2, 22, 45; DLB 77
Grahame, Kenneth 1859-1932 ... TCLC 64; DAB
  See also CA 108; 136; CLR 5; DLB 34, 141, 178;
  MAICYA; YABC 1
Grant, Skeeter
  See Spiegelman, Art
Granville-Barker, Harley 1877-1946 ... TCLC 2;
  DAM DRAM
  See also Barker, Harley Granville
  See also CA 104
Grass, Guenter (Wilhelm) 1927- CLC 1, 2, 4, 6,
  11, 15, 22, 32, 49, 88; DA; DAB; DAC; DAM
  MST, NOV; WLC
  See also CA 13-16R; CANR 20; DLB 75, 124;
  MTCW
Gratton, Thomas
  See Hulme, T(homas) E(rnest)
Grau, Shirley Ann 1929- ...... CLC 4, 9; SSC 15
  See also CA 89-92; CANR 22; DLB 2; INT CANR-
  22; MTCW
Gravel, Fern
  See Hall, James Norman
Graver, Elizabeth 1964- .... CLC 70
  See also CA 135
Graves, Richard Perceval 1945- .... CLC 44
  See also CA 65-68; CANR 9, 26, 51
Graves, Robert (von Ranke) 1895-1985 CLC 1, 2,
  6, 11, 39, 44, 45; DAB; DAC; DAM MST,
  POET; PC 6
  See also CA 5-8R; 117; CANR 5, 36; CDBLB 1914-
  1945; DLB 20, 100; DLBY 85; MTCW; SATA
  45
Graves, Valerie

See Bradley, Marion Zimmer
Gray, Alasdair (James) 1934- .... CLC 41
  See also CA 126; CANR 47; INT 126; MTCW
Gray, Amlin 1946- .... CLC 29
  See also CA 138
Gray, Francine du Plessix 1930- CLC 22; DAM
  NOV
  See also BEST 90:3; CA 61-64; CAAS 2; CANR
  11, 33; INT CANR-11; MTCW
Gray, John (Henry) 1866-1934 .... TCLC 19
  See also CA 119; 162
Gray, Simon (James Holliday) 1936- CLC 9, 14,
  36
  See also AITN 1; CA 21-24R; CAAS 3; CANR
  32; DLB 13; MTCW
Gray, Spalding 1941- CLC 49; DAM POP; DC 7
  See also CA 128
Gray, Thomas 1716-1771 ... LC 4, 40; DA; DAB;
  DAC; DAM MST; PC 2; WLC
  See also CDBLB 1660-1789; DLB 109
Grayson, David
  See Baker, Ray Stannard
Grayson, Richard (A.) 1951- .... CLC 38
  See also CA 85-88; CANR 14, 31, 57
Greeley, Andrew M(oran) 1928-. CLC 28; DAM
  POP
  See also CA 5-8R; CAAS 7; CANR 7, 43; MTCW
Green, Anna Katharine 1846-1935 ..... TCLC 63
  See also CA 112; 159
Green, Brian
  See Card, Orson Scott
Green, Hannah
  See Greenberg, Joanne (Goldenberg)
Green, Hannah 1927(?)- .... CLC 3
  See also CA 73-76; CANR 59
Green, Henry 1905-1973 .... CLC 2, 13, 97
  See also Yorke, Henry Vincent
  See also DLB 15
Green, Julian (Hartridge) 1900-
  See Green, Julien
  See also CA 21-24R; CANR 33; DLB 4, 72;
  MTCW
Green, Julien .... CLC 3, 11, 77
  See also Green, Julian (Hartridge)
Green, Paul (Eliot) 1894-1981 .... CLC 25; DAM
  DRAM
  See also AITN 1; CA 5-8R; 103; CANR 3; DLB 7,
  9; DLBY 81
Greenberg, Ivan 1908-1973
  See Rahv, Philip
  See also CA 85-88
Greenberg, Joanne (Goldenberg) 1932- CLC 7,
  30
  See also AAYA 12; CA 5-8R; CANR 14, 32; SATA
  25
Greenberg, Richard 1959(?)- .... CLC 57
  See also CA 138
Greene, Bette 1934- .... CLC 30
  See also AAYA 7; CA 53-56; CANR 4; CLR 2;
  JRDA; MAICYA; SAAS 16; SATA 8
Greene, Gael .... CLC 8
  See also CA 13-16R; CANR 10
Greene, Graham (Henry) 1904-1991 CLC 1, 3, 6,
  9, 14, 18, 27, 37, 70, 72; DA; DAB; DAC;
  DAM MST, NOV; SSC 29; WLC
  See also AITN 2; CA 13-16R; 133; CANR 35, 61;
  CDBLB 1945-1960; DLB 13, 15, 77, 100, 162;
  DLBY 91; MTCW; SATA 20
Greene, Robert 1558-1592 .... LC 41
  See also DLB 62, 167
Greer, Richard
  See Silverberg, Robert
Gregor, Arthur 1923- .... CLC 9

CLC 1, 2, 3, 4, 7, 9, 14, 15, 27, 49
See also CA 1-4R; CANR 2, 47, 64; DLB 2, 7;
DLBY 80; MTCW

Hawking, S. W.
See Hawking, Stephen W(illiam)

Hawking, Stephen W(illiam) 1942-**CLC 63, 105**
See also AAYA 13; BEST 89:1; CA 126; 129;
CANR 48

Hawthorne, Julian 1846-1934 .... **TCLC 25**

Hawthorne, Nathaniel 1804-1864 **NCLC 39; DA;
DAB; DAC; DAM MST, NOV; SSC 3, 29;
WLC**
See also AAYA 18; CDALB 1640-1865; DLB 1,
74; YABC 2

Haxton, Josephine Ayres 1921-
See Douglas, Ellen
See also CA 115; CANR 41

Hayaseca y Eizaguirre, Jorge
See Echegaray (y Eizaguirre), Jose (Maria
Waldo)

Hayashi Fumiko 1904-1951 .... **TCLC 27**
See also CA 161; DLB 180

Haycraft, Anna
See Ellis, Alice Thomas
See also CA 122

Hayden, Robert E(arl) 1913-1980**CLC 5, 9, 14, 37;
BLC; DA; DAC; DAM MST, MULT, POET;
PC 6**
See also BW 1; CA 69-72; 97-100; CABS 2; CANR
24; CDALB 1941-1968; DLB 5, 76; MTCW;
SATA 19; SATA-Obit 26

Hayford, J(oseph) E(phraim) Casely
See Casely-Hayford, J(oseph) E(phraim)

Hayman, Ronald 1932- .... **CLC 44**
See also CA 25-28R; CANR 18, 50; DLB 155

Haywood, Eliza (Fowler) 1693(?)-1756 .... **LC 1**

Hazlitt, William 1778-1830 .... **NCLC 29**
See also DLB 110, 158

Hazzard, Shirley 1931- .... **CLC 18**
See also CA 9-12R; CANR 4; DLBY 82; MTCW

Head, Bessie 1937-1986**CLC 25, 67; BLC; DAM
MULT**
See also BW 2; CA 29-32R; 119; CANR 25; DLB
117; MTCW

Headon, (Nicky) Topper 1956(?)- .... **CLC 30**

Heaney, Seamus (Justin) 1939-**CLC 5, 7, 14, 25,
37, 74, 91; DAB; DAM POET; PC 18; WLCS**
See also CA 85-88; CANR 25, 48; CDBLB 1960 to
Present; DLB 40; DLBY 95; MTCW

Hearn, (Patricio) Lafcadio (Tessima Carlos) 1850-
1904 .... **TCLC 9**
See also CA 105; DLB 12, 78

Hearne, Vicki 1946- .... **CLC 56**
See also CA 139

Hearon, Shelby 1931- .... **CLC 63**
See also AITN 2; CA 25-28R; CANR 18, 48

Heat-Moon, William Least .... **CLC 29**
See also Trogdon, William (Lewis)
See also AAYA 9

Hebbel, Friedrich 1813-1863 .... **NCLC 43; DAM
DRAM**
See also DLB 129

Hebert, Anne 1916- **CLC 4, 13, 29; DAC; DAM
MST, POET**
See also y CA 85-88; DLB 68; MTCW

Hecht, Anthony (Evan) 1923-**CLC 8, 13, 19; DAM
POET**
See also CA 9-12R; CANR 6; DLB 5, 169

Hecht, Ben 1894-1964 .... **CLC 8**
See also CA 85-88; DLB 7, 9, 25, 26, 28, 86

Hedayat, Sadeq 1903-1951 .... **TCLC 21**
See also CA 120

Hegel, Georg Wilhelm Friedrich 1770-1831

NCLC 46
See also DLB 90

Heidegger, Martin 1889-1976 .... **CLC 24**
See also CA 81-84; 65-68; CANR 34; MTCW

Heidenstam, (Carl Gustaf) Verner von 1859-1940
TCLC 5
See also CA 104

Heifner, Jack 1946- .... **CLC 11**
See also CA 105; CANR 47

Heijermans, Herman 1864-1924 .... **TCLC 24**
See also CA 123

Heilbrun, Carolyn G(old) 1926- .... **CLC 25**
See also CA 45-48; CANR 1, 28, 58

Heine, Heinrich 1797-1856 .... **NCLC 4, 54**
See also DLB 90

Heinemann, Larry (Curtiss) 1944- .... **CLC 50**
See also CA 110; CAAS 21; CANR 31; DLBD 9;
INT CANR-31

Heiney, Donald (William) 1921-1993
See Harris, MacDonald
See also CA 1-4R; 142; CANR 3, 58

Heinlein, Robert A(nson) 1907-1988**CLC 1, 3, 8,
14, 26, 55; DAM POP**
See also AAYA 17; CA 1-4R; 125; CANR 1, 20,
53; DLB 8; JRDA; MAICYA; MTCW; SATA
9, 69; SATA-Obit 56

Helforth, John
See Doolittle, Hilda

Hellenhofferu, Vojtech Kapristian z
See Hasek, Jaroslav (Matej Frantisek)

Heller, Joseph 1923- . **CLC 1, 3, 5, 8, 11, 36, 63;
DA; DAB; DAC; DAM MST, NOV, POP;
WLC**
See also AAYA 24; AITN 1; CA 5-8R; CABS 1;
CANR 8, 42; DLB 2, 28; DLBY 80; INT CANR-
8; MTCW

Hellman, Lillian (Florence) 1906-1984**CLC 2, 4,
8, 14, 18, 34, 44, 52; DAM DRAM; DC 1**
See also AITN 1, 2; CA 13-16R; 112; CANR 33;
DLB 7; DLBY 84; MTCW

Helprin, Mark 1947- .. **CLC 7, 10, 22, 32; DAM
NOV, POP**
See also CA 81-84; CANR 47, 64; DLBY 85;
MTCW

Helvetius, Claude-Adrien 1715-1771 .... **LC 26**

Helyar, Jane Penelope Josephine 1933-
See Poole, Josephine
See also CA 21-24R; CANR 10, 26; SATA 82

Hemans, Felicia 1793-1835 .... **NCLC 29**
See also DLB 96

Hemingway, Ernest (Miller) 1899-1961**CLC 1, 3,
6, 8, 10, 13, 19, 30, 34, 39, 41, 44, 50, 61, 80;
DA; DAB; DAC; DAM MST, NOV; SSC 25;
WLC**
See also AAYA 19; CA 77-80; CANR 34; CDALB
1917-1929; DLB 4, 9, 102; DLBD 1, 15, 16; DLBY
81, 87, 96; MTCW

Hempel, Amy 1951- .... **CLC 39**
See also CA 118; 137

Henderson, F. C.
See Mencken, H(enry) L(ouis)

Henderson, Sylvia
See Ashton-Warner, Sylvia (Constance)

Henderson, Zenna (Chlarson) 1917-1983**SSC 29**
See also CA 1-4R; 133; CANR 1; DLB 8; SATA 5

Henley, Beth .... **CLC 23; DC 6**
See also Henley, Elizabeth Becker
See also CABS 3; DLBY 86

Henley, Elizabeth Becker 1952-
See Henley, Beth
See also CA 107; CANR 32; DAM DRAM, MST;
MTCW

Henley, William Ernest 1849-1903 .... **TCLC 8**

See also CA 105; DLB 19

Hennissart, Martha
See Lathen, Emma
See also CA 85-88; CANR 64

Henry, O. .... **TCLC 1, 19; SSC 5; WLC**
See also Porter, William Sydney

Henry, Patrick 1736-1799 .... **LC 25**

Henryson, Robert 1430(?)-1506(?) .... **LC 20**
See also DLB 146

Henry VIII 1491-1547 .... **LC 10**

Henschke, Alfred
See Klabund

Hentoff, Nat(han Irving) 1925- .... **CLC 26**
See also AAYA 4; CA 1-4R; CAAS 6; CANR 5,
25; CLR 1; INT CANR-25; JRDA; MAICYA;
SATA 42, 69; SATA-Brief 27

Heppenstall, (John) Rayner 1911-1981 . **CLC 10**
See also CA 1-4R; 103; CANR 29

Heraclitus c. 540B.C.-c. 450B.C. .... **CMLC 22**
See also DLB 176

Herbert, Frank (Patrick) 1920-1986**CLC 12, 23,
35, 44, 85; DAM POP**
See also AAYA 21; CA 53-56; 118; CANR 5, 43;
DLB 8; INT CANR-5; MTCW; SATA 9, 37;
SATA-Obit 47

Herbert, George 1593-1633 . **LC 24; DAB; DAM
POET; PC 4**
See also CDBLB Before 1660; DLB 126

Herbert, Zbigniew 1924-**CLC 9, 43; DAM POET**
See also CA 89-92; CANR 36; MTCW

Herbst, Josephine (Frey) 1897-1969 ..... **CLC 34**
See also CA 5-8R; 25-28R; DLB 9

Hergesheimer, Joseph 1880-1954 .... **TCLC 11**
See also CA 109; DLB 102, 9

Herlihy, James Leo 1927-1993 .... **CLC 6**
See also CA 1-4R; 143; CANR 2

Hermogenes fl. c. 175- .... **CMLC 6**

Hernandez, Jose 1834-1886 .... **NCLC 17**

Herodotus c. 484B.C.-429B.C. .... **CMLC 17**
See also DLB 176

Herrick, Robert 1591-1674 ... **LC 13; DA; DAB;
DAC; DAM MST, POP; PC 9**
See also DLB 126

Herring, Guilles
See Somerville, Edith

Herriot, James 1916-1995 .. **CLC 12; DAM POP**
See also Wight, James Alfred
See also AAYA 1; CA 148; CANR 40; SATA 86

Herrmann, Dorothy 1941- .... **CLC 44**
See also CA 107

Herrmann, Taffy
See Herrmann, Dorothy

Hersey, John (Richard) 1914-1993**CLC 1, 2, 7, 9,
40, 81, 97; DAM POP**
See also CA 17-20R; 140; CANR 33; DLB 6;
MTCW; SATA 25; SATA-Obit 76

Herzen, Aleksandr Ivanovich 1812-1870 . **NCLC
10, 61**

Herzl, Theodor 1860-1904 .... **TCLC 36**

Herzog, Werner 1942- .... **CLC 16**
See also CA 89-92

Hesiod c. 8th cent. B.C.- .... **CMLC 5**
See also DLB 176

Hesse, Hermann 1877-1962**CLC 1, 2, 3, 6, 11, 17,
25, 69; DA; DAB; DAC; DAM MST, NOV;
SSC 9; WLC**
See also CA 17-18; CAP 2; DLB 66; MTCW;
SATA 50

Hewes, Cady
See De Voto, Bernard (Augustine)

Heyen, William 1940- .... **CLC 13, 18**
See also CA 33-36R; CAAS 9; DLB 5

Heyerdahl, Thor 1914- .... **CLC 26**

See also DLB 57
Huysmans, Charles Marie Georges 1848-1907
  See Huysmans, Joris-Karl
  See also CA 104
Huysmans, Joris-Karl .... **TCLC 7, 69**
  See Huysmans, Charles Marie Georges
  See also DLB 123
Hwang, David Henry 1957-**CLC 55; DAM DRAM; DC 4**
  See also CA 127; 132; INT 132
Hyde, Anthony 1946- .... **CLC 42**
  See also CA 136
Hyde, Margaret O(ldroyd) 1917- .... **CLC 21**
  See also CA 1-4R; CANR 1, 36; CLR 23; JRDA; MAICYA; SAAS 8; SATA 1, 42, 76
Hynes, James 1956(?)- .... **CLC 65**
Ian, Janis 1951- .... **CLC 21**
  See also CA 105
Ibanez, Vicente Blasco
  See Blasco Ibanez, Vicente
Ibarguengoitia, Jorge 1928-1983 .... **CLC 37**
  See also CA 124; 113; HW
Ibsen, Henrik (Johan) 1828-1906 **TCLC 2, 8, 16, 37, 52; DA; DAB; DAC; DAM DRAM, MST; DC 2; WLC**
  See also CA 104; 141
Ibuse Masuji 1898-1993 .... **CLC 22**
  See also CA 127; 141; DLB 180
Ichikawa, Kon 1915- .... **CLC 20**
  See also CA 121
Idle, Eric 1943- .... **CLC 21**
  See also Monty Python
  See also CA 116; CANR 35
Ignatow, David 1914-1997 .... **CLC 4, 7, 14, 40**
  See also CA 9-12R; 162; CAAS 3; CANR 31, 57; DLB 5
Ihimaera, Witi 1944- .... **CLC 46**
  See also CA 77-80
Ilf, Ilya .... **TCLC 21**
  See also Fainzilberg, Ilya Arnoldovich
Illyes, Gyula 1902-1983 .... **PC 16**
  See also CA 114; 109
Immermann, Karl (Lebrecht) 1796-1840**NCLC 4, 49**
  See also DLB 133
Inchbald, Elizabeth 1753-1821 .... **NCLC 62**
  See also DLB 39, 89
Inclan, Ramon (Maria) del Valle
  See Valle-Inclan, Ramon (Maria) del
Infante, G(uillermo) Cabrera
  See Cabrera Infante, G(uillermo)
Ingalls, Rachel (Holmes) 1940- .... **CLC 42**
  See also CA 123; 127
Ingamells, Rex 1913-1955 .... **TCLC 35**
Inge, William (Motter) 1913-1973 **CLC 1, 8, 19; DAM DRAM**
  See also CA 9-12R; CDALB 1941-1968; DLB 7; MTCW
Ingelow, Jean 1820-1897 .... **NCLC 39**
  See also DLB 35, 163; SATA 33
Ingram, Willis J.
  See Harris, Mark
Innaurato, Albert (F.) 1948(?)- .... **CLC 21, 60**
  See also CA 115; 122; INT 122
Innes, Michael
  See Stewart, J(ohn) I(nnes) M(ackintosh)
Innis, Harold Adams 1894-1952 .... **TCLC 77**
  See also DLB 88
Ionesco, Eugene 1909-1994**CLC 1, 4, 6, 9, 11, 15, 41, 86; DA; DAB; DAC; DAM DRAM, MST; WLC**
  See also CA 9-12R; 144; CANR 55; MTCW; SATA 7; SATA-Obit 79

Iqbal, Muhammad 1873-1938 .... **TCLC 28**
Ireland, Patrick
  See O'Doherty, Brian
Iron, Ralph
  See Schreiner, Olive (Emilie Albertina)
Irving, John (Winslow) 1942- .. **CLC 13, 23, 38; DAM NOV, POP**
  See also AAYA 8; BEST 89:3; CA 25-28R; CANR 28; DLB 6; DLBY 82; MTCW
Irving, Washington 1783-1859 **NCLC 2, 19; DA; DAB; DAM MST; SSC 2; WLC**
  See also CDALB 1640-1865; DLB 3, 11, 30, 59, 73, 74; YABC 2
Irwin, P. K.
  See Page, P(atricia) K(athleen)
Isaacs, Susan 1943- .... **CLC 32; DAM POP**
  See also BEST 89:1; CA 89-92; CANR 20, 41; INT CANR-20; MTCW
Isherwood, Christopher (William Bradshaw) 1904-1986**CLC 1, 9, 11, 14, 44; DAM DRAM, NOV**
  See also CA 13-16R; 117; CANR 35; DLB 15; DLBY 86; MTCW
Ishiguro, Kazuo 1954-**CLC 27, 56, 59; DAM NOV**
  See also BEST 90:2; CA 120; CANR 49; MTCW
Ishikawa, Hakuhin
  See Ishikawa, Takuboku
Ishikawa, Takuboku 1886(?)-1912**TCLC 15; DAM POET; PC 10**
  See also CA 113; 153
Iskander, Fazil 1929- .... **CLC 47**
  See also CA 102
Isler, Alan (David) 1934- .... **CLC 91**
  See also CA 156
Ivan IV 1530-1584 .... **LC 17**
Ivanov, Vyacheslav Ivanovich 1866-1949**TCLC 33**
  See also CA 122
Ivask, Ivar Vidrik 1927-1992 .... **CLC 14**
  See also CA 37-40R; 139; CANR 24
Ives, Morgan
  See Bradley, Marion Zimmer
J. R. S.
  See Gogarty, Oliver St. John
Jabran, Kahlil
  See Gibran, Kahlil
Jabran, Khalil
  See Gibran, Kahlil
Jackson, Daniel
  See Wingrove, David (John)
Jackson, Jesse 1908-1983 .... **CLC 12**
  See also BW 1; CA 25-28R; 109; CANR 27; CLR 28; MAICYA; SATA 2, 29; SATA-Obit 48
Jackson, Laura (Riding) 1901-1991
  See Riding, Laura
  See also CA 65-68; 135; CANR 28; DLB 48
Jackson, Sam
  See Trumbo, Dalton
Jackson, Sara
  See Wingrove, David (John)
Jackson, Shirley 1919-1965**CLC 11, 60, 87; DA; DAC; DAM MST; SSC 9; WLC**
  See also AAYA 9; CA 1-4R; 25-28R; CANR 4, 52; CDALB 1941-1968; DLB 6; SATA 2
Jacob, (Cyprien-)Max 1876-1944 .... **TCLC 6**
  See also CA 104
Jacobs, Harriet 1813(?)-1897 .... **NCLC 67**
Jacobs, Jim 1942- .... **CLC 12**
  See also CA 97-100; INT 97-100
Jacobs, W(illiam) W(ymark) 1863-1943**TCLC 22**
  See also CA 121; DLB 135
Jacobsen, Jens Peter 1847-1885 .... **NCLC 34**
Jacobsen, Josephine 1908- .... **CLC 48, 102**
  See also CA 33-36R; CAAS 18; CANR 23, 48
Jacobson, Dan 1929- .... **CLC 4, 14**

See also CA 1-4R; CANR 2, 25; DLB 14; MTCW
Jacqueline
  See Carpentier (y Valmont), Alejo
Jagger, Mick 1944- .... **CLC 17**
Jahiz, Al- c. 776-869 .... **CMLC 25**
Jahiz, al- c. 780-c. 869 .... **CMLC 25**
Jakes, John (William) 1932-**CLC 29; DAM NOV, POP**
  See also BEST 89:4; CA 57-60; CANR 10, 43; DLBY 83; INT CANR-10; MTCW; SATA 62
James, Andrew
  See Kirkup, James
James, C(yril) L(ionel) R(obert) 1901-1989 **C L C 33**
  See also BW 2; CA 117; 125; 128; CANR 62; DLB 125; MTCW
James, Daniel (Lewis) 1911-1988
  See Santiago, Danny
  See also CA 125
James, Dynely
  See Mayne, William (James Carter)
James, Henry Sr. 1811-1882 .... **NCLC 53**
James, Henry 1843-1916**TCLC 2, 11, 24, 40, 47, 64; DA; DAB; DAC; DAM MST, NOV; SSC 8; WLC**
  See also CA 104; 132; CDALB 1865-1917; DLB 12, 71, 74; DLBD 13; MTCW
James, M. R.
  See James, Montague (Rhodes)
  See also DLB 156
James, Montague (Rhodes) 1862-1936 . **TCLC 6; SSC 16**
  See also CA 104
James, P. D. .... **CLC 18, 46**
  See also White, Phyllis Dorothy James
  See also BEST 90:2; CDBLB 1960 to Present; DLB 87
James, Philip
  See Moorcock, Michael (John)
James, William 1842-1910 .... **TCLC 15, 32**
  See also CA 109
James I 1394-1437 .... **LC 20**
Jameson, Anna 1794-1860 .... **NCLC 43**
  See also DLB 99, 166
Jami, Nur al-Din 'Abd al-Rahman 1414-1492**LC 9**
Jammes, Francis 1868-1938 .... **TCLC 75**
Jandl, Ernst 1925- .... **CLC 34**
Janowitz, Tama 1957- .... **CLC 43; DAM POP**
  See also CA 106; CANR 52
Japrisot, Sebastien 1931- .... **CLC 90**
Jarrell, Randall 1914-1965**CLC 1, 2, 6, 9, 13, 49; DAM POET**
  See also CA 5-8R; 25-28R; CABS 2; CANR 6, 34; CDALB 1941-1968; CLR 6; DLB 48, 52; MAICYA; MTCW; SATA 7
Jarry, Alfred 1873-1907 .... **TCLC 2, 14; DAM DRAM; SSC 20**
  See also CA 104; 153
Jarvis, E. K.
  See Bloch, Robert (Albert); Ellison, Harlan (Jay); Silverberg, Robert
Jeake, Samuel, Jr.
  See Aiken, Conrad (Potter)
Jean Paul 1763-1825 .... **NCLC 7**
Jefferies, (John) Richard 1848-1887 .. **NCLC 47**
  See also DLB 98, 141; SATA 16
Jeffers, (John) Robinson 1887-1962**CLC 2, 3, 11, 15, 54; DA; DAC; DAM MST, POET; PC 17; WLC**
  See also CA 85-88; CANR 35; CDALB 1917-1929; DLB 45; MTCW
Jefferson, Janet
  See Mencken, H(enry) L(ouis)

Jefferson, Thomas 1743-1826 .... NCLC 11
See also CDALB 1640-1865; DLB 31
Jeffrey, Francis 1773-1850 .... NCLC 33
See also DLB 107
Jelakowitch, Ivan
See Heijermans, Herman
Jellicoe, (Patricia) Ann 1927- .... CLC 27
See also CA 85-88; DLB 13
Jen, Gish .... CLC 70
See also Jen, Lillian
Jen, Lillian 1956(?)-
See Jen, Gish
See also CA 135
Jenkins, (John) Robin 1912- .... CLC 52
See also CA 1-4R; CANR 1; DLB 14
Jennings, Elizabeth (Joan) 1926- ...... CLC 5, 14
See also CA 61-64; CAAS 5; CANR 8, 39; DLB
27; MTCW; SATA 66
Jennings, Waylon 1937- .... CLC 21
Jensen, Johannes V. 1873-1950 .... TCLC 41
Jensen, Laura (Linnea) 1948- .... CLC 37
See also CA 103
Jerome, Jerome K(lapka) 1859-1927 .. TCLC 23
See also CA 119; DLB 10, 34, 135
Jerrold, Douglas William 1803-1857 ... NCLC 2
See also DLB 158, 159
Jewett, (Theodora) Sarah Orne 1849-1909 T C L C
1, 22; SSC 6
See also CA 108; 127; DLB 12, 74; SATA 15
Jewsbury, Geraldine (Endsor) 1812-1880 N C L C
22
See also DLB 21
Jhabvala, Ruth Prawer 1927- . CLC 4, 8, 29, 94;
DAB; DAM NOV
See also CA 1-4R; CANR 2, 29, 51; DLB 139; INT
CANR-29; MTCW
Jibran, Kahlil
See Gibran, Kahlil
Jibran, Khalil
See Gibran, Kahlil
Jiles, Paulette 1943- .... CLC 13, 58
See also CA 101
Jimenez (Mantecon), Juan Ramon 1881-1958
TCLC 4; DAM MULT, POET; HLC; PC 7
See also CA 104; 131; DLB 134; HW; MTCW
Jimenez, Ramon
See Jimenez (Mantecon), Juan Ramon
Jimenez Mantecon, Juan
See Jimenez (Mantecon), Juan Ramon
Joel, Billy .... CLC 26
See also Joel, William Martin
Joel, William Martin 1949-
See Joel, Billy
See also CA 108
John of the Cross, St. 1542-1591 .... LC 18
Johnson, B(ryan) S(tanley William) 1933-1973
CLC 6, 9
See also CA 9-12R; 53-56; CANR 9; DLB 14, 40
Johnson, Benj. F. of Boo
See Riley, James Whitcomb
Johnson, Benjamin F. of Boo
See Riley, James Whitcomb
Johnson, Charles (Richard) 1948-CLC 7, 51, 65;
BLC; DAM MULT
See also BW 2; CA 116; CAAS 18; CANR 42;
DLB 33
Johnson, Denis 1949- .... CLC 52
See also CA 117; 121; DLB 120
Johnson, Diane 1934- .... CLC 5, 13, 48
See also CA 41-44R; CANR 17, 40, 62; DLBY 80;
INT CANR-17; MTCW
Johnson, Eyvind (Olof Verner) 1900-1976CLC 14
See also CA 73-76; 69-72; CANR 34

Johnson, J. R.
See James, C(yril) L(ionel) R(obert)
Johnson, James Weldon 1871-1938 TCLC 3, 19;
BLC; DAM MULT, POET
See also BW 1; CA 104; 125; CDALB 1917-1929;
CLR 32; DLB 51; MTCW; SATA 31
Johnson, Joyce 1935- .... CLC 58
See also CA 125; 129
Johnson, Lionel (Pigot) 1867-1902 ..... TCLC 19
See also CA 117; DLB 19
Johnson, Mel
See Malzberg, Barry N(athaniel)
Johnson, Pamela Hansford 1912-1981 CLC 1, 7,
27
See also CA 1-4R; 104; CANR 2, 28; DLB 15;
MTCW
Johnson, Robert 1911(?)-1938 .... TCLC 69
Johnson, Samuel 1709-1784 .. LC 15; DA; DAB;
DAC; DAM MST; WLC
See also CDBLB 1660-1789; DLB 39, 95, 104, 142
Johnson, Uwe 1934-1984 .... CLC 5, 10, 15, 40
See also CA 1-4R; 112; CANR 1, 39; DLB 75;
MTCW
Johnston, George (Benson) 1913- .... CLC 51
See also CA 1-4R; CANR 5, 20; DLB 88
Johnston, Jennifer 1930- .... CLC 7
See also CA 85-88; DLB 14
Jolley, (Monica) Elizabeth 1923-CLC 46; SSC 19
See also CA 127; CAAS 13; CANR 59
Jones, Arthur Llewellyn 1863-1947
See Machen, Arthur
See also CA 104
Jones, D(ouglas) G(ordon) 1929- .... CLC 10
See also CA 29-32R; CANR 13; DLB 53
Jones, David (Michael) 1895-1974CLC 2, 4, 7, 13,
42
See also CA 9-12R; 53-56; CANR 28; CDBLB
1945-1960; DLB 20, 100; MTCW
Jones, David Robert 1947-
See Bowie, David
See also CA 103
Jones, Diana Wynne 1934- .... CLC 26
See also AAYA 12; CA 49-52; CANR 4, 26, 56;
CLR 23; DLB 161; JRDA; MAICYA; SAAS 7;
SATA 9, 70
Jones, Edward P. 1950- .... CLC 76
See also BW 2; CA 142
Jones, Gayl 1949- . CLC 6, 9; BLC; DAM MULT
See also BW 2; CA 77-80; CANR 27; DLB 33;
MTCW
Jones, James 1921-1977 .... CLC 1, 3, 10, 39
See also AITN 1, 2; CA 1-4R; 69-72; CANR 6;
DLB 2, 143; MTCW
Jones, John J.
See Lovecraft, H(oward) P(hillips)
Jones, LeRoi .... CLC 1, 2, 3, 5, 10, 14
See also Baraka, Amiri
Jones, Louis B. .... CLC 65
See also CA 141
Jones, Madison (Percy, Jr.) 1925- .... CLC 4
See also CA 13-16R; CAAS 11; CANR 7, 54; DLB
152
Jones, Mervyn 1922- .... CLC 10, 52
See also CA 45-48; CAAS 5; CANR 1; MTCW
Jones, Mick 1956(?)- .... CLC 30
Jones, Nettie (Pearl) 1941- .... CLC 34
See also BW 2; CA 137; CAAS 20
Jones, Preston 1936-1979 .... CLC 10
See also CA 73-76; 89-92; DLB 7
Jones, Robert F(rancis) 1934- .... CLC 7
See also CA 49-52; CANR 2, 61
Jones, Rod 1953- .... CLC 50
See also CA 128

Jones, Terence Graham Parry 1942- ... CLC 21
See also Jones, Terry; Monty Python
See also CA 112; 116; CANR 35; INT 116
Jones, Terry
See Jones, Terence Graham Parry
See also SATA 67; SATA-Brief 51
Jones, Thom 1945(?)- .... CLC 81
See also CA 157
Jong, Erica 1942-CLC 4, 6, 8, 18, 83; DAM NOV,
POP
See also AITN 1; BEST 90:2; CA 73-76; CANR
26, 52; DLB 2, 5, 28, 152; INT CANR-26;
MTCW
Jonson, Ben(jamin) 1572(?)-1637 LC 6, 33; DA;
DAB; DAC; DAM DRAM, MST, POET; DC
4; PC 17; WLC
See also CDBLB Before 1660; DLB 62, 121
Jordan, June 1936- CLC 5, 11, 23; DAM MULT,
POET
See also AAYA 2; BW 2; CA 33-36R; CANR 25;
CLR 10; DLB 38; MAICYA; MTCW; SATA 4
Jordan, Pat(rick M.) 1941- .... CLC 37
See also CA 33-36R
Jorgensen, Ivar
See Ellison, Harlan (Jay)
Jorgenson, Ivar
See Silverberg, Robert
Josephus, Flavius c. 37-100 .... CMLC 13
Josipovici, Gabriel 1940- .... CLC 6, 43
See also CA 37-40R; CAAS 8; CANR 47; DLB 14
Joubert, Joseph 1754-1824 .... NCLC 9
Jouve, Pierre Jean 1887-1976 .... CLC 47
See also CA 65-68
Jovine, Francesco 1902-1950 .... TCLC 79
Joyce, James (Augustine Aloysius) 1882-1941
TCLC 3, 8, 16, 35, 52; DA; DAB; DAC; DAM
MST, NOV, POET; SSC 3, 26; WLC
See also CA 104; 126; CDBLB 1914-1945; DLB
10, 19, 36, 162; MTCW
Jozsef, Attila 1905-1937 .... TCLC 22
See also CA 116
Juana Ines de la Cruz 1651(?)-1695 .... LC 5
Judd, Cyril
See Kornbluth, C(yril) M.; Pohl, Frederik
Julian of Norwich 1342(?)-1416(?) .... LC 6
See also DLB 146
Juniper, Alex
See Hospital, Janette Turner
Junius
See Luxemburg, Rosa
Just, Ward (Swift) 1935- .... CLC 4, 27
See also CA 25-28R; CANR 32; INT CANR-32
Justice, Donald (Rodney) 1925- CLC 6, 19, 102;
DAM POET
See also CA 5-8R; CANR 26, 54; DLBY 83; INT
CANR-26
Juvenal c. 55-c. 127 .... CMLC 8
Juvenis
See Bourne, Randolph S(illiman)
Kacew, Romain 1914-1980
See Gary, Romain
See also CA 108; 102
Kadare, Ismail 1936- .... CLC 52
See also CA 161
Kadohata, Cynthia .... CLC 59
See also CA 140
Kafka, Franz 1883-1924TCLC 2, 6, 13, 29, 47, 53;
DA; DAB; DAC; DAM MST, NOV; SSC 5,
29; WLC
See also CA 105; 126; DLB 81; MTCW
Kahanovitsch, Pinkhes
See Der Nister
Kahn, Roger 1927- .... CLC 30

See also CA 25-28R; CANR 44; DLB 171; SATA 37

Kain, Saul
See Sassoon, Siegfried (Lorraine)

Kaiser, Georg 1878-1945 .... **TCLC 9**
See also CA 106; DLB 124

Kaletski, Alexander 1946- .... **CLC 39**
See also CA 118; 143

Kalidasa fl. c. 400- .... **CMLC 9**

Kallman, Chester (Simon) 1921-1975 ..... **CLC 2**
See also CA 45-48; 53-56; CANR 3

Kaminsky, Melvin 1926-
See Brooks, Mel
See also CA 65-68; CANR 16

Kaminsky, Stuart M(elvin) 1934- .... **CLC 59**
See also CA 73-76; CANR 29, 53

Kane, Francis
See Robbins, Harold

Kane, Paul
See Simon, Paul (Frederick)

Kane, Wilson
See Bloch, Robert (Albert)

Kanin, Garson 1912- .... **CLC 22**
See also AITN 1; CA 5-8R; CANR 7; DLB 7

Kaniuk, Yoram 1930- .... **CLC 19**
See also CA 134

Kant, Immanuel 1724-1804 .... **NCLC 27, 67**
See also DLB 94

Kantor, MacKinlay 1904-1977 .... **CLC 7**
See also CA 61-64; 73-76; CANR 60, 63; DLB 9, 102

Kaplan, David Michael 1946- .... **CLC 50**

Kaplan, James 1951- .... **CLC 59**
See also CA 135

Karageorge, Michael
See Anderson, Poul (William)

Karamzin, Nikolai Mikhailovich 1766-1826
NCLC 3
See also DLB 150

Karapanou, Margarita 1946- .... **CLC 13**
See also CA 101

Karinthy, Frigyes 1887-1938 .... **TCLC 47**

Karl, Frederick R(obert) 1927- .... **CLC 34**
See also CA 5-8R; CANR 3, 44

Kastel, Warren
See Silverberg, Robert

Kataev, Evgeny Petrovich 1903-1942
See Petrov, Evgeny
See also CA 120

Kataphusin
See Ruskin, John

Katz, Steve 1935- .... **CLC 47**
See also CA 25-28R; CAAS 14, 64; CANR 12; DLBY 83

Kauffman, Janet 1945- .... **CLC 42**
See also CA 117; CANR 43; DLBY 86

Kaufman, Bob (Garnell) 1925-1986 .... **CLC 49**
See also BW 1; CA 41-44R; 118; CANR 22; DLB 16, 41

Kaufman, George S. 1889-1961 .. **CLC 38; DAM DRAM**
See also CA 108; 93-96; DLB 7; INT 108

Kaufman, Sue .... **CLC 3, 8**
See also Barondess, Sue K(aufman)

Kavafis, Konstantinos Petrou 1863-1933
See Cavafy, C(onstantine) P(eter)
See also CA 104

Kavan, Anna 1901-1968 .... **CLC 5, 13, 82**
See also CA 5-8R; CANR 6, 57; MTCW

Kavanagh, Dan
See Barnes, Julian (Patrick)

Kavanagh, Patrick (Joseph) 1904-1967 . **CLC 22**
See also CA 123; 25-28R; DLB 15, 20; MTCW

Kawabata, Yasunari 1899-1972 . **CLC 2, 5, 9, 18, 107; DAM MULT; SSC 17**
See also CA 93-96; 33-36R; DLB 180

Kaye, M(ary) M(argaret) 1909- .... **CLC 28**
See also CA 89-92; CANR 24, 60; MTCW; SATA 62

Kaye, Mollie
See Kaye, M(ary) M(argaret)

Kaye-Smith, Sheila 1887-1956 .... **TCLC 20**
See also CA 118; DLB 36

Kaymor, Patrice Maguilene
See Senghor, Leopold Sedar

Kazan, Elia 1909- .... **CLC 6, 16, 63**
See also CA 21-24R; CANR 32

Kazantzakis, Nikos 1883(?)-1957 **TCLC 2, 5, 33**
See also CA 105; 132; MTCW

Kazin, Alfred 1915- .... **CLC 34, 38**
See also CA 1-4R; CAAS 7; CANR 1, 45; DLB 67

Keane, Mary Nesta (Skrine) 1904-1996
See Keane, Molly
See also CA 108; 114; 151

Keane, Molly .... **CLC 31**
See also Keane, Mary Nesta (Skrine)
See also INT 114

Keates, Jonathan 19(?)- .... **CLC 34**

Keaton, Buster 1895-1966 .... **CLC 20**

Keats, John 1795-1821 **NCLC 8; DA; DAB; DAC; DAM MST, POET; PC 1; WLC**
See also CDBLB 1789-1832; DLB 96, 110

Keene, Donald 1922- .... **CLC 34**
See also CA 1-4R; CANR 5

Keillor, Garrison .... **CLC 40**
See also Keillor, Gary (Edward)
See also AAYA 2; BEST 89:3; DLBY 87; SATA 58

Keillor, Gary (Edward) 1942-
See Keillor, Garrison
See also CA 111; 117; CANR 36, 59; DAM POP; MTCW

Keith, Michael
See Hubbard, L(afayette) Ron(ald)

Keller, Gottfried 1819-1890 .... **NCLC 2; SSC 26**
See also DLB 129

Kellerman, Jonathan 1949- **CLC 44; DAM POP**
See also BEST 90:1; CA 106; CANR 29, 51; INT CANR-29

Kelley, William Melvin 1937- .... **CLC 22**
See also BW 1; CA 77-80; CANR 27; DLB 33

Kellogg, Marjorie 1922- .... **CLC 2**
See also CA 81-84

Kellow, Kathleen
See Hibbert, Eleanor Alice Burford

Kelly, M(ilton) T(erry) 1947- .... **CLC 55**
See also CA 97-100; CAAS 22; CANR 19, 43

Kelman, James 1946- .... **CLC 58, 86**
See also CA 148

Kemal, Yashar 1923- .... **CLC 14, 29**
See also CA 89-92; CANR 44

Kemble, Fanny 1809-1893 .... **NCLC 18**
See also DLB 32

Kemelman, Harry 1908-1996 .... **CLC 2**
See also AITN 1; CA 9-12R; 155; CANR 6; DLB 28

Kempe, Margery 1373(?)-1440(?) .... **LC 6**
See also DLB 146

Kempis, Thomas a 1380-1471 .... **LC 11**

Kendall, Henry 1839-1882 .... **NCLC 12**

Keneally, Thomas (Michael) 1935- **CLC 5, 8, 10, 14, 19, 27, 43; DAM NOV**
See also CA 85-88; CANR 10, 50; MTCW

Kennedy, Adrienne (Lita) 1931- . **CLC 66; BLC; DAM MULT; DC 5**
See also BW 2; CA 103; CAAS 20; CABS 3; CANR 26, 53; DLB 38

Kennedy, John Pendleton 1795-1870 .... **NCLC 2**
See also DLB 3

Kennedy, Joseph Charles 1929-
See Kennedy, X. J.
See also CA 1-4R; CANR 4, 30, 40; SATA 14, 86

Kennedy, William 1928- **CLC 6, 28, 34, 53; DAM NOV**
See also AAYA 1; CA 85-88; CANR 14, 31; DLB 143; DLBY 85; INT CANR-31; MTCW; SATA 57

Kennedy, X. J. .... **CLC 8, 42**
See also Kennedy, Joseph Charles
See also CAAS 9; CLR 27; DLB 5; SAAS 22

Kenny, Maurice (Francis) 1929- **CLC 87; DAM MULT**
See also CA 144; CAAS 22; DLB 175; NNAL

Kent, Kelvin
See Kuttner, Henry

Kenton, Maxwell
See Southern, Terry

Kenyon, Robert O.
See Kuttner, Henry

Kerouac, Jack .... **CLC 1, 2, 3, 5, 14, 29, 61**
See also Kerouac, Jean-Louis Lebris de
See also CDALB 1941-1968; DLB 2, 16; DLBD 3; DLBY 95

Kerouac, Jean-Louis Lebris de 1922-1969
See Kerouac, Jack
See also AITN 1; CA 5-8R; 25-28R; CANR 26, 54; DA; DAB; DAC; DAM MST, NOV, POET, POP; MTCW; WLC

Kerr, Jean 1923- .... **CLC 22**
See also CA 5-8R; CANR 7; INT CANR-7

Kerr, M. E. .... **CLC 12, 35**
See also Meaker, Marijane (Agnes)
See also AAYA 2; CLR 29; SAAS 1

Kerr, Robert .... **CLC 55**

Kerrigan, (Thomas) Anthony 1918- .... **CLC 4, 6**
See also CA 49-52; CAAS 11; CANR 4

Kerry, Lois
See Duncan, Lois

Kesey, Ken (Elton) 1935- **CLC 1, 3, 6, 11, 46, 64; DA; DAB; DAC; DAM MST, NOV, POP; WLC**
See also CA 1-4R; CANR 22, 38; CDALB 1968-1988; DLB 2, 16; MTCW; SATA 66

Kesselring, Joseph (Otto) 1902-1967 ... **CLC 45; DAM DRAM, MST**
See also CA 150

Kessler, Jascha (Frederick) 1929- .... **CLC 4**
See also CA 17-20R; CANR 8, 48

Kettelkamp, Larry (Dale) 1933- .... **CLC 12**
See also CA 29-32R; CANR 16; SAAS 3; SATA 2

Key, Ellen 1849-1926 .... **TCLC 65**

Keyber, Conny
See Fielding, Henry

Keyes, Daniel 1927- .. **CLC 80; DA; DAC; DAM MST, NOV**
See also CA 17-20R; CANR 10, 26, 54; SATA 37

Keynes, John Maynard 1883-1946 ...... **TCLC 64**
See also CA 114; 162; DLBD 10

Khanshendel, Chiron
See Rose, Wendy

Khayyam, Omar 1048-1131 ...... **CMLC 11; DAM POET; PC 8**

Kherdian, David 1931- .... **CLC 6, 9**
See also CA 21-24R; CAAS 2; CANR 39; CLR 24; JRDA; MAICYA; SATA 16, 74

Khlebnikov, Velimir .... **TCLC 20**
See also Khlebnikov, Viktor Vladimirovich

Khlebnikov, Viktor Vladimirovich 1885-1922
See Khlebnikov, Velimir

Mehta, Ved (Parkash) 1934- .... **CLC 37**
  See also CA 1-4R; CANR 2, 23; MTCW
Melanter
  See Blackmore, R(ichard) D(oddridge)
Melikow, Loris
  See Hofmannsthal, Hugo von
Melmoth, Sebastian
  See Wilde, Oscar (Fingal O'Flahertie Wills)
Meltzer, Milton 1915- .... **CLC 26**
  See also AAYA 8; CA 13-16R; CANR 38; CLR
  13; DLB 61; JRDA; MAICYA; SAAS 1; SATA
  1, 50, 80
Melville, Herman 1819-1891**NCLC 3, 12, 29, 45,
  49; DA; DAB; DAC; DAM MST, NOV; SSC
  1, 17; WLC**
  See also CDALB 1640-1865; DLB 3, 74; SATA 59
Menander c. 342B.C.-c. 292B.C. **CMLC 9; DAM
  DRAM; DC 3**
  See also DLB 176
Mencken, H(enry) L(ouis) 1880-1956 . **TCLC 13**
  See also CA 105; 125; CDALB 1917-1929; DLB
  11, 29, 63, 137; MTCW
Mendelsohn, Jane 1965(?)- .... **CLC 99**
  See also CA 154
Mercer, David 1928-1980 .. **CLC 5; DAM DRAM**
  See also CA 9-12R; 102; CANR 23; DLB 13;
  MTCW
Merchant, Paul
  See Ellison, Harlan (Jay)
Meredith, George 1828-1909**TCLC 17, 43; DAM
  POET**
  See also CA 117; 153; CDBLB 1832-1890; DLB
  18, 35, 57, 159
Meredith, William (Morris) 1919-**CLC 4, 13, 22,
  55; DAM POET**
  See also CA 9-12R; CAAS 14; CANR 6, 40; DLB
  5
Merezhkovsky, Dmitry Sergeyevich 1865-1941
  TCLC 29
Merimee, Prosper 1803-1870**NCLC 6, 65; SSC 7**
  See also DLB 119
Merkin, Daphne 1954- .... **CLC 44**
  See also CA 123
Merlin, Arthur
  See Blish, James (Benjamin)
Merrill, James (Ingram) 1926-1995**CLC 2, 3, 6, 8,
  13, 18, 34, 91; DAM POET**
  See also CA 13-16R; 147; CANR 10, 49, 63; DLB
  5, 165; DLBY 85; INT CANR-10; MTCW
Merriman, Alex
  See Silverberg, Robert
Merritt, E. B.
  See Waddington, Miriam
Merton, Thomas 1915-1968**CLC 1, 3, 11, 34, 83;
  PC 10**
  See also CA 5-8R; 25-28R; CANR 22, 53; DLB
  48; DLBY 81; MTCW
Merwin, W(illiam) S(tanley) 1927-**CLC 1, 2, 3, 5,
  8, 13, 18, 45, 88; DAM POET**
  See also CA 13-16R; CANR 15, 51; DLB 5, 169;
  INT CANR-15; MTCW
Metcalf, John 1938- .... **CLC 37**
  See also CA 113; DLB 60
Metcalf, Suzanne
  See Baum, L(yman) Frank
Mew, Charlotte (Mary) 1870-1928 .... **TCLC 8**
  See also CA 105; DLB 19, 135
Mewshaw, Michael 1943- .... **CLC 9**
  See also CA 53-56; CANR 7, 47; DLBY 80
Meyer, June
  See Jordan, June
Meyer, Lynn
  See Slavitt, David R(ytman)

Meyer-Meyrink, Gustav 1868-1932
  See Meyrink, Gustav
  See also CA 117
Meyers, Jeffrey 1939- .... **CLC 39**
  See also CA 73-76; CANR 54; DLB 111
Meynell, Alice (Christina Gertrude Thompson)
  1847-1922 .... **TCLC 6**
  See also CA 104; DLB 19, 98
Meyrink, Gustav .... **TCLC 21**
  See also Meyer-Meyrink, Gustav
  See also DLB 81
Michaels, Leonard 1933- .... **CLC 6, 25; SSC 16**
  See also CA 61-64; CANR 21, 62; DLB 130;
  MTCW
Michaux, Henri 1899-1984 .... **CLC 8, 19**
  See also CA 85-88; 114
Micheaux, Oscar 1884-1951 .... **TCLC 76**
  See also DLB 50
Michelangelo 1475-1564 .... **LC 12**
Michelet, Jules 1798-1874 .... **NCLC 31**
Michener, James A(lbert) 1907(?)-1997**CLC 1, 5,
  11, 29, 60; DAM NOV, POP**
  See also AITN 1; BEST 90:1; CA 5-8R; 161;
  CANR 21, 45; DLB 6; MTCW
Mickiewicz, Adam 1798-1855 .... **NCLC 3**
Middleton, Christopher 1926- .... **CLC 13**
  See also CA 13-16R; CANR 29, 54; DLB 40
Middleton, Richard (Barham) 1882-1911**TCLC 56**
  See also DLB 156
Middleton, Stanley 1919- .... **CLC 7, 38**
  See also CA 25-28R; CAAS 23; CANR 21, 46;
  DLB 14
Middleton, Thomas 1580-1627 .... **LC 33; DAM
  DRAM, MST; DC 5**
  See also DLB 58
Migueis, Jose Rodrigues 1901- .... **CLC 10**
Mikszath, Kalman 1847-1910 .... **TCLC 31**
Miles, Jack .... **CLC 100**
Miles, Josephine (Louise) 1911-1985 . **CLC 1, 2,
  14, 34, 39; DAM POET**
  See also CA 1-4R; 116; CANR 2, 55; DLB 48
Militant
  See Sandburg, Carl (August)
Mill, John Stuart 1806-1873 .... **NCLC 11, 58**
  See also CDBLB 1832-1890; DLB 55
Millar, Kenneth 1915-1983 . **CLC 14; DAM POP**
  See also Macdonald, Ross
  See also CA 9-12R; 110; CANR 16, 63; DLB 2;
  DLBD 6; DLBY 83; MTCW
Millay, E. Vincent
  See Millay, Edna St. Vincent
Millay, Edna St. Vincent 1892-1950 **TCLC 4, 49;
  DA; DAB; DAC; DAM MST, POET; PC 6;
  WLCS**
  See also CA 104; 130; CDALB 1917-1929; DLB
  45; MTCW
Miller, Arthur 1915-**CLC 1, 2, 6, 10, 15, 26, 47,
  78; DA; DAB; DAC; DAM DRAM, MST; DC
  1; WLC**
  See also AAYA 15; AITN 1; CA 1-4R; CABS 3;
  CANR 2, 30, 54; CDALB 1941-1968; DLB 7;
  MTCW
Miller, Henry (Valentine) 1891-1980**CLC 1, 2, 4,
  9, 14, 43, 84; DA; DAB; DAC; DAM MST,
  NOV; WLC**
  See also CA 9-12R; 97-100; CANR 33, 64; CDALB
  1929-1941; DLB 4, 9; DLBY 80; MTCW
Miller, Jason 1939(?)- .... **CLC 2**
  See also AITN 1; CA 73-76; DLB 7
Miller, Sue 1943- .... **CLC 44; DAM POP**
  See also BEST 90:3; CA 139; CANR 59; DLB 143
Miller, Walter M(ichael, Jr.) 1923- .. **CLC 4, 30**
  See also CA 85-88; DLB 8

Millett, Kate 1934- .... **CLC 67**
  See also AITN 1; CA 73-76; CANR 32, 53;
  MTCW
Millhauser, Steven (Lewis) 1943- ... **CLC 21, 54**
  See also CA 110; 111; CANR 63; DLB 2; INT 111
Millin, Sarah Gertrude 1889-1968 .... **CLC 49**
  See also CA 102; 93-96
Milne, A(lan) A(lexander) 1882-1956 ... **TCLC 6;
  DAB; DAC; DAM MST**
  See also CA 104; 133; CLR 1, 26; DLB 10, 77, 100,
  160; MAICYA; MTCW; YABC 1
Milner, Ron(ald) 1938- ..... **CLC 56; BLC; DAM
  MULT**
  See also AITN 1; BW 1; CA 73-76; CANR 24;
  DLB 38; MTCW
Milnes, Richard Monckton 1809-1885 **NCLC 61**
  See also DLB 32, 184
Milosz, Czeslaw 1911-**CLC 5, 11, 22, 31, 56, 82;
  DAM MST, POET; PC 8; WLCS**
  See also CA 81-84; CANR 23, 51; MTCW
Milton, John 1608-1674 . **LC 9; DA; DAB; DAC;
  DAM MST, POET; PC 19; WLC**
  See also CDBLB 1660-1789; DLB 131, 151
Min, Anchee 1957- .... **CLC 86**
  See also CA 146
Minehaha, Cornelius
  See Wedekind, (Benjamin) Frank(lin)
Miner, Valerie 1947- .... **CLC 40**
  See also CA 97-100; CANR 59
Minimo, Duca
  See D'Annunzio, Gabriele
Minot, Susan 1956- .... **CLC 44**
  See also CA 134
Minus, Ed 1938- .... **CLC 39**
Miranda, Javier
  See Bioy Casares, Adolfo
Mirbeau, Octave 1848-1917 .... **TCLC 55**
  See also DLB 123
Miro (Ferrer), Gabriel (Francisco Victor) 1879-
  1930 .... **TCLC 5**
  See also CA 104
Mishima, Yukio 1925-1970**CLC 2, 4, 6, 9, 27; DC
  1; SSC 4**
  See also Hiraoka, Kimitake
  See also DLB 182
Mistral, Frederic 1830-1914 .... **TCLC 51**
  See also CA 122
Mistral, Gabriela .... **TCLC 2; HLC**
  See also Godoy Alcayaga, Lucila
Mistry, Rohinton 1952- .... **CLC 71; DAC**
  See also CA 141
Mitchell, Clyde
  See Ellison, Harlan (Jay); Silverberg, Robert
Mitchell, James Leslie 1901-1935
  See Gibbon, Lewis Grassic
  See also CA 104; DLB 15
Mitchell, Joni 1943- .... **CLC 12**
  See also CA 112
Mitchell, Joseph (Quincy) 1908-1996 ... **CLC 98**
  See also CA 77-80; 152; DLBY 96
Mitchell, Margaret (Munnerlyn) 1900-1949
  TCLC 11; DAM NOV, POP
  See also CA 109; 125; CANR 55; DLB 9; MTCW
Mitchell, Peggy
  See Mitchell, Margaret (Munnerlyn)
Mitchell, S(ilas) Weir 1829-1914 .... **TCLC 36**
Mitchell, W(illiam) O(rmond) 1914- ... **CLC 25;
  DAC; DAM MST**
  See also CA 77-80; CANR 15, 43; DLB 88
Mitford, Mary Russell 1787-1855 .... **NCLC 4**
  See also DLB 110, 116
Mitford, Nancy 1904-1973 .... **CLC 44**
  See also CA 9-12R

Powell, Dawn 1897-1965 .... CLC 66
See also CA 5-8R
Powell, Padgett 1952- .... CLC 34
See also CA 126; CANR 63
Power, Susan 1961- .... CLC 91
Powers, J(ames) F(arl) 1917- ... CLC 1, 4, 8, 57;
SSC 4
See also CA 1-4R; CANR 2, 61; DLB 130; MTCW
Powers, John J(ames) 1945-
See Powers, John R.
See also CA 69-72
Powers, John R. .... CLC 66
See also Powers, John J(ames)
Powers, Richard (S.) 1957- .... CLC 93
See also CA 148
Pownall, David 1938- .... CLC 10
See also CA 89-92; CAAS 18; CANR 49; DLB 14
Powys, John Cowper 1872-1963 CLC 7, 9, 15, 46
See also CA 85-88; DLB 15; MTCW
Powys, T(heodore) F(rancis) 1875-1953 TCLC 9
See also CA 106; DLB 36, 162
Prado (Calvo), Pedro 1886-1952 .... TCLC 75
See also CA 131; HW
Prager, Emily 1952- .... CLC 56
Pratt, E(dwin) J(ohn) 1883(?)-1964 CLC 19; DAC;
DAM POET
See also CA 141; 93-96; DLB 92
Premchand .... TCLC 21
See also Srivastava, Dhanpat Rai
Preussler, Otfried 1923- .... CLC 17
See also CA 77-80; SATA 24
Prevert, Jacques (Henri Marie) 1900-1977 C L C
15
See also CA 77-80; 69-72; CANR 29, 61; MTCW;
SATA-Obit 30
Prevost, Abbe (Antoine Francois) 1697-1763 LC 1
Price, (Edward) Reynolds 1933- CLC 3, 6, 13, 43,
50, 63; DAM NOV; SSC 22
See also CA 1-4R; CANR 1, 37, 57; DLB 2; INT
CANR-37
Price, Richard 1949- .... CLC 6, 12
See also CA 49-52; CANR 3; DLBY 81
Prichard, Katharine Susannah 1883-1969 C L C
46
See also CA 11-12; CANR 33; CAP 1; MTCW;
SATA 66
Priestley, J(ohn) B(oynton) 1894-1984 CLC 2, 5,
9, 34; DAM DRAM, NOV
See also CA 9-12R; 113; CANR 33; CDBLB 1914-
1945; DLB 10, 34, 77, 100, 139; DLBY 84;
MTCW
Prince 1958(?)- .... CLC 35
Prince, F(rank) T(empleton) 1912- .... CLC 22
See also CA 101; CANR 43; DLB 20
Prince Kropotkin
See Kropotkin, Peter (Alekseievich)
Prior, Matthew 1664-1721 .... LC 4
See also DLB 95
Prishvin, Mikhail 1873-1954 .... TCLC 75
Pritchard, William H(arrison) 1932- ... CLC 34
See also CA 65-68; CANR 23; DLB 111
Pritchett, V(ictor) S(awdon) 1900-1997 CLC 5, 13,
15, 41; DAM NOV; SSC 14
See also CA 61-64; 157; CANR 31, 63; DLB 15,
139; MTCW
Private 19022
See Manning, Frederic
Probst, Mark 1925- .... CLC 59
See also CA 130
Prokosch, Frederic 1908-1989 .... CLC 4, 48
See also CA 73-76; 128; DLB 48
Prophet, The
See Dreiser, Theodore (Herman Albert)

Prose, Francine 1947- .... CLC 45
See also CA 109; 112; CANR 46
Proudhon
See Cunha, Euclides (Rodrigues Pimenta) da
Proulx, E. Annie 1935- .... CLC 81
Proust, (Valentin-Louis-George-Eugene-) Marcel
1871-1922 TCLC 7, 13, 33; DA; DAB; DAC;
DAM MST, NOV; WLC
See also CA 104; 120; DLB 65; MTCW
Prowler, Harley
See Masters, Edgar Lee
Prus, Boleslaw 1845-1912 .... TCLC 48
Pryor, Richard (Franklin Lenox Thomas) 1940-
CLC 26
See also CA 122
Przybyszewski, Stanislaw 1868-1927 . TCLC 36
See also CA 160; DLB 66
Pteleon
See Grieve, C(hristopher) M(urray)
See also DAM POET
Puckett, Lute
See Masters, Edgar Lee
Puig, Manuel 1932-1990 ... CLC 3, 5, 10, 28, 65;
DAM MULT; HLC
See also CA 45-48; CANR 2, 32, 63; DLB 113;
HW; MTCW
Pulitzer, Joseph 1847-1911 .... TCLC 76
See also CA 114; DLB 23
Purdy, Al(fred Wellington) 1918- CLC 3, 6, 14,
50; DAC; DAM MST, POET
See also CA 81-84; CAAS 17; CANR 42; DLB 88
Purdy, James (Amos) 1923- CLC 2, 4, 10, 28, 52
See also CA 33-36R; CAAS 1; CANR 19, 51; DLB
2; INT CANR-19; MTCW
Pure, Simon
See Swinnerton, Frank Arthur
Pushkin, Alexander (Sergeyevich) 1799-1837
NCLC 3, 27; DA; DAB; DAC; DAM DRAM,
MST, POET; PC 10; SSC 27; WLC
See also SATA 61
P'u Sung-ling 1640-1715 .... LC 3
Putnam, Arthur Lee
See Alger, Horatio, Jr.
Puzo, Mario 1920- .. CLC 1, 2, 6, 36, 107; DAM
NOV, POP
See also CA 65-68; CANR 4, 42; DLB 6; MTCW
Pygge, Edward
See Barnes, Julian (Patrick)
Pyle, Ernest Taylor 1900-1945
See Pyle, Ernie
See also CA 115; 160
Pyle, Ernie 1900-1945 .... TCLC 75
See also Pyle, Ernest Taylor
See also DLB 29
Pym, Barbara (Mary Crampton) 1913-1980 C L C
13, 19, 37
See also CA 13-14; 97-100; CANR 13, 34; CAP 1;
DLB 14; DLBY 87; MTCW
Pynchon, Thomas (Ruggles, Jr.) 1937- CLC 2, 3,
6, 9, 11, 18, 33, 62, 72; DA; DAB; DAC; DAM
MST, NOV, POP; SSC 14; WLC
See also BEST 90:2; CA 17-20R; CANR 22, 46;
DLB 2, 173; MTCW
Pythagoras c. 570B.C.-c. 500B.C. .... CMLC 22
See also DLB 176
Qian Zhongshu
See Ch'ien Chung-shu
Qroll
See Dagerman, Stig (Halvard)
Quarrington, Paul (Lewis) 1953- .... CLC 65
See also CA 129; CANR 62
Quasimodo, Salvatore 1901-1968 .... CLC 10
See also CA 13-16; 25-28R; CAP 1; DLB 114;

MTCW
Quay, Stephen 1947- .... CLC 95
Quay, Timothy 1947- .... CLC 95
Queen, Ellery .... CLC 3, 11
See also Dannay, Frederic; Davidson, Avram;
Lee, Manfred B(ennington); Marlowe,
Stephen; Sturgeon, Theodore (Hamilton);
Vance, John Holbrook
Queen, Ellery, Jr.
See Dannay, Frederic; Lee, Manfred
B(ennington)
Queneau, Raymond 1903-1976 CLC 2, 5, 10, 42
See also CA 77-80; 69-72; CANR 32; DLB 72;
MTCW
Quevedo, Francisco de 1580-1645 .... LC 23
Quiller-Couch, Arthur Thomas 1863-1944 TCLC
53
See also CA 118; DLB 135, 153
Quin, Ann (Marie) 1936-1973 .... CLC 6
See also CA 9-12R; 45-48; DLB 14
Quinn, Martin
See Smith, Martin Cruz
Quinn, Peter 1947- .... CLC 91
Quinn, Simon
See Smith, Martin Cruz
Quiroga, Horacio (Sylvestre) 1878-1937 . TCLC
20; DAM MULT; HLC
See also CA 117; 131; HW; MTCW
Quoirez, Francoise 1935- .... CLC 9
See also Sagan, Francoise
See also CA 49-52; CANR 6, 39; MTCW
Raabe, Wilhelm 1831-1910 .... TCLC 45
See also DLB 129
Rabe, David (William) 1940- CLC 4, 8, 33; DAM
DRAM
See also CA 85-88; CABS 3; CANR 59; DLB 7
Rabelais, Francois 1483-1553 . LC 5; DA; DAB;
DAC; DAM MST; WLC
Rabinovitch, Sholem 1859-1916
See Aleichem, Sholom
See also CA 104
Rachilde 1860-1953 .... TCLC 67
See also DLB 123
Racine, Jean 1639-1699 LC 28; DAB; DAM MST
Radcliffe, Ann (Ward) 1764-1823 .... NCLC 6, 55
See also DLB 39, 178
Radiguet, Raymond 1903-1923 .... TCLC 29
See also CA 162; DLB 65
Radnoti, Miklos 1909-1944 .... TCLC 16
See also CA 118
Rado, James 1939- .... CLC 17
See also CA 105
Radvanyi, Netty 1900-1983
See Seghers, Anna
See also CA 85-88; 110
Rae, Ben
See Griffiths, Trevor
Raeburn, John (Hay) 1941- .... CLC 34
See also CA 57-60
Ragni, Gerome 1942-1991 .... CLC 17
See also CA 105; 134
Rahv, Philip 1908-1973 .... CLC 24
See also Greenberg, Ivan
See also DLB 137
Raine, Craig 1944- .... CLC 32, 103
See also CA 108; CANR 29, 51; DLB 40
Raine, Kathleen (Jessie) 1908- .... CLC 7, 45
See also CA 85-88; CANR 46; DLB 20; MTCW
Rainis, Janis 1865-1929 .... TCLC 29
Rakosi, Carl .... CLC 47
See also Rawley, Callman
See also CAAS 5
Raleigh, Richard

See Lovecraft, H(oward) P(hillips)
Raleigh, Sir Walter 1554(?)-1618 ...... **LC 31, 39**
　　See also CDBLB Before 1660; DLB 172
Rallentando, H. P.
　　See Sayers, Dorothy L(eigh)
Ramal, Walter
　　See de la Mare, Walter (John)
Ramon, Juan
　　See Jimenez (Mantecon), Juan Ramon
Ramos, Graciliano 1892-1953 .... **TCLC 32**
Rampersad, Arnold 1941- .... **CLC 44**
　　See also BW 2; CA 127; 133; DLB 111; INT 133
Rampling, Anne
　　See Rice, Anne
Ramsay, Allan 1684(?)-1758 .... **LC 29**
　　See also DLB 95
Ramuz, Charles-Ferdinand 1878-1947 **TCLC 33**
Rand, Ayn 1905-1982 **CLC 3, 30, 44, 79; DA; DAC;**
　　DAM MST, NOV, POP; WLC
　　See also AAYA 10; CA 13-16R; 105; CANR 27;
　　MTCW
Randall, Dudley (Felker) 1914- ... **CLC 1; BLC;**
　　DAM MULT
　　See also BW 1; CA 25-28R; CANR 23; DLB 41
Randall, Robert
　　See Silverberg, Robert
Ranger, Ken
　　See Creasey, John
Ransom, John Crowe 1888-1974 **CLC 2, 4, 5, 11,**
　　24; DAM POET
　　See also CA 5-8R; 49-52; CANR 6, 34; DLB 45,
　　63; MTCW
Rao, Raja 1909- .... **CLC 25, 56; DAM NOV**
　　See also CA 73-76; CANR 51; MTCW
Raphael, Frederic (Michael) 1931- ... **CLC 2, 14**
　　See also CA 1-4R; CANR 1; DLB 14
Ratcliffe, James P.
　　See Mencken, H(enry) L(ouis)
Rathbone, Julian 1935- .... **CLC 41**
　　See also CA 101; CANR 34
Rattigan, Terence (Mervyn) 1911-1977 .. **CLC 7;**
　　DAM DRAM
　　See also CA 85-88; 73-76; CDBLB 1945-1960;
　　DLB 13; MTCW
Ratushinskaya, Irina 1954- .... **CLC 54**
　　See also CA 129
Raven, Simon (Arthur Noel) 1927- .... **CLC 14**
　　See also CA 81-84
Rawley, Callman 1903-
　　See Rakosi, Carl
　　See also CA 21-24R; CANR 12, 32
Rawlings, Marjorie Kinnan 1896-1953 . **TCLC 4**
　　See also AAYA 20; CA 104; 137; DLB 9, 22, 102;
　　JRDA; MAICYA; YABC 1
Ray, Satyajit 1921-1992 **CLC 16, 76; DAM MULT**
　　See also CA 114; 137
Read, Herbert Edward 1893-1968 .... **CLC 4**
　　See also CA 85-88; 25-28R; DLB 20, 149
Read, Piers Paul 1941- .... **CLC 4, 10, 25**
　　See also CA 21-24R; CANR 38; DLB 14; SATA
　　21
Reade, Charles 1814-1884 .... **NCLC 2**
　　See also DLB 21
Reade, Hamish
　　See Gray, Simon (James Holliday)
Reading, Peter 1946- .... **CLC 47**
　　See also CA 103; CANR 46; DLB 40
Reaney, James 1926- **CLC 13; DAC; DAM MST**
　　See also CA 41-44R; CAAS 15; CANR 42; DLB
　　68; SATA 43
Rebreanu, Liviu 1885-1944 .... **TCLC 28**
Rechy, John (Francisco) 1934- **CLC 1, 7, 14, 18,**
　　107; DAM MULT; HLC

See also CA 5-8R; CAAS 4; CANR 6, 32, 64;
　　DLB 122; DLBY 82; HW; INT CANR-6
Redcam, Tom 1870-1933 .... **TCLC 25**
Reddin, Keith .... **CLC 67**
Redgrove, Peter (William) 1932- ...... **CLC 6, 41**
　　See also CA 1-4R; CANR 3, 39; DLB 40
Redmon, Anne .... **CLC 22**
　　See also Nightingale, Anne Redmon
　　See also DLBY 86
Reed, Eliot
　　See Ambler, Eric
Reed, Ishmael 1938- . **CLC 2, 3, 5, 6, 13, 32, 60;**
　　BLC; DAM MULT
　　See also BW 2; CA 21-24R; CANR 25, 48; DLB 2,
　　5, 33, 169; DLBD 8; MTCW
Reed, John (Silas) 1887-1920 .... **TCLC 9**
　　See also CA 106
Reed, Lou .... **CLC 21**
　　See also Firbank, Louis
Reeve, Clara 1729-1807 .... **NCLC 19**
　　See also DLB 39
Reich, Wilhelm 1897-1957 .... **TCLC 57**
Reid, Christopher (John) 1949- .... **CLC 33**
　　See also CA 140; DLB 40
Reid, Desmond
　　See Moorcock, Michael (John)
Reid Banks, Lynne 1929-
　　See Banks, Lynne Reid
　　See also CA 1-4R; CANR 6, 22, 38; CLR 24; JRDA;
　　MAICYA; SATA 22, 75
Reilly, William K.
　　See Creasey, John
Reiner, Max
　　See Caldwell, (Janet Miriam) Taylor (Holland)
Reis, Ricardo
　　See Pessoa, Fernando (Antonio Nogueira)
Remarque, Erich Maria 1898-1970 **CLC 21; DA;**
　　DAB; DAC; DAM MST, NOV
　　See also CA 77-80; 29-32R; DLB 56; MTCW
Remizov, A.
　　See Remizov, Aleksei (Mikhailovich)
Remizov, A. M.
　　See Remizov, Aleksei (Mikhailovich)
Remizov, Aleksei (Mikhailovich) 1877-1957
　　TCLC 27
　　See also CA 125; 133
Renan, Joseph Ernest 1823-1892 .... **NCLC 26**
Renard, Jules 1864-1910 .... **TCLC 17**
　　See also CA 117
Renault, Mary .... **CLC 3, 11, 17**
　　See also Challans, Mary
　　See also DLBY 83
Rendell, Ruth (Barbara) 1930- **CLC 28, 48; DAM**
　　POP
　　See also Vine, Barbara
　　See also CA 109; CANR 32, 52; DLB 87; INT
　　CANR-32; MTCW
Renoir, Jean 1894-1979 .... **CLC 20**
　　See also CA 129; 85-88
Resnais, Alain 1922- .... **CLC 16**
Reverdy, Pierre 1889-1960 .... **CLC 53**
　　See also CA 97-100; 89-92
Rexroth, Kenneth 1905-1982 **CLC 1, 2, 6, 11, 22,**
　　49; DAM POET; PC 20
　　See also CA 5-8R; 107; CANR 14, 34, 63; CDALB
　　. 1941-1968; DLB 16, 48, 165; DLBY 82; INT
　　CANR-14; MTCW
Reyes, Alfonso 1889-1959 .... **TCLC 33**
　　See also CA 131; HW
Reyes y Basoalto, Ricardo Eliecer Neftali
　　See Neruda, Pablo
Reymont, Wladyslaw (Stanislaw) 1868(?)-1925
　　TCLC 5

See also CA 104
Reynolds, Jonathan 1942- .... **CLC 6, 38**
　　See also CA 65-68; CANR 28
Reynolds, Joshua 1723-1792 .... **LC 15**
　　See also DLB 104
Reynolds, Michael Shane 1937- .... **CLC 44**
　　See also CA 65-68; CANR 9
Reznikoff, Charles 1894-1976 .... **CLC 9**
　　See also CA 33-36; 61-64; CAP 2; DLB 28, 45
Rezzori (d'Arezzo), Gregor von 1914- .. **CLC 25**
　　See also CA 122; 136
Rhine, Richard
　　See Silverstein, Alvin
Rhodes, Eugene Manlove 1869-1934 ... **TCLC 53**
R'hoone
　　See Balzac, Honore de
Rhys, Jean 1890(?)-1979 **CLC 2, 4, 6, 14, 19, 51;**
　　DAM NOV; SSC 21
　　See also CA 25-28R; 85-88; CANR 35, 62; CDBLB
　　1945-1960; DLB 36, 117, 162; MTCW
Ribeiro, Darcy 1922-1997 .... **CLC 34**
　　See also CA 33-36R; 156
Ribeiro, Joao Ubaldo (Osorio Pimentel) 1941-
　　CLC 10, 67
　　See also CA 81-84
Ribman, Ronald (Burt) 1932- .... **CLC 7**
　　See also CA 21-24R; CANR 46
Ricci, Nino 1959- .... **CLC 70**
　　See also CA 137
Rice, Anne 1941- .... **CLC 41; DAM POP**
　　See also AAYA 9; BEST 89:2; CA 65-68; CANR
　　12, 36, 53
Rice, Elmer (Leopold) 1892-1967 **CLC 7, 49; DAM**
　　DRAM
　　See also CA 21-22; 25-28R; CAP 2; DLB 4, 7;
　　MTCW
Rice, Tim(othy Miles Bindon) 1944- ..... **CLC 21**
　　See also CA 103; CANR 46
Rich, Adrienne (Cecile) 1929- **CLC 3, 6, 7, 11, 18,**
　　36, 73, 76; DAM POET; PC 5
　　See also CA 9-12R; CANR 20, 53; DLB 5, 67;
　　MTCW
Rich, Barbara
　　See Graves, Robert (von Ranke)
Rich, Robert
　　See Trumbo, Dalton
Richard, Keith .... **CLC 17**
　　See also Richards, Keith
Richards, David Adams 1950- ..... **CLC 59; DAC**
　　See also CA 93-96; CANR 60; DLB 53
Richards, I(vor) A(rmstrong) 1893-1979 **CLC 14,**
　　24
　　See also CA 41-44R; 89-92; CANR 34; DLB 27
Richards, Keith 1943-
　　See Richard, Keith
　　See also CA 107
Richardson, Anne
　　See Roiphe, Anne (Richardson)
Richardson, Dorothy Miller 1873-1957 **TCLC 3**
　　See also CA 104; DLB 36
Richardson, Ethel Florence (Lindesay) 1870-1946
　　See Richardson, Henry Handel
　　See also CA 105
Richardson, Henry Handel .... **TCLC 4**
　　See also Richardson, Ethel Florence (Lindesay)
Richardson, John 1796-1852 .... **NCLC 55; DAC**
　　See also DLB 99
Richardson, Samuel 1689-1761 **LC 1; DA; DAB;**
　　DAC; DAM MST, NOV; WLC
　　See also CDBLB 1660-1789; DLB 39
Richler, Mordecai 1931- **CLC 3, 5, 9, 13, 18, 46,**
　　70; DAC; DAM MST, NOV
　　See also AITN 1; CA 65-68; CANR 31, 62; CLR

See also CA 128

Skram, Amalie (Bertha) 1847-1905 .... **TCLC 25**

Skvorecky, Josef (Vaclav) 1924-**CLC 15, 39, 69; DAC; DAM NOV**
See also CA 61-64; CAAS 1; CANR 10, 34, 63; MTCW

Slade, Bernard .... **CLC 11, 46**
See also Newbound, Bernard Slade
See also CAAS 9; DLB 53

Slaughter, Carolyn 1946- .... **CLC 56**
See also CA 85-88

Slaughter, Frank G(ill) 1908- .... **CLC 29**
See also AITN 2; CA 5-8R; CANR 5; INT CANR-5

Slavitt, David R(ytman) 1935- .... **CLC 5, 14**
See also CA 21-24R; CAAS 3; CANR 41; DLB 5, 6

Slesinger, Tess 1905-1945 .... **TCLC 10**
See also CA 107; DLB 102

Slessor, Kenneth 1901-1971 .... **CLC 14**
See also CA 102; 89-92

Slowacki, Juliusz 1809-1849 .... **NCLC 15**

Smart, Christopher 1722-1771**LC 3; DAM POET; PC 13**
See also DLB 109

Smart, Elizabeth 1913-1986 .... **CLC 54**
See also CA 81-84; 118; DLB 88

Smiley, Jane (Graves) 1949- **CLC 53, 76; DAM POP**
See also CA 104; CANR 30, 50; INT CANR-30

Smith, A(rthur) J(ames) M(arshall) 1902-1980 **CLC 15; DAC**
See also CA 1-4R; 102; CANR 4; DLB 88

Smith, Adam 1723-1790 .... **LC 36**
See also DLB 104

Smith, Alexander 1829-1867 .... **NCLC 59**
See also DLB 32, 55

Smith, Anna Deavere 1950- .... **CLC 86**
See also CA 133

Smith, Betty (Wehner) 1896-1972 .... **CLC 19**
See also CA 5-8R; 33-36R; DLBY 82; SATA 6

Smith, Charlotte (Turner) 1749-1806 **NCLC 23**
See also DLB 39, 109

Smith, Clark Ashton 1893-1961 .... **CLC 43**
See also CA 143

Smith, Dave .... **CLC 22, 42**
See also Smith, David (Jeddie)
See also CAAS 7; DLB 5

Smith, David (Jeddie) 1942-
See Smith, Dave
See also CA 49-52; CANR 1, 59; DAM POET

Smith, Florence Margaret 1902-1971
See Smith, Stevie
See also CA 17-18; 29-32R; CANR 35; CAP 2; DAM POET; MTCW

Smith, Iain Crichton 1928- .... **CLC 64**
See also CA 21-24R; DLB 40, 139

Smith, John 1580(?)-1631 .... **LC 9**

Smith, Johnston
See Crane, Stephen (Townley)

Smith, Joseph, Jr. 1805-1844 .... **NCLC 53**

Smith, Lee 1944- .... **CLC 25, 73**
See also CA 114; 119; CANR 46; DLB 143; DLBY 83; INT 119

Smith, Martin
See Smith, Martin Cruz

Smith, Martin Cruz 1942-**CLC 25; DAM MULT, POP**
See also BEST 89:4; CA 85-88; CANR 6, 23, 43; INT CANR-23; NNAL

Smith, Mary-Ann Tirone 1944- .... **CLC 39**
See also CA 118; 136

Smith, Patti 1946- .... **CLC 12**

See also CA 93-96; CANR 63

Smith, Pauline (Urmson) 1882-1959 ... **TCLC 25**

Smith, Rosamond
See Oates, Joyce Carol

Smith, Sheila Kaye
See Kaye-Smith, Sheila

Smith, Stevie .... **CLC 3, 8, 25, 44; PC 12**
See also Smith, Florence Margaret
See also DLB 20

Smith, Wilbur (Addison) 1933- .... **CLC 33**
See also CA 13-16R; CANR 7, 46; MTCW

Smith, William Jay 1918- .... **CLC 6**
See also CA 5-8R; CANR 44; DLB 5; MAICYA; SAAS 22; SATA 2, 68

Smith, Woodrow Wilson
See Kuttner, Henry

Smolenskin, Peretz 1842-1885 .... **NCLC 30**

Smollett, Tobias (George) 1721-1771 .... **LC 2**
See also CDBLB 1660-1789; DLB 39, 104

Snodgrass, W(illiam) D(e Witt) 1926- **CLC 2, 6, 10, 18, 68; DAM POET**
See also CA 1-4R; CANR 6, 36; DLB 5; MTCW

Snow, C(harles) P(ercy) 1905-1980**CLC 1, 4, 6, 9, 13, 19; DAM NOV**
See also CA 5-8R; 101; CANR 28; CDBLB 1945-1960; DLB 15, 77; MTCW

Snow, Frances Compton
See Adams, Henry (Brooks)

Snyder, Gary (Sherman) 1930-**CLC 1, 2, 5, 9, 32; DAM POET; PC 21**
See also CA 17-20R; CANR 30, 60; DLB 5, 16, 165

Snyder, Zilpha Keatley 1927- .... **CLC 17**
See also AAYA 15; CA 9-12R; CANR 38; CLR 31; JRDA; MAICYA; SAAS 2; SATA 1, 28, 75

Soares, Bernardo
See Pessoa, Fernando (Antonio Nogueira)

Sobh, A.
See Shamlu, Ahmad

Sobol, Joshua .... **CLC 60**

Soderberg, Hjalmar 1869-1941 .... **TCLC 39**

Sodergran, Edith (Irene)
See Soedergran, Edith (Irene)

Soedergran, Edith (Irene) 1892-1923 .. **TCLC 31**

Softly, Edgar
See Lovecraft, H(oward) P(hillips)

Softly, Edward
See Lovecraft, H(oward) P(hillips)

Sokolov, Raymond 1941- .... **CLC 7**
See also CA 85-88

Solo, Jay
See Ellison, Harlan (Jay)

Sologub, Fyodor .... **TCLC 9**
See also Teternikov, Fyodor Kuzmich

Solomons, Ikey Esquir
See Thackeray, William Makepeace

Solomos, Dionysios 1798-1857 .... **NCLC 15**

Solwoska, Mara
See French, Marilyn

Solzhenitsyn, Aleksandr I(sayevich) 1918- **C L C 1, 2, 4, 7, 9, 10, 18, 26, 34, 78; DA; DAB; DAC; DAM MST, NOV; WLC**
See also AITN 1; CA 69-72; CANR 40; MTCW

Somers, Jane
See Lessing, Doris (May)

Somerville, Edith 1858-1949 .... **TCLC 51**
See also DLB 135

Somerville & Ross
See Martin, Violet Florence; Somerville, Edith

Sommer, Scott 1951- .... **CLC 25**
See also CA 106

Sondheim, Stephen (Joshua) 1930- **CLC 30, 39; DAM DRAM**

See also AAYA 11; CA 103; CANR 47

Song, Cathy 1955- .... **PC 21**
See also CA 154; DLB 169

Sontag, Susan 1933- **CLC 1, 2, 10, 13, 31, 105; DAM POP**
See also CA 17-20R; CANR 25, 51; DLB 2, 67; MTCW

Sophocles 496(?)B.C.-406(?)B.C. . **CMLC 2; DA; DAB; DAC; DAM DRAM, MST; DC 1; WLCS**
See also DLB 176

Sordello 1189-1269 .... **CMLC 15**

Sorel, Julia
See Drexler, Rosalyn

Sorrentino, Gilbert 1929- . **CLC 3, 7, 14, 22, 40**
See also CA 77-80; CANR 14, 33; DLB 5, 173; DLBY 80; INT CANR-14

Soto, Gary 1952-**CLC 32, 80; DAM MULT; HLC**
See also AAYA 10; CA 119; 125; CANR 50; CLR 38; DLB 82; HW; INT 125; JRDA; SATA 80

Soupault, Philippe 1897-1990 .... **CLC 68**
See also CA 116; 147; 131

Souster, (Holmes) Raymond 1921-... **CLC 5, 14; DAC; DAM POET**
See also CA 13-16R; CAAS 14; CANR 13, 29, 53; DLB 88; SATA 63

Southern, Terry 1924(?)-1995 .... **CLC 7**
See also CA 1-4R; 150; CANR 1, 55; DLB 2

Southey, Robert 1774-1843 .... **NCLC 8**
See also DLB 93, 107, 142; SATA 54

Southworth, Emma Dorothy Eliza Nevitte 1819-1899 .... **NCLC 26**

Souza, Ernest
See Scott, Evelyn

Soyinka, Wole 1934-**CLC 3, 5, 14, 36, 44; BLC; DA; DAB; DAC; DAM DRAM, MST, MULT; DC 2; WLC**
See also BW 2; CA 13-16R; CANR 27, 39; DLB 125; MTCW

Spackman, W(illiam) M(ode) 1905-1990 **CLC 46**
See also CA 81-84; 132

Spacks, Barry (Bernard) 1931- .... **CLC 14**
See also CA 154; CANR 33; DLB 105

Spanidou, Irini 1946- .... **CLC 44**

Spark, Muriel (Sarah) 1918- **CLC 2, 3, 5, 8, 13, 18, 40, 94; DAB; DAC; DAM MST, NOV; SSC 10**
See also CA 5-8R; CANR 12, 36; CDBLB 1945-1960; DLB 15, 139; INT CANR-12; MTCW

Spaulding, Douglas
See Bradbury, Ray (Douglas)

Spaulding, Leonard
See Bradbury, Ray (Douglas)

Spence, J. A. D.
See Eliot, T(homas) S(tearns)

Spencer, Elizabeth 1921- .... **CLC 22**
See also CA 13-16R; CANR 32; DLB 6; MTCW; SATA 14

Spencer, Leonard G.
See Silverberg, Robert

Spencer, Scott 1945- .... **CLC 30**
See also CA 113; CANR 51; DLBY 86

Spender, Stephen (Harold) 1909-1995**CLC 1, 2, 5, 10, 41, 91; DAM POET**
See also CA 9-12R; 149; CANR 31, 54; CDBLB 1945-1960; DLB 20; MTCW

Spengler, Oswald (Arnold Gottfried) 1880-1936 **TCLC 25**
See also CA 118

Spenser, Edmund 1552(?)-1599 ... **LC 5, 39; DA; DAB; DAC; DAM MST, POET; PC 8; WLC**
See also CDBLB Before 1660; DLB 167

Spicer, Jack 1925-1965 .... **CLC 8, 18, 72; DAM POET**

See also CA 110; 143; DLB 9, 102; SATA 17

Tarkovsky, Andrei (Arsenyevich) 1932-1986 **CLC 75**
See also CA 127

Tartt, Donna 1964(?)- .... **CLC 76**
See also CA 142

Tasso, Torquato 1544-1595 .... **LC 5**

Tate, (John Orley) Allen 1899-1979 **CLC 2, 4, 6, 9, 11, 14, 24**
See also CA 5-8R; 85-88; CANR 32; DLB 4, 45, 63; MTCW

Tate, Ellalice
See Hibbert, Eleanor Alice Burford

Tate, James (Vincent) 1943- .... **CLC 2, 6, 25**
See also CA 21-24R; CANR 29, 57; DLB 5, 169

Tavel, Ronald 1940- .... **CLC 6**
See also CA 21-24R; CANR 33

Taylor, C(ecil) P(hilip) 1929-1981 .... **CLC 27**
See also CA 25-28R; 105; CANR 47

Taylor, Edward 1642(?)-1729 . **LC 11; DA; DAB; DAC; DAM MST, POET**
See also DLB 24

Taylor, Eleanor Ross 1920- .... **CLC 5**
See also CA 81-84

Taylor, Elizabeth 1912-1975 .... **CLC 2, 4, 29**
See also CA 13-16R; CANR 9; DLB 139; MTCW; SATA 13

Taylor, Frederick Winslow 1856-1915 **TCLC 76**

Taylor, Henry (Splawn) 1942- .... **CLC 44**
See also CA 33-36R; CAAS 7; CANR 31; DLB 5

Taylor, Kamala (Purnaiya) 1924-
See Markandaya, Kamala
See also CA 77-80

Taylor, Mildred D. .... **CLC 21**
See also AAYA 10; BW 1; CA 85-88; CANR 25; CLR 9; DLB 52; JRDA; MAICYA; SAAS 5; SATA 15, 70

Taylor, Peter (Hillsman) 1917-1994 **CLC 1, 4, 18, 37, 44, 50, 71; SSC 10**
See also CA 13-16R; 147; CANR 9, 50; DLBY 81, 94; INT CANR-9; MTCW

Taylor, Robert Lewis 1912- .... **CLC 14**
See also CA 1-4R; CANR 3, 64; SATA 10

Tchekhov, Anton
See Chekhov, Anton (Pavlovich)

Tchicaya, Gerald Felix 1931-1988 .... **CLC 101**
See also CA 129; 125

Tchicaya U Tam'si
See Tchicaya, Gerald Felix

Teasdale, Sara 1884-1933 .... **TCLC 4**
See also CA 104; DLB 45; SATA 32

Tegner, Esaias 1782-1846 .... **NCLC 2**

Teilhard de Chardin, (Marie Joseph) Pierre 1881-1955 .... **TCLC 9**
See also CA 105

Temple, Ann
See Mortimer, Penelope (Ruth)

Tennant, Emma (Christina) 1937- ... **CLC 13, 52**
See also CA 65-68; CAAS 9; CANR 10, 38, 59; DLB 14

Tenneshaw, S. M.
See Silverberg, Robert

Tennyson, Alfred 1809-1892 . **NCLC 30, 65; DA; DAB; DAC; DAM MST, POET; PC 6; WLC**
See also CDBLB 1832-1890; DLB 32

Teran, Lisa St. Aubin de .... **CLC 36**
See also St. Aubin de Teran, Lisa

Terence 195(?)B.C.-159B.C. ..... **CMLC 14; DC 7**

Teresa de Jesus, St. 1515-1582 .... **LC 18**

Terkel, Louis 1912-
See Terkel, Studs
See also CA 57-60; CANR 18, 45; MTCW

Terkel, Studs .... **CLC 38**

See also Terkel, Louis
See also AITN 1

Terry, C. V.
See Slaughter, Frank G(ill)

Terry, Megan 1932- .... **CLC 19**
See also CA 77-80; CABS 3; CANR 43; DLB 7

Tertz, Abram
See Sinyavsky, Andrei (Donatevich)

Tesich, Steve 1943(?)-1996 .... **CLC 40, 69**
See also CA 105; 152; DLBY 83

Teternikov, Fyodor Kuzmich 1863-1927
See Sologub, Fyodor
See also CA 104

Tevis, Walter 1928-1984 .... **CLC 42**
See also CA 113

Tey, Josephine .... **TCLC 14**
See also Mackintosh, Elizabeth
See also DLB 77

Thackeray, William Makepeace 1811-1863 **NCLC 5, 14, 22, 43; DA; DAB; DAC; DAM MST, NOV; WLC**
See also CDBLB 1832-1890; DLB 21, 55, 159, 163; SATA 23

Thakura, Ravindranatha
See Tagore, Rabindranath

Tharoor, Shashi 1956- .... **CLC 70**
See also CA 141

Thelwell, Michael Miles 1939- .... **CLC 22**
See also BW 2; CA 101

Theobald, Lewis, Jr.
See Lovecraft, H(oward) P(hillips)

Theodorescu, Ion N. 1880-1967
See Arghezi, Tudor
See also CA 116

Theriault, Yves 1915-1983 **CLC 79; DAC; DAM MST**
See also CA 102; DLB 88

Theroux, Alexander (Louis) 1939- .... **CLC 2, 25**
See also CA 85-88; CANR 20, 63

Theroux, Paul (Edward) 1941-. **CLC 5, 8, 11, 15, 28, 46; DAM POP**
See also BEST 89:4; CA 33-36R; CANR 20, 45; DLB 2; MTCW; SATA 44

Thesen, Sharon 1946- .... **CLC 56**

Thevenin, Denis
See Duhamel, Georges

Thibault, Jacques Anatole Francois 1844-1924
See France, Anatole
See also CA 106; 127; DAM NOV; MTCW

Thiele, Colin (Milton) 1920- .... **CLC 17**
See also CA 29-32R; CANR 12, 28, 53; CLR 27; MAICYA; SAAS 2; SATA 14, 72

Thomas, Audrey (Callahan) 1935- **CLC 7, 13, 37, 107; SSC 20**
See also AITN 2; CA 21-24R; CAAS 19; CANR 36, 58; DLB 60; MTCW

Thomas, D(onald) M(ichael) 1935- **CLC 13, 22, 31**
See also CA 61-64; CAAS 11; CANR 17, 45; CDBLB 1960 to Present; DLB 40; INT CANR-17; MTCW

Thomas, Dylan (Marlais) 1914-1953 **TCLC 1, 8, 45; DA; DAB; DAC; DAM DRAM, MST, POET; PC 2; SSC 3; WLC**
See also CA 104; 120; CDBLB 1945-1960; DLB 13, 20, 139; MTCW; SATA 60

Thomas, (Philip) Edward 1878-1917 ... **TCLC 10; DAM POET**
See also CA 106; 153; DLB 19

Thomas, Joyce Carol 1938- .... **CLC 35**
See also AAYA 12; BW 2; CA 113; 116; CANR 48; CLR 19; DLB 33; INT 116; JRDA; MAICYA; MTCW; SAAS 7; SATA 40, 78

Thomas, Lewis 1913-1993 .... **CLC 35**

See also CA 85-88; 143; CANR 38, 60; MTCW

Thomas, Paul
See Mann, (Paul) Thomas

Thomas, Piri 1928- .... **CLC 17**
See also CA 73-76; HW

Thomas, R(onald) S(tuart) 1913- **CLC 6, 13, 48; DAB; DAM POET**
See also CA 89-92; CAAS 4; CANR 30; CDBLB 1960 to Present; DLB 27; MTCW

Thomas, Ross (Elmore) 1926-1995 .... **CLC 39**
See also CA 33-36R; 150; CANR 22, 63

Thompson, Francis Clegg
See Mencken, H(enry) L(ouis)

Thompson, Francis Joseph 1859-1907 .. **TCLC 4**
See also CA 104; CDBLB 1890-1914; DLB 19

Thompson, Hunter S(tockton) 1939- **CLC 9, 17, 40, 104; DAM POP**
See also BEST 89:1; CA 17-20R; CANR 23, 46; MTCW

Thompson, James Myers
See Thompson, Jim (Myers)

Thompson, Jim (Myers) 1906-1977(?) .. **CLC 69**
See also CA 140

Thompson, Judith .... **CLC 39**

Thomson, James 1700-1748 **LC 16, 29, 40; DAM POET**
See also DLB 95

Thomson, James 1834-1882 **NCLC 18; DAM POET**
See also DLB 35

Thoreau, Henry David 1817-1862 **NCLC 7, 21, 61; DA; DAB; DAC; DAM MST; WLC**
See also CDALB 1640-1865; DLB 1

Thornton, Hall
See Silverberg, Robert

Thucydides c. 455B.C.-399B.C. .... **CMLC 17**
See also DLB 176

Thurber, James (Grover) 1894-1961 . **CLC 5, 11, 25; DA; DAB; DAC; DAM DRAM, MST, NOV; SSC 1**
See also CA 73-76; CANR 17, 39; CDALB 1929-1941; DLB 4, 11, 22, 102; MAICYA; MTCW; SATA 13

Thurman, Wallace (Henry) 1902-1934 . **TCLC 6; BLC; DAM MULT**
See also BW 1; CA 104; 124; DLB 51

Ticheburn, Cheviot
See Ainsworth, William Harrison

Tieck, (Johann) Ludwig 1773-1853 . **NCLC 5, 46**
See also DLB 90

Tiger, Derry
See Ellison, Harlan (Jay)

Tilghman, Christopher 1948(?)- .... **CLC 65**
See also CA 159

Tillinghast, Richard (Williford) 1940-. **CLC 29**
See also CA 29-32R; CAAS 23; CANR 26, 51

Timrod, Henry 1828-1867 .... **NCLC 25**
See also DLB 3

Tindall, Gillian (Elizabeth) 1938- .... **CLC 7**
See also CA 21-24R; CANR 11

Tiptree, James, Jr. .... **CLC 48, 50**
See also Sheldon, Alice Hastings Bradley
See also DLB 8

Titmarsh, Michael Angelo
See Thackeray, William Makepeace

Tocqueville, Alexis (Charles Henri Maurice Clerel Comte) 1805-1859 .... **NCLC 7, 63**

Tolkien, J(ohn) R(onald) R(euel) 1892-1973 **CLC 1, 2, 3, 8, 12, 38; DA; DAB; DAC; DAM MST, NOV, POP; WLC**
See also AAYA 10; AITN 1; CA 17-18; 45-48; CANR 36; CAP 2; CDBLB 1914-1945; DLB 15, 160; JRDA; MAICYA; MTCW; SATA 2, 32; SATA-Obit 24

160; JRDA; MAICYA; SATA 12

White, Terence de Vere 1912-1994 .... **CLC 49**
See also CA 49-52; 145; CANR 3

White, Walter F(rancis) 1893-1955 .... **TCLC 15**
See also White, Walter
See also BW 1; CA 115; 124; DLB 51

White, William Hale 1831-1913
See Rutherford, Mark
See also CA 121

Whitehead, E(dward) A(nthony) 1933- .... **CLC 5**
See also CA 65-68; CANR 58

Whitemore, Hugh (John) 1936- .... **CLC 37**
See also CA 132; INT 132

Whitman, Sarah Helen (Power) 1803-1878 **NCLC 19**
See also DLB 1

Whitman, Walt(er) 1819-1892 **NCLC 4, 31; DA; DAB; DAC; DAM MST, POET; PC 3; WLC**
See also CDALB 1640-1865; DLB 3, 64; SATA 20

Whitney, Phyllis A(yame) 1903- **CLC 42; DAM POP**
See also AITN 2; BEST 90:3; CA 1-4R; CANR 3, 25, 38, 60; JRDA; MAICYA; SATA 1, 30

Whittemore, (Edward) Reed (Jr.) 1919- .. **CLC 4**
See also CA 9-12R; CAAS 8; CANR 4; DLB 5

Whittier, John Greenleaf 1807-1892 **NCLC 8, 59**
See also DLB 1

Whittlebot, Hernia
See Coward, Noel (Peirce)

Wicker, Thomas Grey 1926-
See Wicker, Tom
See also CA 65-68; CANR 21, 46

Wicker, Tom .... **CLC 7**
See also Wicker, Thomas Grey

Wideman, John Edgar 1941- **CLC 5, 34, 36, 67; BLC; DAM MULT**
See also BW 2; CA 85-88; CANR 14, 42; DLB 33, 143

Wiebe, Rudy (Henry) 1934- **CLC 6, 11, 14; DAC; DAM MST**
See also CA 37-40R; CANR 42; DLB 60

Wieland, Christoph Martin 1733-1813 **NCLC 17**
See also DLB 97

Wiene, Robert 1881-1938 .... **TCLC 56**

Wieners, John 1934- .... **CLC 7**
See also CA 13-16R; DLB 16

Wiesel, Elie(zer) 1928- ... **CLC 3, 5, 11, 37; DA; DAB; DAC; DAM MST, NOV; WLCS 2**
See also AAYA 7; AITN 1; CA 5-8R; CAAS 4; CANR 8, 40; DLB 83; DLBY 87; INT CANR-8; MTCW; SATA 56

Wiggins, Marianne 1947- .... **CLC 57**
See also BEST 89:3; CA 130; CANR 60

Wight, James Alfred 1916-
See Herriot, James
See also CA 77-80; SATA 55; SATA-Brief 44

Wilbur, Richard (Purdy) 1921- **CLC 3, 6, 9, 14, 53; DA; DAB; DAC; DAM MST, POET**
See also CA 1-4R; CABS 2; CANR 2, 29; DLB 5, 169; INT CANR-29; MTCW; SATA 9

Wild, Peter 1940- .... **CLC 14**
See also CA 37-40R; DLB 5

Wilde, Oscar (Fingal O'Flahertie Wills) 1854(?)-1900 **TCLC 1, 8, 23, 41; DA; DAB; DAC; DAM DRAM, MST, NOV; SSC 11; WLC**
See also CA 104; 119; CDBLB 1890-1914; DLB 10, 19, 34, 57, 141, 156; SATA 24

Wilder, Billy .... **CLC 20**
See also Wilder, Samuel
See also DLB 26

Wilder, Samuel 1906-
See Wilder, Billy
See also CA 89-92

Wilder, Thornton (Niven) 1897-1975 **CLC 1, 5, 6, 10, 15, 35, 82; DA; DAB; DAC; DAM DRAM, MST, NOV; DC 1; WLC**
See also AITN 2; CA 13-16R; 61-64; CANR 40; DLB 4, 7, 9; MTCW

Wilding, Michael 1942- .... **CLC 73**
See also CA 104; CANR 24, 49

Wiley, Richard 1944- .... **CLC 44**
See also CA 121; 129

Wilhelm, Kate .... **CLC 7**
See also Wilhelm, Katie Gertrude
See also AAYA 20; CAAS 5; DLB 8; INT CANR-17

Wilhelm, Katie Gertrude 1928-
See Wilhelm, Kate
See also CA 37-40R; CANR 17, 36, 60; MTCW

Wilkins, Mary
See Freeman, Mary Eleanor Wilkins

Willard, Nancy 1936- .... **CLC 7, 37**
See also CA 89-92; CANR 10, 39; CLR 5; DLB 5, 52; MAICYA; MTCW; SATA 37, 71; SATA-Brief 30

Williams, C(harles) K(enneth) 1936- **CLC 33, 56; DAM POET**
See also CA 37-40R; CAAS 26; CANR 57; DLB 5

Williams, Charles
See Collier, James L(incoln)

Williams, Charles (Walter Stansby) 1886-1945 **TCLC 1, 11**
See also CA 104; DLB 100, 153

Williams, (George) Emlyn 1905-1987 .. **CLC 15; DAM DRAM**
See also CA 104; 123; CANR 36; DLB 10, 77; MTCW

Williams, Hugo 1942- .... **CLC 42**
See also CA 17-20R; CANR 45; DLB 40

Williams, J. Walker
See Wodehouse, P(elham) G(renville)

Williams, John A(lfred) 1925- **CLC 5, 13; BLC; DAM MULT**
See also BW 2; CA 53-56; CAAS 3; CANR 6, 26, 51; DLB 2, 33; INT CANR-6

Williams, Jonathan (Chamberlain) 1929- **CLC 13**
See also CA 9-12R; CAAS 12; CANR 8; DLB 5

Williams, Joy 1944- .... **CLC 31**
See also CA 41-44R; CANR 22, 48

Williams, Norman 1952- .... **CLC 39**
See also CA 118

Williams, Sherley Anne 1944- .. **CLC 89; BLC; DAM MULT, POET**
See also BW 2; CA 73-76; CANR 25; DLB 41; INT CANR-25; SATA 78

Williams, Shirley
See Williams, Sherley Anne

Williams, Tennessee 1911-1983 **CLC 1, 2, 5, 7, 8, 11, 15, 19, 30, 39, 45, 71; DA; DAB; DAC; DAM DRAM, MST; DC 4; WLC**
See also AITN 1, 2; CA 5-8R; 108; CABS 3; CANR 31; CDALB 1941-1968; DLB 7; DLBD 4; DLBY 83; MTCW

Williams, Thomas (Alonzo) 1926-1990 . **CLC 14**
See also CA 1-4R; 132; CANR 2

Williams, William C.
See Williams, William Carlos

Williams, William Carlos 1883-1963 **CLC 1, 2, 5, 9, 13, 22, 42, 67; DA; DAB; DAC; DAM MST, POET; PC 7**
See also CA 89-92; CANR 34; CDALB 1917-1929; DLB 4, 16, 54, 86; MTCW

Williamson, David (Keith) 1942- .... **CLC 56**
See also CA 103; CANR 41

Williamson, Ellen Douglas 1905-1984
See Douglas, Ellen

See also CA 17-20R; 114; CANR 39

Williamson, Jack .... **CLC 29**
See also Williamson, John Stewart
See also CAAS 8; DLB 8

Williamson, John Stewart 1908-
See Williamson, Jack
See also CA 17-20R; CANR 23

Willie, Frederick
See Lovecraft, H(oward) P(hillips)

Willingham, Calder (Baynard, Jr.) 1922-1995 **CLC 5, 51**
See also CA 5-8R; 147; CANR 3; DLB 2, 44; MTCW

Willis, Charles
See Clarke, Arthur C(harles)

Willy
See Colette, (Sidonie-Gabrielle)

Willy, Colette
See Colette, (Sidonie-Gabrielle)

Wilson, A(ndrew) N(orman) 1950- .... **CLC 33**
See also CA 112; 122; DLB 14, 155

Wilson, Angus (Frank Johnstone) 1913-1991 **CLC 2, 3, 5, 25, 34; SSC 21**
See also CA 5-8R; 134; CANR 21; DLB 15, 139, 155; MTCW

Wilson, August 1945- **CLC 39, 50, 63; BLC; DA; DAB; DAC; DAM DRAM, MST, MULT; DC 2; WLCS**
See also AAYA 16; BW 2; CA 115; 122; CANR 42, 54; MTCW

Wilson, Brian 1942- .... **CLC 12**

Wilson, Colin 1931- .... **CLC 3, 14**
See also CA 1-4R; CAAS 5; CANR 1, 22, 33; DLB 14; MTCW

Wilson, Dirk
See Pohl, Frederik

Wilson, Edmund 1895-1972 ... **CLC 1, 2, 3, 8, 24**
See also CA 1-4R; 37-40R; CANR 1, 46; DLB 63; MTCW

Wilson, Ethel Davis (Bryant) 1888(?)-1980 **CLC 13; DAC; DAM POET**
See also CA 102; DLB 68; MTCW

Wilson, John 1785-1854 .... **NCLC 5**

Wilson, John (Anthony) Burgess 1917-1993
See Burgess, Anthony
See also CA 1-4R; 143; CANR 2, 46; DAC; DAM NOV; MTCW

Wilson, Lanford 1937- ..... **CLC 7, 14, 36; DAM DRAM**
See also CA 17-20R; CABS 3; CANR 45; DLB 7

Wilson, Robert M. 1944- .... **CLC 7, 9**
See also CA 49-52; CANR 2, 41; MTCW

Wilson, Robert McLiam 1964- .... **CLC 59**
See also CA 132

Wilson, Sloan 1920- .... **CLC 32**
See also CA 1-4R; CANR 1, 44

Wilson, Snoo 1948- .... **CLC 33**
See also CA 69-72

Wilson, William S(mith) 1932- .... **CLC 49**
See also CA 81-84

Wilson, Woodrow 1856-1924 .... **TCLC 73**
See also DLB 47

Winchilsea, Anne (Kingsmill) Finch Counte 1661-1720
See Finch, Anne

Windham, Basil
See Wodehouse, P(elham) G(renville)

Wingrove, David (John) 1954- .... **CLC 68**
See also CA 133

Wintergreen, Jane
See Duncan, Sara Jeannette

Winters, Janet Lewis .... **CLC 41**
See also Lewis, Janet

Young, Collier
See Bloch, Robert (Albert)
Young, Edward 1683-1765 .... **LC 3, 40**
See also DLB 95
Young, Marguerite (Vivian) 1909-1995 . **CLC 82**
See also CA 13-16; 150; CAP 1
Young, Neil 1945- .... **CLC 17**
See also CA 110
Young Bear, Ray A. 1950- **CLC 94; DAM MULT**
See also CA 146; DLB 175; NNAL
Yourcenar, Marguerite 1903-1987 **CLC 19, 38, 50, 87; DAM NOV**
See also CA 69-72; CANR 23, 60; DLB 72; DLBY 88; MTCW
Yurick, Sol 1925- .... **CLC 6**
See also CA 13-16R; CANR 25
Zabolotskii, Nikolai Alekseevich 1903-1958 **TCLC 52**
See also CA 116
Zamiatin, Yevgenii
See Zamyatin, Evgeny Ivanovich
Zamora, Bernice (B. Ortiz) 1938- **CLC 89; DAM MULT; HLC**
See also CA 151; DLB 82; HW
Zamyatin, Evgeny Ivanovich 1884-1937 **TCLC 8, 37**
See also CA 105
Zangwill, Israel 1864-1926 .... **TCLC 16**
See also CA 109; DLB 10, 135
Zappa, Francis Vincent, Jr. 1940-1993
See Zappa, Frank
See also CA 108; 143; CANR 57
Zappa, Frank .... **CLC 17**
See also Zappa, Francis Vincent, Jr.
Zaturenska, Marya 1902-1982 .... **CLC 6, 11**
See also CA 13-16R; 105; CANR 22
Zeami 1363-1443 .... **DC 7**
Zelazny, Roger (Joseph) 1937-1995 ...... **CLC 21**
See also AAYA 7; CA 21-24R; 148; CANR 26, 60; DLB 8; MTCW; SATA 57; SATA-Brief 39
Zhdanov, Andrei A(lexandrovich) 1896-1948 **TCLC 18**
See also CA 117
Zhukovsky, Vasily 1783-1852 .... **NCLC 35**
Ziegenhagen, Eric .... **CLC 55**
Zimmer, Jill Schary
See Robinson, Jill
Zimmerman, Robert
See Dylan, Bob
Zindel, Paul 1936- **CLC 6, 26; DA; DAB; DAC; DAM DRAM, MST, NOV; DC 5**
See also AAYA 2; CA 73-76; CANR 31; CLR 3, 45; DLB 7, 52; JRDA; MAICYA; MTCW; SATA 16, 58
Zinov'Ev, A. A.
See Zinoviev, Alexander (Aleksandrovich)
Zinoviev, Alexander (Aleksandrovich) 1922- **CLC 19**
See also CA 116; 133; CAAS 10
Zoilus
See Lovecraft, H(oward) P(hillips)
Zola, Emile (Edouard Charles Antoine) 1840-1902 **TCLC 1, 6, 21, 41; DA; DAB; DAC; DAM MST, NOV; WLC**
See also CA 104; 138; DLB 123
Zoline, Pamela 1941- .... **CLC 62**
See also CA 161
Zorrilla y Moral, Jose 1817-1893 .... **NCLC 6**
Zoshchenko, Mikhail (Mikhailovich) 1895-1958 **TCLC 15; SSC 15**
See also CA 115; 160
Zuckmayer, Carl 1896-1977 .... **CLC 18**
See also CA 69-72; DLB 56, 124
Zuk, Georges
See Skelton, Robin
Zukofsky, Louis 1904-1978 **CLC 1, 2, 4, 7, 11, 18; DAM POET; PC 11**
See also CA 9-12R; 77-80; CANR 39; DLB 5, 165; MTCW
Zweig, Paul 1935-1984 .... **CLC 34, 42**
See also CA 85-88; 113
Zweig, Stefan 1881-1942 .... **TCLC 17**
See also CA 112; DLB 81, 118
Zwingli, Huldreich 1484-1531 .... **LC 37**
See also DLB 179

Literary Criticism Series
Cumulative Topic Index

This index lists all topic entries in Gale's *Classical and Medieval Literature Criticism, Contemporary Literary Criticism, Literature Criticism from 1400 to 1800, Nineteenth-Century Literature Criticism,* and *Twentieth-Century Literary Criticism.*

characteristics of Australian literature, 21-33
historical and critical perspectives, 33-41
poetry, 41-58
fiction, 58-76
drama, 76-82
Aboriginal literature, 82-91

Beat Generation, Literature of the TCLC 42: 50-102
overviews, 51-9
the Beat generation as a social phenomenon, 59-62
development, 62-5
Beat literature, 66-96
influence, 97-100

***The Bell Curve* Controversy** CLC 91: 281-330

***Bildungsroman* in Nineteenth-Century Literature** NCLC 20: 92-168
surveys, 93-113
in Germany, 113-40
in England, 140-56
female *Bildungsroman,* 156-67

Bloomsbury Group TCLC 34: 1-73
history and major figures, 2-13
definitions, 13-7
influences, 17-27
thought, 27-40
prose, 40-52
and literary criticism, 52-4
political ideals, 54-61
response to, 61-71

Bly, Robert, *Iron John: A Book about Men and Men's Work* CLC 70: 414-62

The Book of J CLC 65: 289-311

Buddhism and Literature TCLC 70: 59-164
eastern literature, 60-113
western literature, 113-63

Businessman in American Literature TCLC 26: 1-48
portrayal of the businessman, 1-32
themes and techniques in business fiction, 32-47

Catholicism in Nineteenth-Century American Literature NCLC 64: 1-58
overviews, 3-14
polemical literature, 14-46
Catholicism in literature, 47-57

Celtic Mythology CMLC 26: 1-111
overviews, 2-22
Celtic myth as literature and history, 22-48
Celtic religion: Druids and divinities, 48-80
Fionn MacCuhaill and the Fenian cycle, 80-111

Celtic Twilight
See **Irish Literary Renaissance**

Chartist Movement and Literature, The NCLC 60: 1-84
overview: nineteenth-century working-class fiction, 2-19
Chartist fiction and poetry, 19-73
the Chartist press, 73-84

Children's Literature, Nineteenth-Century NCLC 52: 60-135
overviews, 61-72
moral tales, 72-89
fairy tales and fantasy, 90-119
making men/making women, 119-34

Civic Critics, Russian NCLC 20: 402-46
principal figures and background, 402-9
and Russian Nihilism, 410-6
aesthetic and critical views, 416-45

Colonial America: The Intellectual Background LC 25: 1-98
overviews, 2-17
philosophy and politics, 17-31
early religious influences in Colonial America, 31-60
consequences of the Revolution, 60-78
religious influences in post-revolutionary America, 78-87
colonial literary genres, 87-97

Colonialism in Victorian English Literature NCLC 56: 1-77
overviews, 2-34
colonialism and gender, 34-51
monsters and the occult, 51-76

Columbus, Christopher, Books on the Quincentennial of His Arrival in the New World CLC 70: 329-60

Comic Books TCLC 66: 1-139
historical and critical perspectives, 2-48
superheroes, 48-67
underground comix, 67-88
comic books and society, 88-122
adult comics and graphic novels, 122-36

Connecticut Wits NCLC 48: 1-95
general overviews, 2-40
major works, 40-76
intellectual context, 76-95

Crime in Literature TCLC 54: 249-307
evolution of the criminal figure in literature, 250-61
crime and society, 261-77
literary perspectives on crime and punishment, 277-88
writings by criminals, 288-306

Czechoslovakian Literature of the Twentieth Century TCLC 42: 103-96
through World War II, 104-35
de-Stalinization, the Prague Spring, and contemporary literature, 135-72
Slovak literature, 172-85
Czech science fiction, 185-93

Dadaism TCLC 46: 101-71
background and major figures, 102-16
definitions, 116-26
manifestos and commentary by Dadaists, 126-40
theater and film, 140-58
nature and characteristics of Dadaist writing, 158-70

Darwinism and Literature NCLC 32: 110-206
background, 110-31
direct responses to Darwin, 131-71
collateral effects of Darwinism, 171-205

de Man, Paul, Wartime Journalism of CLC 55: 382-424

Detective Fiction, Nineteenth-Century NCLC 36: 78-148

Topic Index

44

Topic Index

CMLC Cumulative Nationality Index

CMLC Cumulative Title Index

Title Index

Title Index

Title Index

See *Partiones oratoriae*
Parzival (Wolfram von Eschenbach) 5:293-94, 296-302, 304-05, 307-10, 312, 314-17, 320-23, 325-26, 333-45, 347, 350-54, 357-58, 360, 362, 366, 369-71, 373, 376, 380-83, 385-86, 390-92, 395-96, 400-01, 403-04, 409, 411, 416-17, 419-23, 425, 429-32
Pasiphae (Euripides) 23:203
"Passing the Huai" (Su Shih) 15:413
The Pastorals of Daphnis and Chloe (Longus)
 See *Daphnis and Chloe*
Patrologia Graeca (Origen) 19:231
"The Pavilion of Flying Cranes" (Su Shih) 15:382
"The Pavilion to Glad Rain" (Su Shih) 15:382
Peace (Aristophanes)
 See *Eirene*
The Peace (Demosthenes)
 See *On the Peace*
"Peacock and Crane" (Aesop) 24:36
Pearl 19:275-407
"A Peasant and a Dung-Beetle" (Marie de France) 8:174
"The Peasant Who Saw His Wife with Her Lover" (Marie de France) 8:190
Pedeir Keinc y Mabinogi 9:144-98
"Peleus and Thetis" (Catullus)
 See *"Poem 64"*
Peliades (Euripides) 23:116
Penelope (Aeschylus) 11:124
Pentachronon (Hildegard von Bingen) 20:163
Perception (Epicurus) 21:73
Perceval (Chretien de Troyes) 10:133, 137, 139, 143, 145-46, 150, 157, 159, 161-66, 169, 178-79, 183, 189-90, 195-96, 199, 206-09, 216-20, 223-26, 228-40
Perceval le Gallois (Chretien de Troyes)
 See *Perceval*
Percevax le viel (Chretien de Troyes)
 See *Perceval*
"Perchance: Two Poems" (Po Chu-i) 24:343
Peri hermeneias (Apuleius) 1:24
Perikeiromene (Menander) 9:207, 210-11, 213, 215, 217, 221, 223, 225, 228, 230, 232, 238-39, 246-48, 250-52, 260, 267, 269-71, 276-77, 281, 288
Perr Archon (Origen)
 See *De Principiis*
Persa (Plautus) 24:170-73, 175, 187, 219, 220-21, 247, 262, 269
Persae (Aeschylus)
 See *Persians*
Persian (Plautus)
 See *Persa*
Persians (Aeschylus) 11:77, 85, 88, 96, 102, 112-13, 117-18, 121, 127, 133-35, 139, 151-53, 156, 158-60, 179, 181-84, 191, 193-95, 198, 200, 202-03, 205, 211, 215-20
Perspective (Bacon)
 See *De Scientia Perspectiva*
Phaedo (Plato) 8:204-07, 209, 233, 235-36, 239, 261, 268, 305-07, 312, 320, 322-25, 328, 331, 340-41, 358, 361-62
Phaedra (Seneca) 6:341, 366, 368-70, 377, 379-81, 389, 403-06, 413-16, 418, 424-26, 432, 448
Phaedrus (Plato) 8:205, 210, 220, 230, 232-33, 241, 244, 254-55, 259, 262, 264-66, 270, 275, 283, 299, 306-07, 317, 322-25, 331, 334, 355,

359, 362, 364
Phaenomena (Euclid) 25: 1-86, 97-8, 108, 144, 168, 258-66
Philebus (Plato) 8:248, 260, 264-68, 270, 306, 310, 333, 341, 361, 363-64
Philippic I (Demosthenes) 13:137, 148-9, 152, 165, 171, 183, 190-2, 195, 197
Philippic II (Demosthenes) 13:138, 148-9, 151, 160, 165, 172
Philippic III (Demosthenes) 13:138, 143-5, 148, 161, 166, 172, 177, 180, 192-3, 195
Philippic IV (Demosthenes) 13:162, 166
Philippics (Cicero) 3:192-93, 196, 198-99, 229-30, 253, 268, 271-73
Philippics (Demosthenes) 13:139, 142-3, 149-52, 158, 161-2, 172, 174, 180, 183, 189
Philoctetes (Aeschylus) 11:125, 140
Philoctetes at Troy (Sophocles) 2:341
Philoktetes (Sophocles) 2:289, 294-95, 302-05, 314, 316, 318, 320, 325, 338, 341, 346, 352-54, 357, 367-68, 377, 385-87, 397-408, 415-16, 419, 426
Philomena (Chretien de Troyes) 10:137
Philosopher (Plato) 8:259
Phineus (Aeschylus) 11:159, 174
The Phoenician Women (Euripides) 23:112, 121, 124-25, 189, 206-07, 219-21
The Phoenician Women (Seneca)
 See *Phoenissae*
Phoenissae (Euripides)
 See *The Phoenician Women*
Phoenissae (Seneca) 6:363, 366, 379-80, 402, 413, 421, 432, 437
"Phoenix Song" (Li Po) 2:152
Phormio (Terence) 14:303, 306-07, 311, 313-18, 320, 333, 335, 340, 341, 347-49, 352-53, 356-57, 364, 376-80, 383-85, 389-90
Phrixus (Euripides) 23:207
Phychostasia (Aeschylus)
 See *Weighing of Souls*
"Phyllis" (Ovid) 7:311
Physica (Albert the Great) 16:4, 36, 61
Physica (Hildegard von Bingen) 20:154
Physicorum (Albert the Great) 16:
Physics (Albert the Great)
 See *Physica*
The Pillow Book of Sei Shonagon (Sei Shonagon)
 See *Makura no soshi*
Pillow Sketches (Sei Shonagon)
 See *Makura no soshi*
Pinakes (Callimachus) 18: 38, 45-8, 62-4, 68-70
"Pine Wine of the Middle Mountains" (Su Shih) 15:382
"The Pious Black Slave" 2:40
Planctus (Abelard) 11:55, 68
"Planher vuelh en Blacatz" (Sordello) 15:332, 337, 343, 365, 375, 377
"Planting Flowers at the Eastern Slope" (Po Chu-i) 24:340
Plants (Albert the Great)
 See *De vegetabilibus*
"Playfully Enjoying the Chrysanthemums at East Garden" (Po Chu-i) 24:327
"Playing with Pine and Bamboo" (Po Chu-i) 24:342
Ploutos (Aristophanes) 4:44, 46, 62, 67, 76, 90, 94, 111, 115, 124-26, 147-48, 153, 161, 165-68, 174-75, 177-80
"The Plunder of the Home of Salur-Kazan" 8:97,

103, 109
Plutus (Aristophanes)
 See *Ploutos*
"Poem 1" (Catullus) 18: 104, 108, 110-11, 117, 122-23, 130-32, 150, 167-78, 185-93
"Poem 2" (Catullus) 18: 116, 161, 178, 187-93, 196
"Poem 3" (Catullus) 18: 166, 174, 178, 187-88
"Poem 4" (Catullus) 18: 108, 117, 167, 180, 187-88
"Poem 5" (Catullus) 18: 102, 137-38, 141, 159, 166, 179, 186, 188, 196-97
"Poem 6" (Catullus) 18: 99, 106, 122, 125-27, 129-30, 133, 138, 188, 195-96
"Poem 7" (Catullus) 18: 102, 108, 118, 137-38, 140, 150, 160-61, 166, 181, 186, 188, 196-97
"Poem 8" (Catullus) 18: 138, 153, 160-61, 166, 188, 192
"Poem 9" (Catullus) 18: 121, 128, 186, 188
"Poem 10" (Catullus) 18: 99, 107, 122-26, 129-30, 188
"Poem 11" (Catullus) 18: 99, 116, 119, 126, 133, 162, 166-67, 179, 181-82, 185, 187-88, 192, 194
"Poem 12" (Catullus) 18: 122, 181, 188
"Poem 13" (Catullus) 18: 102, 109, 127, 180, 186
"Poem 14" (Catullus) 18: 99-101, 166, 186, 188
"Poem 14b" (Catullus) 18: 122, 193
"Poem 15" (Catullus) 18: 119, 133-34, 188-90, 193-95, 197
"Poem 16" (Catullus) 18: 119, 132, 134, 137, 167, 186, 188-90, 193-97
"Poem 17" (Catullus) 18: 122, 129-30, 181
"Poem 18" (Catullus) 18:127 18:127
"Poem 18" (Filderman) 18: 127
"Poem 21" (Catullus) 18: 119, 134, 181, 188
"Poem 22" (Catullus) 18: 100-01, 145
"Poem 23" (Catullus) 18: 99, 119, 133-34, 181, 188
"Poem 24" (Catullus) 18: 99, 132, 134, 188
"Poem 25" (Catullus) 18: 132-33, 166
"Poem 26" (Catullus) 18: 99, 119, 134, 188
"Poem 28" (Catullus) 18: 99, 121, 132, 188
"Poem 29" (Catullus) 18: 99, 118, 144, 166, 181, 187-88
"Poem 30" (Catullus) 18: 99, 125, 169, 171
"Poem 31" (Catullus) 18: 103, 117, 146, 166-67, 186-88
"Poem 32" (Catullus) 18: 115, 122-23, 130, 133, 137-38, 146, 181
"Poem 33" (Catullus) 18: 122, 132-33, 146
"Poem 34" (Catullus) 18: 110-11, 166-67, 176, 181-82
"Poem 35" (Catullus) 18: 93, 99-102, 122, 128, 130, 147, 167, 186
"Poem 36" (Catullus) 18: 100-01, 121, 127, 145, 167, 186
"Poem 37" (Catullus) 18: 118-20, 133
"Poem 38" (Catullus) 18: 99, 181
"Poem 39" (Catullus) 18: 106, 118-19, 131, 133
"Poem 41" (Catullus) 18: 122, 129-30, 146
"Poem 42" (Catullus) 18: 131, 187
"Poem 43" (Catullus) 18: 118, 122-23, 130, 177, 188
"Poem 44" (Catullus) 18: 166
"Poem 45" (Catullus) 18: 122, 126, 130, 166, 181, 188
"Poem 46" (Catullus) 18: 132, 177, 181, 187-88

Title Index

CMLC Cumulative Critic Index

Critic Index

Critic Index

Critic Index

Lawrence, William Witherle
Beowulf 1:75

Lawton, W. C.
Hesiod 5:79

Layamon
Layamon 10:311, 314

Leach, Anna
Arabian Nights 2:16

Leaman, Oliver
Averroes 7:66

Le Bossu, Rene
Aeneid 9:298
Iliad 1:278
Odyssey 16:187

Lecky, W. E. H.
Bacon, Roger 14:11

Lee, Alvin A.
Beowulf 1:140

Lee, Guy
Catullus 18:185

Leech, Kenneth
Llull, Ramon 12:124

Leff, Gordon
Abelard 11:22
Augustine, St. 6:88

Lefkowitz, Mary R.
Sappho 3:481

Le Gentil, Pierre
The Song of Roland 1:203

Legge, James
Confucius 19:3

Legouis, Emile
Layamon 10:319

Leibniz, Gottfried Wilhelm
Augustine, St. 6:8
Averroes 7:5
Plato 8:220

Leiter, Louis H.
The Dream of the Rood 14:256

Leon, Harry J.
Cicero, Marcus Tullius 3:218

Lerer, Seth
Boethius 15:124

Lesky, Albin
Aeschylus 11:158, 190
Demosthenes 13:162
Hesiod 5:112
Odyssey 16:304
Pindar 12:317
Sophocles 2:378

Lessing, Gotthold Ephraim
Sophocles 2:294

Letts, Malcolm
Mandeville, Sir John 19:108

Lever, Katherine
Aristophanes 4:123
Menander 9:227, 233

Levy, G. R.
Epic of Gilgamesh 3:313

Levy, Howard S.
Po Chu-i 24:296

Lewis, C. S.
Aeneid 9:364
Apuleius 1:32
Beowulf 1:87
Boethius 15:43
The Book of Psalms 4:403
Chretien de Troyes 10:147
Layamon 10:343
Romance of the Rose 8:387
Sir Gawain and the Green Knight
  2:221

Lewis, George Cornewall
Thucydides 17:243

Levy, Reuben
Avicenna 16:180

Lewis, Geoffrey
Book of Dede Korkut 8:103

Lewis, Rev. Gerrard
Poem of the Cid 4:228

Liebeschuetz, W.
Boethius 15:47
Livy 11:357

Likhachov, Dmitry
The Igor Tale 1:523

Lindberg, David C.
Bacon, Roger 14:106
Euclid 25:148

Lindsay, Jack
Bertran de Born 5:55
Longus 7:229

Lindsay, Thomas B.
Juvenal 8:17

Littell, Robert
Murasaki, Lady 1:419

Littleton, C. Scott
Eastern Mythology 26:121

Liu Wu-chi
Confucius 19:42
Li Po 2:143

Livy
Livy 11:311
Cato, Marcus Porcius 21:4

Lloyd, G. E. R.
Presocratic philosophy 22:36

Lloyd-Jones, Hugh
Aeschylus 11:168
Menander 9:231
Odyssey 16:321
Pindar 12:342

Locke, John
Aesop 24:4

Lodge, Thomas
Seneca, Lucius Annaeus 6:335

Lofmark, Carl
Wolfram von Eschenbach 5:358

Long, A. A.
Epicurus 21:163

Long, J. Bruce
Mahabharata 5:270

Longfellow, Henry Wadsworth
Beowulf 1:57
Inferno 3:23

Longinus
Aeschylus 11:83
Cicero, Marcus Tullius 3:174
Odyssey 16:192
Plato 8:206
Sappho 3:379
Sophocles 2:292

Longus
Longus 7:216

Lonnrot, Elias
Kalevala 6:208, 210

Loomis, Roger Sherman
Arthurian Legend 10:57, 90, 110
Layamon 10:341

Lord, Albert B.
Iliad 1:363
Odyssey 16:259

Louth, Andrew
Origen 19:254

Lowe, J. C. B.
Plautus 24:238

Lowell, Amy
Murasaki, Lady 1:417

Lowth, Robert
The Book of Psalms 4:352
Song of Songs 18:238

Lucas, F. L.
Epic of Gilgamesh 3:309
Li Po 2:135
Seneca, Lucius Annaeus 6:363

Luck, Georg
Ovid 7:346

Luke, J. Tracy
Epic of Gilgamesh 3:343

Luscombe, D. E.
Abelard 11:48, 61

Lu-shih, Lin
Lao Tzu 7:155

Luther, Martin
The Book of Psalms 4:347
Cicero, Marcus Tullius 3:185
Song of Songs 18:230

Luttrell, Claude
Chretien de Troyes 10:195

Lyne, R. O. A. M.
Catullus 18:148

Lyons, Deborah
Greek Mythology 26:265

Macaulay, Thomas Babbington
Catullus 18:99
Greek Historiography 17:2
Ovid 7:292

MacCana, Proinsias
Celtic Mythology 26:2, 68

MacCulloch, John Arnott
Norse Mythology 26:327

Macdonell, Arthur A.
Mahabharata 5:185

Mackail, J. W.
Aeneid 9:327
Cato, Marcus Porcius 21:25
Iliad 1:315
Odyssey 16:243
Sappho 3:389
Seneca, Lucius Annaeus 6:344
Sophocles 2:317
Terence 14:302

MacKay, L. A.
Apuleius 1:32

MacKillop, James
Celtic Mythology 26:96

Macrae-Gibson, O. D.
The Dream of the Rood 14:278

Macrobius, Ambrosius Theodosius
Aeneid 9:294
Apuleius 1:3
Cicero, Marcus Tullius 3:178

Maeterlinck, Maurice
Arabian Nights 2:17

Magnus, Albertus
Albert the Great 16:65

Magnus, Leonard A.
The Igor Tale 1:480

Magnusson, Magnus
Njals saga 13:332

Magoun, Francis Peabody, Jr.
Cædmon 7:101
Kalevala 6:246

Mahaffey, John Pentland
Xeonophon 17:322

Critic Index

Critic Index

Critic Index

Critic Index